W9-ALU-551

American
Jewish
Year Book

The American Jewish Committee acknowledges with appreciation the foresight and wisdom of the founders of the Jewish Publication Society (of America) in the creation of the AMERICAN JEWISH YEAR BOOK in 1899, a work committed to providing a continuous record of developments in the U.S. and world Jewish communities. For over a century JPS has occupied a special place in American Jewish life, publishing and disseminating important, enduring works of scholarship and general interest on Jewish subjects.

The American Jewish Committee assumed responsibility for the compilation and editing of the YEAR BOOK in 1908. The Society served as its publisher until 1949; from 1950 through 1993, the Committee and the Society were co-publishers. In 1994 the Committee became the sole publisher of the YEAR BOOK.

American

Jewish

Year Book 2003

VOLUME 103

Editors

DAVID SINGER

LAWRENCE GROSSMAN

THE AMERICAN JEWISH COMMITTEE

NEW YORK

ISBN 0-87495-126-7

Library of Congress Catalogue Number: 99-4040

PRINTED IN THE UNITED STATES OF AMERICA
BY MAPLE-VAIL BOOK MANUFACTURING GROUP, BINGHAMTON, N.Y.

Preface

Volume 103 of the AMERICAN JEWISH YEAR BOOK covers the events of the year 2002. It was a year in which the attentions of world Jewry increasingly centered on events in and around the State of Israel, and their global repercussions.

As the YEAR BOOK article on Israel demonstrates in detail, violence between Palestinians and Israelis continued with little hope of a settlement. In an essay specially commissioned for this volume, the eminent demographer Sergio DellaPergola addresses the Israeli-Palestinian conflict from the standpoint of population trends and their implications.

A sharp rise in manifestations of anti-Semitism in many countries—vandalism, physical attacks, verbal abuse, hostile editorials, and biased reporting—was inextricably linked to opposition toward Israel. These disturbing events are carefully described in the YEAR BOOK's regular articles on individual countries.

Yet another way that Israel's importance in Jewish life emerged in 2002 is implicit in the YEAR BOOK's data on world Jewish population—the Jewish state was on the verge of becoming home to the largest Jewish community in the world. American Jewry, meanwhile, argued over the facts of its own demographic profile, as delineated, from different perspectives, in a number of articles in this volume.

Carefully compiled directories of national Jewish organizations, periodicals, and federations and welfare funds, as well as obituaries and religious calendars, round out the 2002 AMERICAN JEWISH YEAR BOOK.

We gratefully acknowledge the assistance of our colleagues, Cyma M. Horowitz and Michele Anish, of the American Jewish Committee's Blaustein Library.

THE EDITORS

Contributors

TOBY AXELROD: Correspondent, Jewish Telegraphic Agency and *Jewish Chronicle* (London); Berlin, Germany.

SERGIO DELLAPERGOLA: Professor and head, Division of Jewish Demography and Statistics, Avraham Harman Institute of Contemporary Jewry, Hebrew University of Jerusalem, Israel.

RICHARD T. FOLTIN: Legislative director and counsel, Office of Government and International Affairs, American Jewish Committee.

ELISE FRIEDMANN: Editor in chief, *Nieuw Israelitische Weekblad*; Amsterdam, Holland.

THOMAS GERGELY: Professor, French literature, and director, Institute of Jewish Studies, Free University of Brussels, Belgium.

ZVI GITELMAN: Professor, political science, and Preston R. Tisch Professor of Judaic Studies, University of Michigan.

LAWRENCE GROSSMAN: Editor, AMERICAN JEWISH YEAR BOOK; associate director of research, American Jewish Committee.

RUTH ELLEN GRUBER: European-based American journalist and author, specialist in contemporary Jewish affairs; Morre, Italy.

GEORGE E. GRUEN: Adjunct professor, international affairs, Middle East Institute and School of International and Public Affairs, Columbia University.

LIONEL E. KOCHAN: Historian; Wolfson College, Oxford, England.

MIRIAM L. KOCHAN: Free-lance journalist and translator; Oxford, England.

JEFFREY LESSER: Professor, history, and director, Latin American and Caribbean Studies Program, Emory University.

COLIN L. RUBENSTEIN: Executive director, Australia/Israel and Jewish Affairs Council; honorary associate, Monash University, Melbourne, Australia.

GEORGES SCHNEK: President, Jewish Museum of Belgium; former president, Jewish Central Consistory of Belgium; emeritus professor, biochemistry, Free University of Brussels, Belgium.

MILTON SHAIN: Professor, Hebrew and Jewish studies, and director, Kaplan Centre for Jewish Studies and Research, University of Cape Town, South Africa.

HANAN SHER: Senior editor, *The Jerusalem Report;* Jerusalem, Israel.

MURRAY GORDON SILBERMAN: Adjunct professor, Austrian Diplomatic Academy, Vienna, Austria.

BRIGITTE SION: Former secretary general, CICAD, the Committee against anti-Semitism and Defamation; Geneva, Switzerland.

MEIR WAINTRATER: Editor in chief, *L'Arche,* the French Jewish monthly, Paris, France.

HAROLD M. WALLER: Professor, political science, McGill University; director, Canadian Centre for Jewish Community Studies, Montreal, Canada.

Contents

OTHER COUNTRIES

DIRECTORIES, LISTS, AND OBITUARIES

Special Article

Demographic Trends in Israel and Palestine: Prospects and Policy Implications

By Sergio DellaPergola

WHILE PUBLIC DEBATE tends to focus on issues of security and politics, the past, present, and future of the Israeli-Palestinian conflict are intimately and crucially related to the way demographic variables affect population size and composition. Therefore, a demographic perspective is essential in the search for a resolution.[1]

The conflict stems from ideological, historical, religious, and political differences that are rooted in ancient cultural traditions. It was during the nineteenth and twentieth centuries that the two sides provided new symbolic meanings, added new contentious frameworks, and reinforced old disagreements, rendering solutions more difficult. At the core of the contemporary confrontation, two peoples—Jews and Arabs—claim rights of settlement and political sovereignty over the same territory they both view as homeland. The very name of that land—in Arab: *Falastin,* in Hebrew: *Eretz Yisrael*—is itself the subject of controversy.

Around this principal bone of contention, two additional tiers further complicate the conflict. The first reflects the general hostility of Arab societies toward the State of Israel. This regional dimension has been demonstrated by repeated, direct interventions by Middle Eastern countries and political movements in support of the Palestinian side of the conflict. The second tier relates to

[1]Early versions of this paper were presented at the XXIV General Population Conference of the International Union for the Scientific Study of Population, Salvador de Bahia, Session 64, *Population Change and Political Transitions* (Chair: Massimo Livi Bacci; Discussant: Alan Hill), August 2001; and at the David Patterson Seminar, Oxford Centre for Hebrew and Jewish Studies, Yarnton, October 2002. Research was carried out at the Division of Jewish Demography and Statistics, the Avraham Harman Institute of Contemporary Jewry, the Hebrew University of Jerusalem. Population projections for world Jewry were supported by the Israel Humanitarian Fund, New York. The author thanks Dalia Sagi for assistance with data processing. While aiming at objectivity, the author takes responsibility for stressing an Israeli point of view in some of the judgments expressed below.

the broader conflict between Islam and Western civilization. Evident at least since Khomeini's Islamic revolution in Iran in the late 1970s, its full intensity became clear with the deadly assaults on American targets on September 11, 2001. This global dimension can be demonstrated, or at least inferred, through the array of contemporary conflicts that Islamic groups are fighting against other forces in Asia, Africa, Europe, and America, and by the explicit or implicit ideological ties among them all. In this last respect, Israel does not stand out on its own, but is rather part of a cluster of other Western, Christian, or otherwise non-Islamic entities that extremist Islam views as adversaries.

In an attempt to solve the core Arab-Jewish conflict, on November 29, 1947, the UN General Assembly approved Resolution 181(II) providing the legal foundations to partition the territory of the former British Mandate over Palestine by establishing separate Arab and Jewish states. Further provisions concerned the international status of the Jerusalem and Bethlehem area.[2] Faced with this UN resolution, representatives of the Jewish side declared their acceptance of territorial partition.[3] The State of Israel was declared on May 14, 1948, thus implementing the claim to a Jewish state in Palestine. Representatives of the Arab side, however, rejected the UN resolution,[4] and thus no parallel declaration of in-

---

[2]Part I, A, 3 of Resolution 181 states that "independent Arab and Jewish States and the Special International Regime for the City of Jerusalem . . . shall come into existence in Palestine . . . not later than 1 October 1948." See: http://www.us-israel.org/jsource/History/partition.html.

[3]Before the vote on the UN partition resolution, Dr. Abba Hillel Silver of the Jewish Agency for Palestine said that the Jewish Agency favored all the resolution's 11 recommendations but one—the exclusion of Jerusalem from the projected Jewish state. "Jerusalem," he went on, "held a unique place in Jewish life and religious traditions. It was the ancient capital of the Jewish nation and its symbol through the ages. . . . The Jewish section of modern Jerusalem, outside the walls, should be included in the Jewish state." Nevertheless, said Silver, "If that heavy sacrifice was the inescapable condition of a final solution, if it made possible the establishment of the Jewish State . . . then the Jewish Agency was prepared to recommend the partition solution. . . ." Ruth Lapidoth and Moshe Hirsch, *The Arab-Israeli Conflict and Its Resolution: Selected Documents* (Dordrecht, 1992), pp. 55–56.

[4]Mr. Husseini of the Arab Higher Committee said: "One other consideration of fundamental importance to the Arab world was that of racial homogeneity. The Arabs lived in a vast territory, stretching from the Mediterranean to the Indian Ocean, spoke one language, had the same history, tradition and aspirations. Their unity was a solid foundation for peace in one of the most central and sensitive areas of the world. It was illogical, therefore, that the United Nations should associate itself with the introduction of an alien body into that

dependence of an Arab state in Palestine followed, although such an intention has been repeatedly claimed ever since. The reasons why an independent Arab state in Palestine was not declared in 1948—at least in a form that would command clear international recognition—are complex and cannot be discussed here.

Warfare between the Arab and Jewish sides in Palestine erupted immediately after the UN partition decision—actually an extension of violence that had already been going on between the two sides—and continued intermittently over the following decades.[5] War between neighboring Arab countries and Israel also erupted in 1948, motivated, at least officially, by the Israeli-Arab conflict within Palestine. By the time cease-fire agreements were reached with the neighboring countries in 1949, Israel had extended its control over some areas that, in the 1947 UN partition plan, were assigned to the would-be Arab state. A major Arab-Israeli war followed two decades later, in 1967, in which Israel occupied the Gaza Strip, the West Bank, and the Golan Heights. The profound demographic implications of 1948–49 and 1967 are discussed in detail below. In 1973, war erupted again, followed by only minor changes in the cease-fire lines with Syria and a major Israeli military redeployment on the Egyptian front. Besides these two full-scale wars, Israel launched major retaliation campaigns in 1956 against Egypt—leading to full-scale invasion of, and temporary control over, the Sinai Peninsula and the Gaza Strip—and in 1982 into Lebanon.[6] During the 1991 Gulf War, Iraq launched a missile strike against Israel.[7]

Cease-fire agreements were signed between Israel and its neigh-

---

established homogeneity. . . . The future constitutional organization of Palestine should be based on . . . the establishment on democratic lines of an Arab State comprising all Palestine. . . ." Ibid., pp. 57–58.

[5]For a historical account see Benny Morris, *Righteous Victims: A History of the Zionist-Arab Conflict, 1881–1999* (New York, 1999).

[6]UN Security Council Resolution 242 of November 22, 1967, called for "withdrawal of Israeli armed forces from territories occupied in the recent conflict." UN Security Council Resolution 338 of October 22, 1973, called "upon the parties concerned to start immediately after the ceasefire implementation of Security Council resolution 242." UN Security Council Resolution 425 of March 19, 1978, following the Litani operation, called "upon Israel immediately to cease its military action against Lebanese territorial integrity and withdraw forthwith its forces from all Lebanese territory." The same principle was reiterated following the entry of Israeli forces into Lebanon in 1982.

[7]Iraq remains the only belligerent country that has not signed a cease-fire agreement with Israel.

bors—Egypt, Jordan, Syria, and Lebanon—in 1949, 1967, and 1974, each reflecting battlefield results and achieving (temporary) boundary definition between the parties inside and outside Palestine. Peace treaties were signed between Israel and Egypt in 1979 and between Israel and Jordan in 1994. With the withdrawal of occupying Israeli forces from Lebanon in 2000, the UN established the exact international boundary between the two countries. An agreement of intent was signed in 1993 between Israel and the Palestinian Authority based on the so-called Oslo Accords, but subsequent negotiations did not lead to a peace treaty. In 1987, and again in September 2000—after negotiations brokered by the U.S. collapsed—the Palestinians initiated an intifada (popular uprising); the second intifada, and Israeli military response to it, are still under way at the time of this writing.

In the prevailing situation of prolonged and unresolved political and military confrontation, observation of demographic trends in Israel and Palestine unveils the deeper layer of political, cultural, religious, social, economic, and environmental factors that underlie the conflict. Because of the crucial connection between population variables and socioeconomic and environmental development in a small and densely settled territory, Jewish and Arab population trends in Palestine are best analyzed through an integrated approach. Looking at the two parties not only as separate and hostile entities but also as one integrated regional societal system may sharpen perception of the complexities of the problems at stake and also help in discerning possible mechanisms to reduce tensions.

One way to assess the significant role of demography in the Israeli-Palestinian context is to elaborate different scenarios of future Jewish and Arab population development for both the short term and the longer run. This essay reviews some of the main demographic trends among Jews and Arabs in Israel and Palestine, presents various population projections for the period 2000–2050, and discusses some possible policy implications of the emerging demographic scenarios. In the following, new projections are presented based on official baseline data released by the State of Israel and by the Palestinian Authority. The analysis and interpretation, however, reflect our independent research. Assumptions for the population scenarios rely on assessment and evaluation of past trends with regard to health and mortality, fertility, international migration, and territorial population redistribution. Cultural, communal, and institutional variables also receive significant attention.

Beyond a general expectation of rapid population growth within a relatively small territory, population projections indicate the important role of differential growth for the different ethnoreligious subpopulations, geographical regions, and functional age groups. Prospective changes in Jewish and Palestinian population sizes, densities, manpower characteristics, and mutual ethnoreligious balance may be primary factors in exacerbating conflict, but may also stimulate innovative thinking about ways to contain conflict.

Demography is a primary force in shaping the political, environmental, socioeconomic, and sociocultural interests of the contending parties. Political boundaries and the very viability of the respective countries are powerfully related to ethnic and religious composition, population densities, environmental constraints, and socioeconomic development. Possible policy interventions may concern fertility, international migration, the population's geographical mobility and distribution, and investments in public facilities and economic infrastructure. From the different perspectives of the two main parties to the Israeli-Palestinian conflict, a serious appraisal of prospective demographic trends might lead to policy decisions that ease the path toward conflict resolution, or at least help keep the situation from deteriorating.

POPULATION CHANGE IN ISRAEL/PALESTINE: FRAMEWORKS AND PATTERNS

Territory

Boundaries of the territory known, among other appellations, as *Kna'an* (the biblical Hebrew word translated in English as Canaan), *Eretz Yisrael,* The Holy Land, and Palestine have changed repeatedly through history. At times, the relevant land formed one single political unit or was at the core of a significantly more extended one. During other periods, it was divided between different foreign powers or constituted a relatively distant and peripheral province controlled by one or more of them.

The geographical concept of *Palestine*—more accurately, Western Palestine—refers to the whole territory between the Mediterranean Sea and the Jordan River. This area formed the British Mandate between 1922 and 1948,[8] and comprises some 28,000 km² (table 1). Of this total, 20,444 km² of land plus 474 km² of lakes are included in the State of Israel, reflecting armistice or cease-fire agreements with Lebanon and Syria, and more recent peace treaties with Egypt and Jordan. In addition, soon after the Six-Day War of June 1967, Israel incorporated into the Jerusalem municipality a total of 73 km² that included the eastern part of the city and adjacent land, areas that, between 1948 and 1967, were ruled by the Hashemite Kingdom of Transjordan, later Jordan. Afterward, Israel also extended its legal jurisdiction over 1,154 km² of the Golan Heights, captured from Syria in 1967. Not included in the State of Israel are the *Palestinian Territories*.[9] These include the

---

[8]The Balfour Declaration, issued November 2, 1917, stated that "the British Government views with favor the establishment in Palestine of a National Home for the Jewish People . . . it being clearly understood that nothing shall be done which may prejudice the civil and religious rights of existing non-Jewish communities in Palestine, or the rights and political status enjoyed by Jews in any other country." These principles were incorporated in the Preamble and Article 2 of the Terms of the Mandate for Palestine, July 24, 1922. On September 16, 1922, the Council of the League of Nations approved a British memorandum stating that provisions aimed at securing the establishment of the Jewish national home in Palestine were not applicable to the area east of the Jordan River—Eastern Palestine—which was to be separately administered by the British. See Palestine Royal Commission, *Report Presented by the Secretary of State for the Colonies to Parliament by Command of His Majesty, July 1937* (London, 1937).

[9]The UN Population Division's 2000 revised population projections adopted the caption "Occupied Palestinian Territories" in place of the previous label, "West Bank and Gaza." This change reflected discussions at several UN bodies—its Legal Office, Department of Political Affairs, Office of the Secretary General, and General Assembly—following a request from the Palestinian Authority that was supported by the Arab states. That led to a 1999 instruction to the Population Division to report statistics according to the new denomination. The decision is documented in a series of internal memoranda based on a more general decision by the General Assembly that does not refer specifically to statistical reporting. Quite aside from its obvious political orientation, the label "Occupied Palestinian Territories" is neither geographically clear nor accurate. In the current political-military reality of the whole territory of Palestine between the Mediterranean Sea and the Jordan River, and following the 1993 Oslo agreements, there are four types of geopolitical situations: 1. *The State of Israel:* Full Israeli sovereignty; 2–4. *The Palestinian Territories,* subdivided into: 2. *The "A" zones:* these areas, including all the main Palestinian cities in the West Bank and Gaza Strip and 64 percent of the population in the Palestinian Territories, are in the full administrative and security control of the Palestinian Authority, and host no Israeli military or civilian settlement; 3. *The "B" zones:* 33 percent of the population, Palestinian administrative responsibility, Israeli army security responsibility; 4. *The "C" zones:* 3 percent of the population, full responsibility in the hands of the Israeli army. See Philippe Fargues "Des cartes dans quel jeu? Les accords israëlo-palestiniens et la démographie,"

West Bank (of the Jordan River), comprising 5,506 km^2 (governed by Jordan between 1948 and 1967), and the Gaza Strip, comprising 378 km^2 (under Egyptian military rule between 1948 and 1967).

TABLE 1. ISRAEL AND PALESTINE, LAND SURFACE, SQUARE KM AND MILES

Surface	Total Israel[a]	West Bank	Gaza	Total Palestinian Territories	Grand Total
Sq. Km	21,671[b]	5,506	378	5,884	27,555
Sq. Miles	8,371	2,127	146	2,273	10,644

[a]Including Golan Heights and East Jerusalem.
[b]According to the UN partition plan, the Jewish state was to have a surface of 16,114 km^2.

Although comparatively small—the equivalent of a medium-size region in a typical European country or one of the smallest states in the United States[10]—the territory of Palestine (Israel plus the Palestinian-ruled areas) comprises significant variations of morphological and climatic regions. The main territorial areas include the Mediterranean coastal plane to the west, the hilly north-south central backbone, and the Jordan Valley to the east. Israel's southern part, the Beersheba Subdistrict— 12,946 km^2 of mostly desert or arid land—makes up 58 percent of Israel's total area. For all of Palestine, then, extremely

Revue d'Études Palestiniennes 75, Spring 2000, pp. 53–64. The "B" and "C" zones, hosting both a military and a civilian Israeli presence, can accurately be described as "occupied territory," but, as noted, most Palestinians live in the "A" zones. To be faithful to the UN terminology, two separate sets of statistical data should be provided for "Occupied Palestinian Territories" and "Autonomous Palestinian Territories." To be sure, in Middle Eastern political rhetoric the State of Israel itself has often been referred to as "Occupied Palestinian Territory." It may be noted that the notion of "occupied territory" may apply to many other places around the world featuring territorial conflict—at least from the point of view of one of the contending parties. Use by the UN—including its Population Division—of the term *exclusively* for parts of Palestine neither enhances scientific clarity nor adds to data reliability. An alternative label for "West Bank and Gaza" would be "Palestinian Territories" or simply "Palestine." The Palestinian Authority's Central Bureau of Statistics (PCBS) in Ramallah refers to the relevant areas as "Palestinian Territory."

[10]The total area of the State of Israel without the Territories is larger than New Jersey and smaller than Massachusetts. The total area of the West Bank approximates that of Delaware.

variable land and climate conditions influence potential and actual settlement patterns.

Past Population Trends

Available evidence indicates that historically, the total population of Palestine—whatever the internal political divisions—shifted significantly in size and composition. The rough reconstruction in table 2 reflects prevailing scholarly assumptions of a relatively large population size—probably ranging between 1 and 2.5 million—during the early centuries C.E.; significant population decline after the fifth century; long-term population stagnation until the beginning of the nineteenth century; and rapid growth ever since.[11] In the modern period, the total population of Palestine repeatedly doubled, from 275,000 in 1800 to over half a million in 1890, over a million in 1931, about two million in 1947, and four million toward the end of the 1960s. More recently, population again doubled from over 4.5 million in 1975 to 9.3 million in 2000, and probably stands in the vicinity of 10 million in 2003. Over the period 1800–2000, Palestine's total population grew by a factor of nearly 34 times. Between 1947, the year of the UN partition plan, and 2000, total population grew by 4.7 times.

Population distribution by main ethnoreligious groups shows an uninterrupted presence of Jews, and subsequently Christians and Muslims, over most of the last two millennia, along with significant changes over time in the absolute and relative size of these groups. Archaeological and documentary evidence points to the early prevalence of Jewish population, political organization, and culture. Then, between the fourth and seventh centuries—the Byzantine period—the majority of the population was Christian. With the rise of Islam after the seventh century, a Muslim majority emerged. This lasted through 1947, when, out of an estimated total population of about 2 million, close to 1.2 million (60 percent) were Muslims, about 650,000 (32 percent) Jews, and about 150,000 (7 percent) Christians.[12]

---

[11]Roberto Bachi, *The Population of Israel* (Jerusalem, 1977). For population estimates in antiquity, see Colin McEvedy and Richard Jones, *Atlas of World Population History* (Harmondsworth, 1978); and Magen Broshi, *Bread, Wine, Walls and Scrolls* (London, 2001), pp. 80–109.

[12]Bachi, *Population of Israel*, pp. 4–5.

TABLE 2. POPULATION IN PALESTINE WEST OF JORDAN RIVER, BY RELIGIOUS GROUPS, FIRST CENTURY — 2000 (ROUGH ESTIMATES, THOUSANDS)

Year	Jews	Christians	Muslims	Total[a]
First half 1st century C.E.	Majority	—	—	1,000 – 2,500
5th century	Minority	Majority	—	>1st century
End 12th century	Minority	Minority	Majority	>225
14th cent.				
pre-black death	Minority	Minority	Majority	225
post-black death	Minority	Minority	Majority	150
1533 – 39	5	6	145	157
1690 – 91	2	11	219	232
1800	7	22	246	275
1890	43	57	432	532
1914	94	70	525	689
1922	84	71	589	752
1931	175	89	760	1,033
1947	630	143	1,181	1,970
1960	1,911	85	1,090	3,111
1967	2,374	102	1,204	3,716
1975	2,959	116	1,447	4,568
1985	3,517	149	2,166	5,908
1995	4,522	191	3,241	8,112
2000	4,969	217	3,891	9,310

[a]Including "Others": Druze, other small religious minorities, and, since 1990, immigrants from the former USSR without religious affiliation.
Sources: until 1975, Roberto Bachi, *The Population of Israel* (Jerusalem, 1977); after 1975, author's estimates based on Israel Central Bureau of Statistics and Palestinian Central Bureau of Statistics.

Following Israel's 1948 War of Independence and the far-reaching political changes that came in its wake, a Jewish majority emerged again in the whole territory of historic Palestine. One of the determinants of this shift was the flight from Palestine of 625,000–675,000 Arabs, according to Israeli sources,[13] or 700,000–850,000, according to Palestinian sources.[14] These have

[13]Ibid., pp. 401–02.
[14]See Edward Hagopian and A.B. Zahlan, "Palestine's Arab Population: The Demography of the Palestinians," *Journal of Palestine Studies* 12, Summer 1974, pp. 32–73; and G.F. Kossaifi, *The Palestinian Refugees and the Right to Return* (Washington, D.C., 1996).

been recognized, together with their descendants, as the Palestinian refugees.[15] Another key determinant of population change beginning with Israeli independence was large-scale, unrestricted Jewish immigration, which amounted to 2,850,000 between 1948 and 2000. Differential natural increase of the main ethnoreligious groups further contributed to the changes in population size and composition.

At the end of 2000, the total population of Palestine from the Mediterranean Sea to the Jordan River was estimated at 9.3 million, about 5 million (53 percent) Jews, close to 3.9 million (42 percent) Muslims, and over 200,000 (2 percent) Christians. Of the grand total of 9.3 million, Israel's population — including Jewish residents of the West Bank and Gaza Strip — amounted to about 6,350,000. Of these, 4,969,000 were Jews, 199,000 non-Jews related to the recent large-scale Jewish immigration from Eastern Europe, and 1,178,000 Arabs and others, mostly Muslim Palestinians, but also Christians and Druze (practitioners of a religion that originated as an offshoot of Islam). The total population of the Palestinian Territories approached 3 million — 1,845,000 on the West Bank and 1,128,000 in the Gaza Strip.

Homelands and Diasporas

One of the most significant aspects of population dynamics in Israel and Palestine has been a continuous interaction between trends occurring locally and developments in the much broader framework of the Jewish and Palestinian diasporas. Of particular salience has been the role of international migration, leading to large-scale and, in a sense, reverse processes of concentration and dispersion of Jews and Arabs worldwide — Jews moving from diaspora to homeland; Arabs moving from homeland to diaspora.

Interactions between a Jewish population core in Palestine and an ancient and globally dispersed diaspora helped shape the very essence of Jewish history, identity, and culture. In modern times, Jewish population patterns in Israel were crucially affected by

---

[15]We cannot enter here into a discussion of the causes and modalities of the great Palestinian flight of 1948. The main Palestinian thesis argues that there was forced expulsion by the Israeli army, while the main Israeli thesis is that there was voluntary flight in response to encouragement by Arab leadership in the framework of a war Israel did not initiate.

heavy and, in the initial stages, very heterogeneous immigration. The essential process driving Jewish population trends has been the transition of Jews from being part of a multitude of communities representing small minorities in their respective diaspora countries of residence, to forming the majority of the State of Israel's population. Complex processes of absorption in a new societal context and growing sociodemographic homogenization were foreshadowed and justified by the prescriptive Zionist societal goals of "the ingathering of the exiles" and "fusion of the diasporas." In actual experience, large-scale immigration and absorption involved considerable social friction, the accumulation of social gaps, and, occasionally, the exploitation of these by political interests. Even so, the predominant pattern was one of convergence between different immigrant groups.[16] At the same time, the remaining Jewish diaspora continued to constitute a potential source of Jewish population growth and—at least in the prevailing normative ethos of Israeli society—contributed to a broad perception of Jewish peoplehood transcending geographical boundaries.

The Palestinian migration experience was, in a sense, symmetric and reversed, a large-scale diaspora emerging only recently. International dispersal of population mostly followed the 1948 war and, to a lesser extent, the 1967 war. The Palestinian case is similar to that of Israel, however, in that the prevailing normative ethos looks to the diaspora as a substantial reservoir for potential immigration. Just as Israel's Zionist ideology speaks of a Jewish return to the homeland, the Palestinians speak of the return of the Palestinian refugees.[17]

---

[16]U.O. Schmelz, Sergio DellaPergola, and Uri Avner, *Ethnic Differences Among Israeli Jews: A New Look* (Jerusalem and New York, 1991).

[17]The question of who is a refugee and who is not, besides being politically overcharged, is complex and requires intensive scrutiny. According to the UN Refugees Relief and Work Agency in the Near East (UNRWA), a Palestinian refugee is "anyone who was living in Palestine two years before the 1948 war and migrated to one of the areas in which UNRWA operates (Jordan, Syria, Lebanon, West Bank, and Gaza Strip) and became 'financially' in need." According to the Palestinian National Convention, Palestinian refugees are "Arab citizens who were living in Palestine until 1947, whether displaced by force outside Palestine or remaining inside Palestine. The definition also includes all of their descendants born to an Arab father inside or outside Palestine after that date." Rather than enter into the specific question of the demographic development of Palestinians holding the status of refugee, we quote available population estimates that basically refer to Palestinian refugees, but address the total Palestinian population as such. Every Palestinian falls into one of the following categories: Registered refugees—holding refugee registration cards issued by

Table 3 presents a rough reconstruction of the size and geographic distribution of worldwide Jewish and Arab Palestinian populations on the eve of Israel's independence in 1948, and in 2000.[18] In 1948, the total world Jewish population was estimated at 11.2 million, of which 650,000 (6 percent) lived in Palestine, 945,000 (8 percent) in Middle Eastern and North African countries, and the other 86 percent in Eastern European and Western countries. Israel's independence and the large-scale international migration it allowed had a huge impact on the geographical dis-

---

UNRWA; Non-registered refugees—not holding refugee cards issued by UNRWA; Non-refugees—Palestinians not categorized under either of the two aforementioned statuses. See http://www.pcbs.org/english/miscelln/definition.htm. According to the Palestinian Central Bureau of Statistics in Ramallah, "the updating of UNRWA data depends on the refugees themselves," and is therefore of unknown validity. See http://www.pcbs.org/miscelln/reading.htm. Issues demanding clarification concern the exact procedures for the recording of vital events among refugees, especially cases of death, since UNRWA benefits associated with refugee status might be lost in case of death. Also, in case of marriage between a refugee and a non-refugee, evaluation of the advantages associated with belonging to either status, and transferability to spouses and descendants, may affect the choice of status. Indeed, the current belonging of (former refugee) Palestinians to refugee or non-refugee status in the West Bank and Gaza reflects individual decisions and processes of social mobility that escape rigid accountancy rules. These and other issues make the definitional boundaries of the refugee population and the accountancy of Palestinian refugees and their descendants an exemplary case in the study of *poorly defined subpopulations*. Many of the same research issues apply to certain Jewish populations, namely those who left Arab countries and immigrated to Israel. The majority of Jews who ever immigrated to Israel would indeed qualify for the status of refugees, having lost most of their belonging and being unable to return to the countries of origin. A significant difference is that Jewish immigrants in Israel were incorporated through a major public effort of absorption within the mainstream of Israeli society. In the case of the Palestinians, a major effort was instead invested in refraining from solving the social problems of immediate relevance, postponing and subordinating those issues to the final solution of the Israeli-Arab conflict.

[18]Jewish population figures derive from a systematic, country-by-country evaluation of sources of data and estimates. See Sergio DellaPergola "World Jewish Population," *American Jewish Year Book* (hereafter AJYB), yearly publication; idem, "Projections démographiques: combat de chiffres," in J.C. Sebag, ed., *L'arrière-plan démographique de l'explosion de violence en Israël-Palestine* (Paris, 2000), pp. 25–31; and Sergio DellaPergola, Uzi Rebhun, and Mark Tolts, "Prospecting the Jewish Future: Population Projections 2000–2080," AJYB 2000, pp. 103–46. Palestinian population figures need to undergo a similar critical evaluation, as they partly reflect estimates by individual researchers or such public bodies as the Office for Statistics and Natural Resources in Damascus. See Hasan Abu Libdeh, "Palestinian Territories: Demographics," in S. Della Seta, ed., *The Price of Non-Peace: The Need for a Strengthened Role for the European Union in the Middle East* (Brussels, 1999), pp. 170–77; PASSIA (Palestinian Academic Society for the Study of International Affairs), *Agenda 1998* (Jerusalem, 1998); Palestinian Central Bureau of Statistics, *Population, Housing and Establishments—Census 1997* (Ramallah, 1999); UNRWA, *Annual Report,* 2000; and http://www.pcbs.org/english/miscelln/method.htm.

tribution of world Jewish population and also on the balance of natural increase and Jewish identification (retention vs. assimilation). It should be noted, however, that world Jewish population grew rather slowly after World War II, and, since the mid-1970s, has been close to zero population growth. In 2000, out of a world total of about 13 million Jews, 4.9 million (38 percent) lived in Israel, only 38,000 remained in Muslim countries (amounting to virtual ethnic cleansing), and the balance (61 percent) mostly lived in North America and elsewhere in the West.[19]

TABLE 3. WORLD JEWISH AND PALESTINIAN POPULATIONS BY MAJOR REGIONS, NUMBERS (THOUSANDS, ROUGH ESTIMATES) AND PERCENTS, 1948–2000

Region	Jews				Palestinians			
	Number		Percent		Number		Percent	
	1948[a]	2000[b]	1948[a]	2000[b]	1948[a]	2000[b]	1948[a]	2000[b]
Total world	11,185	12,900	100.0	100.0	1,664	8,956	100.0	100.0
Israel/Palestine, total	650	4,952	5.8	38.4	1,404	4,356	84.4	48.6
Israel	645	4,582	5.8	35.5	806[c]	1,131	48.5	12.6
West Bank[d], Gaza	5	370	0.0	2.9	598[e]	3,225	35.9	36.0
Middle East[f], North Africa	945	38	8.4	0.3	160[g]	4,100	9.6	45.8
Other countries	9,590	7,910	85.8	61.3	100[g]	500	6.0	5.6

[a]May 15.
[b]December 31.
[c]Assuming 650,000 Palestinians left as refugees.
[d]Including East Jerusalem.
[e]Difference between figures in two preceding lines.
[f]Including Turkey, Syria, Lebanon, Jordan, Iraq, Gulf States, Saudi Arabia, Egypt, and other countries in the region.
[g]Author's rough estimate.
Sources: Bachi (1977); DellaPergola (2001); DellaPergola, Rebhun, Tolts (2000); PASSIA (1998); UNRWA (2000).

The great majority of Palestinian Arabs lived in Palestine on the eve of partition in 1948, though some emigrant communities already existed both in the Middle East and in several Western countries. It can be roughly estimated that the total Palestinian popu-

---

[19]Sergio DellaPergola, "World Jewish Population 2000," AJYB 2000, pp. 484–95.

lation worldwide grew from about 1.7 million in 1948 to about 9 million in 2000, reflecting significant natural increase in the intervening period. A major factor of local, regional, and global population redistribution was the exodus connected with the 1948 war. In 1949, about 156,000 Arabs were left in the areas that had become the State of Israel. A further flight of Palestinians from the West Bank followed with the 1967 war. In 2000, about half of the whole Palestinian people — over 4.3 million, or 49 percent — lived on the territory of historic Palestine, whether in the State of Israel (13 percent), or in the West Bank and Gaza (36 percent).[20] Another estimated 4.1 million (46 percent) were living in neighboring Muslim countries in the Middle East and North Africa, over 60 percent of them in Jordan. The balance (5 percent) lived in other, mostly Western, countries.

Under the current terms of Israeli-Arab conflict in Palestine, diaspora populations constitute a frequently mentioned potential for immigration, and hence a relevant element in the evaluation of possible future population trends in the area. Whether or not actually motivated to move back to Israel/Palestine, diasporas have represented, and continue to represent, a powerful factor in the mobilization of public support and economic resources both internally — within the respective Jewish and Arab constituencies — and vis-à-vis external actors in the international community such as foreign governments, the world media, the United Nations, and other nongovernmental organizations (NGOs). Thus Jews and Palestinians in their respective diasporas have played, and will continue to play, a significant role in the overall development of population trends in Israel and Palestine, if not directly, at least indirectly.

Territorial Aspects of Population Distribution

The Palestine partition plan of 1947 envisioned dividing the land into six areas, three with a Jewish majority, three with an

---

[20]Regardless of citizenship, refugee or non-refugee status, and whether or not living in their localities of birth. In 2001, the number of registered refugees was estimated at 607,770 on the West Bank (33 percent of the total Palestinian population there), of which 163,139 in camps; and 852,626 in the Gaza Strip (73 percent of the total population), of which 460,031 in camps. See http://www.un.org, United Nations Relief and Work Agency for Palestine Refugees in the Near East (2001).

Arab majority, and the Jerusalem-Bethlehem area as a *corpus separatum* under UN administration. Following the 1948 war and the 1949 armistice agreements, the Jewish-Israeli side expanded its territorial hegemony at the expense of the Arab side, with several enclaves of what was to have been Arab territory passing under direct Israeli rule. The 1967 war produced further territorial changes, namely the expansion of Israeli rule (civil or military) over the whole of historic Palestine. As noted, Israel annexed East Jerusalem and surrounding territory in 1967, and Israeli legal jurisdiction was subsequently extended to the Golan Heights. However, in the West Bank and Gaza areas the Israeli administration did not suspend application of the preexisting Jordanian or Egyptian legal frameworks under which the local population had been governed. At the same time, Israel promoted an extensive network of Jewish settlements throughout the West Bank, the Gaza area, and the Golan Heights. Consequently, each part of Palestine ended up having both Jews and Arabs, though the respective proportions varied greatly.[21]

Table 4 provides an approximate classification scheme of Jewish and Arab population distribution over the different political and administrative units of the whole territory that was submitted to various modes and frameworks of Israeli rule after the 1967 war.[22] Within the State of Israel proper, 36 of the 45 natural regions[23] had Jewish majorities in 2000. They contained an enlarged Jewish population[24] of 4.6 million, 93 percent of the total population of these areas. The nine other natural regions continued to display an Arab majority, reflecting the underlying assumptions of the 1947 partition plan and the noted consequences of the 1948 war. There were about 610,000 Arabs in these areas, representing

---

[21]For a more detailed analysis of territorial population distributions of Jews and Arabs within Israel and the Palestinian Territories see Arnon Sofer, *Israel, Demography 2000–2020: Risks and Opportunities* (Haifa, 2001).

[22]Residential segregation between Jews and Arabs is extremely high within single localities, and within residential neighborhoods in the few localities with a mixed Jewish-Arab population. The following discussion refers to population distribution by administrative units.

[23]Natural regions are territorial subdivisions of the 14 administrative subdistricts, which are, in turn, subdivisions of Israel's six major districts.

[24]All of the Jewish population data reported here are "enlarged," meaning they include non-Jewish members of Jewish households, mostly immigrants from the former Soviet Union. See below for further discussion.

a majority of over 76 percent; Jews were less than 24 percent of the population. These majority-Arab areas were in the northwestern and central parts of Galilee in Israel's north, and in the so-called "Triangle" bordering the West Bank.[25]

TABLE 4.   AREAS IN ISRAEL AND IN THE PALESTINIAN TERRITORIES, BY JEWISH[a] AND ARAB[b] POPULATION DISTRIBUTION, 2000

Area	Number (thousands)			Percent		
	Jewish	Arab	Total	Jewish	Arab	Total
GRAND TOTAL	5,180.6	4,213.7	9,394.3	55.1	44.9	100.0
Total Israel	**4,982.4**	**1,188.7**	**6,171.1**	**80.7**	**19.3**	**100.0**
(without Pal. Territories)						
Pre-1967 borders	*4,794.6*	*965.3*	*5,759.9*	*83.2*	*16.8*	*100.0*
Natural regions with Jewish majority	4,608.4	355.6	4,964.0	92.8	7.2	100.0
Natural regions with Arab majority	186.2	609.7	795.9	23.4	76.6	100.0
Added post-1967	*187.8*	*223.4*	*411.2*	*45.7*	*54.3*	*100.0*
Golan Heights	15.8	19.0	34.8	45.4	54.6	100.0
East Jerusalem	172.0	204.4	376.4	45.7	54.3	100.0
Total Palestinian Territories	**198.2**	**3,025.0**	**3,223.2**	**6.1**	**93.9**	**100.0**
West Bank	191.5	1,878.0	2,214.5	8.6	91.4	100.0
Gaza	6.7	1,147.0	1,153.7	0.6	99.4	100.0

[a]Including non-Jewish members of Jewish households, referred to below as the "enlarged Jewish population."
[b]Including others.
Source: Israel Central Bureau of Statistics (2001); Palestinian Central Bureau of Statistics (1997); DellaPergola (2001).

As for the areas directly administered by Israel since the 1967 war, at the end of 2000 the Golan Heights had a total population of 35,000 (55 percent Arab Druze and 45 percent Jews), and the East Jerusalem area had a total population of 376,000 (54 percent Arabs of which 4 percent Christians, and 46 percent Jews). The ag-

---

[25]The Arab-majority natural regions were Eastern Lower Galilee, Kokhav Plateau, Nazareth-Tiran Mountains, Shefar'am Region, Karmi'el Region, Yehi'am Region, Elon Region, all in the Northern District; Alexander Mountain in the Haifa District; and East Sharon in the Central District. There are another three natural regions with Arab majorities on the Golan Heights.

gregate population of Israel—the land within the pre-1967 borders plus the directly ruled territories added after 1967—was 6,171,000, of which 81 percent were Jews and 19 percent Arabs.

In the Palestinian Territories, the total population of the West Bank and Gaza at the end of 2000 was estimated at about 3 million Arabs (94 percent of the total) and about 200,000 Jews (6 percent). Jewish residents of the Palestinian Territories constituted 9 percent of the total population on the West Bank and less than 1 percent in the Gaza Strip. Following partial implementation of the Oslo agreements in the 1990s and withdrawal of Israeli military forces, the majority of Palestinians lived in autonomous districts subject to the Palestinian Authority. However, the current wave of violence, beginning in late 2000, elicited an ongoing military reaction from Israel. As a result, the Palestinian Territories are now highly fragmented, and Israeli forces impose strict limits on travel across the area.

In sum, the grand total population of Israel and Palestine—the area encompassing the old British Mandate plus the Golan Heights—was about 9.4 million in 2000, 55 percent Jewish and 45 percent Arab. This mosaic of interspersed Jewish- and Arab-majority areas stands at the center of a complex and often bloody arena of human interaction and political clash, whose demographic implications constitute one of the most sensitive issues in the region.

DEMOGRAPHY IN COMPARATIVE CONTEXT: PAST AND PROSPECTIVE

International Migration

As already noted, international migration has operated as a leading mechanism of population growth in Palestine. Riddled with apparent contradictions when viewed in strictly political or normative terms, the patterns of this migration constitute important building blocks in the long-term evaluation of population growth.

While events developed in totally different ways for Jews and for Palestinians, it is important to keep in mind the continuing socioeconomic osmosis that prevailed over time across religioethnic boundaries. During most of the twentieth century, Jewish immigration constituted a main engine of economic growth and modernization in the whole area. Not only did this immigration function as a self-reinforcing mechanism expanding the economy to allow for the absorption of further Jewish immigration, but the economic change it stimulated also provided large-scale employment for Palestinian Arabs, and in that way, especially during the British Mandate, encouraged Arab immigration from neighboring countries.[26]

The consequence for Israel was that an Arab labor force became one of the essential prerequisites for the construction of a modern Jewish state. And as far as the Palestinians were concerned, were it not for the existence of the State of Israel, a large share of the Palestinian labor force, unable to find employment locally, would have been forced to migrate elsewhere in search of work. Indeed, about 140,000 Palestinians emigrated from the West Bank during the 1960s—ruled, at the time by Jordan—looking for jobs. Afterwards, from the 1967 Israeli occupation until 1989, 171,000 Palestinians left the West Bank and 114,000 the Gaza area in search of the new opportunities opening up in the booming economies of the Gulf States. After the 1991 Gulf War, about 30,000 returned, and another 30,000—mostly people related to members of the Palestinian Authority's administration and military forces—came back to Palestine after the Oslo agreements.[27]

Between 1967 and 1987, a growing number of Palestinian commuters—perhaps as many as 200,000—were employed within Israel's territory.[28] But with the 1987 (first) intifada, they came to be seen as a security risk, and Israel drastically curtailed their number. The result was a dramatic decline in Palestinian income levels and standard of living.

The most recent chapter in the intertwined relationship between Jewish and Palestinian economies and migrations concerns, once

---

[26]Jacob Metzer, *The Divided Economy of Mandatory Palestine* (Cambridge, 1998).

[27]Elia Zureik, "The trek back home: Palestinians returning home and their problems of adaptation," in A. Hovdenak et al., eds., *Constructing an Order: Palestinian Adaptation to Refugee Life* (Oslo, 1997), pp. 79–102.

[28]According to Israeli data, the 105,000 officially registered Palestinians who worked in Israel in 1989 constituted 37 percent of the total Palestinian labor force. They represented 7 percent of the total Israeli work force, 17 percent of all workers in agriculture, and 44 percent of all construction workers. Central Bureau of Statistics, *Statistical Abstract of Israel* (Jerusalem, 1989).

again, the consequences of political tensions. After a few years' partial recovery, the 2000 (second) intifada brought the Israeli-Palestinian labor-force interaction to a virtual end. Seeking manpower to substitute for the Palestinians, the Israeli economy found it in a growing number of foreign workers, some on temporary contracts who remained illegally in the country. In 2000, their number was estimated at 200,000–250,000.

The mechanisms governing Jewish international migration—immigration to Israel in particular—responded to the variable conditions of Jewish communities worldwide, within the context of general political and socioeconomic change at the global, national, and local levels.[29] Migration policies in the sending and receiving countries played a key role, such as the quotas imposed on immigration by the U.S. beginning in the early 1920s and by the British in Palestine in the 1930s, or the ban on Jewish emigration long imposed by the Soviet Union. Since 1948, Israel's Law of Return has allowed nearly unlimited immigration of Jews, their children and grandchildren, and spouses. Large-scale, push-dominated Jewish emigration translated into repeated waves of migrants, mostly from less developed or less politically emancipated countries, to Israel and to various Western countries.

Figure 1 illustrates the changing volume of Jewish immigration to Palestine/Israel between 1919 and 2002. In absolute terms, there were two major waves. The first, in 1948–51, included the mass transfer of Jews from Muslim countries and of survivors of the World War II destruction of European Jewry. The second, since 1990, has been dominated by the major exodus from the former Soviet Union. Emigration from Israel reached an estimated 15–20 percent of the total volume of immigration—a comparatively low amount in comparison to other countries that have experienced major immigration.

Largely as a consequence of migration, the geographic distribution of the Jewish diaspora tended to become increasingly aligned with the more stable and affluent countries, those where the factors stimulating migration were weak. Hence, the potential for future Jewish migration would appear to be rapidly declining. A pro-

---

[29]Sergio DellaPergola, "The Global Context of Migration to Israel," in Elazar Leshem and Judith T. Shuval, eds., *Immigration to Israel: Sociological Persepctives* (New Brunswick, 1998), pp. 51–92.

FIGURE 1.   ALIYAH TO PALESTINE/ISRAEL, 1919–2002

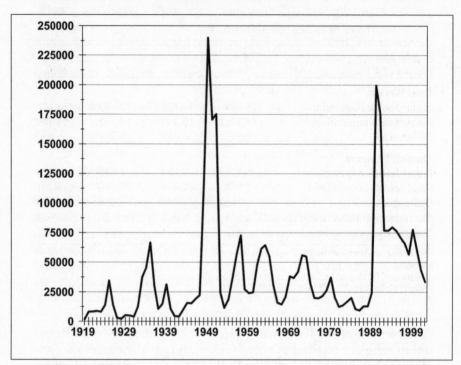

jection assuming continuation of the emigration rates that prevailed during the 1990s in the major current countries of residence of Jews predicts a sharp decline of net migration to Israel, down to a few thousand per year over the first half of the twenty-first century (see table 5). Nevertheless, past experience suggests that we cannot rule out the possibility that new disruptive factors might emerge at some future time in geographical areas that are currently attractive to diaspora Jewish communities. Also, emigration from Israel has been primarily related to long- and short-term economic trends in the country, which also are subject to change.[30]

As for the future of Palestinian migrations, the possibility of an influx of refugees and others into the areas now governed by the State of Israel and by the Palestinian Authority is a major topic

---

[30]Ibid.

TABLE 5. WORLD AND DIASPORA JEWISH POPULATION, BY MAIN FACTORS OF
CHANGE, ASSUMING MIGRATION AND FERTILITY RATES AS OF LATE
1990s, 2000–2050 (THOUSANDS)[a]

Region and Factors of Change	2000–2010	2010–2020	2020–2030	2030–2050
Total World				
Initial Jewish population	13,109	13,428	13,847	14,125
Final Jewish population	13,428	13,487	14,145	14,480
Difference	319	419	298	355
Thereof: Diaspora				
Initial Jewish population	8,235	7,863	7,619	7,250
Final Jewish population	7,863	7,619	7,250	6,251
Difference	−372	−244	−369	−999
Net migration balance with Israel	−105	−49	−28	−34
Natural and other change[b]	−267	−195	−341	−965

[a]Beginning of year estimates. Projection baseline: 1995. Minor discrepancies are due to rounding.
[b]Balance of births, deaths, and changes in Jewish identification.
Source: DellaPergola, Rebhun, and Tolts (2000).

of current political discourse.[31] Large-scale return of former Palestinian refugees to what is now Israel stands at the center of contention, but does not seem compatible with the Israeli position on a final peace agreement. The actual likelihood of such migration is not clear, especially if a plan of economic compensation as an alternative to "return" can be worked out in the framework of a political settlement. The demographic implications of a small-scale influx of Palestinian refugees to Israel will be discussed below. Arab emigration from Israel/Palestine has been occurring on a relatively minor scale, and it is hard to see how it might increase substantially, given the difficulty in locating possible countries of destination.

---

[31]Article 11 of UN General Assembly Resolution 194 of December 11, 1948, "resolves that the refugees wishing to return to their homes and wishing to live at peace with their neighbours should be permitted to do so at the earliest practicable date, and that compensation should be paid for the property of those choosing not to return and for loss of or damage to property which, under principles of international law or in equity, should be made good by the Governments or authorities responsible." See http://www.us-israel.org/jsource/UN/unga194.html.

Our main assumption in the following population projections is that the political and socioeconomic configuration of the global system will not undergo significant change, and that international migration will therefore not play as significant a role as other demographic determinants. Were major change to occur, of course, as in the recent case of the fall and dismemberment of the Soviet Union, international migration—including Jewish migration—would again reflect the pressures and opportunities created by the new circumstances.

Health and Longevity

Ironically—in the prevailing context of Arab-Jewish conflict—the two groups are genetically similar to each other. Recent research in population genetics based on DNA comparisons reveals that Sephardi (Mediterranean/Middle Eastern) and Ashkenazi (Central/Eastern European) Jews share common ancestries with Arab populations of the Middle East, especially the Palestinians.[32] This is so despite wide-ranging international migrations, physical separation, and inbreeding over the centuries.

Contemporary gaps in mortality rates between Jews and Arabs largely reflect cultural, socioeconomic, and environmental differences between the respective populations. Early in the twentieth century, mortality levels were extremely high among the native population in Palestine. Life expectancy at birth for Muslims during the 1930s was less than 40 years.[33] Health patterns in Palestine dramatically improved—beginning with a decline in infant mortality—following Jewish immigration and the superior infrastructures developed by the British administration. Immigrants brought with them higher standards of personal health and hygiene than existed among the veteran population, and they and the British introduced better medical and health training as well as new and more efficient health services.

[32]Michael Hammer et al., "Jewish and Middle Eastern non-Jewish populations share a common pool of Y-chromosome biallelic haplotypes," *Proceedings of the National Academy of Sciences of the USA* 97, June 6, 2000, pp. 6769–74; Almut Nebel et al., "The Y chromosome pool of Jews as part of the genetic landscape of the Middle East," *American Journal of Human Genetics* 69, Nov. 2001, pp. 1095–1112.

[33]Bachi, *Population of Israel,* p. 247.

Jewish immigrants arriving after 1948 from less developed countries—mainly in Asia and Africa—quickly closed the life-expectancy gap with the earlier immigrant communities. On average, life expectancy at birth among Israeli Jews steadily increased by about one additional year of life every five calendar years. Israeli Arabs, starting at a much lower life-expectancy level, followed suit, consistently narrowing the gap. Their infant mortality rates, while twice those of the Jews, are now the lowest in the Arab world, with the possible exception of Kuwait. The overall health of Arabs in the Palestinian Territories after 1967 improved as well, though at a slower pace. Recent measurements of life expectancy indicate smaller gaps between Jews and Arabs in Israel than between Arabs in Israel and those in the Palestinian Territories.

Over the second half of the twentieth century, the health and mortality patterns of Israel/Palestine placed it in the category of the more developed countries, and thus they are likely to share the latter's course of development. Perhaps the clearest indication of this, both for Israelis and Palestinians, is the narrow gap between male and female longevity. Examined in the context of other sociodemographic and economic indicators, it appears to result from especially low male mortality rather than high female mortality.[34]

It can be assumed that ongoing improvements in health will continue to produce declines in age-specific and in most cause-specific mortality rates. In our projections, initial life expectancies at birth for the Israeli population were set at the figures for the second half of the 1990s—76.3 years for Jewish men and 80.2 for Jewish women; 74.2 years for Arab men and 77.4 for Arab women. In the West Bank, the projection's initial life expectancies were 71.4 years for men and 75.5 for women; and in the Gaza area, 70.4 and 73.4, respectively. Our assumption in all the population projections that follow is that, as in the recent past, life expectancy at birth will continue to increase by about one year every five calendar years.

Marriage and Fertility

Reviewing recent demographic trends in Israel and Palestine, one is struck by two factors: (a) the persistence of high-to-

---

[34]United Nations Development Programme (UNDP), *Human Development Report 2001* (New York and Oxford, 2001), pp. 201–13.

moderately-high fertility levels over time; and (b) an apparent lack of consistency between measures of fertility and other key demographic indicators. By the mid-1990s, the Total Fertility Rate (TFR)[35] among Israeli Jews was 2.6 children, only moderately down from its highest level of 4 in 1951, and higher than among the total population of any other developed country (see figure 2). Overall Jewish fertility levels in Israel resulted from the convergence of a significant lowering of the fertility of immigrants from Asia and Africa, on the one hand, and measurable increases among immigrants from Europe and America, on the other.

The TFR among Israel's Christian Arabs was nearly the same as that of the Jews, and the TFR of Israeli Druze was quickly converging at the same level. Israel's Muslim population, which had a TFR of nearly 10 during the 1960s, declined to slightly above 4.5 by the mid-1980s, and stayed steady at that level thereafter. Within this Muslim population, the TFR of Bedouins—an originally nomadic group now increasingly relocating to permanent settlements, mostly in Israel's Southern District (the Negev)—is still estimated at above 10 by Israel's Central Bureau of Statistics, probably the highest fertility currently on record worldwide. Interestingly, during the 1990s, Israel's Jews maintained stable TFRs notwithstanding declining propensities to marry, and Israeli Muslims did the same in spite of rising propensities to marry.[36]

In the Palestinian Territories, TFR was estimated in 1995 at 5.4 in the West Bank and 7.4 in the Gaza area—the latter figure one of the highest on record internationally. A 1997 estimate pointed to TFRs of 5.6 in the West Bank and 6.9 in Gaza, and an estimate for 1997–99 suggested some fertility decline, to 4.5 in the West Bank and 5.4 in Gaza.[37]

While within a general theory of demographic transition the levels of mortality, fertility, and socioeconomic development tend to form one coherent cluster, this has not necessarily been the case for the Jewish and Muslim populations of Israel and the Palestin-

---

[35]The TFR is a measure of the number of children expected on average, assuming indefinite continuation of currently observed age-specific fertility levels.

[36]Sergio DellaPergola, "Demographic Changes in Israel in the Early 1990s," in Y. Kop, ed., *Israel Social Services, 1992–93* (Jerusalem, 1993), pp. 57–115.

[37]All the data come from the Palestinian Central Bureau of Statistics. See http:/pcbs2.org/english/populati/tables5.htm; and http://www.pcbs.org/inside/selcts.htm.

ian Territories. In other words, the Israeli and Palestinian societies are demographically unlike other communities that share roughly the same fertility patterns.

Table 6 exemplifies the respective fertility levels in 1995–2000

FIGURE 2.　TOTAL FERTILITY RATES IN ISRAEL (JEWS, MUSLIMS, CHRISTIANS, DRUZE) AND IN PALESTINIAN TERRITORIES, 1949–2001

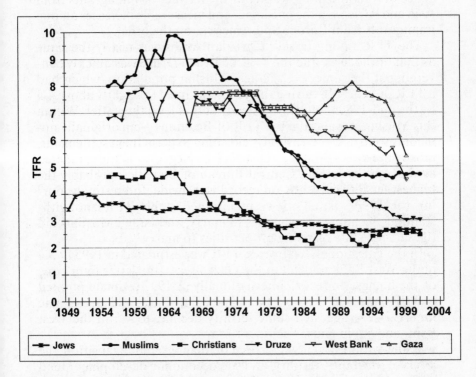

and matches them with similar fertility levels observed among other contemporary populations worldwide. The Israeli Jewish TFR was matched by similar levels in 20 other countries; the Israeli Muslim TFR had 10 matches worldwide; the West Bank's TFR had 12 matches; and Gaza's TFR had 6. But a comparison of Israeli and Palestinian infant mortality rates with the average rates in these matching countries reveals distinctly higher levels among the latter: matched countries had infant mortality rates three to seven times higher, on average, than the respective Israeli/Palestinian rates. Conversely, a comparison of GNP per capita shows levels two to ten times higher in Israel/Palestine than in the matched countries.[38]

If one views fertility levels as the product, or at least a correlate,

TABLE 6.   SELECTED DEMOGRAPHIC AND SOCIOECONOMIC CHARACTERISTICS,
ISRAEL JEWS AND MUSLIMS, PALESTINIAN TERRITORIES, AND
MATCHED COUNTRIES, 1995-2000

Country	TFR	TFR[a]	Infant Mortality[a]	GNP per capita US$[a]
Israel Jews	**2.6**	**2.62**	**5.0**	**17,000[b]**
Matched countries[c]	2.4–2.8	2.62	26.1	3,164
Ratio Israel Jews/Matched		1.00	0.19	5.37
No. of countries		20	20	16
Israel Muslims	**4.7**	**4.67**	**9.2**	**8,000[b]**
Matched countries[d]	4.5–4.9	4.67	65.5	758
Ratio Israel Muslim/Matched		1.00	0.14	10.43
No. of countries		10	10	10
West Bank	**5.4**	**5.44**	**25.5**	**1,618**
Matched countries[e]	5.2–5.6	5.40	78.4	891
Ratio West Bank/Matched		1.01	0.33	2.34
No. of countries		12	12	11
Gaza	**7.4**	**7.41**	**30.2**	**1,468**
Matched countries[f]	7.0+	7.36	115.9	284
Ratio Gaza/Matched		1.01	0.26	5.16
No. of countries		6	6	5

[a]Average of selected countries.
[b]Author's rough estimates.
[c]Albania, Argentina, Bahamas, Bahrain, Brunei, Chile, Colombia, Costa Rica, French Polynesia, Guyana, Jamaica, Mexico, Mongolia, New Caledonia, Panama, St. Lucia, Turkey, Uruguay, Uzbekistan, Vietnam.
[d]Ghana, Jordan, Kenya, Lesotho, Nepal, Papua New Guinea, Samoa, Sudan, Swaziland, Vanuatu.
[e]Bhutan, Cambodia, Central Africa, Comoros, Gabon, Iraq, Laos, Namibia, Pakistan, Senegal, Solomon Isl., Tanzania.
[f]Angola, Mali, Niger, Somalia, Uganda, Yemen.
Sources: Israel Central Bureau of Statistics (2001); Palestinian Central Bureau of Statistics (1997, 1998); United Nations (2001); Population Reference Bureau (2001).

---

[38]Separate income figures for Israeli Jews and Arabs are the author's estimates, based on Israel Central Bureau of Statistics, *Statistical Abstract of Israel* (Jerusalem, 2001). Figures

of several other variables—such as health patterns and socioeconomic development—recent TFRs in Israel and Palestine are definitely out of the range of behaviors normally observed in the international community. Such an intriguing difference can be described as an excess of fertility over the average fertility level of those countries whose other demographic characteristics are comparable.

The apparently anomalous fertility patterns of Israelis and Palestinians can only be explained by a rare combination of factors that counteract the tendencies to limit family size that characterize modern societies.[39]

First, strong pronatalist attitudes are rooted in, or derived from, religious and cultural traditions shared by the vast majority of the population, both Jewish and Muslim.[40] Traditional moral imperatives, widespread conventions, and, last but not least, the competitive logic of political-military conflict, have encouraged fami-

---

for the Palestinian Territories were adapted by the author based on Palestinian Central Bureau of Statistics, *Labor Force Survey, Annual Report* (Ramallah, 1998).

[39]Sergio DellaPergola, "Aspects socio-démographiques de l'intégration des minorités en Israël: convergences ou divergences?" in J.L. Rallu, J. Courbage, and V. Piché, eds., *Old and New Minorities—Anciennes et nouvelles minorités* (Paris, 1997), pp. 229–50; DellaPergola, "Jerusalem's Population, 1995–2020: Demography, Multiculturalism and Urban Policies," *European Journal of Population* 17, Jan. 2001, pp. 165–99; Philippe Fargues, "Protracted National Conflict and Fertility Change: Palestinians and Israelis in the Twentieth Century," *Population and Development Review* 26, 2000, pp. 441–82.

[40]For analyses and outlooks on Jewish fertility trends see Sergio DellaPergola, "Some Effects of Religion on Population Trends," *Pro Mundi Vita Studies* 5, 1988, pp. 40–48; Dov Friedlander and Carol Feldmann, "The Modern Shift to Below-Replacement Fertility: Has Israel's Population Joined the Process?" *Population Studies* 47, 1993, pp. 295–306; Ilana Ziegler, "Family Growth in Israel and the 'Critical Child' " (Ph.D. diss., The Hebrew University of Jerusalem, 1995); Barbara S. Okun, "Religiosity and Contraceptive Method Choice: The Jewish Population of Israel," *European Journal of Population* 16, 2000, pp. 109–32. For the Palestinian side see Dov Friedlander, Zvi Eisenbach, and Calvin Goldscheider, "Modernization Patterns and Fertility Change: The Arab Populations of Israel and the Israel-Administered Territories," *Population Studies* 33, 1979, pp. 239–54; A.G. Hill, "The Palestinian Population of the Middle East," *Population and Development Review* 9, 1983, pp. 293–316; Hasan Abu Libdeh, Geir Ovensen, and Helge Brunborg, "Population Characteristics and Trends," in M. Heiberg and G. Ovensen, eds., *Palestinian Society in Gaza, West Bank and Arab Jerusalem: A Survey of Living Conditions* (Oslo, 1993), pp. 35–97; and Palestinian Central Bureau of Statistics, *The Demographic Survey in the West Bank and Gaza* (Ramallah, 1997). For data on both sides see Eric Peritz and Mario Baras, *Studies in the Fertility of Israel* (Jerusalem, 1992); Fargues, "Protracted National Conflict and Fertility Change"; and Dov Friedlander, "Fertility in Israel: Is the Transition to Replacement Level in Sight?" in United Nations Secretariat, Division of Economic and Social Affairs, Population Division, *Expert Group Meeting on Completing the Fertility Transition* (New York, 2002).

lies—Jewish, and, even more so, Muslim—to have more children.[41] Among the Muslims, in fact—and this holds for the more traditional sectors of the Jewish population as well—women were often discouraged from seeking employment and career rewards, and pushed toward early marriage and reproduction.

Second, Israel's relative economic well-being provides the means for both Jews and Arabs to afford more children, and national policies encourage this through a complex of public incentives and constraints. The Israeli household's comparatively favorable situation enables accumulation of income, durable goods, and other resources, thus allowing Israelis to "purchase" large families. Furthermore, Israel's pronatalist policies include a package of mother-child allowances, extensive public-educational facilities (including tax-supported preschool), and other provisions to ease the situation of working women. This is part of a broader system of transfer payments, as appropriate to a modern welfare state. Israel has also developed a well-articulated and universally accessible public-health system, consistent with its identity as a developed society. Other things being equal, good healthcare for adults and children allows for prolonged and fecund reproductive spans, translating into more children.

The Israeli national commitment to pronatalism operates across the board, devoid of any ethnoreligious bias that might promote differential growth of specific population groups. For example, legislation enacted in Israel in 2000 strongly increased child allowances for the fifth child and above. By that provision, about 40 percent of child-allowance benefits went to the families of Israeli Arab newborns, at a time when Israeli Arabs constituted only about 20 percent of the Israeli population (not including the Palestinian territories).[42] Another mechanism indirectly affecting fertility has been a system of public subventions

---

[41]What the actual effect might be of the rhetoric of the "war of cradles" is not easily quantifiable. See Mati Steinberg, "The Demographic Dimension of the Struggle With Israel As Seen by the PLO," *Jerusalem Journal of International Relations*, 11, 1989, pp. 27–51; and Youssef Courbage, "Reshuffling the Demographic Cards in Israel/Palestine," *Journal of Palestine Studies* 28, 1999, pp. 21–39.

[42]The package of economic reforms approved by the Israeli Knesset in May 2003 included a significant cut in child allowances and a provision for gradual downward equalization of the amounts paid to each successive child. See Zvi Zarhiah, "Gam vikuhim bakoalitzia 'ikvu et hahatzba'ah," *Haaretz,* May 29, 2003.

for education and housing channeled through particular ethnoreligious communities rather than directly to individuals. By
lowering the cost of child rearing for designated subpopulations,
these provisions tend to support the birthrates and higher fertility of these groups.

The combined impact of these pronatalist factors apparently
outweigh the effects of the considerable improvement in educational attainment of both Jewish and Arab women, a trend that,
in other modern societies, exerts a rationalizing influence toward
smaller and more efficiently planned families. One can also con-
jecture that prolonged years of religious education for many men
and women in Israel and Palestine—something rare in Western
countries—reinforce the religiocultural influences supportive of
larger families. Indeed, even the secular education given women
may, in a way, promote fertility by enabling the women to find employment, thus increasing family incomes and making larger families more affordable.

Looking to the future, the proven resilience of religiocultural
patterns and of derived political mechanisms underlying fertility
suggest that changes in fertility levels will be relatively slow. Table
7 indicates several possible fertility scenarios designated for the
population projections, which are discussed below. For Israel's
Jewish population, the possibilities are either continuation, or
moderate declines or increases, of the currently observed TFR levels. Hypothesized changes would stem from either a rise or decline
in current fertility patterns, or else compositional changes within
the Jewish population by subpopulations whose fertility behaviors
have been widely at variance. In this connection it is important to
note that Jewish fertility in fact ranges from very high among the
more religiously oriented, to rather low among the more secular
sections of society, including some of the recent immigrants from
the former Soviet Union.[43] The latter, however, are quickly catch-
ing up to the norms of veteran Jewish Israelis.

Fertility scenarios for Palestinians, whether in Israel or in the
West Bank and Gaza, encompass a broader range of variation. One
possibility would be a gradual convergence of Palestinians to the

---

[43]A study of demographic differentials in Jerusalem during the mid-1990s estimated the
range of variation of Jewish TFRs between 6.5 in the more religious neighborhoods and
1.4 in the least religious. See DellaPergola, "Jerusalem's Population."

TABLE 7. FERTILITY ASSUMPTIONS FOR POPULATION PROJECTIONS, BY MAJOR
ETHNORELIGIOUS ORIGINS AND TERRITORIAL DIVISIONS, ISRAEL AND
PALESTINE, 2000–2050

Population	TFR 2000	High	Medium	Low
Jews	2.6	2.9 instant	As in 2000	2.1 instant
Non-Jewish fringe	1.9	2.9 instant	2.4 instant	As in 2000
Israel Arabs	4.0	As in 2000	2.6 by 2050	2.6 instant
West Bank	5.4	As in 2000	2.6 by 2050	2.6 instant
Gaza	7.4	As in 2000	2.6 by 2050	2.6 instant

Source: S. DellaPergola, The Hebrew University of Jerusalem.

fertility standards of the Jewish population. This was, in fact, one
of the hypotheses typically suggested in previous population projections (see below), but it has never, to this point, materialized.
Here, as a medium scenario, the process of adaptation to the Israeli
Jewish norm is hypothesized to occur slowly, over a period of 50
years. A high scenario would consider uninterrupted continuation
of current fertility levels. Although apparently untenable on conventional theoretical grounds, such a scenario corresponds to the
actual situation over the last 20 years among large sections of the
Palestinian constituency, and it should not necessarily be ruled out.
A low scenario—though quite untenable—is also suggested: the
instant convergence of Palestinian TFRs to the level of Israeli Jews.
The suggested high-low range is thus not a prediction of things to
come, but is rather intended to create a conceivable maximum-
minimum range of projected population sizes for further discussion.

POPULATION PROJECTIONS, 2000–2050

Earlier Experiences with Population Projections

Before embarking on a new round of population projections for
Israel and the Palestinian Territories, it may be useful briefly to review the assumptions and predictive ability of such attempts in the
past. As early as the 1920s and 1930s, in the context of debates
about the political future of post-Mandatory Palestine, scholars
and British government administrators began elaborating various
population scenarios and discussing the emerging policy implica-

tions.[44] Nearly all of these efforts shared three assumptions: that population change reflects the variable levels of two leading determinants—fertility and international migration; that differential growth of various ethnoreligious sectors tends to generate significant changes in population size and composition, which, in turn have far-reaching political implications for the present and future prospects of the region; and that there is some "feedback" between the size of population achieved and the additional population growth that the emerging socioeconomic situation will make possible.

Rather than review the successes or failures of past analysts in predicting population trends, it is interesting to note some of their typical analytic foci. The crucial role of migration in generating long-term consequences for population growth was almost universally recognized, and quite certainly led the British authorities to introduce stringent limitations on Jewish immigration during the last years of the Mandate.

Most population scenarios focused on fixed amounts of immigration, ranging from nil to several tens of thousands a year. The different amounts reflected very different opinions about the potential and resilience of Jewish migration, from very low to moderately high—the emphasis being on migration momentum as such, rather than on a detailed consideration of what forces determine migration. There was almost no attempt to view international migration as powerfully fluctuating in response to the variable intensity of determinants in the countries of origin and destination—as, indeed, has been powerfully demonstrated by the Jewish experience over the past 120 years. Only one such attempt proved accurate, predicting the shift from an Arab to a Jewish majority in Palestine's total population before 1960, which is what ac-

---

[44]Liebmann Hersch, "La population de la Palestine et les perspectives du Sionisme," *Metron* 7, 1928, pp. 115–36; Palestine Royal Commission, *Report,* pp. 280–82; Helmut Mühsam, "Bevölkerungsprobleme Palästinas," *Metron* 13, 1938, pp. 175–201; Roberto Bachi, "Marriage and Fertility in the Various Sections of the Jewish Population and Their Influence on its Future," in D. Gurevich, A. Geertz, and R. Bachi, *The Jewish Population of Palestine* (Jerusalem, 1944), pp. 245–48 (Hebrew); Frank W. Notestein and Ernest Jurkat, "Population Problems of Palestine," *Milbank Memorial Fund Quarterly* 23, 1945, pp. 307–52. Since the 1967 war, there has been renewed emphasis among Israeli scholars on population projections. See Bachi, *The Population of Israel;* Dov Friedlander and Calvin Goldscheider, *The Population of Israel* (New York, 1979), pp. 189–217; and U.O. Schmelz, *World Jewish Population—Regional Estimates and Projections* (Jerusalem, 1981).

tually happened.[45] Another element virtually ignored in past population projections was large-scale emigration, which, as noted, crucially contributed to the post-1948 establishment of a Jewish majority.

With regard to fertility assumptions, the two main challenges were correctly predicting the main changes in fertility levels and discerning the patterns of convergence or divergence between different subpopulations. Generally, assumptions about moderate change better complied with reality than assumptions of rapid change. The predominant assumption of eventual convergence of Muslims to the lower Jewish levels of fertility did not materialize, resulting in significant underestimates of the Arab subpopulation in most projections. Nor did high Muslim fertility levels remain unchanged, as was assumed in several other population projections. Fertility of different Jewish immigrant groups converged more rapidly than was often assumed, while the contrary occurred to fertility levels of Palestinian Arabs in the State of Israel as compared to those in the West Bank and Gaza. Overall—considering the techniques and data available at the time—these earlier attempts to project Palestine's population provide a wealth of relevant and not-entirely-superseded insights. The most interesting projections were those that carefully considered population trends prevailing in the Jewish diaspora as a predicting factor in future demographic changes in Palestine/Israel, and appropriately considered age composition as a crucial intervening factor in population movements.

What demographers consistently did not—indeed could not—achieve was the prediction of macroscopic political events, such as World War II, the Shoah, the 1948 Arab-Israeli war, or the dissolution of the Soviet Union. The demographic consequences of these events were crucial elements in the population equation of the Middle East. This clearly points to the volatility of sociodemographic processes in unstable political environments—such as Israel and Palestine—and their dependence on a much broader range of geopolitical and cultural factors than is the case in the conventional experience of most other populations.

---

[45]Mühsam, "Bevölkerungsprobleme Palästinas."

Contemporary Population Projections

Attempts to project the population of Israel/Palestine are routinely carried out by international organizations,[46] national central statistical agencies,[47] and independent investigators.[48] These often differ over definitions of the territorial units and/or time frames for analysis, and may also reflect the analysts' varying political approaches.[49]

In any case, they generally agree in assuming a continuation of current trends, with higher and lower scenarios reflecting different assumptions about the likelihood of fertility decline in Israel and the Palestinian Territories, and about future immigration. These assumptions can sometimes be questioned. For example, the UN Population Division projects an eventual convergence between Jewish and Arab fertility rates at or below replacement level, largely on the basis of expected rising levels of education among the Palestinians. But, as noted above, ideological factors can render the relationship between education and rate of population growth rather tricky in Israel and Palestine, making it difficult to infer whether and how prospective changes in educational attainment affect fertility levels and population trends.[50]

Nevertheless, the majority of the recent population projections do not give a sense of a "war of data." On the contrary, their findings tend in the same overall direction. Results obtained by dif-

---

[46]United Nations, *World Population Prospects: The 2000 Revision—Highlights* (New York, 2001); Population Reference Bureau, *2000 World Population Data Sheet of the Population Reference Bureau* (Washington, D.C., 2001); World Bank, *World Development Report 2000/2001* (Washington, D.C., 2000).

[47]Israel Central Bureau of Statistics, *Population, Demography and Households 1999* (Jerusalem, 2001); Palestinian Central Bureau of Statistics, *Population in the Palestinian Territory, 1997–2025* (Ramallah, 1999).

[48]Yousef Courbage, *Nouveaux horizons démographiques en Mediterranée* (Paris, 1999); idem, "Israël et Palestine: combien d'hommes demain?" *Population & Sociétés* 362, 2000; Fargues, "Protracted National Conflict"; DellaPergola, Rebhun, and Tolts, "Prospecting the Jewish Future"; DellaPergola and Rebhun, "Projecting a Rare Population: World Jews 2000–2080," paper presented at Population Association of America, Washington, D.C., 2001.

[49]One example is whether to include East Jerusalem in the projections for Israel or for the West Bank. In this paper, all of Jerusalem is computed together with Israel.

[50]One example of multistate population projections is in Anne Goujon, *Population and Education Prospects in the Western Mediterranean Region (Jordan, Lebanon, Syria, the West Bank and the Gaza Strip)* (Laxenburg, 1997).

ferent researchers—despite their possibly warring political allegiances—point, first, to rapid population growth, and, second, to significant differences in the scenarios for Jews and Arabs in Israel/Palestine.[51]

Expected Population Size

We now proceed to present the results of our own analysis of the expected consequences of current population trends in Israel and Palestine. Tables 8–13 and figure 3 show selected findings from a new set of projections for the period 2000–2050.[52] The data emphasize the possible implications of variations in current fertility levels, with the role of international migration ignored or assumed to operate at moderate and declining levels. As noted above, fertility assumptions tend to create a range between minimum and maximum likely scenarios. The figures for Israel are based on Central Bureau of Statistics projections until 2020. All figures for the Palestinian Territories, as well as the 2050 projections for Israel, derive from my own work.[53]

The category "non-Jewish fringe" in the tables represents non-Jews who are mostly part of immigrant Jewish nuclear families from the former Soviet Union, and are therefore socially integrated within the Jewish section of Israeli society.[54] Together, Jews and the associated "fringe" form an "Enlarged Jewish Population." Nearly all other non-Jewish citizens in Israel, whether Muslims or Christians, are Palestinian Arabs from the point of view of their national cultural identity. The Druze minority is also included in this group for the purpose of data analysis. All the inhabitants of the West Bank and Gaza are Palestinian Arabs with the exception of the Jewish residents of these areas, who are included in Israel's Jewish population data. The data are presented in a way that allows for

---

[51]For a typical example of a recent projection that assumed faster fertility decline than actually occurred see Israel Central Bureau of Statistics, *Projections of Population in Israel up to 2003 based on the Population in 1993* (Jerusalem, 1995). The TFRs expected by 2003 were 2.3 for Jews and 3.7 for Moslems, as compared to actual TFRs of 2.6 and 4.7, respectively, in 2001.

[52]The baseline for all projections is end-1995 data and estimates.

[53]I take full responsibility for all the data presented hereafter.

[54]At the end of 2001, this group comprised 231,000 persons with "religion undeclared" plus 25,000 "non-Arab Christians."

modular reconstruction and comparisons of the main ethnoreligious (Jews vs. Palestinians) or territorial (Israel vs. Palestinian Territories) aggregates.[55]

Table 8 shows the alternative population-projection scenarios for the different Jewish and Arab subpopulations in Israel and Palestine between 2000 and 2050. The 2000 medium figure includes about 9.3 million people — 6.3 million in Israel (including East Jerusalem, the Golan Heights, and the Israeli inhabitants of the West Bank and Gaza), and about 3 million in the Palestinian Territories. By 2020, the total population would range between 12.1 and 15.6 million, with a medium projection of 14.4 million. The Jewish population (enlarged to include the non-Jewish "fringe") would range between 6.3 and 6.9 million, as part of a total State of Israel population of 8.2–9.0 million. The Palestinian Territories would reach a population ranging between 4.0 and 6.6 million,[56] and, with the addition of Israel's Arabs, the total Palestinian population would range between 5.8 and 8.7 million.

By 2050, according to the same assumptions, the following ranges would obtain: for the enlarged Jewish population, 7.3–10.4 million with a medium value of 8.8 million; for the State of Israel's total population, including both Jews and Arabs, 9.4–14.8 million with a medium value of 11.9 million; for the total of the Palestinian Territories, 6.0–21.7 million (half in the West Bank and half in Gaza) with a medium value of 11.6 million; and for the total Palestinian population in Israel and the Territories, 8.1–26.1 million with a medium value of 14.7 million. The total population of Israel and Palestine would thus range between 15.4 and 36.5 million with a medium value of 23.5 million.

Admittedly, some of these figures stagger the imagination — especially the higher scenarios for 2050. In fact, both the high and the low scenarios require quite extreme assumptions about the future of current fertility levels — indefinite continuation, on the one hand, and instant reduction, on the other. Medium scenarios, in contrast, assume a blend of demographic transformations that

---

[55]The projections do not include the temporary resident foreign workers and their families, who totaled about 200,000–250,000 in 2000.

[56]The medium projections of the Palestinian Central Bureau of Statistics (1999) fairly match our independently obtained results and fall between our high and medium projections.

TABLE 8. POPULATION OF ISRAEL AND PALESTINE, BY MAJOR ETHNORELIGIOUS AND TERRITORIAL DIVISIONS, 2000–2050 (VARIOUS PROJECTIONS, THOUSANDS)

Year and Projection	Jews	Non-Jewish Fringe	Total Enlarged Jewish	Israel Arabs	Total Israel	West Bank	Gaza	Total Palestinian Territories	Total Palestinians	Grand Total
	(a)	(b)	(c)=(a)+(b)	(d)	(e)=(c)+(d)	(f)	(g)	(h)=(f)+(g)	(i)=(d)+(h)	(j)=(e)+(h)
										(j)=(c)+(i)
2000										
High	5,000	201	5,201	1,185	6,386	1,878	1,147	3,024	4,209	9,410
Medium	4,969	199	5,168	1,178	6,346	1,845	1,128	2,973	4,151	9,319
Low	4,938	197	5,135	1,171	6,306	1,703	993	2,696	3,867	9,002
2010										
High	5,784	281	6,065	1,574	7,639	2,676	1,776	4,452	6,026	12,091
Medium	5,689	291	5,980	1,555	7,535	2,518	1,645	4,163	5,718	11,698
Low	5,574	236	5,810	1,535	7,346	2,049	1,191	3,240	4,775	10,586
2020										
High	6,521	381	6,902	2,092	8,994	3,789	2,782	6,570	8,662	15,564
Medium	6,368	329	6,697	1,976	8,673	3,338	2,342	5,680	7,656	14,353
Low	6,057	239	6,296	1,855	8,151	2,492	1,483	3,975	5,830	12,126
2050										
High	9,741	650	10,391	4,419	14,810	10826	10829	21,655	26,074	36,465
Medium	8,230	550	8,780	3,121	11,901	6,414	5,146	11,560	14,681	23,461
Low	6,873	450	7,323	2,065	9,388	3,752	2,267	6,019	8,084	15,407

Source: S. DellaPergola, The Hebrew University of Jerusalem.

better comply with the demographic experience of the last 50 years in Israel and Palestine. The question still awaiting an answer is why, and under what conditions, a significant departure from the current trends might occur. At the same time, the finding that, under medium assumptions, the total population of Israel/Palestine might increase by about 5 million between 2000 and 2020 stands to reason, and calls for further elaboration.

We now turn to a more detailed examination of some of the main findings of these projections.

Territorial Distribution

One key issue concerns the implications of population growth for population densities, the environment, and natural resources. Such concerns are hardly new, as the question of what might be

Palestine's maximum "economic capability" or "carrying capacity" constituted one of the main themes in the political debate during the British Mandate.[57]

In the 1930s, political leaders and population experts wildly underestimated future population growth and typically suggested "high" scenarios not much above 2 million. The current (2003) total population of roughly 10 million for the same area clearly indicates how technological advances and changes in political assumptions have drastically overturned the opinions of 70 years ago.[58] By the same token, one may today ask similar questions about Palestine's maximum possible population. While the determination of such a maximum would seem necessary given the area's scarcity of such essential resources as drinkable water, a final answer might depend on the nature of future technological development.

In table 9, the population figures presented in table 8 are translated into current and expected population densities per km^2. Figure 3 portrays the expected development of population densities in Israel and Palestine against the background of selected examples of contemporary countries and large metropolitan areas.

In 2001, Israel's population density stood at 294 per km^2—a comparatively high level that is also met in several Western European countries and in the European part of Turkey. The countrywide average density, though, may be misleading because of the very unequal patterns of population distribution over Israeli territory. Population densities ranged between a high of 6,788 per km^2 in the Tel Aviv District, wholly occupied by the central part of the Greater Tel Aviv metropolitan area, and 39 per km^2 in the Beersheba Subdistrict, which includes large tracts of arid desert land and represents 58 percent of Israel's total territory. Leaving out the Beersheba Subdistrict, Israel's population density was 664 per km^2.[59]

---

[57]Palestine Royal Commission, *Report;* Friedlander and Goldscheider, *Population of Israel;* Ilan Troen, "Calculating the 'Economic Absorptive Capacity' of Palestine: A Study of the Political Use of Scientific Research," *Contemporary Jewry* 10, 1989, pp. 19–38.

[58]A population capability of 10 million on both sides of the Jordan River was suggested by Zionist leaders David Ben-Gurion and Yitzhak Ben-Zvi in 1918, in a statement clearly influenced by ideological motives and political hopes. Ben-Gurion and Ben-Zvi, *Eretz Israel in the Past and in the Present*, trans. from Yiddish by D. Niv (Jerusalem, 1979).

[59]Central Bureau of Statistics, *Statistical Abstract of Israel* 53, 2002, table 2.4. The Beersheba Subdistrict comprises 12,946 of Israel's total 21,671 km^2 of land surface.

TABLE 9. POPULATION PER KM², ISRAEL AND PALESTINE, 2000–2050
(VARIOUS PROJECTIONS)

Year and Projection	Total Israel	West Bank	Gaza	Total Palestinian Territories	Grand Total
2000					
High	295	341	3,034	514	341
Medium	293	335	2,984	505	338
Low	291	309	2,627	458	327
2010					
High	352	486	4,698	757	439
Medium	348	457	4,352	708	425
Low	339	372	3,151	551	384
2020					
High	415	688	7,360	1,117	565
Medium	400	606	6,196	965	521
Low	376	453	3,923	676	440
2050					
High	683	1,966	28,648	3,680	1,323
Medium	549	1,165	13,614	1,965	851
Low	433	681	5,997	1,023	559

Source: S. DellaPergola, The Hebrew University of Jerusalem

Regarding the Palestinian Territories, the West Bank's initial population density matches the Israeli countrywide average. Despite steady growth, it remains within the known range of contemporary societies. The Gaza area, however, has a density of about 3,000 people per km². Significantly higher population densities were recently observed in cities such as Hong Kong and Singapore, but the level of socioeconomic development there was significantly more advanced than in Gaza. Prospectively, the medium and high scenarios for Gaza lead to densities comparable only to the densest of contemporary large urban areas.

It is not the outcome that is impossibly high, but rather the clear imbalance between population size and the available urban infrastructure. A population density like that in the city of Paris — about 20,000 per km², similar to the maximum expected in the Gaza area — is conceivable in the context of a leading capital city founded on a developed urban and highly technological infra-

FIGURE 3.   POPULATION DENSITIES PER KM^2 IN ISRAEL, WEST BANK, AND
GAZA, 2000–2050

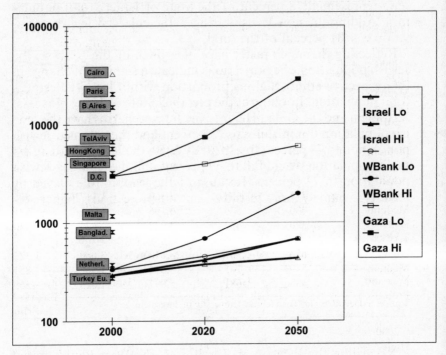

structure, and having at its disposal a large national hinterland. These conditions obviously do not apply to Gaza at present, nor are they likely to come into existence in the near future. The scenario of very high population densities extending over Gaza's 378 km^2 of territory and the excruciating social problems and high human costs involved deserve serious reflection.

Ethnoreligious Population Composition

A second issue of major import concerns the implications of population trends for the ethnoreligious population balance in Israel and Palestine. Table 10 presents the expected percentage of Jews out of total population according to different projection scenarios, different territorial divisions in the State of Israel alone or the whole of Israel and the Palestinian Territories, and different definitions of the Jewish population—the latter either including or excluding non-Jewish members of Jewish households. In 2000, Jews represented 78 percent of the State of Israel's total population. Adding the non-Jewish "fringe," the enlarged Jewish population was 81 percent of the total.

Reflecting the much faster pace of growth of the Arab vs. the Jewish population, the projections indicate a significant change in the respective ethnoreligious proportion within Israel/Palestine's total population. Looking at the pre-1967 State of Israel plus East Jerusalem and the Golan Heights, medium scenarios have the Jewish population diminishing to 73 percent and the enlarged Jewish population to 77 percent, by 2020. By 2050, the Jewish share of Israel's population would fall to 69 percent and the enlarged Jewish population to 74 percent. Because of the leading role played by fertility—namely Arab fertility—in our projections, higher sce-

TABLE 10. PERCENT OF JEWS AMONG ISRAEL AND PALESTINE TOTAL
POPULATION, 2000–2050 (VARIOUS SCENARIOS)

Year and Projection	Israel		Israel and Territories	
	Jewish	Enlarged Jewish[a]	Jewish	Enlarged Jewish[a]
2000				
High	78.3	81.4	53.1	55.3
Medium	78.3	81.4	53.3	55.5
Low	78.3	81.4	54.9	57.0
2010				
High	75.7	79.4	47.8	50.2
Medium	75.5	79.4	48.6	51.1
Low	75.9	79.1	52.7	54.9
2020				
High	72.5	76.7	41.9	44.3
Medium	73.4	77.2	44.4	46.7
Low	74.3	77.2	50.0	51.9
2050				
High	65.8	70.2	26.7	28.5
Medium	69.2	73.8	35.1	37.4
Low	73.2	78.0	44.6	47.5

[a]Including non-Jewish members in Jewish households (column b in Table 8).
Source: S. DellaPergola, The Hebrew University of Jerusalem

narios produce lower percentages of Jews, and lower scenarios produce higher percentages.

Within Israel's territorial framework (basically without the West Bank and Gaza occupied in 1967), a Jewish majority appears to be firmly established at least until the mid-twenty-first century. However, an emerging Israeli Arab minority in the range of 30 percent calls to mind international comparisons with other ethnically split societies. In the case of Cyprus, which went through bitter conflict and eventually a territorial and political split, the minority group was far smaller—the ethnic balance during the 1960s was 82 percent Greek vs. 18 percent Turkish.[60] Other recent examples of ethnically split societies can be found in most of the republics that constituted the former Yugoslavia. In these cases, too, ethnic cleavages have triggered harsh struggles.

Looking now at the grand total of Israel plus the Palestinian Territories in 2000, there was a scant Jewish majority of 53 percent (55 percent using the enlarged definition of Jewish population). According to the medium projections, this majority will be gone before 2010 or very soon thereafter (whether according to the strictly Jewish or the enlarged population definition). By 2020, Jews would constitute 44–47 percent of the total population of Palestine, and by 2050 their share might further diminish to 35–37 percent—reverting to a situation very similar to the Jewish-Arab population division in the mid-1940s, toward the end of the British Mandate.

Age Composition

Further analysis of the projected results by major age groups sharpens the findings and their implications. Age composition obviously constitutes not only one crucial result of demographic change, but also operates as a critical mediating variable in other processes, not all of them demographic.

For example, age composition is intimately linked with political memory. As noted above, one of the decisive events that shaped the current geopolitics of the Middle East was the war of June 1967

---

[60]According to the 1960 census, the share of Greeks within the total population in the different districts of Cyprus varied between a maximum of 86.4 percent and a minimum of 75.6 percent. See Cyprus Republic, *Summary of Main Statistical Data* (Nicosia, 1964).

and the subsequent Israeli occupation of the Palestinian Territories. A simple calculation of the percent of current population that lived in Israel or Palestine at that date reveals that it barely reaches 25 percent on both sides. This low proportion of actual witnesses to the events of 1967 reflects the size of contemporary Jewish and Palestinian population cohorts born after that date, as well as the volume of subsequent Jewish immigration. In other words, some three out of four actors and spectators in the current conflict did not directly experience one of its most crucial developments, and thus appear to be enacting roles they have learned through mediating sources of information—with intriguing consequences for their understanding of facts, underlying causes, and practical implications.

Table 11 presents current and expected population composition by age. Since overall population distribution was significantly affected by high, or comparatively high, fertility levels in the past, children and young adults tended to outnumber older adults and the elderly, whose share within the total population was comparatively low. Among Jews, past large-scale immigration determined peculiar concentrations of younger adults at the time of major migration waves. These tended to move throughout the age ladder, determining a unique configuration of sudden changes in the size of successive birth cohorts. The future rhythm of change in the size of specific age groups will continue to reflect these peculiarities, and, within each ten-year time span, will tend to be quite unequal for different age groups. Table 11, confined to the medium projections, assumes overall stability or moderation in fertility levels, and therefore foreshadows a gradual process of population aging through slower growth of the younger age groups and faster growth of the elderly.

Table 12 shows percentages of Jews (by both the strictly Jewish and the enlarged definitions) among the total population of different age groups within the State of Israel, and in the grand total of Israel plus the Palestinian Territories. Reflecting the higher fertility of Palestinians, the Jewish share of total population is systematically smaller at the younger than at the older end of the age distribution. In turn, percentages of Jews among the younger age groups at one date tend to anticipate their percentage among the total population at a later date. In 2000, Jews represented 71–74 percent of Israel's children aged 0–14, and 92–94 percent of the

TABLE 11.   POPULATION OF ISRAEL AND PALESTINE, BY AGE, MAJOR ETHNORELIGIOUS
AND TERRITORIAL DIVISIONS, 2000–2050 (MEDIUM PROJECTION,
THOUSANDS)

Year and Age	Jews	Non-Jewish Fringe	Total Enlarged Jewish	Israel Arabs	Total Israel	West Bank	Gaza	Total Palestinian Territories	Total Palestinians	Grand Total
	(a)	(b)	(c)=(a)+(b)	(d)	(e)=(c)+(d)	(f)	(g)	(h)=(f)+(g)	(i)=(d)+(h)	(j)=(e)+(h) (j)=(c)+(i)
2000										
Total	4,969	199	5,168	1,178	6,346	1,848	1,128	2,973	4,151	9,319
0–14	1,297	52	1,349	482	1,831	799	564	1,363	1,845	3,194
15–24	840	39	879	233	1,112	386	216	602	835	1,714
25–44	1,297	67	1,364	310	1,674	425	228	653	963	2,327
45–64	949	38	97	117	1,104	166	87	253	370	1,357
65+	576	13	589	36	625	69	33	102	138	727
2010										
Total	5,689	291	5,980	1,555	7,535	2,518	1,645	4,163	5,718	11,698
0–14	1,421	68	1,489	603	2,092	1,038	771	1,809	2,412	3,901
15–24	858	42	900	297	1,197	498	344	842	1,139	2,039
25–44	1,555	97	1,652	404	2,056	641	352	993	1,397	3,049
45–64	1,213	63	1,276	193	1,469	251	127	378	571	1,847
65+	642	21	663	58	721	91	42	133	191	854
2020										
Total	6,368	329	6,697	1,976	8,673	3,338	2,342	5,680	7,656	14,353
0–14	1,521	72	1,593	682	2,275	1,298	1,042	2,340	3,022	4,615
15–24	939	44	983	386	1,369	643	470	1,113	1,499	2,482
25–44	1,710	93	1,803	518	2,321	873	553	1,426	1,944	3,747
45–64	1,303	84	1,387	298	1,685	402	214	616	914	2,301
65+	895	36	931	92	1,023	123	62	185	277	1,208
2050										
Total	8,230	550	8,780	3,121	11,901	6,414	5,146	11,681	14,681	23,461
0–14	1,819	120	1,939	852	2,791	1,877	1,639	3,516	4,368	6,307
15–24	1,177	72	1,249	528	1,777	1,141	995	2,136	2,664	3,913
25–44	1,909	132	2,041	849	2,890	1,788	1,468	3,256	4,105	6,146
45–64	1,720	119	1,839	574	2,413	1,085	770	1,855	2,429	4,268
65+	1,605	107	1,712	318	2,030	524	274	798	1,116	2,828

Source: S. DellaPergola, The Hebrew University of Jerusalem.

elderly, aged 65 and over. Relative to the total for Israel plus the
Palestinian Territories, Jews represented 41–42 percent of the children and 79–81 percent of the elderly. By 2050, according to this
medium projection, Jews would constitute 65–69 percent of the

TABLE 12. PERCENT OF JEWS AMONG TOTAL POPULATION IN ISRAEL AND PALESTINE, BY AGE GROUPS (MEDIUM PROJECTION)

Year and Age	Israel		Israel and Territories	
	% Jewish	% Enlarged J	% Jewish	% Enlarged J
2000				
Total	78.3	81.4	53.3	55.5
0–14	70.8	73.7	40.6	42.2
15–24	75.5	79.0	49.0	51.3
25–44	77.5	81.5	55.7	58.6
45–64	86.0	89.4	69.9	72.7
65+	92.2	94.2	79.2	81.0
2010				
Total	75.5	79.4	48.6	51.1
0–14	67.9	71.2	36.4	38.2
15–24	71.7	75.2	42.1	44.1
25–44	75.6	80.4	51.0	54.2
45–64	82.6	86.9	65.7	69.1
65+	89.0	92.0	75.2	77.6
2020				
Total	73.4	77.2	44.4	46.7
0–14	66.9	70.0	33.0	34.5
15–24	68.6	71.8	37.8	39.6
25–44	73.7	77.7	45.6	48.1
45–64	77.3	82.3	56.6	60.3
65+	87.5	91.0	74.1	77.1
2050				
Total	69.2	73.8	35.1	37.4
0–14	65.2	69.5	28.8	30.7
15–24	66.2	70.3	30.1	31.9
25–44	66.1	70.6	31.1	33.2
45–64	71.3	76.2	40.3	43.1
65+	79.1	84.3	56.8	60.5

Source: S. DellaPergola, The Hebrew University of Jerusalem

0–14 age group and 79–84 percent of the 65-and-over age group in Israel. The respective percentages within the grand total population would be 29–31 percent at 0–14 years of age, and 57–61 percent at 65 and over. The latter would be the last remnant of a Jewish majority among any age group within the grand total population of Israel plus the Palestinian Territories.

One particular aspect of age composition immediately relevant to an assessment of the Israeli-Palestinian conflict is the absolute size of the cohorts of young adults that can potentially confront each other militarily, either as part of the Palestinian intifada or as members of Israel's armed forces. Perhaps surprisingly, the number of Jews and Palestinians aged 15–24 in the year 2000 was quite similar; both groups had 800,000–900,000 young men and women of that age (whether or not actively involved). Of course this does not imply an equivalence of forces and means between the two contending parties. Nevertheless, demography provides a visual angle of some military interest at least at the level of tactics, if not strategy, in assessing the current confrontation.

Socioeconomic Effects

Age compositional changes, in both absolute and relative terms, bear significant implications for the varying types of services and public interventions generally used at the different stages of the lifecycle. Changing cohort sizes imply public and private investments focused on each functional age group: educational facilities for the student population; employment and socioeconomic development for the labor force; and social services geared toward the elderly for the retired. The rhythm of variation of these investments over time for specific age groups is significantly higher and less regular than among the population as a whole. Figure 4 provides an illustration of some of the issues involved by showing prospective changes in the size of relevant age groups in the shorter term, the period 2000–2010.

In the grand total population aggregate of the State of Israel plus the Palestinian Territories, the two fastest growing sectors will be, first, the 25–44 age group, typically demanding employment, and the 0–14 age group, typically demanding education. An increase of about 700,000 (an average of 70,000 per year) is expected for each age group.

Between 2000 and 2010, over 60 percent of the necessary investments in educational facilities and nearly half of the new openings in the labor market will be needed in the Palestinian Territories. Within the State of Israel without the Territories, about half of the investment for the school-age population will be needed for the Arab sector simply to maintain the current situation—with-

FIGURE 4. EXPECTED POPULATION INCREMENTS IN ISRAEL (JEWS AND ARABS) AND PALESTINIAN TERRITORIES, BY AGE, 2000–2010 (THOUSANDS)

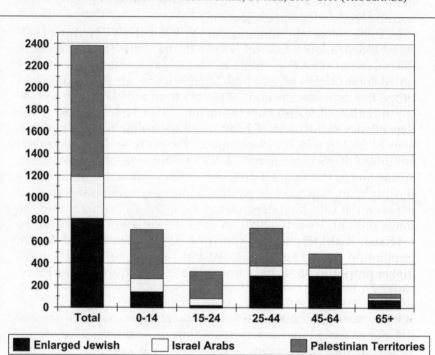

out even moving to close existing gaps in the quality of educational systems for the two groups. In contrast, close to 60 percent of the increase in the older segment of the labor force (aged 45–64) and the elderly (aged 65+) will occur within the Jewish population of Israel. The Palestinian Territories are expected to absorb nearly 75 percent of the total growth in the number of younger adults, aged 15–24, whose critical role in political and security developments was already noted. And within that age group, the growth in the number of Israeli Arabs over the 2000–2010 period will be three times higher than among Israeli Jews.

A synthetic measure of the age distribution may provide a final outlook on expected trends in the allocation of socioeconomic burdens across the different ethnoreligious and territorial subpopulations. Table 13 illustrates the possible long-range development of dependency ratios—the number of children and the elderly as compared to the number of people of working age—according to the medium projection.[61]

In 2000, the total population in the Palestinian Territories featured a dependency ratio of 97 (88 in the West Bank and 112 in Gaza), one of the world's highest,[62] mostly as a result of the already noted combination of very high fertility and quite low infant mortality. The dependency ratio for Israel's total population was 63 (60 for the enlarged Jewish population and 79 for Israeli Arabs). High dependency ratios, even if heavily skewed owing to high percentages of children in the population, obviously underlie a general condition of socioeconomic underdevelopment, or at least stress. According to the medium projection, assuming stable or declining fertility rates, a process of gradual convergence might be expected between the very high dependency ratios of Palestinians and the lower ones of Jews. By 2050, in fact, the situation might even be reversed, with dependency ratios of 71 for the enlarged Jewish population and 60 for the total of Palestinians, reflecting a much higher proportion of elderly among the Jews than among the Palestinians.

TABLE 13. DEPENDENCY RATIOS[a] AMONG THE POPULATION OF ISRAEL AND PALESTINE, BY MAJOR ETHNORELIGIOUS AND TERRITORIAL DIVISIONS, 2000–2050 (MEDIUM PROJECTION)

Year	Jews	Non-Jewish Fringe	Total Enlarged Jewish	Israel Arabs	Total Israel	West Bank	Gaza	Total Palestinian Territories	Total Palestinians	Grand Total
	(a)	(b)	(c)=(a)+(b)	(d)	(e)=(c)+(d)	(f)	(g)	(h)=(f)+(g)	(i)=(d)+(h)	(j)=(e)+(h) (j)=(c)+(i)
2000	60.7	45.1	60.0	78.5	63.1	88.8	112.4	97.1	91.5	72.6
2010	56.9	44.1	56.2	73.9	59.6	81.2	98.8	87.8	83.8	68.6
2020	61.1	48.9	60.5	64.4	61.4	74.1	89.2	80.0	75.7	68.3
2050	71.2	70.3	71.2	60.0	68.1	59.8	59.2	59.5	59.6	63.8

[a]Ratio of ages $((0-14)+(65+))\div(15-64)$
Source: Table 11.

---

[61]In spite of its somewhat unrealistic portrayal of the functional division between major age groups (children, adults, the elderly), a conventional dependency ratio is computed here as the ratio of the sum of population at age 0–14 and 65+, divided by population at age 15–64.

[62]United Nations, *World Population Prospects*.

Higher fertility levels, as hypothesized in the high projections, would obviously produce much higher—and problematic—dependency ratios.

DISCUSSION: PAINFUL TRANSITIONS

General Policy Assumptions

The Israeli-Palestinian conflict draws heavily on ethnoreligious differences, and these serve to heighten the importance of numbers in the conduct of the conflict.[63] Systematic appraisal of demographic trends is essential not only for understanding the causes and issues involved, but also for formulating suggestions about policies that might lead to peace.

There have been five basic approaches to the conflict's fundamental essence and its possible solution:

1. *Historical Rights.* Each party claims legitimate and exclusive rights over the whole contested territory from "time immemorial," or at least since the twentieth century. Each party can bring conspicuous evidence supporting the argument of having been the earlier, more permanent, or more relevant settler in the disputed land. These claims intimately relate to the primordial roots of each party's historical experience and religiocultural identity. Since ancient rights of precedence cannot be rated or ranked, conflict cannot be solved by the sole use of historical argumentation.

2. *Prevalence of Force.* Each party tries to overcome the other through the use of force, military or otherwise, with or without the help of external powers. Over the last several decades the Israeli side, more often than not, has prevailed over its opponents in strictly military terms. However, while one party may claim victory over its rival, the other may never acknowledge defeat or ever give up. Conflict cannot be permanently solved by the sole use of force.

3. *Colonization by Third Party.* Political and cultural hegemony may be imposed from the outside, substituting for the now prevailing Jewish-Israeli and Arab-Muslim-Palestinian frames of reference, and thus making the Israeli-Palestinian conflict obsolete or

---

[63]N. Choukri, *Population and Conflict: New Dimension of Population Dynamics* (New York, 1983).

irrelevant. One example would be conquest or colonization by a third power. The prime example of this during the twentieth century—the British Mandate over Palestine between 1922 and 1948—clearly points to the failure of third-party rule or interference in solving the conflict.

4. *End of Identities.* Several scenarios may be elaborated in which one or both parties give up their own unique religious, ethnic, and cultural identities. Hypothetical examples would include ethnoreligious merger through frequent intermarriage; one particular social class establishing full hegemony and overcoming ethnic differences; or local or imported cultural influences creating an entirely new societal paradigm. However, considering the recent revival of ethnoreligious identifications globally and in the Middle East in particular, and the prevailing patterns of ethnoreligious segregation in Israel/Palestine, these scenarios for conflict resolution appear most unlikely, at least in the short run.

5. *Compromise.* The two contending parties, Jewish and Arab, may achieve compromise by each acknowledging a legitimate contemporaneous presence of the other on the contested land of Palestine. Such compromise may be achieved either through (a) functional partition within one joint sovereign political framework inclusive of both parties—a "binational" state—or, (b) territorial partition and the creation of two separate, sovereign, national frameworks. The obvious preconditions for compromise are an explicit decision to put an end to conflict and a formal acceptance of the main solution modalities by both relevant parties.

Assuming that the preferred line of thought should aim at a solution of the Israeli/Palestinian conflict rather than at its endless perpetuation—an assumption that, under present political circumstances, cannot universally be taken for granted—the latter option, division into two sovereign states, appears the more realistic of the two alternatives for compromise. The first option, a binational state, would require transition from conflict to fully integrated cooperation and division of labor. This is a far more complex and less likely scenario than simple partition along the lines of "two states for two peoples," which might be followed at some later date by coordination between the parties.[64]

---

[64]A two-state solution is mentioned in UN Security Council Resolution 1397 and called for in the proposed "road map" discussed below, pp. 229–30.

Although recent scholarship has demonstrated the often fanciful and imaginary elements that lie at the roots of contemporary nationhood, nationalism, and nation-states,[65] ethnoreligious identities in the Israeli-Palestinian conflict are rooted in a powerful complex of historical and contemporary factors that cannot be reasonably neutralized in the foreseeable future. Their cumulative strength in the light of real experiences—namely, those directly related to the conflict—is so strong as to amount to cogent empirical reality for the vast majority of the concerned populations. Israeli and Palestinian national identities are here to stay. Indeed, the argument can be made that national-religious identities may even help the search for peace insofar as they translate into a dynamic and positive popular force in the building of new societies—provided that their more extremist and destructive fringes are kept under control.

To be sure, such nationalism is not looked upon favorably in Europe today, since, in the experience of most European nation states, this societal model has clearly implied one ethnoreligious group dominating over others. In the case of Nazi Germany, Fascist Italy, and other similar nationalist regimes, it entailed the ruthless suppression of cultural minorities, Jews prominently among them. More recently, particularly since the collapse of the Soviet empire at the beginning of the 1990s, bitter intergroup conflicts have arisen over control of postcommunist governments. There is, therefore, a widespread assumption that the older model of a unitary nation-state is obsolete, its place to be taken by multicultural entities such as the European Union and the United Nations.[66] The multicultural model, however, which so far has represented more a declarative model than political reality in Europe itself, is hardly a realistic proposition for solving the Israel-Palestine conflict, where ethnocultural differences are even sharper. The presence of two states, one Israeli and the other Palestinian, is the more plausible solution.

Zionism, the national liberation movement of the Jewish people, proposed that a Jewish state would provide a solution to the his-

---

[65]See Benedict Anderson, *Imagined Communities* (London and New York, 1991). For a discussion of demography as an important agent in nation building, see Calvin Goldscheider, *Israel's Changing Society: Population, Ethnicity and Development* (Boulder, 1996).

[66]Mark Lilla, "The End of Politics: Europe, the Nation-State, and the Jews," *New Republic*, June 23, 2003, pp. 29–34.

torical problems of the Jewish people. A natural correlate of this assumption is that the State of Israel should be politically and culturally configured so as to give primary expression to the multiform interests and values of a Jewish constituency. At the same time, its 1948 Declaration of Independence stated Israel's commitment to a democratic system ensuring full equality to all citizens regardless of religion and ethnic origin. While the Israeli judicial system and other government and law-enforcement agencies have generally maintained the rights of individuals, the inherent conflict between being a *Jewish* and a *democratic* state is unavoidably entangled with the question of ethnoreligious population composition.[67]

The aspiration of Palestinians to their own sovereign nationhood—whatever might be said of the methods used to bring it into being—has achieved irreversible momentum. The primary aims of an independent Palestine, from the standpoint of world opinion, are to satisfy the aspirations of the Palestinian national liberation movement through full-scale sovereignty, develop an adequate economic infrastructure, and gain international recognition. Concerns about the state's democratic framework, pluralism, or the rights and equality of religious and ethnic minorities, while not neglected, have been minor themes in recent public discourse.

The Israeli-Jewish interest in maintaining a society founded on recognizable Jewish cultural patterns—hence based on a permanent Jewish majority—implies giving up claims to the whole territory of Palestine and redeployment to boundaries conceptually similar to those of 1967. To contribute to the creation of a stable regional political system, parity between a Jewish-Israeli and an Arab-Palestinian state should be founded on a clear ethnic, religious, and cultural definition of each.[68]

---

[67]See Ruth Gavison, "The Significance of Israel In Modern Jewish Identities," in E. Ben-Rafael, Y. Gorni, and Y. Ro'i, eds., *Contemporary Jewries: Convergence and Divergence* (Leiden-Boston, 2003), pp. 118–29.

[68]We may recall, in this context, the respective contentions of both sides in favor of "ethnic cleansing." On the Arab side, the slogan "to throw the Zionists into the sea" was a popular propaganda item after 1948, but came to a halt when the 1967 war proved it impossible. On the Jewish side, the right-wing objective of removing Palestinians eastward and making Jordan into "Palestine," known as "transfer," is clearly impractical on logistical grounds, even leaving aside ethical considerations. And even were it practical, any steps to carry it out would arouse strong international protest and legal sanctions against Israel, with powerful consequences in the light of the ongoing revision and expansion of interna-

The existence within each state of significant ethnoreligious minorities that differ culturally and socioeconomically from the majority inherently brings social friction, legal contentiousness, and—quite possibly—popular unrest. This has certainly been the case with regard to the Arab minority in Israel, which has long felt itself the object of discrimination on the part of the Jewish majority. A similar if not more acute situation would probably emerge in a Palestinian state hosting a substantial minority of Jewish inhabitants—i.e., the "settlers." Nor does the formula sound plausible of partition between a multiethnic, multicultural, binational (Jewish-Arab) Israeli state alongside a monoethnic, monoreligious, uninational (Arab-Muslim) Palestinian state.

The "security fence" that Israel is building as of this writing, designed to separate Israeli from Palestinian territories, is, more than anything else, a symbolic reminder of the unavoidability of separation. Its construction, demanded by Israeli public opinion, is being carried out by a Likud-led government despite complaints from many on the political right that it will create a de facto border by effectively transferring West Bank territory outside the "fence" to a Palestinian state. This may be an important reason for the apparently reluctant pace of its construction, and, hence, its current inefficiency. The fence's function will cease completely the day a real peace agreement is reached.

We now turn to a brief discussion of some environmental, socioeconomic, and policy implications of current and expected demographic trends.

Political and Demographic Scenarios

We illustrated above the powerful momentum of population trends in Israel and Palestine, and their relevance, explicit or at least implicit, for the future of the conflict. Several inescapable paradoxes underline the intertwined sociodemographic relationship between Jews and Palestinians. From the Palestinian point of view, the es-

---

tional law-enforcement tools and of already existing anti-Israeli sentiments in many quarters. For a short overview of the broader legal context of the emerging anti-Israel attitudes, see Irwin Cotler, *Human Rights and the New Anti-Jewishness* (Jerusalem, 2002), JPPI Alert Paper 1, issued by the Jewish People Policy Planning Institute.

tablishment of the State of Israel, large-scale Jewish immigration, and large-scale Palestinian emigration may have constituted undue disruption of the natural social order. On the other hand, were it not for Israel and the conditions its creation allowed for improvements in health, fertility, education,[69] and employment, the Palestinian population would be conspicuously smaller,[70] less healthy, less educated—and less focused on its own national identity.

Future demographic shifts through differential population growth could have disruptive political consequences for the multiethnic societal complex of Israel and Palestine. Enhancing maximum ethnoreligious homogeneity within, and maximum diversity between, each of Israel/Palestine's future sovereign territorial entities—an *Arab state* and a *Jewish state,* in the spirit of UN Resolution 181 of 1947—would at least partially defuse the disrupting effect of prospective demographic trends by optimizing benefits and minimizing liabilities.

The fundamental objective should be to preserve a clearly distinguished and recognizable ethnocultural collective profile for each state. Clearly, there is a political price attached for both parties. For Israel, it is return of territory, for the Palestinians it is settling for less than full "right of return" to Israel proper. Table 14 and figure 5 summarize the possible demographic implications of different political scenarios for the future population distribution among Jews and non-Jews in Israel and Palestine. Two scenarios involve, respectively, a partial return of Palestinian refugees, and limited territorial exchange.

Partial Return of Palestinian Refugees

One scenario mentioned at various stages of the Israeli-Palestinian negotiations in the late 1990s assumed that, in the framework of a final peace agreement, the State of Israel would agree to readmit a symbolic contingent of 100,000 Palestinian refugees onto its territory. For the sake of simplicity we have as-

---

[69] A full-scale higher education system was allowed in the West Bank and Gaza only after Israel's occupation in 1967.

[70] The Palestinian Territories currently have the highest rate of natural increase in the world. See Gilles Pison, "Tous les pays du monde (2001)," *Population & Sociétés* 370, 2001.

TABLE 14.   PERCENT OF JEWS[a] AMONG TOTAL POPULATION IN ISRAEL AND
PALESTINE, ACCORDING TO VARIOUS SCENARIOS, 2000–2050
(MEDIUM PROJECTION)

Year	Israel+ Palestinian Territories	Israel without Territories	Israel+ 100,000 refugees	Israel+ territorial exchange
	(a)	(b)	(c)	(d)
2000	55	81	80	87
2010	51	79	78	86
2020	47	77	76	84
2050	37	74	72	81

[a]Including non-Jewish members in Jewish households (column b in Table 8). Not including foreign workers and illegal residents.
Source: S. DellaPergola, The Hebrew University of Jerusalem

sumed here that this group's age distribution and demographic behaviors would be similar to those of the weighted average of total
Palestinians in Israel and the Palestinian Territories. That initial
contingent would, in absolute numbers, double by the year 2020
and triple by 2050. But according to the assumptions of our projections, their impact on the ethnoreligious equilibrium would be
minimal, a decrease of about 1–2 percent in the Jewish share of
the Israeli population. If the initial contingent of repatriated Palestinian refugees were mainly elderly people who had witnessed the
1948 exodus, the impact on population trends would be much less.
Larger and younger contingents of returning Palestinian refugees,
not assumed in our projections, would exert a much more dramatic
impact on the ethnoreligious composition of Israel's population,
as well as on its absolute size.

Territorial Exchange

A further scenario assumes that some territorial exchanges might
be negotiated between Israel and a future Palestinian state. Minor
portions of Israel's territory within the pre-1967 boundaries now
hosting a predominantly Arab population might be exchanged for
some equally small areas in the Palestinian Territories now hosting large concentrations of Jews.

FIGURE 5. PERCENT JEWISH (INCLUDING NON-JEWISH FAMILY MEMBERS)
AMONG TOTAL POPULATION IN ISRAEL AND PALESTINE, BY
ALTERNATIVE SCENARIOS, 2000–2050

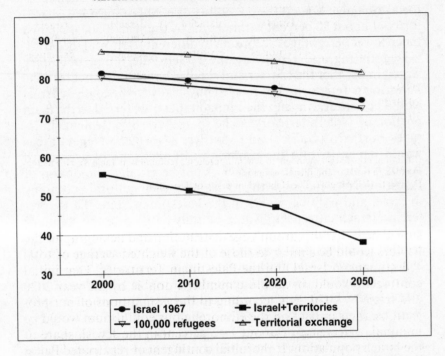

At the end of 2000, about 207,000 Arabs lived in the area popularly known as the "Triangle"[71] on Israeli territory next to the 1967 boundary. Another 210,000 Arabs lived in the eastern quarters of Jerusalem. This population of 417,000 constituted about a third of the total Arab population in Israel, and lived within slightly more than 1 percent of Israel's total territory (not including the West Bank and Gaza Strip). This territory and population might be transferred to the Palestinian Authority or a hypothetical Palestinian state, in return for the areas near Jerusalem and in the western parts of the West Bank close to the northeastern out-

[71]An area forming part of the Alexander Mountain and Hadera natural regions in the Haifa District, and Eastern Sharon, Southern Sharon, and Petah Tikvah natural regions in the Central District.

skirts of Greater Tel Aviv, where the bulk of the Jews living on the West Bank are situated.[72]

Readjusting the population projections allowing for such territorial exchange suggest the possibility of maintaining a Jewish majority of about 80 percent within Israel by the year 2050, as against much lower percentages according to different territorial scenarios.

Negotiating and redrawing the Israeli-Palestinian boundary would imply that the sparser and smaller Israeli settlements in the Palestinian Territories not relayed physically to the State of Israel would be withdrawn, and their inhabitants transferred to the main portion of Israel's territory.[73] The sparser Arab settlements in Israel's northern (Galilee) and southern (Northern Negev) areas would remain within the framework of the State of Israel. All Arabs within the State of Israel would be granted the option of Palestinian citizenship, with provision for their cultural autonomy in Israel and political rights in the Palestinian State. Those preferring Israeli citizenship would be fully entitled to the standard package of Israeli rights and duties, including full exposure to the regular Israeli school curriculum and military service or equivalent civil service—from which they are now exempt.[74]

An alternative might be suggested that would allow Jewish residents in the Territories not annexed to Israel the option of stay-

---

[72]Some 264,000 Jews lived in these areas as of 2000, 172,000 in the eastern neighborhoods of Greater Jerusalem and 92,000 within a ring of about 15 km from Jerusalem, including Ma'aleh Adumim, Beitar Ilit, Giv'at Ze'ev, Efrat, Gush Etzion, and several other localities. That same ring in the West Bank also included an estimated 349,000 Palestinians. Another 100,000 Jews lived elsewhere on the West Bank.

[73]This would include all Jews living in the Gaza Strip, estimated at 7,000 in 2000. Whether Israel would keep control of territory between the Gaza area and Egypt is a security matter outside the scope of this article.

[74]It may be interesting to note provisions regarding political rights and citizenship options for Jewish residents in the Arab state (which did not come into existence) and for Arab residents in the Jewish state, according to UN Resolution 181 enacted in 1947. Part I, C, Chapter 3, 1, states that "persons over the age of eighteen years may opt, within one year from the date of recognition of independence of the State in which they reside, for citizenship of the other State, provided that no Arab residing in the area of the proposed Arab State shall have the right to opt for the citizenship in the proposed Jewish State and no Jew residing in the proposed Jewish State shall have the right to opt for citizenship in the proposed Arab State. The exercise of this right of option will be taken to include the wives and children under 18 years of age of persons so opting. Arabs residing in the areas of the proposed Jewish State and Jews residing in the area of the proposed Arab State who have signed a notice of intention to opt for citizenship of the other State shall be eligible to vote in the Constituent Assembly of that State, but not in the Constituent Assembly of the State in which they reside."

ing there and maintaining Israeli citizenship, in the same way that Israeli Arabs would be given the option of staying in Israel with citizenship in the Palestinian state. One objection, however, is the uncertain security that would follow the dependence of these settlers on Palestinian (and not Israeli) security forces. Furthermore, unlike Arabs in Israel, they would constitute a tiny minority of the total population of the Palestinian state, even if rapidly growing thanks to a robust natural increase. And the noninclusion of these future several hundred thousand Jews within the territory of Israel would mean a lower percentage of Jews out of the total population of the State of Israel.

The exchanges of *land, population,* and *civil rights* for peace envisaged above would be far less disruptive than large-scale mutual population transfer, a well-known model for solving international conflicts with an ethnoreligious component.[75] According to the scenario discussed here, relatively few people—principally the inhabitants of small and sparse Jewish localities in the Palestinian Territories—would have to relocate, and the main changes would derive from redrawing borders and shifting citizenship and related civil rights.

As for the status of Jerusalem, a conventional solution would be partition, allocating the Jewish sections to the Israeli state and the Arab sections to the Palestinian state. A better solution—if it were only feasible—would be the creation of a Greater Jerusalem Authority, with local autonomy for Jewish and Palestinian neighborhoods and a joint Israeli-Palestinian Authority for the governance of the holy sites—primarily the Temple Mount/Haram al-Sharif, or even of Jerusalem's entire walled Old City.[76]

---

[75]Since 1947, for example, an estimated 16–17 million people crossed between India and Pakistan as a result of the partition of the subcontinent and the violence associated with it. In 1922–23, some 1.2 million Greeks from Anatolia fled to Greece. About a million Turks were repatriated from the Balkans between the two world wars. See Myron Weiner, "Political Demography: An Inquiry into the Political Consequences of Population Change," in R. Revelle, ed., *Rapid Population Growth: Consequences and Policy Implications* (Baltimore, 1971), pp. 567–617.

[76]For an Israeli perspective on the future of Jerusalem see Sarah Hershkovitz et al., *Strategic Masterplan for Jerusalem 2020* (Jerusalem, forthcoming). For a Palestinian perspective see Z. al-Qaq, "Post-1967 Palestinian Strategies for Jerusalem?"in *Brussels-Jerusalem: Conflict Management and Conflict Resolution in Divided Cities* (Jerusalem and Brussels, 1997), pp. 339–68. For an overall perspective see Abraham (Rami) Friedman and Rami Nasrallah, eds., *Divided Cities in Transition* (Jerusalem, 2003).

Environmental Policies

The suggested solution assumes some shared responsibility and agreed division of labor between Jews/Israelis and Arabs/Palestinians in the handling of human and other resources over Palestine's whole territory. Assuming the political feasibility of such cooperation, several major policy implications of demographic scenarios follow.

The first relates to the consequences of rapid population growth for future population densities. The changing equilibrium between population and physical environment touches on issues of common interest, and requires strict coordination and agreed allocation of resources between the Israeli and Palestinian parties. In particular, scarce resources like drinkable water, arable land, even sand, call for urgent regulation to prevent excessive or inefficient consumption that will lead to shortages. Similar problems exist in regard to other types of resources as well—such as air—that require constant monitoring to prevent degradation. Joint initiatives will also be required to locate resources that are as yet unexploited, develop new renewable or nonrenewable resources locally, or import them when feasible. Such crucially urgent initiatives require long-term planning, regional cooperation, and the allocation of massive investments from international agencies.

A further area of concern is the future of physical planning for residential uses, and, even more significantly, for the development of adequate transportation and other types of infrastructure, such as sewage disposal, in an increasingly dense environment. To keep pace with the projected population growth, there is an urgent need to develop a common Israeli/Palestinian approach to environmental resources. This is especially true in the case of large metropolitan areas such as Jerusalem, which, in any future political scenario, will continue to include substantially intertwined Jewish and Palestinian populations and economic infrastructures.[77]

---

[77]See Ron Froumkin and Tamar Ahiron-Froumkin, *Environmental Aspects of Agreements and Development Programs in Regional Cooperation: Current Situation and Recommendations for the Future* (Jerusalem, 2003), in Hebrew.

Socioeconomic Policies

One undesirable aspect of the Israeli-Palestinian conflict has been the focusing of public debate on a narrow range of mostly political and security-oriented issues, while other important matters related to daily life are given less attention, if not entirely ignored. The maintenance of civil society and the provision of its social and economic needs—behind and beyond war and peace—have not been adequately addressed, making it harder to plan for the future.[78] In this regard, one key aspect of the population scenarios presented above is their implications for future manpower size and composition.

The huge socioeconomic investments needed to develop educational networks and employment opportunities cannot reasonably occur unless substantial budgetary resources are diverted from current military and defense uses to civilian purposes. Moreover, the massive amount of foreign investment necessary will only materialize if there are strong enough guarantees for stability and future growth in the region.

A major problem in the socioeconomic structure of the Palestinian population is the lack of a middle class, an element that is absolutely essential to lead economic development in a modernizing society. The problem is sharpened by the contrast between a comparatively well-educated Palestinian population, on the one hand, and, on the other, limited occupational opportunities at appropriate professional levels. To be sure, once statehood is achieved the Palestinians will develop a steadily growing central administrative bureaucracy. Even so, the sharp increase in the younger Palestinian labor force projected at least through 2010 needs to be absorbed within an expanding economic and administrative system, or else it will exacerbate existing political tensions. Failure of the Palestinian Authority to fill basic social needs such as education and employment will surely be exploited by other centers of power, such as is already happening in the form of the social

---

[78]A useful overview is S. Della Seta, ed., *The Price of Non-Peace: The Need for a Strengthened Role for the European Union in the Middle East* (Brussels, 1999). See also Ephraim Kleiman, "Some Basic Problems of the Economic Relationship Between Israel, the West Bank and Gaza," in S. Fischer, D. Rodrik, and E.H. Tuma, eds., *The Economics of the Middle East Peace* (Cambridge, Mass., 1993).

services—together with fundamentalist indoctrination—provided by Hamas.

In Israel, too, the question of economic absorption of a growing labor force must be addressed within the context of the interrelation between the economy, security, and peace. As a modern market economy strongly connected internationally, Israel depends on foreign investments—including tourism. As clearly demonstrated by the financial and economic upturns and downturns of the 1990s and early 2000s in Israel, the international economic community is extremely sensitive to the long-term prospects for peace in the region. Only a climate of optimism fueled by advances in the political process toward peace will allow for renewal of the steady economic growth that prevailed in Israel over most of the 1990s. Failure to develop the economy at a rhythm at least equal to that of the inevitable population growth will mean growing unemployment, leading, in the end, to an increase of emigration— which will herald a further weakening of Israel's demographic standing.

Moreover, in light of projected demographic changes in Israel, a large part of the necessary educational and manpower investments will have to go to the Israeli Arab sector, proportionally and even absolutely more than to the Jewish majority. Otherwise, Israel will face sharpened social unrest on the part of those who feel they have been allocated far less than their fair share.

Given the complementarity that, in spite of everything, still exists between the Israeli and Palestinian economies, economic decline in Israel would necessarily produce negative consequences for Palestine. The common vested interest of Israelis and Palestinians in sustained economic growth sufficient at least to absorb the expected population growth and the ensuing increasing demand for employment, should powerfully motivate the two sides in a quest for political solutions and economic cooperation.

Demographic Policies

Demographic trends reflect cultural and socioeconomic factors as well as policy interventions. Some control over population size and distribution may be achieved, at least in theory, by manipulating the various operative variables responsible for demographic change, as well as through administrative policy. International migration balances and fertility levels are highly sensitive to changes in the quality of life. Thus policies affecting employment, housing, physical environment, public services, and personal and collective security may have significant effects on propensities for in-migration and out-migration. Fertility levels and differentials may also be expected to respond to these intervening factors.

Causal mechanisms linking quality-of-life opportunities and demographic response (population size and composition) are easily specified and understood, although there can be no full control over the amount and direction of actual response. In principle, a more attractive, peaceful, and economically developed society in Israel and Palestine will more likely produce more immigration and less emigration. In a social environment still densely imbued with traditional values, social stability and growth do not stand against the natural course of family values in promoting marriage and planned fertility.

Policy interventions more specifically tied to demographic trends have been the subject of debate in Israel. Without entering here into a review of rationales and arguments, the consensus is that, over the years, government policies have directly or indirectly affected population trends.[79] Admittedly, whatever the goals, even the most successful policies can expect only partial and mixed results in the demographic development of a heterogeneous population such as that in Israel/Palestine. The major challenge lies in fully appreciating the relationship between demographic behaviors and the deeper roots of existing conflicts in the regional context. Defusing of political and cultural tensions may be the fundamental prerequisite for a cooling down of demographic trends, particularly with regard to achieving a gradual lowering of fertility levels. If current fertility rates reflect, among other things, the militant ambition to prevail over one's rival through the power of numbers, political normalization may empty that particular argument of much of its appeal.

Normalization involves, in the first place, mutual agreement on a regional peace framework covering the multiple facets of the Israeli-Palestinian conflict—and crucially, as already noted, a

---

[79]Sergio DellaPergola and Leah Cohen, eds., *World Jewish Population: Trends and Policies* (Jerusalem, 1992).

clear definition of national boundaries between Israel and the Palestinian Authority.

A further policy goal is achieving harmony between different antagonistic religiocultural sectors within each of the two major parties, the Jews and the Arabs. In the Palestinian camp, there are cleavages between the Muslim majority and the Christian minority, and between the different Christian denominations. The main cleavage in the Jewish camp is between the *haredi*[80] minority on the one hand, and the moderately religious, traditionalist, and secular majority, on the other.

One important matter of contention among the Jewish groups involves the procedure for conversion of the hundreds of thousands of non-Jewish members of Jewish households—mostly immigrants from the FSU. Finding an agreed solution for their incorporation into the Jewish mainstream of Israeli society constitutes one of the crucial items on the Israeli public agenda, and would have significant consequences for the demographic balance, as shown in our preceding discussion. In the case of the Jews, the idea of a new "social contract" has been advocated to establish rules of respectful political discourse between the factions and among their representatives.[81] This approach would facilitate agreement, or at least mutual noninterference, on topics of potential conflict, and might have long-term consequences in the demographic behaviors of each of the groups.

The key goal of interventions aimed at fertility should be a reduction in the present intergroup and intragroup fertility gaps, rather than the achievement of a specific family size. In the analysis of family and fertility in both Jewish and Palestinian contexts, conventional socioeconomic explanations are not sufficient; the impact of ideas and values should be more carefully evaluated.

An intriguing point is the demographic effect of the ongoing tension on both sides over security, particularly in regard to marriage—a significant intervening determinant of fertility levels. Among the Palestinians, the economic crisis created by the breakdown of security might lead to a reduction in the price of brides, hence more feasible and younger marriages, hence continuing high

---

[80]From the Hebrew *hared*, meaning fearful (of God), used to describe the most religious Jews, estimated at about 7 percent of Israeli Jews in 2000.

[81]For the recent example of the Kinneret Covenant, see below, pp. 271–72.

fertility levels. Excessive deterioration of economic resources and the lack of employment, however, might lead to the opposite effect of unfeasible and delayed marriages, generating fertility decline. Among the Jewish population, a continuing crisis would more likely erode marriage propensities, and some downward effects of continuing insecurity on fertility may ensue. Peace and prosperity, as already noted, might generate opposite effects.

What is called for is a policy of fertility regulation, with an emphasis on the reproductive health of women. A similar process is clearly under way in most of the Muslim countries, including some of the religiously more rigorous such as Iran.[82] Given the persistent preference for medium-size nuclear families in Israel and Palestine, social policies on both sides directly addressing fertility might choose to give strong incentives for the third and fourth children, minor support for the second and fifth, and sharply less for births of a higher order.

Moreover, it is imperative to close the gaps that still prevail between different subpopulations in regard to the role of women in society and in the community. Palestinian women should be granted the same degree of access as Israeli women to all existing health, education, training, and employment facilities and rights. And the available package, in turn, should be expanded to allow fuller participation of women from all groups in economic production and decision making.[83]

Turning to international migration, the situation of the Jewish diaspora indicates a drying-up of the traditional emigration basins and a likely diminution in the volume of migration to Israel over the next decades. The only way this could be reversed would be an unlikely scenario of significant political and economic disruption in the major societies of the West that now host the largest Jewish

---

[82]In 2001, reflecting a marked downward trend during the 1990s, the TFR was estimated at 2.5 in Lebanon, 2.6 in Iran, 3.5 in Egypt, 3.6 in Jordan, and 5.7 in Saudi Arabia. See Pison, "Tous les pays du monde."

[83]The previously mentioned very high dependency ratios reflect, among other things, extremely low rates of labor force participation among Palestinian women. In 2001, 60 percent of Jewish men and 53 percent of Jewish women (in both cases, over age 15) were in the labor force; the corresponding figures for Israeli Arabs were 62 percent for men and 24 percent for women. Among Palestinians of the same age in the West Bank and Gaza in 1997, 76 percent of men and 9 percent of women were working. These figures come from Israel Central Bureau of Statistics, *Statistical Abstract of Israel,* and Palestine Central Bureau of Statistics, *1997 Population Census.*

communities worldwide. Barring that, future Jewish population growth in Israel is bound to slow. Another tool for slowing Jewish population growth would be some restrictive revision of the currently very liberal definition of people eligible for Israeli citizenship under the Law of Return.

On the Palestinian side, as noted above, current growth rates, reflecting high fertility, lead to surrealistic results if not checked — such as 11 million people in Gaza by 2050, according to the high scenario — and the impossibility of absorbing such population growth in a viable economic framework. The consequence would be a spiral of impoverishment and political instability in the future Palestinian state.

Clearly, the call for return and absorption of an unlimited number of Palestinian refugees and their second- and third-generation descendants in the projected Palestinian state is not grounded in a realistic vision of future demographic and social developments — whatever the state's eventual boundaries. Nor is the realization of such an influx within the State of Israel, as it would imply a drastic change in Israel's cultural profile that would be tantamount to termination of the Jewish state. The implausibility of planning the demise of Israeli society necessitates moderation in Palestinian rhetoric about a right of return.[84]

At the same time, there must be a plan of action to solve the housing and other socioeconomic problems in Palestinian refugee camps through compensation, resettlement elsewhere, and development. On these issues, the international community could play a positive role by educating to promote the policy transitions, providing serious financial support to make them possible, and refraining from proclaiming doctrinaire "right of return" views and maintaining the punitive attitudes toward Israel it has often expressed in the past.

---

[84]A survey conducted by Dr. Khalil Shikaki, director of the Palestinian Center for Policy and Survey Research, suggests that 10 percent, at most, of the refugees would insist on permanent residence in Israel. More than half, he found, would accept financial compensation and residence in the West Bank or Gaza, or in land Israel might transfer to the Palestinian state in return for West Bank land. James Bennet, "Palestinian Mob Attacks Pollster," *New York Times,* July 14, 2003. As the title of this article indicates, disseminating the actual views of the refugees, which are apparently quite moderate, can arouse the ire of those Palestinians who insist on a literal "right of return."

Conclusion

The much-hoped-for transition toward terminating conflict in Israel/Palestine has to deal—among many other things—with a nearly insurmountable circular demographic conundrum. In order to defuse excessive and unbalanced population growth, it is necessary to solve, or at least tone down, the conflict. On the other hand, it is exactly the disruptive demographic phenomena that exacerbate the conflict. Given this background, careful study of demographic trends and perspectives may stimulate the elaboration of sensitive social-policy solutions that do not necessarily accord with declared political programs or with popular ideologies.

Even assuming that people who prefer reasonable and honorable compromise solutions will predominate over the strategists of permanent tension and continuous struggle, the two sides in the conflict do have different goals and may prefer different strategies. Looking at the present in historical perspective, certain trends that have appeared with some regularity since the beginning of the Israeli-Arab conflict should teach us about the limits of feasible change. The persistence of political, cultural, national, and religious values as determinants of population trends indicates that not everything can be explained through the logic of rational choice in the Middle East. Values, passions, contradictions, and paradoxes play a central role in the Israeli-Palestinian demographic equation.

More broadly, in any conflict there are often two truths. The truth of Israeli repression of normal civil life and stringent limitations on the free circulation of people and goods in the Palestinian Territories is countered by the truth of Palestinian terrorism against Israeli civilians. In a broad assessment of the future of population and society, one cannot ignore these contradictions and their effects on the psychology of the actors.

The State of Israel's interest is to preserve itself as a democratic state—which it is—with a predominance of Jewish culture and values—to which it aspires. The Palestinian interest is to reach statehood promptly, give expression to national aspirations, and start implementing in its sovereign state the long-frustrated hope for normal civil life. Both interests demand clear territorial and political separation between the two entities. In terms of population, separate growth would at least reduce the impact of demography in magnifying the existing conflict. Coordination between the two parties, crucially needed to solve urgent environmental and socioeconomic problems stemming from rapid population growth, might develop over time if a sense of mutual respect, tolerance, and cultural pluralism can gradually emerge.

Still unclear at the time of this writing is whether or not there is enough goodwill and leadership to make possible the transition to end the conflict. The answer could mean the difference between vision and disaster for the intertwined populations and societies of Israel and Palestine.

Review
of
the
Year

UNITED STATES

United States

National Affairs

IN 2002—THE YEAR AFTER 9/11—America's agenda was largely defined by the war against terrorism. The Republican sweep in the November midterm election was only one indication of the profound implications for American policies and politics both at home and around the world. For American Jews, the response to terrorism had an additional dimension of fear and anger, as Palestinian militants and a complicit Palestinian leadership continued their campaign of terrorism against Israeli civilians, and as global anti-Semitism rose to levels not seen in many decades. The Jewish community's sense of crisis was only somewhat alleviated by the knowledge that Israel still had strong friends in the White House and in Congress.

To be sure, domestic issues of relevance to Jews, such as church-state separation, remained relevant, and Jewish communal agencies grappled with the implications of tax cuts and the president's faith-based initiative for providing social services to those in need. But the domestic agenda drew far less Jewish attention—and fewer advocacy resources—than had been the case in the past, and there was no indication that this priority shift would be reversed any time soon.

THE POLITICAL ARENA

Election 2002

With razor-thin margins in both houses of Congress—Republicans controlling the House of Representatives and Democrats the Senate—political analysts focused for much of the year on the question of whether either or both house would "flip" in the November election. The answer would clearly hinge on the results in a few "swing" states and districts.

By Election Day, analysts were fairly certain that the Democrats would not make the net gain of six seats they needed for a House majority. The decennial redistricting conducted earlier in the year protected incumbents of both parties and, by restricting the field of competitive races, benefited the GOP. But in one notable exception to the incumbency protection associated with redistricting, veteran Rep. Benjamin Gilman (R., N.Y.), the unofficial dean of the House's "Jewish caucus," was squeezed out of a chance for reelection since New York State had to drop two seats from its delegation. When it became clear that Gilman's district would be divided among those of other incumbents, he reportedly considered running for reelection as a Democrat, but in early July Gilman announced that he would be resigning "with great remorse." Leaders of the Jewish community expressed regret at this turn of events, pointing to the leadership role Gilman had played over the years on a range of foreign-policy issues such as support for Israel and the Soviet Jewry movement. Especially notable was his tenure as chairman of the House International Relations Committee from 1995 to 2001, and, after that, as chairman of the committee's Subcommittee on the Middle East and South Asia.

Control of the Senate remained uncertain until the very end, as the Republicans needed a net gain of only one seat to regain the majority. When the 107th Congress first convened, Democrats and Republicans were deadlocked at 50 seats apiece, with Republican control ensured by virtue of Vice President Cheney's tie-breaking vote. It tilted to a tenuous Democratic majority in June 2001 when Sen. Jim Jeffords of Vermont bolted the Republicans to identify as an Independent, and agreed to vote with the Democratic caucus.

By late evening on Election Day, it was evident that the Republicans had widened their majority in the House and taken control of the Senate in defiance of the historic norm that the party holding the White House loses ground in Congress during midterm elections. After run-off races and late-breaking results were tallied, Republicans held 229 seats in the incoming Congress, up from 223, and Democrats held 205 seats, down from 211. The number of Independents in the new House remained one — Vermont's Bernard Sanders, who generally voted Democratic. On the Senate side, once the results of a December 7 run-off in Louisiana were reported, Republicans held 51 seats, a gain of two, compared to the Democrats' 48 plus Jeffords, the Independent. Judging by the election returns, national-security issues invoked by Republicans had particular resonance at a time when the United States had recently suffered an egregious attack and faced the prospect of further threats.

The one bright note for Democrats on Election Day was a gain in the number Democratic governors, including victories in such big-state Republican strongholds as Michigan, Illinois, and Pennsylvania. To be sure, Republicans had their share of gubernatorial victories in Democratic strongholds—Massachusetts and Maryland in particular—and thus retained control of a bare majority of state executive mansions (as of the beginning of 2003, the margin was 26 to 24).

Five Jewish candidates competed for seats in the U.S. Senate in 2002. Democratic Senator Paul Wellstone's campaign for reelection in Minnesota pitted him against a fellow Jew, Republican Norman Coleman, a former mayor of St. Paul. With the outcome in doubt as Election Day approached, both men were drawing support from Minnesota's Jewish community of about 45,000. But Wellstone was killed a few days before the election—together with his wife, a daughter, three campaign staffers, and two pilots—in the crash of a small plane. His sudden death drew expressions of grief from across the nation, within the Jewish community and without, from political allies as well as adversaries. The nation recalled Wellstone's willingness to be a lone voice in support of his liberal convictions, and his basic decency as a person (see the obituary below, p. 715). Wellstone's demise led to a remarkable one-week campaign in which Democrat Walter Mondale, a former vice president and former Minnesota senator, was drafted to run against Coleman. When Coleman defeated Mondale, he became the third Jew in a row to hold that Senate seat—after Wellstone and Rudy Boschwitz, the Republican Wellstone had unseated 12 years before.

Coleman's victory, that of returning Senate veteran Frank Lautenberg (D., N.J.), the reelection of Carl Levin (D., Mich.), and the defeat of Alan Blinken—a Jewish Democrat who ran an uphill battle in Idaho against the incumbent, Republican Larry Craig—meant there would be 11 Jewish senators, a net increase of one. Lautenberg was himself a late entry into the field, chosen by New Jersey Democrats to run after the incumbent, Robert Torricelli, dropped out of the race shortly before Election Day in the wake of ethical questions. Levin, the only incumbent Jewish senator running, opted not to retire at the end of the 107th Congress because of the threat he saw to Democratic control of the Senate. He was certainly correct in that assessment; Levin was handily reelected, but when the 108th Congress convened, he was a member of the minority. In addition to Levin, the eight other incumbent Jewish senators were Barbara Boxer (D., Cal.); Russell Feingold (D., Wis.); Dianne Feinstein (D., Cal.); Herb Kohl (D., Wis.); Joseph Lieberman (D., Conn.); Charles Schumer (D., N.Y.); Arlen Specter (R., Pa.); and Ron Wyden (D., Oreg.).

In a New Hampshire Senate race of great interest to the Jewish community, Rep. John Sununu, the Republican, defeated Democratic governor Jean Shaheen. Sununu's legislative record concerned pro-Israel advocates: among other things, he voted against a resolution criticizing the UN for passing an anti-Israel resolution, and against another that urged the State Department to demand information from Lebanon, Syria, and the Palestinian Authority about three Israelis missing in action. Because of this dubious record, pro-Israel political groups first supported Sununu's primary opponent, Sen. Bob Smith, the incumbent, and then Governor Shaheen in the general election. In a postelection analysis, the American Jewish Committee drew some solace, noting that though "Senator-elect Sununu's record in the House presents, as an understatement by an official of the Republican Jewish Coalition put it, a 'less than stellar record of support' for Israel. . . . Nevertheless, in a campaign position paper, he affirmed his commitment to foreign aid and stressed the need to maintain Israel's military superiority in the Middle East and protect Israel's security."

In Georgia, Rep. Saxby Chambliss, a Republican who had served four terms in the House, unseated first-term incumbent Sen. Max Cleland, a Democrat. Cleland had come under fire from Chambliss's Jewish supporters, who claimed that Cleland did nothing when Democratic Representative Cynthia McKinney antagonized the Jewish community (see below). But others Jews in Georgia endorsed Cleland, noting his consistent pro-Israel stance.

On the other side of Capitol Hill, 35 Jewish candidates competed for congressional seats. With the victory of Democrat Rahm Emanuel, a former Clinton White House aide, in the fifth district of Illinois, and the retirement of Rep. Gilman, the number of Jews in the House remained at 26. Winning reelection, often with no or only token opposition, were California Democrats Howard Berman, Susan Davis, Bob Filner, Jane Harman, Tom Lantos, Adam Schiff, Brad Sherman, and Henry Waxman; Florida Democrats Peter Deutsch and Robert Wexler; Jan Schakowsky (D., Ill.); Ben Cardin (D., Md.); Barney Frank (D., Mass.); Sander Levin (D., Mich.); Shelley Berkley (D., Nev.); Steve Rothman (D., N.J.); New York Democrats Gary Ackerman, Eliot Engel, Steve Israel, Nita Lowey, Jerry Nadler, and Anthony Weiner; Martin Frost (D., Tex.); Eric Cantor (R., Va.); and Bernard Sanders (Ind., Vt.).

With the retirement of Ben Gilman, Rep. Cantor was the only Jewish member of the House's majority party. In December, the House leadership announced that Cantor, a staunch supporter of Israel, had been appointed chief deputy whip, a meteoric ascent for a congressman just concluding his freshman term. In contrast to Gilman, who was seen as a moderate on domestic social issues, Cantor's record was more in line with the conservative mainstream of his party, and therefore not in consonance with many of the positions taken by the bulk of the organized Jewish community. Nevertheless, the Jewish Telegraphic Agency quoted Jewish leaders welcoming the appointment to a leadership position of someone whose "door is always open to us," and reported on speculation that Cantor's elevation was, in part, a reflection of a canny GOP effort at "making inroads into the Jewish community."

In California's 27th district, Democratic incumbent Brad Sherman defeated Republican challenger Robert Levy in the only House race pitting Jewish candidates against each other. In Florida's new 13th district, Jan Schneider, a Jewish Democrat, lost to the Republican, Secretary of State Katherine Harris, who had received national attention for her role in the turmoil surrounding the 2000 election in that state. Two Jewish candidates, both Democrats—Harry Jacobs and Roger Kahn—lost bids for congressional seats in new districts in the South, Florida's 24th and Georgia's 11th, respectively. Democrat David Fink failed in his bid to unseat incumbent Republican Joe Knollenberg in Michigan's ninth district.

Some of the most interesting congressional races played out in the primaries. Reps. Cynthia McKinney (D., Ga.) and Earl Hilliard (D., Ala.), African Americans who were widely regarded as anti-Israel, lost their seats in the Democratic primaries to challengers whose campaigns, while run on a variety of issues, attracted support from pro-Israel groups and individuals. Hilliard, and especially McKinney—she was drawn to conspiracy theories about U.S. foreign policy and even more hostile to Israel than Hilliard—received support from advocates of the Palestinian cause. McKinney was defeated for the Democratic nomination by Denise Majette, and Hilliard by Artur Davis, both of them also African Americans who went on to triumph in the general election. During and after these primary races, the heavy pro-Israel push for ousting the two incumbents raised considerable discussion about the implications for black-Jewish relations (see below, pp. 96–97).

Two Jews competed for, and won, gubernatorial seats. Ed Rendell, the former Democratic mayor of Philadelphia, won in Pennsylvania, and Linda Lingle a Republican, triumphed in Hawaii. They became the first Jewish governors since 1994, when Bruce Sundlun was governor of Rhode Island. Lingle, an active member of the Republican Jewish Coalition, was the second Jewish woman to serve as a state governor. (Madeleine Kunin, the first, governed Vermont from 1985 to 1991.)

As the majority party, Republicans would assume control of every Senate committee when the new Congress convened in January 2003. Jewish Democrats stepping down from chairmanships of full committees were Carl Levin of Michigan, who forfeited Armed Services, and Joseph Lieberman of Connecticut, who lost his post on Government Affairs. Similarly, Charles Schumer of New York would no longer serve as chairman of the Senate Judiciary Subcommittee on Administrative Oversight and the Courts. On the other hand, Republican Arlen Specter of Pennsylvania was slated to take the helm at Veterans Affairs.

The new Congress would see no such sweeping changes on the House side since the leadership remained in Republican hands, but one change in a House committee chairmanship was of particular note. With Gilman retiring, it was unclear at year's end who would chair the House International Relations Subcommittee on the Middle East and South Asia, a panel created when Gilman was forced—under House leadership term-limit rules—to step down from his position as chair of the full committee. It was also conceivable that the new Congress would dissolve the subcommittee.

Significant changes in the House leadership occurred in the week following the election. Rep. Tom DeLay (R., Tex.), formerly House majority whip, was elected majority leader for the 108th Congress, replacing fellow Texas Democrat Dick Armey, who was retiring. Rep. Nancy Pelosi (D., Cal.) became House minority leader following the decision of Rep. Richard Gephardt (D., Mo.) to step down from his leadership post in the wake of the election results. Both of these changes maintained leadership that was widely regarded as supportive of Israel. (Martin Frost, a Jewish Democrat from Texas, was originally in contention with Pelosi for the leadership position, but withdrew when it became clear that he did not have the votes.)

In addition to these shifts in leadership, the Republican gains also enhanced the authority of President Bush, coming as they did while popular support for the war on terrorism was at its height. This became evident very quickly when Sen. Trent Lott (R., Miss.), expected to be the incoming Senate majority leader, asserted that he did not like lame-duck sessions, preferring that unfinished business be left for the next Congress. But Lott had to change his mind when the president, two days after the election, publicly insisted that Congress vote to create a Homeland Security Department and pass bills on terrorism insurance before it adjourned for the year. Congress did exactly what the president wanted. It did not, however, complete work on appropriations for the fiscal year that had already begun on October 1, meaning that the federal government would operate in the interim largely on the basis of continuing resolutions that maintained funding at the levels of fiscal year 2002.

How Jews voted in the 2002 elections was of great interest to the candidates, the parties, and observers of the American Jewish community. Since Jewish turnout at the polls is often disproportionately high, the Jewish vote could prove pivotal, especially in close races, and wealthy Jews were prominent contributors to political campaigns. Analysts speculated before Election Day that Jewish support could be highly significant for the reelection hopes of three governors—George Pataki (R., N.Y.), Jeb Bush (R., Fla.), and Gray Davis (D., Cal.). Some believed that the Jewish vote would show a swing toward the Republican column because of the administration's generally pro-Israel stance, the president's handling of the war on terrorism, and what was widely perceived as a trend toward conservatism among younger Jews. In fact the Republican Jewish Coalition launched a massive issue-advocacy campaign in South Florida, including television, radio, mail, phone, and newspaper advertising, to inform the Jewish community of Governor Bush's pro-Israel views.

After the elections, claims were made about the Jewish vote in specific races. One report had it that more than 80 percent of the Jewish vote in New Jersey went to Frank Lautenberg, the Democratic candidate for senator. A staffer for George Pataki, citing an analysis of the vote in heavily Jewish New York neighborhoods, told the *New York Jewish Week* that the Republican governor had garnered more than 50 percent of the state's Jewish vote, and, in the staffer's words, that "has to be a record for a statewide Republican."

The Voter News Service—an organization created by a consortium of ABC, CBS, NBC, CNN, Fox, and the Associated Press, that, among other things, did exit polling to determine how voters viewed the issues and how certain groups voted—declined, at first, to release exit polling data for 2002, declaring it unreliable. Months later the service announced that 35 percent of Jewish voters had supported Republican candidates in 2002, a substantial increase over the 21–26 percent that had voted Republican in midterm and presidential elections since 1992.

In an unexpected turn of events, Senator Lott, the Republican minority leader who had been expected to regain his former position as majority leader when the new Congress convened, announced in late December that he would step down from his leadership role. The decision came in the wake of a firestorm over statements he had made at a dinner earlier that month feting outgoing Senator Strom Thurmond (R., S.C.). In his remarks, Lott seemed to endorse the segregationist platform on which Thurmond had campaigned when he ran for president as a minor-party candidate in 1948. Several Jewish groups condemned the remarks.

Following Lott's announcement, Senate Republicans named Bill Frist of Tennessee majority leader. Jewish groups were unfamiliar with this physician-turned-politician, but, based on his past votes and history, they noted that Frist could be expected to support Israel. At a speech before a 2001 conference of the American Israel Public Affairs Committee (AIPAC), Frist had reflected on an earlier visit to the Jewish state, and said: "If every American could only go to Israel and have these experiences, the very few challenges to U.S. commitments that we have today, I think they would go away." On the domestic front, however, the incoming leader's positions on such issues as vouchers, charitable choice, and hate-crimes legislation were expected to run counter to those of much of the organized Jewish community.

President Bush and the Jewish Community

For the second year in a row—and just the second time in history—leaders of the American Jewish community came to the White House on December 4, 2002, for a Hanukkah celebration, complete with the lighting of a menorah, and kosher-catered latkes and jelly doughnuts. The event, coming even as the administration prepared to unveil the "road map" for Middle East peace developed together with the European Union, Russia, and the UN (see below, pp. 229–30), followed meetings that same day between a number of Jewish leaders and high-ranking administration officials.

At the party, President Bush said that the spirit of the Maccabees continued "in the lives of the State of Israel and throughout the Jewish community, and among all people who fight violence and terror," and he reaffirmed his commitment to end the threat of terrorism against the United States and Israel. All in all, the Jewish leaders in attendance saw the celebration—"not just a party, but a very powerful, symbolic event," in the words of American Jewish Committee executive director David Harris—as reflecting a steadily warming relationship between the Jewish community and the president. Rooted in a common ground of support for Israel and the war against terrorism, it flourished notwithstanding some significant differences that much of the community had with the administration on certain domestic issues.

Earlier in the year American Jews were not quite so certain that the administration was unequivocally on Israel's side. The massive national pro-Israel rally in Washington on April 15 (see below, p. 115) was largely motivated by fears that the president, under State Department influence, might have the U.S. join with the European powers in pressuring Israel to make territorial concessions without any real Palestinian renunciation of violence. It was that sense of Jewish unease that induced a small number of the demonstrators to boo Secretary of Defense Paul Wolfowitz when, after saying that "President Bush wants you to know that he stands in solidarity with you," he alluded to the suffering of the Palestinians and the contemplated establishment of a Palestinian state.

What largely assuaged Jewish fears was the president's speech of June 24 (for the full text see below, pp. 212–16). Rather than call on Israel to adhere to a firm timetable of actions to ease the condition of the Palestinians—as the State Department had reportedly advised—Bush made any such Israeli moves contingent on the Palestinians holding new parliamentary elections, choosing new leaders "not compromised by terror," conducting comprehensive governmental reform, and taking effective steps to stop terrorism. The broad mainstream of the organized Jewish community applauded the speech, and its perceived pro-Israel message served the administration well in the American Jewish community through the remainder of the year.

Preparing for Election 2004

As the year ended, it seemed certain that Senator Joseph Lieberman (D., Conn.)—the man who made history in 2000 as the first Jewish major-party nominee for vice president—would soon make history once again by announcing his candidacy for the Democratic presidential nomination in 2004. After the bitterly disputed 2000 election, Lieberman had pledged not to run for the presidential nomination against former vice president Albert Gore, his 2000 running mate, were Gore to seek it. But in a surprise announcement on December 15, Gore said that he would sit out the upcoming election, thus opening the door for Lieberman, who had already been preparing for this eventuality. Had he sought the nomination, Gore would have been the clear front-runner, but his withdrawal threw the race wide open.

THE POLICY ARENA

Terrorism

In the wake of September 11, 2001, the nation had quickly closed ranks behind President Bush as he took quick and vigorous action to pursue Al Qaeda forces into their Afghanistan redoubt, and brought down the Taliban regime that had given them sanctuary (see AJYB 2002, pp. 159–61). But divisive domestic issues related to the terrorist threat that had begun to play out in the last months of 2001 became themes that resonated in 2002 for the American Jewish community and for the rest of the nation. As the Bush administration adopted measures intended to forestall another terrorist attack, was it fighting terrorism "smart," or simply taking action for the sake of taking action? And, did some of the administration measures designed to protect national security go too far in infringing on civil liberties and due process?

These questions were brought to the fore first in October 2001, when Congress passed the sweeping USA-PATRIOT Act, which led civil-liberties groups to raise a host of concerns (see AJYB 2002, pp. 162–63). Then, reports emerged that approximately 1,200 aliens—mostly of Middle Eastern or South Asian origin (including some 60 Israelis)—had been taken into custody by police and immigration officials on visa violations, many of whom were subsequently deported. Immigrant-rights groups and other advocacy organizations raised questions about these detentions—including the government's apparent reluctance to release information as to the number of detainees and their identities, violations of due process, and racial profiling.

Many more such issues arose as 2001 ended and 2002 wore on. In November 2001, for example, President Bush issued a directive to the Department of Defense to establish procedures for military tribunals to try noncitizen detainees held at Guantanamo Bay. Most of these people, captured in Afghanistan, were considered "unlawful combatants" in the eyes of the U.S., and thus not subject to the procedural safeguards normally available to prisoners of war. That same month, Attorney General John Ashcroft issued a directive authorizing law enforcement officials to listen in on conversations between detainees and their attorneys under certain circumstances. Another Ashcroft directive, in May 2002, revised and loosened the standards under which federal officials might conduct surveillance of activities otherwise protected under the First Amendment. During 2002, the administration had two American citizens arrested on U.S. soil and held them incommunicado, maintaining that since the men were illegal enemy combatants, they could therefore be held without charges and prevented from seeing their lawyers.

Beginning with the proposal of the USA-PATRIOT Act in late 2001, Reform Judaism's Religious Action Center (RAC) staked out a role as the Jewish community's most outspoken critic of many of the administration's measures; other national Jewish organizations generally supported the war against terrorism while raising questions about specific actions.

This split in the Jewish community came to the fore at the annual conference of the Jewish Council for Public Affairs (JCPA) in February 2002, where the RAC offered a resolution criticizing the administration for drawing the wrong balance between civil liberties and national security in three specific ways—subjecting attorney-client communications to eavesdropping even on a limited basis; creating military tribunals; and detaining aliens suspected of involvement in terrorism for an indefinite period. A number of the major national Jewish organizations—including the American Jewish Committee, the Anti-Defamation League, B'nai B'rith, and Hadassah—opposed the resolution as premature and as sending the wrong message at a time of great national peril. But the RAC resolution carried, supported overwhelmingly by the Jewish community-relations councils, joined by the National Council of Jewish Women and several other national organizations. Balancing its critique of the administration, the JCPA passed an additional resolution noting that so long as "basic constitutional rights" were safeguarded, it favored "strengthening domestic antiterrorism measures that enhance law enforcement capabilities."

Some of the groups voting against the JCPA resolution did find other venues for voicing their concerns within the context of overall support for the administration. Thus on January 8, 2002, President Harold Tanner and Executive Director David A. Harris of the American Jewish Committee wrote Secretary of Defense Donald Rumsfeld urging inclusion of a set of due-process safeguards as part of the procedures to be established pursuant to the president's directive on military tribunals. AJC recommended specific assurances that the accused would be informed of the charges against them, have the right to choose counsel, be judged according to a specified burden of proof, have a right to appeal to the federal courts, and be subject to the death penalty only when the judges' verdict was unanimous. These procedures were largely included in the Department of Defense's implementing order of March 21, with one significant exception—appeals would be taken to a three-member review panel appointed by the secretary of defense, not to the federal courts.

On the legislative front in 2002, Congress's attention focused first on a proposal to create a new cabinet-level Department of Homeland Security into which would be folded various security-related functions, including immigration control. The first to suggest such a department was Sen. Joseph Lieberman (D., Conn.), who introduced the idea in May; it was endorsed by the Democratic-controlled Governmental Affairs Committee of the Senate that same month. At the time, the administration did not express support, but it soon changed course. In a speech to the nation on June 6, President Bush called on Congress to upgrade the Office of Homeland Security to a federal cabinet-level body, consolidating 22 different agencies and 170,000 employees in what would be the most significant reorganization of the federal government in many decades.

Responding to the president's request, both Democrats and Republicans vowed to pass legislation creating the new department before the first anniversary of the terrorist attacks. However, homeland-security legislation was stalled prior to the November elections by a dispute over civil-service protections for the new department's employees. In the aftermath of the Republican electoral victories, the dynamic changed markedly. On November 13, a new "compromise" version of H.R.5710, the Homeland Security Act of 2002, was introduced in Congress, largely hewing to President Bush's demands. The House passed it by 299 to 121, and the Senate subsequently approved by 90 to 9. The bill was signed into law on November 25. Not only did the legislation consolidate the many federal agencies into the new department, but it also created new resources for the battle against terrorism, such as a National Bio-weapons Defense and Analysis Center within the Defense Department to develop countermeasures against potential terrorist attacks that used weapons of mass destruction. Implementation of the act was to take place through much of 2003.

H.R.5710 included provisions pertinent to the civil liberties concerns of a number of Jewish organizations. First, the act included a provision specifically stating that it was not intended to authorize the development of a national identification system or card. Second, it prohibited implementation of the TIPS (Terrorism Information Prevention System) plan announced by Attorney General Ashcroft earlier in the year. TIPS, which would have encouraged bus and truck drivers, meter readers, port workers, letter carriers, and other persons without law-enforcement training to report "suspicious activities," aroused opposition from conservative Republicans such as Dick Armey (R., Tex.), the retiring House majority leader, and Rep. Bob Barr (R., Ga.), as well as from liberal Democrats such as Rep. John Conyers (D., Mich.). The critics charged that TIPS would "promote citizens spying on one another" — a concern echoed by the Religious Action Center of Reform Judaism and the American Jewish Committee. In the end, Armey and Barr succeeded in including a ban on implementation of TIPS in the final version of the legislation.

Some civil libertarians were unhappy about inclusion in the Homeland Security Act of a provision for the creation of a Directorate for Information Analysis and Infrastructure Protection. This body was accorded extensive and unprecedented surveillance powers "to access, receive, and analyze law enforcement information, intelligence information, and other information from agencies of the federal government, state and local government agencies (including law-enforcement agencies), and private sector entities." The act also called for the appointment of a privacy officer to address privacy issues and complaints, and assure compliance with fair-information practices as set out in the Privacy Act of 1974.

In a related development, H.R.3210, the Terrorism Risk Protection Act, passed both houses of Congress in November 2002 during the lame-duck session. The president subsequently signed it into law, singling this bill out as a priority for action in a postelection press conference. It addressed two issues of substantial interest to the Jewish community. First, the measure's major thrust was to assure the insurance industry of a federal backstop in the event of a future terrorist attack, and thus enabled coverage against such attack to be included in newly written policies at reasonable rates. Notwithstanding an FBI alert in June that Jewish organizations were potential targets for terrorist attack, it was not clear that they were facing any greater increases in insurance costs than others. Nonetheless, the legislation would serve to contain the prospect of spiraling insurance costs for all public facilities.

A second key provision of H.R.3210 was often referred to as the Justice for Victims of Terrorism Act. Introduced in various forms by Sens. Christopher Dodd (D., Conn.) and Tom Harkin (D., Iowa), and Reps. Peter Hoekstra (R., Mich.) and Vito Fossella (R., N.Y.), it provided for payments to terror victims from the nondiplomatic frozen assets of terrorists, terrorist organizations, and state sponsors of terrorism. Guidelines for a presidential waiver were included, requiring determination, on an asset-by-asset basis, that a waiver was necessary on national-security grounds. Previous legislation had secured such relief for certain victims of terrorism, but failed to cover all such victims, and potentially left American taxpayers, rather than the state sponsors of terrorism, paying the bills for such judgments.

Speaking at the American Jewish Committee's 2002 annual meeting, Sen. Arlen Specter (R., Pa.) indicated that, due to the unprecedented speed with which the USA-PATRIOT antiterrorism law was enacted, Congress would have to reexamine some of the bill's provisions to address civil-liberties concerns, particularly as those impacted on immigration procedures. Both AJC and the ADL indicated support for Sen. Specter's initiative and worked closely with his office to craft a new bill that maintained the law's core provisions while ameliorating the problematic civil-liberties issues.

Refugees and Immigration

It was hardly surprising that the need for intensified scrutiny of immigrants following the events of September 11, 2001, brought a virtual freeze on admissions to the United States at the end of that year, and, in 2002, a dramatic drop in admissions as compared to prior years. As of the close of fiscal year 2002 on September 30, refugee admissions were at a record low, only some 27,000 admissions out of an authorized level of 70,000.

Several hundred Iranian Jewish refugees, caught by this slowdown, were stranded for months in Vienna, some living in squalid conditions. In their case, the delay was due to the FBI's post-9/11 enhanced security reviews of Middle Eastern nationals bound for the United States. These refugees—141 men traveling along with another 191 family members— awaited the FBI's "security advisory opinions," required for all males between the ages of 16 and 50 seeking to enter the United States from countries known to harbor or sponsor terrorists (the changes in procedure also affected Iranian Christians, Zoroastrians, and Bahais). The plight of the Iranian Jewish refugees was the subject of a White House meeting late in 2001, as representatives of the State Department, National Security Council, Domestic Policy Council, and refugee agencies sought to ameliorate what had become a vexing humanitarian problem. Jewish and immigrant groups urged the Department of State and the FBI to expedite the security examination of these individuals and of other refugees fleeing religious and ethnic persecution in their home countries. In early December, the Immigration and Naturalization Service (INS) announced it would send specially trained agents abroad to interview applicants for refugee status and to resolve asylum claims. This was hailed by the Hebrew Immigrant Aid Society (HIAS) as an important contribution to refugee processing, although Mark Hetfield, HIAS director of international operations, termed it "a silver lining in a very dark cloud," given the growing tendency to view refugees—and immigrants in general— within a security context, as reflected by the impending inclusion of the INS in the new Department of Homeland Security.

Another indication that immigration and border control had become identified with the security agenda was President Bush's signature, on May 14, to H.R.3525, the Enhanced Border Security and Visa Entry Reform Act of 2001. First introduced in the Senate in November 2001 by Sens. Edward Kennedy (D., Mass.), Sam Brownback (R., Kans.), Dianne Feinstein (D., Cal.), and Jon Kyl (R., Ariz.), and in the House that December by Rep. James Sensenbrenner (R., Wis.), chair of the House Judiciary Committee, the act required the attorney general to monitor electronically foreign visitors and students in the U.S. The measure built, as well, on immigration provisions in the USA-PATRIOT law of October 2001 by requiring tighter monitoring of foreign students and the use of tamper-resistant travel documents with biometric identifiers, such as retina scans and fingerprints. The bill also authorized another 200 inspectors for the INS immediately and 200 more annually through fiscal year 2006. Since, unlike the controversial USA-PATRIOT Act, pro-immigration groups viewed this proposal as a consensus measure, it was endorsed not only by Jewish groups, but also by the National Immigration Forum, an immigration-advocacy umbrella organization to which the American Jewish Committee, Anti-Defamation League, and HIAS, among other Jewish groups, belong.

With passage of the Homeland Security Act soon after the November election, the INS was slated to go out of existence in 2003. Long criticized as bloated and inefficient, it was to be replaced by two separate immigration agencies within the new Department of Homeland Security. One, the Bureau of Border Security (BBS), was to handle enforcement of the immigration laws, including border patrol, detention and removal, intelligence, investigations, inspections, and the establishment and administration of rules governing the granting of visas. The other, the Bureau of Citizenship and Immigration Services (BCIS), would assist immigrants in their transition to life in the U.S., and would have jurisdiction over immigrant visas, naturalization, asylum and refugee applications, service-center functions, and all other adjudication previously performed by the INS. Within the BCIS, an Office of Citizenship was to promote instruction and training on citizenship.

The legislation included a "sense of Congress" provision asserting that the missions of the BCIS and BBS were equally important and merited adequate funding, and that functions transferred from the old INS should not operate at levels below those in effect prior to the creation of the Department of Homeland Security. Another "sense of Congress" provision called for improving the quality and efficiency of immigration services. The law ordered, as well, a pilot initiative to eliminate backlog of immigration applications, and called for the appointment of an ombudsman to report on the impact of the new procedures on the government's processing of immigration.

Earlier in the year, pro-immigration groups expressed several concerns about placing the functions of the old INS in the new department. First, the move suggested that immigrants were a security threat. Second, creation of the new department would undermine efforts already underway to reform the INS so as to place equal emphasis on its two components, enforcement and services. And third, subsuming the Bureau of Citizenship and Immigration Services in a massive terrorism-fighting department would further hamper the effective delivery of immigrant services. Thus some pro-immigrant organizations had pushed for immigration services to remain under the jurisdiction of the Department of Justice even after the enforcement functions were transferred to the Department of Homeland Security. Others had hoped that if both enforcement and immigration functions were transferred to the new department, they would be coordinated by one "immigration czar," and expressed disappointment at the legislation's failure to provide for such a high-level official. These groups also criticized H.R.5710's failure to create the position of inspector general for civil rights, a high-level, Senate-confirmed post, with investigative authority over constitutional and related violations within the new Department of Homeland Security.

On February 13, 2002, the Senate passed S.1731, a comprehensive farm bill sponsored by Sen. Harkin, chairman of the Senate Agriculture, Nutrition and Forestry Committee, that included an amendment offered by Sens. Richard Durbin (D., Ill.) and Richard Lugar (R., Ind.) restoring food-stamp eligibility to many legal immigrants, including children and those who had resided in the U.S. for at least five years—a benefit eliminated in 1996. Earlier, the Bush administration had announced its support for this restoration of benefits, and the House-Senate conference committee ultimately incorporated the amendment into the final version of the farm bill. The president signed it into law on May 13.

Foreign Aid and U.S.-Israel Relations

Since the onset of the Palestinian war of terror against Israel toward the end of 2000, Israel had faced a sizeable increase in security spending; in 2001 alone, its security budget rose by almost $800 million. To assist Israel through this trying time, the White House's Office of Management and Budget (OMB) suggested additional aid to Israel in the amount of $200 million, as part of a proposed overall increase in foreign aid commensurate with heightened demands on America's global leadership. But after pressure from the State Department, the administration omitted the money for Israel from the $27-billion supplemental package it sent to Congress in January 2002.

Nevertheless, on May 24, by a vote of 280-138, the House passed a

$29.4-billion supplemental measure that included the additional $200 million for Israel. On June 7, the Senate passed its $31.5-billion supplemental package by a vote of 71-22, and it also included the additional aid to Israel. House and Senate conferees reached agreement on July 18 to trim the supplemental measure to $28.9 billion so as to avoid a likely presidential veto, but they retained the additional aid to the Jewish state. On July 23, the House adopted the conference report by 397-32, and the Senate cleared it the next day, 92-7. President Bush signed the measure into law on August 2. However, the language of the bill did not make the aid to Israel automatic; it was dependent on the president sending a special determination of "emergency need" within 30 days, and only then would the funds be released. Pro-Israel groups urged that such a determination be made, but it was not forthcoming

In the meantime, work continued on legislation for foreign-operations appropriations for fiscal year 2003. The House bill, H.R.5410, reported out of that body's appropriations committee on September 17, 2002, provided for the $600 million in economic support and $2.1 billion in military aid requested by the president in his budget submission earlier in the year, and included as well the $200 million in supplemental aid. The Senate appropriations bill reported out of that body's appropriations committee (S.2779) followed suit. Committee reports for both bills emphasized that the level of assistance for Israel—and for Egypt as well—was based in great measure upon their continued adherence to the Camp David Accords and the Egyptian-Israeli peace process. The reports also urged other Arab League members to end their boycott of Israel and normalize relations with it.

The House bill, but not the Senate's, conditioned U.S. support for Palestinian statehood on Palestinian adherence to the conditions laid out by President Bush in his speech of June 24, 2002, which had become the basis of U.S. policy in the region. They included the requirements that Palestinians elect a new leadership committed to peaceful coexistence with Israel, dismantle the terrorist infrastructure, and join in the creation of a new, cooperative security entity (for the full text of the speech, see below, pp. 212–16). The House version included provision for a presidential waiver to afford flexibility in case of extraordinary or unpredictable circumstances. The American Israel Public Affairs Committee (AIPAC), as well as a number of other pro-Israel organizations, supported this language as simply codifying President Bush's June 24 speech into law.

The language echoing the president's June 24 speech was widely seen as a successor to S.2194, the Arafat Accountability Act, introduced in the spring by Sens. Dianne Feinstein (D., Cal.) and Mitch McConnell (R., Ky.) in the Senate, and the parallel measure, H.R.4693, introduced by Rep. Roy Blunt (R., Mo.) in the House. This initiative was designed to hold Palestinian leadership accountable for its failure to comply with the Oslo Accords and deter terrorism. It incorporated most of the sanction provisions directed against the Palestine Liberation Organization (PLO) and the Palestine Authority (PA) contained in the Middle East Peace Commitments Act (MEPCA), introduced in 2001 in both chambers. In addition, it sought to impose sanctions directly on Arafat himself, deny visas to PA and PLO officials, and "symbolically" lower the status of the Palestinian leadership's Washington office. Finally, the bill would have frozen all PA and PLO assets, as well as Arafat's assets, in the U.S.

Even with an extraordinary lame-duck session, neither the House nor the Senate acted on its foreign appropriations bill, or, indeed, on most other outstanding appropriations bills, even though fiscal year 2003 had already begun on October 1. Spending levels for operations covered by the pending appropriations bills were maintained past the commencement of the new fiscal year at 2002 levels by continuing resolution, an action that left open the question of when the contemplated supplemental funds for Israel would be forthcoming.

Also left unresolved was the disposition of a request made by Dov Weisglass, Israeli prime minister Sharon's bureau chief, of National Security Adviser Condoleezza Rice at a meeting on November 11 for at least $10 billion in loan guarantees, cash, additional military assistance, and a larger proportion of military aid that could be spent inside Israel. The timing of this new request created a complication, coming as it did just prior to the Likud Party's primary elections, which would be followed by Israeli national elections in February 2003. The White House was reportedly wary of appearing to interfere in Israel's internal politics.

ANTI-SEMITISM AND DOMESTIC TERRORISM

Terrorism and the American Jewish Community

On Friday, June 21, as many Jewish organizations prepared to close early for the oncoming Sabbath and synagogues made ready to receive worshipers, the FBI issued a warning to Jewish institutions, based on intelligence information that Al Qaeda operatives had discussed the possibility of attacking them with bomb-laden gasoline trucks. As news of the warning spread throughout the country, the national Jewish agencies cautioned against overreaction even as they called for heightened wariness, noting that the FBI alert did not refer to specific targets or dates, and was uncorroborated. Nevertheless, concern was much in evidence, particularly after the following Sunday, when Al Qaeda announced that it took credit for the fatal April 11 truck bombing of a synagogue on the Tunisian island of Djerba. Jewish communal and religious organizations proceeded to adopt new security procedures and improved their lines of communication with law-enforcement authorities.

Within days of the FBI's warning, that agency and the Jewish community confronted an incident that seemed to place them on opposite sides over how to define an act of terrorism. On July 4, Hesham Mohamed Hadayet, an Egyptian-born resident of Irvine, California, went on a shooting spree at the El Al counter at Los Angeles International Airport, killing Yaakov Aminov, an Israeli-born American, and Victoria Hen, an El Al ticket agent. Hadayet's murderous rampage was stopped when El Al security guards tackled him; unable to subdue him, they shot him to death.

Israeli officials were quick to pronounce the event a terrorist attack, pointing to the fact that "the gunman skipped dozens of other foreign airline counters to target El Al." American Jewish organizations agreed, and noted that the definition of "terror" in the FBI guidelines was "unlawful use of force and violence" in furtherance of "social or political objectives." Their perspective seemed reinforced by news reports emerging soon after the attack that Hadayet had previously expressed virulently anti-Israel opinions, and by the FBI's acknowledgement the day after the attack that Hadayet evidently had gone to the airport intending to kill people. At least initially, however, FBI agents and local law-enforcement officials saw the crime as "an isolated incident," though they would not "rule out" that the attack might be a "hate crime" or even "terrorism."

As days became weeks and the FBI still declined to term the attack a terrorist act, Rabbi Avi Weiss, head of Amcha—The Coalition for Jewish Concerns, threatened to sue the FBI for its alleged failure to adhere to its own guidelines for determining what was a terrorist event. While the mainstream Jewish organizations distanced themselves from the idea of a lawsuit, they spoke of a troubling failure by authorities to confront the obvious, with important implications for the resources to be made available to the investigation. Among others, Daniel Pipes, director of the Middle East Forum, compared the FBI's hesitancy to term the attack an instance of terror to previous cases, such the 1994 Brooklyn Bridge attack on a van carrying Hassidic youngsters that resulted in the death of one boy. The FBI initially classified that incident as "road rage," only to reverse itself in 2000 and recognize it as terrorism.

In August, responding to a letter from Rep. Eliot Engel (D., N.Y.) expressing concern that the FBI had not called the El Al attack terrorism, an FBI spokesman indicated that "terrorism has certainly not been ruled out in this case, and we do not intend this interim period of information gathering to imply that it has been. It is, in fact, being investigated as such." In an interview with the Jewish Telegraphic Agency, Engel termed the FBI's new account of its investigation a "flip-flop."

Unfinished Business

On January 7, a federal court of appeals overturned the convictions of Lemrick Nelson, Jr., and Charles Price for civil-rights violations in connection with the killing of Yankel Rosenbaum, a Hassidic Jew, during the 1991 riots in Crown Heights, Brooklyn. The court found that the defendants had not received a fair trial because the trial judge had manipulated the jury selection process in an effort to create a racially and religiously balanced jury. The appellate court rejected, however, a challenge to the constitutionality of the federal hate-crimes law under which Nelson and Price had been charged. A new trial was ordered.

Also in January, Irv Rubin, chairman of the Jewish Defense League, and Earl Krugel, a JDL member, were indicted in federal court and then arraigned. They had been arrested in December 2001 for conspiring to blow up the King Fahd Mosque in Los Angeles and the offices of an Arab American congressman, Darrell Issa (R., Cal.), in Orange County. A list of targets prepared by the alleged plotters originally included the offices of the Muslim Public Affairs Council in Los Angeles as well, but that site had been removed. The JDL, founded by the late Rabbi Meir Kahane in 1968, had a reputation for using violence and intimidation as a means of responding to anti-Semitism, although the organization had been inactive in recent years. Rubin's lawyer denied the charges, terming the arrests an "overreaction" triggered by the events of September 11. Rubin never came to trial: he died in November in a Los Angeles jail, an apparent suicide.

Assessing Anti-Semitism

On January 24, the American Jewish Committee released a study of the attitudes of Americans toward a wide variety of religious, racial, and ethnic groups. Conducted by Tom Smith, director of the General Social Survey at the University of Chicago's National Opinion Research Center (NORC), it showed that Jews were held in very high esteem by other Americans for being intelligent, hardworking, and strongly committed to their families. In fact, Jews were perceived in more positive terms than whites in general.

More good news for Jews followed in April, when the Anti-Defamation League's annual audit of anti-Semitism came out. It indicated that 1,432 anti-Semitic incidents had been reported in the U.S. during 2001, an 11-percent decline from the previous year. According to these figures, substantial drops in the number of incidents had occurred in both New York and California. Acts of anti-Semitic vandalism nationwide were down from 729 in 2000 to 555 in 2001, the lowest number reported in two decades. All of this stood in marked contrast to the sharp increase in attacks on Jews and Jewish institutions elsewhere in the world, and what the ADL report described as the "mainstreaming" of global anti-Semitism, including acceptance of outlandish theories of Jewish and Israeli conspiracies (see below, in the various articles about other countries). Reflecting on the contrast between the U.S. and Europe, ADL national director Abraham Foxman said: "There's always been a difference between the U.S. and the rest of the world. Political anti-Semitism has been a part of European tradition for hundreds of years."

Yet the ADL's hopeful portrayal of the U.S. had to be modified in June, when that organization released the results of a survey demonstrating an increase in anti-Semitic attitudes, if not incidents. Based on interviews conducted in late April and early May 2002, soon after Israel's incursion into the Jenin refugee camp (see below, p. 201), the survey found a jump in the number of people agreeing with such statements as "Jews have too much power in the U.S. today" and "Jews have too much power in the business world." Even though those endorsing these statements remained a minority (20 percent of respondents agreed with the former statement and 24 percent with the latter), these still amounted to increases of some 3–4 percent. Moreover, the survey concluded that 17 percent of respondents had agreed with enough anti-Semitic statements to be classified as "strongly" anti-Semitic, an increase of 5 percent from 1998. The ADL report also noted an 11-percent rise in the number of anti-Semitic incidents for May 2002 as compared to May 2001.

Hate-Crimes Legislation

Introduced in 2001 by Sens. Edward Kennedy (D., Mass.) and Gordon Smith (R., Oreg.), and by Reps. Connie Morella (R., Md.) and John Conyers (D., Mich.), the Local Law Enforcement Enhancement Act

(LLEEA) extended the category of federal hate crimes beyond the existing criteria of crimes committed on the basis of race, color, religion and national origin to encompass also those motivated by sexual orientation, disabilities, and gender. The measure required that strict certification requirements be met before federal jurisdiction could be invoked, so that federal hate-crime jurisdiction would not intrude on local law enforcement, and provided federal grants for personnel, investigation, and prosecution of hate crimes at the local level.

The Senate began floor debate on the measure immediately after the 2002 Memorial Day break. On June 11, a cloture motion vote came up aimed at limiting debate, part of a Democratic effort to stave off anticipated Republican amendments that would have killed the bill. But Majority Leader Tom Daschle (D., S.D.) pulled the bill from the floor after the Senate voted 54-43 on cloture, failing to reach the 60 votes needed to wrap up debate and move the bill to a final vote. An effort by Rep. Conyers to move the bill forward in the House by filing a motion to discharge from the Rules Committee for consideration also fell short, as the discharge petition garnered only 178 of the requisite 218 signatures for further action. While other strategies were considered for moving the measure through the Senate, including attaching it to the defense-authorization bill, Congress adjourned with no further movement, even though the bill had 50 cosponsors in the Senate and 208 in the House. With continued stiff opposition expected from the House leadership in the new 108th Congress and an uphill battle awaiting in a Senate about to come under Republican control, supporters of hate-crimes legislation were left with a daunting scenario for 2003.

Campus Battles

In a form of trench warfare that often placed the youngest adults in the Jewish community on the front lines, 2002 saw a variety of efforts on America's college campuses to place the policies of the State of Israel beyond the pale. Sometimes these efforts crossed the line from criticism of the Israeli government to denial of Israel's right to exist, and even to outright anti-Semitism.

Divestment campaigns at various universities calling on the school administrations to terminate all financial investments in Israel—modeled on the divestment measures directed at apartheid-era South Africa—received much coverage, at least in the Anglo-Jewish press, when classes resumed in the fall, but little traction. Although a divestment petition at

Harvard University garnered several hundred signatures, a counterpetition terming the divestment effort "a one-sided attempt to delegitimize Israel" was signed by nearly 6,000 Harvard faculty, students, and alumni. The Harvard campaign also received a sharp rebuff from university president Lawrence Summers who, in a speech in September 2002, characterized the effort as anti-Semitic in result if not intent, and linked it to an international movement in which "profoundly anti-Israel views are increasingly finding support in progressive intellectual communities." Petition supporters at Harvard, however, responded that the divestment campaign was a legitimate tool against Israeli policies.

Although they did not express themselves as sharply as Summers, the presidents of Columbia University and Barnard College also opposed a faculty-sponsored divestment petition at their schools spearheaded by, among others, Columbia professor Edward Said. In a written statement also issued in September, Columbia president Lee Bollinger said: "The petition alleges human rights abuses and compares Israel to South Africa at the time of apartheid, an analogy I believe is both grotesque and offensive." Barnard president Judith Shapiro issued a statement "to make clear her opposition to a divestment demand that singles out one country in an unsupportable way. The approach taken by the divestment petition does not begin to do justice to the historical complexity of the current crisis."

In a related development in October, a consortium of pro-Palestinian organizations gathered for the Second National Student Conference on the Palestinian Solidarity Movement. Held on the campus of the University of Michigan at Ann Arbor, the event had the avowed purpose of condemning "the racism and discrimination inherent in Zionism" and demanding an end to American support for and investment in Israel, premised, again, on the allegation that Israeli policies were based in "apartheid and discrimination." The inclusion of Sami Al-Arian as a panelist drew particular attention, since the former University of Florida professor had been fired earlier in the year after being linked to the terrorist Islamic Jihad organization. In the end, the conference refused to condemn Palestinian terrorism because "it is not our place to dictate the strategies or tactics adopted by the Palestinian people in their struggle for liberation." Asked *Detroit News* editorial-page editor Nolan Finley, "How would the university react had the Klan or some other extremist group spouting racist, sexist or homophobic hate speech asked for a platform on campus? And when did anti-Semitism lose its seat on the bus of political correctness?"

In September, arguing that many putative Middle East scholars were utilizing American university resources to promote "disinformation, incitement and ignorance" about the Israeli-Palestinian conflict, Daniel Pipes, director of the Middle East Forum, announced the creation of Campus Watch. This was a national project to monitor and publicize unbalanced and ahistorical teaching about that conflict at institutions of higher education, often under the imprimatur of university departments of Middle East studies. Palestinian sympathizers immediately condemned the endeavor as a form of "McCarthyism" for ostensibly smearing and blacklisting those with "unacceptable" views. The American-Arab Anti-Discrimination Committee asserted: "The organizational campaign to silence academic criticism of Israel is incompatible with the cherished American values of free speech and inquiry." Defenders of Campus Watch responded that it was Middle East studies departments that had routinely blacklisted pro-Israel scholars.

Confronting International Anti-Semitism: The Case of Egypt

Americans in general, and the U.S. Congress in particular, were rare allies of the Jewish community in responding to the alarming resurgence of global anti-Semitism that continued through 2002. Egypt, the cultural capital of the Arab world and a Middle East peace partner, was among the worst offenders. Beginning on November 6, the first night of the Muslim holy month of Ramadan, Egyptian television began showing the virulently anti-Semitic "Horseman Without a Horse." This 41-episode series was based on the insidious *Protocols of the Elders of Zion,* a fictitious conspiracy theory devised in Czarist Russia to scapegoat Jews for a variety of social problems and indoctrinate anti-Semitism.

Egypt's Ministry of Information reviewed the scripts of all television shows and had the final say on what could and could not ultimately hit the airwaves. Despite numerous requests to cancel the series, including one from the U.S. embassy in Cairo, the Media and Culture Committee of Egypt's parliament refused to call for the elimination of this so-called "comedy." To protest the anti-Semitic series, Rep. Henry Waxman (D., Cal.) circulated a "Dear Colleague" letter to the entire House of Representatives for signatures. Cosponsored by Rep. Ben Gilman (R., N.Y.), the letter called on Egyptian president Hosni Mubarak to cancel the broadcast. Although many representatives said they agreed with the letter, some were unable to sign it by the tight deadline, set in order to deliver the letter before the series premier, because they were on the road for last-minute campaigning before the elections. As a result, the letter to Mubarak had a respectable but hardly overwhelming 46 signatures.

Then, on November 4, 130 people gathered in front of the Egyptian embassy in Washington to protest the series. This rally featured a broad spectrum of speakers and demonstrators, including Rabbi Stuart Weinblatt of Congregation B'nai Tzedek, Dr. Paul Marshall of the Center for Religious Freedom, Reverend Roy Howard of St. Mark Presbyterian Church, and Ambassador Alfred H. Moses, who had served as ambassador to Romania and president of the American Jewish Committee, and a statement of support from the Lawyers Committee for Human Rights. Speakers expressed grave concern about the hate and violence that the television series might incite, as well as their hopes for peace and tolerance in the Middle East and throughout the world. The demonstrators concluded with a song for peace.

On November 15, 2002, Sen. Bill Nelson (D., Fla.) introduced S.Con.Res.158, a concurrent resolution urging the government of Egypt and other Arab regimes not to allow their government-controlled television stations to broadcast any program that lent legitimacy to the *Protocols of the Elders of Zion*. The measure, which had ten cosponsors, passed the Senate (as S.Res.366) by unanimous consent on November 20. "The broadcast of this series," stated the resolution, "takes place in the context of a sustained pattern of vitriolic anti-Semitic commentary and depictions in the Egyptian government-sponsored press, which has gone unanswered by the government of Egypt . . . . The use of such heinous propaganda, especially in the Arab world, serves to incite popular sentiment against the Jewish people and the State of Israel rather than promoting religious tolerance and preparing Arab populations for the prospect of peace with Israel." On November 22, Rep. Steven Israel (D., N.Y.) introduced a parallel resolution in the House, H.Con.Res.521, which was referred to the International Relations Committee, but no further action was taken on it.

The Murder of Daniel Pearl

On January 23, 2002, *Wall Street Journal* reporter Daniel Pearl, in Pakistan researching a story on Islamic extremists, was kidnapped and killed by some of those very people. They videotaping the act of slitting his throat, preceded by his "confession" that his parents were Jews and that he was a Jew. When the videotape was released toward the end of February, the press quoted Pearl's abductors as saying that he had been kidnapped and killed because he was "anti-Islam and a Jew." Leaders from around the world quickly condemned the killing.

It remained unclear, however, whether Pearl had been hunted down specifically because he was Jewish, or whether he was picked up because he was a Western journalist, and the Jewish angle was coincidental. Tim Weiner, a *New York Times* reporter and a friend of Pearl's, told the Jewish Telegraphic Agency that he did not believe that Pearl had been singled out for his religion. The crime, Weiner felt, was "primarily an act of hatred against the United States and the West," but the killers "found it useful for their own twisted propaganda purposes to make an issue or try and make headlines out of his religion." Rabbi Marvin Hier, dean of the Simon Wiesenthal Center in California, disagreed, suggesting that Pearl had been targeted as "an American and a Jew." Whatever the original motivation for the act, Yehudit Barsky, director of the American Jewish Committee's division on international terrorism, termed the killing "a red alert for Jews" since "Islamic radicalism has now proclaimed very, very publicly that their goal is to kill Jews. All Jews and all Americans are now targets."

It was subsequently learned that during the period between Pearl's kidnapping and the time his murder became known—when the fate of Daniel Pearl was a worldwide story—international media were prevailed upon not to report details about Pearl's religious background, in particular that his parents had dual American-Israeli citizenship.

INTERGROUP RELATIONS

Black-Jewish Relations

Out-of-state pro-Israel groups and individuals afforded strong support to candidates Denise Majette and Artur Davis in their primary challenges to, respectively, Reps. Cynthia McKinney (D., Ga.) and Earl Hilliard (D., Ala.), both of whom friends of Israel viewed as hostile to the Jewish state (see above, p. 75). But this support brought out, in turn, countervailing efforts on behalf of the incumbents from out-of-state Muslims and Arabs, and other sympathizers with the Palestinian cause. This was particularly true in the case of McKinney, after Davis defeated Hilliard 56 to 44 percent in a June 25 primary.

Throughout the two campaigns, the incumbents and their supporters were not shy in suggesting that there was something untoward about pro-Israel groups backing their opponents, and, after the results came, in blaming Jewish money for their defeat. But others noted that there were clearly issues other than Israel that motivated voters in districts whose population included relatively few Jews. Thus the campaign against Hilliard was marked by a combination of long-simmering charges that he had been an ineffective congressman, a House Ethics Committee reprimand the previous year for mishandling campaign funds, and controversial positions he had taken on a range of issues unrelated to the Israel-Arab conflict, such as Libya and Cuba.

The campaign against McKinney, in a district with more Jewish constituents than Hilliard's, did invoke her long record of what were construed as anti-Israel remarks and votes—culminating in her May 2002 "no" vote, one of only 21 in the House, on a resolution expressing solidarity with Israel and condemnation of Palestinian terrorism. And yet that vote rankled not only pro-Israel activists, but also constituents sensitive, in the wake of September 11, to any softness on terrorism. Other actions raising similar concerns were McKinney's letter to a Saudi prince in October 2001 offering—ostensibly on behalf of the state of Georgia—to accept a $10-million-dollar check for disaster relief that Rudy Giuliani, then mayor of New York, had rejected when it came to light that the prince was drawing a connection between the September 11 attacks and American support for Israel, and, more recently, McKinney's accusation that the Bush administration had knowingly failed to prevent the attacks. Just a week before her August 21 primary, a number of contributors to the McKinney campaign were named as defendants in a $1-trillion lawsuit brought by victims of September 11. In the end, McKinney went down to defeat, Majette prevailing by some 18,000 votes.

During and after these races, concern was voiced about the implications for black-Jewish relations. Rep. Maxine Waters (D., Cal.), for example, charged that the campaign against Hilliard had singled out a member of the Congressional Black Caucus (even though challenger Davis was also an African American). "No one special interest group should be able to take us out," Waters said. Other leaders of the caucus were quick to disclaim any long-lasting impact of these primaries on black-Jewish relations, a theme that was picked up by Jewish members of Congress and community leaders.

Latino-Jewish Relations

It had become almost a commonplace in the Jewish community over the last several years that the rapid growth of America's Latino population—now the largest minority in the U.S.—and that community's concomitant growing political influence, made strengthening Latino-Jewish relationships a priority for American Jewry. 2002 saw some important movement in that direction.

Groundwork was laid for bringing into existence, in 2003, a Latino-Jewish Leadership Council, an umbrella organization of national Jewish and Latino groups. The concept had been agreed upon at the Latino-Jewish Summit convened by B'nai B'rith International in March 2001. The council was expected to include B'nai B'rith, the Anti-Defamation League, and the American Jewish Committee, along with the National Council of La Raza, LULAC, and the Congressional Hispanic Caucus Institute, along with several other groups on both the Latino and Jewish sides. It would focus on dialogue and the formulation, where feasible, of joint policy initiatives in the areas of education, economic development and philanthropy, foreign affairs and immigration, and media issues.

Also in 2002, the Foundation on Ethnic Understanding announced plans to focus more on Latino-Jewish relations, as well as to open an office in Washington, D.C., that would work with members of both the Congressional Black Caucus and the Congressional Hispanic Caucus.

Catholic-Jewish Relations

In line with the prevalent trend in Catholic thinking, the U.S. Catholic Bishops' Committee for Ecumenical and Interreligious Affairs issued a statement in August denying the need to convert Jews since they "already dwell in a saving covenant with God." Strongly disagreeing was the well-known Catholic commentator William F. Buckley, who, in his syndicated column (Sept. 18), quoted the New Testament to show that all people, Jews emphatically included, could attain salvation only through Jesus. Jews active in Christian-Jewish relations expressed dismay at Buckley's words. Rabbi A. James Rudin, for example, senior interreligious affairs advisor for the American Jewish Committee, charged that "Buckley is still committed to the spiritual annihilation of Jews and Judaism."

Another Catholic intellectual, Father Richard John Neuhaus, editor of the influential conservative journal *First Things,* also ruffled Jewish feathers when, in the August-September issue of his magazine, he expressed annoyance that "so many Jews and Jewish publications" were "preoccupied" with "the fringe phenomenon of Holocaust denial, and with emphatically non-trivial pursuits such as attacks on Pius XII and the Catholic Church, and on serious Jewish-Christian theological dialogue." Neuhaus mentioned *Commentary* magazine—the well-known conservative monthly published by the American Jewish Committee—as particularly at fault. *Commentary* editor Neal Kozodoy commented that he was "a longtime admirer of Father Neuhaus and his work" and was "especially loath to be drawn into an exchange of this sort" (*Forward,* Oct. 11).

Resolving one of sore points in Jewish-Catholic relations to which Neuhaus alluded—the role of the papacy during the Holocaust—had come increasingly to center around opening the relevant Vatican archives. The continuing impasse over scholarly access to the Holocaust-era archives saw some progress early in 2002, albeit not enough to satisfy Jewish groups. In mid-February, the Vatican announced that, in the interest of bringing an end to "unjust and thankless speculation" about the wartime role of Pope Pius XII, it would make available to scholars during the coming year selected archives from the period 1922–39, when the future pontiff served as the papal representative in Germany and as Vatican secretary of state. Documents relating to Vatican-German relations during Pius XII's papacy were to follow in approximately three years. Seymour Reich, chair of the International Jewish Committee for Interreligious Consultations (IJCIC), welcomed the announcement as "an important development." Cautioning that the Vatican statement left unclear whether some documents might be held back, he urged that "all documents be released and made available to scholars." By year's end, the Vatican indicated that the promised first release of documents would take place in February 2003.

Evangelical Christian-Jewish Relations

On October 11, the surge of evangelical Christian support for Israel in its time of trouble was strongly evident when thousands of participants in a Christian Coalition conference in Washington, D.C., held a rally to "tell the world that Christians stand firmly behind the Jewish state and are unalterably opposed to trading land for a paper peace." The Anti-Defamation League, which had run an ad in May in the *New York Times* and other outlets reprinting a letter of support for Israel from former Christian Coalition head Ralph Reed, expressed appreciation for the rally, even as ADL national director Abraham Foxman noted that there was no alliance of the two Jewish communities, but a "relationship based on this one, specific issue."

The meaning of even this one-issue relationship and whether or not it was "good for the Jews" showed every sign of snowballing into yet another tumultuous issue within the American Jewish community. Some agreed with Foxman, and were bolstered in this position by Israeli prime minister Ariel Sharon and other Israeli officials, who were quick to term evangelical Christians "friends" and to suggest that Jews had sufficient "self-confidence in their own identity not to fear or be intimidated by Christian groups that are supportive of Israel." Others were less sanguine, as exemplified by a new advocacy group, Jewish Women Watching, which sent out a mailing with a condom enclosed, warning Jewish leaders not to get "in bed" with conservative Christians. The group feared that Jewish voters might be swayed to back the domestic agenda of the Christian Coalition and similar organizations in exchange for their support of Israel. There were also voices in the Jewish community warning that the evangelical agenda still included conversion efforts directed at Jews, as well as a theological perspective that required Jews to be gathered in the Holy Land at the end of days for a final, apocalyptic scenario.

In advance of the October 11 rally, a Christian Coalition spokesman denied the notion of a quid pro quo. Rabbi Yechiel Eckstein, president of the International Fellowship of Christians and Jews, an organization dedicated to furthering Jewish-evangelical relations, noted a marked shift in Jewish attitudes toward evangelicals in just the last several months. He suggested that "the Jewish community is starting to get it. Our friends are these Christians." Days before the rally, his organization issued a poll of evangelical Christians indicating that more than half of them supported Israel because it was a democracy and a U.S. ally in the battle against terrorism, not out of theological motivations. The poll did indicate, however, that some 35 percent of evangelical Christians supported Israel for theological reasons.

Whether or not hopes for conversion were at the root of evangelical support for Israel, commitment to proselytization remained at the core of that Christian community's mission. Thus, following a statement in August by U.S. Catholic bishops that they would no longer target Jews for conversion (see p. 98), the World Evangelical Association reaffirmed the legitimacy of such efforts, adding that no person "can enjoy God's favor apart from the mediation of Jesus Christ." At the same time, the statement condemned anti-Semitism and acknowledged the historic role of the Christian churches in fomenting it.

In February 2002, the National Archives released a 30-year-old tape of a conversation between the Rev. Billy Graham, the legendary evangelical preacher, and Richard Nixon, president at that time, in which Graham spoke of the need to do something about alleged Jewish domination of the American media. Graham, now 83 years old, quickly issued an apology, saying on March 1: "Although I have no memory of the occasion, I deeply regret comments I apparently made in an Oval Office conversation with President Nixon." Rabbi Arnold Resnicoff, interreligious-affairs director for the American Jewish Committee, accepted the apology, noting that Graham's "words and . . . actions since have shown him to be a friend and someone who is working for good across religious lines." But ADL national director Abraham Foxman pronounced the apology "mealy-mouthed," noting that the 1972 remarks reflected a "classic anti-Semitic canard" of Jewish control over the media.

Muslim-Jewish Relations

Relations between the American Jewish community and its Arab and Muslim counterparts remained tenuous, even bitter, as national Jewish organizations refused to work with certain Muslim and Arab groups that they viewed as apologists for terrorism even on matters of common interest. For example, spokespersons for both the Anti-Defamation League's Midwest office and the Council on American Islamic Relations (CAIR) protested when the Cook County sheriff's office in Chicago barred a Muslim woman and a Jewish man from wearing head coverings at work. Yet the ADL refused to collaborate with CAIR on this issue, maintaining that the latter condoned terrorism. CAIR, in turn, denied the charge and called on the ADL to join it in denouncing all terrorism, including "Israeli terrorism." (The sheriff's office eventually agreed to allow the employees in question to wear their respective head coverings while on duty.)

The contention that certain Muslim leaders supported terrorism also came up early in the year when Jewish groups protested a State Department invitation to Salam Al-Marayati, executive director of the Los Angeles-based Muslim Public Affairs Council, to participate in a session of the department's ongoing Open Forum lecture series. Soon after September 11, 2001, Al-Marayati gained notoriety for suggesting that Israel should be a suspect for the day's events because the attacks served to divert attention from its "apartheid activities" (see AJYB 2002, p. 181). The session went ahead as scheduled, and one of Al-Marayati's most outspoken Jewish critics, Morton Klein, president of the Zionist Organization of America, was invited to speak at a later session.

Jewish-Muslim contacts did not cease entirely. For one thing, there remained some national Muslim organizations with which the Jewish groups maintained relations, and for another, some of the national Jew-

ish bodies—the Religious Action Center of Reform Judaism was one—
continued to cooperate with some of the Muslim groups that other Jewish organizations shunned. By and large, however, instances of contact
were more likely to be found on the local level. In February, for example,
members of Valley Beth Shalom, a Los Angeles-area Conservative synagogue, visited the neighboring King Fahd Mosque for services marking
the beginning of the three-day Eid al-Adha festival commemorating
Abraham's willingness to sacrifice his son on God's command. Rabbi
Harold Schulweis termed the visit "a celebration of the common humanity underlying different theologies."

CHURCH AND STATE

Charitable Choice

"Charitable choice," an approach to government funding of social services that seeks to expand funding for, and loosen restrictions on, the
social-service work of faith-based institutions, remained a priority of
the Bush administration and of the Republican leadership in Congress.

The courts continued to wrestle with the constitutional questions posed
by charitable choice, mostly in the context of state, not federal, funding
of faith-based social-service providers. On January 8, a federal district
court held that Wisconsin's "unrestricted, direct" funding of an initiative
called Faith Works was unconstitutional because Christianity was such
an integral part of the substance-abuse and job-training program. Notably, the program's employee handbook stated: "The addict learns that
he has a deep 'soul sickness,' and it is only by connecting to God through
profession, confession, prayer, and involvement in a worshiping community that he has any hope of sustaining a life in recovery." During his
presidential campaign, George W. Bush had cited Faith Works as the type
of program that his faith-based initiative was intended to support. But
the "as applied" nature of the court's ruling (that is, the court struck down
only the funding of the particular agency, not the underlying state program) meant that the decision had only limited implication for the federal faith-based concept. Thus, Nathan Diament, director of the Institute for Public Affairs of the Union of Orthodox Jewish Congregations
of American (Orthodox Union, or OU), a supporter of "charitable
choice," noted that the court ruling underlined the need "to very carefully
structure legislation."

On the national legislative front, Democratic control of the Senate ensured that a full-blown charitable choice bill would have no chance of passage. Sen. Rick Santorum (R., Pa.) joined with Sen. Joseph Lieberman (D., Conn.) to finalize and introduce the Charity Aid, Recovery, and Empowerment (CARE) Act of 2002, a "compromise" bill intended to implement those aspects of the president's faith-based initiative deemed uncontroversial. Thus the bill omitted provisions found in H.R.7, approved by the House in 2001 and found in earlier "charitable choice" initiatives passed by Congress, that had allowed government funds to flow to pervasively religious organizations such as houses of worship, and had explicitly extended the right of certain religious organizations to make employment decisions on the basis of religion to cover people such organizations hired to provide the government-funded services (see AJYB 2002, pp. 184–85).

Recognizing that H.R.7 was not going to make it through the Senate, President Bush threw his support behind the CARE bill. It included provisions, widely supported in the Jewish community, for tax incentives for charitable donations and substantial increases in social-service funding. Nevertheless, provisions of CARE's Title III, intended to assure "equal treatment" of religious organizations, continued to raise church-state concerns among "separationist" Jewish groups and their coalition partners, concerns that became more vocal in the course of the year.

For months, the CARE bill was stalled in the Senate Finance Committee since it was unclear from where its funding would come. On June 18 the committee finally reported CARE favorably, but, for jurisdictional reasons, it only weighed in on CARE's tax provisions, leaving consideration of Title III for the Senate floor. Majority Leader Daschle promised to bring the CARE bill up for a vote in a form that included Title III after Congress returned from its August recess. In a boon for the bill, United Jewish Communities (UJC), the umbrella body of the local Jewish federations that had opposed H.R.7, came out in support of CARE. UJC concluded that the most problematic church-state aspects of the former initiative had been removed, and that the positive features of CARE, including the substantial infusion of additional funds, outweighed whatever problematic elements remained.

Key Democrats, led by Jack Reed (D., R.I.) and Dick Durbin (D., Ill.), still objected to the bill, arguing that it would blur the line between church and state by providing federal funding for programs run by private religious groups without adequate safeguards for church-state separation. These Democrats wanted the opportunity to offer amendments that would, among other things, bar discrimination in hiring for projects that received federal grants and preclude funding of pervasively religious organizations. The bill's sponsors, however, insisted that CARE was already a "compromise" measure, and therefore should come up for consideration under unanimous consent, precluding amendments. Meanwhile, complaints from the Republican side about paying for the bill's tax incentives also militated against passage. In the end, the CARE bill died as the 107th Congress closed.

On December 12, with the CARE bill—much less full-blown "charitable choice"—stalled for the year in Congress, President Bush implemented key elements of his faith-based initiative by executive order, including some elements of H.R.7 and the CARE bill. Citing the need to treat all charities equally regardless of their religious affiliations, the president signed an order opening additional Centers for Faith-Based and Community Initiatives at the Department of Agriculture and the Agency for International Development, and announced the publication of *Guidance to Faith-Based and Community Organizations on Partnering with the Federal Government,* a short handbook to help organizations apply for federal grants. In a separate order, Bush modified a long-standing earlier executive order so as to remove restrictions on the right of faith-based organizations to discriminate in hiring based on a candidate's religion for jobs with programs covered by a government contract. That same month, the Department of Health and Human Services issued proposed rules intended to implement charitable choice provisions enacted by Congress during the Clinton Administration in connection with three specific programs—the Temporary Assistance for Needy Families (TANF) welfare reform program, a major substance abuse program, and block grants for community services.

Jewish organizations largely objected to the president's unilateral actions, the American Jewish Committee, for example, issuing a statement expressing alarm over a policy that "bypasses congressional action, and advances the use of taxpayer dollars to fund social services provided by religious institutions without adequate church-state safeguards and anti-discrimination provisions." The OU, however, hailed the president's moves, which, said Nathan Diament, reflected an endorsement of "the principle of government neutrality towards religion as opposed to government hostility toward religion." He praised, in particular, the portion of one of the executive orders providing that the Federal Emergency Management Agency (FEMA) would revise its policy on emergency relief so that religious nonprofit groups might qualify for assistance after natural disasters. This was a particular grievance of the OU following FEMA's determination, two years earlier, to deny the Seattle Hebrew Academy emergency funds following a severe earthquake, because of the school's religious character. Indeed, that specific directive to FEMA was probably the least controversial part of the president's actions, drawing no comment, pro or con, from the Jewish organizations that protested its other aspects.

Vouchers and Zelman

The issue of "school choice" had been placed on the back burner in 2001 as President Bush worked together with Democrats to produce landmark legislation for educational reform, the No Child Left Behind Act (see AJYB 2002, p. 188). But the issue returned front and center in the administration's proposed budget for fiscal year 2003, sent to Capitol Hill on February 4, 2002. It included a proposal for tax credits of up to $2,500 per year for parents with children in schools determined to be failing under the standards set out in the 2001 law.

The Jewish community responded with its accustomed split on such funding issues. The OU lauded the proposal and called for the tax credit to be made available to low-income families generally, not only to parents with children in public schools. Much of the rest of the organized Jewish community, however, sensed that even if tax credits and vouchers might pass muster as a matter of constitutional analysis, there were strong public-policy grounds to oppose them. Mark Pelavin, for example, associate director of the Religious Action Center of Reform Judaism, asked, "What is this going to do to public schools? Tax credits are a danger." The budget also included a request for $50 million to fund research and a demonstration project on school choice.

In the most anticipated church-state development of the year, the U.S. Supreme Court rendered a decision in *Zelman v. Simmons-Harris* in June 2002, just before leaving for summer recess, on the constitutionality of the city of Cleveland's voucher program. Already in comments made to the Jewish Telegraphic Agency at the time of oral argument in February, Marc Stern, assistant national director and counsel for the American Jewish Congress—who, together with Judge Marvin Frankel, represented parties on the anti-vouchers side of the case before the Supreme Court—observed that the court had shifted its church-state jurisprudence. Rather than relying on precedents strictly prohibiting government aid for religious schools, he suggested, the judges were now prepared to evaluate these cases on the basis of whether funds were being made available to schools based on individual choice and government neutrality with respect to religion. Stern proved correct. The court's 5-4 ruling, in an opinion written by Chief Justice William Rehnquist, declared the program constitutional because it was neutral with respect to religion and provided assistance to students attending any school.

Heralding the decision, House Majority Leader Dick Armey (R., Tex.) lost no time introducing, that same day, the District of Columbia Student Opportunity Scholarship Act of 2002 (H.R.5033). This would provide education "scholarships" of up to $5,000 to children from families with incomes below the poverty line living in the District of Columbia. On August 1, Sen. Judd Gregg (R., N.H.) introduced a companion measure, S.2866. (In 1997, Rep. Armey had introduced a similar bill that passed both houses but was vetoed by President Clinton.) Neither bill moved to passage before the end of the year.

Other Church-State Matters

Proponents of charitable choice pointed to the *Zelman* decision as reinforcement for the constitutionality of their approach to government funding of faith-based social services. But opponents countered that the vouchers decision was distinguishable: charitable choice entailed direct government funding of houses of worship and similar pervasively religious organizations, while vouchers provided only indirect funding. In addition, they noted, there was no universally available system of social-service provision comparable to the system of public education that afforded parents in Cleveland a "true and voluntary" alternative to religious schools. Against this background, it was unlikely that *Zelman* would eliminate pending lawsuits challenging charitable choice programs; indeed, they were likely to multiply as the administration and local jurisdictions implemented them.

One federal lawsuit, brought by the American Jewish Congress and the Texas Civil Rights Project, challenged funding by Texas of an evangelical Christian program for job training and placement. The plaintiffs claimed that such state funding violated the constitutional principle of separation of church and state because it included religious proselytizing (participants were told that "change can only be accomplished through a relationship with Jesus Christ"). A U.S. Court of Appeals decision in May allowed the litigation to go forward.

In contrast to the debate over government funding, another conservative priority, the Houses of Worship Political Speech Protection Act of 2002, found little backing in the Jewish community, evoking only vocal opposition (from "separationist" groups) or statements of concern (from the OU). This bill, H.R.2357, introduced in the House in 2001 by Reps. Walter Jones (R., N.C.) and John Hostettler (R., Ind.) with over 125 cosponsors, would amend the Internal Revenue Code of 1986 to permit churches and other houses of worship, unlike other nonprofit institutions, to endorse or oppose candidates for political office without forfeiting their tax-exempt status. H.R.2357 went down to defeat, however, failing to garner even a majority of votes in its favor, when it was brought up on the House floor on October 2 under suspension of the rules, a parliamentary procedure requiring a two-thirds vote for passage. Proponents promised to push the initiative again in 2003. (A parallel Senate bill saw no movement in 2002.)

Jewish groups and others opposing this bill argued that exempting churches and other houses of worship from the provision barring nonprofits from engaging in partisan political campaigns would undermine a valuable safeguard for the integrity of both the religious institutions and the political process.

Even those in the Jewish community most supportive of a stringent reading of the First Amendment's prohibition of an establishment of religion had mixed feelings when, in May 2002, a federal appeals court upheld an earlier federal trial court ruling that New York State's kosher law was unconstitutional. While the OU and Agudath Israel, not surprisingly, had filed briefs in support of the law's constitutionality, most of the "separationist" camp stayed out of the case, with the notable exception of the American Jewish Congress, which weighed in to argue that the law breached the separation of church and state. The U.S. Court of Appeals for the Second Circuit found that the law, which outlawed the sale of products labeled kosher if they did not conform to the Orthodox definition of the Jewish dietary laws, unconstitutionally established the Orthodox form of Judaism, to the exclusion of Conservative or other Jewish standards.

In October 2002, the American Jewish Committee and the Religious Action Center of Reform Judaism joined with the Baptist Joint Committee, the Interfaith Alliance, and the National Council of Churches in issuing a revised version of *A Shared Vision: Religious Liberty in the 21st Century,* a statement reaffirming the commitment of these organizations to "maintaining church-state separation as the best means of assuring robust religious liberty and creating a climate of mutual respect in a religiously diverse culture." As did the original statement issued in 1994, the new version documented issues of constitutional history and interpretation relating to religion and politics, religion and public institutions, and government aid to religious institutions, all from the "separationist" standpoint.

"Free-Exercise" Developments

On May 23, 2002, Sens. John Kerry (D., Mass.) and Rick Santorum (R., Pa.) reintroduced the Workplace Religious Freedom Act (S.2572), intended to assure that employers have a meaningful obligation to reasonably accommodate their employees' religious practices. While the bill had the backing of a bipartisan group of 15 additional sponsors and incorporated changes reflecting organized labor's position on the issue, it was not passed in either house before the adjournment of Congress.

Soon, however, advocates could point to an important success at the state level. On October 13, 2002, New York governor George Pataki signed a state Workplace Religious Freedom Act into law. It expanded on existing New York law requiring employers to accommodate employees' Sabbath and holiday observances, absent undue hardship, by protecting employees required by their faith to wear distinctive garb. The law also effectively overrode a series of state court cases that had interpreted the existing law in a fashion that made it unduly difficult for employees to prevail against their employers.

HOLOCAUST-RELATED MATTERS

Restitution

On June 4, the House of Representatives passed H.R.4823, the Holocaust Restitution Tax Fairness Act of 2002, sponsored by Rep. Clay E. Shaw (R., Fla.), by 392-1, with the Senate following suit on November 20, with passage by voice vote. The act, signed into law by President Bush on December 17, made permanent a provision enacted in 2001 categorizing restitution payments received by Holocaust victims as nontaxable income. The original measure had not been permanent because, when originally enacted, it was part of President Bush's $1.35-trillion tax cut, written so as to expire in ten years. The new law applied not only to Jewish Holocaust victims, but also to others who were persecuted on the basis of race, religion, physical or mental disability, or sexual orientation.

In October, the International Commission on Holocaust Era Insurance Claims (ICHEIC)—an umbrella organization of Jewish groups, Israeli officials, several large European insurers, and American and European insurance regulators—signed a final agreement with the German insurance industry. This marked a turning point in the long and tedious effort of Holocaust survivors and their heirs to recover on unpaid Holocaust-era insurance claims. The signing opened the door to the release of some $100 million to pay valid insurance claims against German companies, with another $50 million in reserve if needed, plus approximately $175 million to be used for humanitarian purposes. The agreement set up a procedure whereby claims would be reviewed under less stringent standards than the norm, and also provided that Jewish former residents of Germany and their heirs would have access to a comprehensive listing of insurance policies issued to Jews before and during the Nazi era.

Achievement of this agreement came as something of a surprise, given the heavy criticism that had been directed at ICHEIC. At a hearing of the House Government Reform Committee in 2001, members of Congress and Holocaust survivors had joined in calling ICHEIC a failure, and in early 2002 the ICHEIC chairman, former U.S. secretary of state Lawrence Eagleburger, threatened to resign his post over frustration with the stalled negotiations. Now, Eagleburger hailed the agreement as a "major achievement," and Ambassador Randolph Bell, the State Department's special envoy for Holocaust affairs, pronounced the settlement one that "should be given the opportunity to succeed." Several other, non-German insurance companies were expected to continue negotiating with ICHEIC toward a settlement of Holocaust-era claims, but there remained many companies in Eastern Europe that, even at this late date, were not participating.

Nazi War Criminals

The Justice Department's Office of Special Investigations (OSI) continued its efforts to deport Nazi war criminals living in the U.S. before death could take these elderly men out of its jurisdiction. On January 14, OSI began proceedings for denaturalization and deportation of Illinois resident Peter John Bernes, formerly Petras Bernotavicius of Lithuania, on the charge of collaboration in removing Jewish prisoners from a town jail to a site where they were shot to death. In May, Nikolaus Schiffer, a former concentration camp guard, was deported to Romania following court proceedings in which an immigration judge found that he had lied about his wartime activities when he entered the U.S.

In the meantime, OSI's decades-long effort to deport John Demjanjuk, alleged to be the infamous Nazi war criminal known as Ivan the Terrible, reached a significant milestone on February 21, when U.S. District Judge Paul Matia revoked Demjanjuk's American citizenship, the second time that had happened. The first time was in 1981, but in February 1998 Judge Matia had Demjanjuk's citizenship restored. That followed an appellate decision that the Justice Department had knowingly withheld information that Demjanjuk could have used in his 1981 defense, and a determination by the Israeli Supreme Court in 1993 that the identification of Demjanjuk as Ivan the Terrible had not been proven beyond a reasonable doubt—that identification being the basis on which he was deported to Israel and tried there.

In restoring Demjanjuk's citizenship, Judge Matia had left the door open for the Justice Department to file new denaturalization and deportation proceedings, an invitation that the OSI took up in filing a new complaint in 1999. This alleged, in effect, that even if Demjanjuk was not Ivan the Terrible, he was still a war criminal. In his February ruling, Matia found that Demjanjuk, now 81, had fraudulently acquired U.S. citizenship, failing to disclose that he had been a guard at several Nazi concentration camps where he had "willingly" been part of "the process by which thousands of Jews were murdered by asphyxiation with carbon monoxide." Although, in OSI director Eli Rosenbaum's words, the decision was a victory for "this government's determination to serve a measure of justice on behalf of those who perished," it was far from the final word. Demjanjuk's son-in-law indicated that the ruling would be appealed, and Demjanjuk could not be deported until the appeal was heard. In addition, even if a deportation was in order, there remained the question of where he would be sent, with both France and Demjanjuk's native Ukraine among the possibilities.

RICHARD T. FOLTIN

Jewish Communal Affairs

T AKING SERIOUSLY ITS ROLE as the world's largest and most powerful Jewish community, organized American Jewry concentrated its energies outward in 2002, focusing on the threats to Israel's security and the alarming rise of anti-Israel and anti-Semitic sentiment elsewhere in the world. Domestically, controversy swirled over the basic demographic facts of American Jewish life and their meaning, while the downturn of the American economy placed serious constraints on Jewish organizations as they sought to carry on their work.

FOCUS ON THE MIDDLE EAST

Gauging the Administration

The events of September 11, 2001, generated apprehension in the ranks of many pro-Israel organizations. That day's catastrophe, the theory went, would induce the U.S. to bolster relations with the world of mainstream Islam so as to isolate and attack Al Qaeda and other Islamic extremists, and the most obvious way to accomplish this was pressure on Israel to offer new concessions to the Palestinians. But this anticipation also gave new life to the more dovish sectors of the American Jewish community, which had never been comfortable with the hard-line policies of the Sharon government in Israel.

As the year 2002 began, Michael Lerner, editor of *Tikkun* magazine and long-time supporter of the Israeli left, announced the founding of the Tikkun Community, "a new multi-issue national organization of liberal and progressive Jews" for which Israeli concessions were part of a far broader agenda. Its inaugural conference took place January 19–21 in New York. Drawing over 500 participants, the event focused on the need for Israel to evacuate all of the territories so that a Palestinian state could be established there, attacked the Bush administration on many fronts, and called for global "economic justice." Lerner hurt his cause two months later, however, with a full-page Tikkun Community advertisement in the *New York Times* (Mar. 22). As part of developing "a New Planetary Consciousness," the ad—with black scholar Cornel West listed as cochair along with Lerner—blasted Israel's "oppressive" occupation of the territories and lauded Israeli reservists who refused to serve there, but did not criticize the Palestinians. Several members of the organization's advisory board immediately resigned, charging that they had not approved the text of the ad before Lerner printed it with their names on it, and two of them, rabbis of Congregation B'nai Jeshurun in Manhattan, withdrew permission for Tikkun to hold its next meeting in the synagogue. The next month, Lerner and some followers got themselves arrested in Washington while protesting at the State Department against Israeli occupation of the Territories.

Far more helpful to the peace camp was the personal diplomacy initiated by *New York Times* columnist Thomas Friedman. In his February 17 column, Friedman disclosed that, at a dinner in Saudi Arabia with Crown Prince Abdullah bin Abdul Aziz al-Saud, he had suggested that the Arab League offer "full normalization" of relations with Israel in return for evacuation of the Territories. The crown prince enthusiastically retorted that this was exactly the suggestion he was planning to propose to the Arab League at its next meeting. Friedman called this an "intriguing signal." Four days later, the *Times* ran an op-ed by Henry Siegman, the former director of the American Jewish Congress known for his dovish views, who related that other Saudi officials had told him the same thing, even suggesting that the Western Wall and Jewish neighborhoods in East Jerusalem could conceivably remain in Israeli hands once peace was achieved.

These apparent indications of Arab willingness to compromise encouraged anti-Likud elements of American Jewry. In late February, with the "Saudi initiative" still fresh, Americans for Peace Now publicly criticized Sen. Hillary Rodham Clinton (D., N.Y.) for meeting only with Israeli officials on a recent visit to the Middle East and shunning the Palestinian leadership. In mid-March, Seymour Reich, a former chairman of the Conference of Presidents of Major American Jewish Organizations (the umbrella body of Jewish groups on matters related to Israel), harshly castigated Israel's troop movements into Palestinian areas, accusing Prime Minister Ariel Sharon of "flagrant disregard of his best friend, George W. Bush." Reich insisted that "Israel cannot afford to hurt the United States when this country has other goals that are consistent with Israel's objectives."

The pro-peace wing of the Jewish community expressed satisfaction when President Bush called, in an April 4 speech from the White House Rose Garden, for a freeze on settlements in the Territories at the same time that he denounced Palestinian terrorism. Within days, Israel pulled its troops out of West Bank towns. The April 7 meeting of the Israel Policy Forum (IPF) was a virtual love-in for the administration. Featured speaker George Mitchell, the former Maine senator and author of the Mitchell Report for renewing Israeli-Palestinian negotiations, exuded optimism about the chances for peace and was applauded when he called on Israel to "freeze all settlement activity."

Apprehension about U.S. pressure on Israel, however, had not disappeared entirely in Jewish circles, muted though it was by admiration for the president's condemnation of Palestinian violence and his leadership in the war on terror. On March 24, about 500 people rallied at the 92nd Street Y in New York City under the theme "We Stand With Israel Now and Forever," and 100 other communities across North America took part by satellite hookup. This was actually a rescheduling of a pro-Israel event that had been planned by the Conference of Presidents, United Jewish Communities, and local federations for the previous September, but had to be postponed due to September 11. While the Jewish leaders who spoke at the 92nd Street Y—and Prime Minister Sharon, on the phone from Israel—praised the administration as a friend of the Jewish state, the common theme that Israel had the absolute right to defend its citizens was a clear if implicit sign of worry about American intentions.

Three days before, on March 21, the Conference of Presidents issued a statement that managed to achieve an American Jewish consensus only by avoiding points of conflict—it simply expressed solidarity with the state and people of Israel. To obtain approval from the more dovish constituent organizations, there was no reference to support for the *government* of Israel, while the price for assent from the hawkish groups was the absence of any call on Israel to return to negotiations.

Mobilizing American Jewry

A new upsurge in Palestinian suicide bombings culminating in the "seder massacre" in Netanya on March 27 that killed 29 (see below, pp. 198–99), led—but only slowly and gradually—to an altered balance of forces in the American Jewish community.

On April 1, with Israeli troops conducting Operation Defensive Shield—storming into Palestinian areas to find and destroy terrorists and their bases—Prime Minister Sharon spoke via conference call to the Conference of Presidents. He called on American Jews to mobilize on Israel's behalf. "We need you today," Sharon said. "There must be a supreme effort to contradict false accusations against Israel. We need you to express public support, talk to people and groups who influence public opinion, demonstrate your love and support by visits to Israel." Seconding him was Deputy Prime Minister Natan Sharansky, who notified the *New York Jewish Week* (Apr. 5): "With all of the information we have we know there are hundreds—if not thousands—of people actively involved in the terrorist infrastructure. The world must understand and not try to stop us in the middle of the war. That is the challenge for American Jews."

But at that point, as the Israeli daily *Ha'aretz* noted in an article tellingly titled "The Silence of the Lambs" (Apr. 8), there was no sense of crisis among American Jews. "We're ratcheting everything up," said Stephen Hoffman, head of the United Jewish Communities, but he was referring to a new Israel Emergency Fund campaign (it raised $16 million within a few days) and a leadership mission to Israel, not to any dramatic statement or public event to influence American public opinion or policy. Alon Pinkus, Israel's consul general in New York, noted that on the single day of March 29, two days after the massacre in Netanya, he gave 14 separate radio and television interviews. "As long as I am confronting Palestinian representatives, I have no problem," he told *Ha'aretz*. "When I'm invited to appear opposite an American Arab . . . I ask myself why there is no American Jewish leader to oppose him." One possible reason for the muted response may have been that many American Jews, and leaders of their organizations, were away from home for Passover vacation, but observers sensed a deeper problem—a widespread feeling that Israeli policies were to some extent to blame for the situation.

With the American Jewish establishment seemingly passive, Rabbi Avi Weiss, a veteran communal gadfly, filled the leadership vacuum. In days, with backing from just a few small right-wing groups, Weiss managed to bring some 10,000 demonstrators to UN headquarters in New York on Sunday, April 7, to rally for Israel. Both impressed and somewhat shamed by Weiss's accomplishment, the Conference of Presidents invited Weiss to a meeting the next day, and afterwards announced a national rally for Israel in Washington, D.C., for Monday, April 15. Two key points were clear from the outset—this was to be an ecumenical demonstration, not just a Jewish rally, and it would not be used to attack the administration. But the very short time left for planning the event left many details up in the air: How would Jewish organizations get the word out to their constituents? How would transportation from across the country be arranged? Where would the money come from? Who would be the featured speakers? And, most crucially, would attendance be large enough to impress the government and not embarrass the organizers?

All these questions were somehow answered, and the effect was stunning. Some 100,000–200,000 people came on April 15 and stood for hours in 88-degree heat— Jews running the gamut from dovish left to extreme right, secularists, Reform, Conservative, Modern Orthodox, and Hassidim, as well as non-Jewish friends of Israel—presenting a powerful display of pro-Israel solidarity. Only groups on the two extremes of the community did not participate—the sectarian Orthodox Agudath Israel refrained from officially endorsing the rally (see below, pp. 130–31), as did some small dovish groups that feared it would be seen as justifying Sharon's policies. Indeed, some confrontations did take place at the rally between pro-Sharon demonstrators and those carrying "End the Occupation" signs. A far greater potential embarrassment for the organizers was the booing that greeted Deputy Secretary of Defense Paul Wolfowitz, speaking on the president's behalf, when he made passing reference, in the course of his pro-Israel remarks, to the sufferings of the Palestinians and the need for a Palestinian state.

The Israeli government cooperated with the American administration over the next two weeks and, on April 21, finally withdrew from the West Bank towns it had entered. Later, it allowed Yasir Arafat to leave his compound in Ramallah after five months of confinement. The official position of the organized American Jewish community was that the U.S. was not pressuring Israel. Yet its underlying anxiety became evident in the days leading up to a planned Sharon visit to Washington in early May, where he was to meet with President Bush. AIPAC, fearing that Bush was about to press Sharon to negotiate with Arafat and commit to dismantling settlements and withdrawing from territories in line with the Saudi peace plan, geared up for a showdown with the White House by convincing both houses of Congress to pass, overwhelmingly, a resolution on May 2 strongly supporting Israel's military incursions. Pleas from the White House to delete harsh language about the Palestinians from the resolution were ignored.

But Sharon's visit was cut short after just one meeting with Bush when a suicide bomb attack in Rishon Lezion forced the Israeli prime minister to return home. Jewish leaders cited this most recent bombing as evidence for the continuing unwillingness of the Palestinians to disavow violence. Indeed, public-opinion polls taken at this time indicated a rise in public support for Israel, as ordinary Americans associated the suicide bombings with the events of the previous September 11. Mortimer Zuckerman, chairman of the Conference of Presidents, sought to exploit the poll numbers on Israel's behalf when he told a television interviewer that it was the State Department that was pressing Israel for concessions against the will of the president, and that Bush's principled stand against terrorism could very well gain him a majority of the Jewish vote in his 2004 reelection bid.

The horrifying toll the terror attacks were taking in Israel led some American Jews to consider new approaches to the problem. Nathan Lewin, a distinguished constitutional lawyer in Washington, went so far as to suggest a public warning to would-be suicide bombers that their close relatives would be executed if the bombers went ahead with their plans, a proposal that elicited widespread outrage (*Forward,* June 7). On June 10, taking a far less radical tack, United Jewish Communities (UJC), the fund-raising umbrella body of American Jewry whose mandate was to aid needy Jews anywhere in the world, reversed a 35-year-old policy and announced that it would send funds across the Green Line to Jews living in Gaza and the West Bank. "Our dollars are following people, not institutions and organizations," said UJC president Stephen Hoffman. The reason given for the change was the need to help victims of the terrorist incidents that were proliferating in the Territories. The shift in communal opinion about such funding was evident in the muted reaction of the left-of-center groups that had previously mounted adamant opposition to sending UJC money over the Green Line. The New Israel Fund, for example stated that it would continue to confine its donations to Israel within the line, but it had no comment on the UJC move.

The Bush Speech and After

By this time, however, the constellation of forces in the U.S. had shifted once again in the wake of Israel's military offensive into the West Bank. Secretary of State Colin Powell publicly called for an interim Palestinian state, and a Gallup poll showed — for the first time in months — that a plurality of Americans felt that the U.S. was too supportive of Israel. With President Bush reportedly working on a major Middle East policy pronouncement, the annual policy conference of AIPAC (American Israel Public Affairs Committee, the preeminent pro-Israel lobby) released a statement warning that a Palestinian state would necessarily be a terrorist state. And Aaron David Miller, senior adviser on Arab-Israel negotiations for the State Department, was booed and heckled when he told the right-wing Zionist Organization of America (ZOA) in Washington of the "futility" of a military solution to the conflict and said that Palestinians yearned for a state rooted in "democratic, pluralistic, humanistic values."

In this atmosphere of foreboding, the Bush speech of June 24 on the Middle East came as a great relief to the broad mainstream of American Jews (for full text see below, pp. 212–16). Despite the president's call on Israel to freeze settlements and his support for a Palestinian state, Bush's insistence that the Palestinians would have to end acts of terrorism and reform the Palestinian Authority—a clear signal that Arafat had to go— seemed to assuage lingering Jewish concerns. The widespread Jewish feeling that disaster had narrowly been averted was evident in the official reaction of the Conference of Presidents to the Bush address: "The president's speech called for rewarding an end to terrorism and not, as some had speculated, a reward for terrorism."

The Conference of Presidents, which for some years had attracted criticism for alleged pro-Likud bias, ran into the same complaint again in July 2002. That was when Israel closed the offices of Sari Nusseibeh, the PLO representative in Jerusalem. The action, ordered by the Israeli government on the grounds that Nusseibeh and his office had connections with pro-terror elements, was controversial even within the Israeli cabinet, since Nusseibeh, the president of Al Quds University, was reputed to be a moderate opposed to violence. Without consulting its member organizations, the Conference of Presidents issued a written statement on July 11 entitled "Facts About Nusseibeh Belie Image," defending the closure with alleged quotations from Nusseibeh that seemed to indicate radical leanings. This infuriated the more left-leaning members of the conference, who charged that the umbrella organization should not have taken a position absent a consensus of the membership, and that this incident was one more proof that the conference had become a tool of the Israeli right wing. Executive Vice President Malcolm Hoenlein defended the statement, pointing out that it simply reprinted documented remarks by Nusseibeh that were on the public record, which Americans needed to know in order to understand Israel's action.

Critics of the conference picked up more ammunition on August 23, when the organization's "daily alert" used quotation marks in referring to Israel's "occupation" of the West Bank and Gaza, and its "settlements." For dovish American Jews who indeed believed that Israel was conducting an occupation and that the settlements were settlements, the suggestion that both of these were merely "so-called," as it were, was another instance of right-wing bias in what was supposed to be a consensus organization. And toward year's end, as the countdown to war with Iraq began, the conference drew more criticism as Mortimer Zuckerman, its chairman, editorialized for war in *U.S. News and World Report,* the magazine he owned, despite earlier promises that he would not publish his private views about issues relating to Israel so long as he chaired the conference.

In the fall, more dovish voices in the American Jewish community spoke out forcefully once again, encouraged by renewed U.S. criticism of Israeli military actions on the West Bank and the administration's proposed "road map" toward a two-state solution, as well as the prospect of new elections in Israel. Americans for Peace Now, citing a study showing that most Israeli settlers chose to live beyond the Green Line for practical rather than ideological reasons, suggested paying the settlers money to leave their homes and relocate to Israel proper. The New Israel Fund launched a media campaign drawing attention to threats to Israeli democracy, such as the treatment of Arabs. Paul Menitoff, executive director of the Reform movement's Central Conference of American Rabbis (CCAR), called on the U.S. to threaten a cutoff of U.S. aid to Israel and the Palestinians so as to induce them both to make concessions for peace, and this suggestion of moral equivalence evoked anguished and angry debate in Reform circles (see below, p. 135). When the Israeli Labor Party nominated outspoken dove Amram Mitzna to head its ticket in the March 2003 election, Charney Bromberg, director of Meretz USA, expressed the hope of many centrist and left-leaning American Jews that the vote would be a "referendum on the occupation."

The American Jewish rank and file seemed to be moving in the same direction as the dovish leaders. In November, Zogby International released the results of a poll showing an astounding 85 percent of American Jews agreeing with the statement, "Palestinians have a right to live in a secure independent state of their own." (The number had been 63 percent in answer to a similar question in an American Jewish Committee poll in July.) Little wonder, then, that the Zionist Organization of America (ZOA) found itself alone in the Jewish organizational world (it did, however, have Christian fundamentalist support) when it launched a campaign in late November to oppose the creation of a Palestinian state mandated by the administration "road map."

And yet the widespread assumption—and hope—on the left that the administration planned to pressure Israel into concessions was thrown into doubt in early December, when the president appointed Elliott Abrams director of Middle East affairs at the White House. Abrams was a politically conservative, pro-Israel hard-liner, and the choice, according to the *New York Times* (Dec. 7), "thrilled those who had criticized the administration for being too tough on Israel and too deferential to the Palestinians. But it dismayed those, especially at the State Depart-

ment, who want Israel to ease its crackdown in the West Bank and Gaza."
Veteran diplomat Martin Indyk noted: "It does seem that the White
House has decided to back off. If the administration were preparing for
a new push on the road map, this would be an unusual appointment."

Israel's Image and the Media

Complaints about alleged anti-Israel bias in the American media
started soon after the outbreak of the second intifada in late 2000. Whatever degree of truth inhered in the criticism, the extreme sensitivity of
American Jews to how the news from Israel was reported undoubtedly
also reflected a sense of frustration at not being able to do much tangi-
bly to help Israel.

In the early days of the intifada, National Public Radio (NPR) was
among the more notorious media villains in the eyes of the pro-Israel
public. In Boston, an organized movement to stop individuals from donating to, and companies from underwriting, WBUR, the local NPR affiliate, cost the station over a million dollars—nearly 4 percent of its annual budget—and convinced the management to commit itself to greater
care in its reporting.

Criticism of the media reached new heights in the spring of 2002, when
Israeli troops moved into Palestinian territory to root out terrorist cells
on the West Bank in the wake of a series of suicide bombings, and charges
that Israel had perpetrated a "massacre" in Jenin were heard. Jewish
grievances were less about the editorial comment than over what was perceived as slanted news coverage that portrayed Palestinians as victims and
Israelis as oppressors. Presenting the journalists' side of the story, CBS
anchor Dan Rather explained on April 2 that "this situation in immensely
complicated. . . . When you do your best to be an honest broker of information . . . particularly in this region with all the emotion and hatred,
you always run the risk that someone will misrepresent what you said"
(*Forward,* Apr. 26).

A grassroots group in Los Angeles organized by rabbis and calling itself "Stand With Us" organized a one-day boycott of the *Los Angeles
Times* for April 17, Israel Independence Day, that about 1,200 people
joined. John Carroll, the editor, responded to the boycott by saying:
"Some readers may take objection to specific articles, but I am confident
that, over time, careful readers of this newspaper will get a full, balanced
account of these unsettling events." But four days later the paper failed
to cover the city's Israel Independence Day Festival, an event that drew

some 30,000 people, an omission the *Times* called an oversight and Jews considered deliberate.

In Minneapolis, "Minnesotans Against Terrorism," started by two men, took out ads in the *Minneapolis Star Tribune* to protest the paper's Middle East coverage—specifically, that it censored out the word "terrorism" from stories it took from other news sources that used the word in relation to suicide bombings. More than 350 people signed on to the ad, including nearly every major elected official in the state and a number of Christian leaders. A spokesman for the newspaper explained that the *Star Tribune* took "extra care to avoid the term 'terrorist' in articles about the Israeli-Palestinian conflict because of the emotional and heated nature of the that dispute."

The *Chicago Tribune* and leaders of the Chicago Jewish community handled matters differently, avoiding open confrontation. In the wake of complaints in 2001 that the *Tribune* refused to use the word "terrorist" to describe Hamas, Islamic Jihad, or Hezballah, the paper held two public forums for local Jews to express their grievances, and the Jewish Federation of Metropolitan Chicago commissioned a study of the *Tribune*'s Middle East coverage. But it did not release the study's findings, instead holding private meetings with the paper's management. Michael Kotzin, executive vice president of the federation, said that such an approach was "more effective." James O'Shea, managing editor of the *Tribune,* said that the overall coverage of his paper was in fact balanced, and that the critics were merely "finding headlines, pictures, looking at the placement of a story and picking apart those elements."

Ironically, in the case of Atlanta-based CNN—whose hostility toward Israel was evident from the outset of the intifada—public manifestation of that hostility by its founder in 2002 brought a turnaround. In an interview published in a British newspaper, Ted Turner asked, "Aren't the Israelis and the Palestinians both terrorizing each other? The Palestinians are fighting with human suicide bombers, that's all they have. The Israelis . . . they've got one of the most powerful military machines in the world. The Palestinians have nothing. So who are the terrorists? I would make a case that both sides are involved in terrorism." Though he later apologized, the moral equivalency he had evoked between Israelis and Palestinians seemed to fit all too well the nature of CNN coverage. CNN quickly distanced itself from Turner's views, but Israelis reacted angrily, one cable company dropping CNN and replacing it with Fox News. CNN tried to repair the damage, apologizing for giving too much airtime to the family of a suicide bomber and broadcasting a new series of interviews with terror victims on Israeli TV. In the U.S., meanwhile, CNN chairman Walter Isaacson met with editors of Jewish media outlets to make clear that the cable network was not anti-Israel.

Since New York was the center of American Jewish life and the *New York Times*—long owned by the Jewish Ochs-Sulzberger family—the nation's "paper of record," Jews meticulously scrutinized the way the *Times* covered the Israeli-Palestinian dispute, and many found it wanting. In 2001, hundreds of readers followed the lead of Rabbi Haskel Lookstein and suspended their subscriptions to the paper between Rosh Hashanah and Yom Kippur in protest of its coverage of the intifada (see AJYB 2002, p. 226). In the spring of 2002, Rabbi Lookstein, particularly incensed at the paper's publication of a photo of the New York Israel Day Parade that highlighted the few anti-Israel demonstrators rather than the numerous pro-Israel marchers, announced plans for a more ambitious boycott to start May 9, Jerusalem Day, and to run "for at least 30 days." It would include not only cancellation of subscriptions but also an end to the placement of advertisements and obituary notices in the *Times*. The announcement acknowledged that the *Times* "may not be the worst offender but it's certainly the most influential" (*New York Jewish Week,* May 3). The *Times* acknowledged that subscriptions were canceled but would not give a number. Executive Editor Howell Raines said: "We respect our readers' right to express their opinion. We are unhappy whenever we lose a single reader." Raines expressed confidence that his paper covered the Middle East with "fairness and balance" and pledged that "we will remain vigilant to make sure that continues to be the case."

Support for the *Times* boycott seemed strong in the Orthodox community but weak beyond it. Abraham Foxman, national director of the Anti-Defamation League (ADL), questioned the "obsession" many Jews had with the *Times* and noted that "ADL has always fought boycotts." Hebrew Union College went ahead with plans to honor controversial *Times* columnist Thomas Friedman (proponent and quasi-initiator of the Saudi peace plan—see above, p. 112) for "commitment to the betterment of humanity" on May 30. The *New York Jewish Week,* the major Jewish paper in the city, opposed the boycott, editorializing (May 10): "We need more constructive criticism, more marshaling of information, more voices speaking out for fair reporting, not a call to shut ourselves off from reporting and opinions we don't want to deal with."

During the summer, the American Jewish Committee devoted considerable attention to Israel's image in the U.S. The AJC's annual Survey of American Jewish Opinion, conducted by pollster Stanley Greenberg in

July and released in August, indicated no erosion in Jewish support for Israel and in fact showed a higher level of American Jewish "closeness" to the Jewish state than ever. At the same time, 63 percent of respondents favored the establishment of a Palestinian state and only 33 percent opposed it.

The AJC was also a partner in another venture that reported its findings in August, the Israel PR Project, which was also backed by Israel 21C—a group of pro-Israel high-tech professionals in the Silicon Valley—and United Jewish Communities. Using conventional polling as well as sessions with focus groups having different demographic characteristics around the U.S., the project found far more sympathy for Israel than for the Palestinians, but also an escalating "plague upon both your houses" feeling—an overriding revulsion with what many Americans perceived as an unending cycle of war for which both sides deserved blame. The pollsters responsible for the project—Greenberg, Frank Luntz, and Jennifer Laszlo Mizrahi—met with Israeli government officials and American Jewish organizations, advising them to score public-relations points by stressing the common values of Israel and the U.S., and Israel's willingness to make concessions for peace.

In September, AJC and Israel 21C followed up with 30-second ads on cable television—first in New York and Washington, then in the top 100 markets (CNN refused to carry them)—hammering home the American-style freedoms that Israel guaranteed its citizens. David Harris, AJC's executive director, noted that this was a new departure for his organization, which had previously relied on print and radio advertising. "There had been so many visual images presented," he told the *New York Times* (Oct. 1), "that we felt that we had to go to television as well. We could not rely on television reporting to do our work for us."

Battle for the Campus

2002 saw a sharpening of the ideological struggle between pro-Israel and pro-Palestinian groups on American college campuses. In particular, critics of Israel in the academic community escalated efforts to strike at Israel's economy by convincing universities to divest themselves of any holdings they might have in the Jewish state—on the model of the divestment campaign that helped end apartheid in South Africa. In February, for example, the National Student Conference on the Palestinian Solidarity Movement, convening at the University of California at Berkeley, launched a national drive to push divestment, an end to American aid to Israel, and the "right of return" of all Palestinians to Israel. Although Hillel—the Jewish campus organization—the Jewish Agency, and Jewish federations located near campuses sought to combat the pro-Palestinian forces by providing speakers and educational materials, there was a widespread feeling that Jewish students at many universities around the country lacked the information and/or motivation to take on Israel's detractors.

Israel's military move into Palestinian territories in April aroused anti-Israel feeling on campus even more, and on April 9—which Jews were commemorating as Holocaust Memorial Day—there were pro-Palestinian rallies on several campuses. Again it was Berkeley that grabbed the headlines, as hundreds of demonstrators called not simply for changes in Israeli policies but for treating Israel like white-ruled South Africa and dismantling it. Signs accused Israel of genocide and compared both President Bush and Prime Minister Sharon to Hitler. By the end of the day 78 of the demonstrators had been arrested for occupying a university building and disrupting academic activity. Jewish students at Berkeley told a reporter that even before April 9 there had been a number of disturbing incidents, such as anti-Semitic graffiti, and that they had repeatedly been rebuffed when they tried to engage in dialogue with the pro-Palestinians (*Forward,* Apr. 12).

Petitions urging divestment from Israel circulated on a number of campuses, including Ivy League and other elite institutions, and they sometimes attracted long lists of signatures, including those of left-leaning Jewish academics. But since counter-petitions opposing divestment generally drew greater support, and Jews were prominent on the boards of many universities, no institution took the step of divesting from Israel (see above, pp. 92–93).

Another controversial issue on campus was the cancellation by many universities of their travel-abroad programs in Israel. Such decisions, motivated by security considerations, hurt Israel's economy by strengthening the widespread assumption that Israel was an unsafe place to visit, and also played into the hands of those elements on campus eager to stigmatize and isolate the Jewish state. At the State University of New York (SUNY) it took the intervention of Governor George Pataki himself to reverse an administrative decision to cancel the study-in-Israel program of the university's Albany campus.

Birthright Israel, the project begun in 1999 to provide every young Jewish adult with a free ten-day trip to Israel with the aim of bolstering the participants' identification with the Jewish state and the challenges that faced it, was an important tool in the campus struggle. However the uneasy security situation in the summer of 2002 cut deeply into registration for Birthright: some youth groups that had participated regularly in the program brought over far fewer people than in previous years, some canceled entirely, and others switched their itineraries to sites in the U.S. or Europe. Something of a scandal erupted when the national office of March of the Living, a popular program that brought teenagers to visit Auschwitz and then Israel, announced that it was canceling the Israel leg of the trip due to security concerns. The *Jerusalem Post* renamed it "March of the Timid," and Gary Rosenblatt, editor of the *New York Jewish Week,* asked (Apr. 5): "Are we, the American Jewish community, telling our children it is safer to visit a death camp in Poland than the eternal capital of the Jewish people?" Several local March of the Living affiliates defied the national office and sent their participants from Poland on to Israel.

The organized Jewish community geared up for the start of the fall semester—and September 28, the second anniversary of the outbreak of the intifada. Hillel, AIPAC, and other Jewish organizations—coordinating their activities under the banner of the Israel on Campus Coalition, a new umbrella group funded by the Charles and Lynn Schusterman Family Foundation—convened several meetings for Jewish campus activists with Israelis and American Jewish leaders to prepare them to advocate Israel's cause. On another front of the campus battle that September, Daniel Pipes, director of Middle East Forum, launched a Web site, www.campus-watch.org, to identify academics who were biased against Israel (see above, p. 94).

The campaign to challenge the predominant pro-Palestinian atmosphere in academia received an unexpected boost on September 17, when Harvard president Lawrence Summers publicly stated that "profoundly anti-Israel views are increasingly finding support in progressive intellectual communities. Serious and thoughtful people are advocating and taking actions that are anti-Semitic in their effect if not in their intent." Subsequently, about 300 university presidents signed an American Jewish Committee ad denouncing the anti-Israeli campus campaign for encouraging an atmosphere of intimidation.

One manifestation of what Summers and the other presidents had in mind was yet another National Student Conference on the Palestinian Solidarity Movement, held October 12–14 at the University of Michigan (see above, p. 93). Some 400 pro-Palestinian sympathizers came from about 70 campuses around the country. To ward off the inevitable charge of anti-Semitism, the conference made sure to highlight the presence of anti-Israel Jews such as Professor Ilan Pappe of Haifa University and Adam Shapiro, the American Jew who had achieved celebrity in the spring by joining the besieged Yasir Arafat in his Ramallah compound. The conference reiterated the demand for divestment, though some differences among the participants were evident over the legitimacy of suicide bombings and over whether Zionism was inherently racist. Jewish reaction was divided, Hillel taking a nonconfrontational approach and holding a separate pro-Israel rally, and a more militant group, led by Rabbi Avi Weiss of New York, picketing the pro-Palestinian event.

Observers noted that most Jewish students at Michigan seemed ambivalent about the debate swirling around them. Journalist Matthew Purdy noted the same mood at Yale in November, where he found that even Jewish members of pro-Israel organizations empathized with the plight of the Palestinians. James Ponet, the campus rabbi, told Purdy: "They can't look at the world through one lens. The world's too complex. It doesn't refract down to a clear point" (*New York Times,* Nov. 17). By year's end, anti-Israel activity on college campuses seemed to have diminished, probably due to a combination of the failure of the divestment movement, a reduction in Middle East violence, and the emergence of a new rallying cry on the left — opposition to war with Iraq.

American Jews and Iraq

Despite imputations of heavy Jewish influence on the decision to invade Iraq, American Jews were hardly beating the drums for war when the administration first threatened hostile action in August 2002. Although the organized Jewish community was unanimous in its condemnation of Saddam Hussein's regime, Jews worried not only about possible Iraqi retaliation against Israel but also about a worldwide Islamic backlash against both the U.S. and Israel. However, even as the Conference of Presidents was in the process of polling its 52 member organizations by telephone about their views on a possible war, Mortimer Zuckerman, the conference chairman, angered some of those organizations by publishing an editorial in *U.S. News and World Report,* the magazine he owned, supporting war against Iraq.

Nevertheless, the conference itself did not endorse Zuckerman's views and maintained a position of neutrality. Even in the fall, after Congress voted President Bush broad authority to mount an attack on Iraq, the conference approved a resolution supporting the government's efforts to have Iraq give up its weapons of mass destruction but said nothing about war or "regime change." The Jewish Council for Public Affairs (JCPA), the public-policy umbrella organization for the federations and national Jewish groups, was more explicit about its reservations, voting to "support current U.S. diplomatic efforts to disarm Iraq of weapons of mass destruction and to only use force as a last resort." The two major national Jewish organizations, the American Jewish Committee and the Anti-Defamation League, declined to comment on the issue, while the American Jewish Congress and B'nai B'rith favored explicit backing for the president to take whatever action necessary. AIPAC, the powerful pro-Israel lobby, went so far as to assert that it would support the president should he launch an attack, and would, in such an eventuality, seek to mobilize support for the administration in Congress.

On the other hand, there were elements of the Jewish community that argued openly against war. The Workmen's Circle/Arbeter Ring, a member of the Conference of Presidents, bluntly opposed military action, as did Rabbi Ismar Schorsch, chancellor of the Jewish Theological Seminary and, by virtue of his position, the leading figure in the Conservative movement in the eyes of most American Jews. Schorsch took the position that only a UN resolution could justify hostilities, a position that a number of other Conservative leaders disputed. Unilateral American action, Schorsch cautioned, could unleash a "tidal wave of terrorism that could come from the Arab street" (*Forward,* Sept. 20). The Reform movement was split over the issue. The Union of American Hebrew Congregations (UAHC), representing its lay leadership, passed a resolution on September 24 backing unilateral American action if necessary, but there was far less enthusiasm for war among the Reform rabbis.

DENOMINATIONAL DEVELOPMENTS

Orthodox Judaism

Although Orthodoxy constituted only some 10 percent, at most, of American Jewry, its visibility and prestige in American Jewish life continued to grow as its more moderate elements proved willing and able to work in concert with the rest of the community. On the pro-Israel front, more than half of those attending the April 15 rally for Israel in Washington were Orthodox, and AIPAC's annual policy conference, held in Washington the following week, gave ample evidence of growing Orthodox influence in that high-powered body. Also, as American Jewry worried increasingly about maintaining the Jewish identification of its youth, it tended to perceive the Orthodox as role models for success in this endeavor. This was the reason for the prominence of Modern Orthodox speakers at the annual General Assembly (GA) of the United Jewish Communities (UJC), held this year in Philadelphia on November 18–19, which focused on Jewish continuity.

The new Jewish year that began in the fall marked the onset of the 100th year since the birth of Rabbi Joseph B. Soloveitchik as well as the tenth year since his death. The void in the leadership of Modern Orthodoxy created by his passing had still not been filled, and the first two of what would surely be many public commemorations took place in December, one at the convention of the Union of Orthodox Jewish Congregations (Orthodox Union, or OU), the other at a conference of the Combined Jewish Philanthropies of Greater Boston, the city where the rabbi had lived.

The future direction of Yeshiva University (YU), Modern Orthodoxy's flagship educational institution where Soloveitchik had taught for almost 50 years, seemed unclear through much of 2002 as it struggled to find a new president to succeed Dr. Norman Lamm, who had held the post for a quarter-century (see AJYB 2002, pp. 237–38). In its March 8 issue, the *New York Jewish Week* broke the story that a search committee, after working in secrecy for nine months, had come up with a surprise candidate. He was Dov Zakheim, undersecretary of defense, whose experience managing the multibillion-dollar Pentagon budget apparently attracted the enthusiasm of YU leaders eager to improve the managerial efficiency and financial accountability of their institution, whose annual budget was $470 million.

Zakheim could hardly have been more unlike Lamm, who, in addition to extensive experience in the Jewish community as rabbi of a major synagogue, was, like the two previous YU presidents, a respected Jewish scholar and academician. Although it appeared that Zakheim had, at some point, been granted private rabbinical ordination, he could make no claim to expertise in the texts of traditional Judaism, and clearly would not be able to serve as *rosh hayeshivah,* head of the YU rabbinical school, a position that had previously gone along with the office of university president. In addition, though Zakheim had a Ph.D., he had worked as an administrator of a government bureaucracy rather than as an academic, and thus had no experience in university politics or fundraising, where networking and glad-handing worked better than giving orders. Finally, while serving in the Defense Department under the Reagan and first Bush administrations, Zakheim had been vilified by many in the Jewish community for opposing Israel's development of the Lavi jet fighter. Although his stated reason for this was that the Lavi would cost too much money, his opponents charged at the time that Zakheim was acting against Israeli interests in order to protect the American F-16 from competition.

On Sunday, March 9, just after the *Jewish Week* story came out, Zakheim met with the board of the rabbinical school. According to some who were there, the session did not go well. Aware, also, of the degree of opposition to his nomination on campus—more than 400 students signed a petition calling for the new president to be a rabbinic scholar—he decided two days later, to withdraw his candidacy.

Since the search committee had been so certain of Zakheim's suitability that it had not prepared a list of alternate choices, another search would be necessary, and a new committee was formed to conduct it. Although the 74-year-old Lamm had announced his retirement for August, he agreed, in May, to stay on as president until a successor was named. After the trial balloons of several new candidates rose and fell over the next few months, 52-year-old Richard Joel was named to fill the position in late November, the official designation coming on December 5. Joel, national director of Hillel, the network of Jewish campus organizations, was even less of an academic or Jewish scholar than Zakheim: he possessed a law degree but neither rabbinical ordination nor a Ph.D. He was very highly regarded at Hillel, however, for his fund-raising and interpersonal skills. Since Joel, like Zakheim, did not have the expertise to oversee the rabbinical school, Lamm would stay on indefinitely both as *rosh hayeshivah* and chancellor of the university—the latter a largely ceremonial role.

Still, several of the rabbinic faculty maintained their opposition to the choice of a non-rabbi, and hundreds of students signed a petition against Joel—a good number even gathering, together with some faculty rabbis, to recite chapters from the Book of Psalms to "ward off" the evil decree. Even after the university board chose Joel as president, the separate rabbinical school board, in the end, named him not president, but CEO.

One challenge that had dogged YU for four years was a lawsuit filed by students at the university's prestigious Albert Einstein College of Medicine seeking to invalidate the school's housing policy on the grounds of discrimination against homosexuals. To many, the dilemma that the case presented went to the very essence of the university's ambiguous dual mission as both a secular university and a Modern Orthodox institution. Two lesbian students at Einstein barred from living with their non-student partners in university housing charged the university with discrimination. Indeed, Orthodox Jewish law prohibited homosexuality, but, as an officially nondenominational school that received government funding, the medical school was bound not to discriminate. Two courts had accepted YU's argument that the policy of allowing an unmarried couple to live together only if both were students was not discriminatory since it applied to heterosexuals as well, but the New York State Court of Appeals reinstated the suit. To put a halt to the drawn-out litigation, which had cost the university considerable money as well as bad publicity in liberal circles, YU announced a change in policy in August, allowing students to room with anyone with whom they had an "interdependent" or "long-term" relationship. This came as a great disappointment to many Orthodox Jews who had hoped that YU would fight to defend its religious values. It remained unclear whether students at any other of the university's schools would make similar housing requests.

Another Modern Orthodox institution under heavy public scrutiny was the Orthodox Union (OU), a major synagogue body with a constituency of over 1,000 congregations. It had undergone an upheaval in 2001 after an outside investigative panel, chaired by Richard Joel, verified charges that its officials had turned a blind eye to physical and emotional abuse committed by a staff member, Rabbi Baruch Lanner, against teenagers who participated in the organization's National Conference of Synagogue Youth (NCSY). Although Lanner had been fired as soon as the charges were aired, a lawsuit filed against him in New Jersey for similar abuse of students while he had served as principal of a day school — matters having nothing to do with NCSY or the OU — kept the Lanner affair in the public eye (see AJYB 2002, p. 238). In late June, 2002, Lanner was convicted, and in October he was sentenced to seven years in jail. His lawyers appealed, and Lanner was released on bail. At the OU's December convention, its leaders made a commitment to greater openness and, in tacit response to the charge that the lack of female role models encouraged an institutional culture where young women were afraid to come forward with complaints of abuse, had a woman deliver the keynote address.

In the area of religious practice, traditional Orthodox restrictions on the role of women in the synagogue came under challenge. A number of prayer groups in Israel had been experimenting for some time with women leading some parts of the service and being called up to the Torah, and in 2002 a half-dozen American groups, most of them on the Upper West Side of Manhattan, were doing the same. The basis in Jewish law for allowing such an innovation was laid out in an article in the journal of the Modern Orthodox organization Edah, and the arguments set forth there were supported by the noted Israeli scholar Rabbi Daniel Sperber in a presentation to the Jewish Orthodox Feminist Alliance (JOFA) in November. Even so, no established Orthodox congregation or well-known rabbi was ready to sanction the change.

The sectarian Orthodox, institutionally represented by Agudath Israel, continued to struggle with the impact of American values on Jewish tradition. Although a modest lifestyle was, in theory, essential to the Orthodox way of life, pressures generated by material success, consumerism, and "keeping up with the Schwartzes" were driving the costs of weddings, bar mitzvahs, and other lifecycle events ever higher. This problem was real for all sectors of American Jewry, as attested by a headline in the *Forward* (Feb. 22), " 'Today I Am a Master Card': Bar Mitzvahs Break the Bank." But the large number of children (ten or more was not uncommon) among the sectarian Orthodox, and the tightly knit nature of their communities, where everyone felt obligated to invite everyone else, only compounded the situation.

In March 2002, guidelines for spending at weddings, formulated by Agudath Israel rabbinic leaders from New York and New Jersey the previous November, went into effect: no more than 400 guests, meals consisting of no more than three courses plus dessert, a limit of $1,800 to be spent on flowers, a maximum of five musicians, and no bar (wine and liquor bottles to be placed on the tables). As an inducement for families to stick to the regulations, the well-known rabbis who signed the guidelines announced that they would not attend weddings that did not comply. It was hoped that if these rules were effective in holding down costs, they would be adopted elsewhere in the country as well.

Far more divisive for the world of Agudath Israel was determining the appropriate stance that sectarian Orthodoxy should take regarding the State of Israel. Although the organization still remained true to its non-Zionist origins by officially rejecting the legitimacy of secular Jewish nationalism, the participation of sectarian Orthodox political parties in numerous Israeli governments and the widespread emotional identification with the Jewish state among virtually all sectors of American Orthodoxy created a potential conflict with official ideology. This came to the fore when the American Jewish community planned its massive national pro-Israel rally in Washington, D.C., for April 15. Agudath Israel decided not to participate, claiming that it could not involve itself in public events where it was not certain that the program fit Orthodox criteria. (It organized a separate event, a prayer vigil for Israel, which drew 40,000–50,000 people in New York City on April 21.) This position was interpreted as allowing individuals and groups to attend the Washington rally so long as Agudath Israel was not seen as giving formal endorsement. And yet the decision to withhold official participation unleashed an unprecedented degree of disappointment and anger from the rank and file. Editors of the *Jewish Press*—the American Jewish newspaper with the largest circulation in the country, whose readership was overwhelmingly Orthodox—reported that the sheer number of critical letters, many from veteran Agudath Israel members, was unprecedented in the paper's history.

The strains implied in Agudath Israel's balancing act—striving to maintain its sectarian Orthodox posture, which required a degree of social separation, while, at the same time, Americanizing—formed the background for in important roundtable discussion at the organization's annual convention on December 27. There, activists from several different communities pointed out that what looked like anti-Semitism directed against them could sometimes be more accurately described as fear that the Orthodox were taking over. If Orthodox families moving into new neighborhoods, they noted, set up what amounted to isolationist enclaves, and looked out single-mindedly for their own interests, they themselves might be to blame for the consequent resentment expressed by other residents.

The year 2002 marked the centennial of the birth of Rabbi Menachem Mendel Schneerson, the late charismatic leader of the Chabad-Lubavitch Hassidic movement. Since the death of the childless rabbi in 1994, his followers had not chosen a successor, but had gone on propagating his teachings around the world, with considerable success. More controversially, an indeterminate number of Chabad Hassidim believed that their rabbi was the promised messiah who would rise from the grave and bring redemption. In 2001, David Berger, a professor at Brooklyn College, wrote a book, *The Rebbe, the Messiah, and the Scandal of Orthodox Indifference,* calling on the Orthodox mainstream to treat Chabad messianism—which, he argued, had virtually taken over the movement—as heresy (see AJYB 2002, pp. 238–39). The debate continued into 2002, with Berger attacking Chabad at every opportunity, and its supporters responding that authoritative Jewish texts did mention the possibility of the Jewish messiah rising from the dead.

Conservative Judaism

For the first time in the history of the movement, all five of Conservative Judaism's national organizations held their annual meetings in one place, Washington D.C., at one time, mid-February. The United Synagogue of Conservative Judaism, the Rabbinical Assembly, the Cantors Assembly, the Jewish Educators Assembly, and the North American Association of Synagogue Executives convened with a total attendance of about 1,500. The meetings showcased Judy Yudof, the first woman to hold the presidency of the United Synagogue, and Rabbi Reuven Hammer, the first Israeli rabbi to head the Rabbinical Assembly. Both were seen as harbingers of the movement's future—an enhanced role for women and the increasing centrality of Israel.

Rabbi Jerome Epstein, executive vice president of the United Synagogue, sparked controversy in Washington by publicly proposing what he called a "Conservative Compact of Jewish Commitment." Suggesting that it was unrealistic to expect the Conservative laity to adopt the discipline of Jewish law in its entirety—a goal to which the movement was officially committed—Epstein proposed setting minimal demands. For example, a Jew not ready to adopt the kosher laws (only about a quarter of Conservative Jews said they kept them) might refrain just from pork and shellfish, while one feeling unable to relocate to Israel might visit there, or even just put aside money for someone else to visit. If Epstein thought he was offering a practical way to move Conservative Jews somewhat closer to traditional practices, others were offended at what seemed to them a "dumbing-down" of Judaism. One rabbi, referring to Epstein, told the *Forward* (Mar. 1): "This is a movement that's lost nearly all its principles, and now he's planning to abandon the last of them." Chancellor Ismar Schorsch of the Jewish Theological Seminary rebuked Epstein for delivering his remarks without prior consultation with the movement's other leaders, and argued that an upswing in the Jewish observance patterns of younger Conservative Jews signaled a need for setting higher rather than lower standards.

Another controversial issue, this one coming up at the Rabbinical Assembly meeting, was over the heavy participation of Israeli Conservative rabbis in Rabbis for Human Rights, a pro-peace organization that, among its other activities, raised money to replant olive trees uprooted by Israeli forces to prevent terrorists from hiding behind them. In 2001, Conservative rabbis in Israel opposed to the group charged that it gave aid and comfort to Israel's enemies (see AJYB 2002, p. 240), but when their colleagues who were members ignored them, they decided to bring their complaint to the 2002 convention.

One issue not on the formal agenda in Washington but a prominent subject of talk in the corridors was the movement's position on homosexuals—specifically, whether their commitment ceremonies might be performed by Conservative rabbis and whether gays themselves might receive rabbinical ordination. The Reform movement had already given its approval to both, while the Conservatives had only gone so far as to welcome gays into the synagogue and support their civil equality. In the early 1990s, the movement's Committee on Law and Standards had debated the issue and came up with a number of differing opinions, but agreed, in 1992, not to sanction any formal change in the traditional position. Student sentiment at the Jewish Theological Seminary was reportedly strongly supportive of gay rights. But Chancellor Schorsch, responding to a question from a *Washington Post* reporter during the convention (Feb. 13), said that following the Reform position on homosexuality would both violate traditional Jewish law and fracture the Conservative movement.

By the end of the year, however, the issue was out in the open, as United Synagogue president Judy Yudof said she was preparing a letter to the Committee on Law and Standards urging it to rethink the matter, though she did not so far as to suggest explicitly that it reverse the existing policy. Yudof shrugged off the fears of Schorsch that reopening the issue could split the movement, and explained that she was reflecting sentiments she had heard from numerous Conservative laypeople.

The Jewish Theological Seminary came in for some embarrassment when it became known that Prof. Judith Hauptman, a noted talmudist on the seminary faculty, was pursuing rabbinic ordination not at JTS, but at the nondenominational Academy for Jewish Studies. She had received her Ph.D. at JTS, taking many of the same courses offered to the rabbinical students, but that was before 1983, when the seminary began ordaining women. Chancellor Schorsch had turned down her request to finish up the required coursework for JTS ordination on the grounds that it was inappropriate for a faculty member to attend classes together with her own students.

Etz Hayim, the first officially commissioned Bible commentary of the Conservative movement, had appeared toward the end of 2001 (see AJYB 2002, p. 240), but its full impact only began to be felt in 2002, when it won the Jewish Book Council's National Jewish Book Award for nonfiction and was the subject of a major article in the "arts and ideas" section of the *New York Times* ("A New Torah for Modern Minds," Mar. 9). By mid-February, when the Conservative organizations met together in Washington, over 100,000 copies had been sold. As noted by a number of reviewers, *Etz Hayim* embodied both the strengths of Conservative Judaism and its inherent intellectual ambivalence—the English translation and running commentaries elucidating the basis for Jewish religious observance in the modern world, and its appended scholarly essays on theological and archaeological topics suggesting serious doubts about the Bible's historicity.

Reform Judaism

After the heated arguments in recent years over the endorsement of higher standards of adherence to Jewish ritual and over rabbinic officiation at same-sex commitment ceremonies, 2002 was a relatively quiet year for the Reform movement.

Despite Reform's liberal approach to intermarriage—its congregations welcomed intermarried Jews and their families, Reform rabbis were free to perform intermarriages (many did), and Jews married to non-Jews taught in Reform religious schools—the movement drew the line at ordaining intermarried rabbis. The responsa committee of the Central Conference of American Rabbis (CCAR), which provided guidance on Jewish legal issues for the movement, ruled that despite Reform's commitment to reach out to the intermarried, "the ideal toward which we rabbis strive, teach, and lead is that Jews should marry Jews. Since one of the ways in which we convey our teaching is through personal example, a rabbi's life and home should embody this ideal."

Rabbi Eric Yoffie, president of the Union of American Hebrew Congregations (UAHC), Reform's synagogue body, announced as his priority the improvement of congregational afternoon schools. The inadequacy of supplementary Jewish education had long been acknowledged in all of the movements, and interest in Jewish all-day schools had been felt throughout the Jewish community, including its Reform sector. But the UAHC, whose 914 congregations educated some 120,000 children in afternoon programs, understood that the day school was not a realistic alternative for the great majority of its families, and Yoffie asked that "instead of taking potshots at Hebrew schools," congregations should launch an initiative to revitalize them.

The centerpiece of the plan was a new, unified curriculum called Chai Learning for Jewish Life, based on the three Jewish principles of Torah study, ritual performance, and good deeds. It would replace the previous decentralized system in which there was no overarching shape to the different synagogues' curricula. Educational specialists placed in each of the UAHC's 13 regional offices would help individual afternoon schools. Other elements of the new system would be improved recruitment and training of teachers—including on-line courses for professional development—the participation of lay leaders in teaching, and a requirement that parents attend class with their children at least six times a year.

In May, Women of Reform Judaism, the organization of congregational sisterhoods, announced plans for a women's commentary on the Torah. To be edited by Prof. Tamara Cohn Eskenazi of the HUC branch in Los Angeles and written entirely by women, it was expected to take five years to prepare. Any Jewish woman, whether Reform or not, was welcome to submit material. Although a number of other commentaries from women's perspectives were already on the market, this was expected to be the first that would cover the entire Torah.

Reform Judaism's generally dovish stance on Israel and the Palestinians subtly shifted in the wake of the new round of Palestinian violence. In June 2001, Rabbi Yoffie had publicly acknowledged that the movement had "been wrong about Palestinian intentions," though he remained opposed to Israel's "occupation" of the Territories (see AJYB 2002, p. 226), and that December the UAHC passed a resolution denying that Israel had overreacted in responding to terror, while reiterating Reform support for the establishment of a Palestinian state alongside Israel.

In September 2002, however, Rabbi Paul Menitoff, executive vice president of the CCAR, in a public letter in his own name but on CCAR stationery, urged the U.S. to threaten economic sanctions against Israel and the Palestinians if either or both proved reluctant to move toward peace. In early October, 34 Reform rabbis responded with a newspaper ad expressing support for the Israeli position, and soon afterward more than 120 Reform rabbis from several countries put out a 23-point statement rejecting any solution imposed on Israel from the outside and stating that "Yasir Arafat is clearly unable or unprepared to take the necessary steps to reach an agreement with Israel." Rabbi John Moscowitz of Toronto, who signed both the ad and the statement, told the *Forward* (Oct. 25), "There's an intellectual orthodoxy that says if you're a Reform rabbi you take a certain position. That is now being busted apart."

In December, UAHC board members meeting in Phoenix voted unanimously to recommend a change in the name of their 129-year-old organization. The original "Union of American Hebrew Congregations" had been formed with the expectation that it would not just be a denominational body but would, indeed, encompass a *union* of virtually all American congregations—and that clearly had not come to pass. And as for *Hebrew,* the word had been considered less offensive to Christian sensitivities that *Jewish* in the year 1873. The suggested new name, Union for Reform Judaism, would be voted on by the organization's next biennial conference in 2003. A similar name change had been effected a few years earlier by the United Synagogue, the Conservative congregational group, which became the United Synagogue of Conservative Judaism.

Reconstructionist Judaism

After ten years as president of the Reconstructionist Rabbinical College (RRC), Rabbi David Teutsch stepped down to return to teaching. During his tenure the number of students had doubled to 90 and the college's endowment had multiplied nearly six times, to $12 million. Teutsch was succeeded on July 1 by Rabbi Dan Ehrenkrantz, a former pulpit rabbi and the first RRC alumnus to head the 34-year-old institution.

Reconstructionists could point to two major accomplishments in 2002. One was the publication of the fifth and final volume of *Kol Haneshama,* the series of Reconstructionist prayer books. Like the preceding volumes, this one, consisting of prayers for the house of mourning, was egalitarian and excluded traditional references to a personal messiah, miracles, and the chosen people. The other accomplishment—the fulfillment of a long-held dream within the movement—was the establishment of a Reconstructionist summer camp for children: Camp JRF would open in June near Chicago with 40–60 youngsters.

Denominational Relations

As so often in the past, the "who is a Jew" question in Israel aroused Jewish denominational ire in the U.S. In March, Shas, the Sephardi Orthodox party, called on the Israeli Knesset to overturn a Supreme Court decision recognizing non-Orthodox conversions performed in Israel, and Prime Minister Sharon set up a committee to formulate a proposal to that effect (see below, p. 271). The American Conservative movement, warning that passage of such legislation would lead to the nonrecognition of Reform and Conservative conversions even if performed outside Israel, immediately called on its members to send letters of complaint to Prime Minister Sharon. In this instance, however, unlike the major "who is a

Jew" battles of the past, Israel's perilous security situation and the priority American Jewry gave to rallying support for Israel's diplomatic course made the bulk of the community reluctant to follow the Conservative course of public protest.

In a dramatic and well-publicized move, Hebrew Union College (HUC), the Reform rabbinical school, made a statement of Jewish ecumenism by honoring leaders of the Orthodox and Conservative streams of Judaism at the graduation ceremonies of its New York school on May 9. On the initiative of HUC president David Ellenson, Rabbi Ismar Schorsch, chancellor of the Jewish Theological Seminary (Conservative), gave the major address to the newly ordained Reform rabbis and cantors, while both Schorsch and Rabbi Emanuel Rackman, chancellor emeritus of Bar-Ilan University in Israel and a long-time prominent figure in American Orthodoxy, received honorary degrees. Noting that the increased interest in Jewish ritual practice within Reform seemed to signal something of a convergence between it and his own movement, Schorsch saw nothing problematic in addressing the graduates. Rackman, on the other hand, predicted that he would be vilified in certain Orthodox circles for his participation.

Indeed, the degree of Orthodox sensitivity to any sign of "recognition" of the other streams seriously embarrassed the OU in June, when an ad sponsored by the Jewish Agency appeared in Jewish newspapers expressing support for American Jews "who have made the most meaningful decision to make Aliyah." These sentiments were expressed in the name of all three major denominations and signed by the executives of the Reform, Conservative, and Modern Orthodox synagogue bodies. The latter, Rabbi Tzvi Hersh Weinreb, the OU's executive vice president, was sharply criticized by the more sectarian Orthodox for seeming to legitimize the rival groups by including his signature along with those of their leaders. The OU responded that it considered Reform and Conservatism inauthentic forms of Judaism, it had not seen the final wording of the ad before publication, and it had asked the Jewish Agency to discontinue the ad. Nevertheless, the OU saw nothing wrong with interdenominational cooperation on such nonreligious matters as support for Israel, and Weinreb said he would sign a new ad if the text were changed to eliminate possible inferences that Orthodoxy recognized non-Orthodox Judaism.

Another sign of differences within Orthodoxy over how to respond to the other movements was the reaction to the Conservative *Etz Hayim* Torah commentary (see above). Rabbi Avi Shafran, spokesman for Agudath Israel, said that by casting doubt on the historical truth of biblical history, it was "no less shocking" than the Arab anti-Semitic libel that Jews used human blood to bake Purim hamantaschen. The OU and the Rabbinical Council of America, representing Modern Orthodoxy, distanced themselves from Shafran's analogy.

Eagerly anticipated as a landmark in interdenominational relations, *One People, Two Worlds: A Reform Rabbi and an Orthodox Rabbi in Search of Common Ground* was published in October amid considerable publicity. The brainchild of a literary agent, the book consisted of e-mails exchanged between Rabbi Ammiel Hirsch, executive director of the Association of Reform Zionists of America, and Rabbi Yosef Reinman, an Orthodox scholar rooted in the yeshivah world of sectarian Orthodoxy, Hirsch arguing that there were many legitimate ways to be Jewish and Reinman insisting that Orthodoxy was synonymous with Judaism. Despite their deep disagreements, the two rabbis became close friends in the course of working on the book. Hirsch explained to reporters that he considered it important to present a serious theological defense of liberal Judaism, while Reinman, who said that he had requested and received approval from prominent Orthodox leaders to participate in the project, said that the book was not for Orthodox Jews, but solely for non-Orthodox readers, to acquaint them with the Orthodox perspective and possibly influence them to adopt it.

However, the rabbinical council of Agudath Israel and Beth Medrash Govoha, the yeshivah in Lakewood, New Jersey, that had ordained Reinman, both denounced the book for giving the impression that Reform Judaism, as a legitimate dialogue partner, was a possible alternative to Orthodoxy. Accepting their assessment, Reinman pulled out of a 17-city promotional tour that had been scheduled by the publisher, Schocken Books. Some observers compared this exertion of Orthodox pressure on one of their own rabbis to the verbal attacks on Chief Rabbi Jonathan Sacks in Great Britain that forced him to withdraw and alter his latest book (see below, p. 372).

THE AMERICAN JEW IN 2002

Debating Demography

For over a decade American Jews concerned with the future of their community had been living under the cloud of the 1990 National Jewish Population Survey (NJPS), which depicted an aging American Jewry with widespread intermarriage and low fertility. In the late 1990s, the prospect of a demographically stagnant Jewish community took on a political dimension, as the evident growth of Islam in America raised the eventual possibility of more Muslims than Jews in the country and a consequent challenge to American support for the State of Israel.

During the 1990s, the Jewish community initiated numerous programs of education and outreach to promote what came to be called "Jewish continuity," and the planned 2000 NJPS, commissioned by United Jewish Communities (UJC, the successor body to the Council of Jewish Federations, sponsor of the 1990 survey), was expected to indicate whether these initiatives had helped reinvigorate the community. Numerous complications arose, however, due both to a desire to reach a large and representative sample, and the need to address conflicting priorities of various constituencies in the UJC and outside it. The $6-million survey was delayed, and the year 2002 dawned with no findings yet released.

A different survey of American Jewry was published in February, based on data collected the previous year. *American Jewish Identity Survey 2001* was the work of a team led by social scientists Egon Mayer and Barry A. Kosmin. Kosmin, principal investigator of the 1990 NJPS, objected to the UJC's decision not to use the same battery of questions in NJPS 2000. Convinced that the lack of comparability between the two surveys would render the UJC's 2000 product of little use, he and Mayer designed *American Jewish Identity Survey 2001* to replicate the methodology and sampling of the 1990 survey.

What they found was more or less a continuation of patterns noted in 1990. The "core" Jewish population—those who regarded themselves as Jewish by religion or said they were of Jewish parentage or upbringing but had no religion—declined from 5.5 million in 1990 to about 5.3 million in 2001. Just 40 percent of Jews who married since 1990 had spouses born Jewish; 9 percent married converts to Judaism; and the other 51 percent married non-Jews. The impact of intermarriage could be seen in the rise of the number of people living in a household that had at least one Jewish member, from some 8 million in 1990 to nearly 10 million. Fully 81 percent of cohabiting adults who said they were Jewish were living with a partner not born Jewish. Perhaps the most controversial finding was that a large sector of the Jewish population—far more, proportionately, than among other religious groups—defined itself as "secular."

A second survey was released during the summer, a study of American Jewish college freshmen conducted by the Cooperative Institutional Research Program of the University of California for Hillel, the national organization of Jewish college students. It found that among the sample of freshmen with two Jewish parents, over 90 percent considered themselves Jewish, as did almost 40 percent of those with just a Jewish mother, and less than 16 percent of those with just a Jewish father. Of all the children of intermarriage surveyed, 40 percent described their religion as "none," a higher proportion than self-described Jews or Christians. More than a quarter of the entire freshman sample said their parents were intermarried, just about matching the figure for children of the intermarried found in the 1990 NJPS. This seemed to indicate that the ramified programs launched since 1990 to ensure the Jewish affiliation of such children were not working.

On October 8, 2002, the UJC finally released the first findings from the 2000 NJPS, and they roughly corresponded with those of Mayer and Kosmin. The number of American Jews, according to the NJPS, had fallen from 5.5 million in 1990 to 5.2 in 2000, and the growth of the overall American population by some 33 million during that time meant that Jews now constituted just 2 percent of all Americans. The aging of American Jewry had continued apace, the median age of Jews rising from 37 to 41 over the course of the decade. Only 21 percent of Jews were children, as compared to 26 percent in American society as a whole. Jewish divorce rates were comparable to those of other Americans. As for fertility, Jewish women approaching the end of their childbearing years had an average of 1.8 children—below the replacement rate of 2.1—and 52 percent of Jewish women aged 30–50 were childless, as compared to 27 percent in the general population. Jews had a median household income about $8,000 higher than other Americans, and were, on the average, far more likely to earn both bachelor's and graduate degrees than others.

Those involved in the survey stressed that by contacting 177,000 people and interviewing 9,000 of them, this NJPS was by far the most thorough study ever conducted of America's Jews. Stephen Hoffman, president and CEO of the UJC, said that "using state-of-the-art research and technology, our team went to unprecedented lengths to present the broadest picture yet of the American Jewish community." Other survey results, dealing with Jewish identity and affiliation (including the much-anticipated intermarriage rate), were scheduled for release at the UJC's annual General Assembly (GA), to be held in Philadelphia in November.

A battle for "spin control" followed. The Jewish Telegraphic Agency (JTA) headlined the story "A Smaller, Graying American Jewry Poses New Challenges for Community," and quoted sociologist Frank Mott of Ohio State University, cochair of the survey's National Technical Advisory Committee, saying: "It doesn't look good," since without "some significant changes" Jews "are not going to replace themselves." But the UJC, in its own press release, sought to head off the doomsayers, and ran the headlines "U.S. Jewish Population Fairly Stable over Decade . . . " and "Older, Better Educated, More Diverse Community." The *Forward,* also eager to promote optimism, editorialized (Oct. 11) that "the decline isn't necessarily a decline, the 5.2 million isn't exactly 5.2 million, and the definitions of 'Jew' used in the 1990 and 2002 surveys may not even be comparable."

Disagreement over how to interpret the data was one thing, but outright rejection of the findings was something else entirely. Gary Tobin, president of the Institute for Jewish and Community Research, based in San Francisco, charged that the NJPS had come up with "utter nonsense" since it had used screening questions that excluded numerous Jews by immediately asking about Jewishness instead of leading up to it with preliminary queries. Tobin had conducted his own survey of 250 Jewish households, released the week before the NJPS preliminary report, on the basis of which he came up with 6.7 million American Jews, another 2.5 million "connected non-Jews," and yet another 4.1 million people with some Jewish ancestry. Tobin spoke out against the NJPS in no uncertain terms, saying: "Given the political climate, how destructive is it to put it that Jews are a declining population when exactly the opposite is true? It sends a terrible psychological message to the Jewish community, and also to anyone who might be considering joining the community." Writing in the *Forward* (Oct. 4), Tobin mocked "the business of despair" carried out by "prophets of doom" and urged American Jews to "take some satisfaction and pride in our ability both to adapt and endure" in America.

The demographic debate provided a platform for different ideological factions to promote their views about how to ensure the Jewish future. Predictably, the Orthodox advocated a return to Jewish tradition; proponents of outreach to the intermarried argued that the allegiance of the children of mixed-religion families was crucial for Jewish survival; and the Jewish People Policy Planning Institute, an arm of the Jewish Agency for Israel, convened an "international emergency conference" on world Jewish population decline to discuss immigration to Israel and improved Jewish education in the diaspora.

But there was also a new voice in the mix, that of Douglas Rushkoff, author of the only op-ed on NJPS that the *New York Times* chose to print (Nov. 20). Rushkoff, identified as professor of communications at New York University and author of the forthcoming book *Nothing Sacred:*

The Truth About Judaism, claimed that numbers were irrelevant to Jewish life. "It is only by liberating ourselves from these metrics that we become able to understand how Judaism is not on the brink of extinction at all, but poised for renaissance." It was misguided, he argued, to promote Zionism and fight intermarriage, as if Judaism were a race or a tribe interested only in self-preservation. Instead, Judaism had to be seen as the ethical ideal of social justice that "can happen anywhere, between anyone." To judge by the invitations Rushkoff received to speak before Jewish audiences, such sentiments struck a chord with many younger, unaffiliated Jews, for whom the controversy between demographers and the competition between Jewish ideologies had little meaning.

Yet another dramatic episode in the saga of NJPS 2000 occurred on November 13, one week before the opening of the GA, where the rest of the findings were scheduled for release. That day, UJC announced it was dropping all sessions from the conference program relating to the NJPS, since it had learned that data had been "lost" two years earlier by Roper ASW, the outside research company that conducted the fieldwork for the study. Stephen Hoffman, the UJC head, appointed a new task force to investigate, saying that he had "lost total confidence" in the existing technical advisory committee, apparently for not telling him sooner about the mishap. The cochairs of that committee, Frank Mott of Ohio State University and Vivian Klaff of the University of Delaware, responded that the lost material was methodological rather than substantive, that it was insignificant, and that the findings should be released. But Hoffman, in an e-mail message to UJC leaders, explained: "I was faced with the choice of muddling through next week and answering critics on the fly, or pausing to understand what may be happening."

UJC promised that the findings would be released once the technical problems were resolved, but gave no indication of when that might be. Meanwhile, as rumors swirled — unsubstantiated, to be sure — that the findings were being withheld because they offended or jeopardized the funding of one or another interested party, the only thing on which everyone involved could agree was that the delay could seriously undermine the survey's credibility.

Should Interfaith Families Have a Voice?

The American economic climate during the year did not encourage the creation of new organizations. The only significant one that saw the light of day in 2002 was based on a Web site and called the Interfaith-Family.com Network. Its originator, Edmund Case, who had set up the

Web site some time before, explained that the new membership organization would function as a pressure group to get more rabbis to perform mixed marriages, and synagogues and Jewish organizations to be more open toward mixed-religion families. Case, who received grants from two San Francisco family foundations, one for $80,000 and the other for $95,000, to create the new organization, set a goal of 2,500 members over the first year.

Jewish communal leaders opposed to intermarriage had long attacked Case and his Web site for working to make mixed marriage normative in the Jewish community. One of the most outspoken of the critics was Jack Wertheimer, provost of the Jewish Theological Seminary, who described the new membership group as a "lobby" in the full sense of the word, seeking to use political clout to erode and eventually erase the traditional Jewish taboo on intermarriage. Wertheimer considered this "a battle of ideas and a battle of values," and predicted that the mobilization of the intermarried would generate a strong countermovement in support of Jewish endogamy.

Reaching Young Jewish Adults

It was already a truism of American Jewish life—supported by survey and focus-group research—that the fastest growing segment of American Jewry consisted of secular young adults deeply steeped in American popular culture and its values but possessing only a shallowly rooted Jewish identity. This had been the target audience for the community's outreach efforts—special programming, free trips to Israel, innovative prayer services—during the 1990s.

The year 2002 saw the launch of a new three-issue-a-year publication aimed at such young Jews, *Heeb: The New Jew Review*. Its founder was Jennifer Bleyer, a 26-year-old graduate of Columbia University, who received a $60,000 grant for the project from the Joshua Venture, a foundation partially funded by Steven Spielberg and the Bronfman family to encourage young Jews to develop innovative Jewish projects. Explaining that she got the idea for *Heeb* because "there were no magazines for Jews like me," Bleyer described it as "the bastard love child of Emma Goldmann and Lenny Bruce" and said that it would be about "interesting Jews doing interesting things." The first issue, which came out in February, cost $4.50 and was available at bookstores and newsstands in several large cities. It contained articles about poet Allen Ginsberg, the gay Orthodox Jew Sandi DuBowski, a five-page pictorial spread of "Jewfro" hairstyles, a centerfold featuring Neil Diamond, and a discussion of whether the

Krusty the Clown character on "The Simpsons" TV show was "good for the Jews." A second issue appeared in July.

The unceasing search for modes of Jewish identification that might inspire the kind of young, "hip" Jews targeted by *Heeb* to be proud of their Jewishness took some surprising directions during the year.

Leonard Nimoy, the legendary actor known for his portrayal of Mr. Spock on "Star Trek," was a strongly identified Jew who involved himself in numerous Jewish causes and cultural projects, and Mr. Spock's trademark two-finger greeting was Nimoy's version of the biblical priestly benediction. Pursuing his interest in Jewish spirituality, Nimoy published a book of photographs in 2002, *Shekhina,* an "intensely personal photographic inquiry into the feminine manifestation of God." As several of the photos were of nude or barely clad women wearing prayer shawls and tefillin, the Rabbinical Council of America called on its members around the country to protest the "offensive" material. Several federations and other Jewish institutions canceled appearances that Nimoy's publisher had arranged for him to promote the book.

If Nimoy's luster was tarnished, a fresh Jewish celebrity emerged from a new entertainment genre, reality TV, for a brief period of fame. The strikingly handsome 28-year-old Ethan Zohn won $1 million by being the sole survivor of "Survivor: Africa." On the show, he pointedly refused to eat ham. Zohn subsequently accepted several invitations to address groups of young Jews about his Jewish identity, emphasizing that he had won the competition, which placed a premium on selfishly forming and breaking alliances with other competitors, without sacrificing his ethical standards.

No one imagined that Sarah Hughes was Jewish, even after the Great Neck teenager won the gold medal for figure skating at the 2002 Winter Olympics. But eventually a Miami Jewish newspaper broke the story that her mother was Jewish and that Sarah had been brought up with some attachment to Judaism. "The danger in counting Jews is that sometimes you miss one," lamented Lisa Hostein, editor of the Jewish Telegraphic Agency, "and this time we missed a big one" (*Forward,* Mar. 8.)

Ari Fleischer, President Bush's press secretary, the most visible Jew in the administration and allegedly one of the most eligible bachelors in Washington, got married in November. The bride was Rebecca Davis, a Catholic. The interfaith wedding, incorporating Jewish and Catholic elements, was co-officiated by Rabbi Harold White and Rev. Michael Kelley. Rabbi White told the *Forward* (Nov. 15): "I have the feeling from what I've heard is that the children will be raised as Jews."

On August 18, the *New York Times* announced that its "Weddings" section in the Sunday edition would now be called "Weddings/Celebrations," and would include announcements of the commitment ceremonies of gays and lesbians. The first same-sex couple to make it into the listings (Sept. 1) were Steven Goldstein and Daniel Gross. The two men had a Jewish commitment ceremony officiated by a Reconstructionist rabbi followed by a civil ceremony in Vermont, the only state where it was legal. Goldstein told the *Forward* (Sept. 6): "It means so much to us that the first same-sex announcement was a Jewish couple. It didn't have to be us. We are so deeply proud of Judaism, its teachings, its commitment to healing the world; how appropriate that it was a Jewish couple."

LEGACIES OF THE HOLOCAUST

Commemoration and Restitution

On March 8, President George W. Bush selected 55-year-old Fred Zeidman, a Houston businessman and friend of the president, to a five-year term as chair of the U.S. Holocaust Memorial Council, which oversaw the enormously popular Holocaust Memorial Museum in Washington. It was widely expected that the president would eventually replace all 12 council members.

Unlike his predecessor, Rabbi Irving Greenberg, a Clinton appointee, Zeidman was not a Holocaust scholar. Observers were hopeful that Zeidman's business experience and his personal ties to Bush would enable him to overcome the infighting that had hampered the smooth functioning of the council in recent years (see, for example, AJYB 2002, pp. 244–45). Zeidman told reporters that he wanted to "keep us out of the newspapers" and "just get everyone's focus back on the museum and not on their own agendas." Addressing concerns that its status as a government-supported institution (it received $36 million in federal funds in 2002) might move the museum away from its prime focus on the Nazi Holocaust and toward a more universal involvement with instances of inhumanity around the world, Zeidman said that "this museum will always have a Jewish soul."

Among Zeidman's first problems was controversy over the site of Belzec, one of the Nazi death camps in Poland where some 350,000 Jews had been killed. The open area of the camp had been left as it was when the war ended until, in the mid-1990s, the museum reached agreement with the government of Poland to construct a memorial in such a way that the victims' remains would be treated with respect. In July 2002, however, Rabbi Avi Weiss, a veteran Jewish activist in the U.S., charged that the Polish workers were desecrating the dead by disturbing ashes and bone fragments, and called for the museum to bring the work to a halt. Others, who had actually seen the work being done for the memorial, denied Weiss's charges.

There was sharp controversy in 2002 over how to allocate Holocaust restitution money. Early in the year, the debate centered on the choice of new leadership for the Conference on Jewish Material Claims Against Germany—commonly known as the Claims Conference—the primary Jewish body dealing with Holocaust restitution. Its retiring president, Rabbi Israel Miller, headed an international nominating committee that picked Israel Singer of the World Jewish Congress as president, and two other Americans as chairman and treasurer. Israeli officials complained that there had been insufficient Israeli representation on the nominating committee, in turn arousing resentment on the part of some Americans that Israelis, seeming to consider their country the heir of the victims, were seeking to appropriate a larger share of restitution money at the expense of actual survivors.

Another difference of opinion arose over the treatment of Holocaust survivors living in the U.S. A new American organization, the Holocaust Survivors Foundation, complained that disbursements from the class-action settlement for dormant Swiss bank accounts had gone disproportionately to Jews outside the U.S. at a time when about 40 percent of the 127,000–145,000 American survivors lacked the money to pay for home and medical care, according to a study conducted by the Association of Jewish Family and Children Services. The Holocaust Survivors Foundation also called for reevaluating the procedure, formalized in 1994, of allocating 20 percent of unclaimed reparations money for Holocaust education, documentation, and research, with the aim of redirecting much of it to needy survivors. Claims Conference officials, however, defended the appropriations to projects of Holocaust education and scholarship, and suggested that the broader American Jewish community, through its local federations, could better address the material needs of American survivors than the Claims Conference.

"Mirroring Evil"

The Jewish Museum in New York City set March 17 as the opening date for a new exhibition, "Mirroring Evil: Nazi Imagery/Recent Art." Already in January, however, after the *Wall Street Journal* reported on the exhibition catalog, a firestorm of protest erupted in the Jewish community. The nature of the upcoming exhibition outraged many New York Jews, who compared it to the Brooklyn Museum's "Sensation" exhibition in 1999 that had offended Catholics with a portrayal of the Virgin Mary smeared with animal dung, inducing Rudy Giuliani, the mayor at the time, to withhold city funding. There were calls for cancellation of "Mirroring Evil," and, if it opened, to boycott it.

"Mirroring Evil" presented the work of 13 American, European, and Israeli artists in their 20s and 30s, four of them Jewish. Four of the works drew particular criticism: an image of Lego boxes with photographs on the front of Nazi camps built out of Lego pieces; "Giftgas Giftset," with cardboard imitation gas canisters decorated with Chanel and Tiffany logos; an image of artist Alan Schechner holding a can of Diet Coke, superimposed on a photograph of Buchenwald inmates; and collages featuring a nude image of the female artist together with pictures of movie actors portraying Nazis. Lawyer Menachem Rosensaft, a son of survivors, a member of the U.S. Holocaust Memorial Council, and founding chair of the International Network of Children of Jewish Holocaust Survivors, said: "This is not a First Amendment issue. It's a matter of moral judgment and discretion. A Lego concentration camp? To me, that relegates Auschwitz to a game." Nobel Laureate Elie Wiesel, the living embodiment of Holocaust memory for many Americans, commented that "the kitsch and vulgarization of the Holocaust has taken a big step forward—or backward . . . . I don't understand the artists, nor do I understand the Jewish Museum."

In the introduction to the exhibition catalog, curator Norman Kleeblatt noted that the focus was on the Nazis, not their victims, and that in these artworks "viewers would encounter the perpetrators face to face in scenarios in which ethical and moral issues cannot be easily resolved." The exhibition was intended to be "transgressive," noted Kleeblatt. "There is no safe distance. These works make us see ourselves in them," he wrote. Museum director Joan Rosenbaum asserted that survivors had been consulted in preparing the show, which had, in fact, been delayed a year so as to get sufficient input from numerous constituencies. She told *New York Times* art critic Michael Kimmelman (Jan. 29) that the museum was not endorsing the particular artworks, but rather "the goals of the work, to make us think how easy it is to put distance between our lives in the present and what occurred in the past." In a letter to Ismar Schorsch, chancellor of the Jewish Theological Seminary—under whose auspices the museum operated—Rosenbaum claimed that the controversial exhibit was "very much in the tradition of the Jewish Museum, whose great distinction is that it is indeed a 'museum that makes you think.'" The museum scheduled a dozen public programs to help elucidate the exhibition's implications.

Once it was clear that "Mirroring Evil" would open on schedule, boycott plans escalated. In a public speech on February 13, Rosensaft called on synagogues, Jewish schools, and churches not to visit the museum from March 17 through June 30, the day the exhibition was to close. The American Gathering of Holocaust Survivors endorsed the boycott, as did New York State Assemblyman Dov Hikind, whose Brooklyn district was home to many survivors (he called museum officials "intellectual whores"), and the Catholic League for Religious and Civil Rights, a conservative group whose president, William Donohue, explained that "usually it's the Catholics whom the 'creative types' in the artistic community like to offend. Now it's the Jews." Several Jewish institutions that had scheduled events at the museum shifted them to other locations.

Intensive negotiations to head off a boycott produced concessions on the museum's part: warning signs near the more controversial exhibits and a new exit allowing visitors to leave before seeing two works that had received the heaviest criticism. But the opposition remained adamant, Rosensaft declaring: "This does not in any way solve or ameliorate the problem."

On March 10, a week before the opening, the *New York Times* Sunday magazine ran an interview with one of the artists, Tom Sachs, which deprived the exhibition of much of its credibility. Sachs made it clear that neither he nor, he thought, the other featured artists had any interest in the Holocaust or, for that matter, in anything Jewish. "I'm using the iconography of the Holocaust to bring attention to fashion," Sachs said. "Fashion, like fascism, in about loss of identity. . . . The death camps are examples of amazing German engineering and design. And there are strong links between military products and consumer products." "Mirroring Evil," it turned out, was all about the evils of consumerism.

About 100 protesters stood outside the Jewish Museum on opening day, March 17, shouting "don't go in" and "shame on you" to the 1,300 people waiting in line to enter. But the storm quickly blew over, largely because the art critics panned the show. Kimmelman of the *Times,* for example, noted that: "The strange ritual of the art wars, which exhibitions like this always provoke, is to treat as significant what hardly deserves our attention in the first place." Jerry Smith, in the *Village Voice,* pointed to the irony "that none of the art in 'Mirroring Evil' is worth protesting, except on artistic grounds."

The boycott ended after one day and the exhibition quickly disappeared from the headlines, but not before revealing a deep split within the New York Jewish community between a highly educated sector steeped in postmodernism that (mistakenly) believed itself sophisticated and avant-garde in matters artistic, and another, primarily of an older generation, for whom the Holocaust was still much too close to be subjected to "transgressive" treatment.

Another Holocaust?

By any measure, anti-Semitism did not constitute a problem for American Jews in 2002 (see above, pp. 90–91). And yet the extraordinary upsurge in anti-Israel sentiment and attacks on Jewish targets elsewhere in the world, fueled by the ongoing bloodshed in Israel and the Territories— and sometimes impossible to distinguish from classical Jew-hatred— evoked a mood of deep pessimism in many Jewish intellectuals, who warned of a new wave of global anti-Semitism.

"The Return of Anti-Semitism" was the title of an article by Hillel Halkin, an American expatriate living in Israel, in the February issue of *Commentary.* "The new anti-Israelism," Halkin declared, "is nothing but the old anti-Semitism in disguise." Answering the claim that hostility toward the Jewish state had to do with its policies rather than its Jewishness, Halkin asked: "Who at London dinner parties makes nasty remarks about Hindus because India has militarily occupied Muslim Kashmir for half a century?"

The atmosphere turned even grimmer in the spring, as Israel's military thrust into the Palestinian territories in response to a spate of suicide bombings sent anti-Israel sentiment in Europe to new levels. The *New York Times,* not given to hyperbole on this issue, wondered, in a lead editorial (Apr. 20), "whether, six decades after the Holocaust, we are witnessing a resurgence of the virulent hatred that caused it." Ron Rosenbaum, writing in the *New York Observer* (Apr. 15), indeed claimed that a "Second Holocaust" was "a phrase we may have to begin thinking about." In Rosenbaum's view, "almost without exception every European nation was deeply complicit in Hitler's genocide." And therefore, "at some deep level, there is a need to blame someone *else* for the shame of 'European civilization.' To blame the victim. To blame the Jews." Rosenbaum went so far as to predict a doomsday scenario: "a nuclear weapon is detonated in Tel Aviv." Rosenbaum claimed to have no doubt that this was coming; "it's not *whether,* but *when.*"

There were American Jews who believed that the coming anti-Semitic wave might inundate America as well. The cover story for the May 6 issue of *New York* magazine was "Crisis for American Jews." Writing about "How the War Came Home," Amy Wilentz quoted *Village Voice* columnist Nat Hentoff saying, "if a loudspeaker goes off and a voice says: 'All Jews gather in Times Square,' it could never surprise me." Wilentz reported that many American Jews she spoke with, including those who had previously favored far-reaching concession to the Palestinians, were deeply fearful, and "when Jews are frightened, the specter of the Holocaust is always in the background."

Paul Berman picked up the theme in the *Forward* (May 24), noting how pro-Palestinian and antiglobalization rallies all over the country were condoning mass murder by justifying the suicide bombers. And he cited at length the writings of two respected intellectuals—Portuguese Nobel laureate José Saramago and New York University professor Tony Judt—who, in the course of attacking Israeli policies, argued that a Jewish state, like South Africa under apartheid, was racist by its very nature. This charge, Berman felt, denied the right of Jews to survive as a people. Berman recalled a time when "it was pretty unusual to stumble across diatribes against Judaism or anti-Semitic phrases in the intellectual press. But look what has happened. Something has changed."

"Has a new and potent form of anti-Semitism come to life in the world?" asked Gabriel Schoenfeld in the June issue of *Commentary*. His answer was yes. After cataloging some of the incidents of anti-Jewish violence that occurred during the spring in Europe, Schoenfeld turned to the rhetoric that accompanied it. "The themes are also the same everywhere," he noted. "Israel, a country victimized by terrorism, stands accused of perpetrating terrorism; the Jews, having suffered the most determined and thoroughgoing genocide in history, stand accused of perpetrating genocide." In Schoenfeld's view, the hostility to Israel was so unfair, disproportionate, and one-sided that anti-Semitism was "the right and only word" for it.

The first serious challenge from within the American Jewish community to such fears came from Leon Wieseltier, literary editor of the *New Republic*. His cover story for the May 27 issue of the magazine bore the title "Hitler Is Dead: The Case against Ethnic Panic." Surveying American Jewry, Wieseltier found a "community sunk in excitability, in the imagination of disaster. . . . Death is at every Jewish door." Wieseltier considered such nightmare scenarios absurd since the Israeli-Palestinian conflict upon which they were based was over territory, not over the survival of the Jewish people. And he went so far as to accuse pro-Likud American Jews of conflating Arafat with Hitler in order to deligitimize any compromise with the Palestinians. Predictably, Wieseltier's attempt to calm the waters drew attacks from those who took the threat of anti-Semitism more seriously. Abraham Foxman, national director of the Anti-Defamation League, sent a letter to the *New Republic* insisting that Jews were living through "the most significant wave" of anti-Semitism since World War II. And Harvard professor Ruth Wisse responded in *Commentary* (Oct.) that in 2002, as in the 1930s, "when deadlier forms of anti-Semitism are on the rise, there is massive intellectual resistance to acknowledge the threat, and most political analysts still treat anti-Semitism like a hiccup that will soon give way to regular breathing."

The difficulty in assessing the new wave of hostility to Israel and to Jews was evident at a two-day scholarly conference at New York University in early December aptly entitled "Confusion—Questioning Anti-Semitism, Anti-Americanism and Other Modes of Conspiracy." Some of the participants warned of the rise of a resurrected fascism, sociologist Gerda Lerner asserting: "It does not take much imagination to see another specter of genocide on the horizon." Others, however, blamed Israeli policies toward the Palestinians for evoking hostility, one Israeli academic asserting the existence of "Israeli fascism, Israeli terror and Israeli criminality" (*Forward,* Dec. 6).

THE ORGANIZATIONAL WORLD

Hard Times

The ongoing weakness of the American economy had profoundly negative effects on the organized Jewish community. Already hurt by competition from the increasing popular Jewish family foundations, Jewish communal organizations of all kinds found it harder to attract philanthropic dollars, and those that had relied on government aid had to cope with a dwindling supply of such funds.

Many looked for ways to cut their budgets. As the year began, Hadassah, the women's Zionist organization, carried out a 10-percent across-the-board cut in the staff of its New York office, eliminating 200–300 employees. Around the same time, United Jewish Communities, the largest Jewish charitable network in America, was reportedly considering a 40-percent cut, as much as $20 million out a budget of $44.7 million (in the end, however, much to the chagrin of many local federations, UJC adopted a budget only $2.2 million lower than that of 2001). Many of the large federations around the country, their endowments shrinking because of the declining stock market, reduced their overseas allocations so as to keep more money at home for local needs. Even so, a good number of the agencies funded by federations were forced into serious cutbacks, and some contemplated the possibility of shutting down.

The malaise of the Jewish organizational world, however, went far beyond finances. In 2002, the two large Jewish umbrella organizations—the Conference of Presidents of Major American Jewish Organizations, which dealt with Israel-related issues, and the UJC, which focused on philanthropy, were subjected to serious substantive criticism.

Conference of Presidents

The Conference of Presidents, as noted above (p. 117), had repeatedly come under criticism for allegedly toeing the Likud line uncritically. In August, Eric Yoffie, president of the UAHC and one of the critics, publicly called on the conference to revise its procedures so as to democratize its decisions. He suggested establishing a standing executive committee "with the largest organizations serving as permanent members and smaller organizations serving rotating terms." This would have the effect of limiting the powers of the chair and the executive vice president—both positions held by people suspected of Likud sympathies—who, Yoffie felt, had heretofore made too many decisions without consultation (*Forward,* Aug. 2).

Two of the largest component organizations in the conference, the Anti-Defamation League and the United Synagogue of Conservative Judaism, announced their support for the idea, while the Orthodox bodies and the American Jewish Congress, which were smaller and would lose power under the Yoffie plan, stated their opposition. Harvey Blitz, president of the Orthodox Union, warned that "the more structure you have the more chance you have to appear divided." The stakes for the conference were very high. As the *Forward* noted in an editorial (Aug. 9), all it would take for the umbrella body to collapse would be for one of the major organizations to walk out. Indeed, Theodore Mann, a former conference chair, called for the dissolution of the conference because it was "an undemocratic institution and is not worthy of our great Jewish community" (*Forward,* Aug. 23).

No action was taken on Yoffie's suggestion for reform. In December, the conference drew criticism again when, for the fifth straight year, it narrowly rejected the membership application of Meretz USA, the American affiliate of the Israeli left-leaning party. Ostensibly, the reason for the decision was that the group's small budget and membership did not merit recognition as a "major" organization." Meretz USA and its advocates suspected that its link with a primary opposition party in Israel was the real motivation for the rebuff.

United Jewish Communities

UJC had been created in 1999 out of a merger of the old Council of Jewish Federations (CJF), United Jewish Appeal (UJA), and United Israel Appeal (UIA). UJC and the federation system constituted the fifth largest charity in the country, with combined income of over $2.2 billion. In 2002, despite the adverse economic situation, UJC raised $319 million for its Israel Emergency Campaign. But UJC had been the object of criticism from its inception, partly because of its failure to achieve the budgetary savings that had been anticipated, but more importantly, because its detractors felt that it had not come up with a "vision" that might mobilize the energies of the American Jewish community.

It was that alleged failure of "vision," along with "failure of will," "failure of voice," and "failure of spirit," that concerned Richard Wexler of Chicago, who chaired UJC's financial relations committee. On May 21, the *New York Sun* broke the story that Wexler had written a 157-page manuscript making these charges and others, entitled "United Jewish Catastrophes, a Love Story." Wexler told the *Sun,* "I don't know if I'm going to publish this. But I've written it as a cautionary tale of what can happen when people with the best intentions don't execute them, when you take something that could have been extraordinary and make it pedestrian." Wexler named names—including those of a UJC leader who publicly condoned intermarriage and another who allegedly used his position to raise money for the Gore campaign in 2000—and detailed embarrassing events, such as the decision, later countermanded, to give an award for statesmanship to Yasir Arafat.

In the end, Wexler did not publish his manuscript and UJC president and CEO Stephen Hoffman—whom Wexler praised for doing his best to redeem the organization's earlier blunders—named Wexler to chair the UJC's General Assembly (GA) in November. But the GA, held in Philadelphia, was widely considered a disappointment. For one thing, Israeli prime minister Sharon canceled a planned visit, and for another, the long-anticipated unveiling of the National Jewish Population Survey

(NJPS) was aborted when it was discovered that data had been lost (see above, p. 142). Many divisive issues came to the surface at the GA, including the refusal of several important federations to pay their dues (they paid up when threatened with termination), complaints from charities that funded Israeli and other overseas projects that they were not getting the resources they needed, and charges that the UJC budget itself was bloated. Inevitably, calls came for restructuring the UJC.

LAWRENCE GROSSMAN

Jewish Population in the United States, 2002

NJPS Delayed

The 2000–01 National Jewish Population Survey (NJPS), sponsored by United Jewish Communities (UJC), was designed to be the most comprehensive and sophisticated study ever conducted of American Jews. So that the results should be representative of all American Jews, respondents were selected using random-digit-dialing techniques and a complex screening process. Interviews were conducted between August 2000 and August 2001. The questionnaire and overall study design were developed by the UJC Research Department in close collaboration with its National Technical Advisory Committee (NTAC), a distinguished group of 20 academicians and federation professionals with expertise in demography, sociology, religion, geography, economics, education, and other relevant disciplines.

Among the multitude of topics to be explored in NJPS 2000–01 were Jewish population size, socioeconomic characteristics, family structure, fertility, marital history, intermarriage, Jewish identification, religious practices, Jewish education, synagogue affiliation, philanthropic behavior, and relationship to Israel. UJC and others were expected to underwrite a broad range of analyses based on NJPS results to guide the planning and policy-making of the Jewish community.

UJC issued some findings at a press conference on October 8, 2002, and major presentations on various aspects of the NJPS were scheduled for the UJC General Assembly in November. In fact, no further information was released nor was there any indication of when the full study would become available. For an account of the controversy over American Jewish demography that engulfed the community—largely centering around the decision to hold back the data—see the article in this volume, "Jewish Communal Affairs," pp. 138–42 above. For the demographic implications of the NJPS data that were released see the article on "World Jewish Population 2003," p. 599 below.

New York Jewish Community Study

A major study of the Jewish community of the New York City area—the five boroughs plus neighboring Nassau, Suffolk, and Westchester counties—was conducted in 2002 by UJA-Federation of New York. The principal investigators were Jacob B. Ukeles and Ron Miller. Almost 69,000 households were contacted and 6,035 Jewish households were identified, of which 4,533 were subjects of interviews. The initial findings, published under the title *The Jewish Community Study of New York: 2002 Highlights,* also included an explanation of the methodology. It was available from UJA-Federation, which also announced plans to release a complete final report, a profile of neighborhoods, and a special report on Jewish poverty in New York.

The study found that since 1991, when the previous survey of New York Jewry was conducted, the Jewish population of the eight-county region declined slightly, from 1,420,000 to 1,412,000, while the number of Jewish households rose slightly, from 638,000 to 643,000. As in 1991, Jews made up about 15 percent of the New York region's total population in 2002.

But movement to the suburbs led to a 6-percent decline in the number of Jewish households in the five boroughs and a 5-percent drop in the number of Jewish persons: there were now fewer than a million Jews within the city limits, 972,000. The 5-percent decline, however, was far lower than the 11-percent decline in the city's non-Hispanic white population. Jewish households in the three suburban counties increased by 24 percent since 1991, to 188,000, and the Jewish population by 12 percent, to 440,000.

The boroughs of Brooklyn and Manhattan together accounted for 51 percent of the Jewish households in the area and almost 50 percent of the Jewish population. Indeed, Brooklyn itself was home to more Jews than any American city with the exception of Los Angeles. Brooklyn (by 23 percent) and Staten Island (by 27 percent) were the only city boroughs that experienced growth between 1991 and 2002, the others sustaining substantial losses. Westchester Jewry grew by 40 percent and Nassau by 9 percent, while the number for Suffolk fell 8 percent. The 2002 Jewish population figures for the eight counties are listed below, p. 170.

More than half—57 percent—of the adults surveyed were married at the time they were interviewed, 20 percent reported never having married, 12 percent were widowed, 9 percent separated or divorced, and 2 percent living together. Manhattan had the highest percentage of never married (35 percent) and the Bronx the highest percentage of widowed (24 percent). More than a quarter of the Jewish households had at least one child under age 18.

Almost three-quarters of Jewish adults were born in the U.S., but some

92,000 households and 202,000 persons were Russian-speaking (300 respondents filled out the survey in Russian). Of these households, 76,000 included an adult born in the former Soviet Union. Indeed, over 90 percent of Russian-speaking American Jews lived in the New York area. Russian speakers made up 19 percent of the city's Jewish population and 4 percent of the population of the three suburban counties. Brooklyn was home to 62 percent of New York's Russian speakers and Queens to 19 percent. The Russian speakers made up a large part of the Jewish communities in Brooklyn (27 percent), Staten Island (26 percent), and Queens (21 percent).

In terms of denominational identification, the big increases since 1991 were for the Orthodox, up from 13 to 19 percent, and for those identifying as "secular" or "no religion," up from 3 to 10 percent. The Reform numbers dropped from 36 to 29 percent and the Conservative from 34 to 26 percent. The borough with the highest percentage of Orthodox (37 percent) was Brooklyn.

Asked how important being Jewish was in their lives, 65 percent of New York Jews replied it was very important, another 26 percent said it was somewhat important, and just 9 percent felt it was unimportant. Given a list of Jewish values and asked to indicate which were "very important," the top choices were "survival of the State of Israel" (92 percent) and "making the world a better place" (88 percent). As for Jewish communal priorities, the three most popular, all attracting the backing of 86 percent, were helping Jews in distress around the world, supporting Jewish children and families in crisis, and aiding the Jewish poor.

Fully half of all Jewish households belonged to a Jewish organization of some kind, and 43 percent belonged to a synagogue — up from 38 percent in 1991. In Nassau and Suffolk, more than half of Jewish households belonged to synagogues. Younger Jews were slightly more likely than their elders to be synagogue members. Only 17 percent of New York Jews actually attended service at least once a week. Of those Jews who considered it very important to be part of a Jewish community, about a quarter did not have any Jewish communal connection. More than three-quarters of Jews said that Hanukkah candles were lit in their homes and that they attended a Passover seder regularly; almost three-quarters said they fasted on Yom Kippur; Shabbat candles were regularly lit in almost a third of households; and a little over a quarter of respondents said their homes were kosher. On all of these measures, observance was slightly up from 1991.

Of all married Jews in New York, 83 percent had Jewish-born spouses,

4 percent were married to converts, and 13 percent were married to non-Jews. Of all marriages involving Jews, 72 percent were between two Jews, 7 percent between a born-Jew and a convert, and 22 percent between a Jew and a non-Jew. Suffolk County had the highest intermarriage rate and Brooklyn the lowest. The intermarriage rate for the New York area, which rose rapidly in the 1970s, appeared to have stabilized since the 1980s. Of the 370,000 children living in Jewish households (defined as containing at least one Jewish adult), 83 percent were being raised as Jews, 12 percent as non-Jews, and 4 percent as Jews and "something else." Some 61,000 children, 16 percent of the total, were living in intermarried households, and of that number, half were not being raised as Jews.

The New York study found a number of what it called "vulnerable populations." Some 83,000 Jewish seniors lived alone, and almost a third of Jewish households reported an income below $35,000. One of every six Jewish households in the region lived under the poverty line — almost double the 1991 rate — and one in three respondents reported that they were "just managing." The Russian-speaking population had much higher poverty rates than other Jews.

Local Jewish Population

One unanticipated result of the UJC's preoccupation with the delayed NJPS was that, for the first time in decades, its research staff was unable to prepare an updated listing of local Jewish population statistics for the AJYB. As a service to our readers, we reprint the 2001 data published in the 2002 AJYB, with the exception of the New York City area, where the new 2002 numbers made available in the New York UJA-Federation study are substituted. For a description of how the 2001 data were derived, see AJYB 2002, pp. 247–49.

It is expected that the UJC will again furnish updated population figures in future AJYB volumes.

THE EDITORS

APPENDIX

TABLE 1. JEWISH POPULATION IN THE UNITED STATES, 2001

State	Estimated Jewish Population	Total Population*	Estimated Jewish Percent of Total
Alabama	9,000	4,451,000	0.2
Alaska	3,400	628,000	0.5
Arizona	81,500	5,165,000	1.6
Arkansas	1,700	2,678,000	0.1
California	999,000	34,000,000	2.9
Colorado	73,000	4,323,000	1.7
Connecticut	111,000	3,410,000	3.2
Delaware	13,500	786,000	1.7
Dist. of Columbia	25,500	571,000	4.5
Florida	620,000	16,054,000	3.9
Georgia	93,500	8,230,000	1.1
Hawaii	7,000	1,212,000	0.6
Idaho	1,100	1,299,000	0.1
Illinois	270,000	12,436,000	2.2
Indiana	17,500	6,090,000	0.3
Iowa	6,100	2,928,000	0.2
Kansas	14,000	2,692,000	0.5
Kentucky	11,500	4,047,000	0.3
Louisiana	16,000	4,470,000	0.4
Maine	9,300	1,277,000	0.7
Maryland	213,000	5,311,000	4.0
Massachusetts	275,000	6,357,000	4.3
Michigan	110,000	9,952,000	1.1
Minnesota	42,000	4,931,000	0.9
Mississippi	1,500	2,849,000	0.1
Missouri	62,500	5,603,000	1.1
Montana	800	903,000	0.1
Nebraska	7,000	1,713,000	0.4
Nevada	77,000	2,019,000	3.8
New Hampshire	10,000	1,240,000	0.8
New Jersey	485,000	8,429,000	5.7

State	Estimated Jewish Population	Total Population*	Estimated Jewish Percent of Total
New Mexico	11,500	1,821,000	0.6
New York	1,657,000	18,990,000	8.7
North Carolina	26,500	8,077,000	0.3
North Dakota	450	641,000	0.1
Ohio	149,000	11,360,000	1.3
Oklahoma	5,000	3,453,000	0.1
Oregon	32,000	3,429,000	0.9
Pennsylvania	282,000	12,283,000	2.3
Rhode Island	16,000	1,050,000	1.5
South Carolina	11,500	4,023,000	0.3
South Dakota	300	756,000	(z)
Tennessee	18,000	5,702,000	0.3
Texas	131,000	20,947,000	0.6
Utah	4,500	2,242,000	0.2
Vermont	5,500	610,000	0.9
Virginia	66,000	7,104,000	0.9
Washington	43,000	5,908,000	0.7
West Virginia	2,300	1,808,000	0.1
Wisconsin	28,000	5,372,000	0.5
Wyoming	400	494,000	0.1
U.S. TOTAL	**6,155,000	282,125,000	2.2

N.B. Details may not add to totals because of rounding.
* Resident population, April 1, 2001 (*Source:* U.S. Bureau of the Census, Population Division).
** Exclusive of Puerto Rico and the Virgin Islands which previously reported Jewish populations of 1,500 and 350, respectively.
(z) Figure is less than 0.1 and rounds to 0.

TABLE 2. DISTRIBUTION OF U.S. JEWISH POPULATION BY REGIONS, 2001

Region	Total Population	Percent Distribution	Estimated Jewish Population	Percent Distribution
Northeast	53,645,000	19.0	2,850,000	46.3
Middle Atlantic	39,701,000	14.1	2,424,000	39.3
New England	13,944,000	4.9	426,000	6.9
Midwest	64,473,000	22.9	706,000	11.4
East North Central . .	45,210,000	16.0	574,000	9.3
West North Central .	19,263,000	6.8	132,000	2.1
South	100,562,000	35.7	1,265,000	20.6
East South Central . .	17,050,000	6.0	40,000	0.6
South Atlantic	51,964,000	18.4	1,071,000	17.4
West South Central . .	31,548,000	11.1	154,000	2.5
West	63,445,000	22.5	1,334,000	21.7
Mountain	18,267,000	6.5	250,000	4.1
Pacific	45,178,000	16.0	1,084,000	17.6
TOTALS	282,125,000	100.0	6,155,000	100.0

N.B. Details may not add to totals because of rounding.

TABLE 3. RANK-ORDERED METROPOLITAN STATISTICAL AREAS, BY
JEWISH POPULATION, 2001

Metro Area	Estimated Jewish Population	Jewish % of Total Population	% Share of U.S. Jewish Population	Cumulative % Share of Jewish Population
1. New York-Northern NJ-Long Island, NY-NJ-CT-PA*	2,051,000	9.7	33.3	33.3
2. Los Angles-Riverside-Orange County, CA*	668,000	4.1	10.9	44.2
3. Miami-Ft. Lauderdale,FL*	331,000	8.5	5.4	49.6
4. Philadelphia-Wilmington-Atlantic City, PA-NJ-DE-MD*	285,000	4.6	4.6	54.2
5. Chicago-Gary-Kenosha, IL-IN-WI*	265,000	2.9	4.3	58.5
6. Boston-Worcester-Lawrence, MA-NH-ME-CT*	254,000	4.4	4.1	62.6
7. San Francisco-Oakland-San Jose, CA*	218,000	3.1	3.6	66.2
8. West Palm Beach-Boca Raton, FL	167,000	14.8	2.7	68.9
9. Washington, DC-MD-VA-WV	166,000	3.4	2.7	71.6
10. Baltimore, MD	106,000	3.9	1.7	73.3
11. Detroit-Ann Arbor, MI*	103,000	1.9	1.7	75.0
12. Cleveland-Akron, OH*	86,000	2.9	1.4	76.4
13. Atlanta, GA	86,000	2.1	1.4	77.8
14. Las Vegas, NV-AZ	75,000	4.8	1.2	79.0
15. San Diego, CA	70,000	2.5	1.1	80.1
16. Denver-Boulder-Greeley, CO*	67,000	2.3	1.1	81.2
17. Phoenix-Mesa, AZ	60,000	1.8	1.0	82.2
18. St. Louis, MO-IL	54,500	2.1	.9	83.1
19. Dallas-Ft. Worth, TX*	50,000	1.0	.8	83.9
20. Houston-Galveston-Brazoria, TX*	45,500	1.0	.7	84.6
21. Tampa-St. Petersburg-Clearwater, FL	45,000	1.9	.7	85.4
22. Minneapolis-St. Paul, MN-WI	40,500	1.4	.7	86.0

Metro Area	Estimated Jewish Population	Jewish % of Total Population	% Share of U.S. Jewish Population	Cumulative % Share of Jewish Population
23. Pittsburgh, PA	40,500	1.7	.7	86.7
24. Seattle-Tacoma-Bremerton, WA*	40,000	1.1	.6	87.3
25. Hartford, CT	33,500	2.8	.5	87.9
26. Portland-Salem, OR-WA*	27,000	1.2	.4	88.3
27. Cincinnati, OH-KY-IN* .	24,000	1.2	.4	88.7
28. Rochester, NY	23,000	2.1	.4	89.1
29. Columbus, OH	22,000	1.4	.4	89.4
30. Sacramento-Yolo, CA* ..	21,500	1.2	.3	89.8
31. Milwaukee-Racine, WI* .	21,000	1.2	.3	90.1
32. Orlando, FL	21,000	1.3	.3	90.5
33. Tucson, AZ	20,000	2.4	.3	90.8
34. Albany-Schenectady-Troy, NY	19,000	2.2	.3	91.1
35. Kansas City, MO-KS ...	19,000	1.1	.3	91.4
36. Buffalo-Niagara Falls, NY	18,500	1.6	.3	91.7
37. Providence-Fall River-Warwick, RI-MA	17,000	1.4	.3	92.0
38. Sarasota-Bradenton, FL .	15,500	2.6	.3	92.2
39. Austin, TX	13,500	1.1	.2	92.4
40. Norfolk-Virginia Beach-Newport News, VA-NC .	13,500	0.9	.2	92.7
41. Springfield, MA	13,000	2.2	.2	92.9
42. New Orleans, LA	13,000	1.0	.2	93.1
43. Richmond-Petersburg, VA	13,000	1.3	.2	93.3
44. San Antonio, TX	11,000	0.7	.2	93.5
45. Indianapolis, IN	10,000	0.6	.2	93.6
46. Syracuse, NY	9,500	1.3	.2	93.8
47. Charlotte-Gastonia-Rock Hill, NC-SC	9,000	0.6	.1	93.9
48. Louisville, KY-IN	8,500	0.8	.1	94.1
49. Memphis, TN-AR-MS ..	8,500	0.7	.1	94.2
50. Ft. Myers-Cape Coral, FL	8,000	1.8	.1	94.3

Designations for the metropolitan areas are in accordance with the United States Statistical Policy Office, Office of Management and Budget, Bulletin Number 99-04 and established June 30, 1999. All areas are Metropolitan Statistical Areas (MSA) except those designated with an asterisk (*), which are Consolidated Metropolitan Statistical Areas (CMSA). The one exception to this rule is the Washington-Baltimore CMSA, which is separated.
N.B.: Details may not add to totals because of rounding.

TABLE 3. COMMUNITIES WITH JEWISH POPULATIONS OF 100 OR MORE, 2001
(ESTIMATED)

State and City	Jewish Population	State and City	Jewish Population	State and City	Jewish Population
ALABAMA		**CALIFORNIA**		Alameda County,	
*Birmingham	 5,300	Antelope Valley		under S.F. Bay Area)	
Dothan	 100	 3,000		Ontario (incl. in San	
Huntsville	 750	Aptos (incl. in Santa		Gabriel and Pomona	
**Mobile	 1,100	Cruz)		Valleys)	
**Montgomery		Bakersfield-Kern		Orange County[N]	
.... 1,200		County 1,600		 60,000	
Tuscaloosa	 300	Berkeley (incl. in		Oroville (incl. in Chico)	
Other places	 250	Contra Costa County,		Palmdale (incl. in	
		under S.F. Bay Area)		Antelope Valley)	
ALASKA		Carmel (incl. in		Palm Springs[N] .. 17,000	
*Anchorage	 2,300	Monterey Peninsula)		Palo Alto (incl. in	
*Fairbanks	 540	*Chico 750		South Peninsula,	
Juneau	 285	Corona (incl. in		under S.F. Bay Area)	
Kenai Peninsula	... 200	Riverside area)		Paradise (incl. in	
Ketchikan (incl. in		*Eureka	 1,000	Chico)	
Juneau)		Fairfield	 800	Pasadena (incl. in L.A.	
Other places	 100	Fontana (incl. in San		area)	
		Bernardino)		Paso Robles (incl. in	
ARIZONA		*Fresno	 2,300	San Luis Obispo)	
Cochise County	... 350	Lancaster (incl. in		Petaluma (incl. in	
*Flagstaff	 500	Antelope Valley)		Sonoma County,	
Lake Havasu City		Long Beach[N] ... 18,000		under S.F. Bay	
.... 200		Los Angeles area[N]		Area)	
*Phoenix	 60,000	 519,000		Pomona Valley[N] (incl.	
Prescott	 300	*Mendocino County		in San Gabriel and	
Sierra Vista (incl. in		 600		Pomona Valleys)	
Cochise County)		*Merced County	... 190	*Redding area	 150
*Tucson	 20,000	*Modesto	 500	Redwood Valley (incl.	
Yuma	 150	Monterey Peninsula		in Mendocino	
Other places	 100	 2,300		County)	
		Moreno Valley (incl. in		Riverside area	... 2,000
ARKANSAS		Riverside)		Sacramento[N] ... 21,300	
Fayetteville	 175	Murrieta Hot Springs		Salinas	 1,000
Hot Springs	 150	 550		San Bernardino area	
**Little Rock	 1,100	*Napa County	... 1,000	 3,000	
Other places	 250	Oakland (incl. in		*San Diego	 70,000

[N]See Notes below. *Includes entire county. **Includes all of two counties. ***Figure not updated for at least five years.

State and City	Jewish Population	State and City	Jewish Population	State and City	Jewish Population
San Francisco Bay Area[N]	210,000	COLORADO		Manchester (incl. in Hartford)	
Alameda County	32,500	Aspen	750	Meriden (incl. in New Haven)	
Contra Costa County	22,000	Boulder (incl. in Denver)		Middletown	1,200
Marin County	18,500	Breckenridge (incl. in Vail)		New Britain (incl. in Hartford)	
N. Peninsula	24,500	Colorado Springs	1,500	New Canaan (incl. in Stamford)	
San Francisco	49,500	Denver[N]	66,700	New Haven[N]	24,300
San Jose	33,000	Eagle (incl. in Vail)		New London[N]	3,850
Sonoma County	9,000	Evergreen (incl. in Denver)		New Milford (incl. in Waterbury)	
S. Peninsula	21,000	*Fort Collins	1,000	Newtown (incl. in Danbury)	
San Gabriel and Pomona Valleys[N]	30,000	*Grand Junction	320	Norwalk (incl. in Westport)	
*San Jose (listed under S.F. Bay Area)		Greeley (incl. in Fort Collins)		Norwich (incl. in New London)	
*San Luis Obispo	2,000	Loveland (incl. in Fort Collins)		Rockville (incl. in Hartford)	
*Santa Barbara	7,000	Pueblo[N]	425	Shelton (incl. in Bridgeport)	
*Santa Cruz	6,000	Steamboat Springs	250	Southington (incl. in Hartford)	
Santa Maria	500	***Telluride	125	Stamford	9,200
Santa Monica (incl. in Los Angeles area)		**Vail	650	Storrs (incl. in Willimantic)	
Santa Rosa (incl. in Sonoma County, under S.F. Bay Area)		Other places	200	Torrington area	580
Sonoma County (listed under S.F. Bay Area)		CONNECTICUT		Wallingford (incl. in New Haven)	
*South Lake Tahoe	150	Bridgeport[N]	13,000	Waterbury[N]	4,500
Stockton	850	Bristol (incl. in Hartford)		Westport[N]	11,400
Sun City	200	Cheshire (incl. in Waterbury)		Willimantic area	700
Tulare and Kings counties	350	***Colchester	300	Other places	250
Ukiah (incl. in Mendocino Co.)		Danbury[N]	3,200	DELAWARE	
Vallejo area	900	***Danielson	100	Dover (incl. in Kent and Sussex counties totals)	
*Ventura County[N]	15,000	Darien (incl. in Stamford)		Kent and Sussex counties	1,600
Visalia (incl. in Tulare and Kings counties)		Greenwich	4,200	Newark area	4,300
Other places	200	Hartford[N]	32,200	Wilmington area	7,600
		Hebron (incl. in Colchester)			
		Lebanon (incl. in Colchester)			
		Lower Middlesex County[N]	1,600		

	Jewish		Jewish		Jewish
State and City	Population	State and City	Population	State and City	Population

DISTRICT OF COLUMBIA
Washington D.C.[N]
.... 25,500

FLORIDA
Arcadia (incl. in Fort
Myers)
Boca Raton-Delray
Beach (listed under
Southeast Fla.)
Brevard County. . 5,000
Broward County (listed
under Southeast Fla.)
***Crystal River ... 100
**Daytona Beach
.... 2,500
Fort Lauderdale (incl.
in Broward County,
under Southeast Fla.)
**Fort Myers 8,000
Fort Pierce...... 1,060
Gainesville 2,200
Hollywood-S. Broward
County (incl in
Broward County,
under Southeast Fla.)
**Jacksonville.... 7,300
Key West 650
***Lakeland 1,000
*Miami-Dade County
(listed under
Southeast Fla.)
Naples-Collier County
.... 4,200
New Port Richey (incl.
in Pasco County)
Ocala-Marion County
.... 500
Orlando[N] 21,000
Palm Beach County
(listed under
Southeast Fla.)
Pasco County ... 1,000
**Pensacola 975

Pinellas County. 24,200
**Port Charlotte-Punta
Gorda (incl. in Fort
Myers
**Sarasota 15,500
Southeast Florida
.... 498,000
Boca Raton-Delray
Beach...... 93,000
Broward County
.... 213,000
Miami-Dade County
.... 118,000
Palm Beach County
(excl. Boca Raton-
Delray Beach)
.... 74,000
*St. Petersburg-
Clearwater (incl. in
Pinellas County)
Stuart-Port St. Lucie[N]
.... 4,300
Tallahassee 2,200
*Tampa........ 20,000
Venice (incl. in
Sarasota)
*Vero Beach....... 400
***Winter Haven... 300
Other places
.... 100

GEORGIA
Albany area 200
Athens 600
Atlanta Metro Area
.... 85,900
Augusta[N] 1,300
Brunswick 120
**Columbus....... 750
**Dalton 125
Macon......... 1,000
*Savannah....... 3,000
**Valdosta........ 100
Other places...... 250

HAWAII
Hilo 280
Honolulu (incl. all of
Oahu) 6,400
Kauai.......... 100
Maui 210

IDAHO
**Boise 800
Ketchum 100
Lewiston (incl. in
Moscow)
Moscow 100
Other places...... 100

ILLINOIS
Aurora area 750
Bloomington-Normal
.... 500
Carbondale (incl. in S.
Ill.)
*Champaign-Urbana
.... 1,400
Chicago Metro Area[N]
.... 261,000
**Danville 100
*Decatur 130
DeKalb 180
East St. Louis (incl. in
S. Ill.)
Elgin[N]........... 500
Freeport (incl. in
Rockford)
*Joliet............ 210
Kankakee........ 100
Moline (incl. in Quad
Cities)
*Peoria........... 800
Quad Cities-Ill. portion
.... 400
Quincy 100
Rock Island (incl. in
Quad Cities)
Rockford[N] 1,100

State and City	Jewish Population

Southern Illinois[N]
. . . . 500
*Springfield. 1,090
Waukegan 300
Other places 250

INDIANA
Bloomington 1,000
Elkhart (incl. in S. Bend)
Evansville. 400
**Fort Wayne. 900
**Gary-Northwest
Indiana 2,000
**Indianapolis . . 10,000
**Lafayette 550
*Michigan City 300
Muncie. 120
South Bend[N] 1,850
*Terre Haute 200
Other places 200

IOWA
Ames (incl. in Des
Moines)
Cedar Rapids 420
Council Bluffs 150
*Davenport (incl. in
Quad Cities)
*Des Moines 2,800
*Iowa City 1,300
Postville 150
Quad Cities-Iowa
portion 500
**Sioux City 400
*Waterloo 170
Other places 250

KANSAS
Kansas City area-
Kansas portion[N]
. . . . 12,000
Lawrence 200
***Manhattan 425
*Topeka 400

Wichita[N] 1,100
Other places 100

KENTUCKY
Covington-Newport
area 500
Lexington[N] 2,000
*Louisville 8,700
Paducah 150
Other places 150

LOUISIANA
Alexandria[N] 350
Baton Rouge[N] . . . 1,600
Lafayette (incl. in S.
Central La.)
Lake Charles area
. . . . 200
Monroe (incl. in
Shreveport)
**New Orleans . . 13,000
**Shreveport 815
***South Central La.[N]
. . . . 250
Other places 150

MAINE
***Augusta 140
Bangor 3,000
Biddeford-Saco (incl. in
S. Maine)
Brunswick-Bath (incl.
in S. Maine)
Lewiston-Auburn . . 500
Portland (incl. in S.
Maine)
***Rockland area . . 300
Southern Maine[N]
. . . . 6,000
***Waterville 225
Other places 150

MARYLAND
Annapolis area . . 3,000
**Baltimore. 91,400

Columbia (incl. in
Howard County)
Cumberland 275
*Easton 100
*Frederick. 1,200
*Hagerstown 325
*Harford County
. . . . 1,200
*Howard County
. . . . 10,000
Montgomery and
Prince Georges
counties 104,500
Ocean City 200
Salisbury 400
Silver Spring (incl. in
Montgomery County)
Other places 250

MASSACHUSETTS
Amherst area. . . . 1,300
Andover[N] 2,850
Athol area (incl. in N.
Worcester County)
Attleboro area 700
Beverly (incl. in North
Shore, under Boston
Metro Region)
Boston Metro Region[N]
. . . . 227,300
Boston 21,000
Brockton-South
Central 31,500
Brookline 20,300
Framingham . . 19,700
Near West 35,800
Newton 27,700
North Central . 22,900
Northeast 7,700
North Shore . . 18,600
Northwest 13,600
Southeast. 8,500
Brockton (listed under
Boston Metro Region)

State and City	Jewish Population
Brookline (listed under Boston Metro Region)	
Cape Cod-Barnstable County	3,250
Clinton (incl. in Worcester-Central Worcester County)	
Fall River area	1,100
Falmouth (incl. in Cape Cod)	
Fitchburg (incl. in N. Worcester County)	
Framingham (listed under Boston Metro Region)	
Gardner (incl. in N. Worcester County)	
Gloucester (incl. N. Shore, listed under Boston Metro Region)	
Great Barrington (incl. in Pittsfield)	
*Greenfield	1,100
Haverhill	800
Holyoke	600
*Hyannis (incl. in Cape Cod)	
Lawrence (incl. in Andover)	
Leominster (incl. in N. Worcester County)	
Lowell area	2,000
Lynn (incl. in N. Shore, listed under Boston Metro Region)	
*Martha's Vineyard	300
New Bedford[N]	2,600
Newburyport	280
Newton (listed under Boston Metro Region)	
North Adams (incl. in N. Berkshire County)	

State and City	Jewish Population
North Berkshire County	400
North Worcester County	1,500
Northampton	1,200
Peabody (incl. in N. Shore, listed under Boston Metro Region)	
Pittsfield-Berkshire County	4,000
Plymouth area	1,000
Provincetown (incl. in Cape Cod)	
Salem (incl. in N. Shore, listed under Boston Metro Region)	
Southbridge (incl. in S. Worcester County)	
South Worcester County	500
Springfield[N]	10,000
Taunton area	1,000
Webster (incl. in S. Worcester County)	
Worcester-Central Worcester County	11,000
Other places	150

MICHIGAN

State and City	Jewish Population
*Ann Arbor	7,000
Bay City	150
Benton Harbor area	240
**Detroit Metro Area	94,000
*Flint	1,500
*Grand Rapids	1,850
**Jackson	200
*Kalamazoo	1,500
Lansing area	2,100
Midland	120

State and City	Jewish Population
Mt. Clemens (incl. in Detroit)	
Mt. Pleasant[N]	130
*Muskegon	210
*Saginaw	115
Traverse City	200
Other places	350

MINNESOTA

State and City	Jewish Population
**Duluth	485
*Minneapolis	31,500
Rochester	550
**St. Paul	9,200
Other places	150

MISSISSIPPI

State and City	Jewish Population
Biloxi-Gulfport	250
**Greenville	120
**Hattiesburg	130
**Jackson	550
Other places	450

MISSOURI

State and City	Jewish Population
Columbia	400
Joplin	100
Kansas City area-Missouri portion[N]	7,100
*St. Joseph	265
**St. Louis	54,000
Springfield	300
Other places	100

MONTANA

State and City	Jewish Population
*Billings	300
Butte	100
Helena (incl. in Butte)	
*Kalispell	150
Missoula	200
Other places	100

NEBRASKA

State and City	Jewish Population
Grand Island-Hastings (incl. in Lincoln)	

State and City	Jewish Population	State and City	Jewish Population	State and City	Jewish Population
Lincoln......... 700		incl. in Northeastern		Livingston (listed under	
**Omaha....... 6,100		N.J.)........ 83,700		Essex County)	
Other places....... 50		Bridgeton........ 110		Middlesex County (also	
		Bridgewater (incl. in		incl. in Northeastern	
NEVADA		Somerset County)		N.J.)[N]....... 45,000	
Carson City (incl. in		Camden (incl. in		Monmouth County (also	
Reno)		Cherry Hill-S. N.J.)		incl. in Northeastern	
*Las Vegas 75,000		Cherry Hill-Southern		N.J.)......... 65,000	
**Reno 2,100		N.J.[N] 49,000		Morris County (also	
Sparks (incl. in Reno)		Edison (incl. in		incl. in Northeastern	
		Middlesex County)		N.J.)........ 33,500	
NEW HAMPSHIRE		Elizabeth (incl. in		Morristown (incl. in	
Bethlehem 200		Union County)		Morris County)	
Concord......... 500		Englewood (incl. in		Mt. Holly (incl. in	
Dover area 600		Bergen County)		Cherry Hill-S. N.J.)	
Exeter (incl. in		Essex County (also		New Brunswick (incl. in	
Portsmouth)		incl. in Northeastern		Middlesex County)	
Franconia (incl. in		N.J.)[N] 76,200		Newark (incl. in Essex	
Bethlehem)		East Essex 10,800		County)	
***Hanover-		Livingston 12,600		Northeastern N.J.[N]	
Lebanon........ 600		North Essex... 15,600		 417,000	
***Keene 300		South Essex ... 20,300		Ocean County (also	
**Laconia 270		West Orange-Orange		incl. in Northeastern	
Littleton (incl. in		 16,900		N.J.)......... 29,000	
Bethlehem)		*Flemington 1,500		Passaic County (also	
Manchester area		Freehold (incl. in		incl. in Northeastern	
.... 4,000		Monmouth County)		N.J.)......... 17,000	
Nashua area 2,000		Gloucester (incl. in		Passaic-Clifton (incl. in	
Portsmouth area		Cherry Hill-S. N.J.)		Passaic County)	
.... 1,250		Hoboken (listed under		Paterson (incl. in	
Rochester (incl. in		Hudson County)		Passaic County)	
Dover)		Hudson County (also		Perth Amboy (incl. in	
Salem 150		incl. in Northeastern		Middlesex County)	
Other places...... 100		N.J.)........ 11,800		Phillipsburg (incl. in	
		Bayonne....... 1,600		Warren County)	
NEW JERSEY		Hoboken 1,400		Plainfield (incl. in	
Asbury Park (incl. in		Jersey City..... 6,000		Union County)	
Monmouth County)		North Hudson		Princeton area	
**Atlantic City (incl.		County[N]..... 2,800		 3,000	
Atlantic and Cape		Jersey City (listed		Somerset County (also	
May counties) . 15,800		under Hudson		incl. in Northeastern	
Bayonne (listed under		County)		N.J.)........ 11,000	
Hudson County)		Lakewood (incl. in		Somerville (incl. in	
Bergen County (also		Ocean County)		Somerset County)	

State and City	Jewish Population
Sussex County (also incl. in Northeastern N.J.)	4,100
Toms River (incl. in Ocean County)	
Trenton[N]	6,000
Union County (also incl. in Northeastern N.J.)	30,000
Vineland[N]	1,890
Warren County	400
Wayne (incl. in Passaic County)	
Wildwood	330
Willingboro (incl. in Cherry Hill-S. N.J.)	
Other places	200

NEW MEXICO

State and City	Jewish Population
*Albuquerque	7,500
Las Cruces	600
Las Vegas (incl. in Santa Fe)	
***Los Alamos	250
Rio Rancho (incl. in Albuquerque)	
Santa Fe	2,500
***Taos	300
Other places	100

NEW YORK

State and City	Jewish Population
*Albany	12,000
Amenia (incl. in Poughkeepsie-Dutchess County)	
Amsterdam	100
*Auburn	115
Beacon (incl. in Poughkeepsie-Dutchess County)	
*Binghamton (incl. all Broome County)	2,400
Brewster (incl. in Putnam County)	

State and City	Jewish Population
*Buffalo	18,500
Canandaigua (incl. in Geneva)	
Catskill	200
Corning (incl. in Elmira)	
*Cortland	150
Ellenville	1,600
Elmira[N]	950
Fleischmanns	100
Geneva area	300
Glens Falls[N]	800
*Gloversville	300
*Herkimer	130
Highland Falls (incl. in Orange County)	
*Hudson	500
*Ithaca area	2,000
Jamestown	100
Kingston[N]	4,300
Kiryas Joel (incl. in Orange County)	
Lake George (incl. in Glens Falls)	
Liberty (incl. in Sullivan County)	
Middletown (incl. in Orange County)	
Monroe (incl. in Orange County)	
Monticello (incl. in Sullivan County)	
Newark (incl. in Geneva total)	
Newburgh (incl. in Orange County)	
New Paltz (incl. in Kingston)	
New York Metro Area[N]	1,412,000
Bronx	45,000
Brooklyn	456,000
Manhattan	243,500
Queens	186,000

State and City	Jewish Population
Staten Island	42,700
Nassau County	221,000
Suffolk County	90,000
Westchester County	129,000
Niagara Falls	150
Olean	100
**Oneonta	300
Orange County	19,000
Pawling (incl. in Poughkeepsie-Dutchess County)	
Plattsburg	250
Port Jervis (incl. in Orange County)	
Potsdam	200
*Poughkeepsie-Dutchess County	3,600
Putnam County	1,000
**Rochester	22,500
Rockland County	90,000
Rome	100
Saratoga Springs	600
**Schenectady	5,200
Seneca Falls (incl. in Geneva)	
South Fallsburg (incl. in Sullivan County)	
***Sullivan County	7,425
Syracuse[N]	9,000
Troy area	800
Utica[N]	1,100
Walden (incl. in Orange County)	
Watertown	100
Woodstock (incl. in Kingston)	
Other places	600

State and City	Jewish Population	State and City	Jewish Population	State and City	Jewish Population

NORTH CAROLINA
Asheville[N] 1,300
**Chapel Hill-Durham
.... 4,600
Charlotte[N] 8,500
Elizabethtown (incl. in
Wilmington)
*Fayetteville....... 300
Gastonia 210
*Greensboro 2,500
Greenville........ 240
*Hendersonville.... 250
**Hickory 260
High Point (incl. in
Greensboro)
Jacksonville (incl. in
Wilmington)
Raleigh-Wake County
.... 6,000
Whiteville (incl. in
Wilmington)
Wilmington area . 1,200
Winston-Salem.... 485
Other places...... 450

NORTH DAKOTA
Fargo 200
Grand Forks 130
Other places...... 100

OHIO
**Akron 4,000
***Athens 100
Bowling Green (incl. in
Toledo)
Butler County 900
**Canton 1,450
Cincinnati[N] 22,500
Cleveland[N]..... 81,500
*Columbus 22,000
**Dayton 5,000
Elyria 155
Fremont (incl. in
Sandusky)

Hamilton (incl. in
Butler County)
Kent (incl. in Akron)
*Lima............ 180
***Lorain 600
Mansfield........ 150
Marion[N]......... 125
Middletown (incl. in
Butler County)
New Philadelphia (incl.
in Canton)
Norwalk (incl. in
Sandusky)
Oberlin (incl. in Elyria)
Oxford (incl. in Butler
County)
**Sandusky 105
Springfield 200
*Steubenville 115
Toledo[N] 5,900
Warren (incl. in
Youngstown)
Wooster 175
Youngstown[N].... 3,200
*Zanesville........ 100
Other places...... 350

OKLAHOMA
Norman (incl. in
Oklahoma City)
**Oklahoma City
.... 2,300
*Tulsa 2,650
Other places...... 100

OREGON
Ashland (incl. in
Medford)
Bend............ 500
Corvallis......... 500
Eugene 3,250
Grants Pass (incl. in
Medford)
**Medford 1,000

Portland[N]...... 25,500
**Salem......... 1,000
Other places...... 100

PENNSYLVANIA
Allentown (incl. in
Lehigh Valley)
*Altoona 575
Ambridge (incl. in
Pittsburgh)
Beaver Falls (incl. in
Upper Beaver County)
Bethlehem (incl. in
Lehigh Valley)
Bucks County (listed
under Philadelphia
area)
*Butler........... 250
**Chambersburg ... 150
Chester (incl. in
Delaware County,
listed under Phila.
area)
Chester County (listed
under Phila. area)
Coatesville (incl. in
Chester County, listed
under Phila. area)
Easton (incl. in Lehigh
Valley)
*Erie 850
Farrell (incl. in Sharon)
Greensburg (incl. in
Pittsburgh)
**Harrisburg..... 7,000
Hazleton area..... 300
Honesdale (incl. in
Wayne County)
Jeannette (incl. in
Pittsburgh)
**Johnstown 275
Lancaster area
3,000
*Lebanon......... 350

State and City	Jewish Population
Lehigh Valley	8,500
Lewisburg (incl. in Sunbury)	
Lock Haven (incl. in Williamsport)	
McKeesport (incl. in Pittsburgh)	
New Castle	200
Norristown (incl. in Montgomery County, listed under Phila. area)	
**Oil City	100
Oxford-Kennett Square (incl. in Chester County, listed under Phila. area)	
Philadelphia area[N]	206,000
Bucks County	34,800
Chester County	10,100
Delaware County	15,700
Montgomery County	58,900
Philadelphia	86,600
Phoenixville (incl. in Chester County, listed under Phila. area)	
***Pike County	300
Pittsburgh[N]	40,000
Pottstown	650
Pottsville	120
*Reading	2,200
*Scranton	3,100
Shamokin (incl. in Sunbury)	
Sharon	300
State College	700
Stroudsburg	600
Sunbury[N]	200

State and City	Jewish Population
Tamaqua (incl. in Hazleton)	
Uniontown area	150
Upper Beaver County	180
Washington (incl. in Pittsburgh)	
***Wayne County	500
Waynesburg (incl. in Pittsburgh)	
West Chester (incl. in Chester County, listed under Phila. area)	
Wilkes-Barre[N]	3,000
**Williamsport	225
York	1,800
Other places	900
RHODE ISLAND	
Cranston (incl. in Providence)	
Kingston (incl. in Washington County)	
Newport-Middletown	700
Providence area	14,200
Washington County	1,200
Westerly (incl. in Washington County)	
SOUTH CAROLINA	
*Charleston	5,500
**Columbia	2,750
Florence area	220
Georgetown (incl. in Myrtle Beach)	
Greenville	1,200
Kingstree (incl. in Sumter)	
**Myrtle Beach	475
Rock Hill	100

State and City	Jewish Population
*Spartanburg	500
Sumter[N]	140
York (incl. in Rock Hill)	
Other places	450
SOUTH DAKOTA	
Sioux Falls	195
Other places	100
TENNESSEE	
Chattanooga	1,450
Knoxville	1,800
Memphis	8,500
Nashville	6,000
Oak Ridge	250
Other places	200
TEXAS	
Amarillo[N]	200
*Austin	13,500
***Baytown	300
Beaumont	500
*Brownsville	450
***College Station-Bryan	400
*Corpus Christi	1,400
**Dallas	45,000
El Paso	5,000
*Fort Worth	5,000
Galveston	450
Harlingen (incl. in Brownsville)	
**Houston[N]	45,000
Laredo	130
Longview	100
*Lubbock	230
*McAllen[N]	500
Midland-Odessa	200
Port Arthur	100
*San Antonio	11,000
South Padre Island (incl. in Brownsville)	

State and City	Jewish Population	State and City	Jewish Population	State and City	Jewish Population
Tyler	400	Hampton (incl. in Newport News)		**Yakima	150
Waco[N]	300	Harrisonburg (incl. in Staunton)		Other places	350
Wichita Falls	260	Lexington (incl. in Staunton)		WEST VIRGINIA	
Other places	600	Lynchburg area	275	***Bluefield-Princeton	200
UTAH		**Martinsville	100	*Charleston	975
Ogden	150	Newport News-Hampton[N]	2,400	Clarksburg	110
*Salt Lake City	4,200	Norfolk-Virginia Beach	11,000	Huntington[N]	250
Other places	50	Northern Virginia	35,100	Morgantown	200
		Petersburg area	350	***Parkersburg	110
VERMONT		Portsmouth-Suffolk (incl. in Norfolk)		**Wheeling	290
Bennington area	500	Radford (incl. in Blacksburg)		Other places	200
***Brattleboro	350	Richmond[N]	12,500		
**Burlington	2,500	Roanoke	900	WISCONSIN	
Manchester area	325	Staunton[N]	370	Appleton area	100
Montpelier-Barre	550	Williamsburg (incl. in Newport News)		Beloit	120
Newport (incl. in St. Johnsbury)		Winchester[N]	270	Fond du Lac (incl. in Oshkosh)	
Rutland	625	Other places	150	Green Bay	500
**St. Johnsbury	140			Janesville (incl. in Beloit)	
Stowe	150	WASHINGTON		*Kenosha	300
***Woodstock	270	Bellingham	525	La Crosse	100
Other places	100	Ellensburg (incl. in Yakima)		*Madison	5,000
		Longview-Kelso (incl. in Vancouver)		Milwaukee[N]	21,000
VIRGINIA		*Olympia	560	Oshkosh area	170
Alexandria (incl. in N. Virginia)		***Port Angeles	100	*Racine	200
Arlington (incl. in N. Virginia)		*Seattle[N]	37,200	Sheboygan	140
Blacksburg	175	Spokane	1,500	Waukesha (incl. in Milwaukee)	
Charlottesville	1,500	*Tacoma	2,000	Wausau[N]	300
Chesapeake (incl. in Portsmouth)		Tri Cities[N]	300	Other places	300
Colonial Heights (incl. in Petersburg)		Vancouver	600		
Danville area	100			WYOMING	
Fairfax County (incl. in N. Virginia)				Casper	100
Fredericksburg[N]	500			Cheyenne	230
				Laramie (incl. in Cheyenne)	
				Other places	50

Notes

CALIFORNIA

Long Beach—includes in L.A. County: Long Beach, Signal Hill, Cerritos, Lakewood, Rossmoor and Hawaiian Gardens. Also includes in Orange County: Los Alamitos, Cypress, Seal Beach, and Huntington Harbor.

Los Angeles—includes most of Los Angeles County, but excludes those places listed above that are part of the Long Beach area and also excludes the eastern portion that is listed below as part of San Gabriel and Pomona Valleys. Also includes eastern edge of Ventura County.

Orange County—includes most of Orange County, but excludes towns in northern portion that are included in Long Beach.

Palm Springs—includes Palm Springs, Desert Hot Springs, Cathedral City, Palm Desert, and Rancho Mirage.

San Gabriel and Pomona Valleys—includes in Los Angeles County: Alhambra, Altadena, Arcadia, Azusa, Baldwin Park, Bellflower, Bell Gardens, Chapman Woods, Charter Oak, Claremont, Commerce, Covina, Diamond Bar, Downey, Duarte, East Los Angeles, East Pasadena, East San Gabriel, El Monte, Glendora, Hacienda Heights, La Canada Flintridge, La Habra Heights, La Mirada, La Puente, La Verne, Los Nietos, Monrovia, Montebello, Monterey Park, Norwalk, Pico Rivera, Paramount, Pasadena, Pomona, Rosemead, Rowland Heights, San Dimas, San Gabriel, San Marino, Santa Fe Springs, Sierra Madre, South El Monte, South Pasadena, South San Gabriel, South San Jose Hills, South Whittier, Temple City, Walnut, West Covina, West Puente Valley, West Whittier, Whittier, and Valinda. Also includes in San Bernardino County: Alta Loma, Chino, Chino Hills, Mira Loma, Montclair, Ontario, Rancho Cucamonga, and Upland.

Sacramento—includes Yolo, Placer, El Dorado, and Sacramento counties.

San Francisco Bay area—North Peninsula includes northern San Mateo County. South Peninsula includes southern San Mateo County and towns of Palo Alto and Los Altos in Santa Clara County. San Jose includes remainder of Santa Clara County.

COLORADO

Denver—includes Adams, Arapahoe, Boulder, Denver, and Jefferson counties.

Pueblo—includes all of Pueblo County east to Lamar, west and south to Trinidad.

CONNECTICUT

Bridgeport—includes Monroe, Easton, Trumbull, Fairfield, Bridgeport, Shelton and Stratford.

Danbury—includes Danbury, Bethel, New Fairfield, Brookfield, Sherman, Newtown, Redding, and Ridgefield.

Hartford—includes all of Hartford County and Vernon, Rockville, Somers, Stafford Springs in New Haven County and Ellington and Tolland in Tolland County.

Lower Middlesex County—includes Branford, Guilford, Madison, Clinton, Westbrook, Old Saybrook, Old Lyme, Durham, and Killingworth.

New Haven—includes New Haven, East Haven, Guilford, Branford, Madison, North Haven, Hamden, West Haven, Milford, Orange, Woodbridge, Bethany, Derby, Ansonia, Quinnipiac, Meriden, Seymour, and Wallingford.

New London—includes central and southern New London County. Also includes part of Middlesex County and part of Windham County.

Waterbury—includes Bethlehem, Cheshire, Litchfield, Morris, Middlebury, Southbury, Naugatuck, Prospect, Plymouth, Roxbury, Southbury, Southington, Thomaston, Torrington, Washington, Watertown, Waterbury, Oakville, Woodbury, Wolcott, Oxford, and other towns in Litchfield County and northern New Haven County.

Westport—includes Norwalk, Weston, Westport, East Norwalk, Wilton, and Georgetown.

DISTRICT OF COLUMBIA

Washington, D.C.—For a total of the Washington, D.C. metropolitan area, include Montgomery and Prince Georges counties in Maryland, and northern Virginia.

FLORIDA

Orlando—includes all of Orange and Seminole counties, southern Volusia County, and northern Osceola County.

Stuart-Port St. Lucie—includes all of Martin County and southern St. Lucie County.

GEORGIA

Augusta—includes Burke, Columbia, and Richmond counties.

ILLINOIS

Chicago—includes all of Cook and DuPage counties and a portion of Lake County.

Elgin—includes northern Kane County and southern McHenry County.

Rockford—includes Winnebago, Boone, and Stephenson counties.

Southern Illinois—includes lower portion of Illinois below Carlinville.

INDIANA

South Bend—includes St. Joseph and Elkhart counties.

KANSAS

Kansas City—includes Johnson and Wyandotte counties. For a total of the Kansas City metropolitan area, include Missouri portion.

Wichita—includes Sedgwick County and towns of Salina, Dodge City, Great Bend, Liberal, Russell, and Hays.

KENTUCKY

Lexington—includes Fayette, Bourbon, Scott, Clark, Woodford, Madison, Pulaski, and Jessamine counties.

LOUISIANA

Alexandria—includes towns in Allen, Grant, Rapides, and Vernon parishes.

Baton Rouge—includes E. Baton Rouge, Ascension, Livingston, St. Landry, Iberville, Pointe Coupee, and W. Baton Rouge parishes.

South Central—includes Abbeville, Lafayette, New Iberia, Crowley, Opelousas, Houma, Morgan City, Thibodaux, and Franklin.

MAINE

Southern Maine—includes York, Cumberland, and Sagadahoc counties.

MASSACHUSETTS

Andover—includes Andover, N. Andover, Boxford, Lawrence, Methuen, Tewksbury, and Dracut.

Boston Metropolitan region—Brockton-South Central includes Avon, Bridgewater, Brockton, Canton, East Bridgewater, Easton. Foxborough, Halifax, Randolph, Sharon, Stoughton, West Bridgewater, Whitman, and Wrentham. Framingham area includes Acton, Bellingham, Boxborough, Framingham, Franklin, Holliston, Hopkinton, Hudson, Marlborough, Maynard, Medfield, Medway, Milford, Millis, Southborough, and Stow. Northeast includes Chelsea, Everett, Malden, Medford, Revere, and Winthrop. North Central includes Arlington, Belmont, Cambridge, Somerville, Waltham, and Watertown. Northwest includes Bedford, Burlington, Carlisle, Concord, Lexington, Lincoln, Melrose, North Reading, Reading, Stoneham, Wakefield, Wilmington, Winchester, and Woburn. North Shore includes Lynn, Saugus, Nahant, Swampscott, Lynnfield, Peabody, Salem, Marblehead, Beverly, Danvers, Middleton, Wenham, Topsfield, Hamilton, Manchester, Ipswich, Essex, Gloucester, and Rockport. Near West includes Ashland, Dedham, Dover, Natick, Needham, Norfolk, Norwood, Sherborn, Sudbury, Walpole, Wayland, Wellesley, Weston, and Westwood. Southeast includes Abington, Braintree, Cohasset, Duxbury, Hanover, Hanson, Hingham, Holbrook, Hull, Kingston, Marshfield, Milton, Norwell, Pembroke, Quincy, Rockland, Scituate, and Weymouth.

New Bedford—includes New Bedford, Dartmouth, Fairhaven, and Mattapoisett.

Springfield—includes Springfield, Longmeadow, E. Longmeadow, Hampden, Wilbraham, Agawam, and W. Springfield.

MICHIGAN
Mt. Pleasant—includes towns in Isabella, Mecosta, Gladwin, and Gratiot counties.

MISSOURI
Kansas City—For a total of the Kansas City metropolitan area, include the Kansas portion.

NEW HAMPSHIRE
Laconia—includes Laconia, Plymouth, Meredith, Conway, and Franklin.

NEW JERSEY
Cherry Hill-Southern N.J.—includes Camden, Burlington, and Gloucester counties.

Essex County-East Essex—includes Belleville, Bloomfield, East Orange, Irvington, Newark and Nutley in Essex County, and Kearney in Hudson County. North Essex includes Caldwell, Cedar Grove, Essex Fells, Fairfield, Glen Ridge, Montclair, North Caldwell, Roseland, Verona, and West Caldwell. South Essex includes Maplewood, Millburn, Short Hills and South Orange in Essex County, and Springfield in Union County.

Middlesex County—includes in Somerset County: Kendall Park, Somerset, and Franklin; in Mercer County, Hightstown; and all of Middlesex County.

Northeastern N.J.—includes Bergen, Essex, Hudson, Hunterdon, Mercer, Middlesex, Monmouth, Morris, Ocean, Passaic, Somerset, Sussex, Union, and Warren counties.

North Hudson County—includes Guttenberg, Hudson Heights, North Bergen, North Hudson, Secaucus, Union City, Weehawken, West New York, and Woodcliff.

Somerset County—includes most of Somerset County and a portion of Hunterdon County.

Trenton—includes most of Mercer County.

Union County—includes all of Union County except Springfield. Also includes a few towns in adjacent areas of Somerset and Middlesex counties.

Vineland—includes most of Cumberland County and towns in neighboring counties adjacent to Vineland.

NEW YORK
Elmira—includes Chemung, Tioga, and Schuyler counties.

Glens Falls—includes Warren and Washington counties, lower Essex County, and upper Saratoga County.

Kingston—includes eastern half of Ulster County.

New York Metropolitan area—includes the five boroughs of New York City,

Westchester, Nassau, and Suffolk counties. For a total Jewish population of the New York metropolitan region, include Fairfield and New Haven counties, Connecticut; Rockland, Putnam, and Orange counties, New York; Northeastern New Jersey, and Pike County, Pennsylvania.

Syracuse—includes Onondaga County, western Madison County, and most of Oswego County.

Utica—southeastern third of Oneida County.

NORTH CAROLINA

Asheville—includes Buncombe, Haywood, and Madison counties.

Charlotte—includes Mecklenburg County. For a total of the Charlotte area, include Rock Hill, South Carolina.

OHIO

Cincinnati—includes Hamilton and Butler counties. For a total of the Cincinnati area, include the Covington-Newport area of Kentucky.

Cleveland—includes all of Cuyahoga County and portions of Lake, Geauga, Portage, and Summit counties. For a metropolitan total, also include Elyria, Lorain, and Akron.

Toledo—includes Fulton, Lucas, and Wood counties.

Youngstown—includes Mahoning and Trumbull counties.

PENNSYLVANIA

Philadelphia—For total Jewish population of the Philadelphia metropolitan region, include the Cherry Hill- Southern, N.J., Princeton, and Trenton areas of New Jersey, and the Wilmington and Newark areas of Delaware.

Pittsburgh—includes all of Allegheny County and adjacent portions of Washington, Westmoreland, and Beaver counties.

Sunbury—includes Shamokin, Lewisburg, Milton, Selinsgrove, and Sunbury.

Wilkes-Barre—includes all of Luzerne County except southern portion, which is included in the Hazleton total.

SOUTH CAROLINA

Sumter—includes towns in Sumter, Lee, Clarendon, and Williamsburg counties.

TEXAS

Amarillo—includes Canyon, Childress, Borger, Dumas, Memphis, Pampa, Vega, and Hereford in Texas, and Portales, New Mexico.

Houston—includes Harris, Montgomery, and Fort Bend counties, and parts of Brazoria and Galveston counties.

McAllen—includes Edinburg, Harlingen, McAllen, Mission, Pharr, Rio Grande City, San Juan, and Weslaco.

Waco—includes McLennan, Coryell, Bell, Falls, Hamilton, and Hill counties.

VIRGINIA

Fredericksburg—includes towns in Spotsylvania, Stafford, King George, and Orange counties.

Newport News—includes Newport News, Hampton, Williamsburg, James City, York County, and Poquoson City.

Richmond—includes Richmond City, Henrico County, and Chesterfield County.

Staunton—includes towns in Augusta, Page, Shenandoah, Rockingham, Bath, and Highland Counties.

Winchester—includes towns in Winchester, Frederick, Clarke, and Warren counties.

WASHINGTON

Seattle—includes King County and adjacent portions of Snohomish and Kitsap counties.

Tri Cities—includes Pasco, Richland, and Kennewick.

WISCONSIN

Milwaukee—includes Milwaukee County, eastern Waukesha County, and southern Ozaukee County.

Wausau—includes Stevens Point, Marshfield, Antigo, and Rhinelander.

Review
of
the
Year

OTHER COUNTRIES

Israel and the Middle East

Israel

T HE VIOLENCE THAT BEGAN in late 2000 and continued all through 2001—featuring Palestinian suicide bombings aimed at producing a maximum of Israeli casualties, and Israeli reprisals—did not abate in 2002; in fact, it intensified. Tough new measures by the Likud-led coalition, including stepped-up "targeted killings" of terror kingpins and large-scale incursions into Palestinian areas—such as Operation Defensive Shield in the spring—brought only temporary halts to the attacks on Israelis and sharp criticism from around the world.

An exception to the unsympathetic attitude toward Israel in world capitals was that of the American government. Although President George W. Bush became the first president explicitly to call for a Palestinian state, he delivered a speech on June 24 announcing that the Palestinian National Authority would have to undergo democratization, renounce terror, and select new leadership (that is, not Yasir Arafat) first. Toward the end of the year, with a U.S. strike on Iraq looming, the U.S., the UN, the European Union (EU), and the chief European powers promoted a "road map," charting steps that Israel and the Palestinians might take to reach an ultimate settlement.

The security crisis loomed large over Israeli life. The economy, already hard-hit by more than a year of violence, suffered further blows. And while the Labor Party left the coalition and brought down the government on October 30 ostensibly over a budgetary matter, what was really at stake was whether Labor could devise a strategy for stopping the bloodshed that would be both different from Likud's and convincing to the voters.

THE ELUSIVE SEARCH FOR SECURITY

The Karine A

With retired Marine general Anthony Zinni, the U.S. Middle East envoy, returning to the region on January 3, Israel eased its closure of parts of the West Bank. Troops were withdrawn from Jenin and parts of Ramallah, and the military encirclement of Tul Karm, Qalqilya, and Jenin ended. Yasir Arafat, however, remained confined to his compound in Ramallah, where he had been surrounded by Israeli tanks since mid-December 2001. Jibril Rajoub, head of the Palestinian preventive security forces on the West Bank, denounced what he called Israel's "fake withdrawal," designed, he said, to deceive Zinni.

But all of this was overshadowed the next day, January 4, when Israeli chief of staff Shaul Mofaz announced that Israel's navy, the day before, had boarded and seized a ship, the *Karine A,* in the Red Sea. It was carrying some 50 tons of arms intended for the Palestinian National Authority (PNA). The vessel was owned by the PNA and captained by a member of its naval police. The weapons found aboard, mostly of Iranian origin, included Katyusha rockets, antitank missiles, mortars, mines, advanced explosive equipment, rifles, and ammunition. Under the terms of the 1993 Oslo accords, the Palestinians were permitted only a limited amount of light arms for their police force.

The PNA denied the Israeli assertions, claiming that they were concocted to undermine Zinni's mission. Indeed, Israel announced its find as Zinni was meeting with Arafat in Ramallah, after a breakfast meeting with Prime Minister Sharon. The announcement had the immediate effect of shifting public focus away from Zinni to what Israel saw as continuing Palestinian preparations for violence. In a radio interview that day, Dalia Rabin-Pelosoff, Israel's deputy defense minister, said that the seizure of the *Karine A* furnished "further proof that the Palestinian Authority has not changed its intention of achieving its aims through terrorism and violence."

A spokesman for the Israel Defense Force (IDF) provided background information on the ship and its cargo. Apparently, at the start of the intifada in late 2000, Adel Mughrabi, a major buyer for the Palestinian weapons purchasing system, assisted by Juma'a Ghali, commander of the Palestinian naval police, started working with Hezballah and Iran to smuggle weapons. It took about seven months to arrange the shipment, and it was financed by Fuad Shubeiki, an Arafat confidant and financial advisor. According to the report, Mughrabi purchased the *Karine A* in Lebanon and had it sailed, with an ordinary crew, to Sudan, where a Palestinian crew headed by Captain Omar Akawi took over, and, in November 2001, sailed the ship to Hodeida, Yemen. The next month Mughrabi ordered the ship to sail to Qeshm Island, Iran, where a ferry brought out its cargo in 80 large wooden crates. The weapons were stored in special floatable waterproof containers that, the army said, were prepared by Hezballah. The plan was for the ship to traverse the Suez Canal and then rendezvous in the Mediterranean with three smaller vessels, and these were to transport the arms to their final destination. But Israel, which had been monitoring the ship for some time, was not willing to let it get as far as the canal, and sent a force of naval commandos that took over the ship in a lightning operation about 500 km from the canal.

On January 6, Prime Minister Sharon stood at a wharf in Eilat in front of the *Karine A* and a display of the arms it had carried, and told reporters: "When Arafat gave the instructions to purchase the arms discovered on this ship, he made a strategic choice to bring about regional deterioration that could lead to war." Making the case even stronger against Arafat was the testimony of Akawi, the captain, in a prison interview filmed in the presence of Israeli interrogators and broadcast by Fox News. Asked who gave him the orders to pick up the shipment, he gave the name of Adel Awadallah, a top Arafat aide, and continued, "I am an officer in the navy. I am an employee of the Palestinian Authority. I take my salary from them." When asked whether it was possible that Awadallah could have been acting on his own, Akawi answered, "I don't know. I don't think so. One time I asked him why you are doing this and he said I am doing it for Palestine."

Over the next few weeks, American officials repeatedly urged Arafat to clarify his role in the affair. On January 25, Secretary of State Colin Powell told a TV interviewer: "It's a pretty big smoking gun. I can't put it right at [Arafat] personally, but it is clear from all of the information available to us that the Palestinian Authority was involved." Powell said he thought Arafat "ought to acknowledge, as the first step toward moving forward, that this has happened and they bear some responsibility for it happening, and give the international community, and especially the Israelis, some assurance that this kind of activity is going to stop. And do it in a way that will be persuasive. . . ."

With Sharon due to visit Washington on February 7, Powell made it clear that the U.S. would not renew contacts with Arafat until he complied with demands General Zinni had made of him, including the arrest of the three men who organized the *Karine A* arms ship and an end to the transfer of PA money to Hamas and Islamic Jihad. Powell told the Senate Foreign Relations Committee on February 5 that Arafat "must act decisively to confront the sources of terror and choose once and for all the option of peace over violence. He cannot have it both ways."

To be sure, the American administration was not about to let Sharon off the hook. In anticipation of the Bush-Sharon White House meeting, the Americans made it clear that they expected some "creative ideas" from the Israeli side to ease the strain on ordinary Palestinians, including a moratorium on house demolitions, lifting of road closures, and economic aid. Indeed, in late January Sharon met with three high-level Palestinians—Ahmed Qurei (Abu Ala), the PA's number-two man Muhammad Abbas (Abu Mazen), and Muhammad Rashid, Arafat's financial adviser. According to Palestinian sources, the meeting—set up through contacts between Rashid and Sharon's son Omri, and, on a separate track, through businessman (and former Shin Bet official) Yossi Ginossar—took place with Arafat's blessing. Sharon reportedly came with suggestions for reaching a cease-fire and resuming negotiations as well as proposals for a long-term settlement. Agreement was reached on resuming security cooperation, and the two sides said they would convene again after Sharon returned from a planned trip to Washington. Later, Yasir Abd Rabbo, the PA's information minister, cited this meeting as proof that, despite Sharon's repeated declarations that negotiations would not be conducted under fire, "diplomatic talks are taking place."

But with the *Karine A* affair still fresh, Sharon offered no concessions and the Americans did not press him. At the White House meeting, Sharon told Bush that it was essential to encourage the emergence of a different Palestinian leadership. "Arafat is not a partner and will not be a partner," he said to the president. "For an alternative leadership to emerge, Arafat's irrelevance must be made clear. This is a long process, but it could be shortened if the pressure on Arafat is increased." The pressure, he explained, would make Palestinians realize that Arafat is "useless, that he is responsible for the suffering of the Palestinian population." Speaking to the press during the Sharon visit, Bush expressed his displeasure with Arafat, saying: "Obviously, we were, at first, surprised, and then extremely disappointed when the *Karine A* showed up loaded with weapons, weapons that could have only been intended for one thing, which was to terrorize."

Powell received a letter from Arafat on February 10 regarding the *Karine A* affair. Though the text was not released, the secretary of state described it as "somewhat positive"; other reports claimed that in it Arafat accepted "limited responsibility" for the arms ship. Powell said that the administration would remain in contact with Arafat and his top lieutenants in the hope of inducing the Palestinian leadership to do more to stop terror. But the incident, compounded by Arafat's long period of stonewalling before admitting any involvement, seemed to reinforce the increasingly negative American attitude toward the Palestinian leader. And, according to some reports, the *Karine A* episode also influenced Bush to include Iran, together with Iraq and North Korea, among the states included in the "Axis of Evil" in his State of the Union Address.

The Continuing Intifada

Violence, which seemed to have subsided at the end of 2001, flared up again on January 9, when Hamas infiltrators penetrated the Israeli side of the southern Gaza Strip border and killed four members of Israel's Bedouin desert patrol. Hamas called the action retaliation for Israel's "piracy" of the *Karine A,* but the PA swiftly condemned the attack as a violation of Arafat's order of December 16, 2001 to halt Palestinian assaults on Israeli targets. Sharon's office, however, issued a statement holding Arafat and his "coalition of terror" responsible. Israel moved troops into nearby parts of the Gaza Strip, bulldozing dozens of buildings in the Rafah refugee camp, where the attackers came from. An official from the UN Relief and Works Agency (UNRWA) said that 54 houses had been destroyed and more than 500 people left without shelter. After initially denying that any of the destroyed buildings were inhabited, Israel later conceded that many were.

Israel resumed its policy of targeted strikes against terrorist leaders. On January 14, Ra'ed al-Karmi, described by the Israelis as "the leading extremist of a murderous cell" within the Al-Aqsa Martyrs Brigades, died in a roadside explosion near Tul Karm. The Palestinian group issued a statement warning Israel that by killing him "you have opened hell on yourselves." Numerous attacks against Israelis followed, including a shooting at a banquet hall in Hadera during a bat mitzvah party on January 17 in which six people were killed and 20 wounded, a toll that would have been much higher had the attacker been able to set off the explosive belt he was wearing. Israel responded by demolishing a PNA security compound near Tul Karm and the headquarters of the Palestinian Broadcasting Corporation in Ramallah, and moving into Tul Karm, which Israel said had been the launching pad for numerous attacks, including the one in Hadera.

But terror attacks continued. Over the span of just a few days, a shooting incident (January 22) and a bomb (January 27) on the same block off Jaffa Road in Jerusalem killed three and wounded some 150. (Responding to the second incident, Jerusalem police chief Mickey Levy suffered chest pains and had to undergo angioplasty). The bomb was placed between two bus stops and near a popular shoe store by a woman, Wafa Idris, a volunteer with the Palestinian Red Crescent, who was apparently transported to the site, with her bomb, in a PA ambulance. Although some in the media called her the first Palestinian female suicide bomber, it remained unclear from the evidence whether she had meant to kill herself or to leave the bomb and escape. On January 29, Prime Minister Sharon approved a plan for a security cordon around Jerusalem, including construction of a wall along the southern perimeter of the city and the placing of roadblocks on the "seam" between parts of Arab East Jerusalem and the West Jerusalem city center.

In early February, the IDF discovered a cache of homemade, short-range 120-mm. Qassam-2 missile rockets — named after Hamas's military wing, the Izz al-Din al-Qassam Battalions — in a truck on the West Bank, and confirmed earlier reports that Hamas had fired such missiles into Israel from the Gaza Strip. Israel, calling this a "new level of threat," responded with air attacks on Gaza, searches in Beit Hanun, Beit Lahiya, and Deir al-Balah in Gaza to determine where the missiles had been launched, and an investigation in Nablus to locate the factories where they were made and the warehouses where they were stored.

On February 14, Israelis were shocked to learn that a Merkava-3 tank, thought to be the best-protected armored vehicle in the world, had been destroyed by a 100-kg (220-lb.) mine in an ambush in the Gaza Strip. The next day, Lt.-Col. Eyal Weiss, commander of the elite Duvdevan anti-terror unit, was accidently killed when a wall of a house being demolished fell and crushed him during a raid on the village of Saida, in the northern West Bank. On February 19, six soldiers were killed in a well-planned ambush on a military checkpoint in the West Bank, not far from Ramallah. Israel responded with naval and air attacks on Arafat's Gaza headquarters, the first time that building had been targeted. While Arafat, confined by the Israelis to his compound in Ramallah, was not there, four of his presidential guards were killed in the bombardment. Israel also imposed exceptionally severe restrictions on the Palestinian territories, closing virtually all major roads in the northern West Bank.

Diplomatic Maneuvers

Early in the year, differences between Prime Minister Sharon, the leader of the Likud Party, and Foreign Minister Shimon Peres of Labor, its junior partner in the government coalition, gave the appearance of a foreign policy in disarray.

On January 2, Avi Gil, director-general of the Foreign Ministry, complained that the government had issued important pronouncements and made key decisions toward the end of 2001 against the advice of his ministry. Among these he listed the cabinet declaration that Yasir Arafat was "irrelevant"; the arrest of Sari Nusseibeh, the PA official responsible for Jerusalem, for hosting a reception marking the Muslim holy day of Eid El-Fitr on the grounds that the event infringed on Jewish sovereignty over the city; preventing President Moshe Katzav from speaking to the PA legislature in Ramallah as part of a plan to declare a limited cease-fire; Sharon's insistence, in the face of Peres's opposition, on "seven days of quiet" before a renewal of talks with the Palestinians; and barring Yasir Arafat, besieged in Ramallah, from going to Bethlehem for Christmas. Soon thereafter, Sharon vetoed plans by Avraham Burg (Labor), speaker of the Knesset, to address the Palestinian Legislative Council in Ramallah in February or March.

Sharon, for his part, resented being kept in the dark about a draft document that Peres negotiated with Ahmed Qurei (Abu Ala), speaker of the Palestinian Authority's Legislative Assembly, that aimed at renewing peace negotiations. In early February, at the same time that his prime minister was taking a hard line against Arafat in Washington, Peres lobbied for the new plan in Israel. It called for a three-stage process. First, stabilization of the security situation would lead to a complete cease-fire and implementation of the Mitchell and Tenet cease-fire plans put together in 2001, including confidence-building measures (see AJYB 2002, pp. 533–35). Second, Israel and a Palestinian state would recognize each other before the definition of borders, with sovereignty based on the territory already under full control of each side. And third, negotiations for a permanent agreement would commence within eight weeks of the cease-fire, with a deadline of one year for completion.

But the plan went nowhere. Overtures to leaders of Shas—the Sephardi Orthodox party whose 17 Knesset seats made it a vital element in the coalition—to Yosef "Tommy" Lapid, head of Shinui, which had six seats, and to members of Peres's party, Labor, did not produce the desired support. Indeed, his own party leader, Defense Minister Binyamin Ben-Eliezer, angered Peres by saying he did not think the plan was practical. The Prime Minister's Office delivered the coup de grâce when it announced that formal presentation of the plan to the cabinet for approval would be counterproductive.

On February 21, responding to the recent sharp escalation in violence, Sharon delivered a televised address in which he announced plans to construct a "security fence" that would furnish "buffer zones" separating Israel from parts of the Territories. His aides afterwards stressed that the route of the fence had no implications for the political status of the land enclosed within it or left outside, nor did it entail an acceptance of the "Green Line" border demarcating the lines between pre-1967 Israel and the Territories.

Following a bitter cabinet debate, Israeli tanks began pulling back from around the Muq'ata, Arafat's compound in Ramallah, on February 24. Instead of welcoming this, the Palestinians greeted the decision — which still left Arafat confined to Ramallah — as yet another step in Israel's continuing effort to humiliate their leader, and canceled a joint security meeting in protest. At the same time, they continued trying to persuade the Americans to intercede with Israel to let Arafat attend the Arab League summit, due to take place in Beirut in March.

Defense Minister Ben-Eliezer wanted to allow the PA leader freedom of movement. "The continuing imprisonment of Arafat is a mistake that could endanger the moves I am making to calm the Territories," Ben-Eliezer said at a cabinet meeting, referring to an Israeli promise to cease targeted killing and air attacks to see if the Palestinians would live up to their promise to try and curb violence. Ben-Eliezer was backed by Avi Dichter, head of the Shin Bet security agency, who praised the Palestinians for capturing two of the assassins of Rehavam Ze'evi, the tourism minister, the previous October (see AJYB 2002, p. 555). Dichter, however, said that Israel should still press for the arrest of two other men — Fuad Shubeiki, the key figure in the purchase of the *Karine A* weapons ship, and Ahmed Sa'adat, secretary of the Popular Front for the Liberation of Palestine (PFLP), which had carried out the Ze'evi assassination.

The easing of the Muq'ata siege was hardly a sign that Israel was going easy on Arafat or the Palestinians. In late February, Sharon, in an off-the-cuff briefing for Israeli journalists, reportedly said that before substantive talks with the Palestinians could begin "they must be hit hard ... so that they understand terrorism will achieve nothing.... Only after they are beaten will they be able to hold talks, and I want a peace deal." On February 28, Israeli troops moved into the Balata refugee camp near Nablus and another camp near Jenin to root out terror bases. Fighting raged in the camps as Israeli troops carried out house-to-house searches for terror suspects.

Terror continued in the rest of the country as well. Over the first weekend in March, Palestinian attacks killed 22 Israelis, including eight soldiers and five children. One of the attacks, carried out by a 19-year-old youth from the Deheisheh refugee camp near Bethlehem on March 2—which was Shabbat—killed ten, including four members of one family, in Jerusalem's ultra-Orthodox Beit Yisrael neighborhood. Most of the victims were coming out of a synagogue after a bar mitzvah celebration. Speaking to the Knesset two days later, Sharon announced: "It's them or us. Our backs are to the wall but all is not lost. We will win, but this is war, and it will take a long time."

Colin Powell, however, cast doubt on the effectiveness of Sharon's policies, as well as those of Arafat. "If you declare war on the Palestinians and think you can solve the problem by seeing how many Palestinians can be killed, I don't know if that leads anywhere," the secretary of state told a House subcommittee on March 2. Powell also appealed to Arafat, saying that even though the PA leader was confined to Ramallah, he could still pick up the phone and order an end to attacks. A few days later, on March 7, President Katzav took issue with Secretary Powell's criticism of Israeli policy. "No one around the world has any right to condemn us if we use our right to defend ourselves," Katzav told reporters during a visit to Ottawa, the Canadian capital. The Israeli head-of-state denied Powell's assertion that Israel had "declared war" on the Palestinians, saying that channels of communication remained open, and he placed responsibility for ending the violence directly on the Palestinians. If Palestinian violence does not cease, he said, "there will be an escalation and escalation is very bad . . . for us, and a disaster for the Palestinians."

Powell's boss, President Bush, took a different approach, and, like Katzav, placed the onus for the situation on the Palestinians. Speaking to the press after a meeting with Egypt's president Hosni Mubarak—and immediately following the Egyptian's statement to the reporters that Israel must ease up on the Palestinians—Bush said only that Palestinian attacks on Israel had to stop before progress could be made. (During his U.S. visit, Mubarak publicly proposed a summit in Sharm al-Sheikh, the resort at the southern end of Egypt's Sinai peninsula, to be attended by Arafat and Sharon, with Powell as another possible attendee. Powell called the idea "interesting," though nothing materialized from it.)

Zinni Returns

On March 7, President Bush announced that he was sending General Zinni back to the region to promote a new cease-fire initiative under which Israel would drop its demand for a full seven days of quiet in exchange for a U.S. pledge to monitor PA efforts to live up to its promises.

The Americans proposed immediate implementation of the Tenet cease-fire plan even without a drop in violence, so as to begin implementing the Mitchell Plan's blueprint for resumed negotiations. Zinni was to stay on in the region to monitor PA compliance with its obligations, including the collection of illegal weapons and the arrest of terrorists. The American plan also included support for the Saudi peace initiative, which proposed full recognition for Israel in exchange for withdrawal to the 1967 borders and an effort to rebuild the Palestinian economy (see below). For his part, Sharon—whom Bush, in his speech, referred to as "my friend"—expressed a willingness to forego the seven-days-of-quiet requirement and said he would bring the Mitchell and Tenet plans before the cabinet, a clear sign that he wanted Israel to accept them formally.

Pressure on Sharon to lift the siege on Arafat continued. During the second week of March, Powell relayed a message to Sharon stating that he did not believe that Arafat's virtual house arrest had achieved any-thing. Another voice raised in favor of ending Arafat's confinement came from Ben-Eliezer, who said that the arrest of Majdi al-Rimawi, the fourth suspect in the Ze'evi murder, meant that Israel's conditions for lifting travel restrictions on the PA leader had been met. Sharon agreed, and the government announced that Arafat was now free to move about the Pales-tinian territories, though he would still need Israeli permission to travel abroad. Arafat was unlikely to apply for such permission, since once he left the country Israel might not let him return. Sharon's concessions alarmed the right-wing elements in his coalition. Avigdor Lieberman, head of the National Union-Yisrael Beitenu bloc, attacked the govern-ment for giving in to pressure and releasing Arafat from confinement, and called Sharon's decision to drop the seven-day requirement "bizarre." Lieberman even asked Washington not to send Zinni back to the region since "Israel cannot be the only one giving up all the time on principles that it itself has set." On March 15, National Union-Yisrael Beitenu left the government.

Zinni was due to arrive on March 14. The week before, on March 8, Israeli forces began rounding up Palestinians. According to Palestinian sources, some 2,000 men from Tul Karm, Qalqilya, and the Deheisheh refugee camp were stopped, handcuffed, and detained while soldiers checked their papers against a list of wanted militants. In a broadcast three days later, Arafat singled out the IDF's conduct in Tul Karm, where the detainees had been marked with identifying numbers on their arms, as amounting to "new Nazi racism." Complaints about such markings came from Israelis as well, including Shinui leader "Tommy" Lapid, a Holocaust survivor, and the IDF put a stop to it.

On March 11–12, large numbers of Israeli tanks and combat troops pushed into Ramallah and the adjacent al-Amari and Qadura refugee camps and the Jabalya camp in the Gaza Strip in the biggest Israeli military action since the 1982 invasion of Lebanon. Its official purpose was to protect "the citizens, the cities, and the State of Israel." There were dozens of Palestinian deaths. Another casualty of the operation was Italian photographer Raffaele Ciriello, shot dead by an Israeli tank in Ramallah on March 13. An army spokesman expressed "deep sorrow," adding that Ciriello had exposed himself to grave risk by entering a closed military zone.

International pressure was brought to bear. On March 12, the UN Security Council adopted Resolution 1397, sponsored by the U.S., which for the first time endorsed the idea of a Palestinian state. The resolution affirmed "a vision of a region where two states, Israel and Palestine, lived side by side within secure and recognized borders." It called on both sides to implement the 2001 Mitchell and Tenet proposals aimed at securing a cease-fire and eventual peace talks, and also welcomed the Saudi peace plan. The first U.S.-sponsored resolution on the Middle East in some 25 years, it passed 14-0, with Syria, a nonpermanent member of the council, abstaining. Shimon Peres praised the resolution for endorsing an end to terrorism and incitement, while a spokesman for Arafat called it positive "because the whole world is behind a Palestinian state."

On March 13, the day prior to Zinni's arrival in the Middle East, President Bush said that Israel's military operations in the West Bank were hindering U.S. efforts to attain a cease-fire. "Frankly, it's not helpful what the Israelis have done, in order to create conditions for peace," he told a White House press conference. Sharon replied that he was ready to implement a cease fire when Zinni reached the area, but that meanwhile the continuing operation had a few more missions to complete.

As Zinni arrived on March 14, Israel began to withdraw its tanks from Ramallah. Bloodshed continued, however, some of it between Palestinians: in Bethlehem and Nablus four alleged collaborators with Israel were killed and their bodies dragged through the streets by members of the Al-Aqsa Martyrs Brigades. (This was not the first instance of intra-Palestinian violence in 2002. On February 5, a Palestinian mob, enraged at what they considered lenient sentences handed down by a Palestinian court in Jenin to three young men convicted of murdering a PA security officer—himself accused of killing two Palestinians suspected of collaboration with Israel—stormed the courthouse and killed them.)

Zinni immediately began talks with senior Israeli officials, including Sharon, Peres, Ben-Eliezer, and the heads of the military and intelligence. The following day he held further talks with Peres and Ben-Eliezer before traveling to Ramallah, where he spoke with Arafat. Later, Zinni described his meetings as "extremely positive" and said that both sides were "committed to getting out of this terrible situation."

As Zinni shuttled between Israeli officials in Jerusalem and Tel Aviv and their Palestinian counterparts in Ramallah, hopes of a cease-fire were briefly raised on the evening of March 16 when Sharon's office announced a meeting with the Palestinians. But it was canceled an hour later after it became clear that the Palestinians insisted on a full Israeli withdrawal as a precondition for the talks. The next day, however, in the first sign of progress for the Zinni mission, Israeli and Palestinian military commanders began security talks about the handing over of authority in parts of Area A that Israel was vacating. This was significant, since the Palestinians had demanded a full Israeli withdrawal from PA areas as a condition for declaring a cease-fire and implementing the Tenet plan. The next day, Israel began to withdraw from Bethlehem and Beit Jala.

Zinni was not the only important American official to visit the Middle East at this time. On March 10, Vice President Dick Cheney embarked on a ten-state tour of the region aimed at shoring up support for the American war on terrorism—and more specifically, U.S. plans to remove Iraqi president Saddam Hussein. According to some reports, both President Mubarak of Egypt and Crown Prince Abdullah of Saudi Arabia had made it known to the administration that Cheney's mission would be met with a wall of resistance without parallel progress in curbing Israeli-Palestinian violence. Some analysts believed that the Americans would have to make certain pro-Palestinian gestures in order to secure the tacit compliance—if not the participation—of its Arab allies in an eventual offensive against Iraq. Cheney arrived in Israel on March 18. While denying any linkage between the Israeli-Palestinian crisis and his quest for Arab support in the war against terror, Cheney did recognize that the Israel-PA conflict had become "a preoccupation for everyone" in the region. The vice president's talks in Israel touched on Washington's plans to topple the Iraqi regime of Saddam Hussein, Israel's requests for advance warning of a U.S. attack on Iraq and for additional funding of the Arrow antimissile system, Sharon's idea for a kind of "Marshall Plan" to create 100,000 jobs in the Territories, and the results so far of Zinni's mission.

Several more suicide attacks in the Jerusalem area induced the Israelis to cancel a second round of security talks with the Palestinians that had been scheduled for March 21 (they would resume, with Zinni's participation, three days later). Also on March 21, the U.S. announced that it was designating the perpetrator organization, Al-Aqsa Martyrs Brigades, a "foreign terrorist organization" to which it was illegal to provide funds or "material support." Arafat condemned the attacks and pledged to "take the appropriate measures."

But his words did not satisfy the Americans. Vice President Cheney had set aside time to meet Arafat at the Arab summit in Beirut a few days later, and this would have placed enormous pressure on Israel to let him leave the country. But in light of the most recent bloodshed Cheney canceled the meeting because Arafat had not taken the actions against violence that the Americans had sought. "Arafat could have done what was needed to guarantee that he would be allowed to depart from the Territories, and have the meeting with Cheney, and then travel to Beirut" (for the Arab summit), unnamed U.S. officials were quoted as saying in the Israeli daily *Ha'aretz*. "But he did nothing, and now he will have to placate Sharon in order to leave. That will be a lot tougher than satisfying Cheney." The officials suggested that the Palestinians had once again "missed an opportunity"—an obvious reference to former foreign minister Abba Eban's famous dictum that the Palestinians "never miss an opportunity to miss an opportunity." The Palestinians, the officials were quoted as saying, "always want to notch some diplomatic gain, and a meeting with Cheney would have given them such a chance. But they related only to the invitation, and not to the demands that were submitted to them." Sean McCormack, a spokesman for the U.S. National Security Council, characterized the U.S. demands on Arafat as "very specific," and added: "Arafat knows what he has to do to stop the violence. He must take these steps now."

On March 26, the conflict claimed the lives of two apparently unintended victims—Catherine Berruex of Switzerland and Maj. Cengiz Soytunc of Turkey, both members of the Temporary International Presence in Hebron (TIPH), an international observer force. Presumably mistaken for Israelis by Palestinian terrorists, they were shot to death while driving down a road near Hebron. They were the first members of TIPH, established in 1997 to help ease tensions after the partition of Hebron into Israeli and Palestinian zones, to be killed.

The Saudi Initiative

March was also the month of the Saudi Arabian peace initiative, floated by Crown Prince Abdullah in a February interview with *New*

York Times columnist Thomas Friedman, offering Israel normalization in return for its withdrawal from all territories captured in the 1967 Six-Day War. It came soon after CIA director George Tenet and Assistant Secretary of State for the Near East William Burns both visited Saudi Arabia for talks with Abdullah. The Saudi formula, which basically came down to "land for peace," faced resistance in the Arab world on two fronts. First, hard-line states that objected to any recognition of Israel saw it as a capitulation. In addition, countries hosting Palestinian refugees, eager to be rid of them, insisted on full implementation of the so-called "right of return" of refugees to Israel proper, an element not explicitly spelled out in the Saudi plan; Lebanon in particular, with its large population of unabsorbed Palestinian refugees living in camps in the Beirut area and in the south of the country, expressed concern.

Still, the Saudi initiative was the main topic when the 22 members of the Arab League held their 14th summit in Beirut on March 27–28, preceded by a two-day meeting of foreign ministers. The summit was marred, however, by the absence of Arafat, whom Israel did not permit to attend, as well as Egypt's Mubarak and Jordan's King Abdullah II, the leaders of the two countries that had signed peace treaties with Israel. Palestinian delegates walked out of the conference hall during the opening session, after Lebanese officials refused their request for Arafat to address the delegates live by satellite from his office in Ramallah. Lebanese officials said they feared that Israel would break into the transmission to beam pictures of Sharon into the hall. Arafat eventually delivered his speech over the al-Jazeera satellite TV network instead.

On its final day, the summit adopted a resolution including the following:

> Emanating from the conviction of the Arab countries that a military solution to the conflict will not achieve peace or provide security for the parties, the council:
> 1. Requests Israel to reconsider its policies and declare that a just peace is its strategic option as well.
> 2. Further calls upon Israel to affirm:
> (i) Full Israeli withdrawal from all the territories occupied since 1967, including the Syrian Golan Heights, to the June 4, 1967, lines as well as the remaining occupied Lebanese territories in the south of Lebanon.
> (ii) Achievement of a just solution to the Palestinian refugee problem to be agreed upon in accordance with UN General Assembly Resolution 194.
> (iii) The acceptance of the establishment of a sovereign independent Palestinian state on the Palestinian territories occupied since

June 4, 1967, in the West Bank and Gaza Strip, with East Jerusalem as its capital.

3. Consequently, the Arab states affirm the following:

(i) Consider the Arab-Israeli conflict ended, and enter into a peace agreement with Israel, and provide security for all the states of the region.

(ii) Establish normal relations with Israel in the context of this comprehensive peace.

4. Assures the rejection of all forms of Palestinian patriation which conflict with the special circumstances of the Arab host countries.

5. Calls upon the government of Israel and all Israelis to accept this initiative in order to safeguard the prospects for peace and stop the further shedding of blood, enabling the Arab countries and Israel to live in peace and good neighborliness and provide future generations with security, stability, and prosperity.

Thus the plan became an official pan-Arab program dubbed the Arab Peace Initiative. In its specifics, the proposal demanded full Israeli pullback—including from the Golan Heights and the Shebba Farms area at the foot of Mt. Hermon, an area known as Jebel Roos in Arabic and Har Dov by Israel that Israel had taken from Syria in 1967 but was claimed by Lebanon—and establishment of a Palestinian state in the West Bank and Gaza, with East Jerusalem as its capital. As adopted by the summit, the plan did not use Abdullah's original formulation of "normalization" with Israel, offering instead to "enter into a peace agreement with Israel and provide security for all states in the region," at the same time promising "normal relations" with Israel in the context of an overall peace. The resolution's handling of the issue of Palestinian refugees reflected recognition of the grievances of Lebanon and other Arab countries harboring refugees. The reference to a "just solution to the Palestinian refugee problem" mentioned UN General Assembly Resolution 194, which envisioned either repatriation or compensation as options. But it also flatly rejected "all forms of patriation that conflict with the special circumstances of the Arab host countries." Those phrases, wrote Israeli journalist Yossi Klein Halevi, was an example of the "doublespeak" that had become routine for many Arab leaders. For Halevi, they made "just solution to the refugee problem" "a code phrase for inundating the Jewish state with Palestinian refugees hostile to Israel's existence, rather than resettling them in a Palestinian state."

Israel's response to the initiative was unenthusiastic. Aides to Sharon said that the term "normal relations" was too vague, objected to the idea that withdrawal from occupied territories had to be complete and total, and rejected any right of return. A Foreign Ministry spokesman commented that Israel "cannot accept, on the one hand, to have negotiations on the creation of a Palestinian state, an independent Palestinian state, and on the other hand, have all the Palestinians come into Israel. . . . This means the destruction of the State of Israel and obviously we cannot agree."

But Foreign Minister Peres, speaking to the press on March 28, was more upbeat. He said: "Israel views positively every initiative aimed at arriving at peace and normalization. In this respect, the Saudi step is an important one, but it is liable to founder if terrorism is not stopped. We cannot, of course, ignore the problematic aspects which arose at the Beirut summit and the harsh and rejectionist language used by some of the speakers. It is also clear that the details of every peace plan must be discussed directly between Israel and the Palestinians, and to make this possible, the Palestinian Authority must put an end to terror. . . ."

In a related development, the case against Arafat as the key mover in the Palestinian terror campaign seemed to be strengthened on March 24, when an aide to Public Security Minister Uzi Landau, one of the staunchest right-wingers in the Likud, released papers confiscated in mid-2001 from Orient House, the closed PA headquarters in East Jerusalem, showing economic and operational links between Arafat and key terror operatives of the Fatah-Tanzim militia, among them Atef Abayat of the Bethlehem area, who had been assassinated by Israel in October 2001. Among the documents released by Landau's office was a letter asking Arafat to finance Tanzim operatives, including Abayat, and an order by Arafat to the PA Finance Ministry to pay out the sum of $300 each to Abayat and other Tanzim fighters. Other papers allegedly established a working connection between Faisal al-Husseini, the PA's chief Jerusalem representative who died of a heart attack in 2001, and Tanzim field commanders.

Seder Massacre and "Defensive Shield"

The deadliest attack since the start of the intifada occurred on the night of March 27, the first night of Passover, the holiday marking Jewish national liberation. A suicide bomber from Tul Karm managed to slip past police cordons guarding the town of Netanya, as well as the private security guard employed by the Park Hotel, and blew himself up in the dining room where guests had gathered for the seder. The toll came to 29 dead and over 100 injured; many of the victims were elderly people.

The next day Arafat made a vain attempt to avert the inevitable Israeli retaliation. He said he was prepared to offer Israel a cease-fire "without conditions." But the wave of terror continued with a string of horrifying attacks: the killing of three Israelis in Eilon Moreh, near Nablus; the stabbing of two more at Netzarim in the Gaza Strip; and, on March 29, a suicide bombing at the Supersol supermarket in Jerusalem's working-class Jewish neighborhood, Kiryat Hayovel. The Supersol bombing was committed by a female member of the Al-Aqsa Martyrs Brigades, 18-year-old Ayat al-Akhras, who came from a refugee camp on the outskirts of Bethlehem. One of the victims was Rachel Levy, 17, who had gone to shop for a few items before the start of Shabbat. (The similarity in age between the two would cause the *New York Times* and some other foreign publications to draw parallels between them—galling the Israeli girl's heartbroken mother, who complained that her daughter, the victim, was being compared to the perpetrator.)

Israel responded to this latest spate of attacks on March 29 by calling up 20,000 reservists and launching Operation Defensive Shield. The declared aim of the operation, as laid out by Sharon and Chief of Staff Mofaz, was to destroy the terrorist infrastructure using a variety of means, including house-to-house searches for key terrorists in towns and refugee camps. But another effect of the Israeli initiative—its main purpose, according to some observers—was to weaken the PA as a viable government body. Palestinian sources estimated the cost of the direct physical destruction of PA infrastructure during the operation at $800 million–$1 billion, and the loss of GNP at billions of dollars. A third facet of the operation was Israel's apparent determination to strike personally at Yasir Arafat. According to *Ha'aretz,* even before the Passover bombing Sharon had been preparing the political basis for the expulsion of Arafat from the Territories—a goal he had come to share with his chief rival for the Likud leadership, former prime minister Benjamin Netanyahu. Netanyahu—still formally in political retirement, though making more and more public appearances—had been pushing for such a move for months.

With the government declaring Arafat to be Israel's "enemy" who had to be "isolated," Israeli troops took control of Arafat's entire Muq'ata complex in Ramallah except for a few rooms occupied by Arafat, his advisers, and a number of men sought for terror offenses who were hiding there. Palestinian casualties reached 30 dead and some 60 wounded; the Palestinans claimed that some of their officers had been executed in cold blood, but Israel denied the charge. Over 700 Palestinian men, aged

14–45, were arrested and held on the outskirts of the city. The IDF destroyed seven buildings in Arafat's compound, including the PA's intelligence headquarters. Holed up in a windowless basement, Arafat vowed to die rather than surrender, conveying to the outside world the following message: "Allahu Akhbar [God is great]. Don't you know me by now? I am a martyr in the making. May Allah honor me with martyrdom." Pictures of the bearded Palestinian chieftain using a candle for light were flashed around the world. In Bethlehem, Israeli soldiers surrounded a large group of terrorists, who took refuge in the Church of the Nativity.

On March 30, the UN Security Council adopted Resolution 1402 expressing grave concern at the deterioration of the situation. But Israeli public opinion turned even more strongly in favor of aggressive action the next day, March 31, when, despite the heavy IDF presence in the West Bank and tight curfews, suicide attacks continued, killing 16 people in a Haifa restaurant and four more on the outskirts of Efrat, a Jewish city in the West Bank. In all, more than 120 Israelis, most of them civilians, lost their lives in terror attacks during the bloody month of March.

Sharon went on TV to call Arafat an "enemy of the free world." Foreign Minister Peres announced that Israel had moved into the Territories "in order to do the things that the Palestinian Authority was supposed to do and was committed to do so—namely, to bring an end to violence and terror, to arrest the troublemakers, to collect the illegal arms, to control the traffic of violence in the West Bank and Gaza." Maj.-Gen. Giora Eiland, coordinator of Israeli activities in the Territories, told a press conference on March 31:

The goal of this operation, as was said, is not to reoccupy the Palestinian areas, but to control a wide part of the Palestinian areas for a significant period of time, as long as is needed, in order to achieve two things:
1. To reduce the possibility of access of Palestinian terrorists to Israel. During the last operation in Ramallah about two weeks ago . . . no successful Palestinian operation was launched from Ramallah, simply because we were there. And we hope that if we do something like this, not only in Ramallah, but in some other cities, we can reduce the number of terrorist attacks as we experience right now.
2. To arrest as many terrorists as we can. In Ramallah we are quite successful. We managed to capture several hundred people, some of them are not only suspects, they are real important people who have been involved in many activities in the past few weeks. Just one example is the man that sent the suicide bomber to blow himself up on King George Street here in Jerusalem a few days ago, an operation in which an Israeli couple—husband and wife—were killed. Their

two children, aged seven and four are now alone. The man who sent this suicide bomber is in our hands now.

On April 4, the IDF invaded the city of Nablus and the Jenin refugee camp, strongholds of the Palestinian militias, and the UN Security Council passed Resolution 1403 expressing grave concern over the further deterioration of the situation. Over the next five days Israeli tanks, helicopters, and troops destroyed the main PA institutions in Nablus, laid siege to the city's three refugee camps, and stormed the Casbah, where Palestinian fighters had sought refuge among some 30,000 civilians. After ambulances were allowed into Nablus on April 9 to collect the dead and the injured, there were reports that 74 Palestinians had been killed, many of them civilians.

The deadliest combat of the operation took place in the Jenin refugee camp—established in 1953, now home to 13,000 and a stronghold of Islamic Jihad. The army met heavy resistance as soon as it entered the camp. A total of 23 Israeli soldiers were killed during the operation there, 13 of them in an elaborate ambush involving a suicide bomber and a booby-trapped house on April 9. The Palestinian death toll could only be guessed at that point, but it was certainly much higher: civilians were killed by artillery and air attacks, and others died when Israeli bulldozers demolished their houses in order to cut swathes through the densely populated camp. Israeli troops finally took control of the Jenin camp on April 10, as surviving Islamic Jihad fighters, having run out of food and ammunition, gave themselves up.

Three days earlier, on April 7, President Bush publicly called on Israel to stop the offensive. Describing himself as "a committed friend of Israel," he said that "Israel is facing a terrible and serious challenge. For seven days it has acted to root out terrorist nests. America recognizes Israel's right to defend itself from terror. Yet to lay the foundations for future peace, I ask Israel to halt incursions into Palestinian-controlled areas and begin the withdrawal from territory it has recently occupied." The next day, with U.S. pressure mounting, Israel began moving troops out of the West Bank towns of Tul Karm and Qalqilya, where it said operations had been completed. Sharon allowed General Zinni to meet with some of Arafat's advisers—something that the Israelis had not permitted since the start of Defensive Shield—in the hope that Zinni could get Arafat to accept a cease-fire proposal made in late March and accepted by Israel. At the same time, however, Sharon turned down a U.S. request to loosen the siege around Arafat in the Muq'ata.

Colin Powell visited the area once more. Sharon reported on his talks with the secretary of state in a speech to a high-tech conference in Tel Aviv. According to Sharon, he raised the idea of a regional peace conference and Powell was receptive. "I said we are ready to have a regional conference in which a number of countries would participate—Israel, Egypt, the Saudis, Jordan, Morocco, and Palestinian representatives. It doesn't have to be limited to these," Sharon reported. "The conference would be hosted by the United States. This idea is acceptable to the United States and I estimate that within a short period of time the conference will indeed convene." But Sharon made it clear that Arafat would not be on the guest list.

In response, Arafat told Fox News that he welcomed the idea if President Bush did, but only after a complete withdrawal of Israeli forces from Palestinian territories. "I am ready for an immediate conference, but at the same time immediate withdrawal," Arafat said. But senior Palestinian negotiator Sa'eb Erakat called the idea a waste of time, saying it was no substitute for accepting the Saudi plan. He declared: "If Sharon wants to talk about peace, he can accept the Arab peace initiative or agree to end the occupation and withdraw to the June 4, 1967 lines."

Israeli opposition leader Yossi Sarid, head of the dovish Meretz Party, dismissed Sharon's proposal as a "PR trick that has nothing to it." He said Sharon made the suggestion because "he understands that he must present something of a diplomatic nature at the end of the 'rolling military operation' in the West Bank." Sarid continued: "I don't think it will be possible to convene a conference without Arafat, not because I personally miss Arafat especially, but because the lack of his presence is unnatural. It is an Israeli diktat that cannot be accepted, and that everyone will reject."

Even the Americans—who, according to Sharon, found the idea "acceptable"—cast doubt on the efficacy of a peace summit without Arafat. During his visit to the region, Powell met with Arafat at the latter's office in Ramallah and urged Arafat to "think about" the conference idea, at the same time raising other options, including bilateral Palestinian-Israeli talks or tripartite discussions with U.S. involvement. According to Palestinian sources, the American also laid out a three-stage security, economic, and political package to bring an end to the crisis atmosphere around Operation Defensive Shield. The Palestinians, though, said they were less than satisfied with the meeting because it did not bring with it any guarantees of an Israeli withdrawal.

Powell left on April 17 with one substantial accomplishment—he had obtained a timetable for IDF withdrawal from PA areas, including Nablus and Jenin, to go into effect a few days after his departure. "I came here not knowing how long the operation would go on," the secretary told a press conference in Jerusalem. "We had heard everything from a couple more weeks to a couple more months. I leave here able to say to the president, it wasn't immediate but it is now coming to an end." He added that Arafat's promise to condemn terror was not sufficient: "I have made it clear to him that the world is waiting for him to make a strategic choice and lead his people away from violence. . . . Statements, as we all know, are not enough."

Two days later, Bush praised Israel for keeping its promise to pull out its troops. Bush called Sharon "a man of peace" and lauded Powell's accomplishments on his mission, which had started two weeks earlier, when the region was at a "boiling point." At the same time, the president said he understood why Israel had kept its troops in Bethlehem and particularly in Ramallah, where the men accused of murdering Ze'evi were holed up in Arafat's Muq'ata compound. "These people are accused of killing an official of the government. I can understand why the prime minister wants them brought to justice," Bush said. "They should be brought to justice if a man is killed in cold blood."

What Happened in Jenin?

Even while fighting was still going on at the Jenin refugee camp, Foreign Minister Peres predicted that the Palestinian propaganda machine was likely to depict the events as a massacre. He was right. Palestinians alleged, on the basis of "eyewitness" testimony, that the IDF had massacred as many as 500 civilians and fighters, deliberately destroyed ambulances or fired upon their crews so that they could not reach wounded civilians, and, to cover up the killings, had transported the victims' bodies to mass graves in the Golan Heights and the Jordan Valley. Chief Palestinian negotiator Sa'eb Erakat said on April 12 that "a major war crime" had been committed in Jenin. Peter Hansen, head of UNRWA, said that Israel was compounding the tragedy even after the end of hostilities by not allowing his personnel into the refugee camp. He said that UNRWA's "persistent and unrelenting efforts to gain access to the camp and to start the gruesome task of burying the dead, evacuating the wounded, and bringing urgently needed food and water to the population have so far proved unsuccessful" and that the humanitarian situation in the camp was "fast turning into a catastrophe."

On the other side, the IDF argued that its use of infantry had risked Israeli lives to minimize Palestinian civilian casualties, which would have been considerably higher had the camp been bombarded with armor, artillery or air power. IDF spokesman Ron Kitrey noted that Islamic Jihad had deliberately chosen to fight it out from "the environment of civilian neighborhoods, civilian areas. That is the way guerrilla and terror warfare is carried out around the world, and this made it especially difficult for us, because of the methods that we could use in such a vicinity. We know there are civilians there, that's why we didn't use more efficient means. We understand that we paid . . . a very bitter price because of that reason." Kitrey also cited reports from officers in the field that the Palestinians actually refused Israeli offers to assist them in evacuating the wounded and burying the dead. As for barring UNRWA from the site, the Israelis claimed that security in the camp was still too precarious for civilians to enter. Col. Gal Hirsch, operations officer of the army's Central Command, told reporters on April 12 that Palestinian claims about mass graves were "lies" and insisted that "it was not a massacre but a battle." Later in the month, the IDF estimated that 90 Palestinians had died in the Jenin camp fighting. The International Committee of the Red Cross (ICRC) gave provisional figures of 160–200 dead, 600 injured, and 3,000 made homeless.

On April 12, UN secretary-general Kofi Annan said: "My own view is that the situation is so dangerous and the humanitarian and human rights situation so appalling that I think the proposition that a force should be sent in here to create a secure environment . . . can no longer be deferred." In an April 15 resolution adopted 40-5, the UN Human Rights Commission "strongly condemned the war launched by the Israeli army against Palestinian towns and camps, which has so far resulted in the deaths of hundreds of Palestinian civilians." That same day, officials of the International Red Cross and the UN entered the camp. In a statement, the ICRC said that "part of the camp looks as if it has been hit by an earthquake, with houses partially or completely destroyed, and streets filled with rubble." And UN Middle East envoy Terje Roed-Larson, who visited the Jenin camp on April 18, described the conditions he found there—including people using their hands to search for relatives buried under the rubble of destroyed buildings—as "horrific and shocking beyond belief."

Israel declared its offensive over on April 21. The next day, Annan appointed Martti Ahtisaari, a former president of Finland, to lead a high-level fact-finding team to investigate the events in Jenin. The team also included Sadako Ogata, the former UN High Commissioner for Refugees (UNHCR), and Cornelio Sommaruga, a former president of the ICRC. However, on April 26, Sharon's office announced that it believed that the team's declared intentions did not correspond to its mandate from the Security Council, a decision endorsed on April 30 by the cabinet, which issued the following statement: "Israel has raised essential issues before the UN for a fair examination. As long as these terms have not been met, it will not be possible for the clarification process to begin." Annan disbanded the team on May 1.

It took another three months — until August 1 — for Annan to issue an official UN report on Jenin and Operation Defensive Shield. It stated that by April 18, when the IDF finally lifted its curfew and withdrew from the Jenin camp, "at least 52 Palestinians, of whom up to half may have been civilians," and 23 Israeli soldiers were dead. Palestinian allegations that 500 or more had been killed "were not substantiated by the evidence that subsequently emerged." In all, the report said, about 500 Palestinians had been killed during Israeli operations in the West Bank between the end of March and May 7, a period that included all of Defensive Shield. In a press statement, the UN said that Annan "expresses his confidence that 'the picture painted in this report is a fair representation of a complex reality,' as well as his belief that the events described show how urgent it is that the parties return to the peace process." Israel's Foreign Ministry praised the report, which, it said "overwhelmingly negates this Palestinian fabrication and repudiates the malicious lies spread regarding the issue." In addition, the Foreign Ministry stressed that the report "clearly establishes that the Palestinian Authority did nothing to prevent terrorism and had failed to fulfill its responsibility and commitment to confront terrorism, noting that this failure was due to the PA's assumption that terrorism would force Israeli acquiescence."

On October 2, an IDF board of inquiry issued its report on the Jenin camp battle, focusing especially on the circumstances of the deaths of the 13 soldiers killed on April 9. It said that Israeli forces, and particularly reservists, had been properly trained and equipped for the operation. At the same time it criticized the inadequate intelligence preparations for the force that went into the camp, faulty coordination between commanders, underestimation of the number of Palestinians present, mistakes in the deployment of forces so that they were not spread out sufficiently, and lack of proper cover for rescue operations for the Israeli wounded. As for the charges of "massacre," Maj.-Gen. Yitzhak Eitan, head of the army's Central Command and responsible for the operation, was quoted as saying that in destroying an important part of the terror infrastructure, the reservists had adhered to the codes of conduct and values of the IDF.

The Nativity Siege

As part of Operation Defensive Shield, Israeli troops had moved into Bethlehem on April 1, and two days later an estimated 200 Palestinians—many of them armed—sought refuge in the Church of the Nativity in Manger Square, which, in Christian tradition, marked the birthplace of Jesus. Already in the compound were about 35 friars, monks, and nuns who lived there. Israel set up a military cordon around the church because the "refuge-takers" included some 35–40 senior members of Hamas, Islamic Jihad, and Tanzim. For more than a month Israeli troops played cat-and-mouse with the Palestinians inside, not entering one of Christianity's holiest places so as not to defile or damage it, all the while suspecting that the Christian clergy inside were being held hostage. There were, however, intermittent exchanges of small-arms and sniper fire in which several Palestinians were killed and Israeli soldiers wounded. On April 8, the Vatican issued a statement expressing "extreme worry" at the situation in Bethlehem. During the course of the siege sporadic negotiations took place between Israeli and Palestinian officials to lift it—often with the intervention of U.S. or Vatican officials. In mid-April Israel allowed medicine and other supplies to be provided to the people in the complex, and on several occasions permitted wounded Palestinians and church officials to be evacuated from the building. But talks conducted April 23–24 reached an impasse as Israel insisted on the right to arrest any wanted terrorists found inside, and the Palestinians countered that only they had jurisdiction over the people in the church.

The siege was finally lifted on May 10, reportedly through the intervention of the CIA's Tel Aviv station chief and several European diplomats. Under the terms of the agreement reached between the two sides, 13 wanted men who were inside the compound were to go into exile. They were bused to Ben-Gurion Airport and flown, on a British military transport plane, to Cyprus, which had offered to hold them temporarily until a final destination was determined. Another 26 lower-level Palestinian militants were transferred to the Gaza Strip. Then the 84 people remaining—Palestinian police officers, clerics, and civilians (including ten American and European "peace activists")—left the building. On May 21, the EU reached agreement on the final destinations for the 13

Palestinians held in Cyprus: Spain and Italy each accepted three, Greece and Ireland two each, and Portugal and Belgium one apiece. They were to be held under conditions roughly equivalent to house arrest.

It took two more weeks for the siege of Arafat's compound in Ramallah to end, after Israel agreed to allow six men who had holed up in the complex—the four killers of Ze'evi, PFLP head Ahmed Sa'adat (who had ordered the Ze'vi killing in retaliation for Israel's 2001 assassination of his predecessor, Abu Ali Mustafa), and Fuad Shubeiki, a mastermind of the *Karine A* affair—to be transferred to a jail in Jericho, where they would be held under British and American supervision. A few days prior to the deal, a hastily set up PA "court" operating in the besieged Muq'ata had convicted the four assassins in the killing. In Israel's view, the conviction was an attempt to keep Israel from extraditing the four; in addition, Israel feared that without international supervision, the convicted men would be released quickly, in accordance with the PA policy of jailing those wanted by Israel for terror and then rapidly freeing them. In addition, Israel wanted assurances that Sa'adat and Shubeiki, who had not yet been tried, would be tried in the near future by a PA court. (A little more than a month later, the Palestinian High Court of Justice ordered Sa'adat's release on the grounds that there was not enough evidence against him to support a conviction for a role in Ze'evi's murder. But on June 3, the Palestinian cabinet said that it would ignore the court's order, which would have triggered a new crisis on the eve of a visit by CIA director George Tenet for separate talks with Sharon and Arafat to discuss reform of the Palestinian security services.)

The Bloodshed Continues

Operation Defensive Shield appeared to slow down the pace of violent incidents, but did not bring them to an end. In a resumption of Israel's policy of targeting known terrorist kingpins, Marwan Zaloum, a leader of the Tanzim in Hebron, was killed on April 23 when a missile fired from a helicopter hit his car. Zaloum was responsible for organizing attacks on Israeli targets, including an April 12 suicide bombing in Jerusalem. The next Palestinian strike did not take place until May 7, but it was deadly: a suicide bomber killed 16 and wounded 57 by blowing himself up at a pool hall/gambling club in Rishon Lezion. Though Palestinian security forces sought to head off Israeli retaliation by rounding up 23 low-level Hamas members in Gaza it said it suspected of involvement, Israeli troops massed on the border with the Gaza Strip and seemed ready to launch a major operation. But no attack ensued. Some observers suggested that with the recent events in Jenin still fresh, Israeli authorities did not want to risk another round of close-quarter fighting and the inevitable heavy casualties on both sides.

On May 22, Israeli tanks firing on the Balata refugee camp on the outskirts of Nablus killed local Al-Aqsa Martyrs Brigades commander Mahmoud Titti. In the following days there were suicide-bomb attacks in Rishon Lezion and Petah Tikvah, both near Tel Aviv, and an attempt— with a remote-control bomb—to blow up a fuel tanker truck at the Pi Glilot fuel depot, in a densely populated area of northern Tel Aviv.

On June 5, Islamic Jihad detonated a car bomb that blew up a bus at the Megiddo junction in the north of the country, killing 17. Four days later Palestinian security forces arrested Sheikh Abdallah Shami, a leader of Islamic Jihad, and 14 other members of the group that carried out the Megiddo attack. But the men were later freed as part of what Israel had long called the PA's "revolving door" practice of briefly jailing terrorists to create the appearance of fighting terror, and then letting them go. On June 11 a bomb killed a 15-year-old girl and wounded more than a dozen other Israelis in Herzliya; on June 18 a Hamas bus bomb killed 19 in Jerusalem; and on June 20, PFLP terrorists managed to get into Itamar, a settlement near Nablus, and killed five Israelis.

Israel began constructing a security fence around the West Bank on June 16 in the hope of preventing further suicide attacks. The electronically monitored fence, with different types of barriers depending on the varying terrains of the country, was expected to take a year to build. The first segment was to stretch for about 115 km along the northwest of the West Bank. But since Jewish settlements were interspersed with Arab communities in the region, demarking the lines would be no easy matter. Palestinians accused Israel of building the fence in such a way as to divide the territory of what they considered the future Palestinian state into separate Jewish and Arab cantons; settler residents of the West Bank (and their right-wing supporters) opposed the fence as the precursor of what would, in effect, be a new border for Israel, with a good number of the settlers on the outside.

After the June 19 Jerusalem bus bombing, Sharon's office said that Israel would henceforth respond to acts of terror "by capturing territory" and holding it for "as long as terror continues. Additional acts of terror will lead to the taking of additional areas." Following the announcement, Israeli forces moved into the towns of Jenin, Qalqilya, and Nablus, arresting about a dozen Palestinians. At least nine Palestinians died on

June 21 as the Israeli army stepped up its military response to the recent attacks. The dead included three Palestinian children and a teacher killed in Jenin in what Israeli military sources described as an error.

As the army continued to sweep through the West Bank and large numbers of reservists were called up, Defense Minister Ben-Eliezer said on June 23 that the recent Palestinian attacks demanded a "deep and thorough" military response. However, he denied reports in the press that the army was planning a permanent reoccupation of large tracts of the West Bank. Israeli forces moved into Ramallah on June 24. The next day soldiers moved into Hebron, completing the takeover of seven of the eight major Palestinian towns on the West Bank (the exception was Jericho, which had remained quiet).

The Bush Speech

On May 2, a few days before Sharon was due to arrive in Washington to see President Bush and other top officials—this was the fifth Bush-Sharon meeting during this presidency—Congress strengthened Sharon's hand by passing a resolution expressing solidarity with Israel's war against terror. The resolution was sponsored in the House by Tom Lantos (D., Cal.), a Holocaust survivor, and Republican whip Tom DeLay of Texas, and in the Senate by Joseph Lieberman (D., Conn.) and Gordon Smith (R., Ore.). The resolution passed despite delaying tactics by the White House, which traditionally objected to efforts by Congress to mix in foreign policy.

The day before Sharon's arrival, Bush's two top foreign-policy advisors differed publicly over Jewish settlements in the Territories, one of the key issues on the agenda. "Something has to be done about the problem of the settlements. . . . [which] continue to grow and to expand," Secretary of State Powell told "Meet The Press" on May 5. But National Security Advisor Condoleezza Rice, interviewed on Fox News at about the same time, took a different tack. "Let's take one thing at a time. Settlements will eventually be an issue, but I think we have to get the context right here. We need to end terror," she said.

Sharon arrived on May 6, but had to leave for home the next day after the terror attack in Rishon Lezion. Sharon had came with a report prepared by Minister Without Portfolio Danny Naveh, a Likud politician often considered to be an ally of Sharon's rival Netanyahu, that seemed to prove Arafat's personal involvement in directing terror activities. Among the items in the report was evidence that in January, Marwan

Barghouti, the head of Fatah-Tanzim who had been captured in Operation Defensive Shield, wrote in his own handwriting to Arafat requesting payment of "a thousand dollars for each of the fighter brethren"— all Fatah operatives from Tul Karm involved in lethal attacks against Israelis. Arafat cut Barghouti's request to $350 per terrorist, and then put his signature in Arabic on the Barghouti document approving payment. In Naveh's view, the new information should bar the Palestinian leader from involvement in any future talks.

Following up on a U.S. agreement that no progress could take place without significant changes in the PA, Sharon told the Knesset on May 14 that the Palestinian Authority "must be reformed in every respect" before Israel would enter into negotiations with it. Arafat responded the next day in a speech to the Palestinian Legislative Assembly by promising a "complete revision" of the political system and immediate preparation for fresh elections. A senior Arafat aide followed up by declaring that his boss had decided to hold presidential and legislative elections within six months as part of a broader reform package—though Arafat himself, in another speech on May 17, insisted that elections could not be held until Israeli forces withdrew from the West Bank and Gaza Strip. President Mubarak of Egypt visited Washington June 7–8 to suggest establishment of a Palestinian state perhaps as early as 2003, but Bush said that Washington was "not ready to lay down a specific calendar."

Sharon returned to the U.S. on June 10, and the president endorsed his demand that the Palestinian leadership be overhauled before meaningful peace talks could restart. Another sign of which way the Washington wind was blowing came from Condoleezza Rice, who was quoted by Britain's left-leaning *Guardian* newspaper on June 17 as saying that the PA was a corrupt body "that cavorts with terror."

The Bush and Rice statements set the stage for the president's landmark address on the Middle East, delivered in the White House Rose Garden on June 24. In it, Bush declared that the Palestinian people would only achieve a state of their own if they initiated "new leadership, new institutions, and new security arrangements." He called on the Palestinians to "elect new leaders, leaders not compromised by terror" and implicitly accused Arafat—whom he did not mention by name—of heading an authority that was rife with "official corruption" and was "encouraging, not opposing, terrorism." If the Palestinians undertook reforms and ensured Israeli security, Bush said that negotiations could begin on borders, refugees, and the future of Jerusalem as part of final-status talks. He also repeated calls for an Israeli military withdrawal to positions held before the start of the new intifada in September 2000, and an end to settlement activity in the Territories.

Israeli officials hailed the speech as a sign that Bush was lining up behind Sharon. Almost immediately after its delivery, the Prime Minister's Office in Jerusalem issued a statement that said, in part: "Israel is a country that desires peace. Prime Minister Ariel Sharon has said on numerous occasions that when there is a complete cessation of terror, violence and incitement, and when the Palestinian Authority enacts genuine reforms, including new leadership at the top, such that a different Authority is created, then it will be possible to discuss how to make progress on the political tracks."

Zalman Shoval, a senior Likud political figure and former ambassador to the U.S., called it a "remarkable" speech and said that Bush was "backing up the Israeli position that the key to progress on the political track must be an end to terror and violence — not just a reform, not just something cosmetic, but a real change in the Palestinian leadership." David Landau, a left-leaning journalist and English-language editor of *Ha'aretz,* conceded that the speech was a triumph for Sharon. "Yasir Arafat, the seemingly immortal leader of the Palestinian national movement, was politically assassinated Monday by President George W. Bush. His role as Israel's prospective partner in any future diplomatic process was effectively snuffed out by a stern-sounding American president, delivering his verdict on two years of violent intifada and his recipe for a turnabout towards peace in this war-torn region," Landau wrote, adding: "At the end of last year, the Israeli prime minister seemed either naive or perverse, or both, when he pledged to render Arafat 'irrelevant.' Now, he can cogently contend, he has won his case convincingly before what for Israel is the highest court of world opinion: the U.S. government."

Palestinian officials reacted to the speech with dismay. Though Planning Minister Nabil Shaath tried to put on an optimistic face by saying that Bush had made numerous demands on Israel, Sa'eb Erakat, the senior Palestinian negotiator, called Bush's call for a new leadership unacceptable. Arafat himself, speaking on June 25, dismissed Bush's call, asserting that only the Palestinian people could decide on their leaders. The next day — with Bush off to the G-8 summit in Canada where his demand to oust Arafat was a major topic of discussion — Erakat was already saying that elections would be held in January 2003. (On December 22, however, the PA would announce that the elections — which had, in the interim, been scheduled for January 20, 2003 — were postponed indefinitely.)

Ari Fleischer, the White House spokesman, emphasized that Bush's speech was merely an outline, and that there was still much to be done. Fleischer said: "The president has planted the seeds of peace. Now it's up to the parties to nurture those seeds."

FULL TEXT OF THE SPEECH

"For too long, the citizens of the Middle East have lived in the midst of death and fear. The hatred of a few holds the hopes of many hostage. The forces of extremism and terror are attempting to kill progress and peace by killing the innocent. And this casts a dark shadow over an entire region. For the sake of all humanity, things must change in the Middle East. It is untenable for Israeli citizens to live in terror. It is untenable for Palestinians to live in squalor and occupation. And the current situation offers no prospect that life will improve. Israeli citizens will continue to be victimized by terrorists, and so Israel will continue to defend herself.

"In the situation the Palestinian people will grow more and more miserable. My vision is two states, living side by side in peace and security. There is simply no way to achieve that peace until all parties fight terror. Yet, at this critical moment, if all parties will break with the past and set out on a new path, we can overcome the darkness with the light of hope. Peace requires a new and different Palestinian leadership, so that a Palestinian state can be born. I call on the Palestinian people to elect new leaders, leaders not compromised by terror. I call upon them to build a practising democracy, based on tolerance and liberty. If the Palestinian people actively pursue these goals, America and the world will actively support their efforts. If the Palestinian people meet these goals, they will be able to reach agreement with Israel and Egypt and Jordan on security and other arrangements for independence. And when the Palestinian people have new leaders, new institutions, and new security arrangements with their neighbors, the United States of America will support the creation of a Palestinian state whose borders and certain aspects of its sovereignty will be provisional until resolved as part of a final settlement in the Middle East.

"In the work ahead, we all have responsibilities. The Palestinian people are gifted and capable, and I am confident they can achieve a new birth for their nation. A Palestinian state will never be created by terror—it will be built through reform. And reform must be more than cosmetic change, or veiled attempt to preserve the status quo. True reform will require entirely new political and economic institutions, based on democracy, market economics, and action against terrorism. Today, the elected Palestinian legislature has no authority, and power is concentrated in the hands of an unaccountable few. A Palestinian state can only serve its citizens with a new constitution which separates the powers of government. The Palestinian parliament should have the full authority of a legislative body. Local officials and government ministers need authority of their own and the independence to govern effectively.

"The United States, along with the European Union and Arab states, will work with Palestinian leaders to create a new constitutional framework, and a working democracy for the Palestinian people. And the United States, along with others in the international community, will help the Palestinians organize and monitor fair, multi-party local elections by the end of the year, with national elections to follow. Today, the Palestinian people live in economic stagnation, made worse by official corruption. A Palestinian state will require a vibrant economy, where honest enterprise is encouraged by honest government. The United States, the international donor community and the World Bank stand ready to work with Palestinians on a major project of economic reform and development. The United States, the EU, the World Bank, and the International Monetary Fund are willing to oversee reforms in Palestinian finances, encouraging transparency and independent auditing. And the United States, along with our partners in the developed world, will increase our humanitarian assistance to relieve Palestinian suffering. Today, the Palestinian people lack effective courts of law and have no means to defend and vindicate their rights. A Palestinian state will require a system of reliable justice to punish those who prey on the innocent. The United States and members of the international community stand ready to work with Palestinian leaders to establish, finance, and monitor a truly independent judiciary.

"Today, Palestinian authorities are encouraging, not opposing, terrorism. This is unacceptable. And the United States will not support the establishment of a Palestinian state until its leaders engage in a sustained fight against the terrorists and dismantle their infrastructure. This will require an externally supervised effort to rebuild and reform the Palestinian security services. The security system must have clear lines of authority and accountability and a unified chain of command. America is pursuing this reform along with key regional states. The world is prepared to help, yet ultimately these steps toward statehood depend on the Palestinian people and their leaders. If they energetically take the path of reform, the rewards can come quickly. If Palestinians embrace democracy, confront corruption and firmly reject terror, they can count on American support for the creation of a provisional state of Palestine.

"With a dedicated effort, this state could rise rapidly, as it comes to terms with Israel, Egypt, and Jordan on practical issues, such as security. The final borders, the capital, and other aspects of this state's sovereignty will be negotiated between the parties, as part of a final settlement. Arab states have offered their help in this process, and their help is needed. I've said in the past that nations are either with us or against us in the war on terror. To be counted on the side of peace, nations must act. Every leader actually committed to peace will end incitement to violence in official media, and publicly denounce homicide bombings. Every nation actually committed to peace will stop the flow of money, equipment, and recruits to terrorist groups seeking the destruction of Israel—including Hamas, Islamic Jihad, and Hezballah. Every nation actually committed to peace must block the shipment of Iranian supplies to these groups, and oppose regimes that promote terror, like Iraq. And Syria must choose the right side in the war on terror by closing terrorist camps and expelling terrorist organizations. Leaders who want to be included in the peace process must show by their deeds an undivided support for peace. And as we move toward a peaceful solution, Arab states will be expected to build closer ties of diplomacy and commerce with Israel, leading to full normalisation of relations between Israel and the entire Arab world.

"Israel also has a large stake in the success of a democratic Palestine. Permanent occupation threatens Israel's identity and democracy. A stable, peaceful Palestinian state is necessary to achieve the security that Israel longs for. So I challenge Israel to take concrete steps to support the emergence of a viable, credible Palestinian state. As we make progress towards security, Israeli forces need to withdraw fully to positions they held prior to September 28, 2000. And consistent with the recommendations of the Mitchell Committee, Israeli settlement activity in the occupied territories must stop. The Palestinian economy must be allowed to develop. As violence subsides, freedom of movement should be restored, permitting innocent Palestinians to resume work and normal life. Palestinian legislators and officials, humanitarian and international workers, must be allowed to go about the business of building a better future. And Israel should release frozen Palestinian revenues into honest, accountable hands. I've asked Secretary Powell to work intensively with Middle Eastern and international leaders to realize the vision of a Palestinian state, focusing them on a comprehensive plan to support Palestinian reform and institution-building.

"Ultimately, Israelis and Palestinians must address the core issues that divide them if there is to be a real peace, resolving all claims and ending the conflict between them. This means that the Israeli occupation that began in 1967 will be ended through a settlement negotiated between the parties, based on U.N. Resolutions 242 and 338, with Israeli withdrawal to secure and recognized borders. We must also resolve questions concerning Jerusalem, the plight and future of Palestinian refugees, and a final peace between Israel and Lebanon, and Israel and a Syria that supports peace and fights terror. All who are familiar with the history of the Middle East realize that there may be setbacks in this process. Trained and determined killers, as we have seen, want to stop it. Yet the Egyptian and Jordanian peace treaties with Israel remind us that with determined and responsible leadership, progress can come quickly. As new Palestinian institutions and new leaders emerge, demonstrating real performance on security and reform, I expect Israel to respond and work toward a final status agreement. With intensive effort by all, this agreement could be reached within three years from now. And I and my country will actively lead toward that goal.

"I can understand the deep anger and anguish of the Israeli people. You've lived too long with fear and funerals, having to avoid markets and public transportation, and forced to put armed guards in kindergarten classrooms. The Palestinian Authority has rejected your offer at hand, and trafficked with terrorists. You have a right to a normal life; you have a right to security; and I deeply believe that you need a reformed, responsible Palestinian partner to achieve that security. I can understand the deep anger and despair of the Palestinian people. For decades you've been treated as pawns in the Middle East conflict. Your interests have been held hostage to a comprehensive peace agreement that never seems to come, as your lives get worse year by year. You deserve democracy and the rule of law. You deserve an open society and a thriving economy. You deserve a life of hope for your children. An end to occupation and a peaceful democratic Palestinian state may seem distant, but America and our partners throughout the world stand ready to help, help you make them possible as soon as possible. If liberty can blossom in the rocky soil of the West Bank and Gaza, it will inspire millions of men and women around the globe who are equally weary of poverty and oppression, equally entitled to the benefits of democratic government.

"I have a hope for the people of Muslim countries. Your commitments to morality, and learning, and tolerance led to great historical achievements. And those values are alive in the Islamic world today. You have a rich culture, and you share the aspirations of men and women in every culture. Prosperity and freedom and dignity are not just American hopes, or Western hopes. They are universal, human hopes. And even in the violence and turmoil of the Middle East, America believes those hopes have the power to transform lives and nations. This moment is both an opportunity and a test for all parties in the Middle East: an opportunity to lay the foundations for future peace; a test to show who is serious about peace and who is not. The choice here is stark and simple. The Bible says, 'I have set before you life and death; therefore, choose life.' The time has arrived for everyone in this conflict to choose peace, and hope, and life.

"Thank you very much."

The Fallout

In meetings he held in early July with top French and Italian security officials, Shin Bet security service head Avi Dichter passed on the impression that despite Bush's statement, Arafat had not accepted the idea that he was going to be pushed out. In fact, according to a report in *Ha'aretz* on July 14, Arafat believed he could "leave the head intact and attach a new body underneath it, rather than the other way around," wrote Amir Oren, a commentator on defense and security affairs. Dichter told Nicholas Sarkozy, the French interior minister, that Arafat's mental function had deteriorated and that his behavior was increasingly marked by faulty judgement. Still, there were signs that Arafat was moving—perhaps only for appearance's sake—in the direction of reform. In early July, he dismissed four of his most senior security chiefs and put the various Palestinian forces under one command. Reportedly assisting the Palestinians in carrying out this reform were the CIA and officials from Egypt, Jordan, and Saudi Arabia.

The most prominent of those dismissed was Col. Jibril Rajoub, formerly head of the Fatah-controlled Preventive Security Force (PSF). Rajoub had not only established sound relations with Israeli, U.S., and European intelligence services, but had also headed one of the few Palestinian security agencies not actively engaged in fighting the Israelis in some way or other. One theory was that Rajoub had gained Arafat's disfavor during Operation Defensive Shield when he allowed Israel to enter his headquarters in Beituna, near Ramallah. In a statement issued July 5, the Palestinian National Authority said that Arafat had decided to "relieve" Rajoub of his responsibilities as commander of the PSF and to replace him with Zuheir Manasra, a former governor of Jenin. Rajoub initially described his dismissal as "disrespectful" and accepted it only after a 48-hour stand-off. On July 6 he told reporters that senior officers within the PSF would not accept Manasra as their commander, and demanded that someone from "inside the PSF" be appointed to replace him. Amid calls throughout the West Bank for Rajoub's reinstatement, Arafat met with him on July 7 and offered him a number of high-ranking posts, including deputy interior minister, minister without portfolio, and presidential security adviser.

Also dismissed as part of the reform process was Gen. Ghazi Jabali, the chief of the Palestinian police, and Mahmoud Abu Mazouq, the head of civil defense. Both were hated by local Palestinians for their corruption and for their tough way of dealing with political opponents. Jabali was replaced by his deputy, Col. Salim Bardini. It was also reported that Tawfiq Tirawi, who had recently been placed on Israel's "most wanted" list, had been dismissed as the West Bank's intelligence chief.

A fresh international diplomatic initiative was launched in New York in mid-July at a meeting of the Quartet—EU representative for foreign and security affairs Javier Solana, Russian foreign minister Igor Ivanov, UN secretary-general Kofi Annan, and Powell. The Quartet reportedly considered a number of new proposals, including the appointment of a prime minister to take on the day-to-day responsibilities of running the PA, leaving Arafat as a figurehead; the appointment of a Security Council envoy to oversee implementation of PA political reforms and establish security cooperation with Israel; and increased "burden-sharing" between the U.S. and the EU in resolving the conflict, a proposal put forward by German foreign minister Joschka Fischer. The Quartet, and later Bush, also met with the foreign ministers of Jordan, Egypt, and Saudi Arabia. Bush took the opportunity to reiterate the call he made in his June speech for a new Palestinian leadership. The issue, he said, "was much bigger than one person."

In early August, Secretary of Defense Donald Rumsfeld seriously upset the Palestinians. At a meeting with Department of Defense workers at the Pentagon, Rumsfeld questioned the idea of Israel handing over territory to the PA if the latter "cannot or will not" enforce security measures. And he added: "My feelings about the so-called occupied territories are that there was a war, Israel urged neighboring countries not to get involved in it once it started, they all jumped in, and they lost a lot of real estate to Israel because Israel prevailed in that conflict."

Powell and Rice held talks on civil reform efforts and security cooperation with a delegation of Palestinian cabinet ministers—including Erakat, Interior Minister Abd al-Razaq al-Yahya, and Trade and Industry Minister Maher al-Masri—in Washington on August 8–9. It was the highest-level U.S.-Palestinian Authority meeting since Bush's speech in June. According to the Palestinians, Powell reaffirmed U.S. support for the creation of a Palestinian state within three years, but sidestepped the issue of Arafat's leadership.

A Violent Summer

Israel maintained its tight military siege on Palestinian towns, villages, and refugee camps through the summer, justifying the policy as necessary to deter would-be terrorists from crossing over into Israel. The curfews and disruption of travel had a devastating impact on the Palestinian economy, and there were reports of hunger and malnutrition.

Israel continued its policy of targeted assassinations. On June 30, Muhamad Taher, of Nablus, was killed by a tank shell. He was reportedly the mastermind of the June 18 suicide bomb attack on a Jerusalem bus as well as the attack on the Tel Aviv Dolphinarium on June 1, 2001 that killed 20 young Israelis. Sharon called the liquidation of Taher "a very important operation" of self-defense, but Hamas leader Abd al-Aziz Rantisi considered it "a dirty crime" and warned of retaliation. On July 23, Salah Shehadeh, the leader in Gaza of the Izz al-Din al-Qassam Battalions—the military wing of Hamas—was killed when his home was bombed from an airplane. Twelve others were also killed, including Shehadeh's wife and three of his children, and an estimated 140 were injured, 16 critically. Rantisi this time threatened that "retaliation will come very soon. Nor will there be only one retaliation. After this even Israelis in their homes will be targeted." Others criticized the attack for its apparent indifference to the fate of innocent civilians. Arafat called it a "massacre," the U.S. described it as a "heavy-handed action" that did not "contribute to peace," and Kofi Annan charged that Israel was legally and morally culpable for the heavy civilian toll. Some questioned the timing of Israel's action since it appeared to undermine tentative diplomatic developments under way since early July—talks between Foreign Minister Peres and a number of Palestinian ministers, and others between various Palestinian factions over reaching a cease-fire.

Two days later, July 25, Israeli troops were back on one of a series of increasingly frequent incursions into PA areas of Gaza, reacting to Hamas missile and mortar attacks by hitting at buildings where the ammunition had been manufactured. On the West Bank, a number of drive-by shootings killed five Israelis over two days, including three members of one family near Hebron. Settlers in Hebron's small Jewish enclave retaliated by going on a rampage through adjacent Arab areas; Palestinians said that one girl was killed and nine other people wounded by the settlers, who had the reputation of being some of the most radical living in the Territories. On July 30, two Israelis were shot dead by Palestinian gunmen when they entered the West Bank village of Ja'main, apparently to sell fuel to the villagers.

Seven people were killed when a bomb exploded in the Frank Sinatra cafeteria at the Hebrew University's Mt. Scopus campus in Jerusalem on July 31. About 80 others were wounded in the attack, which took place during the busy lunchtime hour. The person responsible was Hamas operative Muhammad Oudeh, 29, of the village of Silwan, east of the Temple Mount, who worked at the university: he tossed the bomb over a fence onto the grounds of the university the day before, and, the next day, picked it up and placed it in the cafeteria. Oudeh was part of a five-man East Jerusalem Hamas cell—it became known as the Silwan gang—which security forces arrested on August 17. The cell was responsible as well for a number of other incidents that had killed 37 Israelis and injured hundreds—including the May attack in Rishon Lezion and the March bombing of the Moment Café in Jerusalem. Four of its members, as residents of East Jerusalem, held blue Israeli identity cards, allowing them free movement not only in Jerusalem but throughout Israel. (On December 15, the Jerusalem District Court would sentence them to terms ranging from 60 years to life.)

Nine Israelis, including six soldiers, were killed, and over 50 others injured on August 4 in a suicide-bomb attack on a bus near Safed in northern Israel, close to the border with Lebanon. A Sharon aide said the incident proved, again, that "Palestinian terrorists view terrorism against innocent Israeli civilians as a feeding frenzy and their appetite for murder is never quite satisfied." In the U.S., President Bush said he was "distressed" by the attack and called upon "all nations to do everything they can to stop these terrorist killers." Israel ratcheted up restrictions on the Territories, imposing a total closure on the West Bank, and continued its policy of targeted elimination of key figures in the infrastructure of terror, killing the Al-Aqsa Martyrs Brigades Tul Karm commander Ziad Daas; Hussein Nimr, the son of senior Gaza Hamas figure Ahmed Nimr; and Nasr Jarrar, a leader of Izz al-Din al-Quassam, in Tubas, near Jenin.

August was also the month of "Gaza first," the suggestion of Defense Minister Ben-Eliezer that a withdrawal from parts of Area A occupied by Israel over the previous month should begin in Gaza and in the West

Bank town of Bethlehem. This, he said, would be a pilot scheme to test whether Palestinian security forces alone could control the militants. The proposal appeared to catch the Palestinian leadership off guard, and there were conflicting initial comments from ministers. Palestinian and Israeli security officials met on August 8 to discuss Ben-Eliezer's proposal in greater detail. At the end of the meeting, the Palestinian side accused the Israelis of reneging on an offer to extend the trial to Bethlehem, and the plan appeared in danger. However, the Defense Ministry announced on August 18 that agreement had been reached to implement the plan on condition that "the Palestinian side takes responsibility to calm the security situation and reduce violence." The deal was sealed at a meeting between Ben-Eliezer, Palestinian interior minister Yehiye, and top PA security official Muhammad Dahlan.

Accordingly, Israeli forces withdrew from Bethlehem on August 19 and were reported to be poised to withdraw from parts of the Gaza Strip as well. But tensions rose on August 20, when Israeli commandos from the elite Duvdevan antiterror unit, which sometimes carried out operations in traditional Arab dress, shot dead Mohammed Sa'adat at his home in Ramallah. Sa'adat was the younger brother of Ahmed Sa'adat, secretary general of the Popular Front for the Liberation of Palestine (PFLP), who had been held in a Palestinian prison in Jericho since May as part of the agreement that had led to the end of an Israeli siege of Arafat's headquarters in Ramallah. According to Israeli reports, the intention had been to arrest Sa'adat, but he attempted to flee, pulled a weapon and began firing at the Israelis, who were dressed in civilian clothes. The soldiers fired back, killing him. The PFLP vowed revenge.

On August 23, additional attacks by Palestinians forced Israeli officials to announce that implementation of "Gaza first" had been "frozen." Speaking on August 26, Defense Minister Ben-Eliezer said that there would be no further withdrawals at least until the end of the Jewish High Holy Days in September. Two days later, Ben-Eliezer called off a fresh round of scheduled security talks after Palestinians shelled a settlement in Gaza with mortars.

On August 27, Israel announced that seven Israeli Arabs, all from one clan in the northern village of Ba'na, had been arrested on charges of assisting the Hamas suicide bomber who had carried out the bus attack in Safed on August 4. In particular, two young men—Ibrahim Bakri and his cousin Yassin Bakri—helped the suicide bomber choose a target and location for the attack, hid him in their village before the attack, and even bought the batteries used to detonate the bomb. Earlier, police had arrested Yasra Bakri, who, with her friend Samiya Assedi, had gotten off the bus after the suicide bomber, when he got on, warned her that something bad was about to happen. The two women, students at a college in Safed, left the bus 20 minutes before the blast took place without warning anyone else. Yasra Bakri was charged with failure to prevent a crime.

Two weeks later, on September 9, Israel for the first time revoked the citizenship of an Israeli Arab, Nahad Abu Kishaq, accusing him of helping Hamas attackers enter Israel to carry out suicide attacks. Abu Kishaq's Israeli identity card had enabled him to move around Israel legally, it said.

Revelations that some Israeli Arabs were tied to terrorism sent shock waves through the Israeli public, raising the possibility that the message of the militant Palestinian organizations had made deep inroads into the Arab population dwelling inside the pre-1967 borders (as opposed to the Arabs of East Jerusalem, who were Israeli residents only post-1967 and therefore never trusted as loyal Israelis). Right-of-center Israeli politicians reacted strongly. National Religious Party MK Zevulun Orlev blamed his Arab colleagues in the Knesset, whose expressions of support for terrorism, he charged, encouraged Israeli Arabs to get involved in such activities. "These leaders cannot absolve themselves of responsibility," he said. Herut MK Michael Kleiner went further, claiming that most Israeli Arabs were loyal not to the state, but to the Palestinian struggle. "The Palestinian problem does not stop at the Green Line," he said. Kleiner suggested the adoption of the death penalty for citizens involved in terrorism, and called for encouraging "hostile citizens" to emigrate.

At the same time that the involvement of some Israeli Arabs in terror angered Israeli Jews, rumors of Palestinians helping Israel set off similar feelings among Palestinian militants, though the results were bloodier—members of the Al-Aqsa Martyrs Brigades killed two "collaborators," both women, in Tul Karm. On August 24, they dragged Ikhlas Khouli, 35, a mother of seven, from her home and shot her dead in a public square. She was reported to be the first Arab woman to be executed during the intifada for collaboration. The second woman, Rajah Ibrahim, 18, was killed on August 30. Palestinian sources said that Ibrahim had provided information to Israeli security services that allowed troops to track down and kill Ra'ed al-Karmi in mid-January.

Eleven Palestinians were killed in several violent incidents over the August 31–September 1 weekend. These included two small children playing outside their home when they were struck by an errant missile aimed at a terrorist leader in Tubas, near Nablus, and four men shot near

Hebron who, Palestinians said, were unarmed workers returning from a night shift in a nearby quarry. Defense Minister Ben-Eliezer ordered the army to investigate these incidents.

Though the number of successful attacks on Israeli targets was lower than the levels reached during the blood-filled spring, efforts to mount such attacks continued. What could easily have been the bloodiest attack ever was averted on September 5, when two border policemen and four border police volunteers intercepted two vehicles in the Wadi Ara area in northern Israel. One of them was packed with about 600 kg (1,300 lbs.) of high explosives, two containers of fuel, metal objects designed to maximize casualties, a cell phone—apparently to detonate the bomb—and a video camera to record the event—as Hezballah terrorists used to do against Israeli troops in Lebanon, before the May 2001 withdrawal. Police sappers detonated the bomb, which was too dangerous to move. The blast was huge, but there were no injuries. Foreign Minister Peres said that had it reached its probable target in a major population center, the bomb could have caused "such a loss of life that it would have changed almost the entire political situation in one moment."

A Deteriorating Situation

On September 9, Arafat, who had not left his Muq'ata compound in Ramallah in months, condemned "every act of terror against Israeli civilians" in a speech to the Palestinian Legislative Council. "We have to reiterate our condemnation of attacks against Israeli civilians and at the same time of any attacks against Palestinian civilians," he said. At the same time, Arafat, transparently attempting to divert the pressure on his leadership created by the Bush speech of June 24, called on the council to hold a special session to review the reforms that the Palestinian cabinet had adopted, as well as his cabinet shake-up, which had drawn criticism for not going far enough. He affirmed a January date for presidential and legislative elections. Dore Gold, the American-born former Israeli ambassador to the UN now serving as a Sharon policy adviser and spokesperson, said he saw little new in Arafat's remarks. "A partner who is responsible will not have security services manned by operatives of terror organizations," Gold said. "We expect transparency in the use of international funds. None of that was heard in this speech. It was very little new in what was said."

A few days later, Arafat suffered a major humiliation when his cabinet was forced to resign to avoid losing a vote of no-confidence in the Palestinian Legislative Council. "President Arafat has accepted the resignation of the cabinet, so there is no need to bring the cabinet to a vote," Tayeb Abdel Rahim, secretary of the Palestinian presidency, told legislators. "In the next 14 days, President Arafat will appoint a new cabinet." This challenge to Arafat's autocratic leadership came on the third day of the first meeting of the Palestinian Legislative Council to be held in more than 18 months, and was directed against the 21-member cabinet Arafat had only appointed on June 9. One of the leaders of the no-confidence initiative, Abdel Jawad Saleh, who had resigned from the cabinet two years earlier, said: "Arafat is trying to buy the Fatah people. I hope they vote against the government." The rebels wanted Arafat to sack ministers seen as inefficient and corrupt, or face rejection of the entire cabinet. (Arafat would finally appoint a new cabinet on October 29, and get the PA legislators to approve by telling them that a vote against it would be a vote for Israel and the Americans. The most noteworthy change in the cabinet was the replacement of Abd al-Razaq al-Yahya, who supported reform and was well-liked by the Americans, with long-time PLO apparatchik Hani al-Hassan at the Interior Ministry.)

In mid-September, the lull in suicide-bomb attacks, which had lasted more than a month since the Safed bus bombing, resumed. A police officer was killed by a bomb near the northern Arab town of Umm al-Fahm on September 18, and the next day five Israelis and a British student were killed and 50 others hurt by a bus bomb in central Tel Aviv. Israel responded by sending tanks and troops into Arafat's compound in Ramallah. Using amplifiers, Israeli soldiers called for the surrender of 20 wanted men who had taken refuge in the compound, including Tawfiq Tirawi, commander of West Bank intelligence. Arafat, now isolated from the outside world and confined to the only building left standing in the Muq'ata, called for international intervention. The siege was criticized by several foreign leaders including President Bush, who said it was "not helpful." In Israel, some critics called the action counterproductive since it only enhanced Arafat's prestige.

UN Security Council Resolution 1435, sponsored by Bulgaria, France, Norway, Ireland, and the United Kingdom, was approved on September 24. It called for an immediate end to the Israeli measures "in and around Ramallah including the destruction of Palestinian civilian and security infrastructure" and the "expeditious withdrawal of the Israeli occupying forces from Palestinian cities towards the return to the positions held prior to September 2000," while also urging the PA to fulfill its earlier commitment to bring terrorists to justice. The U.S., which abstained on the resolution, also called on Israel to pull back. Israel lifted the siege of Arafat's compound on September 29. Moments after emerging, Arafat criticized the Israeli withdrawal as merely "cosmetic." An Israeli cabinet statement said that the decision had been made because of "the deep friendship between Israel and the United States" and Israel's desire to do all it could "to enhance . . . strategic cooperation and relations" with the Americans.

Jewish settlers killed a Palestinian farmer and wounded another while the Palestinians were picking olives in a village near the West Bank town of Nablus and the Jewish settlement of Akraba on October 6. In a separate clash the same day, Israeli police arrested a settler near the West Bank village of Luban al-Sharkiyeh on charges of shooting and wounding a Palestinian. Three other Israelis were also arrested.

As many as 15 people were killed on October 7, when an Israeli helicopter fired a rocket into a crowd of Palestinians in Khan Yunis in the Gaza Strip. Palestinians said that the helicopter had, without provocation, fired a rocket into a crowd of people who had emerged from their houses thinking that an earlier Israeli raid had ended. But the Israelis claimed that Palestinian gunmen had shot at them as they retreated, and that they were returning fire. The Palestinians said that the dead were all civilians; the Israeli army said all but one were militants. As the wounded were arriving in hospital, Palestinians charged, Israeli troops opened fire, killing one man and injuring three others.

Shortly afterwards, four more Palestinians died during an outbreak of fighting between Hamas members and Palestinian security forces loyal to Arafat. What set off the Hamas-PA battle was the kidnapping and killing of a senior Palestinian police commander, Col. Rajeh Abu Lehiya, by Hamas gunmen. Hamas leaders said that the killing was part of a private blood feud and denied any involvement.

On October 9, Israeli troops shot dead two youths and wounded 18 other people in the Rafah refugee camp in southern Gaza. An Israeli woman was killed and 16 people injured the next day when a Hamas suicide bomber blew himself up near a bus outside Tel Aviv after the driver and a passenger foiled his attempt to board. Two Palestinians, one a boy aged three, were killed and more than 30 wounded in the Gaza Strip on October 13, when Israeli troops demolished houses in the Rafah camp.

Israeli security forces reportedly used a booby-trapped public telephone outside a hospital in Bethlehem to blow up and kill Mohammed Abayat, a member of the Al-Aqsa Martyrs Brigades, which had links with Arafat's mainstream Fatah faction, on October 14. Palestinian officials claimed that the intended target had actually been Nasser Abayat, the commander of Tanzim, the military wing of Fatah, in Bethlehem. Israeli tank shells killed at least six Palestinians and wounded 50 others in the Rafah camp in the Gaza Strip on October 17, after gunmen reportedly fired at army bulldozers.

Israeli troops withdrew from the West Bank town of Jenin on October 18 after digging a trench around part of the town to stop would-be suicide bombers from leaving in cars. The move meant that Israeli forces, which had invaded seven West Bank cities and towns in June, had now pulled back from two—Jenin and Bethlehem—while continuing to occupy the others.

At least 14 people were killed and more than 50 injured on October 21 when Palestinian bombers detonated explosives in a car next to a bus near the northern Israeli city of Hadera. The attack was claimed by Islamic Jihad, which had carried out a similar car bombing in June at Megiddo junction, which killed 17 people (see above, p. 208). Many of those killed in the latest attack were soldiers traveling from northern Israel near the Lebanese border to Tel Aviv. Israel reacted by canceling a planned partial withdrawal from Hebron. It also imposed a ban on Palestinians drilling for water—insisting that the PNA was conducting a "water intifada"—and barred olive picking at the height of the harvest. However, amid reports of U.S. concerns that escalating violence could disrupt plans for possible military action against Iraq, Israel refrained from immediate military retaliation. But on October 25, Israeli soldiers, backed by tanks and armored vehicles, moved back into Jenin, tightening their grip on the West Bank city from which they had withdrawn a week earlier. The army said it was pursuing terrorists. At the same time, the army withdrew from parts of Hebron, retaining control only of the divided city's strategic heights.

A suicide bombing at Ariel in the West Bank on October 27 killed three Israeli reserve soldiers and wounded at least 18 others. The bomber, Mohammed Ishkair from Nablus, who had been on Israel's most-wanted list and was an Al-Aqsa member, blew himself up outside a gas station. Further north, Israeli troops shot dead two Al-Aqsa activists driving through Nablus. An IDF spokesman said that the soldiers had told the two to stop, but they opened fire and were killed in the exchange.

A lone gunman infiltrated Kibbutz Metzer, south of Haifa, on the night of November 10, killing five Israelis and escaping. This attack came as a particular shock because of the kibbutz's good relations with surrounding Arab villages. In response, Israel sent troops back into Tul

Karm and Nablus, accompanied by tanks and helicopters, where they arrested dozens of terror suspects.

Twelve Israelis—all soldiers or security guards—were killed and 20 others injured in a November 14 ambush on a procession of settlers walking back to Kiryat Arba from Friday night prayers at the Machpelah Cave, the Tomb of the Patriarchs, in Hebron, along a route known locally as Worshipers' Lane. The dead included Col. Dror Weinberg, the army's Hebron commander and the highest-ranking Israeli officer to be killed in the current intifada. Weinberg and the other Israelis died during a 90-minute gun battle after being ambushed by three Islamic Jihad men. Israeli forces imposed a curfew on Hebron, a divided city with 450 Jewish settlers and 130,000 Palestinians. On the following Saturday night, about 1,500 settlers demonstrated in Hebron demanding that the three civilians who died in the attack be given a military burial. The men "fought like soldiers and should be buried like soldiers," said Kiryat Arba local council head Zvi Katzover. Meanwhile, Prime Minister Sharon said he favored taking control of land along the Worshipers' Lane so as to establish territorial contiguity between Hebron and the outlying Kiryat Arba.

A 13-year-old girl on her way to school and an eight-year-old boy and his grandmother were among the 11 victims of a suicide bombing in Jerusalem's Ir Ganim-Kiryat Menachem neighborhood, not far from the Hadassah Medical Center in Ein Karem, on November 21. The next day, Israeli troops moved back into Bethlehem and imposed a curfew. That was the same day that British aid worker Iain Hook, 54, was killed by an Israeli sniper during a clash with terrorists holed up in the UNRWA compound in the Jenin refugee camp. Israel admitted that Hook had been killed by mistake.

Terror, Foreign and Domestic

Three Israelis, two of them children, and ten Kenyans were killed and dozens wounded in a two-pronged Al Qaeda terror attack on Israeli vacationers in Mombasa, Kenya, on November 28. An SUV filled with explosives drove into the Paradise Beach, an Israeli-owned hotel on the Indian Ocean coast just outside Mombasa, and blew it up just as a group of Israelis was arriving. At about the same time, two surface-to-air anti-aircraft missiles were fired at an Arkia Airlines chartered Boeing 767 carrying 261 other Israelis back from a week's beach vacation at the Paradise and nearby hotels. The crew of the Israeli airliner said that they spotted the deadly missiles only after they had passed the plane, but some published reports suggested that they may have used some kind of antimissile protective device, such as metal chaff or flares, to divert the missiles from their course. The plane arrived home on schedule.

A few days later, Kenyan officials—who had called in Israel to help investigate and to protect the Paradise Beach survivors before they were evacuated to Israel—found two more unfired missiles at another end of the airport runway. Serial numbers on the missiles and other evidence pointed to the involvement of Al Qaeda. Indeed, in a statement a week later, Osama bin Laden's terror group claimed credit for the attack and threatened to target more Israelis and Jews in the future. Sharon vowed that Israel would not let the attack go without a response. "We will not give in to terror," the prime minister said. "Israel will go after those who spilled the blood of its citizens." The Israeli survivors of the Paradise Beach outrage were airlifted out by Israel Air Force Hercules transport planes.

It had long been feared that terrorists would try to fire shoulder-held missiles at commercial airliners, and immediately after the incident, demands were heard—particularly in the United States—for a system that would protect civilian airliners. In late November, Transport Minister Ephraim Sneh told a press conference that such a system was in the final stages of development and would be deployed on Israeli airliners in the near future. Later, both Israel Aircraft Industries and Israel Military Industries were reported to be working on various missile-defense systems for airliners. Briefing foreign ambassadors on November 29, newly appointed Foreign Minister Benjamin Netanyahu, calling the Mombasa attack a wake-up call akin to September 11, 2001, noted that this was not only an Israeli problem, but a global one. "What we see from these attacks is that terror has no boundaries. It has no physical boundaries—it can attack anywhere. It has no boundaries on the nationalities of its victims—we have had Africans killed, Israelis, Russians, Americans, Australians, anyone. And now we see, once again, that terror has no moral boundaries, because indeed yesterday was the crossing of a threshold," he said.

November 28 was also the day of the Likud primary, when party members elected a prime ministerial candidate for the general elections to be held January 28, 2003 (see below, p. 257). That afternoon two Al-Aqsa Martyrs Brigades gunmen attacked the Likud headquarters in Beit She'an, south of Lake Kinneret, and the nearby central bus station, as voters were casting their ballots. Six Israelis—and the two attackers—were killed. The next day, Israeli troops demolished the homes of the attackers in the West Bank village of Jalbun, near Jenin. The incident was described to Army Radio by Galit Cohen, an eyewitness who lived near the Likud office. She said one of the gunmen laughed as he sprayed people with automatic fire. "I opened the window and I simply saw the terrorist standing, smiling, laughing, and shooting in all directions. He simply didn't stop and shot and shot and shot." Local residents noted that the two killers were able to get to Beit She'an very easily because there was no fence on the nearby "Green Line" border between the West Bank and Israel proper. Beit She'an's mayor, Pini Kaballo, demanded that a fence be built along that stretch.

Fatima Hassan Abeida, 95, was killed on December 3 when Israeli troops opened fire on a minibus traveling on a road near Ramallah that was off-limits to Palestinian vehicles. Palestinian sources said they thought the woman was the oldest person killed in the 27 months since the onset of the intifada.

Israel's targeted elimination of terror masterminds continued on December 4, when helicopters hit a Gaza building and killed Mustafa Sabah, said to be the developer of the powerful bombs used several times against Israeli tanks in the Gaza Strip. On December 6, though, Ayman Shishnieh, a leader of the Gaza-based Palestinian Popular Resistance Committee, escaped an Israeli sweep into the al-Burej refugee camp, in an operation where ten Palestinians, five of them identified by Israel as wanted terrorists, were killed. Palestinians, on the other hand, claimed that seven of the men and the one woman killed were innocent civilians. Palestinians also complained that the attack came on the Muslim holiday of Eid El-Fitr. An IDF spokeswoman responded that Palestinians seemed to respect neither Jewish holidays, attacking on Passover in Netanya, nor Muslim ones, since several attacks were launched during Ramadan, the Muslim holy month.

Israel announced in early December that the Shin Bet security force and the army had recently arrested Muhammad Mahmoud Amrou, the Palestinian sniper suspected of killing ten-month-old Shalhevet Pas in Hebron in March 2001 (see AJYB 2002, p. 549). Amrou, 26, a Tanzim activist, reportedly confessed that on the day of the murder Marwan Zaloum, the Tanzim head in Hebron until his death (at the hands of Israel) in April 2002, came to his house and ordered him to carry out a terrorist attack as soon as possible. The fatal shots were fired from the Abu Sneina hill in Hebron, under PA control, into the small Jewish settler colony in the center of the city; Shalhevet was in her father's arms where she was shot. A short time after the murder, the PA had arrested Amrou for several hours, but subsequently released him. But soon after Amrou's capture there was more bad news from Hebron: on December 12, two members of a border police unit guarding Worshipers' Lane, scene of the November ambush that killed 12 Israelis, were killed by a Palestinian who worked his way close to their guard post.

Three Islamic Jihad members from Sur Bahr, in southeastern Jerusalem, were charged on December 15 with planning to fire a missile at a helicopter at the Knesset helipad, ambush a car driving to the prime minister's residence, and set off large bombs at bus stops near a shopping center in Jerusalem.

Israeli troops who moved into Bethlehem in November after a Jerusalem suicide bombing pulled back from the town for a brief Christmas respite on December 24. When they moved back in two days later, heavy fighting broke out and eight Palestinians were reported killed. On December 27, two Islamic Jihad terrorists slipped into Otniel, a settlement in the Hebron hills, and killed four yeshivah students.

The "Road Map"

Despite the seemingly endless violence, negotiations aimed at resumption of a peace process continued. Sharon visited the U.S. again in mid-October for talks with Bush and other senior U.S. leaders. On October 16, Bush and Sharon agreed to back "the gradual return and scheduled transfer" of Palestinian taxes to the PNA, so long as the funds were not used for terrorist activities. U.S. officials also reportedly asked Sharon to curb Israeli military responses to Palestinian violence as Washington was attempting to enlist the support of Arab countries for a possible strike against Iraq.

William Burns, assistant secretary of state for the Near East, visited the region in late October for talks with Israeli and Palestinian officials on the proposed three-phase "road map" to negotiations and a final peace settlement developed by the Quartet in mid-September. Sharon told the Knesset Foreign Affairs and Security Committee in early November that Israel accepted the road map's principles, but that a total freeze on settlement activity was unacceptable. Sharon said that when he would meet with American officials in early 2003 to discuss the road map, he would cite several major points that, in his view, required clarification. These, according to a report in Ha'aretz, included the need for PA compliance with Israeli security demands as a precondition to progress; an understanding that Israel would not move forward on the road map unless the PA met all its obligations; and agreement that final-status issues would not be discussed in the early stages of negotiations.

In early December, Sharon reiterated his willingness to accept a Palestinian state, though he did not define exactly what that meant. In a speech to a national security conference in Herzliya, north of Tel Aviv, the prime minister also outlined his support for the staged process outlined by Bush in the president's June 24 speech and refined by the Quartet. Sharon placed particular emphasis on the sequential nature of the plan's implementation, saying that transition from one phase to the next "is determined on the basis of performance. Only once a specific phase had been implemented will progress into the next phase be possible."

The beginning of that sequence, Sharon reiterated, involved reform of the PA and replacement of its leader. He said that "the U.S. administration, with the world following in its footsteps, has already accepted our unequivocal position that no progress will be possible with Arafat as the chairman of the Palestinian Authority. This man is not—and never will be—a partner to peace. He does not want peace." Sharon said that security reform would include dismantling the current multiple apparatuses, many of which were involved in terror, and their replacement with no more than two or three security organizations under a single command; the outlawing of terror organizations; and the collection and destruction of illegal weapons in Palestinian hands.

The Quartet was due formally to adopt the road map at a meeting in Washington on December 20. But on December 12, the United States announced that in deference to a request from Sharon, the initiative would be placed on hold until after the Israeli elections, scheduled for January 28, 2003, and the formation of a new Israeli government. An understanding to that effect had been reached a few days earlier at a Washington meeting between National Security Adviser Rice and Dov Weisglass, Sharon's bureau chief.

Also on December 12, Secretary of State Powell unveiled the Middle East Partnership Initiative, aimed at promoting regional economic and political reform. Powell said that the U.S. would provide $29 million towards funding the program, aimed at integrating Middle Eastern countries more closely into the global economy by offering aspiring World Trade Organization (WTO) members, such as Saudi Arabia, Lebanon, and Yemen, technical assistance; beginning negotiations on a free-trade agreement with Morocco; and working with Egypt and Bahrain to build on bilateral trade relationships.

The Northern Border

The September 1982 massacres by Christian Phalangist militia of about 800 Muslims in the Lebanese refugee camps of Sabra and Shatilla—a black mark on the record of Israel, which controlled the area at the time, and of Ariel Sharon, the then-defense minister—returned to the front pages on January 24, 2002. On that day, Elie Hobeika, the Phalangist officer who sent the troops into the camp, was assassinated. He was on his way to go skin-diving when a booby-trapped vehicle exploded next to his car, killing him and his three bodyguards. The blast also ignited three oxygen tanks in Hobeika's car, intensifying the blast and damaging several nearby buildings in the East Beirut neighborhood where he lived.

Lebanese officials immediately blamed Israel for the blast, suggesting that Hobeika could have been a key witness in the pending war crimes case against Prime Minister Sharon in Belgium (see below, p. 409). The Israeli government indignantly denied the charge. Hobeika had been saying that he had "revelations" to make that would clear his name and "tell a very different story" than that of Israel's Kahan Commission, which had probed the massacre and found that Sharon had only indirect responsibility for the heinous crime. An anti-Syrian group in Lebanon claimed credit for the killing, saying Hobeika was a Syrian agent who had betrayed his country. In refugee camps south of Beirut, news of Hobeika's death prompted spontaneous celebrations from Palestinian residents, who had nursed deep hatred for him for over two decades.

Tensions remained high along the Lebanese border throughout the year. There was an upsurge of fighting between Israel and Hezballah in southern Lebanon in early April, particularly around the Shebba Farms area, on the slopes of Mt. Hermon. Israeli officials suggested that Hezballah was planning to open a second front to put military pressure on the Israeli army in the north, while forces to the south were aiding Palestinian terror groups in the West Bank and Gaza.

The two sides exchanged fire on a daily basis for a while, but Israel exercised restraint out of concern that tougher action might ignite wider hostilities in the area. Secretary of State Powell canceled a scheduled visit to the border region, but called on "all states that can influence Hezballah, especially Syria, to do what is in their power to restrain the group and stop these actions, before the conflict expands, and has destructive consequences for the region." After a Lebanese announcement that Syria would redeploy its estimated 20,000 troops in Lebanon to areas near the Syrian border—in line with provisions of the 1989 Taif accord ending the Lebanese civil war—Prime Minister Sharon warned that Syria was "not immune" from Israeli military action in the region.

Lt.-Col. Omar al-Hayb, from a well-known Bedouin family whose members had a long record of service in the Israeli army, went on trial for treason, aiding the enemy, grave espionage, and drug dealing. He had served as chief tracking officer for the Northern Command until he left the army in mid-2002, well after his alleged espionage activities began, and also had been in charge of enlisting Bedouin soldiers into the IDF. Al-Hayb, who protested his innocence and declared his loyalty to the state, lost an eye while pursuing terrorists in southern Lebanon in the mid-1990s, but was allowed to stay in the army at his own request. Nine other Bedouin soldiers from the same extended family in the northern village of Zarzir were also arrested in the case. The ten were accused of providing Hezballah with classified maps of the northern border, details of troop movements and tank deployments, and information regarding the location of senior military commanders, in exchange for drugs.

Nissim Nasser, 35, a native of Lebanon who moved to Israel ten years before, was sentenced to six years in jail as a Hezballah spy in a plea-bargain deal on December 11. Nasser, whose mother was Jewish and father Lebanese, said he acted to "protect his family" in Lebanon.

Palestinian Toll

According to the B'Tselem human rights organization, 953 Palestinians were killed by Israeli action during 2002. Of those, 135 were minors—a number slightly larger than the total of minors killed during the first 15 months of the intifada (the last three months of 2000 and all of 2001). B'Tselem also listed 65 Palestinians killed as a result of Israeli "targeted eliminations" or assassinations. Conceding that most of the 65 fit the Israeli definition of terrorists, the human rights group noted that a number of small children and other innocent victim also lost their lives.

The targeted killings were controversial among Israelis. Critics argued that such actions—particularly spectacular hits on charismatic leaders—made matters worse by inflaming the terrorists' desire for revenge, pointing to the upsurge in attacks that followed the assassination of Hamas bomb-maker Yehiye Ayyash, better known as "the Engineer," in 1996, and those, in 2002, of Ra'ed al-Karmi of Tul Karm in January and of Salah Shehadeh in July. But the government and its supporters countered that the terror groups were so filled with hate that they needed no new reason for murder, and that removing key men in the Palestinian infrastructure of terror was necessary to preempt attacks.

Victims of Terror Attacks, 2002

About 450 people were killed by Palestinian attacks during the year:

January 9—Four members of Israel's Bedouin desert patrol—Maj. Ashraf Hawash, 28, Sgts. Ibrahim Hamadieh, 23, Hana (Eli) Abu-Ghanem, 25, and Mofid Sawaid, 25, are killed and two other members of the unit wounded when two armed Hamas terrorists from the southern Gaza Strip, carrying explosive belts, assault rifles, and grenades, and dressed in Palestinian Authority police uniforms, infiltrate Israeli territory near Keren Shalom.

January 14—Sgt. Elad Abu-Gani, 19, is killed and an officer wounded by gunfire in a terrorist ambush between Nablus and Tul Karm. Fatah claims responsibility.

January 15—The bullet-riddled body of Avraham (Avi) Boaz, 71, of Ma'ale Adumim, kidnapped at a PA security checkpoint in Beit Jala, near southern Jerusalem and Bethlehem, is found in a car in Beit Sahur, in the Bethlehem area. The Fatah's Al-Aqsa Martyrs Brigades claims responsibility. Boaz, a U.S. citizen, had done business with Palestinians for years, and, despite the danger, continued to visit Palestinian friends in the Bethlehem area during the course of the intifada.

January 15—Yoela Chen, 45, of Givat Ze'ev, is shot and killed by Palestinian terrorists near the gas station at the entrance to the town, a Jerusalem suburb just northwest of the capital in Israel-controlled Area A, shortly before 8 P.M. Her aunt, with her in the car, is injured. Fatah's Al-Aqsa Martyrs Brigades claims responsibility; the assassins escape, apparently to the nearby Ramallah area.

January 16—Shahada Dadis, 30, an Arab resident of Beit Hanina in East Jerusalem, is found dead in a car bearing Israeli license plates south of Jenin in the West Bank. He was apparently mistaken for an Israeli and killed in a drive-by shooting.

January 17—Edward Bakshayev, 48, Anatoly Bakshayev, 63, Aharon Ben Yisrael-Ellis, 32, Dina Binayev, 48, Boris Melikhov, 56, and security guard Avi Yazdi, 25, are killed and 35 other guests hurt when a terrorist bursts into a bat mitzvah reception in a banquet hall in Hadera shortly before 11 P.M., opening fire with an M-16 assault rifle. The Fatah Al-Aqsa Martyrs Brigades claims responsibility. The family celebrating the bat mitzvah had immigrated from the Caucasus region.

January 22—Sarah Hamburger, 79, and Svetlana Sandler, 56, are killed and 40 people injured when a Palestinian terrorist opens fire with an M-16 assault rifle near a bus stop on Jaffa Road in the center of Jerusalem. The Fatah Al-Aqsa Martyrs Brigades claims responsibility.

January 27—Pinhas Tokatli, 81, is killed and over 150 people wounded, four seriously, in a suicide bombing outside a shoe store on Jaffa Road, in the center of Jerusalem, a few meters from the site of the January 22 attack. The bomb, consisting of over 10 kg. of explosives, was carried by a woman, who is dubbed the first female suicide bomber. Doubts surface, however, as to whether the woman, Wafa Idris, actually intended to blow herself up, or whether she intended to place the bomb and then flee before it detonated.

February 6—Miri Ohana, 45, and her handicapped daughter, Yael, 11, are shot and killed by a terrorist wearing an IDF uniform who infiltrates into Moshav Hamra, in the portion of the Jordan Valley that is in the West Bank, and breaks into the Ohana home. Responsibility is claimed by both Fatah and Hamas. Army reserve Sgt. Moshe Majos Meconen, 33, of Beit She'an, stationed on the moshav to do guard duty, is also killed in the attack.

February 8—Moran Amit, 25, of Kibbutz Kfar Hanasi, is stabbed to death by four teenage Palestinians, aged 14 to 16, while strolling with her boyfriend on the Sherover Promenade in Jerusalem's Armon Hanatziv neighborhood on Friday afternoon. Bystanders, including members of the security forces, give chase, and one of the assailants collapses and dies from what an autopsy disclosed to be a gunshot wound. The other killers, from the nearby mixed Arab and Jewish Abu Tor neighborhood, are later apprehended.

February 9—Atalla Lipobsky, 78, of the town of Ma'ale Ephraim on the edge of the Jordan Valley in the West Bank, is shot dead driving home after Shabbat on the Trans-Samaria Highway with her son. Palestinian gunmen open fire on the car, apparently from ambush, as it passes between Ariel and the Tapuah Junction.

February 10—Lt. Keren Rothstein, 20, and Cpl. Aya Malachi, 18, are killed in a shooting attack on a snack bar-bakery just outside the entrance to the IDF Southern Command headquarters in Beersheba. Four others are wounded, one critically. One of the terrorists is killed at the scene; the second, wearing an explosives belt, flees in the direction of a nearby school but is shot and killed by a soldier and a police officer. Hamas claims responsibility.

February 14—Sgts. Ron Lavie, 20, Moshe Peled, 20, and Asher Zaguri, 21, are killed and four soldiers injured when a powerful mine explodes under a Merkava tank near Netzarim, an isolated settlement at the edge of Gaza City. The tank is lured into the area by shots fired on Israeli vehicles; it is later disclosed that the tankers had removed heavy protective plating on the underside of their vehicle to improve its maneuverability.

February 15—Sgt. Lee Nahman Akunis, 20, is shot and killed by gunmen on Friday night at a roadblock north of Ramallah. The Fatah's Al-Aqsa Martyrs Brigades claims responsibility.

February 16—Nehemia Amar and Keren Shatsky, both 15, are killed and about 30 people wounded, six seriously, when a suicide bomber blows himself up on Saturday night at a pizzeria in the shopping mall in the settlement of Karnei Shomron in Samaria, the area of the West Bank north of Jerusalem. Rachel Thaler, 16, of Ginot Shomron dies of her wounds on February 27. The Popular Front for the Liberation of Palestine (PFLP) claims responsibility.

February 18—Police officer Ahmed Mazarib, 32, of the Bedouin village Beit Zarzir in the Galilee, is killed by a suicide bomber he had stopped for questioning on the Ma'ale Adumim-Jerusalem road. The terrorist succeeds in detonating the bomb in his car. The Fatah Al-Aqsa Martyrs Brigades claims responsibility.

February 18—Ahuva Amergi, 30, of Moshav Ganei Tal, is killed and a 60-year-old man injured when a Palestinian terrorist opens fire on her car in the Gush Katif settlement area of the southern Gaza Strip. Maj. Mor Elraz, 25, and Sgt. Amir Mansouri, 21, are killed while pursuing the attacker, who is killed by other security forces. Fatah Al-Aqsa Martyrs Brigades claims responsibility.

February 19—Lt. Moshe Eini, 21, St.-Sgt. Benny Kikis, 20, Sgt. Mark Podolsky, 20, Sgt. Erez Turgeman, 20, Sgt. Tamir Atsmi, 21, and St.-Sgt. Michael Oxsman, 21, are killed and one other wounded in an attack near a roadblock west of Ramallah. Several terrorists open fire at soldiers at the roadblock, including three off-duty soldiers who are inside a structure at the roadblock, killing them at point-blank range. Fatah Al-Aqsa Martyrs Brigades claims responsibility.

February 22—Valery Ahmir, 59, of Beit Shemesh, is killed by terrorists in a drive-by shooting on the Atarot-Givat Ze'ev road north of Jerusalem as he returns home from work in the North Jerusalem Atarot industrial area. Fatah claims responsibility.

February 25—Avraham Fish, 65, and Aharon Gorov, 46, are killed in a terrorist shooting attack between Tekoa and Nokdim in the West Bank south of Bethlehem. Fish's daughter, nine-months pregnant, is seriously injured, but delivers a baby girl. Fatah al-Aqsa Brigades claims responsibility.

February 25—Police officer Galit Arbiv, 21, dies after being shot at a bus stop in northern Jerusalem. Eight others are injured, two seriously. The Fatah Al-Aqsa Brigades claims responsibility.

February 27—Gad Rejwan, 34, is shot and killed early in the morning by one of his Palestinian employees in a factory in the Atarot industrial area, north of Jerusalem. Two Fatah groups issue a joint statement taking responsibility.

February 28—Sgt. Haim Bachar, 20, is killed during clashes with Palestinians in the Balata refugee camp near Nablus, when Israeli forces enter the camp to search for wanted terrorists.

March 1—Sgt. Ya'acov Avni, 20, is killed by Palestinian sniper fire in the Jenin refugee camp.

March 2—The bullet-ridden body of Jerusalem police detective Moshe Dayan, 46, is discovered next to his motorcycle near the Mar Saba Monastery in the Judean Desert. Fatah Tanzim claims responsibility.

March 2—A total of 11 people die and over 50 are injured, four critically, as a result of a suicide bombing at 7:15 P.M. on Saturday evening near a yeshivah in the ultra-Orthodox Beit Yisrael neighborhood in the center of Jerusalem, where people were gathered for a bar-mitzvah celebration. The terrorist detonates the bomb next to a group of women waiting with their baby carriages for their husbands to leave the nearby synagogue. The victims: Shlomo Nehmad, 40, his wife Gafnit 32, and their daughters Shiraz, 7, and Liran, 3; Shaul Nehmad, 15; Lidor Ilan, 12, and his sister Oriah, 18 months; Tzofia Ya'arit Eliyahu, 23, and her son Ya'akov Avraham, 7 months; later dying of their injuries are Avi Hazan, 37, on March 4, and Avraham Eliahu Nehmad, 7, on June 20. Fatah Al-Aqsa Martyrs Brigades claims responsibility.

March 3—Ten Israelis—seven soldiers and three civilians—are killed and six others injured when a lone terrorist, using a World-War-II-vintage Lee-Enfield bolt-action rifle, opens fire at an army roadblock near Ofra, in the northern West Bank. The victims are Capt. Ariel Hovav, 25; Lt. David Damelin, 29; Sgt. Rafael Levy, 42; Sgt. Avraham Ezra, 38; Sgt. Eran Gad, 24; Sgt. Yochai Porat, 26; Sgt. Kfir Weiss, 24; and civilians Sergei Butarov, 33, Vadim Balagula, 32, and Didi Yitzhak, 66. Fatah Al-Aqsa Martyrs Brigades claims responsibility

March 3—Sgt. Steven Kenigsberg, 19, is killed and four other soldiers hurt when a Palestinian gunman opens fire near the Kissufim crossing in the Gaza Strip. Islamic Jihad and Tanzim claim responsibility.

March 5—Police officer Salim Barakat, 33, of Yarka; Yosef Habi, 52, of Herzliya; and Eli Dahan, 53, of Lod are killed and over 30 people wounded when a Palestinian terrorist opens fire with an assault rifle and throws grenades at the Seafood Market restaurant on Tel Aviv's busy Dereh Petah Tikva, not far from the *Ma'ariv* newspaper building, shortly after 2 A.M. The Fatah Al-Aqsa Martyrs Brigades claims responsibility. The assailant is killed, and security forces, apprehending other members of the gang later, learn that the perpetrators had originally planned to stage an attack in Jerusalem, but, finding nothing open, moved on to Tel Aviv, spotted the lights in the busy eatery where an engagement party was going on, and opened fire.

March 5 — Devorah Friedman, 45, is killed and her husband injured in a shooting attack on the Bethlehem bypass "tunnel road" south of Jerusalem. The Fatah Al-Aqsa Martyrs Brigades claims responsibility.

March 5 — Maharatu Tagana, 85, an Ethiopian immigrant from Upper Nazareth, is killed and a large number of people injured, most of them lightly, when a suicide bomber explodes in an Egged bus no. 823 as it enters the central bus station at Afula, in the Jezreel Valley of northern Israel. Islamic Jihad claims responsibility.

March 6 — Lt. Pinhas Cohen, 23, is killed near the southern Gaza town of Khan Yunis in the course of antiterrorist activity. In a separate incident, reservist Alexander Nastarenko, 37, is killed when Palestinian gunmen cross the border fence and ambush an army jeep on the patrol road near Kibbutz Nir Oz, on the border of the Gaza Strip.

March 7 — Five students — Arik Krogliak, Tal Kurtzweil, Asher Marcus, Eran Picard, and Ariel Zana, all 18 — are killed and 23 others injured, four seriously, when a Hamas gunman penetrates the premilitary training academy in the Gush Katif settlement of Atzmona, in the Gaza Strip.

March 8 — Sgt. Edward Korol, 20, is killed by a Palestinian sniper in Tul Karm.

March 9 — Avia Malka, 9 months, of South Africa, and Israel Yihye, 27, are killed and about 50 people injured, several seriously, when two Palestinians open fire and throw grenades at cars and pedestrians in the coastal city of Netanya, close to the city's boardwalk and hotels, after the end of Shabbat. The terrorists are killed by border police. The Fatah Al-Aqsa Martyrs Brigades claims responsibility.

March 9 — Eleven Israelis — Limor Ben-Shoham, 27, Nir Borochov, 22, Danit Dagan, 25, Livnat Dvash, 28, Tali Eliyahu, 26, Uri Felix, 25, Dan Imani, 23, Natanel Kochavi, 31, Baruch Lerner, 29, Orit Ozerov, 28, and Avraham Haim Rahamim, 28 — are killed and 54 injured, ten of them seriously, when a suicide bomber explodes at 10:30 on Saturday night in the crowded Moment Café at the corner of Aza and Ben-Maimon streets in the Rehavia neighborhood of central Jerusalem, less than two blocks from the prime minister's residence.

March 10 — Sgt. Kobi Eichelboim, 21, dies of wounds suffered when a Palestinian gunman disguised as a worker opens fire at the entrance to Netzarim, an isolated settlement in the Gaza Strip.

March 12 — Security officer Eyal Lieberman, 42, is killed and another person wounded in a shooting attack near Kiryat Sefer east of Modi'in, about halfway between Tel Aviv and Jerusalem.

March 12 — Yehudit Cohen, 33, Ofer Kanarick, 44, Alexei Kotman, 29, Lynne Livne, 49, and her daughter Atara, 15, and Lt. German Rozhkov, 25, are killed when two terrorists wearing IDF uniforms open fire from an ambush on Israeli vehicles traveling between Shlomi and Kibbutz Metzuba near the northern border with Lebanon. Seven others are injured. Israeli forces kill the two gunmen and carry out wide-scale searches for more terrorists.

Mar 13 — Lt. Gil Badihi, 21, dies of his injuries after being shot in the head by Palestinian gunmen while standing outside his tank in Ramallah.

March 14 — Three soldiers — Sgts. Matan Biderman, 21, Ala Hubeishi, 21, and Rotem Shani, 19 — are killed and two soldiers injured early in the morning when a tank escorting a civilian convoy on the Karni-Netzarim road in the Gaza Strip drives over a land mine and terrorists hiding in a nearby mosque detonate the remote-controlled explosive charge. The Democratic Front for the Liberation of Palestine and the Fatah's Al-Aqsa Martyrs Brigades both claim responsibility.

March 17 — Noa Auerbach, 18, is killed and 16 people injured when a terrorist opens fire on passersby in the center of Kfar Saba, northeast of Tel Aviv. The gunman is shot and killed by police.

March 19 — Lt. Tal Zemach, 20, is killed and three soldiers injured when Palestinian terrorists open fire on them in the Jordan Valley. Hamas claims responsibility.

March 20 — Seven Israelis — Sgt. Michael Altfiro, 19, Sgt. Shimon Edri, 20, Senior Warrant Officer Meir Fahima, 40, Cpl. Aharon Revivo, 19, Alon Goldenberg, 28, Mogus Mahento, 75, and Bella Schneider, 53 — are killed and about 30 people wounded, several seriously, in a suicide bombing of an Egged bus no. 823 traveling from Tel Aviv to Nazareth at the Musmus junction on Highway 65 (Wadi Ara) near Afula. Islamic Jihad claims responsibility.

March 21 — Gadi (34) and Tzipi (29) Shemesh, of Jerusalem, and Yitzhak Cohen, 48, of Modi'in, are killed and 86 people injured, three of them seriously, in a suicide bombing on King George Street in the center of Jerusalem. The terrorist detonates the bomb, packed with metal spikes and nails, in the center of a crowd of shoppers. The Fatah Al-Aqsa Martyrs Brigades claims responsibility.

March 24 — Esther Kleiman, 23, of Neve Tzuf, is killed in a shooting attack northwest of Ramallah, while traveling to work in a reinforced Egged bus.

March 24 — Avi Sabag, 24, of Otniel, is killed in a terrorist shooting south of Hebron.

March 27—29 people are killed and 140 injured—20 seriously—in a suicide bombing in the Park Hotel in the coastal city of Netanya, in the midst of a Passover seder attended by 250 guests. Hamas claims responsibility. The victims: Shula Abramovitch, 63, of Holon; David Anichovitch, 70, of Netanya; Sgt.-Maj. Avraham Beckerman, 25, of Ashdod; Shimon Ben-Aroya, 42, of Netanya; Andre Fried, 47, of Netanya; Idit Fried, 47, of Netanya; Miriam Gutenzgan, 82, of Ramat Gan; Ami Hamami, 44, of Netanya; Perla Hermele, 79, of Sweden; Dvora Karim, 73, of Netanya; Michael Karim, 78, of Netanya; Yehudit Korman, 70, of Ramat Hasharon; Marianne Myriam Lehmann Zaoui, 77, of Netanya; Lola Levkovitch, 85, of Jerusalem; Furuk Na'imi, 62, of Netanya; Eliahu Nakash, 85, of Tel Aviv; Irit Rashel, 45, of Moshav Herev La'et; Yulia Talmi, 87, of Tel Aviv; St.-Sgt. Sivan Vider, 20, of Bekaot; Ernest Weiss, 79, of Petah Tikva; Eva Weiss, 75, of Petah Tikva; Meir (George) Yakobovitch, 76, of Holon. Later dying of their injuries: Hanah Rogan, 92, of Netanya; Zee'v Vider, 50, of Moshav Bekaot; Alter Britvich, 88, and his wife Frieda, 86, of Netanya, on April 2–3; Sarah Levy-Hoffman, 89, of Tel-Aviv, on April 7; Anna Yakobovitch, 78, of Holon, on April 11; Eliezer Korman, 74, of Ramat Hasharon, on May 5.

March 28—Rachel and David Gavish, both 50, their son Avraham Gavish, 20, and Rachel's father Yitzhak Kanner, 83, are killed when a terrorist infiltrates the community of Elon Moreh in Samaria, enters their home, and opens fire. Hamas claims responsibility.

March 29—Tuvia Wisner, 79, of Petah Tikva, and Michael Orlansky, 70, of Tel Aviv, are killed when a Palestinian terrorist infiltrates the Netzarim settlement in the Gaza Strip.

March 29—Lt. Boaz Pomerantz, 22, of Kiryat Shmona and St.-Sgt. Roman Shliapstein, 22, of Ma'ale Efraim, are killed in the course of the IDF antiterrorist action in Ramallah (Operation Defensive Shield).

March 29—Rachel Levy, 17, and Haim Smadar, 55, a security guard, both of Jerusalem, are killed and 28 people injured, two seriously, when a female suicide bomber blows herself up in the Kiryat Yovel supermarket in a western Jerusalem neighborhood. The Fatah Al-Aqsa Martyrs Brigades claims responsibility.

March 30—Sgt.-Maj. Constantine Danilov of the border police, 23, of Or Akiva, is shot and killed in Baka al-Garbiyeh during an exchange of fire with two Palestinians trying to cross into Israel to carry out a suicide attack. The Fatah Al-Aqsa Martyrs Brigades claims responsibility.

March 30—Rachel Charhi, 36, of Bat Yam, is seriously injured in a suicide bombing in a café on the corner of Allenby and Bialik streets in Tel Aviv, and, on April 4, dies of her wounds. Some 30 others are also injured in the attack. The Fatah Al-Aqsa Martyrs Brigades claims responsibility.

March 31—15 people are killed and over 40 injured in a suicide bombing in Haifa, in the Matza restaurant near the Grand Canyon shopping mall. Hamas claims responsibility. The victims: Haifa residents Dov Chernobroda, 67; Shimon Koren, 55, and his sons Ran, 18, and Gal, 15; Moshe Levin, 52; Danielle Manchell, 22; Orly Ofir, 16; Aviel Ron, 54, his son Ofer, 18, and daughter Anat, 21; Ya'akov Shani, 53; Adi Shiran, 17; and Daniel Carlos Wegman, 50. Suheil Adawi, 32, of Turan, and Carlos Yerushalmi, 52, of Karkur, die on April 1 of wounds sustained in the attack.

April 1—Sgt.-Maj. Ofir Roth, 22, of Gan Yoshiya, an IDF reserve soldier, is killed at a roadblock near Jerusalem's Har Homa neighborhood by a Palestinian sniper firing from Beit Sahur, near Bethlehem.

April 1—Tomer Mordechai, 19, of Tel Aviv, a policeman, is killed in Jerusalem when a Palestinian suicide bomber driving toward the city center blows himself up after being stopped at a roadblock. The Fatah Al-Aqsa Martyrs Brigades claims responsibility.

April 3—IDF reservist Maj. Moshe Gerstner, 29, of Rishon Lezion is killed in Jenin during antiterrorist action (Operation Defensive Shield).

April 4—Border police Supt. Patrick Pereg, 30, of Rosh Ha'ayin, head of operations in an undercover unit, is killed while attempting to arrest a wanted member of Fatah's Al-Aqsa Martyrs Brigades.

April 4—Sgt.-Maj.(res.) Einan Sharabi, 32, of Rehovot; Lt. Nissim Ben-David, 22, of Ashdod; and St.-Sgt. Gad Ezra, 23, of Bat Yam are killed during the IDF antiterrorist action in Jenin (Operation Defensive Shield).

April 5—Sgt. Marom Moshe Fisher, 19, of Moshav Avigdor; Sgt. Ro'i Tal, 21, of Ma'alot; and Sgt. Oded Kornfein, 20, of Kibbutz Ha'on are killed in exchanges of fire between IDF troops and Palestinian gunmen in Jenin (Operation Defensive Shield).

April 6—Sgt. Nisan Avraham, 26, of Lod, is killed and five other soldiers lightly injured when two Palestinian gunmen open fire and throw grenades at the entrance to Rafiah Yam in the Gaza Strip. The Palestinians, members of Islamic Jihad, ae killed.

April 8—Sgt. Matanya Robinson, 21, of Kibbutz Tirat Zvi, and Sgt. Shmuel Weiss, 19, of Kiryat Arba, are ambushed and killed by Palestinian gunfire in the Jenin refugee camp (Operation Defensive Shield).

April 9—Palestinians terrorists, detonating explosive devices and shooting from the rooftops of buildings, ambush an IDF patrol of reserve soldiers in the Jenin refugee camp; 13 soldiers are killed and seven injured. Those killed: Maj.(res.) Oded Golomb, 22, of Kibbutz Nir David; Capt.(res.) Ya'akov Azoulai, 30, of Migdal Ha'emek; Lt.(res.) Dror Bar, 28, of Kibbutz Einat; Lt.(res.) Eyal Yoel, 28, of Kibbutz Ramat Rachel; 1st Sgt.(res.) Tiran Arazi, 33, of Hadera; 1st Sgt.(res.) Yoram Levy, 33, of Elad; 1st Sgt.(res.) Avner Yaskov, 34, of Beersheba; Sgt. 1st Class (res.) Ronen Alshochat, 27, of Ramle; Sgt. 1st Class (res.) Eyal Eliyahu Azouri, 27, of Ramat Gan; Sgt. 1st Class (res.) Amit Busidan, 22, of Bat Yam; Sgt. 1st Class (res.) Menashe Hava, 23, of Kfar Sava; Sgt. 1st Class (res.) Shmuel Dani Mayzlish, 27, of Moshav Hemed; Sgt. 1st Class (res.) Eyal Zimmerman, 22, of Ra'anana.

April 9—Maj. Assaf Assoulin, 30, of Tel Aviv, is killed in an exchange of fire in Nablus.

April 9—St.-Sgt. Gedalyahu Malik, 21, of Jerusalem is killed and 12 soldiers injured in Jenin when an explosive charge is thrown at a patrol.

April 10—Avinoam Alfia, 26, of Kiryat Ata; Sgt.-Maj.(res.) Shlomi Ben Haim, 27, of Kiryat Yam; Sgt.-Maj.(res.) Nir Danieli, 24, of Kiryat Ata; border police Lance Cpl. Keren Franco, 18, of Kiryat Yam; Sgt.-Maj.(res.) Ze'ev Hanik, 24, of Karmiel; border police Lance Cpl. Noa Shlomo, 18, of Nahariya; Prison Warrant Officer Shimshon Stelkol, 33, of Kiryat Yam; and Sgt. Michael Weissman, 21, of Kiryat Yam are killed and 22 people injured in a suicide bombing on Egged bus no. 960, en route from Haifa to Jerusalem, which explodes near Kibbutz Yagur, east of Haifa. Hamas claims responsibility.

April 12—Lt. Dotan Nahtomi, 22, of Kibbutz Tzuba, died of wounds sustained earlier in the week during IDF operations in Dura (Operation Defensive Shield).

April 12—Border policeman St.-Sgt. David Smirnoff, 22, of Ashdod, is killed and another four Israelis wounded when a Palestinian gunman opens fire near the Erez crossing, in the Gaza Strip. One Palestinian worker is killed and three wounded in the same shooting spree. Islamic Jihad claims responsibility.

April 12—Nissan Cohen, 57; Rivka Fink, 75; Suheila Hushi, 48; and Yelena Konrab, 43, all of Jerusalem; and Ling Chang Mai, 34, and Chai Siang Yang, 32, both foreign workers from China, are killed and 104 wounded when a female suicide bomber detonates a powerful charge at a bus stop on Jaffa Road at the entrance to Jerusalem's Mahane Yehuda open-air market. The Al-Aqsa Martyrs Brigades claims responsibility.

April 20—Border policeman St.-Sgt. Uriel Bar-Maimon, 21, of Ashkelon, is killed in an exchange of fire near the Erez industrial park in the northern Gaza Strip. Israeli forces pursue the Palestinian gunman and kill him, and find an explosive belt on his body. The Fatah Al-Aqsa Martyrs Brigades claims responsibility.

April 22—Sgt. Maj. Nir Krichman, 22, of Hadera, is killed in an exchange of gunfire, when IDF forces entered the village of Asira a-Shamaliya, north of Nablus, to arrest known Hamas terrorists.

April 27—Danielle Shefi, 5; Arik Becker, 22; Katrina (Katya) Greenberg, 45; and Ya'acov Katz, 51, all of Adora, a settlement west of Hebron, are killed when terrorists dressed in IDF uniforms and combat gear cut through the settlement's defensive perimeter fence, enter several homes, and fire upon people in their bedrooms. Seven other people are injured, one seriously. Hamas and the PFLP claim responsibility.

May 3—IDF officer Major Avihu Ya'akov, 24, of Kfar Hasidim, is killed and two other soldiers injured in Nablus in a raid against a terror cell that was planning a suicide attack in Israel.

May 7—15 people are killed and 55 wounded in a crowded club in Rishon Lezion, southeast of Tel Aviv, when a suicide bomber detonates a powerful charge, causing part of the building to collapse. Hamas claims responsibility. The victims: Esther Bablar, 54, of Bat Yam; Yitzhak Bablar, 57, of Bat Yam; Avi Bayaz, 26, of Nes Ziona; Regina Malka Boslan, 62, of Jaffa; Edna Cohen, 61, of Holon; Rafael Haim, 64, of Tel Aviv; Pnina Hikri, 60, of Tel Aviv; Nawa Hinawi, 51, of Tel Aviv; Rahamim Kimhi, 58, of Rishon Lezion; Nir Lovatin, 31, of Rishon Lezion; Shoshana Magmari, 51, of Tel Aviv; Dalia Masa, 56, of Nahalat Yehuda; Rassan Sharouk, 60, of Holon; Israel Shikar, 49, of Rishon Lezion; Anat Teremforush, 36, of Ashdod.

May 12—Nisan Dolinger, 43, of Pe'at Sadeh in the southern Gaza Strip, is shot and killed by a Palestinian laborer, who is apprehended.

May 19—Yosef Haviv, 70, Victor Tatrinov, 63, and Arkady Vieselman, 40, all of Netanya, are killed and 59 people injured—ten seriously—when a suicide bomber disguised as a soldier blows himself up in the market in Netanya. Both Hamas and the PFLP claim responsibility.

May 22—Elmar Dezhabrielov, 16, and Gary Tauzniaski, 65, both of Rishon Lezion, are killed and about 40 people wounded when a suicide bomber detonates himself in the Rothschild Street downtown pedestrian mall of Rishon Lezion.

May 24—Reserve Sgt. Oren Tzelnik, 23, of Bat Yam is killed and two soldiers wounded when terrorists open fire on their vehicle during a counterterrorist operation in Tul Karm.

May 27—Ruth Peled, 56, of Herzliya and her infant granddaughter Sinai Keinan, aged 14 months, of Petah Tikva, are killed and 37 people injured, some seriously, when a suicide bomber detonates himself near an ice-cream parlor outside a shopping mall in Petah Tikva. The Fatah Al-Aqsa Martyrs Brigades claims responsibility.

May 28—Albert Maloul, 50, of Jerusalem, is killed and his cousin wounded when shots are fired at the car in which they are traveling south on the Ramallah bypass road, returning home to Jerusalem from Eli, where they operate the swimming pool. The Fatah Al-Aqsa Martyrs Brigades claims responsibility.

May 28—Netanel Riachi, 17, of Kochav Ya'akov; Gilad Stiglitz, 14, of Yakir; and Avraham Siton, 17, of Shilo—three yeshivah high-school students—are killed and two others wounded in Itamar, southeast of Nablus, when a Palestinian gunman infiltrates the community and opens fire on the teenagers playing basketball. The killer is shot dead by a security guard. The Fatah Al-Aqsa Martyrs Brigades claims responsibility.

June 5—17 people are killed and 38 injured when a car packed with a large quantity of explosives strikes Egged bus no. 830, traveling from Tel Aviv to Tiberias, at the Megiddo junction near Afula. The bus bursts into flames and is completely destroyed and the terrorist, driving the car, is killed in the blast. Islamic Jihad claims responsibility. The victims: From Hadera— Zion Agmon, 50; Cpl. Liron Avitan, 19; Cpl. Dennis Blumin, 20; St.-Sgt. Eliran Buskila, 21; St.-Sgt. Zvi Gelberd, 20; Sgt. Violetta Hizgayev, 20; St.-Sgt. Ganadi Issakov, 21; Cpl. Vladimir Morari, 19; Sgt. Dotan Reisel, 22; and Cpl. Avraham Barzilai, 19. From Netanya—Sgt. Sariel Katz, 21; Sgt. Yigal Nedipur, 21; and St.-Sgt. David Stanislavksy, 23. Also, Sgt. Sivan Wiener, 19, of Holon; Adi Dahan, 17, of Afula; and Shimon Timsit, 35, of Tel Aviv. The body of the 17th victim, Eliyahu Timsit, 32, of Sderot, is not identified until December.

June 6—Erez Rund, 18, of Ofra, north of Ramallah, dies of gunshot wounds to the chest sustained in a shooting attack near his hometown, when Palestinian terrorists open fire from ambush.

June 8—St.-Sgt. Eyal Sorek, 23, of Carmei Tzur, in the Gush Etzion region, his nine-months-pregnant wife Yael, 24, and St.-Sgt.-Maj.(res.) Shalom Mordechai, 35, of Nahariya, are killed and five others injured when terrorists infiltrate Carmei Tzur and open fire at 2:30 A.M. on Shabbat morning. Hamas claims responsibility.

June 11—Hadar Hershkowitz, 14, of Herzliya, is killed and 15 others wounded when a Palestinian suicide bomber sets off a relatively small pipe bomb at a shwarma restaurant in Herzliya.

June 15 — St.-Sgt. Haim Yehezkel (Hezki) Gutman, 22, of Beit El, and St.-Sgt. Alexei Gladkov, 20, of Beersheba, are killed and four soldiers wounded by terrorists near Alei Sinai and Dugit in the northern Gaza Strip. Hamas claims responsibility. Lt. Anatoly Krasik, 22, of Petah Tikva, dies of his wounds on June 22.

June 18 — A total of 19 people are killed and 74 injured — six seriously — in a suicide bombing at the Patt junction in Egged bus no. 32A, traveling from Gilo to the center of Jerusalem with many students on their way to school. The bus is completely destroyed. Hamas claims responsibility. The victims: Jerusalemites Boaz Aluf, 54; Shani Avi-Zedek, 15; Leah Baruch, 59; Mendel Bereson, 72; Rafael Berger, 28; Michal Biazi, 24; Tatiana Braslavsky, 41; Galila Bugala, 11; Raisa Dikstein, 67; Dr. Moshe Gottlieb, 70; Baruch Gruani, 60; Orit Hayla, 21; Helena Ivan, 63; Shiri Negari, 21; Gila Nakav, 55; Yelena Plagov, 42; Liat Yagen, 24; Rahamim Zidkiyahu, 51; and Iman Kabha, 26, of Barta.

June 19 — Noa Alon, 60, of Ofra; Gal Eisenman, 5, of Ma'ale Adumim; Michal Franklin, 22, of Jerusalem; Tatiana Igelski, 43, of Moldova; Hadassah Jungreis, 20, of Migdal Haemek; Gila Sara Kessler, 19, of Eli; and Shmuel Yerushalmi, 17, of Shilo, are killed and 50 people injured — three of them in critical condition — when a suicide bomber blows himself up at a crowded bus stop and hitchhiking post at the French Hill intersection in northern Jerusalem shortly after 7:00 P.M., as people are returning home from work. The Fatah Al-Aqsa Martyrs Brigades claims responsibility.

June 19 — Maj. Shlomi Cohen, 26, of Rehovot, and St.-Sgt. Yosef Talbi, 20, of Yehud, are killed and four soldiers wounded in Kalkilya when Palestinian gunmen open fire while the soldiers are pursuing two terrorists inside a building.

June 20 — A terrorist enters the home of Rachel Shabo, 40, in Itamar, south of Nablus, shooting and killing her and three of her sons — Neria, 16, Zvika, 12, and Avishai, 5 — as well as a neighbor, Yosef Twito, 31, who comes to their aid. Two other children are injured, as well as two soldiers. IDF forces kill the terrorist. The PFLP and the Fatah Al-Aqsa Brigades both claim responsibility.

July 10 — IDF officer Capt. Hagai Lev, 24, of Jerusalem, deputy commander of a Givati reconnaissance unit, is killed by Palestinian sniper fire while conducting a search for tunnels used for weapons smuggling in Rafah, in the southern Gaza Strip. The Fatah Al-Aqsa Martyrs Brigades claims responsibility.

July 16 — Nine people are killed and 20 injured in a terrorist attack on Dan bus no. 189 traveling from Bnei Brak to Emmanuel in

Samaria. The perpetrators, waiting in ambush and reportedly wearing IDF uniforms, detonate an explosive charge next to the bullet-resistant bus, and then open fire. Four terror organizations claim responsibility, but the attack is so similar to the one carried out on the same bus route on December 12, 2001, that the responsible party is apparently the same Hamas cell. The victims: Emmanuel residents Galila Ades, 42; Yonatan Gamliel, 16; Keren Kashani, 29; Sarah Tiferet Shilon, eight months; Gal Shilon (her father), 32; Ilana Siton, 35; and Zilpa Kashi (her grandmother), 65, of Givatayim. The premature infant delivered after its mother, Yehudit Weinberg, is seriously injured dies overnight. Yocheved Ben-Hanan, 21, of Emmanuel, critically wounded, dies July 18.

July 17—Lt. Elad Grenadier, 21, of Haifa, is killed and three soldiers wounded in an early-morning exchange of gunfire with the terrorists responsible for the attack in Emmanuel the day before.

July 17—Adrian Andres, 30, of Romania; Boris Shamis, 25, of Tel Aviv; and Xu Hengyong, 39, of China, are killed and 40 injured in a double suicide bombing on Neve Shaanan Street near the old central bus station in Tel Aviv. Two of those critically wounded subsequently die of their injuries: Li Bin, 33, of China (July 24), and Dmitri Pundikov, 33, of Bat Yam (July 25). Islamic Jihad claims responsibility.

July 25—Rabbi Elimelech Shapira, 43, of Peduel, is killed and another civilian injured in a shooting attack near the West Bank community of Alei Zahav, west of Ariel. The Fatah Al-Aqsa Martyrs Brigades claims responsibility.

July 26—St.-Sgt. Elazar Lebovitch, 21, of Hebron; Rabbi Yosef Dikstein, 45, of Psagot, his wife Hannah, 42, and their nine-year-old son Shuv'el Zion were killed in a shooting attack south of Hebron. Two other of their children were injured. The Fatah Al-Aqsa Martyrs Brigades claims responsibility.

July 30—Shlomo Odesser, 60, and his brother Mordechai, 52, both of Tapuach in Samaria, are shot and killed when their truck comes under fire in the West Bank village of Jama'in, near Ariel. The Fatah Al-Aqsa Martyrs Brigades claims responsibility.

July 31—Nine people—four Israelis and five foreign nationals—are killed and 85 injured, 14 of them seriously, when a bomb explodes in the Frank Sinatra student center cafeteria on the Hebrew University's Mt. Scopus campus. The explosive device, planted inside the cafeteria, demolishes it. Hamas claims responsibility. The victims: David Diego Ladowski, 29, of Jerusalem; Levina Shapira, 53, of Jerusalem; Marla Bennett, 24, of California; Benjamin Blutstein, 25, of Pennsylvania; Dina Carter, 37, of Jerusalem (a U.S. immigrant);

Janis Ruth Coulter, 36, of Massachusetts; and David Gritz, 24, of Jerusalem (dual U.S.-French citizenship). Later dying of their wounds are Daphna Spruch, 61 (August 10) and Revital Barashi, 30 (August 13), both of Jerusalem.

August 1—The body of Shani Ladani, 27, of Moshav Olash, is found bound and shot west of Tul Karm near the Green Line, in the industrial zone where he worked.

August 4—Nine people are killed and some 50 wounded in a suicide bombing of Egged bus no. 361 traveling from Haifa to Safed, at the Meron junction in northern Israel. Hamas claims responsibility. The victims: Mordechai Yehuda Friedman, 24, of Ramat Beit Shemesh; Sari Goldstein, 21, of Karmiel; Maysoun Amin Hassan, 19, of Sajur; Marlene Menahem, 22, of Moshav Safsufa; Sgt.-Maj. Roni Ghanem, 28, of Maghar; Sgt. Yifat Gavrieli, 19, of Mitzpe Adi; Sgt. Omri Goldin, 20, of Mitzpe Aviv; Adelina Kononen, 37, of the Philippines; and Rebecca Roga, 40, of the Philippines.

August 4—Yekutiel Amitai, 34, of Jerusalem, a security guard, and Nizal Awassat, 52, of the Jabel Mukaber neighborhood in East Jerusalem, are killed and 17 wounded when a Palestinian terrorist opens fire with a pistol near the Damascus Gate of Jerusalem's Old City. Border police exchange fire with the gunman, killing him. The Fatah Al-Aqsa Martyrs Brigades claims responsibility.

August 5—Avi Wolanski, 29, and his wife Avital, 27, of Eli, in the northern West Bank, are killed, and their three-year-old child injured when terrorists open fire on their car as they are traveling on the Ramallah-Nablus road. The Martyrs of the Palestinian Popular Army, a splinter group associated with Arafat's Fatah movement, claims responsibility.

August 10—Yafit Herenstein, 31, of Moshav Mechora in the Jordan Valley, is killed, and her husband, Arno, seriously wounded when a Palestinian terrorist infiltrates the moshav and opens fire outside their home. The terrorist is killed by soldiers.

August 20—Sgt. Kevin Cohen, 19, of Petah Tikva, is killed by a sniper near Khan Yunis in the Gaza Strip.

September 5—Lt. Malik Grifat, 24, of the Bedouin town of Zarzir, is killed and another soldier wounded when a Palestinian terrorist opens fire from a crowded school towards a patrol near Nitzanit in the northern Gaza Strip. The terrorist is killed.

September 5—Sgt. Aviad Dotan, 21, of Moshav Nir Galim near Haifa, is killed and three soldiers wounded when a bomb weighing over 100 kgs. explodes under a Merkava tank near the Kissufim crossing in central Gaza Strip. An umbrella group representing several Palestinian factions claims responsibility.

September 18—The charred body of David Buhbut, 67, of Ma'ale Adumim, shot in the head, is found near el-Azzariya, a Palestinian village near his hometown, east of Jerusalem.

September 18—Yosef Ajami, 36, of Jerusalem, is killed when terrorists open fire on his car near Mevo Dotan, north of Jenin in the West Bank. The other occupant of the car, a foreign worker, is lightly injured. The Fatah Al-Aqsa Martyrs Brigades claims responsibility.

September 18—Police Sgt. Moshe Hezkiyah, 21, is killed and three people wounded in a suicide bombing at a bus stop at the Umm al-Fahm junction, not far from Haifa. The bomber, apparently planning to detonate the bomb after boarding a bus, sets the charge off early when approached by police for questioning. Islamic Jihad claims responsibility.

September 19—Six people—Solomon Hoenig, 79, of Tel Aviv; Yossi Mamistavlov, 39, of Or Yehuda; Yaffa Shemtov, 49, of Tel Aviv; Rosanna Siso, 63, of Gan Yavneh; Ofer Zinger, 29, of Moshav Petzael in the Jordan Valley; and Jonathan (Yoni) Jesner, 19, of Glasgow, Scotland, are killed and about 70 people wounded when a terrorist detonates a bomb in Dan bus no. 4 on Allenby Street, opposite the Great Synagogue in Tel Aviv. Hamas claims responsibility.

September 23—Shlomo Yitzhak Shapira, 48, of Jerusalem, is killed and three of his children wounded, one seriously, in a shooting attack near the Cave of the Patriarchs in Hebron. The family, from Jerusalem, had come to Hebron to celebrate Sukkot.

September 26—Naval Commando Capt. Harel Marmelstein, 23, of Mevasseret Zion, is killed while leading a search for wanted terrorists in the West Bank village of Labed near Tul Karm. Israeli soldiers kill senior Hamas terrorist Nisa'at Jaber in the action.

September 30—Sgt. Ari Weiss, 21, of Ra'anana, north of Tel Aviv, is killed and another soldier from the engineering battalion of the Nahal Brigade wounded when Palestinian gunmen open fire on an army position in the Nablus casbah. Islamic Jihad claims responsibility.

October 8—Oded Wolk, 51, of Modi'in, about halfway between Jerusalem and Tel Aviv, is critically wounded in an ambush shooting south of Hebron. He dies of his wounds the following day. Three other Israelis are injured in the attack when Hamas gunmen open fire on their car.

October 10—Sa'ada Aharon, 71, of Ramat Gan, is killed and about 30 people wounded when a suicide bomber blows himself up while trying to board Dan bus no. 87 across from Bar-Ilan University on the Geha highway east of Tel Aviv. Hamas claims responsibility.

October 21—Fourteen people are killed and some 50 wounded when a car bomb containing about 100 kgs. of explosives is detonated next to an Egged no. 841 bus from Kiryat Shmona to Tel Aviv traveling along Wadi Ara on Route 65 toward Hadera. The bus had pulled over at a bus stop when the Islamic Jihad bomber, from Jenin, driving a jeep, approaches from behind and explodes. The victims: Osnat Abramov, 16, of Holon; Indelou Ashati, 54, of Hadera; St.-Sgt. Liat Ben-Ami, 20, of Haifa; Ofra Burger, 56, of Hod Hasharon; Cpl. Ilona Hanukayev, 20, of Hadera; Suad Jaber, 23, of Taibe; Iris Lavi, 68, of Netanya; Sgt.-Maj.(res.) Eliezer Moskovitch, 40, of Petah Tikva; St.-Sgt. Nir Nahum, 20, of Carmiel; Sgt. Esther Pesachov, 19, of Givat Olga; St.-Sgt. Aiman Sharuf, 20, of Ussfiyeh; Sergei Shavchuk, 35, of Afula; Anat Shimshon, 33, of Ra'anana; and Cpl. Sharon Tubol, 19, of Arad.

October 27—Maj. (res.) Tamir Masad, 41, of Ben Shemen; Lt. Matan Zagron, 22, of Itamar; and Sgt.-Maj. Amihud Hasid, 32, of Tapuah, are killed and about 20 people wounded in a suicide bombing at the Sonol gas station at the entrance to Ariel in the northern West Bank. The three are killed while trying to prevent the Hamas terrorist from detonating the bomb.

October 29—Three residents of the West Bank settlement of Hermesh—Orna Eshel, 53, and Linoy Saroussi and Hadas Turgeman, both 14—are killed and two others wounded when a terrorist armed with a Kalashnikov assault rifle and wearing an explosives belt opens fire after infiltrating the settlement. The Al-Aqsa Brigades terrorist is shot dead.

November 4—Security guard Julio Pedro Magram, 51, of Kfar Sava, and Gastón Perpiñal, 15, of Ra'anana, both recent immigrants from Argentina, are killed and about 70 people wounded in a suicide bombing at a shopping mall in Kfar Sava. Islamic Jihad claims responsibility.

November 6—Assaf Tzfira, 18, of B'dolah, and Amos Sa'ada, 52, of Rafiah Yam, in the Gaza Strip, are killed by a terrorist who opens fire in a hothouse and textile factory at Pe'at Sadeh in the southern Gaza Strip. A security officer kills the Hamas terrorist.

November 9—Sgt.-Maj. Madin Grifat, 23, of Beit Zarzir, is killed when a mine explodes during a routine patrol northeast of Netzarim in the Gaza Strip. The Givati Brigade company commander is wounded. Islamic Jihad claims responsibility

November 10—Revital Ohayon, 34, and her two sons, Matan, 5, and Noam, 4, as well as Yitzhak Dori, 44—all of Kibbutz Metzer—and Tirza Damari, 42, of Elyachin, are killed when a terrorist infiltrates the kibbutz, located east of Hadera near the Green Line, and opens fire. This kibbutz is known for its good relations with its neighbors on both sides of the Green Line frontier. Fatah Al-Aqsa Martyrs Brigades claims responsibility.

November 15—Twelve people—nine soldiers and three civilians from the Kiryat Arba emergency response team—are killed and 15 others wounded in Hebron when Palestinian terrorists open fire and throw grenades at a group of Jewish worshipers and their guards as they are walking home from Sabbath prayers at the Cave of the Patriarchs. Three terrorists are killed in the attack, which is claimed by Islamic Jihad. The victims: Col. Dror Weinberg, 38, of Jerusalem; border police officer Samih Sweidan, 31, of Arab al-Aramsha; Sgt. Tomer Nov, 19, of Ashdod; Sgt. Gad Rahamim, 19, of Kiryat Malachi; St.-Sgt. Netanel Machluf, 19, of Hadera; St.-Sgt. Yeshayahu Davidov, 20, of Netanya; Sgt. Igor Drobitsky, 20, of Nahariya; Cpl. David Marcus, 20, of Ma'aleh Adumim; and Lt. Dan Cohen, 22, of Jerusalem. The three local civilians killed are Yitzhak Buanish, 46; Alexander Zwitman, 26; and Alexander Dohan, 33.

November 18—Esther Galia, 48, of Kochav Hashahar, is killed in a shooting attack near Rimonim, on the Allon Road that runs along the eastern edge of the West Bank hills, some 15 kilometers northeast of Ramallah.

November 21—Eleven people are killed and some 50 wounded by a suicide bomber on Mexico Street in the Kiryat Menahem neighborhood of Jerusalem while riding on an Egged no. 20 bus filled with passengers, including schoolchildren, traveling toward the center of the city during rush hour. Hamas claims responsibility. The dead: Jerusalemites Hodaya Asraf, 13; Marina Bazarski, 46; Hadassah (Yelena) Ben-David, 32; Sima Novak, 56; Kira Perlman, 67; her grandson, Ilan Perlman, 8; Yafit Revivo, 14; Ella Sharshevsky, 44; her son Michael Sharshevsky, 16; and Dikla Zino, 22; and Mircea Varga, 25, a tourist from Romania.

November 22—Army tracker Sgt.-Maj. Shigdaf (Shai) Garmai, 30, of Lod, is killed when an IDF Givati Brigade patrol near Tel Qateifa, in the Gaza Strip, comes under fire. Hamas claims responsibility.

November 28—Noy and Dvir Anter, aged 12 and 14, of Ariel, and Albert (Avraham) de Havila, 60, of Ra'anana, are killed along with ten Kenyans when a car bomb explodes in the lobby of the Israeli-owned beachfront Paradise Hotel, frequented almost exclusively by Israeli tourists, near Mombasa, Kenya; 21 Israelis are among the 80 wounded. Al Qaeda claims responsibility for the attack as well as for the unsuccessful attempt, at nearby Mombasa Airport, to shoot down a Boeing airplane chartered by Arkia, the Israeli airline, with more than 250 people aboard, by firing Soviet-made surface-to-air missiles.

November 28—Haim Amar, 56; Ehud (Yehuda) Avitan, 54; Mordechai Avraham, 44; Ya'acov Lary, 35; and David Peretz, 48—

all of Beit She'an; and Shaul Zilberstein, 36, of Upper Nazareth, are killed and about 40 wounded when two Al-Aqsa Martyrs Brigades terrorists open fire and throw grenades at the Likud polling station in Beit She'an, near the central bus station, where party members are voting in the Likud primary election.

December 12—Cpl. Keren Ya'akobi, 19, of Hadera, and Sgt. Maor Halfon, 19, of Kiryat Yam, are killed while on guard near the Tomb of the Patriarchs in Hebron. The killing takes place on Worshipers Way, near the spot where 12 Israelis were killed in an ambush on November 15.

December 20—Rabbi Yitzhak Arama, 40, of Netzer Hazani in Gush Katif, in the Gaza Strip, is shot and killed on the Kissufim corridor road while driving with his wife and six children to attend a pre-wedding Sabbath celebration. Islamic Jihad claims responsibility.

December 27—Four yeshivah students—Sgt. Noam Apter, 23, of Shilo; Pvt. Yehuda Bamberger, 20, of Karnei Shomron; Gavriel Hoter, 17, of Alonei Habashan; and Zvi Zieman, 18, of Re'ut—are killed in Otniel, south of Hebron, while working in the yeshivah kitchen serving Shabbat meals to some 100 students in the adjacent dining room. The two terrorists from Islamic Jihad, which claims responsibility, are killed by Israeli forces. Ten other Israelis, including six soldiers, are wounded in the attack.

Other Security Matters

PHALCON SALE SETTLED

In March, Israel and China signed a deal settling a two-year-old dispute over the cancellation of the $500 million sale of the Phalcon airborne command post to Beijing. The original agreement—which included no American components or technology, and so gave Washington no automatic veto right over it—was canceled by then-prime minister Ehud Barak in 2000 under American pressure (see AJYB 2001, pp. 505–06). In June, however, the U.S. warned Israel against future arms sales to China, particularly if the weapons sold might affect American military operations in the Far East.

ANTI-EXTRADITION

In early August, Israel and the U.S. signed an agreement limiting the extradition of their citizens to the International Criminal Court (ICC) in The Hague. The agreement banned automatic extradition to the court, which came into being in July. Although both countries signed the international court charter at the end of 2000, neither ratified it. Israel feared that the ICC might be used to bring cases against the Israeli army for operations in the Territories, and against settlement activities. In June, Foreign Ministry legal adviser Alan Baker explained that Israel was "fully supportive" of the idea of such a court, but worried about implementation. "A major concern," he said, "is that the court will be subjected to political pressures and its impartiality will be compromised. Israel has recently witnessed many international bodies, established for the highest goals such as protecting human rights and fighting racism, cynically abused and turned into political tools." He added that Israel would watch closely to see if the court met the test of impartiality.

Spy Satellite

Ofek 5, an Israeli intelligence-gathering satellite, was launched into earth orbit on May 28 from the Palmahim military base on the seacoast south of Rishon Lezion. The satellite—which gave Israel the observation capacity lost when Ofek 3 "died" in 2000 and Ofek 4 failed to enter orbit—was built by the government-owned Israel Aircraft Industries and set aloft by a launch vehicle manufactured by the Rafael Arms Development Authority.

Hijack Attempt?

Tawfik Foukra, 23, an Israeli Arab, was taken into custody in Istanbul on November 17 after he had reportedly attempted to hijack an Israeli El Al airliner just before landing at Atatürk International Airport. Foukra was overpowered by guards after allegedly attacking a flight attendant with a pocket knife and trying to enter the cockpit. According to some reports, Foukra told his Turkish interrogators that he intended to force the pilot to return to Israel and crash the plane into one of Tel Aviv's skyscrapers, September 11-style. During the flight, Foukra raised suspicion by his frequent trips to the bathroom.

Foukra's relatives—and the suspect himself—subsequently denied the charges. According to some reports, Foukra was not even holding the knife when two armed El Al security guards tackled him in the plane's business section. Though Israel asked for the man's extradition, Turkish officials held Foukra and he was due to stand trial there in January 2003.

TERROR AND THE LAW

Police said on May 26 that the soldier who shot a handicapped man thinking he was a terrorist was acting properly. The man, with a heavy beard and wearing a thick coat, tried to board a bus traveling from Kfar Saba to Tel Aviv, paid his fare with a new 50-shekel banknote, refused to respond when spoken to, and failed to sit down when there were empty seats on the bus. As the man was getting off the bus and lifting his shirt to show he had no explosive belt, the commotion wakened a sleeping soldier, who shot the man in the thigh.

On September 4, Israel expelled Intisar and Kifah Ajouri from their homes in the Assacre refugee camp near Nablus and transferred them to Gaza, one day after the Supreme Court approved the action. The two sisters were accused of hiding and acting as look-outs for their brother, Ali Ajouri—a man who had planned several suicide bombings, including one in Tel Aviv that claimed five lives, and had been killed in an Israeli military operation on August 6. Attorney General Elyakim Rubinstein argued for the expulsion on the grounds that the women had a direct connection with the terror acts. The Supreme Court ruled that the move did not come under the category of "collective punishment" barred by the Fourth Geneva Convention on the treatment of civilians under military occupation, but rather represented an "assigned residence" permissible under the convention. Although, the judges said, every person has a basic right to remain in his or her place of residence, the convention recognizes circumstances where this right may be overridden for "imperative reasons of security."

Nevertheless, the court did not allow the expulsion of a third Palestinian, Abd al-Nasser Assida, who, it ruled, had not aided in the perpetration of a terrorist crime, but had merely given his brother, Nassar al-Din Assida, food and clean clothes in his home. In its judgement, the court said: "Our role as judges is not easy. We are doing all we can to balance properly between human rights and the security of the area. In this balance, human rights cannot receive complete protection, as if there were no terror, and state security cannot receive full protection, as if there were no human rights. A delicate and sensitive balance is required. This is the price of democracy."

This explanation did not prevent Yasir Arafat from calling the expulsions a "crime against humanity that violates all human and international laws," or Fred Eckhard, a spokesman for UN secretary-general Kofi Annan, from proclaiming that "such transfers are strictly prohibited by international humanitarian law and could have very serious political and security implications."

The army's use of what it called the "neighbor practice," in which local people were forced to go to the door of suspected terror hideouts in the West Bank and Gaza, attracted a good deal of criticism during Operation Defensive Shield in the spring. A number of human-rights groups, including the Association for Civil Rights in Israel and the B'Tselem group, which monitored the situation in the Territories, argued that the practice was, in effect, the employment of human shields. In August, the IDF said it had suspended the practice, but the human-rightst groups, citing evidence to the contrary, petitioned the Supreme Court. In December, the court issued an injuction forbidding it.

A MASTER TERRORIST DIES

Palestinian master terrorist Sabri al-Bana, better known by his nom de guerre, Abu Nidal, committed suicide in Baghdad, Iraq, on August 16. Abu Nidal had been leader of the Revolutionary Council of Fatah (also known as the Abu Nidal Group), a radical Palestinian organization responsible for attacks on Israelis, Westerners, and rival Palestinians. The head of Iraqi intelligence, Taher Jaleel al-Haboush, said that Abu Nidal shot himself after Iraqi security officers attempted to arrest him for illegally entering the country, and that coded messages had been found at Abu Nidal's apartment showing that he had been on the payroll of a country that al-Haboush would not identify. According to some Western news reports, Abu Nidal had been plotting with Kuwait to overthrow the government of President Saddam Hussein. A statement issued by the Revolutionary Council of Fatah said that Abu Nidal had been assassinated by "an intelligence apparatus."

POLITICAL DEVELOPMENTS

Reshuffling the Coalition

The Likud-led coalition government entered the year with the backing of 81 of the 120 members of Knesset. The first defections came on March 15, when the seven MKs from the right-wing National Union-Yisrael Beitenu withdrew and its two men in the cabinet—Infrastructure Minister Avigdor Lieberman and Tourism Minister Benny Elon—resigned.

The faction said it was leaving because Sharon had caved in on the principle of not negotiating under fire, going back on the demand for seven days of quiet as a prior condition for political negotiations.

But Sharon reinforced his government the next month, on April 9, when he took in two parties that had been in opposition—the National Religious Party (NRP), with five seats, and Gesher, a breakaway from what had been Ehud Barak's One Israel in the 2001 election, with three. Three new ministers-without-portfolio were named: Efi Eitam, the newly chosen leader of the NRP, a former army officer who had become religious rather recently; former NRP leader Yitzhak Levy; and Gesher's David Levy, the former Likud foreign minister who had left the party in the late 1990s. Eitam was by far the most controversial of the three, having taken some extreme positions on security and territorial issues. Referring to Eitam, Meretz leader Yossi Sarid went so far as to say that he was "ashamed as a Jew" to live in a country where a "racist" sat in the government.

On May 20, two ultra-Orthodox parties that were members of the government—Shas, the 17-MK Sephardi party, and the five-MK United Torah Judaism (UTJ)—violated coalition discipline as enough of their MKs voted with the opposition or abstained to defeat Sharon's emergency economic program, the so-called Economic Defensive Shield. Both parties opposed provisions to cut by 24 percent government child allowances for families in which neither of the parents had served in the army, a proposal that hit directly at the ultra-Orthodox—and at Arab Israelis. Sharon retaliated by dismissing the four Shas cabinet ministers—Eli Yishai, Interior; Asher Ohana, Religious Affairs; Nissim Dahan, Health; and Shlomo Benizri, Labor and Social Affairs (as a matter of principle, UTJ held no cabinet positions). The two parties left the government, bringing the strength of Sharon's coalition down from 82 seats to 60, one less than a majority.

Ironically, the move actually strengthened the government. Sharon's tough stand, especially vis-à-vis Shas—widely disliked by the secular public for squeezing financial concessions from many Israeli governments for its own pet programs and organizations—won him public and parliamentary support. The identical budget proposal that was defeated 47-44 on May 20, passed 65-26 in a new first reading on May 22. Even many parliamentarians who said they opposed the cuts in social welfare programs praised Sharon for standing up to Shas's pressure.

But it did not take long before Shas and its ministers were back inside the coalition. On June 3, the party agreed to support the economic austerity program the next time it came up in the Knesset, though Sharon granted it the right to raise its objections in Knesset committees before the final vote.

The Road to New Elections

Labor's decision to enter Sharon's unity government in March 2001 had been controversial within the party, with some fearing that it would prevent Labor from articulating a political vision distinct from that of Likud (see AJYB 2002, p. 530). Although the party leadership insisted that remaining inside the government provided some leverage over policy decisions, Labor uneasiness with the coalition situation continued on into 2002. Its most dramatic display came in June, when Labor MK Yossi Beilin, one of Labor's leading doves and an architect of the Oslo peace process with the Palestinians, formed a new political movement, Shahar (Dawn), which some observers saw as the potential beginning of a new social democratic party.

The decision to pull out of the government—and bring it down—was finally made by the man most instrumental in forging the coalition in the first place, Labor leader and Defense Minister Binyamin Ben-Eliezer, who led his party out of Ariel Sharon's 17-month-old national unity government on October 30. The withdrawal of the 26 Labor members denied the ruling coalition the necessary majority of 61 seats in the 120-member Knesset. Sharon, eager to preserve his national unity coalition, was unable to convince Ben-Eliezer to stay.

The ostensible reason for Labor's exit was its objection to the 2003 budget, which was up for Knesset approval: Labor voiced opposition to severe cuts in social programs, including payments from the National Insurance Institute, the Israeli equivalent of social security. But the real reason, observers said, was Ben-Eliezer's standing in the battle for the leadership of Labor. The party primary was to be held three weeks later, and Ben-Eliezer was trailing far behind challenger Amram Mitzna, the mayor of Haifa, and he needed a dramatic gesture to turn the race around.

After the Labor resignations took effect, Sharon set about rebuilding his government, naming former prime minister Netanyahu—who would be his own rival in the Likud leadership election at the end of November—as foreign minister in place of Shimon Peres, and tapping Shaul Mofaz, a hard-line general who had left the army as chief of staff in July, to replace Ben-Eliezer as defense minister.

Though he survived three no-confidence votes in the Knesset on November 4, only because the right-wing National Union-Yisrael Beitenu abstained so as not to automatically trigger new elections, Sharon saw that he could not cobble together anything more than a razor-thin majority for any coalition he might form, and that the survival of any such government would constantly be at the mercy of small parties inside the cabinet. So on November 5, Sharon gave up plans to form a new coalition and informed President Katzav that he wished to dissolve the Knesset and hold fresh elections within 90 days. Sharon explained that he was unwilling to accede to the demands of National Union-Yisrael Beitenu that, as a condition for its entering the government, he reject the "road map" advanced by the U.S. and the other members of the Quartet, and the future establishment of a Palestinian state.

On November 11, the Knesset reached agreement on January 28, 2003, as the date for elections to the 16th Knesset. The 15th Knesset, now coming to an end, had been elected in May 1999; Sharon became prime minister in February 2001, in a special election for the prime minister only, under a law for the direct election of the prime minister, which had subsequently been repealed. Thus in the 2003 elections, Israel's voters would cast a single ballot for a party list, with the leader of the largest party, or the party able to put together a coalition, as prime minister. That system had been in effect for the first 13 Knesset elections; a dual-ballot system, including direct election of the prime minister and a separate vote for the Knesset, was in effect only for the 1996 election, won by Netanyahu, and the 1999 victory of Ehud Barak over Netanyahu.

The Primaries

Amram Mitzna, a newcomer to Israeli national politics, won the Labor leadership in the party's primary election on November 19, with 57 percent of the ballots cast. Ben-Eliezer, the incumbent leader, was second with 35 percent, and veteran Labor politician and former minister Haim Ramon came in third with 8 percent. In the party's Knesset primaries, MKs Yossi Beilin and Yael Dayan—outspoken opponents of the recent coalition with Likud—failed to win "safe" places on the Labor Knesset list, and joined the left-wing party Meretz in December.

Mitzna, Haifa's mayor for a decade, had been a high-ranking military officer and headed the Central Command. He had publicly and emphatically differed with Sharon before and during the Lebanon war. Although public-opinion polls showed him doing better against Sharon than any other potential Labor candidate, he was given little chance of leading Labor to victory in the general election. It was expected that Labor would win around 20 seats in the 120-member Knesset, trailing far behind Likud, which anticipated well over 30 and perhaps as many as 40 seats. Mitzna's platform included a pledge to make a strong effort to reach agreement with the Palestinians within a year, and, if that did not happen, to withdraw from the West Bank and Gaza and dismantle many, though not all, of the Israeli settlements in the Territories.

Former prime minister and current foreign minister Benjamin Netanyahu challenged Sharon in the Likud primaries. Less than two years previously, Netanyahu probably could have won the contest for leadership of the Likud, and then faced the free-falling Ehud Barak in the February 2001 special election for prime minister. But Netanyahu backed out of the race at that time, saying he would run only if there were also a general election for the Knesset; becoming prime minister with the parliamentary constellation that then existed in the Knesset would be an exercise in futility, Netanyahu reasoned, leaving the field open to Ariel Sharon.

During 2001, Netanyahu led Sharon in the opinion polls, and even as late as the middle of 2002, Netanyahu and his supporters were confident that they could unseat Sharon in the November 29 Likud leadership primary, where about 300,000 registered Likud members would made the decision, and then lead the party in the next national elections, then scheduled for the fall of 2003. On May 12, 2002, in an impressive display of their clout within the Likud leadership, the Netanyahu forces got the 2,500-strong Likud Central Committee to adopt a resolution stating that the party would never accept the creation of a Palestinian state. This was considered a major blow to Sharon, who had often publicly said he did not oppose the creation of such a state—though his view of the nature of a Palestinian state differed significantly from that of the Palestinians and that of the Labor Party.

But by the week of the primary contest, the once-confident Netanyahu backers, citing the media and pollsters, recognized the foregone conclusion of a drubbing at the ballot box. Sharon cruised to a landslide triumph, capturing over 60 percent of the vote. This decisive win, observers said, was due largely to the many new rank-and-file party members recruited by the Sharon camp in recent months. Widespread expectations that the prime minister would score a decisive victory over Netanyahu served to mute responses to the Sharon victory, as did public concern over the terror attacks at Beit She'an and Mombasa.

Scandals and Controversies

The Likud held its internal primary, to choose its list of Knesset candidates, on December 8. The election of the slate, by 2,940 members of the party's Central Committee, was billed as a "celebration of democracy"; instead, it turned into an ugly spectacle of corruption and malfeasance that, at least briefly, cut into the party's strong lead in the public-opinion polls and seemed to endanger its chances in the 2003 elections. Almost inexplicably, relative unknowns came in ahead of national figures in the voting, strongly suggesting foul play. (Relative placement on the party list is important, sometimes vital, in Israel's unique electoral system, where if, say, a party wins 15 Knesset seats, candidates numbered 1–15 are elected, while number 16 is out in the cold.) For example, Inbal Gavrieli, 27, whose previous experience was as a waitress but whose family owned casinos, placed 28th on the party's list, and Ruhama Avraham, former office manager to Benjamin Netanyahu, was 18th, while Ehud Olmert, the mayor of Jerusalem mooted as a leading candidate for a senior ministerial post in the next Sharon government, came in 32nd. There were charges of cash payments by candidates or their supporters to "vote contractors" in exchange for large blocs of votes, and suggestions that candidates had treated prospective voters to long weekends at hotels and other illegal favors.

The first to go public with a complaint was Nehama Ronen, who had joined the Likud after serving as director general of the Environment Ministry in the mid-1990s, was an MK from the now-defunct Center Party in the outgoing Knesset, and had not won a spot in the primaries. She said that several Central Committee members told her that if she paid them money they would not only vote for her but also make sure that other members loyal to them would do so as well. Another losing candidate, Haim Cohen, reportedly told authorities that a committee member demanded a $70,000 bribe—the man allegedly approached him and "made a sign with his fingers that he wanted cash"—to guarantee a "safe" spot.

On December 14, Attorney General Elyakim Rubinstein instructed National Police Chief Shlomo Aharonishky to start a criminal investigation into the accusations. Shortly thereafter, police arrested and held two Likud members for interrogation. The two—Gil Haddad and Haim Naim—were named by former MK Akiva Nof as demanding bribes for some 45 votes they claimed to control. Police sources said one of the key elements of corruption in Likud was the entrenched system of collecting money from candidates to pay for campaign expenses, and that it would not be easy to translate such practices into criminal counts. Police also reported "enormous" pressure by senior Likud officials against anyone from the party giving evidence.

Investigators summoned Deputy Infrastructure Minister Naomi Blumenthal, a serving Likud MK, to talk about reports that she had paid for several rooms at the posh City Tower Hotel in Ramat Gan for Central Committee members on the night before the primaries. Blumenthal, who had finished ninth on the Likud list, refused to testify, invoking her right to remain silent.

The scandal also swirled around alleged mob figures who had gained posts in the Likud party infrastructure, though not the Knesset list, including convicted racketeer Moussa Alperon, a new member of the Likud election committee, and Shlomi Oz, who had served 32 months in prison for extortion and conspiracy. Commentators called the Likud vote "crimaries" and warned of the danger to the entire society. Menachem Amir, professor of criminology at the Hebrew University of Jerusalem, said this was the first time "that criminal elements so bluntly promoted people to enter into the Knesset. There is a threat to democracy if your legislators represent crime groups. The very symbol of democracy is the legislator." Amir Oren, writing in *Ha'aretz,* argued: "The problem is not the means of procuring seats in Knesset, but its purpose. Organized crime has spawned a political wing, and is penetrating the government echelons. It is literally taking the law into its own hands. Its influence will be felt in legislation, votes (for the Judicial Selection Committee, the president — the vital partner in the pardoning process — and the state comptroller) and the immunity granted from surveillance of home, office, car and telephones registered in the name of an MK. . . . "

There were also reports that Sharon's son, Omri, who placed 26th on the Likud list, had links with Oz and other crime figures. The prime minister strongly denied the charges against his son. "My son Omri had nothing to do with criminal elements who managed to get into the central committee," Sharon told the government-owned Channel One, as polls showed Likud voters drifting away. Analysts who had originally seen a large Likud victory as a foregone conclusion began hedging their bets. "The question is how many solid seats the Likud has, how low the party can go, and how high up in the party ranks the police investigation will reach," said *Ma'ariv* political analyst Hemi Shalev.

In mid-December, the Central Elections Committee (CEC) had to deal with petitions brought to remove several Knesset candidates from the contest, under provisions of a section of the law that allowed the disqualification of parties or candidates that denied the legitimacy of the State of Israel as a Jewish and democratic state, incited to racism, or supported the armed struggle of an enemy state or a terrorist organization against the State of Israel. One petition, brought by Attorney General Rubinstein, sought to disqualify controversial Arab MK Azmi Bishara and his Balad (National Democratic Assembly) list; others, brought by members of right-wing parties in the Knesset, requested the disqualification of MKs Abdulmalk Dehamshe of the United Arab List and Ahmad Tibi of Ta'al, and of both the United Arab List and the joint list presented by Ta'al and the (mostly Arab) Democratic Front for Peace and Equality. Another request sought to eliminate the candidacy of Baruch Marzel, who was second on the Herut list of MK Michael Kleiner (Kleiner's faction had taken the historical name of the party founded by the legendary Likud leader, Menachem Begin) because of Marzel's association with the banned Kach movement.

The CEC, chaired by Supreme Court Justice Mishael Cheshin, was made up of 41 representatives of all the parties in the outgoing Knesset—8 Labor, 6 Likud, 5 Shas, 3 Meretz, 2 Shinui, 2 Center, 2 National Union, 2 United Torah Judaism, and one each for all the other parties, including five representatives of the Arab parties. This was to be the first time the CEC would decide on the eligibility of individual candidates, under an amendment to the Basic Law passed in May 2002.

ECONOMIC DEVELOPMENTS

Economy in the Doldrums

At the end of 2002, the Central Bureau of Statistics (CBS) reported that in terms of the key economic indicator of growth, the past year had been the worst in Israel's economic history since 1953. The Gross Domestic Product, the total value of goods and services created by the economy over the year, fell by 1 percent, following a decline of 0.9 percent in 2001. The last time the economy had suffered two consecutive years of negative GDP growth had been 1952–53, during the difficult period after the creation of the state in 1948. The decline continued in 2002 despite the passage of two emergency plans during the course of the year—Operation Economic Defensive Shield in May, and a second budgetary revision in July.

The Labor Party was quick to jump on the figures and use them to criticize Likud. The Laborites blamed "the worst year in half a century" on the failure of the Likud finance minister, Silvan Shalom, to manage the economy. In response, Prime Minister Sharon called in the head of the CBS, which subsequently issued a "clarification" noting the difference between the primitive economic conditions that existed in 1953, when Israel was an infant state, and the developed, sophisticated economy of 2002. The CBS now also noted that GDP growth was just one of many statistics that ought to be considered when judging the performance of the Israeli economy.

Political nuances aside (the debate took place less than a month before the Knesset elections) no one doubted that the performance of the economy was dismal, and that actual economic growth was, in fact, much lower than the official figure of –1 percent, which did not account for a population growth of about 2 percent in 2002. The really significant figure was not GDP, but per capita GDP. That fell by 3 percent in 2002. Standing at $15,600 for the year, it was far behind the $17,000 of the late 1990s, though still an improvement over the $12,000 recorded at the start of that decade. Other key figures followed a similar downward trend. Business GDP was down 3.1 percent, and private consumption declined 0.6 percent due to the continuing recession, while unemployment remained at over 10 percent.

One key factor in this dismal picture was the continuing violence of the Palestinian intifada, which had started in October 2000 and continued unabated through all of 2001 and 2002. Particularly hard-hit was the tourism industry, which in the good days of the mid-to-late 1990s had produced income in excess of $1.5 billion, and created tens of thousands of jobs. But there were two other elements as well—the worldwide recessionary trend, particularly in the aftermath of the September 11 terror attacks, and the growing crisis in high-tech industries, which had previously been an engine of rapid growth in exports. Taken together, these three factors undermined many of the economic accomplishments of the previous decade. The erosion in financial and political stability, naturally, was not lost on international rating agencies and investors, who became more cautious about placing their money in Israel.

Inflation and Deficits

But there were major differences between 2002 and other recession years, largely because of the inflation rate. The Consumer Price Index, as calculated by the CBS, rose by 6.5 percent for all of 2002—more than double the government's planned rate of 3 percent as envisioned in the annual budget. This was the highest rate since 1998, and it would have been even higher had the CPI not dropped by 0.8 percent in November and 0.3 percent in December. Inflation is particularly worrisome in a recession, when low demand usually keeps prices—and a rise in the cost of living—down.

The main reason for the high inflation was the shekel's decline against major foreign currencies—by 25 percent against the euro, 21 percent against the British pound sterling and 10 percent against the dollar. There were other factors as well. One was a 1-percent increase in the Value Added Tax (sales tax) as part of the July austerity program, and increases in the cost of energy (24.5 percent for electricity, 18.6 percent for household gas, 51 percent for kerosene). The shekel's decline was also influenced by a natural weakening of the currency in the faltering economy. But the interest-rate policy of the governor of the Bank of Israel, David Klein, also played a role. Klein had drastically lowered basic interest rates in late 2001 as part of a deal he struck with Finance Minister Silvan Shalom and Prime Minister Sharon, who had promised that the reduction would be accompanied by major cuts in government spending. Klein made the mistake of acting first. His lowering of interest (without a compensatory budget cut) in January and February 2002 tempted local and foreign investors, who had been putting their money into shekels to take advantage of relatively high interest, to switch to dollars and other foreign currencies. Those moves away from the shekel caused the Israeli currency to lose value, and Klein had to act to shore it up with several sharp increases in interest. Between the end of December 2001 and mid-July 2002, interest rose from 3.8 percent to 9.1 percent.

At the end of 2002, the government announced that its deficit for all of the year amounted to 3.9 percent of GDP, due largely to a continuing decline in tax revenues (itself a product of slowing economic activity), which dropped by 5 percent during the year. The government's original deficit target, 2.4 percent of GDP, was revised to 3.9 percent over the course of 2002. Accountant General Nir Gilad said that the latter target, amounting to $4.085 billion, was reached despite a delay in the arrival of U.S. aid, a $1.9 billion shortfall in tax collection, and delays in certain legislative steps that the government had approved during 2002. In 2001, the government had missed its 1.75-percent target and ended up with an annual deficit worth 4.6 percent of GDP, attributed to a delay in American aid that arrived during 2002.

When the 2002 deficit data were released, some economists and political figures expressed doubts at the size of the deficit, suggesting that it was only as low as the published figure because some expenses from 2002 had been deferred to the following year. Such a maneuver, they said, made the economic situation look better than it actually was, in advance of the upcoming elections. These suspicions were to some extent confirmed by the January and February 2003 deficit figures, which, in addition to low tax revenues, showed higher than anticipated government expenditures, a situation suggesting the deferment of some 2002 payments to 2003.

Business and Investment

Israel's foreign trade performance reflected the long recession. Exports of goods and services fell by 5.4 percent in real terms—that is, taking into account the fluctuation in shekel exchange rates. Even worse, exports to the European Union and the United States, Israel's main trading partners, fell by $1.2 billion, or 5.7 percent, and exports to Japan (whose economy shrank by 0.5 percent during the year) fell by $129 million, or 23 percent. Nevertheless, a recession-caused decline in the import of goods and services meant that the trade deficit declined by $642 million for the year.

The United States led all export destinations, with $6 billion in goods and services during 2002 (31 percent of total exports), ahead of the $5.6 billion (30 percent) to the European Union. Exports to Asia totaled $5.1 billion (14 percent), and to the European Free Trade Association (EFTA—Iceland, Norway, and Switzerland) $433.9 million (1 percent). As usual in recent years, the trade balance with the U.S. was about equal ($6.1 billion in imports, $6 billion in exports), while Europe sold Israel much more than it bought ($13.5 billion as compared to $5.6 billion).

Exports to Arab countries dropped by 6 percent to $106 million in 2002, predominantly due to the ongoing violence. These figures, however, did not include some $10 million in exports to these places via third countries. The largest declines were to Egypt, Lebanon, and Morocco. Exports to Arab countries consisted mostly of textiles, wood, furniture, paper, rubber and plastic goods, chemicals, and machinery. Imports from Arab countries increased by 10 percent in 2002 to $69 million, the Israel Export Institute said.

Total foreign investment in Israel fell by some 38 percent to 2.6 billion in 2002, from $4.2 billion in 2001 and a record $11.1 billion in 2000, according to the Bank of Israel. Since its height in 2000, foreign investment plummeted 76.5 percent, led primarily by a fall in direct investments—the kind that give the investor voting rights on the firm's board of directors. In 2002, direct investments totaled some $1.2 billion, as compared to $3.1 billion in 2001 and $4.5 billion in 2000. On the Tel Aviv Stock Exchange (TASE), foreign investment rose from 2001's $268 million to some $900 million in 2002, still far below 2000's record $5 billion. Israeli companies listed on foreign stock exchanges—primarily the NASDAQ—saw issues totaling only $200 million in 2002, compared with $1.6 billion in 2001 and $4.9 billion in 2000.

According to the CBS, industrial output fell by 10 percent since the start of Palestinian violence in late September 2002. Following a 5.4-percent drop in 2001, it declined by 3.5 percent in 2002. The Bank of Israel's "S," or State of the Economy, Index fell by 4 percent during 2002; the 2001 decline had been 2.4 percent. The components of this index were manufacturing production; imports, excluding capital goods; trade and services revenue; and the number of business-sector employee positions. The index stood at 106.8 points in December—a seven-year low.

Venture capital investment in Israeli and Israeli-related high-tech companies declined by 43 percent, from $2 billion in 2001 to $1.14 billion in 2002. A report by the Israel Venture Capital Association's research unit said that 352 companies raised capital during the year, down by a third from 2001. The survey was based on reports from 159 venture investors, including 91 Israeli venture-capital funds and 68 other, mostly foreign, investment entities. At the same time, the shortage of new money was reflected in the figure of $481 million invested by Israeli venture-capital firms, down 40 percent from the $812 million invested in 2001. Quarterly investments became progressively smaller throughout the year, as they had in 2001.

The number of new dwellings sold on the private market (not including government-built housing) for the year amounted to 14,210, a drop of 2 percent from 2001 sales figures. The number of unsold homes on the private market at the end of 2002 stood at 11,900, a drop of 24 percent from the "stock" of available homes at the end of 2001. Both figures graphically portrayed the continued recession: prior to the start of the slump in 2000, demand for new houses amounted to about 40,000 a year. The slowdown in the housing market seemed likely to continue. Housing starts for 2002 amounted to only 31,480 units, the lowest number since 1989 (in 2001, work was started on 31,640 new dwellings). Of the 2002 housing starts, 24,710 were by private contractors, and 6,760 were units of public housing built by the government.

Some 54,000 businesses closed down in 2002 and only 47,000 opened, according to the CBS. The net drop of 7,000 businesses followed increases of new enterprises in 2001, when business starts exceeded closings by 3,000, and 2000, when the net increase in the number of new businesses stood at 6,500. The great majority of the businesses that closed—about 50,000——were small businesses, the Organization of Independent Businessmen said. That was a rise of 30 percent over the 35,000 that closed during 2001. The group added that it anticipated another 60,000 small businesses shutting down in 2003. It ascribed the trend to delays in payment from the Defense Ministry, which, at the end of the year, had reached four months beyond the due date. Types of small businesses hardest hit were tourism (80 percent), furniture sales (30–40 percent), clothing and culture (30 percent), and food and electronics (15–20 percent).

Agricultural output reached a value of 15.1 billion shekels in 2002, an increase of 1.2 percent over 2001. The change was largely due to higher prices on foreign markets: While farm exports dropped 7.3 percent in volume, the income from those exports rose by 19.3 percent.

Employment

Joblessness due to the recession remained high throughout 2002, though there was an apparent (but not necessarily a real) dip toward the end of the year. Seasonally adjusted unemployment was 10.1 percent in the fourth quarter of 2002, compared with 10.3 percent in the two preceding quarters and 10.6 percent in the first quarter, the CBS reported. The year-end number of unemployed was 259,000, seasonally adjusted, compared with 263,000 in the second and third quarters, and 268,000 in the first.

The decline in unemployment in the fourth quarter was mostly technical, due to unemployed people who had stopped going to government labor exchanges in search of jobs. Another reason for the decline was the hiring of thousands of the unemployed, many of them university graduates, as security guards. In the fourth quarter, 136,300 men were unemployed (a rate of 9.8 percent) and 122,700 women (10.4 percent). Nevertheless, the average weekly number of unemployed in 2002 was 262,000, 12 percent more than in 2001. And the Bank of Israel predicted a continued increase in unemployment, ascribing this to the lack of a plan to reduce the number of foreign workers, of whom there were more than 200,000. The bank said that unemployment in 2003 could reach 11.5–12 percent, which would translate into more than 300,000 jobless people. Participation by Israelis aged 18–65 in the civilian labor force fell from 54.3 percent in 2001 to 54.1 percent in 2002. The steepest decline was in the industrial sector's workforce, which contracted by 15,000 workers.

In a related development, the Ministry of Labor and Social Affairs reported that the number of job-seekers registering with its employment service rose by 5.2 percent during 2002 to a monthly average of 196,400, as compared to averages of 165,000 in 2000 and 187,000 in 2001. Some 193,100 Israelis signed up for work and unemployment benefits in the last month of 2002. Officials of the ministry noted a decline during the year in the number of senior citizens and academics searching for work. The number of families receiving "income support" welfare payments from the National Insurance Institute because their unemployment benefits had run out or because the wages they earned were below minimal levels, amounted to about 84,000, less than in previous years. Stricter enforcement of National Insurance Institute regulations and unemployment benefit criteria led to a drop in registrants.

2002 was marked by layoffs in Israeli high-tech, caused by the global tech crisis and the NASDAQ crash. Employment in the leading high-tech sectors fell from 128,400 in December 2001 to 122,800 at the end of 2002, a 4.4-percent drop amounting to 5,600 fewer employees. Of these, 2,700 were in computers, 1,700 in electronic communications, 600 in medical science and equipment, and 600 in R&D. The steepest drop was in electronic communications, where employment fell 10 percent to 15,500.

Despite salary cuts implemented in 2002, high-tech employees earned 2–2.5 times the average Israeli wage. Electronic communications employees had the highest pay, averaging $3,296 per month in November, while medical science and equipment workers earned $3,242, computer employees $3,076, and R&D personnel $2,784.

Travel and Tourism

According to the CBS, Israelis reduced their travel abroad in 2002, for the first time in a decade. Only 3.27 million exits from Israel by Israeli citizens were recorded during the year as compared with 3.56 million in 2001, an 8-percent decline after years in which the annual increase averaged 4 percent. In addition to the continuing recession and the intifada, the CBS attributed the decline to devaluation of the shekel, which made foreign travel more expensive.

For the first time since 1982, the number of foreign visitors to Israel dropped below a million, to 862,300, 29 percent lower than the number of visitors in 2001, and just one-third of the figure for 2000. As a consequence, the number of bed-nights in Israeli hotels declined by 3 percent, to 14.6 million, with a 31-percent decline in foreign tourist bed-nights substantially offset by a 6-percent rise in the number of Israeli bed-nights.

Since the outbreak of the current intifada in September 2000, the Israeli-Palestinian conflict had cost Israel an estimated $2.3 billion in tourism revenues, according to a report in the *Globes* business daily. The $1 billion lost in 2001 was topped by losses of another $1.3 billion in 2002. Tourism revenues amounted to $2.1 billion in 2002 compared with $2.4 billion in 2001, an 11-percent drop, and when compared to the $3.4 billion earned in 2000, the decline amounted to 38 percent. Spending by Israelis traveling abroad declined by 4 percent to $3.2 billion.

Standard of Living

The CBS reported that the average salary in Israel at the end of 2002 was $1,411, which was 5.4 percent less than in 2001. The 10 percent of Israeli families with the highest incomes earned 22.4 times the bottom 10 percent, according to the CBS. The gross monthly income of a family in the top bracket averaged $7,604 in 2002, while a family in the bottom bracket averaged only $340.

The CBS data also indicated that the gap between rich and poor had widened over the previous 40 years. While the proportion of total spending on food, clothing, and footwear had declined in that same period, the proportion spent on housing, transportation, and communications rose. For example, spending on food dropped from 42 percent of total spending 40 years before to just 17 percent, and spending on clothing and footwear declined from 12 percent to 3 percent. At the same time, the proportion spent on housing rose from 12 to 23 percent, while spending on transport and communications leaped from 3 to 20 percent. According to the figures, over seven of every ten Israeli households owned their own homes, over half of Israel households had a home computer, and 23 percent were Internet subscribers, while 74 percent owned at least one cellphone and 38 percent had at least two.

According to the Ministry of Housing, Israel experienced a marked drop in new-apartment sales in the second half of 2002. Sales of both privately and publicly built apartments averaged 2,014 a month in the first seven months of the year, but dropped by 32 percent from August through December to 1,366 apartments monthly, reflecting a 12-percent decline from 2001, despite attractive prices. Since 1996, there had hardly been any real rise in the prices of apartments. In 1997, they went up by 0.3 percent and in 1998 by 1.6 percent, but beginning in 1999 they fell cumulatively by some 11 percent. Since 1988, apartment prices went up in real terms by 70.1 percent— an average of 4 percent annually.

Another sign of the recession was the increased average age of Israelis' cars—7.4 years at the end of 2002, compared to 7.2 in 2001. Savyon, the upper-crust town east of Tel Aviv, had the most cars per capita, 568 per 1,000 people, but even that was down from 583 in 2001. Tel Aviv had 445 cars per 1,000 residents, Haifa 274, Eilat 201, Jerusalem 158, and Ariel in the West Bank 104. The bottom ten cities, topped by Dimona with 133, include four Israeli-Arab cities, as well as Beit Shemesh with 113 and Neve Dekalim, in the southern Gaza Strip, with 106. At the end of 2002, Israel had just over 2 million motor vehicles, about three-quarters of them private cars.

The Treasury Ministry's Customs & VAT (Value Added Tax) Division reported that imports of cars and electrical appliances dropped steeply in 2002. Israelis spent $1.38 billion on cars and electrical goods, as compared to $1.66 billion in 2001. The number of imported cars was down 18 percent, and imported electrical goods dropped 17 percent.

OTHER DOMESTIC MATTERS

Israel by the Numbers

At the end of 2002, Israel's population stood at 6.7 million people— up 150,000, or just over 2 percent, from the end of 2001, and more than eight times the 806,000 population at the time that statehood was declared in May 1948. The 5.4 million Jews in the country made up 38 percent of the world Jewish population of 13.3 million. Of Israel's 1.3 million non-Jews, 82 percent were Muslim, 9 percent Christian, and 9 percent Druze. Israel had 4.3 million eligible voters (over the age of 18) living in the country. The CBS estimated that another 420,000 Israelis—over 9 percent of those with the right to vote—lived abroad. The CBS reported that although Jerusalem was the country's largest city, Tel Aviv had the largest number of eligible voters (including those thought to be living abroad), 354,000 to Jerusalem's 325,000, because Jerusalem had a disproportionate number of children and Palestinians. Haifa was third with 235,000 eligible voters.

The number of immigrants arriving in Israel in 2002 was 33,500, a decline of 23 percent from the 43,000 who came in 2001. Though the number was the smallest since the start of the wave of aliyah triggered by the collapse of the Soviet Union in the late 1980s, the CBS noted that it was still higher than the numbers registered during the 1970s and 1980s, when an average of about 15,000 people arrived each year. Of those coming in 2002, about 18,500—55 percent of the total—were from the former Soviet Union.

The workforce totaled 2.569 million people, 2.31 million of whom were employed and 259,000 unemployed. According to CBS estimates, there were 238,000 foreign workers resident in Israel, up 4 percent from 2001. About half of them were in the country illegally, many having come as tourists. During the year, 33,000 foreign workers arrived in Israel with legal work permits—the lowest number of such entries since 1995.

A total of 18,247 traffic accidents with injuries were recorded in Israel proper—not including the West Bank and Gaza—during the year. Of the 37,387 casualties in them, 524 died and 2,358 were injured. Appalling as the figures were, they represented drops of 3.6 percent in the number of accidents and 2.4 percent in the number of fatalities from the year before. The number of accidents with at least one fatality was 456, down 4 percent from 2001. The percentage of Arabs killed in accidents was 23 percent, 4 percent higher than the 19 percent of Arabs in Israel's population. And although women constituted 39 percent of all licensed drivers in the country, only 22 percent of the drivers involved in reported accidents were female. At the end of 2002, about 1.96-million motor vehicles were registered in Israel, up 2.4 percent from a year before. Of those, 1.497 million were private passenger vehicles.

Israel spent 45-billion shekels (about $10 billion) on health services for its residents in 2002. This represented 8.8 percent of the GDP. According to the CBS, that percentage of GDP was comparable to what was spent on health in Sweden, Holland, and Denmark, and lower than what was spent in the United States (13.9 percent) and in Germany, Canada, Switzerland, France, Greece, Portugal, Iceland, and Belgium, countries where health expenditures ranged between 9 and 11 percent of GDP.

Religion and State

As the year began, a group of MKs from across the political spectrum proposed legislation to redraw government regulations over which public activities were prohibited for Jews on Shabbat. Seeking to put an end to ongoing strife about government enforcement of Shabbat restrictions, as well as to accommodate the often conflicting demands of the religious and secular sectors, the bill formalized the existing ban on most business and commerce, but allowed "cultural" activities—including the operation of restaurants, theaters, and movies. In addition, restrictions would be lifted on the operation of public transportation not subsidized by the government. The proposal received considerable praise for formulating a possible modus vivendi between religious and secular Israelis, but drew opposition from the more doctrinaire elements on both sides—secularists opposed to any Sabbath restrictions, and religionists unwilling to legalize "cultural" violations of the Sabbath. The proposal—a "private member's bill" not sponsored by any party—went nowhere.

On February 20, the Supreme Court ruled that people who converted to Judaism under Reform and Conservative auspices in Israel should be listed as Jews in the Interior Ministry's population registry. (Those who converted abroad already enjoyed this status.) The decision not only affected the small number of such converts in the country, but also carried potential implications for the 250,000 immigrants from the former Soviet Union who had been granted immediate Israeli citizenship under the Law of Return, which considered "Jewish" for the purpose of this law anyone with at least one Jewish grandparent, or whose spouse or another first-degree family member had one Jewish grandparent. The bulk of these people had been unwilling or unable to undergo Orthodox conversion; they could now convert under non-Orthodox guidance and be considered Jews.

The court had been petitioned by the Conservative (Masorti) and Reform movements to compel the ministry, controlled by the ultra-Orthodox party Shas, to stop its practice of registering only those Israeli converts who had undergone an Orthodox conversion procedure. The landmark ruling, written by Supreme Court president Aharon Barak, relied on longstanding precedent that the ministry's population registry must list, and not question, the details regarding personal status given to it by Israeli citizens. Interior Minister Eli Yishai, the Shas leader, denounced the ruling as "strengthening a marginal stream that encourages assimilation and assists in the contraction of the Jewish people."

The decision was also condemned by Orthodox bodies in the U.S. The Union of Orthodox Jewish Congregations of America (OU) and the Rabbinical Council of America (RCA), in a joint statement, voiced concern that "the Supreme Court has transcended its jurisdiction and has trespassed into the domain of the religious authority of the Chief Rabbinate. Whereas the court maintains that its decision is limited to statistical procedures pertaining to citizens' identity cards, we agree with the dissenting opinion of Supreme Court Justice Yitzhak Englard that 'this is not merely a matter of statistics but rather a sharp ideological dispute. Conversion is a matter of Torah law as formulated in the Jewish Halakhah throughout the generations.'" The OU-RCA statement warned that the ruling harmed Jewish unity in that "the decision of the court may eventually lead to the division of the People of Israel into two camps. There will be a group of halakhically valid Jews and a group of people who are Jewish only by the ruling of the Supreme Court. Inevitably this myopic decision will be tragic for all of Israel, but especially for those who have been misled by the court to think that they are Jewish."

The ruling is "obviously a complete and total victory," Rabbi Andrew Sacks, executive head of Israel's Masorti movement told the Jewish Telegraphic Agency. Sacks said the court emphasized the importance of not enshrining one stream of Judaism above others, and thus "all those people who converted with us and are listed as Ukranian or Peruvian or whatever, now they can have Jewish listed on their identity cards." Rabbi Uri Regev, head of the Reform movement's World Union for Progressive Judaism, cited the decision's "historical consequence because it strengthens Jewish pluralism in Israel. It effectively repels the Orthodox establishment that holds that Reform and Conservative converts aren't worthy of being recognized because of the liberal identities of the rabbis that convert them."

But the Israeli Orthodox parties were not about to accept defeat. MK Avraham Ravitz, head of the Degel Hatorah non-Hassidic wing of UTJ—the Ashkenazi ultra-Orthodox bloc—dismissed the ruling out of hand. "So what if they have an identity card that says they're Jewish," said Ravitz. "It doesn't mean they're recognized by Jewish law as being Jewish. It's just bureaucratic." Almost immediately, the Shas Knesset faction was circulating a legislative proposal that would bypass the court decision. Under the Shas plan, conversions could not be finalized until they received the Chief Rabbinate's approval—and this would apply even to conversions performed overseas, which heretofore had been accepted by the government.

Kinneret Covenant

The religious/secular divide was perhaps the sharpest but surely far from the only serious fissure in Israeli Jewish society. In January, a group of some 60 Israeli intellectuals, calling itself the Forum for National Responsibility, released a document seeking to bridge these gaps. The result of a yearlong series of discussions under the auspices of the Yitzhak Rabin Center for Israel Studies, it was called the Kinneret Covenant (it was hammered out at a hotel in Tiberias, located on the shore of that lake). Phrased like the Declaration of Independence of 1948, the covenant sought to affirm what all Israeli Jews held in common, which necessitated ignoring or glossing over some real divisions. For example, it justified the creation of Israel neither on the basis of secular Zionism nor of God's will, but rather as "a sublime existential need" rooted in "the devotion of the People of Israel to its heritage, its Torah, its language, and its country." The document also asserted that Israel must remain both Jewish and democratic, but, on the vexed question of how to maintain a Jewish majority, it could only suggest that it be done through "moral means."

Attacks on the Kinneret Covenant followed predictable lines: both the far left and far right castigated it for papering over the country's real ideological cleavages. One particular complaint of the left was the absence of any Israeli Arabs from the list of participants and the vague treatment of their grievances in the covenant's text.

Israeli Arabs

The Or Commission had met intermittently through 2001 to investigate the killing of 13 Israeli Arabs during the Arab riots of October 2000 (see AJYB 2002, pp. 570–72). On February 27, 2002, it sent out warning letters to 14 people involved in those events—including former prime minister Ehud Barak, former public security minister Shlomo Ben-Ami, Alik Ron, the Northern District police commander at the time of the riots, and three Israeli Arabs—MKs Azmi Bishara and Abdulmalik Dehamshe, and Sheikh Ra'ad Salah, the controversial and outspoken Northern District head of Israel's Islamic Movement. The significance of these letters was that the appearances of these men before any subsequent proceedings of the commission would be conducted like a criminal trial, with cross-examination permitted. The Or Commission wound up its public hearings in mid-August, with Barak as the final witness. Its report was due in the spring of 2003.

On March 8, 2000, the Supreme Court had ruled that the state could neither allocate land strictly to Jews on the basis of religion nor prevent the sale of land to Arab citizens because they were Arabs (see AJYB 2001, pp. 524–25). In an attempt to bypass the decision, the Knesset, on June 7, 2002, passed a law allowing the exclusion of Arabs from buying land in areas the Jewish Agency earmarked for Jewish communities. This came to be known as the "Druckman bill" after Rabbi Haim Druckman, the strongly right-wing MK from the NRP who originally proposed it.

The law drew heavy criticism from legal experts, the Labor Party, and political right-winger Benny Begin, the former minister and son of the late prime minister Menachem Begin, all of whom considered it racist and discriminatory. Amid the public furor, Attorney General Elyakim Rubinstein, who originally had verified the bill's legality, reversed his stand, prompting Druckman to ask: "What happened to the attorney general, who is disowning a bill to which he himself is a signatory?" The legislation was nullified on July 7.

Slurring the American Ambassador

On January 8, the Knesset Ethics Committee decided not to penalize National Union MK Zvi Hendel for calling U.S. ambassador Daniel Kurtzer, a Jew, "a jewboy." But the committee condemned Hendel's statement, saying that it not only insulted the foreign envoy but also hurt Israel and Jews everywhere. Hendel, a leader of the settlers in the Gaza Strip, made the comment about Kurtzer from the Knesset floor after the envoy was reported to have stated, in a speech, that Israel would be better off spending money on the handicapped and the poor, rather than on settlements. Hendel sent Kurtzer a letter of apology that said: "A mistake came out of my mouth when I said 'a jewboy.' Of course, my meaning was not in the derogatory connotation of the term, which has been used by the worst of Israel-haters. If anyone has been hurt by this, I sincerely apologize." One of the many to criticize Hendel's slur was Sen. Frank Lautenberg (D., N.J.), also Jewish, who commented: "If someone said that to me I would punch him in the nose."

Shani Resignation

Uri Shani, head of the Prime Minister's Bureau, resigned his post on April 19 after 13 months on the job. Shani's letter of resignation cited a heavy workload, but insiders suggested that the long-time confidant of Prime Minister Sharon felt his influence was on the wane as Sharon turned increasingly to his son, Omri, and to public-relations man Reuven Eldar for advice on political and personal issues. "He felt isolated and sometimes neutralized, and saw that occasionally Arik was bypassing him," one Likud source told the daily *Ha'aretz*. The paper also reported that Shani disagreed with what he considered Sharon's disparaging treatment of Labor, whose presence in the unity government Shani considered vital for the country. Shani was later replaced by attorney Dov Weisglass, another long-time confidant of Sharon and also his personal lawyer.

North American Aliyah

531 new immigrants from the U.S. and Canada arrived in Israel together in July, members of over 100 families. This aliyah was part of a special program sponsored by Nefesh B'Nefesh — a new organization promoting North American aliyah — Rabbi Yechiel Eckstein's International Fellowship of Christians and Jews, the Jewish Agency and the Absorption Ministry. Part of the package was an agreement by Israel to furnish the newcomers absorption grants comparable to the "basket" given to newcomers from the former Soviet Union, Argentina, and other countries outside the West, then not available to North American immigrants. Later in the year the government instituted a "basket" system for all North American immigrants, which became operational in December.

Fuel Dump Closes

The cabinet decided on May 26 to close the Pi Glilot fuel depot, located in the northern part of Tel Aviv. The decision came after an unsuccessful terror attack there, in which an explosive device was attached to a tanker truck while it was delivering fuel, and detonated when it reached the depot (see above, p. 208). The resulting fire was relatively small and was put out by safety crews. But it raised public awareness of the danger of a major disaster, with hundreds or thousands of people affected, had the thousands of gallons of inflammable fuels stored there ignited. With the closing of Pi Glilot, fuel would be shifted to other depots near Kiryat Ata in the Haifa area, and at Ashkelon and Ashdod.

Kibbutz Land Decision

In late August, the Supreme Court sitting as the High Court of Justice (it does so when dealing with matters of justice that do not fall under the jurisdiction of any other court) overruled three 1995 rulings by the Israel Lands Administration (ILA) — the trustee for state land — giving kibbutzim and their members a large chunk of the proceeds from the sale to developers of state-owned kibbutz agricultural land in the center of the country and near cities. The ILA had ruled that kibbutzim could get 27 percent of the proceeds of such land sales, or, alternatively, 27 percent of the land that was rezoned for residential purposes. As a result, many kibbutz members became instant millionaires. Petitioning against the ILA rules were the Society for the Preservation of Nature in Israel and New Dialogue—an organization of Sephardi intellectuals better known as the Mizrahi Democratic Rainbow—which argued that they were so inequitable as to be unreasonable and illegal. The petitioners argued that the ILA had ignored the need to preserve open spaces, and had discriminated in favor of the kibbutz communities by awarding them compensation far above the standard rate for the sale of agricultural land.

Road Opening

The first stretch of the Trans-Israel Highway, a toll road running east of the major urban centers, opened in early August, and other sections of the road followed later in the year. In this early stage, the electronic toll system for recording license plates and charging the drivers automatically for use of the road was not yet operational. The project, in the works for several years, came under heavy fire from environmental groups that complained it would destroy a large swath of the country's green area, and that improvements in public transportation should be substituted instead. One 2-km section of the road that passed near the West Bank town of Qalqilya, where it was exposed to possible sniper fire, was protected by an eight-meter-high walk.

Mad Cow

Bovine Spongiform Encephalopaty (Mad Cow Disease) was detected in a cow that died in the Golan Heights in June. This was the first confirmed case of the disease in Israel, The Veterinary Service responded with stringent regulations, including banning the slaughter of all cattle over the age of 30 months. The restrictions were lifted later in the year, since no more cases of the disease were found.

Charges, Investigations, Convictions

On May 28, police announced that criminal charges would be brought against four top managers of Ehud Barak's successful 1999 prime ministerial campaign (see AJYB 2000, p. 438). Accused of violating campaign financing laws by running electioneering efforts through fictitious nonprofit organizations were Doron Cohen, Barak's brother-in-law; lawyer Yitzhak (Buzi) Herzog, former cabinet secretary and son of the late ex-president Chaim Herzog; campaign manager Tal Zilberstein; and MK Weizman Shiri.

Attorney General Elyakim Rubinstein decided on June 24 not to institute criminal proceedings against Prof. Jacob Frenkel, former governor of the Bank of Israel, for taking excessive payment when he left the bank by cashing in vacation time, sick leave, and academic benefits after serving two terms in the central bank's top spot. Frenkel, who was now international head of the Merrill-Lynch investment firm, denied all wrongdoing.

In mid-December, Attorney General Rubinstein ordered police to look into business ties between Yossi Ginossar, a former Shin Bet official who often served as a go-between in political dealings with the Palestinians, and the PA. According to reports in the daily papers Ma'ariv and Ha'aretz, Ginossar and his former business partner, Ozrad Lev, managed Swiss bank accounts and shell companies on behalf of Arafat and his financial adviser, Muhammad Rashid, and transferred large sums for them to unknown destinations. Ginossar explained that his business ties with PA personnel, especially with Rashid, were public knowledge, entailed no illegal actions, and were found useful by four Israeli prime ministers. "Muhammad Rashid never dealt in terrorism," Ginossar assured TV interviewers after the story broke.

A three-member parole board decided on July 12 to release Arye Deri, after the former Shas leader had served two-thirds of a three-year sentence for bribery and fraud (see AJYB 2000, pp. 476–77). Emerging triumphantly from the hearing at Ma'asiyahu Prison, Deri said he would "devote a lot of time to public work" and to his family.

On August 7, a parole board approved the early release of Yona Avrushmi, sentenced to life for throwing the hand grenade that killed Peace Now activist Emil Grunzweig and hurt nine others at a 1983 demonstration against the war in Lebanon. He had served 19 years.

In mid-September, State Attorney Edna Arbel announced that she would not ask police to investigate a recent letter to the Supreme Court by one of the complainants in the case against former defense minister Yitzhak Mordechai, in which she withdrew her accusation against him. In 2001, Mordechai had been convicted on one count of committing an indecent act in aggravated circumstances and one of committing an indecent act, and received an 18-month suspended sentence (see AJYB 2002, p. 591). Despite the letter, the Supreme Court denied Mordechai's appeal to reopen his case.

Indictments against Ofer Maximov in a $60-million embezzlement from Tel Aviv's Trade Bank, allegedly carried out by his sister Etti Alon, were filed in Tel Aviv District Court on July 8. Maximov, extradited from Romania, was charged with aggravated fraud, conspiracy to commit a felony, and money-laundering. Alon and Maximov's father, Avigdor Maximov, were also indicted. The Maximovs were accused of stealing the money from the bank to pay Ofer Maximov's gambling debts, some of them run up at Israeli-owned casinos in Eastern Europe, and of paying usurious "gray-market" interest to cover those debts. Also charged were two "gray-market" lenders, Benny Ravizada and Aharon Ohev-Zion.

Seven persons were indicted in the May 2001 collapse of the Versailles banquet hall in Jerusalem, in which 23 people died (see AJYB 2001, pp. 595–96). The accused included Eli Ron, inventor of the Pal-Kal floor and ceiling system used in the building, his assistant Uri Pessah, building contractor Yaakov Adiv, and the four owners of the doomed hall.

Felix Abutbul, 50, the alleged crime king of Netanya, was gunned down on August 11 on the steps of a casino he owned in Prague. Abutbul had served ten years in a British jail for his role in the kidnapping of a Nigerian politician in London in 1984.

Charges of fixed soccer matches were raised by the Israel Football Association in March, after a player for the Hapoel Haifa team was accused of deliberately fouling a player on rival Maccabi Haifa in order to give that team a penalty kick to score the winning goal. Over the course of the year, the probe also spread to some referees.

The "Analyzer," Israeli computer whiz Ehud Tennenbaum, 23, had been convicted in 1998 of hacking into the computer systems of the FBI, NASA, the Pentagon, and others, and sentenced to half a year of service and a 75,000-shekel fine. In 2002, the Tel Aviv District Court accepted a government appeal of the original sentence and lengthened the jail term to one-and-a-half years.

Yaakov Nimrodi, board chairman of the *Ma'ariv* newspaper, and author Aryeh Krishak were convicted by a Tel Aviv court on September 1 of harassing witnesses, obstruction of justice, and breach of trust—offenses committed during the 2001 trial of Nimrodi's son Ofer, the ex-publisher of *Ma'ariv,* on witness-tampering charges.

Four hundred and fifty-one safe-deposit boxes in the Israel Discount Bank branch on Yehuda Halevy Street, in the middle of the Tel Aviv financial district, were broken into and looted on the weekend of July 19–20. The break-in, said to be a professional job, was thought to be one of the biggest bank robberies in Israel's history, although no official estimate of the contents of the lock-boxes was published.

Sports

Russian-born Israeli tennis star Anna Smashnova (now known as Pistolesi, after marrying her coach) won three Women's Tennis Association tournaments in 2002—at Canberra, Vienna, and Shanghai—for a career total of 15, more than any other Israeli man or woman. During the course of the year, in which she pushed her winnings over the $1-million mark, Smashnova became the first Israeli woman to reach the semifinals of a major tournament, the German Open, where she lost to Serena Williams.

The Maccabi Haifa soccer team won its first-round European Champions League match against Manchester United, one of the world's leading soccer clubs, by 3-0. One of Israeli sport's greatest victories, the game was played in Cyprus, after the European soccer organization decided that no games in the various European cup competitions would be played in Israel, due to the security situation. Despite the victory, Haifa failed to move on from the first round of 32 to the second qualifying round of the Champions League, Europe's premier club soccer competiton.

Russian-born Israeli pole-vaulter Alex Averbukh won the gold medal at the 2002 European Champonships with a jump of 5.85 meters; Galit Chait and Sergei Sahanovsky won a bronze medal at the World Ice Dancing Championships in Japan; and Vered Borochovsky won the bronze medal for her 26.38-second 50-meter butterfly at the World Short Course Swimming Championships in Moscow, making her the first Israeli woman swimmer ever to medal at these championships

Personalia

APPOINTMENTS, HONORS, AWARDS

Lt.-Gen. Moshe (Bogie) Ya'alon, 51, officially became Israel's 17th chief of staff on July 9. Defense Minister Ben-Eliezer chose him on March 10 over three other candidates—Maj.-Gens. Uzi Dayan, Dan Halutz, and Amos Malka.

David Ivry, the ambassador to the U.S., completed his term in April. He was replaced by prime ministerial political adviser Danny Ayalon, 47.

Salai Meridor, brother of former finance and justice minister Dan Meridor, was elected to a second term as chairman of the Jewish Agency on June 17. Meridor was the only candidate after Gideon Patt, a former Likud minister, withdrew.

Tel Aviv University professor Uzi Even became the first openly gay member of the Knesset in December, filling a vacancy in the Meretz parliamentary delegation.

Nasser Abu-Taheh was appointed a Magistrate's Court judge in Beersheba, becoming the first Bedouin to be appointed to the Israeli bench.

The Israel Prizes for 2002 were awarded on Israel Independence Day to humorist-author Ephraim Kishon, Teva Pharmaceutical Industries founder and CEO Eli Hurvitz, and the Jewish National Fund (all for lifetime achievement); Nahum Rakover (religious literature); Moshe Brawer (geography); Menashe Harel and Shmuel Safrai (Israel studies); Asher Koriat (psychology); Dov Judkowsky (communications); Ram Carmi (architecture); David Tratkover (design); Abraham Haim Halevi (agriculture); Avraham Biran (archeology); Jacob Frenkel and Ariel Rubinstein (economic research); and Ada Yonat and Itamar Wilner (chemistry).

The 2002–03 Wolf Prizes, awarded by the Israel-based Wolf Foundation set up by the late Dr. Ricardo Wolf, went to R. Michael Roberts of the University of Missouri and Fuller Bazer of Texas A&M (agriculture); Mikio Sato of the University of Tokyo and Elias Stein of Princeton (mathematics); Ralph Brinster of the University of Pennsylvania, Mario Capecchi of the University of Utah, and Oliver Smithies of the University of North Carolina (medicine); Bertrand Halperin of Harvard and Anthony Legget of the University of Illinois (physics); and New York-based sculptor Louise Bourgeois (art).

The Konrad Adenauer Prize for Peace and Tolerance was awarded to Adina Shapiro of Jerusalem and Ghassan Abdullah of Ramallah, founders of the Middle East Children Association (MECA), a cooperative education program that continued even during the intifada. Left-wing film director Avi Mograbi won the prestigious Peace Prize at the 52nd annual Berlin Film Festival for *August,* a film about Israelis coping with difficult realities. The Marc and Henia Liebhaber Prize for the Promotion of Religious Tolerance and Cultural Pluralism in Israel for the year 2001 went to Dr. Aryeh Geiger, founder and principal of the Reut School in Jerusalem, which emphasized pluralistic and democratic education. The title "honorary citizen of Jerusalem" was given to Charles R. Bronfman, philanthropist and first president of the United Jewish Communities (UJC), and to his wife, Andrea Morrison Bronfman, herself a leading philanthropist.

DEATHS

Abba Eban, the distinguished South African-born and Cambridge-educated Middle Eastern scholar, orator, and diplomat, died on November 17 at the age of 87. Eloquent in ten languages and projecting an aristocratic British manner, Eban was less popular with the Israeli electorate than he was abroad, where he came to be known as "the voice of Israel." He served as ambassador to the UN and the U.S., Knesset member, minister of education, foreign minister, and deputy prime minister. He also wrote several books and narrated three TV series on Jewish and Israeli history.

Dr. Zerah Warhaftig, one of the two surviving signers of Israel's Declaration of Independence, died on September 26 at the age of 96. Warhaftig served in the Knesset for nine terms as an NRP member, and was minister of religious affairs from 1961 to 1974.

Other notable Israelis who died during 2002: Yekutiel X. Federman, 87, founder of the Dan hotel chain and active in Israeli-Palestinian coexistence efforts, in January; Haim Haberfeld, 71, secretary general of the Histadrut labor federation, in February; Yehoshua Rozin, 83, former Maccabi Tel Aviv basketball coach and for over 40 years a fixture of Israeli basketball, in February; Romanian-born Prof. Moshe Lancet, 75, gynecologist and sex-education pioneer, in April; human-rights champion Haim Cohn, 91, a former state attorney, attorney general, Supreme Court justice, and president of the Association for Civil Rights in Israel, in April; Chaike Belchatowska Spiegel, 81, one of the last surviving fighters of the 1943 Warsaw Ghetto uprising, in April; Benny Berman, 63, journalist, singer, and songwriter, whose 1960s hits included "The Clown Song" and "Not Everyday Is Purim," in April; Avraham (Buma) Shavit, 75, industrialist, former president of the Israel Manufacturers Association, and chairman of El Al 1979–81, in May; Ida Milgrom, 94, who for 12 years battled the Soviet authorities for the release from prison of her son, Natan (Anatoly) Sharansky, in May; Benny Peled, 76, one of the architects of Israel's destruction of Arab air forces in the first days of the 1967 Six-Day War and air force commander in the 1973 Yom Kippur War, in July; Uzi Gal, 79, inventor of the Uzi submachine gun, in September; Ehud Sprinzak, 62, dean of the Lauder School of Government, Policy and Diplomacy at the Interdisciplinary Center in Herzliya and an expert in extremist political movements, in October; Ya'akov Farkash ("Ze'ev"), 79, renowned cartoonist, in October; Israel Amir, 99, first commander of Israel's air force, in November; and Yeruham Meshel, 89, MK and head of the Histadrut labor federation 1973–84, in November.

HANAN SHER

Turkey

National Affairs

For THE MORE THAN 67 million inhabitants of the Turkish Republic, 2002 was a year of deepening economic distress and growing anxiety over the impact of impending war in neighboring Iraq. Adding to these concerns at year's end was speculation over the real objectives of the new Justice and Development Party (AKP), whose roots were Islamist, which won the November parliamentary elections in an unexpected landslide.

The country's small Jewish community, some 18,000 strong, shared these national concerns. But it—like the broader world Jewish community—was especially worried about how the AKP victory would affect Turkey's close and growing strategic and economic ties with Israel, its position on the Arab-Israeli conflict, its pro-Western and secular orientation, and the status of the country's small remaining non-Muslim groups—particularly the Jews. The new government took reassuring steps, and by year's end Jewish anxiety was considerably muted.

THE "POLITICAL EARTHQUAKE"

Turkey is geographically situated in a region that is periodically subject to devastating earthquakes. Fittingly, many observers termed the landslide victory of the new Justice and Development Party (Adalet ve Kalkinma Partisi=AKP) in the elections of November 3, 2002, a "political earthquake." The AKP, whose leaders had been associated with previously banned Islamist parties, won a stunning two-thirds majority, 363 of the 550 seats in the Grand National Assembly, Turkey's parliament. Equally surprising, some 90 percent of incumbent parliamentarians lost their seats, and all three of the veteran political parties that had governed the country in a fractious ruling coalition were swept completely out of the parliament, as were nearly all the opposition parties. In fact, the only party other than the AKP to win representation was the staunchly secularist Republican People's Party (CHP), led by Deniz Baykal, which won 19.4 percent of the vote and 178 seats. The remaining nine seats were won by independents.

The AKP victory profoundly shook up the complacent Turkish political establishment. Among foreign observers, it raised questions about Ankara's relations with the United States, prospects for Turkey's entry into the European Union, resolution of the Cyprus dispute, the future of Ankara's close strategic ties with Israel, and the role of the Turkish army in a possible confrontation with neighboring Iraq.

To put matters into perspective, the AKP received only 34.3 percent of the vote, and its lopsided parliamentary majority had much to do with the peculiar nature of the Turkish electoral system, which set a very high 10-percent threshold for a party to enter parliament. (By way of contrast, the threshold for a seat in the Israeli Knesset was only 1.5 percent.) Furthermore, the more traditional Islamist party, Saadet (Felicity), recently founded by former prime minister Necmettin Erbakan, received only 2.5 percent of the vote. Thus more than 60 percent of Turkey's electorate voted for one of the 16 officially secular parties that contested the election, but the secular vote was so fractured that only one of those parties, the CHP, achieved representation.

Moreover, 47-year-old Recep Tayip Erdoğan, the popular Islamist former mayor of Istanbul who led the AKP, worked strenuously during the campaign to play down the party's Islamist roots, and thus its success was no indication that Turkish voters had suddenly jumped on a fundamentalist Islamic bandwagon and abandoned the strict separation of religion and state enshrined in the country's constitution. The AKP had been formed as a breakaway group from the outlawed Islamic-leaning Virtue Party. However, in the 2002 elections it put forward candidates representing the entire center-right spectrum of Turkish politics, ranging from liberal, to nationalist, to conservative, to religious. Erdoğan and Abdullah Gül, the Western-educated economist and English-speaking deputy party leader, went out of their way to stress that their party was a traditional, values-based conservative party to which the designation "Islamic" applied only in the sense that "Christian" was part of the name of Christian Democratic parties that had long functioned in, and governed, Western European democracies.

While the AKP undoubtedly drew support from traditional Islamic elements in the Turkish population, the consensus of political observers was that its victory had little to do with its Islamic roots. Andrew Mango, the distinguished British analyst of Turkish affairs and author of a recent comprehensive biography of Mustafa Kemal Atatürk, the founder of modern Turkey, told a BBC interviewer that the AKP "has been elected on a protest vote." Mehmet Ali Birand, a well-regarded Turkish political commentator, wrote that the election results "amount to a civilian coup. This is the response given by millions who are saying, 'You have failed to listen to me. You have failed to govern me well. You have impoverished me. You have treated me in a condescending manner.'"

More specifically, the AKP victory was an indictment of the previous government's failure to deal with the series of economic crises that shook the country in November 2000 and February 2001, a situation exacerbated in 2002 by the continuing global economic recession, a decline in tourism to Turkey attributed to fear of terrorism in the Middle East, and the likelihood of an imminent war in neighboring Iraq. Journalist Gerald Robbins, an expert in Turkish affairs, reported that the country's economy "shrank 6.5 percent" in 2002, "with 70 percent inflation and unemployment officially listed at 11 percent but estimated to be twice that amount." Robbins cited a recent survey by Ankara's Middle East Technical University that found that "approximately 10 percent of Turkey's population don't have a regular income and that another 25 percent of Turkish society, although drawing a regular paycheck, still live at the poverty level" (*ATS Report,* Jan. 2003). Another sign of Turkey's economic malaise was that the once strong Turkish lira was trading at around 1,500,000 to one U.S. dollar.

The collapse of the previous three-party coalition began earlier in the year, when it became increasingly clear that Prime Minister Bülent Ecevit was too old and ill to attend important government meetings on a regular basis. While it would have been logical for the governing parties to band together and present a united front in the November elections, longstanding and in some cases bitter personal rivalries among their leaders, not any serious ideological differences, stood in the way. In the end, of the three coalition parties, the Democratic Left Party (DSP) received only 1.2 percent of the vote, the ultranationalist Nationalist Movement Party (MHP) 8.3 percent, and the center-right Motherland Party (ANAP) 5.1 percent. The center-right True Path Party (DYP), which was outside the coalition and led by former prime minister Tansu Çiller, received 9.6 percent, narrowly failing to reach the 10-percent threshold.

Among the legal changes adopted by the Turkish Grand National Assembly in 2002 had been the granting of limited cultural rights to Turkish Kurds—who made up some 20 percent of the total population—including the right to publish and broadcast in Kurdish, but these were only slowly implemented. Though the pro-Kurdish People's Democracy Party (HADEP) had steadily risen in strength from 4.2 percent of the national vote in December 1995, to 4.8 percent in April 1999, and 6.2 percent in

November 2002, that still left it short of the parliamentary threshold. (Indeed, there was widespread suspicion that a primary reason for setting the threshold so high was to keep the pro-Kurdish party out.) Nevertheless, HADEP captured many mayoral posts in cities and towns in the heavily Kurdish-speaking southeastern Anatolia.

There was reason to believe that the AKP received a substantial number of votes from the Kurdish community. According to this line of reasoning, the personal religious piety of the AKP leadership was attractive to Kurdish voters since it might serve to unite the Turkish people under the banner of a common Islamic identity, blurring divisive distinctions between Turkish, Kurdish, and Arab national movements.

WHO IS ERDOĞAN?

Turkey's secular elite—especially the military leaders who saw themselves as guardians of the secularizing and modernizing principles established by Mustafa Kemal Atatürk—remained suspicious of the AKP's objectives. Its leader, Erdoğan, had been a very popular mayor of the cosmopolitan city of Istanbul. Although he was elected mayor as the candidate of the Islamist Welfare Party, his popularity had less to do with piety than with his efforts to improve the welfare of the city's ten million inhabitants. There was widespread agreement that his administration had accomplished a great deal, cleaning up Istanbul both politically, by greatly reducing the level of official corruption, and physically, by improving garbage collection.

But he also did things to arouse the suspicions of secularists. Soon after his election as mayor, he tried to stop the serving of alcoholic beverages in city-owned cafés, and authorized the use of the large public square next to the Blue Mosque (Sultan Ahmet) for a great circumcision party. The square was filled with colorfully decorated beds on which young boys in Islamic blue nightgowns lay as they recovered from their circumcisions, while they and their families were provided with refreshments and entertainment by the municipality—in the eyes of the critics, an illegal use of public space for religious purposes.

Another controversial step that Erdoğan took while serving as mayor was to announce the construction of a massive new mosque at Taksim Square, near Istanbul's fashionable cultural and shopping district. The secularists saw a hidden Islamist agenda, since there was no shortage of mosques in Istanbul. Perhaps, they suggested, its erection at Taksim Square, at whose center stood a large monument to Atatürk and which was situated at the crossroads of "Independence" and "Republic" avenues, was intended symbolically to challenge, overshadow, and dwarf the legacy of the founder of modern, secular Turkey.

But what made Erdoğan a particular target of the secularist military establishment was a speech he gave in Siirt, an impoverished, religious district in southeastern Anatolia, near the city of Diyarbakir, in 1997. He began by reciting a quatrain from a well-known poem by Ziya Gökalp, a leading ideologist of modern Turkish nationalism: "The mosques are our barracks, the domes are our helmets, the minarets are our bayonets, and the faithful are our army" (according to another translation, the last line means "and the believers are our soldiers"). In April 1998, he was brought before a State Security Court to face charges of illegally using religion as a political weapon. (Those brought before such tribunals were usually suspected Kurdish guerrillas and terrorists.) The prosecutors asserted that, by quoting the poem, Erdoğan was praising fundamentalism and violating a law that banned provoking enmity and hatred among the people. In his defense, Erdoğan said that he had merely repeated lines from a classic poem and had aimed them at no person or target.

The State Security Court ruled that Erdoğan's speech violated the acceptable framework of political and religious expression and was part of a pernicious campaign by the Islamist Welfare Party to undermine the republic's secular institutions and replace them with a religious system based on Islamic law. He was convicted and sentenced to a fine and ten months in jail. On appeal, his prison term was reduced to five months, but the fact of his conviction barred him from political office. Thus Erdoğan could not stand as a candidate for parliament in the 2002 national elections even though he was the leader of the new AKP, and therefore his deputy, Abdullah Gül, would be named prime minister.

Not surprisingly, the conviction and jail sentence enhanced Erdoğan's popularity among religious Turks, thousands of whom accompanied him to the prison gate. Ironically, however, it also drew sympathy for him from many secular Turks as well as human-rights advocates outside the country, who found it disturbing that a man could be jailed simply for making a speech. Experts noted that far from being an Islamist, Ziya Gökalp, the Ottoman intellectual who wrote the poem that Erdoğan recited, was influenced by the European Enlightenment and the French (Jewish) sociologist Émile Durkheim, and supported the union of all Turkic-speaking peoples under a government that separated religion and state.

In later interviews, Erdoğan said that the time he spent in prison caused his political views to mature, so that in 2002 he firmly believed in the separation of religion and state. The fact that the Islamist Welfare Party was outlawed and that, shortly before the November elections, the public prosecutor said he planned to seek the banning of the AKP as well, undoubtedly also had something to do with Erdoğan's new thinking.

THE NEW GOVERNMENT

The AKP had to walk a very fine line between religion and secularism. Although the wives of both AKP leaders, Erdoğan and Gül, followed the Islamic practice of covering their hair with headscarves in public, the party was careful to select only those female candidates for office who either did not normally wear a headscarf, or were willing to remove it before entering the parliament or other government offices, as required by current regulations. But not all AKP politicians were so careful. A storm of controversy arose soon after the elections when Bülent Arinç, speaker of the parliament, was accompanied by his headscarf-covered wife as they went to the airport to formally bid farewell to President Ahmet Sezer before his departure for a NATO conference in Prague. (Under the Turkish constitution, the speaker becomes acting president when the president is out of the country.) The powerful and staunchly secular leaders of the Turkish military reportedly expressed deep displeasure about this when they confronted AKP leaders at the monthly meeting of the National Security Council, the country's highest policymaking body.

Indeed, the demand by some Islamist activists for the right of women to wear the headscarf in public schools and government offices remained one of the most heated issues in Turkish politics. While militant secularists saw the headscarf as a dangerous symbol of reactionary Islamic activism, human-rights advocates in Turkey, Western Europe, and the U.S. considered it a matter of individual religious choice. The Provincial Board for Human Rights in Istanbul reported that 351 of the 457 personal applications it received from the time it opened in November 2000 through the end of 2002 were complaints from university students about the ban on headscarves. Erdoğan—who had sent his own daughters to study at American universities where the headscarf would not be an issue—said he would avoid an immediate confrontation on the matter.

Clearly, Erdoğan and the AKP were determined not to repeat the mistakes that Islamist Welfare Party leader Necmettin Erbakan made when he became prime minister in July 1996. Erbakan was elected on a platform of a Muslim common market, Turkish withdrawal from its Western alliances, and an end to diplomatic relations with Israel (indeed, combining the two latter themes, he charged that Jews controlled the European Common Market.) The first official foreign visit of his administration was to the Islamic Republic of Iran, and this was followed by trips to two more Muslim states, Indonesia and Libya. Within a year of his election, Erbakan was eased out of office by the Turkish military.

After the 2002 election, both Erdoğan and Prime Minister Gül reiterated their firm commitment to the secular principles of the Turkish Republic. In sharp contrast to Erbakan, Erdoğan proclaimed as his highest foreign-policy priority the advancement of Turkey's admission to the European Union. His first trip abroad was not to Islamic Iran but to Greece, Turkey's important Christian neighbor. He proceeded to make the rounds of other European capitals, including Rome, Madrid, London, and Brussels. While in Rome, Erdoğan quipped that he sought to arrange a Catholic marriage between Turkey and Italy, meaning an unbreakable relationship not subject to divorce.

The new Turkish leadership persisted in efforts to convince the European Union to set a date for accession talks, and enlisted the support of the United States toward that end. The Americans, for their part, were eager to secure the use of Turkish bases for their planned invasion of Iraq. Erdoğan met with President Bush at the White House in December and received U.S. backing for Turkey's efforts to enter the EU, though Erdoğan was apparently noncommittal about Iraq. (When Erdoğan and his aides met with the president, Bush reportedly startled the Turks by declaring: "You believe in the Almighty, and I believe in the Almighty. That's why we'll be great partners.")

Ankara nevertheless faced an uphill battle getting into the EU, as evidenced by former French president Valéry Giscard-D'Estaing's statement in November that Turkey did not belong since it was not really a European country, and that admitting Turkey would "be the end of the European Union." One problem was that Turkey's economy lagged far behind those of the EU countries, even that of neighboring Greece. Another matter was raised by Anders Rasmussen, the Danish prime minister, who was to chair the Copenhagen summit of the EU. On a pre-summit visit to London on December 5, he told a reporter that it would be "too early at Copenhagen to produce a final statement about the next steps in Turkey's candidacy" since Turkey had first to fulfill political and human-rights conditions for entry. While progress had been made, there was "a need to see clear implementation."

But the new political leadership in Ankara suspected that more than economic and human-rights difficulties were involved and that the issue was one of hostility toward a predominantly Muslim country. After reports in early December that Germany and France had suggested deferring the start of any talks with Turkey until July 2005, Erdoğan warned that failure of the Copenhagen summit to set a firm and early date would fan Muslim anger. The *Times* of London, in fact, quoted Erdoğan as sayings that a delay would confirm his people's perception of the EU as a "Christian club." The EU, he said, should "take the chance to unite civilizations, not set them clashing." Nevertheless, at its Copenhagen summit in December 2002, the EU failed to give Ankara a firm date for the opening of accession talks, though it did so for several Eastern European countries that had applied more recently.

Israel and the Middle East

Turkish-Israeli relations had entered a new era with the beginning of direct Arab-Israeli negotiations at the Madrid peace conference in 1991, which prompted Turkey to raise its diplomatic ties with Israel and the PLO to the ambassadorial level. There was a further rapid development of Turkish-Israeli ties after the signing of the Oslo Accords in 1993. Ankara took the position that its interests were best served by supporting Israel and those Arab states prepared to make peace—notably Egypt and Jordan—against hostile Arab states and militant organizations. Over the years, Israel sold high-tech military equipment to the Turkish army and conducted joint training operations with it. Bilateral trade between the two countries, bolstered by a free-trade agreement, amounted to close to $1.2 billion, and Turkey, just a 90-minute plane ride away, was a popular vacation spot for Israelis.

In 2002, Turkey tried to play a mediating role in the Israeli-Palestinian dispute. Foreign Minister Ismail Cem and his Greek counterpart, George Papandreau, embarked on a joint mission to the Middle East on April 24–25. They met with Israeli and Palestinian leaders with the aim of calming the situation. Turkey was the only Middle Eastern state that both Israel and the Palestinian Authority could agree upon to participate in the Temporary International Presence in Hebron (TIPH). At an emergency UN Security Council session on March 29, following the Passover eve massacre in Netanya that evoked a massive Israeli antiterrorist campaign, Turkey's representative stressed that his country "is increasingly worried about this tragic cycle of violence." He made special mention of "the cold-blooded murder of a ranking Turkish member of the TIPH, along with a Swiss member, while another Turkish member was wounded" (see above, p. 195).

Another area of Turkish involvement with Israel had to do with the export of water from Turkey to the largely arid countries of the Middle East. Not only Israel, but also Jordan, the Turkish Republic of Northern Cyprus, and the Water Authority of the Palestinian Authority expressed interest in obtaining Turkish water. There was much speculation that Ankara's decision to award a $688-million contract to upgrade its American-supplied M-60 tanks to Israel's state-owned Israeli Military Industries (IMI), rather than to the competing large American or European companies, was facilitated by Israel's agreement in principle to purchase fresh water from Turkey's Manavgat River. This, in turn, would generate enough income for Turkey to pay off the $150-million cost of the Manavgat installations, and offset some of the costs paid to IMI for the tank upgrade project.

On March 22, 2002, Israel's economic cabinet decided to purchase the Turkish water "as soon as possible." On August 6, Prime Minister Ariel Sharon assured the visiting Turkish energy minister that Israel would purchase 50 million cubic meters (MCM) of water annually over 20 years. A joint Turkish-Israeli committee was formed to work out the details. Israel's Finance Ministry had opposed the project, arguing that the estimated cost-per-cubic-meter of importing the Turkish water would be nearly double the cost of desalination. Avigdor Yitzhaki, director general of the Prime Minister's Office, conceded that "the decision is not an economic one" but rather a "strategic and political" calculation based on Israel's desire to maintain close ties with Turkey. However, by the end of 2002 Ankara and Jerusalem had not yet reached agreement on the price of the water and other details of the proposed contract.

Public opinion in Turkey turned sharply against Israel at the end of March, after the Israeli army moved into Palestinian towns to root out militants after several suicide attacks against Israeli civilians. This was an awkward time for the Turkish government, since it had just given the contract to IMI, the Israeli firm, to modernize its U.S.-made tanks. Reports circulated, later found to be exaggerated, of excessive Israeli violence, even a "massacre," against Palestinians in Jenin. Prime Minister Ecevit declared that Israeli forces had engaged in "genocide," an intemperate remark for which he quickly apologized, but similar denunciations of Israeli actions came from other political leaders. Temel Karamollaoğlu, spokesman for Erbakan's Felicity Party, demanded that Ankara recall its ambassador from Tel Aviv and call off joint military exercises. He declared that Palestinian suicide bombers were not terrorists, and warned that Sharon had expansionist ambitions threatening Turkey, since the Southeastern Anatolia Project (GAP) region was included in the land promised to the Jews in the Bible. Bülent Arinç, a senior lawmaker from the AKP who would become speaker of the parliament after the November elections, told journalists on April 2: "If Turkey is to hold its head up, it should review the [tank] tender at this stage and use its right to cancel it." On the same day, in a heated special parliamentary debate on the latest Middle East crisis, Arinç declared: "Recent developments have revealed that there was not any difference between Adolf Hitler and Israeli prime minister Ariel Sharon."

Arinç's views were clearly not shared by Erdoğan, his party leader. Immediately after the November elections, Erdoğan affirmed that strategic ties with Israel would continue. In an interview with Israel Radio, he reassured his Israeli listeners: "Israeli-Turkish relations in the military, defense, and economic areas will not be hurt. The relationship between us will remain good because it is a very strong interest of the two countries, backed by the United States.

The significance that the new Turkish government attached to its relations with Israel was dramatically highlighted during Erdoğan's official visit to Washington on December 10. Even before meeting with President Bush in the White House, he met with representatives of major national Jewish organizations at a gathering convened by the American Jewish Committee. Erdoğan assured the Jewish leaders that his government would maintain good relations with Israel. He added that in his contacts with Arab countries he would try to convince them to combat manifestations of anti-Semitism. The idea of a meeting with the American Jewish representatives had been suggested by the State Department and was strongly endorsed by O. Faruk Logoğlu, Turkey's ambassador to the U.S., who also made sure that the new government's platform would explicitly endorse Turkish-Israeli relations.

Turkey's strategic cooperation with Israel on many fronts, including the war on terrorism, continued throughout the year. These included a variety of sophisticated defense-industry projects and periodic joint training exercises involving U.S., Turkish, and Israeli military units. In December 2002, for example, Turkey hosted several high-level, well-publicized visits from Israeli leaders, including Yoav Biran, acting director general of the Foreign Ministry, and Lt. Gen. Moshe Ya'alon, the army chief of staff.

Deborah Sontag, in a *New York Times* piece on Erdoğan (Sunday Magazine, May 11, 2003), suggested that the new Turkish leader had learned the importance of maintaining Jewish support through his ties with the country's business elite. In particular, Erdoğan had struck up a relationship with Ishak Alaton, a prominent member of Turkey's Jewish community and chairman and cofounder of the Alarko Group of Companies—a Turkish industrial conglomerate and appliance manufacturer that won major construction projects in Turkey and many foreign countries. Alaton introduced Erdoğan to the Turkish and American Jewish leadership and helped convince him of the importance for Turkey of maintaining good relations with Israel. Sontag noted that this required a little reeducation first. Speaking of the AKP leadership, Alaton told her, "They had this impression that the world was run by Jews." But Erdoğan, he suggested, was a practical man of good will who represented the forces of change in Turkey. "Erdoğan shouldnt be punished," the Turkish Jewish leader said. "Maybe people of good faith should understand how important he is."

But the prospect of an American invasion of Iraq in 2003 cast a shadow on the future of Turkey's relations with Jews, Israel, and the U.S. For one thing, such an invasion would be widely seen in Turkey as part of a Western assault on Islam (not to mention a venture that served Israel's interests), and it would be hard for the AKP, with its Islamist roots, to support it. Even more important, the hostilities might plunge Iraq into anarchy, inducing the Kurdish areas bordering on Turkey to secede from Iraq and tempting the Turkish Kurds to follow suit—a nightmare scenario for Turkey's powerful military establishment.

JEWISH COMMUNITY

A New Chief Rabbi

Just as Turkey elected new leadership in 2002, so did its Jewish community. Chief Rabbi (*Hahambaşı* in Turkish) David Asseo, who had been ill for several months, died on July 14, 2002, at the age of 88. Born in 1914 in Istanbul, he had worked as a teacher in Jewish schools before joining the office of the rabbinate in 1936, and was elected chief rabbi in 1961. Thus, for the first time in more than four decades, the community had to choose a new chief rabbi.

The selection was conducted in a two-stage democratic process. On October 20, all registered members of the Jewish community over the age of 18, women and men, could cast ballots for their local delegates to a lay leadership council of 120. This represented a significant enlargement of the pool of eligible voters from the previous election 41 years earlier, when only male members above the age of 21 could vote. For the 2002 election, the number of delegates from each congregation or community was determined by the size of its Jewish population. Thus Istanbul, with an estimated Jewish population of around 20,000, chose 105 of the 120 delegates, divided proportionally among the different local synagogues on the basis of membership size. Izmir, with an estimated Jewish population of 2,000, chose ten delegates. *Şalom* (Shalom), the Istanbul Jewish weekly, reported that only about 18.5 percent of those eligible voted. Women fared well in the balloting. The two largest Istanbul synagogues, each allotted 31 delegates — Neve Şalom and Ortaköy — elected six women apiece. (Another woman, Lina Filiba, one of the two executive vice presidents of the Turkish Jewish community, retained that position after the election.)

On October 21, a total of 12 religious delegates were chosen (a number set at 10 percent of the 120 communal delegates), ten from Istanbul and two from Izmir. Those voting were the religious professionals — rabbis, cantors, ritual slaughterers, and *mohalim* (performers of ritual circumcision). Community regulations required that the *Hahambaşı* must have attained the age of 40, and there were only three Turkish rabbis who fulfilled that qualification: Yehuda Adoni, Moshe Benvenisti, and Izak Haleva, all of whom were among the 12 religious delegates.

On October 24, Rabbi Haleva was chosen by acclamation after the two others withdrew. Haleva was known in the broader community for teaching popular courses on religion and philosophy at the Divinity School of Istanbul's Marmara University, and for promoting interfaith dialogue with his Muslim and Christian Turkish counterparts as well as with visiting foreign religious leaders.

Haleva was installed in a festive ceremony at the Neve Shalom Synagogue on December 19, marked by the blowing of the shofar. The doors of the Ark were opened by Rabbi Eliahu Bakshi-Doron, the visiting Israeli Sephardi chief rabbi, together with Bensiyon Pinto, president of the Turkish Jewish community. Istanbul mayor Ali Müfit Gürtuna attended, along with high-ranking Turkish officials, leaders of the country's different religious communities, and Israeli representatives. Among the foreign Jewish visitors, *Şalom* singled out Rabbi Pinchas Goldschmidt, chief rabbi of Moscow. A heavy snowstorm prevented most officials from Ankara from attending, but many sent congratulatory messages. Recep Tayyip Erdoğan, at the time chairman of the AKP, wrote: "It is my heartfelt belief that the esteemed [Chief Rabbi] Haleva's profound cultural as well as philosophical knowledge will be a source for advancing the peace and well-being not only of our Jewish community, but of all the sectors of our country."

An Aging and Shrinking Community

The Turkish Jewish community was organized under the authority of the chief rabbi according to a tripartite structure. First, a Bet Din (religious court) consisting of five rabbis adjudicated matters of Jewish law. Second, there was a 50-member lay council—its president was currently Bensiyon Pinto, a business consultant—with a smaller executive board of 18. And third, a Council of Representatives, whose membership had ranged from 220 to 250 in recent years, consisted of delegates from the various synagogues, foundations, welfare associations, and youth clubs.

The selection of delegates to the council that chose the new chief rabbi brought renewed attention to the serious drop in the Jewish population of the Turkish Republic (in 1965, the Turkish census stopped asking about religion, and so no direct government data was available.) Only one delegate each was selected from Ankara—Turkey's capital—Adana, Antioch (Antakya), Bursa, and Çanakkale because none of them had an estimated Jewish population exceeding 100. Since there had been little recent emigration—only some 40–50 persons left Turkey annually—the main reason for the ongoing decline was the aging of the community: the ratio of births to deaths was estimated at around 1:3. According to an overview of the Jewish community prepared by Lina Filiba, the number of annual births peaked at 250 in 1981 and stabilized at around 125 during the 1990s. Only 20 percent of Turkish Jews were under 25 years of age, 29 percent were between 25 and 44, 33 percent between 45 and 65, and some 18 percent 65 or older. This age profile differed markedly from that of the majority Muslim society, which had a very young average age and was rapidly growing.

There were believed to be only a few Jews still living in Edirne, Gelibolu, and Kırklareli. The absence of Edirne (Adrianople) from the list of cities selecting delegates to participate in electing the new chief rabbi confirmed the sad fact that this once flourishing Jewish community—which had 6,098 Jews according to the official Turkish census of 1927 and still some 400 in 1965—had effectively ceased to exist. Its magnificent main synagogue had begun to fall into ruin a decade earlier, and a plan to restore it and turn it into a museum run by the municipality was not implemented for lack of funds. In Ankara, the old wooden synagogue in the city's historic district had been extensively renovated in the early 1990s, but it is was now open only for the High Holy Days because the small Jewish community lacked the funds to provide security.

Lifting Restrictions on Synagogues

In August, as part of Ankara's efforts to meet the entry requirements of the European Union, the Turkish parliament adopted a series of laws designed to strengthen human rights and bring Turkey's treatment of religious and ethnic minorities more closely in line with Western European standards. One of these laws, having to do with the powers of religious foundations, was of great importance to the Jewish community.

Beginning in 1926, when Turkish Jewry relinquished its corporate legal status as a national Jewish community, every synagogue (sometimes, a group of synagogues) had to be separately incorporated as a *Vakıf,* a religious charitable foundation, each of which might dispose of its property as it saw fit. However, under a Turkish law enacted in 1935, any *Vakıf* property that no longer had a functioning community to take care of it and had not held board elections for four years would come under the authority of the *Vakıflar Müdürlüğü* (General Directorate of Charitable Foundations). Since there was virtually no area in Turkey without a functioning local Muslim community, this law in practice affected only the religious properties of the small remaining Jewish, Armenian, and Greek Orthodox minorities. Over the years, as many Jewish communities in Turkey declined, synagogues were left with no one to care for them. Since, under the law, each synagogue was a separate legal entity, assets of the neglected synagogues could not be transferred to other, functioning Jewish congregations, and instead came under the control of the *Vakıflar Müdürlüğü.*

Furthermore, in fulfillment of the 1935 law on charitable foundations, the Turkish Jewish community the next year issued a declaration listing the buildings and institutions that they possessed, but did not spell out the rules and regulations that would govern the activities of the Jewish foundations. Since it did not specify that the foundations could buy buildings or land, the Turkish authorities had ruled that they did not have the right to do so.

For years, attempts on the part of the Jewish community to have the laws changed got nowhere. Even though Turkish officials told Jewish leaders that they would like to exempt Jewish synagogues from these provisions, they did not want to set a precedent that might benefit the Armenian and Greek Orthodox communities, which controlled far larger holdings than the Jews and were seen as far greater threats to the Muslim majority.

The 2002 law gave permission to all religious community foundations to: a) acquire new buildings with the permission of the cabinet, and b) within six months from August 2002, to register in their names all buildings acquired before August 2002 for which registration rights were not previously given. While this was a positive development in principle, the need for cabinet approval and a set of heavy bureaucratic regulations adopted in October to implement the law proved extremely onerous for the Jewish community. Jewish leaders reached the conclusion that to compile all the required documents would impose upon them "an almost impossible task."

After the AKP's triumph in the November elections, party leader Tayyip Erdoğan expressed understanding for the Jewish community's predicament, and the new government took steps to abrogate the clause requiring cabinet approval for registering community-owned buildings and to cancel the complex regulations. Jewish leaders publicly expressed their gratitude.

Facing Economic Crisis

The Jewish community of Turkey, whose origins could be traced back 2,300 years, had sustained a self-sufficient and vibrant Jewish life for more than 500 years under the Ottoman Empire and 80 years in the modern Turkish Republic. The Jewish community benefited from the positive attitude of the government, which saw it as a loyal and productive element in Turkish society. Especially in recent years, Ankara came to recognize that the close fraternal and economic ties between Turkish Jews and other influential Jewish communities—notably those in the U.S. and Western Europe—could help Turkey improve its own relations with the West, and possibly gain it eventual entry into the European Union.

But this generally positive situation offered no protection from Turkey's economic crisis, which hit the predominantly middle-class Jewish community particularly hard. Once sufficiently prosperous to fund its own communal institutions and take care of the small number of families in need of financial assistance, Turkish Jewry saw its situation sharply deteriorate. By the end of 2002, over 800 members of the Jewish community, most of them businessmen over the age of 50, were unemployed with no source of income, some having to close their businesses and others forced into bankruptcy. In Turkey, where the social safety net was woefully inadequate, they could hope for virtually no public assistance.

The community responded to the crisis by establishing a special unit to deal with the economic situation, appointed lay leaders to supervise it, and began a search for a professional coordinator. With modest financial and professional assistance from the American Jewish Joint Distribution Committee (JDC), the unit provided employment counseling and advice for small-business initiatives. The JDC also established contacts for members of the Jewish community with the Manpower International Employment Agency's office in Istanbul. Training programs were implemented with JDC guidance, including a strategic-planning seminar for community leaders, a fund-raising course, and assistance in grant and proposal writing.

The economic crisis had an immediate effect on the financial health of Jewish institutions in the country. The community could no longer count on collecting regular membership dues as easily as in the past, and many who had pledged funds could not fulfill their obligations. At the same time, there were more Jewish families in need of financial aid. Health care was a particular problem. Since government-sponsored medical services were inadequate, families had purchased private health insurance at very high cost, which many were now no longer able to pay. The Jewish community had to cover the costs for the treatment of a number of complicated medical cases in 2002.

Nevertheless, outside assistance enabled the Jewish community to maintain institutions that provided services to the ill and aged. The century-old, 100-bed Or Hahayim Hospital and Jewish Home for the Aged in Istanbul, used primarily as a nursing home, underwent major renovations with the help of substantial grants from the Harry and Jeanette Weinberg Foundation. The JDC augmented this, bringing in an Israeli occupational therapist to improve the programs and activities. The Weinberg Foundation was also planning a new building for Or Hahayim with a wing for use as a psycho-geriatric center, for which the JDC-ESHEL affiliate in Israel would provide technical assistance. Another JDC project was assisting the Istanbul Jewish community to develop its "golden age club," with 200 elderly participants who met in two locations.

The problem of financing vital community institutions also affected Jewish education. The modern Jewish day school in the fashionable Ulus district of Istanbul, with places for more than 600 students in classes from kindergarten through high school, had been running an annual deficit of around $1 million for years. In the past, prosperous community members provided the funds for students' scholarships, teachers' salaries, and maintenance of the building. But the economic crisis cut sharply into the available scholarship money, forcing many students to leave, and enrollment dropped from 582 in 1998–99 to around 430 in 2002–03. Three Jewish afternoon schools (Talmud Torahs) continued to function in Šišli, Ortaköy, and Caddebostan for elementary and high-school students, and there were also after-school and weekend educational programs for children and parents in Istanbul and Izmir. Among the other informal Jewish educational activities coordinated by the Chief Rabbinate's board of education during 2002 were preschool programs, Hebrew language and discussion groups for all ages, preparation for bar/bat mitzvah, and preparation-for-marriage sessions for engaged couples.

The JDC played a particularly crucial role for the young Jews of Izmir, the second-largest Jewish community in Turkey, which had steadily declined in numbers. In 1992, after the city's only Jewish elementary school closed down, the JDC had sent a member of its Jewish Service Corps for a year of volunteer work with the city's Jewish youth. He organized programs on Jewish subjects for unaffiliated young adults, activated youth activities in nearby Çeşme, Izmir's summer resort, and led Izmir's first group of campers to the International Summer Camp in Szarvas, Hungary, cosponsored by the JDC and the Ronald S. Lauder Foundation. Since then, the JDC continued to provide scholarships for Izmir teenagers to attend the camp, which brought together Jewish teens from around the world, and to do follow-up activity with the participants after they come home. In 2002, Izmir sent 20 campers there. For 2002–03, the JDC placed two new volunteers in Turkey, one based in Istanbul and the other in Izmir, with the aim of strengthening the connection between the two communities and also reestablishing contact with the smaller Jewish communities in other cities.

The JDC also worked with the Turkish Jewish leadership to develop ties with Jewish communities in the neighboring Black Sea countries. In May 2002, Bulgaria hosted the first annual Black Sea Gesher Student Seminar, bringing together Jewish students from Bulgaria, Turkey, Romania, Ukraine, and the former Yugoslavia. The second seminar was to be hosted by Turkey in May 2003.

Cultural Life

Despite the economic difficulties, the Turkish Jewish community continued to publish its weekly newspaper *Şalom* (Shalom). It covered major political developments in Turkey, Israel, and the U.S., and also included movie reviews, historical articles on Jewish leaders and communities around the world, and a rabbi's comment on the weekly Torah reading. All but one of its 12–16 pages was in Turkish, and the other in Judeo-

Spanish, but written in the modified Turkish Latin script. Other books and pamphlets on Jewish subjects were published by Gözlem Publications of Istanbul.

The new Quincentennial Foundation (marking 500 years since the foundation of the Jewish community under the Ottoman Empire) sponsored the Jewish Museum, housed in the renovated Zulfaris synagogue, which opened to the public in November 2001.

Los Pašaros Sefaradis, a musical group founded in 1978 in Istanbul to research, collect, and perform the traditional music of the Sephardim, had produced five albums of Judeo-Spanish secular songs. In 2001, it began a new project dedicated to the liturgical music of the Istanbul synagogues. With the encouragement and professional guidance of four leading rabbis of the community, the group produced a new CD in 2002, *Zemirot: Turkish-Sephardic Synagogue Hymns.* It was accompanied by a colorful 72-page booklet in Turkish, Hebrew, and English that not only provided and explained the texts of the hymns and prayers, but also included illustrations of Turkish Jewish composers and orchestras that performed in the 1920s and 1930s. The group performed at many Jewish and non-Jewish cultural centers throughout Europe, the U.S., and Mexico. On December 9, 2002, for example, Karen Gerson Şarhon, the lead vocalist, participated in and performed at a day-long conference at Brandeis University on "Jewish Women in Turkey: Living in Multiple Worlds."

The Turkish Jewish community had long encouraged Jewish involvement in sports. Indeed, the first Maccabi Club was founded in Istanbul in 1895. The club remained an active member of the European Maccabi Confederation and hosted the tenth European Maccabi Congress, held in Istanbul from October 31 to November 3, 2002.

GEORGE E. GRUEN

The Americas

Canada

National Affairs

CANADA ENJOYED A PEACEFUL YEAR marked by robust economic growth, modest inflation, and a marginal increase in the value of the currency against the U.S. dollar. The central political event was Prime Minister Jean Chrétien's announcement in August that he would retire in February 2004. After nine years in office, Chrétien faced increased restlessness from within his Liberal Party, especially from supporters of his presumptive successor, Paul Martin. Although Martin was widely credited with steering the country toward fiscal responsibility as finance minister, he was never a favorite of the prime minister, who sacked him in June. As soon as Chrétien's impending retirement was announced, Martin immediately became the front-runner to succeed him. In addition to the Liberals, two other parties were looking for new leaders, the Progressive Conservatives and the New Democrats.

Herb Gray, the senior Jewish member of Parliament, resigned his seat in the House of Commons after a January cabinet shuffle. He had entered Parliament in 1962, was the first Jewish cabinet minister at the federal level, and, most recently, served as deputy prime minister. Upon his departure he was awarded the title of Right Honourable, a rare distinction for an MP who had not served as prime minister.

In November, Senator Jerry Grafstein introduced a resolution condemning anti-Semitic violence in Europe and Canada. He was concerned about the increase of arson attacks on Jewish institutions and other anti-Semitic incidents, and the weakness of the Canadian government's response. In a Senate speech, he declared that "silence is acquiescence. Acquiescence breeds license. License breeds legitimacy. Legitimacy leads to fear, scorn, loathing, and then violence." Grafstein's Senate colleagues appeared surprised at his revelation of the extent of anti-Semitic manifestations in Canada in recent years.

The Montreal office of MP Irwin Cotler was taken over by protesters in April. Seven young men and women, opposed to what they termed Canadian government support for Israel, staged what Cotler denounced as "an illegal occupation." They called on the government to toughen its stand against what they labeled Israeli human rights violations, using Cotler's reputation as a champion of human rights to draw attention to their cause. All were arrested.

In October, Cotler took on the Federal Electoral Boundaries Commission, which was redrawing legislative districts in the wake of the 2001 census. The commission proposed to change the boundaries of Cotler's Mount Royal riding (district) in Montreal, which was also the constituency with the highest proportion of Jews. Cotler objected to the dilution of the Jewish community's political weight, the imposition of artificial lines that would arbitrarily divide elements of the community and ignore natural geographic boundaries, and the separating, for electoral purposes, of key Jewish institutions from the main part of the Jewish community. In making his case, he cited the law requiring that community identity and historical patterns must be taken into account in determining district lines.

Observant Jews in Ontario were concerned about their effective disenfranchisement as the Ontario Progressive Conservative Party prepared to select a new leader (and provincial premier as well) in March. The process involved voting by party members throughout the province. The vote was scheduled for the Sabbath and party rules did not allow absentee ballots or advance voting. The only option to voting in person was to utilize a proxy vote, but several Toronto rabbis ruled that proxy voting was also a violation of the Sabbath. Despite intervention by the Canadian Jewish Congress (CJC), no allowance was made, but the party decided to allow advance polling for future leadership votes held on Saturday.

TERRORISM

In the aftermath of the September 11 terror attacks in the United States, Canada became concerned about possible threats within its own territory. Most of the debate throughout the year concerned which terrorist organizations would be included on the government's official list, and since placement on the list carried penalties—such as freezing financial assets—decisions were significant. The government was wary of entering too deeply into the Middle East political thicket, and it therefore proved difficult to have groups linked with the Palestinians listed.

In August, Solicitor-General Lawrence MacAulay announced the names of seven groups officially listed as terrorist, according to criteria contained in the Anti-Terrorism Act. But MP Irwin Cotler quickly pointed out the omission of Hamas, Islamic Jihad, and Hezballah, which he termed "an affront to the moral, juridical, diplomatic, and political struggle against terrorism" that "undermines our counterterrorism law and policy." Both CJC and the Simon Wiesenthal Center joined in the criticism, pointing out that these groups perpetrated homicide bombings against Israel. Later in August, representatives of several national Jewish organizations met with Foreign Minister Bill Graham to press the point. Graham later argued, however, that because of the lawyers, doctors, teachers, and social workers of Hezballah, "all of whom are doing good work," the social and political wings of that group should not be labeled terrorist. Opposition foreign-affairs critic Stockwell Day countered with the case of a Lebanese-Canadian, Fauzi Ayoub, to demonstrate the need for tougher action. Ayoub had been arrested in Israel and charged with being a Hezballah agent dispatched to foment terror attacks.

Cotler continued to pursue the issue during the fall, speaking out in the House of Commons and meeting himself with Graham and with Chrétien. In a speech in the House, Cotler denounced the three organizations as "transnational genocidal terrorists" that seek "the destruction of Israel and the killing of Jews everywhere." He later described the dilatory treatment of Hezballah as "unconscionable." Harvard law professor Alan Dershowitz added his voice in a Toronto speech in November castigating Graham: "Your foreign minister is on the wrong side of history, the wrong side of morality, the wrong side of experience." By December, the opposition Canadian Alliance had joined the fray, stepping up the pressure on the government. In this it was aided by a report that appeared in the *National Post* in November, based on Canadian Security Intelligence Service documents, that Hezballah was raising funds, laundering money, and buying military equipment in Canada. Operatives were reported to be in Montreal, Toronto, and Vancouver. The government finally gave in and banned all Hezballah activities in the country. CJC blamed the prime minister and foreign minister for the delay, charging them of trying to improve relations with Lebanon at the cost of turning a blind eye to terrorism

One of the victims of a Hamas attack on a yeshivah in the Gaza community of Atzmona in March was Asher Marcus, who held dual Canadian and Israeli nationality. Responding to the generally heightened danger posed by terrorists, the Canadian government issued warnings in August urging citizens to avoid all tourist travel to Israel.

A Toronto attorney, Sergio Karas, spurred to action by the fact that most of the September 11 hijackers were Saudis, took on the government over the Canadian policy of visa-free entry for Saudi Arabian citizens. He noted that citizens of other Arab countries required visas, that few other Western nations allowed Saudi citizens in without visas, and that the existing policy constituted a serious threat to Canada's security and especially to its Jewish citizens. In September, the government changed its visa policy in line with Karas's request. While expressing satisfaction, Karas lamented the lack of support he received from Jewish MPs and organizations.

Israel and the Middle East

While acknowledging periodic disagreements, Israeli ambassador Haim Divon characterized the Canada-Israel relationship as basically strong. He referred to Canada as "one of our closest friends." But in March, *Canadian Jewish News* columnist Morton Weinfeld identified some ongoing problems. For one thing, many politicians and government officials viewed Israel's presence in the West Bank and Gaza Strip as the "root cause" of the Palestinian terror war, a perspective that made them interpret Palestinian terrorism as a fight for freedom. Also, Arabs and other Muslims in Canada were gaining political clout, and there was no "peace camp" among them. Stockwell Day, the former leader of the opposition Canadian Alliance, attacked the government's Middle East stand. Speaking in Montreal in February, he called on Canada to suspend all financial support for the Palestinian Authority because of Yasir Arafat's continuing tolerance of terrorist activities. Day expressed skepticism about Arafat's proclamations against terrorism, pointing out that "he allows Hamas, Hezballah, and Islamic Jihad to openly operate in his own territory," described Canada's policy as unbalanced, and urged his country to "stand with the U.S. and Israel against this 'axis of evil.'"

In March, the prime minister addressed the annual parliamentary dinner of the Canada-Israel Committee (CIC) in Ottawa. In the presence of Israeli president Moshe Katzav, Chrétien denounced "the use of violence for political objectives by any state or group." He also urged Israel to seek a just and lasting peace notwithstanding the continuing terrorist attacks, but he framed that remark in the context of a call for a "full guarantee of a safe and secure Israel." Foreign Minister Graham also addressed the CIC meeting. While generally supportive of Israel and its right to respond to terrorism, he raised questions about the way it exercised that right. He argued that "Israel's image as a vital and compassionate nation" might suffer as it inflicted casualties on civilians while defending itself. Graham also denied that Palestinian educational materials funded by a Canadian government agency contained anti-Jewish and anti-Israel ideas. One issue that Graham downplayed in his speech was Canada's voting record in the UN, a topic that many in the audience had wanted to hear about. The prime minister, in his remarks, undertook that "Canada will oppose the effort to undermine the legitimacy of Israel at the United Nations or at any other international forums."

Canada's voting record in the UN remained a sore point throughout the year. Since the country was a staunch advocate of the UN as a force for world peace, Canadians closely followed their government's role in the world body. For years Canadian Jews had charged that the close ties between Israel and Canada and their shared values were not reflected in Canada's performance at the UN. Indeed, the *Canadian Jewish News* contended editorially that "the truth about Canada's voting record at the United Nations is that it is unjustifiably, inexcusably, irredeemably shameful." Over the course of 2002, however, Canada appeared less inclined to support blatantly anti-Israel resolutions.

In February, Canada abstained in a General Assembly vote to implement some of the decisions of the 2001 World Conference Against Racism, held in Durban, South Africa, which was widely perceived as hostile to Israel. In a statement following the vote, the government emphatically dissociated itself from anything that emerged in Durban relating to the Middle East. Israel's UN ambassador, Yehuda Lancry, urged Canada to take a lead role in the UN Commission on Human Rights (UNCHR) and praised Canada for always being "immediately behind the United States in helping to support and defend Israel." Community leaders were pleased when Canada voted against two UNCHR resolutions in April, one on sending a fact-finding mission to the West Bank and the other condemning Israel for mass killings. Canada abstained again in May on a General Assembly resolution criticizing Israel's retaliatory military operations in the territories and its refusal to work with UN factfinders probing events in the Jenin refugee camp. In December, the General Assembly passed six resolutions on the Middle East that Israel opposed as one-sided attempts to prejudge the contents of a solution between it and the Palestinians. Canada voted in favor of three of them and abstained on the other three. On most of these votes, few countries joined Israel and the United States in opposition. Canada's voting pattern, in fact, was similar to those of many European countries.

Israel's military response to the Passover seder bombing in Netanya (see above, p. 199) drew criticism from the Canadian government. At the beginning of April, the Foreign Ministry condemned Israel for its "disproportionate" use of force. That was followed by calls on Israel from both the prime minister and the foreign minister to withdraw from Palestinian cities taken over during the retaliatory offensive. Chrétien blamed Israel for not complying with UN Security Council Resolution 1402 in that regard, and called for the creation of a Palestinian state "eventually, as soon as possible." Graham, in a conference call with reporters, denounced suicide bombings but appeared to classify Israeli responses as part of a cycle of violence that made the achievement of peace more difficult. Jewish leaders were quick to criticize statements they believed lacked empathy for the predicament that Israel faced. CIC chair Joseph Wilder characterized the prime minister's remarks as "unfortunate," while CJC president Keith Landy contended that "this is hardly the time for Canada" to be playing its traditional even-handed role. B'nai Brith Canada (BBC) president Rochelle Wilner contrasted the government's approval of the U.S. response to the 9/11 suicide bombings to its condemnations of Israel's response to the same type of provocation.

Graham paid his first visit to the Middle East as foreign minister in May, making stops in Israel, Egypt, Jordan, and the Palestinian Authority. After meeting with his Israeli counterpart, Shimon Peres, he expressed understanding for Israel's actions to counter terrorism, observing that such moves "can be helpful if in fact they are specifically designed to deal with the terrorist menace." He also came out strongly against collective punishment for innocent Palestinian civilians, and envisioned a peaceful future between the two peoples living next to each other in independent states. He asked each side to recognize that the other needed to live in peace and security.

The government responded equivocally to President George W. Bush's June 24 speech on the route to Israeli-Palestinian peace. Prime Minister Chrétien at first expressed support for Bush's idea of replacing Arafat as leader of the Palestinians, but then backtracked, saying that it was "up to the people of Palestine" to choose their leader.

The CJC sharply criticized the prime minister for his comments at the summit of La Francophonie (an international organization of French-speaking communities) in Beirut in October. Chrétien gave his speech while Hezballah head Sheik Hassan Nasrallah was sitting just a few feet away, but he seemed oblivious to the presence of the terrorist leader. A spokesperson later claimed that he had been unaware of the sheik's identity. But CJC president Landy was "flabbergasted that Jean Chrétien would be speaking in the presence of the sheik," and further disturbed that he had failed to react to a provocative anti-Israel tirade by Lebanon's president, Émile Lahoud. When reporters asked Chrétien how he was able to shake Lahoud's hand after such a speech, Chrétien replied that "it's not my opinion. But I say the violence on both sides must stop. Call violence by one name or another, for me it's violence." After reviewing the record of the summit, CJC's national executive committee passed a resolution saying it was "appalled" at the prime minister's failure to respond to Lahoud and at his explanatory comments afterward.

In November, the CIC charged that money that Canada contributed to UNRWA, the UN agency that maintained Palestinian refugee camps, helped pay for school books for Palestinian students that "demonize, delegitimize and deny Israel's place in the region." UNRWA denied the allegations, while Canadian officials claimed to be investigating them.

Canada criticized Egypt for allowing the broadcast of a television series based on the *Protocols of the Elders of Zion*. Marie-Christine Lilkoff, a spokesperson for the Ministry of Foreign Affairs, declared in November that the government was "appalled," since the 41-part series "contains strongly anti-Semitic undertones. Such messages are simply unacceptable." She added that the Canadian ambassador to Egypt had spoken to Egyptian officials about the matter and that other Canadian diplomats in the Middle East had frequently spoken out against anti-Semitism.

The tax department—Canada Customs and Revenue Agency (CCRA)—gave Canadian Friends of Magen David Adom for Israel (CMDA) quite a bit of difficulty by seeking to withdraw its eligibility to receive tax deductible contributions because of various alleged improprieties that cast doubt upon its charitable status. The Federal Court of Appeal ruled in a split decision in September that one of the allegations, that CMDA did not retain ownership of the ambulances sent to Israel, was meritorious. On the other hand, the use of the ambulances over the Green Line—in the territories—was found not to be contrary to public policy, as CCRA had claimed. That aspect of the ruling had positive implications for other Canadian charitable bodies that carried out activities in the territories. In the end, CMDA, facing revocation of its charitable status over the issue of ownership of the ambulances, struck a deal with the CCRA that provided for CMDA's retention of ownership.

Throughout the year, the MP considered most hostile to Israel was Svend Robinson, foreign affairs critic for the New Democratic Party (NDP). Jewish animosity toward Robinson was so deep that a portrait of him, part of an art exhibit at the Vancouver Jewish Community Center, was removed in response to community protests. In April, his party leader stripped Robinson of responsibility for the Middle East because of his anti-Israel bias.

Despite friction over the Palestine issue, other aspects of the Canada-Israel relationship functioned smoothly. The Department of Foreign Affairs and International Trade published a report in April documenting rapid growth in bilateral trade. As a result of a free-trade agreement between the two countries that sharply reduced or eliminated duties on many products, the value of the trade had doubled in five years to more than $1 billion annually. About two-thirds of it consisted of Canadian imports from Israel. In addition, a Canadian firm was a major participant in building the Cross-Israel Highway. In October, El Al and Air Canada concluded a code-sharing agreement that benefited both airlines and afforded greater flexibility for travelers.

For budgetary reasons, the Israeli Foreign Ministry decided in July to make the Montreal consulate one of eight around the world that would be closed. However, after strong protests from the Canadian and Quebec governments and from the Montreal Jewish community, the ministry announced in September that the consulate would remain open. Outgoing consul general Shlomo Avital declared that "it's a good day for the Jewish community and all our friends in Quebec." It was reported that the final decision was made by Prime Minister Sharon. A similar closure plan had been aborted in 1998.

PUBLIC OPINION AND THE MEDIA

The role of the media in shaping public attitudes about the Arab-Israeli conflict became a subject for debate. In February, Ghila Sroka, editor of *Tribune Juive,* attacked the French-language media in Quebec for their anti-Israel bias, which, she said, had worsened since 9/11 and the terrorist campaign mounted by the Palestinians. She singled out the government-owned radio and television network Radio-Canada (the French-language CBC) as the worst offender. In November, her magazine titled its issue, "Montréal: capitale de la Palestine." In the lead story Sroka lamented the emergence of a "judéophobie perverse" in the universities, the media, and the unions, where "anti-Jewish ideas circulate freely without encountering the least resistance."

Israel Asper, owner of a number of significant media properties, lashed out at the international media for bias against Israel. Speaking in Montreal in October, he blamed journalists for ignorance or sloppiness at best, anti-Semitism at worst. "The result is that the biggest casualties of the Palestinian-Israeli war are truth and the integrity of the media," contended the founder of CanWest Global Communications. He charged that many in the media "have adopted Palestinian propaganda as the context of their stories. They have become partisans in, and not providers of, knowledge about this war against Israel." Asper went on to cite fundamental lies and misleading representations that routinely colored the presentation of Middle East news. He singled out the government-owned CBC and its correspondent in Israel, Neil Macdonald, for special opprobrium, focusing on Macdonald's handling of the alleged massacre in Jenin and his refusal to "label the Palestinian murderers as terrorists."

In July, York University professor Eric Lawee wrote in the *National Post* about his correspondence with the CBC over its refusal to use the word "terrorist" in connection with the Palestinian suicide bombers. In response, CBC ombudsman David Bazay wrote that to comply would mean taking sides and embracing "the Israeli government's position and its definition of terrorism, which denies the legitimacy of Palestinian resistance." But Lawee showed that the network used the term in other, non-Palestinian contexts, such as in reference to Al Qaeda, which also claimed to be a movement of "resistance," and that the CBC's position was therefore inconsistent and hypocritical. Bazay and Lawee both clarified their positions in August in the pages of the *Canadian Jewish News*. Bazay claimed that he had been misinterpreted; correspondents could use the disputed word "terrorist," but had to be extremely careful about doing so in connection with the Palestinians, since there was a tendency in Israel "to equate Palestinian resistance [such as attacks against soldiers] with terrorism." Lawee responded that, after extensive research, he had not found a single example of a CBC reporter describing a Palestinian attack, even against civilians, as "terrorist." He was not asking that Palestinians be routinely referred to as terrorists, only that the term be used when terrorist acts were committed.

The debate intensified in September when CIC media specialist Paul Michaels contended that Neil Macdonald was indeed taking sides in his coverage of the conflict, and that CBC reports generally lacked balance. The CIC proposed several concrete steps to increase the fairness of the CBC's coverage, including more documentaries sensitive to the Israeli perspective, more reporting on Arab and Muslim hostility toward Israel, more balance in each report, and a greater willingness to label terrorism accurately. In response, CBC executive Tony Burman rejected the bias charges and blamed critics for exaggerating the issue of "terrorism" terminology. He cited internal reports by Bazay that found that Macdonald's work was not systematically anti-Israel, and concluded that the CBC's overall reporting was "generally well-balanced, giving fair and reasonable voice to both the Israeli and Palestinian points of view." Shimon Fogel, the top CIC professional, expressed great disappointment with the network's response, and, in December, the CIC threatened to raise the issue of balance with Parliament and with the nation's broadcast regulator.

Norman Spector, a former ambassador to Israel, opened up another front against the national broadcaster in December. In an open letter in the *Ottawa Citizen* to the CBC's top news anchor, followed up by an article in the *Victoria Times-Colonist,* he accused the CBC of employing a double moral standard by using "terrorist" to describe the perpetrators of the Bali bombing, but not when writing about Palestinians attacking Israelis. In an allusion to 9/11, Spector charged that "aside from being irresponsible and amoral, your failure to call Hamas a terrorist organization betrays another double standard. When the blood on the sidewalk is Israeli, it's one thing, when American, it's another." He went on to identify numerous inconsistencies in the application of CBC policy to the detriment of Israel, and criticized Neil Macdonald for his lack of knowledge about Israel. Spector also challenged Burman, the CBC executive, to an open debate on his network's policies.

A number of religious organizations took stands critical of Israel during the year. The Canadian Ecumenical Justice Initiative, known as KAIROS, called on the government to side with the Palestinians in March—before the Passover bombing in Netanya and the subsequent major Israeli incursion into the West Bank—and also to help impose a settlement that would end Israel's "illegal" occupation of "Palestinian territories." KAIROS, formed in 2001, included "peace and social justice" elements from the Catholic, Anglican, Reformed, Mennonite, Lutheran, Presbyterian, Quaker, and United churches. Also in March, John Baycroft, the retired Anglican bishop of Ottawa, compared Israel to South Africa in a speech at a screening of a pro-Palestinian film. "What we see happening in the Holy Land is official oppression—evil being done." A far more balanced statement was issued in April by the Canadian Conference of Catholic Bishops, lamenting the escalation of conflict in the Middle East, condemning war and terrorism, and urging the Canadian government to help achieve peace.

Labor unions also got involved. The Central des Syndicats du Québec (CSQ), a large labor federation, circulated a petition among its members in May sharply condemning Israel's response to terrorist attacks and urging the government to pressure Israel to withdraw unilaterally from Palestinian territory. The one-sided petition criticized Israel's policies since 1967, characterized the occupation as the fundamental cause of the continuing "crisis in Palestine," and termed Israel's control of the Territories as apartheid. Later that month, the Ontario region of the Canadian Union of Public Employees (CUPE) adopted a resolution that referred to an Israeli "invasion" of the territories in 1967 and called for the government to demand action by Israel (but no action from the other side). Carolyn Roberts, president of a union local representing Jewish community workers, denounced the resolution as biased.

Notwithstanding her intercession, in June the Canadian Labour Congress (CLC) convention in Vancouver passed a resolution calling upon Israel to withdraw from Palestinian areas, and it was accompanied by a statement from the executive that compared Israel to South Africa's former apartheid regime. CJC dismissed it as "simplistic and replete with inaccuracies and just plain errors," while former Ontario premier Bob Rae said the apartheid label "indicates a level of ignorance and animosity toward the state which to me is over the line." Former CLC president Dennis McDermott criticized the organization for "coming down on Israel like a ton of bricks, and by association, Jewish people everywhere," and expressed concern that anti-Semitism was creeping into the labor movement. In September, a union official carried the CUPE flag in a Toronto demonstration against an appearance by former prime minister Benjamin Netanyahu.

Former MP Warren Allmand, who headed the International Centre for Human Rights and Democratic Development until mid-year, wrote to Foreign Minister Graham on behalf of his organization asking for Canadian pressure on Israel to withdraw to the pre-1967 lines. He also called for an international peacekeeping force, and upbraided the government for voting against a proposed investigation by the UN Commission on Human Rights into Israeli actions in the territories (see above, p. 204). David Matas, a human-rights expert and a member of the group's board, criticized Allmand for his letter. In June, Louise Harel, speaker of the Quebec National Assembly, marched in a pro-Palestinian demonstration sponsored by the Coalition for Peace and Justice in Palestine and told a newspaper that "what is happening over there is inhumane." In October, the CSQ and this coalition held a press conference to call for a boycott of Israeli products. As the Christmas holiday approached, a Liberal MP from Quebec sent out cards to his constituents with a picture of him and Arafat on the cover.

Somewhat surprisingly, in light of the pro-Palestinian tendencies evident in the media, organized labor, and other Canadian institutions, the results of national public-opinion polls were modestly encouraging for supporters of Israel. In March, an Ipsos-Reid poll showed that 16 percent supported Israel, 12 percent the Palestinians, 17 percent both, and 48 percent neither. Israel found its greatest support in British Columbia and Alberta, while Quebecers were the most likely to support the Palestinians. A COMPAS poll in April found that 74 percent of Canadians saw Yasir Arafat as a terrorist, and that a majority blamed the Arabs for tensions with Israel.

THE CAMPUSES

Montreal's Concordia University was the focal point of radical anti-Israel and anti-Jewish action by militant Arab students. Clashes between them and Jewish students had erupted in past years, and pro-Israel students already lived within a pervasive atmosphere of hostility and intimidation. A legally independent Concordia Student Union (CSU) that avidly supported the Palestinian cause, combined with a weak and indecisive administration, created a volatile setting in which academic freedom was at risk. In 2001, students who were dissatisfied with the direction of their student government organized to force new elections. However the moderate slate that won the election was disqualified on a technicality and new elections were ordered for March 2002 (see AJYB 2002, p. 293).

The victors this time were once again aligned with the pro-Palestinian radicals, some of whom now gained official positions. Only about 10 percent of the students voted, and the last of the three days of voting coincided with the first day of Passover, which probably contributed to diminishing the vote of Jewish students. A request to allow advance polling to accommodate the Jewish students was rejected by the CSU council. The campaign was marked by what a Jewish student termed "the hatred, anti-Semitism and anti-Israel undercurrent," including a provocative display of mock Palestinian gravestones by the Solidarity for Palestinian Human Rights (SPHR).

Matters came to a head in September over a scheduled lecture by former Israeli prime minister Benjamin Netanyahu, who was invited by Hillel to provide a strong Israeli voice in response to the propaganda emanating from the SPHR and CSU. The anti-Israel groups vowed to prevent him from speaking, leading the administration to institute unprecedented security arrangements at the main campus building, the chosen venue. On the day of the lecture, violent protesters created a ruckus that campus security and Montreal police were unable to control. Things got out of hand, and rioters smashed glass windows, threw chairs and other objects at police, and abused and assaulted people on their way into the lecture. Under the circumstances and on the advice of law enforcement, the administration canceled the event and imposed a moratorium on Middle East-related events that was not lifted until late November.

These violent protests were organized by the Quebec Coalition for a Just Peace in the Middle East, and a key role was played by Aaron Mate, a vice president of CSU. Five people were arrested in connection with the riot and faced criminal charges. In addition, the university instituted disciplinary proceedings against 12 identifiable ringleaders. Jewish leaders criticized both the police and the administration for failing to provide adequate security, the CJC calling it acquiescence to mob rule. Netanyahu, who had remained at a nearby hotel during the melee, declared that "what we had was a coercive riot to prevent the airing of the truth . . . our facts against their myths." Later, the Montreal police chief explained that his forces had been unprepared for the violent protest.

The riot energized the local Jewish community, which vowed not to be intimidated. At a rally a few days later at a local synagogue, Rabbi Chaim Steinmetz referred to the events as a "miniature Kristallnacht," Montreal Hillel president Yoni Petel promised that Jewish students would not be driven out of Concordia, and Israeli consul general Shlomo Avital evoked the image of the intifada spreading to university campuses. Separately, Petel criticized the university moratorium on Middle East-related events for making law-abiding pro-Israel students suffer for the actions of their opponents.

Concordia rector Frederick Lowy, however, defended the moratorium as a needed cooling-off period. He and Concordia Hillel president Patrick Amar were booed at a campus forum on free speech when they defended the decision to invite Netanyahu. In an address to the Federation CJA annual meeting a few weeks later, Lowy urged his audience not to abandon Concordia despite the provocations. "It hurts especially to be vilified by Jewish organizations, the Jewish press, and from some synagogue pulpits, given [the] historic role of Concordia in educating the Jewish community and promoting Judaic studies." Simon Wiesenthal wrote a letter to Lowy from Vienna asking the university to invite Netanyahu again, since "failure to do so will only further embolden those who see violence as the only way to achieve results." No decision was forthcoming as the year ended.

Campus antagonisms took a new turn in December when the CSU, citing allegedly unauthorized flyers found on an information table, suspended Hillel's right to function as a student organization. The suspension was pushed through a late-night CSU council meeting under questionable circumstances. The decision denied Hillel access to about $3,000 annually in funding and, more importantly, the permission to book university facilities for its activities. A substitute resolution a week later that eased some of the sanctions but did not reverse the decision entirely condemned Hillel for distributing information about Mahal, a program for Diaspora Jews to serve for a year in the Israel Defense Force. It demanded that Hillel sign an agreement to cease recruitment for any military or paramilitary organization, a demand rejected by Hillel. Later in December, Hillel filed suit against CSU for $100,000 in punitive damages, claiming that the suspension was illegal and its constitutional rights had been violated. Hillel also named the university as a corespondent for failing to "assert its authority over its facilities and university life," and for not standing up to the CSU. Subsequently, the CJC and BBC sought intervener status on the case, CJC president Landy proclaiming that "CJC will not stand idly by as Jewish students are persecuted and their organizations disenfranchised."

Issues arose at other universities as well. As the new academic year approached in late summer, the Arts and Sciences Student Union (ASSU) at the University of Toronto—the undergraduate student society—published an "Anti-Calendar" dedicated "to the memory of the Innocents in Afghanistan and Palestine, murdered." (The Anti-Calendar was an annual guide to courses and professors.) ASSU refused to apologize as requested by Jewish students, and said that the reference to Palestine was meant to "include everyone in the region," rejecting the suggestion that Israeli victims of terrorism had been excluded from the category of "innocents." Adam Cutler, a Hillel leader, vowed to continue to press for an apology even though a university race-relations officer found that the publication was not racist.

At the Ontario Institute for Studies in Education, affiliated with University of Toronto, Jewish leaders complained in April that a professor—Sherene Razack, who headed the school's Centre for Anti-Racism Studies—was using university facilities to circulate an anti-Israel petition. This petition, accompanied by a cover letter, suggested that Israeli troops might have perpetrated crimes against humanity at Jenin and Nablus and referred to "atrocities beyond belief." After pressure from BBC, the university deleted a link between its Web site and the petition, and publicly dissociated itself from Razack's activities.

In December, the Université du Québec à Montréal (UQAM) flip-flopped on the matter of a lecture by Israeli-French journalist Gideon Kouts. At first the administration canceled it on a technicality, presumably fearing violence such as what had transpired at Concordia. But after considerable adverse publicity, the administration relented and allowed the lecture to go on. Kouts recounted his experiences in Beirut in October, when he was barred from covering the summit meeting of the Francophonie (see below, pp. 390–91). He found his UQAM experience comparable, though on a smaller scale—both threatened the "free exchange of ideas."

Laval University's Annette Paquot published an op-ed in *Le Devoir* in the summer condemning the attempted international academic boycott of Israel and its citizens. Asking why Israel was being singled out and why most of her colleagues were so indifferent to such an injustice, she suspected an element of "hidden anti-Semitism." The Society for Academic Freedom and Scholarship also condemned the boycott and declared "any such actions contemptible, political attacks that violate academic freedom. . . ." In a related move, York University translation professor Candace Seguinot resigned from the editorial board of *The Translator* to protest the journal's British editor's sacking of two Israeli professors as part of the academic boycott (see below, p. 364).

Anti-Semitism and Racism

Anger toward Israel spilled over into hostility toward Jews. After a long period during which Canadian anti-Semitism had appeared under control or even on the wane, expressions of anti-Semitism, sometimes in the guise of anti-Zionism, became more common in 2002. Perhaps the most shocking event of the year was the cold-blooded, unprovoked murder of David Rosenzweig, who was obviously Jewish in appearance, in front of a kosher pizza parlor in Toronto late on a Saturday night in July. Although the killer appeared to be a skinhead and there was no previous connection between him and the victim, authorities remained unconvinced that anti-Semitism provided the motivation. Among Jews, however, there was a widespread perception that Rosenzweig had been targeted because he was Jewish. Witnesses reported that the killer had cursed at Jews shortly before the attack. Ed Morgan, Ontario Region Chair of the CJC, asked, "Why else would a skinhead be at a kosher restaurant other than to harass the Jewish customers? When an Orthodox man is killed for no reason whatsoever, it seems like a hate crime."

U.S. intelligence sources compiled a list of 22 Canadian sites believed to be high-priority targets of Al Qaeda. The *National Post* published the list in November, and it included four synagogues, two in Toronto and one each in Winnipeg and Montreal. One synagogue that was actually bombed was Quebec City's Beth Israel Ohev Shalom, in May. The person who planted the pipe bomb was not apprehended. There were also several attacks of vandalism early in April, during Israel's incursion into West Bank towns. They occurred at Temple Israel in Ottawa, Reena, a social-service agency in the Toronto suburb of Thornhill, a Jewish community center in Toronto, and a synagogue in Saskatoon. The last, Agudas Israel, suffered $130,000 of damage from a firebomb. Also in April, Dr. Bernard Goldman, a physician, happened upon some 1,000 pro-Palestinian demonstrators marching to the Israeli consulate in Toronto on Land Day. After denouncing suicide bombers to a protester, Goldman was shoved against a parked car and suffered a broken shoulder. Charges were brought against his Palestinian assailant. A Toronto synagogue, Anshe Minsk, suffered a mysterious fire in April, and arson was suspected. At Toronto's Ryerson University, there was an outbreak of viciously anti-Semitic graffiti in January.

Another kind of incident occurred in April. After a pro-Israel rally attended by thousands of Jews outside the Parliament buildings in Ottawa, two young participants were arrested in the nearby Rideau Centre, a shopping mall, allegedly for refusing to put away an Israeli flag that they were carrying. The two men claimed that security guards had made abusive comments about them as Jews and about the flag. Mall officials denied the accusations and said that the men had violated a policy that barred the display of any flag in the mall. Subsequent investigations failed to sustain the claim of abusive or racist statements. A similar incident involving the Israeli flag occurred in Montreal the same month, also after a pro-Israel demonstration, when the owner of a coffee shop refused to serve three young women who were carrying the flag. In that case the corporate headquarters of Second Cup quickly apologized for the actions of its franchisee. In May, someone removed "March to Jerusalem" posters from lampposts in a Montreal suburb, piled them on the front lawn of a synagogue, and burned them.

David Ahenakew, an aboriginal leader from Saskatchewan, told a reporter in December that Hitler was right to try to annihilate the Jews of Europe, whom he termed a "disease." The ensuing uproar induced Ahenakew to apologize and to resign his position with the Federation of Saskatchewan Indian Nations. There were also calls to revoke his membership in the Order of Canada. Matthew Coon Come, chief of the Assembly of First Nations, reached out to the Jewish community in the aftermath of the Ahenakew affair. He attended Sabbath services at Montreal's Spanish and Portuguese Synagogue, expressed his outrage about the anti-Semitic remarks, and praised Jewish involvement in the struggle for human rights. In a letter to the *Canadian Jewish News,* Coon Come characterized Ahenakew's comments as "repugnant, hateful, ignorant and slanderous."

The alarming rise in anti-Semitic incidents led B'nai Brith Canada (BBC) to accelerate its reporting. Instead of waiting until the year was over to issue its *Audit of Antisemitic Incidents,* it produced a mid-year report in July. It catalogued 197 incidents during the first half of the year, compared to 121 for the same period in 2001 and 286 for all of that year. Most occurred in the two largest cities—Toronto had 96 and Montreal 49. There was a noticeable percentage increase in Winnipeg, even though the absolute number, 14, was small. The annual audit for 2002, released after the end of the year, tallied 459 anti-Semitic incidents, the highest number ever reported in the 20-year history of the audit and an increase of 60.48 percent over 2001. Twenty-nine of the incidents involved physical violence, including the murder of Rosenzweig. More than a third of all the year's incidents took place in April and May, after the bombing in Netanya, when Israeli troops were operating in Palestinian territory.

The Canadian judicial system showed little tolerance for racism and anti-Semitism. The case against Ernst Zundel's Web site (see AJYB 2001, pp. 287–88) concluded in January when a human-rights tribunal found that the site "viciously targeted" Jews and exposed them to hatred or contempt, and ordered Zundel to remove all anti-Semitic material from it. The CJC's Ed Morgan said he was "quite pleased they found that Holocaust denial is the equivalent of hate propaganda" against Jews. Former Toronto-area public-school teacher Paul Fromm lost his grievance against his dismissal for consorting with racists. In March, an arbitration panel ruled 2-1 that his position as a teacher justified restrictions on his freedom of expression. Jordanian-born Yousef Sandouga was sentenced to one year in jail for the 2000 firebombing of Beth Shalom Synagogue in Edmonton (see AJYB 2001, p. 288). He had pleaded guilty to one count of arson, declaring that his motivation was anger toward Israel. The Crown appealed the sentence, and a three-judge panel of the Alberta Court of Appeal increased his term to 30 months, concluding, "Sandouga's act of revenge-based arson was a terrorist act, a hate crime and an act of religious intimidation." In a civil action, former Quebec politician Yves Michaud lost his defamation lawsuit against a professor who had termed remarks he made about Jews in 2000 anti-Semitic. The judge found that Marc Angenot's observations in a 2001 television interview were "fair comment in light of [Michaud's] previous remarks." British author David Icke, accused of promoting anti-Semitic conspiracy theories, found that theaters in Vancouver were unwilling to rent their space to him for a proposed public seminar in February.

A national survey, commissioned by BBC and carried out in February by Conrad Winn of COMPAS, showed that 14 percent of Canadians believed that Jews had "too much" power—virtually identical to the figure in 1986—and that the same figure, 14 percent, had "empathy" for Jews, a significant rise from 6 percent in 1986. French-speaking Quebecers were more likely than other Canadians to harbor feelings of antagonism toward ethnic minorities, especially Jews. Among Francophones, 26 percent believed that Jews were at least partially responsible for the Holocaust, as compared to 15 percent of other Canadians. Some 26 percent of the Francophones also agreed with the statement that Jews had too much power, far more than the 10 percent of other Canadians who thought so. The study noted that the general tendency for education to lessen prejudice did not hold for the Quebecers; in fact "the data suggest that education may even be reinforcing such sentiments." Thus those with university degrees living in the province were much more likely to believe that Jews had too much power (30 percent) than those with a high school education or less (20 percent).

The historical roots of anti-Semitism in the province were probed in a controversial documentary that was finally televised in April, after some networks declined to show it. *Je Me Souviens* (I Remember), directed by Eric Scott, was based on scholarly research into the period of the 1930s and 1940s by Esther Delisle, and also focused on the hostile reaction her studies had generated within the intellectual elite of Quebec.

Canadian Jewry pondered how to respond to the increase in anti-Semitism in 2002. CJC's Jack Silverstone urged his colleagues to revive the activist approach utilized so successfully during the halcyon days of the Soviet Jewry movement. More concretely, MP Irwin Cotler helped establish the International Commission to Combat Anti-Semitism, of which he and Per Ahlmark, formerly deputy prime minister of Sweden, were the initial cochairs. The new organization appealed to prominent non-Jews to take a stand against what Cotler called "an exploding new anti-Jewishness" worldwide. He noted especially the use of anti-Zionism, which denied equality to Jews as a people, as a cover for anti-Semitism. The noted human-rights lawyer asserted: "in a world in which human rights has emerged as the new secular religion of our time, the portrayal of Israel as the metaphor for a human rights violator exposes Israel as the 'new anti-Christ'—with all the teaching of contempt for this 'collective Jew among the nations' that this new anti-Semitism implies."

The same theme was aired at two public forums late in the year. In October, the University of Toronto hosted a panel discussion sponsored by Canadians Against Anti-Semitism. Former Ontario premier Bob Rae, a panelist, accused many critics of Israeli policies of promoting anti-Semitism by taking the position that "Israel does not have a right to exist as a member of the world order and that Jews do not have the right to their own state. Don't tell me that isn't anti-Semitism, because I can think of no greater threat to the life of the Jewish people." Toronto *Globe and Mail* columnist Margaret Wente, another speaker, noted that "the only hate speech on campus that is tolerated is hate speech about Israel and America, and they are linked." In November, three panelists at a Canadian Zionist Federation program in Montreal agreed with MP Cotler's assessment that anti-Semites were using anti-Zionism as a camouflage. Prof. Fred Krantz, director of the Canadian Institute for Jewish Research, noted the irony of Israel, envisioned as the solution to the Jewish question, now becoming the object of Jew-hatred.

Nora Gold, a professor at the Ontario Institute for Studies in Education, released the results of a survey she had done of the attitudes of Jewish women. Gold found that many of the women were "clearly frightened by anti-Semitism, and told painful, terrible stories." Indeed, they were more upset about anti-Semitism than about sexism, which they had also experienced. "The difference, however, is that the women felt that sexism, unlike anti-Semitism, is recognized, and to some degree acknowledged within the society at large."

Holocaust-Related Matters

Canada and Germany signed a treaty in August granting pension rights to Jews of German ancestry who had lived in Eastern Europe. Although few Canadians would benefit, CJC president Landy contended that "for us this is a moral issue that transcends numbers." Jews in Israel and the United States who came from similar backgrounds were already receiving German pensions.

Daniel Leipnik produced an 11-part television series, "My Mother, My Hero," which focused on female survivors of the Holocaust and the way they raised their own children in Canada, the U.S., and Australia after the war. Leipnik interviewed mothers and their adult children about how the mothers' experiences affected their child rearing. He found that "these kids have such intense passion, and that is one of the positive offshoots of being raised by Holocaust survivors." Canada's longest Holocaust documentary series, it premiered in British Columbia in the fall.

The wheels of justice continued to grind slowly for the aging men accused of Nazi war crimes. Hearings commenced in November in the case of Michael Seifert, an SS officer and prison guard during the Nazi era who had been convicted in absentia in Italy of murder, rape, and torture of prisoners, and sentenced to life imprisonment. The government was trying to extradite him to Italy, but his attorney raised questions about his fitness to proceed with the hearing due to mental deterioration that resulted from a fall earlier in the year. A separate legal process to denaturalize Seifert was also underway.

Walter Obodzinski, facing denaturalization proceedings, appealed to the Supreme Court of Canada to stop the case on the grounds that he was too sick to face the charges of lying about his past when he applied to immigrate to Canada after the war. In February, the court declined to take the appeal, thus clearing the way for a lower court to consider the merits of the case. Obodzinski was alleged to have been a member of a Nazi police unit in Ukraine. Meanwhile, the case of Vladimir Katriuk dragged on. In 1999 the Federal Court found that he had concealed his membership in an SS unit based in Ukraine, and yet the cabinet, which had the final say on denaturalization, had yet to follow through by stripping him of his Canadian citizenship.

Another accused war criminal living in Canada, Joseph Kisielaitis, was denied entry into the U.S. in February; he had been placed on a watch list after admitting to being a member of a Nazi-backed Lithuanian battalion that killed thousands of Jews. Even so, Canada had not yet acted against him. War-crimes investigator Steve Rambam expressed puzzlement at the government's inaction and the fact that it appeared not to feel "the slightest embarrassment" over the situation.

In September, there were reports in the media that the government would discontinue moves to deport war criminals after their citizenship was revoked. But a spokesman for Denis Coderre, the minister in charge, asserted that existing policy would not change.

The fifth annual report of the government's war-crimes-prosecution program, issued in November, showed that only one case (that of Seifert) had been launched during 2002. There had been 18 cases since 1995, with 11 concluded and seven still being litigated. Of the 18 there had been eight convictions, six of the accused had died, three had their citizenship revoked, and one proceeding was just getting underway. Seventy-eight people were still under investigation. CJC executive vice president Jack Silverstone opined that "the stuff is moving at a glacial pace," an assessment that reinforced a conclusion of the Simon Wiesenthal Center in Jerusalem, which rated Canada "B" (on a scale from "A" to "F") for its investigation and prosecution of war criminals in 2001–02.

JEWISH COMMUNITY

Demography

Data from the 2001 census began to come out just before the end of 2002, with the full report to be released during 2003. The census showed about a 10-percent decline in the number of people who listed Yiddish as their mother tongue, from 21,420 in 1996 to 19,295 in 2001, reflecting the passing of an older generation of European-born Jews. While the percentage of Jews with Yiddish as their mother tongue could not be calculated until the full population figures were known, it was estimated at about 5 percent. Comparable numbers from selected past years were: 1931—96 percent, 1961—33 percent, and 1981—11 percent. Current Yiddish speakers lived mainly in Montreal (9,280) and Toronto (7,210). The number of people listing Hebrew as their mother tongue also declined, from 13,125 in 1996 to 12,435 in 2001. The bulk of the native Hebrew speakers was in Toronto (7,390), with most of the rest in Montreal (2,945).

The annual meeting of the American Academy of Religion, held in Toronto in December, included a panel discussion about the Toronto Jewish community. York University sociologist Rina Cohen reported on Jews from the former Soviet Union living in Toronto, who numbered, she said, about 25,000–30,000, and some 40 percent were over age 65. Cohen found that, unlike earlier Jewish arrivals, these Soviet Jews constituted a distinctive subcommunity that was not integrating into the larger Jewish community. Israelis living in Toronto, she added, constituted another such subcommunity. Alex Pomson, an education professor at York, reported that about one-third of Toronto's Jewish children attended Jewish day schools. In recent years, he noted, there has been a proliferation of what he termed "boutique" schools catering to very narrow clienteles, and these had drawn students away from the larger, mainline day schools, which were suffering declining enrollments.

The president of the Montreal Federation CJA, Steven Cummings, told his community in October to expect an influx of thousands of immigrants—possibly as many as 10,000 annually—over the next two years, primarily from Argentina and France. If his projection were to prove accurate, there would be a substantial increase in the city's Jewish population, estimated at between 80,000 and 100,000. A delegation of community leaders had recently returned from Buenos Aires, where they had gone to assess the economic distress of the Jewish community.

Communal Affairs

The Montreal YM-YWHA hosted the JCC-Maccabi Games in August, one of five venues on the American continent. The approximately 1,500 teen participants came from the United States, United Kingdom, Israel, Mexico, Venezuela, and Australia, as well as from across Canada. Security was unusually tight because of the threat of terrorism. A media blackout about the event, in effect for months, was lifted only after the games began.

A new organization, United Chesed of Greater Toronto, was formed in July to coordinate and increase the efficiency of communal programs offered by 26 synagogues and other Jewish groups—home and hospital visits to the ill, supplying medical equipment, finding jobs for the unemployed, and emergency fund-raising.

The Quebec government gave $910,000 to the Montreal Holocaust Memorial Centre, which came to about 20 percent of the $4.5-million cost of renovation and expansion of the facility. The balance came from private and corporate donors and other levels of government. Quebec communications minister Diane Lemieux said that her government was contributing toward the construction of a world-class facility that would be "one of Quebec's great museums." The Centre, located in the federation building, featured "living testimonies" of survivors as well as exhibits chronicling the nature of prewar Jewish life in Europe and the Nazi efforts to exterminate the Jews.

The Atlantic Jewish Council, representing the Jewish communities of the four eastern provinces, held its biennial convention in Moncton, New Brunswick, in November. The main concern of the delegates, given the tendency of younger Jews to move to cities, was how to preserve Jewish life in small communities. Incoming president Mark Rosen expressed the "fear that there may not be enough [Jews] to do the work in the future that we are doing now." But his predecessor, Sheva Medjuck, assured the delegates that the council was doing everything possible to insure that "our communities survive and prosper."

Montreal's Jewish Hospital of Hope Foundation (JHH) and the Jewish Eldercare Centre (JEC) went to court to resolve a bitter dispute resulting from a merger of the two institutions in 2000 (see AJYB 2002, p. 292). Despite the merger, their respective fund-raising arms remained separate. The JEC had sought to prevent the foundation from using the JHH name but failed to obtain a court injunction, leaving the JHH Foundation free to raise funds on its own, even though the JHH was now part of the JEC.

Israel-Related Matters

The community sent 19 delegates to the World Zionist Congress in Jerusalem in June. For the third time in a row, elections were dispensed with so as to save money. Instead, the constituent groups of the Canadian Zionist Federation were allocated delegate slots based on membership numbers: United Torah Coalition—4, Arza Canada—4, Mercaz Canada—3, Labor Zionist Coalition—3, Herut-Likud Canada—3, Zionist Organization of Canada—1, and Mizrachi—1.

Data released in 2002 indicated that Canadian Jewish tourism to Israel remained strong despite the security situation. The proportion of Jews among tourists from Canada increased from about 22 percent in 2000 to 41 percent in 2001, when some 33,000 Canadians visited the Jewish state. It was believed that this was a higher Jewish percentage than for most other countries. Data from the first half of 2001 showed that 35 percent of Canadian Jewish tourists to Israel were Orthodox, 33 percent Conservative, and 9 percent Reform.

Several times during the year, Jews in various Canadian cities held rallies to express solidarity with Israel. Many were quite large. Some 300 people showed up in downtown Montreal in March to protest a wave of terrorist attacks earlier that month. Raymonde Folco, a Liberal MP, speaking on behalf of the government, stood up "to condemn terrorism in the strongest possible terms," while Quebec National Assembly member André Boulerice declared that "the Israeli people have the right to live, to live in peace." A similar rally in Toronto, also in March, was organized by the Israel Now Consortium, a network of over 100 community organizations.

Large rallies were held again in Ottawa, Montreal, Vancouver, and elsewhere in April, following the controversial Israeli incursion into Jenin. As many as 25,000 people converged on Ottawa's Parliament Hill on April 21. They came from as far away as Calgary and Vancouver and represented communities across Ontario as well as Montreal. Christians participated as well. Although many MPs were invited, only Toronto's Joe Volpe and Montreal's Irwin Cotler showed up. Volpe assured the crowd that his colleagues believed that "the people of Israel, the Jews of Canada and elsewhere, symbolize those values which we promote every day. . . . This is the time that Canada stands for Israel." Cotler contended that Israel "is not just a Jewish cause but a just cause. . . ." Israel's deputy foreign minister, Michael Melchior, told the crowd that its voice was being heard in Jerusalem and that "this war which has been forced upon us is a crucial war, not just for Israel but for civilization itself."

Several days earlier, Montreal Jewry held a march and rally downtown that produced a remarkable turnout of 20,000 or more from a community of 100,000 at most. Rabbi Reuben Poupko declared it to be one of the largest and most emotional events in Canadian Jewish history. Melchior reiterated Israel's determination to stand up to the Palestinians' terror, while Poupko upheld the conduct of the Israeli army: "their hearts are pure and their hands are clean. The Jewish people and the Jewish state are here to stay."

Many communities launched substantial emergency fund-raising campaigns for Israel, supplementing their normal federation campaigns. Communities supported Israel commercially as well. To help an Israeli economy hurt by the loss of tourist dollars, Israeli merchants were brought to Canada to offer their products for sale at special events organized for that purpose. In Toronto, for example, Olive Branch for Israel held a "*shuk* [marketplace] in the park" in July for the sale of Israeli goods. In August, the Toronto Zionist Federation, BBC, and UJA Federation set up an Israel Mall in the city that lasted several days and attracted thousands of shoppers. Similar events were held in Montreal the same month.

In an op-ed article in the *Canadian Jewish News* in August, David Goldberg and Tillie Shames of the CIC advocated greater community support for "the pro-Israel community at Canadian universities and colleges." They pointed out how efforts to delegitimize Israel were making headway at academic institutions. As a response to the growing pressures, they urged the community to disseminate information, arrange speaking tours, establish academic chairs in Israel and Jewish studies, revive academic exchanges with Israeli universities, and create an organization of pro-Israel academics. In their words, "Nothing less than the integrity of the intellectual discourse among Canadian scholars is at stake." Three scholars—Irving Abella of York University, Ed Morgan of the University of Toronto, and Gil Troy of McGill University—responded, reminding community leaders that there had been a program of academic exchanges and an organization that did precisely what Goldberg and Shames asked, the Canadian Professors for Peace in the Middle East. Both, however, had to shut down when federation leaders withdrew funding over a decade ago.

One Canadian pro-Israel organization with academic roots was the Canadian Institute for Jewish Research, established in 1987. One of its most successful projects was a daily briefing, in which relevant articles and news items were disseminated worldwide by e-mail. The founder, Prof. Fred Krantz of Concordia University, also worked to develop a cadre of student leaders with editorial and organizational experience in Israel advocacy.

Canadian Jewry took new steps to bolster its activities for Israel. The Jewish Federation of Greater Toronto announced the creation of a pro-Israel quarterly to be called *Counterpoint* that would be distributed at the University of Toronto. The Montreal community's pro-Israel activity was reorganized in December with the establishment of the Quebec-Israel Public Affairs Committee. Its chair, Michael Frankel, expected it to be more representative and better funded than its predecessor, the Quebec branch of CIC.

As a protest against the *Toronto Star*'s Middle East coverage, the two leading Jewish funeral homes in Toronto decided in April to cease placing advertisements and death notices in the paper. Benjamin Park Memorial Chapel and Steeles Memorial Chapel switched their business to the *National Post,* which strongly supported Israel. Other pro-Israel advertisers—real estate developers and business-owners—followed suit.

Religion

The touchy issue of the status of Jews married to non-Jews came up at Adath Israel Congregation, a Conservative synagogue in Toronto. The policy of the congregation was not to accept intermarried Jews as members, and there were two cases in which membership and access to seats for the High Holy Days were denied on that basis in 2002, although seats in alternate services were offered. Other Conservative synagogues in Toronto, however, allow intermarried Jews to be members.

A bitterly contested synagogue merger in Montreal led to a court case. The directors of Congregation Anshei Ozeroff, a synagogue with aging and low-income worshipers that could no longer support the cost of operation, agreed to merge with Adath Israel Poalei Zedek Synagogue. However members of Anshei Ozeroff opposed to the merger—many of whom were Russian Jews who felt that they had no good alternative to the existing synagogue—sued to block it. By year's end the merger appeared to be off, the Anshei Ozeroff building was locked, and the worshipers had moved their minyan to other premises.

Three venerable synagogues in Winnipeg's North End—Rosh Pina, Bnay Abraham, and Beth Israel—merged into a new Congregation Etz Chaim. The Jewish population of the North End was in decline, as most Jews had moved to the southern part of the city. The new synagogue, which would use the Rosh Pina building, began with 800 members.

The Reconstructionist movement, which held its biennial convention in Montreal in November, created a new task force on Israeli policies. Although some observers contended that the initiative would weaken the movement's ties to Israel, Rabbi Ron Aigen and leaders of the host congregation, Dorshei Emet, asserted that the task force would actually strengthen such ties. They cited numerous provisions of Reconstructionist policies that stressed commitment to Israel and Zionism. But some speakers at the convention advocated reassessing those traditional ties. Moti Rieber, who worked for the Jewish Reconstructionist Federation in the U.S., contended that there was a growing gap between the views of North American Reconstructionists and the Israeli government. He declared: "In question is the entire Zionist enterprise. If the cost is so high in terms of our values . . . do we wish to support an Israel that does not live up to our ideals?"

Beth Jacob v'Anshei Dridz Congregation (Orthodox) in Toronto held a seminar in October on Judaism and the modern world. Rabbi Jay Kelman lamented the reluctance of many Orthodox Jews to discuss internal problems for fear of criticism by the other movements, and decried the reluctance of the Orthodox rabbinate to dialogue with the non-Orthodox. Rabbi Tzvi Hersh Weinreb, executive vice president of the Orthodox Union, noted that Orthodoxy constituted a minority among Jews and that "our goal must be to deal with [all] Jews and not be sanctimonious." Rabbi Michael Skobac, educational director of Jews for Judaism, an organization that countered Christian missionary activity, claimed that the unspiritual atmosphere of many synagogues—a situation tolerated, he said, by rabbis—drove many people away from Judaism.

Homosexuality became a controversial issue in the Orthodox community. Rabbi Benjamin Hecht of Nishma, an international educational outreach program, mentioned it in a talk he delivered in Toronto in June about how to explain Orthodoxy to the non-Orthodox. Divine commandments such as the ban on homosexuality, he said, must be followed out of a sense of religious obligation, irrespective of modern sensibilities. Rabbi Mordechai Glick, a clinical psychologist participating in a panel discussion at Montreal's Congregation Shaar Hashomayim in July, advocated "reparative therapy" that might enable some gays and lesbians to become heterosexual. Acknowledging that his position was politically incorrect and would be met with opposition, he stressed that "one can choose not to be homosexual. Glick nevertheless urged that homosexuals be welcomed in synagogues and at community activities. The congregation's rabbi, Barry Gelman, welcomed gays and lesbians as synagogue members and supported the idea of civilly recognized unions for them, but rejected the sanctification of such unions in synagogue ceremonies.

Conservative rabbis debated the role of women in synagogue services at a debate at Beth Tzedec Congregation in Toronto in November. Rabbi Baruch Frydman-Kohl contrasted practices in Toronto with those in the United States, which were more egalitarian. "We are trying to maintain what I think are some traditional borders," he said. Rabbi Steven Saltzman suggested that "the future of the Jewish people lies in the complex balancing act between what we're prepared to accept from the modern culture and what we need to reject to insure we survive as a Jewish people." Beth Shalom Synagogue in Ottawa changed its affiliation from the Orthodox Union to the Union for Traditional Judaism (an offshoot of Conservative Judaism), based on a 70-percent majority in a membership vote in June. The synagogue, trying to reverse a decline in membership, hoped that the resultant expansion of the role of women in the congregation would help attract new members.

The new Conservative Torah commentary, *Etz Hayim,* proved controversial in Canada. At a symposium held in Toronto in December, several rabbis evaluated the new publication, with views ranging from enthusiasm to dislike. Critics pointed out that not all Conservative congregations had adopted it. Rabbi Martin Berman, however, lauded the translation and the "sensitive biblical critical studies," while Rabbi Frydman-Kohl singled out the topical essays at the back of the book for praise.

Education

As the result of an agreement between the Grand Rabbinat du Québec and the Université de Montréal, a new program in Jewish theology leading to a master's degree was established. Chief Rabbi David Sabbah said that the program was unique in North America. Rabbis with the appropriate academic credentials would teach the Judaic courses.

The Ontario Institute for Studies in Education, which trained teachers, created a new diploma program in Holocaust and genocide education. Its goal was to make sure that teachers graduating from the institution would be knowledgeable about the Holocaust. Carol Ann Reid, cochair of the program, remarked that "the Holocaust didn't just take place in Jewish history. It took place in non-Jewish history because the non-Jews were the anti-Semites who did the killing."

The Ontario government disappointed many in the Jewish community by instituting a one-year delay in the further implementation of tax credits for religious education. The program, initiated in 2001, was frozen at 10 percent for another year instead of going up to the previously announced 20 percent (see AJYB 2002, p. 295).

Jeff Itcush, president of the union representing teachers in Montreal Jewish day schools, warned that unless workloads were eased many teachers would seek employment in the public sector. The warning came in the fall, shortly before the opening of negotiations for a new contract. Itcush claimed that the union's teachers put in 18 percent more class time than their public-sector counterparts.

Representatives of three secular humanist Jewish Sunday schools in Toronto, Vancouver, and Winnipeg met in Winnipeg in March to coordinate some of their educational programming.

Community and Intergroup Relations

University of Toronto history professor Michael Marrus, who served on the recently disbanded Catholic-Jewish panel investigating the Roman Catholic Church's conduct during the Holocaust, warned in January that beatifying the wartime Pope Pius XII would seriously undermine the

Catholic-Jewish dialogue. Marrus said that beatification should not be considered until historians came to a consensus about the pope's role.

To protest lack of support for Israel among its interlocutors and their silence about the rising tide of anti-Semitism in Canada, CJC refused to participate in the spring meeting of the Canadian Christian-Jewish Consultation. According to CJC president Landy, the last straw was a one-sided statement by Anglican primate Michael Peers that blamed Israel for the crisis with the Palestinians. Other religious denominations that participated in the consultation were the Presbyterian, Roman Catholic, Lutheran, and United churches. On the other hand, BBC forged an alliance with Christians for Israel. The two groups traveled to Israel on a joint solidarity mission in June.

Imam Moin Ghauri, head of a mosque near Montreal, visited Temple Emanu-El–Beth Shalom in December to show solidarity and promote peace in a place of worship that had been named as a possible target of Islamic terrorists. The imam told the congregation that no true Muslim would attack a synagogue, and spoke at length about Muslim-Jewish religious relations.

The Atlantic Jewish Council withdrew from the Nova Scotia Multi-cultural Festival in Halifax in June because its security needs were not met. It had requested special security at its booth.

In July, after Keith Norton, chair of the Ontario Human Rights Commission, compared public funding for religious schools to support for apartheid, a Jewish attorney filed a complaint with the commission demanding his resignation because he had "clearly overstepped his bounds and has offended several minority religious groups in one fell swoop." Norton explained that he feared that the tax credit for religious education announced by the provincial government in 2001 would lead to a proliferation of small independent schools without adequate government supervision. Norton added that his remarks were prompted by the sight of anti-Israel artwork in a rented heritage language classroom and in a school headed by someone with Al Qaeda ties. CJC Ontario Region chair Ed Morgan appeared satisfied with the explanation.

The Windsor Public Library became the center of controversy in May with a window display titled "Palestine: The Great Injustice." Harvey Kessler, executive director of the local federation, termed the exhibit offensive and said that "some people viewed it as probably being propaganda and hateful towards our community." He urged the management to develop new guidelines to prevent a recurrence.

In April, the Quebec Court of Appeal upheld a lower court ruling that sustained a condominium regulation barring the erection of sukkot on balconies. The decision was based on the terms of the contract that all owners had signed.

The Federal Court of Canada ruled in May against Chosen People Ministries (CPM), a conversionary organization, in a case involving the question of whether the menorah is a legally protected symbol. In 1999, the Registrar of Trademarks granted the group official trademark status for its logo that included a menorah. CJC challenged that decision on the grounds that granting such protection to a group that was antagonistic toward Judaism and was out to convert Jews would be "scandalous and immoral." The court agreed, holding that "the menorah is a distinctly Jewish symbol" that had been "the official emblem of the Jewish faith and its people since antiquity." The CPM filed an appeal in September.

In a case in Quebec Superior Court, a man was denied his petition to gain custody of two sons from his estranged wife, who, the man claimed, had abducted them. Judge Herbert Marx ruled in May that the plaintiff had delayed his request for nearly a year while trying to extract money from his wife's family in exchange for granting her a get (religious divorce). Citing both Israeli and Jewish legal precedents, Marx granted a civil divorce and ordered the husband to pay $75,000 in damages.

Two commercial bus companies, Greyhound and Adirondack, appealed to the Quebec Transport Commission in December to stop Tov Travel from offering regular bus service between Montreal and New York because it lacked a commercial license. The near-daily charter bus service, in existence for about 20 years, served a primarily Hassidic clientele.

In January, the Toronto District School Board decided that it would no longer distribute the *District 12 Voice* after the union newsletter published an article in 2001, titled "Why America is Hated," that had anti-Semitic content. The board members passed a four-part resolution in February dissociating themselves from the article, which had been proposed as a teaching tool.

Norman Finkelstein, the notorious Holocaust revisionist and author of *The Holocaust Industry,* was interviewed on a Toronto radio station in January. CJC protested his appearance and the failure of host Andrew Krystal to challenge him more aggressively.

In an effort to be more inclusive, the Royal Ontario Museum announced that it would start using C.E. (Common Era) and B.C.E. (Before Common Era) instead of B.C. (Before Christ) and A.D. (Anno Domini) to identify historical dates.

Culture

A French production of the musical *Les Dix Commandements* had its North American premiere in Montreal in March, and an English version opened in Toronto in July. Solly Levy presented his new work, *La Cantata Yamim Noraim,* an exposition of Sephardi liturgy for the High Holy Days, in Montreal in October. A Yiddish concert in Toronto in July drew 1,000 people.

Montreal's Dora Wasserman Yiddish Theater performed *Double Identity,* adapted from a Sholom Aleichem play, with words and music by Miriam Hoffman and Ben Schaechter respectively, during May and June. *Whiskey Serenade,* a play by Ralph Small and Eli Lukawitz, had its world premiere at the Toronto Centre for the Arts in October. Among the presentations at the Toronto Fringe Festival in July were Aviva Ravel's *Dance Like a Butterfly* and Gideon Forman's *Death of My Dentist.*

A number of documentaries appeared during the year. *Dear Clara,* shown on television in January, told about Clara Greenspan Blum and her efforts, from 1938 to 1947—against considerable bureaucratic hostility—to bring her husband to join her in Canada. Leo Lowy's life story was depicted in *Leo's Journey: The Story of the Mengele Twins.* In the film, Lowy travels to his Hungarian birthplace (now in Ukraine) and to Auschwitz, and documents the grisly experiments that Dr. Josef Mengele performed on twins. In September, CBC Television presented *The Life and Times of Barbara Frum,* the well-known journalist. Ina Fichman produced *Undying Love: True Stories of Courage and Faith,* about survivors' attempts to love after the Holocaust. The film, directed by Helene Klodawsky, premiered at the Montreal World Film Festival in August. *Y.I.D.* (Yehudim in the Diaspora), by Igal Hecht and Ron Furman, compared the lives of Jews in Israel and Canada. Merrily Weisbord and Tanya Ballantyne Tree produced *Ted Allan: Minstrel Boy of the Twentieth Century,* about the screenwriter and playwright. It premiered on television in March. Evan Beloff, Max Wallace, and Ari Cohen made a farcical docudrama based on Jewish aspects of the saga of Elvis Presley. *Schmelvis: Searching for the King's Jewish Roots* had its premiere in April at the Toronto Jewish Film Festival.

The Montreal Jewish Film Festival in May featured several films that dealt with Jewish resistance to the Nazis. Among them was one by Shelley Saywell, *Out of the Fire,* telling the story of Faye Schulman and her work as a saboteur with the partisans. *Conflict,* by Elad Winkler, won the best documentary award at the Montreal World Film Festival in August.

Winkler, an Israeli who moved to Canada as a child, returned to Israel to investigate the impact of the intifada in 2000. Amos Gitai's *Kedma* premiered at the Toronto International Film Festival in September.

The Ashkenaz Festival of New Yiddish Culture was held at Toronto's Harbourfront at the end of August. Its events included the Canadian debut of the Cracow Klezmer Band, Di Naye Kapelya from Hungary, theatrical productions, dance works, and films. Artistic director Mitchell Smolkin termed it "the most unique and comprehensive look at contemporary Yiddish and Jewish culture in Canada and North America."

The Canadian Jewish Virtual Museum, sponsored by several synagogues and other institutions and funded to a substantial extent by the federal government, opened in October. It featured over 1,000 on-line archives, documents, photographs, and oral histories covering many aspects of the Canadian Jewish experience. It was hosted by Congregation Shaar Hashomayim in Montreal.

Boulevard St. Laurent in Montreal, the center of life for Jewish and other immigrants for decades, was designated a National Historic Site. In June, the Royal Ontario Museum presented an exhibit of Italian Judaica, including Bibles and Haggadot.

The Conservatory for Judaic Performing Arts was announced in January, its opening planned for Montreal in 2003. The founder, Dr. Hy Goldman, envisioned the conservatory as an outgrowth of his successful KlezKanada festival. The first major program would be a summer school.

A memorial meeting, consisting of dramatic readings from the works of Mordecai Richler, marked the first anniversary of the writer's death in July. It was held at the Monument National in Montreal and featured such personalities as Richard Dreyfuss, Robert MacNeil, and Ted Kotcheff, family members, and other writers.

Exodus, an English language newspaper for Russian immigrants, was launched in Toronto in June. The monthly, with an initial circulation of 5,000, was published by the Jewish Russian Community Centre.

Publications

Two books chronicled the days in the first half of the last century when Jewish doctors and academics in Toronto faced severe limitations on their ability to pursue their chosen careers. *Medicine: My Story,* by Barnet Berris, told how the author became the first Jew to serve on the full-time medical school faculty at the University of Toronto in 1951, and provided insights into the struggle of Toronto Jewish doctors for equal treatment. Martin Friedland's *The University of Toronto: A History* described the rampant anti-Semitism in the medical school, associated hospitals, and a prestigious social club as late as 1970. The career of the country's first Jewish governor of the central bank was told by Bruce Muirhead in *Against the Odds: The Public Life and Times of Louis Rasminsky.* English translations of articles from Canada's premier Yiddish newspaper were presented in *Through the Eyes of the Eagle: The Early Montreal Yiddish Press 1907–1916,* edited by Pierre Anctil. Naim Kattan's *A. M. Klein: Poet and Prophet* appeared in an English translation from the French by Edward Baxter. Laurel Sefton MacDowell wrote about an early advocate of working-class causes in Toronto in *Renegade Lawyer: The Life and Times of J.L. Cohen.*

Other books on Canada and Canadian Jewry included *Memories on the March* by Tyler Trafford, about Jewish war veterans in Alberta; Ruth Panofsky's *Adele Wiseman: Essays on her Works; Personal Policy Making: Canada's Role in the Adoption of the Palestine Partition Resolution* by Eliezer Tauber; *You Don't Have to Be Jewish: A Commentary on Selected Jewish Films* by Bill Stern; *Shabbos Goy: A Catholic Boyhood on a Jewish Street in Protestant Toronto* by Ted Schmidt; *Not Bad for a Sergeant: The Memoirs of Barney Danson,* about Canada's first Jewish minister of defense; Sondra Gotlieb's *Dogs, Houses, Gardens, Food and Other Addictions; Four Hundred Brothers and Sisters* by Judy Gordon, about Jewish orphanages in Montreal; Alan Morantz's *Where Is Here? Canada's Maps and the Stories They Tell;* Mirl Fish Kelman's *Mother's Memoir and Family Recollections;* and *Mama and Her Mitzvahs: Stories and Reminiscences* by Sophie Stransman.

Books on aspects of the Holocaust included *Hitler's Inferno* by Vera Schiff, an account of eight concentration camp inmates who were forced to do reprehensible acts in order to survive; *Never Far Away: The Auschwitz Chronicles of Anna Heilman;* Morris Schnitzer's *My Three Selves;* Karin Doerr and Robert Michael's *Nazi-Deutsch/Nazi German: An English Lexicon of the Language of the Third Reich; Hana's Suitcase* by Karen Levine; and Hanna Spencer's *Hanna's Diary.* Joe King wrote a handbook for activists on Middle East issues—*The Case for Israel: Background to Conflict in the Middle East.*

Among books on Judaism and Jewish studies were two by David Mendel Harduf, *Rabbinical Exegesis of Biblical Names and Narratives,* and *Biblical and Midrashic Hebrew in the Writings of S. Y. Agnon;* Sharon Green's *Not a Simple Story: Love and Politics in a Modern Hebrew Novel; Scattered Among the Peoples: The Jewish Diaspora in Ten Portraits* by

Allan Levine; *Isaac Abarbanel's Stance Toward Tradition: Defense, Dissent and Dialogue* by Eric Lawee; *Ten Green Bottles: Jewish Refugees in Shanghai from Vienna* by Vivian Jeanette Kaplan; Michael Carin's *The Future Jew; La puissance du regard: Le mauvais oeil et le bon oeil* by Rabbi Haim Moryoussef; *Best-Kept Secrets of Judaism* by Rabbi Reuven Bulka; *The Creation According to the Midrash Rabbah* by Rabbi Wilfred Shuchat; *Walking Humbly with God* by Rabbi Maurice Cohen; *The Rescue of Jerusalem* by Henry Aubin; James Arthur Diamond's *Maimonides and the Hermeneutics of Concealment: Deciphering Scripture and Midrash in the Guide of the Perplexed;* and *Metissages, De Arcimboldo a Zombi* by Alexis Nouss.

Nancy-Gay Rotstein published *This Horizon and Beyond: Poems Selected and New.* Works of fiction included *A Draught for a Dead Man* by Caroline Rose, *Children of Paper* by Martha Blum, and *The Bolshevik's Revenge* by Allan Levine.

The Canadian Jewish Book Awards in Toronto in June went to Emma Richler for *Sister Crazy,* William Weintraub for *Getting Started,* Cary Fagan for *The Market Wedding,* Rabbi Erwin Schild for *The Very Narrow Bridge,* Eric Lawee for *Isaac Abarbanel's Stance Toward Tradition,* Morton Weinfeld for *Like Everyone Else . . . But Different,* Simchah Simchovitch for *The Song That Never Died,* Janine Stingel for *Social Discredit,* and Joseph Sherman for *American Standard.* In Montreal in November, the J.I. Segal Awards were presented to Yossel Birstein for *A Face in the Clouds,* Norman Ravvin for *Not Quite Mainstream: Canadian Jewish Short Stories,* Morton Weinfeld for *Like Everyone Else . . . But Different,* Pierre Lasry for *Une Juive en Nouvelle France,* Pierre Anctil for his translation of Yehuda Elberg's *L'Empire de Kalman l'infirme,* Janine Stingel for *Social Discredit,* and Gary Beitel for his film *My Dear Clara.*

Personalia

A number of Jews were appointed to the Order of Canada. Companions: Reuben Cohen and Phyllis Lambert. Officers: Bluma Appel, Samuel Belzberg, and Alvin G. Libin. Members: Bernard Ghert, Carole Grafstein, Gerald Halbert, and Roel Buck. Herb Gray, who resigned after nearly 40 years in the House of Commons, was appointed to the International Joint Commission. Mel Cappe was appointed high commissioner to the United Kingdom, Martin Freedman became a judge on the Manitoba Court of Appeal, and Victor Goldbloom was appointed chair of the Montreal Regional Health Board. David Levine was appointed junior health minister in Quebec. Michael Crelinsten became a member of the Immigration and Refugee Board.

France named Naim Kattan a chevalier of the Legion of Honor. Barbara Steinman won the Governor General's Award in visual and media arts. Judy Feld Carr received the Wiesenthal Award for Tolerance, Justice and Human Rights. Fred Gitelman and Joseph Silver were among six team members who won the Olympic Gold Medal at the International Olympic Committee Grand Prix of bridge in Salt Lake City just before the Winter Olympics. Edward Greenspan became editor-in-chief of the *Globe and Mail.*

Appointments and elections within the Jewish community included Shira Herzog and Julia Koschitzky as directors of the Jewish Telegraphic Agency, Rochelle Levinson as president of Canadian Hadassah-WIZO, Barry Steinfeld as president of the Canadian Council of Jewish Community Centres, Ian Goldstine as president of the Jewish Federation of Winnipeg, Paul Kochberg as president and Denise Gold as executive director of the United Synagogue of Conservative Judaism–Canada, Rabbi Irwin Witty as director of the Albert and Tammy Latner Jewish Public Library in Toronto, Linda Kislowicz as executive director of the Montreal YM-YWHA, Selim Moghrabi as president of the Synagogue Council of Greater Montreal, and Bernard Shapiro as head of the task force of the United Jewish Communities in the U.S. to examine problems with the recent national survey.

Members of the community who died this year included famous comedian and television personality Frank Shuster, in January, aged 85; Labor Zionist leader and Yiddishist David Newman, in January, aged 82; economist and educator Noah Meltz, in January, aged 67; Ben Kayfetz, writer, broadcaster, community professional, and authority on Canadian Jewry, in February, aged 85; Hamilton community leader Sam Lax, in February, aged 86; spiritual leader and teacher Rabbi Jacob Mendel Kirshenblatt, in March, aged 98; Warsaw Ghetto survivor and resistance fighter Chaike Spiegel, in April, aged 81; philanthropist Morris Wosk, in April, aged 84; publisher and pro-Israel advocate Dan Nimrod, in April, aged 78; community professional Bill Emery, in April, aged 45; Srul Irving Glick, choir director and the leading composer of Jewish music in Canada, in April, aged 67; businessman and philanthropist Morris Emer, in April, aged 75; Shulamis Yelin, noted writer and poet, in June, aged 89; Hersh Zentner, pioneer Holocaust educator, in June, aged 64; murder victim David Rosenzweig, in July, aged 49; Sidney Spivak, former Manitoba Progressive Conservative leader and cabinet member, in July, aged 74; journalist Lou Seligson, in July, aged 88; community professional Fran Yacoubov, in August, aged 48; lawyer, musician, and community leader Sam Taylor, in September, aged 86; Rabbi Seth Binnus, congregational leader and teacher, in September, aged 30; day-school educator Aviva Heller, in October, aged 61; realtor Lisa Posluns, in November, aged 38; advertising executive and folksinger Jerry Goodis, in November, aged 73; accountant and educational leader Harold Dessen, in November, aged 81; Israeli journalist Sam Orbaum, in December, aged 46; and philanthropist and patron-of-the-arts Irving Zucker, in December, aged 82.

HAROLD M. WALLER

Brazil

National Affairs

Aᴄᴄᴏʀᴅɪɴɢ ᴛᴏ ᴛʜᴇ ᴍᴏꜱᴛ recent census, completed in 2000, Brazil had a population of approximately 169,000,000. Multiethnic and multicultural, Brazil counted the largest populations of African and Japanese descent of any country in the world. Many Brazilians are of European and Middle Eastern background, and in recent years the country attracted significant immigration from Korea and China as well as large numbers of Palestinians. The common description of Brazil as the world's largest Catholic country was somewhat misleading. Many who self-identified as Catholic also practiced syncretistic Afro-Catholic religions. In addition, the Protestant population had been growing rapidly, and in some cities there were more non-Catholic Christians than Catholics. Other religions represented in large numbers—concentrated in specific parts of the country—were Buddhism and the so-called New Japanese Religions (in São Paulo) and Islam (in the deep south of Brazil, notably the city of Foz de Iguaçú).

In 2002, the two-term presidency of Fernando Henrique Cardoso came to a close. He was barred from a third term by law, and Brazil held elections to choose a successor. Cardoso, a former university professor who had been forced into exile during the military dictatorship of 1964–88, did much to strengthen democracy in the country. Taking political reform seriously, he noticeably reduced the entrenched power of regionally based politicians. Perhaps his most important democratic legacy was simply serving out his two terms and then handing over the office of president to a democratically elected successor.

While Brazil faced many economic, political, and social crises in 2002, none reached the level of those in Argentina (a disintegrating economy), Venezuela (political instability under the Chavez regime), and Colombia (continued and growing civil war). Cardoso had committed the country to open markets, an export/import-based economy, and a relatively free-floating currency. This led to a year of modest inflation. The Brazilian economy ended 2002 with a growth rate of approximately 2 percent, with better than 4-percent growth predicted for 2003. Cardoso privatized many formerly state-owned industries, and this, along with a commitment to budget containment, led to much hardship for the middle classes, government employees, and workers in the newly privatized industries who were no longer guaranteed "jobs for life."

Brazil continued to have one of the most unequal societies in the world, whether measured by income, health, land ownership, or education, and the resentments arising from this fact fueled interest in the hotly contested 2002 presidential elections. Much of Brazil's electioneering takes place on television, with each political party allotted its share of free time on all the stations.

One major candidate for president was Luis Inacio Lula da Silva, the perennial standard-bearer of the Workers' Party (PT). This time, the charismatic union leader transformed his public image, emerging as a well-dressed neo-social democrat à la Tony Blair or Bill Clinton, whose main aim was the welfare of the Brazilian people. Another leading candidate was Senator José Serra of the Partido da Social Democracia (Social Democracy, PSDB), which was Cardoso's party. A classic Marxist activist as a university student, he, like Cardoso, spent considerable time in exile. By 2002, however, his political posture was that of a center-right technocrat. While Serra sought to appeal to voters by portraying himself as a leftist opposition figure within the previous administration, Lula was clearly the opposition candidate. Other serious contenders for the presidency were Anthony Garotinho, governor of the state of Rio de Janeiro, and Ciro Gomes, a former governor of the state of Ceará and Cardoso's first finance minister. Underlining his commitment to the democratic process, President Cardoso played a nonpartisan role in the election, maintaining relationships with all candidates.

Brazil's presidential electoral system demanded a majority of votes cast, and thus runoffs were often required. That is what happened in 2002. In the first round, held October 6, Lula won 46 percent of the vote, with 23 percent for Serra, 17 percent for Garotinho, and 12 percent for Ciro Gomes. The second round, pitting the two top finishers against each other, occurred a month later. It was a landslide for Lula and the Workers' Party, which won 61 percent, versus 39 percent for José Serra.

While Lula had promised to modify Brazil's neoliberal economic model with a more social-democratic perspective, he had also made a commitment to hold to International Monetary Fund agreements. Thus despite fears expressed by some vociferous anti-Lula politicians, the Brazilian unit of currency, the real, did not fall against the dollar in the wake of the election, and remained in the 3.5:1 range.

One of the toughest issues Lula would face, as Cardoso did before him, was the problem of landlessness and the growing strength of the Movimento dos Trabalhadores Rurais Sem Terra (Landless Rural Workers' Movement, or MST). While the 1988 Brazilian constitution strengthened provisions stating that unutilized lands could be taken over by the government and distributed to landless people, few landless people in Brazil had the financial resources to take advantage of the opportunity and farm the land. Cardoso's administration—under pressure from the MST, which organized "land invasions" throughout Brazil—distributed land to more families than had been settled in decades. This did not satisfy the MST, however, which wanted Brazil to put an end to large commercial agriculture by redistributing all farms of over 1,000 hectares to the landless.

Some MST leaders sought to link their plight to that of the Palestinians. In March 2002, Brazilian television showed film of Palestinian Authority president Yasir Arafat, confined to his compound in Ramallah by the Israelis, receiving an MST flag from Mario Lill, a member of the MST directorate of the state of Rio Grande do Sul.

Some other Jewish-related issues emerged during the election contest. Presidential candidate Anthony Garotinho, an evangelical Christian, frequently brought his faith into the campaign, and some Jewish leaders suggested that his policies as governor of Rio de Janeiro had unfairly benefited evangelicals. Another candidate, Ciro Gomes, said that he admired Adolf Hitler's determination, even though it was toward a bad end. As for the two front-runners, both Lula's and Serra's vice-presidential candidates (José de Alencar and Rita Camata respectively) made pro-Palestinian remarks in discussing the crisis in the Middle East. Alencar went so far as to say that the only solution was for Israelis to "leave the Middle East." This led Rabbi Henry Sobel, a national figure and leader of the Congregação Israelita Paulista, Latin America's largest synagogue, to demand and receive an apology from Alencar, who expressed regret that he had been insensitive and uninformed. Indeed, just a few days after the remarks, during Yom Kippur, Alencar, Lula, and São Paulo mayor Marta Suplicy (a member of the Workers' Party whose husband was Jewish), visited Sobel's congregation.

While these incidents raised some initial concern in the Jewish community, there was little evidence to suggest that they represented a larger anti-Semitic trend. First, they were isolated, apparently spontaneous statements, not part of any discernible anti-Jewish or anti-Israel platform. Second, all the candidates considered the Brazilian "Jewish vote" important enough to warrant politicking in Jewish spaces, such as synagogues and community centers. Third, Jewish leaders almost uniformly understood the comments as stemming from ignorance of the complexity of the issues. Jews from a wide range of class backgrounds and of varying degrees of religious practice supported numerous presidential candidates, but most noticeably Lula and Serra. While some Jews worried that Brazil's leftist movements might take a stridently anti-Semitic turn, Brazilian political life, in 2002, was characterized by little open anti-Jewish activity.

Israel and the Middle East

Brazil continued along the "middle road" that it had traditionally taken on Middle East issues. In 2002, the government strongly supported UN Security Council resolutions calling for the end, as soon as possible, to Israel's occupation of Palestinian territories. Brazil called for the peaceful creation of a democratic state of Palestine, based on the Beirut Declaration issued by the League of Arab States and the proposals formulated by the "Quartet" (the U.S., the European Union, Russia, and the UN secretary general). Brazil also belonged to the Rio Group, which had consistently called for an immediate cessation of all acts of terrorism, provocation, incitement, and destruction in the Middle East.

Brazil had strong trade relations with Israel, especially in the areas of agriculture, technology, and water usage. Lula, the new president, gave no indication that these economic ties, or Brazil's position on the Middle East situation, would change in 2003. Indeed, in his inaugural address, he made specific mention of the region, saying that the conflict there should be resolved by "negotiated and peaceful means."

Holocaust-Related Issues

Literature denying the Holocaust continued to be published in Brazil, almost all of it privately funded by 71-year-old Siegfied Ellwanger Castan, a wealthy industrialist living in the state of Rio Grande do Sul. Castan's publishing company, Editôra Revisão (Revisionist Publishing House), distributed an unknown quantity of books, for free, to politicians all over Brazil, but there was no sign that they affected policy. Castan's books were not available in any of the major bookstore chains, but could occasionally be found in independent and second-hand shops. His *Holocaust: Jewish or German?* was said to have reached its 30th edition in 2002, but no one knew how many copies had actually been printed. His *The Lie of the Century,* published in 1993, called the accounts of Nazi murders of Jews "Zionist lies." In 1994, Castan offered a prize to anyone who "has lived in Brazil for 20 years and can prove that any Jew was killed in a gas chamber." A number of Jews took up the offer, but Castan refused to entertain their claims. Castan also reprinted a number of anti-Semitic books originally published in the 1920s, such as the *Protocols of the Elders of Zion* and Henry Ford's *The International Jew.* In spite of its small circulation, Castan's literature was widely attacked, and consequently received disproportionate publicity.

All such publications were actually banned by Brazil's antiracism laws (Brazilian constitution of 1988, Article 5, paragraph XLII). But attempts to enforce the laws and suppress this material were not supported by politicians, and, indeed, when cases were prosecuted, the courts often found for the racists on the basis of Brazil's guarantees of freedom of speech and of the press. Thus, when Editôra Revisão was removed as a member of a publisher's consortium in Rio Grande do Sul, a local judge reinstated it. In April 2002, after a trial lasting several years, Castan received a two-year conditional sentence (served as community service) from a federal high court judge for "inciting racism." In December, however, the Supreme Court threw out the conviction, agreeing with a defense argument that since Jews were not a "race," there could be no racism against Jews in the juridical sense of the term as used in the constitution.

Another problematic publication was the academic journal *Revista Humanus,* which began publication in 2000 in Campinas, home to the prestigious university, UNICAMP. It was published by Oaska—Centro Espiritual Beneficente União do Vegetal. The cover of *Revista Humanus* bore the Nazi rune symbol, and many of its articles extolled Nazi figures and attacked Jews (including this author).

Racism and Anti-Semitism

Racism, especially that targeted against people of African descent, was noticeable in the social and economic spheres. While Brazil's elite had always insisted that the country was a "racial democracy," such claims were increasingly harder to sustain. The correlation between race and income was very high, with darker-skinned people generally belonging to the lower classes. And as Brazilians from the impoverished northeastern part of the country moved south into the large urban centers like São Paulo and Rio de Janeiro, the number of physical attacks on them multiplied.

In contrast, there was little open anti-Semitism. One factor explaining this was the limited contact between the relatively small community of Jews, on the one hand, and the mass of Brazil's impoverished urban and rural people, on the other. Another was that Jewish communal organizations were careful to keep internal Jewish issues (as opposed to ones related to Israel) out of the spotlight. Also, Brazil's strong rhetorical commitment to ethnic, cultural, and racial tolerance was backed up by law, making public anti-Semitism a potential crime. And finally, the wide publicity given to the active involvement of some Jewish community leaders in popular movements to combat hunger, poverty, and discrimination presented Brazil's Jews in a favorable, socially conscious, light.

Outright anti-Semitic movements in Brazil attracted only a tiny number of participants. One moribund old group, the Integralist Party, based in the interior of the state of São Paulo, revived with the return to democracy in 1988. Back in the 1930s, its precursor and namesake, the Ação Integralista Brasileira, had some members who engaged in a virulently anti-Semitic campaign that was tolerated by the government. At their height, those Integralists claimed one million members, but in late 1937 they were banned along with all other political parties. The new Integralist Party appeared to be supported by a few hundred people, at most.

There was a formal neo-Nazi political party, the Brazilian National Revolutionary Party (PNRB), which had about 200 sympathizers. A number of other groups popularly associated with neo-Nazism were Carecas do Suburbio, Carecas ABC, Carecas do Brasil, SP Oi!, Carecas, White Power, S.P.F., and Neo-Nazis. While their discourse was frequently anti-Semitic, these groups seemed to have non-specific bigoted ideological roots, and were committed to little more than generic thuggery. Much of the "evidence" that some observers used to suggest a growth in Brazil's neo-Nazi movement was the result of better reporting techniques and an increasing unwillingness, among both Jews and others, to let anti-Semitic rhetoric or actions pass without comment.

The small extremist groups were based in the industrial suburbs surrounding Brazil's largest cities, where the economic crisis of the previous half-decade created high levels of unemployment. During 2002, skinhead groups appeared to grow as well (although they may simply have been more frequently noticed), but their attacks were random, not specifically targeted at Jews. The victims tended to be migrants from Brazil's impoverished northeastern states, those of African descent, and homosexuals (Brazil had the highest rate of recorded homosexual murders in the world between 1980 and 1999).

JEWISH COMMUNITY

Demography

The Jewish community of Brazil, formed primarily after 1920, was ethnically diverse, encompassing Ashkenazim (primarily of Polish and German descent) and Sephardim (the largest plurality was of Egyptian descent). Preliminary information collected for the 2000 Census showed a Jewish population of 86,825, almost all of whom lived in urban areas. Some Jewish organizations in Brazil disputed this figure and placed the number between 120,000 and 140,000. Probably the most reliable estimate came from Israeli demographer Sergio DellaPergola, who placed the 2002 number at 97,300, a slight decline from the 1980 figure of 100,000. This made Brazilian Jewry the 11th largest Jewish community in the world. Early breakout numbers from the census suggested that the population self-identifying as Jewish was diminishing, in large part because of intermarriage.

The largest Jewish community in Brazil was in São Paulo, Brazil's largest city. In 2002, the Albert Einstein Jewish Hospital sponsored a study of the Jewish community of São Paulo. It showed a Jewish population of 60,000 out of a total population of 10.4 million, significantly higher than the official census figure of 44,000. The findings of this study must be used with caution, however, since DellaPergola, a consultant on the project, has suggested publicly that the methodologies used were not fully reliable. According to the Einstein data, some 60 percent of Jews in São Paulo attended synagogue only on High Holidays or for social activities, 13 percent never attended, about 14 percent attended weekly, and 3 percent—representing, in large part, a small but growing Orthodox community—went every day. The study also indicated a low number of students in Jewish day schools.

The second largest Jewish community was in Rio de Janeiro (25,000–30,000 Jews out of a population of 5.85 million), the third largest was in Porto Alegre, Rio Grande do Sul (10,000–12,000 Jews in a population of about 1.36 million), and there were other significant communities in Belo Horizonte, Curitiba, Santos, and Recife.

Communal Affairs

As in many other countries with relatively large Jewish populations, there were numerous nationwide and local community organizations seeking to represent Jews. The central body representing all the Jewish federations and communities in Brazil was the Confederação Israelita do Brazil (CONIB), founded in 1951. This umbrella body included 200 organizations engaged in promoting Jewish and Zionist activities, as well as groups involved in Jewish education, culture, and charity. The Jewish Federation of São Paulo had a standing commission dedicated to fighting racism. The Latin American Jewish Committee Section for Interreligious Affairs, in the same city, actively combated racial hatred with support from the Brazilian National Commission for Catholic-Jewish Dialogue, an affiliate of the National Conference of Brazilian Bishops. There was a special police unit specializing in the investigation of racial crimes in São Paulo, and the Federação Israelita do Estado de São Paulo (Jewish Federation of São Paulo) had a permanent member on the unit's advisory board. All the major international Zionist organizations and Zionist youth movements were represented in Brazil. Brazilian Jews published a number of newspapers and journals in Portuguese, and much Jewish activity took place in "Hebraica" clubs, which were Jewish community centers.

Culture

Books about Jews and Jewish issues were published regularly in Brazil. Books about Brazilian Jewry tended to be either hagiographic or to engage in debates about varying interpretations of Brazilian immigration policy during World War II. Two important scholarly works published in 2002 were Fábio Koifman's *Quixote nas Trevas O Embaixador Souza Dantas e os refugiados do nazismo,* about Brazil's ambassador to France who provided visas to Jews during the Holocaust, and the translation from Yiddish of Meir Kucinski's memoir on life as an immigrant in São Paulo beginning in the 1920s, entitled *Imigrantes, Mascates & Doutores.*

The major cities held Jewish film festivals that presented a wide range of features and documentaries from around the world on Jewish themes. The Israeli film *Promises* was certainly the most successful such film in 2002, running for months in major art-house cinemas in São Paulo and Rio de Janeiro. In addition, the film version of Moacyr Scliar's novel, *Sonhos Tropicais* (Tropical Dreams), drew considerable interest.

An important event during the year was the inauguration of the new site of the Casa de Cultura de Israel in São Paulo. In its new premises, this Jewish cultural center expanded its activities in 2002 to include a significant number of courses, lectures, and films. It also began publication of a new, high-quality, Jewish cultural review, *Revista 18.*

Brazilian Jewry, like many other Jewish communities in the Americas, experienced a wave of "Sephardism" that attracted interest from Jews (both Ashkenazi and Sephardi) and non-Jews. In Brazil, much of the cultural fascination had to do with the myth that most of the Portuguese explorers of the country were actually secret Jews, a notion that found its way into elite and middle-class culture. In 2002, CONFARAD, the First Sephardi Conference in Brazil, was held in São Paulo, with good attendance and much publicity.

Jewish studies was growing as a field of research at major Brazilian universities, as evidenced by the impressive proliferation in M.A. and Ph.D. theses in Brazil on Jewish topics. In 2002, the Latin American Jewish Studies Association held its research conference in Rio de Janeiro, with strong support from the local universities.

Personalia

Rabbi Henry Sobel of the Congregação Israelita Paulista was perhaps the best known Jewish leader in Brazil, in large part because of his active stance against discrimination and poverty, and his engagement in interreligious dialogue. Rabbi Nilton Bonder of Rio de Janeiro's Congregação Judaica do Brasil, known as the "green rabbi," was a prize-winning and best-selling author who used Jewish tradition and mysticism to discuss a wide variety of spiritual matters, and social issues such as the environment. Dr. Celso Lafer, one of Brazil's most important diplomats, served as minister of foreign affairs beginning in 2001. José Mindlin, now retired as director of Metaleve Industries, a large international producer of metal products such as pistons, bearings, and oil pumps, did much to preserve rare Brazilian books. His own book, *Uma vida entre livros* (A Life among Books), was published in 2002 to great acclaim. The Safras, former owners of Banco Safra, constituted one of the most prominent Sephardi families in Brazil. Silvio Santos ("Señor Abravanel"), Brazil's most popular television personality, increasingly asserted his Jewish identity publicly, even though his wife and daughter were evangelical Christians. This came to public attention after the kidnapping of Santos's daughter, which was followed by the kidnapper invading Santos's home and holding him hostage before a Brazilian television audience.

JEFFREY LESSER

Argentina

National Affairs

AFTER THREE-AND-A-HALF years of economic recession, the Argentinean economy went into free-fall in December 2001. Both the budget deficit and the external debt were out of control, nearly a fifth of the workforce was unemployed, and an estimated 2,000 Argentineans slipped below the poverty line each day. To prevent a massive run on the banks, strict limitations were placed on the amount of money that account-holders might withdraw. Angry people—workers and members of the middle class—took to the streets, and 28 were killed in rioting. The government of President Fernando de la Rúa (Radical Party) fell on December 20. Within a few months de la Rúa's economy minister would be jailed for corruption, and his state security secretary for violent repression of demonstrators.

The first president the national Congress elected to serve out de la Rúa's term resigned quickly, and was replaced by Adolfo Rodríguez Saá of the Justicialista Party (Perónist). Saá defaulted on $155 billion in interest payments on the country's debt, the largest single default by any sovereign nation in history. But he was out of office within a week. After one more president rose and fell, Eduardo Duhalde took office on January 2, 2002. A Perónist with a populist reputation who represented Buenos Aires Province in the national Senate, Duhalde was an experienced politician. He had been vice president from 1989 through 1991, and then served as governor of Buenos Aires Province, where he drew criticism for police bungling of, and possible ties to, the still unsolved 1994 bombing of the AMIA building, the central headquarters of Jewish life in the country (see below). Duhalde ran for president in 1999 but lost to de la Rúa.

Quite aside from the strictly economic challenges facing the new regime, there were political dangers as well. Not only were Duhalde's opponents in the national Congress waiting for the opportunity to oust this unelected president, but the powerful governments of Argentina's 24 provinces, determined to avoid cuts in their own budgets, were unlikely to be very cooperative. The possibility that the country could descend into anarchy and chaos was not out of the question.

On January 6, the new government devalued the peso to a fixed rate of 1.40 to the dollar, and announced a new two-tier system of exchange rates—an official rate set by the country's monetary authority for trade in goods, and a floating rate for everything else. To protect citizens from the impact of the devaluation, bank deposits of up to $100,000 would be translated into pesos at the old one-to-one ratio, with the losses to the banks partially compensated for with money from a new tax on oil, an industry that stood to gain from the cheaper exchange rate. The government clamped down even further on bank deposits, freezing accounts with more than $10,000 in them. The regime hoped that such steps would help persuade the International Monetary Fund (IMF) to lend Argentina $15–20 billion, and to work out a repayment agreement with the country's foreign creditors. But the freeze on bank accounts triggered a new round of middle-class rage, and on January 25, thousands blocked highways and gathered at rallies against the new government; in Buenos Aires, riot police fired tear gas to disperse the crowds.

By the beginning of March, when IMF representatives arrived in Argentina to negotiate the possibility of new loans, President Duhalde could point to an economic accomplishment—on February 28 he had convinced Congress to pass a budget 14 percent lower than that of the previous year. But this was not enough to convince the IMF that Argentina was on the road to fiscal responsibility, and new loans were not forthcoming. Duhalde's economy minister resigned, and the situation continued to deteriorate. GDP for the first quarter of 2002 was 16 percent lower than it was for the same period in 2001. Inflation reached 41 percent, and the cost of the basket of basic products increased by 75 percent. Unemployment reached 25 percent—even higher in some areas of the country—and estimates of how many people lived below the poverty live were as high as 60 percent. About a fourth of the population supported themselves on less than $100 a month. People who had previously belonged to the solid middle class were reduced to living off charity.

Argentina having defaulted on its loans, there was no new outside investment coming into the country. Two foreign banks closed their subsidiaries in Argentina, with more threatening to follow suit. President Duhalde, meanwhile, bowing at least symbolically to rising public demands for new elections to provide a democratically elected government, moved up the date of the scheduled national election from September 2003 to March. On June 26, there were again riots in the streets.

In early July, a number of leaders of other Latin American nations met with Duhalde in Buenos Aires and came away issuing supportive statements. Argentinean officials continued their consultations with the IMF, and while the latter helped prop up the economies of neighboring Brazil and Uruguay with loans, it refused to do so for Argentina. The key sticking point was the refusal of Congress to approve Duhalde's proposal, backed by the IMF, to convert the frozen bank deposits into bonds, so that undoing the freeze would not trigger a sudden spike in inflation; the majority in Congress, reflecting the feelings of their constituents, supported a simple end to the freeze. Complicating matters further, the nation's Supreme Court ruled a number of the government's economic measures unconstitutional, at least partly out of pique at Duhalde's unsuccessful attempt to impeach all its members. The *Economist* (Sept. 5) noted that "the prospect of Argentina recovering from its shocking economic collapse seems to recede like a mirage on an endless Pampas road."

In the fall, hopeful sounds about the Argentinean economy hitting bottom and being poised to inch upward were dashed by news that the government was defaulting on the country's debts to the World Bank. On November 14, it repaid just $79.2 million out of the $805 million it owed. Only 18 countries had previously defaulted on World Bank loans in the 58 years of the bank's existence. Argentina was its fourth-biggest debtor, and the amount left unpaid was larger than that of all the earlier defaulting countries together. Meanwhile, political jockeying between and within the Perónist factions over whom to back in the 2003 election added another element of uncertainty to the situation.

Anti-Semitism

Argentina had been settled by immigrants from many different countries, and its society encompassed a wide variety of ideological tendencies. Yet there emerged, over time, a certain shared vision of Argentinean society requiring immigrant groups to integrate into the cultural model already set by the earlier arrivals. This attitude encouraged Jews to become part of the Argentinean collective, but harbored potential antagonism to the retention of a distinctive Jewish identity.

This assimilationist view was espoused not only by right-wing Catholic nationalists, who disapproved of immigrants who might threaten the religious uniformity of the country, but also by the bourgeois democratic streams and the socialist left, which demanded that Jews and other immigrants abandon traits differentiating them from other members of society, or, in the case of the socialists, from the rest of the proletariat. (The Communist Party was the only group to dissent from this position, allowing the formation of special Jewish and Italian sections.)

Throughout the twentieth century, Jews entered nearly every field of Argentine life; the only two sectors off-limits were the middle and senior levels of the military, and the senior foreign service. Jews were prominent in academia, business and industry, the sciences, the arts, and communications. Some were active in political life, and in the second half of the twentieth century Jews began to win election to the provincial and national legislative bodies as representatives of the Socialist, Radical, and Perónist parties. A number of Jews became cabinet ministers and provincial governors. To be sure, there was often informal bias against Jews even in those sectors of Argentine life that did not expressly discriminate.

Expressions of ideological anti-Semitism appeared in intellectual and journalistic circles as early as the 1880s and have continued since. Jews were attacked for being leftists, revolutionaries, and anarchists; for being bourgeois, capitalist, and imperialist; for being a separate nation within the "Argentine nation"; for participating in an international plot together with the freemasons; for being descendents of Jesus's murderers; for their unbelief and for remaining loyal to their beliefs. The teachings of the Catholic Church often lay behind popular anti-Semitism, and there was also continuous dissemination of anti-Semitic literature modeled on the *Protocols of the Elders of Zion.*

In the 1930s, a right-wing military junta took power that drew on Catholic and nationalist sentiments in the country. It set limits on Jewish immigration to Argentina, and these remained in effect for years. Also, the Nazi government in Germany spread anti-Semitic propaganda throughout Latin American, and Argentinean army officers trained in Germany came back home imbued with Nazi anti-Jewish ideology. Since then, the army retained an anti-Jewish bias, one that surfaced again from 1976 to 1983, when the military suspended the constitution and took power. While the regime outlawed public manifestations of anti-Semitism—just as it banned all independent political activity— Jews were harassed and tortured more than others in the official detention centers and clandestine prisons.

When democracy returned to Argentina in 1983, anti-Semitic groups resumed open activity, continuing with their propaganda and mounting physical attacks against Jewish organizations. In the 1990s some of them succeeded in organizing two political parties. While these trends alarmed Argentine Jews and contributed to Argentina's image as an anti-Semitic country, they did not endanger Jewish existence in Argentina. In fact hostility from some sectors of the population united the Jewish community to fight publicly against potential or actual attacks.

In the 1960s a new variant of anti-Semitism emerged, originating in the

Arab world, and it continued to have great resonance in 2002. In this case, the hatred of Jews was tied together with anti-Zionism and antagonism toward Israel. Paradoxically, while the Arab variety of anti-Semitism tended to identify with the radical left, its practitioners often allied themselves with Argentinean nationalist groups, finding common ground in anti-Semitism. Anti-Jewish organizations continue to disseminate their literature in 2002. For example, the book *El Kahal de Oro* (The Gold Kahal) by Hugo Wast—pseudonym of the Catholic anti-Semitic writer Gustavo Martínez Zuviría—was exhibited at the fourth annual Exhibition of the Catholic Book in La Plata, in November. This book, originally published in the late 1930s, was a popular classic of Argentinean anti-Semitism.

Remarkably, the social and economic crisis that Argentina experienced in 2001–02 produced no anti-Semitic reaction either in the political arena or in the popular protests. For a short time, indeed, an Argentine-Israeli economist, Mario Blejer—an observant Jew—was governor of the Central Bank. Public discussion about his performance focused on his policies and the fact that for many years he had worked for the International Monetary Fund. Not only did he attract no anti-Semitic comments, but, like all of the prominent Jews in politics in recent years, the fact of his Jewishness went unmentioned.

An instance of anti-Jewish discrimination in politics did come up in 2002, but it had nothing to do with the economic situation and had a happy ending. The country's new constitution of 1994 canceled the previous requirement that only a Catholic could be elected president, vice president, or president of the Senate. But this change was not introduced into the provincial constitutions. In December 2002, when the possibility rose that the Justicialista Party would choose Senator José Alperovich, a Jew, as its candidate for governor of Tucumán Province, the archbishop of Tucumán, Luis Alberto Villalba, together with candidates from the opposition, expressed outrage. They pointed out that the provincial constitution required the governor and lieutenant governor, upon taking office, to swear their loyalty to "God, the Nation, and the Holy Gospels." An intense public debate ensued in which Jewish organizations, representatives of the Muslim community, and the Evangelist Christian Council—a union of 200 non-Catholic churches—demanded repeal of the discriminatory requirement. In a public survey carried out in Tucumán toward the end of the year, 52.8 percent of the people favored the constitutional change while 45.3 percent opposed it. Despite the constitutional provision, the voters of the province, in a remarkable rejection of religious bigotry, elected Alperovich governor in June 2003.

This complex framework of relationships between the Jewish community and other sectors of Argentine society was reflected in reactions to the terrorist attack on the Israeli embassy in Buenos Aires in 1992 that left 29 dead, and, especially, the attack two years later, July 18, 1994, on the building of the Asociación Mutual Israelita Argentina (Argentine Israelite Mutual Aid Association, AMIA), the headquarters of most of the organizations of the Jewish community, that killed 85 and injured hundreds more.

The spontaneous popular reaction, after the AMIA bombing, was to identify with the victims in a mass demonstration a few days after the attack. Tens of thousands, including the president of Argentina and leaders of the Jewish community, gathered in Plaza Congreso for expressions of solidarity by different sectors of the society. And yet it was not until September 2001, more than seven years later, that 20 Argentine men, four of them police officers, went on trial for allegedly providing local help for the attackers, who were assumed to be foreigners. On July 22, 2002, the *New York Times* revealed that an Iranian defector had provided information linking Iran to both the Israeli embassy and the AMIA attacks. Ever since the atrocities took place and continuing during the ongoing trial of the 20 Argentineans, suspicions were voiced about the possible collaboration of politicians, members of the judiciary, and police officers in obstructing the investigation.

Beginning in 1994, the Jewish community tightened its security considerably. Most buildings belonging to Jewish organizations, such as synagogues, schools, and social and sports clubs, were surrounded by barricades, and Jewish institutions hired guards to supplement the police or gendarmerie officials patrolling outside the buildings, a state of affairs similar to Jewish communities in Europe and elsewhere.

A public-opinion survey in 2000 sponsored by the American Jewish Committee and AMIA showed that only 15 percent of Argentineans would "prefer not" to have Jews as neighbors, and that the same proportion of people who thought Jews had "too much" influence in society—roughly a quarter—believed that Jews had "too little" influence. Multinational corporations, the Catholic Church, the mass media, banks, politicians, and the military were all considered more powerful than Jews. Some 28 percent of the sample considered anti-Semitism a "very serious problem" in Argentina, and another 35 percent considered it "somewhat of a problem." Seventy-two percent agreed with the statement that there "are groups in our society that espouse Nazi ideology." Asked about the AMIA bombing, 52 percent thought it was targeted at "Jews generally," 31 percent that it was targeted at "all Argentines," and only 7 percent that it was aimed specifically at AMIA.

Holocaust-Related Matters

A major change in Argentina's attitude toward the Holocaust occurred in 1995, when the government approved funding for the Fundación Memoria del Holocausto (Holocaust Memorial Foundation), and provided it a building. In 1999, Congress granted the foundation a 99-year lease on the property. That same year, the Ministry of the Interior issued a book on the Holocaust, *Seis millones de veces uno—el Holocausto* (Six Million Times One—the Holocaust), edited by Eliyahu Toker and Anita Weinstein, that was distributed to public schools to educate the country's young people about the subject. In addition, April 19, the date of the Warsaw Ghetto uprising, was set aside for the public schools to honor cultural diversity. That day, called Día de la Convivencia en la Diversidad Cultural en Recordación del Levantamiento del Ghetto de Varsovia (Day of Coexistence and Cultural Diversity in Recollection of the Warsaw Ghetto Uprising), was devoted totally to the study of subjects related to the Holocaust.

Steps were also taken at that time to bring to light Argentina's historical role during World War II and the Holocaust. At the initiative of Guido Di Tella, who was then foreign minister, the government established the Comisión para el Esclarecimiento de las Actividades del Nazismo en la Argentina (Commission for the Clarification of Nazi Activities in Argentina, or CEANA), which sponsored research and published two compilations of articles resulting from it in 1999 and 2000. Working independently, journalist Uki Goñi studied archives in Germany, Belgium, Chile, Denmark, the U.S., Great Britain, and Switzerland—in addition to those of Argentina—and in 2002 published *La auténtica Odessa—La fuga nazi a la Argentina de Perón* (The Authentic Odessa—The Nazi Escape to Perón's Argentina), about the escape routes that Nazi war criminals used to reach Argentina, with Perón's express support. There has also been some historical scholarship on the involvement of some of these Nazi refugees in industry, commerce, and scientific and military research in Argentina. But nothing has yet been published about their role in the security forces and their ideological influence upon officials in the various branches of the military, or their active participation in military and police repression of the civilian population.

The opinion poll undertaken by the American Jewish Committee and AMIA in 2000 indicated that over 70 percent of Argentineans wanted the memory of the Holocaust kept alive and that Holocaust denial had had a negligible impact on the country. Nevertheless, Argentineans, on the whole, had meager factual knowledge about the Holocaust.

JEWISH COMMUNITY

Demography

The Jewish population of Argentina was estimated at about 180,000 in 2002. At its peak, in the 1960s, the community had numbered 300,000, but had steadily declined since. One reason was the low birthrate. As in other predominantly urban and middle-class Jewish communities around the world, a low birthrate meant an aging Jewish population. The average age, which was 25–27 in 1930, 31 in 1947, and 35 in 1960, jumped to over 40 in the 1970s, and continued rising. In addition, a growing number of Jews abandoned the community, many through exogamous marriages, which increased steadily. While no exact statistics are available, the intermarriage rate was estimated at 30–40 percent in the mid-1980s, and certainly went up in the interim. There was also a negative migratory balance. The rate of aliyah was proportionally among the highest in the Jewish diaspora, and there was also considerable emigration to the U.S., other countries in the Western Hemisphere, and, to a lesser extent, Western Europe.

The Jewish population of Argentina—about 80 percent Ashkenazi— was mostly urban. Memories of Jewish agricultural settlement and the "Jewish gaucho" retained their places of honor in communal consciousness—reinforcing the idea that Jews were an old and legitimate element in predominantly Catholic Argentine society—and in the country's tourist industry, which was eager to use the image to lure American Jews to visit. But they had no relation to current reality. Until 1905, 66 percent of Jews lived in agricultural settlements, but as early as 1935 the number had plummeted to 10 percent.

In 2002, more than 80 percent of the Jewish community lived in Buenos Aires (Capital Federal and the suburbs), and another 10 percent in cities that had more than a million inhabitants (Córdoba, Rosario, Tucumán, and La Plata).

Communal Affairs

La Asociación Mutual Israelita Argentina (Argentine Israelite Mutual Aid Association, AMIA), whose origins dated back to the 1930s when the Ashkenazi Jews of Argentina formed a burial society, coordinated the religious, cultural, and social-welfare activities of the Ashkenazi community, on the model of the European *kehilla*. The 20 percent of Argentine Jews who were Sephardi had three separate organizations, depending if they came from Aleppo, Damascus, or Morocco. A Sephardi umbrella organization encompassing them disbanded in 1998, and in October 2002 a new one was launched, La Federación Sefaradí de la República Argentina (Sephardi Federation of the Argentine Republic, FESERA), with 66 institutions participating.

La Federación de Comunidades Israelitas Argentinas—Vaad Hakehilot b'Argentina (Federation of Argentine Jewish Communities), included all the Jewish institutions in Argentina—Ashkenazi and Sephardi—under a federative umbrella. AMIA, which was instrumental in organizing the federation, continued to play a dominant role. While constituents from the provinces sometimes complained that the Buenos Aires administration maintained excessive control, the federation remained the only body dealing with widely different services—spiritual and religious, cultural, educational, and social welfare—throughout the country.

The key political umbrella organization of the Jewish community was La Delegación de Asociaciones Israelitas Argentinas (Delegation of Israelite Argentine Associations, DAIA), founded in 1935. Responsible for defending Jewish interests before the civil society and the government, DAIA also functioned as the Latin American representative of the World Jewish Congress, and, in 1964, took the initiative in founding the Latin American Jewish Congress. DAIA fought anti-Semitism, racism, and other forms of discrimination in Argentina, and belonged to the advisory council of Argentina's National Institute Against Discrimination, Xenophobia, and Racism (INADI), established in 1997.

The DAIA managed to maintain itself through almost seven decades of political, social, and economic upheaval by sticking to a self-imposed limitation: no identification with any Argentinean party or political faction. To be sure, DAIA's silence during the period of the military junta, 1976–83, which used kidnapping, torture, and murder to maintain power, drew criticism from within the Jewish community, although DAIA's supporters responded that outright defiance of the junta would make things even worse for Jews. More recently, a sharp debate arose over whether the DAIA's response to the terrorist attacks against the Israeli embassy in 1992 and the AMIA building in 1994 was sufficiently vigorous (the DAIA's offices were located on the fifth floor of the AMIA building). The Memoria Activa group, highly critical of what it saw as the DAIA's too cozy relationship with the authorities, continued its regular demonstrations in front of the main courthouse in Buenos Aires every Monday at 9:53 A.M., the day and exact time of the AMIA attack. The man who was DAIA' s president in 1994, Rubén Beraja, had to resign his position in 1998 because of irregularities in the administration of the bank he owned, Banco Mayo.

Elections for officers of AMIA and DAIA were often accompanied by vigorous political activity. Many of the competing Jewish factions appealed across the Ashkenazi-Sephardi boundary, identifying themselves with one or another Israeli political party (Abraham Kaul, current president of AMIA, supported the Labor Party), various social and political ideologies, sports clubs, or specific leaders.

Religion and Secularism

The Jewish community of Argentina was overwhelmingly secular. For many, synagogue attendance on Shabbat or Jewish holidays was not a religious expression but instead a mode of social and national identification with the Jewish people and its culture. Yet even while the large majority of Jews and their leaders lived secular lives, the central institutions of the community remained officially Orthodox.

One controversial religious issue with potentially profound implications for Argentine Jewry as a whole was conversion. With the high rate of intermarriage, some non-Jewish spouses were willing to convert to Judaism, be formally incorporated into the community, and raise their children as Jews. As early as the 1920s, however, suspicions that many "conversions" did not fulfill the requirements of Halakhah led some Orthodox rabbis to ban all conversions in the country, but not every rabbinical authority abided by the ban. In 2002 there were still many Jews in Argentina, including people who were not themselves religiously observant, who insisted that non-Jews converted by local rabbis were not yet Jews and should go to Israel, the U.S., or Europe to be converted by rabbis there before the community could recognize them.

The Masorti movement, which identified with Conservative Judaism and performed its own conversions, began its activity in Argentina in

1960, and in 2002 had dozens of affiliated congregations there. The Reform movement, which also performed conversions, had a very limited presence in Argentina and very few followers. Most Jews of Argentina, whose Judaism was a matter of social and ethnic identity and who emphasized active participation in Jewish life and the upbringing of children as members of the Jewish people rather than following Halakhah, were satisfied with Conservative and Reform conversions.

According to some estimates, about half of all Jews in Argentina who maintained relatively continuous contact with a synagogue were identified with the Masorti movement. In 1962, Masorti established the Seminario Rabínico Latinoamericano (Latin American Rabbinical Seminary) in Buenos Aires, an institution of higher learning to train rabbis and other religious leaders. In 2002, more than 60 graduates of the seminary were serving as rabbis in Argentina, elsewhere in Latin America, the U.S., and around the world.

Recently, a growing number of young Jews, especially from Aleppo, Syria, as well as some Ashkenazim, had "returned" to religious Orthodoxy. They observed Jewish law strictly and studied rabbinical literature in the traditional way. But this trend had very little impact on the broader community.

More significant was the growth of the Chabad-Lubavitch Hassidic group. Chabad's entry into the Argentine Jewish community began in the late 1960s, and by the end of the 1990s it had 20 centers in the country, two-thirds of them in the Buenos Aires metropolitan area. Part of Chabad's strategy, not only in Argentina but worldwide, was to establish a public presence by celebrating holidays like Hanukkah, Sukkot, and Lag Ba'omer in public, non-Jewish spaces, and many Jews responded positively to such demonstrations of Jewish pride. Chabad's original appeal in Argentina was to the poorer Jews—a steadily growing group under the economic conditions of 2001–02—who appreciated the economic help it furnished them. It also attracted a number of wealthy people to help support its activities. It was unclear, however, how many of those who identified with Chabad or received financial aid from it adopted the fully observant Chabad lifestyle, since the movement did not insist on strict conformity to Halakhah on the part of those who found their way into its orbit.

Education

Jewish schools, among the most vital factors enhancing Jewish socialization and community organization in Argentina, traditionally reflected the various streams of Jewish thought in the community. Until the late 1960s these were afternoon schools that children would attend after the public-school day. There were schools for Ashkenazim and Sephardim, as well as those with religious, traditional, leftist, secular, Zionist, non-Zionist, and anti-Zionist ideologies. A central educational organization for the Ashkenazim was founded in 1935. In the early days Yiddish was the language of instruction for most Ashkenazi schools, even the Zionist ones. The number of students in Jewish schools rose from 5,300 in 1940 to 17,500 in 1965. The ideological map shifted as well during these years, most schools declaring a Zionist identification and adopting Hebrew as the language of instruction.

When the public educational system changed its schedule to a longer day in the late 1960s leaving no time for the afternoon Jewish schools, the community transformed them into private day schools offering both a general and a Jewish curriculum. This put pressure on the schools to excel in their general programs so that parents would not remove their children and send them to public school. While tending to relegate the Jewish program to a secondary place, this strategy did succeed in retaining Jewish students. In addition to formal Jewish education, Jewish schools offered an informal social framework with events connected to the Hebrew calendar and Israel-related activities such as dance groups and choirs. For students in the higher grades there was the opportunity for educational trips to Israel.

A survey carried out in 1997 found that nearly half of all Jewish families in Argentina with children aged 13–17 and two-thirds of those with children aged 6–12 sent them to Jewish day schools. These schools taught the mandated national curriculum along with a Jewish cultural program that took up between five and 20 hours per week. A total of 19,248 students attended classes in 56 nursery schools, 52 elementary schools, and 29 high schools.

By 2002, however, the numbers apparently dropped—a new study showed just 14,700 students in 40 elementary schools and 22 high schools. Although the two surveys conducted five years apart had different methodologies and were therefore not necessarily comparable, it is likely that the difference reflected a real downturn, the natural result of a low birthrate, assimilation, and emigration. Indeed, since the bulk of Jewish emigration took place in the second half of the year and was not yet reflected in the 2002 data, the actual decline was probably greater. The high tuition charges were also a deterrent under the grim economic circumstances, even though local Jewish institutions, the Jewish Agency, and Israel's Ministry of Education established financial aid programs.

Recognizing that other educational alternatives were necessary for those not in day schools, the community, in cooperation with the Jewish Agency, established supplementary programs with classes two or three days a week. Chabad developed a similar strategy, offering children attending public school an enriched after-school curriculum in computers, English, and other subjects, together with Jewish studies.

Economic Catastrophe and Emigration

The Jewish community's economic troubles had begun in 1998, when two Jewish-owned banks, Mayo and Patricios, where money belonging to Jews and Jewish institutions had been invested, went bankrupt. Then, the collapse of 2001 devastated the primarily middle-class Jews of Argentina. An estimated 30 percent of Jews were unemployed, and one-fourth lived below the poverty line. Those who could not pay their utility bills had their gas and electricity cut off. Some had no food to eat, and the community worried about the possibility of suicides. Jewish welfare agencies in Buenos Aires struggled to keep up with the rising demands of families in need, especially those living in the countryside. Many synagogues and community centers opened emergency soup kitchens.

The Jewish community of Argentina could not itself handle the heavy new welfare burden. In December 2001, the Inter-American Development Bank granted $1.73 million to AMIA for its job placement service, which was receiving 500 work applications a month as compared to 1,000 for all of 2000. The AMIA's Tzedaka Foundation, founded to help the community's needy, could not do so on its own, and relied on a heavy infusion of funds from the American Jewish Joint Distribution Committee (JDC), the U.S. Jewish organization that funded overseas relief, to pay for the distribution of food packages and vouchers, medicine, clothing, and cash assistance. The JDC's chief social worker in Buenos Aires said: "I feel that poverty is consuming us one by one. First went the business employees, then the business owners, then the professionals: lawyers, doctors, architects, then property owners—and the end is not yet near." By the time Passover came, there were so many Jews who could not afford a seder that the JDC and Tzedaka organized several massive communal seders—hundreds of people attended each one—in Buenos Aires. In all, the JDC spent $6.7 million on Argentina in 2002.

When the economic crisis broke, the Jewish Agency declared the Jewish community of Argentina—along with those of France and South Africa—"endangered," and stepped up its program to encourage aliyah with promises of jobs, language training, free health insurance, and a

$20,000 living allowance. The agency's office in Buenos Aires reported a 300-percent increase in inquiries about opportunities in Israel. Argentina was fertile soil for calls of aliyah: over the previous ten years about 14,000 Jews had moved from Argentina to Israel, a number equal to 8 percent of the Argentinean Jewish population.

During 2002, Israeli political leaders visited Argentina to encourage Jews to leave, several mayors of Israeli cities advertising the benefits of life in their hometowns. Some 1,500 Jews had gone on aliyah in 2001, and Israel reportedly hoped to double or even triple that number in 2002. Prime Minister Sharon personally greeted a planeload of Jews from Buenos Aires who landed in Israel on January 23. In February, reports circulated that Sharon had met with American Jewish leaders to request $200 million to fund aliyah from Argentina. He did not get such an astronomical sum, but a United Jewish Communities (UJC) press release on February 27 announced it was giving the Jewish Agency $35 million to bring 5,000 Jews from Argentina to Israel during 2002. This was in addition to a $5-million allocation to the JDC for aid to Jews in Argentina. By March, the Jewish Agency raised its sights, announcing a "master plan" to absorb 20,000 Jews from Argentina (more than 10 percent of the community) over three years.

By year's end, 5,931 Argentinean Jews had left for Israel—most of them in the second half of the year—nearly four times as many as in 2001. Although there were no statistics for Jewish emigration to other countries, their number was estimated as roughly equal to those who chose aliyah. HIAS (Hebrew Immigrant Aid Society), based in New York, played an indispensable role in facilitating the migration of Argentinean Jews.

One factor that might have made some Jews in Argentina think twice about the policies of the State of Israel was a lingering uncertainty over the role that the Israeli government had played during the dictatorship of 1976–83 in their country. While Israel helped more than 300 Jews leave Argentina at the time (HIAS saved hundreds as well, both Jews and others), relatives of some of the Jews who "disappeared" claimed that their requests for intercession by the Israeli embassy had not been honored, and since Israel was helping Argentina militarily in those days, they thought that more could have been done to save the imperiled Jews. Israeli diplomats, however, claimed that they had presented the military government with lists of hundreds of names of "disappeared" Jews, but that the junta had not responded.

In 2000, the Israeli Knesset established an interministerial commission, including two representatives of the families, to investigate the charges. By the end of 2002 it had heard testimony from some 100 victims of the

junta, its staff had combed through the relevant archives of the Foreign
Ministry and the Jewish Agency, and it discreetly requested the current
Argentinean government to check its records. The commission's final re-
port was due for release in 2003.

Culture

Jews constituted an integral part of Argentine cultural life. Jewish participation was evident in every sphere of culture—literature, journalism,
theater, cinematography and television, the visual arts, and classical and
popular music. Furthermore, Jews generally made up a disproportionate
part of the audience at cultural events and scholarly conferences.

Two of the best known Agentinean writers were Jewish. Marcos Agui-
nis, whose Spanish-language novels, short stories, and essays demonstrated the breadth of his erudition in medicine, psychoanalysis, literature, and history, was the recipient of numerous awards and attracted
international acclaim. Perla Suez was one of the most important writers
of children's books in the country, and she also wrote and lectured on the
role that reading played in the imaginative life of the child.

Milá Publishing House, sponsored by AMIA, published many works
of Jewish interest, most in the original Spanish, as well as a number of
translations, particularly from Yiddish.

Two original creative works that appeared during the year deserve special mention. One was *Recreando la cultura judeoargentina, 1894-2001: en
el umbral del Segundo siglo,* (Recreating Jewish-Argentine Culture,
1894–2001: On the Verge of the Second Century), a compilation of papers delivered at a conference in Buenos Aires in August 2001. Presenting diverse views about the cultural inquietude that generates creativity,
it focused on the transmission of Argentine Jewish culture, and included
the perspectives of Argentinean Jews who wrote or performed in Spanish but whose work was especially popular in Israel and the U.S.

The second was a film, *Aquellos niños* (And We Were Children), which
documented the experiences of people who underwent the Holocaust as
children, and explored the deep imprint the experience left in their souls.
This was one of the first works in Argentina to document the Holocaust
and its spiritual legacy. Previously, Argentinean audiences had been exposed to film treatments of the Holocaust only via imports from the
U.S., Europe, and Israel.

Demonstrating its conviction that the history of the Jews in Argentina
was a valued and integral part of the country's culture, the prestigious

Academia Nacional de la Historia (National Historical Academy) elected Raanan Rein as a member. Rein, director of Tel Aviv University's Institute of Latin American History and a native of Argentina, was the author of nine books on Jewish and Israeli relations with Spain and Latin America. In 2002 he also won the Latin American Jewish Studies Award for Outstanding Research for his latest work, *Argentina, Israel, and the Jews: From the Partition of Palestine to the Eichmann Affair.*

Personalia

César Milstein, a co-winner of the 1984 Nobel Prize for Physiology or Medicine, died in England on March 24. Born in Argentina in 1927, Milstein attended the University of Buenos Aires. In 1958 he went to Cambridge University to complete his Ph.D., returned to Argentina in 1961 to head the molecular biology division at the National Institute of Microbiology, but left two years later and went back to Cambridge to protest the dismissal of many of his colleagues by the regime. The Nobel Prize, which he shared with two others, was for the development of a technique to produce monoclonal antibodies, accomplished in 1975.

Two important Argentine Jewish educators passed away in December. Rajel Bogopolsky de Hodara, born in 1939 in Buenos Aires, died in Jerusalem. A member of the Zionist youth movement Ijud Habonim, Bogopolsky de Hodara graduated from the Hebrew University of Jerusalem with a degree in Bible and Hebrew. She taught mostly Spanish-speaking adults in the Jewish communities of Latin America and in Israel, and was an especially favored speaker for Mexican Jewish organizations. A Ph.D. candidate at the time of her death, she had published scholarly articles on women during the Holocaust.

Jaime Barylko was born in 1936 in Buenos Aires, where he died. A graduate of the Teacher's Seminary in Moisesville, he taught in Jewish schools in the interior of the country as well as in Buenos Aires. He directed the Rambam secondary school and, later, the Vaad Hachinuch Hamercazi (Central Council of Jewish Education). Earning a Ph.D. in philosophy from La Plata University, Barylko was a professor in various Argentine universities and dean of humanities in the private university Maimónides in Buenos Aires. He wrote many books on philosophy, psychology, and pedagogy, lectured for Jewish organizations, and appeared on many radio and television programs.

THE EDITORS

Western Europe

Great Britain

National Affairs

FROM AN ECONOMIC STANDPOINT, the year ended much as it began, but with some suggestion of difficulties ahead. Interest rates remained at about 4 percent all year, a 38-year low, leading to a rise in house prices and a boom in consumption. Employment was at a record high as retailers and the public sector continued to recruit heavily, and the number of unemployed reached a two-year low in November. Average earnings from August to October rose 3.7 percent and remained well below the 4.5-percent rate the Bank of England considered consistent with its 2.5-percent inflation target. However, the rapid rise in house prices brought year-end inflation to 2.8 percent, the highest in four years, creating a potential problem. Also worrisome was the government's vastly increased need to borrow. In his prebudget report in November, Chancellor of the Exchequer Gordon Brown noted that the tax revenue forecast in his April budget had not been reached due to disappointing growth in the economy, falling stock prices, and lower profits for investment banks and brokers. The deficit was forecast to reach £20 billion by the end of the year, £9 billion more than predicted in April and more than in any year since Brown became chancellor in 1997. Also in his November report, Brown revealed that he had set aside £1 billion toward the cost of war in Iraq. Rather than raise taxes or cut spending, he announced that the government would cover the deficit by borrowing.

The increased appropriations in the April budget were aimed primarily at improving standards and facilities in the National Health Service and the state educational system. These objectives enjoyed wide public support that compensated politically for the signs of governmental disarray evident in the resignations of the unpopular ministers for transport and education. Thus the Labor lead over the Tories, which fell to 7–9 percentage points in March, was up to 12 percent by November. A survey that month showed 42 percent Labor; 30 percent Conservative; and 21 percent Liberal Democrat—virtually no change since the 2001 election.

Israel and the Middle East

The main lines of British policy emerged in March, when Prime Minister Tony Blair and Foreign Secretary Jack Straw supported a UN Security Council resolution calling for an end to Middle East violence and the establishment of a Palestinian state alongside Israel. Israel's right to a secure existence had to be acknowledged "by all the Arab world," Blair told the House of Commons, and Israel and the international community had to accept "a viable Palestinian state." In April, sources reported Britain's readiness to seek a Security Council resolution based on Saudi crown prince Abdullah's land-for-peace proposals. In June, Britain welcomed the two-state solution envisaged by President George Bush, including the notion of a peace treaty within three years. But while sharing Bush's frustration at the leadership of Palestine Authority president Yasir Arafat, British diplomats did not go so far as to advocate his removal, asserting that the Palestinians should choose their own leaders. And whereas Bush pointedly refused to meet with Arafat, Blair had met with him some dozen times in recent years. In June, Straw announced that Britain planned to give more than £30 million in aid to the Palestinians in 2002.

Prominent British politicians met with Israeli and Palestinian leaders on numerous occasions, condemning acts of terror, urging restraint, and appealing for an end to violence. In January, Foreign Office minister Ben Bradshaw met with Arafat and "very firmly" expressed Britain's dissatisfaction at how few terrorists the PA had arrested. In February, Foreign Secretary Straw visited Israel, the Palestinian Authority, and Turkey to show concern over the growing violence. Mike O'Brien, who replaced Bradshaw in May, was in Ramallah in June urging Arafat to take decisive action against terrorism. Whitehall persisted in refusing to grant Israel export licenses for military hardware lest it be used against Palestinians. Already in March, Straw accused Israel of contravening an undertaking not to use British-supplied military equipment, such as Centurion tanks, in the West Bank and Gaza Strip.

Britain generally condemned acts of violence by either side. The Foreign Office described the suicide car bombing near Megiddo in June as "appalling" and urged the PA to do more to crack down on terror, but made equally clear its opposition to Israeli incursions into the West Bank. In July, Straw called Israel's air strike on Gaza, aimed at a top Hamas terrorist, "completely unjustified." Describing the strike as the "slaughter of innocents," O'Brien called on Israel to impose an immediate freeze on settlement activity. In November, Straw condemned an ambush that killed 12 Israeli soldiers and security guards, but warned Sharon against expanding settlements in the Hebron area, which Britain considered illegal and an obstacle to peace.

In the spring, Britain expressed readiness to play a more proactive role in the peace process. After backing a Security Council resolution in March calling on Israel and the Palestinians to agree to a cease-fire, in April Britain said it was willing to send observers to the Middle East to monitor the cease-fire and ensure that terrorists were kept behind bars. The same month a team of Foreign Office experts traveled to the West Bank to prepare for the arrival of British and U.S. security personnel to guard prisoners in a Jericho jail who were accused of murdering Israel's tourism minister in 2001.

British policy became even more assertive toward the end of the year, signaling what Israeli officials saw as a shift in favor of the Palestinians. In October, Great Britain's ambassador to Israel, Sherard Cowper-Coles, called the West Bank and Gaza "the largest detention camp in the world." Britain hosted a visit by Syrian president Bashar al-Assad in December, despite protests from the Jewish community and Israeli officials. Assad received a glittering welcome in London, meeting both Blair and Queen Elizabeth, though one Whitehall official described the atmosphere as "cool," and major differences between the two countries remained, particularly regarding terrorist organizations based in Syria.

Britain gave supporters of Israel further cause for concern when it neither informed nor consulted Israel about its decision to convene a conference on Palestinian political reform, to be held in London in January 2003. It would be chaired by Straw, and participants would include the PA, Egypt, Saudi Arabia, and Jordan, as well as the "Quartet"—the U.S., the European Union, Russia, and the UN. The conference, Blair told Arab leaders, would focus on ways the international community could help the Palestinians prepare for independence, setting the stage for implementation of the Quartet's "road map" for peace once the new Israeli government was in place. That the Palestinian delegates to the conference would be nominated by Arafat—a man regarded as irrelevant by Israeli leaders—heightened Israel's unease. It made talk of genuine PA reform pointless, Israeli foreign minister Benjamin Netanyahu told Straw when he visited London in December to "a less than friendly" welcome. The fact that Amram Mitzna, the new leader of the opposition Labor Party in Israel, had been invited to visit London the following month did not improve the atmosphere.

THE MEDIA AND PUBLIC OPINION

On the cover of the January 14 issue of the weekly *New Statesman* appeared the title of the lead article—"A Kosher Conspiracy?"—concerning alleged Zionist control of the media, illustrated with a large Star of David standing atop the Union Jack. The editor denied any anti-Semitic intent, but, acknowledging that the publication's Web site had received laudatory anti-Semitic messages, issued an apology. Also in January, Harrods, the large, upscale department store owned by Mohamed Al Fayed, acceded to a request from the Council for the Advancement of Arab-British Understanding (CAABU) and removed from its shelves Israeli products that might have originated in Gaza or the West Bank. In the wake of strong protests, however, Harrods once again stocked the products, but with stickers affixed noting where they came from. In March, the Scottish Palestinian Forum launched a "Boycott Israeli Goods" campaign.

Other signs of anti-Israel sentiment showed in connection with the Israeli occupation of West Bank cities in the spring, particularly the events in Jenin. The British media gave almost unanimous credence to atrocity stories that were later proved to be fabrications, the popular London tabloid the *Sun* standing virtually alone in defending the Jewish state. In an editorial, the *Guardian* called the actions of the Israeli army "every bit as repellent" as September 11. The columnist for the *Evening Standard* wrote "of massacre, and a cover-up, of genocide," and accused Israel of poisoning Palestinian water supplies (a few months earlier he had "reluctantly" concluded that Israel had no right to exist). Phil Reeves, Jerusalem correspondent for the London *Independent,* uncritically quoted local Palestinians who spoke of "mass murder" and "executions." Tom Paulin, a poet who taught at Oxford, went further, telling an Egyptian newspaper that U.S.-born Jews living in the West Bank were Nazis, and should be "shot dead." Iain Duncan Smith, leader of the Conservative opposition in Parliament, called Paulin and his ilk "salon anti-Semites" whose actions were "unforgivable." Yet even months later, after the allegations of Israeli crimes had been shown to be false, no apologies were forthcoming from Paulin or the newspapers.

In June, the Jewish community protested remarks by Cherie Blair, the prime minister's wife, which seemed to show understanding of Palestinian suicide bombers. Mrs. Blair said that her words had been misinterpreted—she had not meant to justify the bombers, and her sympathy lay with the victims. The controversy subsided at the end of the month, when Mrs. Blair hosted a charity event at 10 Downing Street to benefit Israeli terror victims.

Hostility toward Israel was noticeable on university campuses. Although an anti-Israel motion at Manchester University failed to gain the necessary two-thirds majority in February, Jewish students there faced "vicious anti-Semitism of a level unseen for years on campus," according to the campaign organizer for the Union of Jewish Students (UJS). In March, the annual conference of the Association of University Teachers (AUT) passed an anti-Israel resolution. Motions committing student unions to boycott Israeli academics and products were rejected at York University but passed unanimously at London University's School of Oriental and African Studies (SOAS), where a talk at the Islamic Society in May was titled "Sharon: A New Hitler for a New Age."

Campus controversy over Israel's policies accelerated in May and June, after the incursion into Jenin. The student union at the University of Central England in Birmingham passed a motion banning anti-Israel literature on campus; a resolution at Oxford University calling on Israeli forces to withdraw from West Bank Palestinian towns was rescinded on legal grounds; anti-Semitic and anti-Israel posters appeared at Bristol University; and Liverpool University's ban on anti-Zionist literature on campus, passed unanimously in March, was overturned. These controversies resumed again toward the end of the year. In November, University of East London students pledged to raise funds to send a delegation to Palestine to demonstrate solidarity; Jewish students at SOAS were harassed; a motion at Sussex University accusing Israel of human-rights abuses was defeated; and a Cambridge University motion supporting a boycott of Israeli academics and goods was passed. In December, anti-Israel motions were defeated at the London School of Economics and at Warwick and Cambridge universities.

A dispute arose in June, when, as part of the campaign to boycott Israeli scholars and universities, two Israeli academics were removed from the boards of British translation journals that were edited and published privately by Egyptian-born Mona Baker of the University of Manchester Institute of Science and Technology (UMIST). In July, Ian Haworth, that institution's director of external relations, announced that "UMIST does not agree with the boycott of the editorial committee members" and announced an investigation. A House of Commons early-day motion condemning the sackings called on university authorities and the government to ensure that academic life in Britain was not "disfigured by prejudice and persecution." But in November, the Campaign for Academic Freedom and Standards petitioned UMIST's chancellor to drop the inquiry into the dismissals. As the year ended, the university had not yet taken any action.

In August, following the dismissals, the Board of Deputies of British Jews, the community's representative body, announced plans to lobby educational institutions—including universities—to combat discrimination, and in October the board warned university vice chancellors of the dangers of academic boycotts. The National Association of Teachers in Further and Higher Education, whose annual meeting in June urged British schools to consider cutting academic links with Israel until its forces withdrew from the territories, issued a statement condemning anti-Semitism and agreed that anyone distributing inflammatory literature attacking Jews be prosecuted. Jo Wagerman, president of the Board of Deputies, said that the National Union of Teachers (NUT) had committed itself to oppose any boycott of Israel.

The annual Blackpool conference of the Trades Union Congress (TUC) in September was suffused with an anti-Israel atmosphere, David Mencer, director of Trades Union Friends of Israel (TUFI) calling it "the nastiest" he had ever experienced. Already before the conference opened, Sir Ken Jackson, the TUFI chair, was narrowly defeated by a left-wing candidate for the position of general secretary of Amicus, one of the country's largest unions. The conference called for an "immediate termination of Israel's occupation of Palestinian territories and of its settlement policy," and it was with great difficulty that the pro-Israel forces managed to add language urging the Palestinian Authority to halt "terror bombings" against Israeli citizens. Afterwards, in November, Britain's largest union, Unison, joined the Palestinian Solidarity Campaign and other groups in a pro-Palestinian lobby of Parliament to mark the UN International Day of Solidarity with the Palestinians.

An ADL survey released in June found that 13 percent of people in Great Britain sympathized with Israel in the Middle East conflict, 30 percent with the Palestinians, 27 percent with neither, 17 percent with both, and the rest had no opinion.

Anti-Semitism and Racism

The ADL report also compared attitudes toward Jews in five European countries. It found that the British as a whole were less likely to have anti-Semitic attitudes than the residents of the other four nations studied: Belgium, Denmark, France, and Germany. Even so, the numbers for Great Britain were hardly encouraging: 21 percent felt that Jews had too much power in the business world, 34 percent that they were more loyal to Israel than to Britain, 11 percent that Jews were more likely than others to use "shady practices," and 10 percent that Jews did not care about anyone but "their own kind."

The Community Security Trust (CST) reported 350 anti-Semitic incidents in 2002—an average of one a day—marking a 13-percent rise from the 2001 figure of 310. Although this was still far less than the total of 405 in 2000, the CST noted that the community faced a "general upward trend" of incidents since the 1990s. Just as the worst period in 2001 followed the events of 9/11, so too 94 of the 2002 incidents—more than a quarter of the annual total—occurred in April and May, the time of the Israeli incursion in Jenin. Mike Whine, who headed the CST, noted that the upsurge was "a direct consequence of tensions in the Middle East." The shift noted in the 2001 report, away from verbal and written anti-Semitism to physical attacks on Jews and on communal property, continued in 2002. Forty-seven of the incidents were violent assaults—a 15-percent rise since 2001—and 55 incidents involved damage to Jewish institutions. 56 percent of all incidents happened in London. The number of cases of distribution of anti-Semitic literature dropped from 20 in 2001 to 14 in 2002.

In March, British Jewry was placed on highest alert after attacks in France and Belgium "created a mood of apprehension in Britain, the like of which I have never known," said Mike Whine. In April, when 51 anti-Semitic attacks were reported—the second worst monthly total on record—the Nottingham Holocaust memorial was defaced, 80 Jewish gravestones in Hull were smashed, and Finsbury Park Synagogue (North London) was ransacked. The synagogue at Swansea was desecrated in July and two of its Torah scrolls burned, and the next month 300 Jewish vacationers there were pelted with rocks and racial abuse.

The extreme right-wing British National Party (BNP) organized its biggest campaign in several years in the May local elections, contesting 68 seats and winning three in Burnley. A local government by-election in Blackburn in November won it a fourth East Lancashire seat.

After Nottingham University students voted against adopting the policy of the National Union of Students that refused racists a platform, Forum, the university's student-union-financed debating society, invited Holocaust denier David Irving to address it in January. Protests by the Board of Deputies and the local Beit Shalom Holocaust study center were in vain, and the invitation was withdrawn only because of the high cost of policing the meeting. In March, Irving had to declare bankruptcy due to the legal costs of his failed libel action against Penguin Books and American historian Deborah Lipstadt (see AJYB 2001, p. 310).

The role of extremist Islam in fomenting group hatred received considerable attention. In February, a Muslim cleric, Sheik Abdullah al Faisal, was arrested under the Offenses Against the Person Act that had been passed in 1986. He was charged with incitement to murder, based on allegations that he urged his followers to kill Jews. In April, Southwark crown court found Iftikhar Ali guilty of possessing and distributing material with intent to foment racial hatred, actions barred under the Public Order Act of 1986. Ali, who had distributed leaflets advertising a meeting of the radical Muslim, anti-Israel, anti-gay, anti-Western Al-Muhajiroun group, was fined and sentenced to 200 hours of community service. In August, three law lords (functioning as the nation's highest appeals court) confirmed an April decision of the Court of Appeal to maintain the ban on Nation of Islam leader Louis Farrakhan from entering Britain. Home Secretary Blunkett supported maintenance of the ban. In December, the charity commissioners ordered the removal of Sheikh Abu Hamza from his position with a mosque in Finsbury Park, North London, on the grounds that his open support for the Taliban conflicted with the mosque's status as a charitable institution. The sheikh's assets had already been frozen when he was accused of links with terror groups. Also in December, Al-Muhajiroun received a summons from the Greater London Authority to appear in court in January 2003 to answer charges arising from its march through Central London on August Bank Holiday Sunday in defiance of a ban by London mayor Ken Livingstone.

Following private meetings with Chief Rabbi Sacks in November, the prime minister condemned campus racism and anti-Semitism as well as moves to impose an academic boycott on Israel. Home Secretary David Blunkett, for his part, pledged tough action against any individuals or groups on campus who targeted Jews or other minorities. With this government backing, the Union of Jewish Students teamed up with the

National Union of Students and with black and African groups to campaign against racism and extremism in the universities. The same month, London police arrested dozens of suspected racists in a series of raids. "The purpose of such a high profile day," said Commander Cressida Dick, "was to demonstrate our commitment to cutting out hate crime."

Attempts to improve intergroup relations continued throughout the year. In January, Prime Minister Blair hosted a series of meetings with leaders of different religions to stimulate dialogue. In January too, plans were announced to "twin" Jewish and Muslim communities in Britain. This initiative was the brainchild of Rabbi Tony Bayfield, chief executive of the Reform Synagogues of Great Britain (RSGB), and Sir Sigmund Sternberg, cofounder of the Three Faiths Forum. In June, the forum combined with the Leo Baeck College Center for Jewish Education to sponsor shared study of religious texts by Christians, Jews, and Muslims, and in November, Central London's City University launched a program for Israelis and Palestinians to study together.

Nazi War Criminals

The government issued a white paper on immigration policy in February that, among other provisions, proposed stripping suspected Nazi war criminals living in the country of their British citizenship so that they could be expelled. Home Secretary Blunkett explained that this would enable the immigration and nationality authorities to "target both convicted and suspected war criminals" and "avoid repeating the mistakes of history." The document came at a time when Scotland Yard Special Branch officers were investigating a Nottingham pensioner named by the *Daily Telegraph* as Julius Damasevicius. The Simon Wiesenthal Center claimed that he had belonged to the German-backed Lithuanian police battalion that committed atrocities against slave laborers while overseeing construction of a highway in the Ukraine during World War II.

In April, the Wiesenthal Center's Israeli office described British efforts to bring suspected war criminals to justice as "insufficient and unsuccessful." Over the previous year, the center charged, British authorities had initiated six investigations under the 1991 War Crimes Act of which none had led to a prosecution, and no new cases were currently under investigation.

JEWISH COMMUNITY

Demography

Data on Jews from the 2001 British census was not yet available, and since the census question on religion was voluntary, the official numbers, when released, would undercount the Jewish population. The Board of Deputies estimated that there were 285,000 Jews in the country. Demographic statistics of Anglo-Jewry for 2001 published by the Board of Deputies Community Research Unit reflected a community in decline. Numbers of synagogue marriages recorded in 2001 fell to 845 from 907 the previous year, and only the Reform sector registered a rise, from 104 to 118. The number of gittin (religious divorces) went down as well, from a revised figure of 270 in 2000 to 256 in 2001. Burials and cremations under Jewish religious auspices fell from 3,791 in 2000 to 3,610 in 2001.

Although statistics based on figures for circumcision showed births rising from 2,509 in 1999 to 2,647 in 2000, the Research Unit did not believe that the increase affected the persistent overall downward trend of the 1990s. This mirrored the national trend, but in exaggerated form: births in England and Wales in 2000 were 93 percent of those in 1991; for the Jewish community, the comparable proportion was 76 percent.

The religious court of the Reform Synagogues of Great Britain converted 87 proselytes in 2002 as compared with 112 in 2001.

Communal Affairs

In January, the Board of Deputies moved its offices into the first building of its own, in central London's Bloomsbury Square. Almost immediately it got caught up in a controversy over the commemoration of Holocaust Memorial Day, which took place on January 27. In February, a memo was leaked, allegedly written by board vice president Jerry Lewis, challenging the chief rabbi's representative role at the ceremony. When Lewis refused to resign, the board decreed that he be denied access to any sensitive information. A second embarrassing leak occurred in March, when a private letter written by board president Jo Wagerman criticizing Home Secretary Blunkett's failure to attend the Manchester launch of Holocaust Memorial Day found its way into the *Jewish Chronicle*. Wagerman apologized for her "angry language" in the letter.

Several charities opted for a new look. In April, Norwood-

Ravenswood, British Jewry's main children and family service, announced a name change and makeover to increase community awareness of its services and attract younger supporters. In July, the organization reverted to its former name of Norwood and opened a £1.25-million residential home for people with learning difficulties, its 45th residential home. In June, Jewish Care, the community's largest social-service organization, sought to improve its image with a new logo. In February, it bought a 16-acre site in Stanmore, Middlesex, where, in conjunction with the Jewish Association for the Mentally Ill, it opened its first residential home for young Jewish adults with mental health problems in October. In September, the United Jewish Israel Appeal (UJIA) also "rebranded," changing the titles of its twin missions of supporting Israel and Anglo-Jewish education from "Rescue" and "Renewal" to "Israel Now" and "Jewish Future." UJIA's income rose from £13.9 million in 2000 to £14.8 million in 2001, mainly due to its Victim Support Campaign for Israeli victims of terrorism.

Concern for the community's future needs elicited three reports. *Facing the Future: The Provision of Long-term Care for Older Jewish People in the United Kingdom,* prepared by Oliver Valins and published in May, was part of a larger project, Planning for Jewish Communities, launched by the Institute for Jewish Policy Research (JPR). This report found that increasing longevity and a low birth rate would bring a 50-percent rise in the number of British Jews aged 90 or over by the year 2012. Already, almost a quarter of British Jews were 65 or over, far more than the national average of 16 percent, and approximately 14 percent were 75 or over, as compared with 7 percent in the general population. The report warned that reduced levels of state funding would put increasing pressure on Jewish charities. Another in the same JPR series, *A Portrait of Jews in London and the South-East: A Community Study,* appeared in December. It found London Jewry for the most part middle-aged, relatively affluent, and possessing typically middle-class values and lifestyle. While 83 percent belonged to a synagogue, more than half felt more secular than religious. A closer look at a specific London area was *Torah, Worship and Acts of Loving Kindness,* a study of the Haredi (strictly Orthodox) community in Stamford Hill, North London. Published in November and based on research by members of De Montfort University in Leicester, the report found an average family size of 5.9 persons as compared to the national average of 2.4, and noted that 53 percent of families had four or more children, whereas the national rate was only 2 percent.

Religion

There were 362 congregations in the United Kingdom in 2001 with a membership of 87,790 households, as compared with 359 with a membership of 93,684 in 1996, the last time that such a survey was made, a Community Research Unit report found. *British Synagogue Membership in 2001,* by Marlena Schmool and Frances Cohen, showed that 70 percent of these households and 56 percent of the congregations were situated in the Extended London area.

The mainstream Orthodox sector, which included inter alia the United Synagogue (US) and the Federation of Synagogues, comprised 182 congregations (a decline from 192 in 1996) and 50,043 household members (a drop of 12 percent from the 1996 level of 56,895). Still, US members constituted about 57 percent of total British synagogue membership. All other groups either grew or remained relatively stable during that time span. In 2001, the Union of Orthodox Hebrew Congregations (Haredi Orthodox) had 86 congregations and 7,509 members; Reform 41 congregations and 17,745 members; the Liberals 30 congregations and 7,941 members; there were 15 Sephardi congregations with 3,096 members; and eight congregations with 1,456 members affiliated with Masorti Judaism, roughly equivalent to the American Conservative movement.

Meanwhile, the US itself reported in July that membership had risen from 39,033 in 2000 to 39,139 in 2001. Although the number of male members fell from 20,385 to 20,332, the number of females increased from 18,648 to 18,807. In January, the 65th US synagogue opened in Shenley, Hertfordshire. In February, the US treasurer predicted a £254,000 surplus, primarily from selling its synagogue in Hammersmith, West London, for an estimated £1.2 million. In January, June, and November, the US raised money by selling books and manuscripts from its Bet Din (religious court) library at New York auctions.

Jewish women's religious role showed only "patchy" improvement, according to Diana Welsher, whose book, *Jewish Women in the Twenty-first Century,* came out in January. The book, which acknowledged the US's wish to improve women's status in the religious sphere, was sponsored by the Women in the Jewish Community Greater London Update Committee, formed to monitor implementation of Chief Rabbi Sacks's suggestions for enhancing the role of women, issued in 1994. Rabbi Sacks accepted one important recommendation in the book — the establishment of a liaison committee of rabbis and women to implement change — but he assigned this task to the Association of United Synagogue Women rather than to Women in the Jewish Community.

The predicament of women who might become *agunot* ("chained" wives, whose husbands would not give them Jewish divorces) was ameliorated in July when the Divorce (Religious Marriages) Bill passed into law. A private member's bill, it permitted spouses to apply to a judge to delay a civil divorce if the religious marriage was not yet dissolved.

During the summer, a new book by Chief Rabbi Sacks, *The Dignity of Difference*, came under criticism on theological grounds, and in October, the London Bet Din, made up of Orthodox rabbinic scholars, found that parts of it were "open to an interpretation inconsistent with basic Jewish beliefs." The specific charge was that Sacks's suggestion that religions other than Judaism might possess some element of spiritual truth undermined belief in the uniqueness of the Torah. In November, Rabbi Yosef Shalom Elyashiv of Jerusalem, widely considered the leading Orthodox authority in the world, condemned these passages as heretical (though, knowing no English, he could not have read the book himself). Thereupon Sacks instructed his publisher to cease printing and promoting the book, and promised an amended version shortly.

British Jews and Israel

The Jewish community was divided about Israeli policies. In March, Board of Deputies president Jo Wagerman urged solidarity and claimed that the community supported Israel in all its efforts against terrorism. But she made these remarks in response to an ad placed in the *Jewish Chronicle* by British Friends of Peace Now urging Israel to start withdrawing from the Territories, signed by some 300 prominent Jews—including Lady Levy, wife of the prime minister's envoy to the Middle East. On April 16, veteran Labor MP Gerald Kaufman, a Jew and a former shadow foreign secretary, said on the floor of the House of Commons that Ariel Sharon was a "war criminal" leading a "repulsive government."

In April, 100 Orthodox rabbis signed a letter to Sharon declaring support for Israel's "war against terror," and more than 5,000 people attended a Solidarity with Israel/Israel Independence Day celebration inside Wembley (Middlesex) conference center, while outside, anti-Zionist Jews demonstrated side by side with pro-Palestinian Muslims. There was a major Solidarity with Israel rally in Trafalgar Square in May attended by some 55,000 people, and the speakers included Benjamin Netanyahu and Chief Rabbi Sacks. Yet members of Jews for Justice for the Palestinians and of the Palestine Solidarity Campaign attending the rally waved their banners in protest. Some Jewish groups also backed a pro-Palestinian demonstration in London the following week. In October and November, British Friends of Peace Now organized meetings addressed by Courage to Refuse, a group of Israeli soldiers who refused to serve in the Territories, and also sponsored another ad in the *Jewish Chronicle* signed by prominent personages criticizing Sharon and calling for Israel to evacuate the West Bank and Gaza.

Chief Rabbi Sacks, already under attack for his new book (see above), found himself engulfed in another controversy in late summer when the *Guardian* newspaper (Aug. 27) published an interview with him under the front-page headline: "Israel set on tragic path, says Chief Rabbi." Among the comments the article attributed to Sacks was that some Israeli policies "make me uncomfortable as a Jew." The Board of Deputies issued a statement that "the chief rabbi's views do not necessarily reflect the opinions held by every section of the community," while the right-wing Zionist youth group Betar called on Sacks to resign. Rabbi Sacks's office claimed that his words had been taken out of context and that his real message was his "passionate support for Israel."

Education

Race riots in the north of England during the summer of 2002 coupled with the lingering impact of the events of September 11, 2001, raised serious questions about the wisdom of encouraging more "faith schools"—schools run by religious denominations with government funding—since they might inculcate intergroup hostility. In April, the annual conference in Scarborough of the National Association of Schoolmasters/Union of Women Teachers passed a motion opposing faith schools. Since 1997, when the present government assumed office, six Jewish primary schools had obtained state funding. A JPR survey of multicultural education in Jewish schools found that some of them failed to deal effectively with this topic.

In July, plans for a new Orthodox Jewish secondary school that was to open in Hertfordshire by September 2005 hit a snag. The US-backed Hertsmere Jewish High School Trust was challenged by another group that wanted a cross-communal rather than an Orthodox school, meaning that children recognized as Jewish by any mainstream synagogue body—including those with Jewish fathers and non-Jewish mothers—would be admitted. The controversy still raged as the year ended.

In September, The Jewish Free School, Britain's oldest and largest Jewish secondary school, moved to new £43-million premises in Kenton, North London.

In February, Dr. Abner Weiss resigned as principal of the cash-strapped London School of Jewish Studies (LSJS, formerly Jews' College), citing stress over LSJS's fate and the community's indifference, as well as personal considerations. The South-African-born Weiss, who came to London from Los Angeles in September 2000, also resigned as rabbi of London's Western Marble Arch Synagogue, and returned to the U.S. Despite vigorous efforts by Chief Rabbi Sacks, who became acting head of LSJS, a plan to rescue the school by splitting it into two separate organizations failed to win the required unanimous support of the leadership. A sale in New York of Hebrew manuscripts and books from LSJS in December raised record sums, but the survival of the school remained in doubt.

The number of students at the Leo Baeck College Center for Jewish Education (Progressive) rose from 60 in 2001 to a record 75 in 2002, with 23 in the five-year rabbinic ordination program and 23 working for degrees in Jewish education.

In March, the Heritage Lottery Fund awarded Southampton University library £951,000 for the upkeep and enhancement of its Jewish collection. That same month London University's School of Oriental and African Studies (SOAS) axed Britain's only M.A. program in Yiddish.

Foreign Aid

Aid to East European communities was both financial and hands-on. In January, Belarus United, a group of businessmen and medics, visited Belarus to offer help to the Pinsk Jewish community. In June, Leeds World Jewish Relief contributed towards Lviv's Chesed community center. In March, Norwood-Ravenswood ran a training program for staff from Belarus orphanages. In June, children from Harrow and Wembley Progressive Synagogue donated pocket money to help poor Jews in the Ukraine in a "Kippers for Kiev Kids" campaign, and on June 15 the Radlett (Hertfordshire) Reform congregation hosted children from Grodno, Belarus. In August, Northwood and Pinner Liberal Synagogue sent £1000 to help flood-stricken Jews in Prague.

Some British communities identified closely with specific Eastern European communities. North London's Hampstead Garden Suburb Synagogue, which had supported the Lviv community in Ukraine for more than eight years, raised more funds for it at a concert in January, and, in June, entertained children from that community in London. Also in June, Dunstan Road Congregation, Golders Green, North London, adopted the 20,000-member community in Zaporozhye, where World Jewish Relief supported a Jewish day school as well as communal and welfare projects.

Publications

The 2002 Jewish Quarterly-Wingate literary award for fiction went to the late W. G. Sebald for his novel *Austerlitz,* and the nonfiction award to Oliver Sacks for *Uncle Tungsten: Memories of a Chemical Boyhood.*

The year yielded a large number of books on the Holocaust. These included *Holocaust and Rescue* by Pamela Shatzkes; *The Hidden Life of Otto Frank* by Carol Ann Lee; *Nicholas Winton and the Rescued Generation* by Muriel Emanuel and Vera Gissing; *The Villa, the Lake, the Meeting: Wannsee and the Final Solution* by Mark Roseman; *Flares of Memory: Stories of Children during the Holocaust,* edited by Anita Brostoff; *"Bystanders" to the Holocaust: A Re-Evaluation* by David Cesarani and Paul A. Levine; *Hitler and the Holocaust* by Robert S. Wistrich; *Holocaust: A History* by Debórah Dwork and Robert Jan van Pelt; *Telling Lies about Hitler: The Holocaust, History and the David Irving Trial* by Richard J. Evans; *The Gold Train: The Destruction of the Jews and the Second World War's Most Terrible Robbery* by Ronald Zweig; *Saved by My Face* by Jerzy Lando; *Pope Pius XII and the Holocaust,* edited by Carol Rittner and John K. Roth; *Storeys of Memory,* edited by Ben Barkow, Katherine Klinger, and Melissa Rosenbaum, a collection of reflections delivered at the 2001 Holocaust Memorial Day at London's Wiener Library; *Desperate Journey* by Freddie Knoller with John Landaw; and *The Righteous — The Unsung Heroes of the Holocaust* by Martin Gilbert, who also published *Letters to Auntie Forie,* explaining Judaism in simple terms, and the heavily illustrated *From the Ends of the Earth: The Jews in the Twentieth Century.*

Publications on religious themes were *Deconstructing the Bible: Abraham Ibn Ezra's Introduction to the Torah* by Irene Lancaster; *The Jewish Prophet: Visionary Words from Moses and Miriam to Henrietta Szold and A. J. Heschel* by Michael Shire; *The Eternal Journey: Meditations on the Jewish Year* by Jonathan Wittenberg; *Revelation Restored* by David Weiss-Halivni; *Companion to the High Holy-Days Prayer Book* by the late Immanuel Jakobovits, who was the subject of a biography, *Immanuel Jakobovits: A Prophet in Israel,* compiled and edited by Meir Persoff;

Reader's Guide to Judaism, edited by Michael Terry; *The Blackwell Reader in Judaism*, edited by Jacob Neusner and Alan J. Avery-Peck; *The Philosophy of the Talmud* by Hyam Maccoby; *The Dignity of Difference: How to Avoid the Clash of Civilizations* by Jonathan Sacks (for the controversy over this book see above); *The Shabbat Elevator and Other Sabbath Subterfuges* by Alan Dundes; *Ignaz Maybaum: A Reader*, edited by Nicholas de Lange; *The Shabbat Siddur Companion* by Harvey Belovski; *He Kissed Him and They Wept*, an introduction to Catholic-Jewish dialogue edited by Tony Bayfield, Sidney Brichto, and Eugene Fisher; *A Rabbi's Journal* by Yitzchak Reuven Rubin; *Judaism: Key Facts* by Nissan Dovid Dubov; and *Tree of Life, Tree of Knowledge* by Michael Rosenak. *The Rebbe, the Messiah and the Scandal of Orthodox Indifference* by David Berger challenged the Chabad-Lubavitch movement, and *The Messiah Problem: Berger, the Angel and the Scandal of Reckless Indiscrimination* by Chaim Rapoport responded.

Works of biography and autobiography included *Claude Montefiore: His Life and Thought* by Daniel R. Langton; *The Jerusalem Diary: Music, Society and Politics 1977 and 1979* by Hans Keller, with drawings by Millein Cosman, edited by Christopher Wintle and Fiona Williams; *Disraeli's Jewishness*, compiled and edited by Todd Endelman and Tony Kushner, based on papers from a conference at Southampton University in 1994; *Where Did It All Go Right?* by Al Alvarez; and *Nazi Hunter: The Wiesenthal File* by Alan Levy.

Books on Israel were *The Land beyond Promise: Israel, Likud and the Zionist Dream* by Colin Shindler; *Holy Land, Unholy War: Israelis and Palestinians* by Anton La Guardia; *A History of Israel* by Ahron Bregman; *Breaking Ranks: Turbulent Travels in the Promised Land* by Ben Black; *The Lost Testament* by David Rohl; *Historical Atlas of Jerusalem* by Meir Ben-Dov; and *The Palestine-Israeli Conflict: A Beginner's Guide* by Dan Cohn-Sherbok and Dawoud El-Alami. Cohn-Sherbok also published another volume, *Antisemitism*.

Fiction published in 2002 included *From Here to Obscurity* by Yoel Sheridan; *Coralena* by Michael Mail; *Nothing I Touch Stands Still* by Jane Spiro; *The Book of Israel* by Jeremy Gavron; *Nine Lives* by Bernice Rubens; *The Song of Names* by Norman Lebrecht; *Impossible Love: Ascher Levy's Longing for Germany* by Roman Frister; *The Autograph Man* by Zadie Smith; *Dorian* by Will Self; *Still Here* by Linda Grant; *Who's Sorry Now* by Howard Jacobson; and *The Strange Case of Dr. Simmonds and Dr. Glas* by Dannie Abse. Collections of short stories were *Cherries in the Icebox: Contemporary Hebrew Short Stories*, edited by Marion

Baraitser and Haya Hoffman; *Meet the Wife* by Clive Sinclair; and *The Complete Short Stories* by Muriel Spark. Poetry published included *Carrying the Elephant,* prose poems by Michael Rosen on the death of his son; *An English Apocalypse* by George Szirtes; *Stranger in the House* by Eric Donner; and *If That Spoon Could Only Speak* by Joan Gordan.

Collections of articles and essays were *Personal Terms* by Frederic Raphael; *Scenes and Personalities in Anglo-Jewry 1800–2000,* the third volume of Israel Finestein's collected essays; *British Romanticism and the Jews,* edited by Sheila A. Spector; and *The Shtetl,* edited by Joachim Neugroschel.

Varied aspects of English life were covered in *Waddesdon Manor: The Heritage of a Rothschild House; East End 1888* by William J. Fishman; *Nightingale: The Story since 1840,* which traces the development of the Nightingale House home for the aged; and *Capturing Memories: The Art of Reminiscing* by Jewish Care volunteers Jeanie Rosefield, Sue Gordon, Pat Stanton, and Vivienne Wolf.

Other notable publications were *Sunlight and Shadow: The Jewish Experience of Islam* by Lucian Gubbay; *Henry Ford and the Jews* by Neil Baldwin; *The Lost Tribes of Israel: The History of a Myth* by Tudor Parfitt; and *From Falashas to Ethiopian Jews* by Daniel P. Summerfield.

Personalia

Honors conferred on British Jews in 2002 included knighthoods to Nicholas Winton for his work rescuing Jewish children in World War II; Howard Bernstein, chief executive of Manchester City Council, for services in the reconstruction of Manchester and for helping secure it the 17th Commonwealth Games; Alan Fersht, the Herchel Smith professor of organic chemistry, Cambridge University, for discoveries in protein science; Lawrence Freedman, professor of war studies, King's College, London; and David Garrard, chairman of Minerva, a commercial property company, for charitable work.

Notable British Jews who died in 2002 included Joseph Finklestone, on the staff of the *Jewish Chronicle* for 40 years and ultimately its assistant editor, in London, in January, aged 77; Harry Rabinowicz, rabbi and expert on Hassidism, in London, in January, aged 82; Barry Weinberg, musician, in London, in January, aged 53; Arthur Shenkin, psychiatrist, poet, and Jewish scholar, in Glasgow, in January, aged 86; Basil Bard, scientist, lawyer, and communal leader, in London, in February, aged 87; Ruth Goldschmidt-Lehmann, for 25 years librarian at Jews' College, the first woman to hold that post, in London, in February, aged 71; Trude Dub, writer and teacher, in Leicester, in February, aged 91; Rita Rosemarine, Manchester communal leader, in Manchester, in March, aged 78; Chaim Lipshitz, youth leader and teacher, in London, in March, aged 96; Israel Kolvin, child psychiatrist, in London, in March, aged 72; Nancy Hurstbourne, communal professional and life-long worker for Jewish Child's Day, in London, in March, aged 88; César Milstein, biochemist and joint Nobel prizewinner, in Cambridge, in March, aged 75; Joseph Witriol, linguist and translator, in London, in March, aged 89; Solomon Evans, minister to congregations in northern and western cities for over 60 years, in Leeds, in April, aged 89; Henry Pack, Association of Jewish Ex-Servicemen and Women (AJEX), welfare expert, in London, in May, aged 82; Sydney Davis, AJEX general secretary for 25 years, in London, in May, aged 80; Eva Mitchell, first woman chair of the council of Reform Synagogues of Great Britain, in London, in June, aged 73; Donald Silk, Zionist and communal activist, in Oxford, in June, aged 73; Lionel "Rusty" Bernstein, antiapartheid fighter, in Kidlington, Oxfordshire, in June, aged 82; Harold Miller, former chair of British Poale Zion and Zionist Federation, in London, in June, aged 90; Martin Savitt, major Jewish communal figure and defense expert, in London, in June, aged 81; Arnold Lord Weinstock, electrical and electronic tycoon, in Bowden, Wiltshire, in July, aged 77; Caesar Aronsfeld, scholar and historian, in London, in July, aged 92; Robert Halle, executive chairman of B'nai B'rith Hillel Foundation, in London, in September, aged 88; Beatrice, Baroness Serota, civil servant and politician, in London, in September, aged 83; Myrella Cohen, eminent judge, in London, in September, aged 74; Michael Cohen, photographer for the antifascist magazine *Searchlight,* in London, in September, aged 67; Zina Cohen, long-time member of the Board of Deputies, in London, in September, aged 86; Frank Allaun, left-wing Labor MP for Salford East for nearly 30 years, in Manchester, in November, aged 89; Saul Amias, founding father of Rosh Pinah Jewish primary school and Edgware (Middlesex) Synagogue, where he was minister for more than 40 years, in London, in December, aged 95; Boris Schapiro, bridge champion, in Long Crendon, Buckinghamshire, in December, aged 93; and David Elias, patron of London's Indian and Far Eastern Jewish communities, in December, in London, aged 86.

MIRIAM & LIONEL KOCHAN

France

National Affairs

T HE CENTRAL POLITICAL EVENT of 2002 in France was the presidential election, which took place in two rounds, on April 21 and May 5. Under the French constitution, the president is elected by all citizens through direct universal suffrage. If no one receives a majority in the initial balloting, the people vote again two weeks later to decide between the two top candidates. Since getting on the ballot was not difficult, the field of candidates could be quite large—in 2002, there were 16—making it very difficult to achieve a majority on the first ballot and almost insuring a run-off.

On April 21, in the first round, conservative incumbent Jacques Chirac received 19.88 percent of the vote. His principal adversary, the Socialist prime minister Lionel Jospin, won 16.18 percent. But another candidate, Jean-Marie Le Pen of the far-right National Front, just managed to beat out Jospin for second place with 16.86 percent. A difference of slightly less than 200,000 votes was enough to eliminate Jospin and get Le Pen into the second round, ensuring a resounding victory for Chirac on May 5.

The vote for Le Pen was no doubt significant: one in six French voters supported a man who had been denounced by his adversaries, starting with Chirac and Jospin, as racist and anti-Semitic. But Le Pen's showing was not an isolated phenomenon. The National Front had played a role in French politics over many years, and Le Pen had received 15 percent of the vote in the previous presidential election, in 1995. It was true that the party has no seats in Parliament, but that was due to the single-member-district system for electing representatives, which put fringe groups at a disadvantage. In fact, the National Front had succeeded in electing representatives whenever the vote was on a proportional basis by party, either within a region or in France as a whole. This was the case for the French representatives in the European Parliament and in the representative assemblies of France's 22 regions.

What was unusual about this election was less Le Pen's strong performance than the poor showing of Jospin, who would have needed only another 0.68 percent to make it to the second ballot. The missing votes were those of many on the left who, confident that Jospin would face Chirac in the second round or unhappy with Jospin's government, chose to stay home or to vote for other left-wing candidates. Thus the little-known Christiane Taubira, candidate of the Left Radical Party (one of the smaller players in Jospin's parliamentary coalition), received 2.32 percent of the vote. Had her party withdrawn her candidacy before the first round, Jospin would certainly have made it to the second.

Taken together, the seven candidates of the left and far left (three Trotskyists, one Communist, one environmentalist, and two from the center-left) other than Jospin who ran in the first round obtained 26.71 percent of the vote. Thus, fewer than four of every ten voters who supported left-wing candidates voted for Jospin. This division on the left, showing up the weakness of the man who sought to be its leader, was politically much more significant than the small vote gain that allowed Le Pen to "steal" Jospin's place in the second round.

First and foremost, the election represented the defeat of Jospin, and he paid the price, announcing that very night that he would leave political life (he was replaced by one of his loyalists, François Hollande). But the election also marked the end of an era of Socialist ascendancy that began when François Mitterrand was elected president in 1981 and continued with the left controlling the National Assembly, the lower house of Parliament, for two decades, except for two interruptions totaling six years. The Socialist record, while certainly respectable, did not excite the voters in 2002. The left's internal divisions, evidenced by the multiplicity of candidates, were symptomatic of its lack of clear direction. Leftist rhetoric still bore the stamp of revolutionary ideology, but the left's behavior in government did not differ from that of center-left parties elsewhere in Europe. This inconsistency — which François Mitterrand, in his time, knew how to play to his advantage — came back to haunt the Socialists, who were not "left" enough to please a good part of their constituency, but too "left" for the majority of voters.

The presence in the second round of Jean-Marie Le Pen, leader of the far-right National Front, came as a shock to most people in France and around the world. Was the country threatened with a turn toward fascism? Had racism and anti-Semitism gained legitimacy in a France that still considered itself the homeland of human rights? In Paris and other large cities, demonstrators turned out by the hundreds of thousands to "defend democracy." Much of the political left called on French voters to "confront the danger posed by the far right" by backing the incumbent president, Jacques Chirac, candidate of the "parliamentary right" —

that is, unlike Le Pen's far right, it was represented in Parliament. In the end, Chirac was reelected with more than 82 percent of the vote.

For people outside France, the (relative) rise in power of the National Front was big news. It seemed for a brief moment that France was divided between the traditional right and the far right. Some thought that the demons of the past, from the Dreyfus Affair to Pétain's Vichy regime during World War II, had returned. In reality, things were more complicated. Viewing the first round as an opinion poll of the entire electorate, the left as a whole was in the minority: all the different leftist tendencies together (including the three Trotskyist streams) received only 43 percent of the vote. In this respect the first round was the continuation of a deeply rooted French political phenomenon in which the left is structurally a minority, whose victories are exceptions that happen when centrist elements lend support.

But even with the left in a minority position, the right too was seriously divided between the 38 percent of French voters who supported one of the "parliamentary right" candidates in the first round, and the 19 percent who voted for a far-right candidate (either Le Pen or his former second-in-command, now a rival, Bruno Mégret). Ironically, the "parliamentary right" was even more a minority than the left because it refused to ally itself with the far right. This situation had been going on for years. It was brought to the light of day only in the spring of 2002 because of the "technical" incident that deprived Lionel Jospin of his chance in the second round, but the problem ran much deeper. The persistent presence of the far right, incapable of attaining power but endowed with a real talent for playing the spoiler, revealed a national malaise. And this malaise directly concerned the Jews—not the Jews alone by any means, but the Jews along with others.

The French were not particularly sympathetic to far-right ideologies, with their antidemocratic, racist, and anti-Semitic elements. The current wisdom, reinforced by all the public-opinion polls, had it that the French were no different in this respect from most other Europeans. Where they seemed to differ, however, was in feeling more insecure. This sentiment had many dimensions—insecurity with regard to France's place in the world, insecurity about the future of French identity, and, increasingly, insecurity in the conduct of everyday life. Le Pen's special talent for capitalizing on these insecurities enabled him to benefit from the weaknesses of politicians from the right and the left.

In the year preceding the presidential election, the public had been affected by the rise of urban violence, a phenomenon hitherto largely unknown in France. While it rarely resulted in deaths, it convinced many in France that the authorities were not doing their jobs. The perpetrators were frequently identified as belonging to the Arab-Muslim community, and the politicians of the left who were in power were suspected of purposely minimizing the magnitude of the problem for fear of subjecting a population already suffering from social disadvantage and racism to further disapproval. One of the most shocking aspects of this new insecurity involved incidents in the public schools—traditionally a bastion of French republican ideology—where, according to numerous reports, students terrorized their fellow classmates and even their teachers.

Anti-Semitism—expressed by a marginal but not negligible element of the Muslim population, and with the Israeli-Palestinian conflict as a backdrop—played a role in all of this. There were attacks against Jewish sites and Jewish people of all ages, and even pressure in classrooms not to talk about the Dreyfus Affair or the Holocaust. But if the way in which Jews were targeted was particularly shocking, the physical and verbal violence of which they were victims arose within a general climate that was increasingly unhealthy. In a country where cities had for several generations been considered quite safe, and where people customarily responded to news of violence in American cities and schools with a mixture of surprise and irony, this sudden eruption of brutality came as a shock.

Faced with an increasing number of press reports of violence, some left-wing politicians, including members of the government, responded with simple denials. "Psychological" interpretations that made insecurity an essentially subjective phenomenon proliferated. These words were meant to calm, but among those most directly touched by the violence they strengthened animosity toward the "caviar left," whose members were assumed to be living in the most comfortable neighborhoods, sending their children to private schools, and ignoring the real problems of ordinary people. Le Pen benefited from the tide of protest this mood engendered—though not very much, since his vote, as noted above, was only marginally higher than in the previous election. The main victim was Jospin, whose failure to address the new urban violence in any serious way led some traditional left-wing voters to stay home in the first round.

The weak government response to incidents that seriously alarmed many French people undoubtedly stemmed from ideology. Immigrants from North Africa and sub-Saharan Africa were perceived as "new proletarians" and as representatives of the "South," the portion of humanity mired in suffering, and leftist politicians found it difficult to distance themselves from this group. Another factor was the guilt the French left felt over the ambiguous positions taken by a large number of its representatives during the colonial period. Finally, electoral considerations clearly played a role. Pascal Boniface, an academic and member of the Socialist Party, had suggested in an internal memo to leaders of his party in 2001 that since Arab-Muslims were much more numerous than Jews, it was important to move closer to them as the election drew near (see AJYB 2002, pp. 331–34).

Public manifestation of bitterness toward the Socialist Party did not end with the presidential contest. A month after Chirac's reelection the French returned to the polls to choose their representatives to the National Assembly. The left, previously in the majority, was crushed as the Union for a Presidential Majority (UMP), a party that was hurriedly constituted to bring together most of the right-wing politicians loyal to Chirac, obtained 64 percent of the seats, 369 out of 577. The National Front, without enough support in any one district to gain a seat, remained shut out. But the new government, led by Prime Minister Jean-Pierre Raffarin, understood that if it wanted to escape the pressure from the far right once and for all it would have to prove to the French people that democratic politicians—of the left or the right—could ensure their security. Nicolas Sarkozy, the new minister of the interior and, in that capacity, overall chief of police services, became personally responsible for carrying out this commitment.

The night the results of the first round were announced and it became clear that Le Pen would face Chirac in the run-off, a minor incident occurred that had long-lasting repercussions. A reporter for the Israeli daily *Ha'aretz* interviewed Roger Cukierman, president of CRIF (Conseil Représentatif des Institutions Juives de France), the Representative Council of Jewish Institutions of France, about the likely effect of Le Pen's presence on the second-round ballot. Cukierman's response, according to the Israeli journalist, was that this development would be "a message to the Muslims to keep quiet." Immediately taken up by the French media, this was interpreted by some as support for Le Pen.

But this was not Cukierman's intent. The CRIF president—a retired banker with little experience in political matters or in dealing with the press—spoke as if he and the reporter were having a private conversation, forgetting for the moment that he was a public figure. Furthermore, he spoke in English with the Israeli journalist, his remarks were translated into Hebrew to appear in *Ha'aretz,* then retranslated from Hebrew to English for the paper's international edition, and then translated again from English to French for the French newspapers. Thus Cukierman's response had no chance of being understood with any degree of subtlety or nuance. While he might indeed have attributed Le Pen's strong showing to resentment against Arabs and Muslims, he strongly asserted that Le Pen was an anti-Semite, and, like virtually all French political figures right and left, urged people to vote for Jacques Chirac.

Adding to the misapprehension, French television broadcast a quote from Jo Goldenberg, owner of a well-known Jewish restaurant in Paris, which was also widely interpreted—inaccurately again—as expressing support for Le Pen. Despite later clarifications, the damage was done, and the allegation that the president of CRIF and large numbers of French Jews supported Le Pen was added to the arsenal of criticisms of the Jewish community. This naturally raised the question of why they would have done so. Those who were relatively well informed said it was a reaction to the attacks on Jews that had proliferated in France during April and had made Jews more receptive to accusations against "the Arabs." Others, less sophisticated or more partisan, accused the Jewish community of turning to the far right in order to support Israeli government policy.

Israel and the Middle East

The two main political streams in France—Chirac's right-of-center neo-Gaullists, and the Socialists, led by Jospin and then François Hollande—had similar policies with regard to Israel. Though the details might vary according to the person and the circumstances, the basics were: friendship toward the Jewish state and affirmation of its right to live in peace and security; support as well for the Palestinians' right to an independent state; and a desire for a peace agreement that would include Arab recognition of Israel and Israeli withdrawal from the Territories.

However, Israel's image in the eyes of the French public was severely damaged in 2002. The change happened in April, when the fighting in Jenin and the occupation of the Church of the Nativity in Bethlehem were presented as expressions of Israeli brutality toward the Palestinians (see above, pp. 201–04). The media, which had given little coverage to the attacks against Israelis in February and March, now devoted considerable attention to stories and images depicting the suffering of the Palestinian population.

At the same time, far-left elements—the Communist Party, some of the Greens, and at least two of the Trotskyist factions—engaged in strong pro-Palestinian, anti-Israel agitation. They were motivated by several related factors. One was an "anti-imperialist" ideology in which Israel, representing the West, stood against the "just cause" of the "oppressed," represented by the Palestinians. Another was principled anti-Zionism, fed by the personal resentment felt by some activists of Jewish origin and the anti-Jewish prejudices of some non-Jews. A third was an open desire to win the favor of young Muslims who, making up some 10 percent of their generation of French people, represented a future electoral force not to be ignored. Two additional elements also came into play: agitation carried out by Palestinian, Arab, and Muslim organizations representing a variety of allegiances, and the activism of human-rights and other general-interest groups whose leaders, for various personal or political reasons, were also drawn to "the Palestinian cause." Often "ad hoc" committees, tied to one or another of the tendencies mentioned above, would be formed to organize a specific action.

The results were not long in coming. Competition between all these streams resulted in a kind of rhetorical bidding war, with propaganda statements reverberating endlessly as if in an echo chamber. A rumor about "Israeli atrocities" put on the Internet by an unknown source would turn up months later in newspapers, on radio and television, in pamphlets, and sometimes even in books. Young journalists working in mainstream media outlets, often knowing nothing of the realities of the Middle East, were influenced by propagandists (who, being of a similar age and education level, shared similar values and assumptions) and recycled these themes for the public at large. The myth of a "Jenin massacre" anchored itself in people's consciousness, in turn justifying more anti-Israel prejudices. That the bearers of such slogans were almost always sincere, convinced that they were acting in the name of peace and harmony between peoples, only increased the effectiveness of the message.

Little by little the center of gravity for public debate moved from the Middle East to the international scene—most notably through denunciation of the "pro-Likud neoconservatives" who allegedly influenced American policies—and to France itself. The hydra of "world Zionism," a term hitherto used only by small far-right groups and in the most unrestrained Arab propaganda, was suddenly a legitimate topic in publications identifying themselves as on the far left. With disarming good faith, people truly believed that secret organizations dictated the laws that governments passed and the words the media published. Even in the minds of the most rational, the threefold figure of Zionist, Jew, and Israeli became the object of very strange reveries.

An excellent illustration of the misunderstandings (and fantasies) surrounding the image of Israel in France occurred early in 2002. Rabbi Michael Melchior, leader of the left-wing religious party Meimad, was at the time a member of the Israeli government with the title of deputy minister of foreign affairs, responsible for relations with the Jewish diaspora. In this capacity, he called a meeting to set up a body to monitor the state of global anti-Semitism. An Agence France Presse report dated January 6, 2002, quoted Melchior as saying, "France has the worst record of all the Western countries in terms of the number of anti-Semitic attacks and incidents." This statement was made in response to a question posed by journalists at a press conference. Factually accurate, it was confirmed a few months later by a spate of anti-Semitic attacks in France.

Rabbi Melchior's remark passed unnoticed in Israel. But in France, it elicited a virtual storm. President Chirac set the tone at an informal meeting with the press to mark the new year. "There is no anti-Semitism in France," he declared to journalists. "Those who say there is have ulterior political motives." People close to Chirac said that he was devoid of any anti-Jewish prejudice and that he took the characterization of his country as anti-Semitic as a personal insult. However, his reference to "ulterior political motives" was an allusion to the Middle Eastern situation, a connection that was immediately taken up by the press.

Rabbi Melchior tried to clarify his words, in response to a journalist from the Jewish newsweekly *Actualité juive* (Jan. 17, 2002): "I do not think that France is an anti-Semitic country. I do not think that French society is anti-Semitic. I did not accuse the French government. But the numbers are indisputable." However, no one wanted to hear this. Just a few months before a presidential election, the reality of the numbers of anti-Jewish attacks was taboo for both the right and the left. Nor were commentators interested in delving into the rabbi's personal motivations (he was an open, moderate politician of the left), preferring not to see beyond his title of deputy minister and his *kippah* and beard.

A paranoid interpretation took hold and spread throughout the French media and political circles, and even into senior levels of the French government, according to which Melchior's remark had three objectives: 1) to smear France's image in Western countries and especially in the U.S., since the real source of anger at France was its refusal to support the policies of the Sharon government toward the Palestinians; 2) to turn public attention away from the allegedly reprehensible actions of the Israeli army in the Territories; and 3) to create a sense of panic among French Jews so that they would move to Israel and become a counterweight to

Palestinian population pressure. At this very time, word came that in Israel, the Jewish Agency had characterized the Jews of France, Argentina, and South Africa as "communities in danger," a designation entitling French Jews immigrating to Israel to special financial support. The French press highlighted this news as additional proof of Rabbi Melchior's mischievous intentions.

Anyone at all familiar with Israeli reality could attest that the image — fed by the title "deputy minister responsible for the diaspora" — of a Jerusalem-based mechanism to activate the Jewish diaspora was pure fantasy. But in the collective French imagination, Rabbi Melchior had become the representative of a grand Israeli scheme to disgrace France. A few months later, Michael Melchior was no longer deputy minister; instead he sat in the Knesset on the opposition benches, along with the MKs from the Labor Party. But for those in France caught up in the story, he continued to symbolize the Israeli far right, religious and nationalist, and his very name was anathema. He was the one who said that anti-Semitism existed in France at a moment when no one wanted to hear this truth.

The idea that anti-Jewish violence could happen on a regular basis in France was odious to many French people not only because of concern for their country's image but also because of a sincere aversion to anti-Semitism. But the people committing these acts were generally Muslim immigrants or their sons, a group that only the far right always felt comfortable criticizing. Resisting anti-immigrant racism was part of French "political correctness," just as resisting anti-Semitism was. How could the two be reconciled? One way was to blame Israel.

And so it was that the antiglobalization leader José Bové, when questioned about anti-Semitic violence in France on his return from a "solidarity visit" with Yasir Arafat, was quoted in the daily newspaper *Libération* (Apr. 3) as saying that one must ask "whom the crime benefits." He explained that "the Israeli government and its agencies have an interest in creating a kind of psychosis, to make people believe that an anti-Semitic climate has taken hold in France, so as to better divert their attention." Strongly criticized for this statement, Bové did not apologize until several months later, and even then without retreating from his anti-Israel activism. Supporters of the Peasant Confederation founded by Bové and of Attac, the antiglobalization organization of which he was a leader, remained absolutely convinced that anti-Semitic violence in France was really the work of the Israeli Mossad.

What worried the Jewish community was that Bové was not an isolated case. People had been associating French Jews with the Israeli-Palestinian problem for a long time, but with the outbreak of the intifada in late 2000 this association had acquired a highly emotional, even frightening dimension. The question, "How can the Jews do to others what was done to them?" had become common, and hardly anyone pointed out that even asking such a question both distorted the current reality and denied the enormity of the Holocaust.

Caught in this sea of rhetoric, most French Jews were stunned. Whether or not they identified with the policies of the Israeli government, they deeply resented the way that Israel was portrayed in their country and, by extension, the way that they themselves had come under attack. (Without much exposure to the foreign press, they generally had no idea that they were not alone. From one European country to the next, the nature of the anti-Zionist obsession varied somewhat; an allegation that was shocking in one place might be commonplace in another. But the intensity of the obsession was more or less constant.)

Simply invoking the name of Ariel Sharon conjured up the specter of evil, and representatives of the Jewish community were suspected of collusion with the government identified by that name before they even opened their mouths to speak. Called on to endorse grossly exaggerated accusations against Israel or to disavow crimes that might well be imaginary, they chose the path of silence. And the experience of the public representatives of the community was increasingly extended to every Jew — even down to schoolchildren who were called on by classmates and sometimes by teachers to account for "the Sharon government's policies."

Put on the defensive in this atmosphere of paranoia, many Jews reacted with a kind of counter-paranoia. It seemed to them that the whole world had become hostile toward Israel, and that this hostility was nothing other than a horrendous resurgence of age-old anti-Semitism. Some people stopped reading newspapers, watching television or listening to the radio. Others, by contrast, started monitoring the media compulsively, searching out the smallest mistakes and then sending belligerent (and not very effective) responses to the editors or producers. Most of these ferocious Jewish wolves had previously been lambs, filled with the milk of human kindness, wishing ardently for a world of peace and harmony. Confronted with patent lies that were repeated as if they were gospel truth, wounded incessantly by malicious remarks that seemed to echo the hostility that had been directed against Jews since time immemorial, they no longer had a reference point for distinguishing between bitter enemies and inept friends. In their ardor to defend Israel and the Jews at any cost, they only intensified the conflict.

To complicate matters even further, there were also Jews who, whether out of conviction, cynicism or ignorance combined with a desire to do good, added fuel to the fire by taking on the role of the "courageous Jew" who was willing to denounce Israel. In doing this, they (consciously or not) tarred all Jews who would not denounce Israel—that is, the over-whelming majority—with the same brush: as running dogs of evil. In short order, citing "courageous Jews" became a necessary complement to any anti-Israel polemic. This ritualized reference made it possible for the speaker to avoid any suspicion of anti-Semitism or even a priori opposi-tion to Israel.

There could be no doubt, however, about how the great majority of French Jews felt. On April 7, a demonstration in Paris organized by CRIF brought out an impressive crowd (53,000 according to the police, 150,000 according to the organizers). Given that some 300,000 Jews lived in and around Paris, a significant proportion of the adult Jewish popu-lation turned out that day. Well-known Jewish writers and actors joined the demonstration, along with some politicians, generally from the right. At the same time, tens of thousands were marching in other cities, in-cluding Strasbourg, Lyon, Toulouse, Montpellier, Nice, Marseille, and Bordeaux.

CRIF chose the slogan "Against Anti-Semitism, For Israel" for the march. At the time, anti-Jewish violence was on the rise throughout France (police recorded 56 "serious" incidents in the first week of April), and Israel was the object of strong public attacks (the battle in Jenin was still going on, and no one knew until later that accusations of an Israeli massacre were unfounded). Some Jews and many non-Jews criticized the juxtaposition of the two themes "Against Anti-Semitism" and "For Is-rael." They would have preferred a demonstration against anti-Semitism that could also draw support from people who were against the govern-ment of Israel. Most Jewish leaders replied that it was more important to support Israel at a time when it was under attack, regardless of per-sonal policy preferences. According to them, it was impossible to march against anti-Semitism while ignoring the threats and attacks against Is-rael (the suicide bombing that killed 29 people at a Passover seder in Ne-tanya on March 27 was still fresh in people's minds).

In truth, most Jews saw the two causes as being inextricably linked. It would have been practically impossible for Jewish leaders to establish a common front against racism with organizations on the far left, several of which were involved in anti-Israel actions that were in turn con-tributing to anti-Jewish violence. Furthermore, had the April 7 march been organized solely as a demonstration against anti-Semitism, it would undoubtedly have been disrupted by people within the march wanting to express their unconditional support for Israel.

Tensions were high during the march. Jewish extremists confronted a group of young North Africans, some with Palestinian flags, who had positioned themselves near the demonstration. Just before and not far away from the CRIF march, several thousand people took part in another demonstration organized by French Friends of Peace Now (complementary to and not in competition with the CRIF march, explained organizers, and timed so that demonstrators could subsequently join the main group). This demonstration also came under attack, and a police officer who intervened was stabbed, no doubt by an unidentified Jewish extremist.

On July 31, 2002, David Gritz, a French student, was killed in a bomb explosion at the Hebrew University in Jerusalem. The only child of a Jewish American father and a Catholic Croatian mother who had settled in Paris, David Gritz was born and had grown up in France. An exceptionally bright student and a talented violinist, he had embarked on a path toward Judaism, as could be seen in his journal, in which an entry dated July 27 and written in Hebrew read, "Little by little, I am going back." With the help of a scholarship from Maskilim, a French organization that supported the study of Jewish thought, the young man had arrived in Jerusalem in mid-July for a one-year program at the Hartman Institute. He had planned to work on his doctoral dissertation in philosophy on "the politics of Creation," taking his inspiration from the Tower of Babel story as the first example of "the political problem of human coexistence within the City." Gritz died two weeks after arriving in Jerusalem, at the age of 24. In an announcement published in the daily newspaper *Le Monde,* his parents wrote, "May the circle of love that surrounded David triumph over the hate of which he was a victim."

La Francophonie, an international organization bringing together France with other countries where French was widely spoken, met in October 2002 in Beirut. (Israel, which had several hundred thousand French-speaking residents, had always been blocked from participating by the Arab countries). Jacques Chirac attended the event, which was in fact more diplomatic than cultural. One of the many journalists accompanying the president was Gideon Kouts, a French reporter representing the Jewish monthly *L'Arche*. Kouts was also the Paris correspondent for an Israeli television station, to which he filed a report on the summit on his portable telephone. The Lebanese daily *As-Safir* printed an indignant article about this on October 18, and Arab journalists harassed Kouts when he arrived at the press center. Kouts was then expelled and escorted by French agents to his hotel, where he remained under a kind of house arrest for more than two days. The Lebanese minister of justice accused Kouts of committing a "crime" by establishing a telephone link with Israel, and for a time there was some doubt regarding his position under Lebanese law. The French press took the side of the Franco-Israeli journalist threatened with being held hostage in Lebanon. Finally, after a tense period — during which the official French delegation, by President Chirac's express order, looked out for his safety — Gideon Kouts was allowed to return to Paris.

Anti-Semitism and Racism

The year 2002 was marked by an unprecedented flare-up of anti-Jewish violence. According to police statistics cited by the Ministry of the Interior in the annual report of the National Consultative Commission of Human Rights (CNCDH) — an agency attached to the prime minister's office — 193 acts of anti-Semitic violence (defined as acts "presenting a certain degree of seriousness") were identified in the course of the year. Three of these were bombings, 57 acts of arson, 75 of vandalism, and 58 of "aggression." In all, 17 people were injured, and no one was killed. The attacks were directed against synagogues, Jewish schools, school buses, and individuals of all ages. In addition, the same police sources identified 731 anti-Semitic "threats" — insults, pamphlets, anonymous letters, etc.

These figures were significant from two perspectives. First, in relation to previous years, they constituted an all-time record. And second, in relation to all acts subsumed under the category of "racist or anti-Semitic" violence, the 193 anti-Semitic acts constituted 62 percent of the 313 acts tabulated by the Ministry of the Interior for the year. This latter figure would be even higher if acts of xenophobic violence in Corsica, arising out of a very specific conflict based on separatist nationalism, were eliminated from the calculation. Using only figures from "continental" France, the total number of incidents dropped to 240, so that the 193 anti-Semitic acts amounted to more than 80 percent. The racist "threats" showed an equally striking predominance of anti-Semitism: the 731 threats directed against Jews represented 74 percent of the total of 992 acts of racist intimidation or threat tabulated in 2002.

Who were the perpetrators? The far right was barely involved at all. Of the 193 acts of violence, only three were attributed to the far right. As the 2002 report of the CNCDH, again citing analyses by the Ministry of the Interior, expressed it, "The perpetrators of the tabulated incidents are adolescents or young adults, who to a large extent come from 'sensitive' neighborhoods where their parents, who are often North African immigrants, live." The report emphasized that these young people were "often delinquents with respect to the law" and that the acts of anti-Jewish aggression "have been vigorously condemned by authorities in France's Muslim communities, except for a minority of Islamist radicals." Although it was impossible to establish any systematic link with political organizations, especially Islamist ones, the official report noted that the aggressors "seek to exploit the Middle East conflict." But ideology appeared to play only a secondary role. The perpetrators were primarily young people, long accustomed to carrying out acts of violence and breaking the law, whose deep-seated hostility to Jews was exacerbated by the manner in which events in the Middle East were reported in the French media and in other sources of information—Arabic radio and television, Web sites, reports, and pamphlets.

The strongest wave of anti-Semitic violence was recorded in April, when, as noted above, both the mass media and activist organizations intensified their anti-Israel messages. Of the 193 acts of violence committed during the year, 118, more than 60 percent of the total, took place in April. However, the special circumstances prevailing in April 2002 did not explain everything. Even during the other 11 months of the year, 75 of the 109 acts of racist violence in continental France recorded by the Interior Ministry—69 percent of the total—were directed against Jews.

That Jews should be singled out as targets of racist violence was even more extraordinary in light of the fact that they represented only a small proportion of potential victims of racism in France. The 500,000–600,000-strong Jewish community was dwarfed by the Muslim community, which had between five and six million members. Adding non-Muslim Africans, Roma, and a few other minority groups yielded a total of almost ten million people in France who ran the risk of being targets of racist acts. That a large majority of such acts were directed against the half-million Jews indicated the peculiar way that the "Jewish question" manifested itself in France in 2002.

While anti-Semitic violence occurred in all regions of France, it was especially concentrated in a limited number of localities and neighborhoods where Jews lived side-by-side with Arabs and Muslims. Many French people living elsewhere, including Jews, became aware of these incidents only indirectly, and this explained—although it did not justify—their relative indifference. Comfortable neighborhoods in large cities were not greatly affected, and Jews who did not wear *kippot* or other noticeable articles of clothing ran few risks. Schools where Jewish students were regularly harassed by classmates (to the point where some had to change schools at the request of principals powerless to ensure their safety) and where history teachers had to stop inviting Jewish Holocaust survivors to give presentations for fear that students would insult them, were also located in areas that most middle-class people rarely saw.

Some characterized the incidents as a "war of communities" on French soil. It was no such thing, if only because the war was in one direction only—according to the Ministry of the Interior's statistics, there were "about ten" Jewish acts of "self-defense or vengeance" in response to 190 acts of anti-Jewish violence carried out by Arabs and Muslims. The need to propose a (spurious) moral equivalence was rooted in guilt over France's colonial history in North Africa and current anti-Arab racism in the country. The fact that violent denunciation of the State of Israel was often the context for verbal or physical aggression against Jews also greatly contributed to the perception of these acts as normal. Cabinet ministers were heard to say that since young Jews stood up for Israel, it was natural that young Arabs should stand up for the Palestinians.

The number of those guilty of anti-Jewish attacks was unknown, but could hardly have been more than a few thousand in an Arab-Muslim community of several million. Any Jew living in France had daily contact with Arab or Muslim fellow citizens who were far from being extremists in any sense, desiring nothing more than to build a better future for themselves and their children and feeling no hostility toward Jews. Yet the extent to which a small minority could wreak havoc was graphically demonstrated in *Les territoires perdus de la République* (The Lost Territories of the Republic), a book published by Fayard/Mille et Une Nuits in September 2002. In it, a group of teachers described how many schools had been ravaged by the behavior of small groups of students who combined anti-Semitism and Holocaust denial with racist and sexist attitudes.

Polls consistently indicated that anti-Semitism was a marginal phenomenon in French society. In a BVA Institute poll, carried out between November 29 and December 6, 2002, 89 percent of a representative sample of the population agreed with the statement that "Jewish French people are French people like anybody else" (63 percent "agreed completely" and 26 percent "agreed somewhat"). Only 9 percent disagreed (6 percent "somewhat" and 3 percent "completely"). By comparison, 74 percent agreed that "Muslim French people are French people like anybody else," while 25 percent disagreed. Commenting on the poll for the CNCDH, political researcher Nonna Mayer noted that when the same question had been asked in 1946, a little more than a third of French people answered that a French person of Jewish origin was "as French as anybody else"; in 2000, a little over two-thirds answered affirmatively; and by 2002, the figure was approaching 90 percent. Acceptance of Jews within French society had made rapid progress.

Though Mayer did not address the issue, there was room to wonder what significance such "acceptance" held at a time when Jews were being singled out through anti-Zionist propaganda and anti-Semitic violence. Thus, when Daniel Vaillant, the Socialist minister of the interior in the Jospin government, received Jewish leaders who complained about the rise of anti-Semitism, he told them that their fears were exaggerated, and it was a long time before he took specific measures to protect Jews. President Chirac, as noted earlier, was also opposed to any acknowledgement of French anti-Semitism. The consensus embodied in the statement that "Jews are French people like anybody else" thus masked a refusal to see expressions of malice indicating that Jews were not precisely like anybody else. Indeed, the hostility of which Jews were targets could even be turned against them, since by their very presence they had the capacity to disturb the serenity of a world in which all citizens were supposed to be "French people like anybody else."

In her commentary published by the CNCDH, Mayer also drew attention to another recent poll, a major survey surrounding the 2002 presidential and legislative elections. One question in it asked people to agree or disagree with the assertion that "Jews have too much power in France." This statement, considered a good indicator of anti-Semitism, was rejected in various polls carried out between 1998 and 2000 by slightly more than 50 percent of French people. During this period there was also a substantial drop in the "no answer" category, along with a rise in the number of affirmative responses from 21 to 34 percent. Analyzing this phenomenon in an earlier article, Mayer had noted a climate favoring "free expression of anti-Semitic views," a phrase that was widely quoted. In 2002, however, Mayer noted that the number of people rejecting this form of anti-Semitic prejudice had increased drastically, from 54 percent in 2000 to 59 percent just before the first round of the 2002 presidential election, and to 66 percent immediately after the second round. And the number of people who agreed that "Jews have too much power in France" dropped from 34 percent in 2000 to 25 percent in 2002. She interpreted these results to mean that the situation was developing "as if repeated acts of violence against the Jewish community, far from inflaming anti-Semitism or making it seem normal, had raised awareness of the danger it represents."

The question on "Jewish power" in the survey tied to the election could be correlated with political preference, and thus be used to gauge the strength of anti-Semitic sentiments on the far left and far right. Ironically, the far right, responsible for almost none of the anti-Jewish violence in the country, was far more susceptible to the anti-Semitic stereotype than the left. Of those supporting Le Pen's National Front, nearly 40 percent clung to the myth of Jewish power, far higher than the 25-percent figure among the French population as a whole. And yet that still left 60 percent of Le Pen's backers who were not, by this criterion, anti-Semites. Supporters of the far-left parties were neither more nor less likely than other French people to subscribe to the notion that Jews were especially powerful.

For voters on both of the political extremes, of course, the presence or absence of a belief in "Jewish power" did not rule out their leaders' recourse to racist or anti-Israel rhetoric that could have negative practical consequences for Jews. In psychoanalytic terms, acts of anti-Semitic violence, carried out by marginal elements that are often attracted to all forms of violence, could be *passages à l'acte,* an acting out of more broadly held ideas, and hence tolerated and even authorized, if not actually desired by society as a whole. According to various accounts, some of the perpetrators experienced their acts of violence in precisely this way.

In November, a novel entitled *Rêver la Palestine* (Dreaming Palestine) was published in Paris by Flammarion. It was a French translation of a novel for young readers originally published in March in Italy under the title *Sognando Palestina* (see below, p. 442). The author, Randa Ghazy, was an Italian of Egyptian origin who was 15 years old when she wrote the book, which told the story of a band of young Palestinians who fall into violence. *Rêver la Palestine* portrayed Israeli soldiers as violent, bloody, and immoral, and justified the Palestinians' recourse to violence, including suicide bombings. Given what was happening in France—indeed, in Europe generally—such a book could be expected to incite young people of Arab origin to acts of violence against Jews. However, the publisher rejected all protests against the book, and the press, on the whole, remained indifferent to its message of hate.

Holocaust-Related Matters

The annual memorial day for victims of anti-Semitic persecution, mandated by law, took place on July 21, 2002. On this occasion, Prime Minister Jean-Pierre Raffarin reiterated President Chirac's 1995 acknowledgement of the French state's responsibility for the arrest of Jews and their transfer to German hands. "Yes," the prime minister said, "the Vel d'Hiv, Drancy, Compiègne [places where Jews were interned in France], and all the transit camps, those antechambers of death, were organized, managed, and guarded by French people. Yes, the first act of the Holocaust was played here, with the complicity of the French state." Referring directly to anti-Jewish violence in France in 2002, Raffarin said, "To attack the Jewish community is to attack France, and to attack the values of our Republic, which can allow no place for anti-Semitism, racism, and xenophobia."

On September 18, 2002, Maurice Papon left the prison where he had been held for just under three years. A civil servant in the Vichy government under the German occupation and later a cabinet minister, Papon had been sentenced to ten years in prison for "complicity in crimes against humanity"—helping the Germans arrest Jews in the Bordeaux region. His lawyers had tried various strategies to get him out of prison, including a request for a presidential pardon, but in vain. He finally obtained his freedom through a law passed on March 4, 2002, allowing for the early release of prisoners for health reasons. While the law was not passed with his case in mind, Papon, 92 years old and suffering from heart trouble, was the first to benefit from it. The Court of Appeal granted Papon's early release on the basis of medical reports and against the advice of the government's representative. Strong feelings surrounded the decision, with the seriousness of Papon's crimes weighing on one side, and the application of a humanitarian law on the other. Even the lawyers for Papon's victims were divided.

An international conference was held in Strasbourg, October 17–18, on the representation of the Holocaust in the plastic arts, film, television, theater, literature, and museums. When it was over, education ministers of the Council of Europe met and ratified a decision to establish an official day devoted to Holocaust remembrance and the prevention of crimes against humanity. In France, the date chosen was January 27, the anniversary of the liberation of Auschwitz.

On October 24, the public television network France 2 broadcast Thomas Gilou's *Paroles d'étoiles* (Words of Stars), a film devoted to testimony by Jews who, as children during the World War II, had been hidden by French families. The same stories were also told in two books with the same title released at the same time, one in illustrated format and the other in paperback.

Four important French films on the Holocaust were released during 2002. Early in the year, *Amen,* by the Greek-born French director Constantin Costa-Gavras, came to the theaters. Inspired by Rolf Hochhuth's play *The Deputy,* which condemned Pope Pius XII's silence during the Holocaust, and with a screenplay by Costa-Gavras and the writer Jean-Claude Grumberg, the film gave a balanced presentation of the reasons why the pope chose not to speak publicly against Nazi Germany's treatment of Jews. It was generally well received, both for its cinematographic qualities and for the way it dealt with a historical debate that had aroused strong feelings. The only controversial element was the poster for the film, designed by a leading Italian graphic artist, which showed a swastika turning into a Christian cross (or vice versa). The poster's presence all over the walls of France's large cities elicited protests, including one from 22 leading Jewish figures who issued a joint statement terming the mixture of the two symbols "unhealthy." But only a far-right Catholic organization urged that the poster be banned, a request rejected by a Paris court on February 21.

Gérard Jugnot's *Monsieur Batignole* was released in March. It recounted the adventure of an ordinary Frenchman who, Jugnot said, could have been himself two generations earlier. Knowing nothing about Jews and not particularly well disposed toward them, through a combination of circumstances this character finds himself saving a Jewish child under the Nazi occupation.

The Pianist was screened at the Cannes Film Festival in June. Directed by Roman Polanski, who had been born in Poland, lived in the United States, and fled to France to avoid a rape charge, the film told the story of a Jew who survived the Warsaw Ghetto partly due to his musical ability. It was awarded the Palme d'Or at Cannes and went on to win Oscars for best director and best actor. In addition to its outstanding formal qualities, *The Pianist* expressed a feeling of humanity that deeply affected the French public.

Late in the year Michel Deville's *Un monde presque paisible* (An Almost Peaceful World) was released. Adapted from Robert Bober's 1993 novel *Quoi de neuf sur la guerre?* (What's New on the War?), the film portrayed a women's fashion workshop in Paris just after the war. The characters, almost all of them Jewish (and almost all played by non-Jews), learn to live again after the Holocaust, remembering the dead and hoping for a different world.

JEWISH COMMUNITY

Demography

In December 2002, the results of a study of the Jews of France carried out under the leadership of the French-Israeli sociologist Erik Cohen were published in *L'Arche*. Commissioned by the FSJU (Fonds Social Juif Unifié, the United Jewish Philanthropic Fund), it was the first of its kind since 1988. Surnames were used to construct a sample of France's Jewish population, addresses were chosen at random on the basis of that list, and only the names of 1,132 heads of families who reported that they were Jewish were retained for the rest of the survey. In addition, 842 individuals whose names were on the list of Jewish surnames reported that they were not Jewish, and 1,130 refused to participate before answering the initial question about their self-definition as Jews. This rate of non-participation was substantially higher than in the previous survey conducted according to the same method, probably reflecting a rising feeling of discomfort about Jewish identity in France, the present condition of French Jews, or both.

The study found some 500,000 Jews currently living in France, or 575,000 counting the non-Jewish spouses of people identifying as Jews. Since people with at least one Jewish parent who refused to self-identify as Jews were not included in the survey, it was plausible to assume the existence of a broader "Jewish galaxy" whose boundaries reached beyond the core Jewish population, as was the case in all diaspora countries. The new study, then, dealt with the "recognizable" Jews in France.

The majority of these French Jews were born in France. This was a new phenomenon, since many of the older generation of Jews in France tended to be immigrants from Eastern Europe and, later, from North Africa. While about 50 percent of French Jews had identified as Sephardim in 1988, the figure was now 70 percent. Neither immigration nor natural increase explained this phenomenon. Rather, it reflected the loss of Jewish identity by a portion of the "old" Ashkenazi Jewish population, which was therefore less heavily represented in the new survey. Not only were an overwhelming majority of the Jews (96 percent) French nationals, but few of the generation now reaching adulthood had ever lived in another country. Asked which Jewish identity they would choose if they could be born again, 42 percent chose to be diaspora Jews and 38 percent Israeli Jews. More than half of French Jews lived in and around Paris. Their demographic indicators (age, number of children) were similar to those of the French population as a whole. Almost 48 percent of the Jews surveyed reported having attended university, and this figure rose to more than 60 percent in the Paris region. Politically, Jews were more likely to be on the left (59 percent) than on the right (41 percent).

On the key question of choice of spouse, the evolution of attitudes in France was similar to that in other countries, although with a time lag: 70 percent of French Jews in permanent relationships had partners who were Jewish either by birth or conversion, while 30 percent were married or living with non-Jews. Among Jews under 30, however, the proportions were 60 and 40 percent respectively, the same as for those who had completed at least four years of university education. Only 36 percent of those interviewed said they would try to prevent their children from marrying non-Jews, another 21 percent said they would not resist this eventuality but would be "troubled" by it, and 42 percent saw no problem.

A little over a quarter of all Jews reported having registered their children in Jewish day schools. (The close correspondence between this figure and available data on enrollment in Jewish schools strengthened the credibility of the survey.) There was a broader consensus on the importance of Jewish education — 56 percent considered it "very important" and another 30 percent considered it "somewhat important." Moreover, if conditions were favorable, 70 percent said they would enroll their children in Jewish schools.

A degree of religious practice still appeared to be the norm. Shabbat candles were lit and kiddush said on a regular basis in 50 percent of Jewish homes in France. Only 29 percent of the sample identified themselves as "non-practicing," 51 percent identified as "traditionalist," 15 percent as "liberal" (not necessarily indicating affiliation with the Reform movement, which referred to itself as "Liberal" in France), and 5 percent as "orthodox."

Attachment to Israel was an important element in the identity of French Jews, 48 percent saying they felt "very close" and 38 percent "rather close" to Israel. A factor contributing to this attachment was that more than half of French Jews had close relatives, including children, in Israel, while only 16 percent had neither relatives nor friends there. Among those surveyed, 18 percent were considering making their homes in Israel, while 81 percent said they would be happy if their children did so. One of the survey questions dealt with Israeli policy: "Should Israel trade land for peace?" A significant plurality (48 percent) answered "yes" to this question, 39 percent answered "no," and 13 percent felt that "it's not up to a Jew living in France to say."

Religion

The AJCF (l'Amitié Judéo-Chrétienne de France), France's Jewish-Christian friendship organization, gave its 2002 award to Father Jean-Baptiste Gourion, abbot of the monastery in Abu Ghosh near Jerusalem. The presentation took place in late October when a delegation of some 30 people went to Israel where the speaker of the Knesset and France's ambassador to Israel received them. The honor given to Father Gourion, a Jewish-born Catholic priest, was all the more remarkable in that it came only a short time after the Jewish origins of another priest, Jean-Marie Lustiger, had been a source of unease in the Jewish community (see below). In fact, the only discordant voices this time came from another direction—pro-Palestinian Catholics who suspected the award's initiators of trying to make a political point by suggesting Christian support for Israeli policies.

This accusation appeared to be part of a wider debate within the Catholic Church about the legitimacy of the Jewish people's relationship with its historic homeland. Another manifestation of the same controversy was the appearance of *Paix sur Jérusalem* (Peace over Jerusalem), a book consisting of speeches and writings by Michel Sabbah, Latin patriarch of Jerusalem—the Vatican's representative to the Christians in the Holy Land—edited by Yves Teyssier d'Orfeuil. The book contained vigorous criticism of "the theology of the mystery of Israel," which, in the patriarch's view, led to justification of the actions of the State of Israel. The volume also included a bizarre appeal to Christians to take into account "the theology of the mystery of Palestine." Sabbah, a Palestinian, seemed to speak less as a church leader than as a spokesperson for Palestinian nationalism, especially when he justified "resistance" to the Israeli occupation.

But his words came as a shock for Catholics who remembered that, since the Second Vatican Council, deepening the significance of the "mystery of Israel" had been a central element in the church's *aggiornamento* with the Jews. While the resulting controversy had little impact among the general public, it made its mark in the French Catholic world and among Jews active in promoting Jewish-Christian ties. Some observers pointed to the paradox that while support for the Palestinians was generally linked with a "progressive" political position, Sabbah had now tied it to a questioning of the church's new attitude toward the people of Israel, and therefore with highly retrograde theological conceptions.

Related issues were raised by the publication of Jean-Marie Lustiger's book *La Promesse* (The Promise), which created uneasiness in both Christian and Jewish circles. Significantly, the cover illustration was a photograph of Pope John Paul II in front of the Western Wall, and the subject of the book was the place of the Jewish people in the divine plan. The author was cardinal archbishop of Paris and one of the central figures in the Catholic Church in France, but no one forgot—least of all Cardinal Lustiger himself—that he had been born Aron Lustiger, that both his parents were Jewish, and that his mother died in an Auschwitz gas chamber. In the book, consisting partly of "spiritual interviews" intended for French nuns a quarter-century earlier and partly of more recent speeches before Jewish and Israeli audiences, the cardinal presented a Christian vision of Judaism that some Jews regarded as too Christian and some Christians saw as too respectful of Judaism. Cardinal Lustiger, unlike Patriarch Sabbah, did not discuss the political situation in the Middle East, but he left no doubt that the "mystery of Israel" remained alive in his interpretation of Catholic doctrine.

Publications

Many books of Jewish interest were published in France during 2002. In the realm of ideas: Alain Finkielkraut's *L'imparfait du présent* (The Imperfect Present); Betty Rojtman's *Une rencontre improbable* (An Improbable Meeting); Pierre Birnbaum's *Sur la corde raide* (On the Tightrope); and Shmuel Trigano's *L'ébranlement d'Israël: philosophie de l'histoire juive* (The Trembling of Israel: Philosophy of Jewish History). Historical works: *Regards sur la culture judéo-alsacienne* (Perspectives on Jewish-Alsatian Culture), edited by Freddy Raphaël; Laurent Joly's *Darquier de Pellepoix et l'antisémitisme français* (Darquier de Pellepoix and French anti-Semitism); Marian Apfelbaum's *Retour sur le ghetto de Varsovie* (Reflection on the Warsaw Ghetto); and Serge Klarsfeld's *La Shoah en France* (The Holocaust in France). Current affairs: Benoît M. Billot, Zuhair Mahmood, and Michel Serfaty's *Le moine, l'imam et le rabbin* (The Monk, the Imam and the Rabbi); Elie Barnavi and Luc Rosenzweig's *La France et Israël: une affaire passionnelle* (France and Israel: A Passionate Affair); Ghaleb Bencheikh and Philippe Haddad's *L'islam et le judaïsme en dialogue* (Islam and Judaism in Dialogue); Marianne Rubinstein's *Tout le monde n'a pas la chance d'être orphelin* (Not Everyone is Lucky Enough to be an Orphan); and Salomon Malka's *Emmanuel Lévinas, la vie et la trace* (Emmanuel Lévinas: His Life and Legacy). Novels: Elie Wiesel's *Le temps des déracinés* (The Time of the Uprooted); Henri Raczymow's *Le plus tard possible* (As Late as Possible); and Jacquot Grunewald's *L'homme à la bauta* (The Man in the Bauta). Translations: Henri Meschonnic's *Au commencement* (a translation of the Book of Genesis) and *Gloires* (a translation of Psalms). Art books: Esaias Baitel's *Jérusalem* and Sonia Fellous's *Histoire de la Bible de Moïse Arragel* (The Story of Moses Arragel's Bible). Cartoon: Joann Sfar's *Le Chat du Rabbin* (The Rabbi's Cat).

Personalia

Marcel Greilsammer, one of the leading figures in the Liberal (Reform) Jewish movement in France, celebrated his 100th birthday on November 26. Greilsammer had been born in Paris to a family of Alsatian origin, and graduated from one of France's most prestigious engineering schools. He played an important role in France's Jewish community both as president of the Rue Copernic Liberal congregation and as vice president of the FSJU. When he was 88 years old, he and his wife left France to settle in Israel, where their four children were already living.

Among the notable French Jews who passed away in 2002:

Louis Mitelberg, born in 1919 in Kaluszyn, Poland, died on January 7. Under the pseudonym "Tim," he became one of the leading cartoonists in the French press. His most famous cartoon appeared in *Le Monde* in response to President Charles de Gaulle's statement after the 1967 Six-Day War that the Jews were "an elite people, sure of themselves and dominating." It showed a Jew in inmate's clothing, proudly striking a Napoleonic pose on the barbed-wire fence of a concentration camp.

Francis Lemarque, whose real name was Nathan Korb, was a composer, lyricist, and singer, born in Paris in 1917. Paris was the subject of many of his songs, which remained a central part of the French popular repertoire. He died on April 20.

Devi Tuszynski, born in 1915 in Brzeziny, near Plock, Poland, was a talented miniaturist. Much of his work was devoted to the Jewish heritage and the memory of Eastern European Judaism. He died on December 16.

MEIR WAINTRATER

Belgium

National Affairs

BELGIUM HAD A POPULATION of almost 10.3 million in 2002. Its population density of 336 inhabitants per square kilometer made it one of the most densely populated countries in Europe. The fertility index was low, only 1.62 children per woman of childbearing age. The long life expectancy (75 years for men and almost 82 for women) and the consequent aging of the population were characteristic of an industrialized country with extensive modern hospital facilities and health care.

The two major groups in Belgium were the Flemings, who spoke Dutch and various Dutch dialects and tended to live in the northern part of the country, and the Walloons, who spoke French, Picard, and Walloon dialects and lived primarily in southern Belgium. The inhabitants of the eastern cantons of Eupen and Malmedy, near the German border, were largely German-speaking.

Since its origins in 1830, Belgium has been a constitutional monarchy. The titular head of state in 2002, whose powers were ceremonial and symbolic, was King Albert II. Beginning in the 1970s Belgium had moved toward the adoption of a federal structure of government. Article 1 of the Belgian constitution now stated, "Belgium is a Federal State composed of communities and regions." Policy decisions were no longer made entirely by the central government but rather by a variety of bodies that wielded independent powers in the specific areas assigned to them.

The distribution of powers followed two major axes, the first connected to language and culture, and the second to geography and economic aspirations. "Communities" denoted groups united by language and cultural ties: the Dutch Community, the French-speaking Community (which was renamed the "Wallonia-Brussels Community"), and the German-speaking Community. Dutch, French, and German were all official languages. The three "Regions" of the country were roughly comparable to the states in the U.S., though they enjoyed a greater degree of autonomy. They were the Flemish Region, Brussels-Capital Region, and Walloon Region. The country was also subdivided into ten provinces and 589 municipalities.

The federal government retained powers in many areas, such as foreign

403

affairs (including relations with NATO and the European Union), national defense, justice, finance, social security, and large parts of public health and domestic affairs (through the Department of the Interior). The Communities and Regions were nevertheless empowered to establish relations with foreign states in matters over which they had jurisdiction.

Federal legislative power was in the hands of a Parliament composed of two chambers, the House of Representatives and the Senate. Proposed legislation had to be approved by both chambers and signed by the king's ministers (the cabinet had to contain an equal number of French- and Dutch-speaking ministers). While the House of Representatives was elected by universal suffrage, virtually the entire Senate was chosen by a complicated system of proportional representation for the different Communities.

Since 1999 Belgium had been governed by a so-called "rainbow majority" composed of the two traditional big secular parties, Socialists (PS) and Liberals (VLD), and the recently founded Ecolo, a "green" party made up of defectors from the Communist Party (itself now practically nonexistent) and left-wing Christians. The prime minister was Guy Verhofstadt of the VLD. National elections were scheduled for 2003.

On the regional and local levels in Flanders, Wallonia, and Brussels power was in the hands of similar alliances of "greens" (Ecolo), "reds" (Socialists), and "blues" (Liberals). In Flanders the government also included a party created on a Flemish-language platform, the Volksunie, which splintered early in 2002 into two parties. As was the case on the national level, the two Christian parties—the CVP in Flanders and the PSC in Wallonia and Brussels—were in the opposition. What is more, the PSC underwent a partial split with the birth of the MCC (Mouvement du Changement Citoyen, or Civic Change Movement), which joined forces with the FDF (Front des Francophones) and Liberal Party to form a united political front in some local election districts.

The far-right National Front, which had practically disappeared in Wallonia and Brussels, enjoyed a new lease on life in Flanders, especially Antwerp Province, under the banner of the Vlaamse Blok, a Flemish nationalist party. This party, itself a radical offshoot of the Volksunie that was in the Flemish government, made spectacular gains, winning 10 percent of the vote in 1999, and 15 seats in the House of Representatives. Indeed, in towns such as Antwerp and Mechelen, up to 20 percent of the voters supported the Flemish far right. While this trend certainly reflected a xenophobic reaction to rising immigration, it also indicated heightened concern about personal safety, especially a rise in the number of attacks on elderly people.

The Belgian government strongly supported the concept of a united Europe, seeing it as a potential global power that projected "European values" and served to counterbalance American power. Belgium's capital, Brussels, was the headquarters of the European Commission, the administrative heart of the European Union, and on January 1, 2002, Belgium, along with 11 other EU members, adopted the euro as its currency.

Domestically, Belgians debated further steps on the road toward a decentralized federalism. The downturn in the global economy, which affected Belgium as well, exacerbated the grievances of those living in the Flemish area, since there was a large net flow of money from it to the less productive French-speaking part of the country, largely to pay for social welfare programs (the unemployment rate in Wallonia was 15 percent, far higher than the 4.9 percent in Flanders). A number of leading mainstream Flemish politicians called for a separate Flemish constitution that would provide, among other things, an autonomous welfare system for Flanders. Leaders of French-speaking Belgium reacted with dismay and warned that such a move was a recipe for splitting Belgium into two separate states. Journalists began referring to the ethnically divided country as "Belgoslavia."

The long-drawn-out Dutroux affair came to public attention again in January when a Flemish-language television station broadcast an interview with Marc Dutroux that had been taped by a reporter smuggled into Dutroux's prison cell. In 1996, Dutroux had been arrested for abducting, raping, and killing four young girls, and the bodies of two of them were found under his house. At the time, it became clear that the police had been negligent in their investigation, and hundreds of thousands of Belgians demonstrated in the streets to call for reform of the law-enforcement system. Rumors that political influence was being applied on Dutroux's behalf gained credibility when his trial was delayed several times; it was now scheduled for 2003. In his television interview, Dutroux admitted the kidnapping charge but denied the murders. He acknowledged belonging to a pedophile ring, "however," he added, "the law does not want to investigate this lead." Dutroux's comments added to speculation that prominent members of the Belgian establishment were part of the ring, and were doing what they could to cover up their involvement.

Belgium held the EU presidency during the second half of 2001, and on February 18, 2002, Prime Minister Verhofstadt delivered an address to the Transatlantic Journalists Forum on his nation's role in the war on terrorism in the wake of the events of September 11. He expressed some skepticism about the American administration's "unilateralism and even simplicity" in addressing the issue, and doubted whether it was possible to root out international terrorism entirely. While backing American military efforts in Afghanistan and ensuring Belgium's full cooperation in hunting down Al Qaeda operatives, the prime minister also advocated dealing with what he considered a root cause of the problem, "to make failed states work again." Thus he advocated "dialogue with the so-called antiglobalists, who have a point in stressing that globalization does not always work."

Belgium took the lead in seeking the arrest of Victor Bout, a well-known but elusive international arms trafficker of Russian nationality suspected of supplying weapons to Al Qaeda and the Taliban. In February, Belgium issued an arrest warrant for Bout on the charge of money laundering, the first formal move by any country to go after him. It was the climax of a four-year probe into allegations that he had moved millions of dollars of profits from illicit arms sales into Belgium. But Bout could not be found, and remained at large as the year ended.

Nizar Trabelsi, a native of Tunisia who had been arrested in Belgium on September 13, 2001, confessed in November 2002 that Osama bin Laden had taught him how to build bombs in Afghanistan, and that he had been planning an attack for spring 2002 on the Kleine-Brogel air base in Belgium, where about 100 U.S. Air Force personnel were stationed. That base, rumored to hold U.S. nuclear warheads, was a popular site for protests by Belgian antinuclear activists.

Belgium took a major step toward addressing the dark side of its colonialist past on February 6, when it released the results of a two-year investigation into its role in the assassination of Patrice Lumumba, prime minister of the Republic of the Congo—formerly the Belgian Congo—in 1961. When the Congo achieved independence in 1960, it became Belgian policy to ensure that the resource-rich Katanga province secede and become a Belgian puppet state. The investigators found that after Lumumba was captured by Belgian-led rebel forces, his execution was supervised by a Belgian captain. Foreign Minister Louis Michel said: "some members of the government and some Belgian actors at the time bear an irrefutable part of the responsibility for the events that led to Patrice Lumumba's death." Michel issued a formal apology and announced the creation of a fund in Lumumba's memory to promote democracy in the Congo.

Reaching even further back into Belgium's history as an imperial power, the Royal Museum for Central Africa, located near Brussels, announced that it was sponsoring the first full-scale historical study of the colonial period, in preparation for a major exhibition on the subject that was to open in 2004. Guido Gryseels, director of the government-owned museum, explained the need for the study: "My generation was brought up with the view that Belgium brought civilization to the Congo, that we did nothing but good out there. I don't think that during my entire education I ever heard a critical word about our colonial past."

Israel and the Middle East

Israel's image in Europe, Belgium in particular, began to deteriorate in the 1980s, and the downturn accelerated after the outbreak of the second intifada in September 2000. This often spilled over into antagonism toward Jews, and the word "Judeophobia" was sometimes used to describe the atmosphere.

Over the course of 2002 the overwhelming majority of the media continued to hound Israel, sometimes in vulgar fashion. Both the press—especially *Le Soir,* the French-language newspaper with the largest circulation—and the electronic media tended to ignore the broader context of events in the Middle East, displaying scenes of violence and Palestinian suffering that could readily lead to one-sided and partial judgments. For many Belgians, there was a sense of schadenfreude, the enjoyment of others' moral distress: Jews, the constant victims throughout history, had now allegedly turned into their erstwhile bloodthirsty oppressors, the Nazis.

An additional factor was the presence of some 450,000 practicing Muslims in the country, making Islam Belgium's second most popular religion, next to Catholicism. Anti-Israel feeling was encouraged in Belgium by the Arabic press and virulent sermons in mosques and Muslim schools, as well as at pro-Palestinian demonstrations.

The Belgian government officially supported a two-state solution to the Israeli-Palestinian conflict, but, in the UN and other international forums, Belgium consistently supported resolutions critical of Israeli policies. In fact, many politicians on both the left and the right—and not just the extremists—voiced anti-Israel sentiments. In April, hostility to the Jewish state reached a new level after Israeli troops moved into Palestinian towns to hunt down terrorists and destroy their infrastructure. Foreign Minister Michel announced a suspension of Belgian military sales to Israel. As noted above, the three regions of Belgium had the power to conduct certain aspects of foreign policy for themselves, and the council of the Brussels Region voted to suspend the cooperation agreement it had signed with Israel in 2000. The proposal received widespread backing across the political spectrum. In December 2001, the Flemish Region had approved a similar resolution. Throughout the country, ordinary Belgian Jews reported feeling pressured to distance themselves from the policies of the Israeli government in order to maintain their acceptance in Belgian society.

The Belgian Jewish community took steps to counteract hostility toward Israel and convince the public that the Jewish state sought peace. The Coordinating Committee of Belgian Jewish Organizations (CCOJB) placed pro-Israel op-eds in newspapers and argued Israel's case on radio and television. The CCOJB also organized pro-Israel rallies on April 2, May 29, June 19, and November 27. The May 29 demonstration was the largest, sponsored by all the major Jewish umbrella organizations and including Jews from several other European countries. Toward the end of the year the CCOJB met several times with government officials to advocate steps to ensure that Palestinian textbooks published with Belgian financial support include maps of Israel and acknowledge the Jewish state's existence and legitimacy.

THE SHARON PROSECUTION

In 1993, Belgium had adopted legislation incorporating the principle of "universal jurisdiction" for war crimes and crimes against humanity into Belgian law. This meant that anyone of any nationality suspected of carrying out such crimes anywhere in the world could be tried in Belgium. Only once, however, had anyone been successfully prosecuted under the law: in 2001, four Rwandans were convicted of involvement in crimes of genocide against the Tutsi minority during the 1994 civil war in that country.

In June 2001, survivors of the September 1982 massacres in the Sabra and Shatilla refugee camps for Palestinians near Beirut filed suit in Belgium against Israeli prime minister Ariel Sharon and a number of others. The charges were war crimes, crimes against humanity, and genocide. (The Kahan Commission, which Israel set up at the time to investigate the massacres, had ruled that as defense minister, Sharon bore indirect responsibility, and he had to resign his post.) But even though Lebanese

Christian militiamen carried out the killings, the Belgian and Lebanese lawyers for the plaintiffs argued that Sharon, as the government minister in charge of Israeli forces at the time, was in control of the area where the massacres occurred and therefore bore criminal responsibility.

Sharon's lawyers countered that the case was politically motivated. They pointed out that war-crimes charges had been brought in Belgium against 30 other world leaders, including Yasir Arafat, Saddam Hussein, and Fidel Castro, but only Sharon's case had been expedited for prosecution. They also noted that none of the Lebanese militia leaders who had actually perpetrated the massacres had been charged, and that the plaintiffs had waited until Sharon became prime minister to launch their complaint. The Belgian government, for its part, was unhappy with the prosecution, a spokesman for the Ministry of Foreign Affairs commenting that it caused "diplomatic embarrassment" for Belgium and made it more difficult for the country to play an evenhanded role in the Middle East.

Several pretrial hearings were held during 2001 to determine the admissibility of the case. On January 23, 2002, came the announcement that an appeals court would rule on the complaint on March 6. In defiance of the separation between judicial and legislative branches mandated by Belgian law, two members of the country's Senate, Vincent van Quickenborne and Josy Dubie, were especially eager to help the prosecution (the former, a lawyer and the youngest person ever elected to the Senate, originally expressed eagerness to argue the case against Sharon in court himself). The two men traveled to Lebanon in January to persuade witnesses to come to Belgium and testify.

One of the people they met with, Elie Hobeika, reputedly the militia leader who actually ordered the massacres but who was not named in the suit, told them that he would like to testify and present "irrefutable proof" of his own innocence and Sharon's guilt, but that he felt "threatened." Two days later, on January 24, Hobeika was killed by a car bomb planted by unknown parties. Sharon's detractors immediately suggested an Israeli hand in the car bombing, but Hobeika had many enemies who might have wanted him dead.

The appeals court decision was postponed until June 26. On that day—after a delay of nearly two hours—the court issued a 22-page ruling voiding the complaint against Sharon. It was based on a provision of Belgian law dating back to 1878 stating that proceedings could be initiated only if the crime took place on Belgian soil or if the suspect was himself located in Belgian territory at the time of prosecution. Israel and its supporters applauded the decision as a triumph of justice over anti-Israel prejudice, while Palestinians and their sympathizers complained that American Jewish and U.S. government pressure on the judges had thwarted the demands of justice. The decision in fact followed the precedent set by the recent case of Ndombasi Yerodia, a former foreign minister of the Republic of the Congo, whose prosecution for inciting racial hatred in his home country had been thrown out in April because he was not then on Belgian soil.

The plaintiffs immediately launched an appeal to the Court of Cassation in Brussels, Belgium's supreme court for criminal cases—with backing from Amnesty International and other nongovernmental human-rights agencies—maintaining that the principle of universal jurisdiction was at stake. Meanwhile, legislators sympathetic to the Palestinians announced that they would propose repeal of the 1878 law barring criminal prosecutions for actions outside the country if the suspect was not situated in Belgium.

Those pressing the case against Sharon were heartened in November, when the Court of Cassation overturned the appeals court ruling in the Yerodia case and reinstituted criminal proceedings against the former Congolese minister. Also, the high court postponed ruling on the appeal of the Sharon case, a move widely interpreted as providing time for the Belgian Parliament to pass legislation canceling the 1878 provision and explicitly introducing universal jurisdiction into the country's law code.

Anti-Semitism

Unlike several other European countries, Belgium had no bureau or organization that monitored incidents of anti-Semitism. Nevertheless, no one could doubt the fact of an upsurge in violence against Jews during 2002 that created an exceedingly hostile climate for them. To a great extent this was linked to the Israeli-Palestinian conflict, and perhaps triggered particularly by the Sharon prosecution. There were some in the Jewish community who refused to call what was happening anti-Semitism, preferring to ascribe the incidents solely to Middle Eastern tensions. Already in December 2001, Belgian Jews were shocked to learn that Rabbi Albert Guigi of Brussels had been roughed up by young men of Moroccan descent. The following catalog of incidents for 2002, far from complete, provides a representative sample:

January 25 — Swastikas and anti-Semitic slogans were found plastered over the baggage of El Al passengers at Brussels National Airport. According to authorities, the deed was committed in the off-limits, "secure" area of the airport.

March 4 — Local youths threw stones at the synagogue in Rue de la Clinique, in the Brussels borough of Anderlecht, shattering several windows.

April 1 — Five firebombs were launched on that same synagogue around midnight. No witnesses were found. Luckily, the fire brigade doused the fire quickly and the damage was contained.

April 3 — Molotov cocktails were hurled at the back of the Bouwmeesterstraat Synagogue in Antwerp, which belonged to the strictly Orthodox Shomre Hadass community and was the city's oldest synagogue.

April 22 — Charleroi's synagogue was hit by shots from an automatic rifle, apparently fired from a car. Eighteen holes made by 9-mm bullets were found on the building.

May 3 — Several Molotov cocktails were thrown at the Sephardi Synagogue (Rue du Pavillon) in Brussels during the night. The bottles hit the synagogue wall but failed to explode or do any damage.

May 5 — As the European Rabbinical Conference was meeting in Brussels, a group of rabbis who had gotten off a train at the Central Station was insulted and called "dirty Jews." A youth of North African descent spit on them.

May 14 — The wall of a playground in the Saint Gilles borough of Brussels was defaced with graffiti reading "TSAHAL=SS" and "SHARON=ASSASSIN." (TSAHAL was the Hebrew acronym for the Israel Defense Force.)

August 29 — An anonymous call to the French-language state broadcasting network warned that a bomb was going to explode in one of the synagogues in the Brussels Region at 1:30 in the afternoon. The synagogues went on alert, but nothing happened.

September 8 — A Jewish family was attacked on Place de Bethléem (Bethlehem Square!), in Brussels. The incident began with insults, and when the father responded, the assailants punched him and his children.

October 3 — A Brussels family with a subscription to the *Jerusalem Post* received its mailed copy covered with swastikas.

October 19 — The windows of three cars belonging to people attending a pro-Israel event in the Brussels borough of Schaerbeek, organized by Israel Bonds, were smashed, and swastikas were carved on the cars.

In 2002 the Jewish community continued to rely on its collaborative relationship with the police and gendarmerie (paramilitary federal police) that had been in place for over two decades, to provide heightened surveillance for the country's Jewish institutions and their buildings. These officials worked in tandem with the Jewish community's own security service, set up by the Central Consistory, which had a staff of paid professionals assisted by several dozen young volunteers trained in self-defense and antiterrorism tactics. On February 18, the Orthodox community of Schaerbeek and the Sephardi community of Brussels organized a brief ceremony of tribute to Schaerbeek's police force—its canine brigade in particular—to thank them for ensuring the community's safety.

Holocaust Restitution and Remembrance

The 1995 commemoration of the 50th anniversary of the country's liberation and the end of World War II triggered a new awareness of the Holocaust. It also coincided with the opening of government archives that had remained closed for 50 years under the laws governing the declassification of official documents.

Belgium voluntarily contributed the equivalent of $1 million to the compensation fund set up in the aftermath of the conference on gold stolen by the Nazis that took place in London in December 1997. This sum was subsequently paid out to the Jewish community and split between the country's two Jewish museums, the Jewish Museum in Brussels and the Museum of the Deportation and Resistance in Mechelen. The Belgian Jewish community and the Belgian government participated in several subsequent international conferences on the Holocaust.

On July 6, 1997, the Belgian government, following the precedent set by France and the Netherlands, created a National Study Commission to determine what happened to Jewish-owned assets during the Holocaust era. It consisted of five senior civil servants representing government ministries; representatives of the country's war victims; a retired judge; two historians; and four representatives of Belgian Jewry.

Its final report, submitted in July 2001, detailed the role played by the country's banks, insurance companies, and government officials in the disposal of the assets and the approximate worth of what was taken by each sector. To implement the report, the government proposed a bill providing for the restitution of the stolen assets to the victims and their heirs in the Jewish community. It called for the creation of a new commission to examine the validity of all submitted claims and the conditions for returning assets or paying out compensation. A portion of the sums collected from banks, insurance companies, and the Belgian state would go toward the creation of a foundation, managed jointly by representatives of the country's Jewish institutions and government appointees, that would use the interest generated by its endowment to finance social, cultural, and educational projects. This legislation was adopted in November 2001. The exact amount of the endowment was not yet known, but the Belgian Jewish community's National Commission for Restitution was already meeting regularly in preparation for the foundation's creation, and negotiating with banks, insurance companies, and government bodies.

In addition, a law passed in December 1998 provided that Jews living in Belgium during World War II who were not Belgian nationals could henceforth claim the status of political prisoners, a designation with moral but no financial implications. The Jewish community had earlier secured government recognition of this status for hidden children, hidden adults, and the orphans of deportees. In 2001, however, the community demanded compensation for the Jewish orphans as well as for other children and adults who lived in hiding during the war. The number of surviving Jews who had lived in Belgium at some time between 1940 and 1945 was not expected to exceed 5,000, including 300 deportees and 3,000 hidden children (1,800 of them orphaned). France and the Netherlands already provided such compensation.

In 2002, the National Commission for Restitution finalized an agreement for the creation of the national foundation that would manage the balance of funds that could not be returned to descendents of the despoiled families. Moreover, the government recognized a special legal status for hidden children and Jewish deportees that would place them on the same footing as political deportees, with the same privileges and benefits. The status of the country's Jewish war orphans remained to be settled.

A number of public events related to the Holocaust took place during the year. The CCOJB organized a ceremony at the Memorial to the Jewish Martyrs of Belgium on March 8, the day officially marked in Belgium for commemorating the Holocaust. Prime Minister Verhofstadt and other top officials addressed the gathering. In October, several members of Parliament held a press conference to announce the launching of an investigation into the responsibility of Belgian authorities for the deportation of the country's Jews. Later that month, at a ceremony on the 60th anniversary of the beginning of the deportations, the prime minister said that the country must acknowledge and assume responsibility for them.

The Auschwitz Foundation brought 87 Belgian teachers on its annual study trip to Auschwitz in April. The foundation also provided schools and organizations with speakers on the topic of the Holocaust — some of them camp survivors — maintained a traveling exhibit about the concentration camps, and ran a cycle of four seminars for teachers to delve deeply into the Nazi genocide.

JEWISH COMMUNITY

Demography

The Jewish population of Belgium was estimated at around 31,400. While the fall of the Berlin wall and the collapse of the communist regimes stimulated Jewish immigration from the East, this influx was more than offset by the emigration of young people to North America and Israel, and the low Jewish birthrate. The rate of intermarriage was estimated at around 50 percent.

As Jewish activities came increasingly to be concentrated in the large urban centers of Brussels and Antwerp, each home to about 15,000 Jews, smaller Jewish communities such as those of Liège and Charleroi grew smaller. The community was rapidly aging overall, though more so in Brussels than in Antwerp, where the large Orthodox presence included many young families.

Religion

The Belgian constitution guaranteed freedom of religion and provided for government financial support to all recognized faiths. Even before Belgian independence in 1830, when the country was under the control of Napoleonic France, Jewish communities were organized under the consistorial system that had been established for French Jews in 1808. That framework, the Jewish Central Consistory of Belgium, comprised 16 communities in 2002, two of them Sephardi (one in Brussels, the other in Antwerp) and the rest Ashkenazi. Consistorial policy was set by an assembly whose 40 delegates were elected democratically by their respective communities.

The Central Consistory was the uncontested religious and moral authority of Belgian Jewry, and not only because it was the oldest Jewish institution in the country. By encompassing all of Belgium it brought together in one federation all Jewish communities despite their varied ideological currents—from Orthodoxy to moderate religious liberalism—and thus included the vast majority of the Jewish population. The Central Consistory also personified the model of Jewish integration into modern Western society. As the representative institution of Judaism in Belgium, it engaged in dialogue with other religions, and, like the representative institutions of all the recognized faiths, the Consistory was given radio and television slots for broadcasts in French and Dutch.

Belgium hosted the 23rd annual European Conference of Rabbis, held in the Charlemagne Building of the European Communities, May 2–5, 2002. This exceptional event brought together rabbis not only from all over Europe but also from Israel and the U.S. This year's topic was "The Concept of the Jewish Family in Europe." The conference was conducted under the patronage of Prof. Romano Prodi, president of the European Commission, who addressed the participants, as did Viviane Reding, the EC commissioner in charge of education, culture, youth, the media, and sports. Immediately after the conference, on May 5–6, the Central Consistory—Union of Jewish Communities of France held its European Council Meeting of Synagogue Organizations there.

The last official chief rabbi of Belgium retired in 1980. To help fill the rabbinical vacuum, the Consistory had prevailed upon the Justice Ministry in 1996 to create the position of regional chief rabbi. In 2001 there were four such governmentally recognized rabbis, two in Brussels—one for the general community and the other for the strictly Orthodox—and two in Antwerp, one for each of the main Orthodox communities. In addition, Rabbi Albert Guigui, rabbi of the Brussels general community since 1983 and thus one of the regional rabbis, was given special responsibility as rabbinic advisor to the Consistory, making him, in effect, a de facto chief rabbi.

BRUSSELS

The Great Synagogue, built in 1878, was the center of religious life for the Jewish Community of Brussels (JCB). Recognized by the government as a national historic landmark, the synagogue was also the site for major communal ceremonies. Even though it was Orthodox, it had traditionally featured organ music on Sabbath and holidays, as well as a mixed male-female choir. Albert Guigi, however, the present rabbi, eliminated both practices, arguing the need to bring the JCB into line with other Orthodox Jewish communities.

Rabbi Israël Chaikin, the other "regional rabbi" in Brussels, led the Orthodox communities of the boroughs of Saint Gilles and Schaerbeek, and presided over Beth Israel Synagogue. In addition, the Maale community had become attractive to a number of young Jewish academics who were sympathetic to the Orthodox tradition. The Sephardi Synagogue of Brussels was noted for taking the initiative in meeting with Muslims. In 1999 the Sephardi chief rabbi of Israel came to Brussels to install Rabbi Chalom Benizri as the city's Sephardi chief rabbi.

The borough of Forest had the greatest concentration of Orthodox Jews. There were two relatively new *shtieblach* (prayer rooms) run by Orthodox Sephardi Jews, one sponsored by Chabad. An ultramodern *mikveh* (ritual bath) was located in this borough, installed in the headquarters of the Brussels Bet Din (religious court), which supervised it. There was also a Sephardi Community Center set up primarily for educating Jewish children living in the area.

The Liberal Jewish community in Brussels, whose synagogue, Beth Hillel, was also in Forest, grew gradually after World War II at the initiative of a group of American Jews, and most of the current officers were formerly affiliated with the Great Synagogue in the city. Though the Ministry of Justice recognized this community, thus putting it on a par with the Orthodox communities, it was not accredited by the Consistory. Nevertheless, its activities that were not of a religious nature were represented within the Coordinating Committee of Belgian Jewish Organizations (CCOJB).

ANTWERP

Three Antwerp communities were represented within the Consistory, all labeled "Orthodox." The largest was Shomre Hadass, which supervised important religious activities as well as the Tachkemoni School. Machsike Hadass was a federation of all the city's Hassidic groups and considered itself more strictly Orthodox than Shomre Hadass. It had its own kashrut certification system. The "Portuguese" community, smaller that the other two, was supported by many Sephardi Jews.

Jewish Education

The Consistory played a key role in Jewish education. Two of its appointees, rabbis who held the title of "religious inspectors," supervised the teaching of Jewish religion to Jewish students in the nation's public schools. These classes were voluntary, but the right to attend them was guaranteed by Belgian law. About 60 percent of public-school children from Jewish families in Brussels and 30 percent in Antwerp attended them. In addition, the Consistory largely funded, directly or indirectly, the three large Jewish schools in Brussels (attended by some 2,000 children) and all the Jewish schools in Antwerp (attended by some 5,000 children). A significant percentage of Belgian Jewish children attended Jewish schools (the ratio in Antwerp outstripped that in Brussels), and it was probably the highest of any European Jewish community.

Of the three schools in Brussels, the Maimonides Athenaeum was the most religiously traditional and had the most intensive program of Jewish studies. It had a large nursery school, a primary school, and a secondary school. The Ganenou Athenaeum, which had grown exponentially over the previous few years, had started primarily to service the children of Israelis living in the country. It now had a secondary school offering excellent preparation for university study. The third and newest school, Beth Aviv, consisted of a nursery school and a primary school.

In Antwerp more than 3,000 children attend the city's two main Jewish schools, Tachkemoni and Yesode Hatora. The latter was for the children of Orthodox families only, and boys and girls were taught separately. Both institutions had secondary schools, and Yesode Hatora also had a program for training future elementary-school teachers. Yavne, a third large Jewish school in Antwerp, was run by Modern Orthodox Jews, and included the teaching of Zionism. The Hassidic Jews of the Belz and Satmar movements had their own schools in Antwerp, attended by nearly 800 kindergarten and primary-school pupils. The Jewish community also supported Tikvatenu, a school and center for children with mental and physical disabilities servicing more than 100 children.

There was an Orthodox yeshivah in the Brussels borough of Forest that had been functioning for over 20 years. In Antwerp there were two such yeshivahs, attended primarily by Hassidic youths, as well as a weekly *kollel* (intensive seminar) that brought together erudite adult scholars for the study of Jewish texts.

The Jewish Studies Institute (originally known as the Martin Buber Institute), the first school of its kind to be established in Europe, operated under the auspices of Brussels Free University (ULB), and some of its academic courses were recognized as part of the regular curriculum of the university. Besides the regular two-year curriculum leading to a degree, the institute held seminars on Jewish topics for secondary-school teachers and summer classes in Yiddish. The institute's Dutch section, originally located at the ULB's sister institutions, the Vrije Universiteit Brussel (VUB), was moved to Antwerp's university center (Instituut voor Joodse Studies at the UIA) and was expected to become gradually more independent from the Brussels section.

In addition, almost all of the Belgian universities had programs in Jewish studies.

Communal Institutions

The Coordinating Committee of Belgian Jewish Organizations (CCOJB) had 41 affiliates in 2002. It was recognized, along with the Central Consistory, as a representative spokesman for Belgium's Jewish community in dealings of a political nature with Belgian and foreign official bodies, such as, for example, on the question of Holocaust restitution.

Most of Antwerp's Jewish institutions, however, stayed out of the CCOJB and founded the Forum der Joodse Organisaties (Forum of Jewish Organizations) in 1994 to represent Dutch-speaking Jews to the authorities of the Flemish Community. Both it and the CCOJB participated in the Central Consistory.

In the area of social welfare, the Brussels-based Centrale des Oeuvres sociales juives (Central Administration of Jewish Welfare Organizations) was primarily a fund-raising body, much like the federation system in the U.S. The money raised went to the Jewish Social Service (equivalent to Jewish family and children's services in the U.S. and open to all, regardless of religion), an old people's home, the three Jewish schools in Brussels, two cultural centers, an athletic center, summer camps, and an education loan fund, all of which also sought to raise money on their own. The Central Administration published a cultural magazine, *La Centrale*.

A similar coordinating role in Antwerp, where bad economic conditions and the 1996 collapse of the Fischer Bank had greatly increased the number of people needing assistance, was played by the Central Beheer van Joodse Weldadigheid en Maatscheppelijk Hulpbetton (Central Administration for Social Welfare Organizations). Its most recent achievement was the creation of the Queen Elisabeth Residence, consisting of studio apartments for elderly persons.

The *Belgisch Israëlitisch Weekblad* (BIW) was the only regular Jewish newspaper in the country. A weekly, it was published in Antwerp by Louis Davids, who was also the head of an association to promote the Flemish language in the Jewish community. The paper reported on Jewish life in Antwerp and avidly defended Israel.

The Cercle Ben Gurion (Ben-Gurion Circle) was founded in 1977 by socialist Zionists in Brussels to counteract anti-Israel propaganda. Among its activities were a youth center with seminars, festivals, tournaments, Hebrew and Bible classes, Sabbath dinners, and trips. In 1987 it began publishing a monthly on Jewish issues. Most important, the circle created the first Jewish community radio station in Europe, Radio Judaica, on March 11, 1980, and it quickly became a force to reckon with in Belgium and elsewhere in Europe. It broadcast on matters of interest to the Jewish community, providing a forum for the expression of diverse points of view, round the clock Sunday through Friday. In a sense, Radio Judaica became the voice of Belgium's Jewish community.

A number of other pro-Israel organizations operated in Belgium. The Centre d'Information et de Documentation (Center for Information and Documentation, or CID), created in the aftermath of the Yom Kippur War, promoted understanding of Israel and its security concerns, especially in the media. Since the start of the second intifada, Solidarité avec Israel (Solidarity with Israel) had collected funds for Israeli projects. L'Aide médicale à Israël, an association of doctors and members of the allied paramedical professions, created in 1967 and now working under the aegis of Solidarité avec Israël, raised money for Israel's hospitals and health-care projects. There were also groups allied with specific Israeli educational and social institutions, and with the different Israeli political parties. Finally, the Maccabis, the country's oldest Jewish athletic association, organized in a Brussels section and an Antwerp section, promoted sports in the Jewish community and participated regularly in the international Maccabiahs in Israel.

The Jewish Secular Community Center (CCLJ), founded by former communists, was the most important voice of secular Judaism, and its headquarters was one of the most active meeting places for Brussels Jewry. The CCLJ organized lectures, colloquia, and seminars on ethnic, historical, and cultural topics outside the traditional religious structure, as well as Yiddish and Hebrew courses. Its members tended to be political leftists, favoring a negotiated peace in the Middle East and the creation of a Palestinian State. The CCLJ prepared children for a "secular bar mitvah" at age 13 and published the magazine *Regards,* the most widely read Jewish magazine in the community.

The Union of Jewish Progressives of Belgium (Union des Progressistes Juifs de Belgique, or UPJB) was situated even farther to the left than the CCLJ and had a much smaller following, most of whom belonged to the Ecolo and Socialist parties. The organization was not only pro-Palestinian but openly supportive of the PLO. Like the CCLJ, it sponsored activities centered on Jewish history and culture, and the Yiddish language. Its monthly, *Points Critiques* (Critical Points), and its quarterly, *Entre Points Critiques* (Between Critical Points), had very limited circulation. The Jewish community of Belgium excluded the UPJB from federative institutions such as the CCOJB.

L'Union des Etudiants juifs de Belgique (UEJB, Jewish Students' Union of Belgium) was created in the wake of World War II to bring the Jewish students of the entire country under one organizational structure. Most of the current leaders of the community had been active in the UEJB when they were students. In 2002 it had several hundred members from the country's main universities, and constituted a chapter of the World Union of Jewish Students.

The Conseil des Femmes Juives (Jewish Women's Council), an affiliate of the International Council of Jewish Women, defended of the rights of Jewish women, particularly in regard to the problem of the *agunot* (women whose husbands refused to give them a Jewish divorce).

Interreligious Relations

CHRISTIANS

The Central Consistory remained deeply involved in relations with Belgian Christians, especially the Roman Catholic Church, which claimed the allegiance of some 90 percent of the population. The Consistorial Commission for Pluralistic Relations had conducted these activities for more than a quarter-century.

There was another organization, Organe de Concertation entre Juifs et Chrétiens (OCJB), a consensus-building body for Jews and Christians. It promoted regular "summit meetings" among Protestants, Catholics, and Jews to review issues facing them, especially on educational matters and on major international events. An ongoing aim of the Belgian Jewish community was to ensure that schoolbooks did not include negative Christian stereotypes about Jews. The OCJB worked with the International Jewish Committee on Interreligious Consultations (IJCIC) in Europe and globally to carry on dialogue between Jews and Christians.

Jewish-Catholic dialogue groups existed in the main cities of Belgium where Jews lived. Seminars, colloquia, and other meetings were held regularly in a climate of mutual respect. The Brussels chapter of B'nai B'rith also organized a number of Jewish-Christian dialogue groups in coordination with the Consistory.

Jews participated in a number of joint events with the Sisters of Zion group during 2002, all designed to enhance Christian-Jewish understanding and promote peace in the world. On November 25, the CCOJB presented a medal to the Sisters of Zion for their interfaith work.

MUSLIMS

After World War II, Belgium brought in immigrant workers from North Africa and Turkey to work in its mines, steel mills, and other heavy industries. Two-thirds of this group were of Moroccan descent; the remaining third were primarily Turkish nationals, but also included Algerians, Tunisians, Pakistanis, Albanians, and others. There were some 300 mosques in Belgium.

The Executive of Muslims of Belgium (EMB), the Muslim equivalent of the Central Consistory of the Jews, was created in 1998. It was the official representative, to the government and to the Jewish community, of all those claiming the Islamic faith, with the right to recognize mosques and certify the credentials of imams and religious teachers. There was also a Federation of Unions of Mosques, made up of eight associations of mosques totaling 140 individual mosques in Belgium. It represented only North African, mostly Moroccan, mosques. There was a separate federation of Kurdish and Turkish mosques.

Despite the growing number of incidents of young Muslim men vandalizing Jewish property and attacking Jews, relations between the Muslim and Jewish communities and institutions were generally proper and peaceful. Personal relations between the rabbis (who were often themselves of Moroccan descent and spoke Arabic fluently) and the imams were courteous. One or another imam at the Great Mosque of Brussels had received representatives of the Jewish community on several occasions, just as Jewish leaders received representatives of the EMB at the Consistory. Each time an incident occurred, such as the attack on Rabbi Guigui in December 2001, the president of the Consistory and the president of the Muslim Executive issued a statement calling for calm and mutual respect.

During 2002, the CCOJB held several meetings with leaders of the Muslim community in the hope of cementing good relations between the two religious groups. The official reopening of the Orthodox Synagogue of Brussels on April 20, the day commemorating the Warsaw Ghetto uprising, turned into an ecumenical demonstration against group hatred as a dozen Muslim leaders and several Belgian political figures participated. And yet observers noted a palpable change as the year wore on, as Muslim leaders, expressing intense anger over Israel's policies toward the Palestinians, tended to withdraw somewhat from their earlier engagement with the Jewish community.

Culture

On March 10, as part of its ongoing series on Halakhah and modernity, the Consistory's Women's Commission held a colloquium on the role of women in Jewish liturgy. It took place on the campus of Brussels Free University (ULB).

The Jewish Social Service continued to run its programs in Yiddish for senior citizens—one of the last remaining places in Brussels where Yiddish remained a living language. Many of the lectures and discussion groups in 2002 were devoted to the theme of the return of Jewish property stolen during World War II. Jewish Social Service also set up a permanent exhibition on the photographic work and writings of Luc and Viviane Rabine.

The Jewish Museum of Belgium, initiated by leaders of the Consistory in 1980 to display the art and history of the Belgian Jewish community, teach visitors something about the Jewish religion, and demonstrate the Jewish contribution to Belgian life, was now run by a nonprofit organization, Pro Museo Judaico. On November 4, 2002, an agreement was signed with the government giving the museum the right to occupy all buildings at 21 Rue des Minimes. The next evening, the first exhibition at the new site opened, "Setting Up a New Museum." It was attended by leaders of the Jewish community, political figures, and leading academics.

The Jewish Museum of Deportation and Resistance was located in Mechelin on the site of the Dossin Barracks holding camp where Belgian Jews and Gypsies had been taken to await deportation. Some 30,000 people visited the museum annually, the great majority of them high-school seniors brought by their schools. As it did each year, the museum participated in European Jewish Culture Day, which, in 2002, took place in June. Its aim was to introduce the public—Jews and non-Jews—to the variety of Jewish culture. In July, the museum participated in Flemish Museum Night, which attracted many visitors. The museum also organized two concerts of Jewish music under the aegis of the Flanders Festival. The first, in October, featured liturgical music sung by the choir of Antwerp's municipal synagogue, accompanied by its cantor. At the second, in November, the music was klezmer. From September through November, the museum hosted a major exhibition on the history of the Jews of Lithuania, with the help of the Lithuanian embassy and Mechelen's Municipal Cultural Center.

The Contemporary Memory Foundation (La Fondation de la Mémoire contemporaine) sponsored a number of research projects in 2002, among them studies of the illegal immigration of Belgian Jews into Palestine before 1948 and of Jewish education under the Nazi occupation. Catherine Massange's manuscript on the history of Jewish Social Service since 1944 was published in 2002 under the title *Bâtir le Lendemain— L'aide aux Israélites victimes de la guerre et le Service Social Juif de 1944 à nos jours*. The foundation also prepared for publication the fourth volume in its *Cahiers de la Mémoire Contemporaine* series, and made progress on its project to establish a map of Jewish memory in Belgium, *Lieux de Mémoire—pour une géographie de la mémoire juive de Belgique*. This involved a methodical search through the country's archives to establish a list of towns, villages, and other sites of significance in Belgian Jewish history.

The Jewish Secular Community Center (CCLJ) sponsored numerous events during the year focusing on Jewish cultural topics and on the situation in the Middle East. Among the featured speakers were Foreign Minister Louis Michel; Theo Klein, honorary president of CRIF and founding president of the European Jewish Congress; Elie Barnavi, Israel's ambassador to France; Shaul Amor, Israel's ambassador to Belgium; Jacques Attali, author of a new book on the connection between Jews and money; and Yossi Beilin, Israel's former justice minister. Over several days at the end of November, the center held a colloquium on "Where is Israel Heading: We Are All Concerned."

Personalia

Baron Jean Bloch, an outstanding figure in Belgian Jewish life, passed away March 30, 2002. Among other positions, he had served as president of the Central Administration of Jewish Welfare Organizations (Centrale d'oeuvres sociales) and the Jewish Central Consistory. As a young man, Bloch fled to England after Belgium capitulated at the start of World War II, and became a company commander in the independent Belgian Legion. He participated, with the famous Piron Brigade, in the Normandy campaign and the liberation of Brussels. In the last years of his life, this exceptional eyewitness worked on a book that would relate the Jewish community's role in the fight against Hitler. He completed the manuscript a few days before his death, and it was published in December 2002 under the title *Epreuves et Combats 1940–1945 — Histoires d'hommes et de femmes issus de la collectivité juive de Belgique.*

The last surviving chief rabbi of Belgium, Robert Dreyfus, died in Israel on April 12, close to 90 years old. He was the oldest of the 25 French-born rabbis living in Israel, and one of the few whose rabbinical career had begun before World War II.

GEORGES SCHNEK
THOMAS GERGELY

The Netherlands

National Affairs

THE NETHERLANDS REMAINED the most densely populated country in Europe even though its net population growth decreased from 118,000 in 2001 to 88,000 in 2002. The number of immigrants arriving in the country during the year was 124,000, down from 133,000 in 2001, and emigration out of the Netherlands increased.

The influx of Muslim immigrants from countries like Morocco and Turkey, however, remained fairly stable, and the population growth of non-Western inhabitants was eight times the overall rate. Many lived in the poorer inner-city neighborhoods. In 2002, their number was estimated at 1.6 million, or 10 percent of the general population. Because of a higher birthrate and a tendency to "import" relatively young spouses from their countries of origin, this percentage was even higher in the younger age brackets, and would undoubtedly continue to rise.

The assimilation of such immigrants into Dutch society was high on the priority list of Pim Fortuyn, the right-wing populist whose rise and fall dramatically shook up Holland's normally stable politics in 2002.

The ruling government coalition, made up of Labor (PvdA), Conservative Liberals (VVD), and the small center-left Democrats 1966 (D'66), had begun its tenure in August 1998. Wim Kok, PvdA leader for 15 years, was due to be succeeded by Ad Melkert after the May 15 elections. But on April 16 the government abruptly resigned over the findings of a report of what happened in the Balkans seven years earlier. Dutch troops had been guarding the Muslim enclave of Srebrenica in July 1995 when it was taken by Bosnian Serbs, who then massacred some 7,400 men whom the Dutch were supposed to protect. Kok was vice premier at the time. The 2002 report from the Dutch Institute for Wartime Documentation did not blame the Dutch government and troops for failing to prevent the massacre. But critics said the report was both too lenient and too late: the 1995 government should have taken appropriate action, and its successors should have investigated.

Thus the major political parties went into the elections under a cloud, most with new leaders. PvdA candidate Melkert was much less popular than Kok had been; Christian Democrat leader Jan Pieter Balkenende was nicknamed "Harry Potter." Pim Fortuyn, the flamboyant leader of a new party called Livable Netherlands, made mincemeat of them in public debates.

Fortuyn "has the guts to say what we think," his followers said. The 54-year-old former Marxist held fiercely anti-immigrant views, calling for a halt to immigration on the grounds that Holland was "full up." Yet he angrily rejected comparisons between himself and other European far-right leaders, notably Austria's Jörg Haider and France's Jean-Marie Le Pen. He said of Le Pen: "I am appalled by his anti-Semitic thoughts. A man who describes the Holocaust as a footnote in history is beyond my comprehension." Fortuyn charged that Muslims posed a threat to such Dutch national values as full rights for women and gays. Islam was clearly what he had in mind when he claimed that Holland was much too tolerant towards intolerant cultures. Openly gay himself, he called Islam a "retarded culture" that rejected modern values, and said that antiracism clauses should be struck from the national constitution because they impeded the freedom of speech.

On February 9, Livable Netherlands removed its popular leader for airing these views in a newspaper interview, but two days later he had his own party, the List Pim Fortuyn (LPF). In the Rotterdam municipal election on March 6, the LPF went from zero to being the largest party in the city council. National polls predicted that the LPF might get one-fifth of the May 15 vote. But on the evening of May 6, just one week before the national elections, Fortuyn was assassinated by a left-wing environmental activist, Volkert van der Graaf. This was the first political murder in the Netherlands since 1672, and the Dutch public, still appalled by the violence of September 11, 2001, was in a state of shock. Thousands came to a memorial service for Fortuyn, and the pavement in front of his house was covered with flowers. Fortuyn's followers accused the media, the political establishment, and left-wing groups of "demonizing" their leader. After threats were made against politicians, many of them hired bodyguards.

Dutch Jews, while echoing the sense of national shock at the assassination, also conveyed deep ambivalence about Fortuyn's political views. Some Jews had joined his party, but others abhorred it. Ronny Naftaniel, a member of the Netherlands Central Jewish Organization, highlighted the assassinated leader's contradictory impact on the country's Jewish population. "Fortuyn was one of very few politicians who was definitely pro-Israel," he said. "On the other hand, he also called wartime restitution money 'our money,' claiming that Dutch leaders were 'giving in to the Jewish lobby.'" Orthodox Rabbi Shmuel Spiero said that he "wouldn't have voted for Fortuyn." But he added: "It's a great shame. His views about Israel won't be heard anymore." A Jewish law student in Amsterdam explained that he had intended to vote for Fortuyn: "He's anti-Muslim. We lost an ally," he said.

The now leaderless LPF was the big winner on May 15, going from 0 to 26 seats in the 150-member lower house of parliament. The Christian Democrats (CDA), also winners, became the largest party, but still needed others to form a majority coalition. PvdA, VVD, and D'66, which had made up the previous government, all lost dramatically. After difficult negotiations, CDA's Jan Pieter Balkenende formed a government of CDA, VVD, and LPF. But conflicts were rife among the inexperienced "new politicians" in the LPF. On October 16, Balkenende's government disintegrated due to a conflict between two of its LPF ministers. It had lasted 87 days. For the remainder of 2002, the country was ruled by a wobbly minority government left over from Balkenende's cabinet.

The Jewish community was traditionally close to the Dutch royal family, and Jewish leaders were invited to the marriage of Crown Prince Willem Alexander to Maxima Zorreguieta. Some attended even though the ceremony took place in an Amsterdam church on the Sabbath, February 2. The death on October 6 of Prince Claus, husband of Queen Beatrix, deeply affected many members of the community. Beatrix's marriage to the German-born Claus had originally met with much resistance in the Jewish community, particularly since he once had been a member of the Hitler Youth. Claus, however, never sought to deny his past, expressed his regret, and befriended many members of the Jewish community.

The Dutch economy, which had already slowed significantly in 2001, ground to a standstill as the international economic situation deteriorated. By the end of 2002, the projected rate of economic growth for 2003 was set at 0.75 percent, as compared to as much as 4 percent in recent years. Unemployment, which had declined from half a million in 1996 to a quarter million in 2001, went up by 50,000 to reach 300,000, a level last seen in 1999. Unemployment among immigrants, though declining, was still much higher than among the general population (among those of Moroccan origin, it was three times as high). More people fell below the poverty line, and, with prices rising due to the introduction of the euro currency, even some who were not poor found it increasingly difficult to make ends meet.

In May, the euro received the Karel Award for promoting European co-operation. The award was presented to Wim Duisenberg, the Dutch president of the European Central Bank.

Israel and the Middle East

Tourism to Israel was still down at the beginning of 2002, and reached an all-time low when the IDF reentered the territories after the Passover suicide bombing in Netanya (see above, pp. 198–99). Dutch Jews who had been spending Passover in Israel returned to a severe culture shock. The media, the politicians, and ordinary Dutch citizens appeared to have forgotten the many terror attacks against civilians that provoked the IDF actions, and rumors about a massacre in Jenin were widely believed. Former foreign minister Hans van den Broek (CDA) called Sharon "the Nero of Israel" and implicitly compared him to Hitler. Prime Minister Kok held Israel—and particularly Sharon—responsible for the "escalating violence," and supported the efforts of his foreign minister, Jozias van Aartsen (VVD), to convince the EU and the U.S. to issue a joint reprimand. The atmosphere had become more anti-Israel than ever, and it spilled over into anti-Semitism.

In Amsterdam on April 13, demonstrators against the Israeli occupation of the Territories burned Israeli flags and carried anti-Semitic banners. They even attacked those they recognized as Jews, chasing an American tourist into the Krasnapolsky Hotel, which they then pelted with stones. A small group of Jewish young people later presented members of parliament with photos, banners, and burned flags taken from the scene. Almost (but not quite) all the parties voiced concern about this new anti-Semitism. (One member of the left-wing Jewish dissident group Another Jewish Voice, however, who had joined the demonstration and was seen standing beneath a swastika, said he hadn't noticed anything anti-Semitic.)

The demonstration included not only Moroccan youngsters who identified with Palestinians, but ordinary Dutch citizens as well. One of the latter was Wim Duisenberg's wife, Gretta, carrying a Palestinian flag she had bought over the Internet for the occasion. It was to be the beginning of her activist career. After the demonstration, the 60-year-old Mrs. Duisenberg hung the PLO flag from the balcony of her house in an affluent Amsterdam neighborhood and left it there for six weeks. When her Jewish neighbors complained, she told them that "the rich Jews in America" enabled Israel to continue the "colonial oppression of the Palestinian people." A local Jewish lawyer filed a formal complaint against her for anti-Semitism and incitement. The case was dismissed, but Gretta Duisenberg soon provoked a second one. In June, she founded a new organization, "Stop the Occupation." When a Dutch radio interviewer asked her how many signatures she hoped to collect for the new group, she responded "six million," and laughed. This prompted a group of Jewish lawyers to file a second complaint with the Dutch attorney general. Duisenberg denied she was referring to the six million Jewish Holocaust victims. Again, the claim was dismissed, although the attorney general said that Duisenberg was "poisoning the atmosphere."

In a telling indication of popular sympathies in the Middle East conflict, Mrs. Duisenberg was elected "Amsterdammer of 2002" by the readers of a national daily, and her husband, Wim, was widely admired for stating that he fully supported his wife. Still, some non-Jews, mainly evangelical Christians, joined a solidarity demonstration "for peace and against terrorism" in Amsterdam on April 21. Organized by students and heavily guarded by riot police, it drew about 1,500 people.

Anti-Semitism and Extremism

The Center for Information and Documentation on Israel (CIDI), which tracked anti-Semitic incidents, found that the increase in number and gravity of incidents that started in 2001 continued in 2002. In the first four months of 2002 alone, the number of incidents recorded, 110, was almost four times the number for the whole of 2001, 31. For the first (recorded) time after World War II, a Jew was threatened at gunpoint. Still, the situation was nowhere near as bad as in France and Belgium.

Anti-Semitic incidents were clearly related to the situation in Israel. Especially after the alleged Jenin "massacre," the number of incidents rose considerably. They included verbal abuse, anti-Semitic e-mails, and physical threats. Many, though not all, of the incidents took place in Amsterdam—the city with the largest number of (recognizable) Jews. Orthodox Jewish men adjusted to the situation by wearing hats or caps in public—hardly anyone wore a *kippah* in the center of town.

There were many incidents (experts estimated as many as three out of every four) that went unrecorded, as Jews who sought police help and did not receive it gave up trying to report anti-Semitic occurrences to law-enforcement authorities. Incidents involving young people also often went unreported as Jewish children became used to the phenomenon. For example, a youth soccer team with recognizably Jewish players was subjected to verbal and physical abuse by a Turkish-Moroccan team called Orient, in a game in Amsterdam. The referee ignored the situation, pretending not to see or hear what was going on. When two of the Jewish players had to be helped off the field — one with a torn ligament and the other with a concussion — Orient players waved them out with Hitler salutes. After the game, while they were in the showers, Orient players barricaded the door, and the Jewish team had to be "rescued" by adult members of their club who were called by mobile phone. The chairman of the Jewish club invited the Orient board to a meeting, but did not report the incident to the police.

This type of incident was not restricted to the streets and playing fields. Jewish children in non-Jewish schools met with varying reactions when reporting anti-Semitic abuse to school authorities, they told the Dutch Jewish weekly *Nieuw Israelitisch Weekblad* (NIW). Some principals took firm and immediate action, but others ignored the incidents or even suggested that Jewish students provoked them. Anecdotal evidence indicated that the phenomenon was widespread, but no statistics were available.

In the last week of February, the Dutch Domestic Security Service published a report on Muslim schools. The service had been asked to undertake an investigation in 2001, in the wake of claims that some schools were inciting hatred; in one, for example, a copy of the magazine *Al Tawheed,* containing blatant anti-Semitism, had been circulated. The report, however, concentrated on the problem of integrating Muslim children into Dutch culture; anti-Semitism was only mentioned in a footnote.

One worrisome development was the rising popularity among young Dutch Moroccans of the Belgian-based Arab European League (AEL), which had already evoked tensions and anti-Semitic incidents in Belgium. At the end of 2002, AEL leader Abu Jahjah announced plans to establish Dutch branches of the organization in cities such as Utrecht and Amsterdam, which had large numbers of youngsters of Moroccan descent. In the Netherlands, the AEL appealed to those who felt threatened by the growing pressure to integrate into Dutch society, which they saw as forcing them to assimilate totally and give up their own Muslim culture. This was the very same group of malcontents who identified with Palestinians and were responsible for most of the anti-Semitic incidents in Holland.

Interestingly, some of the AEL's greatest adversaries were also to be found in the Moroccan community. Its leader, Abu Jahjah, an Arab from Lebanon, propagated "Arab pride," but a large percentage (some said 90 percent) of Moroccans living in the Netherlands were not Arabs, but rather Berbers from the Rift Mountains, most of whom did not speak Arabic. Many resisted the "Arabization" of their own culture in Morocco—though they are Muslims—and continued to do so in the Netherlands. For the same reason, they did not particularly identify with the Palestinians.

Countering ethnic tensions and anti-Semitism in Dutch society were intercultural initiatives that brought together worried Jews, Christians, and Muslims in the hope of jointly countering both Islamophobia and anti-Semitism. The (Jewish) mayor of Amsterdam, Job Cohen, set up one such interfaith group. There were other examples: a group of Jewish and Muslim students organized communal meals and discussions; Moroccan "neighborhood fathers" worked to get wayward youngsters back in line in inner-city neighborhoods where tensions had risen; and antiracist groups started projects to counteract prejudice and anti-Semitism in Dutch schools.

Holocaust Restitution

Many of the international and national restitution schemes that had been set in motion in 2000 continued.

In April, there was a "second distribution round" of restitution monies to individual Dutch survivors. The monies were put up by the government, banks, insurance companies, and the stock exchange in 2000 (see AJYB 2001, pp. 347–48). About $235 million was available for distribution among an anticipated 50,000 Dutch survivors of the Holocaust, each of whom would receive $5,500 from the fund. In those cases where a survivor died after the war, the money would go to the surviving spouse or be divided among the children. As of January 2002, about 26,000 claims had been satisfied. Just over 18,600 went to survivors and the rest to 14,000 heirs sharing a portion. Clearly, not all survivors or their families had been reached.

Of the unclaimed money, 20 percent was to be distributed to Jewish institutions for communal purposes, and the remainder went to individuals who qualified in the "second round." However, dividing the money destined for communal purposes—"Jewish infrastructure"— in the Netherlands proved a lengthy process. Preparations continued all through 2002, and payments looked unlikely to start before the end of 2003 at the earliest. One problem was that only 28 percent of Dutch Jews were synagogue members, and a large majority of the rest was not associated with any Jewish organization at all. To assess the demand for Jewish activities, a survey was held among some 250 organizations. Forms were sent out in the first week of January, but recommendations on how to distribute the money were not ready until the fall. Because of the small number of active Jewish leaders in the country and the relatively large number of organizations, most candidates for positions on a board to distribute the money had a vested interest in at least one organization that was hoping to make a claim. Detailed rules were clearly necessary for distribution, and discussions about these rules were still going on at the end of the year.

On March 19, the Jewish Humanitarian Fund started its operations with a capital of about $22.6 million. The board—including Dutch Jewish leaders, politicians, and Avi Beker, secretary general of the World Jewish Congress—was to allocate part of the money returned to the Dutch Jewish community to humanitarian projects outside the Netherlands. Most of the sponsored projects were educational programs for Jews in Central and Eastern Europe; the only exceptions were two projects in Argentina, where students were dropping out of school because their parents were unable to pay for bus fares, tuition fees, and even lunch.

In the area of art restitution, Project Origins Unknown continued researching the provenance of 449 paintings in Dutch museums that had been stolen, confiscated, or sold to Germany from the Netherlands during the war, and later retrieved. Research into the drawings, graphic art, and applied arts was due to be completed in 2003. The project was started in 1997, when the secretary of state at the time, Aad Nuis, opened an investigation into the identity of the original owners of these works. In November, the names of many Jewish original owners were made public, along with the circumstances under which they had lost their property, and, in some cases, how they had tried, unsuccessfully, to recover the artworks after the war. Recommendations issued by the Ekkart Commission for the restitution of looted art had been adopted, and claims were slowly beginning to be processed (see AJYB 2002, pp. 368–69).

JEWISH COMMUNITY

Demography

A demographic survey of the Jews in the Netherlands published in 2001—the first in 35 years—estimated the Jewish population of the country at 44,000, or 0.275 percent of the total Dutch population of 16 million. In 2002, the general population rose to 16.2 million, but the Jewish community undoubtedly grew at a lower rate. According to the 2001 survey, Dutch Jews were postponing marriage to a later age than the general population. More Jewish women remained childless, and those who did have children had fewer (1.5) than the national average (1.9).

Fully 30 percent of the community in 2001 was not Jewish according to Halakhah, traditional Jewish law, because they were children of Jewish fathers and non-Jewish mothers. (Among the bona fide Jews—those with Jewish mothers—24 percent had non-Jewish fathers.) Intermarriage was accelerating. Among younger married Jews, 76 percent of men and 68 percent of women were married to non-Jews. Even of the roughly 46 percent who had two Jewish parents, fully half were themselves married to non-Jews.

Communal Affairs

Perhaps because Dutch society was becoming increasingly less tolerant of minority cultures, the government intervened in the affairs of the Jewish community on several occasions in 2002.

The kosher slaughter of heavy bulls was halted temporarily several times by the Dutch Veterinary Inspection, and ordered stopped on May 8. The vet supervising all ritual slaughter claimed that because of their thick skin, ritual slaughter of these particular bulls (called "limousine bulls") took too long and caused "unnecessary suffering." The Inspection proposed new rules for ritual slaughter to make the slaughter of these bulls impossible. The threat was removed at the very last moment after the Board of Orthodox Communities in the Netherlands (NIK) demonstrated to the outgoing agriculture minister, Laurens Jan Brinkhorst, that the new rules were more restrictive than those in any other European Union country. Slaughter of all permitted animals was restored in July. A revised set of instructions for kosher slaughter became operative, which the Jewish community "accepted on pragmatic grounds," according to a statement.

Brinkhorst had only agreed to meet with NIK representatives after much political pressure, including a letter to the official then in charge of forming a new government coalition warning that religious freedom was at risk. This was the Jewish community's first attempt in centuries to influence party negotiations regarding the formation of a government coalition.

Beside the proposed restriction on the Jewish community's freedom to choose which types of cattle to slaughter, the outgoing government also wanted to do away with an exception to the Dutch burial laws that guaranteed that Jewish graves would never be disturbed. After a certain number of years, according to the suggested revision, Jewish graves might be "cleared," just like other graves in Holland. The NIK intervened again, pointing out that the new rule would require Orthodox Jews to bury their dead outside the country. The new government, distracted by other matters, took no further action.

A third potential threat to religious freedom was the proposed restriction on "importing" spouses from abroad. Targeted at badly integrated foreigners from Muslim countries, the law could also affect Orthodox Jews unable to find suitable spouses among Holland's small population of halakhic Jews—a mere 30,000—many of whom were not religiously observant. Further debate on this issue was certain for 2003.

Despite the influx of 30 new people, the "Portuguese" Sephardi Congregation still hovered between 400 and 500 members in the whole of Holland, with most of the active members attending the "secondary minyan"in Amstelveen rather than the historic 17th-century Esnoga in the center of nearby Amsterdam. The community was barely able to afford the enormous costs of maintaining that monumental building.

The Ashkenazi Jewish community of Amsterdam continued to struggle with the high costs of kosher slaughter, and meat prices were sky-high. In 2001, the ritual slaughterer had resigned and returned to Israel, and the community continued to fly a replacement in from Israel periodically through 2002. This caused the community's budget deficit to rise to about $172,000, far higher than the $73,000 previously agreed by the board. The community's capital decreased by $96,000 to $7.3 million. In 2001, 146 new members joined the community, but another 147 resigned or died, leaving membership constant at just under 2,900.

In other communal news, the Jewish community of Amersfoort celebrated the 275th anniversary of its synagogue. In June, the board of the Federation of Netherlands Zionists held its first meeting in over two years and installed several new members, including three of the younger generation. The meetings had been discontinued in 2000; the board members then said they had no time to devote to the cause, but could not resign since there were no available replacements. In Utrecht, the kosher (and organic) bakery closed due to the health problems of owner/baker Eli van Leeuwen, who died later in the year, leaving a wife and three young children. The number of kosher bakers outside Amsterdam was thus reduced to two, one in The Hague and one in Amersfoort. This accelerated the general trend in recent years, which saw more and more religious Jews moving to Amsterdam, where such amenities as kosher shops and restaurants, community buildings, and Jewish schools were to be found, while such establishments closed down elsewhere in the country.

Yet a revival was beginning to show in smaller communities such as Haarlem, and in newly constructed towns like Almere, where small numbers rejoined synagogues they had not visited in years or started new synagogues. Many had been made more aware of their Jewish roots by publications about Holocaust restitution, and the situation in Israel may also have been a factor in reawakening Jewish feelings. Their reentry was eased by the Jewish community's outreach programs, which had been stepped up in response to dwindling membership outside Amsterdam, and to the results of the population survey of 2001 that predicted a further decrease in numbers.

Another positive development saw young Jews, many of them students, getting together in small, informal groups. One such group organized the solidarity demonstration with Israel. Others organized a huge concert in Amsterdam to raise funds for Israeli terror victims, visited high schools to share information about Israel, or monitored media reports on the Middle East, setting the record straight by writing to apparently misinformed papers and politicians. Most of the participants in and around Amsterdam knew each other from the Jewish youth movement. Several said they were not ready to join Jewish communal institutions, but were propelled into action by the general anti-Israel atmosphere.

Publications

British historian Carol Ann Lee's biography of Anne Frank's father, Otto, was widely criticized for inaccuracies and even dubbed "a study in character assassination" by some reviewers. Lee named a new suspect in the betrayal of the Frank family and claimed that Otto Frank allowed himself to be blackmailed into protecting this man, because, said Lee, Frank had done business with the suspect and with the German occupation army during the war. The National Institute of Wartime Documentation later announced that it would evaluate Lee's sources, and a report would be ready in 2003. It would not, however, investigate the betrayal of the Frank family.

The International Institute of Social History in Amsterdam placed its Yiddish collection on the Internet, including all the printed works of the Jewish Labor Bund, and pictures of Yiddish poets, revolutionaries, and artists (see www.iisg.nl, and under "search" enter "Yiddish").

An exceptionally large number of new books chronicled prewar Jewish life in small country towns—including Veenendaal, Ede, Edam, Alphen aan den Rijn, Amersfoort, Vriezenveen, The Hague, and Haaksbergen—and "Jewish neighborhoods" in Amsterdam. These latter included Henriëtte Boas's posthumously published memoirs of her childhood neighborhood, *Terug in de Den Texstraat. Sarphati, een biografie* chronicled the life and work of Samuel Sarphati (1813–66), who greatly influenced social projects and new housing developments in Amsterdam. In *Minhagé Amsterdam,* Rabbi Jehoeda Brilleman minutely described religious customs peculiar to the various Ashkenazi Amsterdam congregations through the ages, and attempts to unify their rituals. Ab Caransa's *Vrijmetselarij en jodendom. De wereld een tempel* described the (not always positive) relationship between Dutch Jews and freemasons. *Storm in the Community. Yiddish Polemical Pamphlets of Amsterdam Jewry 1797–1798,* by Jozeph Michman and Marion Aptroot, elucidated the differences of opinion in Yiddish pamphlets between "old" and "new" congregations just prior to the emancipation of Dutch Jewry.

Hebreeuwse en Jiddisje woorden in het Nederlands set down rules for transliteration into Dutch of Hebrew and Yiddish words. *Dutch Jewry – Its History and Secular Culture (1500–2000)* consisted of 17 articles on a wide range of aspects of Dutch Jewish history. In *Kopgeld* (Head Money), Ad van Liempt revealed that Dutch "Jew hunters" caught over 8,000 Jews during World War II (and not just under 3,000, as was previously presumed). This earned them a premium amounting to about $37.50 per head, the money taken from property stolen from Jews. *Eksters* (Magpies) was part three of historian Gerard Aalders's trilogy describing wartime robbery and postwar restitution of Jewish property; this volume covered the Nazi robbery of 146,000 kilos of monetary gold from the Dutch National Bank. *Binnenskamers* (Behind Closed Doors) and *Polderschouw* (View of the Flatlands) were parts three and four of a series launched in 2001 about the reception of various groups—including Jewish survivors—who returned to the Netherlands after the war.

Personalia

Rivka Weiss-Blok resigned as director of the Jewish Historical Museum in Amsterdam. She was succeeded by the Dutch-born Joel Cahen, formerly head conservator of Beth Hatefutsoth, the Diaspora Museum, in Tel Aviv.

Historian Evelien Gans was awarded the prestigious Henriëtte Roland

Holtsprijs for her study of Jewish social democrats and socialist Zionists in the Netherlands. On September 1, she became professor of contemporary Judaism at the University of Amsterdam.

Henri Markens resigned as chairman of the Orthodox community of the Netherlands. He remained the principal of one of Holland's two Jewish high schools.

Author Leon de Winter was awarded the prestigious Welt-Literaturpreis, a German prize, for his collective works.

The death of Pee Koelewijn, an evangelical Christian who organized many solidarity events for Israel, was mourned by many in the Jewish community.

Prominent Jews who died in 2002 included: author Siegfried E. van Praag, 102, whose postwar books (he published more than 50) described Jewish dilemmas; author and criminologist Andreas Burnier (Dessaur), 71, a women's-rights activist who, after a visit to Dachau in 1989, studied Judaism and Hebrew and published a new translation of the Psalms; Martin van Amerongen, 60, journalist and editor of *Vrij Nederland,* one of Holland's leading weeklies; Boudewijn Büch (Buch), 53, author, critic, and art collector; Sem Dresden, 87, former professor of French literature and comparative literature and author of erudite essays, including his best-known work on how to read literary testimonies of war and destruction, who, just before his death, received the P.C. Hooft Award for his collective works; Annie van der Heijden-Lob, 91, the "grand old lady of Jewish childcare" in the Netherlands; Bram Jacobs, 92, who helped rebuild Jewish life in The Hague after the war; Bob Levisson, 87, a leader of the Liberal movement in The Hague and founder of CIDI; Joop Al, 54, attorney general at the court of Amsterdam and expert in Jewish family law; Simon Meerschwam, 88, greatly mourned by members of "his" small Gerrit van der Veenstraat-synagogue, a hugely successful businessman who quietly supported many individuals and Jewish institutions; and Chaim Natkiel, 85, much-decorated Jewish resistance fighter and chairman of the Committee Jewish Resistance.

ELISE FRIEDMANN

Italy and the Vatican

National Affairs

IN JANUARY, PRIME MINISTER Silvio Berlusconi of the center-right coalition also assumed the post of foreign minister after Renato Ruggiero quit over a dispute with other cabinet members skeptical of the euro, which was introduced as Italy's currency on January 1. Berlusconi served as foreign minister until November, when he appointed Franco Frattini to the post.

Berlusconi remained firmly in the saddle despite an economic slow-down (including heavy losses for the giant automaker, Fiat), strikes, and mass protests against his government. In April, millions of Italians staged the biggest strike in decades to protest the government's plans to reform labor laws and make it easier to fire newly hired workers. The strike came just two weeks after the main architect of the reform, economist Marco Biagi, was assassinated by left-wing terrorists.

The center-left opposition was weak and divided. Fed up with tradi-tional leftist politicians, some prominent intellectuals and artists—such as film director Nanni Moretti—sparked the formation of a grassroots left-wing movement. The type of peaceful street demonstrations it orga-nized in many cities was called the *girotondo* (the Italian name for the chil-dren's game ring-around-a-rosy), because demonstrators linked hands to form "protective" circles around a building or square.

Deputy Prime Minister Gianfranco Fini, leader of the right-wing Na-tional Alliance (AN) and chosen by the prime minister to be Rome's rep-resentative at the convention on the Future of the European Union, moved further to distance himself from the AN's fascist roots. In Janu-ary, he retracted an earlier comment that fascist dictator Benito Mussolini was the greatest statesman of the twentieth century, and during the course of the year Fini proved himself one of Israel's staunchest supporters. In September, Fini publicly apologized for Italy's persecution of Jews under Mussolini. In an interview with the Israeli daily *Ha'aretz,* Fini said that "fascism quashed human rights, and racial laws created one of the great-est atrocities in the history of humanity." He added, "As an Italian I have to accept responsibility, in the name of the Italians. This is something I must do. The Italians bear responsibility for what happened after 1938, after the racial laws were legislated. They bear a historic responsibility, a responsibility that is inscribed in history, a responsibility to issue declarations and ask for forgiveness. I am speaking of national, not personal responsibility." The apology was seen as a run-up to a hoped-for invitation to Israel.

Fini's apology was followed by a similar public statement by Prince Vittorio Emanuele of Savoy, son of the last king of Italy, Umberto II. In July, Parliament passed a constitutional amendment allowing the male heirs to the Italian throne to return to the country, and in December, Vittorio Emanuele, his wife, and his son made a four-hour trip to Rome, where they had a private audience with the pope. A referendum had abolished the monarchy in 1946, and Italy's 1948 constitution banned all male members of the Savoy family from the country, since the king had collaborated with Mussolini.

In November, an appeals court shocked Italy by convicting former prime minister Giulio Andreotti of ordering the Mafia to kill a journalist in 1979, and sentencing him to 24 years in prison. The verdict overturned a 1999 acquittal on the same charges.

During the year, Jews and Muslims protested a proposed bill, sponsored by the anti-immigrant Northern League, to hang crucifixes in public offices, schools, and train stations.

Israel and the Middle East

Repercussions from the Middle East conflict, threats of global terrorism in the wake of September 11, and the possibility of war with Iraq had a powerful impact on Italian politics. Italy was at the center of several investigations targeting alleged Al Qaeda operatives or cells. In February, for example, authorities investigated whether holes found in the walls of a utility tunnel near the U.S. embassy in Rome were linked to a group of Moroccan men suspected of planning an attack on the embassy. In July, police in Milan arrested eight men for allegedly aiding Al Qaeda by preparing and distributing forged documents. Also in July, a heavy police presence guarded the historic Venice ghetto for three days following an unspecified terrorist threat.

The question of how to deal with a growing immigrant population, many of whom were Muslims, remained a high priority. Hundreds of illegal immigrants entered Italy by boat, often smuggled in by organized-crime gangs. A poll of 3,000 Italians between the ages of 15 and 34 was released in April. More than 75 percent of the respondents agreed with the view that there were too many immigrants in the country, 40 percent agreeing "strongly." In addition, some 21 percent of respondents "strongly" agreed that most immigrants were involved in illegal or criminal activity. At the same time, however, 68.1 percent said they felt a sense of solidarity and a duty to help the immigrant population.

A movement opposed to possible war in Iraq grew over the course of the year, attracting many mainstream Italians as well as anti-Americans, pro-Palestinians, and antiglobalization forces. In November, more than half a million people staged an antiwar demonstration in Florence. This protest climaxed the first European Social Forum, a four-day meeting of antiglobalization campaigners from all over Europe. Some placards depicted President Bush as Hitler and Berlusconi as Mussolini.

Italy tried to mediate in the Middle East. At an EU summit in March in Barcelona, Berlusconi outlined plans for a 6.2-billion-euro aid package for Palestinians that was based on the post-World War II Marshall Plan for the economic recovery of Europe. Italy strongly backed the creation of a Palestinian state and Israel's right to exist in security, though it criticized Israel's hard-line response to the intifada that began in 2000. Leftist parties and movements were generally antagonistic toward the Sharon government and its policies. Right-wing parties, including the National Alliance, were more supportive of Israel. The small Radical Party formally called for Israel to be admitted to the European Union. On separate official visits in December, Israel's president, Moshe Katzav, and its foreign minister, Benjamin Netanyahu, called Prime Minister Berlusconi one of Israel's firmest friends in Europe. While serving as foreign minister earlier in the year, Shimon Peres also visited Italy. In late December, Palestinian representatives complained to the media that Italy had become too supportive of Israel.

Berlusconi made several trips to the Middle East and also met with Middle Eastern leaders in Rome. In February, Syrian president Bashar al-Assad met Berlusconi and other Italian leaders on his first visit to Europe since the September 11 attacks. Jewish groups, human rights activists, the Radical Party, and the Greens protested the visit. Berlusconi, on a one-day visit to Libya in October, met with that country's leader, Col. Muammar Qaddafi. Italy was Libya's leading trade partner, and Libya supplied one-quarter of Italy's energy needs.

Rome Mayor Walter Veltroni sponsored several Middle East peace initiatives. Under his auspices, the city of Rome opened an Office for Peace in Jerusalem, in cooperation with the Rome representatives of both the Italy-Israel and Italy-Palestine associations. The city of Rome and those two associations also organized a peace march on March 20 whose slogan was "Peace and Security in the Middle East: Two Peoples and Two States." In May, Veltroni offered Rome as a possible location for an international peace conference on the Middle East, and a peace concert in the ancient Colosseum brought together Israeli and Palestinian artists. In June, a Rome cultural association, in association with the Italian foreign ministry and the Dutch-based Education for Life organization, hosted a three-day brainstorming session for an influential group of 25 Israelis and 25 Palestinians. Veltroni revealed in July that, under his auspices, representatives of Israel and the Palestinians had held secret talks in Rome in 2001. In September, Veltroni hosted an event sponsored by the Israeli-Palestinian Coalition for Peace. Featured speakers were Yasir Abd Rabbo, the Palestinian Authority's minister for culture and information, and former Israeli justice minister Yossi Beilin.

An Italian Center for Peace in the Middle East operated in Milan. In January, it set up a "twinning" arrangement between a Milan high school, the Terra Sancta College in Bethlehem, and the Nisui Experimental College in Jerusalem. Some 150 teenagers in the three schools exchanged letters, tapes, and gifts. In October, five Milan families hosted five Israeli and five Palestinian teenagers. They attended a concert, "Voices of Peace," which was organized by an Israeli and a Lebanese, and included choral renditions of Jewish, Muslim, and Christian songs. In June, 20 Israeli and Palestinian children took part in a floral-painting festival near Rome whose theme was "symbols of peace and solidarity."

Jewish observers believed that much of the media demonstrated a pro-Palestinian bias. Criticism of Israeli policy mounted sharply with Israel's military incursions into the West Bank in the spring. A political cartoon in *La Stampa* newspaper showed the baby Jesus in a manger, threatened by an Israeli tank and saying, "They don't want to kill me again, do they?" Another cartoon by the same artist, published during the Israeli siege of the Church of the Nativity in Bethlehem, where 200 Palestinian gunmen were holed up (see above, p. 206), showed the pope, crucified against flames and bursting bombs. "How's this?" he says, referring to the siege. "You fire on the house where my God was born, you shoot at his tomb, you target the statue of his mother, you terrorize my priests and my nuns in order to get rid of a few Palestinian ragamuffins . . . and if I protest, you call me an anti-Semite??!!"

Italian pacifists embraced the Palestinian point of view, and for months pro-Palestinian demonstrators maintained a permanent camp just off central Rome's main square, Piazza Venezia.

The pro-Palestinian cause became part of the leftist, anti-establishment youth culture. Members of a rock band, for example, were part of a group of Italians who traveled to the West Bank at the end of March to protest Israel's military operations. (They were among hundreds of pro-Palestinian foreigners who went to Ramallah as "human shields" for Palestinians fearing a massive Israeli military response to the suicide bombing in Netanya that killed 29 people at a Passover seder.) A leftist music magazine wrote up their experiences, portraying Israelis as aggressors. One group from a "Young Communist" organization unfurled a huge pro-Palestinian banner on their return to Rome's Fiumicino airport. Likewise, a book, *Sognando Palestina* (Dreaming Palestine), aimed at teenage readers, was published in the spring. Written by Randa Ghazy, a 15-year-old Egyptian-Italian girl who had never been to Israel or the Palestinian territories, it sympathetically described a group of young Palestinians fighting against Israeli troops. A theme throughout the book was that Israel was persecuting the Palestinians in the same brutal way that Jews had previously been persecuted. (In December, the Simon Wiesenthal Center and other Jewish organizations protested against the French version of the book.)

Various leftist "peace demonstrations" with an anti-Israel slant were held. One, in Rome on April 6, turned into a display of anti-Israel invective so vicious that most of the political organizations that sponsored it pulled out. Youths dressed as suicide bombers marched alongside others carrying placards equating Prime Minister Ariel Sharon of Israel with Hitler.

This rally prompted the organization of an "Israel Day" counter-demonstration a few days later under the slogan "Israel Must Live." The driving force behind it was the newspaper *Il Foglio,* which had promoted a "USA Day" rally in November 2001 to show solidarity with America following the September 11 attacks. This was believed to be the first pro-Israel demonstration in Italy organized by people from outside the Jewish community. More than 10,000 demonstrators walked through downtown Rome carrying Israeli flags.

Also in reaction to the April 6 march, journalist Oriana Fallaci published a scathing indictment of Italy, Italians, the Catholic Church, the left wing, and Europeans in general for abandoning Israel and fomenting a "shameful" new wave of anti-Semitism (see below, p. 447). At the same time, some 260 prominent Italians—Christians and Jews—issued an open letter expressing concern over the new wave of anti-Semitism in Europe and the media's role in fostering it.

Vatican-Mideast Relations

A number of times during the year, Pope John Paul II condemned terrorism and bloodshed, called on the parties in the Middle East conflict to return to the negotiating table, and stressed that religion must not be used as an excuse for killing. The pontiff set the tone in his New Year's Day message (Catholics mark January 1 as the World Day of Peace) in which he called on monotheistic religions to condemn the use of violence. No one, for any reason, he said, had the right to kill in the name of God. And, he went on, a "cry of blood" in the Holy Land must persuade Christians, Muslims, and Jews, "all sons of the same Patriarch Abraham," to seek peace. The pope added that the September 11 attacks on the United States and their aftermath had shaken the world. "Perverse interests," he said, threatened to turn the world into a "theater of war."

Three weeks later, speaking four days ahead of an interfaith Day of Prayer for Peace in the World scheduled for January 24 in Assisi, he declared that Palestinians and Israelis appeared to have entered a "blind alley" of conflict with no apparent way out.

In March, Israel's deputy foreign minister, Michael Melchior, was among a group of Catholic, Jewish, and Muslim leaders who attended a general audience with the pope. The group had recently signed a declaration against violence. During the audience, the pope appealed for an end to Israeli-Palestinian bloodshed.

The pope reiterated his appeal for peace in the Holy Land in his Easter message on March 31. On April 7, he led Roman Catholics around the world in prayers for peace in the Middle East and called for a resumption of negotiations. This latest appeal was made five days after about 200 Palestinian gunmen and unarmed civilians stormed into the Church of the Nativity in Bethlehem to escape Israeli soldiers. The Palestinians remained in the church with about 40 priests, Franciscan monks, and nuns, for 39 days as Israeli troops ringed the complex. Israel said that the armed Palestinians included terrorists wanted for killing Israeli soldiers and civilians.

This siege of one of the holiest sites in Christianity strained relations between the Vatican and Israel. According to Israel, the Palestinians were using the church as a sanctuary and the clergy inside as hostages; even so, Israel said that its troops were under orders not to fire at holy places. The Christian clergy inside, however, denied that they were hostages. A day after the siege began, the Vatican denounced acts of terrorism targeting Israel, but also sharply criticized Israel for imposing "unjust conditions and humiliations" on the Palestinians. It summoned the Israeli and U.S. ambassadors to the Holy See to discuss the crisis, and also called in a representative of the Arab League to demand an end "to indiscriminate acts of terrorism" against Israel.

On April 8, the Vatican issued a statement saying it was following events with "extreme worry," and warned Israel and the Palestinians to respect religious sites in the Holy Land that were central to the Christian, Jewish, and Muslim faiths. The Vatican called on Israel to give the Palestinians in the church safe passage to the Gaza Strip. Israeli president Katzav told the pope, in a letter, that Israeli forces would not permit armed Palestinians it considered terrorists to escape from the church. Katzav also indicated that Israel was ensuring that the church did not "become a focus of hostilities." Sporadic gun battles flared during the siege.

The standoff ended May 10 with an agreement to deport 13 Palestinian militants to Europe—three of them to Italy—and to send another 26 to Gaza. Soon after the Palestinians left the church, the Israeli army pulled out of Bethlehem. (The siege provided the backdrop for an Italian television drama, aired in December, in which the hero, an Italian TV cameraman, helps a Palestinian woman holed up in the church to give birth, and smuggles her baby out to a hospital. The film depicted Israelis as well-armed and intimidating soldiers.)

In June, the pope denounced a suicide bombing of a bus in Jerusalem that killed 19 Israelis. Expressing frustration that his pleas had gone unheeded, he said, "I tell those who plot and plan these acts of barbarity that they will have to answer before God."

In November, the Vatican announced it was giving $400,000 to Roman Catholic causes in Israel and the West Bank so as to improve life for Christians in the region and persuade them not to flee. The Vatican's charity arm noted that many Christians wanted to leave the Holy Land not only due to the fighting, but also because of economic hardships linked to the sharp drop in religious tourism.

In February, Syrian president Assad had an audience with the pope at the Vatican. In December, Moshe Katzav became the first Israeli president to visit the Holy See. He had a 15-minute audience with the pope and also met with the Vatican secretary of state. The Israeli embassy to the Vatican called the papal audience "warm and cordial" and reported that the pope said he felt the meeting could be a "turning point" in relations, possibly leading to a deepening of ties. The Vatican reiterated to Katzav that it supported both an Israeli and a Palestinian state, and urged Israel to allow "free access" to Bethlehem over Christmas. Israeli troops had reoccupied the city after a suicide bomb killed 11 Israelis in Jerusalem. According to the Israeli embassy, Katzav promised an Israeli troop withdrawal from Bethlehem "if there will not be warnings of terror operations." Meanwhile, it said, the Israeli president pledged that the army would "do everything possible to enable pilgrims to celebrate the Christmas holiday as appropriate."

At Christmas, the pope again reiterated his call for peace. He also came out against a possible war in Iraq.

Holocaust-Related Developments

January 27 was Holocaust Memorial Day in several European countries, including Italy. Dozens of cultural, commemorative, and educational events took place on or around that date, which marked the anniversary of the liberation of Auschwitz in 1945. Many schools scheduled special programs. In a televised interview, President Carlo Azeglio Ciampi said it was "our duty to remember. The force of memory must be passed on to our children and grandchildren." A project to set up a national museum in Ferrara to commemorate the Shoah advanced in the Chamber of Deputies, the lower house of Parliament. As part of the observances, a cache of valuables confiscated from a local Jew before World War II was restituted to the Jewish community in Trento, northern Italy. In Rome, the Jewish Culture Center, the German Goethe Institute, and the German embassy sponsored two days of events focusing on the Terezin ghetto. On January 28–29, Italian state television aired a two-part miniseries based on the life of Giorgio Perlasca, an Italian businessman who saved Jews in the Budapest ghetto during World War II. An exhibition devoted to Perlasca opened in the town of Abano Terme on February 3. Milan's Center for Contemporary Jewish Documentation published a comprehensive new book detailing the Shoah in Italy.

Two weeks before this outpouring of commemorative events, however, Amos Luzzatto, president of the Union of Italian Jewish Communities (UCEI), accused the government of being indifferent to Holocaust Memorial Day.

Tensions over historical revisionism that had been simmering in Italy for several years came to the fore during the January 27 observances in Trieste, the site of the only Nazi death camp to have operated on Italian soil. The Risiera di San Sabba served mainly as a transit camp, but as many as 1,000 Jews were killed there, in addition to thousands more Croats, Slovenes, and antifascist Italians. In 2001, the new rightist mayor of Trieste had appointed Roberto Menia, a leading figure in the National Alliance who had been a hard-line activist in the old neofascist MSI party, to be the city's chief cultural assessor, and thus head of the commission governing the Risiera, now a memorial museum.

Menia presided over the January 27 Holocaust memorial ceremonies at the Risiera, but his presence created controversy. Several thousand people attended the event. They included Amos Luzzatto, who gave a speech urging that bridges be built between religious and ethnic groups, and warning: "If we want a different future, we cannot lower a veil of forgetfulness over a past that is still all too present." Local Jews and members of other minority groups had asked Luzzatto to take part as a counterbalance to Menia. Still, about 300 left-wing demonstrators heckled Menia from outside the gates and waved posters bearing old photographs of him giving the fascist salute. About 100 of Trieste's 600 Jews boycotted the ceremony altogether, and instead held their own commemoration in the city's Jewish cemetery.

Nostalgia for fascism and for Mussolini remained a troubling issue. In April, thousands of posters bearing a photograph of Mussolini were plastered on walls all over Rome. Other posters put up at the same time, carrying the name of the neofascist National Social Front, urged citizens to place memorial flowers at an obelisk in Rome erected by Mussolini. The posters were apparently displayed to protest the commemorations of April 25, marking the liberation of Italy from Nazi occupation in 1945. During Liberation Day ceremonies this year, President Ciampi branded revisionism "unacceptable."

During a state visit to Italy in April, German president Johannes Rau paid homage to Italian victims of the Nazis in World War II. Accompanied by President Ciampi, he visited the village of Marzabotto where, in September 1944, nearly 2,000 Italian civilians were massacred by Nazi soldiers for allegedly harboring antifascist partisans. Also in April, Italy's highest appeals court upheld a life sentence for former SS officer Erich Priebke, who was sentenced in 1998 to life in prison for his role in the March 1944 execution of 335 Roman men and boys (75 of them Jewish) in reprisal for a partisan attack that killed 33 German military police. In his mid-80s and in ill health, Priebke was serving his sentence under house arrest.

As part of ceremonies on October 16 marking the anniversary of the deportation of Roman Jews to Auschwitz, the Survivors of the Shoah Visual History Foundation and the Italian Central State Archive announced they would join forces to catalog some 400 Italian-language testimonies of Holocaust survivors. These would be made available to educate Italian young people about the Shoah. Other events marking the anniversary included a torchlight march through downtown Rome, religious services, an exhibition on art and memory, and a conference on anti-Semitism held at City Hall. The main piazza in the old Rome ghetto was renamed "October 16, 1943 Piazza."

Anti-Semitism and Racism

Jewish leaders and individuals expressed deep and continuing concern about a pro-Palestinian, anti-Israel bias in the local media, and its likely connection to what they perceived as a growing atmosphere of anti-Semitism in everyday discourse.

In her attack on anti-Semitism in April, Oriana Fallaci (not herself Jewish) warned of "the resurgence of a new fascism, a new Nazism" (see above, p. 442). The thousands of participants at the Israel Day rally on April 15 cheered her article. Some politicians applauded her, but others condemned her tone as inflammatory and accused her of sowing racial and religious hatred.

UCEI president Amos Luzzatto warned often during the year about the rise of a culture of anti-Semitism rooted in Catholicism, Islam, and a left-wing mentality uncritically supportive of third-world countries and causes. He and other Italian Jews feared that pro-Palestinian political sentiments were bringing back classic anti-Semitic rhetoric in both public discourse and private conversation.

In June, in an address to the UCEI Congress, Pierfernando Casini, speaker of the Chamber of Deputies, minimized these concerns. Anti-Semitism, he said, "could be the expression of a crazed and criminal fragment of society, but not certainly a mass phenomenon. To evoke the presence of anti-Semitism in our society, or in some political forces, or in the Catholic Church, demonstrates a mistaken image of our country."

Italy did not suffer the wave of anti-Semitic violence that hit other countries, such as France, but there were a few confrontations. In June, Yasha Reibman, a Jewish member of the pro-Israel Radical Party, was roughed up by a group of extreme left-wingers for carrying an Israeli flag during a gay pride march in Milan. Also in June, several dozen young Roman Jews jeered and harassed a leading Italian pro-Palestinian activist when he tried to have lunch in a restaurant in Rome's old Jewish ghetto quarter. Riot police led Vittorio Agnoletto to safety after he was trapped in the restaurant for more than two hours. Agnoletto was the spokesman for Italy's main antiglobalization movement. In April, he and other members of a pro-Palestinian Italian delegation had been turned back by Israeli authorities when they landed at Ben-Gurion Airport.

In July, vandals smashed about three dozen tombs in the Jewish section of Rome's Verano cemetery on the eve of Tisha B'Av. The desecration shocked the Jewish community and drew sharp condemnation from government leaders, the pope, and international Jewish organizations. Jewish groups and officials initially viewed the desecration as part of a wave of attacks on Jews and Jewish institutions in several countries, linked to the conflict in the Middle East. Police, however, focused their investigation on local cemetery-maintenance rackets, and at the end of July charged an unauthorized cemetery worker with extortion, contempt, desecration, and damaging of tombs, and placed five other people under investigation. At the time of the attack, U.S. Anti-Defamation League national director Abraham Foxman was in Rome to meet with Prime Minister Berlusconi as part of a series of consultations with European leaders on how to combat the new wave of anti-Semitism.

Traditional extreme right-wing anti-Semitism remained a problem. A big gathering of skinheads from all over Europe was held in February in the village of Sarentino, in northern Italy. In May, the tiny fringe neo-fascist Ordine Nuovo group held a meeting in Trieste. It scheduled another meeting, which it billed as an international convention, in Verona, but local authorities barred the event following protests from the Simon Wiesenthal Center and other groups. It was to have been called "To the Memory of Millions of Civilian Victims of Democracy and Their Lies," and was to have included the participation of Holocaust deniers and anti-Semites. In October, more than 8,000 people gathered in Mussolini's hometown, Predappio, to mark the 80th anniversary of the 1922 march on Rome that brought him to power. About 80 right-wing extremists marked the day with an anti-immigrant march in Rome.

JEWISH COMMUNITY

Demography

About 28,000 Jews were officially registered as members of Italian Jewish communities, but the actual number of Jews in the country was believed to be between 30,000 and 40,000. Three-quarters of Italy's Jews lived in two cities where there was a full infrastructure for an active Jewish life: Rome, with about 15,000 Jews, and Milan, with about 10,000. The rest of the country's Jews were scattered in 19 other towns and cities, mostly in northern and central Italy, in communities ranging from a handful of Jews to a thousand or so. About half of Italy's Jews were native born, and the other half were immigrants who had come over the past few decades. Between one-third and one-half of Rome's Jews were members of families that had emigrated from Libya following the Six-Day War of 1967. At the beginning of 2002, in fact, the Rome Jewish Culture Center held a daylong event, including an exhibition and food-tasting, dedicated to the history and culture of Libyan Jews. The Milan Jewish community included recent arrivals from more than two dozen countries. The largest contingent was Iranian, with most of the rest coming from other Muslim states.

Communal Affairs

Orthodoxy was still the only officially recognized form of Judaism in Italy, encompassing three ritual traditions: Sephardi, Ashkenazi, and Italian, the latter a local rite that evolved from the Jewish community that lived in the country before the destruction of the Second Temple. Most Italian Jews, however, were not strictly observant, and even many of the observant Italian-born Jews were highly acculturated, with a strong Italian as well as Jewish identity. On the other hand, many of the Jewish immigrants from Muslim countries were very observant and not as acculturated. Chabad-Lubavitch maintained its strong presence, particularly in Rome, Milan, and Venice, where the movement ran a yeshivah. Milan was the site of the Chabad-run Rabbinical Center of Europe. In February, nearly 100 Orthodox European rabbis attended a seminar on Jewish law at the center. Also in attendance was Rabbi Israel Meir Lau, the Ashkenazi chief rabbi of Israel.

In February, Dr. Riccardo Di Segni was formally installed as Rome's chief rabbi, at a crowded ceremony in the main synagogue. Di Segni, 52, replaced Elio Toaff, who retired in October 2001 after 50 years in the post. Di Segni, who was also a medical doctor, had been elected the new chief rabbi in November.

Reform and Conservative streams were not recognized by the Union of Italian Jewish Communities and did not officially exist. Nonetheless, Lev Chadash, an independent liberal Jewish association affiliated with the World Union for Progressive Judaism, operated in Milan, and hosted visiting rabbis from London. Over the year it expanded its activities. It opened permanent premises and a prayer room, held regular weekly services, and, in November, received a Torah scroll. Another similar congregation, Beth Shalom, was established in Milan in the fall. Established community leaders criticized the new groups, some warning that they could lead to an outright schism in Italian Jewry.

Italian Jews had a well-organized (though financially troubled) infrastructure of schools, clubs, associations, youth organizations, and other services, including a rabbinical college. The women's organization ADEI-WIZO was active nationwide, sponsoring numerous bazaars, lectures, meetings, and other social, cultural, and fund-raising events. Jewish community and culture centers in Milan and Rome also had a full schedule of such activities. In April, the Union of Italian Jewish Communities held its annual four-day Moked cultural and educational conference. This year's theme was Jewish identity as reflected in the Jewish community and the Jewish family. In June, the Rome Jewish community center hosted a conference, organized by the European Association of Jewish Community Centers, for directors of such centers from all over the continent.

Italian Jews, many of whom had close family ties with Israelis, followed the continuing conflict between Israel and the Palestinians with great concern. Italians were among the dead and injured in terrorist attacks. Israeli soldier Yochai Porat, 26, whose family came from Rome, was killed by a Palestinian sniper on March 3. Danielle Manchell, 22, who died in a terrorist attack on the Matza restaurant in Haifa on March 31, was born in Rome and spent her first ten years there. An Italian student was among those wounded in the terrorist attack at the Hebrew University in July. Furthermore, an Italian photojournalist was killed covering violence in the West Bank in March. During the summer, Italian Jews organized vacations in Italy for dozens of Israelis, including about 60 children, who were victims of terrorism.

Jews worried about the negative portrayal of Israel in the media, the pro-Palestinian stance of many political parties and public figures, and the "one-sided pacifism" of peace advocates who aligned themselves with the Palestinian cause (see above, p. 442). In the spring, a Roman Jewish activist group, I Ragazzi del '48 (The '48 Guys), granted awards to more than a dozen journalists whose reporting, it felt, was unbiased.

These broader issues, and not internal Jewish problems, dominated the national congress of the Union of Italian Jewish Communities in June. The congress is held every four years to elect national officers who chart community policy and also serve as the official political face of Italian Jewry. Amos Luzzatto, a physician and Jewish scholar who had headed the organization for the previous four years, was reelected.

The run-up to the congress showcased political differences within the community over whether Diaspora Jews had the right—some would say the duty—to criticize Israeli policies. Delegates were split between "conservatives," who unreservedly supported the government of Israel, and "progressives," critical of Prime Minister Sharon's course. However, Israel-bashing in the media moved the two groups closer to each other. Two leading media celebrities headed the competing factions in the elections to the union's board. Gad Lerner, a well-known TV personality and longtime leftist activist, led the progressives. In a published open letter and in television commentaries, he accused Italian leftists of anti-Israel bias. The conservative Fiamma Nirenstein, Israel correspondent for Turin's *La Stampa* newspaper, urged greater resistance to granting concessions to the Palestinians. Her book, *L'abbandono — Come l'Occidente ha tradito gli Ebrei* (The Abandonment: How the West Has Betrayed the Jews), caused a stir with its denunciation of Europe's failure to support Israel and to counter rising anti-Semitism. In the end, the number of "progressives" elected to the board was slightly greater than the number of "conservatives."

The congress passed resolutions that condemned official delay in confronting the "new anti-Semitism," and expressed "apprehension" at the "systematic manipulation of information about Israel and the history and nature of the Arab-Israeli conflict." Delegates called "forcefully" on Europe to assume a more balanced position on the Middle East, to ensure the accurate dissemination of information about Israel and the Middle East conflict, and to further authentic peace initiatives.

On October 9, Jews marked the 20th anniversary of the Palestinian terrorist attack on Rome's main synagogue. The attack, on members of the congregation leaving Shemini Atzeret services, killed a toddler, Stefano Tache, and wounded 100 others. A newly established library and the Jewish community's nursery school were named for the boy. Since that attack, police had kept Jewish sites and institutions in Rome under constant armed guard. Coinciding with the anniversary, the October issue of the Rome Jewish monthly, *Shalom,* included a nine-page manual of anti-terrorism security guidelines called "Some Useful Advice on How to Live More Safely." Prepared by Rome Jewish community security director Gianni Zarfati, the brochure provided a 24-hour hotline number for use in case of emergency. This was not the first time that the community had issued security guidelines, but Jewish leaders explained that now the information was being distributed with *Shalom* in order to reach as many Jewish families as possible.

Jewish-Catholic and Interfaith Relations

After the pope, in his New Year's Day message, set the tone by calling on monotheistic religions to condemn the use of violence, there were a number of interfaith initiatives throughout the year.

January 17 marked the Catholic Church's annual Day of Dialogue with the Jews. At a meeting in Rome, the city's new chief rabbi, Riccardo Di Segni, gave a major address in which he asserted that a prerequisite to sincere Christian-Jewish dialogue was Christian agreement that the Jews did not need Jesus to achieve salvation.

To coincide with the Day of Dialogue, the Vatican published a Polish translation of a book-length document, *The Jewish People and the Holy Scriptures in the Christian Bible,* the fruit of years of scholarly work by the Pontifical Biblical Commission. The book had originally appeared in the fall of 2001 without publicity, and only in French and Italian versions. Signed by the Vatican's chief theologian, Cardinal Joseph Ratzinger, prefect of the Congregation for the Doctrine of the Faith, the document said that Catholics should regard what Christians call the Old Testament not just as literature but as a source of moral teachings. In addition, it explicitly stated that "The Jewish wait for the Messiah is not in vain." Jews and Christians, it went on, shared the wait for the messiah, but while Jews waited for the first coming, Christians waited for the second. The text also expressed regret that certain passages in the New Testament condemning individual Jews had been used to justify anti-Semitism. Nowhere in the New Testament, it declared, could one find passages reflecting "an attitude of scorn, hostility or persecution of Jews as Jews." Jewish observers considered the document a potential turning point in the official Roman Catholic view of Jews and their Holy Scriptures.

On January 24, about 200 rabbis, imams, priests, patriarchs and other representatives from a dozen world religions joined the pope in the central Italian town of Assisi to pray for peace and condemn violence committed in the name of God. In the wake of September 11 and the war in Afghanistan, the pope had invited them for a Day of Prayer for Peace in the World. The aim was to stress that religion must never be the excuse for violence, war, or terrorism. During the day, participants read statements recognizing that religions are all too often misused to justify conflict and exploit inequality. In a concluding declaration, they jointly pledged to work for peace and declared their "firm conviction that violence and terrorism are incompatible with the authentic spirit of religion." They committed themselves to "doing everything possible to eliminate the root causes of terrorism" and also pledged themselves to the principles of dialogue and forgiveness.

Also in January, the first Middle East Interfaith Summit took place in Alexandria, Egypt. The two-day meeting, which drew very little publicity, brought together Jewish, Christian, and Muslim religious leaders from across the region. A joint declaration condemned "killing innocents in the name of God" and called for "a religiously sanctioned ceasefire, respected and observed on all sides."

About a week later, the European Jewish Congress organized a high-profile meeting between Jews and Catholics. Attended by senior Vatican officials, it took place at the Paris City Hall.

In early September, Rome's chief rabbi, Israeli minister Dan Meridor, and the Palestinian Sari Nuseibeh, president of Al-Quds University, were among more than 450 representatives of world religions at a three-day seminar in Palermo. This was the annual meeting on Faiths and Cultures within Conflict and Dialogue sponsored by the Roman Catholic Sant'-Egidio community. Seminar topics included "Israelis and Palestinians: Dialogue about the Future," and "Three Faiths and the Book," and there was a roundtable discussion on the theme: "After September 11: An Unavoidable Clash of Civilizations?"

The Jewish world's official dialogue partner with the Vatican changed its leadership. The International Jewish Committee for Interreligious Consultations (IJCIC) elected Rabbi Israel Singer of the World Jewish Congress as its new chairman effective July 1, replacing Seymour Reich. It also named Rabbi Joel Meyers, executive vice president of the Conservative movement's Rabbinical Assembly, as chairman of its governing board.

In August, "Reflections on Covenant and Mission," an unofficial document drafted by a group of American Catholic and Jewish scholars, was posted on the Web site of the U.S. Conference of Catholic Bishops, which cosponsored it along with the National Council of Synagogues. In it, the scholars said that the Church's goal in its relations with Jews should be dialogue, not conversion (see above, p. 100). It explained, "In view of our conviction that Jews are in an eternal covenant with God, we renounce missionary efforts directed at converting Jews."

In October, a conference in Rome marked the 37th anniversary of *Nos-*

tra Aetate, the Second Vatican Council document that opened the way to the contemporary Jewish-Catholic dialogue. *Nostra Aetate* deplored anti-Semitism and repudiated the charge that all Jews throughout the generations were collectively responsible for killing Jesus. During the meeting, Cardinal Walter Kasper, the Vatican official in charge of relations with Jews, affirmed that the Roman Catholic Church was more committed than ever to improving relations with Jews. The conference was organized by the Dionysia Center, a Rome-based cultural institute that promoted dialogue among religions and peoples. Other participants included the Israeli Jewish scholar Rabbi Adin Steinsaltz.

In February, the Vatican announced that it would begin opening some of its secret archives for the period before, during, and immediately after World War II in order to clarify the role of the Holy See and Pope Pius XII during the Holocaust. It said that the first material to be released would be diplomatic documents dealing with relations between the Vatican and Germany from 1922 to 1939, the period when the future Pius XII served as Vatican representative in Germany and then Vatican secretary of state. Documents relating to Vatican-German relations during Pius XII's papacy would begin to become available in about three years.

In December, the Vatican announced that the first documents would be opened to scholars on February 15, 2003. These would include records from the Vatican diplomatic missions in Berlin and Munich, as well as a series of other documents relating to the rise of Nazism and the "condemnation of racism." However, it reported, the Berlin diplomatic archive for the years 1931–34 had been "nearly completely destroyed or dispersed" during the 1945 bombing of the city and a fire at the apostolic nuncio's palace.

Culture

As every year, there were numerous Jewish cultural events, some organized by Jewish communities, some by private organizations, some by civic and state bodies, and some by a combination of sources. The Israeli embassy sponsored performances, exhibits, and appearances by Israeli cultural figures. The following is a small but representative sample of Jewish cultural events throughout the year.

On the annual European Day of Jewish Culture, held this year on June 16, dozens of sites of Jewish heritage, Jewish museums, and other venues in 45 Italian cities and towns were opened to the public, drawing some 18,000 visitors. Special performances, exhibits, and concerts were staged.

In October, tourism officials and local authorities in Trieste introduced a set of Jewish heritage itineraries in the Friuli-Venezia Giulia region.

There were several festivals devoted to aspects of Jewish culture. The annual Klezmer Music Festival took place in Ancona in July. A Jewish culture festival in Turin, September 30–October 6, featured lectures, exhibits, performances, concerts, and food tastings. The fifth annual "Pitifest" Jewish film festival took place in the Tuscan town of Manciano in December. It was sponsored by the Italian Ministry of Culture, local authorities, the Israeli embassy, and Jewish organizations.

There were many concerts of Jewish music by local and foreign Jewish musicians. In February, the Italian Jewish music group Lokshen Quartet gave a concert of klezmer music, Yiddish song, and Jewish liturgical music at the Quirinale Palace, the official residence of Italy's president. A CD of Italian Jewish liturgical music, *Italian Jewish Musical Traditions,* was released in association with Hebrew University and Rome's Accademia Nationale di Santa Cecilia. It was based on recordings made in the 1950s by Italian Jewish ethnomusicologist Leo Levi.

There were numerous Jewish-themed exhibits and performances. In January, *The Death of Klinghoffer,* an opera by American composer John Adams about the killing of American Jewish passenger Leon Klinghoffer during the 1984 hijacking of the Italian cruise ship *Achille Lauro,* was performed in Ferrara and Modena. A series of talks, films, and exhibitions in Rome in February commemorated the writings of Etty Hillesum, a Dutch woman who died in Auschwitz in 1943 at the age of 29 and kept a diary chronicling her Holocaust experiences from March 1941 through September 1942. In the summer, Rome's Palazzo Barberini hosted "Palestina 1927," an exhibition of photographs taken in Palestine in the 1920s by photographer Luciano Morpurgo. In July, top fashion design graduates from Tel Aviv's Shenkar College presented shows in Rome, Gorizia, and Trieste. In October, stage artist Enrico Fink premiered a production based on the biblical story of Jonah. In November, an exhibit of the works of the Italian Jewish painter Clemente Pugiese Levi (1855–1936) opened in his native town, Vercelli. Also in November, popular Jewish performer Moni Ovadia premiered his new production of *Fiddler on the Roof,* which was performed partly in Yiddish.

As usual, numerous books on Jewish topics or by Jewish authors were published, and there were book launches, readings, roundtables, and other literary happenings throughout the year. The Milan bookstore Tikkun, which specialized in Jewish books, sponsored readings and other events, including a series of lectures and performances about Jewish music, from January through March. Several Israeli authors, including David Grossman, Aharon Appelfeld, Alon Altaras, Nava Semel, and Uzi Weill, gave readings and lecture tours in Italy. Appelfeld won the second annual ADEI-WIZO literary prize for his book *That Which I Loved,* published this year in Italian translation. A.B. Yehoshua gave a well-attended series of four lectures at the Roma Tre University in November. He and Grossman inaugurated and closed the first International Festival of Literature, held in Rome May 21–June 20.

In March, *Fossoli: Transito per Auschwitz,* a new book by Danilo Sacchi about the World War II Fossoli transit camp, was discussed at a roundtable at Rome's City Hall, the Campidoglio. A similar panel discussion was held at the Campidoglio in October based on a special issue of the Jewish intellectual journal *La Rassegna Mensile di Israel* that was devoted to the impact on European Jewry of the fall of communism. That same journal issue was the focus of a daylong international seminar at Rome's Goethe Institute in December.

Numerous conferences and seminars took place. In April, in the town of Agira, Sicily, there was a conference on Jews in Sicily. In November, a daylong conference on martyrdom in the Jewish, Christian, and Muslim experiences took place at Milan University. That same month, the Jewish Museum in Bologna hosted a three-day conference of the Association of European Jewish Museums. Representatives of some 23 Jewish museums from 14 European countries attended. Daniel Dratwa, director of the Jewish Museum in Brussels, was elected the new chairman of the association. Work proceeded, meanwhile, on plans to enlarge, modernize, and revamp the Jewish Museum in Rome, changing it from a traditional display of Judaica to a museum that also incorporated narrative history. Donations from a private Catholic study group paid for the restoration of several items in the historical archives of the Jewish community of Rome. In December, a center for Jewish studies was established at Rome's Tor Vergata University, thanks to an agreement between the university and the Rome Jewish community.

Personalia

In January, journalist Fiamma Nirenstein was awarded the Women for Journalism prize. Later in the year, she won several literary prizes for her book *L'abbandono—Come l'Occidente ha tradito gli Ebrei* (The Abandonment: How the West Has Betrayed the Jews). In February, Rome's chief rabbi emeritus, Elio Toaff, 86, was awarded the Golden Livornian award by his hometown, Livorno, for his "high political and human importance." On February 8, Genoveffa Astrologo, the oldest member of the Rome Jewish community, turned 101. Milan's former chief rabbi, Elia Kopciowski, died in July at age 81. Writer Ferruccio Fölker, born in Trieste in 1921, died in Milan in August. In October, American producer and director Bruce Paltrow, father of Oscar-winning actress Gwyneth Paltrow, died at age 58 while vacationing in Italy. Prominent journalist Willy Molco died in December, aged 59.

During the year, Yad Vashem in Jerusalem recognized several Italians as Righteous Gentiles. In April, writer Umberto Eco received an honorary degree from Hebrew University. In July, the Golden Dove of Peace award was given in Rome to Italian Luisa Morgantini, along with Palestinian Suhad Amery and Israeli Terry Greenblatt, for their involvement in the peace group Donne in Nero (Women in Black). In December, UCEI president Amos Luzzatto was awarded the San Giusto d'Oro award from the city of Trieste. This award honors people born in Trieste or with Triestine origins who "honor the city in Italy and the world."

RUTH ELLEN GRUBER

Switzerland

National Affairs

T HE YEAR WAS ONE OF closure for Switzerland, but also one of a new openness. What closed was the Holocaust chapter in Swiss history, as most of the special agencies that had been created to address Switzerland's role during World War II and the "dormant accounts" of Jews in Swiss banks completed their work. The new openness was signaled by a decision of the Swiss people to join the United Nations: Switzerland became the 190th member of the world body on September 10, 2002.

Switzerland still struggled over its refugee policy. In October, Swiss citizens rejected by a narrow margin (3,422 votes) an initiative of the Swiss People's Party (SVP/UDC) "against abuses in asylum laws" that would have barred refugees living in bordering countries—France, Germany, Italy, and Austria—from requesting asylum in Switzerland.

Israel and the Middle East

The general climate of opinion turned increasingly against Israel over the course of the year. There were more pro-Palestinian rallies than in previous years, greater distribution of anti-Israel material on streetcorners, and shriller calls for boycotting the Jewish state.

Pro-Palestinian organizations such as Urgence Palestine led weekly demonstrations and vigils where the banners indicated the agenda : "Stop Repression in Palestine," "Stop the Massacre," "Against Imperialism and Zionism." While most of the participants were Muslims, left-wing Swiss citizens and a handful of anti-Zionist Jews attended as well. After many of these demonstrations, graffiti were sprayed on Jewish buildings, including Geneva's Holocaust memorial, located in front of the main synagogue, where swastikas and several inscriptions of the word "Nazis" were written. A growing number of similar graffiti equating Israel, Ariel Sharon, and/or the Magen David (Star of David) symbol with Nazism, fascism, and/or bloodshed were found in school classrooms, on public buildings, and on sidewalks.

Programs offering a unilaterally pro-Palestinian view of the Middle East conflict took place all around the country, featuring Palestinian journalists, left-wing filmmakers, and human-rights activists, always presenting Israel as the aggressor and the Palestinians as victims.

Petitions calling for the boycott of products from the occupied Territories multiplied in 2002. Signatures were often solicited and collected at street stands set up on market days, and in front of well-attended shopping malls. The Swiss media echoed such calls and pretended to investigate whether some fruit grown in the West Bank and Gaza, picked by Palestinian workers, had deceitfully been labeled " made in Israel" so as to evade the boycott. Since no such trail could actually be discovered, consumers were urged : "when in doubt, abstain," that is, not to buy anything bearing the word "Israel." Leaflets were handed out to help customers at food stores identify the bar code of goods of Israeli origin, whether vegetables, fruits, or groceries. Thus, certain Israeli products traditionally sold in Switzerland all year round, such as small potatoes, melons, and strawberries, mysteriously disappeared from supermarkets.

Boycott ideas were voiced at a much higher level in April when the Ministry of Foreign Affairs asked the Ministry of Defense to "examine the means of restricting military cooperation with Israel," and the Ministry of Economy to "draw the consequences" of "possible violations of trade agreements by Israel" — a reference to goods produced in Gaza and the West Bank but allegedly sold under the "made in Israel" label. The two ministries receiving the requests did not take public action, and the issue was not raised again in governmental circles. The reason for backing off might have been the fact that Switzerland stood to lose more money than Israel if trade agreements were suspended, since Switzerland exported many more goods to Israel — high-precision tools, chemical products, metal, machinery — than it imported from the Jewish state.

Criticism of Israel came from politicians and other public figures, and from extremists both on the right and the left, who joined forces in denouncing "imperialist Zionism" and charging that the "Jewish lobby" manipulated the U.S. government to give Israel unconditional support.

Muslim leaders in Switzerland were especially outspoken, among them Tariq and Hani Ramadan, grandsons and followers of Hassan al-Bana, the Egyptian founder of the fundamentalist Muslim Brotherhood. While Tariq defended Islam in sophisticated and moderate-sounding language, Hani, head of the Islamic Center of Geneva, explicitly called for the strict application of the sharia (Muslim law) and advocated an anti-Zionism that bordered on anti-Semitism. While his comparison of Israel to Nazi Germany and his justification of suicide attacks against Israelis drew no outrage, he went too far in September 2002, in an op-ed piece published in the French daily *Le Monde.* There he declared that if the world followed Islamic principles, there would be no AIDS epidemic, and stated that the two Nigerian women convicted under sharia law of adultery should indeed be stoned to death. Complaints both in France and Switzerland induced the Geneva minister of education to suspend him from his teaching position in a French-language junior high school in the city on the grounds that being a teacher—and thus a civil servant—was incompatible with support for execution by stoning. Hani Ramadan appealed the decision, but early in 2003 the government of Geneva confirmed his firing on different grounds, ruling that one cannot be both an imam and a public-school teacher at the same time.

As the general climate in the country turned more anti-Israel, the Jewish community asserted a higher profile in defending the Jewish state. The first sign of this occurred in April, in the wake of media reports about an Israeli "massacre" of Palestinians in Jenin (see above, p. 203). A number of Swiss Jews began media campaigns to denounce the biased coverage, some writing dozens of letters-to-the-editor questioning journalistic ethics, others buying advertising space in newspapers to publicize their opinions. Jewish leaders met with editors and reporters to discuss concrete examples of breaches in professional ethics in the reporting and publication of certain stories.

Following numerous anti-Israel statements by Foreign Minister Joseph Deiss regarding the events in Jenin, the presidents of the Jewish communities of Geneva and Lausanne wrote a letter of protest to Deiss. In his response weeks later, Deiss did not go into detail, but stated that Switzerland's position was based on international law, and that he also condemned Palestinian suicide attacks. The Jewish leaders followed up with a second letter, questioning how the foreign minister could claim to be evenhanded given his singling out of Israel regarding alleged violations of the Fourth Geneva Convention, his systematic critique of Israeli military actions, and the inconsistent nature of his opposition to suicide attacks. In his answer to this letter, Deiss admitted a double standard, clearly stating that respect for international law could not be demanded from the Palestinian Authority as stringently as from Israel.

Alfred Donath, president of the Swiss Federation of Jewish Communities, gave a forceful speech at the annual meeting of the federation in May. He accused Switzerland of indirectly funding, through its financial aid to the UN Relief and Works Agency (UNRWA), which ran Palestinian refugee camps, textbooks that contained anti-Zionist and anti-Semitic content. He was immediately attacked in the press for his charges, and received a considerable amount of hate mail, including threats. Swiss national radio launched an investigation into Donath's charges about the final destination of Swiss humanitarian aid to the Palestinians, but eventually reported that it could not trace the money.

The Zurich-based organization David, Center Against Anti-Semitism and Defamation, filed a suit with the Swiss Press Council after a newspaper called Israeli prime minister Ariel Sharon a war criminal. The council ruled that this did not constitute libel, and found in favor of the newspaper.

The only supporters of Israel outside the Jewish community were Christian evangelicals, more than 1,500 of whom gathered at a pro-Israel rally in Bern. The media, which often reported on pro-Palestinian rallies with fewer than 50 participants, barely covered it.

Anti-Semitism and Extremism

Beside the anti-Semitic fallout of the Israeli-Palestinian conflict, another national debate triggered a serious wave of anti-Jewish feeling: the government-proposed lifting of the longstanding legal prohibition on *shehitah* (Jewish ritual slaughter).

Since 1893, Jews (and Muslims) were forbidden to slaughter animals according to their religious laws. The impetus for this ban was an anti-Semitic attempt to limit Jewish immigration into Switzerland (there being no Muslim immigration to speak of at that time). Since then, kosher and halal meat had to be imported from France and Germany.

In late 2001, the Swiss government decided to repeal the law as a sign of religious tolerance. The popular reaction was unexpectedly hostile, especially from spokespersons for societies protecting animals, who often lapsed into anti-Semitic and racist rhetoric. Jews and Muslims were accused of following inhumane customs stemming from an uncivilized age that were not acceptable in modern Switzerland. Some went so far as to suggest that observant Jews and Muslims "either become vegetarian or leave the country." The media gave considerably more coverage to the opponents of change than to those affected by it, and the government, which had ignited the debate, remained silent. Jewish leaders were mailed hundred of hate letters ("Jews, kill the cows in your kibbutz," "Nazis"), and one received death threats. The threatened woman (the author of this article) sought to file suit against her tormentor in Geneva, but the public prosecutor dismissed the case with the argument that the man who made the threats "never had the intention to kill," and was merely expressing his strong feelings.

At the high point of the debate, in February 2002, two formal initiatives were launched to ban the import of kosher meat into Switzerland, an even greater limitation than the status quo. Each of the initiators had until 2003 (for one the deadline was July, for the other it was September) to collect 100,000 signatures and thus put the issue to a popular referendum, which would occur in 2004 at the earliest. The author of one of the the initiatives was Erwin Kessler, president of Verein gegen Tierfabrik (Association against Animal Factories), who had already been convicted twice for anti-Semitic statements, such as equating kosher slaughter to Nazi treatment of the Jews.

Ritual slaughter was one of the matters addressed by far-right leaders in their publications, among other traditional anti-Semitic themes. For years, the most active far-right group had been Vérité & Justice (Truth and Justice), headed by Jürgen Graf, Philippe Brennenstuhl, and René-Louis Berclaz. It promoted Holocaust denial and allegations of Jewish wealth, greed, and power. Graf escaped to Iran in 2000 to avoid a prison sentence in Switzerland, and the other two men were sentenced to prison terms in 2002 for publishing Holocaust-denial articles in their bulletin, which the judges ruled a form of racial discrimination. Their organization was disbanded by the court.

Veteran neo-Nazi Gaston-Armand Amaudruz, sentenced to a three-month prison sentence in 2001, was due to serve it beginning in January 2003. Until that date, however, and in spite of his conviction, Amaudruz continued to publish his monthly *Courrier du Continent,* a 12-page bulletin advocating racism, anti-Semitism, and Holocaust denial.

In April 2002, Jürg Scherrer, an elected official from the city of Biel, gave an interview to Swiss national radio in which he supported French far-right leader Jean-Marie Le Pen's statement that "gas chambers are a detail of history." Local antiracist groups sued him, but the judge decided that Scherrer's words were too vague to make him liable to prosecution.

Skinheads were also active on the far right. Swiss Federal Police estimated that there were about 1,000 of them in the country, and that their ranks were growing. They held concerts and gatherings, published and distributed propaganda (CDs, films, insigna, clothes, magazines), and collected weapons. However, they still lacked a charismatic leader to unify the scattered groups and give the movement cohesion.

On the intellectual end of the far right, Geneva lawyer Pascal Junod continued to host lectures by extremist figures from France, such as Roger Garaudy and Pierre Vial. Like skinhead events, Junod's evenings were by personal invitation only, and, under the Swiss law banning public expressions of racism, one could not be sued for racist statements uttered at private gatherings.

Some other ongoing anti-Semitic publications that had small but loyal readerships were Geneviève Aubry's *L'Atout,* Ernst Indlekofer's *Recht + Freiheit,* and Claude and Mariette Paschoud's *Le Pamphlet.*

Holocaust-Related Matters

The year 2002 saw the culmination of Switzerland's reckoning with the record of its actions regarding Jews during and after the Holocaust.

In March, the historical commission headed by Professor Jean-François Bergier completed publication of its 25-volume, 14,000-page work, covering all aspects of Switzerland's policies during World War II — refugees; Jewish-owned artworks and insurance policies; the provision of electricity, money transfers, armaments, and gold to Germany; the role of its legal system and the press; and much more. The conclusion of the final report provided a nuanced analysis of Switzerland's responsibilities, clearing the nation of some unjustified accusations (no trains carrying deported people ever crossed Switzerland), as well as confirming serious wrongdoing (abuse of neutrality; requiring the J-stamp on passports of German citizens who were Jewish; turning down refugees at the border). The study recommended that Switzerland come to terms with its history and that this five-year research project mark the beginning rather than the end of discussions, debates, and evaluations. The commission was officially dissolved on March 31, 2002.

The Special Fund for needy Holocaust victims completed the distribution of $175 million (298 million Swiss francs) donated for humanitarian purposes by Swiss banks and industries. The fund, headed by Rolf Bloch, identified beneficiaries around the world, among them Jews, political prisoners, gypsies, Christians of Jewish descent, Jehovah's Witnesses, homosexuals, and non-Jews who had helped Jews. The fund was dissolved in December 2002, with the remaining $8 million to be shared between a Jewish organization in Switzerland helping needy Holocaust victims and the Swiss Red Cross Fund for victims of war and torture.

The Swiss Solidarity Foundation, proposed by President Kaspar Villiger in 1997, was intended to use more than $4 billion (7 billion Swiss francs) from the national gold reserves for humanitarian projects. Originally, Holocaust victims were included on the list of proposed beneficiaries, but political and popular pressure later forced them off. In the end it made no difference, since, in a popular referendum held in September 2002, the Swiss people (51.1 percent of them) rejected the entire idea. The nationalist Swiss People's Party (SVP/UDC) proposed that the money go toward social security, but this too was rejected by popular vote. No new suggestions were under consideration for the use of this gold.

The global settlement reached in August 1998 between Swiss banks and the lawyers bringing class-action suits in the name of Holocaust victims or their heirs determined that $1.25 billion would be distributed, $800 million to heirs of dormant-account holders, and the rest distributed to other victims of the Nazis (see AJYB 2000, p. 331). Since many of the potential beneficiaries were very old, new rules were established to accelerate and simplify the distribution process. By the end of 2002, it was expected that 32,000 requests would be honored. Forced laborers would receive $1,450, refugees $3,625, and people incarcerated in Switzerland $750. The Claims Conference would receive $10 million on behalf of survivors who were robbed of their property.

In December, Stuart Eizenstat, the former U.S. undersecretary of state who had handled restitution issues during the Clinton administration, published a book, *Imperfect Justice,* about his experiences negotiating restitution claims. Before the book was even published and its contents discussed, the design for its cover created a major controversy in Switzerland. It showed a Swiss flag (white cross on red background) covered with a swastika made of gold bars. Political leaders, journalists, and historians complained that the design unfairly smeared their country's reputation. Two lawyers filed suits against Eizenstat for defaming the Swiss emblem. Some Swiss reacted hysterically, sending anti-Semitic e-mails to the World Economic Forum, which had invited Eizenstat to speak at its annual meting in Davos, Switzerland, in January 2003. The Swiss Federation of Jewish Communities stated that it too was shocked by the cover, which, it charged, reinforced the very association of Jews with money that it had tried to combat during the controversy over the dormant accounts. Eizenstat gave numerous interviews to the Swiss press in which he stated that he was sorry if the cover shocked some people, but that it did reflect the historical reality of Switzerland's wartime attitude. He added that the content of the book gave a balanced and fair analysis.

JEWISH COMMUNITY

The size of the Jewish community remained stable at around 18,000 people, some 0.25 percent of Switzerland's population of seven million.

In reaction to the media's biased coverage of the Israeli-Palestinian conflict, the Swiss Federation of Jewish Communities created the Jüdisches Medienforum Schweiz (Jewish Forum of Swiss Media) in August. Its goals were to observe and analyze how the Swiss media covered issues related to Israel and Jews, and to counter anti-Semitic statements and attempts to delegitimize Israel. It began its work in the German-speaking part of Switzerland, where it was headed by Prof. Ekkehard W. Stegemann of the University of Basel's theology department.

Yitzhak Dayan, former rabbi of Salonika, was elected rabbi of the Communauté Israélite de Genève, Geneva's traditional congregation.

In December 2002, Minister of Interior Ruth Dreifuss quit the Swiss government in which she had served since 1993. In 1999 she had become the first woman and the first Jew to be president of Switzerland (the president of the country is chosen from among the ministers, on a rotating basis). A biography of her, *Dreifuss ist unser Name* (Dreifuss Is Our Name), by Isabella Maria Fischli, was published upon her resignation.

BRIGITTE SION

Central and Eastern Europe

Germany

National Affairs

WAR ON TERROR

Chancellor Gerhard Schröder had declared himself a committed partner with the United States in the war on terror after September 11, 2001, and Germany was second only to the U.S. in terms of the number of troops sent to Afghanistan. But after barely surviving a no-confidence vote in the Bundestag that November (see AJYB 2002, p. 406), Schröder switched his stance, and in 2002 opposed German military involvement in possible hostilities against Iraq.

Observers suggested that there was another reason beside political calculations for the shift in Schröder's position—fear of terrorist attacks on German soil had subsided. To be sure, Germans were among the victims of the 9/11 attacks as well as attacks in Tunisia and Bali in 2002. The Tunisian incident received considerable press coverage: 15 people, including ten German tourists, were killed by terrorists in the historic La Ghriba synagogue in Jerba. The German media suggested that the attack brought terrorism home to Germans, some suggesting that Germany must play a larger role in trying to resolve the Mideast crisis because so long as the conflict continued the violence could spread into Europe. The danger to the tourist industry in Tunisia was another topic of discussion, since that country was a popular vacation destination for Europeans, and Jewish sites there drew many German visitors. Nevertheless, the German Foreign Ministry did not put out a travel advisory after the attack.

Despite the refusal to cooperate fully with American policy, Germany continued to share intelligence information about potential terrorism with U.S. agencies. Arrests and trials of suspected terrorists and banning of terrorist groups continued through the year. In April, Germany's Federal Crime Bureau warned local bureaus about the possibility of attacks on Jewish venues in Germany, but details were not made public. Otto Schily, the federal interior minister, called on all states of Germany to check their security plans and strengthen them if necessary, but no concrete threats were reported. In August, the *Frankfurter Allgemeine Zeitung* claimed that German car dealers of Arabic background were helping Islamic fundamentalists launder money for the "war against Christians and Jews." The newspaper said it had received this information from the Federal Bureau of Criminal Investigation in Wiesbaden, but the bureau refused comment. Germany's Jewish communities had already increased security after the September 11 attacks in the U.S. Police with machine guns were posted outside most Jewish sites, some of which had been equipped with double metal barricades as well.

At the end of November 2002, the German Supreme Court renewed its year-old ban on the Islamic extremist group Calipha State, based in Cologne, which had about 1,100 members and was reportedly tied to Osama bin Laden. The ban had been made possible under a law passed at the end of 2001 that criminalized membership in, and support of, terrorist organizations abroad, and allowed the banning of religious groups that abused their legal protection and tax advantages by harboring terrorists or promoting extremism. The stated objectives of this particular group were to establish an Islamic state in Turkey and to promote Islamic world domination. Despite the ban, the group continued to broadcast its propaganda on a weekly German television show.

A group with similar goals, Hizb ut-Tahrir, grabbed headlines in October when it sponsored a lecture at Berlin's Technical University. The organization, founded in East Jerusalem in 1953, promoted a "struggle against Jews" in its Turkish-, German-, and Arabic-language magazine; it was outlawed in Muslim countries but had a functioning headquarters in London. The lecture drew leading figures of Germany's right-wing extremist scene, providing ample evidence of their shared attraction to anti-American, anti-Israel, and anti-Semitic rhetoric. German courts banned the group in January 2003.

ELECTION 2002

Preparation for the September 22 national elections dominated German politics during much of 2002. Two long-standing taboos were broken during the campaign as the parties jockeyed to win public support — one against asserting German national pride, the other against injecting anti-Semitism into politics. Both were previously off-limits to mainstream politicians because of their Nazi associations.

The first taboo was broken by Chancellor Schröder, leader of the Social Democratic Party (SPD), who linked the invocation of German national feeling to anti-U.S. sentiment, correctly calculating that the electorate would rally with him against cooperation in America's anti-Iraq policy. Breaking the second taboo, Jürgen Möllemann, vice president of the Free Democratic Party (FDP), used anti-Semitic clichés and anti-Israel jibes, but the tactic failed and his party did not win enough votes to earn a position in the new coalition government.

As the year began, Schröder appeared to have lost the support of the "new middle" that had helped him win in 1998. He seemed vulnerable to his main challenger, Edmund Stoiber, governor of Bavaria, who headed the Christian Social Union (CSU), sister party of the Christian Democratic Union (CDU). Against the background of a faltering economy and fear of war with Iraq, Schröder opened his campaign with a public dialogue with controversial author Martin Walser on the themes of patriotism and national identity. It took place on May 8, the anniversary of the end of World War II. The invitation to this event read, in part, "We in Germany . . . want renewal and we want to stick together. And we want to fulfill our role in a changed in Europe and the world as a normal nation." Jewish leaders and others protested angrily not only at the choice of subject but also at the identity of the chancellor's discussion partner. They noted that Walser, in a 1998 speech, had called Auschwitz a "moral cudgel" used against Germany (see AJYB 1999, p. 345), and, furthermore, that the scheduled moderator of the dialogue, journalist Christoph Dieckmann, had written in *Die Zeit* that "Israel's arrogant belief in its chosenness is a curse."

During the discussion, Schröder said that some of Germany's greatest patriots were those who "resisted the murderous Nazi regime." He defined modern Germany's national identity in terms of its role within Europe, its reintegration of east and west, and its self-definition in terms of values rather than place. Walser, for his part, asserted that national identity was a feeling that largely defied rational definition. He suggested that Hitler might never have come to power had heavy reparations not been demanded of Germany after World War I, and that without Hitler there would have been no Auschwitz. This theory of indirect Allied responsibility for Nazi war crimes was hardly novel—it was, in fact, a common theme among conservative historians in Germany. In the end, the discussion between the 58-year-old Schröder and the 75-year-old Walser revealed how difficult it remained for Germany to define itself, 57 years after the downfall of the Nazi regime.

As the election approached, Germany's major Jewish newspaper, the *Jüdische Allgemeine Zeitung,* asked the leading candidates to answer several questions of Jewish concern. The fact that they responded even though the Jewish vote represented only .05 percent of the electorate indicated that politicians remained sensitive to how they were perceived by the Jewish community. The candidates' replies, however, were predictable. Across the board, from the conservatives to the communists, all condemned anti-Semitism, pledged to help integrate Jewish immigrants from the former Soviet Union, and declared their commitment to the survival of Israel, while at the same time supporting the Palestinians' right to a homeland. Both Stoiber of the CSU and Guido Westerwelle of the FDP stated that it must be permissible to criticize Israel without being accused of anti-Semitism. In fact, mainstream German politicians and journalists regularly criticized Israeli policies. While Schröder raised the possibility of German soldiers taking part in a UN peacekeeping force in the Middle East, Stoiber said he could not envision this given "our historical background."

German-Jewish journalist Richard Chaim Schneider speculated that Jews would hesitate to vote for Stoiber because he would likely choose the FDP as his coalition partner, necessitating a high ministerial position for Westerwelle—the man "who did not have the courage to silence the anti-Semites [i.e. Möllemann] in his own party." Jews were more likely to support Schröder, Schneider felt, but not because of anything to do with the Middle East. Rather, they remembered how he had "rushed to Düsseldorf after the arson attack on the synagogue" in the summer of 2000, and how he pressured German industry to contribute to the $5-billion compensation fund for Nazi-era slave and forced laborers.

There was some fear that the issue of immigration would have an impact on the campaign and bring out nativist sentiments in the electorate. Seven million noncitizens resided in Germany—nearly 9 percent of the country's population of 82 million. Most of them, nearly six million, came from European countries (mostly Turkey, Italy, Greece, and former Yugoslavia). The next largest groups were Asians, Africans, North and South Americans, and Australians. An estimated 200,000 were arriving each year. A law had been proposed by the coalition government in 1998 to streamline regulations for asylum seekers, facilitate the integration of foreigners, and develop a method of determining who might enter the country in order to work, but it had not yet been voted into law. As it turned out, however, Germany's immigration policy did not become a focus of the election.

The anti-Israel, anti-Semitic slogans of Jürgen Möllemann served only to earn the FDP a reputation as a wishy-washy party ready to pander to the questionable fringes. Early in the campaign, party leader Westerwelle said he hoped to attract voters from the far left and the far right to his centrist party. Möllemann, who had previously expressed sympathy for Palestinian suicide bombers, said he wanted to attract Muslims (there were roughly three million Muslims in Germany, but only a minority of them were citizens with the right to vote). This drew criticism from mainstream politicians and Jewish leaders, among them Michel Friedman, vice president of the Central Council of Jews in Germany (CCJG), the representative organization of German Jewry. Möllemann countered that "unfortunately, the politics of [Israeli prime minister Ariel] Sharon and the unbearably aggressive and arrogant manner of Mr. Friedman are liable to stir anti-Israeli and anti-Semitic resentment." Jewish leaders and German politicals figures reacted with outrage to the imputation that Jews were to blame for causing anti-Semitism. Paul Spiegel, president of the CCJG, asserted that this insult of a Jewish leader by a mainstream politician was unprecedented in the postwar era. When Westerwelle did nothing more than verbally slap his deputy chairman on the wrist, several longtime party members quit the FDP. Yet Möllemann was hardly alone in his views: a poll released on May 31 showed that 40 percent of FDP party members (and 28 percent of the general public) agreed with him that Michel Friedman's personality increased anti-Semitism.

In May, the head of the Turkish Community of Germany, together with the Turkish Union of Berlin-Brandenburg, protested what they called attempts by the FDP to attract Muslim voters by swinging toward the right. Members of the union, in fact, joined members of the Berlin Jewish community in a protest demonstration at the party's headquarters. Ayman Mazyek, spokesman for the politically moderate Central Council of Muslims in Germany, told the *Financial Times of Germany* that it was "not enough to express anti-Israeli criticism and to expect that Muslims will rally around the FDP." In September, shortly before election day, Möllemann distributed an anti-Israel, anti-Semitic flyer to some eight million voters in his home state in which he repeated past criticisms of Sharon and Michel Friedman. Again, his tactics brought a reaction of outrage from political leaders and Jews, and this time even FDP chief Westerwelle sternly rebuked his deputy.

In the end, the election turned out to be the closest in German postwar history. Although the SPD and the CDU/CSU ran a dead heat, each winning 38.5 percent of the vote, the Greens' 8.6 percent edged out the FDP's 7.4 percent, ensuring a continuation of the Social Democratic-Green coalition. The postcommunist Party of Democratic Socialism (PDS) got 4 percent.

Some observers viewed the anti-American tone that helped Schröder eke out his victory as not just a passing election-year phenomenon, but rather a sign of profound change in the transatlantic relationship. It was hardly surprising that full-blown anti-Americanism—often linked to anti-Israel and anti-Semitic views—was common on the two political extremes, left and right. What was new was that mainstream society had become generally critical of American policies. According to a survey commissioned by the American Jewish Committee's Berlin office, 77 percent of Germans believed that American foreign policy did not take the interests of U.S. allies into account. A substantial majority, however, said that good relations with the U.S. were important. In fact, when Justice Minister Herta Däubler-Gmelin was reported to have compared President George W. Bush to Adolf Hitler, outrage came not just from the American administration but also from pro-American German intellectuals and politicians, and she was forced to resign her post.

Despite the popularity of his continuing opposition to a war with Iraq, the reelected chancellor was losing public support by the end of 2002 due to the weak economy. The CDU/CSU opposition demanded an investigation into whether the SPD had used fraud to win the election by not informing the public that the budget deficit was much greater than predicted—indeed, that it was above the limit the European Union allowed its members, a situation that might lead to the imposition of fines.

As for the FDP, its poor performance in the election, said critics, proved that an anti-Semitic campaign could not win in Germany. In November, Westerwelle accused Möllemann of "attempting on his own to shift the axis of the FDP against its will" so as to turn it into a right-wing populist party, and asserted that this "caused the Free Democrats serious damage." Political scientist Hajo Funke of the Free University in Berlin commented: "Contrary to Austria, West Germany after the Second World War distanced itself from anti-Semitism and racism, so if you try to play this card again, you shake the basic consensus of postwar federal Germany, the liberal democratic identity. And this was seen after a while by the electorate."

Ultimately, it was not Möllemann's message but his method that caused his downfall. An investigation launched soon after the election into the source of funds he used to print and mail the offending flyers in his home state uncovered a pattern of illegal activity.

IRAQ

Early in 2002, former German culture minister Michael Naumann, who had lived in the United States for many years, criticized President George W. Bush for suggesting that Iraq might be the next target, after Afghanistan, in the war on terror. According to Naumann, Osama Bin Laden was the only person who stood to benefit from an attack on Iraq. Throughout the year, German officials insisted they needed proof that Iraq was a threat before they would participate in any war aimed at the ouster of Saddam Hussein. These sentiments accurately reflected German public opinion.

During the election campaign, Schröder said he would not allow American warplanes to fly over Germany if the U.S. went to war against Iraq without a UN mandate. After the election Schröder modified his stance, saying that he could imagine allowing U.S. jets to fly over and refuel in Germany in case of a war, since the NATO charter apparently mandated such aid. With British prime minister Tony Blair fully supporting the Bush administration's stance on Iraq, Germany found itself increasingly torn between loyalty to the war-wary European Union and the hawkish U.S.-British partnership.

In December, the Green Party passed a resolution calling on Schröder to deny refueling and fly-over rights if the U.S. acted unilaterally. A government spokesperson said that German support would have to be based on a UN mandate. But this stance was further modified by an SPD parliamentary spokesperson for internal affairs, who confirmed that the NATO Treaty required member-states to grant each other fly-over rights and the use of bases. By the end of 2002, Foreign Minister Joschka Fischer (Green Party) said he could not rule out Germany's supporting a UN resolution for war. The remark drew the ire of many figures in the SPD and in his own Green Party, but they were quickly overshadowed by Schröder's unequivocal statement that Germany would not support a war on Iraq. With this as its official position, Germany prepared to take its seat as a nonpermanent member of the UN Security Council in January 2003; it was scheduled to assume the rotating chairmanship of the council in February.

CCJG president Paul Spiegel told the weekly *Bild am Sonntag* newspaper in December that war against Iraq might be necessary to avert even greater horror, since "if Iraqi dictator Saddam Hussein has weapons of mass destruction, he would use them." Though he said he hoped war would not be necessary, the Jewish leader pointed out that democratic politicians during the Nazi era who did nothing to stop Hitler were later justly criticized for allowing the Holocaust to happen, and that "the Nazi concentration camps were not liberated by demonstrators, but by soldiers—hundreds of thousands of whom lost their lives." The United States "played a decisive role" at the time, he stressed. In supporting rapprochement between Germany and the U.S. in defiance of German public opinion, Spiegel was doing something new. Previous postwar Jewish leaders in Germany had generally spoken out only on domestic or Israel-related matters. Spiegel's readiness to address a controversial foreign-policy issue not directly related to Israel suggested a growing confidence among the Jewish leadership in the stability of German democracy.

Israel and the Middle East

The German government's traditional support for the Jewish state, based on recognition of German guilt and responsibility, remained steadfast in 2002 despite pressures from an electorate with growing pro-Palestinian sympathies. Amit Gilad, spokesman for the Israeli embassy, found it encouraging that Chancellor Schröder and Foreign Minister Fischer declared their support for Israel in the event of an Iraqi attack on it, and added that "the German commitment to the ongoing peace process is clear." But Gilad warned of a trend in the media "of being more distant to Israel," and noted that fewer Germans were visiting Israel, largely out of safety concerns.

The coalition government remained committed to helping bring peace to the Middle East. Foreign Minister Fischer's seven-point plan for ending the conflict envisioned a negotiated cease-fire followed by peace talks. Chancellor Schröder, as noted above, favored a UN peacekeeping unit in the area including German troops, but Fischer found the idea of German soldiers on Israeli soil repugnant for historical reasons.

In April, when Israeli troops moved into West Bank cities after a series of Palestinian suicide bombings (see above, pp. 198–201), Germany joined with Britain and Italy in refusing to support a UN Human Rights Commission resolution condemning Israel for "mass killings" of Palestinians. During an earlier EU Commission meeting in Luxembourg, the three countries found fault with the resolution for not clearly condemning suicide bombings against Israeli civilians. However other EU states—

France, Spain, Sweden, Portugal, and Belgium—endorsed the resolution with reservations. It passed the Human Rights Commission 40 to 5 with seven abstentions and one member not present.

Military cooperation between Germany and Israel had been close for years. Israel was Germany's seventh largest military client, and Germany was Israel's second biggest supplier, after the U.S. In 2000, the last year for which figures were available, Germany sold Israel military equipment worth $170 million, including torpedoes and parts for tanks and armored cars. In April 2002, however, in the wake of the Israeli offensive into the West Bank, Germany halted arms sales to Israel, though it pointedly refused to call the action an embargo. Quiet diplomacy between the two countries brought a restoration of arms sales, but controversy erupted in Germany toward the end of the year over whether Israel should receive tanks and Patriot missiles it had requested. The debate centered on whether the tanks would be used to destroy Palestinian homes in the Territories, and on whether delivering any weapons at all would go against Germany's constitutional ban on sending weapons into a war zone. Ultimately, two patriot missiles were delivered on loan for two years.

Two back-to-back demonstrations in Berlin illustrated the divided sympathies of the public. On April 13, some 4,000 people gathered for the largest pro-Palestinian demonstration ever held in Berlin. Observers expressed some surprise at the hate-filled tone of some of the slogans and signs; one demonstrator was later arrested for having dressed his children as suicide bombers. The following day, some 2,000 Jews and non-Jews demonstrated for Israel in a march organized by the nondenominational Association Against Anti-Semitism and Anti-Zionism and endorsed by several Jewish communal organizations. Speakers expressed their frustration that attacks on Israel were explained away while Israel's acts of self-defense were condemned.

Since the start of the second intifada, said CCJG president Spiegel, there had been a dramatic increase in the amount of mail sent to him and other Jewish figures containing anti-Semitism thinly disguised as criticism of Israel. As a particularly shocking example he cited a letter that Norbert Blüm, a former German labor minister, wrote to Shimon Stein, Israel's ambassador in Berlin, describing Israeli military actions as a "relentless war of extermination"—words echoing Nazi rhetoric.

Supporters of Israel felt that Jürgen Möllemann's role in the election campaign was exacerbating the situation, making public expression of anti-Israel views acceptable in German society and blurring the line between criticism of Israeli policies and anti-Semitism. Proof of this was offered in an exhibit at Berlin's Jewish Museum of readers' letters to German Jewish journalist Henryk Broder and to the editor of the *Jüdische Allgemeine Zeitung*. Though some letter writers expressed support for Israel and disgust with Möllemann's election campaign, many others said that Möllemann had given them the courage to express their pent-up anti-Israel views and their dislike of individual Jewish leaders in Germany.

The letters were just the tip of the iceberg. Surveys conducted during the spring showed that Germans were increasingly critical of the Jewish state. A poll by the Emnid firm found that 73 percent of Germans believed that "Israel's tough treatment of the Palestinians" was not justified. A study commissioned by the American Jewish Committee's Berlin office showed that 34 percent of Germans respected Möllemann for his willingness to criticize Israel openly, and 23 percent respected him for having stood up to the leaders of the German Jewish community. It also found that Germans were increasingly likely to question the "special relationship" between Israel and Germany forged in the aftermath of the Holocaust. The weekly news magazine *Der Spiegel* released a study showing that 70 percent of Germans said they were just as ready to criticize Israel as any other country, and only 29 percent felt they should hold back from criticizing Israel due to the tangled historical relationship of Jews with Germany. Furthermore, 25 percent of respondents agreed with the statement that Israel's actions in the Middle East "are principally no different from what the Nazis did to the Jews in the Third Reich," a figure that rose to 35 percent in the 18–29 age group. And an Anti-Defamation League survey revealed that 25 percent of Germans sympathized with the Palestinians as against 17 percent who sympathized with the Israelis.

Media coverage of the Middle East encouraged a distancing between Germans and Israel, according to a study commissioned by the American Jewish Committee, "Mideast Reporting on the Second Intifada in German Print Media," released in June. Affirming what many others had noticed, it concluded that "there is often distortion in the image of Israel, a lack of context and an aggressive tone" in Germany's Middle East reportage. The media coverage came in for tough criticism at Berlin's pro-Israel demonstration in April. There, Matthias Loerbroks, minister of the Protestant parish of Friedrichstadt, decried the use of such terms as "Old Testament-like," "wrathful," and "vengeful" in connection with Israeli policy by reporters who themselves were "not particularly pious."

In February, Jewish students held a well-attended conference in Frankfurt to discuss how better to present the case for Israel on college campuses. Also, a group of Frankfurt Jews launched Honestly Concerned, a

media-watch group that would monitor the German press on its reporting of Israel and other issues of Jewish interest. In September, hoping to
counter negative reporting, the Berlin Jewish Community proposed
putting up posters in 50 subway stations showing the faces of Israelis who
had been murdered by suicide bombers, and the question, "What if it had
been your child?" But Berlin's mass-transit corporation turned down the
request, fearing that the posters would provoke a violent response. "We
don't want to create political propaganda," a spokesperson said.

Among the strongest supporters of Israel in Germany was a small but
steadfast group of Evangelical Christians, and in August they organized
one of the largest pro-Israel demonstrations Germany had seen in years.
Some 4,000 of them assembled in Berlin where they prayed, waved Israeli
flags, and heard speeches critical of a proposed Palestinian state. Jewish
groups did not participate, and the German Jewish Student Union
protested against the anti-Palestinian stance displayed as well as the
Christian fundamentalist view of Judaism as an "incomplete" faith. But
the Israeli embassy welcomed the show of support, and later in the year
Keren Hayesod (United Israel Appeal) and the U.S.-Israel based International Fellowship of Christians and Jews signed an agreement to launch
a major campaign to activate Evangelical Christian support for Israel in
Germany and elsewhere in Europe

In spite of calls for boycotts against Israeli academics, German-Israeli
cultural and scientific exchange continued, according to the Israeli embassy, though fear of terrorism had caused many Germans to "hesitate
to come to Israel."

In December, Israeli president Moshe Katzav paid his first official visit
to Germany, at the invitation of German president Johannes Rau. The
two joined in dedicating a synagogue in the city of Wuppertal, and paid
a visit to the concentration camp memorial at Sachsenhausen. During his
three-day stay, Katzav took issue with German attitudes toward Israel,
saying that he did not understand how one could "equate Palestinian terror and our fight against terror." In Berlin, Katzav told Jewish leaders that
though he worried about anti-Semitism in Europe, he was optimistic
about the future of German-Jewish relations. Katzav did not repeat the
faux pas of his predecessor, Ezer Weizman, who upset the Jewish community during his 1996 visit when he said that all Jews should leave Germany and go to Israel. During Katzav's visit, about 30 neo-Nazis demonstrated against the delivery of weapons to Israel; some 1,000 anti-Nazi
protesters countered them. Paul Spiegel called the Katzav visit a "sym-

bol of solidarity and a sign of the recognition that Germany today is another Germany, in which Jews can live again."

Anti-Semitism and Extremism

According to statistics compiled by the Department for Constitutional Protection, there were no reported cases of murder associated with right-wing extremism during 2002. There were, however, 28 anti-Semitic violent crimes, up from 18 the year before.

The number of right-wing and anti-Semitic incidents rose dramatically in the first half of 2002, according to the midyear report of the Party for Democratic Socialism (PDS), the postcommunist party that regularly requested a breakdown of such incidents from the federal authorities. In the second quarter of the year, police registered 319 such incidents, up from 127 in the first quarter. Most of them involved public expression or display of illegal material, such as swastikas, the raised arm of the "Hitler greeting," the singing of SS songs, and Holocaust denial. For the year 2001, the government had reported 989 anti-Semitic incidents, down from 1,084 in 2000.

The area of the country that had formerly been East Germany saw the steepest rise in such crimes. In the state of Mecklenburg-Pomerania, for example, 33 incidents were recorded in the first half of 2002, as compared to 44 in all of 2001. A number of these attacks targeted Holocaust and death-march memorials in Raben-Steinfeld near Schwerin, as well as in Woebbelin and Boizenburg. (Throughout Brandenburg and Mecklenburg-Pomerania there were markers showing the routes of the death marches conducted toward the end of the war, along which thousands of camp inmates died of exhaustion or were shot by guards.) In a few cases vandals placed pigs' heads on Holocaust memorials. Authorities believed it possibile that these events were linked.

On September 5—the night before Rosh Hashanah—in what one Jewish leader called a clear act of Holocaust denial, arsonists destroyed an exhibition room at a museum about the death march in the Below Forest. Local political and religious leaders joined in condemning the crime, and some 500 residents attended a demonstration the next day to show their disgust. A $10,000 reward was established for information leading to arrests. Around the same time, vandals spray-painted a swastika on a Jewish memorial stone in the town of Grevesmühlen in Mecklenburg-Pomerania. The state department of criminal investigation said that similar red paint was used in the Below Forest crime. A later attack, in November, was also likely connected to those in Below Forest and Grevesmühlen: vandals destroyed a memorial to victims of the Sachsenhausen concentration camp in the former East German town of Leegebruch, north of Berlin.

There was considerable discussion of whether this upsurge of incidents reflected a resurgent German anti-Semitism or a backlash against Israeli policies. In some of these cases the perpetrators were described as appearing to be of Arab background, lending credence to the second interpretation, but in most cases no one saw the vandals' faces. Peter Fischer, who oversaw Jewish communities in former East Germany for the CCJG, said he believed the primary motivation for the latest attacks—which were largely aimed at Holocaust memorial sites—to be plain and simple Holocaust denial.

There were also several anti-Semitic incidents in the capital city of Berlin. In March, an explosive device was detonated near the entrance to a Jewish cemetery in the Charlottenburg district, damaging windows in the chapel. On March 30, two American rabbis visiting Berlin were accosted by about eight young men police described as being "of Arabic background" who beat and kicked one of the rabbis. This happened soon after a number of violent attacks on synagogues and other Jewish sites in France and Belgium, and the perpetrators reportedly first asked their victims if they were Jewish. The Jewish Community of Berlin requested special police protection following this incident. Several days later, a young Jewish woman wearing a Star of David necklace was attacked in similar circumstances at a Berlin subway station. Police said the attackers, who managed to flee, appeared to be of Arab origin.

Also in April, unknown persons threw a Molotov cocktail onto the grounds of a Berlin synagogue. Guards on night patrol were able to extinguish the flames before they could cause any damage. Later that month, a Holocaust memorial on the Pulitzbruecke in Berlin was vandalized. Police reported that swastikas had been painted on the memorial shortly after midnight. Again, the perpetrators were not apprehended. In May, vandals laid waste to the interior of an unused, pre-World War II Jewish hospital in Berlin. Jewish leaders said they had no doubt that the motivation was anti-Semitism. "The destruction of a Jewish historical site cannot be considered a neutral act," said a spokesperson. Alexander Brenner, head of the Jewish Community of Berlin, said that unfair media reports on Israel were partly to blame for such incidents. And Michel Friedman, vice president of the CCJG, said that greater protection for Jewish venues was "urgently needed" since the Hamas movement had declared Jews worldwide "enemy number one."

Reichstag member Ulla Jelpke, the PDS spokesperson for domestic policy, charged in July that anti-Semitic crimes were "clearly encouraged by the anti-Semitic abuses of Möllemann" and the failure of the government to ban the extreme right-wing National Democratic Party of Germany (NPD). The government coalition had indeed been trying to gather support to ban the NPD, which it compared to the Nazi party of the 1920s. But the effort suffered a setback in February, when the German Supreme Court postponed its hearings on the matter after learning that the federal Ministry of the Interior and the Department for Constitutional Protection had used paid government informants to gather evidence, and that these informants were among the "experts" scheduled to testify at the hearings. The court felt that this cast doubt on the strength of the government's case since the NPD could argue that the evidence against it was actually created by provocateurs. The scandal shook public faith in Interior Minister Schily, and opposition parties called for his resignation. Despite this embarrassment, the government reiterated its determination to have the NPD banned. Only two parties had ever been banned in postwar Germany before, a communist party and a neo-Nazi party, both in the 1950s.

In May, the theme of German anti-Semitism took on a new twist with the publication of *Death of a Critic,* a new novel by German author Martin Walser that drew widespread criticism for promoting anti-Semitic stereotypes. Frank Schirrmacher, publisher of the *Frankfurter Allgemeine Zeitung,* which had serialized Walser's earlier books, chose not to run this one. Instead, he published an open letter to Walser calling the book a "document of hate." Specifically, he charged that André Ehrl-König, a character depicted in the novel as a Jewish literary critic, was meant to libel real-life Jewish critic Marcel Reich-Ranicki, the only member of his family to survive the Holocaust. In one passage, for example, the fictional Ehrl-König is described as being fond of little German girls. Reich-Ranicki remained silent for a day or two. Finally, he told *Die Welt* newspaper that he found the novel "deeply shocking, offensive, and hurtful."

In August, another well-known German expressed sentiments that many considered anti-Semitic. Defense Minister Rudolf Scharping, forced to resign his post over accusations of financial irregularities, told a Hamburg audience that President Bush wanted to oust Iraqi leader Saddam Hussein in order to garner the support of "a powerful—perhaps overly powerful—Jewish lobby" with the aim of helping Republicans win the fall gubernatorial races in Florida and New York (the candidate in Florida was Bush's brother, Jeb). Scharping went on to say that congressional redistricting in the U.S. since 2000 had strengthened the electoral power of American Jews.

Old-fashioned right-wing anti-Semitism reared its head again in October, when residents of a street in Berlin protested against the restoration of the street's pre-Nazi name, Jüdenstrasse (Jews' Street). During ceremonies for the renaming of what had been called, since Hitler's time, Kinkelstrasse, some bystanders reportedly interrupted the speech of Alexander Brenner, head of the Jewish Community of Berlin, with statements such as "Jews out," "It's all the fault of you Jews," and "You crucified Jesus." Brenner, who later said he was shocked and nearly broke down, cut short his speech and told the hecklers, "Whether you like it or not, you have aligned yourselves with the Nazis." Police launched an investigation. Reportedly, a good many of the aproximately 40 people in attendance were members of Citizens for Kinkelstrasse, a local group opposed to the street renaming. They wanted to retain the old name, they said, not because of any anti-Semitism, but because the change had been made without consideration of their concerns, such as having to change their addresses.

A major investigation into right-wing extremism was bungled in July, when Berlin police arrested a neo-Nazi who, unknown to them, had been providing information about the extremist music scene to police in the neighboring state of Brandenburg. Toni Stadler, 27, was arrested as his pop group, White Aryan Rebels, was about to give a concert for 100 neo-Nazis in Berlin. Such concerts, illegal under the law forbidding the dissemination of racism and Nazism, were conducted clandestinely. White Aryan Rebels was known for its 2001 CD, *Notes of Hate*. One of the songs on it, "This Bullet Is for You," called for the murder of CCJG vice president Michel Friedman and of the interracial children of tennis star Boris Becker, among others. According to German officials, the popularity of music with racist, anti-Semitic and ultranationalist lyrics was on the increase. To evade the German legal ban, the music was often downloaded from the Internet, particularly through U.S. providers.

The year 2002 saw the release of several polls and studies measuring German attitudes toward Jews and other minority groups. Two surveys released in June seemed to contradict each other. One, published in *Der Spiegel* magazine, found a drop in anti-Semitism in Germany. Some 79 percent of those surveyed said they would not care if they had a Jewish neighbor, and 20 percent said they would actually like having one. Only

1 percent said having a Jewish neighbor would bother them, down from 11 percent six years earlier. While 44 percent of those over age 60 felt that "Jews have too much influence in the world," only 16 percent of those aged 18–29 agreed. Nearly 50 percent of respondents said that Germany still had a special responsibility to Jews because of the Nazi genocide, up 16 percent since 1991.

The second survey, published in the *Frankfurter Rundschau,* purported to show an increase in German anti-Semitic attitudes since 1999. In 2002, 36 percent agreed with the statement, "I can understand that some people find Jews unpleasant." Three years earlier, only 20 percent had agreed. However the *Frankfurter Rundschau* poll showed greater dislike for Arabs than for Jews: 49 percent said they "could understand how some people might find Arabs unpleasant," while 23 percent disagreed.

Later in June, the Anti-Defamation League released a survey of attitudes in Britain, France, Germany, Belgium, and Denmark that found that "classical anti-Semitism, coupled with a new form fueled by anti-Israel sentiment, has become a potent and dangerous mix in countries with enormous Muslim and Arab populations." The ADL survey found that 55 percent of the German respondents considered Jews more loyal to Israel than to their home country, 32 percent thought Jews had too much power in the business world, and 58 percent—the highest figure among the countries surveyed—believed that Jews talked too much about the Holocaust.

In September, researchers at the University of Leipzig conducted a survey that found that anti-Semitism was more common in the western states of Germany than in the east, whereas a more generalized xenophobia tended to predominate in the east.

Finally, a study released by Bielefeld University in November indicated that Germans were becoming increasingly sympathetic to political calls for "law and order" and appeals to xenophobia, anti-Semitism, and anti-Islamic feeling.

Holocaust-Related Matters

On January 20, 2002, Germany marked the 60th anniversary of the Wannsee Conference at which the Nazi high command finalized the plan to kill out Europe's Jews. The 1942 conference resulted in a 16-page protocol, including Adolf Eichmann's alphabetical list of 33 European lands from which the Jewish people were to be eliminated. Calling the Holocaust "the darkest chapter of our history," Chancellor Schröder said the

Wannsee Conference demonstrated the "perversity of the Nazi system." The building where the meeting took place had been turned into a public memorial and education center a decade earlier. Some 60,000 people visited the site annually, about one-third of them from outside Germany.

A new exhibit, "Holocaust: The National Socialist Genocide and the Motifs of Memory," opened in Berlin's German Historical Museum on January 17, timed immediately to precede the annual Holocaust Remembrance Day, January 27. In what was believed to be a first for any German museum, the exhibit traced the development of modern anti-Semitism and racism in Germany through its culmination as the Nazis' "final solution." Included were artifacts such as concentration camp uniforms, early Nazi propaganda, period artworks, and a desecrated Torah scroll from Pultuk, Poland, on loan from the U.S. Holocaust Memorial Museum. "We wanted to demonstrate the causes and the reality of the Holocaust without arguing about it and without moralizing," said museum director Hans Ottomeyer.

In June, the International Auschwitz Committee announced that it would move its headquarters to Berlin in 2003, where it would intensify the battle against all forms of hate by using survivor testimony as the key weapon, especially in classrooms. Christoph Heubner, executive vice president of the committee, said that survivors "felt an urgent need to act. They said, 'At the end of our life we have to go a step forward and be even more energetic with our work in schools, giving younger people the chance to learn from history.' "

Historical sites associated with the Holocaust received increased federal support in 2002, according to Thomas Lutz, director of the memorial museums department at the Topography of Terror Foundation, an archive and memorial on the site of the former Gestapo headquarters in Berlin. Not only had the government earmarked more than $6 million for the preservation and restoration of former concentration camps, but Topography of Terror itself received a verbal pledge of nearly $32.5 million in federal and state funds to build a permanent museum. The flow of money to memorial sites had increased since the unification of Germany in 1990, said Lutz, when the government realized that the exhibits in the former East Germany were marred by socialist propaganda.

On July 7, a conference on Nazi abuse of law opened in Berlin, raising controversial issues about tyranny and justice past and present. The three-day seminar, called "Tyranny, Justice, and the Law," was a joint project of the Touro Law Center in New York, the Free University of Berlin, and Touro's three-year-old Institute on the Holocaust and the Law. In addition, the German-American Lawyers' Association and the Simon Bond Foundation supported the event. The conference dealt with the Nazis' destruction of democratic law, the flawed process of healing after World War II, and attempts to bring war criminals to justice. Looking at the contemporary scene, it examined the role of international criminal courts and the U.S. refusal to endorse them, and the question of whether the circumstances of Al Qaeda prisoners at the U.S. base in Cuba could be compared to the early Nazi concentration camps for political opponents.

In August, work on Germany's planned Holocaust Memorial in Berlin was postponed due to the discovery of irregularities in the bidding process for the contract to construct the 2,700 cement steles, some up to 15 feet high, on a 204,500-square-foot site near the Brandenburg Gate. After the bidding was repeated, it was announced that work would begin in 2003. American architect Peter Eisenman designed the memorial, which was approved in 1999 by the Reichstag after more than ten years of debate and discussion. It was expected to cost some $22 million.

A revamped museum in Peenemünde, on the Baltic, birthplace of both the intercontinental ballistic missile and, hence, of space exploration, reflected a new understanding of the moral ambiguities of local history. Ten years earlier, the nearby town of Usedom had opened a museum and planned to celebrate the 50th anniversary of the first launching of the Nazis' V-2 rocket from Peenemünde without mentioning that some 20,000 slave laborers had died working on the project, or that several thousand people were killed by the bombs themselves in England, Belgium, and the Netherlands. These omissions were rectified in new museum exhibits. The reopening was celebrated in late September with a "concert of healing" featuring conductor Mstislav Rostropovich. German president Johannes Rau spoke at the event.

In October, the Center for Research on Anti-Semitism at Berlin's Technical University marked its 20th year. Since its founding, the center had published more than 500 studies and books on subjects related to anti-Semitism and the Holocaust. The center held conferences on historical and current topics and published a yearbook as well as educational material disseminated to schools across Germany. "I will never say that our work is done," Wolfgang Benz, director of the center since 1990, said. "Every new generation must be taught to recognize the mechanisms that lead to prejudice."

Also in October, the publishing company Bertelsmann admitted that Jews had been forced to work in its printing facilities in Lithuania and Latvia, and that the firm had been a major producer of Nazi propaganda books. Previously, the firm had claimed that the Nazis had closed the company in 1944 because its chairman, Heinrich Mohn, was a devout Christian who published theological texts. Bertelsmann was one of 6,000 German firms paying into a $5-billion fund set up by the German government and its industries for survivors of Nazi forced and slave labor.

October was also the month that controversial American scholar Daniel J. Goldhagen presented the German translation of his new book, *A Moral Reckoning: The Role of the Catholic Church in the Holocaust and its Unfulfilled Duty of Repair,* at the annual Frankfurt book fair. His remarks at the event, and the book itself, drew heavy criticism. *A Moral Reckoning* faulted the Catholic Church for its role in the historical development of anti-Semitism and what he termed its passivity, at best, toward the persecution of Jews in Nazi Germany. Goldhagen proposed radical acts of atonement, including the issuance of new editions of the New Testament purged of anti-Jewish passages. After a court-ordered delay due to a disputed photo caption, the German edition entered the local bookstores. Goldhagen was no stranger to controversy. His 1996 book, *Hitler's Willing Executioners,* which suggested that there was a uniquely German "eliminationist anti-Semitism," was a best-seller in Germany, despite being panned by critics and historians.

In one of the more publicized cases of Holocaust trivialization, Roland Koch, governor of the state of Hessen and a member of the conservative Christian Democratic Union (CDU), came under fire in December for alluding to the Holcaust in a debate about a proposed tax increase. Responding to proponents of the measure who publicly named certain well-to-do citizens who would have to pay a higher tax, Koch accused them of putting "a new form of the star on the chest" of the wealthy. His statement evoked such an uproar that the state parliamentary session had to be interrupted. The obvious comparison to the yellow star Jews were forced to wear during the Nazi era was "an insult to all victims of the Nazi regime," said CCJG president Spiegel. Koch later apologized.

In December, the German Federal Archive released the names of 31,161 victims of the Nazi "euthanasia" program. The names had been filed in an archive in the former East Germany for decades, and it had taken years to computerize the information. Historians believed that some 300,000 people were selected for extermination as "worthless" under this Nazi program that preceded the mass murder of Jews and others.

The American Jewish Committee released a poll on December 17 that found that 52 percent of Germans believed Jews were exploiting the memory of the Holocaust for their own purposes. AJC executive director

David Harris called the finding highly disturbing. This was the third such AJC poll conducted since German unification in 1990.

There were two positive developments during 2002 in the area of Holocaust compensation. Early in the year, negotiations between the German government and the Conference for Jewish Material Claims Against Germany (Claims Conference) resulted in a liberalization of eligibility criteria for payments from the Article 2 Fund (see AJYB 2002, pp. 22–23). This change allowed up to 5,000 additional Holocaust survivors to receive monthly compensation payments. In September, the International Commission on Holocaust Era Insurance Claims (ICHEIC) reached agreement with the German insurance industry on the processing and payment of previously unpaid insurance policies to survivors and their heirs (see above, p. 109). In November, the Claims Conference held a two-day symposium in Berlin to mark the 50th anniversary of the signing of the first compensation agreement with Germany.

Heirs of the Wertheim department-store family fought to gain compensation in 2002 for a large parcel of land in Berlin, worth hundreds of millions of dollars today, which once belonged to the family. They said that German retailer KarstadtQuelle AG lied to the family in 1951 when it offered a low purchase price for the property, claiming the company stock had no value. Located in former East Berlin, the site was taken over by the federal government after German unification, and it refused to compensate the family.

JEWISH COMMUNITY

Communal Affairs

With an influx of immigrants from the former Soviet Union, Germany's Jewish population had risen from about 30,000 in 1990 to over 100,000 in 2002, making it the fastest growing Jewish community in the world. Since 1991, Germany had allowed 5,000 Jews per year to enter from the former Soviet Union in order to help rebuild Germany's destroyed Jewish communities. Germany granted such Jewish immigrants "contingent refugee" status, which gave them residency and full social benefits but not immediate citizenship. The program was to continue indefinitely, and Jewish representatives expected the community to grow to at least 130,000 members over the course of the next decade. The Zentralwohlfahrtstelle (Central Jewish Welfare Office), an arm of the Jewish community, offered numerous classes to educate new immigrants about German culture, the German job market, and basic Judaism.

Germany's 83 local Jewish communities operated under the umbrella of the Einheitsgemeinde, "united community," which oversaw funding for communal needs. Under the law, German citizens who wished to belong to a church or synagogue paid a percentage of their annual income tax into a so-called "church tax" whose funds were channeled through the federal government to the faith communities in proportion to their membership. With the rapidly expanding Jewish population, the need had grown for more language and job-training programs, religious education, synagogues, and community centers. These were beyond the financial capacity of the CCJG, whose annual budget of nearly $1 million reflected the needs of the 1980s, when former chancellor Helmut Kohl created an endowment of nearly $20 million, interest from which funded the community's budget.

In November 2002, after years of negotiations with the CCJG, the German government entered into an unprecedented contractual relationship with the country's Jewish community, equivalent to the arrangement it had with the Catholic and Protestant communities. This left Islam, whose more than three million adherents made it the largest non-Christian minority in the country, as the only major religious group not covered by such a contract, largely because there was no comparable national umbrella organization to oversee the distribution of funds to local Muslim communities.

The contract with the Jewish community included a dramatic increase in financial support—the government would triple its annual budget for the CCJG to nearly $3 million, adjusted annually for inflation. This federal agreement did not replace or affect the contracts that individual German states had with their local Jewish communities. It was approved by the Parliament and was expected to go into effect in early 2003. Paul Spiegel called it an "historical situation, and it proves that the German government is not only aware of the new Jewish community here but also supports it and welcomes it."

The World Union for Progressive Judaism, whose German affiliates were outside of the CCJG, feared it would be shut out by the new contract and wrote to Chancellor Schröder demanding a share of the money. But the government chose not to take a stand, seeing the controversy as an internal matter for the Jewish community. Spiegel said that if the progressive Jewish communities in Germany applied for CCJG membership they would be considered for funding.

Several new synagogues opened in Germany in 2002. In June, the former East German city of Chemnitz dedicated one, designed by Frankfurt architect Alfred Jacoby. The Jewish community there numbered some 500. In 1933, there were 3,000 Jews in Chemnitz. Only 57 returned after the war, among them community president Siegmund Rotstein. The community grew from 11 members in 1989 to its current size due to the influx of Jewish immigrants from the former Soviet Union. In July, the Jewish community of Osnabrück joined with the Lingen Forum for Jews and Christians to restore a 19th-century synagogue in Freren. The site would be used for a chapel and center for interfaith meetings. In December, Israeli president Katzav and German president Rau dedicated a new synagogue in the city of Wuppertal. This was the first time that an Israeli president had taken part in the dedication of a German synagogue.

One of Germany's most famous new synagogues, dedicated in Dresden in November 2001 (see AJYB 2002, p. 423), suffered moderate damage due to the flooding of the Elbe River during the summer of 2002. Some 150 Jewish families in Dresden were left temporarily homeless by the flooded river, whose torrents forced tens of thousands of Dresdeners from their homes, damaged landmark buildings, and hampered communication with and travel to the historic city. Before the floodwaters hit, the Torah scrolls and prayer books were brought to the community house, situated on higher ground. Dresden's original synagogue had been burned down on Kristallnacht, November 9, 1938.

In October, a new group calling itself "A Network of Jewish Women in Economics, Research, Media and Institutions" was launched in Berlin with a conference. The organizers said they aimed to build professional connections, provide mentors and role models, and overcome career obstacles in a society where more than 90 percent of upper-level professionals were men. Furthermore, said Charlotte Knobloch, a vice president of the CCJG and president of the Jewish Community of Munich, "the network has to have Jewish content" and be informed by "Jewish traditions, a Jewish way of life, a life built on Jewish values." The Berlin-based network was the brainchild of Noa Gabriel Lerner, a 37-year-old entrepreneur who founded the Milch und Honig German-Jewish Web site (www.milch-und-honig.com) and a Jewish tourism service in Berlin.

EDUCATION

In July, the Cologne Jewish community signed a contract for its first Jewish primary school since World War II. In September, about 20 first-graders began classes at the Lauder Morijah Elementary School (Morijah had been the name of a Jewish school there in pre-Nazi times). The Ronald S. Lauder Foundation contributed $1.4 million toward building the school and an adjoining new social-service center, a project that had been put on hold for a while because of funding problems. Contributions were also received from the Protestant church and from the state of North-Rhine Westphalia, which paid for security protection. Construction was expected to be completed in 2003. Paul Spiegel called the new school a "sign that Jews have confidence in this country." Ten years earlier, the first postwar Jewish elementary school in North-Rhine Westphalia had been opened in Spiegel's home city of Düsseldorf.

The Lauder Foundation was also active in the Jewish educational projects of other German communities. It financed the reopening of the Talmud Tora School in Hamburg, which had been closed 60 years before by the Nazis. Hamburg's Jewish community now had about 10,000 members, many of them immigrants from the former Soviet Union. The foundation, in conjunction with Jewish Community of Würzburg, set up a new German-Jewish genealogy center in that city in October, called the Ephraim Gustav Hönlein Genealogie Projekt. The Würzburg community also planned to open a new Lauder Chorev Center, a meeting place for Jewish teens.

In November, financial irregularities led to a leadership change at the Institute of Judaic Studies in Heidelberg, as University of Heidelberg theology professor Manfred Oeming replaced Michael Graetz as program director, at the request of the CCJG. Graetz reportedly agreed to step down for the duration of an investigation into allegations that some funding appropriated to the institute was instead placed in a hidden account. Graetz's appointment was to last until 2005. Oeming, 47, a specialist in the Hebrew Bible, said that one of his priorities as director would be to build up the institute's multidenominational rabbinical program, which had opened in October 2001 with three students. There were a total of 164 students enrolled in the institute.

KASHRUT

In January, Jewish and Muslim groups applauded the reversal of a 1995 law that had banned Islamic ritual slaughter in Germany. The decision by the high court in Karlsruhe was seen as an affirmation of religious freedom in Germany and Europe. But German animal-rights groups decried the ruling and said they would not cease their quest for a European-wide ban on forms of ritual slaughter they considered cruel to animals. They intended to take their campaign to the European Union.

Though German law required that an animal be rendered unconscious before slaughter, an exception had long been made for Jewish ritual slaughter on the grounds that a trained and licensed kosher slaughterer was presumed to take precautions against an animal's suffering. But the 1995 law banning Islamic slaughter reflected the view of many lawmakers that Islam was not as clear as Judaism in forbidding the slaughter of an unconscious animal, and that therefore it should be possible for Muslim butchers to produce halal meat under the existing German law. But Muslims had worked to overturn the law by comparing their deprivation to what Jews would have to undergo were kosher slaughter to be banned.

The year 2002 saw the arrival of two new sources of kosher bread in Berlin— Rabbi Yitzchak Ehrenberg, the religious head of the Orthodox community, certified a bakery as kosher, and the Chabad-Lubavitch rabbi, Yehudah Teichtal, took charge of making kosher the oven at an Israeli restaurant for the weekly production of challah, rolls, and pita. Teichtal also supervised a dairy near Berlin so that kosher milk could be produced. In Frankfurt, a new kosher food emporium opened.

REMEMBERING THE MUNICH MASSACRE

In August and September, Germany marked the 30th anniversary of the massacre at the Munich Olympics. On September 5, 1972, members of the Palestinian Black September guerrilla group took Israeli athletes hostage, and then killed them during a botched rescue attempt by German police at the Furstenfeldbruck military airport. Surviving participants as well as 23 family members of the victims took part in a ceremony at a memorial near the Olympic stadium on August 11, during the European athletic championships. Esther Roth, who competed as a hurdler for the Israeli team in 1972, was there. She recalled: "My coach was very happy because I had my best results for him. It was like a dream." That coach, Amitzur Shapira, was one of 11 Israels killed in the attack. "Being around here makes me remember everything that happened 30 years ago," Roth said. "Some pictures you cannot forget. Some pictures are still with you for 30 years." Israel's ambassador to Germany, Shimon Stein, and representatives of the local Jewish community also attended the event, which was organized by the Israeli Light Athletics Association together with its European counterpart. During the one-hour ceremony, a large stone tablet was placed at the bridge linking the former Olympic village to the Olympic stadium, and an Israeli flag was draped across the tablet.

In September, Germany offered a financial settlement to survivors of the murdered athletes, whose compensation claims were based on the inadequate security that Germany provided at the Olympic village, and the bungled rescue attempt.

Culture

MUSEUMS AND EXHIBITS

Berlin's Jewish Museum, which provided an introduction to Jewish traditions and the history of German Jewry, continued to attract record numbers. By May 2002 it had recorded more than 500,000 visitors since its opening on September 9, 2001, maintaining its status as one of Germany's most visited museums (see AJYB 2002, pp. 426–28). It was federally funded, with a budget of about $10 million.

Two collections of photographs brought before the public in 2002 provided insight into the psychological environment of the Nazi state. An exhibit, "Before All Eyes," opened September 5 at the Topography of Terror. It contained some 120 images of deportations of Jews, auctioning of their belongings, and public humiliations of Germans accused of consorting with Jews or slave laborers. The photos, most of which had never been seen by the public before, were culled from 335 images in the book of the same name, published in 2002 by the center's research director, historian Reinhard Ruerup.

A second photo collection illuminated the same subject on the microcosmic level. A long-missing cache of 119 photographs of deportations of Jews from Würzburg and Kitzingen, taken by a member of the Gestapo in 1941 and 1942, was rediscovered by historian Edith Raim of Munich's Institute for Contemporary History. In November 2002 the photos were the subject of a German TV documentary by filmmaker Renate Eichmeier, who interviewed survivors and other eyewitnesses. A traveling exhibit of the photographs was planned for 2003. The project was a cooperative effort of Munich's Institute for Contemporary History and the State Archives of Würzburg. Like the Topography of Terror exhibit, these photos suggested that very few Germans could have avoided witnessing the degradation and abuse of their Jewish neighbors.

In September, Survivors of the Shoah Visual History Foundation, the nonprofit organization that collected video testimonies of Holocaust survivors and other witnesses, opened a collection of survivor testimonies at the Landeswohlfahrtsverband Hessen (LWV) in Kassel, Germany. It included 13 rare interviews with survivors who were subjected to Nazi eugenic crimes and forced-sterilization programs. Lutz Bauer, director of the LWV, said his institution was "the first archive in Europe" to make such material available to the general public.

A controversial exhibit by Berlin artist Anna Adam raised the question of how far one could go in poking fun at philosemitism in Germany. Called "Feinkost Adam," the exhibit—a hit at the Jewish Museum in Fürth—consisted of mock "Jewish" products, such as a tiny sukkah for Jewish birds and a book teaching one how to breathe the Jewish way. A fracas erupted when a local rabbi called Adam and her exhibit anti-Semitic. The controversy served to attract more visitors.

Marking the new year of 2002 at Frankfurt's German Architecture Museum was an exhibit about modern synagogue architecture, featuring the works of local architect Alfred Jacoby, one of which was the newly opened synagogue in Chemnitz.

FILMS

Several Israeli films were screened at the 52nd annual Berlinale Film Festival in February. One of them won the peace award—*August, A Moment Before the Eruption,* by Avi Mograbi, which delved into the everyday realities of tension and mistrust between Jews and Arabs in Israel and had its world premiere at the festival. This award was funded by the Action Group Peace Film Award along with the Heinrich Boll Foundation and the International Physicians for the Prevention of Nuclear War. A second Israeli film, *Mabul* (Flood), was chosen best short film in the children's category by a jury of 11 Berlin children. In it, filmmaker Guy Nattiv portrayed the coming-of-age experience of two teenage brothers. Nattiv, screenwriter Noa Berman Herzberg, and editor Yuval Orr all studied film at the Camera Obscura school in Tel Aviv.

Another film that premiered at the Berlinale was *L'Chayim Comrade Stalin,* a documentary by American filmmaker Yale Strom about the Soviet Jewish autonomous region of Birobidzhan. Both Strom's and Mograbi's films were also shown in June at the eighth annual Jewish Film Festival in Berlin, directed by Nicola Galliner. One of the most remarkable films screened there was German journalist Esther Schapira's 2002 documentary *Three Bullets and a Dead Child,* about the propaganda war over Palestinian children who were either killed in the Israeli-Palestinian conflict or volunteered for suicide missions. American director Pearl Gluck showed her work in progress, *Divan,* a charming and provocative film about her search for a family heirloom couch on which renowned rabbis once slept.

This year the annual two-week Jewish cultural festival in Berlin—one of several such events in Germany—was dedicated to the city of Berlin. It included dozens of programs of theater, music, exhibits, readings, and films. In a new twist, several Berlin-based Jewish filmmakers were asked to produce short films. The resulting works by Sharon Brauner, Dani Levy, Ulrike Ottinger, Esther Slevogt, Arielle Artsztein, and November Wanderin were shown under the title "JEWels."

Germany's first domestically produced comedy TV movie about the Holocaust aired nationwide in November, to mixed reviews. *Goebbels and Geduldig,* by Peter Steinbach, had won several awards in 2001, including two at the New York Film Festival. It told the fictional tale of Harry Geduldig, a Jewish man who looked exactly like Joseph Goebbels, the Nazi propaganda minister (actor Ulrich Mühe played both roles). In the story, the real Goebbels meets his double, and they accidentally switch. Steinbach said he was shocked to hear "that 70 percent of Germans feel they must not laugh about the Nazis." But Nicola Galliner agreed with the naysayers when it came to Holocaust comedy. "You have to be a lot more thoughtful in Germany than in America or England," she said. "You cannot show just anything."

German film director Werner Herzog came out with *Invincible* in 2002, a film about Zishe Breitbart, an Orthodox Jewish blacksmith who became a circus strong man in the early 1930s. German and American fans called him "the strongest man in the world."

Publications

Aufbau, the German Jewish newspaper founded by Jewish immigrants to the United States in 1934, opened a Berlin office in February. The newspaper's publishers were ex-Berliners Manfred George and Ludwig Wronkow. Among the contributors to *Aufbau* in its early days had been Albert Einstein, Thomas Mann, Lion Feuchtwanger, Hannah Arendt, Franz Werfel, and Stefan Zweig. Irene Armbruster, director of the new Berlin office, noted that many Germans expressed surprise that she was not Jewish. She explained to them that Jews and non-Jews had always worked together to produce *Aufbau,* and that the paper hoped to develop a readership in Germany that would go beyond the Jewish community. A new German editorial board member was appointed, historian Julius Schoeps, director of the Moses Mendelssohn Center at the University of Potsdam.

The third edition of *Golem — Europäisch-jüdisches Magazin* (Golem — European-Jewish Magazine), was published in the spring by Philo Verlag in Berlin. The magazine had been launched in 2000 by a group of Berlin-based writers, editors, and artists as a nonprofit venture. All articles were presented in three languages, English, German, and French.

Two works of translation drew considerable attention during the year. *Jews in Berlin* was an English translation of a comprehensive history of Jews in the city that had appeared in German in 2001. The authors were Hermann Simon, director of the Centrum Judaicum Foundation in Berlin, and Rabbi Andreas Nachama, director of the Topography of Terror archive there. A book tour in the U.S. was planned for early 2003. A German translation of Leo Rosten's *The Joys of Yiddish* hit German bookstands in October, 35 years after it first appeared in English. The book's title in German — translatable in English as *Yiddish: A Small Encyclopedia*—did not include the word "joy." Wolfgang Balk, the head of Deutscher Taschenbuch Verlag, which published the book, explained that the word did not convey the seriousness of the work. He called the translation "our most important title this fall. It is very appropriate that a company that calls itself 'German' should show that German and Jewish culture belong together." This was just one indication among many of growing German fascination with Yiddish, part of a more general curiosity about Jews and Judaism.

Other important books on Jewish themes in 2002 included *"Ihr Leben in unserer Hand": Die Geschichte der Jüdischen Brigade im Zweiten Weltkrieg,* a history of the Jewish brigade in World War II by Howard Blum; *"Mein verwundetes Herz": Das Leben der Lilli Jahn 1900–1944,* an epistolary biography of Holocaust victim Lilli Jahn by her grandson, Martin Doerry; *Die Euthanasie und die späte Unschuld der Psychiater: Massenmord, Bedburg-Hau und das Geheimnis rheinischer Widerstandslegende,* a study by Ludwig Hermeler of the role played by Nazi psychiatrists in the "euthanasia" program; *Wegweiser durch das jüdische Mecklenburg-Pomerania,* a guide to Jewish Mecklenburg-Pomerania, the second in a series of books by Irene Diekmann about the history and culture of Jews in the states of the former East Germany; *Antisemitismus in der Region,* about anti-Semitism in several German states from 1870 to

1914, authored by Hansjörg Pötzsch; *Dolgesheimer Mord,* a study of the 1933 murder of Julius Frank, a Jewish resident of a small village, written by Cologne attorney Winfried Seibert; *Errinerungen an die Hagerlocher Juden,* a portrait of the Jewish community of Haigerloch by Utz Jeggle, part of a series published by the University of Tübingen; and *In einem unbewachten Augenblick: Eine Frau überlebt im Untergrund,* the story of a German Jewish woman who survived the Holocaust in hiding, by Mark Roseman.

Personalia

In the fall, Paul Spiegel was reelected to a second four-year term as president of the CCJG. He promised to devote his attention to the integration of the Russian immigrants. Spiegel celebrated his 65th birthday on December 31. In congratulatory messages, Chancellor Schröder, President Rau, and Bundestag president Wolfgang Thierse complimented Spiegel on his dedication to the fight against anti-Semitism and xenophobia, and his commitment to building a better society. Spiegel had been instrumental in creating the "Show Your Face" campaign for civic courage in Germany following a disturbing rise in anti-Semitic and xenophobic crimes in the summer of 2000.

CCJG vice president Michel Friedman was elected to head the European Jewish Congress, becoming the second German Jew to hold that position (the first had been Ignatz Bubis).

Toward the end of the year, after a six-month try-out, Rabbi Ady E. Assabi was hired by the Jewish Community of Berlin to serve the non-Orthodox congregations in the city—Oranienburgerstrasse, Frankelüfer, and Rykerstrasse. Born in Tel Aviv in 1947, he was ordained at the liberal Leo Baeck College in London.

American Jewish businessman Arthur Obermayer presented the third annual Obermayer German Jewish History Awards, for 2002, in Berlin on January 27, 2003, Germany's Holocaust Remembrance Day. The awards honored non-Jewish Germans who contributed toward recording or preserving the Jewish history of their communities. Obermayer was of German-Jewish heritage.

The winners were: Hans-Eberhard Berkemann, an elementary-school teacher who rescued two synagogues from demolition and documented the names of those interred in nine Jewish cemeteries in Bad Sobernheim and Rheinland-Pfalz; Irene Corbach, who, together with her late husband, a Protestant pastor, helped preserve the memory of Jewish life in

Cologne; Carla and Erica Pick, twin sisters and retired schoolteachers who instituted teaching about the history of the local Jewish community in the schools of Borken and Gemen near the Dutch border, where there were no longer any Jews; Gerhard Jochem and Susanne Rieger, who set up a Web site (www.rijo-research.de) on the Jews of Nuremberg; and Heinrich Dittmar, a retired teacher who cared for 16 abandoned Jewish cemeteries in the Hesse region.

The annual Leo Baeck Prize was awarded on September 3, 2002, to German actor Iris Berben. She was recognized for her dedication to tolerance, coexistence, and humanitarian causes, as well as her active commitment to the fight against racism, anti-Semitism, and neo-Nazism in Germany. Berben, who had traveled through Germany reading aloud from the diaries of both Anne Frank and Nazi propaganda minister Josef Goebbels, was the first actor to receive the award since its creation in 1957.

In November, Foreign Minister Joschka Fischer accepted the 14th annual Heinz Galinski award from the Jewish Community of Berlin. He was recognized for his commitment to the security of the State of Israel, and the award was given just one day after two terrorist attacks against Israeli targets in Kenya. "Israel's right to exist is one of the untouchable pillars of our state," said Fischer. In March, Fischer had been the guest speaker at the first major dinner event in the CCJG's history.

German rabbinical student Andreas Jonathan Hinz of Ulm was found murdered in London in July. Hinz had been completing his rabbinical studies at the Leo Baeck College in London and was planning to serve progressive Jewish communities in Germany. Police said the incident was not connected to anti-Semitism.

TOBY AXELROD

Austria

National Affairs

On September 9, after Vice Chancellor Susann Riess-Passer and two other key leaders of the Freedom Party (FPÖ) resigned from the government, Chancellor Wolfgang Schüssel called for new elections. He explained that it was no longer possible to maintain the governing coalition in the face of constant criticism from Jörg Haider, leader of the Freedom Party, the junior partner in the government. The "straw that broke the camel's back" in this case was Haider's strident objection to the government's postponement of promised tax cuts in order to pay for the extensive damage to crops and property brought on by the late-summer floods. The chancellor declared that the Freedom Party had to choose whether it wanted "to govern or oppose. . . . Both are not possible." Following the call from the chancellor, Parliament dissolved itself on September 20, paving the way for elections on November 24.

This brought an end to the increasingly shaky center-right coalition led by Schüssel's People's Party (ÖVP, commonly referred to by its color, blue) and the far-right FPÖ (commonly referred to by its color, black), which had governed the country for two-and-a-half years. After the national elections in late 1999, the conservative ÖVP had struck a deal with Haider, making his party its governing partner. This was the first time in Europe's postwar history that a far-right party shared power at the national level in a member state of the European Union. No sooner had the blue-black coalition been formed in February 2000, however, than it ran into difficulties with the 14 other members of the EU, to whom Haider was anathema because of past remarks praising certain of Hitler's policies, and his unrestrained anti-foreigner views. The EU voted diplomatic sanctions against Austria, but these were withdrawn after seven months, and the coalition partners managed to get along.

That the coalition lasted as long as it did was largely due to Haider's forced resignation from his party's leadership in May 2000. His grip on the party machinery further loosened in February 2002 when he had to quit a national policy-making committee in the coalition government. But Haider remained the dominant force in the Freedom Party, which he effectively controlled from his elected position as governor of the southern province of Carinthia.

Meantime, the fortunes of the Freedom Party began to suffer at the polls after the government made a number of politically unpopular decisions. Though the economy remained buoyant, voters became increasingly disenchanted with painful spending cuts in social and welfare programs. In this changing political climate, the Freedom Party went into free fall, while both the People's Party and the opposition Social Democrats (SPÖ, commonly referred to by their color, red) improved their standing in the provincial elections of 2001. Clearly, joining the government, a long-sought-after goal of Haider's, had cost the Freedom Party much of its appeal as a protest movement. Adding to the party's woes was Haider's bizarre behavior: three visits to Baghdad to attack U.S. policies in the Middle East; several times assuming the party leadership and then resigning—earning him the derisive epithet, "the comeback kid"; and unilaterally naming close allies to key party positions.

It was against this background that Haider, in 2002, launched an attack against the government's taxation policy as well as its support for EU expansion into the former Soviet bloc, policies that more moderate members of his own party—Vice Chancellor Riess-Passer, Finance Minister Karl-Heinz Grasser, and Transport Minister Monika Forstinger—supported. Their resignations induced the chancellor to call for new elections. Most observers believed that Haider deliberately provoked the crisis in the hope of regaining control over the Freedom Party, which, everyone acknowledged, he had almost single-handedly made into a national political force.

The election turned out to be a triumph for Chancellor Schüssel's People's Party, which won 42 percent of the vote. This was the first time since 1966 that the People's Party had come in first. In second place were the Social Democrats at 37 percent. Haider's Freedom Party plunged from its record of 27 percent in November 2000 to just over 10 percent. The Green Party came in last, with 9 percent. The People's Party's strong showing was largely attributed to the chancellor's adroit handling of the economy and of the volatile Haider. Schüssel apparently understood from the beginning that his embrace of the Freedom Party would set off a storm of international criticism. Yet, over time, he had succeeded in splitting the far-right party by persuading its more moderate members to eschew xenophobia and anti-European policies, while at the same time adopting some of the FPÖ's more reasonable positions, such as faster privatization of state-owned industries and retrenchment in government spending.

That the Freedom Party's defeat turned into a rout had much to do with Haider's unusual behavior and extreme rhetoric, and also with the fact that playing the anti-foreigner card, as he had done with much effect in 2000, now failed to fire up latent Austrian xenophobia because the government had already tightened the immigration and asylum laws.

Despite the People's Party's impressive showing, it still needed a coalition partner in order to govern. The question was who that partner would be. The Social Democrats, the Freedom Party, and the Greens each offered potential benefits, but also political problems. Another option was for the People's Party to form a minority government and rule on its own. While that might lead to instability and early calls for a new election, some analysts noted that several Nordic countries had been governed quite satisfactorily by minority governments.

Israel and the Middle East

Relations between Israel and Austria continued to be strained. Jerusalem had withdrawn its ambassador to Vienna following the swearing-in of the new government in February 2000, and only maintained a chargé d'affaires, Avraham Toledo. This action had been taken in response to the Freedom Party's inclusion in the coalition. Israel continued to show its diplomatic displeasure with Vienna even after the EU countries restored normal ties with it in September 2000 (see AJYB 2001, pp. 397–98). Discreet attempts by Austria to normalize relations with Israel went unanswered.

However, as far-right parties made impressive gains in national elections in other European countries, the policy of maintaining limited diplomatic relations with Austria became increasingly untenable. In Italy, the far-right National Alliance of Gianfranco Fini became a member of Silvio Berlusconi's center-right government. In Portugal and the Netherlands as well, far-right parties joined government coalitions, confirming the startling rightward political shift in Western Europe, and yet Israel continued to maintain normal ties with these governments. The patent inconsistency in this policy may well have been the reason why Jerusalem showed signs of reconsidering its position regarding Austria. In July, in an interview with ARD, the German television station, Prime Minister Sharon said: "I have in fact proposed to our foreign minister that he try to restore relations with Austria." Though the Austrian foreign minister stated that Israel would have to take the first step in normalizing ties, Vienna made that possibility easier by maintaining its ambassador, Wolfgang Paul, in Tel Aviv rather than retaliating against Israel's withdrawal of its ambassador by calling him home. When Ambassador Paul completed his term of office in September, Vienna replaced him with another diplomat of equal rank, Kurt Hengl. Following Austria's government crisis in September and the subsequent breakup of the coalition, no further progress was made towards normalizing relations with Israel.

At the UN, Austria joined with other EU countries in voting against Israel on issues relating to Palestine.

As a result of the strained relations between the two countries, only two visits of high-ranking officials took place during the year. Kurt Fischer, president of the Austrian Parliament, came to Jerusalem in January at the invitation of Avraham Burg, speaker of the Knesset. In May, the mayor of Tel Aviv, Ron Hulda'i, was welcomed in Vienna as the guest of Mayor Michael Häupl. In addition, a cultural agreement between Israel and Austria, the third such arrangement, was signed in November. It spelled out a plan for intensified contacts over the coming four years in the areas of film, music, dance, and science. Earlier, in May, an Austrian delegation headed by State Secretary Franz Morak came to Israel and met with Matan Vilnai, Israel's minister of culture. They agreed that the Vienna State Opera would perform in Israel in February 2003, but its appearance was postponed because of security concerns.

An official Austrian exhibition depicting the life and times of Sigmund Freud was held in May at the Beth Hatefutsoth in Tel Aviv, with the cosponsorship of the U.S. Library of Congress. Itamar Rabinovich, president of Tel Aviv University, officially opened the exhibition.

Holocaust Restitution and Compensation

Under terms of the Washington agreement signed on January 17, 2001 (see AJYB 2002, pp. 438–39), the Nationalfond, established in 1995, was to distribute $150 million in an expedited manner to survivors of the National Socialist era. Each claimant was to receive $7,000 for losses of rental apartments, small-business leases, household property, and personal valuables and effects. In the event an eligible person died after October 24, 2000, his or her heirs could apply for the money. As of December 31, 2002, payments had been made to 19,000 survivors or heirs living in many different countries.

Another major component of the agreement called for establishment by the Austrian government of a General Settlement Fund (GSF) so as to acknowledge, through voluntary payments, Austria's moral responsibility for losses and damages inflicted upon Jewish citizens and other victims of National Socialism. Following through on this aspect of the agreement, the Austrian Parliament enacted legislation in January 2002 creating such a fund, in the amount of $210 million. These monies, to be administered by the Nationalfond, were to be provided by the Republic of Austria and by Austrian companies. Persons or associations persecuted by the Nazi regime or forced to leave the country to escape such persecution, and who/which suffered property losses or damages, were eligible to apply. Categories of property for which compensation could be sought were liquidated businesses, real property, bank accounts, stocks, bonds, mortgages, insurance policies, and occupational or educational losses. In addition, applications would be accepted for restitution of real estate and buildings (in the case of Jewish organizations, also tangible movable property) owned by the federal government or the city of Vienna as of January 17, 2001. The deadline for filing was set for May 28, 2003. As of December 31, 2002, 7,000 claims had been filed. A key condition of the agreement was that no money would be paid out of the GSF until all U.S. class-action suits against Austria and/or Austrian companies relating to the National Socialist era were dismissed. As the year ended, there were still two such suits pending in U.S. federal courts, one in New York and the other in Los Angeles.

Under the terms setting up the GSF, claimants turned down by the claims committee might appeal the decision. It would then go to a special three-person arbitration panel, one of whose members would be named by the U.S. government, another by the Austrian government, and the third, chosen jointly by them, would serve as chair. Appeals to the panel had to be filed no later than October 4, 2003 or, at the latest, one year after the Austrian Historical Commission issued its final report (see below).

Another part of the Washington agreement was the allocation of an additional $112 million to be paid out in the form of social benefits to survivors living outside of Austria, including those who were under six years of age in 1938, when Nazi Germany annexed the country. These monies were available, on a case-by-case basis, for nursing care, the retroactive purchase of pension rights, and similar purposes. Responsibility for payment rested with Austria's Ministry of Social Affairs and the administrative authorities of the Austrian pension fund.

Toward the end of 2001, Ariel Muzicant, president of the Israelitische Kultusgemeinde (IKG), the representative body of Austrian Jewry, met with representatives of the federal government and the country's nine provincial governments to resolve outstanding issues that had not been addressed by the Washington accord. Negotiations with the federal authorities centered not only on Holocaust compensation but also on strengthening the IKG's network of social services, such as help for the Jewish elderly and new immigrants, meeting rising security costs, improving Jewish schools, and renovating synagogues. The sum requested was on the order of $22.5 million. While no progress was made in these negotiations, the talks with the provincial authorities yielded positive results in regard to the return of looted artworks and ritual artifacts, upkeep of Jewish cemeteries, and aid for social institutions. In May 2002, an agreement was signed with a committee of four of the provincial governors, representing all nine, on compensating the Federation of Jewish Communities of Austria $18 million over five years. The same condition attached to the GSF disbursements would apply: payments would only begin once the U.S. class-action suits were closed.

Under a plan worked out in U.S. federal court in August, two Austrian banks, Credit Anstalt and Bank Austria AG, made the first payments to settle Holocaust-victim claims arising from the Nazi seizure of the banks over 60 years earlier. A three-member claims committee reviewed some 58,000 claims for the $40-million settlement agreed upon by the two banks. About $30 million were set aside in a fund for survivors and their heirs. The rest was divided into two other funds, one of which would support the Austrian Historical Commission's investigation of Austrian banks' activities during the Nazi era and the publication of its report.

The Holocaust Victims' Information and Support Center (HVISC, or Anlaufstelle), which the IKG established in July 1999, expanded its work of promoting and protecting the interests of Jewish Holocaust victims in and from Austria (see AJYB 2002, p. 441). Through its extensive data banks, research and information programs, and semiannual newsletter, the HVISC, with a small staff, helped survivors and their heirs comply with the complex requirements for obtaining compensation and restitution of properties seized by the Nazis. Two HVISC social workers provided information on how to obtain documents, such as birth and marriage certificates and proof of past membership in the IKG, which were often required to claim compensation. They also assisted people, many of them elderly, in filling out forms and submitting them by the deadlines.

HVISC researchers were often able to locate archival material identifying the personal effects and furniture of people whose apartments were taken over by Austrians after they were forced to emigrate.

This information was stored in a computer database where survivors or their heirs could consult it. The HVISC also developed databases of Jewish associations that had been in existence prior to 1938 but were dissolved by the Nazis and had their assets confiscated. Starting in 2001, it trained lawyers and historians in the use of archival materials so that these resources could be used in processing claims for compensation from the GSF. In June 2002, the IKG concluded an agreement with the U.S. Holocaust Memorial Museum for microfilming the complete collection of archival material covering the National Socialist period as it related to Austria's Jewish population.

The HVISC also worked with the Erste Bank in researching Jewish assets that the bank held during the Nazi regime and thereafter. They found 199 savings accounts of Jewish clients that were looted by the Nazis after the annexation of Austria.

The HVISC was active in securing the restitution of artworks. Four of its representatives sat on the Austrian Commission for the Investigation of the Provenance of Art Objects. Since the 1998 Austrian federal law concerning "Return of Works of Art from Austrian Federal Museums and Collections" did not provide for a search of owners or heirs, the HVISC sometimes carried out its own investigations. It also provided technical support to several of the provinces—notably Styria, Upper Austria, and Vienna—in crafting legislation for restituting artworks from provincial museums and collections, and undertook investigations on behalf of individuals with claims for the restitution of artwork.

On October 1, 1998, the government had set up the Austrian Historical Commission (Historikerkommission) with the mandate ". . . to investigate and report on the whole complex of expropriations in Austria during the Nazi regime and on restitution and/or compensation (including other financial or social benefits) after 1945 by the Republic of Austria." By early 2000, the commission had issued two reports, one on "forced labor" and the other on "withdrawal of rental rights." On June 6, 2002, it submitted six more reports, dealing mostly with the legal and practical implications, on the federal and provincial levels, of Austria's postwar restitution and compensation legislation. Six more interim reports were issued before the end of the year. A final report was expected in March 2003.

In an unprecedented action, Austrian police seized a painting by Egon Schiele just before it was to go on sale at the Dorotheum, Vienna's famed auction house, in November. The seizure was at the request of the IKG, which was acting on behalf of the heirs of Dr. Heinrich Rieger, a Jewish dentist in Vienna, whose collection of early-20th-century Austrian art was among the world's largest. The IKG claimed that the painting, *Wayside Shrine, Houses and Trees,* had been part of an 800-piece collection expropriated in 1938 under the "Aryanization" policy, and taken by Dr. Friedrich Welz, a prominent gallery owner and Nazi party member. Rieger was killed in 1942 in the Theresienstadt concentration camp, and his collection was never returned to the heirs. Even though Austria passed a law in 1998 under which such items were to be given back, this was the first time that authorities had confiscated an art object on grounds that it might have been illegally taken by the Nazis. Since many other paintings from the Rieger collection were held in public and private collections in numerous countries, and the ownership of these artworks might also be contested, the outcome of this case, according to legal experts, could have ramifications throughout the art world.

This tangled web of information about the painting became known through the research of Stephan Templ and Tina Walzer, whose book, sarcastically entitled *Unser Wien* (Our Vienna), was published in Germany in 2001. Indeed, the book's publication was expected to have an impact on the final legal disposition of the case. Previous efforts to recover Nazi-confiscated art in Austria and other European countries were often stymied by a provision of the law, dating back to ancient Roman jurisprudence, stating that a stolen object bought in good faith could not be recovered by the original owner. In this case, however, lawyers for the Rieger heirs were prepared to argue that *Unser Wien* had already established and made public the fact that the Rieger collection was, or could have been, stolen, and that the auction house should have known of this.

Another Schiele painting was likely to be restituted to heirs of the prewar Jewish owner, Daisy Hellman, by the city of Linz. In December 2002, municipal authorities decided to return *Landscape at Krumau,* a $10-million Schiele landscape, completed in 1916 and held in the city's New Gallery museum, to the seven legal heirs. After Hellman fled Austria when the Nazis annexed the country, the Gestapo seized the work. A Vienna auction house sold it to a collector from Berlin, who sold it to the Linz museum in 1953. Although the New Gallery purchased the painting without knowing its provenance and was therefore not legally bound to relinquish it, Franz Dobusch, the mayor of Linz, explained: "Morally, this return is justified." For three years, the IKG had been working to help the heirs regain the painting.

In a landmark decision in California in December, a three-member panel of the U.S. Ninth Circuit Court of Appeals ruled that Maria Altmann, an 87-year-old Los Angeles woman, could sue the Austrian government in U.S. courts to recover six Gustav Klimt paintings. Now valued at $135 million, they had been taken by the Nazis from her uncle, Ferdinand Bloch. Even though, following the war, the family agreed that the paintings belonged to the Austrian National Gallery, Altmann, who fled to California to escape the Nazis, contended in her suit that the family had been coerced into signing away its rights. The court's unanimous decision marked the first time that a federal appeals court required a foreign government to answer in the United States for a Holocaust claim. Federal law, under the doctrine of sovereign immunity, had generally barred lawsuits against foreign governments, although there were certain exceptions. The court ruled that Altmann's case fell under an exception—when rights or property are taken in violation of international law. The attorney representing the Austrian government and the state-run Austrian National Gallery said that his clients were considering an appeal to the U.S. Supreme Court.

A court of lay judges in the town of Feldkirch found journalist and publisher Walter Ochensberger guilty of six counts of Holocaust denial for writing articles claiming that the Holocaust had not happened. The court sentenced him, in January, to a two-year term—eight months to be served in prison and the rest on probation. Long associated with extreme right-wing groups, Ochensberger had previously been convicted of similar charges.

An exhibition documenting atrocities committed by German soldiers during World War II, which had already provoked severe controversy in Berlin (see AJYB 2002, pp. 417–18), went on display in Vienna, running from April 9 through May 26. The exhibition, showing photographs of Wehrmacht soldiers carrying out crimes against civilians, sparked a demonstration by some 180 right-wing protesters who marched in Heldenplatz (Heroes Square) carrying placards charging that the exhibition desecrated the memory of German soldiers. It was in this square that Adolf Hitler addressed masses of Austrians after annexing the country in March 1938. As some 2,000 left-wing counterdemonstrators approached carrying banners reading "Give no inch to the fascists" and "Solidarity with the victims of anti-Semitism," police intervened to avoid violence. For decades after the war, many Germans and others had believed that it was primarily the Nazi SS and Gestapo that carried out Hitler's murderous policies, and that the regular army was not involved.

In solemn ceremonies held in Vienna in April, the body parts of executed opponents of the Nazi regime were put to rest in Vienna's central cemetery. The burial, in a communal grave near the tombs of Beethoven and Schubert, marked an end to a grisly chapter in the history of the University of Vienna. Until just a few years earlier, the university had been using the body parts for research at its anatomy institute. The university launched an investigation after the Yad Vashem Holocaust memorial in Israel alleged that the university had used the corpses of victims from the notorious Mauthausen concentration camp for its celebrated anatomy text, the *Atlas of Topographical and Applied Human Anatomy.* Often referred to as the *Pernkopf Atlas* after its creator, Eduard Pernkopf, an ardent Nazi who became dean of the medical faculty in 1938, this hand-illustrated book was widely used by medical and art students throughout the world.

After a yearlong investigation, historian Gustav Spann concluded that there was no evidence that the cadavers used in preparing the atlas came from Mauthausen, which was some 125 miles away. Rather, Spann said, they came "from just around the corner." Between 1938 and 1945, when Austria was part of the Third Reich, the corpses of 1,377 men and women (eight of them Jewish) went straight from the Vienna guillotine to the university's laboratories. More than half of the victims were executed for opposing the Nazis or for "treason." And, indeed, some of the human tissue was still being used at the university in the mid-1990s. The epitaph on the new tombstone of the victims read: "Here rest the mortal remains of victims not known by name of National Socialist justice whose bodies were unlawfully used for research and teaching in the anatomical and other institutes of the University of Vienna's Faculty of Medicine. The University of Vienna regrets deeply this culpable involvement and commemorates these people with great respect."

In another commemorative ceremony, the remains of children tortured and murdered by the Nazis in the name of medical research were also laid to rest in Vienna's central cemetery, six decades after their death. Between 1940 and 1945, 789 mentally and physically handicapped children were killed at Am Spiegelgrund hospital for leading "worthless lives." The brains of most of these children, preserved in a chemical solution and used for neurological research, remained accessible to the medical profession until only a few months before the burial. In recent years, the Austrian government had come under heavy pressure from families of the victims and survivors of the infanticide program to have a proper interment of the remains. Approximately 600 urns were buried over a two-week period in April, under stone plaques inscribed with each child's name. The headstone on the honorary grave read: "Never forget." Addressing the mourners, Austrian president Thomas Klestil said that his nation had been very late in facing up to this criminal chapter of its history. Austrians, he warned, must ensure that a "cloak of silence" not be spread over what happened, and that those who participated in the Nazi euthanasia program should be brought to justice.

Reality did not match the rhetoric. Dr. Heinrich Gross, one of the chief perpetrators of these crimes against children, remained a free man. Gross became a prominent neurologist and forensic psychiatrist in postwar Austria despite several attempts to bring him to trial. He often appeared as an expert witness on psychiatric matters in Austrian courts, and published dozens of papers on brain deformations, much of it based upon research undertaken on the Spiegelgrund victims. Austria awarded Gross a medal of honor in 1975 for his psychiatric work. Gross was finally brought to trial in 1999 for acting as an accessory to multiple infanticide at the clinic in 1944, but proceedings were suspended after the court heard he was suffering from dementia (see AJYB 2000, pp. 367–68). In May 2002, apparently embarrassed by the publicity attending the burial of the remains of the children and those of the opponents of the Nazi regime, the government stripped the 86-year-old Gross of his medal.

The U.S. Department of Justice carried out the order of an American court to deport Michael Gruber from the U.S. to Austria. Gruber, an Austrian citizen, had served as an armed guard at the Sachsenhausen concentration camp during World War II.

JEWISH COMMUNITY

Demography

The Jewish population registered with the IKG numbered 6,702, an increase of 95 over 2001. Knowledgeable observers, however, placed the actual number of Jews living in the country at 10,000–12,000. Following a long historical pattern, the overwhelming majority of Jews lived in Vienna; only some 300–400 made their homes elsewhere, primarily in the large provincial cities of Salzburg, Graz, Baden, and Linz.

The Jewish community worried about its small numbers; many young Jews were leaving in search of economic opportunities elsewhere, and there was little immigration. In 2000, the IKG had requested the government to waive certain provisions of the country's highly restrictive immigration laws so as to allow the entry of the same number of Jews who left. The government did not respond at the time, and the IKG did not pursue the matter.

Communal Affairs

Elections were held over a three-day period to select members of the IKG governing board. Of 5,198 eligible voters, 3,255, or 62.6 percent, turned out to vote. Eight parties competed in the election, with Atid, the party headed by IKG president Ariel Muzicant, winning 11, a plurality of the 24-member board. The other parties winning seats were Sephardim-Bukharin (3); Federation of Social Democratic Jews (3); Kehal Yisroel (3); Alternative (1); Mizrahi (1); Bloc of Religious Jews (1); and Georgian Jews (1). The new board unanimously reelected Muzicant to another term as president.

With an eye to improving the IKG's efficiency, the board established a special reform commission charged with reviewing the work of the board in all its aspects, and recommending changes in the statutes governing its operations—statutes that had remained in effect virtually unchanged since their enactment in 1896. The commission was to submit its report in two years.

Toward the end of the year, an organizational plan was developed for the establishment of a new research center, to be called the Vienna Wiesenthal Institute for Holocaust Studies. It would bring together relevant archival resources of the Jewish community, the Wiesenthal Documentation Center, and the Austrian Resistance Center, and was expected to open in 2003. Working in collaboration with the Institute of Contemporary History of the University of Vienna, it would offer fellowships, host scholarly lectures, hold seminars in the field of Holocaust studies, and disseminate findings to the broader public. Mayor Häupl of Vienna indicated that the city would provide some initial financial backing, and the IKG planned, at a later stage, to seek federal government support as well.

The IKG negotiated an agreement with the governor of Lower Austria and the mayor of Baden to restore that city's synagogue, desecrated by the Nazis on Kristallnacht, November 9–10, 1938. The work was to be completed in 2004.

As part of a court settlement, Jörg Haider apologized to Ariel Muzicant for making derogatory remarks about his character during the 2001 Vienna state election. In a statement released to the press in January 2002, Haider said he "withdraws" his comments with "an expression of regret and apology." During the campaign, Haider had made mocking reference to Muzicant's first name, which was also the name of a brand of detergent, saying: "I don't understand how someone called Ariel can have so much dirt on his hands" (see AJYB 2002, pp. 434–35).

In a solemn ceremony on November 10, the 64th anniversary of Kristallnacht, a monument was dedicated to the Austrian Jewish victims of the Holocaust. The monument, designed by architect Thomas Feiger and located in the Stadttempel, Vienna's central synagogue, was in the form of a book, with the names of the 65,000 Austrian Jews who perished inscribed on it. Attending the ceremony were President Klestil; Heinz Fischer, president of the National Parliament; Mayor Häupl of Vienna; Avraham Toledo, the Israeli chargé d'affaires; Chief Rabbi Chaim Eisenberg; and IKG president Muzicant.

Among the exhibitions mounted by the Vienna Jewish Museum was one, titled "Music and Poetry," that ran from October 23 through January 6, 2002, featuring manuscripts from the collections of Stefan Zweig and Martin Bodmer. Included were autographed manuscripts of Wolfgang Amadeus Mozart, Ludwig van Beethoven, Franz Schubert, Gustav Mahler, Felix Mendelssohn-Bartholdy, Claude Debussy, Hugo von Hofmannsthal, Arnold Schoenberg, Arthur Schnitzler, and Sigmund Freud. Before his expulsion from Austria, Zweig had been obliged to sell the collection. It was acquired in 1936 by the Swiss academician Martin Bodmer (1899–1971), who added to it and converted it into a foundation consisting of selected manuscripts, books, and works of art going back three millennia — a library, in the full sense of the word, of world literature.

Another exhibition contained pictures and models of works by the architect Ernst Epstein (1881–1938), whose buildings left an indelible mark on the city of Vienna. Epstein was responsible for about 100 structures, mostly middle-class residential buildings, but also simpler apartment houses, villas, and industrial facilities throughout Vienna. His style reflected practically all of the fashionable movements of the age. On May 21, 1938, Epstein, by now a wealthy man and childless widower, took his own life out of fear of arrest by the Gestapo. The exhibition ran from June 30 through September 29.

A third exhibition featured the life and work of the painter and sculptor Ernst Eisenmayer. Born in Vienna in 1920, Eisenmayer was deported to Dachau in 1938, but managed to escape before the war and made his way to London. There he met the famed painter Oskar Kokoschka, who helped him in his artistic development. Eisenmayer's creations are in the classic Modernist style, his early works heavily influenced by life in exile—the subject is often man and his fate, with depictions of oppression, violence, and abuse of power. The exhibition presented a wide range of sculptures, oil paintings, and drawings. Between 1975 and 1988 Eisenmayer lived and worked in Carrara, Italy. In 1996, he returned to his native city of Vienna.

The fourth Vienna International Theodor Herzl Symposium was held April 8–11 under the patronage of President Klestil and Mayor Häupl. Attended by scholars as well as by religious and communal leaders from Israel, the United States, and Austria, it had as its major theme the significance of the Jewish Diaspora and its relationship to Israel.

The Jewish Cultural Weeks Festival, in October and November, offered a wide array of events—music, featuring chamber-music concerts with the Amber Trio and other groups; lectures, notably orchestra conductor Herbert Prikopa speaking on "Jewish Influence on Viennese Song"; plays, such as performances by the Dora Wasserman Yiddish Theater of Montreal; and a variety of films on Jewish life.

Personalia

In April, the International Association of Prosecutors awarded its Medal of Honor—given to figures who promote and defend human rights under the just rule of law—to Nazi-hunter Simon Wiesenthal. Wiesenthal was the third person to receive this honor; his two predecessors were Justice Louise Arbour of the Canadian Supreme Court and the UN war-crimes tribunal in The Hague, and former South African president Nelson Mandela.

MURRAY GORDON SILBERMAN

East-Central Europe

T HE POSTCOMMUNIST COUNTRIES of the region continued to institutionalize their integration with the West. At a NATO summit in Prague in November, Bulgaria, Estonia, Latvia, Lithuania, Romania, Slovakia, and Slovenia were invited to join the 19-nation alliance. The newcomers would assume full membership in 2004. In December, a European Union summit in Copenhagen formally agreed to admit ten new countries to the EU: Cyprus, the Czech Republic, Estonia, Hungary, Latvia, Lithuania, Malta, Poland, Slovakia, and Slovenia. They would officially enter on May 1, 2004.

These landmark decisions came against the background of global developments related to the war on terrorism, the conflict in the Middle East, and the buildup to possible war with Iraq, all of which had an impact on the region. There was also continuing concern over the persistence of racism—directed primarily against Roma (Gypsies)—and anti-Semitism in the region, though anti-Semitism linked to the Palestinian intifada was less of a concern in former communist states than in it was in some Western countries.

NATO made respect for ethnic and religious minorities one of its criteria for joining. In March, representatives of Jewish communities in East-Central Europe met in Bucharest, at the same time that a summit of leaders from postcommunist states aspiring to enter NATO was taking place there. Participants in the Jewish roundtable—organized by the American Jewish Committee—came from Bulgaria, Croatia, Estonia, Latvia, Lithuania, Macedonia, Romania, and Slovenia, as well as from three states that had entered NATO in 1999—Poland, the Czech Republic, and Hungary. The delegates presented status reports on Jewish affairs in their countries, which were circulated to prime ministers and NATO officials at the summit.

Jewish communities continued their own internal development and integration with European and world Jewry. Countries in the region took part in the European Day of Jewish Culture, held June 16, a continent-wide initiative that saw hundreds of Jewish-heritage sites in more than a score of countries opened to the public.

Paris historian Diana Pinto, a leading proponent of the idea of a new pan-European Jewish identity, declared that now, 13 years after the fall of communism opened the way for Jewish revival, it was "bar mitzvah time"—a moment to reflect on achievements already made and to plan for the future. In Prague in November, representatives from Jewish communities in some 40 countries attended a "meeting of presidents" sponsored by the European Council of Jewish Communities. Debate centered on the impact of rising anti-Semitism; global terrorism; Islamic fundamentalism; Holocaust revisionism; and widespread support for the Palestinian side in the Middle East conflict and the consequent demonization of Israel. There was also considerable hands-on discussion of internal issues related to Jewish communal development.

Bosnia-Herzegovina

In April, Bosnia-Herzegovina marked ten years since the outbreak of its 1992–95 war and international recognition of its independence from the former Yugoslavia. In general elections held October 5, nationalist parties representing rival Serbs, Muslims, and Croats made a strong showing. Vienna's *Die Presse* newspaper called the vote a clear rebuke to efforts to foster closer coexistence between these communities, and said that the international community should now rethink its strategy in Bosnia.

In July, the presidents of Yugoslavia, Bosnia, and Croatia held a landmark summit in Sarajevo. The first top-level three-way meeting of the main countries involved in the Bosnian and Croatian wars, it was aimed at rebuilding links, trust, and cooperation.

In December, coinciding with Hanukkah, the 14th-century Sarajevo Haggadah went on permanent public display for the first time in its history. Handwritten in Spain and brought to Sarajevo after the expulsion of the Spanish Jews in 1492, it had long symbolized the Jewish presence in the Balkans. A gala ceremony inaugurated the exhibition of the priceless 109-page manuscript in a secure, new, climate-controlled room in the Sarajevo National Museum, where it was displayed along with valuable religious texts of the same period produced by Bosnia's other faiths: Islam, Catholicism, and Orthodoxy. The $150,000 project to restore the Haggadah and prepare the new exhibition room was spearheaded by Ambassador Jacques-Paul Klein, special representative of the UN secretary general to Bosnia-Herzegovina. It was facilitated by grants from the UN mission to Bosnia, the Bosnian Jewish community, the Joint Distribution Committee (JDC), and two foundations—Yad Hanadiv and Wolfenson. Representatives of the other faiths, including the chief Muslim imam of Bosnia, joined Jewish leaders and government officials for the impressive inauguration ceremony.

When Klein left his post in December, Jakob Finci, president of the Bosnian Jewish community, sent him a letter of appreciation thanking Klein for his "generous personal contribution" to the Haggadah project as well as his assistance in restoring Sarajevo's Old Synagogue. Finci wrote: "From the very beginning you have championed mutual understanding and respect as the means to bring disparate ethnic and religious communities in our country together. We do not know of any other international statesman who has taken the time and the effort that you have to explore the underpinnings of our life and faith."

Bulgaria

Bulgaria remained one of Europe's poorest nations, with an average annual monthly salary of little more than $100, and fraud and corruption were widespread. President Georgi Parvanov took office on January 22.

Jewish leaders expressed concern during the year at increasing anti-Semitism, including graffiti and anti-Semitic publications. While not quite calling it an organized phenomenon, one Jewish leader said, "at least as a publishing activity, anti-Semitism has become more than just a pattern of infrequent, isolated episodes." At a news conference in February, the leaders of five Evangelical churches in Bulgaria denounced rising anti-Semitism, noting the recent publication of material with an anti-Semitic character or espousing Holocaust denial, as well as skinhead threats against Roma and other minorities. One publication specifically noted was *The Boomerang of Evil* by the deputy editor of the *Monitor,* a daily newspaper that ran anti-Jewish material. The book, they said, was a collection of classic anti-Semitic stereotypes.

March 9 was designated as the official Day of Commemoration of Holocaust Victims and the Rescue of Bulgarian Jews. At a ceremony on March 10 in Plovdiv, in front of a Holocaust monument, President Parvanov described it as "a day of deserved national pride." It was on March 9, 1943, that preparations were being finalized by the Nazi-allied government to deport 8,500 Jews to Auschwitz. But protests by parliamentary deputies, clergymen, intellectuals, and ordinary citizens prevented the deportation. One of those Jews who was to have been deported with that group was Emanuel Zisman, a native of Plovdiv, who now served as Israel's ambassador to Bulgaria.

On March 12, Yad Vashem named Metropolitans Stefan of Sofia and Kiril of Plovdiv as Righteous Among the Nations in recognition of the role the Bulgarian Orthodox Church played in the rescue of the country's 50,000 Jews from the Nazis. On April 9, coinciding with Yom Hashoah,

Holocaust Remembrance Day, the National Assembly, Bulgaria's parliament, unanimously adopted a declaration condemning all manifestations of racism, xenophobia, and anti-Semitism as threats to a democratic civil society and as contradicting human, moral, and Euro-Atlantic values. The National Assembly's speaker recalled the role of wartime legislators, headed by Dimitâr Peshev, in helping foil the deportations. He also underscored the role of the king at the time, Boris III, the father of the current prime minister, Simeon Saxecoburggotski. In October, a museum was opened in honor of Peshev, in the house in the town of Kjustendil where he was born in 1894. It was funded by the Israeli embassy and private donations, mostly from Bulgarian Jews who lived in Israel.

In May, the third biannual Sephardi cultural event, Esperansa, took place near Sofia. About 1,600 people from Bulgaria, Romania, Ukraine, Turkey, Greece, Israel, and the former Yugoslavia attended the four-day celebration of song, dance, theater, and cuisine. A delegation of board members of the JDC, the main organizer of the event, also attended. The festival concluded with six couples, ranging in age from 45 to 55, renewing their matrimonial vows under six wedding canopies, in the kind of traditional Jewish ceremony that had been forbidden under communism.

In June, Israeli foreign minister Shimon Peres made a two-day official visit to Bulgaria. He met with the president, prime minister, and foreign minister. During the year, the Bulgarian government began implementing a long-term strategy to revive relations with Arab countries. Thus there were high-level official contacts with Libya, Jordan, and Syria, and Prime Minister Saxecoburggotski and Foreign Minister Solomon Passy both visited the Middle East.

In the summer, Passy, who is Jewish, was named an honorary member of the International Raoul Wallenberg Foundation, in recognition of Bulgaria's wartime rescue of its Jews. The foundation, established in 1966 to promote dialogue, understanding, and peace among nations, carried out research on, and publicized the work of, people who rescued Jews and others during World War II.

In July, Prime Minister Saxecoburggotski urged the National Assembly to adopt a legal framework that would guarantee the right "to a religious faith and religious freedoms."

Croatia

In January, David Granit, Israel's ambassador to Croatia, honored ten Croatian individuals or families as Righteous Among the Nations for saving Jews during the Holocaust, when Croatia was ruled as a Nazi puppet state by the fascist Ustashe movement. The ceremony—which was streamed over the Internet—took place at a Zagreb high school. The students wrote stories about each of those honored, which were published in the school newspaper and given to the families of the honorees. Granit urged young Croats to learn more about the Holocaust, and President Stipe Mesic, who attended the ceremony, urged Croats to take pride in their countrymen who showed courage and saved Jews. The ceremony was part of a Holocaust education program spearheaded by Natasha Jovicic of the Ministry of Education, who also initiated several pilot programs to introduce Holocaust education into Croatian schools. The Jewish community of Zagreb was granted $20,000 from the Claims Conference to train educators to teach about the Holocaust, but the funds had not yet been utilized as the year ended. Another Claims Conference grant enabled the Jewish community in Osijek to initiate a Holocaust research project that included publication of a book on the history of the Jews of Vinkovci.

In December, Jovicic—newly named the director of the recently reopened museum at the former Ustashe-run Jasenovac concentration camp—announced the disturbing findings of a study she had initiated of how Croatian textbooks dealt with the Holocaust. A group of high-school teachers analyzed 23 texts used in Croatian elementary schools, and found a clear tendency to rationalize Croatia's role. One eighth-grade history book, for example, was found to have relativized fascism and the antifascist resistance to the point where they were morally indistinguishable. This book included a picture of Croatian wartime leader Ante Pavelić with a caption describing him as a jurist, politician, and the founder of the Ustashe movement, but making no mention of the war crimes committed under his rule.

Simmering tensions regarding Croatia's role in World War II persisted through 2002. Early in the year, writer Slavko Goldstein and his son, Ivo, came under attack in the media—including the Catholic press and Croatian television—for criticizing Alojzije Stepinac, the archbishop of Zagreb between 1941 and 1945, in a book on the Holocaust in that city. (Slavko Goldstein, now 73, joined the Yugoslav Resistance in 1942, after his father was killed by the Ustashe. He served as president of Zagreb's Jewish community from 1986 to 1990. Ivo Goldstein was professor of medieval history at the University of Zagreb.) In their book, the Goldsteins noted that Stepinac did save some Jews and that after the war he was sentenced to 16 years in jail on trumped-up charges. But they also wrote that he failed to condemn the Ustashe regime or the Nazis until 1943, when his brother was killed by either the Nazis or Ustashe. The book had won praise when it came out in late 2001, and President Mesic spoke at a ceremony at Zagreb's Old City Hall marking its publication.

In April, Prime Minister Ivica Racan took part in a ceremony at Jasenovac honoring hundreds who died in a failed attempt by about 600 prisoners to break out of the camp on April 22, 1945.

In November, at Zagreb's Mimara Art Museum, President Mesic inaugurated an exhibition on the Holocaust, "The Courage to Remember," organized by the Simon Wiesenthal Center and brought to the Croat capital by the Civic Committee for Human Rights, a Zagreb-based NGO concerned with the recent Balkan wars. The exhibit, shown in 19 countries since 1988, consisted of 40 panels documenting the Holocaust from the rise of Nazism in 1933 to the survivors' postwar struggles. A small group of Croatian nationalist demonstrators protested the opening, demanding "Jews out of Croatia."

Concern about nostalgia among young people for the Ustashe regime—exemplified by a concert at a stadium in Split, where some in the crowd of 40,000 wore Ustashe insignia and waved Nazi flags—prompted Croatian legislators to sponsor a bill, in the fall, criminalizing the glorification of Nazi ideology. It was still under debate as the year ended.

Amendments passed in the summer to a property-restitution law stipulated that people who emigrated from Croatia but did not maintain their citizenship would be eligible for restitution of property confiscated by Croatia's wartime fascists or by the postwar communist government. Jewish Holocaust survivors who left Croatia after World War II and Jews who, after the war, emigrated and settled in Israel and were forced to give up their citizenship in order to leave, would be among those benefiting from the changes. Under the law, only direct lineal descendants had the right to be compensated for seized property, and compensation was capped at a maximum of $500,000. A deadline of January 5, 2003, was set for filing claims.

Relations between Croatia and Israel, launched with the establishment of full diplomatic ties five years earlier, were good. One result was an influx of Israeli tourists to Croatia, with some 100,000 coming in 2002.

In May, the leftist *Feral Tribune* newspaper published an editorial accusing the government of not supporting a UN resolution criticizing Israel for "petty pragmatic reasons," such as fear of alienating Israeli tourists. It called on Croatian Jews themselves to criticize Israel's military actions against the Palestinians, which it considered "war crimes," and charged Croatian Jewish intellectuals with turning a deaf ear to what it described as "the terrible events in the Middle East and mass killings of Palestinian civilians in Jenin."

There was a mixed response from the Jewish community. The *Feral Tribune*'s pro-Palestinian stance was nothing new, but, on the other hand, it had for years earned Jewish gratitude by courageously opposing extreme Croatian nationalism and those who tried to downplay Croatia's role in the Holocaust. Sociologist Zarko Puhovski, the head of the Croatian branch of the human-rights group Helsinki Watch, described the *Feral Tribune* editorial as "hate speech." (Puhovski's mother was Jewish but he had never been an active Jew.) Slavko Sajber, however, a Jew who had survived the Holocaust and then was a communist official, condemned "Israeli state terrorism" in an interview with the *Feral Tribune,* and called Israeli prime minister Ariel Sharon "a pathological killer." Slavko Goldstein published an article saying, "One must not draw a line between Auschwitz and Jenin, as we can read in some articles today, but it does not mean that we can remain silent concerning the crime in Jenin, as crime is always crime." This, in turn, prompted criticism from other members of the Jewish community.

JEWISH COMMUNITY

About 2,000 people were registered as members of the Croatian Jewish community, most of them living in Zagreb. But figures from Croatia's 2001 census, issued in 2002, showed only 576 people describing themselves as Jews "by ethnicity" and 475 describing their religion as Judaism. Before the count was conducted, the president of the Zagreb Jewish community, Ognjen Kraus, wrote to community members urging them to identify as Jews on the census form. Croatia recognized Jews as an official minority group who were thus entitled to state aid—including money for a kindergarten, a retirement home, a newspaper, and a variety of Jewish cultural projects. Jewish leaders were concerned that their status with the government could be lost if too few people declared themselves as Jews. It was estimated that more than 90 percent of Croatian Jewish community members were either partners in or children of mixed marriages. Before the breakup of Yugoslavia, most Jews in Croatia had identified as Yugoslav.

In September, more than 200 Jews from all parts of the former Yugoslavia—and also Yugoslav Jews who had emigrated to other places in Europe, to North America, to Israel, or elsewhere—gathered on an island off Croatia's Dalmatian coast for the weeklong Beyahad (Hebrew for "Together") meeting, organized by the Croatian Jewish community. This annual event grew out of the sporadic contacts that the Jews of the former Yugoslavia managed to keep up during the wars of the 1990s, when communications between Zagreb, Sarajevo, and Belgrade were difficult or impossible. Beyahad featured concerts, dancing, performances, literary events, and lectures, as well as excursions, sports, and time on the beach. Each year, guests were invited from a different "outside" Jewish community to provide insight into Jewish intellectual and cultural activities in that foreign location. This year, the Jewish community of Berlin furnished the guests.

Work was carried out in Dubrovnik to expand the 40-member community's facilities and to adopt new security measures. In the building housing the town's historic synagogue, two rooms were refurbished as exhibition halls for the synagogue's precious collection of ritual objects, including valuable silver and textiles, as well as Torah scrolls written in Spain in the thirteenth and fourteenth centuries and brought to Dubrovnik after the expulsion of 1492. In addition, the community moved its office to a nearby building. In August, Dubrovnik was the scene of an international conference on Jewish history and culture in the Eastern Adriatic. The conference—held regularly every other year since 1996—drew scholars from Europe, Israel, and the United States. It coincided with the height of the tourist season and featured a public concert of Sephardi songs performed by two Israeli musicians.

Throughout the year, there was a wide-ranging public debate in Zagreb about what to build on the site of the synagogue, destroyed in World War II and restituted to the Jewish community in 1999. The debate centered on whether to recreate the facade of the demolished landmark, or to put up a modern building.

Meanwhile, Darko Fischer, president of the Jewish community of Osijek, floated the idea of rebuilding the destroyed synagogue in Vukovar as a symbol of tolerance and of the renaissance of a bombed-out city. Vukovar's grand, domed synagogue was damaged during World War II and sold by the Yugoslav Jewish Federation in 1958, its remnants to be used for building material. Vukovar's 500 Jews were deported to Jasenovac and only about ten survived. In 2002, Vukovar also embodied the destruction inflicted by the wars of the 1990s. On the border with Serbia, it had been besieged for three months by the Yugoslav army in 1991 and almost totally destroyed. Its Croatian citizens left en masse, and now Serbs and Croats in the town lived separately.

Czech Republic

Following national elections in mid-June, a center-left government headed by Social Democratic leader Vladimir Spidla took office on July 15. Eleven ministers in the 17-member cabinet were Social Democrats, and the other six were from a two-party centrist alliance. The government had only a one-vote majority in the 200-seat Chamber of Deputies. The country was hit hard by devastating floods in August that wreaked havoc on Prague and other cities and towns (see below for the effect of the flooding on Prague's Jewish community). At the European Union summit in Copenhagen in December, the Czech Republic was confirmed to join the EU in May 2004.

Racist attacks—primarily on Roma—and other manifestations of right-wing extremism caused concern throughout the year. Officials reported that skinhead violence was on the rise. In May, published results of a survey conducted by the Center for Public Opinion Research showed that one-third of Czechs did not "always" tolerate foreigners living in the Czech Republic, and that half were intolerant of people of a different skin color. About three-fourths claimed to display tolerance toward Jews, but only 25 percent were tolerant of the Roma. An analyst told the media that, compared with the center's findings for 2000, tolerance had grown toward all groups except the Roma.

In January, police charged two 16-year-old boys with racial hate crimes after seizing a videotape showing as many as seven teenagers vandalizing more than 50 tombstones at a Jewish cemetery in the Prague suburb of Uhrineves. The video, apparently shot by the teens themselves, showed them giving Nazi salutes and chanting Nazi slogans. In February, the Interior Ministry dissolved the far-right group Republican Youth, saying that parts of the organization's program broke the law by including anti-Roma references. In September, four members of the skinhead rock band Hlas kvre (Voice of the Blood) were charged with promoting a movement disseminating hatred. Police said the band's lyrics "openly propagate ideas of racism, anti-Semitism, and xenophobia."

In June, a smoke bomb was thrown at Chief Rabbi Karol Sidon while he was meeting with a journalist in a bookshop in the town of Liberec. The news media reported that the perpetrator, who managed to run away, looked like a skinhead. At the beginning of July, the synagogue and a Holocaust memorial in the spa town of Karlovy Vary were vandalized. In October, the Supreme Court overturned the conviction of a publisher fined about $60,000 in 2001 for having published a Czech translation of

Mein Kampf without explanatory footnotes or disclaimers. Michal Zitko's conviction for "supporting and promoting a movement aimed at suppressing human rights and freedoms" had been upheld on appeal earlier in the year, but the Supreme Court ruled that Zitko could not have promoted Nazism since the movement did not exist at the time of the alleged crime. The ruling angered Czech Jewish groups as well as government officials. Interior Minister Stanislav Gross described the verdict as "shocking and crazy," and legal experts said that it might set a precedent hindering prosecution of other right-wing extremists.

Both the Czech people and their government were favorably disposed toward Israel. Relations between the intelligence services of the two countries were described as "excellent," and Czech media coverage of the Middle East was generally pro-Israel or even-handed. Milos Zeman, then the prime minister, visited Israel in February. In an interview with the daily *Ha'aretz,* Zeman was quoted as labeling PA chairman Arafat a terrorist and drawing parallels between him and Hitler. Zeman applauded Sharon's policy of not negotiating with Arafat as long as violence persisted. He compared the Palestinians to the ethnic Germans who lived in Czechoslovakia before World War II, whom he called "Hitler's fifth column." Just as those Sudeten Germans should have been expelled from Czechoslovakia to avert World War II, he said, the Palestinians should be expelled for not accepting Israel's peace proposals. Zeman later denied that he had compared Arafat to Hitler. He said that when asked by *Ha'aretz* "about the possibility of such a comparison, I replied: 'Of course it is not my duty to pass judgment on Arafat.' " However, the published text read: "Of course. It is not my duty . . ." suggesting that the Arafat-Hitler analogy was a matter of course. Zeman now added that his government considered a peaceful solution to the conflict in the Middle East as "the only realistic way" out of the Israeli-Palestinian crisis. He said, "I regard as desirable the return of all the parties involved to the negotiating table. The peace negotiations must take into account the Palestinians' legal rights, including the establishment of an independent Palestinian state, and the security needs of the State of Israel."

In April, Zeman told the Czech Parliament that the Palestinians had no right to an independent state unless they halted terrorism against Israel. Also in April, the Czech Republic was one of only five states to vote against a UN Commission on Human Rights resolution, in Geneva, condemning Israel for "gross violations" of humanitarian law in the Territories and "mass killings" of Palestinians. The resolution passed 40-5. In addition to the Czech Republic, the others voting "no" were Germany,

Great Britain, Canada, and Guatemala. Seven countries abstained. The Palestinian Authority's representative in Prague criticized the Czech vote. Foreign Minister Jan Kavan visited Israel in May and conferred with Israeli and Palestinian leaders. While Kavan met with Sharon, he canceled a scheduled meeting with Arafat.

Prague remained a popular destination for Israeli tourists, but the number of Israeli visitors to the Czech Republic dropped sharply in 2002. The Czech statistical office said that in the first nine months of the year there was a 38-percent drop in the number of Israeli tourists as compared with the same period in 2001. Total Israeli visitors for the year were expected to number about 100,000—about half those in 2001. The decline surely had something to do with fears related to the September 11 attacks, but there were two other factors as well: the flooding in August and the continuing tense situation in the Middle East.

JEWISH COMMUNITY

A total of some 3,000 members were registered with the Jewish communities of the Czech Republic, about 1,700 of them living in Prague. Jewish leaders, however, estimated that there were many more unaffiliated Jews in the country. In addition, an estimated 2,000 Israelis lived in Prague, though they had little contact with the local Jewish community. At the beginning of the year, Jan Munk, director of the Terezin Memorial, was reelected to a third three-year term as president of the Czech Federation of Jewish Communities. In November, the Prague Jewish community hosted a meeting of presidents of the European Council of Jewish Communities, which drew leaders and representatives from more than 40 countries.

Early in the year, the federation voted to recognize the Conservative (Masorti) stream of Judaism, opening the way to establish an official Conservative congregation and hire a Conservative rabbi. The federation later passed new rules allowing member communities to accept patrilineal Jews (people with Jewish fathers and non-Jewish mothers), who were not considered Jews by Orthodox criteria. Friction—and some confusion—ensued among Prague's non-Orthodox congregations as the new rules were put into effect.

In September, Bejt Praha, the "open Jewish community," dismissed Rabbi Ronald Hoffberg, a Conservative rabbi it had brought from the United States to serve as its spiritual leader, less than a year into his two-year contract. Bejt Praha said that Hoffberg, who oversaw the conversion to Judaism of a group of Czechs in September, was fired because he "did not fulfil his commitment to the board." Observers suggested that "politics and personality conflicts" were involved in the break, which left bitterness on both sides. (Bejt Praha's director, Peter Gyori, told an interviewer that he had received "disturbing messages and letters.") Despite opposition by the Masorti movement in the U.S. and elsewhere, Bejt Praha began bringing in, periodically, the American-born retired chief rabbi of Sweden to lead services. Hoffberg, however, remained in town. Earlier in the year he had been hired by the Czech Federation of Jewish Communities—with modest state support for his salary—to be available to the outlying communities, and during the second half of 2002 he became quite active in visiting and lecturing in these places.

In October, Hoffberg founded his own Conservative congregation in Prague, which formally affiliated with Masorti Olami, the World Union of Masorti Judaism. Some ten former members of Bejt Praha followed him into the new congregation. Bejt Simcha, a liberal congregation affiliated with the World Union for Progressive Judaism (Reform), engaged Hoffberg to conduct lectures, but later chose Rabbi Michael Dushinsky, described as "a different type of Orthodox rabbi," as its Judaism teacher. In Israel, Dushinsky had been accused, in 1997, of taking money to arrange quick conversions, after which he moved to the town of Ostrava in the Czech Republic. A Czech opponent of Dushinsky got hold of a video filmed by Israeli TV during an undercover sting operation that showed the rabbi accepting a bribe, and he showed it in Prague.

The Prague Jewish community took in $4.7 million in annual revenues, making it one of the wealthiest Jewish communities in Central Europe, community president Tomas Jelinek told an interviewer in August. The main sources of money were rent from restituted properties, income from tourism, and contributions from the state. But the devastating floods that swept Prague and other cities in the Czech Republic shortly after Jelinek's remarks caused hundreds of thousands of dollars of damage to Jewish sites, cut tourism, and strained community resources.

Giant steel barriers and sandbags prevented the Vltava River from overflowing into Prague's low-lying historic Jewish quarter, but several feet of water seeped up through underground drains and channels. Water flooded the 13th-century Old-New Synagogue and floodwater rose to seven feet in the Pinkas Synagogue, damaging some of the 80,000 handwritten names of Czech Holocaust victims inscribed on the walls. The Jewish Museum was also hit by underground flooding, but its priceless relics had all been moved to safety in time, and insurance covered most of the repairs to the building. Terezin, site of the former concentration camp/ghetto north of Prague, was submerged by as much as ten feet of water. A cemetery for some 10,000 Holocaust victims there was totally flooded. President Havel toured the flooded Jewish sites in Prague, and the Jewish community issued an appeal for international help. Individuals, governments, and organizations responded. Among them, Israel's deputy foreign minister, Rabbi Michael Melchior, toured damaged Jewish sites and handed over $50,000 from the Israeli government, and the Claims Conference gave $20,000 to help Czech flood victims who were Holocaust survivors.

The Prague Jewish community recognized that the damage to Jewish sites was minor compared to the damage suffered in other parts of the city, and donated funds to help several schools in the hard-hit Karlin district. With funds from the Weinberg Foundation and several U.S. Jewish federations and individuals, the JDC also undertook three nonsectarian flood-relief projects in Prague and Terezin.

There were a number of commemorative events throughout the year. Holocaust Remembrance Day was marked on January 27, the anniversary of the liberation of Auschwitz, and, for the first time, representatives of the country's Jewish and Romany communities observed the day in a joint ceremony. In April, the town of Plzen (Pilsen) commemorated the 60th anniversary of the Nazi deportation of its 2,600 Jews by creating a memorial consisting of pebbles inscribed with the victims' names. Plzen hosted a number of events to commemorate the Holocaust as part of a project called "Year 2002—Year of Memories." In May, representatives of more than two dozen countries, including U.S. first lady Laura Bush among them, laid wreaths at the annual ceremony commemorating the liberation of Terezin. At an event at the Terezin museum in June, 250 Czech children received prizes for paintings and essays in memory of the Holocaust. That same month, a commemorative ceremony and cultural event marked the completion of the renovation of the synagogue in the small town of Boskovice. Among other things, local high-school students began documenting the Boskovice Jewish cemetery. Also in June, Arthur Avnon, the Israeli ambassador to Prague, honored a group of Czechs as Righteous Among the Nations. In October, more than a dozen Czech Holocaust survivors flew to Israel, led by Rabbi Samuel Abramson of Karlovy Vary, to show their solidarity with the Jewish state.

There were numerous cultural events of Jewish interest. In February, the German motor company Porsche donated to the Prague-based Franz Kafka Society a reconstruction of Kafka's personal library of more than

1,000 books. A seven-day festival honoring Czech- and German-Jewish culture opened in Prague on June 27 with a ceremony commemorating the deportation of Czech Jews to Nazi concentration camps. The third Nine Gates Festival of Czech-German-Jewish Culture featured films, concerts, and lectures, and took place in Prague and other locations. Simhat Torah marked the official launch of www.chewra.com, a Web site devoted to Czech Jewish cemeteries, tombstones, epitaphs, and information about the people buried there. This project was initiated by Jaroslav Achab Haidler, a Czech theater director who wanted to convert to Judaism and had formed the Keshet Foundation several years earlier to document Jewish cemeteries. In October, Prague was the scene of a joint Czech-Argentine project called Golem 2002/5763, which featured films, performances, exhibits, and a seminar about the legendary Golem figure. Also in October, a two-day conference on anti-Semitism was hosted by Radio Free Europe in Prague, and held under the auspices of Prime Minister Spidla and the president of the Czech Senate, the upper house of Parliament. In March, admirers of Thomas Masaryk, the first president of the former Czechoslovakia, presented Chief Rabbi Sidon with an honorary medal on the 152nd anniversary of Masaryk's birth. The medal recognized Sidon's role in maintaining the "spirit" of Masaryk, considered a figure of great moral integrity.

Hungary

In the April general elections, the center-left opposition narrowly ousted Prime Minister Viktor Orban. The ex-communist Socialists and their liberal Free Democrat allies won 198 seats in the 386-seat National Assembly, giving them a ten-seat majority over Orban's conservative alliance centered around his party, FIDESZ. The election was bitterly contested, and the results showed a divided country. During the campaign, Orban used with-us-or-against-us rhetoric to rally "patriotic" Hungarians. The extremist right-wing Hungarian Justice and Life Party (MIEP)—which repeatedly appealed to anti-Semitic sentiments—predicted big gains for itself, but in the end failed to win even the 5 percent of votes necessary to enter Parliament. Socialist Peter Medgyessy, a 59-year-old former finance minister, formed Hungary's new government in May. At a European Union summit in Copenhagen in December, Hungary was confirmed to join the EU in May 2004.

Jewish leaders and others expressed concern about anti-Semitism throughout the year. In January, the Alliance of Hungarian Jewish Communities criticized the Justice Ministry for not introducing legislation against hate speech. Complaining that government officials had not distanced themselves from anti-Semitic discourse in the public media, it suggested that the government might be courting the far right in advance of the elections. During the campaign, however, Orban's foreign minister, János Martonyi, flatly ruled out a government coalition with MIEP.

On January 17, thousands rallied outside the National Assembly building to mark the anniversary of the liberation of Budapest's World War II ghetto in 1945 and to call for action against anti-Semitism and other forms of prejudice. Martonyi and Budapest mayor Gábor Demszky addressed the gathering, and a message from President Ferenc Madl was read. This was the first time that the annual commemoration, usually conducted inside the historic Dohany Street Synagogue, took place in a public space. Péter Tordai, president of the Alliance of Hungarian Jewish Communities, told reporters that this was to show that Jews could appear before the general public without fear. Still, the U.S. State Department's spokesman for European affairs told the *Nepszabadsag* newspaper that Washington remained concerned about anti-Semitic and anti-minority extremist groups in Hungary. He noted that Martonyi had admitted during a visit to Israel that month (see below) that anti-Semitism remained a problem in the country even though the government condemned it and was committed to protecting the rights of minorities.

In February, the Orban government opened a controversial "House of Terror" museum in the downtown building that had been the headquarters of the Hungarian pro-Nazi Arrow Cross in 1944–45 and was taken over by the communist secret police after the war. The museum's aim was to memorialize the victims of totalitarian terror—both those of wartime Hungarian fascism and of postwar communism. However, Jews and other critics charged that it presented all victims as equal and all victimizers as equal, and painted Hungary as one of Nazi Germany's victims rather than an accomplice. They also noted that it devoted only one of nearly two dozen rooms exclusively to the Holocaust, seeming to imply that communism was far worse.

In March, Ferenc Olti, a vice president of the Alliance of Jewish Communities in Hungary, said that bias against Jews had grown dramatically over the past several years. He charged that anti-Semitic publications were being reprinted and sold without restriction, and that anti-Semitism had become part of everyday discourse, including on state-owned radio and television. (In February, Jews raised an outcry when a Hungarian-language edition of Henry Ford's anti-Semitic book, *The International*

Jew, went on sale at outlets of the British supermarket chain Tesco in two Hungarian cities. Tesco apologized and removed the books.) Olti said the government had promised several times to strengthen regulations barring anti-Semitic speech and Holocaust denial; not only had this not happened, but existing laws were not even being enforced. Olti presented his report at the meeting of East-Central European Jewish representatives organized by the American Jewish Committee and held in Bucharest alongside a summit of countries aspiring to enter NATO.

In November, senior World Jewish Congress officials, accompanied by legal experts from several countries, met in Budapest with Hungarian justice minister Peter Barandy and other officials to discuss how to strengthen Hungary's legislation aimed at curbing racism and anti-Semitism.

The activities of Pannon Radio, a commercial station controlled by the extreme-right MIEP, caused particular concern. In January, the National Radio and Television Board fined Pannon Radio the equivalent of $8,400 for broadcasts that promoted MIEP, encouraged hatred and anti-Semitism, and grossly insulted ethnic minorities. Later in the year, the broadcasting board warned Pannon Radio several more times about its overtly pro-MIEP bias. Indeed, some 60 musicians demanded that Pannon Radio stop playing their songs because of the station's "openly racist and anti-Semitic tone."

In June, Lorant Hegedus, a Protestant minister who was a MIEP member of the National Assembly, pleaded innocent to the charge of "incitement against a community." The charge was based on an article he published in 2001 advocating the expulsion of the Jews. Parliament had suspended his parliamentary immunity, making him liable to prosecution (see AJYB 2002, p. 458).

In December, on the sixth night of Hanukkah, a group of more than 100 skinheads disrupted an open-air Chabad-sponsored menorah lighting in Budapest, chanting "Hungary is ours!" There was no physical violence and police did not intervene. Later, the national police chief apologized to the Jewish community, as both groups had been granted permission to hold public meetings on the same square at the same time. Representatives of foreign Jewish organizations were present at the menorah lighting, which took place ahead of a meeting of the European Jewish Congress in Budapest on December 8.

Jews regarded the Hungarian government's policy toward Israel as fair and friendly, with few outstanding issues other than the subject of Hungarian anti-Semitism, which was often raised by Israeli officials. Economic relations were particularly good: Israel had capital-investment projects worth over $1.5 billion in Hungary. In January, Foreign Minister Martonyi made a four-day official visit to Israel and the territory of the Palestinian National Authority. He met with top Israeli and Palestinian leaders, including PA chairman Yasir Arafat, and told reporters that Hungary had offered its assistance in mediation efforts and would be prepared to host negotiations. But, he said, the first step toward resurrecting the peace process would have to be an end to terrorism. He added that the Hungarian government dissociated itself from, and would take action against, anti-Semitic phenomena within the country.

For the most part, the attitude of the general public toward Israel was positive, despite what Jews described as a clear pro-Palestinian bias in the print and broadcast media, which, they felt, was influenced by the way the media in Western Europe covered Middle East news. Anti-Semitic elements in the press blamed Israel for everything wrong in the Middle East and around the world, but even many of the more objective journalists also criticized Israel.

In October, Auschwitz survivor Imre Kertesz, 72, was awarded the Nobel Prize for Literature for his novels describing the Shoah and its aftermath. Kertesz was deported to Auschwitz as a teenager in 1944 and later sent to Buchenwald, where he was liberated in 1945. The honor came as a surprise, as his books had a very small readership in Hungary. His first novel, *Sorstalanság* (Fateless), was a first-person account of a teenage boy in Nazi concentration camps and his attempts to reconcile himself to that experience after the war. Written in the 1960s, it was not published until 1975, when it was greeted with almost total silence. That volume turned out to be the first part of a trilogy of semiautobiographical novels: *A kudarc* (Fiasco), was published in 1988, and *Kaddis a meg nem születetett gyermekért* (Kaddish for a Child Not Born) in 1990. "There is no awareness of the Holocaust in Hungary," Kertesz told the AP after winning the prize. "People have not faced up to the Holocaust. I hope that in the light of this recognition, they will face up to it more than until now."

After the Nobel announcement, editions of his books quickly sold out and Kertesz was hailed as a Hungarian national hero. The president, the prime minister, the speaker of the National Assembly, and many other officials congratulated him personally, Budapest gave him the key to the city, and the National Assembly passed a bill exempting his prize money from taxes. The Culture Ministry said it would send copies of *Sorsta-*

lanság to all schools. The far right, however, criticized the award on the grounds that Kertesz did not represent Hungarian national values.

JEWISH COMMUNITY

Data from the February 2001 census, released in the summer of 2002, showed only 13,000 people identifying themselves as Jewish, even though a recent survey put the actual number of Jews in Hungary at more than 100,000. About 90 percent of them lived in Budapest, the vast majority nonobservant, secular, or totally unaffiliated. Only 6,000 or so were formally registered with the Jewish community, and about 20,000 had some sort of affiliation with Jewish organizations or institutions. The dominant religious affiliation was Neolog, similar to America's Conservative Judaism. There was a very small Orthodox community made up of both Modern Orthodox and Hassidim. During the year, a new Modern Orthodox congregation, composed mainly of young adults, opened. Neolog communities were grouped in the Alliance of Jewish Communities in Hungary (MAZSIHISZ), while the Orthodox operated as the Autonomous Orthodox Community. Sim Shalom, a small Reform congregation established in Budapest in 1992, led by a female rabbi and associated with the World Union for Progressive Judaism, functioned outside these official umbrella structures. There was also an active Chabad-Lubavitch presence.

For some time, the official Jewish leadership had come under criticism from the independent Jewish monthly *Szombat* for autocratic policies, sloppy finances, and personal and political infighting. Similar criticism had been voiced by various individuals, but not publicly. In November, however, Ferenc Olti, vice president of MAZSIHISZ, openly accused the president, Gusztav Zoltai, of "dictatorship" and lack of financial transparency, and called for his resignation. Olti made his accusations at the general meetings of MAZSIHISZ and of the Budapest Jewish community. The latter voted him off its board.

There were three Jewish day schools operating in Budapest in addition to kindergartens, with a total enrollment of 1,800. Budapest also had a Jewish University, which included the Rabbinical Seminary and a teacher-training college. Budapest's Balint Jewish Community Center had an active program of lectures, clubs, courses, and public events. A new program launched in 2002 was a "family day" one Sunday a month, featuring events to attract three generations. The Lauder/JDC international Jewish summer camp at Szarvas in southern Hungary drew about 2,000 Jewish children from all over East-Central Europe. The camp was also used for seminars, such as the fourth Machol Hungaria, which taught Israeli folk dancing. This five-day seminar in May drew 140 participants from 12 countries. The Hungarian Jewish Social Support Foundation coordinated extensive social-welfare programs, including a 360-bed Jewish hospital that also had a hospice center for the terminally ill.

There were a number of commemorative events. During the course of 2002, more than 50 Hungarians were honored for having saved Jews during World War II. In April, there were several programs to mark the national Holocaust Memorial Day, April 16. In May, the newly restored Orthodox synagogue in the town of Mako was renamed in honor of its rabbi, Mozes Vorhand, who was killed by Hungarian Nazis in 1944, shortly before the Jews were deported to Auschwitz. Local officials, members of the National Assembly, and Jewish leaders attended. So did scores of Orthodox Jews originally from Mako, who came regularly from Israel, Europe, and the U.S. on an annual pilgrimage to commemorate the community. In July, a monument to Hungary's wartime Jewish Aid and Rescue Committee and its controversial leader, Rudolf Kasztner, was dedicated in the courtyard of Budapest's main Dohany Street Synagogue. A 30-person delegation came from Israel for the ceremony. Kasztner was murdered in Israel in 1957 after critics accused him of "playing God" in negotiating with the Nazis to win safe passage out of Hungary for 1,684 Jews. In August, a memorial ceremony in Budapest marked the 90th anniversary of the birth of Raoul Wallenberg, the Swedish diplomat who saved thousands of Hungarian Jews during World War II and vanished after being taken into custody by Soviet troops.

In December, Prime Minister Medgyessy laid the cornerstone of what will become the country's Holocaust museum, a multimillion-dollar complex to be located in a disused synagogue just outside the downtown area. The synagogue, built in 1923, was designed by Lipot Baumhorn, Europe's most prolific modern synagogue architect. Also taking part in the ceremony was Tibor Vamos, head of the Holocaust Documentation Center and Memorial Collection, the public foundation behind the project. Due to open in April 2004, the museum was expected to collect and publish historical documents related to the Holocaust, host conferences and seminars, and run educational programs. The state was to contribute $7 million to cover renovation and construction costs. "It is our duty to remember and to remind people about the past," Medgyessy said during the cornerstone ceremony. "The Holocaust was a tragedy for the whole nation."

There were numerous Jewish cultural and social events, including the annual Jewish culture festival in Budapest in August. From April through September, the Jewish Museum in Budapest featured an exhibition on Hungarian Jewish women.

Israel Sela, the JDC country director for Hungary, died in Jerusalem in November at the age of 61 after a four-year battle with cancer. Sela, an Israeli, took up his JDC position in Budapest in 1994.

Macedonia

In October, the Social Democratic Union and the ethnic Albanian Democratic Union for Integration announced the formation of a coalition government headed by Social Democratic leader Branko Crvenkovski.

According to Jewish leaders, the government had a generally positive view of Israel, often holding up Israel as an example for Macedonians both because of its successful economic development and the way it persevered in a hostile environment. The 200-member Jewish community, said these leaders, maintained "very friendly" relations with Macedonia's Islamic community, and had not experienced negative consequences from the intifada.

In early June, eight Macedonians and two couples from Belgrade underwent conversion to Judaism in Skopje. Preparations started early in 2001, when the Belgrade-based Orthodox rabbi Yitzhak Asiel, who also served Macedonia, agreed to give lessons to the candidates. Classes took place both in Skopje and in Belgrade. The Reform bet din (religious court) was led by a U.S. military chaplain, Rabbi Kenneth J. Leinwand, who came from Germany. One of the Belgrade couples, who had been married for many years under Yugoslav civil law, married in a Jewish religious ceremony in the Skopje synagogue after their conversion. The Macedonian converts included seven young women and a young man who was studying with Rabbi Asiel to learn how to conduct services. The Macedonian Jewish community planned eventually to send him to a yeshivah.

At a ceremony in Skopje on August 29, Finance Minister Nikola Gruevski announced that the government would either physically return or provide compensation for Jewish communal properties claimed by the current Jewish community. Furthermore, all heirless private Jewish property or compensation from it would go to a newly created "Holocaust Fund" foundation, jointly administered by the government and the Jewish community. These decisions, based on a 2000 law on the denationalization of property, were hailed as the most sweeping regarding the return or compensation of property enacted in any postcommunist country. The foundation was to use the restituted assets to create a regional Holocaust museum and education center; to finance the repair, restoration, and upkeep of Jewish heritage sites; and to underwrite as-yet-undefined programs in the areas of education and multiethnic understanding. To provide start-up funding, Gruevski said the government would immediately transfer to the Holocaust Fund government bonds worth nearly $500,000 as compensation for four heirless properties assessed in Skopje.

In those cases where the property no longer existed or else belonged to someone other than the state, the Finance Ministry would evaluate the current worth, and the government would give the foundation that amount in interest-bearing, euro-linked, ten-year government bonds. Jewish community officials said that as many as 1,000 sites could be involved. Under the new provisions, compensation for communal property would not be administered as part of the Holocaust Fund, but directly by the Jewish community. Gruevski announced the restitution of several specific communal properties and said that the Jewish community would receive financial compensation for nearly three dozen sites that could not be physically returned.

At a ceremony in Washington in December, U.S. secretary of state Colin Powell and Macedonian foreign minister Ilinka Mitreva signed an agreement regarding the preservation of cultural properties in Macedonia, including places of worship, historic sites, monuments, cemeteries, and cultural archives. The countries pledged to take steps to help protect and preserve properties important to the cultural heritage of citizens of the two nations; to cooperate in identifying and preserving such properties; and to ensure equal treatment of all cultural groups in property preservation and access policies. It also established a Joint Cultural Heritage Commission for bilateral efforts on these issues, which was expected to focus on the cultural property of groups in Macedonia that the Nazis tried to exterminate, and groups that suffered under the communist regime. Warren C. Miller, chairman of the U.S. Commission for the Preservation of America's Heritage Abroad, who negotiated the agreement, said that his commission planned to conduct a survey of Jewish cultural properties in Macedonia. This agreement with Macedonia was the 11th such pact between the U.S. and other countries. A $190,000 project to restore the historic Jewish cemetery in Bitola, partly funded by the Macedonian government, was already under way.

Poland

As Poland implemented market-oriented reforms needed for entry into the European Union, the unemployment rate surged to over 18 percent. Two-thirds of respondents to a survey conducted in April were pessimistic about the country's future. This situation fueled support in the country for populist, "Euro-skeptic" parties and political figures, including the radical farmer Andrzej Lepper, head of the Self-Defense Party. The EU summit in Copenhagen in December confirmed its invitation to Poland to join in 2004. During the year, Poland, which joined NATO in 1999, was a strong supporter of U.S. president George Bush's foreign policy, including the military buildup against Iraq.

In January, Prime Minister Leszek Miller told the Conference of Presidents of Major American Jewish Organizations in New York that he would work to improve Poland's relations with the international Jewish community. His priorities included restitution of Jewish property, broader ties with Israel, support for Jewish culture in Poland, and backing for the creation of a $60-million Museum of Jewish History in Warsaw, which would include a multimedia education center employing computer images, films, databases, dioramas, models, and interactive technology. The museum would stand on the site of the wartime Warsaw Ghetto on a plot donated by the city, just in front of the sculptural Warsaw Ghetto memorial. The museum already had a Web site, www.jewishmuseum.org.pl.

In July, Poland's Institute of National Memory (INM) announced that a nearly two-year-long investigation confirmed that local Poles, not Nazi occupiers, had carried out the 1941 massacre of 1,600 Jews in the village of Jedwabne. However, it would not file charges against anyone for the crime. For decades, the massacre had been attributed to German Nazis. Revelations in 2000 that local Poles were responsible sparked widespread debate about the role of Poland and of Polish people in the Holocaust, and prompted the involvement of the INM, which was charged with investigating and prosecuting perpetrators of Nazi- and communist-era crimes (see AJYB 2001, pp. 424–25; 2002, pp. 463–64). In July, 20 teenagers from Jedwabne were taken on a trip to the United States as part of a program aimed at teaching tolerance. Jedwabne's former mayor, Krzysztof Godlewski, was given an award for openly condemning the 1941 massacre and arranging the memorial ceremony held on its 60th anniversary in 2001. At the time, townspeople had branded him "anti-Polish" and forced his resignation.

The INM also investigated reports of Polish crimes against Jews in other places, and, in November, it published a two-volume report listing incidents in at least two dozen villages. In December, the remains of 13 Jews believed killed by Poles during World War II were ceremonially buried in the Jewish cemetery in Tomaszow Mazowiecki. The remains were discovered in September at a mass grave in a nearby wooded area.

A public-opinion survey conducted in April asked Poles which one group they thought was too influential in Poland. Less than 1 percent of respondents said "Jews," while more than 10 percent said "the Catholic Church," and 26 percent said "businessmen." But when the same survey asked which ethnic groups were too influential, Jews were mentioned the most often, by 19 percent of respondents, and when the remaining 81 percent were asked specifically if Jews had too much power in Poland, 24 percent said "yes." In October, as part of Action Week of Football Against Racism in Europe, a petition against racism in Polish soccer stadiums, signed by 27,000 people, was presented to the president of the Polish Football Association. The petition noted anti-Semitic abuse, neofascist symbols, and frequent hostility to black players. A group called Polish Humanitarian Action and the independent antiracist association Never Again had collected the signatures at stadiums and schools all over Poland.

The Jewish cemetery in Wroclaw was vandalized during the period between Rosh Hashanah and Yom Kippur; about 70 tombstones were toppled or broken into pieces. The Jewish community issued an appeal for aid to repair the damage, and about 200 local volunteers responded.

Jewish restitution claims for communal property seized during World War II got under way in earnest in February, just three months before the May 2002 deadline for filing set by the 1997 restitution law. The Foundation for the Preservation of Jewish Heritage in Poland elected as its cochairs Jerzy Kichler, chairman of the Union of Jewish Religious Communities in Poland (JRCP), and Kalman Sultanik, president of the Federation of Polish Jews in the United States and chairman of the American Section of the World Zionist Organization. It also named Eve Anderson, an American, to be its Warsaw-based executive director, charged with coordinating the process of researching and filing claims for the restitution of thousands of properties that belonged to the pre-Holocaust Jewish community. The foundation was formed as a partnership between the World Jewish Restitution Organization (WJRO) and the

JRCP after wrangling between the two bodies had held up the process for years. Claims for 5,200 properties were filed by the May deadline, but many of them still required the submission of further documentation. Once restitution is made, the foundation will own and manage recovered properties located mainly in areas where no Jews now lived. Properties elsewhere in Poland, where organized Jewish communities existed, were being reclaimed, owned, and managed by the JRCP and the individual communities. Some Jewish leaders came under criticism for their handling of restitution transactions and for lacking an overall strategy for dealing with properties and profits (see below). In the wake of this controversy, the Jewish community of Warsaw held an open meeting in November on the topic, "Where do we get money and what do we spend it on, and what are our plans for the future?" JRCP leaders present discussed the organization's budget and addressed criticism.

Restitution of prewar Jewish private property remained an unresolved, contentious issue. Despite the lack of clear legislation, however, many individuals, including Jews residing outside the country, were already using existing legal mechanisms to get back property that had belonged to them or to their ancestors (see below).

According to a report by Konstanty Gebert, publisher of the Jewish monthly *Midrasz,* the State of Israel "used to enjoy a favorable image in Polish public opinion, as the Arabs were seen as allied with Moscow, Poland's arch-nemesis." Israelis "were not seen as 'Jews,' in the sense of the negative stereotype associated with the latter," he said in the report, presented at a March meeting in Bucharest of Jewish representatives from East-Central Europe. Also, "many Israelis came from Poland, and ties of friendship, or of landsman solidarity, remained." Even the Polish right wing, he said, "saw in Israel a country implementing values and policies Poland should in their eyes emulate: a strong state with a powerful and popular military and a widely accepted national-religious ideology, one that does not let its neighbors push it around." But, Gebert cautioned, some of these positive associations "have since dissipated, as the mainstream media has reported, and often distorted, the plight of the Palestinians. There is a consensus that Israel uses excessive force, and possibly wanton cruelty, in retaliating against Palestinian attacks, and Ariel Sharon is considered a war criminal. Internet chat lists are infused with hatred, with many participants alleging that the reprehensible behavior Israel is charged with stems from the 'nature' of the Jews."

Nonetheless, on the whole, Poland's relations with Israel were good. Israel's ambassador in Warsaw, Shevach Weiss, a Polish Holocaust survivor and former speaker of the Knesset, was very popular, traveling widely around the country and appearing frequently on television and at public events. In March, Polish national security adviser Marek Siwiec made a four-day visit to Israel, where he and Israeli National Security Council chairman Maj. Gen. Uzi Dayan signed a memorandum of understanding on the establishment of bilateral cooperation in the war on terrorism. Israeli foreign minister Shimon Peres visited Warsaw in April, and took part in a conference linked to the creation of the Museum of Jewish History. (During the conference, Polish foreign minister Wlodzimierz Cimoszewicz said that the aim of the museum was "to state the honest truth about the composite nature of Polish-Jewish relations; to show all of their light and dark sides. This is the only way of helping to abolish harmful stereotypes, xenophobic prejudices, and unjust images of each other.") While Peres was in the country, a group of 41 right-wing lawmakers from Self-Defense, the Peasant Party, and the League of Polish Families presented a protest to the Israeli embassy against the "barbaric war on the Palestinian land." Warsaw's mayor visited Israel in May. He donated hundreds of original cobblestones from the Warsaw Ghetto to Yad Vashem, which planned to recreate a ghetto street as an exhibition. In September, Poland's Defense Ministry announced it would buy antitank missiles from the Israeli arms maker Rafael. During a state visit to Washington in July, President Aleksander Kwasniewski said that Poland strongly supported Israel's right to exist in peace, but also wanted to see the creation of a Palestinian state that was democratic and "free from fundamentalism, terror, and crime."

JEWISH COMMUNITY

Estimates of the number of Jews in Poland ranged widely, from the 7,000–8,000 officially registered with the community, belonging to Jewish organizations or receiving aid from the JDC, to the 10,000–15,000 people of Jewish ancestry who showed interest in rediscovering their heritage, to as many as 30,000–40,000 with some Jewish ancestry. The Ronald S. Lauder Foundation ran the country's most extensive Jewish educational programs, including a school in Warsaw with more than 160 pupils and a genealogy project. The Joint Distribution Committee, which provided extensive social-welfare aid, also ran education and leadership-training programs. The Polish Jewish community's Web site, www.jewish.org.pl, provided information about the community and news about cultural, religious, and other activities.

Established Jewish religious communities were grouped under the umbrella of the Union of Jewish Religious Communities in Poland. In addition, a liberal, *havurah*-type congregation, Bejt Warszawa, operated in Warsaw. Though not a member of the umbrella group, it sometimes cooperated with Warsaw's Orthodox congregation—for example, both joined forces at Simhat Torah celebrations this year, for the first time. For the High Holy Days, Bejt Warszawa received a 100-year-old Torah as a gift from the Reform community of Clarksdale, Mississippi. In October, a group of Jews from Cleveland presented a Torah to the Lomdei Mishnayot synagogue in Oswieçim, the town near the Auschwitz death camp. The synagogue was restored and reopened in 2000 as the Auschwitz Jewish Center, with a museum and facilities for Jewish study and prayer.

In December, the board of the nationwide secular Jewish organization, the Social-Cultural Association of Jews of Poland (TSKZ), unexpectedly voted out its longtime leadership, including its president, Szymon Szurmiej, director of Warsaw's state Jewish theater.

During the summer, young Polish Jews attended several Jewish summer-camp programs as well as the Szarvas camp in Hungary. Twenty-one Jewish students from Poland visited Israel as part of the Birthright Israel program, the first time that Polish students had taken part in it. A delegation of Polish Jews also visited the Jewish community in Bulgaria as part of the JDC Buncher leadership-development program.

During the year, tensions emerged between the Orthodox rabbinical establishment and Jews who wanted to join the Conservative (Masorti) stream. These came to a head in September, when 20 residents of Wroclaw underwent Conservative conversion ceremonies conducted by a Masorti bet din (religious court) of rabbis from Israel and the United States. The group was prepared for conversion by Rabbi Ivan Caine, a Conservative rabbi from America who served as the Wroclaw rabbi. Warsaw's American-born rabbi, Michael Schudrich, who was Orthodox, denied permission to use the Warsaw community's *mikveh* (ritual bath) for the conversion, so the group used one in a private hotel in Kraków. There, Sasha Pecaric, an Orthodox rabbi and head of Lauder Foundation activities in the city, organized a demonstration against the group and attempted, unsuccessfully, to bar access to the *mikveh*.

At the beginning of the holiday of Sukkot, two weeks after the conversions, two Wroclaw girls became b'not mitzvah in an egalitarian, Conservative ceremony that was believed to be the first of its kind in Poland. The parents of both girls were leading members of the Wroclaw congregation. But since the mother of one and both parents of the other had been among the group just converted to Judaism in September, neither girl was Jewish, according to Jewish law. Both, therefore, had undergone Conservative conversion in the United States during the summer after studying with Rabbi Caine.

Several Jewish communal scandals made the headlines during the year.

Feliks Lipman, an Auschwitz survivor in his 80s who was chairman of the Jewish community in Katowice and a vice chairman of the Union of Polish Jewish Religious Communities, killed himself at the end of August. In a suicide note, he reportedly cited failed business ventures. The Polish daily *Rzeczpospolita* ran a major article implicating Lipman in shady dealings related to the restitution of both communal and privately owned prewar Jewish property. Media reports and Jewish sources said police were investigating several restitution cases in which Lipman was involved. The revelations followed earlier accusations of fraud connected with private restitution requests elsewhere in Poland. News articles during the year reported that several buildings in Kraków, in particular, had been restituted and later sold on the basis of falsified wills or through proxies. Kraków prosecutors said that organized networks of swindlers were carrying out such scams and asked the Jewish Historical Institute in Warsaw to help trace the legal heirs to properties.

In the fall, the Warsaw Jewish community fired Boleslaw Szernicer, the caretaker of the Jewish cemetery, after police found and destroyed a plot of marijuana growing in the vast graveyard. This sparked an article in the *Polityka* newspaper charging that Szernicer's dismissal was actually the result of broader conflicts involving Jewish quarrels over restitution profits. It quoted a letter Szernicer wrote in August accusing Jewish communal officials of disposing of restituted Jewish heritage sites by selling them off quickly, and of "secrecy" and lack of transparency in the disposition of profits from restituted property. The paper said that Szernicer was attempting to establish a congregation in Warsaw separate from the established community. *Polityka* also dwelt on other instances of independent groups, in Gdansk and Poznan, that were not recognized by the union. In Gdansk, the Independent Community of the Mosaic Faith was headed by Jakub Szadaj, the former chairman of the official Gdansk Jewish community. The union had removed Szadaj in 2000 after accusing him of financial irregularities, including accepting money to allow the building of a gas station on the site of a Jewish cemetery, and of inflating the membership of his community by including fictitious names. Szadaj, however, claimed that his opposition to the union's restitution policy was the cause of the conflict.

There were a number of commemorations during 2002. The Roman Catholic Church in Poland marked its fifth annual Day of Judaism, January 17, with a series of events commemorating the Shoah and exploring Jewish teachings. These included a prayer ceremony in the former Majdanek concentration camp near Lublin and a discussion on Bible passages and their commentaries organized by Józef Zyciñski, the archbishop of Lublin. Among the participants was the chief rabbi of Haifa, Rabbi Shear Yashuv Cohen. Several events commemorated the 60th anniversary of the annihilation of Jewish ghettos in German-occupied Poland. One took place on August 19 in Otwock, near Warsaw. Several hundred townspeople, Jewish representatives, and a Jewish survivor from the town gathered at the train station from which the Otwock Jews were sent to Treblinka, and there they prayed and lit candles. The ceremony was organized by local citizens and the Committee for the Commemoration of Otwock and Karczew Jews, headed by the editor of the Catholic monthly *Wiez* (Link).

In August, a memorial to Janusz Korczak, the Jewish doctor and educator who, in 1942, was killed in Treblinka along with all of the children from his Warsaw Ghetto orphanage, was dedicated in Warsaw's Jewish cemetery.

Numerous Jewish cultural events took place throughout the year, including concerts, exhibitions, seminars, and festivals. The audiences for these were mostly non-Jewish. The annual Jewish Culture Festival in Kraków drew a record number of people to its final concert, parts of which were broadcast live on Polish national television. As usual, the Jewish Culture Center in Kraków sponsored events each month. In September, an exhibit on the participation of Polish Jewish soldiers in World War II opened at the Jewish Historical Institute in Warsaw. Also in September, Roman Polanski's Holocaust movie, *The Pianist,* had its world premiere in Warsaw. School classes were taken to see the film, which was based on the memoirs of pianist Wladyslaw Szpilman, who survived the Warsaw Ghetto. The film won the Palme d'Or at the Cannes Film Festival. Polanski, who himself survived the Holocaust in Kraków as a child, attended the premiere along with Szpilman's widow and children. The fifth annual Warsaw Jewish Book Fair, organized by the Lauder Foundation and the Jewish monthly *Midrasz,* took place in October. Warsaw's mayor opened the five-day event. Lecturers during the book fair included Joanna Olczak-Roniker, whose book, *In the Gardens of Memory,* which told the story of her Jewish family, won Poland's most coveted literary award, the Nike. The city of Warsaw, with the cooperation of Warsaw's

Jewish Historical Institute, set up a new Web site that provided detailed information on Jewish historical and heritage sites in Warsaw, http://jewish.sites.warszawa.um.gov.pl.

In June, Britain's Prince Charles toured Kraków's centuries-old Remuh Synagogue and Old Jewish Cemetery, and met with local Holocaust survivors. His guide was Tadeusz Jakobowicz, the head of the city's 200-member Jewish community.

Dr. Arnold Mostowicz, a resistance fighter who treated fellow Jews in the Lodz Ghetto during World War II before being deported to Auschwitz, died in February, aged 87.

Romania

Most Romanians continued to live in grinding poverty, which fueled rampant corruption and, among some, nostalgia for the regime of communist dictator Nicolae Ceauşescu. In April, a report by PricewaterhouseCoopers, presented at an international conference in Bucharest, said that the widespread corruption and the lack of transparency in the legal and political systems had cost Romania billions of dollars in foreign investment in 2001.

Romania was one of seven postcommunist countries invited to join NATO in November. Earlier, in March, representatives of Jewish communities in East-Central Europe met in Bucharest alongside a summit of postcommunist states that aspired to enter NATO. At a roundtable discussion organized by the American Jewish Committee, they presented status reports on Jewish affairs in their countries, which were circulated to prime ministers and NATO officials at the summit. Participants came from NATO aspirants Bulgaria, Croatia, Estonia, Latvia, Lithuania, Macedonia, Romania, and Slovenia, as well as from Poland, the Czech Republic, and Hungary, which had entered NATO in 1999.

NATO insisted on respect for human rights as a criterion for membership, and this put right-wing nationalist extremism, manifestations of racism and anti-Semitism, and nostalgia for the pro-Nazi World-War-II government of Marshal Ion Antonescu under heightened scrutiny. In February, the chairman of the U.S. NATO Committee told a Romanian newspaper that such phenomena could hinder Romania's efforts to enter NATO. The government attempted to crack down. In mid-March it passed a special ordinance against racism and the Antonescu cult, barring statues or plaques commemorating Antonescu or others condemned for "crimes against peace" and "crimes against humanity," and also prohibiting the naming of streets or other public places in their honor. (This in effect mandated the removal of six Antonescu statues from around the country and the renaming of some 30 streets and parks.) The ordinance also banned the public display of "racist or fascist symbols" and outlawed organizations "of fascist, racist, and xenophobic character" such as the Antonescu Foundation, which promoted the dictator's legacy. Penalties for infractions ranged from fines to five years in prison.

In March, the head of the Dinamo Bucharest soccer team's fan club was fined the equivalent of about $50—an average monthly salary—for having failed to stop fans from unfurling a huge racist banner and a portrait of Antonescu at a match. At the end of March, a bust of Antonescu in Piatra Neamt was dismantled, and in April authorities took down another in Slobozia. During the year, however, reports in the local media suggested some resistance to the new legislation, with local councils in at least two towns voting against government orders to change street names honoring Antonescu.

In March, the government passed an ordinance that mandated stiff penalties for the desecration of Jewish cemeteries, synagogues, and other sites. It said that no construction on historically Jewish sites could be undertaken without the prior approval of the Federation of Jewish Communities (FEDROM), and that such projects must respect Jewish religious practice and traditions. Penalties for violations ranged from fines to 25 years in prison. A government spokesman said that while 600 out of 800 Jewish cemeteries in Romania were no longer in use, they had to be preserved as an important part of the country's heritage.

On March 18, the first course on the Holocaust in Romania was introduced at the National Defense College. It was taught to senior officers by Radu Ioanid, an official of the U.S. Holocaust Memorial Museum. In a message to the participants, Prime Minister Adrian Nastase called on Romania to recognize the role the Antonescu government had played in the Shoah. In the Senate, the upper house of Parliament, on April 2, several right-wing nationalist members rejected Nastase's admission of Romania's responsibility.

The Jewish Studies Institute at Babes Bolyai University in Cluj ran a six-week summer program for Romanian high-school history teachers who taught the Holocaust, one teacher chosen from each Romanian county. The faculty came from Israel, the U.S., France, and Poland, and the entire group visited Auschwitz at the end of the course. At a June 27–July 2 conference in Bucharest, Romanian and Israeli historians took part in three symposia on the role of Romania in the Holocaust.

In July, the Center for Monitoring and Combating Anti-Semitism in Romania (www.antisemitism.ro) called recent government moves against racism and anti-Semitism superficial ploys whose aim was "to recruit Jewish support in the effort to push Romania's interests forward without Romania truly accepting its share of responsibility in the extermination of 20–50 pecent of the Jews living in Romania before the war."

In September, President Ion Iliescu, addressing a student forum in Bucharest, warned against what he saw as the danger of "the rebirth of aggressive nationalism, anti-Semitism, xenophobia, racism, intolerance, and extremism." That month, the license of the private television station OTV was revoked after an on-air appearance by ultranationalist senator Corneliu Vadim Tudor, who made derogatory remarks about Roma and Jews. Tudor, leader of the Greater Romanian Party, was already facing the prospect of several trials on charges of offending ethnic minorities in his newspaper.

In May, vandals desecrated the synagogue in Falticeni. Swastikas and anti-Semitic slogans signed by a previously unknown group, "The Front of Anti-Semitic Struggle," were scrawled on its walls, and a Torah scroll was stolen. Six weeks later, there was a break-in at the synagogue in Vatra Dornei. In October, vandals marked swastikas and anti-Semitic slogans into the facade of the Yiddish theater in Bucharest. FEDROM criticized the police for not taking sufficient measures to prevent "anti-Semitic, xenophobic, and racist" incidents. Culture Minister Razvan Theodorescu called the vandalism "a serious provocation." In the days that followed, anti-Semitic slogans were also found in Cluj.

On May 20, a former Nazi concentration camp guard, Nikolaus Schiffer, was deported from the U.S. to Romania.

In April, Foreign Minister Mircea Geoana toured the Middle East and met with leaders in Egypt, Jordan, and Israel. In Jerusalem he met with Prime Minister Sharon, and in Ramallah with Palestinian Authority chairman Arafat. He gave both a letter from President Iliescu offering Romania's "good services" for mediation in the Israeli-Palestinian crisis. Sharon said that Israel considered relations with Romania to be important. He praised recent measures aimed at preserving the Jewish heritage in Romania and banning the Antonescu cult. In June, President Iliescu came out against removing Arafat from his position as Palestinian leader, saying that such a step could lead to "additional tension, instead of alleviating it." He expressed skepticism about President Bush's plan, announced June 24, to replace Arafat and gradually set up a democratic Palestinian state.

Relations with Israel were close, with growing economic links. Nearly 400,000 Romanian Jews had left for Israel in the postwar decades, and now many non-Jewish Romanians worked in Israel. Nevertheless, Jewish observers felt that the Romanian media, both the mainstream and fringe publications, were biased against Israel. In August, Ephraim Sneh, the Israeli transport minister, came to Bucharest with a delegation of Israeli businessmen and investors to participate in a symposium on Romanian-Israeli cooperation in infrastructure and the construction industry.

Naphtali Lavie, vice chairman of the World Jewish Restitution Organization (WJRO), met with Prime Minister Nastase in Bucharest in November. Nastase said that Romania was "favorable" toward addressing compensation claims for property confiscated during World War II. Lavie said this could represent a turning point in negotiations, which had been going on since 1994.

JEWISH COMMUNITY

Some 11,000–16,000 Jews were believed to live in Romania, about half of them in Bucharest. Most Romanian Jews were elderly, and they were hit hard by the poor economic situation—an average pension amounted to just $20–$30 a month. Educational, religious, and welfare programs were carried out by FEDROM, funded by the JDC. There were ten kosher canteens throughout the country. Thousands received supplemental food packages containing flour, cooking oil, sugar, rice, cheese, powdered milk, eggs, and kosher canned meat. Special deliveries were made for the Jewish holidays. In Bucharest, the meals-on-wheels program had a newly equipped kosher kitchen and delivered 300 kosher meals to the homebound elderly every other day. There were also free medical services for the community, with a full-time ambulance and a staff of 12 doctors. There were three Jewish old-age homes in the country. At the end of the year the biggest of them, the Rosen Home in Bucharest, had 136 residents, most over 85 years of age.

There was also a nationwide Jewish youth movement, OTER (Romanian Youth Organization), funded by the JDC, with 11 branches around the country. Nearly 700 young Jews took part in its seminars, training programs, Jewish camps, and social and religious gatherings. In addition, the Lauder Foundation ran the Lauder Reut Kindergarten and Lower School in Bucharest. At the beginning of the year, a new *mikveh* opened in Bucharest and a bar mitzvah was celebrated in the small northern town of Roman.

In October, three JDC officials—President Eugene J. Ribakoff, Executive Vice President Steven Schwager, and Zvi Feine, the country director in Romania—attended a community celebration at the Choral Synagogue in Bucharest marking 35 years since the JDC returned to Romania in 1967 after a 20-year absence. Ribakoff, Schwager, and Feine toured several Jewish communities and met with government officials.

Numerous commemorative and cultural events took place. In July, President Iliescu awarded Nobel laureate Elie Wiesel the country's highest honor, the Star of Romania. Wiesel, 74, was presented the award in Bucharest after he and his family, accompanied by Iliescu and the Israeli and U.S. ambassadors, paid a visit to his hometown, Sighet, from which he and his family were deported to Auschwitz in 1944. Thousands of townspeople turned out to greet Wiesel in Sighet, where he inaugurated a museum in the house where he lived as a child. In August, members of Parliament, ambassadors, cultural figures, and leaders of other religions joined Jewish community members at a ceremony marking the 70th birthday of Rabbi Menachem Hacohen, the Israel-based rabbi who served as chief rabbi of Romania. In October, there was a government-sponsored festival of Yiddish theater in Iasi.

Bibi Cajal, the wife of FEDROM president Nicolai Cajal, died in January. Ovidius University in Costanza awarded Nicolai Cajal an honorary doctorate in March. Writer and philosopher Henri Wald died in July.

Slovakia

In the September election, a coalition of the Slovak Democratic Party, the Christian Union (SDKU), ethnic Hungarians, Christian Democrats, and the business-oriented New Citizens Alliance (ANO) won 78 out of 150 seats in parliament. The new center-right government took office in October, led by Prime Minister Mikulas Dzurinda, leader of the Slovak Democrats, who began a second term in office. The NATO summit in Prague in November invited Slovakia to join, and the EU summit in Copenhagen in December confirmed Slovakia's admission, set for 2004.

There was concern throughout the year about racist sentiments in the country and neo-Nazi attacks, mainly against Roma. In January, Slovak historians and Jews complained when President Rudolf Schuster awarded Jozef Mikus, 92, a diplomat who served the wartime Slovak fascist puppet state, a high state award, the Pribrina's Cross. On March 14, dozens of skinheads and elderly Slovaks rallied outside the presidential palace in Bratislava to mark the 63rd anniversary of the establishment of the pro-Nazi wartime independent Slovak state. (On the same day, the local Jewish community took Slovak officials on a tour of the site where a new memorial commemorating Jewish Holocaust victims was under construction.) In April, the media quoted police as saying that there were about 2,500 right-wing extremists and sympathizers in Slovakia. The active core was made up of some 500 skinheads, neo-Nazis, and fascists. Also in April, vandals defaced some 135 tombstones at the Jewish cemetery in Košice, causing $35,000 worth of damage. Police later traced the act to three schoolboys, aged 10–12, who could not be charged because of their youth.

In September, the government approved creation of a fund to compensate Holocaust victims who suffered under the Slovak wartime state. Prime Minister Dzurinda and Fero Alexander, executive chairman of the Central Union of Jewish Religious Communities, signed the agreement in October. Under the accord, the government allocated the equivalent of nearly $20 million to the fund, which, with its accrued interest, would be transferred to the union after ten years. A commission made up of four Jewish and three government representatives was to decide on distribution of the money.

There were about 4,000 Jews in Slovakia's 13 Jewish communities. The two main communities were Bratislava and Košice, each with several hundred members.

In July, the underground mausoleum of the revered 19th-century sage Chatam Sofer was reopened after renovation. President Schuster attended the ceremony, along with members of the Slovak government and Jewish representatives. The work was carried out through the efforts of the Bratislava Jewish community, city officials, and the New York-based International Committee for the Preservation of the Gravesites of the Sages of Bratislava.

There were a number of commemorative events during the year. In March, ceremonies marked the 60th anniversary of the first Slovak transport to Auschwitz—March 25, 1942, when 1,000 young women were taken by train from Poprad. The Central Union of Slovak Jews used the occasion to warn against the spread of Holocaust denial. It issued a statement saying, "The number of those who demonstratively dismiss the existence of the Holocaust is growing, despite the large number of witnesses, historical records, archives . . . films, newspapers, and mass graves." This denial, it said, represented "a continuation of the Holocaust. Dead Jews cannot be killed again, the last thing that can be taken from them is the almost forgotten shadow of their former existence."

In June, Slovakia's ambassador to the U.S., Martin Butora, received the American Jewish Committee's Celebration of Freedom Award. The AJC said it was honoring Butora, a sociologist, for advancing freedom in the Slovak Republic and for working to "preserve and protect the surviving Jewish community in Slovakia . . . preserving Jewish landmarks, reestablishing institutions of Jewish education, and strengthening relations with Israel." In November, Slovak director Matej Minac received an International Emmy in New York for his documentary film, *Nicholas Winton—The Power of Good,* which told the story of an English man, now aged 93, who, in 1939, save 669 Czechoslovak Jewish children.

Slovenia

Jewish leaders estimated that approximately 400 Jews lived in Slovenia, about 130 of whom were members of the Jewish community. Chabad rabbi Ariel Haddad, director of the Jewish museum in Trieste, Italy—about an hour's drive from Ljubljana, the Slovenian capital—served as Slovenia's rabbi, traveling to Ljubljana about once a month. Other rabbis and lecturers were also invited from time to time. During the year, the community, with financing from the JDC and the local government, published a lavishly illustrated Passover Haggadah, fully translated into Slovenian. This was the first book ever published in Hebrew in Slovenia, and proceeds from its sale were going to finance the creation of a synagogue in Ljubljana, the only European capital beside Tirana (Albania) that did not have one.

In October, scholars from Europe, North America, and Israel attended an international conference on anti-Semitism in the Balkans, held at the lakeside town of Bled. Topics included contemporary ethnic conflicts and their relevance to anti-Semitism; Holocaust denial and historical revisionism; anti-Semitism and anti-Zionism in public discourse; the survival and perpetuation of common anti-Jewish stereotypes in Balkan folklore, literature, and art; and the connection between the State of Israel, the status of local Jewry, and the evolution of anti-Semitism.

Yugoslavia (Serbia and Montenegro)

Yugoslavia's economic situation was still disastrous, though significantly improved since the ouster of President Slobodan Milosevic in 2000. Inflation had dropped from 125 percent to an estimated 15 percent, and the average monthly wage had risen from 35–40 euros a week to 160. The unemployment rate, however, was still around 50 percent.

In the spring, under a deal brokered by the European Union, Yugoslavia's two constituent republics, Serbia and tiny Montenegro, agreed to transform their relationship into a looser union under which each would exercise almost sovereign authority. Steps to attain this end were taken during the year.

In the fall, Serbians and Montenegrins tried unsuccessfully to elect new presidents. In Serbia, neither Yugoslav president Vojislav Kostunica nor his main opponent, Miroljub Labus, received enough votes in either the first round of voting or the runoff. The pro-Western Labus was backed by Kostunica's bitter rival, Serbian prime minister Zoran Djindjic.

Jews worried about manifestations of anti-Semitism. In February, after protests by Israel and the Yugoslav foreign minister, the synod of the Serbian Orthodox Church condemned anti-Semitic remarks made by a retired Orthodox priest in a New Year's broadcast. In May, vandals marked up the walls of the entrance to the Jewish community offices in Novi Sad with the Star of David, swastikas, and the slogan "Free Palestine," and left feces on the floor. In the summer, after receiving threats, the Jewish community in Zemun installed a new security door. The Jewish cemetery in Belgrade was desecrated in August. During the electoral campaign in the fall, graffiti appeared saying that both candidates were Jewish. In December, the Serbian minister of religion named Davor Salom, secretary of the Federation of Jewish Communities in Yugoslavia, to the consultative council of the ministry.

In March, Serbian prime minister Djindjic, accompanied by the minister of religion, visited the historic synagogue in Subotica, on the Hungarian border. He met there with leaders of the 225-member Jewish community and with members of the board of a new foundation aimed at restoring and reviving the synagogue. He pledged support for these efforts as a symbol of tolerance and multiculturalism. This was Djindjic's first visit as prime minister to a Jewish community, and it coincided with celebrations marking the 150th anniversary of the Subotica Jewish Women's Association. Guests of honor included Princess Katarina— wife of Crown Prince Alexander of Yugoslavia, the pretender to the Serbian throne—and June Jacobs, the outgoing president of the International Council of Jewish Women. The Subotica community was the third largest of Yugoslavia's ten Jewish communities. Only Belgrade, with more than 1,800 members, and Novi Sad, with 600, were bigger. This year, after a hiatus of several decades, a Jewish community was formally reestablished in the town of Kikinda, about 100 km north of Belgrade. Consisting of 42 members, it was admitted as a member of the Federation of Jewish Communities in December.

Yugoslavia's 3,000-or-so Jews were highly integrated into the broader society, mostly secular, and often intermarried. Leaders of the federation urged members to identify as Jews in the national census. In February, nearly 200 Jews from the various parts of former Yugoslavia met for the "Sholet-2002" gathering in Novi Sad, and in June about 200 young people took part in a Maccabee games competition near Zrenjanin. In the summer, ten members of the 45-member community in Nis began a program to visit all the other communities in the country. Their program was based on the insight that "since nobody comes to visit us, we will go and visit everyone else."

Yugoslavia had just one active rabbi, Belgrade-based Yitzhak Asiel. Stevan Lanyi (Ezra ben Jitzhok), a Subotica community member studying at the Rabbinical Seminary of the Jewish University in Budapest, served as religious leader in Subotica and also traveled to other nearby communities. He published a prayer book and Jewish calendar. In May, he began celebrating holiday services in the Subotica Synagogue rather than the smaller community prayer room, which had been used previously. Lanyi led the first communal seder in many years in Zrenjanin. In the town of Zemun, outside Belgrade, about 70 people attended the first communal seder since World War II. In addition, Stefan Sablic served as a cantor in Serbia, and once a month in Skopje, Macedonia. The religious activities of Asiel, Lanyi, and Sablic were subsidized by the JDC. The Italian government financed the reconstruction of a social hall and dining area for the kosher kitchen built under the Belgrade synagogue.

Subotica's Jewish lay leadership was very active, sponsoring a number of civic, religious, educational, and social-welfare activities. But the community, wracked by internal divisions, was also in conflict with the Federation of Jewish Communities. In snap elections in the spring, the community ousted its president, Tomas Halbrohr (who lived part-time in Subotica and part-time in Budapest), and elected a new team headed by activist lawyer Mira Poljakovic. The federation, however, said that the conduct of the election violated its bylaws, and recognized both presidents as members of its board. A community faction backing the ousted leadership accused the new leaders of discrimination and misuse of power. Critics said the community bylaws were undemocratic in that, among other flaws, they did not provide for a secret ballot and they mandated criteria for community president that excluded the majority of members. In November, the Subotica community adopted new bylaws mandating secret balloting.

There were numerous Jewish cultural and commemorative events in Serbia, including lectures, performances, seminars, publications, and courses. In March, some 130 students from Europe, Israel, and the countries of the former Yugoslavia attended a five-day international Jewish seminar in Belgrade. Stefan Sablic, the cantor in Belgrade, performed during the year with his Jewish music group Shira Utfila. Sablic also directed the production of a play, *Visiting Mr. Green,* by the American playwright Jeff Baron and starring two Jewish actors. The play treated the evolution of a friendship between a timid, anguished Jewish homosexual and a lonely, old Jewish man who resists all contact with the outside world. It premiered at the Beyahad gathering in Croatia in September, and afterward became a huge hit at one of the top theaters in Belgrade.

RUTH ELLEN GRUBER

Former Soviet Union

National Affairs

RUSSIA'S ECONOMIC AND POLITICAL evolution was marked by contradictory tendencies during the year. For the first time since the fall of communism, in the second quarter of 2002 more capital flowed into the country than out of it. President Vladimir Putin offered to allow repatriation of funds at low tax rates and with no questions asked, but the positive trend was probably due more to growing confidence in the economy. That confidence, in turn, stemmed from apparent political stability as well as Russia's ability to produce large amounts of petroleum for export at a time of uncertainty in the Middle East. By February, the Russian Federation was the world's largest oil producer, outstripping even Saudi Arabia, as huge Russian companies such as Yukos and Lukoil purchased companies in neighboring countries. However, the state continued to play a major role in the oil industry, as all crude oil leaving Russia passed through a state-owned pipeline to which the government assigned quotas for access.

On the other hand, many Western analysts pointed out ongoing weaknesses in the Russian economy. Wealth was highly concentrated, and small businesses continued to struggle against excessive government regulation, corruption, and onerous taxation. Eight large business groups were said to control 85 percent of the revenue from Russia's 64 largest private companies. World Bank figures showed that while small businesses in the United States produced 60 percent of the country's total economic output, in Russia they generated only 20 percent. In June, the Duma, the lower house of the national legislature, finally passed a law — by a very narrow margin — legalizing the sale and purchase of agricultural land, facilitating the long-postponed privatization of agriculture. But upon the insistence of communists and nationalists, the law forbade the sale of land to foreigners.

In the political arena there were contradictory tendencies as well. A new legal code, enacted in June, codified the principle of habeas corpus, for the most part eliminated double jeopardy, and gave suspects the right to demand a lawyer from the moment of their arrest. Going against years of Russian and Soviet precedent, the new code enshrined the presumption of innocence, strengthened the position of defense attorneys, and somewhat diminished the powers of the prosecutors, which had previously been far greater than those of defense lawyers. The Duma also passed a law that, for the first time, allowed certain restricted categories of conscientious objectors to apply for alternatives to military service. An estimated 10 percent of those eligible for the draft evaded it, and the Russian army continued to be plagued by desertions, suicides, and murders, many caused by very harsh conditions and the mistreatment of subordinates by superiors.

Political murders continued to occur with alarming frequency. Parliamentary deputies — Vladimir Golovlyov, for instance — were assassinated, as were investigative reporters such as Valery Ivanov, who had been investigating organized crime in Togliatti, and law enforcement officials such as General Vitaly Gamov of the border guards, who tried to bring law and order to the Pacific Ocean fishing industry.

Western observers and Russian democrats were troubled by the continuing extension of state control over the mass media. The Moscow Higher Arbitration Court ordered the dissolution of T-6, an independent national television network controlled by Boris Berezovsky from London, where he was living in self-imposed exile. Berezovsky, one of the "oligarchs" who had prospered under former president Boris Yeltsin, continued his criticism of the Putin government, releasing a tape in which he made his case. Berezovsky claimed that the September 1999 explosions in apartment buildings in several Russian cities were caused not by Chechens, as the government claimed, but by the Russian security services themselves, and pointed out that the Duma had, in March 2000, rejected a call for an inquiry into the explosions. Berezovsky did admit that he had given $2 million to Shamil Basayev, then president of Chechnya, in 1997, ostensibly to repair a cement plant, and that he had negotiated the release of kidnapped people in Chechnya.

The closing of TV-6 left two of the three major national networks firmly under state control, and the third run by a state-controlled monopoly. Earlier, in the summer of 2001, the independent network NTV, owned by former "oligarch" and Jewish leader Vladimir Gusinsky, had been shut down when it could not pay its debts to Gazprom, the state-owned natural gas monopoly (see AJYB 2002, p. 481). Gusinksy, like Berezovsky a political enemy of President Putin, also remained outside the country, fearing rearrest. In October, the government rescinded Boris Yeltsin's 1991 decree allowing Radio Free Europe/Radio Liberty to broadcast from Russia.

The breakaway region of Chechnya remained intractable. Chechen and Russian military forces continued their war there, with about 85,000 Russian troops deployed. Official government figures released early in the year admitted to 3,500 Russian dead since the fighting was renewed in October 1999, and claimed that between 10,000 and 13,000 Chechens had died in the conflict. Many observers considered these figures understated. On May 9, the anniversary of the end of World War II in Europe, Chechens killed 41 parade-watchers, including 17 children, in the Russian city of Kaspiisk. In August, an overloaded Mi-26 Russian helicopter, designed to carry cargo, was shot down in Chechnya, and 118 Russian soldiers aboard were killed—about the same number lost in the sinking of the Kursk submarine in 2000. Putin sharply criticized the military for violating a 1997 ban on using the helicopters for troop transport.

The Russian government claimed that Chechen and foreign Muslim fighters were taking shelter in the Pankisi Gorge, a valley in the mountainous region between Russia and Georgia. Russian planes bombed the area, drawing protests from Georgians against what they saw as violation of Georgian airspace. Russia responded by accusing Georgia of harboring terrorists. In September, President Putin threatened to launch military strikes against Chechens who fled to Georgia. This set up a potential conflict with the U.S., which had sent a small contingent of specialists to train Georgian forces.

Aside from the ongoing conflict in Chechnya, another point of social tension was the conflict between the Russian Orthodox Church, which increasingly saw itself as the guardian of Russian values and identity, and the minority Catholic Church. When the latter announced that it was dividing the Russian Federation into four new dioceses serving a total of some 1.3 million Catholics, the Orthodox Church denounced this as an "unfriendly act," and reentry visas were denied to Catholic priests who had left Russia on short visits abroad. Though Pope John Paul II had traveled widely around the world, especially in former communist states, he had never been invited to visit Russia, and Orthodox leaders made quite clear that he was not welcome.

President Putin met with U.S. president George W. Bush in May. They signed a treaty cutting the American and Russian nuclear arsenals by two-thirds over the next decade and agreed to cooperate on developing an antimissile defense. In June, the United States officially recognized Russia as a market economy, facilitating Russian exports to the U.S.

At a meeting of its 19 member states, NATO agreed to allow Russia to participate in the organization's discussions of specific topics, such as nu-

clear nonproliferation, crisis management, missile defense, and counterterrorism. But NATO did not grant Russia membership, leaving the
country outside its collective defense pact.

Ukraine held parliamentary elections in the spring. Though President
Leonid Kuchma, elected to a five-year term in 1999, came under mounting public criticism, his party, For a United Ukraine, won a plurality in
the Rada (parliament) largely because independent regional candidates
agreed to support him and his policies. In September, however, thousands
protested in Kiev against Kuchma's rule, which they called corrupt and
inefficient. Kuchma was accused of arranging murders of political opponents and, most recently, of selling Kolchuga advanced radar systems
to Iraq against the explicit wishes of the United States, even though
Ukraine was the third largest recipient of American foreign aid. Moreover, several disasters had occurred in 2001–02, including the shooting
down by Ukrainian forces of a Russian airliner bound from Israel to
Siberia; a crash at an air show in Lviv that killed 23 children and 53
adults; and a coal mine explosion in July 2001 that killed 35.

Israel and the Middle East

To some extent, the congruence between Russia's problems in Chechnya and Israel's struggle against Palestinian terrorism brought the two
countries together. In March, Israel and Russia signed an agreement on
jointly combating terrorism and organized crime. On June 11, Israel ex-
tradited Andrei Zhuravlev, an Israeli citizen, to Russia, where he was
charged with murder and other serious crimes committed in 1995–98, before he emigrated to Israel. The extradition was an unprecedented move
by Israel, heralding a new level of cooperation between the law enforcement agencies of the two countries.

Israel's military advance into Palestinian territory in the spring met
with Russian disapproval, but this did not even approach the level of anti-
Israel feeling manifested elsewhere in Europe. In April, the Duma
adopted a nonbinding resolution condemning Israeli policies in the Territories and threatening Israel with economic sanctions. The Russian
Foreign Ministry protested Israel's storming of a hostel owned by the
Russian Orthodox Church. Catholicos Garegin II, head of the Armenian Apostolic Church, expressed "extreme concern" about the situation
and called on Israel to return Armenian church properties seized on the
West Bank. Demonstrations criticizing Israel were held at the American
and Israeli embassies in Baku, capital of Azerbaijan.

The atmosphere was quite different in September, when Israeli prime minister Ariel Sharon spent two days in Moscow seeking to dissuade Russian leaders from cooperating with Iraq and Iran, whose policies Israel saw as inimical to its interests. President Putin used the occasion to praise Israel for fighting terrorism, and welcomed the ending of the siege that had kept Yasir Arafat confined to his compound in Ramallah.

Anti-Semitism

According to the Anti-Defamation League, the number of anti-Semitic incidents in Russia during 2002 roughly matched the number for 2001. There were some violent attacks and a number of worrisome political developments.

The most dramatic incident of violence occurred on May 27, near Moscow, when a 28-year-old woman, Tatyana Sapunova, was driving a car and saw a sign reading "Death to the Kikes [zhidy]" along the highway. She tried to remove it, triggering an explosion that caused her serious burns. Sapunova, who had a Jewish grandfather but was not raised as a Jew, was treated in Israel for her injuries. Yuri Chaika, the Russian minister of justice, condemned the act and said it must be "severely punished." President Putin met with Sapunova on July 25 and remarked, "If we let this bacillus of chauvinism and national or religious intolerance develop, we will ruin our country." There were at least seven other incidents similar to the Sapunova case, except that most of the explosive devices were fakes. In July, a box with an anti-Semitic slogan was found near the entrance to a maternity hospital and, in another incident, a pipe bomb bearing the slogan "Death to the Kikes" was thrown on to the balcony of a Moscow apartment where it exploded.

At least nine cases of vandalism of Jewish cemeteries and synagogues took place in 2002. The police, however, found few of the perpetrators, and classified the incidents as "hooliganism" rather than hate crimes, which were punishable under Russian law. In Volgograd and Taganrog buildings housing Jewish organizations were defaced, and, in November, guards at a Jewish school in Volgograd had to beat off a group of men armed with metal pipes. Ten-ruble notes were said to be circulating in Moscow, the phrase "Moscow without Kikes" carefully typewritten on both sides. Officials declared the bills still legal tender, and there was no way to stop their circulation or find out who was spreading them.

In September, the Russian Ministry of Justice registered a new political party called the National Great Power Party of Russia despite its open and radical anti-Semitism. The party's official Web site included the slogan, "Not an ounce of power to the Kikes." Its cochairman, Boris Mironov, had been ousted in 1994 from his post as government press minister for anti-Semitic behavior. Another party leader, Viktor Korshagin, directed a publishing house that had issued several editions of Adolf Hitler's *Mein Kampf.* Another extremist faction, the People's National Party, had been registered in 1994 and claimed 10,000 members nationwide. It called for stripping citizenship from "persons who are not ethnically Russian or not members of the Orthodox faith," and for deporting all foreigners.

Jewish and other ethnic minority leaders pressed for criminal charges to be filed against the Russian Orthodox Church for permitting the sale of anti-Semitic literature, including the *Protocols of the Elders of Zion,* on church premises in Ekaterinburg and other cities.

A Jewish former army officer turned businessman, Vladimir Brikker, ran for the mayoralty of Dzerzhinsk, but was subjected to a great deal of anti-Semitic propaganda. Similar incidents were reported about electoral campaigns in Nizhny Novgorod, Saratov, and elsewhere.

Problems persisted elsewhere in the former Soviet Union as well. In Ukraine, police arrested eight young soccer fans who, following a Saturday game in April, smashed windows in a Kiev synagogue and, according to the rabbi, attacked worshipers and badly beat a Jewish-studies teacher. Police did not arrive until 20–30 minutes after the incident began. In Belarus, vandals desecrated cemeteries in Minsk, Borisov, and Vitebsk, and anti-Semitic graffiti appeared in six cities. President Aleksandr Lukashenka called the cemetery desecrations "a commonplace hooligan action" and denied charges by Jewish activists that anti-Semitism was growing in Belarus. The deputy chairman of the foreign affairs committee of the Belarussian Chamber of Representatives told a newspaper on November 25 that he favored a halt to the reconstruction of destroyed synagogues in Minsk. He declared his opposition to Jewish protestors who wanted to "turn Belarus into a springboard of Zionism," as they already had allegedly done to "Moscow." "America is an absolutely Zionistic-fascist state and now they want to do this in Belarus," he said. "That is why I do not give a damn about these synagogues. I do not care about them just as Ariel Sharon does not care about mosques or Palestinian children."

In June, the Russian Duma adopted its third and final reading of a controversial bill on combating extremism. Defining extremism as any action that used force or other illegal means to impede the functioning of the federal authorities, the bill prohibited "extremist activity" and organizations recognized by a court as "extremist." Some human-rights activists expressed concern that the bill could be used to suppress protest since it also banned "inciting social animosity." A month after the bill's passage a Moscow city court ruled that the newspaper *Russkie Vedomosti,* which claimed a circulation of 10,000, should be shut down because it was publishing extremist, nationalist, and anti-Semitic materials. The paper had already received two warnings. Despite the new law, attacks by skinheads on foreigners, people from the Caucasus, and others went on. Officials in St. Petersburg estimated that there were more than 2,000 skinheads in that city alone.

Holocaust-Related Developments

There were a number of developments in Estonia during 2002 regarding the Holocaust. The Estonian government designated January 27, the day in 1945 that Auschwitz-Birkenau was liberated by the Red Army, a day of remembrance of the Holocaust and other crimes against humanity. A commission established by President Lennart Meri concluded that the 36th Estonian Police Battalion that collaborated with the Nazis during World War II played a role in the massacre of Jews in Nowogrudek (Poland/Belarus) in 1942. City officials in Parnu ordered the redesign of a privately funded monument featuring a soldier clad in a Waffen-SS uniform. Prime Minister Siim Kallas had condemned the monument, which also depicted a gun pointing eastward towards Russia.

Efraim Zuroff, director of the Jerusalem office of the Simon Wiesenthal Center, offered $10,000 for information leading to the trial and conviction of Nazi war criminals living in the Baltic states. The center claimed that 17 residents had already come forth with 51 names of such criminals, 47 of them living in Lithuania. Twelve were known to have died. Some questioned the legality of Zuroff's advertisements in local newspapers and others criticized the idea of offering bounties.

In western Ukraine, authorities in the city of Ivano-Frankivsk recognized 24 veterans of the SS Halychyna (Galicia) division as participants in the struggle for an independent Ukraine. Over 80,000 men had volunteered for the division. These veterans living in Ivano-Frankivsk, most of them disabled after being imprisoned in the Soviet gulag, were now entitled to an increase in their pensions and other benefits. Both Russian and Jewish organizations protested the authorities' decision.

Also in Ukraine, the school program "Lessons of the Holocaust and

Tolerance in Ukrainian Schools" entered its third year. It was sponsored by the Jewish Confederation of Ukraine, the Center for Jewish Education, the Ukrainian Ministry of Education, the Claims Conference, and the Dutch Ministry of Foreign Affairs. The teachers' seminars that were part of the program drew participants from eight of Ukraine's 25 regions.

The American branch of the Wiesenthal Center urged the Belarussian government to ask for the extradition of 79-year-old Michael Gorshkow from the U.S. on the grounds that, as a Gestapo interpreter, he had been directly involved in the mass killings of the Jews of Minsk.

JEWISH COMMUNITY

Emigration

There was a sharp downturn in 2002 in the emigration of Jews from the former Soviet Union. This was due to the improvement of the Russian economy, the escalating violence in and around Israel, and tightened restrictions on immigration imposed by the United States in the aftermath of the attacks of September 11, 2001. Only 2,486 Jews from the FSU arrived in the U.S. in 2002, far less than the 4,978 who arrived the previous year. Whereas nearly 51,000 had immigrated to Israel in 2000 and 34,000 in 2001, only about 18,500 did so in 2002. For the first time, the number of Soviet Jewish immigrants to Germany—about 19,000—surpassed the number resettling in Israel.

In 2000, 2,700 people had left Birobidzhan, the "Jewish Autonomous Oblast" in Russia, for Israel. In 2001, only 250 did so, and 110 former emigrants returned from Israel to Birobidzhan. All told, in 2002 over 1,600 immigrants to Israel returned to the Russian Federation, and others returned to Azerbaijan, Uzbekistan, and Ukraine.

Israeli media reported estimates that some 270,000 immigrants from the FSU were not Jewish according to Halakhah, Jewish law. Of those who arrived in Israel in 2002, some 70 percent were not Jewish according to this traditional definition. About 100 of these non-Jewish immigrants formed a small new organization, the Slav Union of Israel.

Communal Affairs

During the year, the Russian Jewish Congress organized demonstrations in Moscow and 14 other cities against anti-Semitism and terrorism, and in support of Israel. It also withdrew its financial support from the *Mezhdunarodnaya Evreiskaya Gazeta* (International Jewish Newspaper), edited by veteran journalist Tankred Golenpolsky, and announced plans to publish another newspaper, *Evreiskiye Novosti* (Jewish News).

Jewish organizations continued to proliferate and compete with each other. The Federation of Jewish Communities of Russia, dominated by the Chabad-Lubavitch Hassidic movement, held its national congress in Moscow. About 400 delegates from 143 Jewish communities attended. The president of the federation was Mikhail Gluz, a former theater director, and its executive director was historian Valery Engel. Both had been active in the revival of Jewish culture in the early 1990s. Minister of Culture Mikhail Shvidkoi and Israeli ambassador Natan Meron attended the congress, as did a representative of President Putin.

A new Jewish group, the Association of Jewish Public Organizations, was established in Moscow in October by Chabad-affiliated people who felt excluded from the Conference of Leaders of Jewish Organizations, the latter reportedly affiliated with the Russian Jewish Congress and associated with Mikhail Fridman, head of the Alfa Group, one of the major business conglomerates in Russia. As a Jewish communal activist from Orenburg stated at the founding meeting of the association, "I'm here because my organization is poor," implying that he hoped to get funding for local activities from the new body.

Another founding meeting, this of the World Congress of Russian-Speaking Jews, took place in Moscow over two days, and then continued in Jerusalem for another two days. Rabbi Berel Lazar, the Chabad leader recognized by President Putin as the spokesman for Russian Jewry, and Valery Engel spearheaded this meeting. They announced plans to open schools for Russian-speaking children in a number of countries and to publish Russian-language texts and magazines dealing with Jewish history, culture, and contemporary issues.

Finally, a Euro-Asian Jewish Congress announced its formation in April with a celebratory banquet at a luxury Moscow hotel. Its head was Aleksandr Machkevich, a Jewish businessman based in Kazakhstan.

On Lithuania's national independence day in February, the state honored the 4,000 Jews who "voluntarily defended" Lithuania during its struggle for independence, 1918–23. The names of 60 of them who had died in combat were inscribed on new plaques in the restored Jewish museum in the capital city of Vilnius. The Lithuanian Ministry of Defense contributed $3,000 to the memorial.

Religion

The Chabad-Lubavitch Hassidic group continued to make great strides in establishing its influence during 2002. Just before Passover, President Putin met in the Kremlin with 21 Chabad rabbis and, according to them, voiced his gratitude for "the Jews' contribution to Russian society," praised the late Lubavitcher Rebbe, and sent holiday greetings to Russian Jewry. Putin also thanked the Chabad movement for its support in seeking repeal, in the U.S. Congress, of the 1974 Jackson-Vanik amendment. The argument for repeal was that emigration was now a freely available option, so that the amendment, no longer needed, only impeded Russian trade with the U.S. Among those who attended the meeting were Rabbi Berel Lazar, the Chabad "chief rabbi" of Russia, and Lev Leviev, a very wealthy diamond merchant born in Uzbekistan, who was a major funder of Chabad activities in the FSU. The Russian newspaper *Kommersant* (Mar. 20) reported that one decision reached at the meeting was that the Russian Jewish community would seek to establish close ties with Jews who had emigrated from the country.

Further evidence of Chabad's clout was the visit by President George W. Bush to the Chabad-run synagogue in St. Petersburg, where he stayed half an hour longer than scheduled and expressed satisfaction with the end of officially sanctioned Russian anti-Semitism. Bush's visit, which came during a summit meeting with President Putin, was seen as further cementing the relationship between Chabad and the Russian president.

In testimony to the U.S. Congress on March 7, Lawrence Uzell, director of the Keston Institute in England, specializing in the study of religion in former communist countries, decried the close relationship of the Putin administration to only one branch of Russian Jewry, Chabad. He claimed that the governor of Omsk, in Siberia, had approached members of a local synagogue board and asked them to switch their affiliation to the Chabad-controlled Federation of Jewish Communities so that regional government subsidies would follow.

The Reform movement claimed 110 affiliated groups in Russia, Belarus, and Ukraine, 54 of them officially registered in Russia, and some 5,000–10,000 people identifying with the movement. The Institute for Modern Jewish Studies in Moscow, affiliated with Reform, was said to be training 15 students in its one-year program for Jewish communal service, including nine women. Most of these students were not born Jewish according to Halakhah, and planned to convert to Judaism after completing their studies. The Reform movement was also building a new Jewish school in Lviv, western Ukraine, renovating a synagogue building in Evpatoria, Crimea, and registering a community in Kharkiv, Ukraine.

In Kostroma, Russia, a synagogue the Soviet government had seized in the 1930s was returned to the Jewish community. In Minsk, Belarus, about 30 demonstrators mounted a public demonstration demanding the reconstruction of a synagogue built in 1897 in the center of the city, and included in the Nazi-constructed ghetto during World War II. The synagogue was torn down in 2001 and a large apartment building constructed in its place.

Also in Belarus, a coalition of Uniate, Protestant, Jewish, and human-rights groups called on the legislature to reject a bill placing restrictions on small denominations that was meant to insure the domination of the Russian Orthodox Church. The bill banned publications, missionary work, and public prayer by religious groups having fewer than 20 Belarussian citizens as members, and forbade foreign citizens from leading religious organizations in Belarus.

In February, the Lithuanian government handed over 307 Torah scrolls that had been looted by the Nazis to an Israeli delegation. During Stalin's reign, Antanas Ulais, a Lithuanian archivist, had defied government orders to destroy the scrolls and hid them in St. George's Church. Negotiations to release the scrolls had dragged out over six years. Of those saved, 13 scrolls did not go to Israel but were kept in Lithuania as part of the national patrimony.

Jewish Culture

The Russian State Library ("Lenin Library") opened a small Jewish reading room. The library had about 40,000 books in Hebrew; 20,000 in Yiddish; and others in Aramaic, Arabic, Ladino, and other European languages. The Baron David Ginsburg collection included 7,000 books, 2,000 manuscripts, and the third largest collection of incunabula in the world (only the Jewish National and Hebrew University Library and the library of the Jewish Theological Seminary in New York had more).

The Jewish Agency opened a School of Judaica, with free tuition, in Moscow for upper-grade high school and university students. Fifteen high school seniors began the course, which featured eight-day intensive seminars.

The Association of Jewish Principals and Schools of the Commonwealth of Independent States and the Baltic Republics held its 13th national seminar in Moscow in October. The group had a membership of 44 schools, and 39 principals attended the seminar. The association produced curricula for the study of Hebrew, Jewish history, and tradition, and also organized regular seminars for master teachers of Judaic subjects and for teachers and administrators in charge of Jewish studies, some of whom were sent to study for a time in Israel. It also held an in-service seminar in Moscow in June that was attended by 114 teachers from 31 cities. The Ohr Avner foundation, based in Israel, also opened a Jewish studies teacher-training institute in Moscow.

By the end of the year, nearly 1,600 young Jews from the FSU had visited Israel as part of Operation Birthright. The cost of the trips was partially funded by Lev Leviev.

Plans were announced in April to rebuild parts of the World War II ghetto area in Vilnius. Private firms would be given land on which to build, and they would fund the reconstruction and get rights to commercial use. However, they would turn over a third of the space to the municipal authorities, who would, in turn, give it to the Jewish Cultural Fund. Cost of the project was estimated at $78 million.

A small monument to the great Yiddish writer Sholem Aleichem was unveiled in Moscow. It stood not far from the site of the former State Yiddish Theater, where many of his works had been performed.

ZVI GITELMAN

Australia

National Affairs

AUSTRALIA ENTERED 2002 WITH ITS economy outstripping those of most other free-market democracies and with the conservative Liberal-National coalition government of Prime Minister John Howard riding a wave of popularity after its November 2001 election victory. In contrast, the opposition Labor Party entered a period of soul-searching and internal rancor prompted by its lack of success at the national level, despite its complete dominance of the state and territorial governments.

The year also saw the emergence of the Greens as the most influential minority party, gaining support on a wide range of issues including refugee policy and strident opposition to war with Iraq. The Greens were also helped by the weakness of the Labor Party and the bitter infighting that dogged their ideological cousins, the Australian Democrats.

On the far right, the populist and controversy-ridden party One Nation continued to drift into irrelevance, its founding figurehead Pauline Hanson having already resigned as leader of the party and taking an indefinite break from politics. Ongoing legal action by the Australian Electoral Commission against Hanson and former director David Ettridge for fraudulent party registration in 1997 was the only news of note. Senator Len Harris, elected in 1998, languished as the party's sole representative in Federal Parliament and faced a likely exit at the next election.

The ramifications of September 11 for Australian security were already apparent early in the year when Singaporean investigators thwarted a plot by Islamic extremists to destroy the Australian High Commission in Singapore, along with the embassies of the United States, Israel, and Great Britain. Investigators concluded that a dangerous Southeast Asian offshoot of Al Qaeda, Jemaah Islamiah, was already well established across the region in a loose but coordinated network. This was confirmed in October by the shocking terrorist attack on vacationers in Bali, Indonesia, which resulted in nearly 200 deaths, 88 of them Australians. It was the most deadly terrorist attack yet seen in Southeast Asia and the most shocking tragedy suffered by Australia since World War II. In response, Australia took a leading role in assisting the Indonesian investigative team that, by year's end, captured the perpetrators. But there was little confidence that the elusive Jemaah Islamiah had been decisively damaged.

As security concerns progressively assumed center stage in political debates—surpassing worries over the worst drought in decades—the government clearly indicated its support for a U.S.-led action to disarm Iraq. With Australian special-forces troops already in Afghanistan and peacekeepers remaining in East Timor, an advance navy contingent was sent to the Persian Gulf. As in the U.S. and Britain, Australia's presence in "the coalition of the willing"generated political division and widespread public demonstrations at home, but the government remained firm in its conviction that Iraq had to be disarmed.

Australia and Israel

There was considerable political discussion about the Middle East during the year both in connection with the Israel-Palestinian conflict and in regard to the debate over the use of military force against Iraq. Both the government and the opposition in Australia remained largely supportive of Israel. However, some Labor backbenchers as well as representatives of smaller parties in the Australian Parliament vociferously condemned Israel.

The strong commitment of the government, and especially Prime Minister Howard, to Israel was recognized at a ceremony in New York on January 30, 2002, where the American Jewish Committee bestowed on him its Award for Excellence in Public Service. On that occasion Howard pledged "unyielding support and a perpetual protection of secure and defensible borders" for Israel. He accurately described himself as "unapologetic and longstanding friend of Israel and of the Jewish community" from a time predating his entry into politics. Similar positive statements came from Foreign Minister Alexander Downer, who pointed out on October 11, in a speech at a pro-Israel function, that "Yasir Arafat walked away from Camp David in 2000 offering nothing," and defended Israeli responses to Palestinian terrorism.

In the UN General Assembly Australia did vote for resolutions slanted against Israel on "Jerusalem," "peaceful settlement of the question of Palestine," and the "Special Information Programme on Palestine of the Department of Public Information of the Secretariat." It abstained from voting on anti-Israel resolutions regarding "Syrian Golan," the "Division for Palestinian Rights of the Secretariat," and the "Committee on the Exercise of the Inalienable Rights of the Palestinian People." Despite this mixed voting record, Bassim Blazey, counselor of the Australian UN mission, said that Australia was committed to the vision of two states, Israel and Palestine, living side by side within secure and recognized borders. Australia wholeheartedly supported Israel's territorial integrity and its right to live in peace, as well as the right of the Palestinian people to self-determination, a Palestinian state being an inevitable part of a peaceful settlement.

On the Labor opposition side, the party's foreign affairs spokesperson, Kevin Rudd, told a Jewish community function that Ehud Barak's proposal to Arafat at Camp David was "a bloody good offer" and called it "a tragedy of history" that Arafat turned it down. He also expressed "a profound sense of solidarity with the experience of so many with the horror and phenomenon of suicide bombings," adding that Labor's policy of supporting the right of Israel to a secure existence was "rock solid." Labor leader Simon Crean also expressed support for Israeli security and understanding for Israel's need to defend itself.

However some Australian Jews criticized Crean for exercising insufficient control over a number of Labor backbenchers who, critical of Israel in the past, stepped up their attacks in 2002, joined by representatives of such smaller parties in the Senate as the Australian Democrats and the Greens. In a speech in early June, one Labor backbencher insisted that both the city of Nablus and the town of Bethlehem had been "destroyed" by Israel in Operation Defensive Shield in April. Two other Laborites compared Israeli prime minister Sharon to Saddam Hussein, and another branded Israel a "rogue state" in a parliamentary debate on Iraq in September.

In November, yet a fourth Labor backbencher introduced a motion calling for Israel "unconditionally" to withdraw to its 1967 borders. He claimed that Israel's failure to do so violated UN Resolution 242 and demanded that a UN peace-keeping force protect the boundaries of a new Palestinian state to be recognized in all the Territories, after which peace negotiations should resume. His proposal failed to mention Palestinian terrorism or make any demands of the Palestinian side. The motion was debated but not voted on. Meanwhile, the foreign affairs spokesperson for the Australian Democrats, which, though a tiny faction, held the balance of power in the Australian Senate, called on the government to "take a much harder line on Israeli aggression in Palestine."

The Australian government continued to pursue improved relations with a number of Middle East nations, some of them sworn enemies of Israel, with the aim of stimulating increased trade, especially in agricultural products but also in some petroleum-related technological goods and services. Relations with Libya, interrupted in 1987, were renewed in 2002, and Trade Minister Mark Vaile led a major trade mission there in July. Vaile stressed particularly the importance of a meeting he had with Saife Qaddafi, son of Libyan dictator Muammar Qaddafi, which he described as a "watershed event" in Australia-Libya relations.

Australia pursued its long-standing policy of engagement with Iran. Iran's foreign minister, Dr. Kamal Kharrazi, visited Australia in June 2002, the first such visit by an Iranian foreign minister in a decade, and the two countries agreed to establish a "mechanism" for regular dialogue on human rights and regional issues. Trade Minister Vaile led a delegation of more than 50 Australian businessmen to Iran in September and signed a new Investment Protection and Promotion Agreement designed to broaden Australian investment there.

MEDIA BIAS

Australian media coverage of the conflict between Israel and the Palestinians was hardly as anti-Israel as in most European countries, but it still left plenty of room for improvement. There was a general tendency to oversimplify the facts in a way that favored the Palestinian point of view. The myth that Israel was defying UN Security Council Resolution 242 and was therefore "as bad as Iraq" was widely presented as fact.

The year commenced with perennial Israel critic and Arafat biographer Tony Walker, political editor of the *Australian Financial Review,* touring the Middle East. He filed a series of reports that demonized Ariel Sharon, misrepresented Israel's obligations under the U.S.-sponsored Mitchell Plan, downplayed Yasir Arafat's support for terrorism, and described the *Karine A* affair (see above, pp. 183–87) as a "damp squib."

Radio and TV coverage by the Australian Broadcasting Corporation (ABC), the public national broadcaster, tended to favor the Palestinians, often through the use of "experts" hostile to Israel. The radio coverage improved slightly toward the end of the year when correspondent Tim Palmer was reassigned to Indonesia. While stationed in Israel Palmer seemed determined to discredit Israeli tactics in dealing with terror, highlighting perceived failures and downplaying successes while maintaining a constantly critical line in regard to Prime Minister Sharon. On the floor of the New South Wales parliament Palmer was described as "simply a Palestinian spokesman." Supporters of Israel also considered radio talk-show hosts Jon Faine of ABC Radio Melbourne and Vivian Schenker of ABC Radio National as biased in favor of the Palestinian side.

ABC TV's investigative journalism program "Four Corners"replayed a program that was originally aired by the BBC, "The Accused," which sought to label Ariel Sharon a war criminal for his involvement in the Sabra and Shatilla massacres. AIJAC (the Australia/Israel and Jewish Affairs Council) attempted to convince the ABC to provide some balance, such as a panel discussion about responsibility for the massacres. AIJAC's intervention, in turn, was pilloried by David Marr on his program "Media Watch," an ABC weekly show that was supposed to highlight inadequacies in the media, not defend them. The following week, AIJAC's complaints to the ABC about its anti-Israel bias were given similar sarcastic treatment on "Media Watch."

The ABC's Special Broadcasting Service (SBS), the public multicultural network, had an even worse record. It provided inaccurate information, stated facts—about Israeli military actions, for example—without providing the context that would make them understandable, and at times highlighted arguments favorable to the Palestinians while remaining silent about other arguments that might strengthen Israel's position. In September and October, SBS showed a flood of anti-Israel documentaries, the worst of which was veteran Israel-basher John Pilger's rant, "Palestine Is Still the Question."

Israel's Operation Defensive Shield in the spring—and especially the fighting in Jenin—provided a particularly fertile field for anti-Israel bias across the Australian media. The ABC and SBS naturally took a prominent role, and the print media, while far from scrupulously fair, was on the whole more balanced. ABC Radio gave detailed coverage to allegations of Israeli atrocities and massacres in Jenin, but never adequately reported the findings by Human Rights Watch, Amnesty International, and the UN that there was, in fact, no massacre, and that few civilians were killed. They also ignored the humanitarian efforts of the Israelis there. As late as August, ABC Radio foreign editor Peter Cave was still adamant that there had been a "massacre"in Jenin, comparing Israeli conduct following the battle to the Chinese cover-up after Tiananmen Square.

Among the newspapers, the *Sydney Morning Herald* and the *Canberra Times* remained the most problematic. The *Morning Herald* and the *Age,* published in Melbourne—generally regarded as the "quality"broadsheets in Australia's two major cities—consistently used the anti-Israel

British newspaper the *Guardian* as a source for their Middle East coverage. Other papers, such as the *Australian,* the *Herald Sun,* the *Daily Telegraph,* and the *Courier Mail,* were more balanced in their editorials and opinion pieces.

Anti-Semitism and Extremism

During 2002, the Jewish community in Australia logged the highest number of reports of physical assault, property damage, and harassment since annual national records began being tallied. These took several forms: attacks on Jews by groups of assailants, often when the Jews were on their way to or from synagogue; a petrol bomb thrown at a synagogue that had been similarly bombed in 2001, this time requiring a fire brigade to extinguish the blaze; the windows of a Jewish community center smashed by rocks; a fire-cracker thrown at students leaving a Jewish day school; and vandalism of a communal sukkah, the perpetrators screaming, "Kill the Jews" and "Hitler's a legend."

The incidents of harassment—recorded at a little over twice the average for the previous 12 years—included verbal abuse of Jewish children walking home from synagogue; anti-Semitic comments to Jewish participants in public forums, including chants of "Kill the Jews"; street marches and rallies where placards included anti-Jewish slogans; harassment of participants in Jewish ceremonies held in public; and Jews being chased by large groups of men who made it clear that they were after potential Jewish victims.

There was also dramatic growth in the amount of anti-Jewish imagery in publications of extremist organizations—especially on the far left— much of it based on theories of Jewish conspiracies. Mainstream media also carried more anti-Semitic matter than in previous years, as the virulence of some public criticism of Israeli actions crossed the line between political commentary and anti-Jewish incitement. As had been the case for some time, the Internet facilitated the dissemination of hostile statements about Jews.

EXTREMIST GROUPS

Extremist and anti-Semitic groups in Australia varied greatly in their memberships, activities, and target audiences. Most of the better-known Australian groups maintained links with foreign extremists such as militia movements in the U.S., Christian Identity churches, the Lyndon

LaRouche organization, various groups of conspiracy theorists, the Australian League of Rights, and others.

The most vicious anti-Jewish propaganda in Australia was produced by the Adelaide Institute, a loose network of people who admired self-styled Holocaust revisionist Dr. Frederick Toben. Even David Irving, in his *Action Report,* wrote that Toben's Web site was so extreme that it constituted a liability to Holocaust revisionists. In 2002, Toben participated in international gatherings of Holocaust deniers. In addition to his own newsletter and Web site, Toben's material was posted on numerous neo-Nazi and racist sites on the Internet.

The Australian League of Rights was once described by the Australian Human Rights and Equal Opportunity Commission as "undoubtedly the most influential and effective, as well as the best organized and most substantially financed, racist organization in Australia." Its membership — consisting largely of veterans of the moribund Social Credit movement of the 1930s and 1940s — was overwhelmingly elderly, but it continued to hold meetings, conduct action campaigns, and seek publicity for its anti-Semitic assessments of domestic and international affairs. With founder Eric Butler retired and in failing health, Betty Luks, the league's director, continued to publish its weekly newsletters, monthly magazines, and quarterly journal, and to maintain its Web site.

The Citizens Electoral Councils (CEC) continued to distribute large quantities of literature reflecting the views of Lyndon LaRouche. These included allegations of bizarre Jewish conspiracies that also targeted non-Jewish antiracist organizations in Australia. Beside mass mailings, another common tactic was handing out pamphlets and magazines to unsuspecting citizens in shopping areas commonly frequented by Jews. Throughout the year, Jewish leaders in Victoria, Western Australia, and New South Wales complained about CEC activities. An advertisement organized and authorized by the LaRouche cult and signed by hundreds of Australians was published in the *Australian* in June and again in September, claiming that the government wanted to introduce legislation modeled on Hitler's laws.

The deceptively named Australian Civil Liberties Union (ACLU) continued to advocate Holocaust denial, with most of the group's public pronouncements aimed at protecting the "rights" of Holocaust deniers and other extremists. *Your Rights 2002* was the 28th annual edition of the ACLU's handbook. John Bennett, the ACLU's most influential figure, was on the editorial advisory committee of the *Journal of Historical Review,* the Holocaust-denial publication of the notorious Institute for Historical Review in California.

A number of organizations on the neo-Nazi fringe came to attention during 2002. Australian National Action, which declared its enmity toward Jews, non-whites, and immigrants, staged rallies in Melbourne and Adelaide, and published a newsletter. Its members also engaged in direct confrontation with, and harassment of, political opponents. Other similar groups included the Australian Nationalists Movement, White Australian Revolutionaries, the Australian National Socialist Movement, C-18, and the Australian Revolutionary Movement. In most cities there were also small, unorganized groups—little more than gangs—of neo-Nazis, sometimes including violent skinheads. They tended to focus their racist anger on Asian students and on those they perceived to be left-wingers. The Australian public was surprised to learn during the year that three former members of an elite army unit had been members of the Blood Oath, a neo-Nazi band, while serving in the military.

Nazi War Criminals

Australia took no legal action against Nazi war criminals in 2002, despite the fact that in May, the Simon Wiesenthal Center submitted to the authorities a list of 22 suspected Lithuanian Nazi war criminals living in Australia. This same list had previously been supplied to Lithuanian officials, who also passed it on to Australia in 2001. The suspects had entered Australia shortly after World War II. Philip Ruddock, the minister for immigration, stated that these men could not be deprived of their citizenship and deported, but the justice minister, Senator Chris Ellison, promised that the Australian Federal Police would investigate the allegations. In August, the Australian Attorney General's Department informed the Lithuanian prosecutor general that nine of the suspects lived in Australia at known addresses. In December, Attorney General Daryl Williams said that Lithuania had made no extradition requests for any of the suspects, and that the Lithuanians had indicated that they did not have enough evidence to lay charges.

JEWISH COMMUNITY

Demography

Results of the 2001 census indicated that Australia's Jewish community was still growing. The census showed some 84,000 Jews in Australia, 4,000 more than in 1996, amounting to about 0.44 percent of the total population of over 19 million. The actual number of Jews was undoubtedly higher, as the question about religion was optional on the census form and about a quarter of the Australian population did not answer it. Jewish leaders believed that Holocaust survivors might have been particularly reluctant to identify their religion. The actual number of Jews was assumed to be over 100,000.

Melbourne had the nation's largest Jewish population, and Adelaide was the only city to show a decrease in its number of Jews. The census showed that most recent Jewish newcomers were from South Africa. Hebrew was the preferred language for 6,000 Australians and Yiddish for 2,667. Australian Jewish women outnumbered Jewish men, according to the census, 43,600 to 40,300.

Communal Affairs

Jeremy Jones continued in his post as president of the Executive Council of Australian Jewry (ECAJ), the preeminent Jewish representative body, while Ron Weiser continued as president of the Zionist Federation of Australia. Mark Leibler remained national chairman of the Australia/Israel and Jewish Affairs Council (AIJAC), with Dr. Colin Rubenstein as AIJAC's executive director. AIJAC continued its close association with the American Jewish Committee. Stanley Roth continued as federal president of the United Israel Appeal, and Michael Naphtali as head of the Jewish National Fund.

Education

More than half of all Jewish children aged 4–18—including almost 70 percent of those aged 4–12—received full-time Jewish education in the 19 Jewish day schools in Australia. Spanning the religious spectrum, these schools continued to rank at the highest level for academic achievement. This reflected the community's major investment in the schools as a means of preserving Jewish continuity. Day-school enrollments continued to grow, despite ongoing concerns over high costs and the challenge to the community to find new sources of funding.

There was an increased emphasis on adult education, largely under the influence of the Melton Program, which had nearly 500 students in Sydney and Melbourne. Short-term courses utilizing guest lecturers also proved popular. Top priorities for the future, according to Australian Jewish educators, were expanded Jewish studies on the university level and teacher education to train qualified faculty for the day schools.

Interfaith Dialogue

Australian Jewry remained active in interreligious discussions. In most states and territories there was a functioning Council of Christians and Jews. Through its national and regional bodies, the World Conference on Religion and Peace provided a structure for Jewish Australians to engage actively with Christians, Muslims, Buddhists, Hindus, and members of smaller denominations. Faith Communities for Reconciliation, a significant interfaith cooperative venture that brought together official representatives of every substantial religious group in Australia, was chaired by the Jewish community's representative, ECAJ president Jeremy Jones.

For more than a decade the Jewish community and the Uniting Church of Australia—a major Protestant body made up of former Presbyterians, Methodists, and Congregationalists—had been conducting a formal "National Dialogue" of top leaders. A similar national dialogue, known as the "Annual Conversation," had been taking place for six years between the Australian Catholic Bishops Conference and the ECAJ.

In 2002, representatives of the Australian Federation of Islamic Councils, the National Council of Churches in Australia, and the ECAJ met formally for the first time, in three separate sessions, to discuss the creation of a structure which would allow for regular and constructive interaction. This inaugural meeting took place in the Great Synagogue Sydney, the second at the Alexandria Mosque, and the third at the headquarters of the Council of Churches.

Personalia

In January 2002, the government conferred Australia Day Honors on several prominent members of the Jewish community. Prof. Geoffrey Opat of Melbourne was appointed Officer of the Order of Australia (AO) for his contributions to scientific research and the teaching of science in Australia and overseas. In addition, the Medal of the Order of Australia (OAM) was awarded to: Eva Engel of Sydney for her work in community welfare, including the establishment of Child Survivors of the Holocaust and her involvement with the Sydney Jewish Museum as a volunteer guide; Tom Goldman of Sydney, former Maccabi Australia president, for service to the community through sport; Dr. Max Lake, a prominent Sydney winemaker, for promoting the boutique wine industry in Australia; Nathan Gutman of Melbourne for his service to music, particularly as a violin performer and teacher; Henry Nissen of Melbourne, a former Australian boxing champion, for assisting and rehabilitating disadvantaged youth; and Dr. Solomon Rose of Melbourne for his assistance to Jewish war veterans and their families.

The annual Queen's Birthday Honors, awarded in June 2002, recognized the contributions made by several other members of the Australian Jewish community. Jeanne Pratt received the nation's highest honor, being appointed a Companion of the Order of Australia (AC) for outstanding leadership in the arts and service to the community through charitable institutions. Rabbi Pinchus Feldman, dean of the Sydney Yeshivah, was awarded a Medal of the Order of Australia (OAM) for service to the Jewish community for his work in developing spiritual, educational, and welfare facilities. High-profile Sydney lawyer and investment banker David Gonski was appointed an Officer of the Order of Australia (AO) in recognition of his service to the visual and performing arts and for developing government policy to encourage philanthropy. Raymond Weinberg of Melbourne, Olympic athlete, athletics administrator, and coach, was appointed a Member of the Order of Australia (AM) for services to sport and the community. Former North Shore Temple Emanuel vice president Gary Braude received a Medal of the Order of Australia (OAM) for services to the community and his congregation, of which he had been a member for 40 years. West Australian Dr. Nathan Hoffman, a fellow of Edith Cowan University, was awarded an OAM for services to mathematics education and in recognition of his work for the Jewish community of Perth, which he had served in many capacities, including president of the Perth Hebrew Congregation. Former Sydney High School principal Michael Gold was the recipient of an OAM for his services to education, as was prize-winning sculptor Errol Davis of Sydney for his service to the arts.

In 2002, the Australian Jewish community mourned the passing of: Erwin Graf, a Sydney-based property developer and prominent supporter of AIJAC; Sam Fiszman of Sydney, Holocaust survivor, businessman, political fund-raiser, and philanthropist; Dr. Ben Haneman of Sydney, medical practitioner and supporter of the arts—particularly the work of the State Library of New South Wales—who was remembered for his life-long commitment to social justice and who served for many years on the New South Wales Jewish Board of Deputies; Louis Kahan of Melbourne, one of Australia's most celebrated artists, who was awarded the prestigious Archibald Prize for portraiture in 1962 for his depiction of Australia's Nobel laureate in literature, Patrick White; Henry Krongold of Melbourne, Polish-born businessman, patron of the arts, philanthropist, and inaugural federal president of the United Israel Appeal; Linda

Phillips of Melbourne, a composer and music critic who died at the age of 102; and Dr. Solomon Rose of Melbourne, a former president of the Victorian Association of Jewish Ex-Servicemen and Women (VAJEX), who passed away shortly after having been awarded the Medal of the Order of Australia, as noted above.

Rabbi Raymond Apple celebrated 30 years of service as chief minister of Australia's oldest congregation, the Great Synagogue Sydney, in 2002, and his deputy, Rabbi Mendel Kastel, was appointed a member of the inaugural multifaith chaplaincy of the New South Wales Police Service.

COLIN L. RUBENSTEIN

South Africa

THE YEAR 2002 SAW THE continuing transformation of South Africa and the consolidation of power by the African National Congress (ANC), led by President Thabo Mbeki. Substantial attention was given to regional foreign policy. Domestically, the ANC-led government maintained its conservative Growth, Employment, and Redistribution (GEAR) strategy despite the strains this produced with its partners in the coalition—the South African Communist Party (SACP) and the Congress of South African Trade Unions (COSATU).

Notwithstanding the global economic slowdown and regional instability, the GDP grew by 3 percent. Investment rose by 6 percent and manufacturing production—boosted by the 37-percent depreciation of the rand in 2001—was up by 5.4 percent, as compared to 2.8 percent in 2001. But such advances were undermined by a rise in inflation to 10 percent and a continuing unemployment rate of about 40 percent.

Policies aimed at black empowerment, including a mining charter ensuring that mining operations would come under black control, impacted positively on black elites and a burgeoning black bourgeoisie. Nonetheless, *Statistics South Africa* reported that the average income (corrected for inflation) for African blacks decreased from R 32,000 per annum to R 26,000 between 1995 (one year after the first democratic elections) and 2000. During the same period the average income for whites increased from R 137,000 to R 158,000. Furthermore, greater access to electricity, clean water, and sewerage was offset by the loss of over a million jobs.

HIV/AIDS remained a major problem, with an estimated 4.5 million South Africans living with the disease. About 18.4 percent of South African blacks aged 15–49 were HIV positive. An indication of the devastating social impact was that 3.3 percent of households were headed by children aged 12–18. Treatment Action Campaign (TAC), a nongovernmental agency established in 1998, sharply criticized the government's AIDS policy, harnessed substantial public support, and convinced the Constitutional Court to rule that public hospitals must issue anti-retrovirals—a step the authorities had opposed.

Notwithstanding ambitious efforts by the government to improve the efficiency of its justice system, the level of crime remained high, largely due to the poor quality of policing and lack of confidence in the courts, which were viewed as tainted by corruption.

Careful planning and international strategizing prevented the World Summit on Sustainable Development (WSSD), held in Johannesburg in August, from turning into an exercise in Israel-bashing. Jewish groups, including the South African Jewish Board of Deputies (SAJBOD), were involved in the strategy talks, and two months prior to the conference the SAJBOD hosted a media tour of various sustainable development projects under Jewish auspices. There were pro-Palestinian protests and some anti-Israeli chanting at the summit, but the event did not come close to turning into the kind of fiasco that occurred the year before at the UN World Conference Against Racism (WCAR) in Durban (see "Demonization in Durban," AJYB 2002, pp. 85–111).

South Africa's northern neighbor, Zimbabwe, led by Robert Mugabe, was a source of concern and a major problem for President Mbeki. His response to the contested presidential election, erosion of civil rights, and land grabs there was a policy of "constructive engagement" and secret diplomacy that, as the year ended, had not produced results. Instability in Burundi and the Great Lakes area of central Africa also threatened the stability of the region, and South Africa involved itself in peace initiatives, encouraged by the cessation of hostilities in Angola.

South Africa took the lead in replacing the 39-year-old Organization for African Unity (OAU) with the new African Union (AU), which sought to enhance the African continent's influence in relation to the "North"—the industrialized world. Officially founded in Durban in July, the AU was based on the ideology of Mbeki's African Renaissance and the New Partnership for Africa's Development (NEPAD). Nations belonging to the AU were required to commit themselves to democratic principles and respect for human rights.

The *SA Jewish Report* (May 12) devoted an editorial to the implications of the new AU for Israel. Recalling that Israel had played a constructive role in many African countries before the 1973 Yom Kippur War, the paper suggested that the AU's overriding commitment to "the principles of democracy, good governance, and economic development" should lead it to appreciate Israel, "a vibrant, highly developed democratic country in a region where this is a scarce commodity." And it asked, "Is it too much to hope that the AU will break the old pattern of OAU hostility to Israel?"

In October, nine bomb blasts shook Soweto and Bronkhorstspruit in Gauteng Province, resulting in one death. Police suspected that the far right was responsible. "We know who they are," said Police Commissioner Jackie Selebe. A number of suspects were subsequently arrested.

In November, the New National Party (NNP) broke away from the Democratic Alliance (DA) in a bitter divorce and aligned itself instead with the ruling ANC-led government.

The ANC held its 51st conference at Stellenbosch outside Cape Town in December. There was a strong emphasis on black economic empowerment, alleviation of poverty, a comprehensive social-security program, improving public health and education, speeding up land reform, and improving the quality of the judiciary. Before the conference, ANC leaders warned that the "ultra-left" that criticized the government's economic policy would have its wings clipped.

Israel-Related Activity

The South African government remained involved in the Israeli-Palestinian conflict. In January, the government hosted a conference outside Cape Town for Israeli and Palestinian diplomats that focused on how the South African experience of conflict resolution might be useful for Middle East peacemakers. The eight-man Israeli delegation was headed by Yossi Beilin and included Avraham Burg, speaker of the Knesset. Sa'eb Erakat and Ziad Abu Ziad led the Palestinian team. The South African contingent included four ANC ministers—Jeff Radebe, Valli Moosa, Dullah Omar, and Ronnie Kasrils—as well as former National Party stalwarts Pik Botha, Roelf Meyer, and Leon Wessels. President Mbeki was present throughout. Top religious leaders, including Chief Rabbi Cyril Harris and Nudungane Njongonkulu, the Anglican archbishop, also participated. A joint communiqué issued at the conclusion of the conference stated that the conflict could not be resolved through violence; effective channels of communication had to be maintained under all circumstances; each side had to take into consideration the fears of the other; reaching a solution meant that there could be to "winner" or "loser"; and the process could not be held hostage to extremists.

Reactions to the conference varied. Yossi Beilin, in a newspaper interview, said that the South African transition experience held valuable lessons for the Middle East. Israel's ambassador to South Africa, Tova

Herzl, noted that "Israel welcomes anything that might bring the parties together—but we can't disconnect it from anything that happens on the ground." The SAJBOD welcomed the initiative, and the *SA Jewish Report* (Jan. 18) criticized cynics, asking, "isn't it better to allow ourselves to hope that the spirit of that meeting should be carried back to the Middle East and influence others? No stone should be left unturned in the search for peace."

Deputy Minister of Foreign Affairs Aziz Pahad reaffirmed South Africa's relations with Israel at the 45th conference of the South African Zionist Federation (SAZF) in March. Pahad told the meeting that South Africa's policy was predicated on the fundamental principle of unequivocal and unchanging support for the right of Israel to exist within defined borders, in full peace and security with its neighbors. Pahad also acknowledged that the nongovernmental segment of the World Conference Against Racism in 2001 at Durban had been "hijacked and used by some with an anti-Israel agenda to turn it into an anti-Semitic event" (*SA Jewish Report,* Mar. 15).

In April, however, as Israeli troops entered West Bank cities in the wake of a spate of bloody Palestinian suicide bombings (see above, pp. 199–201), the ANC and its coalition partners (the SACP and COSATU), along with the South African Civics Organization, adopted a joint resolution condemning Israeli actions. It accused Israel of aggression against the people of Palestine and of violating UN Human Rights treaties and the Geneva Convention's protocols on the treatment of civilians and prisoners of war. These groups also marched on the embassies of Israel and the United States. Meanwhile, the Nonaligned Movement (NAM) Ministerial Meeting Committee on Palestine, convened in Durban, voted to send a delegation to meet with Yasir Arafat in an "expression of solidarity with the president and the people of Palestine." Led by South African foreign minister Nkosazana Dlamini-Zuma, a delegation of NAM ministers visited Arafat in June and then released a statement expressing "its support for all international efforts aimed at a achieving a just, comprehensive and lasting solution."

There were about 600,000 Muslims in South Africa, 1.5 percent of the total population, and many turned out to participate in pro-Palestinian rallies. Even the historically moderate Muslim Judicial Council, the official voice of the South African Muslim community, recognized Hamas, Islamic Jihad, and Hezballah as "legitimate fighters for the liberation of Palestine" (*Sunday Argus*, Mar. 17). In fact Hanan Ashwari, the Palestinian spokeswoman, informed the SAJBOD that she had traveled the entire Arab world and had never seen such virulent support for Hamas as she had in the Western Cape, which was where the majority of South African Muslims resided.

A senior delegation from the SAJBOD met with President Mbeki in May to discuss the Middle East conflict. The president assured the group that the South African government was committed to playing a constructive role in the quest for a peaceful, negotiated settlement, and Mbeki believed that lessons could be drawn from the South African experience. The SAJBOD, in turn, conveyed the insecurity that Jews felt, particularly when they heard or read about the extreme rhetoric directed against Israel and Jews at pro-Palestinian rallies.

In September, the ANC chairman of the Parliament's Foreign Affairs Committee, Dr. Pallo Jordan, told the Cape Council of the SAJBOD that there was "absolute consensus" in Parliament on Israel's right to exist. The sentiment was repeated by Kgalema Motlanthe, the ANC secretary general, in a keynote address at the SAJBOD's Gauteng Council: Israelis, he stated, had the clear right to live in their own state. He also praised the disproportionate role played by Jews in the struggle against apartheid.

Critics of Israel staged a major protest against Israeli foreign minister Shimon Peres when he addressed the Jewish community at the University of the Witwatersrand in September. Water canon had to be used to break up the demonstration. The SAJBOD, which organized the talk, was blamed for not adequately informing the university of the nature of the event so that proper security could be provided. The SAJBOD, while condemning the hooliganism of the demonstrators, acknowledged that it should have maintained better communications with the university.

Despite strenuous objections from the SAJBOD, E-TV, an independent television network, broadcast a documentary highly critical of Israel, "Palestine is Still the Issue," by British filmmaker John Pilger. The South African Zionist Federation (SAZF) deemed the actions of E-TV "provocative and inciteful." The station did allow for a debate after the documentary between Ronnie Kasrils, South Africa's minister of water affairs and forestry and an opponent of Israeli policies, and Hagai Segal, a British commentator on Middle Eastern affairs.

Anti-Semitism

There were substantial manifestations of anti-Semitism and Holocaust denial during 2002. These came in the form of harassment of individuals, abusive letters and e-mails to Jewish organizations, and journalistic excesses—slanted newspaper coverage, abusive cartoons, and offensive comments on radio talk shows.

Some examples: There was a violent confrontation between Jews and non-Jews at an interfaculty soccer match at the University of the Witwatersrand. At Rand Afrikaans University in Johannesburg, a sukkah was vandalized. Swastikas were daubed on Jewish premises in Johannesburg, and the Cape Town Jewish Center received an anonymous bomb threat. Holocaust denial pamphlets were distributed to households in the northern suburbs of Bloemfontein. The Doors Nightclub in Johannesburg held a "soldiers party" characterized by Nazi paraphernalia, including a doorman with an SS uniform, swastika decorations, and someone shouting, "Heil Hitler." Sometimes the anti-Jewish vitriol was tied to the Middle East conflict, although the rhetoric and motifs were plainly anti-Semitic and not just directed against Israeli policies.

Addressing the Union of Jewish Women on the question of anti-Semitism in the "new South Africa," Marlene Bethlehem, national president of the SAJBOD, noted that hostility had taken a new turn since the birth of democracy in 1994. Whereas before that it had been generally restricted to the white far right, in was now manifest in the Muslim community. Bethlehem believed that the danger posed by Pagad (People Against Gangsterism and Drugs, a mainly Muslim vigilante movement) was far from over. But she cautioned against painting the whole Muslim community with the same brush. "Most are not radicals, and just want to live as peace-loving citizens," she said.

The SAJBOD repeatedly denounced anti-Jewish incitement over the course of the year, including rhetoric and behavior at anti-Israel rallies and marches.

Holocaust-Related Matters

In April, the Constitutional Court handed down judgment in a long-running legal battle between the SAJBOD and the Islamic Unity Convention (IUC). The case originated in 1998, when the SAJBOD complained to the Independent Broadcasting Authority (IBA) about Radio 786, a Muslim community radio station in the Western Cape, for allegedly broadcasting statements that were anti-Semitic because they denied the Holocaust (see AJYB 2002, pp. 511–12). The IUC, in turn, sought to have the relevant section of the code of conduct for broadcasting services declared unconstitutional because its prohibition on broadcasting hate speech infringed on the freedom of expression. While the court found that the sweeping language of the broadcasting code did indeed infringe on the constitutional guarantee on free speech — a ruling that had been anticipated — the court nevertheless upheld the prohibition on the advocacy of hate speech based on race, ethnicity, gender or religion. The SAJBOD expressed satisfaction with the result. Russell Gaddin, chairman of the SAJBOD, noted that "as South Africans we are protected by freedom of speech and protected from hate speech. This is a landmark victory for all South Africans and we will be pursuing the matter against Radio 786 on the grounds set out in the ruling" (*SA Jewish Report*, Apr. 19).

But in November, the Broadcasting Complaints Commission (BCC) dismissed the SAJBOD's complaint. The acting chairman of the BCC, advocate Roland Sutherland, wrote that "the trivializing of the extent of suffering" of Jews during the Second World War was "doubtless perceived by many who accept the accuracy of Holocaust evidence as churlish and insulting. Nevertheless, in my view, it is not the stuff of which reasonable people take offence to the degree it warrants the proscription of the expression of such views." Sutherland ruled that there was no hate speech since there was "no attack in the broadcast on the Jewish religion or Jews as such . . . no exhortation to hatred of any particular religious group or group of individuals." The decision shocked the SAJBOD. "We will pursue every avenue open to us to take this matter further," said Russell Gaddin. "We believe we have a case they have to answer."

Mervyn Smith, chairman of the SAJBOD subcommittee that dealt with the matter, said it was "extremely difficult to accept the dismissive tone throughout the decision" and noted that even the mainstream press had facetiously asked whether Sutherland had gotten his education at the University of Damascus. Referring to Sutherland's use of the phrase "many who accept the accuracy of Holocaust evidence," Smith suggested that Sutherland himself had trivialized the Holocaust and that his ruling was offensive. "What is he saying," asked Smith, "that there are many people who do not accept the evidence of the Holocaust?" This, in Smith's view, was "grist to the mill of Holocaust revisionists; it makes them respectable" (*SA Jewish Report,* Dec. 23).

The BCC did uphold a complaint against another Muslim community radio station, the Johannesburg-based Radio Islam, for two offensive broadcasts in August. The station explicitly attacked Jews and called for their death, and its anti-Israel rhetoric was ruled to be hate speech — Israel, representing world Jewry, was accused of controlling the world and being responsible for the September 11 attacks on the U.S. In making his judgment, Prof. Kobus van Rooyen said that to threaten people with murder amounted to "a severe and serious invasion of their rights of personality." Van Rooyen maintained that it was "no excuse to hide behind an Islamic text, quoted out of context, on air," and that the same would hold for the recitation of violent passages from the Bible quoted out of context for the purpose of inciting violence. As for the anti-Israel rhetoric, Van Rooyen claimed it was "strident, emotive, unforgiving and blatantly accusatorial.. . . One cannot escape the hate that flows forth from the comment and tone thereof." And he added that no opposing views were broadcast, as required by the law on airing controversial statements. The BCC warned Radio Islam that it would be fined if it broadcast similarly in the future.

The Cape Town Holocaust Centre (CTHC) maintained its prominent role in human-rights education. Marlene Silbert, its education director, reported an "ever-growing number of adult groups who are participating in the Centre's programs — university faculties, the military, law enforcement agencies, religious groups of all faiths and backgrounds, and a broad range of groups from civil society." There was also a special program on sensitivity training for the South African Police Services.

The CTHC held two exhibitions during 2002. In February, Esther Surdat displayed "Framing History: Family History and Memory," the story of her family, which came from the shtetl of Kusshan (Kursenai). In December, "Visas for Life" opened. This exhibition celebrated the bravery of diplomats and others who helped Jews escape the clutches of Nazism. "Visas for Life" was seen in some 100 venues around the world.

In August, Professor Christopher Browning, a renowned Holocaust historian and visiting professor at the Kaplan Centre for Jewish Studies and Research at the University of Cape Town, delivered the third anniversary lecture at the CTHC. He discussed the trials of Holocaust deniers David Irving and Ernst Zundel, at both of which he had appeared as an expert witness.

JEWISH COMMUNITY

South African Jews and Israel

Memories were still fresh of the anti-Israel tone of the World Conference Against Racism held in Durban the previous fall and of the harsh criticism of Israel ignited by the Kasrils/Ozinsky declaration presented to Parliament in October 2001 (see AJYB 2002, pp. 509–10). Not surprisingly, Israel dominated the South African Jewish agenda in 2002.

In January, the Jewish Agency declared that South African Jewry—together with those of Argentina and France—was an "endangered" Jewish community. Targeted for aliyah, South African Jews would be entitled to a special subsidized package of benefits if they relocated to Israel. Commenting on the matter, Russell Gaddin, national chairman of the SAJBOD, said that South African Jews had no reason to feel singled out as particularly in danger, though he acknowledged concern over Muslim anti-Semitism in the Western Cape and what he termed the anti-Israel bias of South Africa's Middle East policy. The SAJBOD's attitude, he said, "had always been that Jews should either go home or stay home. We are completely committed to the ideal of aliyah, and those who choose to make their homes in Israel do so with our blessing. At the same time we recognize that we are citizens of South Africa and that it is our duty to put as much as we can into the society that has nurtured us and enabled us to live in peace and prosperity as proud South Africans and proud Jews" (*SA Jewish Report,* Jan. 25).

Speaking at the South African Zionist Federation (SAZF) conference in Johannesburg, Salai Meridor, chairman of the Jewish Agency executive and the World Zionist Organization, disagreed. Meridor contended that Jews could only ensure their Jewishness through aliyah. He praised South African Jews who went to live in Israel and condemned those emigrating to other diaspora countries. At the same conference, Kenny Katz, outgoing chairman of the SAZF, spoke of the challenges facing South African Zionism. In his view the government was biased with regard to the Israeli-Palestinian conflict, and he lamented what the Jewish community had had to witness in Durban at the World Conference Against Racism. Nonetheless, he viewed the future with optimism. The SAZF conference prompted the *SA Jewish Report* (Mar. 15) to editorialize about the worldwide Zionist movement, which, it charged, was in a state of confusion, insisting, on the one hand, that all Jews belonged in Israel, but acting, on the other, as if "Zionism today boils down to 'support' for Israel, financial and moral, but does not translate into the practical reality of actually going to live there."

Israel Independence Day celebrations in April drew large audiences, and in May, a group of South African volunteers (including non-Jews) went to Israel to alleviate the country's manpower shortage created by military call-ups. An editorial in the *SA Jewish Report* (May 10) called on South Africans to "come out and show the South African public and government that support for Israel is widespread and cuts across the entire spectrum of viewpoints including Jews who were active in the anti-apartheid struggle." There were well-attended Israel solidarity meetings in Johannesburg and Cape Town, and a SAZF delegation to the World Zionist Organization in Israel handed a 12,000-signature solidarity petition to President Moshe Katzav.

In August, the SAJBOD met with Archbishop Emeritus Desmond Tutu, the Nobel Peace Prize laureate, in what both parties described as a cordial exchange. The meeting arose out of the archbishop's public statements on the Israeli-Palestinian conflict: he compared Israel's treatment of the Palestinians to South Africa's treatment of blacks under apartheid, and later described disinvestment from Israel as a "necessary move" in opposing her policies. Commenting after the meeting, Russell Gaddin said the discussions concerned "how we could possibly influence peace in the Middle East, bring an end to violence and perhaps introduce the South African peace model to that area of the world."

The SAJBOD's strategy of quiet diplomacy with Tutu was not to the taste of all South African Jews. In an open letter published in the *SA Jewish Report* (Aug. 9), editor Geoff Sifrin accused the prelate of condemning Israeli actions while turning a blind eye to Palestinian atrocities against Israelis. Tutu responded by describing Sifrin's letter as "a thinly veiled sarcastic observation that the South African Jewish community has not heard me castigate the Palestinian bombers enough." Tutu maintained that a careful reading of his remarks on the subject would reveal that "I was quite categorical in my condemnation, first, of what I described as the Arab stupidity in having refused to recognize Israel and committing the Arab nations to her destruction, and secondly, the awfulness of suicide bombers, and thirdly the poisoning of children's minds if it was true that Palestinian children were being taught to hate Jews." Tutu continued, "I am deeply concerned for the Jews and the Palestinians. I want to see them live harmoniously together . . . . Peace is possible based on justice and equity; based on respect for the territorial integrity of Israel as a sovereign state existing side by side with an equally independent and sovereign Palestinian State."

There was widespread outrage among South African Jews in December, when young children dressed up as suicide bombers participated in a march in Cape Town marking Al Quds Day, and an Israeli flag was set on fire to the shout of "Death to Israel, death to Sharon." Russell Gaddin considered the occasion a "disgraceful display of hate speech, incitement, and anti-Semitism." A spokesman for Qibla, the radical Muslim group that organized the march, said the use of children was "completely justified" in order to draw attention to "the murder happening in Palestine." On the other hand, Imam Gassan Solomon, a member of the Muslim Judicial Council, said it was "irresponsible to expose children to a march of this kind" (*SA Jewish Report,* Dec.12).

The "Not in My Name" group, made up of Jews who opposed Israeli policies, held a Peace Hanukkah ceremony at the District 6 Museum. (District 6 was an inner-city area from which the apartheid government had forcefully removed the "colored" [mixed-race] community.) Speakers made repeated comparisons between the apartheid government and Israel's actions in the Territories.

The South African Union of Jewish Students organized a memorial service for the seven students killed in a bomb blast on the campus of the Hebrew University of Jerusalem. The campus chaplain, Rabbi Jonathan Shippel, delivered an interdenominational message to an audience of Jews, Muslims, and Christians.

The Israeli Trade Center underwent a major refurbishing. The center's first secretary for economic affairs, Elad Stav, spoke of refocusing Israel's commercial interests in Africa, and particularly South Africa. Over the last several years Israel's exports to South Africa had shrunk while its imports from the country had skyrocketed, a situation he though the center might help reverse. In another effort to stimulate trade with Israel, the South Africa-Israel Chamber of Commerce appointed the first black ever to its executive, Bonang Mohale. Mohale was director of marketing at Sanlam and had a long association with the Jewish community.

A new Israel Center was launched in June to coordinate all Israel-related issues in the community. Michael Mensky, the director, explained that it would seek to promote a greater awareness of Israel in South Africa, focusing on such matters as Israeli technological advances and lifestyle trends in the Jewish state.

Communal Affairs

The South African Jewish community continued to make progress in consolidating and rationalizing its operations. The latest step in this direction was the establishment by the SAJBOD and the SAZF of "Tachlis from Beyachad," an e-mail newsletter about Jewish world affairs, with primary focus on Israel and South Africa.

Chabad House in Johannesburg inaugurated a drug-awareness campaign aimed at the entire Jewish community. The purpose, explained Rabbi David Masinter, the Chabad House director, was to educate the community "to the dangers and pitfalls of drug abuse."

A number of women were appointed to important communal positions. The Cape Council of the SAJBOD appointed Vivienne Anstey as vice chairman; the SAZF named Islo Brito as its new director; and Suzanne Belling became director of the Cape Council of the SAJBOD.

A new Jewish community center opened in the fast-growing coastal town of Plettenberg Bay. Over 220 Jews lived in the area, and the number regularly swelled during the holiday seasons.

Kosher Mobile Meals were more in demand than ever before in the program's 30-year history. While in 1972 it provided meals for 14 recipients, in 2002 the number had grown to 130. Margaret Cohen, co-convener of the organization, said that she and her colleagues were "there to assist any Jewish person who needs our help."

Indicative of the financial climate was a report by Stan Rothbart, the outgoing president, at the 42nd annual general meeting of the Society for the Jewish Handicapped. "Gone are the days of largesse when people could just supply shortfalls," he told the gathering, and went on to name new targets for fund-raising, including South African Jews who had emigrated elsewhere.

In November, controversy surrounded elections to the committee of the Gauteng Council of the SAJBOD, as accusations of illicit lobbying were raised at its biennial conference in Johannesburg. An editorial titled "Strengthening Internal Jewish Democracy" in the *SA Jewish Report* (Nov. 11) noted the absence of clear "procedures for voting, resolution of disputes, membership criteria and so on." The newspaper went on, "Of course, many people will protest the SAJBOD does have a constitution, and this is true. But the acrimonious fog which characterized the last election, in which 'deals' eventually had to be made between powerful individuals to rescue the outcome, shows that this constitution is not what it needs to be. Strict adherence to the principles of proper 'corporate governance' has never been a strong point of Jewish organizations. But we live in a new era now, where people demand to know how decisions are being made, and who is making them."

Community Relations

At the launch of his new book, *Profile of a Community: South African Jewry,* retired Jewish communal worker Aleck Goldberg urged Jews to reach out to South African blacks. "Too few of us still take pride and joy in living in South Africa," he said. "As a community we should feel more secure, not less secure with the demise of apartheid. We should celebrate it with all South Africans."

There were a number of significant outreach initiatives during 2002. Tikkun, the Jewish organization committed to help the underprivileged of South Africa, announced a new program of scholarships for disadvantaged young people studying technology-related fields at the Peninsula Technikon, Rhodes University, and the University of Potchefstroom. In addition, a new Tikkun/Alexander Forbes Care for the Aged project would concentrate on providing support for the elderly in Alexandra, a black Johannesburg township. Tikkun had a number of other ongoing projects, including help for the inhabitants of the poverty-stricken Orange Farm in Gauteng, with emphasis on eradicating unhygienic conditions and dealing with crime. Tikkun also facilitated a workshop, "Culture Among Cultures," at the South African Jewish Museum in Cape Town, for 25 high-school students from black townships and an equal number of white Jewish students.

Following a meeting with TAC (Treatment Action Campaign), the advocacy organization for HIV/AIDS victims, the SAJBOD joined in the fight to promote a national treatment plan for HIV-positive mothers. National Chairman Russell Gaddin undertook to have the SAJBOD investigate avenues for practical assistance, and requested TAC to submit proposals to help the SAJBOD determine strategy. In August, the SAJBOD met with the ANC Youth League (ANCYL). The two organizations agreed to "cement relationships" and agreed that it was important to deepen democracy, unity, and economic development in the country. Toward that end Jewish youth organizations would work together with the ANCYL to achieve common objectives.

Religion

The Union of Orthodox Synagogues of South Africa (UOS) celebrated its 70th birthday. Lady Amelie Jakobovits, widow of the late Lord Immanuel Jakobovits, former chief rabbi of Great Britain and the Commonwealth, was guest speaker at a banquet celebrating the occasion. The UOS appointed Darren Sevitz executive director and Tobi Einhorn director of education and convener of the conversion program.

Ongoing tensions between the Green and Sea Point Hebrew Congregation of Cape Town and the UOS Bet Din, or religious court (see AJYB

2001, pp. 470–71) continued in 2002. The focus of the dispute was whether the actions of Rabbi E.J. Steinhorn in carrying out the religious functions of the synagogue—primarily decisions about conversions, burial rights, and who might hold office—were within the bounds of Orthodoxy. Some South African Jews saw the matter as a broader struggle between modern Orthodoxy and a resurgent fundamentalism. In August, the congregation called a special meeting to consider a proposal to withdraw from the UOS and establish its own religious court. The congregation's president began the meeting by noting that relations between the synagogue and the Bet Din had "steadily deteriorated" over the years, and that "acrimony" had reached "an untenable level." During the discussion, Rabbi Steinhorn assured those present that he had no intention of transforming the congregation into a Conservative synagogue, as some of his critics had suggested. A letter from Chief Rabbi Cyril Harris was read, warning that the Green and Sea Point Hebrew Congregation would not be recognized as Orthodox if it left the UOS. After considerable debate the motion to secede was withdrawn.

In other developments in the Orthodox community, Johannesburg's Tzeirei Tzion and Mizrachi Young Adults merged into the new Mizrachi Yeshivah Shul in July. A gala dinner was held in Johannesburg to celebrate the contribution of the Adass Yeshurun congregation and its leader, Rabbi Yossi Salzer, to Orthodox Judaism in South Africa. Strictly observant German Jewish immigrants founded the Adass in 1936.

In the Liberal sector of the community, the South African Union of Temple Sisterhoods (SAUTS) celebrated its Golden Jubilee during its biennial conference in Johannesburg in July, and Rabbi Michael Standfield was inducted as minister of Durban's Temple David.

Education

The Johannesburg College of Adult Jewish Education (CAJE) brought together four of the city's congregations—Sydenham, Highlands North, Pine Street, and Range Grove—into a unified adult-education project.

Yeshivah College in Johannesburg celebrated its jubilee in August. Tributes were paid to the principal, Rabbi Avraham Tanzer, the driving force of the institution.

The designers of the South African national school curriculum announced plans to require ninth-graders to study the history of the Holocaust and its moral and ethical dimensions. Gail Weldon, senior curriculum planner for history of the Western Cape Education Department and a member of the National Working Group for the Social Sciences, explained that intimate involvement with the Cape Town Holocaust Centre had convinced her "that the study of the Holocaust has a special impact and relevance in South Africa. Teachers and pupils who have participated in the education programs at the Holocaust Centre have come out with not only a deeper understanding of the Holocaust itself, but also of issues of prejudices and racism, which up till then they have not confronted."

Culture

In a new marketing venture, the *SA Jewish Report* would be made available free of charge at over 300 outlets nationwide beginning in 2003. *Jewish Affairs,* the journal published by the SAJBOD, celebrated its 60th anniversary. David Saks, the editor since 2001, noted that it "is the primary vehicle for Jewish thought in South Africa. Its philosophy is to be the forum in which the Jewish community and the entire South African population can communicate" (*SA Jewish Report,* Feb.15).

The Isaac and Jessie Kaplan Centre for Jewish Studies and Research at the University of Cape Town established a new department dedicated to the study of Jewish migration and genealogy, the first of its kind. Its planned mapping of South African Jewry would be linked up to the South African Jewish Museum so that visitors to the museum might trace their family histories. The initiative for this project came from industrialist and Jewish communal leader Mendel Kaplan.

In July, the South African Jewish Arts and Culture Trust (SAJACT) entered into a partnership with the SAJBOD. Under the arrangement, SAJACT was incorporated within the board's administrative structure and provided with logistical support. The goal of SAJACT was to provide a platform for Jewish artists of all kinds by nurturing and promoting new talent and providing funding.

Some noteworthy publications of Jewish interest were *To Forgive . . . But Not Forget* by Maya Abramowitch; *Joffe Marks — A Family Memoir* by Georgina Jaffe; *The White Life of Felix Greenspan* by Lionel Abrahams; *Yad Avraham* by Dov Tanzer; *Imaging the Unimaginable: Holocaust Memory in Art and Architecture* by Neville Dubow; *No Single Loyalty: A South African Teacher's Life* by Franz Auerbach; *Memories, Realities and Dreams: Aspects of the South African Jewish Experience,* edited by Milton Shain and Richard Mendelsohn; and *Profile of a Community: South African Jewry* by Aleck Goldberg.

Personalia

Helen Lieberman, known as South Africa's Mother Theresa, was awarded an honorary doctorate by the University of Notre Dame in the U.S. Ivan Ferrer, honorary treasurer of the SAZF and chairman of Likud, South Africa, was elected to the board of the Jewish Agency representing the World Likud. Chief Rabbi Cyril Harris received the Jerusalem Prize for Communal Leadership. Simon Jocum was elected to the executive of the World Union for Progressive Judaism (WUPJ) and to its board of governors. Barney Singer was given the Colleagues of Virilist Award by the World Zionist Congress

Among prominent South African Jews who died during 2002 were Rabbi Dr. David Sherman, rabbi emeritus of Temple Israel, Cape Town; Lazer Sidelsky, the attorney who gave Nelson Mandela his first job as an articled clerk; Alicia Lazar, devoted communal worker; Blumie Louis, first honorary life president of the Federation of Synagogues Women's Guilds; Rusty Bernstein, activist and coauthor of South Africa's Freedom Charter; Percy Yutar, state prosecutor in the Rivonia Trial that led to Nelson Mandela's incarceration; Arnie Benjamin, columnist and journalist; and Hans Kramer, patron of classical music. Archie Shandling, communal leader, died at the end of 2001.

MILTON SHAIN

World Jewish Population, 2003

THE WORLD'S JEWISH POPULATION was estimated at 12.95 million at the beginning of 2003—an increase of about 15,000 over the previous year's revised estimate.[1]

The new world Jewish population figure reflects a significant downward revision, mostly related to a new estimate of the Jewish population in the United States (see below). Moreover, new data on Jewish population have become available in several other countries with large Jewish populations, generally confirming our previous estimates but sometimes suggesting upward or downward revisions. New information emerging from national population censuses or special surveys makes it possible to improve and update the worldwide Jewish demographic picture.

Figures on population size, characteristics, and trends are a primary tool in the assessment of Jewish community needs and prospects at the local level and worldwide. The estimates for major regions and individual countries reported in this short overview reflect a prolonged and ongoing effort to study scientifically the demography of contemporary world Jewry.[2] Data collection and comparative research have benefited from the collaboration of scholars and institutions in many countries, including replies to direct inquiries regarding current estimates. It should be emphasized, however, that the elaboration of a worldwide set of estimates for the Jewish populations of the various countries is beset with difficulties and uncertainties.[3] Users of Jewish population estimates

---

[1]The previous estimates, as of January 1, 2002, were published in AJYB 2002, vol. 102, pp. 601–42. See also Sergio DellaPergola, Uzi Rebhun, and Mark Tolts, "Prospecting the Jewish Future: Population Projections 2000–2080," AJYB 2000, vol. 100, pp. 103–46; and previous AJYB volumes for further details on earlier estimates.

[2]Many of these activities are carried out by, or in coordination with, the Division of Jewish Demography and Statistics at the A. Harman Institute of Contemporary Jewry (ICJ), the Hebrew University of Jerusalem. The collaboration of the many institutions and individuals in the different countries who have supplied information for this update is acknowledged with thanks.

[3]For overviews of the subject matter and technical issues see Paul Ritterband, Barry A. Kosmin, and Jeffrey Scheckner, "Counting Jewish Populations: Methods and Problems," AJYB 1988, vol. 88, pp. 204–21; and Sergio DellaPergola, "Demography" in Martin Goodman, ed., *The Oxford Handbook of Jewish Studies* (Oxford, 2002), pp. 797–823.

should be aware of these difficulties and of the inherent limitations of our estimates.

Main Problems in Jewish Population Research

DETERMINANTS OF JEWISH POPULATION CHANGE

Major geopolitical and socioeconomic changes have affected the world scene since the end of the 1980s, particularly the political breakup of the Soviet Union, Germany's reunion, South Africa's change of regime, political and economic instability in several Latin American countries, and the volatile situation in Israel and the Middle East. Jewish population trends were most sensitive to these developments. Large-scale emigration from the former USSR (FSU) and rapid population growth in Israel were the most visible effects, accompanied by other significant Jewish population transfers. Geographical mobility and the increased fragmentation of the global system of nations notwithstanding, over 80 percent of world Jewry live in two countries, the United States and Israel, and 95 percent are concentrated in the ten largest country communities. Six of the G8 countries[4] (the United States, France, Canada, the United Kingdom, the Russian Republic, and Germany) comprise 87 percent of the total Jewish population outside of Israel. The aggregate of these major Jewish population centers virtually determines the assessment of world Jewry's total size and trends.

One fundamental aspect of population in general and of Jewish population in particular is its perpetual change. Population size and composition reflect a well-known array of determinants. Two of these are shared by all populations: (a) the balance of vital events (births and deaths); and (b) the balance of international migration (immigration and emigration). Both these factors affect increases or decreases in the physical presence of individuals in a given place. The third determinant consists of identificational changes (accessions and secessions) and only applies to populations defined by some cultural or symbolic peculiarity, as is the case with Jews. The latter type of change does not affect people's physical presence but rather their willingness to identify with a specific religious, ethnic or otherwise culturally defined group.

The country figures presented here for 2003 were updated from those

---

[4]The eight leading economies in the world, also including Japan and Italy.

for 2002 in accordance with the known or estimated changes in the interval—vital events, migrations, and identificational changes. In our updating procedure, whether or not exact data on intervening changes are available, we consistently apply the known or assumed direction of change, and accordingly add to or subtract from previous Jewish population estimates. If there is evidence that intervening changes balanced each other off, Jewish population remains unchanged. This procedure proved highly accurate in the past. Whenever improved Jewish population figures became available reflecting a new census or survey, our annually updated estimates generally proved on target.

The more recent findings basically confirm the estimates we had reported in previous AJYB volumes and, perhaps more importantly, our interpretation of the trends now prevailing in the demography of world Jewry.[5] Concisely stated, these involve a positive balance of vital events among Jews in Israel and a negative one in nearly all other Jewish communities; a positive migration balance for Israel, the United States, Germany, Australia, and a few other Western countries, and a negative one in Latin America, Eastern Europe, Muslim countries, and some Western countries as well; a positive balance of accessions and secessions in Israel, and an often negative, or, in any event, rather uncertain one elsewhere. While allowing for improvements and corrections, the 2003 population estimates highlight the increasing complexity of the sociodemographic and identificational processes underlying the definition of Jewish populations, and hence the estimates of their sizes. This complexity is magnified at a time of enhanced international migration, often implying double counts of people on the move. Consequently, the analyst has to come to terms with the paradox of the *permanently provisional* character of Jewish population estimates.

SOURCES OF DATA

In general, the amount and quality of documentation on Jewish population size and characteristics is far from satisfactory. In recent years,

---

[5]See Roberto Bachi, *Population Trends of World Jewry* (Jerusalem, 1976); U.O. Schmelz, "Jewish Survival: The Demographic Factors," AJYB 1981, vol. 81, pp. 61–117; U.O. Schmelz, *Aging of World Jewry* (Jerusalem, 1984); Sergio DellaPergola, "Changing Cores and Peripheries: Fifty Years in Socio-demographic Perspective," in Robert S. Wistrich, ed., *Terms of Survival: The Jewish World since 1945* (London, 1995), pp. 13–43; and Sergio DellaPergola, *World Jewry beyond 2000: Demographic Prospects* (Oxford, 1999).

however, important new data and estimates became available for several countries through official population censuses and Jewish-sponsored sociodemographic surveys. National censuses yielded results on Jewish populations in Ireland, the Czech Republic, and India (1991); Romania and Bulgaria (1992); the Russian Republic and Macedonia (1994); Israel (1995); Canada, South Africa, Australia, and New Zealand (1996 and 2001); Belarus, Azerbaijan, Kazakhstan, and Kyrgyzstan (1999); Brazil, Mexico, Switzerland, Estonia, Latvia, and Tajikistan (2000); the United Kingdom, Lithuania, and Ukraine (2001); and the Russian Republic (2002). Permanent national population registers, including information on the Jewish religious, ethnic or national group, exist in several European countries (Switzerland, Norway, Finland, Estonia, Latvia, and Lithuania) and in Israel.

In addition, independent sociodemographic studies have provided most valuable information on Jewish demography and socioeconomic stratification, as well as on Jewish identification. Surveys were conducted over the last several years in South Africa (1991 and 1998); Mexico (1991 and 2000); Lithuania (1993); the United Kingdom and Chile (1995); Venezuela (1998–99); Israel, Hungary, the Netherlands, and Guatemala (1999); Moldova and Sweden (2000); the United States (2000–01); and France and Turkey (2002). Several further Jewish population studies were separately conducted in major cities in the United States (notably New York City in 2002) and in other countries. Additional evidence on Jewish population trends can be obtained from the systematic monitoring of membership registers, vital statistics, and migration records available from Jewish communities and other Jewish organizations in many countries or cities, notably in the United Kingdom, Germany, Italy, Buenos Aires, and São Paulo. Detailed data on Jewish immigration routinely collected in Israel help assess changing Jewish population sizes in other countries. Some of this ongoing research is part of a coordinated effort constantly to update the profile of world Jewry.[6]

---

[6]Following the International Conference on Jewish Population Problems held in Jerusalem in 1987, initiated by the late Roberto Bachi of the Hebrew University and sponsored by major Jewish organizations worldwide, an International Scientific Advisory Committee (ISAC) was established. See Sergio DellaPergola and Leah Cohen, eds., *World Jewish Population: Trends and Policies* (Jerusalem, 1992). A new project called the Initiative on Jewish Demography, sponsored by the Jewish Agency, resulted in an international conference in Jerusalem in 2002, and a plan of data collection and analysis. The newly established Jewish People Policy Planing Institute (JPPPI), chaired by Ambassador Dennis Ross,

DEFINITIONS

A major problem in Jewish population estimates periodically circulated by individual scholars or Jewish organizations is a lack of coherence and uniformity in the definition criteria followed—when the issue of defining the Jewish population is addressed at all. Three operative concepts should be considered in order to put the study of Jewish demography on serious comparative ground.

The *core Jewish population*[7] includes all those who, when asked, identify themselves as Jews; or, if the respondent is a different person in the same household, are identified by him/her as Jews. This is an intentionally comprehensive and pragmatic approach reflecting the nature of most available sources of data on Jewish population. In countries other than Israel, such data often derive from population censuses or social surveys where the interviewees decide how to answer relevant questions on religious or ethnic preferences. Such definitions of a person as a Jew, reflecting subjective feelings, broadly overlap but do not necessarily coincide with Halakhah (rabbinic law) or other normatively binding definitions. They do not depend on any measure of that person's Jewish commitment or behavior in terms of religiosity, beliefs, knowledge, communal affiliation, or otherwise. The *core Jewish population* includes all converts to Judaism by any procedure, as well other people who declare themselves to be Jewish. Also included are persons of Jewish parentage who claim no current religious or ethnic belonging. Persons of Jewish parentage who adopted another religion are excluded, as are other individuals who did not convert out but explicitly identify with a non-Jewish group. In Israel, personal status is subject to the rulings of the Ministry of the Interior, which relies on rabbinical authorities. Therefore the *core* Jewish population in Israel does not simply express subjective identification but reflects definite legal rules, namely Halakhah.

The *enlarged Jewish population*[8] includes the sum of (a) the *core* Jew-

---

provides a framework for policy suggestions in relation to population issues. See Sergio DellaPergola, *Jewish Demography: Facts, Outlook, Challenges,* JPPPI Alert Paper 2 (Jerusalem, 2003).

[7]The term *core Jewish population* was initially suggested by Barry A. Kosmin, Sidney Goldstein, Joseph Waksberg, Nava Lerer, Ariela Keysar, and Jeffrey Scheckner, *Highlights of the CJF 1990 National Jewish Population Survey* (New York, 1991).

[8]The term *enlarged Jewish population* was initially suggested by Sergio DellaPergola, "The Italian Jewish Population Study: Demographic Characteristics and Trends," in U.O. Schmelz, P. Glikson, and S.J. Gould, eds., *Studies in Jewish Demography: Survey for 1969–1971* (Jerusalem-London, 1975), pp. 60–97.

ish population; (b) all other persons of Jewish parentage who are not Jews currently (or at the time of investigation); and (c) all of the respective further non-Jewish household members (spouses, children, etc.). Non-Jews with Jewish background, as far as they can be ascertained, include: (a) persons who have themselves adopted another religion, even though they may claim still to be Jews by ethnicity or religion; and (b) other persons with Jewish parentage who disclaim being Jews. It is customary in sociodemographic surveys to consider the religioethnic identification of parents. Some censuses, however, do ask about more distant ancestry. For both conceptual and practical reasons, this enlarged definition does not include other non-Jewish relatives who lack a Jewish background and live in exclusively non-Jewish households.

The *Law of Return,* Israel's distinctive legal framework for the acceptance and absorption of new immigrants, awards Jewish new immigrants immediate citizenship and other civil rights. According to the current, amended version of the Law of Return, a Jew is any person born to a Jewish mother, or converted to Judaism (regardless of denomination— Orthodox, Conservative, or Reform), who does not have another religious identity. By ruling of Israel's Supreme Court, conversion from Judaism, as in the case of some ethnic Jews who currently identify with another religion, entails loss of eligibility for Law of Return purposes. The law per se does not affect a person's Jewish status, which, as noted, is adjudicated by Israel's Ministry of Interior and rabbinical authorities. The law extends its provisions to all current Jews, their children, and grandchildren, as well as to the respective Jewish or non-Jewish spouses. As a result of its three-generation and lateral extension, the Law of Return applies to a large population, one of significantly wider scope than *core* and *enlarged* Jewish populations defined above.[9] It is actually quite difficult to estimate what the total size of the *Law of Return* population could be. These higher estimates are not discussed below systematically, but some notion of their possible extent is given for the major countries.

The following estimates of Jewish population distribution in each continent (table 1 below), country (tables 2–9), and metropolitan area (table 10) consistently aim at the concept of *core* Jewish population.

---

[9] For a concise review of the rules of attribution of Jewish personal status in rabbinic and Israeli law, including reference to Jewish sects, isolated communities, and apostates, see Michael Corinaldi, "Jewish Identity," chap. 2 in his *Jewish Identity: The Case of Ethiopian Jewry* (Jerusalem, 1998).

PRESENTATION AND QUALITY OF DATA

Until 1999, Jewish population estimates presented in the *American Jewish Year Book* referred to December 31 of the year preceding by two the date of publication. Since 2000 our estimates refer to January 1 of the current year of publication. The effort to provide the most recent possible picture entails a short span of time for evaluation and correction of available information, hence a somewhat greater margin of inaccuracy. Indeed, where appropriate, we revised our previous estimates in the light of newly accrued information on Jewish populations (tables 1 and 2). Corrections were also applied retrospectively to the 2002 figures for major geographical regions so as to ensure a better base for comparisons with the 2003 estimates. Corrections of the latest estimates, if needed, will be presented in future volumes of the AJYB.

We provide separate figures for each country with approximately 100 or more resident *core* Jews. Residual estimates of Jews living in other smaller communities supplement some of the continental totals. For each of the reported countries, the four columns in tables 3–7 provide an estimate of midyear 2002 total population,[10] the estimated 1/1/2003 Jewish population, the proportion of Jews per 1,000 of total population, and a rating of the accuracy of the Jewish population estimate.

There is wide variation in the quality of the Jewish population estimates for different countries. For many diaspora countries it would be best to indicate a range (minimum–maximum) rather than a definite figure for the number of Jews. It would be confusing, however, for the reader to be confronted with a long list of ranges; this would also complicate the regional and world totals. The figures indicated for most of the diaspora communities should be understood as being the central value of the plausible range of the respective core Jewish populations. The relative magnitude of this range varies inversely to the estimate's accuracy.

The three main elements that affect the accuracy of each estimate are the nature and quality of the base data, how recent the base data are, and the method of updating. A simple code combining these elements is used to provide a general evaluation of the reliability of the Jewish population figures reported in the detailed tables below. The code indicates different quality levels of the reported estimates: (A) Base figure derived

---

[10]Data and estimates derived from Population Research Bureau, *2002 World Population Data Sheet* (New York, 2003).

from countrywide census or relatively reliable Jewish population survey; updated on the basis of full or partial information on Jewish population movements in the respective country during the intervening period. (B) Base figure derived from less accurate but recent countrywide Jewish population data; partial information on population movements in the intervening period. (C) Base figure derived from less recent sources, and/or unsatisfactory or partial coverage of a country's Jewish population; updating according to demographic information illustrative of regional demographic trends. (D) Base figure essentially speculative; no reliable updating procedure. In categories (A), (B), and (C), the year in which the country's base figure or important partial updates were obtained is also stated. For countries whose Jewish population estimate for 2003 was not only updated but also revised in the light of improved information, the sign "X" is appended to the accuracy rating.

One additional tool for updating Jewish population estimates is provided by a recent set of demographic projections developed at the Hebrew University of Jerusalem.[11] Such projections extrapolate the most likely observed or expected Jewish population trends over the first decades of the 21st century. Even where reliable information on the dynamics of Jewish population change is not immediately available, the powerful connection that generally exists between age composition of a population and the respective vital and migration movements helps provide plausible scenarios of the developments bound to occur in the short term. Where better data were lacking, we used indications from these projections to refine the 2003 estimates as against previous years. On the other hand, projections are clearly shaped by a comparatively limited set of assumptions, and need to be periodically updated in the light of actual demographic developments.

Global Overview

WORLD JEWISH POPULATION SIZE

The size of world Jewry at the beginning of 2003 is assessed at 12,950,000. World Jewry constitutes about 2.08 per 1,000 of the world's total population of 6,215 million. One in about 480 people in the world is a Jew. According to the revised figures, between the beginning of 2002

---

[11]See DellaPergola, Rebhun, and Tolts, "Prospecting the Jewish Future."

and the beginning 2003, the Jewish population grew by an estimated 14,600 people, or about 0.1 percent. This compares with a total world population growth rate of 1.3 percent (0.1 percent in more developed countries, 1.6 percent in less developed countries). Despite all the imperfections in the estimates, world Jewry continued to be close to "zero population growth," with increase in Israel (1.4 percent) slightly overcoming decline in the diaspora (−0.7 percent).

Table 1 gives an overall picture of Jewish population for the beginning of 2003 as compared to 2002. For 2002 the originally published estimates are presented along with somewhat revised figures that take into account, retrospectively, the corrections made in certain country estimates in the light of improved information. These corrections resulted in a net decrease of the 2002 world Jewry's estimated size by 360,000. Explanations are given below of the reasons for these corrections.

The number of Jews in Israel rose from 5,025,000 at the beginning of 2002 to 5,094,000 at the beginning of 2003, an increase of 69,200 people, or 1.4 percent. In contrast, the estimated Jewish population in the diaspora diminished from 7,910,600 (according to the revised figures) to 7,856,000 — a decrease of 54,600 people, or −0.7 percent. These changes reflect the continuing Jewish emigration from the FSU and other countries, and also the internal decrease typical of the aggregate of diaspora Jewry. In 2002, the estimated Israel-diaspora net migratory balance (immigration minus emigration) amounted to a minimum gain of Jews for Israel.[12] Internal demographic evolution (including vital events and conversions) produced nearly all of the growth among the Jewish population in Israel and nearly all of the decline in the diaspora. Recently, instances of accession or "return" to Judaism can be observed in connection with the emigration process from Eastern Europe and Ethiopia, and the comprehensive provisions of the Israeli Law of Return. The return or first-time access to Judaism of some of such previously unincluded or unidentified individuals contributed to slowing down the pace of decline of the relevant diaspora Jewish populations and some gains for the Jewish population in Israel.

As noted, corrections should be introduced in previously published Jewish population estimates in the light of new information that has became available. Table 2 provides a synopsis of the world Jewish population estimates relating to the period 1945–2002, as first published each

---

[12]Israel, Central Bureau of Statistics, *Monthly Bulletin of Statistics* (Jerusalem, 2003).

TABLE 1. ESTIMATED CORE JEWISH POPULATION, BY CONTINENTS AND MAJOR
GEOGRAPHICAL REGIONS, 2002 AND 2003[a]

| Region | 2002 | | | 2003 | | Yearly % Change 2002–2003 |
	Original Abs. N.	Revised Abs. N.	Percent[b]	Abs. N.	Percent[b]	
World	13,296,100	12,935,600	100.0	12,950,000	100.0	0.1
Diaspora	8,271,100	7,910,600	61.2	7,856,000	60.7	−0.7
Israel	5,025,000	5,025,000	38.8	5,094,200	39.3	1.4
America, Total	6,476,300	6,112,300	47.3	6,071,100	46.9	−0.7
North[c]	6,064,000	5,700,000	44.1	5,670,000	43.8	−0.5
Central	52,500	52,500	0.4	52,100	0.4	−0.8
South	359,800	359,800	2.8	349,000	2.7	−3.0
Europe, Total	1,558,500	1,564,500	12.1	1,550,800	12.0	−0.9
European Union	1,034,400	1,040,400	8.0	1,046,500	8.1	0.6
Other West	19,600	19,600	0.2	19,900	0.2	1.5
Former USSR[d]	410,000	410,000	3.2	389,700	3.0	−5.0
Other East and Balkans[d]	94,500	94,500	0.7	94,700	0.7	0.2
Asia, Total	5,069,900	5,069,900	39.2	5,137,800	39.7	1.3
Israel[e]	5,025,000	5,025,000	38.8	5,100,000	39.3	1.4
Former USSR[d]	25,000	25,000	0.2	23,300	0.2	−6.8
Other[f]	19,900	19,900	0.2	19,500	0.2	−2.0
Africa, Total	87,200	87,200	0.7	83,900	0.6	−0.9
North[f]	7,400	7,400	0.1	7,300	0.1	−1.4
South[g]	79,800	77,300	0.6	76,600	0.6	−0.9
Oceania[h]	104,200	104,200	0.8	106,900	0.8	2.6

[a]January 1.
[b]Minor discrepancies due to rounding.
[c]U.S.A. and Canada.
[d]The Asian regions of Russia and Turkey are included in Europe.
[e]Including West Bank and Gaza.
[f]Including Ethiopia.
[g]South Africa, Zimbabwe, and other sub-Saharan countries.
[h]Australia, New Zealand.

TABLE 2. WORLD JEWISH POPULATION ESTIMATES: ORIGINAL AND CORRECTED, 1945–2003

Year	Original Estimate[a]	Corrected Estimate[b]	Yearly % Change[c]
1945, May 1	11,000,000	11,000,000	
1950, Jan. 1	11,303,400	11,297,000	0.57
1960, Jan. 1	12,792,800	12,079,000	0.67
1970, Jan. 1	13,950,900	12,585,000	0.41
1980, Jan. 1	14,527,100	12,819,000	0.18
1990, Jan. 1	12,810,300	12,868,000	0.04
2000, Jan. 1	13,191,500	12,900,000	0.02
2001, Jan. 1	13,254,100	12,914,000	0.11
2002, Jan. 1	13,296,100	12,935,600	0.17
2003, Jan. 1	12,950,000		0.11

[a]As published in *American Jewish Year Book,* various years. Estimates reported here as of Jan. 1 were originally published as of end of previous year.
[b]Based on updated, revised, or otherwise improved information. Original estimates for 1990 and after, and all corrected estimates: The A. Harman Institute of Contemporary Jewry, The Hebrew University of Jerusalem.
[c]Based on corrected estimates.

year in the *American Jewish Year Book* and as corrected retroactively, incorporating all subsequent revisions. These revised data correct, sometimes significantly, the figures published until 1980 by other authors, and since 1981 by ourselves. Thanks to the development over the years of an improved database, these new revisions are not necessarily the same revised estimates that we published year by year in the AJYB based on the information that was available at each date. It is expected that further retrospective revisions will be necessary reflecting ongoing and future research.

The revised figures in table 2 clearly portray the slowing down of Jewish population growth globally since World War II. Based on a post-Holocaust world Jewish population estimate of 11,000,000, a growth of 1,079,000 occurred between 1945 and 1960, followed by growths of 506,000 in the 1960s, 234,000 in the 1970s, 49,000 in the 1980s, and 32,000 in the 1990s. While it took 13 years to add one million to world Jewry's postwar size, the next 45 years have not been enough to add another million.

POPULATION DISTRIBUTION BY MAJOR REGIONS AND COUNTRIES

About 47 percent of the world's Jews reside in the Americas, with about 44 percent in North America. About 40 percent live in Asia, including the Asian republics of the former USSR (but not the Asian parts of the Russian Republic and Turkey)—most of them in Israel. Europe, including the Asian territories of the Russian Republic and Turkey, accounts for 12 percent of the total. Fewer than 2 percent of the world's Jews live in Africa and Oceania. Among the major geographical regions listed in table 1, the number of Jews in Israel—and, consequently, in total Asia—increased in 2002. Moderate Jewish population gains were also estimated for the European Union (with its 15 member countries), and Oceania. North, Central, and South America, other regions in Europe, Asian countries outside of Israel, and Africa sustained decreases in Jewish population size. These regional changes reflect the trends apparent in the Jewish population in each of the major countries. We now turn to a review of recent trends in the 14 largest Jewish populations.

In the United States (table 3), following publication of the American Jewish Identity Survey (AJIS)[13] and the initial report of the 2000–01 National Jewish Population Survey (NJPS),[14] the total core Jewish population appeared to be in the range of 5.2–5.35 million. The revised estimate was around 400,000 short of the 5.7 million we had projected for 2002 based on the estimate of 5.515 million for mid-1990 from the previous NJPS.[15] The expected Jewish population increase was supposed to reflect the inflow over the 1990s of at least 200,000 new immigrants—from the former Soviet Union, Israel, Latin America, South Africa, Iran, and Western Europe. However—pending thorough analysis and possibly slight revisions in the new database—a continuing low Jewish fertility

---

[13]Egon Mayer, Barry Kosmin, and Ariela Keysar, *American Jewish Identity Survey 2001* (New York, 2002). See also Barry A. Kosmin, Egon Mayer, and Ariela Keysar, *American Religious Identification Survey 2001* (New York, 2001).

[14]Laurence Kotler-Berkowitz, Steven M. Cohen, Jonathon Ament, Vivian Klaff, Frank Mott, Danyelle Peckerman-Neuman, with Lorraine Blass, Debbie Bursztyn, and David Marker, *The National Jewish Population Survey 2000–01: Strength, Challenge, and Diversity in the American Jewish Population* (New York, 2003). See also "U.S. Jewish Population Fairly Stable over Decade, According to Results of National Jewish Population Survey 2000–01," United Jewish Communities press release, Oct. 8, 2002. Following this press release, UJC management conducted a thorough technical check of the survey's methodology and results. The final checked database that was eventually released substantially confirmed the initial Jewish population estimate.

[15]See Kosmin et al., *Highlights of the CJF 1990 National Jewish Population Survey.*

TABLE 3. ESTIMATED CORE JEWISH POPULATION DISTRIBUTION IN THE AMERICAS, 1/1/2003

Country	Total Population	Jewish Population	Jews per 1,000 Population	Accuracy Rating
Canada	31,300,000	370,500	11.8	B 2001 X
United States	287,400,000	5,300,000	18.4	B 2001 X
Total North America[a]	318,827,000	5,670,000	17.8	
Bahamas	300,000	300	1.0	D
Costa Rica	3,900,000	2,500	0.6	C 1993
Cuba	11,300,000	600	0.1	C 1990
Dominican Republic	8,800,000	100	0.0	D
El Salvador	6,600,000	100	0.0	C 1993
Guatemala	12,100,000	900	0.1	A 1999
Jamaica	2,600,000	300	0.1	A 1995
Mexico	101,700,000	40,000	0.4	B 2001
Netherlands Antilles	215,000	200	0.9	B 1998
Panama	2,900,000	5,000	1.7	C 1990
Puerto Rico	3,915,000	1,500	0.4	C 1990
Virgin Islands	114,000	300	2.6	C 1986
Other	22,556,000	300	0.0	D
Total Central America	177,000,000	52,100	0.3	
Argentina	36,500,000	187,000	5.1	C 2002
Bolivia	8,800,000	500	0.1	C 1999
Brazil	173,800,000	97,000	0.6	B 2001
Chile	15,600,000	20,900	1.3	C 1991
Colombia	43,800,000	3,400	0.1	C 1996
Ecuador	13,000,000	900	0.1	C 1985
Paraguay	6,000,000	900	0.2	B 1997
Peru	26,700,000	2,500	0.1	C 1993
Suriname	417,000	200	0.5	B 1986
Uruguay	3,400,000	20,000	5.9	C 2001 X
Venezuela	25,100,000	15,700	0.6	B 1999
Total South America[a]	354,043,000	349,000	1.0	
Total	849,870,000	6,071,600	7.1	

[a]Including countries not listed separately.

rate, the consequent aging in population composition, and continuing erosion in the willingness to identify with Judaism among the younger age groups apparently led to a significantly lower total core population size. We choose an estimate of 5.3 million for U.S. Jewry, intermediate between the figures so far available from the two major surveys. On the other hand, the enlarged total—current Jews, former Jews, and their non-Jewish family members—was between 9.2 and 10 million individuals in 2001, significantly higher than the 8.2 million found in 1990. A 2002 study of the Jews in New York, the major U.S. metropolitan community,[16] pointed to a stable Jewish population of 1.4 million in the extended eight-borough area, but for the first time less than 1 million in New York City's five boroughs.

In Canada, the 2001 population census[17] indicated a decrease in the number of Jews according to ethnicity (including holders of a non-Jewish religion) from 369,565 in 1991 to 348,605 in 2001 (−20,960 or 5.7 percent). Of the latter, 186,475 indicated Jewish as their sole ethnicity, and 162,130 as one of their several ethnic identities. The percentage of single-ethnic Jews thus diminished to 53 percent in 2002, versus 66 percent in 1991. On the other hand, the number of Canada's Jews according to religion increased from 318,070 in 1991 to 329,995 in 2001 (+11,925 or 3.7 percent). Of the latter total, 22,365 Jews immigrated during the ten-year interval between the two censuses. Were it not for this immigration, the Jewish population would have decreased by 10,440 (3.3 percent). Keeping in mind that some ethnic Jews are not Jewish by religion, and that an even greater number of Jews by religion do not declare a Jewish ethnicity, we updated the estimate of Canada's Jewish population from 356,315 in 1991 to 370,520 in 2001. This included some for whom "Jewish" was only one among multiple ethnic identities.

In Latin America, the Jewish population was generally declining, reflecting economic and local security concerns. In Argentina, following a sharpening of the ongoing economic crisis, about 6,000 emigrated to Israel in 2002—the highest figure ever in a single year from that country.[18] While, based on the experience of previous years, 10–20 percent of these migrants were non-Jewish household members in the enlarged population, partial evidence from different sources indicated that less than half

---

[16]See http://www.ujafedny.org/site/PageServer?pagename=jewishcommunitystudy.
[17]See http://www.statcan.ca.
[18]See Israel Central Bureau of Statistics: http://www.cbs.gov.il.

of total Jewish emigration from Argentina went to Israel. We consequently assessed Argentina's Jewish population at 187,000.

The 2000 census of Brazil indicated a stable Jewish population of 86,828, versus 86,416 in 1991.[19] Considering the possible noninclusion of people who failed to indicate a religion, we assessed the total at 97,000. This appeared to be consistent with a systematic documentation effort undertaken by the Jewish Federation of São Paulo, and an assumption that about one half of Brazil's Jews live in that city.

In Mexico, the 2000 census indicated a Jewish population of 45,260 individuals aged five and over.[20] Of these, 32,464 lived in the capital's metropolitan area and, consistently with erratic figures in past censuses, a most unlikely 12,796 appeared to live in states other than the Federal District and Mexico State. Allocation of the 0–4 age group based on a 2000 Jewish survey determined a corrected estimate of about 35,000 Jews in Greater Mexico City, and 40,000 nationwide.

Jewish population in Europe (table 4) tended to be increasingly concentrated in the western part of the continent, and within the European Union particularly. The 15-country EU, bound for expansion to another ten countries in 2004, had an estimated total of 1,1046,500 Jews. The largest community was in France, where a new countrywide survey undertaken at the beginning of 2002 suggested a downward revision to 500,000 Jews and an additional 75,000 non-Jewish members of the enlarged households.[21] Our 2002 Jewish population estimate stood at 519,000. The difference, cumulated over several years, was primarily explained by a growing pace of emigration of French Jews not only to Israel, which received 2,000 in 2002, but also to Canada and other countries. This was due to a feeling of uneasiness about manifestations of anti-Jewish intolerance and physical violence.

In the United Kingdom, for the first time since the nineteenth century a population census provided detailed data about religion.[22] The total Jewish population of 266,741 for England, Wales, Scotland, and Northern Ireland closely approximated our 273,500 estimate for 2002. However, considering that 22.8 percent of the UK population stated no religion and

---

[19]See http://www.ibge.br; and René D. Decol, "Brazilian Jews: a Demographic Profile," paper delivered at the International Conference of Jewish Demography, Jerusalem, 2002.

[20]See Instituto Nacional de Estadística, Geografía e Informatica, *XII Censo General de Población y Vivienda 2000* (Mexico City, 2002).

[21]See Erik H. Cohen, *Les Juifs de France: Valeurs et identité* (Paris, 2002).

[22]See http://statistics.gov.uk; and Barry Kosmin and Stanley Waterman, *Commentary on Census Religion Question* (London, 2002).

another 7.3 percent did not answer the question—even though the organized Jewish community largely supported participation in the census—we suggest the estimate should be raised to 300,000. According to more detailed data on Scotland, 6,448 indicated a current Jewish religion but 7,446 said they were raised as Jews—a net loss of 13 percent.

In Germany, significant Jewish immigration continued. More particularly, in 2002 the enlarged total of Jews and non-Jewish family members who came from the former Soviet Union was 19,262, as against 18,878 who immigrated to Israel. The total number of core Jews registered with the central Jewish community grew to 98,335.[23] Of these, 14,732 were the survivors of the initial pool of 28,081 members that existed at the end of 1990, and the rest were recent immigrants. The age composition of the Jewish old-timers, and even more so of the newcomers, was disproportionately elderly. Allowing for delays in joining the organized community and a possible reluctance on the part of some new immigrants to affiliate, we assess Germany's core Jewish population at 108,000.

In the former Soviet Union, Jewish population continued to decrease rapidly, reflecting an overwhelming imbalance of Jewish births and Jewish deaths, and continuing emigration. Our assessment of the total core Jewish population in the aggregate of the former Soviet Republics was 413,000, of which 389,700 in Europe and 23,300 in Asia. At least as many non-Jewish family members were integrated into the respective enlarged households. In the Russian Republic—pending publication of the 2002 census—we estimated the core population at 252,000. The size of Jewry in Russia was comparatively more stable and resilient than in the other republics, partly as a consequence of Jewish migrations between the various republics, partly due to lower emigration propensities from Moscow and some of the other main urban areas.[24] Nevertheless, a striking imbalance of Jewish births and deaths determined continuing population decline even there.

In the Ukraine, the population census undertaken on December 5, 2001, yielded 103,600 Jews, whereas we had expected 100,000 on January 1, 2002. It should be noted that our baseline for the latter estimate were the 486,300 Jews counted in the previous census of January 1989

---

[23]Zentralwohlfahrtsstelle der Juden in Deutschland, *Mitgliederstatistik; Der Einzelnen Jüdischen Gemeinden und Landesverbände in Deutschland* (Frankfurt, 2002).

[24]Mark Tolts, "Aliya from the Russian Federation: An Analysis of Recent Data," *Jews in Eastern Europe,* 1–2 (new series), Spring/Fall 2002, pp. 5–23.

TABLE 4. ESTIMATED CORE JEWISH POPULATION DISTRIBUTION IN EUROPE, 1/1/2003

Country	Total Population	Jewish Population	Jews per 1,000 Population	Accuracy Rating
Austria	8,100,000	9,000	1.1	B 2001
Belgium	10,300,000	31,400	3.0	C 2002
Denmark	5,400,000	6,400	1.2	C 2001
Finland	5,200,000	1,100	0.2	B 1999
France[a]	59,500,000	498,000	8.4	B 2002 X
Germany	82,400,000	108,000	1.3	B 2002
Greece	11,000,000	4,500	0.4	B 1995
Ireland	3,800,000	1,000	0.3	B 2001
Italy	58,100,000	29,000	0.5	B 2002
Luxembourg	450,000	600	1.3	B 2000
Netherlands	16,100,000	30,000	1.9	B 2000 X
Portugal	10,400,000	500	0.0	C 1999
Spain	41,300,000	12,000	0.3	D
Sweden	8,900,000	15,000	1.7	C 1990
United Kingdom	60,400,000	300,000	5.0	B 2001 X
Total European Union	381,350,000	1,046,500	2.7	
Gibraltar	25,000	600	24.0	B 1991
Norway	4,500,000	1,200	0.3	B 1995
Switzerland	7,300,000	18,000	2.5	A 2000
Other	860,000	100	0.1	D
Total other West Europe	12,685,000	19,900	1.6	
Belarus	9,900,000	23,000	2.3	B 1999
Estonia	1,400,000	1,800	1.3	B 2001
Latvia	2,300,000	9,200	4.0	B 2001
Lithuania	3,500,000	3,500	1.0	B 2001
Moldova	4,300,000	5,200	1.2	C 2000
Russia[b]	143,500,000	252,000	1.8	B 2001
Ukraine	48,200,000	95,000	2.0	B 2001
Total former USSR in Europe	213,100,000	389,700	1.8	

TABLE 4.—*(Continued)*

Country	Total Population	Jewish Population	Jews per 1,000 Population	Accuracy Rating
Bosnia-Herzegovina	3,400,000	500	0.1	C 2001 X
Bulgaria	7,800,000	2,200	0.3	C 2001 X
Croatia	4,300,000	1,700	0.4	C 2001 X
Czech Republic	10,300,000	4,000	0.4	C 2001 X
Hungary	10,100,000	50,000	5.0	C 2001 X
Macedonia (FYR)	2,000,000	100	0.1	C 1996
Poland	38,600,000	3,300	0.1	C 2001 X
Romania	22,400,000	10,600	0.5	B 2001
Serbia and Montenegro	10,700,000	1,500	0.1	C 2001 X
Slovakia	5,400,000	2,700	0.5	C 2001 X
Slovenia	2,000,000	100	0.1	C 1996
Turkey[b]	67,300,000	18,000	0.3	B 2002 X
Total other East Europe and Balkans[c]	188,300,000	94,700	0.5	
Total	795,435,000	1,550,800	1.9	

[a]Including Monaco.
[b]Including Asian regions.
[c]Including Albania.

(not including a few "oriental" Jews).[25] Taking into account the dramatic pace of emigration since 1989, the other major intervening changes among Ukraine's Jewry, and also the continuing emigration at the end of 2001, the census fully confirmed our previous assessment of ongoing demographic trends. Taking into account continuing emigration in 2002, we now assess the core Jewish population at 95,000.

The largest Jewish community in the rest of Central and Eastern Europe is that of Hungary. Our core estimate of 50,000 reflects the expectedly negative balance of Jewish births and deaths in a country whose total population, too, has for years incurred a negative vital balance. While a Jewish survey in 1999 indicated a conspicuously larger enlarged Jewish

---

[25]Ukraine Goskomstat, *Population Census 2001* (Kiyev, 2002); Mark Tolts, *Main Demographic Trends of the Jews in Russia and the FSU* (Jerusalem, 2002).

TABLE 5.   ESTIMATED CORE JEWISH POPULATION DISTRIBUTION IN ASIA, 1/1/2003

Country	Total Population	Jewish Population	Jews per 1,000 Population	Accuracy Rating
Israel[a]	6,631,000	4,879,100	735.8	A 2003
West Bank and Gaza	3,280,000	215,100	65.6	A 2003
Total Israel and Palestine	9,911,000	5,094,200	514.0	
Azerbaijan	8,200,000	7,500	0.9	C 1999
Georgia	4,400,000	4,700	1.1	C 2000
Kazakhstan	14,800,000	4,200	0.3	B 1999
Kyrgyzstan	5,000,000	800	0.2	B 1999
Tajikistan	6,300,000	100	0.0	B 2000
Turkmenistan	5,600,000	500	0.1	C 2000
Uzbekistan	25,400,000	5,500	0.2	C 2000
Total former USSR in Asia[b]	73,500,000	23,300	0.3	
China[c]	1,287,900,000	1,000	0.0	D
India	1,049,500,000	5,200	0.0	B 1996
Iran	65,600,000	11,000	0.2	C 1986
Japan	127,096,000	1,000	0.0	C 1993
Korea, South	48,400,000	100	0.0	C 1998
Philippines	80,000,000	100	0.0	D
Singapore	4,200,000	300	0.1	B 1990
Syria	17,200,000	100	0.0	C 1995
Thailand	62,600,000	200	0.0	C 1988
Yemen	18,600,000	200	0.0	B 1995
Other	853,293,000	300	0.0	D
Total other Asia	3,614,389,000	19,500	0.0	
Total	3,697,800,000	5,137,000	1.4	

[a]Total population of Israel 1/1/2003.
[b]Including Armenia. Not including Asian regions of Russian Republic.
[c]Including Hong Kong.

TABLE 6. ESTIMATED CORE JEWISH POPULATION DISTRIBUTION IN AFRICA, 1/1/2003

Country	Total Population	Jewish Population	Jews per 1,000 Population	Accuracy Rating
Egypt	71,200,000	100	0.0	C 1998
Ethiopia	67,700,000	100	0.0	C 1998
Morocco	29,700,000	5,500	0.2	B 1995
Tunisia	9,800,000	1,500	0.2	B 1995
Other	69,700,000	100	0.0	D
Total North Africa	248,100,000	7,300	0.0	
Botswana	1,541,000	100	0.1	B 1993
Congo D.R.	50,948,000	100	0.0	B 1993
Kenya	31,100,000	400	0.0	B 1990
Namibia	1,800,000	100	0.1	B 1993
Nigeria	129,900,000	100	0.0	D
South Africa	43,600,000	75,000	1.8	B 2001
Zimbabwe	12,300,000	500	0.0	B 1993
Other	320,711,000	300	0.0	D
Total other Africa	591,900,000	76,600	0.1	
Total	840,000,000	83,900	0.1	

population, a demographic extrapolation based on the usually accepted number of post-Holocaust core Jewish survivors and accounting for the known or estimated numbers of births, deaths, and emigrants closely matches our assessment.[26]

As noted, Jewish population in Asia is mostly affected by the trends in Israel (table 5). Israel's core Jewish population reached 5,094,200, to which another 273,000 non-Jewish members of households can be added

---

[26]Andras Kovacs, ed., *Jews and Jewry in Contemporary Hungary: Results of a Sociological Survey* (Budapest, 2002).

TABLE 7.   ESTIMATED CORE JEWISH POPULATION DISTRIBUTION IN OCEANIA, 1/1/2003

Country	Total Population	Jewish Population	Jews per 1,000 Population	Accuracy Rating
Australia	19,700,000	100,000	5.1	B 2001
New Zealand	3,900,000	6,800	1.7	A 2001 X
Other	8,400,000	100	0.0	D
Total	32,000,000	106,900	3.3	

TABLE 8.   COUNTRIES WITH LARGEST JEWISH POPULATIONS, 1/1/2003

			% of Total Jewish Population			
		Jewish	In the World		In the Diaspora	
Rank	Country	Population	%	Cumulative %	%	Cumulative %
1	United States	5,300,000	40.9	40.9	67.5	67.5
2	Israel	5,094,200	39.3	80.3	=	=
3	France	498,000	3.8	84.1	6.3	73.8
4	Canada	370,500	2.9	87.0	4.6	78.5
5	United Kingdom	300,000	2.3	89.3	3.8	82.3
6	Russia	252,000	1.9	91.2	3.2	85.5
7	Argentina	187,000	1.4	92.7	2.4	87.9
8	Germany	108,000	0.8	93.5	1.4	89.3
9	Australia	100,000	0.8	94.3	1.3	90.6
10	Brazil	97,000	0.7	95.0	1.2	91.8
11	Ukraine	95,000	0.7	95.8	1.2	93.0
12	South Africa	75,000	0.6	96.3	1.0	94.0
13	Hungary	50,000	0.4	96.7	0.6	94.6
14	Mexico	40,000	0.3	97.0	0.5	95.1
15	Belgium	31,400	0.2	97.3	0.4	95.5

TABLE 9. WORLD DISTRIBUTION OF CORE JEWISH POPULATION, BY NUMBER,
AND PROPORTION (PER 1,000 POPULATION) IN EACH COUNTRY,
1/1/2003

Number of Jews in Country	Jews per 1,000 Population					
	Total	0.0-0.9	1.0-4.9	5.0-9.9	10.0-24.9	25.0+
	Number of Countries					
Total[a]	93	61	22	6	3	1
100-900	35	31	3	-	1	-
1,000-4,900	21	18	3	-	-	-
5,000-9,900	10	4	6	-	-	-
10,000-49,900	14	7	6	1	-	-
50,000-99,900	4	1	1	2	-	-
100,000-999,900	7	-	3	3	1	-
1,000,000 or more	2	-	-	-	1	1
	Jewish Population Distribution (Absolute Numbers)					
Total[a]	12,950,200	307,600	721,100	1,155,000	5,671,100	5,094,200
100-900	11,600	9,800	1,200	-	600	-
1,000-4,900	50,800	40,800	10,000	-	-	-
5,000-9,900	65,300	23,700	41,600	-	-	-
10,000-49,900	294,600	136,300	138,300	20,000	-	-
50,000-99,900	324,000	97,000	75,000	150,000	-	-
100,000-999,900	1,810,500	-	455,000	985,000	370,500	-
1,000,000 or more	10,394,200	-	-	-	5,300,000	5,094,200
	Jewish Population Distribution (Percent of World's Jews)					
Total[a]	100.0	2.4	5.6	8.9	43.8	39.3
100-900	0.1	0.1	0.0	0.0	0.0	0.0
1,000-4,900	0.4	0.3	0.1	0.0	0.0	0.0
5,000-9,900	0.5	0.2	0.3	0.0	0.0	0.0
10,000-49,900	2.3	1.1	1.1	0.2	0.0	0.0
50,000-99,900	2.5	0.7	0.6	1.2	0.0	0.0
100,000-999,900	14.0	0.0	3.5	7.6	2.9	0.0
1,000,000 or more	80.2	0.0	0.0	0.0	40.9	39.3

[a]Grand total includes countries with fewer than 100 Jews, for a total of 1,200 Jews. Minor discrepancies due to rounding. Israel includes West Bank and Gaza.

to reach an enlarged Jewish population of 5,367,200.[27] Israel's Jewish fertility rate continued to be stable, at 2.6 children per woman, above that of all other developed countries, and probably twice or more as high as that of most Jewish communities in the diaspora. In 2002, 36,700 new immigrants arrived in Israel, 21,800 of them Jewish.[28] Current Jewish emigration reduced this to a net migration balance of 9,300. Some 4,500 new immigrants underwent conversion to Judaism—half of them arrived from Ethiopia. Of the 5,095,200 core Jews in 2003, 4,879,100 lived within the pre-1967 borders plus East Jerusalem and the Golan Heights, and 215,100 lived in the West Bank and Gaza.

Jewish population in Africa is mostly concentrated in South Africa (table 6). Emigration continued at a moderate pace.[29] According to the 2001 census results, the white Jewish population was 61,675. Allowing for non-response and Jews reported among non-whites, we assess the community size at 75,000.

Continuing immigration produced some increase in the size of Jewish populations in Oceania (table 7). Australia's 2001 census indicated a Jewish population of 83,500, up about 4,000 from 1996.[30] Taking into account nonresponse, but also the community's aging composition, we estimate the core Jewish population at 100,000.

DISPERSION AND CONCENTRATION

Reflecting global Jewish population stagnation along with growing concentration in a few countries, 97.3 percent of world Jewry live in the largest 15 communities, and 95.5 percent live in the 14 largest communities of the diaspora—i.e., excluding Israel from the count (table 8). Only nine communities beside Israel constitute at least 5 per 1,000 (or 0.5 percent) of their country's total population (table 9). In descending order by the relative weight (not size) of their Jewish population they were Gibraltar (24.0 Jews per 1,000 inhabitants), the United States (18.4), Canada (11.8), France (8.4), Uruguay (5.9), Australia (5.1), Argentina (5.1), the United Kingdom (5.0), and Hungary (5.0). Jews represented 735.8 per

---

[27]See Central Bureau of Statistics, *Statistical Abstract of Israel,* 54,2003. See also http://www.cbs.gov.il.

[28]Not including foreign workers and illegal residents.

[29]See the initial analysis by David Saks, *Jewish Report,* 2003. See also Barry A. Kosmin, Jaqueline Goldberg, Milton Shain, and Shirley Bruk, *Jews of the New South Africa: Highlights of the 1998 National Survey of South African Jews* (London, 1999).

[30]Australian Bureau of Statistics, *Population Census 2001* (Canberra, 2002).

TABLE 10. METROPOLITAN AREAS WITH LARGEST CORE JEWISH POPULATIONS, 1/1/2003

Rank	Metro Area[a]	Country	Jewish Population	Share of World's Jews %	Cumulative %
1	Tel Aviv[b,c]	Israel	2,626,100	20.3	20.3
2	New York[d]	U.S.	2,051,000	15.8	36.1
3	Los Angeles[d]	U.S.	668,000	5.2	41.3
4	Haifa[b]	Israel	653,800	5.0	46.3
5	Jerusalem[e]	Israel	638,000	4.9	51.2
6	Southeast Florida [d, f]	U.S.	498,000	3.8	55.1
7	Be'er Sheva[b]	Israel	342,800	2.6	57.7
7	Philadelphia[d]	U.S.	285,000	2.2	59.9
9	Paris[g]	France	284,000	2.2	62.1
10	Chicago[d]	U.S.	265,000	2.0	64.2
11	Boston[d]	U.S.	254,000	2.0	66.1
12	San Francisco[d]	U.S.	218,000	1.7	67.8
13	London[h]	United Kingdom	195,000	1.5	69.3
14	Toronto[i]	Canada	175,000	1.4	70.7
15	Buenos Aires[j]	Argentina	168,000	1.3	72.0
16	Washington[k]	U.S.	166,000	1.3	73.3
17	Moscow[l]	Russia	108,000	0.8	74.1
18	Baltimore[k]	U.S.	106,000	0.8	74.9
19	Detroit[d]	U.S.	103,000	0.8	75.7
20	Montreal[i]	Canada	90,000	0.7	76.4
21	Cleveland[d]	U.S.	86,000	0.7	76.4
22	Atlanta[k]	U.S.	86,000	0.7	77.0

[a]Most metropolitan areas include extended inhabited territory and several municipal authorities around central city. Definitions vary by country. Some of the estimates may include non-core Jews.
[b]As newly defined in the 1995 Census.
[c]Includes Ramat Gan, Bene Beraq, Petach Tikwa, Bat Yam, Holon, Rishon Lezlon, Netanya and Ashdod, each with a Jewish population above 100,000.
[d]Consolidated Metropolitan Statistical Area (CMSA).
[e]Revised estimate. Includes the whole Jerusalem District and parts of Judea and Samaria District.
[f]Miami-Ft. Lauderdale and West Palm Beach-Boca Raton CMSA.
[g]Departments 75, 77, 78, 91, 92, 93, 94, 95.
[h]Greater London and contiguous postcode areas.
[i]Census Metropolitan Area.
[j]Capital Federal and Partidos del Gran Buenos Aires.
[k]Metropolitan Statistical Area (MSA).
[l]Territory administered by city council.

1,000 inhabitants in the State of Israel, including East Jerusalem and the Golan Heights, and 65.6 per 1,000 inhabitants in the West Bank and Gaza. The overwhelming urban location of Jewish populations globally is evinced by the fact that 51.2 percent of total world Jewry live in only five metropolitan areas—Tel Aviv, New York, Los Angeles, Haifa, and Jerusalem—and another 25 percent live in the next 15 largest metropolitan concentrations (table 10).

SERGIO DELLAPERGOLA

Directories
Lists
Obituaries

National Jewish Organizations*

UNITED STATES

Organizations are listed according to functions as follows:

COMMUNITY RELATIONS

AMERICAN COUNCIL FOR JUDAISM (1943). PO Box 9009, Alexandria, VA 22304. (703)836-2546. Pres. Stephen L. Naman; Exec. Dir. Allan C. Brownfeld. Seeks to advance the universal principles of a Judaism free of nationalism, and the national, civic, cultural, and social integration into American institutions of Americans of Jewish faith. *Issues of the American Council for Judaism; Special Interest Report.* (WWW.ACJNA.ORG)

AMERICAN JEWISH COMMITTEE (1906). The Jacob Blaustein Building, 165 E. 56 St., NYC 10022. (212)751-4000. FAX: (212) 750-0326. Pres. Harold Tanner; Exec. Dir. David A. Harris. Protects the rights and freedoms of Jews the world over; combats bigotry and anti-Semitism and promotes democracy and human rights for all; works for the security of Israel and deepened understanding between Americans and Israelis; advocates public-policy positions rooted in American democratic values and the perspectives of Jewish her-

---

*The information in this directory is based on replies to questionnaires circulated by the editors. Web site addresses, where provided, appear at end of entries.

itage; and enhances the creative vitality of the Jewish people. Includes Jacob and Hilda Blaustein Center for Human Relations, Project Interchange, William Petschek National Jewish Family Center, Jacob Blaustein Institute for the Advancement of Human Rights, Institute on American Jewish-Israeli Relations. *American Jewish Year Book; Commentary; AJC Journal.* (WWW.AJC.ORG)

AMERICAN JEWISH CONGRESS (1918). Stephen Wise Congress House, 15 E. 84 St., NYC 10028. (212)879-4500. FAX: (212)249-3672. E-mail: pr@ajcongress. org. Pres. Jack Rosen; Exec. Dir. Neil B. Goldstein. Works to foster the creative survival of the Jewish people; to help Israel develop in peace, freedom, and security; to eliminate all forms of racial and religious bigotry; to advance civil rights, protect civil liberties, defend religious freedom, and safeguard the separation of church and state; "The Attorney General for the Jewish Community." *Congress Monthly; Judaism; Inside Israel; Radical Islamic Fundamentalism Update.* (www. AJCONGRESS.ORG)

AMERICAN JEWISH PUBLIC RELATIONS SOCIETY (1957). 575 Lexington Ave., Suite 600, NYC 10022. (212)644-2663. FAX: (212)644-3887. Pres. Diane J. Ehrlich; V-Pres., membership, Lauren R. Marcus. Advances professional status of public-relations practitioners employed by Jewish organizations and institutions or who represent Jewish-related clients, services, or products; upholds a professional code of ethics and standards; provides continuing education and networking opportunities at monthly meetings; serves as a clearinghouse for employment opportunities. *AJPRS Reporter; AJPRS Membership Directory.*

ANTI-DEFAMATION LEAGUE OF B'NAI B'RITH (1913). 823 United Nations Plaza, NYC 10017. (212)885-7700. FAX: (212)867-0779. E-mail: webmaster@adl. org. Natl. Chmn. Glen A. Tobias; Natl. Dir. Abraham H. Foxman. Seeks to combat anti-Semitism and to secure justice and fair treatment for all citizens through law, education, and community relations. *ADL on the Frontline; Law Enforcement Bulletin; Dimensions: A Journal of Holocaust Studies; Hidden Child Newsletter; International Reports; Civil Rights Reports.* (WWW.ADL.ORG)

ASSOCIATION OF JEWISH COMMUNITY RELATIONS WORKERS (1950). 7800 Northaven Road, Dallas, TX 75230. (214)615-5229. FAX: (214)373-3186. Pres. Marlene Gorin. Aims to stimulate higher standards of professional practice in Jewish community relations; encourages research and training toward that end; conducts educational programs and seminars; aims to encourage cooperation between community-relations workers and those working in other areas of Jewish communal service.

CENTER FOR JEWISH COMMUNITY STUDIES (1970). 1515 Locust St., Suite 703, Philadelphia, PA 19102. (215)772-0564. FAX: (215)772-0566. E-mail:*jcpa@net vision.net.il* or cjcs@worldnet.att.net. Jerusalem office:Jerusalem Center for Public Affairs. Pres. Amb. Dore Gold; Dir. Gen. Zvi Marom; Chmn. Bd. of Overseers Michael Rukin. Worldwide policy-studies institute devoted to the study of Jewish community organization, political thought, and public affairs, past and present, in Israel and throughout the world. Publishes original articles, essays, and monographs; maintains library, archives, and reprint series. *Jerusalem Letter/Viewpoints; Jewish Political Studies Review.* (WWW.JCPA.ORG).

CENTER FOR RUSSIAN JEWRY WITH STUDENT STRUGGLE FOR SOVIET JEWRY/SSSJ (1964). 240 Cabrini Blvd., #5B, NYC 10033. (212)928-7451. FAX: (212)795-8867. Dir./Founder Jacob Birnbaum; Chmn. Dr. Ernest Bloch. Campaigns for the human rights of the Jews of the former USSR, with emphasis on emigration and Jewish identity; supports programs for needy Jews there and for newcomers in Israel and USA, stressing employment and Jewish education. As the originator of the grassroots movement for Soviet Jewry in the early 1960s, possesses unique archives.

COALITION ON THE ENVIRONMENT & JEWISH LIFE (1993). 443 Park Ave. S., 11th fl., NYC 10016-7322. (212)684-6950, ext. 210. FAX: (212)686-1353. E-mail: info@ coejl.org. Dir. Mark X. Jacobs. Promotes environmental education, advocacy, and action in the American Jewish community. Sponsored by a broad coalition of Jewish organizations; member of the National Religious Partnership for the Environment. *Bi-annual newsletter.* (www. COEJL.ORG)

COMMISSION ON SOCIAL ACTION OF RE-FORM JUDAISM (1953, joint instrumentality of the Union of American Hebrew Congregations and the Central Conference of American Rabbis). 633 Third Ave., 7th fl., NYC 10017. (212)650-4160. FAX: (212)650-4229. E-mail: csarj@uahc.org. Wash. Office:2027 Massachusetts Ave., NW, Washington, DC 20036. Chmn. Robert Heller; Dir. Rabbi Daniel Polish; Dir. Religious Action Center of Reform Judaism, Rabbi David Saperstein. Policy-making body that relates ethical and spiritual principles of Judaism to social-justice issues; implements resolutions through the Religious Action Center in Washington, DC, via advocacy, development of educational materials, and congregational programs. *Tzedek V'Shalom (social action newsletter); Chai Impact (legislative update).*

CONFERENCE OF PRESIDENTS OF MAJOR AMERICAN JEWISH ORGANIZATIONS (1955). 633 Third Ave., NYC 10017. (212)318-6111. FAX: (212)644-4135. E-mail: info@prescon.org Chmn. Mortimer B. Zuckerman; Exec. V.-Chmn. Malcolm Hoenlein. Seeks to strengthen the U.S.-Israel alliance and to protect and enhance the security and dignity of Jews abroad. Toward this end, the Conference of Presidents speaks and acts on the basis of consensus of its 54 member agencies on issues of national and international Jewish concern.

CONSULTATIVE COUNCIL OF JEWISH ORGANIZATIONS-CCJO (1946). 420 Lexington Ave., Suite 1731, NYC 10170. (212)808-5437. Chmn. Ady Steg & Clemens N. Nathan. A nongovernmental organization in consultative status with the UN, UNESCO, ILO, UNICEF, and the Council of Europe; cooperates and consults with, advises, and renders assistance to the Economic and Social Council of the UN on all problems relating to human rights and economic, social, cultural, educational, and related matters pertaining to Jews.

COORDINATING BOARD OF JEWISH ORGANIZATIONS (1947). 2020 K Street, NW, 7th Floor, Washington, D.C. 20006. (202)857-6540. FAX: (202)857-6689. Exec. V. Pres. Daniel S. Mariaschin. To promote the purposes and principles for which the UN was created.

COUNCIL OF JEWISH ORGANIZATIONS IN CIVIL SERVICE, INC. (1948). 45 E. 33 St., Rm. 601, NYC 10016. (212)689-2015. FAX: (212)447-1633. Pres. Louis Weiser; 1st V.-Pres. Melvyn Birnbaum. Supports merit system; encourages recruitment of Jewish youth to government service; member of Coalition to Free Soviet Jews, NY Jewish Community Relations Council, NY Metropolitan Coordinating Council on Jewish Poverty, Jewish Labor Committee, America-Israel Friendship League. *Council Digest.*

INSTITUTE FOR PUBLIC AFFAIRS (*see* UNION OF ORTHODOX JEWISH CONGREGATIONS OF AMERICA)

INTERNATIONAL LEAGUE FOR THE REPATRIATION OF RUSSIAN JEWS, INC. (1963). 2 Fountain Lane, Suite 2J, Scarsdale, NY 10583. (914)683-3225. FAX: (914)683-3221. Pres. Morris Brafman; Chmn. James H. Rapp. Helped to bring the situation of Soviet Jews to world attention; catalyst for advocacy efforts, educational projects, and programs on behalf of Russian Jews in the former USSR, Israel, and U.S. Provides funds to help Russian Jewry in Israel and the former Soviet Union.

JEWISH COUNCIL FOR PUBLIC AFFAIRS (formerly NATIONAL JEWISH COMMUNITY RELATIONS ADVISORY COUNCIL) (1944). 443 Park Ave. S., 11th fl., NYC 10016-7322. (212)684-6950. FAX: (212)686-1353. E-mail: jcpainfo@thejcpa.org. Chmn. Michael Bohnen;; Exec. Dir. Dr. Hannah Rosenthal. National coordinating body for the field of Jewish community relations, comprising 13 national and 122 local Jewish community-relations agencies. Promotes understanding of Israel and the Middle East; supports Jewish communities around the world; advocates for equality and pluralism, and against discrimination, in American society. Through the Council's work, its constituent organizations seek agreement on policies, strategies, and programs for effective utilization of their resources for common ends. *Insider (Weekly).* (www.JEWISHPUBLICAFFAIRS.ORG)

JEWISH LABOR COMMITTEE (1934). Atran Center for Jewish Culture, 25 E. 21 St., NYC 10010. (212)477-0707. FAX: (212) 477-1918. Pres. Stuart Appelbaum; Exec. Dir. Avram B. Lyon. Serves as liaison between the Jewish community and the trade union movement; works with the U.S. and international labor movement to combat anti-Semitism, promote intergroup relations, and engender support for the State of Israel and Jews in and from the former Soviet Union; promotes teaching in public schools about the Holocaust and Jewish resistance; strengthens support within the Jewish community for the social goals and programs of the labor movement; supports Yiddish-language and cultural institutions. *Jewish Labor Committee Review; Issues Alert; Alumni Newsletter.*

——, NATIONAL TRADE UNION COUNCIL FOR HUMAN RIGHTS (1956). Atran Center for Jewish Culture, 25 E. 21 St., NYC 10010. (212)477-0707. FAX: (212)477-1918. Exec. Dir. Avram Lyon. Works with the American labor movement in advancing the struggle for social justice and equal opportunity, and assists unions in every issue affecting human rights. Fights discrimination on all levels and helps to promote labor's broad social and economic goals.

JEWISH PEACE FELLOWSHIP (1941). Box 271, Nyack, NY 10960. (914)358-4601. FAX: (914)358-4924. E-mail: jpf@forusa.org. Hon. Pres. Rabbi Philip Bentley; Ch. Murray Polner. Unites those who believe that Jewish ideals and experience provide inspiration for a nonviolent philosophy and way of life; offers draft counseling, especially for conscientious objection based on Jewish "religious training and belief"; encourages Jewish community to become more knowledgeable, concerned, and active in regard to the war/peace problem. *Shalom/Jewish Peace Letter.* (WWW.JEWISHPEACEFELLOWSHIP.ORG)

JEWISH WAR VETERANS OF THE UNITED STATES OF AMERICA (1896). 1811 R St., NW, Washington, DC 20009. (202)265-6280. FAX: (202)234-5662. E-mail: jwv@jwv.org. Natl. Exec. Dir. Herb Rosenbleeth; Natl. Commander Daniel Weiss. Seeks to foster true allegiance to the United States; to combat bigotry and prevent defamation of Jews; to encourage the doctrine of universal liberty, equal rights, and full justice for all; to cooperate with and support existing educational institutions and establish new ones; to foster the education of ex-servicemen, ex-servicewomen, and members in the ideals and principles of Americanism. *Jewish Veteran.*

——, NATIONAL MUSEUM OF AMERICAN JEWISH MILITARY HISTORY (1958). 1811 R St., NW, Washington, DC 20009. E-mail: nmajmh@nmajmh.org. (202)265-6280. FAX:(202)234-5662. Pres. Edwin Goldwasser; Archivist Tom Wildenberg. Documents and preserves the contributions of Jewish Americans to the peace and freedom of the United States; educates the public concerning the courage, heroism, and sacrifices made by Jewish Americans who served in the armed forces; and works to combat anti-Semitism. *The Jewish War Veteran).*

NATIONAL ASSOCIATION OF JEWISH LEGISLATORS (1976). 65 Oakwood St., Albany, NY 12208. (518)527-3353. FAX: (518) 458-8512. E-mail: najl01@aol.com. Exec. Dir. Marc Hiller; Pres. Sen. Richard Cohen, Minn. state senator. A nonpartisan Jewish state legislative network focusing on domestic issues and publishing newsletters. Maintains close ties with the Knesset and Israeli leaders.

NCSJ: ADVOCATES ON BEHALF OF JEWS IN RUSSIA, UKRAINE, THE BALTIC STATES AND EURASIA (formerly AMERICAN JEWISH CONFERENCE ON SOVIET JEWRY) (1964; reorg. 1971). 1640 Rhode Island Ave., NW, Suite 501, Washington, DC 20036-3278. (202)898-2500. FAX: (202)898-0822. E-mail: ncsj@ncsj.org. N.Y. office:823 United Nations Plaza, NYC 10017. (212)808-0295. Chmn. Robert J. Moth, M.D.; Pres. Dr. Joel M. Schindler; Eexc. Dir. Mark B. Levin. Coordinating agency for major national Jewish organizations and local community groups in the U.S., acting on behalf of Jews in the former Soviet Union (FSU); provides information about Jews in the FSU through public education and social action; reports and special pamphlets, special programs and projects, public meetings and forums. *Newswatch; annual report; action and program kits; Tekuma.* (WWW.NCSJ.ORG)

——, SOVIET JEWRY RESEARCH BUREAU. Chmn. Denis C. Braham; Pres. Howard E. Sachs. Organized by NCSJ to monitor emigration trends. Primary task is the accumulation, evaluation, and processing of information regarding Jews in the

FSU, especially those who apply for emigration.

NATIONAL JEWISH COMMUNITY RELATIONS ADVISORY COUNCIL (*see* JEWISH COUNCIL FOR PUBLIC AFFAIRS)

NATIONAL JEWISH DEMOCRATIC COUNCIL (1990). 777 N. Capital St., NE, Suite 305, Washington, DC 20002. (202)216-9060. FAX: (202)216-9061. E-mail: info@njdc. org. Chmn. Monte Friedkin; Founding Chmn. Morton Mandel; Exec. Dir. Ira N. Forman. An independent organization committed to strengthening Jewish participation in the Democratic party primarily through grassroots activism. The national voice of Jewish Democrats, NJDC is dedicated to fighting the radical right and promoting Jewish values and interests in the Democratic party. *Capital Communiqué; Extremist Watch.* (WWW. NJDC.ORG)

REPUBLICAN JEWISH COALITION (1985). 50 F Street, NW Suite 100, Washington, DC 20001. (202) 638-6688. FAX: (202)638-6694. E-mail: rjc@rjchq.org. Natl. Chmn. Sam Fox; Hon. Chmn. Max M. Fisher, Richard J. Fox, Lawrence Kadish, George Klein. Promotes involvement in Republican politics among its members; sensitizes Republican leaders to the concerns of the American Jewish community; promotes principles of free enterprise, a strong national defense, and an internationalist foreign policy. *RJC Bulletin.* (WWW.RJCHQ. ORG)

SHALEM CENTER (1994). 5505 Connecticut Avenue, NW, No. 1140, Washington, DC 20015. (877)298-7300. FAX: (888)766-1506. E-mail: shalem@shalem.org.il. Pres. Yoram Hazony (Israel); Academic Director, Daniel Polisar (Israel). The purposes and activities of the Shalem Center are to increase public understanding and conduct educational and research activities on the improvement of Jewish national public life, and to develop a community of intellectual leaders to shape the state of Israel into a secure, free, and prosperous society. *Azure.* (WWW. SHALEMCENTER.ORG)

SHALOM CENTER (1983). 6711 Lincoln Dr., Philadelphia, PA 19119. (215)844-8494. E-mail: shalomctr@aol.com. (Part of Aleph Alliance for Jewish Renewal.) Exec. Dir. Rabbi Arthur Waskow. Na-

tional resource and organizing center for Jewish perspectives on dealing with overwork in American society, environmental dangers, unrestrained technology, militarism, and corporate irresponsibility. Initiated A.J. Heschel 25th Yahrzeit observance. Trains next generation of *tikkun olam* activists. Holds colloquia on issues like environmental causes of cancer. *New Menorah.* (WWW.SHALOMCTR. ORG)

STUDENT STRUGGLE FOR SOVIET JEWRY (*see* CENTER FOR RUSSIAN JEWRY)

UN WATCH (1993). 1, rue de Varembé, PO Box 191, 1211 Geneva 20, Switzerland. (41-22)734.14.72. FAX: (41-22)734.16.13. E-mail: unwatch@unwatch.org. Exec. Dir. Andrew M. Srulevitch; Chm. Amb. Alfred H. Moses. An affiliate of the AJC, UN Watch measures UN performance by the yardstick of the UN's Charter; advocates the non-discriminatory application of the Charter; opposes the use of UN fora to attack Israel and promote anti-Semitism; and seeks to institutionalize at the UN the fight against worldwide anti-Semitism. *The Wednesday Watch (English and Spanish).* (WWW.UNWATCH.ORG)

UCSJ: UNION OF COUNCILS FOR JEWS IN THE FORMER SOVIET UNION (formerly UNION OF COUNCILS FOR SOVIET JEWS) (1970). 1819 H St., NW, Suite 230, Washington, DC 20005. (202)775-9770. FAX: (202)775-9776. E-mail: ucsj@ucsj.com. Pres. Yosef I. Abramowitz; Natl. Dir. Micah H. Naftalin. Devoted to promoting religious liberty, freedom of emigration, and security for Jews in the FSU (former Soviet Union) through advocacy and monitoring of anti-Semitism, neofacism, human rights, rule of law, and democracy. Offers educational, cultural, medical, and humanitarian aid through the Yad L'Yad partnership program pairing Jewish communities in the US and the FSU; advocates for refuseniks and political prisoner. (WWW.FSUMONITOR.COM)

WORLD CONGRESS OF GAY, LESBIAN, BISEXUAL & TRANSGENDER JEWS (1980). 8 Letitia St., Philadelphia, PA 19106-3050. (609)396-1972. FAX: (215)873-0108. E-mail: president@wcgljo.org. Pres. Scott R. Gansl (Philadelphia, PA); V.-Pres. Francois Spiero (Paris, France). Supports, strengthens, and represents over 67 Jewish gay and lesbian organizations across the globe and the needs of gay and lesbian Jews generally. Challenges homophobia and sexism within the Jewish community and responds to anti-Semitism at large. Sponsors regional and international conferences. *The Digest.* (WWW.WCGLJO.ORG/ WCGLJO/)

WORLD JEWISH CONGRESS (1936; org. in U.S. 1939). 501 Madison Ave., 17th fl., NYC 10022. (212) 755-5770. FAX: (212) 755-5883. Pres. Edgar M. Bronfman; Co-Chmn. N. Amer. Branch Prof. Irwin Cotler (Montreal) & Evelyn Sommer; Dr. Avi Beker, Secretary General. Seeks to intensify bonds of world Jewry with Israel; to strengthen solidarity among Jews everywhere and secure their rights, status, and interests as individuals and communities; to encourage Jewish social, religious, and cultural life throughout the world and coordinate efforts by Jewish communities and organizations to cope with any Jewish problem; to work for human rights generally. Represents its affiliated organizations-most representative bodies of Jewish communities in more than 80 countries and 35 national organizations in American section-at UN, OAS, UNESCO, Council of Europe, ILO, UNICEF, and other governmental, intergovernmental, and international authorities. *WJC Report; Boletin Informativo OJI; Dialogues; Dateline: World Jewry; Coloquio; Batfutsot; Gesher.*

CULTURAL

AMERICAN ACADEMY FOR JEWISH RESEARCH (1929). 420 Walnut Street, Philadelphia, PA 19106. (215)238-1290. FAX: (215)238-1540. Pres. Robert Chazan. Encourages Jewish learning and research; holds annual or semiannual meeting; awards grants for the publication of scholarly works. *Proceedings of the American Academy for Jewish Research; Texts and Studies; Monograph Series.*

AMERICAN GATHERING OF JEWISH HOLO-CAUST SURVIVORS. 122 W. 30 St., #205. NYC 10001. (212)239-4230. FAX: (212) 279-2926. E-mail: mail@american gathering.org. Pres. Benjamin Meed. Dedicated to documenting the past and passing on a legacy of remembrance. Compiles the National Registry of Jewish Holocaust Survivors-to date, the records

of more than 165,000 survivors and their families-housed at the U.S. Holocaust Memorial Museum in Washington, DC; holds an annual Yom Hashoah commemoration and occasional international gatherings; sponsors an intensive summer program for U.S. teachers in Poland and Israel to prepare them to teach about the Holocaust. *Together (newspaper).*

AMERICAN GUILD OF JUDAIC ART (1991). 15 Greenspring Valley Rd., Owings Mills, MD 21117. (410)902-0411. FAX: (410)581-0108. E-mail: office@jewishart. org. Pres. David Klass; 1st V.-Pres. Richard McBee. A not-for-profit membership organization for those with interests in the Judaic arts, including artists, galleries, collectors & retailers of Judaica, writers, educators, appraisers, museum curators, conservators, lecturers, and others personally or professionally involved in the field. Helps to promote members' art. *Hiddur (quarterly); Update (members' networking newsletter).* (WWW.JEWISHART. ORG)

AMERICAN JEWISH HISTORICAL SOCIETY (1892). 15 W. 16 St., NYC 10011. (212)294-6160. FAX: (212)294-6161. E-mail: ajhs@ajhs.cjh.org. Pres. Kenneth J. Bialkin; Dir. Dr. Michael Feldberg. Collects, catalogues, publishes, and displays material on the history of the Jews in America; serves as an information center for inquiries on American Jewish history; maintains archives of original source material on American Jewish history; sponsors lectures and exhibitions; makes available audiovisual material. *American Jewish History; Heritage.* (WWW.AJHS.ORG)

AMERICAN JEWISH PRESS ASSOCIATION (1944). Natl. Admin. Off.: 1828 L St. NW, Suite 720, Washington, DC 20036. (202)785-2282. FAX: (202)785-2307. E-mail: toby@ajpa.org. Pres. Aaron Cohen; Exec. Dir. Toby Dershowitz. Seeks the advancement of Jewish journalism and the maintenance of a strong Jewish press in the U.S. and Canada; encourages the attainment of the highest editorial and business standards; sponsors workshops, services for members; sponsors annual competition for Simon Rockower Awards for excellence in Jewish journalism. *Membership bulletin newsletter.*

AMERICAN SEPHARDI FEDERATION (1973). 15 W. 16 St., 6th Floor, NYC 10011. (212)294-8350. FAX: (212)294-8348. E-mail: asf@cjh.org. Hon. Pres. Leon Levy; Exec. Dir. Vivienne Roumani-Denn. The central voice of the American Sephardic community, representing a broad spectrum of Sephardic organizations, congregations, and educational institutions. Seeks to strengthen and unify the community through education, communication, advocacy, and leadership development, creating greater awareness and appreciation of its rich and unique history and culture. *Sephardic Today.* (WWW.ASFONLINE.ORG)

AMERICAN SOCIETY FOR JEWISH MUSIC (1974). c/o The Center for Jewish History, 15 W. 16 St., NYC 10011. (212)294-8328. FAX: (212)294-6161. Pres. Michael Leavitt; V.-Pres. Judith Tischler & Martha Novick; Sec. Fortuna Calvo Roth; Bd. Chmn. Rabbi Henry D. Michelman; Treas. Cantor Nathaniel Benjamin. Promotes the knowledge, appreciation, and development of Jewish music, past and present, for professional and lay audiences; seeks to raise the standards of composition and performance in Jewish music, to encourage research, and to sponsor performances of new and rarely heard works. *Musica Judaica Journal.*

ASSOCIATION OF JEWISH BOOK PUBLISHERS (1962). c/o Jewish Book Council, 15 East 26th Street, 10th Floor, New York, NY 10010. (212)532-4949. FAX: (212)481-4174. Email: arjhill@jewishbooks.com. Pres. Ellen Frankel. As a nonprofit group, provides a forum for discussion of mutual areas of interest among Jewish publishers, and promotes cooperative exhibits and promotional opportunities for members. Membership fee is $85 annually per publishing house.

ASSOCIATION OF JEWISH LIBRARIES (1965). 15 E. 26 St., 10th fl, NYC 10010. (212)725-5359. FAX: (212)481-4174. E-mail: ajl@jewishbooks.org. Pres. Pearl Berger; V.-Pres. Ronda Rose. Seeks to promote and improve services and professional standards in Jewish libraries; disseminates Jewish library information and guidance; promotes publication of literature in the field; encourages the establishment of Jewish libraries and collections of Judaica and the choice of Judaica librarianship as a profession; cocertifies Jewish libraries. *AJL Newsletter; Judaica Librarianship.*

B'NAI B'RITH KLUTZNICK NATIONAL JEWISH MUSEUM (1957). 1640 Rhode Island Ave., NW, Washington, DC 20036. (202)857-6583. FAX: (202)857-1099. A center of Jewish art and history in the nation's capital, maintains temporary and permanent exhibition galleries, permanent collection of Jewish ceremonial objects, folk art, and contemporary fine art, outdoor sculpture garden and museum shop, as well as the American Jewish Sports Hall of Fame. Provides exhibitions, tours, educational programs, research assistance, and tourist information.; *Permanent collection catalogue; temporary exhibit catalogues.*

CENTRAL YIDDISH CULTURE ORGANIZATION (CYCO), Inc. (1943 incorporated) (1948-non profit status). 25 E. 21 St., 3rd fl., NYC 10010. (212) 505-8305. FAX: (212)505-8044. E-mail: cycobooks@earthlink.net. Pres. Dr. Barnett Zumoff; Exec. Officer Hy Wolfe. To promote the Yiddish word that is Cyco's purpose. We do this through the promotion, publication and distribution of Yiddish books, music books, CDs, tapes and albums. All in Yiddish!

CONFERENCE ON JEWISH SOCIAL STUDIES, INC. (formerly CONFERENCE ON JEWISH RELATIONS, INC.) (1939). Bldg. 240, Rm. 103. Program in Jewish Studies, Stanford University, Stanford, CA 94305-2190. (650)725-0829. FAX:(650)725-2920. E-mail: jss@leland.stanford.edu. Pres. Steven J. Zipperstein; V.-Pres. Aron Rodrigue. *Jewish Social Studies.*

CONGREGATION BINA (1981). 600 W. End Ave., Suite 1-C, NYC 10024. (212)873-4261. E-mail: samueldivekar@hotmail.com . Pres. Joseph Moses; Exec. V.-Pres. Moses Samson; Hon. Pres. Samuel M. Daniel; Sec. Gen. Elijah E. Jhirad. Serves the religious, cultural, charitable, and philanthropic needs of the Children of Israel who originated in India and now reside in the U.S. Works to foster and preserve the ancient traditions, customs, liturgy, music, and folklore of Indian Jewry and to maintain needed institutions. *Kol Bina.*

CONGRESS FOR JEWISH CULTURE (1948). 25 E. 21 St., NYC 10010. (212)505-8040. FAX: (212)505-8044. E-mail: kongres@

earthlink.net. Exec. Dir. Shane Baker. Congress for Jewish Culture administers the book store CYCO and publishes the world's oldest Yiddish journal, *The Zukunft.* Currently producing a two volume anthology of Yiddish literature in America. Activities include yearly memorials for the Warsaw ghetto uprising and the murdered Soviet Yiddish writers, also readings and literary afternoons. *The Zukunft; Bulletin: In the World of Yiddish.*

ELAINE KAUFMAN CULTURAL CENTER (1952). 129 W. 67 St., NYC 10023. (212)501-3303. FAX: (212)874-7865. Email: lhard@ekcc.org. Hon. Chmn. Leonard Goodman; Chmn. Elaine Kaufman; Pres. Phyllis Feder; Exec. Dir. Lydia Kontos. Offers instruction in its Lucy Moses School for Music and Dance in music, dance, art, and theater to children and adults, in Western culture and Jewish traditions. Presents frequent performances of Jewish and general music by leading artists and ensembles in its Merkin Concert Hall and Ann Goodman Recital Hall. The Birnbaum Music Library houses Jewish music scores and reference books. *In Harmony (quarterly newsletter); EKCC Events (bimonthly calendar); Bimonthly concert calendars; catalogues and brochures.* (WWW.EKCC.ORG)

HISTADRUTH IVRITH OF AMERICA (1916; reorg. 1922). 426 W. 58 St., NYC 10019. (212)957-6658/9. Fax: (212)957-5811. E-mail: HebrewUSA@aol.com. Pres. Miriam Ostow; Exec. V.P. Moshe Margolin. Emphasizes the primacy of Hebrew in Jewish life, culture, and education; aims to disseminate knowledge of written and spoken Hebrew in N. America, thus building a cultural bridge between the State of Israel and Jewish communities throughout N. America. *Hadoar; Lamishpacha; Tov Lichtov; Sulam Yaakov; Hebrew Week; Ulpan.* (WWW.HEBREWUSA.ORG)

HOLOCAUST CENTER OF THE UNITED JEWISH FEDERATION OF GREATER PITTSBURGH (1980). 5738 Darlington Rd., Pittsburgh, PA 15217. (412)421-1500. FAX: (412)422-1996. E-mail: lhurwitz@ujf.net. Pres. Holocaust Comm. Chair Dr. Barbara Burstin; UJF. Ch. James A. Rudolph; Dir. Linda F. Hurwitz. Develops programs and provides resources to further understanding of the Holocaust and its impact

on civilization. Maintains a library, archive; provides speakers, educational materials; organizes community programs. Published collection of survivor and liberator stories. (WWW.UJFHC.NET)

HOLOCAUST MEMORIAL CENTER (1984). 6602 West Maple Rd., West Bloomfield, MI 48322. (248)661-0840. FAX: (248)661-4204. E-mail: info@holocaust center.org. Founder & Exec. V.-Pres. Rabbi Charles Rosenzveig. America's first free-standing Holocaust center comprising a museum, library-archive, oral history collection, garden of the righteous, research institute and academic advisory committee. Provides tours, lecture series, teacher training, Yom Hashoah commemorations, exhibits, educational outreach programs, speakers' bureau, computer database on 1,200 destroyed Jewish communities, guided travel tours to concentration camps and Israel, and museum shop. Published *World Reacts to the Holocaust; Survey of U.S. Federal, U.S. State and Canadian Provincial Support for Holocaust Education, Newsletter.*

HOLOCAUST MEMORIAL RESOURCE & EDUCATION CENTER OF CENTRAL FLORIDA (1982). 851 N. Maitland Ave., Maitland, FL 32751. (407)628-0555. FAX: (407)628-1079. E-mail: execdir@holocaustedu.org. Pres. Stan Sujka, MD; Bd. Chmn. Tess Wise. An interfaith educational center devoted to teaching the lessons of the Holocaust. Houses permanent multimedia educational exhibit; maintains library of books, videotapes, films, and other visuals to serve the entire educational establishment; offers lectures, teacher training, and other activities. *Newsletter; Bibliography; Holocaust-Lessons for Tomorrow; elementary and middle school curriculum.*

THE HOLOCAUST MUSEUM AND LEARNING CENTER IN MEMORY OF GLORIA GOLDSTEIN (1995) (formerly ST. LOUIS CENTER FOR HOLOCAUST STUDIES) (1977). 12 Millstone Campus Dr., St. Louis, MO 63146. (314)432-0020. FAX: (314)432-1277. E-mail: dreich@jfedstl.org. Chmn. Richard W. Stein; Curator/Dir. Of Ed. Dan A. Reich; Exec. Dir. Barbara Raznick; Dir. Of Admin. & Dev. Brian Bray. Develops programs and provides resources and educational materials to further an understanding of the Holocaust and its impact on civilization; has a 5,000 sq. ft. museum containing photographs, artifacts, and audiovisual displays. *Newsletter.*

INTERNATIONAL ASSOCIATION OF JEWISH GENEALOGICAL SOCIETIES (1988). 4430 Mt. Paran Pkwy NW, Atlanta, GA 30327-3747. (404)261-8662. Fax: (404) 228-7125. E-mail: homargol@aol.com. Pres. Howard Margol. Umbrella organization of more than 70 Jewish Genealogical Societies (JGS) worldwide. Represents organized Jewish genealogy, encourages Jews to research their family history, promotes new JGSs, supports existing societies, implements projects of interest to individuals researching their Jewish family histories. Holds annual conference where members learn and exchange ideas. (WWW.IAJGS.ORG)

INTERNATIONAL JEWISH MEDIA ASSOCIATION (1987). U.S.: c/o St. Louis Jewish Light, 12 Millstone Campus Dr., St. Louis, MO 63146. (314)432-3353. FAX: (314)432-0515. E-mail: stlouislgt@aol.com and ajpamr@aol.com. Israel:PO Box 92, Jerusalem 91920. 02-202-222. FAX: 02-513-642. Pres. Robert A. Cohn (c/o St. Louis Jewish Light); Exec. Dir. Toby Dershowitz. 1828 L St. NW, Suite 402, Washington, DC 20036. (202)785-2282. FAX: (202)785-2307. E-mail: toby@dershowitz.com. Israel Liaisons Jacob Gispan & Lifsha Ben-Shach, WZO Dept. of Info. A worldwide network of Jewish journalists, publications and other media in the Jewish and general media, which seeks to provide a forum for the exchange of materials and ideas and to enhance the status of Jewish media and journalists throughout the world. *IJMA Newsletter; Proceedings of the International Conference on Jewish Media.*

INTERNATIONAL NETWORK OF CHILDREN OF JEWISH HOLOCAUST SURVIVORS, INC. (1981). 13899 Biscayne Blvd. Suite 404, N. Miami, FL 33181. (305)919-5690. FAX: (305)919-5691. E-mail: info@hdec.org. Pres. Rositta E. Kenigsberg; Founding Chmn. Menachem Z. Rosensaft. Links Second Generation groups and individuals throughout the world. Represents the shared interests of children of Holocaust survivors; aims to perpetuate the authentic memory of the Holocaust and prevent its recurrence, to strengthen and preserve

the Jewish spiritual, ideological, and cultural heritage, to fight anti-Semitism and all forms of discrimination, persecution, and oppression anywhere in the world.

THE JACOB RADER MARCUS CENTER OF THE AMERICAN JEWISH ARCHIVES (1947). 3101 Clifton Ave., Cincinnati, OH 45220. (513) 221-1875 ext. 403. FAX: (513)221-7812. E-mail: aja@cn.huc.edu. Exec. Dir. Dr. Gary P. Zola. Promotes the study and preservation of the Western Hemisphere Jewish experience through research, publications, collection of important source materials, and a vigorous public-outreach program. *American Jewish Archives Journal, Monographs, Pamphlets, booklets, educational materials and posters.*

JEWISH BOOK COUNCIL (1946; reorg. 1993). 15 E. 26 St., NYC 10010. (212)532-4949, ext. 297. E-mail: jbc@jewishbooks.org. Pres. Rabbi Maurice S. Corson; Bd. Chmn. Henry Everett; Exec. Dir. Carolyn Starman Hessel. Serves as literary arm of the American Jewish community and clearinghouse for Jewish-content literature; assists readers, writers, publishers, and those who market and sell products. Provides bibliographies, list of publishers, bookstores, book fairs. Sponsors National Jewish Book Awards, Jewish Book Month, Jewish Book Fair Network. *Jewish Book Annual; Jewish Book World.* (WWW.JEWISHBOOKCOUNCIL.ORG)

THE JEWISH FEDERATION'S LOS ANGELES MUSEUM OF THE HOLOCAUST (MARTYRS MEMORIAL) (org. mid-1960s; opened 1978). 6006 Wilshire Blvd., Los Angeles, CA 90036. (323)761-8170. FAX: (323) 761-8174. E-mail: museumiemp@jewishla.org. Chmn. Gary John Schiller; Director Rachel L. Jayoela. A photo-narrative museum and resource center dedicated to Holocaust history, issues of genocide and prejudice, curriculum development, teacher training, research and exhibitions. *PAGES, a newslettr; Those Who Dared; Rescuers and Rescued; Guide to Schindler's List;Anne Frank:A Teaching.*

JEWISH HERITAGE PROJECT (1981). 150 Franklin St., #1W, NYC 10013. (212)925-9067. E-mail: jhpffh@jps.net. Exec. Dir. Alan Adelson. Strives to bring to the broadest possible audience authentic works of literary and historical value relating to Jewish history and culture. With funding from the National Endowment of the Arts, Jewish Heritage runs the National Initiative in the Literature of the Holocaust. Not a grant giving organization. Distributor of the film *Lodz Ghetto,* which it developed, as well as its companion volume *Lodz Ghetto:Inside a Community Under Siege; Better Than Gold: An Immigrant Family's First Years in Brooklyn.*

JEWISH MUSEUM (1904, under auspices of Jewish Theological Seminary). 1109 Fifth Ave., NYC 10128. (212)423-3200. FAX: (212)423-3232. Dir. Joan H. Rosenbaum; Bd. Chmn. Robert J. Hurst. Expanded museum features permanent exhibition on the Jewish experience. Repository of the largest collection of Jewish related paintings, prints, photographs, sculpture, coins, medals, antiquities, textiles, and other decorative arts-in the Western Hemisphere. Includes the National Jewish Archive of Broadcasting. Tours, lectures, film showings, and concerts; special programs for children; cafe; shop. *Special exhibition catalogues; annual report.* (WWW.THEJEWISHMUSEUM.ORG)

JEWISH PUBLICATION SOCIETY (1888). 2100 Arch St., 2nd fl., Philadelphia, PA 19103. (215)832-0600. FAX: (215)568-2017. E-mail: jewishbook@jewishpub.org. Pres. Allan R. Frank; CEO/Ed.-in-Chief Dr. Ellen Frankel. Publishes and disseminates books of Jewish interest for adults and children; titles include TANAKH, religious studies and practices, life cycle, folklore, classics, art, history. *Booklink JPS Catalogue.* (WWW.JEWISHPUB.ORG)

JUDAH L. MAGNES MUSEUM-JEWISH MUSEUM OF THE WEST (1962). 2911 Russell St., Berkeley, CA 94705. (510)549-6950. FAX: (510)849-3673. E-mail: pfpr@magnesmuseum.org. Pres. Fred Weiss; Dir. Susan Morris. Collects, preserves, and makes available Jewish art, culture, history, and literature from throughout the world. Permanent collections of fine and ceremonial art; rare Judaica library, Western Jewish History Center (archives), Jewish-American Hall of Fame. Changing exhibits, traveling exhibits, docent tours, lectures, numismatics series, poetry and video awards, museum shop. *Magnes News; special exhibition catalogues; scholarly books.*

JUDAICA CAPTIONED FILM CENTER, INC. (1983). PO Box 21439, Baltimore, MD 21282-1439. Voice Relay Service (1-800) 735-2258; TDD (410)655-6767. E-mail: lweiner@jhucep.org. Pres. Lois Lilienfeld Weiner. Developing a comprehensive library of captioned and subtitled films and tapes on Jewish subjects; distributes them to organizations serving the hearing-impaired, including mainstream classes and senior adult groups, on a free-loan, handling/shipping-charge-only basis. *Newsletter.*

LEAGUE FOR YIDDISH, INC. (1979). 200 W. 72 St., Suite 40, 5NYC 10023. (212)787-6675. E-mail: mschaecht@aol.com. Pres. Dr. Zuni Zelitch; Exec. Dir. Dr. Mordkhe Schaechter. Encourages the development and use of Yiddish as a living language; promotes its modernization and standardization; publisher of Yiddish textbooks and English-Yiddish dictionaries; most recent book *The Standardized Yiddish Orthography (New York, 200); Afn Shvel (quarterly).* (WWW.METALAB.UNC.EDU/YIDDISH/YIDLEAGUE)

LEO BAECK INSTITUTE, INC. (1955). 15 W. 16 St., NYC 10011-6301. (212)744-6400. FAX: (212)988-1305. E-mail: lbi1@lbi.com. Pres. Ismar Schorsch; Exec. Dir. Carol Kahn Strauss. A research, study, and lecture center, museum, library, and archive relating to the history of German-speaking Jewry. Offers lectures, exhibits, faculty seminars; publishes a series of monographs, yearbooks, and journals. *LBI News; LBI Yearbook; LBI Memorial Lecture; occasional papers.*

LIVING TRADITIONS (1994), (c/o WORKMAN'S CIRCLE) 45 East 33rd Street, New York, NY 10016. (212)532-8202. E-mail: henry@livingtraditions.org. Pres. Henry Sapoznik; V.-Pres. Sherry Mayrent. Nonprofit membership organization dedicated to the study, preservation, and innovative continuity of traditional folk and popular culture through workshops, concerts, recordings, radio and film documentaries; clearinghouse for research in klezmer and other traditional music; sponsors yearly weeklong international cultural event, "Yiddish Folk Arts Program/'KlezKamp.' " *Living Traditions (newsletter).* (WWW.LIVINGTRADITIONS.ORG)

THE MARTIN BUBER FORUM (1990), PMB #22112 365 West 25th Street, #19B., NYC (10001). (212)242-5637. Hon. Chmn. Prof. Maurice Friedman; Pres. Martin Warmbrand. Conducts discussion groups on the life and thought of Buber. *Martin Buber Review (annual)*.

MEMORIAL FOUNDATION FOR JEWISH CULTURE, INC. (1964). 50 West Broadway, 34th Floor, NYC 10004. (212)425-6606. FAX: (212)425-6602. Pres. Prof. Anita Shapira; Exec. V.-Pres. Jerry Hochbaum. Through the grants that it awards, encourages Jewish scholarship, culture, and education; supports communities that are struggling to maintain Jewish life; assists professional training for careers in communal service in Jewishly deprived communities; and stimulates the documentation, commemoration, and teaching of the Holocaust. (WWW.MFJC.ORG)

MUSEUM OF JEWISH HERITAGE—A LIVING MEMORIAL TO THE HOLOCAUST (1984). One Battery Park Plaza, NYC 10004-1484. (212)968-1800. FAX: (212)968-1368. Bd. Chmn. Robert M. Morgenthau; Museum Pres. Dr. Alfred Gottschalk; Museum Dir. David Marwell. New York tri-state's principal institution for educating people of all ages and backgrounds about 20th-century Jewish history and the Holocaust. Repository of Steven Spielberg's Survivors of the Shoah Visual History Foundation videotaped testimonies. Core and special exhibitions. *18 First Place (newsletter); Holocaust bibliography; educational materials*. (WWW.MJHNYC.ORG)

MUSEUM OF TOLERANCE OF THE SIMON WIESENTHAL CENTER (1993). 9786 W. Pico Blvd., Los Angeles, CA 90035-4792. (310)553-8403. FAX: (310)553-4521. E-mail: avra@wiesenthal.com. Dean-Founder Rabbi Marvin Hier; Assoc. Dean Rabbi Abraham Cooper; Exec. Dir. Rabbi Meyer May. A unique experiential museum focusing on personal prejudice, group intolerance, struggle for civil rights, and 20th-century genocides, culminating in a major exhibition on the Holocaust. Archives, Multimedia Learning Center designed for individualized research, 6,700-square-foot temporary exhibit space, 324-seat theater, 150-seat auditorium, and outdoor memorial plaza. (WWW.WIESENTHAL.COM)

NATIONAL CENTER FOR THE HEBREW LANGUAGE (1996). 15 E. 26th St., Ste. 921, NYC 10010. (212)339-6023. FAX: (212)318-6193. E-mail: ivrit@ivrit.org. Pres. Dr. Alvin I. Schiff; Exec. Dir. Dr. Joseph Lowin. The NCHL advocates for Hebrew language and culture; serves as a Hebrew resource center; and is a catalyst for networking in Hebrew language and culture. It coordinates a Mini-Ulpan at the GA, publishes "Directory of Hebrew Classes," organizes "Lunch & Hebrew Lit" nationwide, and runs a Conference of Hebrew Teacher Trainers. *IvritNow/IvritAkhshav.* (WWW.IVRIT.ORG)

NATIONAL FOUNDATION FOR JEWISH CULTURE (1960). 330 Seventh Ave., 21st fl., NYC 10001. (212)629-0500. FAX: (212)629-0508. E-mail: nfjc@jewishculture.org. Pres. Lynn Korda Kroll; Exec. Dir. Richard A. Siegel. The leading Jewish organization devoted to promoting Jewish culture in the U.S. Manages the Jewish Endowment for the Arts and Humanities; administers the Council of American Jewish Museums and Council of Archives and Research Libraries in Jewish Studies; offers doctoral dissertation fellowships, new play commissions, and grants for documentary films, recording of Jewish music, contemporary choregraphy, fiction and non-fiction writing, and cultural preservation; coordinates community cultural residencies, local cultural councils, and national cultural consortia; sponsors conferences, symposia, and festivals in the arts and humanities. *Jewish Culture News; Culture Currents (electronic)*.

NATIONAL MUSEUM OF AMERICAN JEWISH HISTORY (1976). Independence Mall E. 55 N. Fifth St. Philadelphia, PA 19106-2197. (215) 923-3811. FAX: (215) 923-0763. E-mail: nmajh@nmajh.org. Dir./CEO Gwen Goodman. The only museum in the nation to offer education, exhibits, and programs dedicated to preserving the history and culture of the Jewish people in America; located across from the Liberty Bell. (WWW.NMAJH.ORG)

NATIONAL MUSEUM OF AMERICAN JEWISH MILITARY HISTORY (*see* JEWISH WAR VETERANS OF THE U.S.A.)

NATIONAL YIDDISH BOOK CENTER (1980). 1021 West St., Amherst, MA 01002. (413)256-4900. FAX: (413)256-4700. E-mail: yiddish@bikher.org. Pres. Aaron Lansky; V.-Pres. Nancy Sherman. Since 1980 the center has collected 1.5 million Yiddish books for distribution to readers and libraries worldwide; digitized more than 12,000 Yiddish titles, offered a range of educational programs in Yiddish and modern culture, and published *Pakn Treger,* an award-winning English-language magazine. (WWW.YIDDISHBOOK CENTER.ORG)

ORTHODOX JEWISH ARCHIVES (1978). 42 Broadway, New York, NY 10004. (212)797-9000, ext. 73. FAX: (212)269-2843. Exec. V-Pres. Rabbi Shmuel Bloom & Shlomo Gertzullin; Dir. Rabbi Moshe Kolodny. Founded by Agudath Israel of America; houses historical documents, photographs, periodicals, and other publications relating to the growth of Orthodox Jewry in the U.S. and related communities in Europe, Israel, and elsewhere. Particularly noteworthy are its holdings relating to rescue activities organized during the Holocaust and its traveling exhibits available to schools and other institutions.

RESEARCH FOUNDATION FOR JEWISH IMMIGRATION, INC. (1971). 570 Seventh Ave., NYC 10018. (212)921-3871. FAX: (212) 575-1918. Sec./Coord. of Research Herbert A. Strauss; Archivist Dennis E. Rohrbaugh. Studies and records the history of the migration and acculturation of Central European German-speaking Jewish and non-Jewish Nazi persecutees in various resettlement countries worldwide, with special emphasis on the American experience. *International Biographical Dictionary of Central European Emigrés, 1933–1945; Jewish Immigrants of the Nazi Period in the USA.*

SEPHARDIC EDUCATIONAL CENTER (1979). 10808 Santa Monica Blvd., Los Angeles, CA 90025. (310)441-9361. FAX: (310) 441-9561. E-mail: secforever@aol.com. Founder & Chmn. Jose A. Nessim, M.D. Has chapters in the U.S., North, Central, and South America, Europe, and Asia, a spiritual and educational center in the Old City of Jerusalem, and executive office in Los Angeles. Serves as a meeting ground for Sephardim from many nations; sponsors the first worldwide movement for Sephardic youth and young adults. Disseminates information about Sephardic Jewry in the form of motion

pictures, pamphlets, and books, which it produces. *Hamerkaz (quarterly bulletin in English).* (WWW.SECWORLDWIDE.ORG)

SEPHARDIC HOUSE-THE CULTURAL DIVISION OF ASF (1978). 15 West 16th Street, NYC 10011. (212)294-6170. FAX: (212) 294-6149. E-mail: sephardichouse@cjh.org. Pres. Morrie R.Yohai; Dir. Dr. Janice E. Ovadiah. A cultural organization dedicated to fostering Sephardic history and culture; sponsors a wide variety of classes and public programs, film festivals, publication program disseminates materials of Sephardic value; outreach program to communities outside of the New York area; program bureau provides program ideas, speakers, and entertainers; International Sephardic Film Festival every year. *Sephardic House Newsletter; Publication Catalogue.* (WWW.SEPHARDIC HOUSE.ORG)

SIMON WIESENTHAL CENTER (1977). 1399 South Roxbury Drive., Los Angeles, CA 90035-4701. (310)553-9036. FAX: (310) 553-4521. Email: avra@wiesenthal.com. Dean-Founder Rabbi Marvin Hier; Assoc. Dean Rabbi Abraham Cooper; Exec. Dir. Rabbi Meyer May. Regional offices in New York, Miami, Toronto, Paris, Jerusalem, Buenos Aires. The largest institution of its kind in N. America dedicated to the study of the Holocaust, its contemporary implications, and related human-rights issues through education and awareness. Incorporates 185,000-sq.-ft. Museum of Tolerance, library, media department, archives, "Testimony to the Truth" oral histories, educational outreach, research department, international social action. *Response Magazine.* (WWW.WIESENTHAL. COM)

SKIRBALL CULTURAL CENTER (1996), an affiliate of Hebrew Union College. 2701 N. Sepulveda Blvd., Los Angeles, CA 90049. (310)440-4500. FAX: (310)440-4595. Pres. & CEO Uri D. Herscher; Bd. Chmn. Howard Friedman. Dedicated to exploring the connections between four thousand years of Jewish heritage and the vitality of American democratic ideals. It welcomes and seeks to inspire people of every ethnic and cultural identity. Guided by our respective memories and experiences, together we aspire to build a society in which all of us can feel at home. Skirball Cultural Center achieves its mission through pubic programs that explore literary, visual, and performing arts from around the world; through the display and interpretation of its permanent collections and changing exhibitions; through scholarship in American Jewish history and related publications; and through outreach to the community. (WWW.SKIRBALL.ORG)

SOCIETY FOR THE HISTORY OF CZECHOSLOVAK JEWS, INC. (1961). 760 Pompton Ave., Cedar Grove, NJ 07009. (973)239-2333. FAX: (973)239-7935. Pres. Rabbi Norman Patz; V.-Pres. Prof. Fred Hahn; Sec. Anita Grosz. Studies the history of Czechoslovak Jews; collects material and disseminates information through the publication of books and pamphlets; conducts annual memorial service for Czech Holocaust victims. *The Jews of Czechoslovakia (3 vols.); Review I-VI.*

THE SOCIETY OF FRIENDS OF TOURO SYNAGOGUE NATIONAL HISTORIC SITE, INC. (1948). 85 Touro St., Newport, RI 02840. (401)847-4794. FAX: (401)845-6790. E-mail: info@tourosynagogue.org. Pres. M. Bernard Aidinoff; Exec. Dir. Michael L. Balaban. Helps maintain Touro Synagogue as a national historic site, opening and interpreting it for visitors; promotes public awareness of its preeminent role in the tradition of American religious liberty; annually commemorates George Washington's letter of 1790 to the Hebrew Congregation of Newport. *Society Update.*

————, TOURO NATIONAL HERITAGE TRUST (1984). 85 Touro St., Newport, RI 02840. (401)847-0810. FAX (401)847-8121. Pres. Bernard Bell; Chmn. Benjamin D. Holloway. Works to establish national education center within Touro compound; sponsors Touro Fellow through John Carter Brown Library; presents seminars and other educational programs; promotes knowledge of the early Jewish experience in this country.

SPERTUS MUSEUM, SPERTUS INSTITUTE OF JEWISH STUDIES (1968). 618 S. Michigan Ave., Chicago, IL 60605. (312)322-1747. FAX: (312)922-6406. Pres. Spertus Institute of Jewish Studies, Dr. Howard A. Sulkin. The largest, most comprehensive Judaic museum in the Midwest with 12,000 square feet of exhibit space and a permanent collection of some 10,000

works reflecting 5,000 years of Jewish history and culture. Also includes the redesigned Zell Holocaust Memorial, permanent collection, changing visual arts and special exhibits, and the children's ARTIFACT Center for a hands-on archaeological adventure. Plus, traveling exhibits for Jewish educators, life-cycle workshops, ADA accessible. *Exhibition catalogues; educational pamphlets.*

————, ASHER LIBRARY, SPERTUS INSTITUTE OF JEWISH STUDIES, (approx. 1930), 618 S. Michigan Ave., Chicago, IL 60605. (312) 322-1749, FAX (312) 922-6406. Pres. Spertus Institute of Jewish Studeis, Dr. Howard A. Sulkin; Director, Asher Library, Glenn Ferdman. Asher Library is the largest public Jewish Library in the Midwest, with over 100, 000 books and 550 periodicals; extensive collections of music, art, rare books, maps and electronic resources; nearly 1,000 feature and documentary films available on video cassette. Online catalogue access available. Also, the Chicago Jewish Archives collects historical material of Chicago individuals, families, synagogues and organizations. *ADA accessible.*

SURVIVORS OF THE SHOAH VISUAL HISTORY FOUNDATION (1994). PO Box 3168, Los Angeles, CA 90078-3168. (818)777-7802. FAX: (818)866-0312. Exec. Dir. Ari C. Zev. A nonprofit organization, founded and chaired by Steven Spielberg, dedicated to videotaping and preserving interviews with Holocaust survivors throughout the world. The archive of testimonies will be used as a tool for global education about the Holocaust and to teach racial, ethnic, and cultural tolerance.

UNITED STATES HOLOCAUST MEMORIAL MUSEUM (1980; opened Apr. 1993). 100 Raoul Wallenberg Place, SW, Washington, DC 20024. (202)488-0400. FAX: (202)488-2690. Chmn. Fred S. Zeidman; Dir. Sara J. Bloomfeld. Federally chartered and privately built, its mission is to teach about the Nazi persecution and murder of six million Jews and millions of others from 1933 to 1945 and to inspire visitors to contemplate their moral responsibilities as citizens of a democratic nation. Opened in April 1993 near the national Mall in Washington, DC, the museum's permanent exhibition tells the story of the Holocaust through authentic artifacts, videotaped oral testimonies, documentary film, and historical photographs. Offers educational programs for students and adults, an interactive computerized learning center, and special exhibitions and community programs. *United States Holocaust Memorial Museum Update (bimonthly); Directory of Holocaust Institutions; Journal of Holocaust and Genocide Studies (quarterly).* (WWW.USHMM.ORG)

THE WILSTEIN (SUSAN & DAVID) INSTITUTE OF JEWISH POLICY STUDIES (1998). 160 Herrick Road, Newton Centre, MA 02459. (617)559-8790. FAX: (617)559-8791. E-mail: wilstein@hebrewcollege. edu. Dir. Dr. David M. Gordis; Assoc. Dir. Rabbi Zachary I. Heller; Chmn. Howard I. Friedman. The Wilstein Institute's West Coast Center in Los Angeles and East Coast Center at Hebrew College in Boston provide a bridge between academics, community leaders, professionals, and the organizations and institutions of Jewish life. The institute serves as an international research and development resource for American Jewry. *Bulletins, various newsletters, monographs, research reports, and books.*

YESHIVA UNIVERSITY MUSEUM (1973). Center for Jewish History, 15 W. 16 St., NYC 10011-6301. (212)294-8335. E-mail: dgoldman@yum.cjh.org. Dir. Sylvia A. Herskowitz; Chmn. Erica Jesselson. Collects, preserves, and interprets Jewish life and culture through changing exhibitions of ceremonial objects, paintings, rare books and documents, synagogue architecture, textiles, contemporary art, and photographs. Oral history archive. Special events, holiday workshops, live performances, lectures, etc. for adults and children. Guided tours and workshops are offered. Exhibitions and children's art education programs also at branch galleries on Yeshiva University's Main Campus, 2520 Amsterdam Ave., NYC 10033-3201. *Seasonal calendars; special exhibition catalogues; newsletters.*

YIDDISHER KULTUR FARBAND-YKUF (1937). 1133 Broadway, Rm. 820, NYC 10010. (212)243-1304. FAX: (212)243-1305. E-mail: mahosu@amc.one. Pres./Ed. Itche Goldberg. Publishes a bimonthly magazine and books by contemporary and classical Jewish writers; conducts cultural forums; exhibits works by contemporary Jewish artists and materials of Jewish historical value; organizes reading circles. *Yiddishe Kultur.*

YIVO INSTITUTE FOR JEWISH RESEARCH (1925). 15 W. 16 St., NYC 10011. (212) 246-6080. FAX: (212)292-1892. E-mail: yivomail@yivo.cjh.org. Chmn. Bruce Slovin; Exec. Dir. Dr. Carl J. Rheins. Engages in historical research and education pertaining to East European Jewish life; maintains library and archives which provide a major international, national and New York resource used by institutions, individual scholars, and the public; provides graduate fellowships in East European and American Jewish studies; offers Yiddish language classes at all levels, exhibits, conferences, public programs; publishes books. *Yedies-YIVO News; YIVO Bleter.*

———, MAX WEINREICH CENTER FOR ADVANCED JEWISH STUDIES/YIVO INSTITUTE (1968). 15 W. 16 St., NYC 10011. (212) 246-6080. FAX: (212)292-1892. E-mail: mweinreich@yivo.cjh.org. Provides advanced-level training in Yiddish language and literature, ethnography, folklore, linguistics, and history; offers guidance on dissertation or independent research; post-doctoral fellowships available.

YUGNTRUF-YOUTH FOR YIDDISH (1964). 200 W. 72 St., Suite 40, NYC 10023. (212)787-6675. FAX: (212)799-1517. E-mail: ruvn@aol.com. Chmn. Dr. Paul Glasser; V.-Chmn. Marc Caplan; Coord. Brukhe Lang Caplan. A worldwide, nonpolitical organization for young people with a knowledge of, or interest in, Yiddish; fosters Yiddish as a living language and culture. Sponsors all activities in Yiddish:reading, conversation, and creative writing groups; annual weeklong retreat in Berkshires; children's Yiddish play group; sale of shirts. *Yugntruf Journal.*

ISRAEL-RELATED

THE ABRAHAM FUND (1989). 477 Madison Ave., 4th fl., NYC 10022. (212)303-9421. FAX: (212)935-1834. E-mail: info@ AbrahamFund.org. Chmn. Alan B. Slifka, Exec. V.P. Dan Pattir. The Abraham Fund Initiatives (TAFI) seeks to enhance relations between Israel's Jewish and Arab citizens by promoting increased dialogue, understanding, and democracy. Founded in 1989, TAFI has contributed more than $8 million to community-based coexistence projects. TAFI also develops regional and national coexistence programs in partnership with other major institutions in Israel and orchestrates public advocacy campaigns to implement change.

AMERICA-ISRAEL CULTURAL FOUNDATION, INC. (1939). 51 E. 42nd St., Suite 400, NYC 10017. (212)557-1600. FAX: (212)557-1611. E-mail: info@aicf.org. Chmn. Emer. Isaac Stern (in memoriam); Pres. Vera Stern. Supports and encourages the growth of cultural excellence in Israel through grants to cultural institutions; scholarships to gifted young artists and musicians. *Newsletter.* (WWW.AICF.ORG)

AMERICA-ISRAEL FRIENDSHIP LEAGUE, INC. (1971). 134 E. 39 St., NYC 10016. (212) 213-8630. FAX: (212)683-3475. E-mail: aifl@aifl.org. Pres. Mortimer B. Zuckerman, Chmn. Bd. Kenneth J. Bialkin, Exec. V. Pres. Ilana Artman. A non-sectarian, non-partisan, not-for-profit organization which seeks to broaden the base of support for Israel among Americans of all faiths and backgrounds. Activities include educational exchanges, missions to Israel for American leadership groups, symposia and public-education activities, and the dissemination of multi media information. *Newsletter.*

AMERICAN ASSOCIATES, BEN-GURION UNIVERSITY OF THE NEGEV (1972). 1430 Broadway, 8th Floor, New York, NY 10018. (212)687-7721, (800)-AABGU. FAX: (212)302-6443. E-mail: info@aabgu.org. Pres. Zvi Alov; Exec. V-Pres. Seth Moscovitz. Since 1972, the American Associates, Ben—Gurion University of the Negev has played a vital role in building a world-class center for research and education in the desert. A nonprofit cooperation with ten regional offices throughout the United States, AABGU prides itself on its efficiency and effectiveness in raising funds to help Ben-Gurion University bring knowledge to the Negev and to the world. AABGU plays a vital role in helping BGU fulfill its unique responsisbility to develop the Negev, the focus of the future of Israel.(WWW.AABGU. ORG)

AMERICAN COMMITTEE FOR SHAARE ZEDEK MEDICAL CENTER IN JERUSALEM (1949). 49 W. 45 St., Suite 1100, NYC 10036. (212)354-8801. FAX: (212)391-2674. E-mail: pr@szmc.org.il. Natl. Pres. & Chmn. Intl. Bd. of Gov. Menno Ratzker; Chair Erica Jesselson. Increases awareness and raises funds for the various needs of this 100-year old hospital, including new medical centers of excellence, equipment, medical supplies, school of nursing and research; supports exchange program between Shaare Zedek Jerusalem Medical Center and Albert Einstein College of Medicine, NY. *Heartbeat Magazine.*

AMERICAN COMMITTEE FOR SHENKAR COLLEGE IN ISRAEL, INC. (1971). 855 Ave. of the Americas, #531, NYC 10001. (212) 947-1597. FAX: (212)643-9887. E-mail: acfsc@worldnet.att.net. Pres. Nahum G. (Sonny) Shar; Exec. Dir. Charlotte A. Fainblatt. Raises funds and coordinates projects and research with Shenkar College of Engineering and Design, Israel. A unique government academic institute in Israel dedicated to education and reaseach in areas impacting Israel's industries and its artistic and scientific development. Textile, Fashion, Interior and Product design courses are offered with Scientific courses:Plastics, Chemistry, Software and Industrial Management and Marketing. Certified by Israel's Council of Higher Education, it offers continuing education and complete testing facilities for the textile/apparel industry and plastics engineering. *Shenkar News.*

AMERICAN COMMITTEE FOR THE BEER-SHEVA FOUNDATION (1988). PO Box 179, NYC 10028. (212)534-3715. FAX: (973)992-8651. Pres. Ronald Slevin; Sr. V.-Pres. Joanna Slevin; Bd. Chmn. Sidney Cooperman. U.S. fundraising arm of the Beer-Sheva Foundation, which funds vital projects to improve the quality of life in the city of Beer-Sheva: nursery schools for pre-K toddlers, residential and day centers for needy seniors, educational programs, facilities and scholarships (especially for new olim, the physically and mentally challenged), parks, playgrounds, and other important projects. Also offers special services for immigrants—such as heaters, blankets, clothing, school supplies, etc. *Brochures.*

AMERICAN COMMITTEE FOR THE WEIZMANN INSTITUTE OF SCIENCE (1944). 130 E. 59 St., NYC 10022. (212)895-7900. FAX: (212)895-7999. E-mail: info@acwis. org. Chmn. Robert Asher; Pres. Albert

Willner, M.D.; Exec. V.-Pres. Martin Kraar. Through 13 regional offices in the U.S. raises funds, disseminates information, and does American purchasing for the Weizmann Institute in Rehovot, Israel, a world-renowned center of scientific research and graduate study. The institute conducts research in disease, energy, the environment, and other areas; runs an international summer science program for gifted high-school students. *Interface; Weizmann Now; annual report.* (WWW.WEIZMANN-USA.ORG)

AMERICAN FRIENDS OF ALYN HOSPITAL (1932). 51 East 42nd Street., Suite 3088, NYC 10017. (212)869-8085. FAX: (212) 768-0979. E-mail: friends@alynus. org. Pres. Minette Halpern Brown; Exec. Dir. Cathy M. Lanyard. Supports the Alyn Hospital (Woldenberg Family Hospital/Pediatric and Adolescent Rehabilitation Center) in Jerusalem. Treats children suffering from birth defects (such as muscular dystrophy and spina bifida) and traumas (terrorism, car accidents, cancer, and fire), enables patients and their families to achieve independence and a better quality of life. (WWW.ALYNUSA.ORG)

AMERICAN FRIENDS OF ASSAF HAROFEH MEDICAL CENTER (1975). PO Box 21051, NYC 10129. (212)481-5653. FAX: (212) 481-5672. Chmn. Kenneth Kronen; Exec. Dir. Rhoda Levental; Treas. Robert Kastin. Support group for Assaf Harofeh, Israel's third-largest government hospital, serving a poor population of over 400,000 in the area between Tel Aviv and Jerusalem. Raises funds for medical equipment, medical training for immigrants, hospital expansion, school of nursing, and school of physiotherapy. *Newsletter.*

AMERICAN FRIENDS OF BAR-ILAN UNIVERSITY (1955). 235 Park Ave. So., NYC 10003. (212)673-3460. FAX: (212)673-4856. Email: nationaladmin@biuny.com, beverlyf@biuny.com. Chancellor Rabbi Emanuel Rackman; Chmn. Global Bd. Aharon Dahan; Pres. Amer. Bd. Melvin Stein; Exec. V.-Pres. Gen. Yehuda Halevy. Supports Bar-Ilan University, an institution that integrates the highest standards of contemporary scholarship in liberal arts and sciences with a Judaic studies program as a requirement. Located in Ramat-Gan, Israel, and chartered by the Board of Regents of the State of NY. *Bar-Ilan News; Bar-Ilan University Scholar; Heritage Newsletter.*

AMERICAN FRIENDS OF BETH HATEFUTSOTH (1976). 633 Third Ave., 21st fl., NYC 10017. (212)339-6034. FAX: (212)318-6176. E-mail: afbhusa@aol.com. Pres. Stephen Greenberg; Chmn. Sam E. Bloch; Exec. Dir. Gloria Golan. Supports the maintenance and development of Beth Hatefutsoth, the Nahum Goldmann Museum of the Jewish Diaspora in Tel Aviv, and its cultural and educational programs for youth and adults. Circulates its traveling exhibitions and provides various cultural programs to local Jewish communities. Includes Jewish genealogy center (DOROT), the center for Jewish music, and photodocumentation center. *Beth Hatefutsoth (quarterly newsletter).*

AMERICAN FRIENDS OF HAIFA UNIVERSITY (*see* AMERICAN SOCIETY OF THE UNIVERSITY OF HAIFA)

AMERICAN FRIENDS OF HERZOG HOSPITAL/EZRATH NASHIM-JERUSALEM (1895). 800 Second Ave., 8th fl., NYC 10017. (212)499-9092. FAX:(212)499-9085. E-mail: herzogpr@hotmail.com. Co-Pres. Dr. Joy Zagoren , Amir Sternhell; Exec. Dir. Stephen Schwartz. Herzog Hospital is the foremost geriatric and psychiatric health care facility in Israel, and a leading research center in genetics, Alzheimer's and schizophrenia, with expertise in neurogeriatrics, physical rehabilitation, and long-term respiratory care. Its Israel Center for the Treatment of Psychotrauma provides therapy and seminars to help Israelis cope with the ongoing violence. (WWW.HERZOGHOSPITAL. ORG)

AMERICAN FRIENDS OF LIKUD. P.O.Box 8711, JAF Station, NYC 10116. (212)308-5595. FAX: (212)688-1327. E-mail: The likud@aol.com. Natl. Chmn. J. Phillip Rosen, Esq; Pres. Julio Messer,M.D; Natl. V. Pres. Jacques Torczyner; Natl. Treasurer Milton S. Shapiro, Esq.; Exec. Dir. Salomon L. Vaz Dias. promotes public education on the situation in the Middle East, particularly in Israel, as well as advancing a general awareness of Zionism; provides a solid partnership of public support for the State of Israel, its citizens and its democratically-elected governments.

AMERICAN FRIENDS OF NEVE SHALOM/ WAHAT AL-SALAM (1988). 4201 Church Road, Suite 4, NYC 10013. (856) 235-3667. FAX: (856) 235-4674. E-mail: afnswas @oasisofpeace.com. Pres. Deborah First; V.-Pres. Adeeb Fadil; Exec. Dir. Deanna Armbruster. Supports and publicizes the projects of the community of Neve Shalom/Wahat Al-Salam, the "Oasis of Peace." For more than twenty years, Jewish and Palestinian citizens of Israel have lived and worked together as equals. The community teaches tolerance, understanding and mutual respect well beyond its own borders by being a model for peace and reaching out through its educational institutions. A bilingual, bicultural Primary School serves the village and the surrounding communities.

AMERICAN FRIENDS OF RABIN MEDICAL CENTER (1994). 220 Fifth Avenue, Suite 1301, NYC 10001-7708. (212) 279-2522. Fax: (212)279-0179. E-mail: afrmc826@ aol.com. Bd. Chmn. Abraham E. "Barry" Cohen; Exec. Dir. Burton Lazarow. Supports the maintenance and development of this medical, research, and teaching institution in central Israel, which unites the Golda and Beilinson hospitals, providing 12% of all hospitalization in Israel. Department of Organ Transplantation performs 80% of all kidney and 60% of all liver transplants in Israel. Affiliated with Tel Aviv University's Sackler School of Medicine. *New Directions Quarterly.*

AMERICAN FRIENDS OF RAMBAM MEDICAL CENTER (1969). 226 West 26th Street, NYC 10001. (212)644-1049. FAX: (775)562-5399. E-mail: michaelstoler@ princetoncommercial.com. Pres/CEO. Michael R. Stoler. Represents and raises funds for Rambam Medical Center (Haifa), an 887-bed hospital serving approx. one-third of Israel's population, incl. the entire population of northern Israel (and south Lebanon), the U.S. Sixth Fleet, and the UN Peacekeeping Forces in the region. Rambam is the teaching hospital for the Technion's medical school.

TEL AVIV UNIVERSITY: AMERICAN COUNCIL (formerly AMERICAN FRIENDS OF TEL AVIV UNIVERSITY, INC.) (1955). 39 Broadway, 15th Floor., NYC 10006. (212)742-9070. FAX: (212)742-9071. Email: info@tauac.org. Pres. Sam Witkin; Natl. Chmn. Joel Tauber. Promotes higher education at Tel Aviv University, Israel's largest and most comprehensive institution of higher learning. Included in its nine faculties are the Sackler School of Medicine with its fully accredited NY State English-language program, the Rubin Academy of Music, and 70 research institutes, including the Moshe Dayan Center for Middle East & African Studies and the Jaffe Center for Strategic Studies. *Tel Aviv University News; FAX Flash, Connections Newsletter (quarterly).*

AMERICAN FRIENDS OF THE HEBREW UNIVERSITY (1925; inc. 1931). 11 E. 69 St., NYC 10021. (212)472-9800. FAX: (212) 744-2324. E-mail: info@afhu.org. Pres. Ira Lee Sorkin; Bd. Chmn. Keith L. Sachs; Exec. V.-Pres. Adam Kahan. Fosters the growth, development, and maintenance of the Hebrew University of Jerusalem; collects funds and conducts informational programs throughout the U.S., highlighting the university's achievements and its significance. *Wisdom; Scopus Magazine.* (WWW.AFHU.ORG)

AMERICAN FRIENDS OF THE ISRAEL MUSEUM (1972). 500 Fifth Ave., Suite 2540, NYC 10110. (212)997-5611. FAX: (212) 997-5536. Pres. Barbara Lane; Exec. Dir. Carolyn Cohen. Raises funds for special projects of the Israel Museum in Jerusalem; solicits works of art for permanent collection, exhibitions, and educational purposes. *Newsletter.*

AMERICAN FRIENDS OF THE ISRAEL PHILHARMONIC ORCHESTRA (AFIPO) (1972). 122 E. 42 St., Suite 4507, NYC 10168. (212)697-2949. FAX: (212)697-2943. Interim Pres. Lynn Syms; Exec. Dir. Suzanne K. Ponsot. Works to secure the financial future of the orchestra so that it may continue to travel throughout the world bringing its message of peace and cultural understanding through music. Supports the orchestra's international touring program, educational projects, and a wide array of musical activities in Israel. *Passport to Music (newsletter).*

AMERICAN FRIENDS OF THE OPEN UNIVERSITY OF ISRAEL. 180 W. 80 St., NYC 10024. (212)712-1800. FAX: (212)496-3296. E-mail: afoui@aol.com. Natl. Chmn. Irving M. Rosenbaum; Exec.V.-Pres. Eric G. Heffler. *Open Letter.*(WWW. OPENU.AC.IL)

AMERICAN FRIENDS OF THE SHALOM HARTMAN INSTITUTE (1976). One Penn Plaza, Suite 1606, New York, NY 10119. (212) 268-0300. FAX: (212)239-4550. E-mail: afshi@afshi.org. Pres. Richard F. Kaufman; Exec. Dir. Robbi Bensley. Supports the Shalom Hartman Institute in Jerusalem, an international center for pluralist Jewish education and research, serving Israel and world Jewry. Founded in 1976 by David Hartman, the Institute includes:the Institute for Advanced Judaic Studies, with research centers for contemporary halakha, religious pluralism, political thought and peace and reconciliation; the Institute for Teacher and Leadership Training, educating Israeli principals, teachers, graduate students and leaders; and the Institute for Diaspora Education, which offers seminars and sabbaticals to rabbis, educators and lay leaders of diverse ideological commitments. (WWW.HARTMANINSTITUTE. COM)

AMERICAN FRIENDS OF THE TEL AVIV MUSEUM OF ART (1974). 545 Madison Ave., 8th Floor (55 St.), NYC 10022. (212) 319-0555. FAX: (212)754-2987. Email: dnaftam@aol.com. Chmn. Steven P. Schwartz; Exec. Dir. Dorey Neilinger. Raises funds for the Tel Aviv Museum of Art for special projects, art acquisitions, and exhibitions; seeks contributions of art to expand the museum's collection; encourages art loans and traveling exhibitions; creates an awareness of the museum in the USA; makes available exhibition catalogues, monthly calendars, and posters published by the museum.

AMERICAN-ISRAEL ENVIRONMENTAL COUNCIL (formerly COUNCIL FOR A BEAUTIFUL ISRAEL ENVIRONMENTAL EDUCATION FOUNDATION) (1973). c/o Perry Davis Assoc., 25 W. 45 St., Suite 1405, NYC 10036. (212)840-1166. Fax: (212)840-1514. Pres. Alan Silberstein. A support group for the Israeli body, whose activities include education, town planning, lobbying for legislation to protect and enhance the environment, preservation of historical sites, the improvement and beautification of industrial and commercial areas, and sponsoring the CBI Center for Environmental Studies located in Yarkon Park, Tel Aviv. *Yearly newsletter; yearly theme oriented calendars in color.*

AMERICAN ISRAEL PUBLIC AFFAIRS COMMITTEE (AIPAC) (1954). 440 First St., NW, Washington, DC 20001. (202)639-5200. FAX: (202)347-4889. Pres. Lonny Kaplan; Exec. Dir. Howard A. Kohr. Registered to lobby on behalf of legislation affecting U.S.-Israel relations; represents Americans who believe support for a secure Israel is in U.S. interest. Works for a strong U.S.-Israel relationship. *Near East Report.* (WWW.AIPAC.ORG)

AMERICAN-ISRAELI LIGHTHOUSE, INC. (1928; reorg. 1955). 276 Fifth Ave., Suite 713, NYC 10001. (212)686-7110. Pres. Mrs. Leonard F. Dank; Sec. Mrs. Ida Rhein. Provides a vast network for blind and physically handicapped persons throughout Israel, to effect their social and vocational integration into the mainstream of their communities. Center of Services for the blind; built and maintains Rehabilitation Center for blind and handicapped persons (Migdal Or) in Haifa.

AMERICAN JEWISH LEAGUE FOR ISRAEL (1957). 130 E. 59 St., 12th Floor, NYC 10022. (212)371-1583. FAX: (646)497-0093. E-mail: AJLIMS@aol.com. Pres. Dr. Martin L. Kalmanson; Exec. Dir. Jeffrey Scheckner. Seeks to unite all those who, notwithstanding differing philosophies of Jewish life, are committed to the historical ideals of Zionism; works independently of class, party, or religious affiliation for the welfare of Israel as a whole. Not identified with any political parties in Israel. Member of World Jewish Congress, World Zionist Organization. *Newsletter.* (WWW.AMERICANJEWISH LEAGUE.ORG)

AMERICAN PHYSICIANS FELLOWSHIP FOR MEDICINE IN ISRAEL (1950). 2001 Beacon St., Suite 210, Boston, MA 02135-7771. (617)232-5382. FAX: (617) 739-2616. E-mail: apf@apfmed.org. Pres. Sherwood L. Gorbach, M.D.; Exec. Dir. Ellen-Ann Lacey. Supports projects that advance medical education, research, and care in Israel and builds links between the medical communities of Israel and N. Amer.; provides fellowships for Israeli physicians training in N. Amer. and arranges lectureships in Israel by prominent N. Amer. physicians; sponsors CME seminars in Israel and N. Amer.; coordinates U.S./Canadian medical emergency volunteers for Israel. *APF News.*

AMERICAN RED MAGEN DAVID FOR ISRAEL, INC. (1940) (a/k/a ARMDI & RED MAGEN DAVID). 888 Seventh Ave., Suite 403, NYC 10106. (212)757-1627. FAX: (212)757-4662. E-mail: armdi@att.net. Natl. Pres. Robert L. Sadoff, M.D.; Exec. V.-Pres. Benjamin Saxe. An authorized tax-exempt organization; the sole support arm in the U.S. of Magen David Adom (MDA), Israel's equivalent to a Red Cross Society; raises funds for the MDA emergency medical, ambulance, blood, and disaster services which help Israel's defense forces and civilian population. Helps to supply and equip ambulances, bloodmobiles, and cardiac rescue ambulances as well as 45 pre-hospital MDA Emergency Medical Clinics and the MDA National Blood Service Center and MDA Fractionation Institute in Ramat Gan, Israel. *Lifeline.*

AMERICAN SOCIETY FOR TECHNION-ISRAEL INSTITUTE OF TECHNOLOGY (1940). 810 Seventh Ave., 24th fl., NYC 10019. (212)262-6200. FAX: (212)262-6155. Pres. Evelyn Berger; Chmn. Larry Jackier; Exec. V.-Pres. Melvyn H. Bloom. The American Technion Society (ATS) raises funds for the Technion-Israel Institute of Technology. Based in New York City, it is the leading American organization with more than 20,000 supporters and 197 satellite offices around the country, the ATS is driven by the belief that the economic future of Israel is in high technology and the future of high technology in Israel is at the Technion. *Technion USA.* (WWW.ATS.ORG.MAIL)

AMERICAN SOCIETY FOR THE PROTECTION OF NATURE IN ISRAEL, INC. (1986). 28 Arrandale Ave., Great Neck, NY 11024. (212) 398-6750. FAX: (212) 398-1665. E-mail: aspni@aol.com. Co-Chmn. Edward I. Geffner & Russell Rothman. A nonprofit organization supporting the work of SPNI, an Israeli organization devoted to environmental protection and nature education. SPNI runs 26 Field Study Centers and has 45 municipal offices throughout Israel; offers education programs, organized hikes, and other activities; seeks ways to address the needs of an expanding society while preserving precious natural resources. *SPNI News.*

AMERICAN SOCIETY FOR YAD VASHEM (1981). 500 Fifth Ave., Suite 1600, NYC 10110-4299. (212)220-4304. FAX: (212)220-4308. E-mail: yadvashem@aol. com. Chmn. Eli Zborowski; Exec. Dir. Rochel U. Berman; Dev. Dir. Shraga Y. Mekel; Ed. Dir. Marlene Warshawski Yahalom, Ph.D. Development arm of Yad Vashem, Jerusalem, the central international authority created by the Knesset in 1953 for the purposes of commemoration and education in connection with the Holocaust. *Martyrdom and Resistance (newsletter).* (WWW.YADVASHEM.ORG)

AMERICAN SOCIETY OF THE UNIVERSITY OF HAIFA (formerly AMERICAN FRIENDS OF HAIFA UNIVERSITY) (1972). 220 Fifth Ave., Suite 1301, NYC 10001. (212) 685-7880. FAX: (212)685-7883. E-mail: asuhtr@att.net. Pres.Paul Amir; Sec./ Treas. Robert Jay Benowitz. Promotes, encourages, and aids higher and secondary education, research, and training in all branches of knowledge in Israel and elsewhere; aids in the maintenance and development of University of Haifa; raises and allocates funds for the above purposes; provides scholarships; promotes exchanges of teachers and students.

AMERICAN ZIONIST MOVEMENT (formerly AMERICAN ZIONIST FEDERATION) (1939; reorg. 1949, 1970, 1993). 110 E. 59 St., NYC 10022. (212)318-6100. FAX: (212) 935-3578. E-mail: info@azm.com. Pres. Melvin Salberg; Exec. Dir. Karen J. Rubinstein. Umbrella organization for 20 American Zionist organizations and the voice of united Zionism in the U.S. Conducts advocacy for Israel; strengthens Jewish identity; promotes the Israel experience; prepares the next generation of Zionist leadership. Regional offices in Chicago and Dallas. Groups in Detroit, Pittsburgh, Washington, DC. *The Zionist Advocate.* (WWW.AZM.ORG)

AMERICANS FOR A SAFE ISRAEL (AFSI) (1971). 1623 Third Ave., Suite 205, NYC 10128. (212)828-2424. FAX: (212)828-1717. E-mail: afsi@rcn.com. Chmn. Herbert Zweibon; Exec. Dir. Helen Freedman. Seeks to educate Americans in Congress, the media, and the public about Israel's role as a strategic asset for the West; through meetings with legislators and the media, in press releases and publications AFSI promotes Jewish rights to Judea and Samaria, the Golan, Gaza, an indivisible Jerusalem, and to all of Israel. AFSI believes in the concept of "peace for peace" and rejects the concept of "territory for peace." *The Outpost (monthly).* (WWW.AFSI.ORG.AFSI)

AMERICANS FOR PEACE NOW (1984). 1815 H St., NW, Suite 920, Washington, DC 20006. (202)728-1893. FAX: (202)728-1895. E-mail: apndc@peacenow.org. Pres. & CEO Debra DeLee; Chmn. Patricia Barr and Luis Lainer. Conducts educational programs and raises funds to support the Israeli peace movement, Shalom Achshav (Peace Now), and coordinates U.S. advocacy efforts through APN's Washington-based Center for Israeli Peace and Security. *Jerusalem Watch; Peace Now News; Settlement Watch; Fax Facts; Middle East Update (on-line); Benefits of Peace.* (WWW.PEACENOW.ORG)

AMIT (1925). 817 Broadway, NYC 10003. (212)477-4720. FAX: (212)353-2312. E-mail: info@amitchildren.org. Pres. Sondra Sokal; Exec. Dir. Marvin Leff. The State of Israel's official reshet (network) for religious secondary technological education; maintains innovative children's homes and youth villages in Israel in an environment of traditional Judaism; promotes cultural activities for the purpose of disseminating Zionist ideals and strengthening traditional Judaism in America. *AMIT Magazine.*

AMPAL-AMERICAN ISRAEL CORPORATION (1942). 1177 Avenue of the Americas, NYC 10036. (212)782-2100. FAX: (212) 782-2114. E-mail: ampal@aol.com. Bd. Chmn. Daniel Steinmetz; CEO Shuki Gleitman. Acquires interests in businesses located in the State of Israel or that are Israel-related. Interests include leisure-time, real estate, finance, energy distribution, basic industry, high technology, and communications. *Annual report; quarterly reports.*

ARZA/WORLD UNION, NORTH AMERICA (1977). 633 Third Ave., 6th fl., NYC 10017-6778. (212)650-4280. FAX: (212)650-4289. E-mail: arza/wupjna@uahc.org. Pres. Philip Meltzer; Exec. Dir. Rabbi Ammiel Hirsch. Membership organization dedicated to furthering the development of Progressive Judaism in Israel, the FSU, and throughout the world. Encourages Jewish solidarity, promoting religious pluralism and further-

ing Zionism. Works to strengthen the relationship of N. American Reform Jews with Progressive Jewish communities worldwide and to educate and inform them on relevant issues. *Quarterly newsletter.* (WWW.ARZAWUNA.ORG)

BETAR EDUCATIONAL YOUTH ORGANIZATION (1935). 4 East 34th Street, NYC, 10016. (646)742-9364. FAX: (646)742-9666. E-mail: newyork@betar.org. Pres. Dany Danon; Exec. Officer Itzik Simhon. Betar is a Zionist active college students' movement, which dedicates itself to promoting Israeli issues in the American media. Betar was founded in 1923 by Zeev Jabotinsky, among its' famous alumni are Nenachem Begin and Itzhak Shamir. Betar's goal is the gathering of all Jewish people in their ancient land.

BOYS TOWN JERUSALEM FOUNDATION OF AMERICA INC. (1948). 12 W. 31 St., Suite 300, NYC 10001. (212)244-2766. (800) 469-2697. FAX: (212)244-2052. E-mail: btjny@compuserve.com. Raphael Benaroya, Pres. Michael J. Scharf; Hon. Chmn. Josh S. Weston; Chmn. Raphael Benaroya; Exec. V.-Pres. Rabbi Ronald L. Gray. Raises funds for Boys Town Jerusalem, which was established in 1948 to offer a comprehensive academic, religious, and technological education to disadvantaged Israeli and immigrant boys from over 45 different countries, including Ethiopia, the former Soviet Union, and Iran. Enrollment:over 1,000 students in jr. high school, academic and technical high school, and a college of applied engineering. Boys Town was recently designated as the "CISCO Regional Academy," the first center in Jerusalem for the instruction of the CISCO Networking Management Program. *BTJ Newsbrief.*

CAMERA-COMMITTEE FOR ACCURACY IN MIDDLE EAST REPORTING IN AMERICA (1983). PO Box 35040, Boston, MA 02135. (617)789-3672. FAX: (617)787-7853. E-mail: media@camera.org. Pres./ Exec. Dir. Andrea Levin; Chmn. Joshua Katzen. CAMERA monitors media coverage of Israel, responds to error, omissions, and distortion, promotes factual information and works to educate the media and public about key issues related to conflict in the Middle East. CAMERA encourages members to participate in fostering full and fair coverage through communication with the media. *CAMERA Media Report (quarterly); CAMERA on Campus;CAMERA Media Directory, CAMERA Monographs, Action Alerts, Backgrounders.* (WWW.CAMERA.ORG)

COUNCIL FOR A BEAUTIFUL ISRAEL ENVIRONMENTAL EDUCATION FOUNDATION (*see* AMERICAN-ISRAEL ENVIRONMENTAL COUNCIL)

EMUNAH OF AMERICA (formerly HAPOEL HAMIZRACHI WOMEN'S ORGANIZATION) (1948). 7 Penn Plaza, NYC 10001. (212) 564-9045, (800)368-6440. FAX: (212)643-9731. E-mail: info@emunah.org. Natl. Pres. Dr. Marcia Genuth; Exec. V.-Pres. Carol Sufian. Maintains and supports 200 educational and social-welfare institutions in Israel within a religious framework, including day-care centers, kindergartens, children's residential homes, vocational schools for the underprivileged, senior-citizen centers, a college complex, and Holocaust study center. Also involved in absorption of Soviet and Ethiopian immigrants (recognized by Israeli government as an official absorption agency). *Emunah Magazine; Lest We Forget.* (WWW.EMUNAH.ORG)

FEDERATED COUNCIL OF ISRAEL INSTITUTIONS—FCII (1940). 4702 15th Ave., Brooklyn, NY 11219. (718)972-5530. Bd. Chmn. Z. Shapiro; Exec. V.-Pres. Rabbi Julius Novack. Central fund-raising organization for over 100 affiliated institutions; handles and executes estates, wills, and bequests for the traditional institutions in Israel; clearinghouse for information on budget, size, functions, etc. of traditional educational, welfare, and philanthropic institutions in Israel, working cooperatively with the Israeli government and the overseas department of the Council of Jewish Federations. *Annual financial reports and statistics on affiliates.*

FRIENDS OF THE ISRAEL DEFENSE FORCES (1981). 298 5th Avenue, NYC 10001. (212) 244-3118. FAX: (212)244-3119. E-mail: fidf@fidf.com. Chmn. Marvin Josephson; Pres. Jay Zises; Natl. Dir. Brig. Gen. Eliezer Hemeli. Supports the Agudah Lema'an Hahayal, Israel's Assoc. for the Well-Being of Soldiers, founded in the early 1940s, which provides social, recreational, and educational programs for soldiers, special services for the sick and wounded, and summer programs for widows and children of fallen soldiers. (WWW.FIDF.COM)

GESHER FOUNDATION (1969). 25 W. 45 St. Suite 1405, NYC 10036. (212)840-1166. FAX: (212)840-1514. E-mail: gesherfoundation@aol.com. Pres./Founder Daniel Tropper; Chmn. Philip Schatten. Seeks to bridge the gap between Jews of various backgrounds in Israel by stressing the interdependence of all Jews. Runs encounter seminars for Israeli youth; distributes curricular materials in public schools; offers Jewish identity classes for Russian youth, and a video series in Russian and English on famous Jewish personalities.

GIVAT HAVIVA EDUCATIONAL FOUNDATION, INC. (1966). 114 W. 26 St., Suite 1001, NYC 10001. (212)989-9272. FAX: (212) 989-9840. E-mail: mail@givathaviva.org. Chmn. Yvonne Baum Silverman. Supports programs at the Givat Haviva Institute, Israel's leading organization dedicated to promoting coexistence between Arabs and Jews, with 40,000 people participating each year in programs teaching conflict resolution, Middle East studies and languages, and Holocaust studies. Publishes research papers on Arab-Jewish relations, Holocaust studies, kibbutz life. In the U.S., GHEF sponsors public-education programs and lectures by Israeli speakers. *Givat Haviva News; special reports.* (WWW.DIALOGATE.ORG.IL)

HABONIM-DROR NORTH AMERICA (1935). 114 W. 26 St., Suite 1004, NYC 10001-6812. (212)255-1796. FAX: (212)929-3459. E-mail: programs@habonimdror.org. (Mazkir Tnua) Jamie Levin; Shliach Onri Welmer. Fosters identification with progressive, cooperative living in Israel; stimulates study of Jewish and Zionist culture, history, and contemporary society. Sponsors summer and year programs in Israel and on kibbutz, 7 summer camps in N. America modeled after kibbutzim, and *aliyah* frameworks. *B'Tnua (on-line and print newsletter).* (WWW.HABONIMDROR.ORG)

HADASSAH, THE WOMEN'S ZIONIST ORGANIZATION OF AMERICA, INC. (1912). 50 W. 58 St., NYC 10019. (212)355-7900. FAX: (212)303-8282. Pres. June Walker. Largest women's, largest Jewish, and largest Zionist membership organization in U.S. In Israel: Founded and funds Hadassah

Medical Organization, Hadassah College of Jerusalem, Hadassah Career Counseling Institute, Young Judaea summer and year-course programs, as well as providing support for Youth Aliyah and JNF. U.S. programs: Jewish and women's health education; advocacy on Israel, Zionism and women's issues; Young Judaea youth movement, including six camps; Hadassah Leadership Academy; Hadassah-Brandeis Institute for International Research on Jewish Women; Hadassah Foundation. *Hadassah Magazine; Update; Hadassah International Newsletter; Medical Update; American Scene.* (WWW.HADASSAH.ORG)

———, YOUNG JUDAEA (1909; reorg. 1967). 50 W. 58 St., NYC 10019. (212)303-8014. FAX: (212)303-4572. E-mail: info@ youngjudaea.org. Natl. Dir. Doron Krakow. Religiously pluralistic, politically nonpartisan Zionist youth movement sponsored by Hadassah; seeks to educate Jewish youth aged 8-25 toward Jewish and Zionist values, active commitment to and participation in the American and Israeli Jewish communities; maintains six summer camps in the U.S.; runs both summer and year programs in Israel, and a jr. year program in connection with both Hebrew University in Jerusalem and Ben Gurion University of the Negev. College-age arm, Hamagshimim, supports Zionist activity on campuses. *Kol Hat'nua; The Young Judaean; Ad Kahn.* (WWW.YOUNGJUDAEA. ORG)

HASHOMER HATZAIR, SOCIALIST ZIONIST YOUTH MOVEMENT (1923). 114 W. 26 St., Suite 1001, NYC 10001. (212)627-2830. FAX: (212)989-9840. E-mail: mail@ hashomerhatzair.org. Dir. Giora Salz; Natl. Sec. Moran Banai. Seeks to educate Jewish youth to an understanding of Zionism as the national liberation movement of the Jewish people. Promotes aliyah to kibbutzim. Affiliated with Kibbutz Artzi Federation. Espouses socialist-Zionist ideals of peace, justice, democracy, and intergroup harmony. *Young Guard.* (WWW.HASHOMERHAZAIR. ORG)

INTERNS FOR PEACE INTERNATIONAL (1976). 475 Riverside Dr., Room 240., NYC 10115. (212)870-2226. FAX: (914) 686-8896. E-mail: ifpus@mindspring. com. Intl. Dir. Rabbi Bruce M. Cohen;

Intl. Coord. Karen Wald Cohen. An independent, nonprofit, nonpolitical educational program training professional community peace workers. In Israel, initiated and operated jointly by Jews and Arabs; over 250 interns trained in 35 cities; over 80,000 Israeli citizens participating in joint programs in education, sports, culture, business, women's affairs, and community development; since the peace accord, Palestinians from West Bank and Gaza training as interns. Martin Luther King Project for Black/Jewish relations. *IFP Reports Quarterly; Guidebooks for Ethnic Conflict Resolution.* (WWW.INTERNSFORPEACE.ORG)

ISRAEL CANCER RESEARCH FUND (1975). 1290 Avenue of the Americas, NYC 10104. (212)969-9800. FAX: (212)969-9822. E-mail: mail@icrfny.org. Pres. Yashar Hirshaut, M.D.; Chmn. Leah Susskind; Exec. V.P. Donald Adelman. The largest single source of private funds for cancer research in Israel. Has a threefold mission:To encourage innovative cancer research by Israeli scientists; to harness Israel's vast intellectual and creative resources to establish a world-class center for cancer study; to broaden research opportunities within Israel to stop the exodus of talented Israeli cancer researchers. *Annual Report; Research Awards; ICRF Brochure; Newsletter.*

ISRAEL HISTADRUT FOUNDATION (*see* Israel Humanitarian Foundation)

ISRAEL HUMANITARIAN FOUNDATION (IHF) (1960). 276 Fifth Ave., Suite 901, NYC 10001. (212)683-5676, (800)434-5IHF. FAX: (212)213-9233. E-mail: info@ihf. net. Pres. Marvin M. Sirota; Exec.V.-Pres. Stanley J. Abrams. Since 1960, Israel Humanitarian Foundation (IHF) has funded more than 130 social service projects in Israel that provide funds and programs in a diverse range of areas. IHF strives to improve the standard of living of the Israeli population through its support for education, youth in need, elder care, the disables, and medical care & research projects that directly benefit thousands of people in need.

ISRAEL POLICY FORUM (1993). 165 East 56th Street, 2nd Floor, NYC 10022. (212)245-4227. FAX: (212)245-0517. E-mail: ipf@ipforum.org. 1030 15 St., NW, Suite 850, Washington, DC 20005. (202)842-

1700. FAX:(202)842-1722. E-mail: ipf@ipforum.org. Chmn. Jack Bendheim; Pres. Judy Stern Peck; Exec. Dir. Debra Wasserman. An independent leadership institution whose mission is to encourage an active U.S. role in resolving the Arab-Israeli conflict. IPF generates this support by involving leaders from the business, political, entertainment, academic, and philanthropic communitites in the peace effort, and by fostering a deeper understanding of the peace process among the American public. *Forum Fax, Washington Bulletin, Security Watch.* (WWW.IPFORUM.ORG)

THE JERUSALEM FOUNDATION, INC. (1966). 60 E. 42 St., Suite 1936, NYC 10165. (212) 697-4188. FAX: (212) 697-4022. E-mail: info@jfoundation.com. Chmn. Kenneth J. Bialkin; Exec. Dir. Dorothy Kauffman. A nonprofit organization devoted to improving the quality of life for all Jerusalemites, regardless of ethnic, religious, or socioeconomic background; has initiated and implemented more than 1,500 projects that span education, culture, community services, beautification, and preservation of the city's historic heritage and religious sites.

JEWISH INSTITUTE FOR NATIONAL SECURITY AFFAIRS (JINSA) (1976). (202)667-3900. E-mail: info@jinsa.org. Pres. Norman Hascoe; Exec. Dir. Tom Neumann. A nonprofit, nonpartisan educational organization working within the American Jewish community to explain the link between American defense policy and the security of the State of Israel; and within the national security establishment to explain the key role Israel plays in bolstering American interests. (WWW.JINSA.ORG)

JEWISH INSTITUTE FOR THE BLIND-JERUSALEM, INC. (1902, Jerusalem). 15 E. 26 St., NYC 10010. (212) 532-4155. FAX: (212) 447-7683. Pres. Rabbi David E. Lapp; Admin. Eric L. Loeb. Supports a dormitory and school for the Israeli blind and handicapped in Jerusalem. *INsight.*

JEWISH NATIONAL FUND OF AMERICA (1901). 42 E. 69 St., NYC 10021. (212)879-9300. (1-800-542-TREE). FAX: (212)570-1673. E-mail: communications @jnf.org. Pres. Ronald S. Lauder; Exec. V.-Pres. Russell F. Robinson. Jewish National Fund is the American fund-raising arm of Keren Kayemeth LeIsrael, the official land agency in Israel and is celebrating its 100th Anniversary this year. JNF works in the following areas:water resource development, afforestation and ecology, eduction, tourism and recreation, community development and research. (WWW.JNF.ORG)

JEWISH PEACE LOBBY (1989). 8604 Second Avnue, PMB 317, Silver Spring, MD 20910. (301)589-8764. FAX: (301)589-2722. Email: peacelobby@msn.com. Pres. Jerome M. Segal. A legally registered lobby promoting changes in U.S. policy vis-a-vis the Israeli-Palestinian conflict. Supports Israel's right to peace within secure borders; a political settlement based on mutual recognition of the right of self-determination of both peoples; a two-state solution as the most likely means to a stable peace. *Annual Report.*

KEREN OR, INC. JERUSALEM CENTER FOR MULTI-HANDICAPPED BLIND CHILDREN (1956). 350 Seventh Ave., Suite 200, NYC 10001. (212)279-4070. FAX: (212) 279-4043. E-mail: kerenorinc@aol.com. Chmn. Dr. Edward L. Steinberg; Pres. Dr. Albert Hornblass; Exec. Dir. Rochelle B. Silberman. Funds the Keren-Or Center for Multi-Handicapped Blind Children at 3 Abba Hillel Silver St., Ramot, Jerusalem, housing and caring for over 70 resident and day students who in addition to blindness or very low vision suffer from other severe physical and/or mental disabilities. Students range in age from 1 1/2 through young adulthood. Provides training in daily living skills, as well as therapy, rehabilitation, and education to the optimum level of the individual. *Insights Newsletter.*

LABOR ZIONIST ALLIANCE (formerly FARBAND LABOR ZIONIST ORDER) (1913). 275 Seventh Ave., NYC 10001. (212)366-1194. FAX: (212)675-7685. E-mail: labzionA@aol.com. Pres. Jeffry Mallow; Exec. Dir. Ari M. Chester. Seeks to enhance Jewish life, culture, and education in U.S.; aids in building State of Israel as a cooperative commonwealth and its Labor movement organized in the Histadrut; supports efforts toward a more democratic society throughout the world; furthers the democratization of the Jewish community in America and the welfare of Jews everywhere; works with labor and liberal forces in America; sponsors Habonim-Dror labor Zionist youth movement. *Jewish*

Frontier, Yiddisher Kempfer. (WWW.JEWISH FRONTIER.ORG)

MACCABI USA/SPORTS FOR ISRAEL (formerly UNITED STATES COMMITTEE SPORTS FOR ISRAEL) (1948). 1926 Arch St., 4R, Philadelphia, PA 19103. (215)561-6900. Fax: (215)561-5470. E-mail: maccabi@maccabiusa.com. Pres. Toni Worhman. Sponsors U.S. team for World Maccabiah Games in Israel every four years; seeks to enrich the lives of Jewish youth in the U.S., Israel, and the Diaspora through athletic, cultural, and educational programs; develops, promotes, and supports international, national, and regional athletic-based activities and facilities. *Sportscene Newsletter; Commemorative Maccabiah Games Journal; financial report.* (WWW.MACCABIUSA.COM)

MERCAZ USA (1979). 155 Fifth Ave., NYC 10010. (212)533-7800, ext. 2016. FAX: (212)533-2601. E-mail: info@mercazusa.org. Pres. Rabbi Vernon H. Kurtz; Exec. Dir. Rabbi Robert R. Golub. The U.S. Zionist organization for Conservative/Masorti Judaism; works for religious pluralism in Israel, defending and promoting Conservative/Masorti institutions and individuals; fosters Zionist education and *aliyah* and develops young leadership. *Mercaz USA Quarterly Newsletter.* (WWW.MERCAZUSA.ORG)

MERETZ USA FOR ISRAELI CIVIL RIGHTS AND PEACE (1991). 114 W. 26 St., Suite 1002, NYC 10001. (212)242-4500. FAX: (212)242-5718. E-mail: mail@meretzusa.org. Pres. Jeremiah S. Gutman; Exec. Dir. Charney V. Bromberg. A forum for addressing the issues of social justice and peace in Israel. Educates about issues related to democracy, human and civil rights, religious pluralism, and equality for women and ethnic minorities; promotes the resolution of Israel's conflict with the Palestinians on the basis of mutual recognition, self-determination, and peaceful coexistence. *Israel Horizons.* (WWW.MERETZUSA.ORG)

NA'AMAT USA, THE WOMEN'S LABOR ZIONIST ORGANIZATION OF AMERICA, INC. (formerly PIONEER WOMEN/NA'AMAT) (1925). 350 Fifth Ave., Suite 4700, NYC 10118-4799. (212)563-5222. FAX: (212) 563-5710. E-mail: naamat@naamat.org. Natl. Pres. Lynn Wax. Part of the World Movement of Na'amat (Movement of Working Women and Volunteers), the largest Jewish women's organization in the world, Na'amat USA helps provide social, educational, and legal services for women, teenagers, and children in Israel. It also advocates legislation for women's rights and child welfare in Israel and the U.S., furthers Jewish education, and supports Habonim Dror, the Labor Zionist youth movement. *Na'amat Woman magazine.* (WWW.NAAMAT.ORG)

NATIONAL COMMITTEE FOR LABOR ISRAEL (1923). 275 Seventh Ave., NYC 10001. (212)647-0300. FAX: (212)647-0308. E-mail: ncli@laborisrael.org. Pres. Jay Mazur; Exec. Dir. Jerry Goodman; Chmn. Trade Union Council Morton Bahr. Serves as a bridge among Israel's labor sector, including its General Federation of Labor, Histadrut, the American labor movement, the Jewish community and the general public. Brings together Jews and non-Jews to build support for Israel and advance closer Israel-Arab ties. Cooperates with Israels labor sector. National in scope, it conducts education in the Jewish community and among labor groups to promote better relations with labor Israel. Raises funds for youth, educational, health, social and cultural projects in Israel from a constituency which includes labor unions, foundations, government agencies and individual donors and supporters. *Occasional background papers* (WWW.LABORISRAEL.ORG

NEW ISRAEL FUND (1979). 1101 14th St., NW, 6th fl., Washington, DC 20005-5639. (202)842-0900. FAX: (202)842-0991. E-mail: info@nif.org. New York office:165 E. 56 St., NYC 10022. (212)750-2333. FAX: (212)750-8043. Pres. Yoram Peri; Exec. Dir. Norman S. Rosenberg. A partnership of Israelis and North Americans dedicated to promoting social justice, coexistence, and pluralism in Israel, the New Israel Fund helps strengthen Israeli democracy by providing grants and technical assistance to the public-interest sector, cultivating a new generation of social activists, and educating citizens in Israel and the Diaspora about the challenges to Israeli democracy. *Quarterly newsletter; annual report; other reports.* (WWW.NIF.ORG)

PEF ISRAEL ENDOWMENT FUNDS, INC. (1922). 317 Madison Ave., Suite 607, NYC 10017. (212)599-1260. Chmn. Sidney A. Luria; Pres. B. Harrison Frankel; Sec. Mark Bane. A totally volunteer organization that makes grants to educational, scientific, social, religious, health, and other philanthropic institutions in Israel. *Annual report.*

PIONEER WOMEN/NA'AMAT (*see* NA'AMAT USA)

POALE AGUDATH ISRAEL OF AMERICA, INC. (1948). 2920 Avenue J, Brooklyn, NY 11210. (718)258-2228. FAX: (718)258-2288. Pres. Rabbi Fabian Schonfeld. Aims to educate American Jews to the values of Orthodoxy and aliyah; supports kibbutzim, trade schools, yeshivot, moshavim, kollelim, research centers, and children's homes in Israel. *PAI News; She'arim; Hamayan.*

———, WOMEN'S DIVISION OF (1948). Pres. Miriam Lubling; Presidium: Sarah Ivanisky, Tili Stark, Peppi Petzenbaum. Assists Poale Agudath Israel to build and support children's homes, kindergartens, and trade schools in Israel. *Yediot PAI.*

PRO ISRAEL (1990). 1328 Broadway, Suite 435, NYC. (212)594-8996. FAX: (212) 594-8986. E-mail: proisrael@aol.com. Pres. Dr. Ernest Bloch; Exec. Dir. Rabbi Julian M. White. Educates the public about Israel and the Middle East; provides support for community development throughout the Land of Israel, particularly in Judea, Samaria, Gaza, and the Golan Heights. Projects include the Ariel Center for Policy Research and Professors for a Strong Israel.

PROJECT NISHMA (*see* ISRAEL POLICY FORUM)

RELIGIOUS ZIONISTS OF AMERICA (1909). 7 Penn Plaza, Suite 205, NYC 10001. (212)465-9234. FAX: (212)465-9246. Email: mizrachi@rza.org. Pres. Rabbi Simcha Krauss, Exec. V.P. Mandell I. Ganchrow. Disseminates ideals of religious Zionism; conducts cultural work, educational program, public relations; raises funds for religious educational institutions in Israel, including yeshivot hesder and Bnei Akiva. *Voice of Religious Zionism.* (WWW.RZA.ORG)

———, BNEI AKIVA OF THE U.S. & CANADA (1934). 7 Penn Plaza, Suite 205, NYC 10001. (212)465-9536. FAX: (212)465-2155. Shaliah, Rabbi Shaul Feldman; Natl. Dir. Steve Frankel. The only religious Zionist Youth movement in North America, Educating thousands of youths from grade school throughout the US and Canada. We have five summer camps in North America and a summer program in Israel. We educate towards the values of the Religious Zionist Movement which sees the place of all Jews, in Israel, involved in social action, and committed to Orthodox Torah values. *Akivon; Pinkas Lamadrich; Daf Rayonot; Me'Ohalai Torah; Zraim.* (WWW.BNEIAKIVA.ORG)

———, NATIONAL COUNCIL FOR TORAH EDUCATION (1939). 7 Penn Plaza, Suite 205, NYC 10001. (212)465-9234. FAX: (212)465-9246. E-mail: mizrachi@rza. org. Pres. Aaron S. Tirschwell, Chmn. Rabbi Mark Dratch. Organizes and supervises yeshivot and Talmud Torahs; prepares and trains teachers; publishes textbooks and educational materials; organizes summer seminars for Hebrew educators in cooperation with Torah Department of Jewish Agency; conducts ulpan. *Ohr HaMizrach, Torat Yisrael (weekly).* (WWW.RZA.ORG)

SCHNEIDER CHILDREN'S MEDICAL CENTER OF ISRAEL (1982). 130 E. 59 St., Suite 1203, NYC 10022. (212)759-3370. FAX: (212)759-0120. E-mail: mdiscmci@aol. com. Bd. Chmn. H. Irwin Levy; Exec. Dir. Shlomit Manson. Its primary goal is to provide the best medical care to children in the Middle East. *UPDATE Newsletter*

SOCIETY OF ISRAEL PHILATELISTS (1949). 24355 Tunbridge Lane, Beachwood, OH 44122. (216)292-3843. Pres. Robert B. Pildes. MD; Exec. Secry. Howard S. Chapman; Journal Ed. Dr. Oscar Stadtler. Promotes interest in, and knowledge of, all phases of Israel philately through sponsorship of chapters and research groups, maintenance of a philatelic library, and support of public and private exhibitions. *The Israel Philatelist; monographs; books.*

DEVELOPMENT CORPORATION FOR ISRAEL (formerly STATE OF ISRAEL BONDS) (1951). 575 Lexington Ave., 11th Floor, NYC 10022. (212)644-2663. FAX: (212) 644-3887. E-mail: raphael.rothstein@ israelbonds.com. Bd. Chmn. Burton P. Resnick; Pres./CEO Joshua Matza. An international organization offering securities issued by the government of Israel.

Since its inception in 1951 has secured $25 billion in investment capital for the development of every aspect of Israel's economic infrastructure, including agriculture, commerce, and industry, and for absorption of immigrants. *Israel Hadashot-News.* (WWW.ISRAELBONDS.COM)

THEODOR HERZL FOUNDATION (1954). 633 Third Ave., 21st fl., NYC 10017. (212)339-6040. FAX: (212)318-6176. Email: info@midstream.org. Chmn. Kalman Sultanik; Sec. Sam E. Bloch. Offers cultural activities, lectures, conferences, courses in modern Hebrew and Jewish subjects, Israel, Zionism, and Jewish history. *Midstream.*

———, HERZL PRESS. Chmn. Kalman Sultanik; Dir. of Pub. Sam E. Bloch. Serves as "the Zionist Press of record," publishing books that are important for the light they shed on Zionist philosophy, Israeli history, contemporary Israel and the Diaspora and the relationship between them. They are important as contributions to Zionist letters and history. *Midstream.*

TSOMET-TECHIYA USA (1978). 185 Montague St., 3rd fl., Brooklyn, NY 11201. (718)596-2119. FAX: (718)858-4074. E-mail: eliahu@aol.com. Chmn. Howard B. Weber. Supports the activities of the Israeli Tsomet party, which advocates Israeli control over the entire Land of Israel.

UNITED CHARITY INSTITUTIONS OF JERUSALEM, INC. (1903). 1467 48 St., Brooklyn, NY 11219. (718)633-8469. FAX: (718)633-8478. Chmn. Rabbi Charlop; Exec. Dir. Rabbi Pollak. Raises funds for the maintenance of schools, kitchens, clinics, and dispensaries in Israel; free loan foundations in Israel.

UNITED ISRAEL APPEAL, INC. (1925). 111 Eighth Ave., Suite 11E, NYC 10011. (212)284-6900. FAX: (212)284-6988. Chmn. Bennett L. Aaron; Exec. V.-Chmn. Daniel R. Allen. Provides funds raised by UJA/Federation campaigns in the U.S. to aid the people of Israel through the programs of the Jewish Agency for Israel, UIA's operating agent. Serves as link between American Jewish community and Jewish Agency for Israel; assists in resettlement and absorption of refugees in Israel, and supervises flow and expenditure of funds for this purpose. *Annual report; newsletters; brochures.*

UNITED STATES COMMITTEE SPORTS FOR ISRAEL (*see* MACCABI USA/SPORTS FOR ISRAEL)

US/ISRAEL WOMEN TO WOMEN (1979). 45 West 36th Street, 10th Floor, NYC 10018. (917) 351-0920. FAX: (917) 351-0921. E-mail: info@usisraelwomen.org. Ch. Nina Kaufman, esq.; Exec. Dir. Joan Gordon. Provides critical seed money for grassroots efforts advocating equal status and fair treatment for women in all spheres of Israeli life; targets small, innovative, Israeli-run programs that seek to bring about social change in health, education, civil rights, domestic violence, family planning, and other spheres of Israeli life. *Newsletters.* (WWW.USISRAELWOMEN.ORG)

VOLUNTEERS FOR ISRAEL (1982). 330 W. 42 St., Suite 1618, NYC 10036-6902. (212) 643-4848. FAX: (212)643-4855. E-mail: vol4israel@aol.com. Pres. Jeanne S. Schachter; Vice Pres. Carol Stein. Provides aid to Israel through volunteer work, building lasting relationships between Israelis and Americans. Affords persons aged 18 and over the opportunity to participate in various duties currently performed by overburdened Israelis on IDF bases and in other settings, enabling them to meet and work closely with Israelis and to gain an inside view of Israeli life and culture.

WOMEN'S LEAGUE FOR ISRAEL, INC. (1928). 160 E. 56 St., NYC 10022. (212)838-1997. FAX: (212)888-5972. E-mail: wliny@aol.com. Pres. Harriet Lainer; Exec. Dir. Dorothy Leffler. Maintains centers in Haifa, Tel Aviv, Jerusalem, Natanya. Projects include Family Therapy and Training, Centers for the Prevention of Domestic Violence, Meeting Places (supervised centers for noncustodial parents and their children), DROR (supporting families at risk), Yachdav-"Together" (long-term therapy for parents and children), the National Library for Social Work, and the Hebrew University Blind Students' Unit.

WORLD CONFEDERATION OF UNITED ZIONISTS (1946; reorg.1958). 130 E. 59 St., NYC 10022. (212)371-1452. FAX: (212) 371-3265. Co-Pres. Marlene Post & Kalman Sultanik. Promotes Zionist education, sponsors nonparty youth movements in the Diaspora, and strives for an Israel-oriented creative Jewish survival in the Diaspora. *Zionist Information Views (in English and Spanish).*

WORLD ZIONIST ORGANIZATION-AMERICAN SECTION (1971). 633 Third Ave., 21st fl., NYC 10017. (212)688-3197. Chmn. Kalman Sultanik. As the American section of the overall Zionist body throughout the world, it operates primarily in the field of aliyah from the free countries, education in the Diaspora, youth and Hechalutz, organization and information, cultural institutions, publications; conducts a worldwide Hebrew cultural program including special seminars and pedagogic manuals; disperses information and assists in research projects concerning Israel; promotes, publishes, and distributes books, periodicals, and pamphlets concerning developments in Israel, Zionism, and Jewish history. *Midstream.*

———, DEPARTMENT OF EDUCATION AND CULTURE (1948). 633 Third Ave., 21st fl., NYC 10017. (212)339-6001. FAX: (212) 826-8959. Renders educational services to boards and schools: study programs, books, AV aids, instruction, teacher-intraining service. Judaic and Hebrew subjects. Annual National Bible Contest; Israel summer and winter programs for teachers and students.

———, ISRAEL ALIYAH CENTER (1993). 633 Third Ave., 21st fl., NYC 10017. (212)339-6060. FAX: (212)832-2597. Exec. Dir. N. Amer. Aliyah Delegation, Kalman Grossman. Through 26 offices throughout N. Amer., staffed by *shlichim* (emissaries), works with potential immigrants to plan their future in Israel and processes immigration documents. Through Israel Aliyah Program Center provides support, information, and programming for olim and their families; promotes long-term programs and fact-finding trips to Israel. Cooperates with Tnuat Aliyah in Jerusalem and serves as American contact with Association of Americans and Canadians in Israel.

YOUTH RENEWAL FUND. 488 Madison Ave., 10th fl., NYC 10022. (212)207-3195. FAX: (212)207-8379. E-mail: info@youthrenewalfund.org. Pres. Samuel L. Katz; Exec. Dir. Karen L. Berman. The Youth Renewal Fund was established in 1989 to provide supplemental education to disadvantaged youth in Israel. Since inception, YRF has implemented over $10 million in programs that have benefited over 19,500 Israeli children. (WWW.YOUTHRENEWALFUND.ORG)

ZIONA. 641 Lexington Avenu, 24th Floor, New York, NY 10022. (212) 688-2890. FAX: (212) 688-1327. Email: thezionist @aol.com. Pres. Arnie T. Goldfarb; Ex. Vice Pres. Rev. Salomon L. Vaz Dias. ZIONA is a volunteer organization whose members are motivated and inspired to strengthen their partnership with Israel, ensure Jewish continuity, and realize their potential as a dynamic force in American society. In Israel, ZIONA initiates and supports education and youth institutions, and land development to meet the country's changing needs; helps to restore the ancient cemetery on the Mount of Olives in Jerusalem. *The Zionist Update* (WWW.ZIONA.ORG)

ZIONIST ORGANIZATION OF AMERICA (1897). ZOA House, 4 E. 34 St., NYC 10016. (212)481-1500. FAX: (212)481-1515. E-mail: email@zoa.com. Natl. Pres. Morton A. Klein; Exec. Dir. Robert Jancu, Esq. Strengthens the relationship between Israel and the U.S. through Zionist educational activities that explain Israel's importance to the U.S. and the dangers that Israel faces. Works on behalf of pro-Israel legislation; combats anti-Israel bias in the media, textbooks, travel guides, and on campuses; promotes *aliyah.* Maintains the ZOA House in Tel Aviv, a cultural center, and the Kfar Silver Agricultural and Technical High School in Ashkelon, which provides vocational training for new immigrants. *ZOA Report; Israel and the Middle East: Behind the Headlines.*(WWW.ZOA.ORG)

OVERSEAS AID

AMERICAN FRIENDS OF THE ALLIANCE ISRAÉLITE UNIVERSELLE, INC. (1946). 420 Lexington Ave., Suite 1731, NYC 10170. (212)808-5437. FAX: (212)983-0094. E-mail: afaiu@onsiteaccess.com. Pres. Albert Sibony; Asst. Batya Minkowitz. Participates in educational and human-rights activities of the AIU and supports the Alliance system of Jewish schools, teachers' colleges, and remedial programs in Israel, North Africa, the Middle East, Europe, and Canada. *Alliance Review.*

AMERICAN JEWISH JOINT DISTRIBUTION COMMITTEE, INC.—JDC (1914). 711 Third Ave., NYC 10017-4014. (212)687-6200. FAX:(212)370-5467. E-mail:newyork @jdcny.org. Pres. Eugene J. Ribakoff; Exec. V.-Pres. Steven Schwager. Provides assistance to Jewish communities in Europe, Asia, Africa, and the Mideast, including welfare programs for Jews in need. Current concerns include:Rescuing Jews from areas of distress, facilitating community development in the former Soviet Union; helping to meet Israel's social service needs by developing innovative programs that create new opportunities for the country's most vulnerable populations; youth activities in Eastern Europe and nonsectarian development and disaster assistance. *Annual Report; Snapshots: JDC's Activities in the Former Soviet Union; JDC: One People, One Heart.* (WWW.JDC.ORG).

AMERICAN JEWISH PHILANTHROPIC FUND (1955). 122 E. 42 St., 12th fl., NYC 10168-1289. (212)755-5640. FAX: (212)644-0979. Pres. Charles J. Tanenbaum. Provides college scholarship assistance to Jewish refugees through pilot programs being administered by the Jewish Family Service in Los Angeles and NYANA in New York.

AMERICAN JEWISH WORLD SERVICE (1985). 45 West 36th Street., NYC 10018. (212) 736-2597. FAX: (212)736-3463. E-mail:jws@ajws.org. Chmn. Marty Friedman; Pres. Ruth W. Messinger. Provides nonsectarian, humanitarian assistance and emergency relief to people in need in Africa, Asia, Latin America, Russia, Ukraine, and the Middle East; works in partnership with local nongovernmental organizations to support and implement self-sustaining grassroots development projects; serves as a vehicle through which the Jewish community can act as global citizens. *AJWS Reports (newsletter).* (WWW.AJWS.ORG)

AMERICAN ORT, INC. (1922). 817 Broadway, NYC 10003. (212)353-5800/(800)364-9678. FAX: (212)353-5888. E-mail: infor@aort.org. Pres. Robert L. Sill; Exec. Dir. Paul B. Firstenburg. American ORT coordinates all ORT operations in the U.S., in cooperation with Women's American ORT; promotes and raises funds for ORT, a non-political organization and the largest non-governmental global educa-tion and training organization in the world. With past and present activities in over 100 countries, ORT has educated nearly 4 million people in a global network of high schools, colleges, apprenticeship programs and teacher training institutes. This year, ORT's global network enables its 300,000 students in more than 60 countries to pursue fruitful careers and live lives of hope. Students at ORT schools everywhere around the world rely on funds raised by American ORT to help them meet tuition costs, build the most up-to-date learning facilities and furnish them with cutting-edge learning tools, computers, laboratories and other equipment. In Israel, 100,000 students attend 145 schools and training centers; there are 47 ORT schools and centers in the CIS (the former Soviet Union) and in the Baltic States; and in the U.S., over 15,000 students are served by ORT's Technical Institutes in Chicago, Los Angeles, and New York, and in Jewish day school programs in Atlanta, Chicago, Cleveland, Detroit, Florida, Los Angeles, and the National Capital Area (Washington, D.C.). Jewish day school students are served by ORT compute technology programs in Atlanta, Cleveland and Miami. (WWW.AORT.ORG)

———, WOMEN'S AMERICAN ORT (1927). 250 Park Ave. S., NYC 10003-1494. (212)505-7700; (800)51-WAORT. FAX: (212)674-3057. E-mail: waort@waort. org. Pres. Carol Linch; Exec. V.P. & Dir. Alice Herman. Strengthens the worldwide Jewish community by empowering people to achieve economic self-sufficiency through technological and vocational training; educates 290,000 students in 60 countries including the United States, Israel and the former Soviet Union; supports ORT programs through membership, fundraising and leadership development; domestic agenda promotes quality public education, women's rights and literacy. *Women's American ORT Reporter; Women's American ORT Annual Report.* (WWW.WAORT.ORG)

CONFERENCE ON JEWISH MATERIAL CLAIMS AGAINST GERMANY, INC. (1951). 15 E. 26 St., Rm. 906, NYC 10010. (212)696-4944. FAX: (212)679-2126. E-mail: info@ claimscon.org. Pres. Dr. Israel Singer; Exec. V.-Pres. Gideon Taylor. Represents Jewish survivors in negotiations for compensation from the German government and other entities once controlled by the Nazis. Also an operating agency that administers compensation funds, recovers Jewish property and allocates funds to institutions that serve Holocaust survivors. The Claims Conference—made up of the conference on Jewish Material Claims Against Germany and the Committee for Jewish Claims on Austria—is one of the founders of the World Jewish Restitution Organization, Memorial Foundation for Jewish Culture and the United Restitution Organization. *Newsletter; Annual Report; Guide to Restitution and Compensation; Special Update.* (www. CLAIMSCON.ORG)

HIAS, INC. (HEBREW IMMIGRANT AID SOCIETY) (1880; reorg. 1954). 333 Seventh Ave., NYC 10001-5004. (212)967-4100. FAX: (212)967-4483. E-mail:public@hias.org. Chair Neil Greenbaum; Pres. & CEO Leonard Glickman. The oldest international migration and refugee resettlement agency in the United States, dedicated to assisting persecuted and oppressed people worldwide and delivering them to countries of safe haven. As the migration arm of the American Jewish community, it also advocates for fair and just policies affecting refugees and immigrants. Since its founding in 1881, the agency has rescued more than four and a half million people. *Bi-Annual report.*

THE JEWISH FOUNDATION FOR THE RIGHTEOUS (1986). 305 Seventh Ave., 19th fl., NYC 10001. (212)727-9955. FAX: (212) 727-9956. E-mail: jfr@jfr.org. Pres. Paul Goldberger; Exec. V.P. Stanlee J. Stahl. Provides monthly support to 1,700 aged and needy Righteous Gentiles living in 30 countries who risked their lives to save Jews during the Holocaust. The Foundation's education program focuses on educating teachers and their students about the history of the Holocaust and the significance of altruistic behavior for our society. *Newsletter (3 times a year).* (www. JFR.ORG)

NORTH AMERICAN CONFERENCE ON ETHIOPIAN JEWRY (NACOEJ) (1982). 132 Nassau St., Suite 412, NYC 10038. (212)233-5200. FAX: (212)233-5243. E-mail: nacoej@aol.com. Pres. Judith L. Wolf; Exec. Dir. Barbara Ribakove Gordon. Provides programming for Ethiopian Jews in Israel in the areas of education (elementary school, high school and college) and cultural preservation. Assists Ethiopian Jews remaining in Ethiopia. National speakers bureau offers programs to synagogues, schools, and Jewish and non-Jewish organizations. Exhibits of Ethiopian Jewish artifacts, photos, handicrafts, etc. available. *Lifeline (newsletter).* (WWW.NACOEJ.ORG)

RE'UTH WOMEN'S SOCIAL SERVICE, INC. (1937). 130 E. 59 St., Suite 1200, NYC 10022. (212)836-1570. FAX: (212)836-1114. Chmn. Ursula Merkin; Pres. Rosa Strygler. Maintains, in Israel, subsidized housing for self-reliant elderly; old-age homes for more dependent elderly; Lichtenstadter Hospital for chronically ill and young accident victims not accepted by other hospitals; subsidized meals; Golden Age clubs. Recently opened a wing for chronically ill children. *Annual dinner journal.*

THANKS TO SCANDINAVIA, INC. (1963). The American Jewish Committee, 165 East 56th Street, 8th Fl., NYC 10022. (212)891-1403. FAX: (212)838-2120. Email: tts@ajc.org. Pres. Richard Netter; Exec. Dir. Rebecca Neuwirth. Provides scholarships and fellowships at U.S. universities and medical centers and Israeli educational institutions to students/teachers/medical professionals from Denmark, Finland, Norway, and Sweden in lasting appreciation of the rescue of Jews during World War II and to build friendships based on those examples of courage and humanity in history. (WWW.THANKSTOSCANDIAIVIA.ORG)

UJA FEDERATION OF NORTH AMERICA. (1939). (*see* United Jewish Communities)

UNITED JEWISH COMMUNITIES (1999). 111 Eighth Ave., 11th fl., NYC 10011-5201. (212)284-6500. FAX: (212)284-6822. Chmn. James Tisch; Pres./CEO Stephen H. Hoffman. Formed from the merger of the United Jewish Appeal, the Council of Jewish Federations and United Israel Appeal, is the dominant fundraising arm for North American Jewry, and represents 189 Jewish Federations and 400 independent communities across the continent. It reflects the values and traditions of education, leadership, advocacy and social justice, and continuity of community that define the Jewish people.

RELIGIOUS AND EDUCATIONAL ORGANIZATIONS

AGUDATH ISRAEL OF AMERICA (1922). 42 Broadway, NYC, 10004. (212)797-9000. FAX: (646)254-1600. E-mail: shafran@agudathisrael.org. Exec. V.-Pres. Rabbi Shmuel Bloom; Exec. Dir. Rabbi Boruch B. Borchardt. Mobilizes Orthodox Jews to cope with Jewish problems in the spirit of the Torah; speaks out on contemporary issues from an Orthodox viewpoint; sponsors a broad range of projects aimed at enhancing religious living, education, children's welfare, protection of Jewish religious rights, outreach to the assimilated and to arrivals from the former Soviet Union, and social services. *Jewish Observer; Dos Yiddishe Vort; Coalition.*

——, AGUDAH WOMEN OF AMERICA-N'SHEI AGUDATH ISRAEL (1940). 42 Broadway, NYC 10004. (212)363-8940. FAX: (212)747-8763. Presidium Aliza Grund & Rose Isbee; Dir. Hannah Kalish, Esq. Organizes Jewish women for philanthropic work in the U.S. and Israel and for intensive Torah education. Its new division, N'shei C.A.R.E.S., (Community, Awareness, Responsibility, Education, & Support), conducts seminars and support groups promoting the health and well-being of Jewish women and their families.

——, BOYS' DIVISION-PIRCHEI AGUDATH ISRAEL (1925) 42 Broadway, NYC 10004 (212)797-9000. Natl. Coord. Rabbi Shimon Grama. Educates Orthodox Jewish children in Torah; encourages sense of communal responsibility. Branches sponsor weekly youth groups and Jewish welfare projects. National Mishnah contests, rallies, and conventions foster unity on a national level. *Leaders Guides.*

——, GIRLS' DIVISION—BNOS AGUDATH ISRAEL (1921). 42 Broadway, NYC 10004. (646)254-1600. Natl. Dir. Leah Zagelbaum. Sponsors regular weekly programs on the local level and unites girls from throughout the Torah world with extensive regional and national activities. *Kol Bnos.*

——, YOUNG MEN'S DIVISION—ZEIREI AGUDATH ISRAEL (1921) . . . 42 Broadway, NYC 10004. (212)797-9000, ext. 57. Dir. Rabbi Labish Becker. Educates youth to see Torah as source of guidance for all issues facing Jews as individuals and as a people. Inculcates a spirit of activism through projects in religious, Torah-educational, and community-welfare fields. *Am Hatorah; Daf Chizuk.*

AGUDATH ISRAEL WORLD ORGANIZATION (1912) 42 Broadway, 14th Floor, NYC 10004. (212)797-9000. FAX: (212)254-1650. Chmn. Rabbi Yehudah Meir Abramowitz; U.N. Rep. Prof. Harry Reicher, Esq. Represents the interests of Orthodox Jewry on the national and international scenes. Sponsors projects to strengthen Torah life worldwide.

ALEPH: ALLIANCE FOR JEWISH RENEWAL (1963; reorg. 1993). 7000 Lincoln Drive, #B2, Philadelphia, PA 19119-3046. (215)247-9700. FAX: (215)247-9703. E-mail: alephajr@aol.com. Bd. Chmn. David Steinmetz; Rabbinic Dir. Rabbi Daniel Siegel. Serving the worldwide grassroots movement for Jewish spiritual renewal, ALEPH organizes and nurtures communities, trains lay and rabbinic leaders, creates new liturgy and adult learning resources, sponsors conferences, retreats and seminars and works for social and environmental justice. *New Menorah online journal and KolAleph/Or Hador combined quarterly newsletter of the Aleph and the Network of Jewish Renewal Communities (NJRC).* (WWW.ALEPH.ORG)

AM KOLEL JUDAIC RESOURCE CENTER (1990). 15 W. Montgomery Ave., Rockville, MD 20850. (301)309-2310. FAX: (301)309-2328. E-mail: amkolel@aol.com. Pres. David Shneyer. An independent Jewish resource center, providing a progressive Jewish voice in the community. Activities include:religion, educational and cultural programs; classes, workshops and seminars; interfaith workshops and programs; tikkun olam (social action) opportunities. The staff provides training and resources to emerging and independent communities throughout N. America. Am Kolel sponsors Jews United for Justice, the Center for Inclusiveness in Jewish Life (CIJL) and Yedid DC. *Directory of Independent Jewish Communities and Havurot in Maryland, DC and Virginia; Rock Creek Haggadah.*

AMERICAN ASSOCIATION OF RABBIS (1978). 350 Fifth Ave., Suite 3304, NYC 10118. (212)244-3350, (516)244-7113. FAX: (516)344-0779. E-mail: tefu@aol.com.

Pres. Rabbi Jeffrey Wartenberg; Exec. Dir. Rabbi David L. Dunn. An organization of rabbis serving in pulpits, in areas of education, and in social work. *Quarterly bulletin; monthly newsletter.*

AMERICAN STUDENTS TO ACTIVATE PRIDE (ASAP/OU College Affairs) (1993). 11 Broadway, 14th fl., NYC 10004. (212) 563-4000. FAX: (212)564-9058. E-mail: davidfel@ix.netcom.com. Pres. Zelda Goldsmith; Natl. Dir. Rabbi David Felsenthal; Chmn. Bernard Falk. A spiritual fitness movement of Jewish college students promoting Torah learning and discussion. Supports 100 learning groups at over 65 campuses as well as regional and national seminars and shabbatonim. *Good Shabbos (weekly); Rimon Discussion Guide (monthly); Jewish Student College Survival Guide (yearly).*

ASSOCIATION FOR JEWISH STUDIES (1969). MB 0001, Brandeis University, PO Box 549110, Waltham, MA 02454-9110. (781)736-2981. FAX: (781)736-2982. E-mail: ajs@brandeis.edu. Pres. Lawrence H. Schiffman; Exec. Dir. Aaron L. Katchen. Seeks to promote, maintain, and improve the teaching of Jewish studies in colleges and universities by sponsoring meetings and conferences, publishing a newsletter and other scholarly materials, aiding in the placement of teachers, coordinating research, and cooperating with other scholarly organizations. *AJS Review; AJS Perspectives.* (WWW. BRANDEIS.EDU/AJS)

ASSOCIATION FOR THE SOCIAL SCIENTIFIC STUDY OF JEWRY (1971). c/o Prof. Carmel U. Chiswick, Department of Economics (m/c 144), University of Illinois at Chicago, 601 S. Morgan Street, Chicago, Il 60607-7121 (312)996-2683. FAX: (312)996-3344. E-mail: exec@assj.org. Pres. Sherry Israel; V.-Pres. Riv-Ellen Prell; Sec.-Treas. Carmel Chiswick. Journal Ed. Samuel Heilman; Mng. Ed. Uriel Heilman. Arranges academic sessions and facilitates communication among social scientists studying Jewry through meetings, journal, newsletter and related materials and activities. *Contemporary Jewry; Newsletter (electronic).*

ASSOCIATION OF HILLEL/JEWISH CAMPUS PROFESSIONALS (*see* TEKIAH: ASSOCIATION OF HILLEL/JEWISH CAMPUS PROFESSIONALS)

ASSOCIATION OF ORTHODOX JEWISH SCIENTISTS (1948). 25 W. 45ᵗˢᴸ˙ Suite 1405, NYC 10036. (212)840-1166. FAX: (212)840-1514. E-mail: aojs@jerusalemail.com. Pres. Allen J. Bennett, M.D.; Bd. Chmn. Rabbi Nachman Cohen. Seeks to contribute to the development of science within the framework of Orthodox Jewish tradition; to obtain and disseminate information relating to the interaction between the Jewish traditional way of life and scientific developments—on both an ideological and practical level; to assist in the solution of problems pertaining to Orthodox Jews engaged in scientific teaching or research. Two main conventions are held each year. *Intercom; Proceedings; Halacha Bulletin; newsletter.*

B'NAI B'RITH HILLEL FOUNDATIONS (*see* HILLEL)

B'NAI B'RITH YOUTH ORGANIZATION (1924, became independent in 2002). 2020 K Street, NW, 7th Floor, Washington, DC 20006. (202)857-6633. FAX: (212)857-6568. Chmn. Lynn Schusterman; Intl. Dir. Brian Greene. Organized in local chapters, BBYO is a youth led international organization offering leadership opportunities and Jewish programming, which helps Jewish teenagers achieve self-fulfillment and contribute to the community. Assists members acquire a greater knowledge and appreciation for the Jewish religion, culture and the State of Israel. (WWW.BBYO.ORG)

CANTORS ASSEMBLY (1947). 3080 Broadway, Suite 613, NYC 10027. (212)678-8834. FAX: (212)662-8989. E-mail: caoffice@ aol.com. Pres. Sheldon Levin; Exec. V.-Pres. Stephen J. Stein. Seeks to unite all cantors who adhere to traditional Judaism and who serve as full-time cantors in bona fide congregations to conserve and promote the musical traditions of the Jews and to elevate the status of the cantorial profession. *Annual Proceedings; Journal of Synagogue Music.* (WWW. CANTORS.ORG)

CENTER FOR CHRISTIAN-JEWISH UNDERSTANDING OF SACRED HEART UNIVERSITY (1992). 5151 Park Ave., Fairfield, CT 06825. (203)365-7592. FAX: (203)365-4815. E-mail: jhe@sacredheart.edu. Pres. Dr. Anthony J. Cernera; Exec. Dir. Rabbi Joseph H. Ehrenkranz. An educational and research division of Sacred Heart

University; brings together clergy, laity, scholars, theologians, and educators with the purpose of promoting interreligious research, education, and dialogue, with particular focus on current religious thinking within Christianity and Judaism. *CCJU Perspective.*

CENTRAL CONFERENCE OF AMERICAN RABBIS (1889). 355 Lexington Ave., NYC 10017. (212)972-3636. FAX: (212)692-0819. E-mail: info@ccarnet.org. Pres. Rabbi Janet Marder; Exec. V.-Pres. Rabbi Paul J. Menitoff. Seeks to conserve and promote Judaism and to disseminate its teachings in a liberal spirit. The CCAR Press provides liturgy and prayerbooks to the worldwide Reform Jewish community. *CCAR Journal: A Reform Jewish Quarterly; CCAR Yearbook.* (WWW.CCARNET.ORG)

CLAL—NATIONAL JEWISH CENTER FOR LEARNING AND LEADERSHIP (1974). 440 Park Ave. S., 4th fl., NYC 10016-8012. (212)779-3300. FAX: (212)779-1009. E-mail: info@clal.org. Pres. Rabbi Irwin Kula; Chmn. Thomas O. Katz; Exec. V.-Chmn. Donna M. Rosenthal. Provides leadership training for lay leaders, rabbis, educators, and communal professionals. A faculty of rabbis and scholars representing all the denominations of Judaism make Judaism come alive, applying the wisdom of the Jewish heritage to help shape tomorrow's Jewish communities. Offers seminars and courses, retreats, symposia and conferences, lecture bureau and the latest on-line information through CLAL web site. *Sacred Days calendar; monographs; holiday brochures; CLAL Update.* (WWW.CLAL.ORG)

COALITION FOR THE ADVANCEMENT OF JEWISH EDUCATION (CAJE) (1977). 261 W. 35 St., #12A, NYC 10001. (212)268-4210. FAX: (212)268-4214. E-mail: cajeny@caje.org. Pres. Alan Wiener; Exec. Dir. Dr. Eliot G. Spack. The Coalition for the Advancement of Jewish Education (CAJE), the largest membership organization of Jewish educators in North America, hosts annual conferences and offers outreach programming, teacher recruitment, and mentoring, a Job Bank, and a Curriculum Response Service. CAJE has established an Early Childhood Department. Though its Hanukat CAJE Committee, CAJE advocates on behalf of Jewish educators. *Jewish Education News; CAJE Page; timely curricular publications; Hanukat CAJE series.* (WWW.CAJE.ORG)

CONGRESS OF SECULAR JEWISH ORGANIZATIONS (1970). 19657 Villa Dr. N., Southfield, MI 48076. (248)569-8127. FAX: (248)569-5222. E-mail: csjd@csjd.org. Chmn. Alan J. Wiener; V.-Chmn. Karen Knecht; Exec. Dir. Dr. Eliot G. Spack. An umbrella organization of schools and adult clubs; facilitates exchange of curricula and educational programs for children and adults stressing the Jewish historical and cultural heritage and the continuity of the Jewish people. *New Yorkish (Yiddish literature translations); Haggadah; The Hanuka Festival; Mame-Loshn.*

CONVERSION TO JUDAISM RESOURCE CENTER (1997). 74 Hauppauge Rd., Rm. 53, Commack, NY 11725. (631) 462-5826. E-mail: inform@convert.org. Pres. Dr. Lawrence J. Epstein; Exec. Dir. Susan Lustig. Provides information and advice for people who wish to convert to Judaism or who have converted. Puts potential converts in touch with rabbis from all branches of Judaism.

COUNCIL FOR JEWISH EDUCATION (1926) 11 Olympia Lane, Monsey, NY 10952-2829. (845)368-8657, Fax (845)369-6583. E-mail: mjscje@aol.com. Pres. Dr. Morton J. Summer; Editor Rabbi Irwin E. Witty. Fellowship of Jewish education professionals-administrators, supervisors, and teachers in Hebrew high schools and Jewish teachers colleges-of all ideological groupings; conducts national and regional conferences; represents the Jewish education profession before the Jewish community; cooperates with Jewish Agency Department of Education in promoting Hebrew culture and studies. *Journal of Jewish Education.*

EDAH (1996) 47 W. 34 St., Suite 700, NYC 10001. (212) 244-7501. FAX: (212)244-7855. Pres. Dr. Michael Hammer; Dir. Rabbi Saul J. Berman. Gives voice to the ideology and values of modern Orthodoxy, valuing open intellectual inquiry and expression in both secular and religious arenas, engagement with the social, political, and technological realities of the modern world, the religious significance of the State of Israel, and the unity of Clal Yisrael. *Monograph series.* (WWW.EDAH.ORG)

FEDERATION OF JEWISH MEN'S CLUBS (1929). 475 Riverside Dr., Suite 832, NYC 10115. (212)749-8100; (800)288-FJMC. FAX: (212)316-4271. E-mail: international @fjmc.org. Intl. Pres. Bob Levine; Exec. Dir. Rabbi Charles E. Simon. Promotes principles of Conservative Judaism; develops family education and leadership training programs; offers the Art of Jewish Living series and Yom HaShoah Home Commemoration; sponsors Hebrew literacy adult-education program; presents awards for service to American Jewry. Latest innovation-"The Ties that Bind," a motivational and instructional video about Tefillin. *Torchlight; Hearing Men's Voices.* (WWW.FJMC.ORG)

FEDERATION OF RECONSTRUCTIONIST CONGREGATIONS AND HAVUROT (*see* JEWISH RECONSTRUCTIONIST FEDERATION)

HILLEL: THE FOUNDATION FOR JEWISH CAMPUS LIFE (formerly B'NAI B'RITH HILLEL FOUNDATIONS) (1923). Charles and Lynn Schusterman International Center, Arthur and Rochelle Belfer Building, 800 Eight Street, NW, Washington, DC 20001-3724. (202)449-6500. FAX: (202)449-6600. E-mail: info@hillel.org. Chmn. Intl. Bd. Govs. Edgar M. Bronfman; Bd. Dir. Neil M. Moss; Pres. Vacant. The largest Jewish campus organization in the world, Hillel:The Foundation for Jewish Campus Life, is committed to creatively empowering and engaging Jewish students through its network of over 500 regional centers, campus-based foundations, program centers and affiliates. *The Hillel Annual Report; Shavua Tov. Israel Update.* (WWW. HILLEL.ORG)

INSTITUTE FOR COMPUTERS IN JEWISH LIFE (1978). 7074 N. Western Ave., Chicago, IL 60645. (773)262-9200. FAX: (773)262-9298. E-mail: rosirv@aol.com. Pres. Thomas Klutznick; Exec. V.-Pres. Dr. Irving J. Rosenbaum. Explores, develops, and disseminates applications of computer technology to appropriate areas of Jewish life, with special emphasis on Jewish education; creates educational software for use in Jewish schools; provides consulting service and assistance for national Jewish organizations, seminaries, and synagogues.

INTERNATIONAL FEDERATION OF SECULAR HUMANISTIC JEWS (1983). 224 West 35th Street, Suite 410, NYC 10024. (212)564-6711. FAX: (212)564-6721. E-mail: info@ ifshj.org. Co-Ch. Felix Posen (Europe), Yair Tzaban (Israel) & Sherwin Wine (USA). The International Federation of Secular Humanistic Jews provides a voice for secular Jews worldwide in their common goal to foster Secular Humanistic Judaism as an option for modern Jewish identity. The IFSHJ develops awareness of Secular and Humanistic Judaism by serving as a resource and for general information, and developing literature, conferences, and communications that promote philosophy of Secular and Humanistic Judaism in the world community. *Newsletter (Hofesh); Contemplate: International Journal of Secular Jewish Thought.*

INTERNATIONAL INSTITUTE FOR SECULAR HUMANISTIC JUDAISM (1985). 28611 West Twelve Mile Rd., Farmington Hills, MI 48334. (248)476-9532. FAX: (248)476-8509. E-mail: iishj@iishj.org. Chmn. Rabbi Sherwin T. Wine. Established in 1985 in Jerusalem to serve the needs of a growing movement, its two primary purposes are to commission and publish educational materials and to train rabbis, leaders, teachers, and spokespersons for the movement. The Institute has two offices-one in Israel (Jerusalem) and one in N. America and offers educational and training programs in Israel, N. America, and the countries of the former Soviet Union. The N. American office, located in a suburb of Detroit, offers the Rabbinic Program, the Leadership Program, and the Adult Education Program. *Brochure, educational papers, and projects.*

JEWISH CHAUTAUQUA SOCIETY, INC. (sponsored by North American Federation of Temple Brotherhoods) (1893). 633 Third Ave., NYC 10017. (212)650-4100/(800) 765-6200. FAX: (212)650-4189. E-mail: jcs@uahc.org. Pres. Irving B. Shnaider; Chancellor Stuart J. Aaronson; Exec. Dir. Doug Barden. Works to promote interfaith understanding by sponsoring accredited college courses and one-day lectures on Judaic topics, providing book grants to educational institutions, producing educational videotapes on interfaith topics, and convening interfaith institutes. A founding sponsor of the National Black/Jewish Relations Center at Dillard University. *ACHIM Magazine.*

JEWISH EDUCATION IN MEDIA (1978). PO Box 180, Riverdale Sta., NYC 10471. (212)362-7633. FAX: (203)359-1381. Pres. Ken Asher; Exec. Dir. Rabbi Mark S. Golub. Devoted to producing television, film, and video-cassettes for a popular Jewish audience, in order to inform, entertain, and inspire a greater sense of Jewish identity and Jewish commitment. "L'Chayim," JEM's weekly half-hour program, which is seen nationally on NJT/ National Jewish Television, features outstanding figures in the Jewish world addressing issues and events of importance to the Jewish community. (WWW.LCHAYIM. COM)

JEWISH EDUCATION SERVICE OF NORTH AMERICA (JESNA) (1981). 111 Eighth Ave., 11th fl., NYC 10011. (212)284-6950. FAX: (212)284-6951. E-mail: info@jesna. org. Pres. Jonathan S. Woocher; Bd. Ch. Joseph Kanfer. The Jewish Federation system's educational coordinating, planning, and development agency. Promotes excellence in Jewish education by initiating exchange of ideas, programs, and materials; providing information, consultation, educational resources, and policy guidance; and collaborating with partners in N. America and Israel to develop educational programs. *Agenda: Jewish Education; planning guides on Jewish Renaissance; research reports; Jewish Educators Electronic Toolkit.* (WWW.JESNA.ORG)

JEWISH RECONSTRUCTIONIST FEDERATION (formerly Federation of Reconstructionist Congregations and Havurot) (1954). 7804 Montgomery Ave., Suite 9, Elkins Park, PA 19027-2649. (215)782-8500. Fax: (215)782-8805. E-mail: info@jrf.org. Pres. Daniel Cedarbaum; Exec. V.-Pres. Judy Wortman. Provides educational and consulting services to affiliated congregations and havurot; fosters the establishment of new Reconstructionist communities. Publishes *Kol Haneshamah*, an innovative series of prayer books, including a new mahzor and haggadah; provides programmatic materials. Regional offices in New York, Los Angeles, Chicago, Philadelphia, and Washington DC. *Reconstructionism Today.* (WWW.JRF. ORG)

———, RECONSTRUCTIONIST RABBINICAL ASSOCIATION (1974). 1299 Church Rd., Wyncote, PA 19095. (215)576-5210. FAX:

(215)576-8051. E-mail: info@therra.org. Pres. Rabbi Nancy Fuchs-Kreimer; Exec. Dir. Rabbi Richard Hirsh. Professional organization for graduates of the Reconstructionist Rabbinical College and other rabbis who identify with Reconstructionist Judaism; cooperates with Jewish Reconstructionist Federation in furthering Reconstructionism in the world. *Newsletters; position papers.*

———, RECONSTRUCTIONIST RABBINICAL COLLEGE (*see* p. 662)

JEWISH TEACHERS ASSOCIATION—MORIM (1931). 45 E. 33 St., Suite 310, NYC 10016-5336. (212)684-0556. Pres. Phyllis L. Pullman; V.-Pres. Ronni David; Sec. Helen Parnes; Treas. Mildred Safar. Protects teachers from abuse of seniority rights; fights the encroachment of anti-Semitism in education; offers scholarships to qualified students; encourages teachers to assume active roles in Jewish communal and religious affairs. *Morim JTA Newsletter.*

KULANU, INC. (formerly AMISHAV USA) (1993). 11603 Gilsan St., Silver Spring, MD 20902. (301)681-5679. FAX: (301)681-1587. Email: jdzeller@umich. edu. Pres. Jack Zeller; Sec. Karen Primack. Engages in outreach to dispersed Jewish communities around the world who wish to return to their Jewish roots. Current projects include the formal conversion of Shinlung-Menashe tribesmen in India currently practicing Judaism, and supplying materials and rabbis for conversos/marranos in Mexico and Brazil. *Newsletter.*

NATIONAL COMMITTEE FOR FURTHERANCE OF JEWISH EDUCATION (1941). 824 Eastern Pkwy., Brooklyn, NY 11213. (718)735-0200; (800)33-NCFJE. FAX: (718)735-4455. Pres. Dr. Steven Rubel; Bd. Chmn. Rabbi Shea Hecht; Chmn. Exec. Com. Rabbi Sholem Ber Hecht. Seeks to disseminate the ideals of Torah-true education among the youth of America; provides education and compassionate care for the poor, sick, and needy in U.S. and Israel; provides aid to Iranian Jewish youth; sponsors camps and educational functions, family and vocational counseling services, family and early intervention, after-school and preschool programs, drug and alcohol education and prevention; maintains schools in Brooklyn and Queens. Every year distributes 25,000 toys/gifts through Toys for Hospitalized children; runs the Release-time program of Greater NY, offers classes FT/PT through Hadar Hatorah Rabbinal Seminary. *Panorama; Cultbusters; Intermarriage; Brimstone & Fire; Focus; A Life Full of Giving.*

NATIONAL COUNCIL OF YOUNG ISRAEL (1912). 3 W. 16 St., NYC 10011. (212)929-1525. FAX: (212)727-9526. E-mail: ncyi @youngisrael.org. Pres. Shlomo Mostofsky; Exec. V.-Pres. Rabbi Pesach Lerner. Through its network of member synagogues in N. America and Israel maintains a program of spiritual, cultural, social, and communal activity aimed at the advancement and perpetuation of traditional, Torah-true Judaism; seeks to instill in American youth an understanding and appreciation of the ethical and spiritual values of Judaism. Sponsors rabbinic and lay leadership conferences, synagogue services, rabbinic services, rabbinic and lay leader training, rabbinic placement, women's division, kosher dining clubs, and youth programs. *Viewpoint Magazine; Divrei Torah Bulletin; NCYI Suggestion Box; The Rabbi's Letter.* (WWW.YOUNGISRAEL.ORG)

——, AMERICAN FRIENDS OF YOUNG ISRAEL IN ISRAEL—YISRAEL HATZA'IR (1926). 3 W. 16 St., NYC 10011. (212)929-1525. FAX: (212)727-9526. E-mail: ncyi@ youngisrael.org. Pres. Meir Mishkoff. Promotes Young Israel synagogues and youth work in Israel; works to help absorb Russian and Ethiopian immigrants.

——, YOUNG ISRAEL DEPARTMENT OF YOUTH AND YOUNG ADULTS ACTIVITIES (reorg. 1981). 3 W. 16 St., NYC 10011. (212)929-1525; (800)617-NCYI. FAX: (212)243-1222. Email: youth@yiyouth. org. Dir. Bradley Karasik. Fosters varied program of activities for the advancement and perpetuation of traditional Torah-true Judaism; instills ethical and spiritual values and appreciation for compatibility of ancient faith of Israel with good Americanism. Runs leadership training programs and youth shabbatonim; support programs for synagogue youth programs; annual national conference of youth directors; ACHVA summer programs for teens IN Israel and U.S.; Nachala summer program in Israel for Yeshiva H.S. girls and Natzach summer program for Yeshiva H.S. boys. *Torah Kidbits; Shabbat Youth Manual; Y.I. Can Assist You; Synagogue Youth Director Handbook.* (WWW.YIYOUTH.ORG)

NATIONAL HAVURAH COMMITTEE (1979). 7135 Germantown Ave., Philadelphia, PA 19119-1720. (215)248-1335. FAX: (215) 248-9760. E-mail: institute@havurah.org. Ch. Neil Zatz Litt. A center for Jewish renewal devoted to spreading Jewish ideas, ethics, and religious practices through havurot, participatory and inclusive religious mini-communities. Maintains a directory of N. American havurot and sponsors a weeklong summer institute, regional weekend retreats. *Havurah! (newsletter).* (WWW.HAVURAH.ORG)

NATIONAL JEWISH CENTER FOR LEARNING AND LEADERSHIP (*see* CLAL)

NATIONAL JEWISH COMMITTEE ON SCOUTING (Boy Scouts of America) (1926). 1325 West Walnut Hill Lane, PO Box 152079, Irving, TX 75015-2079. (972)580-2000. FAX: (972)580-7870. Chmn. Rabbi Peter Hyman. Assists Jewish institutions in meeting their needs and concerns through use of the resources of scouting. Works through local Jewish committees on scouting to establish Tiger Cub groups (1st grade), Cub Scout packs, Boy Scout troops, and coed venturer crews in synagogues, Jewish community centers, day schools, and other Jewish organizations wishing to draw Jewish youth. Support materials and resources on request.

NATIONAL JEWISH GIRL SCOUT COMMITTEE (1972). 33 Central Dr., Bronxville, NY 10708. (914)738-3986, (718)252-6072. FAX: (914)738-6752. E-mail: njgsc@aol. com. Chmn. Rabbi Herbert W. Bomzer; Field Chmn. Adele Wasko. Serves to further Jewish education by promoting Jewish award programs, encouraging religious services, promoting cultural exchanges with the Israel Boy and Girl Scouts Federation, and extending membership in the Jewish community by assisting councils in organizing Girl Scout troops and local Jewish Girl Scout committees. *Newsletter.*

NATIONAL JEWISH HOSPITALITY COMMITTEE (1973; reorg. 1993). PO Box 53691, Philadelphia, PA 19105. (800)745-0301.

Pres. Rabbi Allen S. Maller; Exec. Dir. Steven S. Jacobs. Assists persons interested in Judaism-for intermarriage, conversion, general information, or to respond to missionaries. *Special reports.*

NORTH AMERICAN ALLIANCE FOR JEWISH YOUTH (199650 West 58th Street, NYC, NY, 10019 (212)494-1023. FAX: (212) 906-9371. E-mail: info@naajewishyouth. org. Chmn. Joseph E. Brenan; Dir. Heather Kibel. Serves the cause of informal Jewish and Zionist education in America; provides a forum for the professional leaders of the major N. American youth movements, camps, Israel programs, and university programs to address common issues and concerns, and to represent those issues with a single voice to the wider Jewish and Zionist community. Sponsors annual Conference on Informal Jewish Education for Jewish youth professionals from across the continent.

OZAR HATORAH, INC. (1946). 625 Broadway, 11th Fl. NYC, 10012. (212)253-7245. FAX: (212) 437-4773. Email: agutman @ozarhatorah.org. Pres. Henry Shalom; Sec. Sam Sutton; Exec. Dir. Rabbi Jean Paul Amoyelle. An international educational network which builds Sephardic communities worldwide through Jewish education.

PARDES PROGRESSIVE ASSOCIATION OF REFORM DAY SCHOOLS (1990). 633 Third Ave., NYC 10017-6778. (212)650-4000. FAX: (480)951-0829. E-mail: educate@ uahc.org. Pres. Zita Gardner; Chmn. Carol Nemo. An affiliate of the Union of American Hebrew Congregations; brings together day schools and professional and lay leaders committed to advancing the cause of full-time Reform Jewish education; advocates for the continuing development of day schools within the Reform movement as a means to foster Jewish identity, literacy, and continuity; promotes cooperation among our member schools and with other Jewish organizations that share similar goals. *Visions of Excellence (manual).*

P'EYLIM-LEV L'ACHIM (1951). 1034 E. 12 St. Brooklyn, NY 11230. (718)258-7760. FAX: (718)258-4672. E-mail: joskarmel @aol.com. Natl. Dir. Rabbi Joseph C. Karmel; Exec. V.-Pres. Rabbi Nachum Barnetsky. Seeks to bring irreligious Jews in Israel back to their heritage. Conducts outreach through 12 major divisions consisting of thousands of volunteers and hundreds of professionals across the country; conducts anti-missionary and assimilation programs; operates shelters for abused women and children; recruits children for Torah schools.

RABBINICAL ALLIANCE OF AMERICA (Igud Harabonim) (1942). 3 W. 16 St., 4th fl., NYC 10011. (212)242-6420. FAX: (212) 255-8313. Pres. Rabbi Abraham B. Hecht; Admin. Judge of Beth Din (Rabbinical Court) Rabbi Herschel Kurzrock. Seeks to promulgate the cause of Torah-true Judaism through an organized rabbinate that is consistently Orthodox; seeks to elevate the position of Orthodox rabbis nationally and to defend the welfare of Jews the world over. Also has Beth Din Rabbinical Court for Jewish divorces, litigation, marriage counseling, and family problems. *Perspective; Nahalim; Torah Message of the Week; Registry.*

RABBINICAL ASSEMBLY (1901). 3080 Broadway, NYC 10027. (212)280-6000. FAX: (212)749-9166. Pres. Rabbi Vernon H. Kurtz; Exec. V.-Pres. Rabbi Joel H. Meyers. The international association of Conservative rabbis; actively promotes the cause of Conservative Judaism and works to benefit *klal yisrael*; publishes learned texts, prayer books, and works of Jewish interest; administers the work of the Committee on Jewish Law and Standards for the Conservative movement; serves the professional and personal needs of its members through publications, conferences, and benefit programs and administers the movement's Joint Placement Commission. *Conservative Judaism; Proceedings of the Rabbinical Assembly; Rabbinical Assembly Newsletter.*

RABBINICAL COUNCIL OF AMERICA, INC. (1923; reorg. 1935). 305 Seventh Ave., Suite 1200, NYC 10001. (212)807-7888. FAX: (212)727-8452. Pres. Rabbi Kenneth Aumann; Exec. V.-Pres. Rabbi Basil Herring. Promotes Orthodox Judaism in the community; supports institutions for study of Torah; stimulates creation of new traditional agencies. *Hadorom; Tradition.* (WWW.RABBIS.ORG)

SOCIETY FOR HUMANISTIC JUDAISM (1969). 28611 W. Twelve Mile Rd., Farmington Hills, MI 48334. (248)478-7610. FAX: (248)478-3159. E-mail: info@shj.org.

Pres. Shari Gelber; Pres. Elect Phillip Gould; Exec. Dir. M. Bonnie Cousens. Serves as a voice for Jews who value their Jewish identity and who seek an alternative to conventional Judaism, who reject supernatural authority and affirm the right of individuals to be the masters of their own lives. Publishes educational and ceremonial materials; organizes congregations and groups. *Humanistic Judaism (quarterly journal); Humanorah (quarterly newsletter).* (WWW.SHJ.ORG)

TEKIAH: ASSOCIATION OF HILLEL/JEWISH CAMPUS PROFESSIONALS (1949). c/o Hillel Foundation of New Orleans, 912 Broadway, New Orleans, LA 70118. (504)866-7060. FAX: (504)861-8909. E-mail: president@tekiah.org. Pres. Rabbi Jeffrey Kurtz-Lendner. Seeks to promote professional relationships and exchanges of experience, develop personnel standards and qualifications, safeguard integrity of Hillel profession; represents and advocates before the Foundation for Jewish Campus Life, Council of Jewish Federations. *Handbook for Hillel Professionals; Guide to Hillel Personnel Practices.* (WWW.TEKIAH.ORG)

TEVA LEARNING CENTER/SHOMREI ADAMAH (1988). 307 Seventh Ave., #900, NYC 10001. (212)807-6376. FAX: (212)924-5112. E-mail: teva@tevacenter.org. Co-Dir. Nili Simhai; Asst. Dir., Noam Dolgin Exists to renew the ecological wisdom inherent in Judaism. Runs Jewish environmental education programs for Jewish day schools, synagogues, community centers, camps, university groups and other organized groups. *Let the Earth Teach You Torah, Ecology and the Jewish Spirit.* (WWW.TEVACENTER.ORG)

TORAH SCHOOLS FOR ISRAEL—CHINUCH ATZMAI (1953). 40 Exchange Pl., NYC 10005. (212)248-6200. FAX: (212)248-6202. Exec. Dir. Rabbi Henach Cohen. Conducts information programs for the American Jewish community on activities of the independent Torah schools educational network in Israel; coordinates role of American members of international board of governors; funds special programs of Mercaz Hachinuch Ha-Atzmai B'Eretz Yisroel; funds religous education programs in America and abroad.

TORAH UMESORAH—NATIONAL SOCIETY FOR HEBREW DAY SCHOOLS (1944). 160 Broadway, NYC 10038. (212)227-1000. FAX: (212)406-6934. E-mail: umesorah @aol.com. Exec. V.-Pres. Rabbi Joshua Fishman. Establishes Hebrew day schools and Yeshivas in U.S. and Canada and provides a full gamut of services, including placement, curriculum guidance, and teacher training. Parent Enrichment Program provides enhanced educational experience for students from less Jewishly educated and marginally affiliated homes through parent-education programs and Partners in Torah, a one-on-one learning program. Publishes textbooks; runs shabbatonim, extracurricular activities; national PTA groups; national and regional teacher conventions. *Olomeinu-Our World.*

——, NATIONAL ASSOCIATION OF HEBREW DAY SCHOOL PARENT-TEACHER ASSOCIATIONS (1948). 160 Broadway, NYC 10038. (212)227-1000. FAX: (212)406-6934. Natl. PTA Coord. Bernice Brand. Acts as a clearinghouse and service agency to PTAs of Hebrew day schools; organizes parent education courses and sets up programs for individual PTAs. *Fundraising with a Flair; PTA with a Purpose for the Hebrew Day School.*

——, NATIONAL CONFERENCE OF YESHIVA PRINCIPALS (1956). 160 Broadway, NYC 10038. (212)227-1000. FAX: (212)406-6934. E-mail: umesorah@aol.com. Pres. Rabbi Rabbi Schneur Aisenstark; Exec. V.-Pres. Rabbi Joshua Fishman. Professional organization of elementary and secondary yeshivah/day school principals providing yeshivah/day schools with school evaluation and guidance, teacher and principal conferences-including a Mid-Winter Conference and a National Educators Convention; offers placement service for principals and teachers in yeshivah/day schools. *Directory of Elementary Schools and High Schools.*

——, NATIONAL YESHIVA TEACHERS BOARD OF LICENSE (1953). 160 Broadway, NYC 10038. (212)227-1000. Exec. V.-Pres. Rabbi Joshua Fishman; Dir. Rabbi Yitzchock Merkin. Issues licenses to qualified instructors for all grades of the Hebrew day school and the general field of Torah education.

UNION FOR TRADITIONAL JUDAISM (1984). 241 Cedar Lane, Teaneck, NJ 07666.

(201)801-0707. FAX: (201)801-0449. Pres. Burton G. Greenblatt; Exec. V.-Pres. Rabbi Ronald D. Price. Through innovative outreach programs, seeks to bring the greatest possible number of Jews closer to an open-minded observant Jewish lifestyle. Activities include Kashrut Initiative, Operation Pesah, the Panel of Halakhic Inquiry, Speakers Bureau, adult and youth conferences, and congregational services. Includes, since 1992, the Morashah rabbinic fellowship. *Hagahelet (quarterly newsletter); Cornerstone (journal); Tomeikh Kahalakhah (Jewish legal responsa).*

UNION OF AMERICAN HEBREW CONGREGATIONS (1873). 633 Third Ave., NYC 10017-6778. (212)650-4000. FAX: (212) 650-4169. E-mail: uahc@uahc.org. Pres. Rabbi Eric H. Yoffie; V.-Pres. Rabbi Lennard R. Thal; Bd. Chmn. Russell Silverman. Serves as the central congregational body of Reform Judaism in the Western Hemisphere; serves its approximately 900 affiliated temples and membership with religious, educational, cultural, and administrative programs. *Reform Judaism.* (WWW.UAHC.ORG)

———, AMERICAN CONFERENCE OF CANTORS (1953). 5591 Chamblee Dunwoody Rd. Bldg. 1360, Ste. 200, Atlanta, GA 30338. (770)390-0006. FAX: (770)390-0020. E-mail: accantors@aol.com. Pres. Richard Cohen, Exec. V.-Pres. Scott E. Colbert Exec. VP; Dir. of Placement Barbara Ostfeld; Admin. Asst. Deborah Barber. Members are invested or certified by accredited seminaries, i.e., Hebrew Union College-Jewish Insitute of Religion School of Sacred Music. Through the Joint Cantorial Placement Commission, the ACC serves Reform congregations seeking cantors. Dedicated to creative Judaism, preserving the past, and encouraging new and vital approaches to religious ritual, liturgical music and ceremony. *Koleinu (monthly).*

———, COMMISSION ON SOCIAL ACTION OF REFORM JUDAISM (see p. 617)

———, COMMISSION ON SYNAGOGUE MANAGEMENT (UAHC-CCAR) (1962). 633 Third Ave., NYC 10017-6778. (212)650-4040. FAX: (212)650-4239. Chmn. Marshall Krolick; Dir. Dale A. Glasser. Assists congregations in management, finance, building maintenance, design, construction, and art aspects of synagogues; maintains the Synagogue Architectural Library.

———, NATA (NATIONAL ASSOCIATION OF TEMPLE ADMINISTRATORS) (1941). 6114 La Salle Ave., Box 731, Oakland, CA 94611. (800)966-6282. FAX: (925)283-7713. E-mail: nataorg@hotmail.com. FTA Elizabeth L. Hirsh. Professional organization for UAHC synagogue administrators. Sponsors graduate training in synagogue management with Hebrew Union College; offers in-service training, workshops, and conferences leading to certification; provides NATA Consulting Service, NATA Placement Service for synagogues seeking advice or professional administrators; establishes professional standards. *NATA Journal.*

———, NATE (NATIONAL ASSOCIATION OF TEMPLE EDUCATORS) (1955). 633 Third Ave., 7th fl., NYC 10017-6778. (212)452-6510. FAX: (212)452-6512. E-mail: nateoff @aol.com. Pres. Julie A. Vanek; Exec. Dir. Rabbi Stanley T. Schickler. Represents educators within the general body of Reform Judaism; fosters the full-time profession of the Jewish educator; encourages the growth and development of Jewish religious education consistent with the aims of Reform Judaism; stimulates communal interest in and responsibility for Jewish religious education. *NATE NEWS.* (WWW.RJ.ORG/NATE)

———, NORTH AMERICAN FEDERATION OF TEMPLE BROTHERHOODS (1923). 633 Third Ave., NYC 10017. (212)650-4100. FAX: (212)650-4189. E-mail: nftb@uahc. org. Pres.Irving B. Shnaider; JCS Chancellor Stuart J. Aaronson; Exec. Dir. Douglas Barden. Dedicated to enhancing the world through the ideal of brotherhood, NFTB and its 300 affiliated clubs are actively involved in education, social action, youth activities, and other programs that contribute to temple and community life. Supports the Jewish Chautauqua Society, an interfaith educational project. *ACHIM (formerly Brotherhood magazine)* (WWW.RJ. ORG/NFTB)

———, UAHC DEPARTMENT OF JEWISH EDUCATION (1923). 633 Third Ave., 7th fl., NYC 10017. (212)650-4112. FAX: (212)650-4229. E-mail: jkatzew@uahc. org. Chmn. Dr. Rabbi Jan Katzew, Robert Heller; Dir. Dr. Rabbi Jan Katzew. Long-range planning and policy development for congregational programs of lifelong education; materials concerning Reform Jewish Outreach, Teacher Development and Reform Day Schools; activities administered by the UAHC Department of Education. *V'Shinantam; Torah at the Center, Family Shabbat Table Talk, Galilee Diary, Jewish Parent Page.*

————, WOMEN OF REFORM JUDAISM— THE FEDERATION OF TEMPLE SISTER-HOODS (1913). 633 Third Ave., NYC 10017. (212)650-4050. FAX: (212)650-4059. E-mail: wrj@uahc.org. Pres. Helene H. Waranch; Exec. Dir. Ellen Y. Rosenberg. Serves more than 600 sisterhoods of Reform Judaism; promotes interreligious understanding and social justice; provides funding for scholarships for rabbinic students; founded the Jewish Braille Institute, which provides braille and large-type Judaic materials for Jewish blind; supports projects for Israel; is the women's agency of Reform Judaism, an affiliate of the UAHC; works in behalf of the Hebrew Union College-Jewish Institute of Religion and the World Union for Progressive Judaism. *Notes for Now; Art Calendar; Windows on WRJ.* (WWW.RJ.ORG/WRJ)

————, YOUTH DIVISION AND NORTH AMERICAN FEDERATION OF TEMPLE YOUTH (1939). 633 Third Ave, NYC 10017-6778. (212)650-4070. FAX: (212)650-4199. E-mail: youthdivision @uahc.org. Dir. UAHC Youth Div. Rabbi Allan L. Smith; Assoc. Dir. UAHC Youth Div. Rabbi Andrew Davids. Dedicated to Jewishly enhancing the lives of the young people of North America's Reform congregations through a program of informal education carried out in UAHC Camp-Institutes (11 camps for grades 2 and up), UAHC/NFTY Israel Programs (summer and semester), European and domestic teen travel, NFTY/Junior & Senior High School Programs (youth groups), and Kesher/College Education Department (Reform havurot on campuses).

UNION OF ORTHODOX JEWISH CONGREGA-TIONS OF AMERICA (1898). 11 Broadway, 14th fl., NYC 10004. (212)563-4000. FAX: (212)564-9058. E-mail: ou@ou.org. Pres. Harvey Blitz.; Exec. V.-Pres. Rabbi Dr. Tzvi Hersh Weinreb. Serves as the national central body of Orthodox syna-gogues; national OU kashrut supervision and certification service; sponsors Institute for Public Affairs; National Conference of Synagogue Youth; National Jewish Council for the Disabled; Israel Center in Jerusalem; Torah Center in the Ukraine; New Young Leadership Division; Pardes; provides educational, religious, and organization programs, events, and guidance to synagogues and groups; represents the Orthodox Jewish community to governmental and civic bodies and the general Jewish community. *Jewish Action magazine; OU Kosher Directory; OU Guide to Kosher for Passover Foods; Keeping Posted (NCSY); Synagogue Trends; Our Way magazine; Yachad magazine; Luach & Limud Personal Torah Study, Leadership Briefing, Behind the Union Symbol.* (WWW.OU.ORG)

————, INSTITUTE FOR PUBLIC AFFAIRS (1989). 11 Broadway, 14th fl., NYC 10004. (212)613-8124. FAX: (212)613-0724. E-mail: ipa@ou.org. Pres. Harvey Blitz; Chmn. Richard Stone; Dir. Nathan Diament; Dir. Intl. Affairs & Comm. Rel. Betty Ehrenberg. Serves as the policy analysis, advocacy, mobilization, and programming department responsible for representing Orthodox/traditional American Jewry. *IPA Currents (quarterly newsletter).*

————, NATIONAL CONFERENCE OF SYNA-GOGUE YOUTH (1954). 11 Broadway, 14th fl., NYC 10004. (212)563-4000. E-mail: ncsy@ou.org. Central body for youth groups of Orthodox congregations; provides educational guidance, Torah study groups, community service, program consultation, Torah library, Torah fund scholarships, Ben Zakkai Honor Society, Friends of NCSY, weeklong seminars, Israel Summer Experience for teens and Camp NCSY East Summer Kollel & Michlelet, Teen Torah Center. Divisions include Senior NCSY, Junior NCSY for preteens, Our Way for the Jewish deaf, Yachad for the developmentally disabled, Israel Center in Jerusalem, and NCSY in Israel. *Keeping Posted with NCSY; Darchei Da'at.*

————, WOMEN'S BRANCH OF THE ORTHO-DOX UNION (1923). 156 Fifth Ave., NYC 10010. (212)929-8857. Pres. Sophie Ebert. Umbrella organization of Orthodox sisterhoods in U.S. and Canada, educating women in Jewish learning and observance; provides programming, leadership, and organizational guidance, conferences, conventions, Marriage Committee and projects concerning mikvah, Shalom Task Force, and Welcoming Guests. Works with Orthodox Union Commissions and outreach; supports Stern and Touro College scholarships and Jewish braille publications; supplies Shabbat candelabra for hospital patients; NGO representative at UN. *Hachodesh; Hakol.*

UNION OF ORTHODOX RABBIS OF THE UNITED STATES AND CANADA (1902). 235 E. Broadway, NYC 10002. (212)964-6337(8). Dir. Rabbi Hersh M. Ginsberg. Seeks to foster and promote Torah-true Judaism in the U.S. and Canada; assists in the establishment and maintenance of yeshivot in the U.S.; maintains committee on marriage and divorce and aids individuals with marital difficulties; disseminates knowledge of traditional Jewish rites and practices and publishes regulations on synagogal structure; maintains rabbinical court for resolving individual and communal conflicts. *HaPardes.*

UNION OF SEPHARDIC CONGREGATIONS, INC. (1929). 8 W. 70 St., NYC 10023. (212)873-0300. FAX: (212)724-6165. Pres. Rabbi Marc D. Angel; Bd. Chmn. Edward Misrahi. Promotes the religious interests of Sephardic Jews; prints and distributes Sephardic prayer books. *Annual International Directory of Sephardic Congregations.*

UNITED LUBAVITCHER YESHIVOTH (1940). 841-853 Ocean Pkwy., Brooklyn, NY 11230. (718)859-7600. FAX: (718)434-1519. Supports and organizes Jewish day schools and rabbinical seminaries in the U.S. and abroad.

UNITED SYNAGOGUE OF CONSERVATIVE JUDAISM (1913). 155 Fifth Ave., NYC 10010-6802. (212)533-7800. FAX: (212) 353-9439. E-mail: info@uscj.org. Pres. Judy Yudof; Exec. V.-Pres. Rabbi Jerome M. Epstein. International organization of 760 Conservative congregations. Maintains 17 departments and 15 regional offices to assist its affiliates with religious, educational, youth, community, and administrative programming and guidance; aims to enhance the cause of Conservative Judaism, further religious observance, encourage establishment of Jewish religious schools, draw youth closer to Jewish tradition. Extensive Israel programs. *United Synagogue Review; Art/Engagement Calendar; Program Suggestions; Directory & Resource Guide; Book Service Catalogue of Publications.* (WWW.USCJ.ORG)

————, COMMISSION ON JEWISH EDUCATION (1930). 155 Fifth Ave., NYC 10010. (212)533-7800. FAX: (212)353-9439. E-mail: education@uscj.org. Chmn. Temma Kingsley; Dir. Rabbi Robert Abramson. Develops educational policy for the United Synagogue of Conservative Judaism and sets the educational direction for Conservative congregations, their schools, and the Solomon Schechter Day Schools. Seeks to enhance the educational effectiveness of congregations through the publication of materials and in-service programs. *Tov L'Horot; Your Child; Shiboley Schechter; Advisories.*

————, COMMISSION ON SOCIAL ACTION AND PUBLIC POLICY (1958). 155 Fifth Ave., NYC 10010. (212)533-7800. FAX: (212)353-9439. Chmn. Hon. Jerry Wagner; Dir. Sarrae G. Crane. Develops and implements positions and programs on issues of social action and public policy for the United Synagogue of Conservative Judaism; represents these positions to other Jewish and civic organizations, the media, and government; and provides guidance, both informational and programmatic, to its affiliated congregations in these areas. *HaMa'aseh.*

————, JEWISH EDUCATORS ASSEMBLY (1951). 426 W. 58 St., NYC 10019. (212)765-3303. FAX: (212)765-3310. Pres. Dr. Mark S. Silk; Exec. Dir. Susan Mitrani Knapp. The Jewish Educators Assembly is the professional organization for the Jewish educators within the Conservative movement. The JEA provides a forum to discuss the trends and challenges within Conservative Jewish education as well as provides professional development and a sense of community for educational directors. Services offered: annual conference, placement service, career services, research grants, personal benefits and *V'Aleh Ha-Chadashot* newsletter.

————, KADIMA (formerly PRE-USY; reorg. 1968). 155 Fifth Ave., NYC 10010-6802. (212)533-7800. FAX: (212)353-9439. E-mail: kadima@uscj.org. Dir. Karen L.

Stein; Dir. of Youth Activities Jules A Gutin. Involves Jewish preteens in a meaningful religious, educational, and social environment; fosters a sense of identity and commitment to the Jewish community and the Conservative movement; conducts synagogue-based chapter programs and regional Kadima days and weekends. *Mitzvah of the Month; Kadima Kesher; Chagim; Advisors Aid; Games; quarterly Kol Kadima magazine.*

———, NORTH AMERICAN ASSOCIATION OF SYNAGOGUE EXECUTIVES (1948). 155 Fifth Ave., NYC 10010. (212)533-7800, ext 2609. FAX: (631)732-9461. E-mail: office@naase.org. Pres. Judith Kranz, FSA, ATz; Hon. Pres. Amir Pilch, FSA; Exec. Dir. Harry Hauser. Aids congregations affiliated with the United Synagogue of Conservative Judaism to further the aims of Conservative Judaism through more effective administration (Program for Assistance by Liaisons to Synagogues—PALS); advances professional standards and promotes new methods in administration; cooperates in United Synagogue placement services and administrative surveys. *NAASE Connections Newsletter; NAASE Journal . . .*

———, UNITED SYNAGOGUE YOUTH (1951). 155 Fifth Ave., NYC 10010. (212)533-7800. FAX: (212)353-9439. E-mail: youth@uscj.org. Pres. Jesse Olitzky; Exec. Dir. Jules A. Gutin. Seeks to strengthen identification with Conservative Judaism, based on the personality, development, needs, and interests of the adolescent, in a mitzvah framework. *Achshav; Tikun Olam; A.J. Heschel Honor Society Newsletter; SATO Newsletter; USY Program Bank; Hakesher Newsletter for Advisors.*

VAAD MISHMERETH STAM (1976). 4907 16th Ave., Brooklyn, NYC 11204. (718)438-4980. FAX: (718)438-9343. Pres. Rabbi David L. Greenfield. A nonprofit consumer-protection agency dedicated to preserving and protecting the halakhic integrity of Torah scrolls, tefillin, phylacteries, and mezuzoth. Publishes material for laymen and scholars in the field of scribal arts; makes presentations and conducts examination campaigns in schools and synagogues; created an optical software system to detect possible textual errors in stam. Teaching and certifying sofrim worldwide. Offices in Israel, Stras-

bourg, Chicago, London, Manchester, Montreal, and Zurich. Publishes *Guide to Mezuzah* and *Encyclopedia of the Secret Aleph Beth. The Jewish Quill; and many other publications.*

PANIM: THE INSTITUTE FOR JEWISH LEADERSHIP AND VALUES (formerly WASHINGTON INSTITUTE FOR JEWISH LEADERSHIP & VALUES) (1988). 6101 Montrose Road, Suite 200, Rockville, MD 20852. (301) 770-5070. FAX: (301) 770-6365. E-mail: info@panim.org. Founder/Pres. Rabbi Sidney Schwarz; Bd. Chmn. Mark Levitt. Institute for Jewish Leadership and Values is a non-profit educational organization dedicated to the renewal of American Jewish life through the integration of Jewish learning, values and social responsibility. Our flagship program, *Panim el Panim*:High School in Washington, each year brings over 1,000 Jewish teens from across the country to Washington, D.C. to learn about political and social activism in the context of Jewish learning and values. We also sponsor the Jewish Civics Initiative, the largest national Jewish service/learning program for teens. The Institute also sponsors a Synagogue Transformation Project, and conducts leadership training. *Jewish Civics: A Tikkun Olam/World Repair Manual; Jews, Judaism and Civic Responsibility.*

WOMEN'S LEAGUE FOR CONSERVATIVE JUDAISM (1918). 475 Riverside Dr., NYC 10115. (212)870-1260. FAX: (212)772-3507. Email: womensleague@wlcj.org Pres. Janet Tobin; Exec. Dir. Bernice Balter. Parent body of Conservative (Masorti) women's synagogue groups in U.S., Canada, Puerto Rico, Mexico, and Israel; provides programs and resources in Jewish education, social action, Israel affairs, American and Canadian public affairs, leadership training, community service programs for persons with disabilities, conferences on world affairs, study institutes, publicity techniques; publishes books of Jewish interest; contributes to support of Jewish Theological Seminary of America. *Women's League Outlook magazine; Ba'Olam world affairs newsletter.*

WORLD COUNCIL OF CONSERVATIVE/MASORTI SYNAGOGUES (1957). 155 Fifth Ave., NYC 10010. (212)533-7800, ext. 2014, 2018. FAX: (212)533-9439. E-mail: worldcouncil@compuserve.com. Pres.

Rabbi Alan Silverstein; Rabbi of Council, Rabbi Benjamin Z. Kreitman. Organize and support Conservative/Masorti congregations in Latin America, Europe, Australia and South Africa. *World Spectrum.*

WORLD UNION FOR PROGRESSIVE JUDAISM (1926). 633 Third Ave. NYC 10017. (212)650-4280. FAX: (212)650-4289. E-mail: arzawupjna@uahc.org. Pres. Ruth Cohen; Exec. Dir. Rabbi Dow Marmur. International umbrella organization of Liberal Judaism; promotes and coordinates efforts of Liberal congregations throughout the world; starts new congregations, recruits rabbis and rabbinical students for all countries; organizes international conferences of Liberal Jews. *World News.* (WWW.WUPJ.ORG)

SCHOOLS, INSTITUTIONS

THE ACADEMY FOR JEWISH RELIGION (1956). 6301 Riverdale Avenue, Riverdale, NY 10471. (718)543-9360. FAX: (718)5431038. E-mail: admin@ajrsem. org. Acting Pres. Rabbi David Greenstein; Dean Rabbi Dr. Ora Horn Prouser. The pluralistic rabbinic and cantorial seminary uniting teachers and students from all streams of Judaism, passionately committed to their own paths, yet respectful and supportive of the paths of others. Emphasis on integrating learning, practice, and spirt through traditional and contemporary approaches. Training for congregations, chaplaincy, education, community work.

ANNENBERG RESEARCH INSTITUTE (*see* CENTER FOR JUDAIC STUDIES)

BALTIMORE HEBREW UNIVERSITY (1919). 5800 Park Heights Ave., Baltimore, MD 21215. (410)578-6900; (888)248-7420. FAX: (410)578-6940. E-mail: mgreenberg @bhu.edu. Pres. Dr. Rela Mintz Geffen; Bd. Chmn. Rabbi Mark Loeb. Offers PhD, MA, BA, and AA programs in Jewish studies, Jewish education, biblical and Near Eastern archaeology, philosophy, literature, history, Hebrew language, literature, and contemporary Jewish civilization; School of Continuing Education; Joseph Meyerhoff Library; community lectures. (WWW.BHU.EDU)

———, BALTIMORE INSTITUTE FOR JEWISH COMMUNAL SERVICE. (410)578-6932. FAX: (410)578-1803. Dir. Karen S. Bern-

stein; Co-Dir. Cindy Goldstein. Trains Jewish communal professionals; offers a joint degree program: an MA from BHU and an MAJE from BHU, an MSW from U. of Maryland School of Social Work, or an MPS in policy sciences from UMBC; MA with Meyerhoff Graduate School and Johns Hopkins U. in nonprofit management.

———, BERNARD MANEKIN SCHOOL OF UNDERGRADUATE STUDIES. Dean Dr. George Berlin. BA program; interinstitutional program with Johns Hopkins University; interdisciplinary concentrations: contemporary Middle East, American Jewish culture, and the humanities; Russian/English program for new Americans; assoc. of arts (AA) degree in Jewish studies.

———, LEONARD AND HELEN R. STULMAN SCHOOL OF CONTINUING EDUCATION. Dean Dr. George Berlin. Noncredit program open to the community, offering a variety of courses, trips, and events covering a range of Jewish subjects. *Elderhostel, Ulpan Modern Hebrew Department.*

———, PEGGY MEYERHOFF PEARLSTONE SCHOOL OF GRADUATE STUDIES. Dean Dr. Barry M. Gittlen. PhD and MA programs; MA in Jewish studies; MAJE in Jewish education; PhD in Jewish studies; a double master's degree with an MA from BHU and an MAJE from BHU, an MSW from the University of Maryland School of Social Work, or an MPS in policy sciences from UMBC; MA with Baltimore Institute and Johns Hopkins U. in nonprofit management.

BRAMSON ORT COLLEGE (1977). 69-30 Austin St., Forest Hills, NY 11375. (718)261-5800. Dean of Academic Services Barry Glotzer. A two-year Jewish technical college offering certificates and associate degrees in technology and business fields, including accounting, computer programming, electronics technology, business management, office technology. Additional locations in Brooklyn.

BRANDEIS-BARDIN INSTITUTE (1941). 1101 Peppertree Lane, Brandeis, CA 93064. (805)582-4450. FAX: (805)526-1398. E-mail: info@thebbi.org. Pres. Dr. Lee T. Bycel; Chair, Bd. Of Dir. Helen Zukin. A Jewish pluralistic, nondenominational educational institution providing programs for people of all ages:BCI (Brandeis Collegiate Institute), a summer leadership program for college-age adults from around the world; Camp Alonim, a summer Jewish experience for children 8-16; Gan Alonim Day Camp for children in kindergarten to 6th grade; weekend retreats for adults with leading contemporary Jewish scholars-in-residence; Jewish music concerts; Family Days and Weekends, Grandparents Weekends, Elderhostel, Young Adult programs, dance weekends, institute for newly marrieds. *Monthly Updates; BBI Newsletter.*

BRANDEIS UNIVERSITY (1948). 415 South St., Waltham, MA 02454. (781)736-2000. Pres. Jehuda Reinharz; Provost Irving Epstein; Exec. V.-Pres./CEO Peter B. French; Sr. V.-Pres. of Devel. Nancy Winship. Founded in 1948 by the American Jewish community, Brandeis University is a private, coeducational, and nonsectarian institution of higher learning and research located in Waltham, Massachusetts, enrolling approximately 3,100 undergraduate students and 1,200 graduate students. While Brandeis maintains a special relationship with the Jewish community, it welcomes students and faculty of all backgrounds and beliefs. The University's principal components are the undergraduate College of Arts and Sciences, the Graduate School of Arts and Sciences, The Heller School for Social Policy and Management, the Graduate School of International Economics and Finance, and the Rabb School of Summer and Continuing Studies. *Various newsletters, scholarly publications.*

———, NATIONAL WOMEN'S COMMITTEE (1948). MS 132, Waltham, MA 02454-9110. (781) 736-4160. FAX: (781)736-4183. E-mail: bunwc@brandeis.edu. Pres. Marcia F. Levy; Exec. Dir. Joan C. Bowen. Provides support for Brandeis University and its Libraries. It connects Brandeis, a non-sectarian university founded by the American Jewish community, to its members and their communities through programs that reflect the ideals of social justice and academic excellence. In addition to its fundraising activities, NWC offers its members opportunity for intellectual pursuit, continuing education, community service, social interaction, personal enrichment and leadership development. Open to all, regardless of race, religion, nationality or gender. *Connecting.*

CENTER FOR JUDAIC STUDIES, School of Arts and Sciences, University of Pennsylvania. 420 Walnut St., Philadelphia, PA 19106. (215)238-1290. FAX: (215) 238-1540. Dir. David B. Ruderman. *Jewish Quarterly Review.*

CLEVELAND COLLEGE OF JEWISH STUDIES (1964). 26500 Shaker Blvd., Beachwood, OH 44122. (216)464-4050. FAX: (216)464-5827. Pres. David S. Ariel; Dir. of Student Services Diane M. Kleinman. Provides courses in all areas of Judaic and Hebrew studies to adults and college-age students; offers continuing education for Jewish educators and administrators; serves as a center for Jewish life and culture; expands the availability of courses in Judaic studies by exchanging faculty, students, and credits with neighboring academic institutions; grants bachelor's and master's degrees.

DROPSIE COLLEGE FOR HEBREW AND COGNATE LEARNING (*see* CENTER FOR JUDAIC STUDIES)

GRATZ COLLEGE (1895). 7605 Old York Rd., Melrose Park, PA 19027. (215)635-7300. FAX: (215)635-7320. Bd. Chmn. Dr. Matti K. Gershenfeld.; Pres. Dr. Jonathan Rosenbaum. Offers a wide variety of undergraduate and graduate degrees and continuing education programs in Judaic, Hebraic, and Middle Eastern studies. Grants BA and MA in Jewish studies, MA in Jewish education (joint program in special needs education with La Salle U.), MA in Jewish music, MA in Jewish liberal studies, MA in Jewish communal studies, certificates in Jewish communal studies (joint program with U. of Penna. School of Social Work and Temple U), Jewish education, Israel studies, Judaica librarianship (joint program with Drexel U.), and Jewish music. Joint graduate program with Reconstructionist Rabbinical College in Jewish education and Jewish music. Netzky Division of Continuing Education and Jewish Community High School. *Various newsletters, annual academic bulletin, scholarly publications, centennial volume, Gratz newsletter and occasional papers.*

HEBREW COLLEGE (1921). 160 Herrick Road, Newton Centre, MA 02459. (617)559-8600. FAX: (617)559-8601. Pres.

Dr. David M. Gordis; Ch. Bd. Dir. Mickey Cail; Hon. Ch. Bd. Trustees Ted Benard-Cutler. Through training in Jewish texts, history, literature, ethics, and Hebrew language, prepares students to become literate participants in the global Jewish community. Offers graduate and undergraduate degrees and certificates in all aspects of Jewish education, Jewish studies, and Jewish music; serves students of all ages through its Prozdor High School, Camp Yavneh, Ulpan Center for Adult Jewish Learning, and *Me'ah*—One Hundred Hours of Adult Jewish Learning. *Hebrew College Today; Likut.* (WWW.HEBREWCOLLEGE.EDU)

HEBREW SEMINARY OF THE DEAF (1992). 4435 W. Oakton, Skokie, IL 60076. (847) 677-3330. FAX: (847)677-7945. E-mail: hebrewsemdeaf@juno.com. Pres. Rabbi Douglas Goldhamer; Bd. Chmn. Alan Crane. Trains deaf and hearing men and women to become rabbis and teachers for Jewish deaf communities across America. All classes in the 5-year program are interpreted in Sign Language. Rabbis teaching in the seminary are Reform, Conservative, and Reconstructionist.

HEBREW THEOLOGICAL COLLEGE (1922). 7135 N. Carpenter Rd., Skokie, IL 60077. (847)982-2500. FAX: (847)674-6381. E-mail: htc@htcnet.edu. Chancellor Rabbi Dr. Jerold Isenberg; Rosh Hayeshiva Rabbi Shlomo Morgenstern. Hebrew Theological College, a fully accredited insitution, includes the Bet Midrash for Men, Blitstein Institute for Women, Kanter School of Liberal Arts and Sciences, Fasman Yeshiva High School, Community Service Devision, Silber Memorial Library, Bellows Kollel, Israel Experience Program and Yeshivas HaKayitz summer camp. *Likutei Pshatim, Or Shmuel, Academic Journal.* (WWW.HTCNET.EDU)

HEBREW UNION COLLEGE—JEWISH INSTITUTE OF RELIGION (1875). 3101 Clifton Ave., Cincinnati, OH 45220. (513)221-1875. FAX: (513)221-1847. Pres. Rabbi David Ellenson; Chancellor Dr. Alfred Gottschalk; V.-Pres. Finance Robert J. Goldsmith; V.-Pres. Devel. Erica S. Frederick; Chmn. Bd. Govs. Burton Lehman; Provost Dr. Norman J. Cohen; V.-Pres. For Communal Dev. Dr Paul M. Steinberg. Academic centers: 3101 Clifton Ave., Cincinnati, OH 45220 (1875), Dean Rabbi Kenneth Ehrlich. 1 W. 4 St., NYC

10012 (1922), Dean Rabbi Aaron Panken. FAX: (212) 388-1720. 3077 University Ave., Los Angeles, CA 90007 (1954), Dean Rabbi Lewis Barth; FAX: (213)747-6128. 13 King David St., Jerusalem, Israel 94101 (1963), Dean Rabbi Michael Marmur; FAX: (972-2)6251478. Prepares students for Reform rabbinate, cantorate, Jewish education and educational administration, communal service, academic careers; promotes Jewish studies; maintains libraries, archives, and museums; offers master's and doctoral degrees; engages in archaeological excavations; publishes scholarly works through Hebrew Union College Press. *American Jewish Archives; Bibliographica Judaica; HUC-JIR Catalogue; Hebrew Union College Annual; Studies in Bibliography and Booklore; The Chronicle; Kesher.* (WWW.HUC.EDU)

———, AMERICAN JEWISH PERIODICAL CENTER (1957). 3101 Clifton Ave., Cincinnati, OH 45220. (513)221-1875, ext. 396. FAX: (513)221-0519. Dir. Herbert C. Zafren. Maintains microfilms of all American Jewish periodicals 1823-1925, selected periodicals since 1925. *Jewish Periodicals and Newspapers on Microfilm (1957); First Supplement (1960); Augmented Edition (1984).*

———, BLAUSTEIN CENTER FOR PASTORAL COUNSELING. 1 West 4th Street, NYC, 10012. (212)824-2238. FAX: (212)388-1720. Email: nwiener@huc.edu. Dir. Nancy Wiener. In partnership with CCAR, prepares spiritual leaderss to sensitively and capably help congregants to deal with the critical issues they face throughout their lives; enables rabbinical students to complete a variety of supervised clinical experiences, including a year of congregational workd as well as pastoral counseling internships, and an academic grounding in psychodynamics and pastoral counseling; and develops new approaches to teaching counseling skills, grounding reflections on practical field work experiences in the teachings of Jewish texts.

———, CENTER FOR HOLOCAUST AND HUMANITY EDUCATION. 3101 Clifton Ave., Cincinnati, OH 45220. (513)221-1875, ext. 355. FAX: (513)221-1842. Email: holocaustandhumanity@huc.edu. Dir. Dr. Racelle R. Weiman. Co-sponsored by Hebrew Union College-Jewish Institute of Religion and Combined Generations of the Holocaust of Greater Cincinnati; offers graduate level courses for educational professionals and clergy; surveys and assesses Holocaust education needs in public and private sectors; innovates curriculum development and evaluation; provides teacher training, pedgogic resources, and programming for general public of all ages and faiths; convenes conferences and symposia; cooperates with university consortium on outreach initiatives; creates traveling exhibits; fosters tolerance education and prejudice reduction in the school system.

——, EDGAR F. MAGNIN SCHOOL OF GRADUATE STUDIES (1956). 3077 University Ave., Los Angeles, CA 90007. (213)749-3424. FAX: (213)747-6128. E-mail: magnin@huc.edu. Dir. Dr. Reuven Firestone. Supervises programs leading to DHS, DHL, and MA degrees; participates in cooperative PhD programs with U. of S. Calif.

——, GRADUATE STUDIES PROGRAM. 1 W. 4 St. NYC 10012. (212)824-2252. FAX: (212)388-1720. E-mail: nysgrad@huc.edu. Dir. Dr. Carol Ochs. Offers the DHL (doctor of Hebrew letters) degree in a variety of fields; the MAJS (master of arts in Judaic studies), a multidisciplinary degree; and is the only Jewish seminary to offer the DMin (doctor of ministry) degree in pastoral care and counseling.

——, HUC-UC CENTER FOR THE STUDY OF ETHICS AND CONTEMPORARY MORAL PROBLEMS (1986). 3101 Clifton Ave., Cincinnati, OH 45220. (513)221-1875, EXT. 367. FAX: (5130221-1842. Email: ethics@huc.edu. Dir. Dr. Jonathan Cohen. Co-sponsored by Hebrew Unon College-Jewish Institute of Religion and the University of Cincinnati; dedicated to the study of contemporary moral problems on the basis of valuews that are at the heart of Judeo-Christian and secular ethical traditions; provides forum for open discussion and reflection on important moral dilemmas that arise in modern life; promotes the incorporation of ethical values in personal life, professional practice, and community development; lauching MA and PhD programs in Jewish and Comparative Law and Applied Ethics; offering development programs for legal, medical, and social work professionals; promoting cooperative research among academic institutions, social service, and not-for-profit organizations in Greater Cincinnati.

——, IRWIN DANIELS SCHOOL OF JEWISH COMMUNAL SERVICE (1968). 3077 University Ave., Los Angeles, CA 90007. (800)899-0925. FAX: (213)747-6128. E-mail: swindmueller@huc.edu. Dir. Dr. Steven F. Windmueller. Offers certificate and master's degree to those employed in Jewish communal services, or preparing for such work; offers joint MA in Jewish education and communal service with Rhea Hirsch School; offers dual degrees with the School of Social Work, the School of Public Administration, the Annenberg School for Communication, Marshall School of Business and the School of Gerontology of the U. of S. Calif. and with other institutions. Single master's degrees can be completed in 15 months and certificates are awarded for the completion of two full-time summer sessions. (WWW.HUC.EDU)

——, JACOB RADER MARCUS CENTER OF THE AMERICAN JEWISH ARCHIVES (*see* p. 623)

——, JEROME H. LOUCHHEIM SCHOOL OF JUDAIC STUDIES (1969). 3077 University Ave., Los Angeles, CA 90007. (213)749-3424. FAX: (213)747-6128. Dir. Dr. Reuven Firestone. Offers programs leading to MA, BS, BA, and AA degrees; offers courses as part of the undergraduate program of the U. of S. Calif.

——, NELSON GLUECK SCHOOL OF BIBLICAL ARCHAEOLOGY (1963). 13 King David St., Jerusalem, Israel 94101. (972)2-6203333. FAX: (972)2-6251478. Dir. Avraham Biran. Offers graduate-level research programs in Bible and archaeology. Summer excavations are carried out by scholars and students. University credit may be earned by participants in excavations. Consortium of colleges, universities, and seminaries is affiliated with the school. Skirball Museum of Biblical Archaeology (artifacts from Tel Dan, Tel Gezer, and Aroer).

——, RHEA HIRSCH SCHOOL OF EDUCATION (1967). 3077 University Ave., Los Angeles, CA 90007. (213)749-3424. FAX: (213)747-6128. Dir. Sara Lee. Offers PhD and MA programs in Jewish and Hebrew education; conducts joint degree programs with U. of S. Calif.; offers courses for Jewish teachers, librarians, and early educators on a nonmatriculating basis; conducts summer institutes for professional Jewish educators.

———, SCHOOL OF EDUCATION (1947). 1 W. 4 St., NYC 10012. (212)824-2213. FAX: (212)388-1720. E-mail: nysed@huc.edu. Dir. Jo Kay. Trains teachers and principals for Reform religious schools; offers MA degree with specialization in religious education.

———, SCHOOL OF GRADUATE STUDIES (1949). 3101 Clifton Ave., Cincinnati, OH 45220. (513)221-1875, ext. 230. FAX: (513)221-0321. E-mail: gradschool@huc.edu. Dir. Dr. Adam Kamesar. Offers programs leading to MA and PhD degrees; offers program leading to DHL degree for rabbinic graduates of the college.

———, SCHOOL OF JEWISH STUDIES (1963). 13 King David St., Jerusalem, Israel 94101. (972)2-6203333. FAX: (972)2-6251478. E-mail: jerusalem@huc.edu. Acting Pres. Dr. Norman J. Cohen; Dean Rabbi Michael Marmur; Assoc. Dean Rabbi Shaul R. Feinberg. Offers first year of graduate rabbinic, cantorial, and Jewish education studies (required) for North American students; graduate program leading to ordination for Israeli rabbinic students; non-degree Beit Midrash/Liberal Yeshivah program of Jewish studies (English language); in-service educational programming for teachers and educators (Hebrew language); Hebrew Ulpan for immigrants and visitors; Abramov Library of Judaica, Hebraica, Ancient Near East and American Jewish Experience; Skirball Museum of Biblical Archaeology; public outreach programs (lectures, courses, concerts, exhibits).

———, SCHOOL OF SACRED MUSIC (1947). 1 W. 4 St., NYC 10012. (212)824-2225. FAX: (212)388-1720. Dir. Cantor Israel Goldstein. Trains cantors for congregations; offers MSM degree. *Sacred Music Press.*

———, SKIRBALL CULTURAL CENTER (*see* p. 626)

INSTITUTE OF TRADITIONAL JUDAISM (1990). 811 Palisade Ave., Teaneck, NJ 07666. (201)801-0707. FAX: (201)801-0449. Rector (Reish Metivta) Rabbi David Weiss Halivni; Dean Rabbi Ronald D. Price. A nondenominational halakhic rabbinical school dedicated to genuine faith combined with intellectual honesty and the love of Israel. Graduates receive "yoreh yoreh" smikhah.

JEWISH THEOLOGICAL SEMINARY (1886; reorg. 1902). 3080 Broadway, NYC 10027-4649. (212)678-8000. FAX: (212)678-8947. Chancellor Dr. Ismar Schorsch; Bd. Chmn. Gershon Kekst. Operates undergraduate and graduate programs in Judaic studies; professional schools for training Conservative rabbis, educators and cantors; the JTS Library; the Ratner Center for the Study of Conservative Judaism; Melton Research Center for Jewish Education; the Jewish Museum; Ramah Camps and the Ivry Prozdor high-school honors program. Other outreach activities include the Distance Learning Project, the Finkelstein Institute for Religious and Social Studies, and the Wagner Institute lay leadership program. *Academic Bulletin; JTS Magazine; Gleanings; JTS News.* (www.JTSA.EDU)

———, ALBERT A. LIST COLLEGE OF JEWISH STUDIES (formerly SEMINARY COLLEGE OF JEWISH STUDIES—TEACHERS INSTITUTE) (1909). 3080 Broadway, NYC 10027. (212)678-8826. Dean Dr. Shuly Rubin Schwartz. Offers complete undergraduate program in Judaica leading to BA degree; conducts joint programs with Columbia University and Barnard College enabling students to receive two BA degrees.

———, GRADUATE SCHOOL OF JTS (formerly INSTITUTE FOR ADVANCED STUDY IN THE HUMANITIES) (1968). 3080 Broadway, NYC 10027-4649. (212)678-8024. FAX: (212)678-8947. E-mail: gradschool @jtsa.edu. Dean Dr. Stephen P. Garfinkel; Asst. Dean Dr. Bruce E. Nielsen. Programs leading to MA, DHL, and PhD degrees in Judaic studies; specializations include Ancient Judaism, Bible and Ancient Semitic Languages, Interdepartmental Studies, Jewish Art and Material Culture, Jewish Education, Jewish History, Jewish Literature, Jewish Philosophy, Jewish Women's Studies, Liturgy, Medieval Jewish Studies, Midrash, Modern Jewish Studies, Talmud and Rabbinics, and Dual Degree Program with Columbia University School of Social Work.

———, H.L. MILLER CANTORIAL SCHOOL AND COLLEGE OF JEWISH MUSIC (1952). 3080 Broadway, NYC 10027. (212)678-8036. FAX: (212)678-8947. Dean Cantor Henry Rosenblum. Trains cantors, music teachers, and choral directors for congregations. Offers full-time programs in sacred music leading to degree of MSM, and diploma of *Hazzan.*

———, JEWISH MUSEUM (*see* p. 624)

———, LIBRARY OF THE JEWISH THEOLOGICAL SEMINARY. 3080 Broadway, NYC 10027. (212)678-8075. FAX: (212)678-8998. E-mail: library@jtsa.edu. Librarian Dr. Mayer E. Rabinowitz. Contains one of the largest collections of Hebraica and Judaica in the world, including manuscripts, incunabula, rare books, and Cairo Geniza material. The 320,000-item collection includes books, manuscripts, periodicals, sound recordings, prints, broadsides, photographs, postcards, microform, videos and CD-ROM. Exhibition of items from the collection are ongoing. Exhibition catalogs are available for sale. The Library is open to the public for on-site use (photo identification required). *Between the Lines.* (WWW.JTSA. EDU/LIBRARY)

———, LOUIS FINKELSTEIN INSTITUTE FOR RELIGIOUS AND SOCIAL STUDIES (1938). 3080 Broadway, NYC 10027. (212)870-3180. FAX: (212)678-8947. E-mail: finkelstein@jtsa.edu. Dir. Rabbi Gerald Wolpe. Since 1938 has maintained an innovative interfaith and intergroup relations program, pioneering new approaches to dialogue across religious lines. Through scholarly and practical fellowship, highlights the relevance of Judaism and other contemporary religions to current theological, ethical, and scientific issues, including the emerging challenge of bioethics.

———, MELTON RESEARCH CENTER FOR JEWISH EDUCATION (1960). 3080 Broadway, NYC 10027. (212)678-8031. E-mail: stbrown@jtsa.edu. Dir. Dr. Steven M. Brown; Admin. Lisa Siberstein-Weber. Develops new curricula and materials for Jewish education; prepares educators through seminars and in-service programs; maintains consultant and supervisory relationships with a limited number of pilot schools; develops and implements research initiatives; sponsors "renewal" retreats. *Gleanings; Courtyard: A Journal of Research and Reflection on Jewish Education.*

———, NATIONAL RAMAH COMMISSION (1947). 3080 Broadway, NYC 10027. (212)678-8881. FAX: (212)749-8251. Pres. Alan H. Silberman; Natl. Dir. Sheldon Dorph. Sponsors an international network of 16 summer camps located in the US, Canada, S. America, Russia, and Israel, emphasizing Jewish education, living, and culture; offers opportunities for qualified college students and older to serve as counselors, administrators, specialists, etc., and programs for children with special needs (Tikvah program); offers special programs in U.S. and Israel, including National Ramah Staff Training Institute, Ramah Israel Seminar, Ulpan Ramah Plus, and Tichon Ramah Yerushalayim. Family and synagogue tours to Israel and summer day camp in Israel for Americans.

———, PROJECT JUDAICA (1992). 3080 Broadway, NYC 10027. (212)678-8983. Dir. Dr. David Fishman. Students in this intensive, five year program sponsored with YIVO and the Russian State University for the Humanities in Moscow pursue the university's general curriculum while majoring in Jewish history and culture taught by JTS faculty and advanced students. Graduates receive a diploma (the equivalent of an MA) or a candidate of sciences degree (the equivalent of a PhD) from RSUH.

———, RABBINICAL SCHOOL (1886). 3080 Broadway, NYC 10027. (212)678-8817. Dean Allan Kensky. Offers a program of graduate and professional studies leading to the degree of Master of Arts and ordination; includes one year of study in Jerusalem and an extensive field-work program.

———, RADIO AND TELEVISION (1944). 3080 Broadway, NYC 10027. (212)678-8020. Produces radio and TV programs expressing the Jewish tradition in its broadest sense, including hour-long documentaries on NBC and ABC. Distributes cassettes of programs at minimum charge.

———, REBECCA AND ISRAEL IVRY PROZDOR (1951). 3080 Broadway, NYC 10027.

(212)678-8824. E-mail: prozdor@jtsa. edu. Principal Rhonda Rosenheck; Community Advisory Board Chmn. Michael Katz. The Hebrew high school of JTS, offers a program of Jewish studies for day school and congregational school graduates in classical texts, Hebrew, interdisciplinary seminars, training in educational leadership, and classes for college credit. Classes meet one evening a week and on Sundays in Manhattan and at affiliated programs. *High School Curricula.*

————, SAUL LIEBERMAN INSTITUTE FOR TALMUDIC RESEARCH (1985). 3080 Broadway, NYC 10027. (212)678-8994. FAX: (212)678D8947. E-mail: liebinst@ jtsa.edu. Dir. Shamma Friedman; Coord. Jonathan Milgram. Engaged in preparing for publication a series of scholarly editions of selected chapters of the Talmud. The following projects support and help disseminate the research:Talmud Text Database; Bibliography of Talmudic Literature; Catalogue of Geniza Fragments.

————, SCHOCKEN INSTITUTE FOR JEWISH RESEARCH (1961). 6 Balfour St., Jerusalem, Israel 92102. (972)2-5631288. FAX: (972)2-5636857. E-mail: sjssg@ vms.huji.ac.il. Dir. Dr. Shmuel Glick. Comprises the Schocken collection of rare books and manuscripts and a research institute dedicated to the exploration of Hebrew religious poetry (*piyyut*). *Schocken Institute Yearbook (P'raqim).*

————, WILLIAM DAVIDSON GRADUATE SCHOOL OF JEWISH EDUCATION (1996). 3080 Broadway, NYC 10027. (212) 678-8030. E-mail: edschool@jtsa.edu. Dean Dr. Aryeh Davidson. Offers master's and doctoral degrees in Jewish education; continuing education courses for Jewish educators and Jewish communal professionals; and programs that take advantage of the latest technology, including distance learning and interactive video classrooms.

MAALOT—A SEMINARY FOR CANTORS AND JUDAISTS (1987). 15 W. Montgomery Ave., Suite 204, Rockville, MD 20850. (301)309-2310. FAX: (301)309-2328. Pres./Exec. Off. David Shneyer. An educational program established to train individuals in Jewish music, the liturgical arts, and the use, design, and application of Jewish customs and ceremonies. Offers classes, seminars, and an independent study program.

MESIVTA YESHIVA RABBI CHAIM BERLIN RABBINICAL ACADEMY (1905). 1605 Coney Island Ave., Brooklyn, NY 11230. (718)377-0777. Exec. Dir. Y. Mayer Lasker. Maintains fully accredited elementary and high schools; collegiate and postgraduate school for advanced Jewish studies, both in America and Israel; Camp Morris, a summer study retreat; Prof. Nathan Isaacs Memorial Library; Gur Aryeh Publications.

NATIONAL CENTER FOR THE HEBREW LANGUAGE (*see* p. 625)

NER ISRAEL RABBINICAL COLLEGE (1933). 400 Mt. Wilson Lane, Baltimore, MD 21208. (410)484-7200. FAX: (410)484-3060. Rosh Hayeshiva, Rabbi Aharon Feldman; Pres. Rabbi Herman N. Neuberger. Trains rabbis and educators for Jewish communities in America and worldwide. Offers bachelor's, master's, and doctoral degrees in talmudic law, as well as teacher's diploma. College has four divisions: Israel Henry Beren High School, Rabbinical College, Teachers Training Institute, Graduate School. Maintains an active community-service division. Operates special programs for Iranian and Russian Jewish students. *Ner Israel Update; Alumni Bulletin; Ohr Hanair Talmudic Journal; Iranian B'nei Torah Bulletin.*

RABBINICAL COLLEGE OF TELSHE, INC. (1941). 28400 Euclid Ave., Wickliffe, OH 44092. (216)943-5300. Roshei Hayeshiva and Pres. Rabbi Zalman Gifter and Rabbi Yitzchok Sorotzkin ; V.-Pres. Rabbi Abba Zalka Gewirtz. College for higher Jewish learning specializing in talmudic studies and rabbinics; maintains a preparatory academy including a secular high school, postgraduate department, teacher-training school, and teachers' seminary for women. *Pri Etz Chaim; Peer Mordechai; Alumni Bulletin.*

RECONSTRUCTIONIST RABBINICAL COLLEGE (1968). 1299 Church Rd., Wyncote, PA 19095. (215)576-0800. FAX: (215)576-6143. E-mail: rrcinfo@rrc.edu. Pres. Dan Ehrenkranz; Bd. Chmn. Donald L. Shapiro; Genl. Chmn. Aaron Ziegelman. Coeducational. Trains rabbis and cantors for all areas of Jewish communal life:synagogues, academic and educational positions, Hillel centers, federation agencies, and chaplaincy for hospitals, hospices, and geriatric centers; confers title of rabbi and cantor and grants degrees of Master and Doctor of Hebrew Letters and Master of Arts in Jewish Studies. *RRC Report; Reconstructionist.* (WWW.RRC.EDU)

SPERTUS INSTITUTE OF JEWISH STUDIES (1924). 618 S. Michigan Ave., Chicago, IL 60605. (312)922-9012. FAX: (312)922-6406. Pres. Howard A. Sulkin; Dean Dr. Dean Bell; Museum Dir. Rhoda Rosen; Lib. Dir. Glenn Ferdman. An accredited institution of higher learning offering one doctor of Jewish studies degree; master's degree programs in Jewish studies, Jewish education, Jewish communal service, and human-services administration; plus an extensive program of continuing education. Major resources of the college encompass Spertus Museum, Asher Library, Chicago Jewish Archives, and Spertus College of Judaica Press.

———, SPERTUS MUSEUM (*see* p. 627)

TOURO COLLEGE (1970). Executive Offices: 27 West 23rd Street., NYC 10010. (212) 4630400. FAX: (212)627-9049. Pres. Dr. Bernard Lander; Bd. Chmn. Mark Hasten. Non-profit comprehensive college with Judaic Studies, Liberal Arts and professional programs leading to BA, BS, MA, MS and JD degrees at campuses in NYC and Long Island; emphasizes relevance of Jewish heritage to Western civilization. Undergraduate and graduate degree programs in Moscow and Jerusalem. California campuses offer DO degree and distance learning BS, MS, MBA and PhD degrees.

———, COLLEGE OF LIBERAL ARTS AND SCIENCES. 27-33 W. 23 St., NYC 10010. (212)463-0400. FAX: (212)627-9144. Exec. Dean Stanley Boylan. Offers comprehensive Jewish studies along with studies in the arts, sciences, humanities, and preprofessional studies in health sciences, law, accounting, business, computer science, education, and finance. Women's Division, 160 Lexington Ave., NYC 10016. (212)213-2230. FAX: (212)683-3281. Dean Sara E. Freifeld.

———, INSTITUTE OF JEWISH LAW. (631) 421-2244, ext. 335. A constituent of Touro College Jacob D. Fuchsberg Law Center, the Institute of Jewish Law provides an intellectual framework for the study and teaching of Jewish law. Coedits *Dinei Israel* (Jewish Law Journal) with Tel Aviv University Law School.

———, JACOB D. FUCHSBERG LAW CENTER (1980). Long Island Campus, 300 Nassau Rd., Huntington, NY 11743. (516) 421-2244. Dean Howard A. Glickstein. Offers studies leading to JD degree.

———, MOSCOW BRANCH. Oztozhenka #38, Moscow, Russia 119837. Offers BS program in business and BA program in Jewish studies.

———, SCHOOL OF GENERAL STUDIES. Midtown Main Campus, 27 W. 23 St., NYC 10010. (212)463-0400; Harlem Main Campus, 240 E. 123 St., NYC 10035; Sunset Park extension, 475 53rd St., Brooklyn, NY 11220; Flushing Extension, 133-35 Roosevelt Ave., Queens, NY 11374. Dean Stephen Adolphus. Associate and bachelor degree programs in human services, education N-6, computing, business and liberal arts; special emphasis on service to non-traditional students.

———, TOURO COLLEGE FLATBUSH CENTER (1979). 1602 Ave. J, Brooklyn, NY 11230. (718)252-7800. Dean Robert Goldschmidt. A division of the College of Liberal Arts and Sciences; options offered in accounting and business, education, mathematics, political science, psychology, special education and speech. Classes are given on weeknights and during the day on Sunday.

———, TOURO COLLEGE ISRAEL. 20 Pierre Koenig St., Jerusalem, Israel. (02)6796666. FAX: (02)6796688. V-Pres., Israel, Matityahu Adler; Dean of Faculty, Israel, Prof. Moshe Lieberman. Touro College Israel offers both undergraduate and graduate degrees in management, marketing, economics, finance, and accounting. Touro College also offers a graduate degree in Jewish Studies. Courses in both these programs are given in Hebrew. In addition undergraduate courses in our one year program are offered in English. (WWW.TOURO.AC.IL)

———, TOURO COLLEGE SCHOOL OF HEALTH SCIENCES (1986). 1700 Union Blvd, Bay Shore, NY 11706. (516)665-1600. FAX:(516)665-6902. E-mail:edwarda @touro.edu. Pres. Dr. Bernard Lander; Dean Dr. Joseph Weisberg. Offers the following programs:MS/MD with Faculty of Medicine, Technion Institute, Israel; BS/MS Occupational Therapy; BS/MS Physical Therapy; MS Public Health; Advanced MS Orthopedic Physical Therapy; MS Forensic Examination; MS Clinical Engineering; MS Early Intervention; MS Gerontology; BS Physician Assistant; AAS Occupational Therapy Assistant; AAS Physical Therapists Assistant.

————, TOURO GRADUATE SCHOOL OF JEWISH STUDIES (1981). 160 Lexington Ave., NYC 10016. (212)213-2230. FAX: (212)683-3281. E-mail: moshesh@touro.edu. Pres. Bernard Lander; Dean Michael A. Shmidman. Offers courses leading to an MA in Jewish studies, with concentrations in Jewish history or Jewish education. Students may complete part of their program in Israel through MA courses offered by Touro faculty at Touro's Jerusalem center.

UNIVERSITY OF JUDAISM (1947). 15600 Mulholland Dr., Los Angeles, CA 90077. (310)476-9777. FAX: (310)476-0347. E-mail: gleuenthal@uj.edu. Pres. Dr. Robert D. Wexler. The College of Arts and Sciences is an accredited liberal arts college for undergraduates offering a core curriculum of Jewish, Western, and non-Western studies, with majors including bioethics (a premedical track in partnership with Cedars-Sinai Medical Center), business, English, Jewish studies, journalism, literature & politics, political science, psychology, and U.S. public policy. Accredited graduate programs in nonprofit business administration (MBA), and Jewish education. The Ziegler School of Rabbinic Studies provides an intensive four-year program with Conservative ordination. Home of the Whizin Center for the Jewish Future, a research and programming institute. Offers the largest adult Jewish education program in the U.S., cultural-arts programs, and a variety of outreach services for West Coast Jewish communities. *Vision.*

WEST COAST TALMUDICAL SEMINARY (Yeshiva Ohr Elchonon Chabad) (1953). 7215 Waring Ave., Los Angeles, CA 90046. (323)937-3763. FAX: (323)937-9456. Dean Rabbi Ezra Schochet. Provides facilities for intensive Torah education as well as Orthodox rabbinical training on the West Coast; conducts an accredited college preparatory high school combined with a full program of Torah-talmudic training and a graduate talmudical division on the college level. *Torah Quiz; Kovetz Migdal Ohr; Kovetz Ohr HaMigdal.*

YESHIVA TORAH VODAATH AND MESIVTA TORAH VODAATH RABBINICAL SEMINARY (1918). 425 E. 9 St., Brooklyn, NY 11218. (718)941-8000. Bd. Chmn. Chaim Leshkowitz. Offers Hebrew and secular education from elementary level through rabbinical ordination and postgraduate work; maintains a teachers institute and community-service bureau; maintains a dormitory and a nonprofit camp program for boys. *Chronicle; Mesivta Vanguard; Thought of the Week; Torah Vodaath News; Ha'Mesifta.*

————, YESHIVA TORAH VODAATH ALUMNI ASSOCIATION (1941). 425 E. 9 St., Brooklyn, NY 11218. (718)941-8000. Pres. George Weinberger. Promotes social and cultural ties between the alumni and the schools through classes and lectures and fund-raising; offers vocational guidance to students; operates Camp Ohr Shraga; sponsors research fellowship program for boys. *Annual Journal; Hamesivta Torah periodical.*

YESHIVA UNIVERSITY (1886). Wilf Campus, 500 W. 185 St., NYC 10033-3201. (212) 960-5400. FAX: (212)960-0055. Chancellor Dr. Norman Lamm; Pres. Richard Joel; Chmn. Bd. of Trustees Ronald P. Stanton. The nation's oldest and most comprehensive independent university founded under Jewish auspices, with 18 undergraduate and graduate schools, divisions, and affiliates; widespread programs of research and community outreach; publications; and a museum. A broad range of curricula lead to bachelor's, master's, doctoral, and professional degrees. Undergraduate schools provide general studies curricula supplemented by courses in Jewish learning; graduate schools prepare for careers in medicine, law, social work, Jewish education, psychology, Jewish studies, and other fields. It has seven undergraduate schools, seven graduate and professional schools, and four affiliates. *Yeshiva University Review; Yeshiva University Today.* (WWW.YU.EDU)

Yeshiva University has four campuses in Manhattan and the Bronx: Wilf Campus, 500 W. 185 St., NYC 10033-3201; Midtown Campus, 245 Lexington Ave., NYC 10016-4699; Brookdale Center, 55 Fifth Ave., NYC 10003-4391; Jack and Pearl Resnick Campus, Eastchester Rd. & Morris Pk. Ave., Bronx, NY 10461-1602.

Undergraduate schools for men at Wilf Campus (212)960-5400: Yeshiva College (Bd. Chmn. Joshua L. Muss; Dean Dr. Norman T. Adler) provides liberal arts and sciences curricula; grants BA degree. Isaac Breuer College of Hebraic Studies (Dean Dr. Michael D. Shmidman) awards Hebrew teacher's diploma, AA, BA, and BS. James Striar School of General Jewish Studies (Dean Dr. Michael D. Shmidman) grants AA degree. Yeshiva Program/Mazer School of Talmudic Studies (Max and Marion Grill Dean Rabbi Zevulun Charlop) offers advanced course of study in Talmudic texts and commentaries. Irving I. Stone Beit Midrash Program (Dean Dr. Michael D. Shmidman) offers diversified curriculum combining Talmud with Jewish studies.

Undergraduate school for women at Midtown Campus (212)340-7700: Stern College for Women (Bd. Chmn. Marjorie Diener Blenden; Dr. Monique C. Katz; Dean Dr. Karen Bacon) offers liberal arts and sciences curricula supplemented by Jewish studies programs; awards BA, AA, and Hebrew teacher's diploma.

Sy Syms School of Business at Wilf Campus and Midtown Campus (Bd. Chmn. Bernard L. Madoff; Dean Dr. Charles Snow) offers undergraduate business curricula in conjunction with study at Yeshiva College or Stern College; grants BS degree.

Universitywide programs serving the community and the nation include the S. Daniel Abraham Israel Program; Joseph Alexander Foundation Program for Enhancemant of Science Education; Samuel H. and Rachel Golding Center for Judaic Studies; Samuel H. and Rachel Golding Institute for Biomedical Education; Carl C. Icahn Foundation Institutes for Child Protection; Irving and Hanni Rosenbaum Aliyah Incentive Fund; Holocaust Studies Program; Yeshiva University Press; Yeshiva University Museum.

———, ALBERT EINSTEIN COLLEGE OF MEDICINE (1955). Eastchester Rd. & Morris Pk. Ave., Bronx, NY 10461-1602. (718)430-2000. Pres. Richard Joel; Ch-

pers. Bd. of Overseers Robert A. Belfer; Marilyn and Stanley M. Katz Dean Dr. Dominick P. Purpura. Prepares physicians and conducts research in the health sciences; awards MD degree; includes Sue Golding Graduate Division of Medical Sciences (Dir. Dr. Anne M. Etgen), which grants PhD degree. Einstein's clinical facilities and affiliates encompass Jack D. Weiler Hospital of Albert Einstein College of Medicine, Jacobi Medical Center, Montefiore Medical Center, Long Island Jewish Medical Center, Beth Israel Medical Center, Bronx-Lebanon Hospital Center, and Rose F. Kennedy Center for Research in Mental Retardation and Developmental Disabilities. *Einstein; Einstein Today; Einstein Quarterly Journal of Biology and Medicine.*

———, ALUMNI OFFICE, 500 W. 185 St., NYC 10033-3201. (212)960-5373. FAX: (212)960-5336. E-mail: alumdesk@ymail. yu.edu. University Dir. Alumni Affairs Robert R. Saltzman. Seeks to foster a close allegiance of alumni to their alma mater by maintaining ties with all alumni and servicing the following associations: Yeshiva College Alumni; Stern College for Women Alumnae; Sy Syms School of Business Alumni; Albert Einstein College of Medicine Alumni; Ferkauf Graduate School of Psychology Alumni; Wurzweiler School of Social Work Alumni; Rabbinic Alumni; Benjamin N. Cardozo School of Law Alumni. *Yeshiva University Review; AECOM Alumni News; Ferkauf Progress Notes; Wurzweiler Update; Jewish Social Work Forum.*

———, AZRIELI GRADUATE SCHOOL OF JEWISH EDUCATION AND ADMINISTRATION (1945). 245 Lexington Ave., NYC 10016-4699. (212)340-7705. FAX: (212) 340-7787. Pres. Richard Joel; Chmn. Bd. Of Dirs. Moshael J. Straus; Dir. Dr. Yitzchak S. Handel. Offers MS degree in Jewish elementary and secondary education; specialist's certificate and EdD in administration and supervision of Jewish education. Block Education Program, subsidized by a grant from the Jewish Agency's Joint Program for Jewish Education, provides summer course work to complement year-round field instruction in local communities.

———, BELFER INSTITUTE FOR ADVANCED BIOMEDICAL STUDIES (1978). Eastchester

Rd. & Morris Pk. Ave., Bronx, NY 10461-1602. (718)430-2801. Dir. Dr. Dennis Shields. Integrates and coordinates the Albert Einstein College of Medicine's postdoctoral research and training-grant programs in the basic and clinical biomedical sciences. Awards certificate as research fellow or research associate on completion of training.

———, BENJAMIN N. CARDOZO SCHOOL OF LAW (1976). 55 Fifth Ave., NYC 10003-4391. (212)790-0200. E-mail:lawinfo@ymail.yu.edu. Pres. Richard Joel; Chmn. Bd. Of Directors Earle I. Mack; Dean Paul R. Verkuil. Offers a rigorous and enriched legal education leading to juris doctor (JD) degree and two LLM programs—in intellectual property and in general law. Programs and services include Jacob Burns Institute for Advanced Legal Studies; Jacob Burns Center for Ethics in the Practice of Law; Bet Tzedek Legal Services Clinic, including the Herman J. Stich Program for the Aged and Disabled; Cardozo International Institute/Uri and Caroline Bauer Israel Program; Leonard and Bea Diener Institute of Jewish Law; Floersheimer Center for Constitutional Democracy; Ford Foundation Program in International Law and Human Rights; Samuel and Ronnie Heyman Center on Corporate Governance; Kukin Program for Conflict Resolution; Romie Shapiro Program in International Law and Human Rights; Stephen B. Siegel Program in Real Estate Law; Sol S. Singer Research Program in Real Property Law; Howard M. Squadron Program in Law, Media, and Society; Center for Professional Development. *Cardozo Life; Cardozo Law Review; Cardozo Arts and Entertainment Law Journal; Cardozo Women's Law Journal; Cardozo Journal of International and Comparative Law; Cardozo Studies in Law and Literature; Post-Soviet Media Law and Policy Newsletter; New York Real Estate Reporter.*

———, BERNARD REVEL GRADUATE SCHOOL OF JEWISH STUDIES (1935). 500 W. 185 St., NYC 10033-3201. (212)960-5253. Pres. Richard Joel; Chmn. Bd. Of Directors Mordecai D. Katz; Dean Dr. Arthur Hyman. Offers graduate programs in Bible, Talmudic studies, Jewish history, and Jewish philosophy; confers MA and PhD degrees. Harry Fischel

Summer Program offers the Revel program during the summer.

———, FERKAUF GRADUATE SCHOOL OF PSYCHOLOGY (1957). Eastchester Rd. & Morris Pk. Ave., Bronx, NY 10461-1602. (718)430-3941. FAX: (718)430-3960. E-mail: gill@aecom.yu.edu. Pres. Richard Joel; Chair Bd. of Governors. Dr. Jayne G. Beker; Dean Dr. Lawrence J. Siegel. Offers MA in applied psychology; PsyD in clinical and school-clinical child psychology; and PhD in developmental and clinical health psychology. Programs and services include the Leonard and Muriel Marcus Family Project for the Study of the Disturbed Adolescent; Max and Celia Parnes Family Psychological and Psychoeducational Services Clinic.

———, (affiliate) PHILIP AND SARAH BELZ SCHOOL OF JEWISH MUSIC (1954). 560 W. 185 St., NYC 10033-3201. (212)960-5353. FAX: (212)960-5359. Dir. Cantor Bernard Beer. Provides professional training of cantors and courses in Jewish liturgical music; conducts outreach; publishes *Journal of Jewish Music and Literature;* awards associate cantor's certificate and cantorial diploma.

———, (affiliate) RABBI ISAAC ELCHANAN THEOLOGICAL SEMINARY (1896). 2540 Amsterdam Ave., NYC 10033-9986. (212) 960-5344. FAX: (212)960-0061. Chmn. Bd. of Trustees Julius Berman; Max and Marion Grill Dean Rabbi Zevulun Charlop. Leading center in the Western Hemisphere for Torah study and rabbinic training. RIETS complex encompasses 15 educational entities and a major service and outreach center with some 20 programs. Grants semikhah (ordination) and the degrees of master of religious education, master of Hebrew literature, doctor of religious education, and doctor of Hebrew literature. Includes Rabbi Joseph B. Soloveitchik Center of Rabbinic Studies; Gabriel Levine Post-Graduate School for Rabbinic Studies; Morris and Nellie L. Kawaler Rabbinic Training Program; Irving I. Stone Rabbinic Internship Program; Aaron, Martha, Isidore N., and Blanche Rosansky Foundation Contemporary Halakhah Program.

Kollelim include Marcos and Adina Katz Kollel (Institute for Advanced Research in Rabbinics); Kollel l'Horaah (Yadin

Yadin) and External Yadin Yadin; Israel Henry Beren Institute for Higher Talmudic Studies (HaMachon HaGavohah L'Talmud); Bella and Harry Wexner Kollel Elyon and Semikhah Honors Program; Ludwig Jesselson Kollel Chaverim; Caroline and Joseph S. Gruss Institute in Jerusalem.

Riets sponsors one high school for boys (Manhattan) and one for girls (Queens).

The Max Stern Division of Communal Services (Acting Dir. Rabbi David A. Israel), provides personal and professional service to the rabbinate and related fields, as well as educational, consultative, organizational, and placement services to congregations, schools, and communal organizations around the world; coordinates a broad spectrum of outreach programs, including Association of Modern Orthodox Day Schools and Yeshiva High Schools, Stone-Sapirstein Center for Jewish Education, Gertrude and Morris Bienenfeld Department of Rabbinic Services, Gindi Program for the Enhancement of Professional Rabbinics, Continuing Rabbinic Education Initiatives, Leadership Education and Development Program (LEAD), Kiruv College Outreach Program, Community Kollel and Beit Midrash and Boardroom Learning Programs, Project Kehillah, Myer and Pauline Senders Off-Campus Lecture Series, Jewish Medical Ethics Consultation Service, National Commission on Torah Education.The Torah U-Madda Project, supported by the Joseph J. and Bertha K. Green Memorial Fund, includes the Orthodox Forum and publishes the *The Torah U-Madda Journal and Ten Da'at*.

Sephardic components are Jacob E. Safra Institute of Sephardic Studies and the Institute of Yemenite Studies; Sephardic Community Program; Dr. Joseph and Rachel Ades Sephardic Outreach Program; Maybaum Sephardic Fellowship Program.

———, SIMON WIESENTHAL CENTER (see p. 626)

———, WOMEN'S ORGANIZATION (1928). 500 W. 185 St., NYC 10033-3201. (212) 960-0855. Chmn. Natl. Bd. Dinah Pinczower. Supports Yeshiva University's national scholarship program for students training in education, community service, law, medicine, and other professions. Its Torah Chesed Fund provides monthly stipends to needy undergraduate students.

———, WURZWEILER SCHOOL OF SOCIAL WORK (1957). 500 W. 185 St., NYC 10033-3201. (212)960-0800. FAX: (212) 960-0822. Pres. Richard Joel; Chair Bd. of Governors David I. Schachne; Dorothy and David I. Schachne Dean Dr. Sheldon R. Gelman. Offers graduate programs in social work and Jewish communal service; grants MSW and PhD degrees and certificate in Jewish communal service. MSW programs are: Concurrent Plan, 2-year, full-time track, combining classroom study and supervised field instruction; Plan for Employed Persons (PEP), for people working in social agencies; Block Education Plan (Dir. Dr. Adele Weiner), which combines summer course work with regular-year field placement in local agencies; Clergy Plan, training in counseling for clergy of all denominations; Silvia and Irwin Leiferman Center for Professional Training in the Care of the Elderly. *Jewish Social Work Forum.*

———, (affiliate) YESHIVA OF LOS ANGELES (1977). 9760 W. Pico Blvd., Los Angeles, CA 90035-4701. (310)772-2424. FAX: (310)772-7661. E-mail: mhmay@ wiesenthal.com. Dean Rabbi Marvin Hier; Bd. Chmn. Samuel Belzberg; Dir. Academic Programs Rabbi Sholom Tendler. Affiliates are Yeshiva University High Schools of Los Angeles, Jewish Studies Institute and Kollel Torah MiTzion.

———, YESHIVA UNIVERSITY MUSEUM (see p. 628)

SOCIAL, MUTUAL BENEFIT

ALPHA EPSILON PI FRATERNITY (1913). 8815 Wesleyan Rd., Indianapolis, IN 46268-1171. (317)876-1913. FAX: (317) 876-1057. E-mail: office@aepi.org. Internatl. Pres. Dr. Jay Levine; Exec. V.-Pres. Sidney N. Dunn. International Jewish fraternity active on over 100 campuses in the U.S. and Canada; encourages Jewish students to remain loyal to their heritage and to assume leadership roles in the community; active in behalf of the State of Israel and Magen David Adom among other causes. *The Lion of Alpha Epsilon Pi (quarterly magazine).*

THE AMERICAN ASSOCIATION OF JEWS FROM THE FORMER USSR, INC. (AAJFSU) (1989). 100 Church Street, Suite 1608, NYC 10007. (212) 964-1946. FAX: (212) 964-1946. E-mail: GeorgeZilberman @yahoo.com. Pres. Yury Zilberman; Bd. Chmn. Mark Gurevich. National not-for-profit, grassroots mutual assistance and refugee advocacy organization, which unites and represents interests of over 600,000 Russian speaking Jewish refugees and legal immigrants from the former Soviet Union. It has chapters and independent associations in seven states, including New York, Ohio, Colorado, New Jersey, Massachusetts, Wisconsin and Maryland. The national organization is a member of the National Immigration Forum and it is affiliated with the United Jewish Communities, Washington Action Office. It has become a founding member of the Jewish Community Relations Council of New York and the New York Immigration Coalition. Local Chapters work in cooperation with Jewish Federation and New York Chapter works in co-operation with JCRC, NYANA, HIAS and UJA-Federation of New York. The AAJFSU assists newcomers in their re-settlement and vocational and cultural adjustment, fosters their Jewish identity and involvement in American civic and social affairs, fights anti-Semitism and vi-olation of human rights in the FSU and the U.S. through cooperation with other human rights organizations and advocacy organizations, supports struggle of Israeli Jews for sustainable peace, collects money for Israeli victims of terror, provides as-sistance in social safety net and natural-ization of the elderly and disabled, provides advocacy in cases of political asylum for victims of anti-Semitism in the FSU. *Chronicles of Anti-Semitism and Nationalism in Republics of the Former USSR (in English, annually); Information Bulletin (in Russian, quarterly).*

AMERICAN FEDERATION OF JEWS FROM CENTRAL EUROPE, INC. (1938). 570 Sev-enth Ave., NYC 10018. (212)921-3871. FAX: (212) 575-1918. Pres. Fritz Wein-schenk; Exec. Asst. Dennis E. Rohr-baugh. Seeks to safeguard the rights and interests of American Jews of German-speaking Central European descent, es-pecially in reference to restitution and indemnification; through its affiliate Re-search Foundation for Jewish Immigra-tion sponsors research and publications on the history, immigration, and accul-turation of Central European émigrés in the U.S. and worldwide; through its affil-iate Jewish Philanthropic Fund of 1933 supports social programs for needy Nazi victims in the U.S.; undertakes cultural activities, publications; member, Council of Jews from Germany, London.

AMERICAN VETERANS OF ISRAEL (1951). 136 E. 39 St., NYC 10016. E-mail: spielgelsi @aol.com. Pres. Samuel Z. Klausner; V-Pres. David Kaplan. Maintains contact with American and Canadian volunteers who served in Aliyah Bet and/or Israel's War of Independence; promotes Israel's welfare; holds memorial services at grave of Col. David Marcus; is affiliated with World Mahal. *Newsletter.*

ASSOCIATION OF YUGOSLAV JEWS IN THE UNITED STATES, INC. (1941). 130 E. 59 St., Suite 1202, NYC 10022. (212)371-6891. V.-Pres. & Chmn. Emanuel Salom; Sec. Dr. Joseph Stock. Assistance to all Jews originally from Yugoslavia— Bosnia, Serbia, Croatia—and new settlers in Israel. *Bulletins.*

BNAI ZION—THE AMERICAN FRATERNAL ZIONIST ORGANIZATION (1908). 136 E. 39 St., NYC 10016. (212)725-1211. FAX: (212)684-6327. Pres. Michael J. Lazar; Exec. V.-Pres. Mel Parness. Fosters prin-ciples of Americanism, fraternalism, and Zionism. The Bnai Zion Foundation sup-ports various humanitarian projects in Is-rael and the USA, chiefly the Bnai Zion Medical Center in Haifa and homes for retarded children-Maon Bnai Zion in Rosh Ha'ayin and the Herman Z. Quittman Center in Jerusalem Ahava Project. Also supports building of new central library in Ma'aleh Adumim. In U.S. sponsors program of awards for ex-cellence in Hebrew for high school and college students. Chapters all over U.S. *Bnai Zion Voice* (quarterly). (www. BNAIZION.ORG)

BRITH ABRAHAM (1859; reorg. 1887). 136 E. 39 St., NYC 10016. (212)725-1211. FAX: (212)684-6327. Grand Master Robert Freeman. Protects Jewish rights and combats anti-Semitism; supports So-viet and Ethiopian emigration and the safety and dignity of Jews worldwide; helps to support Bnai Zion Medical Cen-ter in Haifa and other Israeli institutions;

aids and supports various programs and projects in the U.S.: Hebrew Excellence Program-Gold Medal presentation in high schools and colleges; Camp Loyaltown; Brith Abraham and Bnai Zion Foundations. *Voice.*

BRITH SHOLOM (1905). 3939 Conshohocken Ave., Philadelphia, PA 19131. (215)878-5696. FAX: (215) 878-5699. Pres. Seymour Rose; Exec. Dir. Roy Shenberg; Exec. V. P., Jerome Verlin. Fraternal organization devoted to community welfare, protection of rights of Jewish people, and activities that foster Jewish identity and provide support for Israel. Through its philanthropic arm, the Brith Sholom Foundation (1962), sponsors Brith Sholom House in Philadelphia, nonprofit senior-citizen apartments; and Brith Sholom Beit Halochem in Haifa, Israel, rehabilitation, social, and sports center for disabled Israeli veterans, operated by Zahal. Chmn. Martin Winit; Exec. Dir. Saundra Laub. *Brith Sholom Digest; monthly news bulletin.*

FREE SONS OF ISRAEL (1849). 250 Fifth Ave., Suite 201, NYC 10001. (212)725-3690. FAX: (212)725-5874. Grand Master Arlene Hoberman Kyler; Grand Sec. Ronald J. Laszlo. Oldest Jewish fraternal-benefit society in U.S. Affordable membership men & women (18+). Supports Israel, UJA projects, non-sectarian toy drives/philanthropies. Social Action fights anti-Semitism, supports human rights. Member benefits-IBM Metro Credit Union, scholarships, cemetery, discounted Long Term Care Insurance, educational and social functions, Free Model Seder. *Free Sons Reporter.* (WWW.FREESONS.ORG)

JEWISH LABOR BUND (Directed by World Coordinating Committee of the Bund) (1897; reorg. 1947). 25 E. 21 St., NYC 10010. (212)475-0059. FAX: (212) 473-5102. Acting Pres. Motl Zelmanowics; Sec. Gen. Benjamin Nade. Coordinates activities of Bund organizations throughout the world and represents them in the Socialist International; spreads the ideas of socialism as formulated by the Jewish Labor Bund; publishes books and periodicals on world problems, Jewish life, socialist theory and policy, and on the history, activities, and ideology of the Jewish Labor Bund. *Unser Tsait* (U.S.); *Lebns-Fragn* (Israel); *Unser Gedank* (Australia).

SEPHARDIC JEWISH BROTHERHOOD OF AMERICA, INC. (1915). 97-45 Queens Blvd., Rm. 610, Rego Park, NY 11374. (718)459-1600. Pres. Bernard Ouziel; Sec. Irving Barocas. A benevolent fraternal organization seeking to promote the industrial, social, educational, and religious welfare of its members. *Sephardic Brother.*

SIGMA ALPHA MU FRATERNITY (1909). 9245 No. Meridian St., Ste. 105, Indianapolis, IN 46260. (317)846-0600. FAX: (317)846-9462. E-mail: samhq@sam.org. Sup. Prior Leland P.Manders; Exec. Dir. Aaron M. Girson. Founded at the City College of NY as a fraternity of Jewish men, currently active on 70 campuses across North America. Encourages students to take an active role on campus, offers leadership opportunities and financial aid to members and scholarships to leaders of Jewish youth groups. *Octogonian of Sigma Alpha Mu (quarterly).*

THE WORKMEN'S CIRCLE/ARBETER RING (1900). 45 E. 33 St., NYC 10016. (212)889-6800. FAX: (212)532-7518. E-mail: member@circle.org. Pres. Martin Krupnick; Exec. Dir. Robert Kestenbaum. Fosters Jewish identity and participation in Jewish life through Jewish, especially Yiddish, culture and education, friendship, mutual aid, and the pursuit of social and economic justice. Offices are located throughout the U.S. and Canada. Member services include:Jewish cultural seminars, concerts, theater, Jewish schools, children's camp and adult resort, fraternal and singles activities, a Jewish Book Center, public affairs/social action, health insurance plans, medical/dental/legal services, life insurance plans, cemetery/funeral benefits, social services, geriatric homes and centers, and travel services. *The Call.* (WWW.CIRCLE.ORG)

ZETA BETA TAU FRATERNITY (1898). 3905 Vincennes Rd., Suite 300, Indianapolis, IN 46268. (317)334-1898. FAX: (317)334-1899. E-mail: zbt@zbtnational.org. Pres. Kenneth L. Simon, M.D.; Exec. Dir. Jonathan I. Yulish. Oldest historically Jewish fraternity; promotes intellectual awareness, social responsibility, integrity, and brotherhood among over 5,000 undergrads and 110,000 alumni in the U.S. and Canada. Encourages leadership and diversity through mutual respect of all heritages; nonsectarian since 1954. A brotherhood of Kappa Nu, Phi Alpha, Phi Epsilon Pi, Phi Sigma Delta, Zeta Beta Tau. *The Deltan (quarterly).* (www. ZBT.ORG)

SOCIAL WELFARE

AMC CANCER RESEARCH CENTER (formerly JEWISH CONSUMPTIVES' RELIEF SOCIETY, 1904; incorporated as American Medical Center at Denver, 1954). 1600 Pierce St., Denver, CO 80214. (303) 233-6501. FAX: (303)239-3400. E-mail: edelmanj@amc.org. Pres./CEO Bob R. Baker; Exec. V-Pres. Research Dr. Tom Slaga. A nationally recognized leader in the fight against cancer; employs a three-pronged, interdisciplinary approach that combines laboratory, clinical, and community cancer-control research to advance the prevention, early detection, diagnosis, and treatment of the disease. The exclusive scientific focus of our work is the prevention and control of cancer and other major diseases. *The Quest for Answers; Annual Report.* (WWW.AMC.ORG)

AMCHA FOR TSEDAKAH (1990). 9800 Cherry Hill Rd., College Park, MD 20740. (301)937-2600. Pres. Rabbi Bruce E. Kahn. Solicits and distributes contributions to Jewish charitable organizations in the U.S. and Israel; accredits organizations which serve an important tsedakah purpose, demonstrate efficiency and fiscal integrity, and also support pluralism. Contributors are encouraged to earmark contributions for specific organizations; all contributions to General Fund are forwarded to the charitable institutions, as operating expenses are covered by a separate fund. *Newspaper supplement.*

AMERICAN JEWISH CORRECTIONAL CHAPLAINS ASSOCIATION, INC. (formerly NATIONAL COUNCIL OF JEWISH PRISON CHAPLAINS) (1937). 10 E. 73 St., NYC 10021-4194. (212)879-8415. FAX: (212) 772-3977. (Cooperates with the New York Board of Rabbis.) Supports spiritual, moral, and social services for Jewish men and women in corrections; stimulates support of correctional chaplaincy; provides spiritual and professional fellowship for Jewish correctional chaplains; promotes sound standards for correctional chaplaincy; schedules workshops and research to aid chaplains in counseling and with religious services for Jewish inmates. Constituent, American Correctional Chaplains Association. *Chaplains Manual.*

AMERICAN JEWISH SOCIETY FOR SERVICE, INC. (1950). 15 E. 26 St., Rm. 1029, NYC 10010. (212)683-6178. Email: aud1750@ aol.com. Founder/Chmn. Henry Kohn; Pres. Lawrence G. Green; Exec. Dirs. Carl & Audrey Brenner. Conducts voluntary work-service camps each summer to enable high school juniors and seniors to perform humanitarian service.

ASSOCIATION OF JEWISH AGING SERVICES (formerly NORTH AMERICAN ASSOCIATION OF JEWISH HOMES AND HOUSING FOR THE AGING) (1960). 316 Pennsylvania Ave., SE, Suite 402, Washington, DC 20003. (202) 543-7500. FAX: (202)543-4090. E-mail: ajas@ajas.org. Pres. Jodi L. Lyons; Chmn. Michael Ellentuck. Represents nearly all the not-for-profit charitable homes and housing for the Jewish aging; promotes excellence in performance and quality of service through fostering communication and education and encouraging advocacy for the aging; conducts annual conferences and institutes. *Directory; The Scribe (quarterly newsletter).*

ASSOCIATION OF JEWISH CENTER PROFESSIONALS (1918). 15 E. 26 St., NYC 10010-1579. (212)532-4949. FAX: (212) 481-4174. E-mail: ajcp@jcca.org. Pres. Susan Bender; Exec. Dir. Harvey Rosenzweig. Seeks to enhance the standards, techniques, practices, scope, and public understanding of Jewish community center professionals and kindred agency work. *Kesher.*

ASSOCIATION OF JEWISH COMMUNITY ORGANIZATION PERSONNEL (AJCOP) (1969). 14619 Horseshoe Trace, Wellington, FL 33414. (561)795-4853. FAX: (561)798-0358. E-mail: marlene@ajcop.org. Pres. Rabbi Daniel Allen; Exec. Dir. Louis B. Solomon. An organization of professionals engaged in areas of fund-raising, endowments, budgeting, social planning, financing, administration, and coordination of services. Objectives are to develop and enhance professional practices in Jewish communal work; to maintain and improve standards, practices, scope, and public understanding of the field of community organization, as practiced through local federations, national agencies, other organizations, settings, and private practitioners. *Prolog (quarterly newspaper); Proceedings (annual record of papers and speeches).* (WWW.AJCOP.ORG)

ASSOCIATION OF JEWISH FAMILY AND CHILDREN'S AGENCIES (1972). 557 Cranbury Rd., Suite 2, E. Brunswick, NJ 08816-5419. (800) 634-7346. FAX: (732)432-7127. E-mail: ajfca@ajfca.org. Pres. Bert J. Goldberg; Bd. Chair. Lawrence Abramson. The national service organization for Jewish family and children's agencies in the U.S. and Canada. Reinforces member agencies in their efforts to sustain and enhance the quality of Jewish family and communal life. Operates the Elder Support Network for the national Jewish community. *Tachlis (quarterly); Professional Opportunities Bulletin; Executive Digest (monthly).* (WWW.AJFCA.ORG)

BARON DE HIRSCH FUND (1891). 130 E. 59 St., 12th fl., NYC 10022. (212)836-1358. FAX: (212)453-6512. Pres. Jenny Morgenthal; Mng. Dir. Lauren Katzowitz. Aids Jewish immigrants in the U.S. and Israel by giving grants to agencies active in resettlement, focusing on educational, community development, and vocational training.

B'NAI B'RITH (1843). 1640 Rhode Island Ave., NW, Washington, DC 20036. (202) 857-6600. FAX: (202)857-1099. Pres. Richard D. Heideman; Exec. V.-Pres. Daniel S. Mariaschin. International Jewish organization, with affiliates in 58 countries. Offers programs designed to ensure the preservation of Jewry and Judaism: Jewish education, community volunteer service, expansion of human rights, assistance to Israel, housing for the elderly, leadership training, rights of Jews in all countries to study their heritage. *International Jewish Monthly; B'nai B'rith Today.*

——, ANTI-DEFAMATION LEAGUE OF (see p. 616)

——, HILLEL (see p. 647)

——, KLUTZNICK MUSEUM (see p. 621)

——, YOUTH ORGANIZATION (see p. 645)

CITY OF HOPE NATIONAL MEDICAL CENTER AND BECKMAN RESEARCH INSTITUTE (1913). 1500 E. Duarte Rd., Duarte, CA 91010. (626)359-8111. FAX: (626) 301-8115. E-mail: dhalper@coh.org. Exec. V. P. Krontiris; Medical and Scientific Affairs Theodore. City of Hope is one of the world's leading research and treatment centers for cancer and other life-threatening diseases, including diabetes and HIV/AIDS. A pioneer in the fields of bone marrow transplantation and genetics, City of Hope is a Comprehensive Cancer Center, the highest designation bestowed by the National Cancer Institute, and a founding member of the National Comprehensive Cancer Network. *City of Hope Cancer Research Center Report.*

CONFERENCE OF JEWISH COMMUNAL SERVICE (see JEWISH COMMUNAL SERVICE ASSOCIATION OF N. AMERICA)

COUNCIL OF JEWISH FEDERATIONS (see UNITED JEWISH COMMUNITIES)

INTERNATIONAL ASSOCIATION OF JEWISH VOCATIONAL SERVICES (formerly Jewish Occupational Council) (1939). 1845 Walnut St., Suite 640, Philadelphia, PA 19103. (215) 854-0233. FAX: (215)854-0212. E-mail: coheng@iajvs.org. Exec. Dir. Genie Cohen; Vivian Seigel, President. Not-for-profit membership association of Jewish-sponsored social service agencies in the U.S., Canada, and Israel. Provides member agencies with technical, informational, and communications support; researches funding opportunities, develops collaborative program models, and represents Jewish vocational network nationally and internationally. Sponsors annual conference for members. Member agencies provide a wide range of educational, vocational, and rehabilitation services to both the Jewish and non-Jewish communities. *Executive quarterly newsletter.* (WWW.IAJVS.ORG)

INTERNATIONAL COUNCIL ON JEWISH SOCIAL AND WELFARE SERVICES (1961). c/o American Jewish Joint Distribution Committee, 711 Third Ave., NYC 10017. (NY liaison office with UN headquarters.) (212)687-6200. FAX: (212)370-5467. E-mail: newyork@jdcny.org. Pres. Eugene J. Ribokoff; Exec. V. P. Steven Schwager. Provides assistance to Jewish communities in Europe, Asia, Africa, and the Mideast, including welfare programs for Jews in need. Current concerns include:Rescuing Jews from areas of distress, facilitating community development in the former Soviet Union; helping to meet Israel's social service needs by developing innovative programs that create new opportunities for the country's most vulnerable populations; youth activities in Eastern Europe and nonsectariean development and disaster assistance. *Annual Report, JDC's Activities in the Former Soviet Union; JDC: One People One Heart, Crisis in Argentina Monthly Update.*

JBI INTERNATIONAL (FOUNDED IN 1931 AS THE JEWISH BRAILLE INSTITUTE OF AMERICA, INC.) (1931). 110 E. 30 St., NYC 10016. (212)889-2525. FAX: (212)689-3692. E-mail: sradinsky@jbilibrary.org. Pres. Barbara B. Friedman; Exec. V.-Pres. Dr. Ellen Isler. Provides Jewish books for the visually impaired, blind and reading-disabled on tape, in large print, and in Braille. International program serves clients in more than 50 countries; sponsors special programs in Israel and Eastern Europe. Periodical and journals available to our subscribers include *Moment, Tikkun, the Jerusalem Reporter and Commentary.* (WWW.JBILIBRARY.ORG)

JEWISH CHILDREN'S ADOPTION NETWORK (1990). PO Box 147016, Denver, CO 80214-7016. (303)573-8113. FAX: (303) 893-1447. E-mail: jcan@qwest.net. Pres. Stephen Krausz; Exec. Dir. Vicki Krausz. An adoption exchange founded for the primary purpose of locating adoptive families for Jewish infants and children. Works with some 200 children a year, throughout N. Amer., 85-90% of whom have special needs. No fees charged for services, which include birth-parent and adoptive-parent counseling. *Quarterly newsletter.* (WWW.USERS.QWEST.NET/JCAN)

JEWISH COMMUNAL SERVICE ASSOCIATION OF N. AMERICA (1899; formerly CONFERENCE OF JEWISH COMMUNAL SERVICE). 3084 State Hwy. 27, Suite 9, Kendall Park, NJ 08824-1657. (732)821-1871. FAX: (732)821-5335. E-mail: jcsana@aol.com. Pres. Dr. Audrey S. Weiner; Exec. Dir. Brenda Gevertz. Serves as forum for all professional philosophies in community service, for testing new experiences, proposing new ideas, and questioning or reaffirming old concepts; umbrella organization for 7 major Jewish communal service groups. Concerned with advancement of professional personnel practices and standards. *Journal of Jewish Communal Service; Concurrents.*

JEWISH COMMUNITY CENTERS ASSOCIATION OF NORTH AMERICA (formerly JWB)

(1917). 15 E. 26 St., NYC 10010-1579. (212)532-4949. FAX: (212)481-4174. E-mail: info@jcca.org. Chair Edward H. Kaplan; Pres. Allan Finkelstein. The leadership network of, and central agency for, the Jewish Community Center movement, comprising more than 275 JCCs, YM-YWHAs, and camps in the U.S. and Canada, which annually serve more than one million members and an additional million non-member users. JCC Association offers a wide range of services and resources to strengthen the capacity of its affiliates to provide educational, cultural, social, Jewish identity-building, and recreational programs to enhance the lives of North American Jews of all ages and backgrounds. Additionally, the movement fosters and strengthens connections between North American Jews and Israel as well as with world Jewry. JCC Association is also the only U.S. government-accredited agency for serving the religious and social needs of Jewish military personnel, their families, and patients in VA hospitals through JWB Chaplains Council. *JCC Circle; Chaplines; other newsletters for JCC professionals.* (WWW.JCCA. ORG)

———, JEWISH WELFARE BOARD JEWISH CHAPLAINS COUNCIL (formerly COMMISSION ON JEWISH CHAPLAINCY) (1940). 15 E. 26 St., NYC 10010-1579. (212)532-4949. FAX: (212)481-4174. E-mail: nathanlandman@jcca.com. Chmn. Rabbi David S. Goldstein; Dir. Rabbi David Lapp; Dep. Dir. Rabbi Nathan M. Landman. Recruits, endorses, and serves Jewish military and Veterans Administration chaplains on behalf of the American Jewish community and the major rabbinic bodies; trains and assists Jewish lay leaders where there are no chaplains, for service to Jewish military personnel, their families, and hospitalized veterans. *CHAPLINES newsletter.*

JEWISH FAMILY AND CHILDREN'S PROFESSIONALS ASSOCIATION (*see* Jewish Social Services Professionals Association)

JEWISH FUND FOR JUSTICE (1984). 260 Fifth Ave., Suite 701, NYC 10001. (212) 213-2113. FAX: (212)213-2233. E-mail: jfjustice @jfjustice.org. Bd. Chmn. John Levy; Exec. Dir. Marlene Provizer. The Jewish Fund for Justice is the only national Jewish organization solely committed to fighting the injustice of poverty in America. By assisting on a non-denominational basis grassroots organizations struggling for decent housing, schools and jobs, and by helping Jews develop community-based, social justice partnerships, the Jewish Fund for Justice brings to life the core Jewish values of *tikkun olam* (repair of the world) and *tzedakah* (righteous giving). Giving opportunities include general support, family, wedding, and youth endowment funds and planned giving. *Annual report, newsletter.* (WWW.JFJUSTICE.ORG)

JEWISH FUNDERS NETWORK (1990). 15 E. 26 St., Suite 1038, NYC 10010. (212) 726-0177. FAX: (212) 726-0195. E-mail: jfn@jfunders.org. Pres. Mark Charendoff. International agency providing leadership, programs and services to help Jewish grantmakers be more effective and strategic in their philanthropy. JFN members collaborate and plan so that their money can be used to effectively change the world. Key initiatives:International Conference, regional programs, publications, strategic partnerships, web site, consultation, resources and referral. *Quarterly Newsletter, Reports on Philanthropy.*

JEWISH SOCIAL SERVICES PROFESSIONALS ASSOCIATION (JSSPA) (1965). c/o AJFCA, 557 Cranbury Rd., Suite 2, E. Brunswick, NJ 08816-0549. (800) 634-7346. FAX: (732)432-7127. E-mail: ajfca@ajfca.org. Chmn. Jaclynn Faffer; Chair Elect Norman Keane. Brings together executives, supervisors, managers, caseworkers, and related professionals in Jewish Family Service and related agencies. Seeks to enhance professional skills, improve personnel standards, further Jewish continuity and identity, and strengthen Jewish family life. Provides a national and regional forum for professional discussion and learning; functions under the auspices of the Association of Jewish Family and Children's Agencies. *Newsletter.*(WWW.AJFCA.ORG)

JEWISH WOMEN INTERNATIONAL (1897). 1828 L St., NW, Suite 250, Washington, DC 20036. (202)857-1300. FAX: (202) 857-1380. E-mail: jwi@jwi.org. Pres. Barbara Rabkin; Exec. Dir. Gail Rubinson. Jewish Women International breaks the cycle of violence by developing emotionally healthy adults, empowering women and strengthening families. Jewish Women International accomplishes its goals through direct service programs, education, advocacy and the promotion of "best practice"models. Offers programs in the United States, Canada, and Israel. *Jewish Woman Magazine (quarterly).* (WWW.JEWISHWOMEN.ORG)

JWB (*see* JEWISH COMMUNITY CENTERS ASSOCIATION OF NORTH AMERICA)

LEVI HOSPITAL (1914). 300 Prospect Ave., Hot Springs, AR 71901. (501)624-1281. FAX: (501) 622-3500. E-mail: levi hospital@hsnp.com. Pres. Philip M. Clay; Admin. Patrick G. McCabe. Offers outpatient rehab, including therapy sessions in large thermal heated pool. Other programs:adult/geriatric inpatient and outpatient psychiatric program, child/adolescent psychiatric clinic, hospice care, home health care, osteoporosis clinic, Levi Rehabilitation Unit, a cooperative effort of Levi and St. Joseph's hospitals (inpatient rehab). *The Progress Chart; The Legacy.*

MAZON: A JEWISH RESPONSE TO HUNGER (1985). 1990 S. Bondy Drive, Suite 260, Los Angeles, CA 90025. (310)442-0020. FAX: (310)442-0030. E-mail: mazonmail @mazon.org. Exec. Dir. Eric Schockman, PhD. A grant-making and fund-raising organization that raises funds in the Jewish community and provides grants to nonprofit 501(c)(3) organizations which aim to prevent and alleviate hunger in the United States and abroad. Grantees include food pantries, food banks, multi-service organizations, advocacy, education and research projects, and international relief and development organizations. *Annual Report, 2 newsletters each year.*

NATIONAL ASSOCIATION OF JEWISH CHAPLAINS (1988). 901 Route 10, Whippany, NJ 07981. (973)929-3168. FAX: (973) 736-9193. E-mail: cecille3@juno.com. Pres. Rabbi Stephen Roberts; Natl. Coord. Cecille Allman Asekoff. A professional organization for people functioning as Jewish chaplains in hospitals, nursing homes, geriatric, psychiatric, correctional, and military facilities. Provides collegial support, continuing education, professional certification, and resources for the Jewish community on issues of pastoral and spiritual care. *The Jewish Chaplain.*

NATIONAL COUNCIL OF JEWISH PRISON CHAPLAINS, INC. (*see* AMERICAN JEWISH CORRECTIONAL CHAPLAINS ASSOCIATION, INC.)

NATIONAL COUNCIL OF JEWISH WOMEN (1893). 53 W. 23 St., NYC 10010. (212) 645-4048. FAX: (212)645-7466. E-mail: actionline@ncjw.org. Pres. Jan Schneiderman; Exec. Dir. Susan Katz. Works to improve the lives of women, children, and families in the United States and Israel; strives to insure individual rights and freedoms for all. NCJW volunteers deliver vital services in 500 U.S. communities and carry out NCJW's advocacy agenda through a powerful grassroots network. *NCJW Journal; Washington Newsletter.* (WWW.NCJW.ORG)

NATIONAL INSTITUTE FOR JEWISH HOSPICE (1985). PO Box 48025, Los Angeles, CA 90048. (800)446-4448. 330 Broad Ave., Englewood, NJ 07631. (201)816-7324. FAX: (201)816-7321. Pres. Rabbi Maurice Lamm; Exec. Dir. Shirley Lamm. Serves as a national Jewish hospice resource center. Through conferences, research, publications, referrals, and counseling services offers guidance, training, and information to patients, family members, clergy of all faiths, professional caregivers, and volunteers who work with the Jewish terminally ill. *Jewish Hospice Times.*

NATIONAL JEWISH CHILDREN'S LEUKEMIA FOUNDATION (1990). 172 Madison Avenue, NYC 10016. (212)686-2722. FAX: (212)686-2750. E-mail: leukemia@erols.com. Pres./Founder Zvi Shor. Dedicated to saving the lives of children. Programs:Bone Marrow Donor Search, Stem Cell Banking-freezing cells from babies' umbilical cords for long-term storage, in case of need for bone marrow; Make-A-Dream-Come True-granting wishes for terminally ill children; Referral Service; Patient Advocacy. (WWW.LEUKEMIA FOUNDATION.ORG)

NATIONAL JEWISH MEDICAL AND RESEARCH CENTER (formerly NATIONAL JEWISH HOSPITAL/NATIONAL ASTHMA CENTER) (1899). 1400 Jackson St., Denver, CO 80206. (800)222-LUNG. E-mail: lung line@njc.org. Pres./CEO Lynn M. Taussig, MD; Bd. Chmn. Lawrence Gelfond. The only medical and research center in the United States devoted entirely to respiratory, allergic, and immune system diseases, including asthma, tuberculosis, emphysema, severe allergies, AIDS, and cancer, and autoimmune diseases such as lupus. Dedicated to enhancing prevention, treatment, and cures through research, and to developing and providing innovative clinical programs for treating patients regardless of age, religion, race, or ability to pay. *New Directions; Medical Scientific Update.* (WWW.NATIONAL JEWISH.ORG)

NORTH AMERICAN ASSOCIATION OF JEWISH HOMES AND HOUSING FOR THE AGING (*see* ASSOCIATION OF JEWISH AGING SERVICES)

UNITED JEWISH COMMUNITIES (*see* p. 643)

UNITED ORDER TRUE SISTERS, INC. (UOTS) (1846). 100 State St., Suite 1020, Albany, NY 12207. (518)436-1670, Fax (518) 436-1573. Pres. Marian S. Cohen; Fin. Sec. Betty Peyser; Treas. Rose Goldberg. Charitable, community service, especially home supplies, etc., for indigent cancer victims; supports camps for children with cancer. *Inside UotS.* (WWW.UOTS.ORG)

WORLD COUNCIL OF JEWISH COMMUNAL SERVICE (1966; reorg. 1994). 711 Third Ave., 10th fl., NYC 10017. (212)687-6200. FAX: (212)370-5467. Pres. Howard Charish; Assoc. Pres. Dr. Jack Habib; Exec. V.-Pres. Theodore Comet. Seeks to build Jewish community worldwide by enhancing professional-to-professional connections, improving professional practice through interchange of experience and sharing of expertise, fostering professional training programs, and stimulating research. Conducts quadrennial conferences in Jerusalem and periodic regional meetings. *Proceedings of international conferences; newsletters.*

PROFESSIONAL ASSOCIATIONS*

AMERICAN ASSOCIATION OF RABBIS (Religious, Educational)

AMERICAN CONFERENCE OF CANTORS, UNION OF AMERICAN HEBREW CONGREGATIONS (Religious, Educational)

---

*For fuller listings see under category in parentheses.

AMERICAN JEWISH CORRECTIONAL CHAPLAINS ASSOCIATION, INC. (Social Welfare)

AMERICAN JEWISH PRESS ASSOCIATION (Cultural)

AMERICAN JEWISH PUBLIC RELATIONS SOCIETY (Community Relations)

ASSOCIATION OF HILLEL/JEWISH CAMPUS PROFESSIONALS (Religious, Educational)

ASSOCIATION OF JEWISH CENTER PROFESSIONALS (Social Welfare)

ASSOCIATION OF JEWISH COMMUNITY ORGANIZATION PERSONNEL (Social Welfare)

ASSOCIATION OF JEWISH COMMUNITY RELATIONS WORKERS (Community Relations)

CANTORS ASSEMBLY (Religious, Educational)

CENTRAL CONFERENCE OF AMERICAN RABBIS (Religious, Educational)

COUNCIL OF JEWISH ORGANIZATIONS IN CIVIL SERVICE (Community Relations)

INTERNATIONAL JEWISH MEDIA ASSOCIATION (Cultural)

JEWISH CHAPLAINS COUNCIL, JWB (Social Welfare)

JEWISH COMMUNAL SERVICE ASSOCIATION OF N. AMERICA (Social Welfare)

JEWISH EDUCATORS ASSEMBLY, UNITED SYNAGOGUE OF CONSERVATIVE JUDAISM (Religious, Educational)

JEWISH SOCIAL SERVICES PROFESSIONALS ASSOCIATION (Social Welfare)

JEWISH TEACHERS ASSOCIATION—MORIM (Religious, Educational)

NATIONAL ASSOCIATION OF HEBREW DAY SCHOOL ADMINISTRATORS, TORAH UMESORAH (Religious, Educational)

NATIONAL ASSOCIATION OF JEWISH CHAPLAINS (Social Welfare)

NATIONAL ASSOCIATION OF TEMPLE ADMINISTRATORS, UNION OF AMERICAN HEBREW CONGREGATIONS (Religious, Educational)

NATIONAL ASSOCIATION OF TEMPLE EDUCATORS, UNION OF AMERICAN HEBREW CONGREGATIONS (Religious, Educational)

NATIONAL CONFERENCE OF YESHIVA PRINCIPALS, TORAH UMESORAH (Religious, Educational)

NORTH AMERICAN ASSOCIATION OF SYNAGOGUE EXECUTIVES, UNITED SYNAGOGUE OF CONSERVATIVE JUDAISM (Religious, Educational)

RABBINICAL ALLIANCE OF AMERICA (Religious, Educational)

RABBINICAL ASSEMBLY (Religious, Educational)

RABBINICAL COUNCIL OF AMERICA (Religious, Educational)

RECONSTRUCTIONIST RABBINICAL ASSOCIATION (Religious, Educational)

UNION OF ORTHODOX RABBIS OF THE U.S. AND CANADA (Religious, Educational)

WORLD CONFERENCE OF JEWISH COMMUNAL SERVICE (Community Relations)

WOMEN'S ORGANIZATIONS*

AMIT WOMEN (Israel-Related)

BRANDEIS UNIVERSITY NATIONAL WOMEN'S COMMITTEE (Educational)

EMUNAH WOMEN OF AMERICA (Israel-Related)

HADASSAH, THE WOMEN'S ZIONIST ORGANIZATION OF AMERICA (Israel-Related)

JEWISH WOMEN INTERNATIONAL (Social Welfare)

NA'AMAT USA, THE WOMEN'S LABOR ZIONIST ORGANIZATION OF AMERICA (Israel-Related)

NATIONAL COUNCIL OF JEWISH WOMEN (Social Welfare)

UOTS (Social Welfare)

WOMEN OF REFORM JUDAISM—FEDERATION OF TEMPLE SISTERHOODS, UNION OF AMERICAN HEBREW CONGREGATIONS (Religious, Educational)

WOMEN'S AMERICAN ORT, AMERICAN ORT FEDERATION (Overseas Aid)

WOMEN'S BRANCH OF THE UNION OF ORTHODOX JEWISH CONGREGATIONS OF AMERICA (Religious, Educational)

---

*For fuller listings see under category in parentheses.

WOMEN'S DIVISION OF POALE AGUDATH IS-RAEL OF AMERICA (Israel-Related)

WOMEN'S LEAGUE FOR CONSERVATIVE JU-DAISM (Religious, Educational)

WOMEN'S LEAGUE FOR ISRAEL, INC. (Israel-Related)

WOMEN'S ORGANIZATION, YESHIVA UNI-VERSITY (Religious, Educational)

YOUTH AND STUDENT ORGANIZATIONS*

AGUDATH ISRAEL OF AMERICA (Religious, Educational)

B'NAI B'RITH YOUTH ORGANIZATION (Religious, Educational)

BNEI AKIVA OF NORTH AMERICA, RELI-GIOUS ZIONISTS OF AMERICA (Israel-Related)

HABONIM—DROR NORTH AMERICA (Israel-Related)

HASHOMER HATZAIR, SOCIALIST ZIONIST YOUTH MOVEMENT (Israel-Related)

HILLEL (Religious, Educational)

KADIMA, UNITED SYNAGOGUE OF CONSER-VATIVE JUDAISM (Religious, Educational)

NATIONAL CONFERENCE OF SYNAGOGUE YOUTH, UNION OF ORTHODOX JEWISH CONGREGATIONS OF AMERICA (Religious, Educational)

NATIONAL JEWISH COMMITTEE ON SCOUT-ING (Religious, Educational)

NATIONAL JEWISH GIRL SCOUT COMMITTEE (Religious, Educational)

NORTH AMERICAN ALLIANCE FOR JEWISH YOUTH (Religious, Educational)

NORTH AMERICAN FEDERATION OF TEMPLE YOUTH, UNION OF AMERICAN HEBREW CONGREGATIONS (Religious, Educational)

STUDENT STRUGGLE FOR SOVIET JEWRY—SEE CENTER FOR RUSSIAN JEWRY (Community Relations)

YOUNG JUDAEA/HASHACHAR, HADASSAH (Israel-Related)

YUGNTRUF—YOUTH FOR YIDDISH (Cultural)

CANADA

AISH HATORAH (1981). 949 Clark Ave., W., Thornhill, ONT L4J8G6. (905)764-1818. FAX: (905)764-1606. E-mail: www. Aish. com. Edu. Dir. Rabbi Ahron Hoch; Dr. Allan Seidenfeld. An educational center, a community center, and a network of synagogues throughout Toronto; seeks to reawaken Jewish values, ignite Jewish pride and promote Jewish unity through education; reaches out to Jews from all backgrounds in a friendly, warm and non-judgmental environment. *Shabbat Shalom Fax, Monthly newsletter-Village Shul, Winter, Sping, Summer, Fall Calendars.* (WWW.AISH.EDU)

B'NAI BRITH CANADA (1875). 15 Hove St., Downsview, ONT M3H 4Y8. (416) 633-6224. FAX: (416)630-2159. E-mail: fdimant@bnaibrith.ca. Pres. Rochelle Wilner; Exec. V.-Pres. Frank Dimant. Canadian Jewry's major advocacy and service organization; maintains an office of Government Relations in Ottawa and co-sponsors the Canada Israel Committee; makes representations to all levels of government on matters of Jewish concern; promotes humanitarian causes and educational programs, community projects, adult Jewish education, and leadership development; dedicated to the preservation and unity of the Jewish community in Canada and to human rights. *The Jewish Tribune.*

——, INSTITUTE FOR INTERNATIONAL AF-FAIRS (1987). E-mail: institute@bnai brith.ca. Ch. Rochelle Wilner; Natl. Dir. Ruth Klein. Identifies and protests the abuse of human rights worldwide. Advocates on behalf of Israel and Jewish communities in distress. Monitors national and international legislation dealing with war crimes. Activities include briefs and consultations with governmental and non-governmental organizations, research and public education, advocacy and community mobilization, media monitoring, and international conferences and fact-finding missions. *Ad hoc publications on human rights issues.*

——, LEAGUE FOR HUMAN RIGHTS (1964). Co-Chmn. Marvin Kurz & Dr Harriet Morris. National volunteer asso-

---

*For fuller listings see under category in parentheses.

ciation dedicated to combating racism, bigotry, and anti-Semitism. Educational programs include multicultural antiracist workshops, public speakers, Holocaust education, Media Human Rights Awards; legal and legislative activity includes government submissions, court interventions, monitoring hate-group activity, responding to incidents of racism and anti-Semitism; community liaison includes intergroup dialogue and support for aggrieved vulnerable communities and groups. Canadian distributor of ADL material. *Heritage Front Report: 1994; Anti-Semitism on Campus; Skinheads in Canada; Annual Audit of Anti-Semitic Incidents; Holocaust and Hope Educators' Newsletter; Combatting Hate: Guidelines for Community Action.*

————, NATIONAL FIELD SERVICES DEPARTMENT. Natl. Dir. Pearl Gladman. Services community affordable housing projects, sports leagues, food baskets for the needy; coordinates hands-on national volunteer programming, Tel-Aide Distress Line; responsible for lodge membership; direct-mail campaigns, annual convention and foundation dinners.

CANADIAN FRIENDS OF CALI & AMAL (1944). 7005 Kildare Rd., Suite 14, Côte St. Luc, Quebec, H4W 1C1. (514)484-9430. FAX: (514)484-0968. Pres. Harry J.F. Bloomfield, QC; Exec. Dir. Fran Kula. Incorporates Canadian Association for Labour Israel (Histadrut) and Canadian Friends of Amal; supports comprehensive health care and education in Israel. Helps to provide modern medical and surgical facilities and the finest vocational, technical education to the Israeli people of all ages.

CANADIAN FRIENDS OF THE HEBREW UNIVERSITY OF JERUSALEM (1944). 3080 Yonge St., Suite 5024, Toronto, ONT M4N 3N1. (416) 485-8000. FAX: (416) 485-8565. E-mail: inquiry@cfhu.org. Pres. Stephen Victor, QC; Natl. Dir. Charles S. Diamond. Represents the Hebrew University of Jerusalem in Canada; serves as fund-raising arm for the university in Canada; recruits Canadian students and promotes study programs for foreign students at the university; sponsors social and educational events across Canada.

CANADIAN JEWISH CONGRESS (1919; reorg. 1934). 100 Sparks Street, Suite 650, Ottawa, Ontario K1P 5B7. (613)233-8703. FAX: (613)233-8748. E-mail: canadian jewishcongress@cjc.ca. Pres. Keith M. Landy; Exec. V. Pres./General Counsel Jack Silverstone. The community's national voice on public affairs, Canadian Jewish Congress works with governments, community organizations and other partners to fight antisemitism and racism, to promote positive links to Israel and to other Jewish communities, and to support humanitarian and human rights efforts. *DAIS; National Archives Newsletter; regional newsletters.*

CANADIAN YOUNG JUDAEA (1917). 788 Marlee Ave., Suite 205, Toronto, ONT M6B 3K1. (416)781-5156. FAX: (416) 787-3100. E-mail: cyj@idirect.com. Natl. Exec. Dir. Risa Epstein. Strives to attract Jewish youth to Zionism, with goal of aliyah; educates youth about Jewish history and Zionism; prepares them to provide leadership in Young Judaea camps in Canada and Israel and to be concerned Jews. *Judaean L'Madrich; Young Judaean.*

CANADIAN ZIONIST FEDERATION (1967). 5151 Côte St. Catherine Rd., #206, Montreal, PQ H3W 1M6. (514)739-7300. FAX: (514)739-9412. Pres. Kurt Rothschild; Natl. Sec. Florence Simon. Umbrella organization of distinct constituent member Zionist organizations in Canada; carries on major activities in all areas of Jewish life through its departments of education and culture, aliyah, youth and students, public affairs, and small Jewish communities, for the purpose of strengthening the State of Israel and the Canadian Jewish community. *Canadian Zionist.*

————, BUREAU OF EDUCATION AND CULTURE (1972). Pres. Kurt Rothschild. Provides counseling by pedagogic experts, in-service teacher-training courses and seminars in Canada and Israel; national pedagogic council and research center; distributes educational material and teaching aids; supports annual Bible contest and Hebrew-language courses for adults; awards scholarships to Canadian high-school graduates studying for one year in Israel.

HADASSAH—WIZO ORGANIZATION OF CANADA (1917). 1310 Greene Ave., Suite 900, Montreal, PQ H3Z 2B8. (514)937-9431. FAX: (514)933-6483. E-mail: natoff

@canadian-hadassah-wizo.org. Natl. Pres. Rochelle Levinson; Natl. Exec. V.-Pres. Lily Frank. Largest women's volunteer Zionist organization in Canada, located in 43 Canadian cities; dedicated to advancing the quality of life of the women and children in Israel through financial assistance and support of its many projects, day-care centers, schools, institutions, and hospitals. In Canada, the organization promotes Canadian ideals of democracy and is a stalwart advocate of women's issues. *Orah Magazine.*

HASHOMER HATZAIR (1913). 1111 Finch Ave. W., #456, Downsview, ONT M3J 2E5. (416)736-1339. FAX: (416)736-1405. E-mail: mail@givathaviva.ca. Shlicha-Ora Merin; Pres. Sheryl Neshel; Sec. Lipa Roth. A Zionist youth movement established over 80 years ago with centers all over the world. In Toronto, there are weekly meetings during the school year where children get a strong sense of their Jewish identity and connection to Israel, celebrate Jewish holidays together and learn to be contributing members of the community. Hashomer Hatzair runs a 6-day residential winter camp and a 6-week summer camp for youth ranging from 7-16 on Otty Lake.

INTERNATIONAL JEWISH CORRESPONDENCE (IJC) (1978). c/o Canadian Jewish Congress, 1590 Dr. Penfield Ave., Montreal, PQ H3G 1C5.9 (514)931-7531. FAX: (514)931-0548. E-mail: barrys@cjc.ca. Founder/Dir. Barry Simon. Aims to encourage contact between Jews of all ages and backgrounds, in all countries, through pen-pal correspondence. Send autobiographical data and stamped self-addressed envelope or its equivalent (to cover cost of Canadian postage) to receive addresses.

JEWISH IMMIGRANT AID SERVICES OF MONTREAL (JIAS) (1922). 5500 Westbury, 2nd Floor, Montreal, Quebec H3W-2W8. (514)342-9351. FAX: (514)342-0287. E-mail: jiasmail@aol.com. Pres. Joe Kislowicz; Exec. Dir. Shellie Ettinger. JIAS is a national organization assisting the lawful entry of Jews into Canada, as well as their settlement and integration ... *JIAS News for Clients.*

JEWISH NATIONAL FUND OF CANADA (Keren Kayemeth Le'Israel, Inc.) (1901). 1980 Sherbrooke St. W., Suite 500, Montreal, PQ H3H 1E8. (514)934-0313. FAX: (514)934-0382. E-mail: mtl@jnf.canada. org. Natl. Pres. Sandra Posluns; Exec. V.-Pres. Joe Rabinovitch. Fund-raising organization affiliated with the World Zionist Organization; involved in afforestation, soil reclamation, and development of the land of Israel, including the construction of roads and preparation of sites for new settlements; provides educational materials and programs to Jewish schools across Canada.

LABOUR ZIONIST ALLIANCE OF CANADA (1909). 272 Codsell Ave., Downsview, ONT M3H 3X2. (416)630-9444. FAX: (416)630-9451. Pres. Josef Krystal; City Committee Chmn. Montreal-Harry Froimovitch. Associated with the World Labor Zionist movement and allied with the Israel Labor party. Provides recreational and cultural programs, mutual aid, and fraternal care to enhance the social welfare of its membership; actively promotes Zionist education, cultural projects, and forums on aspects of Jewish and Canadian concern.

MERETZ CANADA (1950s). 1111 Finch Ave. W., Suite 456, Downsview, ONT M3J 2E5. (416)736-1339. FAX: (416)736-1405. Pres. Joseph Podemski., Vice Pres. Lipa Roth. Acts as a voice of Socialist-Democratic and Zionist points of view within the Jewish community and a focal point for progressive Zionist elements in Canada; affiliated with Hashomer Hatzair and the Givat Haviva Educational Center.

MIZRACHI ORGANIZATION OF CANADA (1941). 296 Wilson Ave., North York, ONT M3H 1S8. (416)630-9266. FAX: (416)630-2305. Pres. Jack Kahn. Promotes religious Zionism, aimed at making Israel a state based on Torah; maintains Bnei Akiva, a summer camp, adult education program, and touring department; supports Mizrachi-Hapoel Hamizrachi and other religious Zionist institutions in Israel which strengthen traditional Judaism. *Mizrachi Newsletter.*

NATIONAL COMMUNITY RELATIONS COMMITTEE OF CANADIAN JEWISH CONGRESS (1936). 4600 Bathurst St., Toronto, ONT M2R 3V2. (416)631-5673. FAX: (416) 635-1408. E-mail: mprutschi@ujafed. org. Chmn. Ellen T. Cole; Pres. Keith M. Landy; Dir. Manuel Prutschi. Seeks to safeguard the status, rights, and welfare of Jews in Canada; to combat antisemitism, and promote understanding and goodwill among all ethnic and religious groups.

NATIONAL COUNCIL OF JEWISH WOMEN OF CANADA (1897). 118-1588 Main St., Winnipeg, MAN R2V 1Y3. (204)339-9700. FAX: (204)334-3779. E-mail: info@ncjwc.org. Chmn. Carol Slater; Natl. V.-Pres. Roz Fine & Brenlee Gurvey Gales. Dedicated to furthering human welfare in the Jewish and general communities, locally, nationally, and internationally; through an integrated program of education, service, and social action seeks to fulfill unmet needs and to serve the individual and the community. *National ByLines.*

ORT CANADA (1948). 3101 Bathurst St., Suite 604, Toronto, ONT M6A 2A6. (416)787-0339. FAX: (416) 787-9420. E-mail: info@ort-toronto.org. Pres. Dr. Roger Korman; Exec. Dir. Joel Shapiro. Chapters in 11 Canadian cities raise funds for ORT's nonprofit global network of schools where Jewish students learn a wide range of marketable skills, including the most advanced high-tech professions. *Focus Magazine.*

STATE OF ISRAEL BONDS (CANADA-ISRAEL SECURITIES, LTD.) (1953). 970 Lawrence Ave. W., Suite 502, Toronto, ONT M6A 3B6. (416)789-3351. FAX: (416)789-9436. Pres. Norman Spector; Bd. Chmn. George A. Cohon. An international securities organization offering interest-bearing instruments issued by the government of Israel. Invests in every aspect of Israel's economy, including agriculture, commerce, and industry. Israel Bonds are RRSP-approved.

Jewish Federations, Welfare Funds, Community Councils

UNITED STATES

ALABAMA

BIRMINGHAM

BIRMINGHAM JEWISH FEDERATION (1936; reorg. 1971); Box 130219 (35213-0219); (205)879-0416. FAX: (205)803-1526. E-mail: federation@bjf.org. Exec. Dir. Richard Friedman. (WWW.BJF.ORG)

MOBILE

MOBILE JEWISH WELFARE FUND, INC. (inc. 1966); One Office Park, Suite 219 (36609); (334)343-7197. FAX: (334)343-7197. E-mail: mjwf123@aol.com. Pres. Eileen Susman.

MONTGOMERY

JEWISH FEDERATION OF MONTGOMERY, INC. (1930); 2820 Fairlane Dr. (36120-0058); (334)277-5820. FAX: (334)277-8383. E-mail: jfedmgm@aol.com. Pres. Alan Weil; Admin. Dir. Susan Mayer Bruchis.

ARIZONA

PHOENIX

JEWISH FEDERATION OF GREATER PHOENIX (1940); 12701 N. Scottsdale Rd., Suite 201 (85254); (480)634-4900. FAX: (480)634-4588. E-mail: info@jewishphoenix.org. Pres. Neil Hiller; Exec. Dir. Arthur Paikowsky. (WWW.JEWISHPHOENIX.ORG)

TUCSON

JEWISH FEDERATION OF SOUTHERN ARIZONA (1946); 3822 East River Rd., Suite 100 (85718); (520)577-9393. FAX: (520)577-0734. E-mail: gbarnhill@jfsa.org. Pres. Linda Tumarkin; Exec. Dir. Stuart Mellan. (WWW.JEWISHTUCSON.ORG)

ARKANSAS

LITTLE ROCK

JEWISH FEDERATION OF ARKANSAS (1911); 425 N. University (72205); (501)663-3571. FAX: (501)663-7286. E-mail: jflar@aristotle. net. Pres. Doris Krain; Exec. Dir. Ziva Starr. (WWW.JEWISHARKANSAS.ATFREEWEB.COM)

CALIFORNIA

EAST BAY

JEWISH FEDERATION OF THE GREATER EAST BAY (including Alameda & Contra Costa Counties) (1917); 401 Grand Ave., Oakland (94610-5022); (510)839-2900. FAX: (510) 839-3996. E-mail: admin@jfed.org. Pres. Marjorie Wolf; Exec. V.-Pres. Ami Nahshon. (WWW.JFED.ORG)

FRESNO

JEWISH FEDERATION OF FRESNO; 295 W. Cromwell Ave., Suite 111 (93711-6161); (559)432-2162. FAX: (559)432-0425.

LONG BEACH

JEWISH FEDERATION OF GREATER LONG BEACH AND W. ORANGE COUNTY (1937; inc. 1946); 3801 E. Willow St. (90815); (562)426-7601. FAX: (562)424-3915. E-mail: kgibbs@jewishlongbeach.org. Pres. Richard Lipeles; Exec. Dir. Michael S. Rassler. (WWW.JEWISHLONGBEACH.ORG)

LOS ANGELES

JEWISH FEDERATION COUNCIL OF GREATER LOS ANGELES (1912; reorg. 1959); 6505 Wilshire Blvd., 8th fl. (90048); (323)761-8000. FAX: (323)761-8235. E-mail: webcoordinator@jewishla.org. Pres. Lionel Bell; Exec. V.-Pres. William Bernstein. (WWW.JEWISH LA.ORG)

ORANGE COUNTY

JEWISH FEDERATION OF ORANGE COUNTY (1964; inc. 1965); 250 E. Baker St., Suite A, Costa Mesa (92626); (714)755-5555. FAX: (714)755-0307. E-mail: info@jfoc.org. Pres. Charles Karp; Exec. Dir. Bunnie Mauldin. (WWW.JFOC.ORG)

PALM SPRINGS

JEWISH FEDERATION OF PALM SPRINGS AND DESERT AREA (1971); 255 N. El Cielo, Suite 430 (92262-6990); (760)325-7281. FAX: (760)325-2188. E-mail: msjfedps@gte.net. Pres. Larry Pitts; Exec. Dir. Mitzi Schafer. (WWW.JEWISHPALMSPRINGS.ORG)

SACRAMENTO

JEWISH FEDERATION OF THE SACRAMENTO REGION (1948); 2351 Wyda Way (95825); (916)486-0906. FAX: (916)486-0816. E-mail: jfed2@juno.com. Pres. Skip Rosenbloom; Exec. Dir. Phillis Helene Cohen. (WWW.JEWISHSAC.ORG)

SAN DIEGO

UNITED JEWISH FEDERATION OF SAN DIEGO COUNTY (1936); 4950 Murphy Canyon Rd. (92123); (858)571-3444. FAX: (858)571-0701. E-mail: fedujf@ujfsd.org. Pres. Gary Jacobs; Exec. V.-Pres. Stephen M. Abramson. (WWW.JEWISHINSANDIEGO.ORG)

SAN FRANCISCO

JEWISH COMMUNITY FEDERATION OF SAN FRANCISCO, THE PENINSULA, MARIN, AND SONOMA COUNTIES (1910; reorg. 1955); 121 Steuart St. (94105); (415)777-0411. FAX: (415)495-6635. E-mail: info@sfjcf.org. Pres. Adele Corvin; CEO Samuel Salkin. (WWW. SFJCF.ORG)

SAN GABRIEL AND POMONA VALLEY

JEWISH FEDERATION OF THE GREATER SAN GABRIEL AND POMONA VALLEYS; 258 W. Badillo St. (91723-1906); (626)967-3656. FAX: (626)967-5135. E-mail: sgpvfed @aol.com. (WWW.SGPV.ORG)

SAN JOSE

JEWISH FEDERATION OF GREATER SAN JOSE (incl. Santa Clara County except Palo Alto and Los Altos) (1930; reorg. 1950); 14855 Oka Rd., Suite 2, Los Gatos (95030); (408)358-3033. FAX: (408)356-0733. E-

mail: federation@jfgsj.org. Pres. Bonnie Slavitt Moore; Interim Exec. Dir. Janet Berg. (WWW.JEWISHSILICONVALLEY.ORG)

SANTA BARBARA

SANTA BARBARA JEWISH FEDERATION (1974); 524 Chapala St. (93190); (805)957-1115. FAX: (805)957-9230. E-mail: sbjfed @silcom.com. Pres. Ron Fox; Exec. Dir. Shelly Katz. (WWW.JEWISHSANTABARBARA. ORG)

VENTURA COUNTY

JEWISH FEDERATION OF VENTURA COUNTY; 7620 Foothill Rd. (93004); (805)647-7800. FAX: (805)647-0482. E-mail: ujavtacty@ worldnet.att.net.

COLORADO

DENVER/BOULDER

ALLIED JEWISH FEDERATION OF COLORADO (1936); 300 S. Dahlia St., Denver (80222); (303)321-3399. FAX: (303)322-8328. E-mail: ajfcolo@aol.com. Chmn. Noel Ginsburg; Pres. & CEO:Doug Seserman. (WWW. JEWISHCOLORADO.ORG)

CONNECTICUT

BRIDGEPORT

JEWISH FEDERATION OF EASTERN FAIRFIELD COUNTY. (1936; reorg. 1981); 4200 Park Ave. (06604-1092); (203)372-6567. FAX: (203)374-0770. E-mail: jccs@snet.net. Chmn. Stanley Strouch; Pres. & CEO Daniel P. Baker. (WWW.JCCS.ORG)

DANBURY

THE JEWISH FEDERATION OF GREATER DANBURY, INC. (1945); 105 Newton Rd. (06810); (203)792-6353. FAX: (203)748-5099. E-mail: info@thejf.org. Pres. Daniel Wolinsky; Exec. Dir. Judy Prager. (WWW.THEJF.ORG)

EASTERN CONNECTICUT

JEWISH FEDERATION OF EASTERN CONNECTICUT, INC. (1950; inc. 1970); 28 Channing St., New London (06320); (860)442-8062. FAX: (860)443-4175. E-mail: jfec@ worldnet.att.net. Pres. Myron Hendel; Exec. Dir. Jerome E. Fischer.

GREENWICH

GREENWICH JEWISH FEDERATION (1956); One Holly Hill Lane (06830-6080); (203) 622-1434. FAX: (203)622-1237. E-mail: pezmom3@aol.com. Pres. Jonathan Nelson; Exec. Dir. Pam Zur.

HARTFORD

JEWISH FEDERATION OF GREATER HARTFORD (1945); 333 Bloomfield Ave., W. Hartford (06117); (860)232-4483. FAX: (860) 232-5221. E-mail: aperrault@jewishhartford.org. Pres. Robert Nabolchek; Acting Exec. Dir. Steven Bayer. (WWW.JEWISH HARTFORD.ORG)

NEW HAVEN

JEWISH FEDERATION OF GREATER NEW HAVEN (1928); 360 Amity Rd., Woodbridge (06525); (203)387-2424. FAX: (203)387-1818. E-mail: marinak@megahits.com Pres. David Schaefer; Exec. Dir. Neil Berro. (WWW.JEWISHNEWHAVEN.ORG)

NORWALK

(See Westport)

STAMFORD

UNITED JEWISH FEDERATION (inc. 1973); 1035 Newfield Ave., PO Box 3038 (06905); (203)321-1373. FAX: (203)322-3277. E-mail: office@ujf.org. Pres. Corrine Lotstein; Dir. of Dev. Edith Samers. (WWW.UJF.ORG)

WESTERN CONNECTICUT

JEWISH FEDERATION OF WESTERN CONNECTICUT (1938); 444 Maine St. N., Southbury (06488); (203)267-5121. FAX: (203) 267-3392. E-mail: jfedwtby@aol.com. Pres. Dan Goodman; Exec. Dir. Rob Zwang. (WWW.JFED.NET)

WESTPORT-WESTON-WILTON-NORWALK

UJA/FEDERATION OF WESTPORT—WESTON—WILTON—NORWALK (inc. 1980); 431 Post Road E., Suite 22, Westport (06880); (203)226-8197. FAX: (203)226-5051. E-mail: rkessler@optonline.net. Pres. Ed Goldstein; Exec. Dir. Robert Kessler. (WWW.UJAFEDERATION.ORG)

DELAWARE

WILMINGTON

JEWISH FEDERATION OF DELAWARE, INC. (1934); 100 W. 10th St., Suite 301 (19801-1628); (302)427-2100. FAX: (302)427-2438. E-mail: delawarejfd@jon.cjfny.org. Pres. Barry Kayne; Exec. V. Pres. Samuel H. Asher. (WWW.SHALOMDEL.ORG)

DISTRICT OF COLUMBIA

WASHINGTON

THE JEWISH FEDERATION OF GREATER WASHINGTON, INC. (1935); 6101 Montrose Rd., Rockville, MD (20852); (301)230-7200. FAX: (301)230-7265. E-mail: info@jewish fedwash.org. Pres. Michael C. Gelman; Exec. V.-Pres. Misha Galperin. (WWW.JEWISH FEDWASH.ORG)

FLORIDA

BREVARD COUNTY

JEWISH FEDERATION OF BREVARD (1974); 108-A Barton Ave., Rockledge (32955); (407)636-1824. FAX: (407)636-0614. E-mail: jfbrevard@aol.com. Pres. Gary Singer; Exec. Dir. Joanne Bishins.

BROWARD COUNTY

JEWISH FEDERATION OF BROWARD COUNTY (1943; 1968); 5890 S. Pine Island Rd., Davie (33351-7319); (954)252-6900. FAX: (954)252-6892. E-mail: info@jewishfed-broward.org. Pres. David B. Schulman; Exec. Dir. Gary N. Rubin. (WWW.JEWISH FEDBROWARD.ORG)

COLLIER COUNTY

JEWISH FEDERATION OF COLLIER COUNTY (1974); 1250 Tamiami Trail N., Suite 202, Naples (33940); (941) 263-4205. FAX: (941)263-3813. E-mail: jfccfl@aol.com. Pres. Ann Jacobson. (WWW.JEWISHNAPLES. ORG)

DAYTONA BEACH

(See Volusia & Flagler Counties)

FT. LAUDERDALE

(See Broward County)

GAINESVILLE

JEWISH COUNCIL OF NORTH CENTRAL FLORIDA; 1861 NW 21 St. (32604); (352) 371-3846. E-mail: oberger@gnv.fdt.net.

JACKSONVILLE

JACKSONVILLE JEWISH FEDERATION, INC. (1935); 8505 San Jose Blvd. (32217); (904)448-5000. FAX: (904)448-5715. E-mail: jaxjewishfed@jon.cjfny.org. Pres. Guy Benrubi; Exec. V.-Pres. Alan Margolies. (WWW.JAXJEWISH.ORG)

LEE COUNTY

JEWISH FEDERATION OF LEE AND CHARLOTTE COUNTIES (1974); 6237-E Presidential Court, Ft. Myers (33919-3568); (941) 481-4449. FAX: (941)481-0139. E-mail: jfedswfl@aol.com. Pres. Rozzi Osterman; Exec. Dir. Annette Goodman. (WWW.JEWISH FEDERATIONSWFL.ORG)

MIAMI

GREATER MIAMI JEWISH FEDERATION, INC. (1938); 4200 Biscayne Blvd. (33137); (305) 576-4000. FAX: (305)573-4584. E-mail: info@gmjf.or. Pres. Michael Scheck; Exec. V.-Pres. Jacob Solomon. (WWW.JEWISH MIAMI.ORG)

ORLANDO

JEWISH FEDERATION OF GREATER ORLANDO (1949); 851 N. Maitland Ave.; PO Box 941508, Maitland (32794-1508); (407)645-5933. FAX: (407)645-1172. Pres. James S. Grodin; Exec. Dir. Eric Geboff. (WWW. ORLANDOJEWISHFED.ORG)

PALM BEACH COUNTY

JEWISH FEDERATION OF PALM BEACH COUNTY, INC. (1962); 4601 Community Dr., W. Palm Beach (33417-2760); (561)478-0700. FAX: (561)478-9696. E-mail: info@ jfedpbco.org. Pres. Norman P. Goldblum; Exec. V.-Pres. Jeffrey L. Klein. (WWW.JEWISH PALMBEACH.ORG)

JEWISH FEDERATION OF SOUTH PALM BEACH COUNTY, INC. (1979); 9901 Donna Klein Blvd. Boca Raton (33428-1788); (561)852-3100. FAX: (561)852-3136. E-mail: dstern@ jewishboca.org. (WWW.JEWISHBOCA.ORG)

PENSACOLA

PENSACOLA JEWISH FEDERATION; 800 No. Palafox (32501); (850)434-7992.

PINELLAS COUNTY

JEWISH FEDERATION OF PINELLAS COUNTY, INC. (incl. Clearwater and St. Petersburg) (1950; reincorp. 1974); 13191 Starkey Rd., #8, Largo (33773-1438); (727) 530-3223. FAX: (727)531-0221. E-mail: pinellas@jfed-pinellas.org. Pres. David Abelson; Interim Exec. Dir. Bonnie Friedman. (WWW.JFED-PINELLAS.ORG)

SARASOTA-MANATEE

SARASOTA-MANATEE JEWISH FEDERATION (1959); 580 S. McIntosh Rd. (34232-1959); (941)371-4546. FAX: (941)378-2947. E-mail: jlederman@smjf.org. Pres. Scott Gordon; Exec. Dir. Jan C. Lederman. (WWW. SMJF.ORG)

TALLAHASSEE

APALACHEE FEDERATION OF JEWISH CHARITIES; PO Box 14825 (32317-4825); (850) 877-3989; FAX: (850)877-7989. E-mail: mdlevy@pol.net.

TAMPA

TAMPA JEWISH FEDERATION (1941); 13009 Community Campus Dr. (33625-4000); (813)264-9000. FAX: (813)265-8450. E-mail: tjfjcc@aol.com. Pres. Lili Kaufman; Exec. V.-Pres. Howard Borer. (WWW.JEWISH-TAMPA.ORG)

VOLUSIA & FLAGLER COUNTIES

JEWISH FEDERATION OF VOLUSIA & FLAGLER COUNTIES, INC. (1980); 733 S. Nova Rd., Ormond Beach (32174); (904)672-0294. FAX: (904)673-1316. Pres. Steven I. Unatin; Exec. Dir. Gloria Max.

GEORGIA

ATLANTA

JEWISH FEDERATION OF GREATER ATLANTA, INC. (1905; reorg. 1967); 1440 Spring St., NW (30309-2837); (404)873-1661. FAX: (404)874-7043/881-4027. E-mail: kkaplan @jfga.org. Pres. Dr. Arnold Rubenstein; Exec. Dir. David I. Sarnat. (WWW. SHALOM ATLANTA.ORG)

AUGUSTA

AUGUSTA JEWISH FEDERATION (1937); 898 Weinberger Way, Evans (30809-3636); (706)228-3636. FAX: (706)868-1660/823-3960. E-mail: mpousman@hotmail.com. Pres. Dr. Louis Scharff; Exec. Dir. Michael Pousman.

COLUMBUS

JEWISH FEDERATION OF COLUMBUS, INC. (1944); PO Box 6313 (31906); (706)568-6668. Pres. Murray Solomon; Sec. Irene Rainbow.

SAVANNAH

SAVANNAH JEWISH FEDERATION (1943); 5111 Abercorn St. (31403); (912)355-8111. FAX: (912)355-8116. E-mail: jrgreen4@juno.com. Pres. Dr. Paul Kulbersh; Exec. Dir. Moises Paz. (WWW.SAVJ.ORG)

ILLINOIS

CHAMPAIGN-URBANA

CHAMPAIGN-URBANA JEWISH FEDERATION (1929); 503 E. John St., Champaign (61820); (217)367-9872. FAX: (217)344-1540. E-mail: cujf@shalomcu.org. Pres. Anthony E. Novak; Exec. Dir. Lee Melhado. (WWW. SHALOMCU.ORG)

CHICAGO

JEWISH FEDERATION OF METROPOLITAN CHICAGO/JEWISH UNITED FUND OF METRO-

POLITAN CHICAGO (1900); Ben Gurion Way, 1 S. Franklin St. (60606-4694); (312)346-6700. FAX: (312)444-2086. E-mail: webinfo @juf.org. Chmn. Fred Bondy; Pres. Steven B. Nasatir. (WWW.JUF.ORG)

JOLIET

JOLIET JEWISH WELFARE CHEST (1938); 250 N. Midland Ave. at Campbell St. (60435); (815)741-4600.

PEORIA

JEWISH FEDERATION OF PEORIA (1933; inc. 1947); 2000 W. Pioneer Pwky., Suite 10B (61615-1835); (309)689-0063. FAX: (309) 689-0575. Pres. Jennifer Dolin; Exec. Dir. Eunice Galsky.

QUAD CITIES

JEWISH FEDERATION OF QUAD CITIES (1938; comb. 1973); 1705 2nd Ave., Suite 405, Rock Island (61201); (309)793-1300. FAX: (309)793-1345. E-mail: qcfederation@ juno.com. Pres. Paul Light; Exec. Dir. Ida Kramer.

ROCKFORD

JEWISH FEDERATION OF GREATER ROCKFORD (1937); 1500 Parkview Ave. (61107); (815)399-5497. FAX: (815)399-9835. E-mail: rockfordfederation@juno.com. Pres. Sterne Roufa; Exec. Dir. Marilyn Youman.

SOUTHERN ILLINOIS

JEWISH FEDERATION OF SOUTHERN ILLINOIS, SOUTHEASTERN MISSOURI, AND WESTERN KENTUCKY (1941); 6464 W. Main, Suite 7A, Belleville (62223); (618)398-6100. FAX: (618)398-0539. E-mail: silfed@simokyfed. com. Co-Pres. Harvey Cohen & Carol Rudman; Exec. Dir. Steven C. Low. (WWW. SIMOKYFED.COM)

SPRINGFIELD

SPRINGFIELD JEWISH FEDERATION (1941); 2815 Old Jacksonville Rd., Ste 103A (62704); (217)787-7223. FAX: (217)787-7470. E-mail: sjf@springnet1.com. Pres. Rita Victor; Exec. Dir. Gloria Schwartz.

INDIANA

FORT WAYNE

FORT WAYNE JEWISH FEDERATION (1921); 227 E. Washington Blvd. (46802-3121); (219)422-8566. FAX: (219)422-8567. E-mail: fwjewfed@aol.com. Pres. Doris Fogel; Exec. Dir. Jeff Gubitz. (WWW.SHALOMFW. ORG)

INDIANAPOLIS

JEWISH FEDERATION OF GREATER INDIANAPOLIS, INC. (1905); 6705 Hoover Rd. (46260-4120); (317)726-5450. FAX: (317) 205-0307. E-mail controljfg@aol.com. Pres. Richard Leventhal; Exec. V.-Pres. Harry Nadler. (WWW.JFGI.ORG)

LAFAYETTE

JEWISH FEDERATION OF GREATER LAFAYETTE (1924); PO Box 3802, W. Lafayette (47906); (765)426-4724. E-mail: jfgl1@aol.com. Pres.Earl Prohofsky; Admin. Judy Upton.

NORTHWEST INDIANA

JEWISH FEDERATION OF NORTHWEST INDIANA (1941; reorg. 1959); 2939 Jewett St., Highland (46322); (219)972-2250. FAX: (219)972-4779. E-mail: defwej@aol.com. Pres. Carol Karol; Exec. Dir. David Tein. (WWW.JFEDOFNWI.COM)

ST. JOSEPH VALLEY

JEWISH FEDERATION OF ST. JOSEPH VALLEY (1946); 3202 Shalom Way, South Bend (46615); (219)233-1164. FAX: (219)288-4103. E-mail: mgardner@fedsjv.org. Pres. Dr. Douglas H. Barton; Exec. V.-Pres. Marilyn Gardner. (WWW.JFEDSJV.ORG)

IOWA

DES MOINES

JEWISH FEDERATION OF GREATER DES MOINES (1914); 910 Polk Blvd. (50312); (515)277-6321. FAX: (515)277-4069. E-mail: jcrc@dmjfed.org. Pres. Robert M. Pomerantz; Exec. Dir. Elaine Steinger. (WWW.DMJFED.ORG)

SIOUX CITY

JEWISH FEDERATION OF SIOUX CITY (1921); 815 38th St. (51104-1417); (712)258-0618. FAX: (712)258-0619. Pres. Michele Ivener; Admin. Dir. Doris Rosenthal.

KANSAS

KANSAS CITY

See listing under Missouri

WICHITA

MID-KANSAS JEWISH FEDERATION, INC. (serving South Central Kansas) (1935); 400 N. Woodlawn, Suite 8 (67208); (316)686-4741. FAX: (316)686-6008. E-mail: jpress@ mkjf.org. Pres. Marie Levy; Exec. Dir. Judy Press. (WWW.MKJF.ORG)

KENTUCKY

CENTRAL KENTUCKY

CENTRAL KENTUCKY JEWISH FEDERATION (1976); 340 Romany Rd., Lexington (40502-2400); (606)268-0672. FAX: (606)268-0775. E-mail: ckjf@jewishlexington.org. Pres. Martin Barr; Exec. Dir. Daniel Chejfec. (WWW.JEWISHLEXINGTON.ORG)

LOUISVILLE

JEWISH COMMUNITY FEDERATION OF LOUISVILLE, INC. (1934); 3630 Dutchmans Lane (40205); (502)451-8840. FAX: (502) 458-0702. E-mail: jfed@iglou.com. Pres. Gerald D. Temes MD; Exec. Dir. Alan S. Engel. (WWW.JEWISHLOUISVILLE.ORG)

LOUISIANA

BATON ROUGE

JEWISH FEDERATION OF GREATER BATON ROUGE (1971); 3354 Kleinert Ave. (70806); (504) 387-9744. FAX: (504)387-9487. E-mail: jfedofbr@postoffice.att.net. Pres. Harvey Hoffman.

NEW ORLEANS

JEWISH FEDERATION OF GREATER NEW ORLEANS (1913; reorg. 1977); 3747 W. Esplanade Ave., Metairie (70002-3524); (504) 780-5600. FAX: (504)780-5601. E-mail: shalom@jewishnola.com. Pres. Hugo Kahn; Exec. Dir. Eli Skora. (WWW.JEWISH NEWORLEANS.ORG)

SHREVEPORT

NORTHERN LOUISIANA JEWISH FEDERATION (1941; inc. 1967); 4700 Line Ave., Suite 117 (71106-1533); (318)868-1200. FAX: (318) 868-1272. E-mail: nljfed@bellsouth.net. Pres. Rick Murov; Exec. Dir. Howard L. Ross. (WWW.NLJFED.ORG)

MAINE

LEWISTON-AUBURN

LEWISTON-AUBURN JEWISH FEDERATION (1947); 74 Bradman St., Auburn (04210); (207)786-4201. FAX: (207)783-1000. Pres. Scott Nussinow.

PORTLAND

JEWISH COMMUNITY ALLIANCE OF SOUTHERN MAINE (1942); 57 Ashmont St. (04103); (207)773-7254. FAX: (207)772-2234. E-mail: info@mainejewish.org. Pres. Charlie Miller. (WWW.MAINEJEWISH.ORG)

MARYLAND

BALTIMORE

THE ASSOCIATED: JEWISH COMMUNITY FEDERATION OF BALTIMORE (1920; reorg. 1969); 101 W. Mt. Royal Ave. (21201-5728); (410) 727-4828. FAX: (410)752-1327. E-mail: information@associated.org. Chmn. Barbara L. Himmelrich; Pres. Darrell D. Friedman. (WWW.ASSOCIATED.ORG)

COLUMBIA

JEWISH FEDERATION OF HOWARD COUNTY; 8950 Rte. 108, Suite 115, Columbia (21045); (410)730-4976; FAX: (410)730-9393. E-mail: jfohc@starpower.net. Pres. Toby Knopf; Exec. Dir. Roberta Greenstein. (WWW.EROLS.COM/JFOHC)

MASSACHUSETTS

BERKSHIRE COUNTY

JEWISH FEDERATION OF THE BERKSHIRES (1940); 235 East St., Pittsfield (01201); (413)442-4360. FAX: (413)443-6070. E-mail: jreichbaum@berkshire.net. Pres. Stephen Rudin; Exec. Dir. Jaquelynne Reichbaum. (WWW.BERKSHIREWEB.COM/JEWISH FEDER)

BOSTON

COMBINED JEWISH PHILANTHROPIES OF GREATER BOSTON, INC. (1895; inc. 1961); 126 High St. (02110-2700); (617)457-8500. FAX: (617)988-6262. E-mail: info@cjp.org. Chmn. Cynthia B. Shulman; Pres. Barry Shrage. (WWW.CJP.ORG)

MERRIMACK VALLEY

MERRIMACK VALLEY JEWISH FEDERATION (Serves Andover, Haverhill, Lawrence, Lowell, Newburyport, and 22 surrounding communities) (1988); PO Box 937, Andover (01810-0016); (978)688-0466. FAX: (978) 688-1097. E-mail: jan@mvjf.org. Pres. James H. Shainker; Exec. Dir. Jan Steven Brodie. (WWW.MVJF.ORG)

NEW BEDFORD

JEWISH FEDERATION OF GREATER NEW BEDFORD, INC. (1938; inc. 1954); 467 Hawthorn St., N. Dartmouth (02747); (508)997-7471. FAX: (508)997-7730. Co-Pres. Harriet Philips, Patricia Rosenfield; Exec. Dir. Wil Herrup.

NORTH SHORE

JEWISH FEDERATION OF THE NORTH SHORE, INC. (1938); 21 Front St., Salem (01970-

3707); (978)598-1810. FAX: (978)741-7507. E-mail: mail@jfns.org. Pres. Shepard M. Remis; Exec. Dir. Neil A. Cooper. (www. JFNS.ORG)

SPRINGFIELD

JEWISH FEDERATION OF GREATER SPRINGFIELD, INC. (1925); 1160 Dickinson St. (01108); (413)737-4313. FAX: (413)737-4348. E-mail: cfschwartz@jewishspringfield.org. Pres. Jeffrey Mandell. (WWW.JEWISH SPRINGFIELD.ORG)

WORCESTER

JEWISH FEDERATION OF CENTRAL MASSACHUSETTS (1947; inc. 1957); 633 Salisbury St. (01609); (508)756-1543. FAX: (508)798-0962. E-mail: info@jfcm.org. Pres. Peter Herman; Exec. Dir. Howard Borer. (www. JFCM.ORG)

MICHIGAN

ANN ARBOR

JEWISH FEDERATION OF WASHTENAW COUNTY/UJA (1986); 2939 Birch Hollow Dr. (48108); (734)677-0100. FAX: (734)677-0109. E-mail: info@jewishannarbor.org. Pres. Morley Witus; Exec. Dir. Nancy N. Margolis. (WWW.JEWISHANNARBOR.ORG)

DETROIT

JEWISH FEDERATION OF METROPOLITAN DETROIT (1899); 6735 Telegraph Rd., Suite 30, PO Box 2030, Bloomfield Hills (48301-2030); (248)642-4260. FAX: (248)642-4985. E-mail: jfmd@jfmd.org. Pres. Penny Blumenstein; Exec. V.-Pres. Mark Davidoff. (WWW.THISISFEDERATION.ORG)

FLINT

FLINT JEWISH FEDERATION (1936); 619 Wallenberg St. (48502); (810)767-5922. FAX: (810)767-9024. E-mail: fjf@tm.net. Pres. Dr. Steve Burton; Exec. Dir. Joel B. Kaplan. (http://users.tm.net/flint)

GRAND RAPIDS

JEWISH COMMUNITY FUND OF GRAND RAPIDS (1930); 4127 Embassy Dr. SE (49546-2418); (616)942-5553. FAX: (616) 942-5780. E-mail: jcfgr@iserv.net. Pres. Richard Stevens; Admin. Dir. Rosalie Stein; V.P. Maxine Shapiro. (WWW.JFGGR.ORG)

MINNESOTA

MINNEAPOLIS

MINNEAPOLIS JEWISH FEDERATION (1929; inc. 1930); 13100 Wayzata Blvd., Suite 200,

Minnetonka (55305); (612)593-2600. FAX: (612)593-2544. E-mail: webmaster@ujfc. org. Pres. Michael Horovitz; Exec. Dir. Joshua Fogelson. (WWW.JEWISHMINNESOTA. ORG)

ST. PAUL

UNITED JEWISH FUND AND COUNCIL (1935); 790 S. Cleveland, Suite 227 (55116); (651)690-1707. FAX: (651)690-0228. E-mail: webmaster@ujfc.org. Pres. James Stein; Exec. Dir. Eli Skora. (WWW.JEWISH MINNESOTA.ORG)

MISSOURI

KANSAS CITY

JEWISH FEDERATION OF GREATER KANSAS CITY MO/KS (1933); 5801 W. 115 St., Overland Park, KS (66211-1824); (913)327-8100. FAX: (913)327-8110. E-mail: jessical@jewishkc.org. Pres. Howard Jacobson; Exec. Dir. Todd Stettner. (WWW.JEWISHKANSAS CITY.ORG)

ST. JOSEPH

UNITED JEWISH FUND OF ST. JOSEPH (1915); 1816 Walnut (64503); (816)233-1186. FAX: (816)233-9399. Elliot Zidell; Exec. Sec. Sherri Ott.

ST. LOUIS

JEWISH FEDERATION OF ST. LOUIS (incl. St. Louis County) (1901); 12 Millstone Campus Dr. (63146-9812); (314)432-0020. FAX: (314)432-1277. E-mail: jfedstl@jfedstl.org. Pres. Harvey A. Harris; Exec. V.-Pres. Barry Rosenberg. (WWW.JEWISHSTLOUIS.ORG)

NEBRASKA

LINCOLN

JEWISH FEDERATION OF LINCOLN, INC. (1931; inc. 1961); PO Box 67218 (68506); (402)489-1015. FAX: (402)476-8364. Pres. Herb Friedman; Exec. Dir. Karen Sommer.

OMAHA

JEWISH FEDERATION OF OMAHA (1903); 333 S. 132nd St. (68154-2198); (402)334-8200. FAX: (402)334-1330. E-mail: pmonsk@ top.net. Pres. Steven Pitlor; Exec. Dir. Jan Goldstein. (WWW.JEWISHOMAHA.ORG)

NEVADA

LAS VEGAS

JEWISH FEDERATION OF LAS VEGAS (1973); 3909 S. Maryland Pkwy. # 400 (89119-7520); (702)732-0556. FAX: (702)732-3228.

Bd. Chr. Michael Unger; Exec. Dir. Meyer Bodoff. (WWW.JEWISHLASVEGAS.COM)

NEW HAMPSHIRE

MANCHESTER

JEWISH FEDERATION OF GREATER MANCHESTER (1974); 698 Beech St. (03104-3626); (603)627-7679. FAX: (603) 627-7963. (WWW. JEWISHNH.ORG)

NEW JERSEY

ATLANTIC AND CAPE MAY COUNTIES

JEWISH FEDERATION OF ATLANTIC AND CAPE MAY COUNTIES (1924); 3393 Bargaintown Rd., Box 617, Northfield (08225-0196); (609)653-3030. FAX: (609)653-8881. E-mail: jfedacm@cyberenet.net. Pres. Joseph Rodgers; Exec. V.-Pres. Bernard Cohen. (WWW.JFEDACM.COM)

BERGEN COUNTY

UJA FEDERATION OF BERGEN COUNTY AND NORTH HUDSON (inc. 1978); 111 Kinderkamack Rd., River Edge (07661); (201)488-6800. FAX: (201)488-1507. E-mail: contact @jewishbergen.org. Pres. Dr. Leonard Cole; Exec. V.-Pres. Howard E. Charish. (WWW. JEWISHBERGEN.ORG)

CENTRAL NEW JERSEY

JEWISH FEDERATION OF CENTRAL NEW JERSEY (1940; merged 1973); 1391 Martine Ave., Scotch Plains (07076); (908)889-5335. FAX: (908)889-5370. E-mail: community @jfedcnj.org. Pres. Mark Wilf; Exec. V.-Pres. Stanley Stone. (WWW.JFEDCNJ.ORG)

CLIFTON-PASSAIC

JEWISH FEDERATION OF GREATER CLIFTON-PASSAIC (1933); 199 Scoles Ave., Clifton (07012-1125). (973)777-7031. FAX: (973) 777-6701. E-mail: yymuskin@jfedclifton-passaic.com. Pres. George Kramer; Exec. V.-Pres. Yosef Y. Muskin.

CUMBERLAND COUNTY

JEWISH FEDERATION OF CUMBERLAND COUNTY (inc. 1971); 1063 E. Landis Ave. Suite B, Vineland (08360-3752); (856)696-4445. FAX: (856)696-3428. E-mail: questions@jfedcc.org. Pres. Edward Roth; Exec. Dir. Kirk Wisemayer. (WWW.JFEDCC.ORG)

METROWEST NEW JERSEY

UNITED JEWISH FEDERATION OF METRO-WEST (1923); 901 Route 10, Whippany (07981-1156); (973)929-3000. FAX: (973)

884-7361. E-mail: webmail@ujfmetrowest. org. Pres. Steven Klinghoffer; Exec. V.-Pres. Max L. Kleinman. (WWW.UJFMETROWEST. ORG)

MIDDLESEX COUNTY

JEWISH FEDERATION OF GREATER MIDDLESEX COUNTY (org. 1948; reorg. 1985); 230 Old Bridge Tpk., S. River (08882-2000); (732)432-7711. FAX: (732)432-0292. E-mail: middlesexfed@aol.com. Pres. Roy Tanzman; Exec. Dir. Gerrie Bamira. (WWW.JFGMC.ORG)

MONMOUTH COUNTY

JEWISH FEDERATION OF GREATER MONMOUTH COUNTY (1971); 100 Grant Ave., PO Box 210, Deal (07723-0210); (732)531-6200-1. FAX: (732)531-9518. E-mail: info@ jewishmonmouth.org. Pres. Stuart Abraham; Exec. Dir. David A. Nussbaum. (WWW.JEWISHMONMOUTH.ORG)

NORTH JERSEY

JEWISH FEDERATION OF NORTH JERSEY (1933); One Pike Dr., Wayne (07470-2498); (973)595-0555. FAX: (973)595-1532. Branch Office: 17-10 River Rd., Fair Lawn (07410-1250); (973)794-1111. E-mail: jfnj@aol.com. Pres. George Liss; Exec. Dir. Martin Greenberg.

OCEAN COUNTY

OCEAN COUNTY JEWISH FEDERATION (1977); 301 Madison Ave., Lakewood (08701); (732)363-0530. FAX: (732)363-2097. Pres. David Rosen; Exec. Dir. Alan Nydick.

PRINCETON MERCER BUCKS

UNITED JEWISH FEDERATION OF PRINCETON MERCER BUCKS (merged 1996); 3131 Princeton Pike, Bldg. 2A, Lawrenceville (08648-2207); (609)219-0555. FAX: (609)219-9040. E-mail: mailbox@ujfpmb.org. Pres. Carol Pollard; Exec. Dir. Andrew Frank. (WWW.UJFPMB.ORG)

SOMERSET COUNTY

JEWISH FEDERATION OF SOMERSET, HUNTERDON & WARREN COUNTIES (1960); 775 Talamini Rd., Bridgewater (08807); (908)725-6994. FAX: (908)725-9753. E-mail: info@jfedshaw.org. Pres. Jo Ann Chase; Exec. Dir. Diane S. Naar. (WWW. JFEDSHAW.ORG)

SOUTHERN NEW JERSEY

JEWISH FEDERATION OF SOUTHERN NEW JERSEY (incl. Camden, Burlington, and

Gloucester counties) (1922); 1301 Springdale Rd., Suite 200, Cherry Hill (08003-2769); (856)751-9500. FAX: (856)751-1697. E-mail: imorrow@jfedsnj.org. Pres. Dr. Robert Belafsky; Exec. V.-Pres. Stuart Alperin. (WWW.JFEDSNJ.ORG)

NEW MEXICO

ALBUQUERQUE

JEWISH FEDERATION OF GREATER ALBUQUERQUE (1938); 5520 Wyoming Blvd., NE (87109-3167); (505)821-3214. FAX: (505) 821-3351. E-mail: nmjfga@nmjfga. org. Pres. Steven Sanders; Exec. Dir. Andrew Lipman. (WWW.JEWISHNEWMEXICO.ORG)

NEW YORK

ALBANY

(See Northeastern New York)

Broome County

JEWISH FEDERATION OF BROOME COUNTY; 500 Clubhouse Rd., Vestal (13850); (607) 724-2332; FAX: (607)724-2311. (WWW.TOER. NET/JFEDERATION)

BUFFALO (INCL. NIAGARA FALLS)

JEWISH FEDERATION OF GREATER BUFFALO, INC. (1903); 787 Delaware Ave. (14209); (716)886-7750. FAX: (716)886-1367. Pres. Irving M. Shuman; Exec. Dir. James M. Lodge. (WWW.JFEDBFLO.COM)

DUTCHESS COUNTY

JEWISH FEDERATION OF DUTCHESS COUNTY; 110 Grand Ave., Poughkeepsie (12603); (845)471-9811. FAX: (845) 471-3233. E-mail: info@jewishdutchess.org. Pres. Alan Zucker; Exec. Dir. Bonnie Meadow. (WWW. JEWISHDUTCHESS.ORG)

ELMIRA-CORNING

JEWISH CENTER AND FEDERATION OF THE TWIN TIERS (1942); Grandview Ave. Extension, Elmira (14905-0087); (607)734-8122. FAX: (607)734-8123. Pres. John Spiegler; Admin. Diane Huglies.

NEW YORK

UJA-FEDERATION OF JEWISH PHILANTHROPIES OF NEW YORK, INC. (incl. Greater NY, Westchester, Nassau, and Suffolk counties) (Fed. org. 1917; UJA 1939; merged 1986); 130 E. 59 St. (10022-1302); (212)980-1000. FAX: (212)888-7538. E-mail: contact@ujafedny.org. Pres. Larry Zicklin; Exec. V.-Pres. & CEO John Ruskay. (WWW. UJAFEDNY.ORG)

NORTHEASTERN NEW YORK

UNITED JEWISH FEDERATION OF NORTHEASTERN NEW YORK (1986); Latham Circle Mall, 800 New Loudon Rd., Latham (12110); (518)783-7800. FAX: (518)783-1557. E-mail: info@jewishfedny.org. Pres. Dr. Lewis Morrison; Exec. Dir. Rodney Margolis. (WWW.JEWISHFEDNY.ORG)

ORANGE COUNTY

JEWISH FEDERATION OF GREATER ORANGE COUNTY (1977); 68 Stewart Ave., Newburgh (12550); (845)562-7860. FAX: (914)562-5114. E-mail: jfogoc@aol.com. Pres. Mona Rieger; Admin. Dir. Joyce Waschitz.

ROCHESTER

JEWISH COMMUNITY FEDERATION OF GREATER ROCHESTER, NY, INC. (1939); 441 East Ave. (14607-1932); (716)461-0490. FAX: (716)461-0912. E-mail: info@jewishrochester.org. Pres. Howard Grossman; Exec. Dir. Lawrence W. Fine. (WWW.JEWISH ROCHESTER.ORG)

ROCKLAND COUNTY

JEWISH FEDERATION OF ROCKLAND COUNTY (1985); 900 Route 45, Suite 1, New City (10956-1140); (914)362-4200. Fax: (914)362-4282.

SCHENECTADY

(See Northeastern New York)

SYRACUSE

SYRACUSE JEWISH FEDERATION, INC. (1918); 5655 Thompson Rd. So., DeWitt (13214-0511); (315)445-2040. FAX: (315)445-1559. Pres. Gershon Vincow; Exec. V.-Pres. Richard Friedman. (WWW.SJFED.ORG)

TROY

(See Northeastern New York)

ULSTER COUNTY

JEWISH FEDERATION OF ULSTER COUNTY (1951); 159 Green St., Kingston (12401); (845)338-8131. FAX: (845)338-8131. E-mail: ucjf@ulster.net. Pres. Michelle Tuchman; Exec. Dir. Joan Plotsky. (WWW.UCJF. ORG)

UTICA

JEWISH COMMUNITY FEDERATION AND CENTER OF UTICA (1950; reorg. 1994); 2310 Oneida St. (13501-6009); (315)733-2343. FAX: (315)733-2346. E-mail: jcc1@borg. com. Pres. Ann Siegel; Exec. Dir. Barbara Ratner-Gantshar.

NORTH CAROLINA

ASHEVILLE

WESTERN NORTH CAROLINA JEWISH FEDERATION (1935); 236 Charlotte St. (28801-1434); (828)253-0701. FAX: (828)254-7666. Pres. Stan Greenberg; Exec. Dir. Marlene Berger-Joyce.

CHARLOTTE

THE JEWISH FEDERATION OF GREATER CHARLOTTE (1938); 5007 Providence Rd. (28226-5849); (704)366-5007. FAX: (704)944-6766. E-mail: jfgc@shalomcharlotte.org. Pres. Jill Newman; Exec. Dir. Randy Czarlinsky. (WWW.JEWISHCHARLOTTE.ORG)

DURHAM-CHAPEL HILL

DURHAM-CHAPEL HILL JEWISH FEDERATION & COMMUNITY COUNCIL (1979); 3700 Lyckan Pkwy., Suite B, Durham (27707-2541); (919)489-5335. FAX: (919)489-5788. E-mail: federation@shalomdch.org. Pres. Lew Margolis; Interim Exec. Dir. David Sclove. (http://shalomdch.org)

GREENSBORO

GREENSBORO JEWISH FEDERATION (1940); 5509C W. Friendly Ave. (27410-4211); (336)852-5433. FAX: (336)852-4346. E-mail: mchandler@shalomgreensboro.org. Pres. Nancy Brenner; Exec. Dir. Marilyn Chandler. (WWW.SHALOMGREENSBORO.ORG)

RALEIGH

RALEIGH-CARY JEWISH FEDERATION (1987); 8210 Creedmoor Rd., Suite 104 (27613); (919)676-2200. FAX: (919)676-2122. E-mail: info@rcjf.org. Pres. Jim Maass; Exec. Dir. Judah Segal. (WWW.RCJF.ORG)

OHIO

AKRON

AKRON JEWISH COMMUNITY FEDERATION (1935); 750 White Pond Dr. (44320-1128); (330)869-CHAI (2424). FAX: (330)867-8498. Pres. David Kock; Exec. Dir. Michael Wise. (WWW.JEWISHAKRON.ORG)

CANTON

CANTON JEWISH COMMUNITY FEDERATION (1935; reorg. 1955); 2631 Harvard Ave., NW (44709-3147); (330)452-6444. FAX: (330)452-4487. E-mail: cantonjcf@aol.com. (jewishcanton.org)

CINCINNATI

JEWISH FEDERATION OF CINCINNATI (1896; reorg. 1967); 4380 Malsbary Rd., Suite 200 (45242-5644); (513) 985-1500. FAX: (513)985-1503. E-mail: jfed@jfedcin.org. Pres. Harry B. Davidow; Chief Exec. Officer Rabbi Michael R. Zedek. (WWW.JEWISH CINCINNATI.ORG)

CLEVELAND

JEWISH COMMUNITY FEDERATION OF CLEVELAND (1903); 1750 Euclid Ave. (44115-2106); (216)566-9200. FAX: (216)861-1230. E-mail: info@jcfcleve.org. Exec. V.-Pres. & CEO Joel Fox. (WWW.JEWISH CLEVELAND.ORG)

COLUMBUS

COLUMBUS JEWISH FEDERATION (1926); 1175 College Ave. (43209); (614)237-7686. FAX: (614)237-2221. E-mail: cjf@tcjf.org. Pres. & CEO Marsha Hurwitz. (WWW.JEWISH COLUMBUS.ORG)

DAYTON

JEWISH FEDERATION OF GREATER DAYTON (1910); 4501 Denlinger Rd. (45426-2395); (937)854-4150. FAX: (937)854-2850. Pres. Joseph Bettman; Exec. V.-Pres. Peter H. Wells. (WWW.JEWISHDAYTON.ORG)

STEUBENVILLE

JEWISH COMMUNITY COUNCIL (1938); 300 Lovers Lane (43952); (614)264-5514. FAX:: (740)264-7190. Pres. Curtis L. Greenberg; Exec. Sec. Jennie Bernstein.

TOLEDO

JEWISH FEDERATION OF GREATER TOLEDO (1907; reorg. 1960); 6505 Sylvania Ave., Sylvania (43560-3918); (419)885-4461. FAX: (419)885-3207. E-mail: jftoledo@cjfny.org. Pres. Joel Beren; Exec. Dir. Alix Greenblatt. (WWW.JEWISHTOLEDO.ORG)

YOUNGSTOWN

YOUNGSTOWN AREA JEWISH FEDERATION (1935); 505 Gypsy Lane (44504-1314); (330) 746-3251. FAX: (330)746-7926. E-mail: samkoopl@juno.com. Pres. Dr. Ronald Roth; Dir. Bonnie Deutsch-Burdman.

OKLAHOMA

OKLAHOMA CITY

JEWISH FEDERATION OF GREATER OKLAHOMA CITY (1941); 710 W. Wilshire, Suite C (73116-7736). (405)848-3132. FAX: (405) 848-3180. E-mail: okcfed@flash.net. Pres.

Harriet Carson; Exec. Dir. Edie S. Roodman. (WWW.JFEDOKC.ORG)

TULSA

JEWISH FEDERATION OF TULSA (1938); 2021 E. 71 St. (74136); (918)495-1100. FAX: (918)495-1220. E-mail: federation@jewishtulsa.org. Pres. Andrew M. Wolov; Exec. Dir. David Bernstein. (WWW.JEWISHTULSA. ORG)

OREGON

PORTLAND

JEWISH FEDERATION OF PORTLAND (incl. Northwest Oregon and Southwest Washington communities) (1920; reorg. 1956); 6651 SW Capitol Hwy. (97219); (503)245-6219. FAX: (503)245-6603. E-mail: charlie @jewishportland.org. Pres. Rob Shlachter; Exec. Dir. Charles Schiffman. (WWW.JEWISH PORTLAND.ORG)

PENNSYLVANIA

BUCKS COUNTY

(See Jewish Federation of Greater Philadelphia)

ERIE

JEWISH COMMUNITY COUNCIL OF ERIE (1946); 1611 Peach St., Suite 405 (16501-2123); (814)455-4474. FAX: (814)455-4475. E-mail: jcceri@erie.net. Pres. Robert Cohen; Admin. Dir. Cynthia Penman; Dir. Barbara Singer. (WWW.JCCERI.ORG)

HARRISBURG

UNITED JEWISH COMMUNITY OF GREATER HARRISBURG (1941); 3301 N. Front St. (17110-1436); (717)236-9555. FAX: (717) 236-8104. E-mail: communityreview@ desupernet.net. Pres. Raphael Aronson; Exec. Dir. David Weisberg. (WWW.HBGJEWISH COMMUNITY.COM)

LEHIGH VALLEY

JEWISH FEDERATION OF THE LEHIGH VALLEY (1948); 702 N. 22nd St., Allentown (18104); (610)821-5500. FAX: (610)821-8946. E-mail: ivfed@enter.net. Exec. Dir. Mark Goldstein.

PHILADELPHIA

JEWISH FEDERATION OF GREATER PHILADELPHIA (incl. Bucks, Chester, Delaware, Montgomery, and Philadelphia counties) (1901; reorg. 1956); 2100 Arch St. (19103); (215)832-0500. FAX: (215)832-1510. E-mail: lyouman@philjnet.org. Pres.

Michael R. Belman; Exec. V.-Pres. Harold Goldman. (WWW.JEWISHPHILLY.ORG)

PITTSBURGH

UNITED JEWISH FEDERATION OF GREATER PITTSBURGH (1912; reorg. 1955); 234 McKee Pl. (15213-3916); (412)681-8000. FAX: (412) 681-3980. E-mail: information@ujf.net. Chmn. David Burstin; Pres. Howard M. Rieger. (WWW.UJF.NET)

READING

JEWISH FEDERATION OF READING, PA., INC. (1935; reorg. 1972); 1700 City Line St. (19604); (610)921-2766. FAX: (610)929-0886. E-mail: stanr@epix.net. Pres. Sheila Lattin; Exec. Dir. Stanley Ramati. (www. READINGJEWISHCOMMUNITY.COM)

SCRANTON

JEWISH FEDERATION OF NORTHEASTERN PENNSYLVANIA (1945); 601 Jefferson Ave. (18510); (570)961-2300. FAX: (570)346-6147. E-mail: jfednepa@epix.net. Pres. Louis Nivert; Exec. Dir. Mark Silverberg. (WWW.JFEDNEPA.ORG)

WILKES-BARRE

JEWISH FEDERATION OF GREATER WILKES-BARRE (1950); 60 S. River St. (18702-2493); (570)822-4146. FAX: (570)824-5966. E-mail: wbreport@aol.com. Pres. Murray Ufberg; Exec. Dir. Don Cooper.

RHODE ISLAND

PROVIDENCE

JEWISH FEDERATION OF RHODE ISLAND (1945); 130 Sessions St. (02906); (401)421-4111. FAX: (401)331-7961. E-mail: shalom @jfri.org. Pres. Edward D. Feldstein; Exec. Dir. Steven A. Rakitt. (WWW.JFRI.ORG)

SOUTH CAROLINA

CHARLESTON

CHARLESTON JEWISH FEDERATION (1949); 1645 Raoul Wallenberg Blvd., PO Box 31298 (29407); (843)571-6565. FAX: (843) 852-3547. E-mail: ellenk@jewishcharleston. org. Co-Pres. Wendy Goer and Paul Saltzman; Exec. Dir. Ellen J. Katzman. (www. JEWISHCHARLESTON.ORG)

COLUMBIA

COLUMBIA JEWISH FEDERATION (1960); 4540 Trenholm Rd., PO Box 6968 (29206-4462); (803)787-2023. FAX: (803)787-0475. E-mail: ternercjf@hotmail.com. Pres. Stephen Serbin; Exec. Dir. Steven Terner.

SOUTH DAKOTA

SIOUX FALLS

JEWISH WELFARE FUND (1938); 510 S. First Ave. (57102-1003); (605)332-3335. FAX: (605)334-2298. E-mail: asnh94@prodigy.com. Pres. Laurence Bierman; Exec. Sec. Stephen Rosenthal.

TENNESSEE

CHATTANOOGA

JEWISH COMMUNITY FEDERATION OF GREATER CHATTANOOGA (1931); 3601 Ringgold Rd. (37412); PO Box 8947 (37412); (423)493-0270. FAX: (423)493-9997. E-mail: mdzik@jcfgc.com. Pres. Michael Lebovitz; Exec. Dir. Michael Dzik. (www.JCFGC.COM)

KNOXVILLE

KNOXVILLE JEWISH FEDERATION, INC. (1939); 7800 Deane Hill Dr. (37919); (865)693-5837. FAX: (865)694-4861. E-mail: ajcckjf@aol.com. Pres. Marilyn Lieberman; Exec. Dir. Dr. Bernard Rosenblatt. (WWW.JEWISHKNOXVILLE.ORG)

MEMPHIS

MEMPHIS JEWISH FEDERATION (incl. Shelby County) (1935); 6560 Poplar Ave. (38138-3614); (901)767-7100. FAX: (901)767-7128. E-mail: jfeld@memjfed.org. Pres. Louise Sklar; Exec. Dir. Jeffrey Feld. (www.KORRNET.ORG/MJF)

NASHVILLE

NASHVILLE JEWISH FEDERATION (1936); 801 Percy Warner Blvd. (37205-4009); (615)356-3242. FAX: (615)352-0056. E-mail: jnashjfed@aol.org. Pres. Peter Haas. (WWW.JNASHFED.ORG)

TEXAS

AUSTIN

JEWISH COMMUNTY ASSOCIATION OF AUSTIN (1939; reorg. 1956); 7300 Hart Lane (78731); (512)735-8000. FAX: (512)735-8001. E-mail: austinjfed@jfaustin.org. Pres. Linda Millstone; Exec. Dir. Sandy Sack. (WWW.JFAUSTIN.ORG)

BEAUMONT

BEAUMONT JEWISH FEDERATION; PO BOX 1891 (77704-1981); (409)832-2881.

CORPUS CHRISTI

COMBINED JEWISH APPEAL OF CORPUS CHRISTI; 750 Everhart Rd. (78411-1906); (512)855-6239. FAX: (512)853-9040.

DALLAS

JEWISH FEDERATION OF GREATER DALLAS (1911); 7800 Northaven Rd. (75230-3226); (214)369-3313. FAX: (214)369-8943. E-mail: jharburger@jfgd.org. Pres. Donald Schaffer; Exec. Dir. Gary Weinstein. (www.JEWISHDALLAS.ORG)

EL PASO

JEWISH FEDERATION OF EL PASO, INC. (1937); 405 Wallenberg Dr. (79912-5605); (915)584-4437. FAX: (915)584-0243. Pres. Gary Weiser; Exec. Dir. Larry Harris. (www.JEWISHFED.HUNTLEIGH.NET)

FORT WORTH

JEWISH FEDERATION OF FORT WORTH AND TARRANT COUNTY (1936); 4255 Bryant Irvin Rd. #209 (76008); (817)569-0892. FAX: (817)569-0895. E-mail: jfed@tarrantfederation.org. Pres. Harold Gernsbacher; Exec. Dir. Naomi Rosenfield.

HOUSTON

JEWISH FEDERATION OF GREATER HOUSTON (1936); 5603 S. Braeswood Blvd. (77096-3907); (713)729-7000. FAX: (713)721-6232. E-mail: lwunsch@houstonjewish.org. Pres. Marvin Woskow; Exec. V.-Pres. Lee Wunsch. (WWW.HOUSTONJEWISH.ORG)

SAN ANTONIO

JEWISH FEDERATION OF SAN ANTONIO (incl. Bexar County) (1922); 12500 NW Military Hwy., Suite 200 (78231); (210)302-6960. FAX: (210)408-2332. E-mail: markfreedman@jfsatx. Pres. Alan Petlin; Exec. Dir. Mark Freedman. (WWW.JFSATX.ORG)

WACO

JEWISH FEDERATION OF WACO & CENTRAL TEXAS (1949); PO Box 8031 (76714-8031); (817)776-3740. FAX: (817)776-4424. E-mail: debhersh@aol.com. Pres. Harry Smith; Exec. Sec. Deborah Hersh. (www.AGUDATH-JACOB.ORG/FED.HTM)

UTAH

SALT LAKE CITY

UNITED JEWISH FEDERATION OF UTAH (1936); 2 North Medical Drive (84113); (801)581-0102. FAX: (801) 581-1334. Pres. Robert Wolff; Exec. Dir. Donald Gartman.

VIRGINIA

RICHMOND

JEWISH COMMUNITY FEDERATION OF RICHMOND (1935); 5403 Monument Ave., PO

Box 17128 (23226-7128); (804)288-0045. FAX: (804)282-7507. E-mail: executivedirector@jewishrich.org. Pres. Stewart Kasen; Exec. Dir. Ellen Chernack. (WWW.JEWISH RICHMOND.ORG)

TIDEWATER

UNITED JEWISH FEDERATION OF TIDEWATER (incl. Norfolk, Portsmouth, and Virginia Beach) (1937); 5029 Corporate Woods Dr., Suite 225, Virginia Beach (23462-4370); (757)671-1600. FAX: (757)671-7613. E-mail: ujft@ujft.org. Pres. David Brand; Exec. V.-Pres. Harry Graber. (WWW.JEWISHVA. ORG)

VIRGINIA PENINSULA

UNITED JEWISH COMMUNITY OF THE VIRGINIA PENINSULA, INC. (1942); 2700 Spring Rd., Newport News (23606); (757)930-1422. FAX: (757)930-3762. E-mail: unitedjc@erols. com. Pres. Roy H. Lasris; Exec. Dir. Rodney J. Margolis. (WWW.UJCVP.ORG)

WASHINGTON

SEATTLE

JEWISH FEDERATION OF GREATER SEATTLE (incl. King County, Everett, and Bremerton) (1926); 2031 Third Ave. (98121); (206) 443-5400. FAX: (206)443-0306. E-mail: wendyj@jewishinseattle.org. Pres. Dr. Michael Spektor; Exec. V.-Pres. Barry M. Goren. (WWW.JEWISHINSEATTLE.ORG)

WEST VIRGINIA

CHARLESTON

FEDERATED JEWISH CHARITIES OF CHARLESTON, INC. (1937); PO Box 1613 (25326); (304)345-2320. FAX: (304)345-2325. E-mail: mzltov@aol.com. Pres. Stuart May; Exec. Sec. Lee Diznoff.

WISCONSIN

MADISON

MADISON JEWISH COMMUNITY COUNCIL, INC. (1940); 6434 Enterprise Lane (53719-1117); (608)278-1808. FAX:(608)278-7814. E-mail: mjcc@mjcc.net. Pres. Diane Seder; Exec. Dir. Steven H. Morrison. (WWW.JEWISH MADISON.ORG)

MILWAUKEE

MILWAUKEE JEWISH FEDERATION, INC. (1902); 1360 N. Prospect Ave. (53202); (414)390-5700. FAX: (414)390-5782. E-mail: info@milwaukeejewish.org. Pres. Stephen L. Chernof; Exec. V.-Pres. Richard H. Meyer. (WWW.MILWAUKEEJEWISH.ORG)

CANADA

ALBERTA

CALGARY

CALGARY JEWISH COMMUNITY COUNCIL (1962); 1607 90th Ave. SW (T2V 4V7); (403)253-8600. FAX: (403)253-7915. E-mail: cjcc@cjcc.ca. Pres. Nate Feldman; Exec. Dir. Myrna Linder. (WWW.CJCC.CA)

EDMONTON

JEWISH FEDERATION OF EDMONTON (1954; reorg. 1982); 7200 156th St. (T5R 1X3); (780)487-5120. FAX: (780)481-1854. E-mail: edjfed@net.com.ca. Pres. Stephen Mandel; Exec. Dir. Lesley A. Jacobson.

BRITISH COLUMBIA

VANCOUVER

JEWISH FEDERATION OF GREATER VANCOUVER (1932; reorg. 1987); 950 W. 41st Ave., Suite 200 (V5Z 2N7); (604)257-5100. FAX: (604)257-5110. E-mail: jfed@jfgv.com. Pres. Sondra Green; Exec. Dir. Mark Gurvis. (WWW.JFGV.COM)

MANITOBA

WINNIPEG

JEWISH FEDERATION OF WINNIPEG/COMBINED JEWISH APPEAL (1938; reorg. 1973); 123 Doncaster St., Suite C300 (R3N 2B2); (204)477-7400. FAX: (204)477-7405. E-mail: bfreedman@aspercampus.mb.ca. Pres. Dr. Ian Goldstein; Exec. V.-Pres. Robert Freedman. (WWW.JEWISHWINNIPEG.ORG)

ONTARIO

HAMILTON

UJA/JEWISH FEDERATION OF HAMILTON/WENTWORTH & AREA (1932; merged

1971); PO Box 7258, 1030 Lower Lions Club Rd., Ancaster (L9G 3N6); (905)648-0605 #305. FAX: (905)648-8350. E-mail: hamujajf@interlynx.net. Pres. Bonnie Loewith; Exec. Dir. Gerald Fisher. (WWW.JEWISH HAMILTON.ORG)

LONDON

LONDON JEWISH FEDERATION (1932); 536 Huron St. (N5Y 4J5); (519)673-3310. FAX: (519)673-1161. Pres. Ron Wolf; Off. Mgr. Debra Chatterley. (WWW.JEWISHLONDON.CA)

OTTAWA

UNITED JEWISH APPEAL OF OTTAWA (1934); 21 Nadolny Sachs Private (K2A 1R9); (613)798-4696. FAX: (613)798-4695. E-mail: uja@jccottawa.com. Pres. Barbara Farber; Exec. Dir. Mitchell Bellman. (WWW. JEWISHOTTAWA.ORG)

TORONTO

UJA FEDERATION OF GREATER TORONTO (1917); 4600 Bathurst St. (M2R 3V2); (416)635-2883. FAX: (416)631-5715. E-mail: webmaven@feduja.org. Pres. Joseph Steiner; Exec. V.-Pres. Allan Reitzes. (WWW. JEWISHTORONTO.NET)

UIA FEDERATIONS OF CANADA (1998); 4600 Bathurst St. (M2R 3V2); (416)636-7655. FAX: (416)636-9897. E-mail: mfinkelstein@uiafed.org. Exec. V-Pres. Maxyne Finkelstein. (WWW.JEWISHCANADA.ORG)

WINDSOR

JEWISH COMMUNITY FEDERATION (1938); 1641 Ouellette Ave. (N8X 1K9); (519)973-1772. FAX: (519)973-1774. Pres. Jay Armeland; Exec. Dir. Harvey Kessler. (WWW. JEWISHWINDSOR.ORG)

QUEBEC

MONTREAL

FEDERATION CJA (formerly Allied Jewish Community Services) (1965); 1 Carrie Cummings Square (H3W 1M6); (514)735-3541. FAX: (514)735-8972. E-mail: dcantor@federationcja.org. Pres. Steven Cummings; Exec. V.-Pres. Danyael Cantor. (WWW.FEDERATIONCJA.ORG)

Jewish Periodicals*

UNITED STATES

ALABAMA

DEEP SOUTH JEWISH VOICE (1990) (formerly THE SOUTHERN SHOFAR). PO BOX 130052, Birmingham, 35213. (205) 595-9255. FAX: (205)595-9256. E-mail: dsjvoice@aol.com. Lawrence M. Brook. Monthly. (WWW.DEEPSOUTHJEWISHVOICE. COM)

ARIZONA

ARIZONA JEWISH POST (1946). 2601 N. Campbell Ave., #205, Tucson, 85719. (520)319-1112. FAX: (520) 319-1118. E-mail: pbraun@azjewishpost.com. Editor Phyllis Braun. Fortnightly. Jewish Federation of Southern Arizona.

JEWISH NEWS OF GREATER PHOENIX (1948). 1625 E. Northern Ave., Suite 106, Phoenix, 85020. (602)870-9470. FAX: (602)870-0426. E-mail: editor@jewishaz.com. Editor Rabbi Barry Cohen. Weekly. (WWW.JEWISHAZ.COM)

CALIFORNIA

THE AMERICAN RABBI (1968). 22711 Cass Ave., Woodland Hills, 91364. (818)225-9631. E-mail: amrabbi@pacbell.net. Ed.-in-Ch./Pub. David Epstein; Ed. Harry Essrig. Quarterly.

CENTRAL CALIFORNIA JEWISH HERITAGE (1914). 20201 Sherman Way, Winnetka, 91306. (818) 576-9000. FAX: (818) 576-9910. E-mail: heritagepub@earthlink.net. Dan Brin. Six times a year. Heritage Group.

HERITAGE-SOUTHWEST JEWISH PRESS (1914). 20201 Sherman Way, Suite 204, Winnetka, 91306. (818) 576-9000. FAX: (818) 576-9910. E-mail: heritagepub@earthlink.net. Dan Brin. Weekly. Heritage Group.

JEWISH BULLETIN OF NORTHERN CALIFORNIA (1946). 225 Bush St., Suite 1480, San Francisco, 94104-4281. (415)263-7200. FAX: (415)263-7223. E-mail: info@jbnc. com. Marc S. Klein. Weekly. San Francisco Jewish Community Publications, Inc.

JEWISH COMMUNITY CHRONICLE (1947). 3801 E. Willow St., Long Beach, 90815. (562)426-7601, ext. 1021. FAX: (562)595-5543. E-mail: jchron@surfside.net. Harriette Ellis. Fortnightly except January, July & August/ once per month 21 issues a year. Jewish Federation of Greater Long Beach & West Orange County.

JEWISH COMMUNITY NEWS (1976). 14855 Oka Rd., Suite 2, Los Gatos, 95030. (408)358-3033, ext. 31. FAX: (408)356-0733. E-mail: jcn@jfgsj.org. Eileen Goss; Adv. Lindsay Greensweig (408)286-6669. Monthly. Jewish Federation of Greater San Jose.

JEWISH JOURNAL OF GREATER LOS ANGELES (1986). 3660 Wilshire Blvd., Suite 204, Los Angeles, 90010.(213)368-1661. FAX: (213)368-1684. E-mail:jjla@aol.com. Gene Lichtenstein. Weekly.

JEWISH NEWS (1973). 15060 Ventura Blvd., Suite 210, Sherman Oaks, CA 91403.

---

*The information in this directory is based on replies to questionnaires circulated by the editors. For organization bulletins, see the directory of Jewish organizations.

(818)786-4000. FAX: (818)380-9232. Phil Blazer. Monthly. (Also weekly Sunday TV and radio broadcasts in LA, NY, and Miami.)

JEWISH SOCIAL STUDIES: HISTORY, CULTURE, AND SOCIETY (1939). c/o Program in Jewish Studies, Bldg. 240, Rm. 103, Stanford University, Stanford, 94305-2190. (650)725-0829. FAX: (650)725-2920. E-mail: jss@stanford.edu. Steven J. Zipperstein, Aron Rodrigue. Three times a year. Conference on Jewish Social Studies, Inc.

JEWISH SPORTS REVIEW. 1800 S. Robertson Blvd., #174, Los Angeles, 90035. (800)510-9003. E-mail: shel@jewishsportsreview.com. Shel Wallman/Ephraim Moxson. Bimonthly. (WWW.JEWISHSPORTS REVIEW.COM)

LOS ANGELES JEWISH TIMES (formerly B'nai B'rith Messenger) (1897). 5455 Wilshire Blvd., Suite 903, Los Angeles, 90036. (323)933-0131. FAX: (323)933-7928. E-mail: lajtart@aol.com. Ed.-in-Chief Joe Bobker; Mng. Ed. Jane Fried. Weekly.

ORANGE COUNTY JEWISH HERITAGE. 24331 Muirlands Blvd., Suite D-347, Lake Forest, 92630. Phone/FAX: (949)362-4446. E-mail: ocnews@hotmail.com. Stan Brin. Biweekly.

SAN DIEGO JEWISH PRESS HERITAGE (1914). 3615 Kearny Villa Rd., #111, San Diego, 92123. (619)265-0808. FAX: (619)265-0850. E-mail: sdheritage@home.com. Donald H. Harrison. Weekly.

SAN DIEGO JEWISH TIMES (1979). 4731 Palm Ave., La Mesa, 91941. (619)463-5515. FAX: (619) 463-1309. E-mail: jewishtimes@earthlink.net. Editor Michael Sirota. Fortnightly.

SHALOM L.A. (1988). 16027 Ventura Blvd., #400, Encino, 91436. (818)783-3090. FAX: (818)783-1104. E-mail: news@sholomla.net. Gal Shor. Weekly. Hebrew.

TIKKUN MAGAZINE (1986). 2107 Van Ness Ave., Suite 302, San Francisco, 94109. (415)575-1200. FAX: (415)575-1434. E-mail: magazine@tikkun.org. Michael Lerner. Bimonthly. Institute for Labor & Mental Health. (WWW.TIKKUN. ORG)

WESTERN STATES JEWISH HISTORY (1968). 22711 Cass Ave., Woodland Hills, 91364. (818)225-9631. E-mail: amrabbi@pac-bell.net. Ed.-in-Ch. Gladys Sturman; Ed. David Epstein. Quarterly. Western States Jewish History Association.

COLORADO

INTERMOUNTAIN JEWISH NEWS (1913). 1275 Sherman St., Suite 214, Denver, 80203-2299. (303)861-2234. FAX: (303)832-6942. E-mail: email@ijn.com. Exec. Ed. Rabbi Hillel Goldberg; Pub. Miriam Goldberg. Weekly.

CONNECTICUT

CONNECTICUT JEWISH LEDGER (1929). 740 N. Main St., W. Hartford, 06117. (860)231-2424. FAX: (860)231-2428. E-mail: editorial@jewishledger.com. Lisa Lenkiewicz. Weekly.

JEWISH LEADER (1974). 28 Channing St., PO Box 1468, New London, 06320. (860)442-7395. FAX: (860)443-4175. E-mailjfecmim@aol.com. Ed. Mimi Perl. Biweekly. Jewish Federation of Eastern Connecticut.

DELAWARE

JEWISH VOICE. 100 W. 10th St., Suite 301, Wilmington, 19801. (302) 427-2100. FAX: (302) 427-2438. E-mail: jewishvoic@aol.com. Lynn Edelman. 22 times per year. Jewish Federation of Delaware.

DISTRICT OF COLUMBIA

AZURE (1996). 5505 Connecticut Ave., NW, Suite 1140, Washington, 20015. (877)298-7300. FAX: (888)766-1506. E-mail: patrick@shalemcenter.org. Dan Polisar. Quarterly. Hebrew/English. The Shalem Center. WWW.AZURE.ORG.IL

B'NAI B'RITH INTERNATIONAL JEWISH MONTHLY (1886, under the name Menovah). 2020 K Street, NW, 7th Floor, Washington, DC 20006. (202)857-2708. FAX: (202)857-2781. E-mail: ijm@bnai brith.org. Editor Elana Harris. Quarterly. B'nai B'rith International.

CAPITAL COMMUNIQUÉ (1991). 777 N. Capital St., NE, Suite 305, Washington, 20002. (202)216-9060. FAX: (202)216-9061. Jason Silberberg. Biannually. National Jewish Democratic Council.

THE JEWISH VETERAN (1896). 1811 R St., NW, Washington, 20009-1659. (202)265-6280. FAX: (202)234-5662. E-mail: jwv@jwv.org. Seymour "Sy" Brody. 5

times per year. Jewish War Veterans of the U.S.A. Quarterly

MOMENT (1975). 4710 41 St., NW, Washington, 20016. (202)364-3300. FAX: (202)364-2636. E-mail: editor@moment-mag.com. Hershel Shanks. Bimonthly. Jewish Educational Ventures, Inc.

FSU MONITOR (1990). 1819 H Street, NW, Suite 230, Washington, 20006. (202)775-9770. FAX: (202)775-9776. E-mail: ucsj@ucsj.com. Nickolai Butkevich. Quarterly. Union of Councils for Soviet Jews.

NEAR EAST REPORT (1957). 440 First St., NW, Suite 607, Washington, 20001. (202)639-5254. FAX: (202) 347-4916. Dr. Raphael Danziger. Fortnightly. Near East Research, Inc.

SECURITY AFFAIRS (1976). 1717 K St., NW, Suite 800, Washington, 20006. (202)833-0020. FAX: (202)296-6452. E-mail: info @jinsa.org. Jim Colbert. Quarterly. Jewish Institute for National Security Affairs.

WASHINGTON JEWISH WEEK. *See under* MARYLAND

FLORIDA

THE CHRONICLE (1971). 580 S. McIntosh Rd., Sarasota, 34232. (941)371-4546. FAX: (941)378-2947. Barry Millman. Fortnightly. Sarasota-Manatee Jewish Federation.

HERITAGE FLORIDA JEWISH NEWS (1976). PO Box 300742, Fern Park, 32730. (407)834-8787. FAX: (407)831-0507. E-mail: heritagefl@aol.com. Pub. Jeffrey Gaeser; Asst. Ed. Uim Fischer. Weekly.

JACKSONVILLE JEWISH NEWS (1988). 8505 San Jose Blvd., Jacksonville, 32217. (904)448-5000, (904)262-1971. FAX: (904)448-5715. E-mail: srgnews@aol. com. Susan R. Goetz. Monthly. Jacksonville Jewish Federation.

JEWISH JOURNAL (Palm Beach-Broward-Dade) (1977). 601 Fairway Dr., Deerfield Beach, 33441. (954)698-6397. FAX: (954)429-1207. Alan Gosh. Weekly. South Florida Newspaper Network.

JEWISH PRESS OF PINELLAS COUNTY (Clearwater-St.Petersburg) (1985). PO Box 6970, Clearwater, 33758-6970; 1101 S. Belcher Road, Suite H, Largo, FL 33771. (727)535-4400. FAX:(727)530-3039. E-mail: jewishpress@aol.com. Karen Wolf-

son Dawkins. Biweekly. Jewish Press Group of Tampa Bay (FL), Inc. in cooperation with the Jewish Federation of Pinellas County.

JEWISH PRESS OF TAMPA (1987). PO Box 6970, Clearwater 33758-6970; 1101 S. Belcher Road, Suit H, Largo, FL 33771. (727)535-4400. FAX: (727)530-3039. E-mail: jewishpress@aol.com. Karen Wolfson Dawkins. Biweekly. Jewish Press Group of Tampa Bay (FL), Inc.

SHALOM TODAY (1994) Jewish Federation of Broward County, 5890 S. Pine Island Road, Davie, FL 33328. (954)352-6900. FAX: (954) 252-6893. Editor Ray Levi. Weekly. Jewish Federation of Broward County.

GEORGIA

ATLANTA JEWISH TIMES (1925). 6065 Roswell Rd., Suite 700, Atlanta 30328. (404)252-1600. FAX: (404)252-1172. E-mail: bmenaker@atlantajewishtimes.com. Bob Menaker. Weekly.

ILLINOIS

CHICAGO JEWISH NEWS (1994). 5301 W. Dempster, Skokie, Ill 60077. (847)966-0606. FAX: (847)966-1656. E-mail: info@chicagojewishnews.com. Joseph Aaron. Weekly.

CHICAGO JEWISH STAR (1991). PO Box 268, Skokie, 60076-0268. (847)674-7827. FAX: (847)674-0014. E-mail: chicago-jewish-star@mcimail.com. Ed. Douglas Wertheimer; Assoc. Ed. Gila Wertheimer. Fortnightly.

JEWISH COMMUNITY NEWS (1941). 6464 W. Main, Suite 7A, Belleville, 62223. (618)398-6100/ (877)714-6103. FAX: (618)398-0539. E-mail: silfed@simoky fed.com Steve Low. Quarterly. Jewish Federation of Southern Illinois. (www. SIMOKYFED.COM)

JUF NEWS & GUIDE TO JEWISH LIVING IN CHICAGO (1972). One S. Franklin St., Rm. 701G, Chicago, 60606. (312)357-4848. FAX: (312)855-2470. E-mail: jufnews @juf.org. Aaron B. Cohen. Monthly (Guide, annually). Jewish United Fund/ Jewish Federation of Metropolitan Chicago.

INDIANA

ILLIANA JEWISH NEWS (1975). 2939 Jewett St., Highland, 46322. (219)972-2250.

FAX: (219)972-4779. E-mail: defwej@
aol.com. Editor Carol Karol. Quarterly
(except July/Aug.). Jewish Federation of
Northwest Indiana, Inc.

INDIANA JEWISH POST AND OPINION (1935).
238 S. Meridian St., #502, Indianapolis,
46225. (317)972-7800. FAX: (317)972-
7807. E-mail: jpost@surf-ici.com. Gabriel
Cohen. Weekly.

NATIONAL JEWISH POST AND OPINION
(1932). 238 S. Meridian St., Indianapolis,
46225. (317)972-7800. FAX: (317)972-
7807. E-mail: jpost@surf.ici.com. Gabriel
Cohen. Weekly.

PROOFTEXTS: A JOURNAL OF JEWISH LITER-
ARY HISTORY (1980). Indiana University
Press, 601 N. Morton St., Bloomington,
47404. (812)855-9449. FAX: (812)855-
8507. E-mail: journals@indiana.edu. Ed-
itorial address (for contributors):Dept. of
Hebrew Language, Box 46, Jewish Theo-
logical Seminary, 3080 Broadway, NY,
NY 10027-4649. Alan Mintz, David G.
Roskies. Three times a year.

KANSAS

KANSAS CITY JEWISH CHRONICLE (1920).
7373 W. 107 St., Overland Park, 66212.
(913)648-4620. FAX: (913)381-1402. E-
mail: chronicle@sunpublications.com.
Rick Hellman. Weekly. Sun Publications.

KENTUCKY

COMMUNITY (1975). 3630 Dutchmans Lane,
Louisville, 40205-3200. (502) 451-8840.
FAX: (502) 458-0702. E-mail: jfed@iglou.
com. Shiela Steinman Wallace. Biweekly.
Jewish Community Federation of
Louisville.

KENTUCKY JEWISH POST AND OPINION
(1931). 3701 Bardatown Road, Som-
merville, KY 40205. (502)459-1914.
Gabriel Cohen. Weekly.

LOUISIANA

JEWISH CIVIC PRESS (1965). 804 Main
Street, Suite A-2, Forest Park, GA 30297.
(404)231-2194. E-mail: jewishcivicpress@
yahoo.com. Claire & Abner Tritt, eds. and
pubs. Monthly.

JEWISH NEWS (1995). 3747 W. Esplanade
Avenue, Suite 307, Metairie, LA 70002.
(504)780-5600. FAX: (504)780-5601. E-
mail: jewishnews@jewishnola.com. Gail
Naron Chalew. Fortnightly. Jewish Federation of Greater New Orleans.

MARYLAND

BALTIMORE JEWISH TIMES (1919). 2104 N.
Charles St., Baltimore, 21218. (410)752-
3504. FAX: (410)752-2375. Phil Jacobs.
Weekly.

WASHINGTON JEWISH WEEK (1930, as the
National Jewish Ledger). 1500 East Jefferson St., Rockville, 20852. (301)230-
2222. FAX: (301)881-6362. E-mail: wjweek
@aol.com. Debra Rubin. Weekly.

MASSACHUSETTS

AMERICAN JEWISH HISTORY (1892). 160
Herrick Road, Newton Centre, MA
02459. (671)559-8880. FAX: (671)559-
8881. E-mail: ajhs@ajhs.org. Eli Faber.
Quarterly. American Jewish Historical
Society.

THE JEWISH ADVOCATE (1902). 15 School
St., Boston, 02108. (617)367-9100. FAX:
(617)367-9310. E-mail: editorial@the
jewishadvocate.com. David Nathan.
Weekly.

THE JEWISH CHRONICLE (1927). 131 Lincoln
St., Worcester, 01605. (508)752-2512. E-
mail: chronicle.editor@verizon.net. Pub.
Sondra Shapiro; Ed. Ellen Weingart.
Fortnightly.

JEWISH GUIDE TO BOSTON & NEW ENGLAND
(1972). 15 School St., Boston, 02108.
(617)367-9100. FAX: (617)367-9310.
Rosie Rosenzweig. Irregularly. The Jewish
Advocate.

THE JEWISH JOURNAL/NORTH OF BOSTON
(1976). 201 Washington St., PO Box 555,
Salem, 01970. (978)745-4111. FAX:
(978)745-5333. E-mail: editorial@jewish
journal.org. Judith Klein. Biweekly. Russian section. North Shore Jewish Press Ltd.

THE JEWISH NEWS OF WESTERN MASSA-
CHUSETTS (see Jewish Advocate)

METROWEST JEWISH REPORTER (1970). 76
Salem End Rd., Framingham, 01702.
(508)872-4808. FAX: (508)879-5856.
Marcia T. Rivin. Monthly. Combined
Jewish Philanthropies of Greater Boston.

PAKN-TREGER (1980). 1021 West St.,
Amherst, 01002. (413)256-4900. FAX:
(413)256-4700. E-mail: pt@bikher.org.
Nancy Sherman. Three times a year. National Yiddish Book Center.

SH'MA (1970). 90 Oak Street, 4th Floor,
Newton MA 02459. (781)449-9894. FAX:

(781)449-9825. E-mail: susanb@jflmedia. com. Susan Berrin. Monthly. Jewish Family & Life.

MICHIGAN

DETROIT JEWISH NEWS (1942). 27676 Franklin Rd., Southfield, 48034. (248)354-6060. FAX: (248)354-6069. E-mail: rsklar@thejewishnews.com. Robert Sklar. Weekly.

HUMANISTIC JUDAISM (1968). 28611 W. Twelve Mile Rd., Farmington Hills, 48334. (248)478-7610. FAX: (248)478-3159. E-mail: info@shj.org. M. Bonnie Cousens, Ruth D. Feldman. Quarterly. Society for Humanistic Judaism.

WASHTENAW JEWISH NEWS (1978). 2935 Birch Hollow Dr., Ann Arbor, 48108. (734)971-1800. FAX: (734)971-1801. E-mail: wjna2@aol.com. Susan Kravitz Ayer. Monthly.

MINNESOTA

AMERICAN JEWISH WORLD (1912). 4509 Minnetonka Blvd., Minneapolis, MN 55416. (952)259-5280. FAX: (952)920-6205. E-mail: amjewish@isd.net. Mordecai Specktor. Weekly.

MISSISSIPPI

DEEP SOUTH JEWISH VOICE (see Alabama)

MISSOURI

KANSAS CITY JEWISH CHRONICLE. See under KANSAS

ST. LOUIS JEWISH LIGHT (1947; reorg. 1963). 12 Millstone Campus Dr., St. Louis, 63146. (314)432-3353. FAX: (314)432-0515. E-mail: stlouislgt@aol.com. Robert A. Cohn. Weekly. St. Louis Jewish Light.

NEBRASKA

JEWISH PRESS (1920). 333 S. 132 St., Omaha, 68154. (402)334-6450. FAX: (402)334-5422. E-mail: ckatzman@jewishomaha. org. Carol Katzman. Weekly. Jewish Federation of Omaha.

NEVADA

JEWISH REPORTER (1976). 3909 S. Maryland Pkwy., Suite 400, Las Vegas, 89119-7520. (702)948-5129. FAX: (702)967-1082. E-mail: lvjewishreporter@aol.com. Terri Herman. Bimonthly. Jewish Federation of Las Vegas.

LAS VEGAS ISRAELITE (1965). PO Box 14096, Las Vegas, 89114. (702)876-1255. FAX: (702)364-1009. Michael Tell. Bimonthly.

NEW JERSEY

AVOTAYNU (1985). 155 N. Washington Ave., Bergenfield, 07621. (201)387-7200. FAX: (201)387-2855. E-mail: info@avotaynu. com. Sallyann Amdur Sack. Quarterly.

JEWISH CHRONICLE (1982). 1063 East Landis Ave.,Suite B, Vineland, 08360. (856)696-4445. FAX: (856)696-3428. E-mail: jfedcc@aol.com. Ann Lynn Lipton. Bimonthly. The Jewish Federation of Cumberland County.

JEWISH COMMUNITY NEWS. 1086 Teaneck Rd., Teaneck, 07666. (201) 837-8818. FAX: (201) 833-4959. E-mail: jewish std2@aol.com. Rebecca Kaplan Boroson. Fortnightly. Jewish Federation of North Jersey and Jewish Federation of Greater Clifton-Passaic.

JEWISH COMMUNITY VOICE (1941). 1301 Springdale Rd., Suite 250, Cherry Hill, 08003-2762. (856)751-9500, ext. 217. FAX: (856)489-8253. E-mail: jvcheditor@aol.com. Harriet Kessler. Biweekly. Jewish Federation of Southern NJ.

THE JEWISH JOURNAL (OF OCEAN COUNTY) (1999). 320 Raritan Ave., Suite 203, Highland Park, 08904. (732)393-0023. FAX: (732)393-0026. E-mail: jewish@castle.net. Ron Ostroff. Monthly. Published in co-operation with the Jewish Federation of Ocean County.

JEWISH STANDARD (1931). 1086 Teaneck Rd., Teaneck, 07666. (201)837-8818. FAX: (201)833-4959. Rebecca Kaplan Boroson. Weekly.

JEWISH STAR (1985). 230 Old Bridge Turnpike, South River, 08882-2000. (732)432-7711. FAX: (732)432-0292. E-mail: jfgmc @aol.com. Marlene A. Heller. Fortnightly. Jewish Federation of Greater Middlesex County.

THE JEWISH STATE—THE WEEKLY NEWSPAPER FOR CENTRAL JERSEY'S JEWISH COMMUNITIES (1996). 320 Raritan Ave., Suite 203, Highland Park, 08904. (732)393-0023. FAX: (732)393-0026. E-mail: jewish @castle.net. Ron Ostroff. Weekly.

JEWISH VOICE & OPINION (1987). 73 Dana Place, Englewood, 07631. (201) 569-2845.

FAX: (201)569-1739. Susan L. Rosen-bluth. Monthly.

JEWISH VOICE OF GREATER MONMOUTH COUNTY (1971). 100 Grant Ave., Deal Park, 07723. (732)531-6200. FAX: (732)531-9518. E-mail: pfdnuss@msn. com. Lauren Silver. Monthly. Jewish Federation of Greater Monmouth County and Ocean County Jewish Federation.

JOURNAL OF JEWISH COMMUNAL SERVICE (1899). 3084 State Hwy. 27, Suite 9, Kendall Pk., 08824-1657. (732)821-1871. FAX: (732)821-5335. E-mail: jcsana@aol. com. Gail Naron Chalew. Quarterly. Jewish Communal Service Association of North America.

NEW JERSEY JEWISH NEWS (1947). 901 Route 10, Whippany, 07981-1157. (973) 887-3900. FAX: (973)887-5999. E-mail: 6853202@mcimail.com. Andrew Silow-Carroll.Weekly. United Jewish Federation of MetroWest.

THE SPEAKER (1999). 320 Raritan Ave., Suite 203, Highland Park, 08904. (732)393-0023. FAX: (732)393-0026. E-mail: jewish@castle.net. Ron Ostroff. Monthly. Published in cooperation with the Jewish Federation of Somerset, Hunterdon & Warren Counties.

NEW MEXICO

NEW MEXICO JEWISH LINK (1971). 5520 Wyoming NE, Albuquerque, 87109. (505)821-3214. FAX: (505)821-3351. E-mail: nmjlink@aol.com. Tema Milstein. Monthly. Jewish Federation of Greater Albuquerque.

NEW YORK

AFN SHVEL (1941). 200 W. 72 St., Suite 40, NYC, 10023. (212)787-6675. E-mail: yidleague@aol.com. Mordkhe Schaechter. Quarterly. Yiddish. League for Yiddish, Inc.

AGENDA: JEWISH EDUCATION (1949; formerly Pedagogic Reporter). JESNA, 111 Eighth Ave., Suite 11E, NYC, 10011-5201. (212)284-6950. FAX: (212)284-6951. E-mail: info@jesna.org. Amy Stein. Twice a year. Jewish Education Service of North America, Inc.

ALGEMEINER JOURNAL (1972). 225 E. Broadway, NYC, 10002. (212)267-5561. FAX: (212)267-5624. E-mail: Alge-meiner@aol.com. Gershon Jacobson. Weekly. Yiddish-English.

AMERICAN JEWISH YEAR BOOK (1899). 165 E. 56 St., NYC, 10022. (212)751-4000. FAX: (212)751-4017. E-mail: research @ajc.org. David Singer, Lawrence Grossman. Annually. American Jewish Committee.

AMIT (1925). 817 Broadway, NYC, 10003. (212)477-4720. FAX: (212)477-5213. E-mail: amitmag@amitchildren.org. Rita Schwalb. Quarterly. AMIT (formerly American Mizrachi Women).

AUFBAU (1934). 2121 Broadway, NYC, 10023. (212)873-7400. Voice mail: (212) 579-6578. FAX: (212)496-5736. E-mail: aufbau2000@aol.com. Monika Ziegler/Andreas Mink/Irene Armbruster. Fortnightly. German-English. New World Club, Inc.

BUFFALO JEWISH REVIEW (1918). 15 E. Mohawk St., Buffalo, 14203. (716)854-2192. FAX: (716)854-2198. E-mail: buffjewrev @aoc.com. Harlan C. Abbey. Weekly. Kahaal Nahalot Israel.

THE CALL (1933). 45 E. 33 St., NYC, 10016. (212)889-6800, ext. 225. FAX: (212)532-7518. E-mail: socolove@circle.org. Emily Socolov. Three times a year. The Workmen's Circle/Arbeter Ring.

CCAR JOURNAL: A REFORM JEWISH QUARTERLY (formerly Journal of Reform Judaism) (1953). 355 Lexington Ave., NYC, 10017. (212)972-3636. FAX: (212)692-0819. Ed. Stephen Pearce. Mng. Ed. Elliot Stevens. Quarterly. Central Conference of American Rabbis.

CIRCLE (1943). 15 E. 26 St., NYC, 10010-1579. (212)532-4949. FAX: (212)481-4174. E-mail: info@jcca.org. Miriam Rinn. JCC Circle Quarterly. Jewish Community Centers Association of North America (formerly JWB).

COMMENTARY (1945). 165 E. 56 St., NYC, 10022. (212)751-4000. FAX: (212)891-6700. E-mail: mail@commentarymagazine. com. Ed. Neal Kozodoy; Ed.-at-Large Norman Podhoretz. Monthly. American Jewish Committee.

CONGRESS MONTHLY (1933). 15 E. 84 St., NYC, 10028. (212)879-4500. Rochelle Mancini. Six times a year. American Jewish Congress.

CONSERVATIVE JUDAISM (1945). 3080 Broadway, NYC, 10027. (212)280-6065. FAX: (212)749-9166. E-mail: rapubs@jtsa.edu. Rabbi Martin S. Cohen. Quarterly. Rabbinical Assembly and Jewish Theological Seminary of America.

FORVERTS (Yiddish Forward) (1897). 45 E. 33 St., NYC, 10016. (212)889-8200. FAX: (212)684-3949. Boris Sandler. Weekly. Yiddish. Forward Association, Inc.

FORWARD (1897). 45 E. 33 St., NYC, 10016. (212)889-8200. FAX: (212)447-6406. E-mail: newsdesk@forward.com. J. J. Goldberg. Weekly. Forward Newspaper, L.L.C.

HADAROM (1957). 305 Seventh Ave., NYC, 10001. (212)807-7888. FAX: (212)727-8452. Rabbi Gedalia Dov Schwartz. Annual. Hebrew. Rabbinical Council of America.

HADASSAH MAGAZINE (1914). 50 W. 58 St., NYC, 10019. (212)688-0227. FAX: (212) 446-9521. Alan M. Tigay. Monthly (except for combined issues of June-July and Aug.-Sept.). Hadassah, the Women's Zionist Organization of America.

HADOAR (1921). 426 W. 58 St., NYC, 10019. (212)957-6658/9/8662-HEBREW. FAX: (212)957-5811. E-mail: HebrewUSA @aol.com. Ed. Shlomo Shamir; Lit. Ed. Dr. Yael Feldman. Biweekly. Hebrew. Hadoar Association, Inc., Organ of the Histadruth of America. (WWW.HEBREW USA.ORG)

I.A.J.E. NEWSLETTER (1999). (718)339-0337. E-mail: sanuav@stjohns.edu. Victor D. Sanua. International Association of Jews from Egypt.

JBI VOICE (1978). 110 E. 30 St., NYC, 10016. (212)889-2525, (800)433-1531, FAX (212) 689-3692. Email: dbarbara @jbilibrary.org. Dena Barbara. Ten times a year in U.S. (audiocassettes). English. Jewish Braille Institute of America.

JEWISH ACTION (1950). 11 Broadway, NYC, 10004. (212)613-8146. FAX: (212)613-0646. E-mail: ja@ou.org. Nechama Carmel. Quarterly. Orthodox Union.

JEWISH BOOK ANNUAL (1942). 15 E. 26 St., 10th fl., New York, NY 10010. (212)532-4949, ext. 297. E-mail: jbc@jewishbooks.org. Dr.Stephen H. Garrin. Hebrew & English with bibliography in Yiddish. Jewish Book Council, Jewish Book Annual published by Jewish Book Council.

JEWISH BOOK WORLD (1945). 15 E. 26 St., NYC, 10010. (212)532-4949, ext. 297. FAX: (212)481-4174. E-mail: jbc@jewish books.org. Esther Nussbaum. Three times annually. Jewish Book Council.

JEWISH BRAILLE REVIEW (1931). 110 E. 30 St., NYC, 10016. E-mail:dbarbara @jbilibrary.org. (212)889-2525, (800)433-1531. Dena Barbara. 10 times a year in U.S. (braille). English. Jewish Braille Institute of America.

JEWISH CURRENTS (1946) 22 E. 17St., Suite 601, NYC, 10003-1919. (212)924-5740. FAX: (212)414-2227. Bimonthly. Association for Promotion of Jewish Secularism, Inc.

JEWISH EDUCATION NEWS (1980). 261 W. 35 St., Fl. 12A, NYC 10001. (212) 268-4210. FAX: (212)268-4214. E-mail: publications @caje.org. Mng. Ed. Judi Resnick. Triannually. Coalition for the Advancement of Jewish Education.

THE JEWISH FRONTIER (1934). P.O. Box 4013, Amity Station, New Haven, CT 06525. (203)397-4903. FAX: (212)675-7685. E-mail: jewish-frontier@yahoo. com. Nahum Guttman-Graff. Bimonthly. Labor Zionist Letters, Inc. Managing Editor Bennett Lovett-Graff

JEWISH HERALD (1984). 1689 46 St., Brooklyn, NY 11204. (718)972-4000. E-mail: jewishherald@aol.com. Leon J. Sternheim. Weekly.

JEWISH JOURNAL (1969). 11 Sunrise Plaza, Valley Stream, 11580. (516)561-6900. FAX: (516)561-6971. Ed. Paul Rubens; Pub. Harold Singer. Weekly.

JEWISH LEDGER (1924). 2535 Brighton-Henrietta Town Line Rd., Rochester, 14623. (716)427-2434. FAX: (716)427-8521. Barbara Morgenstern. Weekly.

THE JEWISH OBSERVER (1963). 42 Broadway, NYC, 10004. (212)797-9000. FAX: (646)254-1600. E-mail: nwolpin@aol. com. Rabbi Nisson Wolpin. Monthly (except July and Aug.). Agudath Israel of America.

JEWISH OBSERVER OF CENTRAL NEW YORK (1978). 5655 Thompson Road, DeWitt, NY 13214. (315)445-2040 ext. 116 FAX:

(315)445-1559. E-mail: jocny@aol.com. Bette Siegel. Biweekly. Syracuse Jewish Federation, Inc.

JEWISH POST OF NY (1993). 262 West 38th St., NYC, 10018. (212)398-1313. FAX: (212)398-3933. E-mail: jpost@nais.com. Ed. Gad Nahshon. Monthly. Link Marketing & Promotion, Inc.

JEWISH PRESS (1950). 338 Third Ave., Brooklyn, 11215. (718)330-1100. FAX: (718)935-1215. E-mail: editor@jewish press.com. Jerry Greenwald. Weekly.

JEWISH TELEGRAPHIC AGENCY COMMUNITY NEWS REPORTER (1962). 330 Seventh Ave., 11th fl., NYC, 10001-5010. (212)643-1890. FAX: (212)643-8498. Email: www.jta.org/info@jta.org. Lisa Hostein. Monthly.

JEWISH TELEGRAPHIC AGENCY DAILY NEWS BULLETIN (1917). 330 Seventh Ave., 11th fl., NYC, 10001-5010. (212)643-1890. FAX: (212)643-8498. Exec. Ed. Mark Joffe; Ed. Lisa Hostein. Daily.

JEWISH TELEGRAPHIC AGENCY WEEKLY NEWS DIGEST (1933). 330 Seventh Ave., 11th fl., NYC, 10001-5010. (212)643-1890. FAX: (212)643-8498. E-mail: www. jta.org/info@jta.org. Exec. Ed. Mark Joffe; Ed. Lisa Hostein. Weekly.

JEWISH TRIBUNE. PMB #372, 169 South Main St., New City, 10956; Exec. off. (mailing address): 115 Middle Neck Rd., Great Neck, 11021. (845)352-5151. FAX: (516)829-4776. E-mail: lijeworld@aol. com. Jerome W. Lippman. Weekly. Jewish Tribune; Long Island Jewish World; Manhattan Jewish Sentinel.

JEWISH WEEK (1876; reorg. 1970). 1501 Broadway, NYC, 10036-5503. (212)921-7822. FAX: (212)921-8420. E-mail: editor @jewishweek.org. Gary Rosenblatt. Weekly.

JEWISH WORLD (1965). 3 Vatrano Road, Albany, 12205. (518)459-8455. FAX: (518)459-5289 .E-mail: news@jewishworld-news.org. Sam S. Clevenson. Weekly.

JOURNAL OF JEWISH EDUCATION-CJE (formerly Jewish Education) (1929). 11 Olympia Lane, Monsey, NY 10952. (845)368-8657. FAX: (845)369-6538. E-mail: mjscje@aol.com. Rabbi Irwin E. Witty. Three times a year. Council for Jewish Education.

JOURNAL OF REFORM JUDAISM. *See* CCAR Journal

JTS PUBLICATIONS (1991). 3080 Broadway, NYC 10027. (212)678-8950. FAX: (212)864-0109. E-mail: jowerner@jtsa.edu. Three times a year. The Jewish Theological Seminary. Asst. Dir. of Pub. Jodi Werner.

JUDAISM (1952). 15 E. 84 St., NYC, 10028. (212)360-1500. FAX: (212)249-3672. Editor's address: Kresge Col., U. of California, Santa Cruz, CA, 95064. (831)459-2566. FAX: (831)459-4872. Subscription address: 15 E. 84 St., NYC 10028. (212) 360-1500. E-mail: judaism@cats.ucsc. edu. Prof. Murray Baumgarten. Quarterly. American Jewish Congress.

KASHRUS MONTHLY-YOUR UUDATE ON KOSHER (1990). PO Box 204, Brooklyn, 11204. (718)336-8544. Rabbi Yosef Wikler. Monthly. Kashrus Institute. (editorial @kashrusmagazin.com)

KASHRUS MAGAZINE-THE PERIODICAL FOR THE KOSHER CONSUMER (1980). PO Box 204, Brooklyn, 11204. (718)336-8544. E-mail: editorial@kashrusmagazine.com. Rabbi Yosef Wikler. Five times per year (January, March, May, July, October). Kashrus Institute. (WWW.KASHRUS MAGAZINE.COM)

KOL HAT'NUA (Voice of the Movement) (1975). c/o Young Judaea, 50 W. 58 St., NYC, 10019. (212)303-4576. FAX: (212) 303-4572. E-mail: info@youngjudaea. org. Dov Wilker. Quarterly. Hadassah Zionist Youth Commission-Young Judaea.

KULTUR UN LEBN-CULTURE AND LIFE (1960). 45 E. 33 St., NYC, 10016. (212)889-6800. FAX: (212)532-7518. E-mail: wcfriends@aol.com. Joseph Mlotek. Quarterly. Yiddish. The Workmen's Circle.

LAMISHPAHA (1963). 426 W. 58 St., NYC, 10019. (212)957-6658/9/8862-HEBREW. FAX: (212)957-5811 .E-mail: general@ hist-ivrit.org. Dr. Vered Cohen-Raphaeli. Illustrated. Monthly (except July and Aug.). Hebrew. Histadruth Ivrith of America. (WWW.HEBREWUSA.ORG)

LIKUTIM (1981). 110 E. 30 St., NYC, 10016. (212)889-2525. Joanne Jahr. Two times a year in Israel (print and audiocassettes).

Hebrew. Jewish Braille Institute of America.

LILITH-THE INDEPENDENT JEWISH WOMEN'S MAGAZINE (1976). 250 W. 57 St., #2432, NYC, 10107. (212)757-0818. FAX: (212)757-5705. E-mail: lilithmag @aol.com. Susan Weidman Schneider. Quarterly. (WWW.LILITHMAG.COM)

LONG ISLAND JEWISH WORLD (1971). 115 Middle Neck Rd., Great Neck, 11021. (516)829-4000. FAX: (516)829-4776. E-mail: lijeworld@aol.com. Jerome W. Lippman. Weekly.

MANHATTAN JEWISH SENTINEL (1993). 115 Middle Neck Rd., Great Neck, 11021. (212)244-4949. FAX: (212)244-2257. E-mail: lijeworld@aol.com. Jerome W. Lippman. Weekly.

MARTYRDOM AND RESISTANCE (1974). 500 Fifth Ave., 42nd Floor, NYC, 10110-4299. (212)220-4304. FAX:(212)220-4308. E-mail: yadvashem@aol.com. Ed. Dr. Harvey Rosenfeld; Ed.-in-Chief Eli Zborowski. Bimonthly. International Society for Yad Vashem.

MIDSTREAM (1954). 633 Third Ave., 21st fl., NYC, 10017. (212)339-6020. FAX: (212)318-6176. E-mail: midstreamthf@ aol.com. Leo Haber. Eight times a year. Theodor Herzl Foundation, Inc.

NA'AMAT WOMAN (1925). 350 Fifth Ave., Suite 4700, NYC, 10118-4799. (212)563-5222. FAX: (212)563-5710. Judith A. Sokoloff. Quarterly. English-Yiddish-Hebrew. NA'AMAT USA, the Women's Labor Zionist Organization of America.

OLOMEINU-OURWORLD (1945). 5723 18th Ave., Brooklyn, 11204. (718)259-1223. FAX: (718)259-1795. Email: mail@ tupublications.com. Rabbi Yaakov Fruchter. Monthly. English-Hebrew. Torah Umesorah-National Society for Hebrew Day Schools.

PASSOVER DIRECTORY (1923). 11 Broadway, NYC, 10004. (212)613-8135. FAX: (212) 613-0772. Email: lieberd@ou.org Deborah Lieber. Annually. Union of Orthodox Jewish Congregations of America.

PROCEEDINGS OF THE AMERICAN ACADEMY FOR JEWISH RESEARCH (1920). 51 Washington Sq. South, NYC, 10012-1075. (212)998-3550. FAX: (212)995-4178. Dr. Nahum Sarna. Annually. English-Hebrew-French-Arabic-Persian-Greek. American Academy for Jewish Research.

RCA RECORD (1953). 305 Seventh Ave. NYC, 10001. (212)807-7888. FAX: (212) 727-8452. Rabbi Mark Dratch. Quarterly. Rabbinical Council of America.

REFORM JUDAISM (1972; formerly Dimensions in American Judaism). 633 Third Ave., 6th fl., NYC, 10017. (212)650-4240. Aron Hirt-Manheimer. Quarterly. Union of American Hebrew Congregations. (http://uahc.org/rjmag)

THE REPORTER (1971). 500 Clubhouse Rd., Vestal, 13850. (607)724-2360. FAX: (607)724-2311. E-mail: TReporter@aol. com. Judith S. Huober. Weekly. Jewish Federation of Broome County, Inc.

THE REPORTER (1966). 315 Park Ave. S., NYC 10010. (212)505-7700. FAX: (212)674-3057. E-mail; editor@waort. org. Marlene A. Heller. Semi-Annual. Women's American ORT, Inc.

RESPONSE: A CONTEMPORARY JEWISH REVIEW (1967). Columbia University Post Office, PO Box 250892, NYC, 10025. E-mail: response@panix.com. Chanita Baumhaft. Annual.

RUSSIAN FORWARD (1995). 45 E. 33 St., NYC, 10016. (212)889-8200. FAX: (212)448-9124. E-mail: rforward99@ yahoo.com. Leonid Shkolnik. Weekly. Russian.

SYNAGOGUE LIGHT AND KOSHER LIFE (1933). 47 Beekman St., NYC, 10038. (212)227-7800. Rabbi Meyer Hager. Quarterly. The Kosher Food Institute.

TRADITION (1958). 305 Seventh Ave., NYC, 10001. (212)807-7888. FAX: (212)727-8452. Rabbi Michael Shmidman. Quarterly. Rabbinical Council of America.

UNITED SYNAGOGUE REVIEW (1943). 155 Fifth Ave., NYC, 10010. (212)533-7800. FAX: (212)353-9439. E-mail: info@uscj. org. Lois Goldrich. Semiannually. United Synagogue of Conservative Judaism.

UNSER TSAIT (1941). 25 E. 21 St., 3rd fl., NYC, 10010. (212)475-0059. Bimonthly. Yiddish. Jewish Labor Bund.

VIEWPOINT MAGAZINE (1952). 3 W. 16 St., NYC, 10011. (212)929-1525, ext. 131. E-mail: ncyi@youngisrael.org. Esther Altman. Quarterly. National Council of Young Israel.

VOICE OF THE DUTCHESS JEWISH COMMUNITY (1989). 110 Grand Ave., Poughkeepsie, 12603. (845)471-9811. FAX: (845)471-3233. E-mail: jfeddutchess@mindspring.com. Business off.:500 Clubhouse Rd., Vestal, 13850. (607)724-2360. FAX: (607)724-2311. Sandy Gardner and Judith Huober. Monthly. Jewish Federation of Dutchess County, Inc.

WOMEN'S LEAGUE OUTLOOK MAGAZINE (1930475 475 Riverside Drive, Suite 820, New York, 10115. (212)870-1260. FAX: (212)870-1261. E-mail: rkahn@wlcj.org. Janet Arnowitz. Quarterly. Women's League for Conservative Judaism.

WORKMEN'S CIRCLE CALL. *See* The Call

WYOMING VALLEY JEWISH REPORTER (formerly WE ARE ONE) (1995). 500 Clubhouse Rd., Vestal, 13850. (607)724-2360. FAX: (607)724-2311. E-mail: TReporter @aol.com. Judith S. Huober. Every other week. Wilkes-Barre Jewish Community Board.

YEARBOOK OF THE CENTRAL CONFERENCE OF AMERICAN RABBIS (1890). 355 Lexington Ave., NYC, 10017. (212)972-3636. FAX: (212)692-0819. Rabbi Elliot L. Stevens. Annually. Central Conference of American Rabbis.

YIDDISH (1973). Queens College, NSF 350, 65-30 Kissena Blvd., Flushing, 11367. (718)997-3622. Joseph C. Landis. Quarterly. Queens College Press.

DI YIDDISHE HEIM (1958). 770 Eastern Pkwy., Brooklyn, 11213. (718)735-0458. Rachel Altein, Tema Gurary. Twice a year. English-Yiddish. Neshei Ub'nos Chabad-Lubavitch Women's Organization.

YIDDISHE KULTUR (1938). 1133 Broadway, Rm. 820, NYC, 10010. (212)243-1304. FAX (212)243-1305. E-mail: mahosu@aol.com. Itche Goldberg. Bimonthly. Yiddish. Yiddisher Kultur Farband, Inc.—YKUF.

DOS YIDDISHE VORT (1953). 84 William St., NYC, 10038. (212)797-9000. Joseph Friedenson. Bimonthly, (November-December monthly). Yiddish. Agudath Israel of America.

YIDDISHER KEMFER (1900). 275 Seventh Ave., NYC, 10001. (212)675-7808. FAX: (212) 675-7685. Dr. Jacob Weitzney. Bimonthly. Yiddish. Labor Zionist Alliance.

YIDISHE SHPRAKH (1941). 15 W. 16 St., NYC, 10011. (212)246-6080, ext. 6139. FAX: (212) 292-1892. Dr. Mordkhe Schaechter. Irregularly. Yiddish. YIVO Institute for Jewish Research.

YIVO BLETER (1931). 15 W. 16 St., NYC, 10011. (212)246-6080. FAX: (212)292-1892.E-mail: yivomail@yivo.cjh.org. Dr. David E. Fishman. Biannually. Yiddish. YIVO Institute for Jewish Research.

THE YOUNG JUDAEAN (1909). 50 W. 58 St., NYC, 10019. (212)303-4588. FAX: (212)303-4572. Email: ugoldflam@youngjudaea.org. Uri Goldflam. Quarterly. Young Judaea Zionist Youth Movement/Hadassah.

YUGNTRUF: YIDDISH YOUTH MAGAZINE (1964). 200 W. 72 St., Suite 40, NYC, 10023. (212)787-6675. FAX: (212)799-1517. E-mail: yugntruf@yugntruf.org. Elinor Robinson. Two to four times a year. Yiddish. Yugntruf Youth for Yiddish.

ZUKUNFT (The Future) (1892). 25 E. 21 St., NYC, 10010. (212)505-8040. FAX: (212)505-8044. Chaim Beider & Yonia Fain. Quarterly. Yiddish. Congress for Jewish Culture.

NORTH CAROLINA

CHARLOTTE JEWISH NEWS (1978). 5007 Providence Rd., Charlotte, 28226. (704)944-6765. FAX: (704) 365-4507. E-mail: amontoni@shalomcharlotte.org. Amy Krakovitz. Monthly (except July). Jewish Federation of Greater Charlotte.

JEWISH FEDERATION NEWS (1986). 8210 Creedmoor Rd., Suite 104, Raleigh, 27613. (919)676-2200. FAX: (919)676-2122. Sarah Falk. Monthly. Wake County Jewish Federation.

MODERN JUDAISM (1980). Oxford University Press, 2001 Evans Rd., Cary, 27513. (919)677-0977. FAX: (919)677-1714. E-mail: jnlorders@oup-usa.org. (Editorial address:Center for Judaic Studies, Boston University, 745 Commonwealth Ave., Boston, 02215. (617)353-8096. FAX: (617)353-5441.) Steven T. Katz. Three times a year.

OHIO

AKRON JEWISH NEWS (1929). 750 White Pond Drive, Akron, 44320. (330) 869-2424. FAX: (330)867-8498.E-mail: Toby__Liberman@jewishakron.org. Paula Maggio. Fortnightly. Fifteen times a year. Jewish Community Board of Akron.

AMERICAN ISRAELITE (1854). 906 Main St., Rm. 508, Cincinnati, 45202-1371. (513) 621-3145. FAX: (513)621-3744. E-mail: amisralite@aol.com. Stanley H. Bard. Weekly.

AMERICAN JEWISH ARCHIVES JOURNAL (1948). 3101 Clifton Ave., Cincinnati, 45220-2488. (513)221-1875. FAX: (513) 221-7812. E-mail: aja@cn.huc.edu. Ed. Dr. Gary P. Zola; Mng. Ed. Dr. Frederic Krome. Twice a year. Jacob Rader Marcus Center, American Jewish Archives, HUC-JIR.

CLEVELAND JEWISH NEWS (1964). 3645 Warrensville Center Rd., Suite 230, Cleveland, 44122. (216)991-8300. FAX: (216)991-2088. E-mail: editorial@cjn.org. Cynthia Dettelbach. Weekly. Cleveland Jewish News Publication Co.

INDEX TO JEWISH PERIODICALS (1963). PO Box 18525, Cleveland Hts., 44118. (216)381-4846. FAX: (216)381-4321. E-mail: index@jewishperiodicals.com. Lenore Pfeffer Koppel. Annually. Available in book and CD-ROM form. (WWW.JEWISH PERIODICALS.COM)

JEWISH JOURNAL (1987). 505 Gypsy Lane, Youngstown, 44504-1314. (330)744-7902. FAX: (330)746-7926. E-mail: yojjour-nal@aol.com Sherry Weinblatt. Biweekly (except July/Aug.). Youngstown Area Jewish Federation. (WWW.JEWISHJOURNAL PLUS.COM)

OHIO JEWISH CHRONICLE (1922). 2862 John-stown Rd., Columbus, 43219. (614)337-2055. FAX: (614)337-2059. Email: ojc@insight.rr.com. Judy Franklin. Weekly.

STARK JEWISH NEWS (1920). 2631 Harvard Ave. NW, Canton, 44709. (330)452-6444. FAX: (330)452-4487. E-mail: cantonjcf @aol.com. Linda Sirak. Monthly. Canton Jewish Community Federation;

STUDIES IN BIBLIOGRAPHY AND BOOKLORE (1953). 3101 Clifton Ave., Cincinnati, 45220. (513)221-1875. FAX: (513)221-0519. E-mail: lwolfson@huc.edu. Editor David J. Gilner; Managing Editor Laurel S. Wolfson. Irregularly. English-Hebrew-etc. Library of Hebrew Union College-Jewish Institute of Religion.

TOLEDO JEWISH NEWS (1951). 6505 Sylvania Ave., Sylvania, 43560. (419)724-0363. FAX: (419)724-0423. E-mail: meira@jew ishtoledo.org. Laurie Cohen. Monthly. United Jewish Council of Greater Toledo.

OKLAHOMA

TULSA JEWISH REVIEW (1930). 2021 E. 71 St., Tulsa, 74136. (918)495-1100. FAX: (918)495-1220. Ed Ulrich. Monthly. Jewish Federation of Tulsa.

OREGON

BRIDGES: A JOURNAL FOR JEWISH FEMINISTS AND OUR FRIENDS (1990). PO Box 24839, Eugene, 97402. (541)343-7617. FAX: (541)343-7617. E-mail: clare@ bridgesjournal.org. Mng. Ed. Clare Kinberg.

JEWISH REVIEW (1959). 6680 SW Capitol Highway, Portland, OR 97219. Edit.:(503) 245-4340. FAX: (503) 245-4342. Adv.: (503) 546-9883. FAX: (503) 620-3433. E-mail: news@jewishreview. org. Paul Haist. Regular column in Russian. Fortnightly. Jewish Federation of Portland. (WWW.JEWISHREVIEW.ORG)

PENNSYLVANIA

COMMUNITY REVIEW (1925). 3301 N. Front St. Annex, Harrisburg, 17110. (717)236-9555, ext.3402. FAX:(717)236-2552. E-mail: communityreview@desupernet.net. Carol L. Cohen. Fortnightly. United Jewish Community of Greater Harrisburg.

CONTEMPORARY JEWRY (1974), under the name Jewish Sociology and Social Research). Graduate Center CUNY, Room 6112-13, 365 Fifth Avenue, New York, NY 10016. (212) 817-8772. FAX: (914) 235-6717. E-mail: heilman@qc.edu. Samuel C. Heilman. Annually. Association for the Social Scientific Study of Jewry.

JERUSALEM LETTER/VIEWPOINTS (1978). 1515 Locust St., Suite 703, Philadelphia, 19102. (215)772-0564. FAX: (215)772-0566. Zvi R. Marom. Fortnightly. Jerusalem Center for Public Affairs.

JEWISH CHRONICLE OF PITTSBURGH (1962). 5600 Baum Blvd., Pittsburgh, 15206.

(412)687-1000. FAX:(412)687-5119. E-mail: news@pittchron.com. Lee Chottiner. Weekly. Pittsburgh Jewish Publication and Education Foundation.

JEWISH EXPONENT (1887). 2100 Arch St., Philadelphia, 19103. (215)832-0740. FAX: (215)569-3389. E-mail: jexponent@aol.com. Jonathan S. Tobin. Weekly. Jewish Federation of Greater Philadelphia.

JEWISH POLITICAL STUDIES REVIEW (1989). 1515 Locust St., Suite 703, Philadelphia, 19102. (215)772-0564. FAX: (215)772-0566. Mark Ami-El. Twice a year. Jerusalem Center for Public Affairs.

JEWISH QUARTERLY REVIEW (1910). 420 Walnut St., Philadelphia, 19106. (215)238-1290. FAX: (215)238-1540. E-mail: jqroffice@sas.upenn.edu. Ed. David M. Goldenberg; Mng. Ed. Bonnie L. Blankenship. Quarterly. Center for Advanced Jewish Studies, University of Pennsylvania.

NEW MENORAH (1978). 7318 Germantown Ave., Philadelphia, 19119-1793. (215)247-9700. FAX: (215)247-9703. Rabbi Arthur Waskow, PhD. Quarterly. Aleph: Alliance for Jewish Renewal.

RECONSTRUCTIONISM TODAY (1993). Beit Devora, 7804 Montgomery Ave., Suite 9, Elkins Park, 19027-2649. (215)782-8500. FAX: (215)782-8805. E-mail: jrfnatl@aol.com. Lawrence Bush. Quarterly. Jewish Reconstructionist Federation.

THE RECONSTRUCTIONIST (1935). 1299 Church Rd., Wyncote, 19095-1898. (215)576-5210. FAX: (215)576-8051. E-mail: rhirsh@therra.org. Rabbi Richard Hirsh. Semiannually. Reconstructionist Rabbinical College.

RHODE ISLAND

JEWISH VOICE AND HERALD (formerly jewish voice of rhode island) (1973). 130 Sessions St., Providence, 02906. (401)421-4111. FAX: (401)331-7961. E-mail: voiceherald@jfri.org. Jonathan Rubin. Biweekly. Jewish Federation of Rhode Island.

RHODE ISLAND JEWISH HERALD (1930). 99 Webster St., Pawtucket, 02860. (401)724-0200. FAX: (401)726-5820. Luke O'Neill. Weekly. Herald Press Publishing Company.

RHODE ISLAND JEWISH HISTORICAL NOTES (1951). 130 Sessions St., Providence, 02906. (401)331-1360. FAX: (401)272-6729. E-mail: rjhist@aol.com. Leonard Moss. Annually. Rhode Island Jewish Historical Association.

SOUTH CAROLINA

CHARLESTON JEWISH VOICE (2001). 1645 Wallenberg Blvd., Charleston, 29407. (843)571-6565. FAX: (843)556-6206. Ellen Katzman. Monthly. Charleston Jewish Federation.

TENNESSEE

HEBREW WATCHMAN (1925). 4646 Poplar Ave., Suite 232, Memphis, 38117. (901)763-2215. FAX: (901)763-2216. Herman I. Goldberger. Weekly.

OBSERVER (1934). 801 Percy Warner Blvd., Suite 102, Nashville, 37205. (615)354-1637. FAX: (615)352-0056. E-mail: judy@jewishnashville.org. Judith A. Saks. Biweekly (except July). Jewish Federation of Nashville.

SHOFAR. PO Box 8947, Chattanooga, 37414. (423)493-0270, Ext. 12. FAX: (423) 493-9997. E-mail: shofar@jcfgc.com. Rachel Schulson. Ten times a year. Jewish Federation of Greater Chattanooga.

TEXAS

JEWISH HERALD-VOICE (1908). 3403 Audley Street, Houston, 77098-1923. (713)630-0391. FAX: (713)630-0404. E-mail: jhvht@aol.com. Jeanne Samuels. Weekly. Four special issues:Rosh Hashanah; Passover; Wedding Planner; Bar/Bat Mitzvah Planner.

JEWISH JOURNAL OF SAN ANTONIO (1973). 8434 Ahern, San Antonio, 78213. (210)828-9511. FAX: (210)342-8098. Barbara Richmond. Monthly (11 issues). Jewish Federation of San Antonio.

TEXAS JEWISH POST (1947). 3120 S. Freeway, Fort Worth, 76110. (817)927-2831. FAX: (817)429-0840. 11333 N. Central Expressway, Suite 213, Dallas, 75243. (214)692-7283. FAX: (214)692-7285. Weekly.

VIRGINIA

RENEWAL MAGAZINE (1984). 5041 Corporate Woods Drive, Suite 150, Virginia Beach, 23462. (757)671-1600. FAX: (757) 671-7613. E-mail: news@ujft.org. Reba

Karp. Quarterly. United Jewish Federation of Tidewater.

SOUTHEASTERN VIRGINIA JEWISH NEWS (1959). 5041 Corporate Woods Drive, Suite 150, Virginia Beach, 23462. (757) 671-1600. FAX: (757)671-7613. E-mail: news@ujft.org. Reba Karp. 22 issues yearly. United Jewish Federation of Tidewater.

WASHINGTON

JEWISH TRANSCRIPT (1924). 2041 Third Ave., Seattle, 98121. (206)441-4553. FAX: (206)441-2736. E-mail: jewishtran@aol.com. Donna Gordon Blankinship. Fortnightly. Jewish Federation of Greater Seattle.

WISCONSIN

WISCONSIN JEWISH CHRONICLE (1921). 1360 N. Prospect Ave., Milwaukee, 53202. (414)390-5888. FAX: (414)271-0487. E-mail: milwaukeej@aol.com. Vivian M. Rothschild. Weekly. Milwaukee Jewish Federation.

INDEXES

INDEX TO JEWISH PERIODICALS (1963). PO Box 18525, Cleveland Hts., OH 44118. (216)381-4846. FAX: (216)381-4321. E-mail: index@jewishperiodicals.com. Lenore Pfeffer Koppel. Annually. Available in book and CD-ROM form. (WWW.JEWISHPERIODICALS.COM)

NEWS SYNDICATES

JEWISH TELEGRAPHIC AGENCY, INC. (1917). 330 Seventh Ave., 17th fl., NYC., 10001-5010. (212)643-1890. FAX: (212)643-8498. Mark J. Joffe, Lisa Hostein. Daily.

CANADA

CANADIAN JEWISH HERALD (1977). 17 Anselme Lavigne, Dollard des Ormeaux, PQ H9A 1N3. (514)684-7667. FAX: (514) 684-7667. Ed./Pub. Dan Nimrod. Irregularly. Dawn Publishing Co., Ltd.

THE CANADIAN JEWISH NEWS (1971). 1500 Don Mills Rd., Suite 205, North York, ONT M3B 3K4. (416)391-1836. FAX: (416)391-0829 (Adv.); (416)391-1836.

FAX: (416)391-0829. Mordechai Ben-Dat. 50 issues a year. Some French.

CANADIAN JEWISH OUTLOOK (1963). #3-6184 Ash St., Vancouver, BC V5Z 3G9. (604)324-5101. FAX:(604)325-2470. E-mail: cjoutlook@telus.net. Carl Rosenberg. Six times per year. Canadian Jewish Outlook Society.

DAIS (1985) (formerly Intercom). 100 Sparks St., #650, Ottawa, ONT KIP 5B7. (613)233-8703. FAX: (613)233-8748. E-mail: canadianjewishcongress@cjc.ca. Jack Silverstone. Three times a year. Canadian Jewish Congress.

DIRECTIONS (1998) (formerly Dialogue (1988)). 1 Carré Cummings, Suite 202, Montreal, Quebec H3W 1M6. (514)345-64111. FAX: (514)345-6412. E-mail: etay@cjc.ca. Eta Yudin. Quarterly. French-English. Canadian Jewish Congress, Quebec Region.

JEWISH FREE PRESS (1990). 8411 Elbow Dr., SW Calgary, AB. T2V 1K8. (403)252-9423. FAX: (403)255-5640. E-mail: jewishfp@telus.net. Judy Shapiro. Fortnightly.

JEWISH POST & NEWS (1987). 113 Hutchings St., Winnipeg, MAN R2X 2V4. (204)694-3332. FAX: (204)694-3916. E-mail: jewishp@mts.net. Matt Bellan. Weekly.

JEWISH STANDARD (1928). 1912A Avenue Road, Suite E5, Toronto, ONT M5M 4A1. (416)537-2696. FAX: (416)789-3872. Email: thejewishstandardasympatico.ca. Ed./Pub. Michael Hayman. Monthly.

JEWISH STANDARD (1928). 5184, Chemin de la Cote-des-Neiges, Suite 407, Montreal, Quebec H3T 1X8. Email: thejewish standardasympatico.ca. Ed./Pub. Michael Hayman. Monthly

THE JEWISH TRIBUNE (1950). 15 Hove St., Toronto, ONT M3H 4Y8. (416)633-6224. FAX: (416)633-6299. E-mail: carla@ jewishtribune.ca . Carla Lancit. B'nai Brith Canada, Bimonthly.

JEWISH WESTERN BULLETIN (1930). 301, 68 E. Second Ave., Vancouver, BC V5T 1B1. (604)689-1520. FAX: (604)689-1525. E-mail: jbeditor@istar.ca. Baila Lazarus. Weekly. 57786 BC Ltd.

JOURNAL OF PSYCHOLOGY AND JUDAISM (1976). 1747 Featherston Dr., Ottawa, ONT K1H 6P4. (613)731-9119. Reuven

P. Bulka. Quarterly. Center for the Study of Psychology and Judaism.

OTTAWA JEWISH BULLETIN (1954). 21 Nadolny Sachs Private., Ottawa, ONT K2A 1R9. (613)798-4696. FAX: (613) 798-4730. E-mail: bulletin@jccottawa. com. Barry Fishman. Nineteen times a year. Ottawa Jewish Bulletin Publishing Co. Ltd.

SHALOM (1975). 5670 Spring Garden Rd., Suite 508, Halifax, NS, B3J 1H1. (902) 422-7491. FAX: (902)425-3722. E-mail: jgoldberg@theajc.ns.ca. Jon M. Goldberg. Quarterly. Atlantic Jewish Council.

LA VOIX SÉPHARADE (1975). 5151 Chemin de la Cote, St. Catherine, Montreal, PQ H3W 1M6. (514)733-4998, FAX: (514) 733-3158. E-mail: elieb@fedcjamtl.org. Ed. James Dahan; Pub. Elie Benchitrit. Bimonthly (five times a year). French and occasional Spanish and English. Communauté Sépharade du Québec.

NEWS AND VIEWS (1942) (formerly Windsor Jewish Federation). 1641 Ouellette Ave., Windsor, ONT N8X 1K9. (519)973-1772. FAX: (519)973-1774. Exec. Dir. Harvey Kessler. Quarterly. Windsor Jewish Federation.

THE WORLD OF LUBAVITCH (1980). 770 Chabad Gate, Thornhill, ONT L4J 3V9. (905)731-7000. FAX: (905)731-7005. Rabbi Moshe Spalter. Quarterly. English. Chabad Lubavitch of Southern Ont.

Obituaries: United States*

ALTSCHUL, ARTHUR G., banker, philanthropist; b. NYC, Apr. 6, 1920; d. Centre Island, N.Y., Mar. 17, 2002. Educ.: Yale U. (AB). Served U.S. Marine Corps, WWII. After working as reporter for *N.Y. Times* and analyst for Lehman Brothers, partner, Goldman, Sachs & Co., 1959–76, limited partner, 1977–; bd. chmn., General American Investors Co., 1961–95. Bd. chmn., Barnard Coll., 1977–83; pres., Overbrook Found., 1981–2001; trustee, Whitney Museum of American Art; trustees council, Natl. Gallery of Art; chmn.'s council, Metropolitan Museum of Art; governing bd., Yale U. Art Gallery; member, distrib. com., N.Y. Community Trust.

ANNENBERG, WALTER, publisher, philanthropist; b. Milwaukee, Wis., Mar. 13, 1908; d. Wynnewood, Pa., Oct. 1, 2002. Educ.: Wharton School, U. Pa. Went to work for his father's company, Triangle Publs., 1929, ed. and publisher, 1942–88, running *Philadelphia Enquirer, Philadelphia Daily News, Daily Racing Form;* launched *Seventeen* magazine, 1944, *TV Guide,* 1953; acquired six radio and television stations. U.S. ambassador to Great Britain, 1969–74; pres., Annenberg Found., 1988–. Endowed M.L. Annenberg School for Communication, U. Pa., 1962; M.L. Annenberg School for Communication, U. Southern Cal., 1971; An-

nenberg Inst. (Center for Judaic Studies, U. Pa., successor to Dropsie Coll.), 1986. Bd. member of numerous orgs. and supporter of many causes including Corp. for Public Broadcasting, United Negro Coll. Fund, public education programs in several cities, Metropolitan Museum of Art, Natl. Gallery of Art, State of Israel, Weizmann Inst. of Science, N.Y. UJA-Fed., Jewish Fed. of Greater Philadelphia, Museum of Amer. Jewish History; received many awards, medals, and honorary degrees.

BERLE, MILTON, entertainer; b. NYC, July 12, 1908; d. Los Angeles, Cal., Mar. 27, 2002. At age five, wins Charlie Chaplin look-alike contest (prize: $5), becoming a child actor, performing in vaudeville and silent movies beginning 1914; first Hollywood appearance is in *The Mark of Zorro* (1920) and makes the transition to "talkies," appearing in many motion pictures; first solo performance at Loew's State Theater, 1924, followed by many more; appeared in several Broadway shows during 1930s, including *The Ziegfield Follies* and *Last of the Red Hot Lovers;* popular radio performer with his own show in 1940s; becomes first major television personality with "Texaco Star Theater" broadcast live on NBC, 1948–54, becoming known as "Uncle Miltie" to millions; continued to perform

---

*Including American Jews who died between January 1 and December 31, 2002.

live and on film well into his 80s; throughout his life did benefits for charities and armed forces personnel, hosted telethons. Au.: *Out of My Trunk* (1945); *Earthquake* (1959); *Milton Berle: An Autobiography* (1974). Rec.: Emmy Award (1979); Television Hall of Fame (1984).

BERNSTEIN, THERESA, artist; b. Philadelphia. Pa., Mar. 1, 1890; d. NYC, Feb. 13, 2002. Educ.: Philadelphia School of Design, Art Students League. Prominent member of "Ash Can" school of realistic painting that depicted urban scenes; there were more than 40 solo exhibition of her work, and her paintings are in the permanent collections of the Metropolitan Museum of Art, Library of Cong., Smithsonian Inst., Chicago Art Inst., N.Y. Public Library, Brooklyn Museum, and elsewhere. Rec. of numerous prizes and awards. Au.: *William Meyerowitz: The Artist Speaks* (1986); *The Poetic Canvas* (1988).

BLOCK, IRVING J., rabbi; b. Bridgeport, Conn., Mar. 17, 1923; d. NYC, Sept. 30, 2002. Educ.: U. Conn. (BS); Hebrew Union Coll. (ordination, MHL). Served U.S. Army, WWII; Haganah, Israel War of Independence, 1947–48. Founding rabbi, Brotherhood Synagogue, NYC, 1954–94, sharing building with Village Presbyterian Church until 1974 when dispute over support for Israel induced the synagogue to find new premises. Pioneer in Jewish-Christian brotherhood work and black-Jewish relations; active in NYC civic and Jewish organizations.

CHARGAFF, ERWIN, biochemist; b. Czernowitz, Austria, Aug. 11, 1905; d. NYC, June 20, 2002; in U.S. since 1928. Educ.: U. Vienna (PhD). Research fellow, Yale U., 1928–30; asst., U. Berlin, 1930–33; research assoc., Pasteur Inst., Paris, 1933–34; faculty, Columbia U., 1935–74, prof., biochemistry, 1952–74, dept. chmn., 1970–74, prof. emer., 1974–. His research in the 1940s on DNA and the four bases of which it is composed laid the basis for Crick and Watson's discovery of the double helix. Au.: *Essays on Nucleic Acids* (1963); *Voices in the Labyrinth* (1977); *Heraclitean Fire* (1978); *Serious Questions* (1986); also several books in German and numerous articles in professional journals. Rec.: Guggenheim Fellowship; Pasteur Medal; Neuberg Medal; National Medal of Science;

Columbia U. Distinguished Service Award, and many other awards.

CHYET, STANLEY, historian, archivist; b. Boston, Mass., Apr. 2, 1931; d. Los Angeles, Cal., Oct. 19, 2002. Educ.: Brandeis U. (BA); Hebrew Union Coll. (ordination, PhD). Prof., Jewish history, and assoc. dir., Amer. Jewish Archives, HUC, Cincinnati, 1960–76; Prof., Amer. Jewish history, HUC, Los Angeles, 1976–96, prof. emer., 1996–, dir., graduate studies, 1978–96, dir., rabbinical school, 1980–82, asst. to pres.-sec. to bd. of trustees, Skirball Cultural Center, 1996–. Mem., Assn. for Jewish Studies Exec. Bd.; Amer. Jewish Historical Soc. Academic Council; Jewish Publ. Soc. Publs. Com. Au.: *Lopez of Newport* (1970). Translated and ed.: *Israeli Poetry: A Contemporary Anthology* (1988); *Words in My Lovesick Blood: Poems by Haim Gouri* (1996); *No Sign of Ceasefire: An Anthology of Contemporary Israeli Poetry* (2002).

EDELSON, BURTON I., space-flight administrator; b. NYC, July 31, 1926; d. NYC, Jan. 6, 2002. Educ.: U.S. Naval Acad. (BS); Yale U. (MS, PhD). Engineer with U.S. Navy starting as ensign, 1947, rising to commodore, 1963, and retiring 1967. Deputy dir., Comsat Laboratories, 1967–72, dir., 1972–79, v.-pres., systems and engineering, 1979–82; assoc. administrator, space science and applications, NASA, 1982–87; founding dir., Inst. for Applied Space Research, George Washington U., 1987–. At NASA played a key role in Hubble Space Telescope, Mars exploration. Wrote more than 75 scholarly articles. Awards: Navy Legion of Merit; Wilbur Cross Medal (Yale U.); NASA Exceptional Service Medal.

FEUER, LEWIS, sociologist; b. NYC, Dec. 7, 1929; d. Newton, Mass., Nov. 24, 2002. Educ.: CCNY (BS); Harvard U. (AM, PhD). Served U.S. Army, WWII. Instr., philosophy, CCNY, 1939–42; assoc. prof., Vassar Coll., 1946–51; prof., U. Vermont, 1951–57; prof., philosophy and social science, U. Cal.-Berkeley, 1957–66; prof., sociology, U. Toronto, 1966–76; prof., sociology and govt., U. Virginia, 1976–83, prof. emer., 1983–. Created controversy by analysis of 1960s student activism as generational rebellion; one of first Western scholars to lecture on Marx in USSR, 1963, where he publicly criticized lack of free speech, treatment of Soviet Jews. Au.: *Spinoza and the Rise of Liberalism* (1951); *The Scientific Intellectual* (1963); *The Conflict of Generations* (1969); *Marx and the Intellectuals* (1969); *Einstein and the Generations of Science* (1974); *Ideology and the Ideologists* (1975); *The Case of the Revolutionist's Daughter: Sherlock Holmes Meets Karl Marx* (1983); *Imperialism and the Anti-Imperialist Mind* (1986).

FONER, MOE, labor leader; b. Brooklyn, NY, Aug. 3, 1915; d. NYC, Jan. 10, 2002. Educ.: Brooklyn Coll., CUNY (AB). Served U.S. Army, WWII. Clerk, CCNY registrar's office, fired for Communist Party membership, 1942; educational director, Depart. Store Local 1250, 1945–50; social and cultural dir., Distributive Workers District 65, 1950–52 (when Communists were forced out); educational and cultural dir., Local 1199 (health and human services workers union), 1952–82; exec. sec., Nat. Hospital Union, 1982–83, exec. sec. emer., 1983–. Made 1199 first union to install a permanent art gallery, 1972; key figure in 1199's successful 46-day strike to unionize NYC hospital workers; founded Bread and Roses, union cultural program, 1982; opposition to Vietnam War got him on to President Nixon's "enemies list."

FRANKEL, MARVIN E., jurist; b. NYC, July 26, 1920; d. NYC, Mar. 3, 2002. Educ.: Queens Coll., CUNY (AB); Columbia U. (LLB, ed.-in-chief, law review). Served U.S. Army, WWII. Asst. to U.S. solicitor-genl., 1949–56; partner, Proskauer Rose Goetz and Mendelsohn, NYC, 1956–62, 1978–83; prof., law, Columbia U., 1962–65; U.S. district judge, Southern District of N.Y., 1965–78; partner, Kramer, Levin, Naftalis, Nessen, Kamin and Frankel, NYC, 1983–. Au.: *Criminal Sentences: Law Without Order* (with Gary Naftalis, 1973); *The Grand Jury—In Institution on Trial* (1977); *Partisan Justice* (1980). His critique of criminal sentencing contributed to creation of federal sentencing guidelines, and his Supreme Court brief successfully defending *N.Y. Times* in *Times v. Sullivan* (1964) was a free-speech landmark; campaigned for internat'l. human rights as chmn., Lawyers Com. For Human Rights, 1980–.

GINZBERG, ELI, economist; b. NYC, Apr. 30, 1911; d. NYC, Dec. 12, 2002. Educ.: Columbia U. (AB, AM, PhD). Economics faculty, Columbia U., 1935–79, A. Barton Hepburn prof., Graduate School of Business, 1967–79, prof. emer., 1979–, dir., conservation of human resources project, 1950–90. Special asst. to chief statistician, U.S. War Dept., 1942–44, dir., resource analysis div., 1944–46; member, medical adv. bd. to sec. of war, 1946–48; dir., staff studies, Natl. Manpower Council, 1952–61; served on numerous other govt. and private-sector bodies dealing with employment, health care, and racial discrimination. Au.: *The Illusion of Economic Stability* (1939); *The Unemployed* (1943); *A Pattern for Hospital Care* (1949); *Agenda for American Jews* (1950); *The Uneducated* (1953); *The Negro Potential* (1956); *The Ineffective Soldier* (1959); and many more, including a biography of his father, *Keeper of the Law: Louis Ginzberg* (1966), and two memoirs, *My Brother's Keeper* (1989) and *The Eye of Illusion* (1993). Mem., bd. of govs., Hebrew U., Jerusalem.

GOLDMAN, LILLIAN, philanthropist; b. NYC, Jan. 17, 1922; d. East Hampton, N.Y., Aug. 20, 2002. Worked with her husband, Sol Goldman, in his real estate business, which became one of the largest private landlords in NYC. Established Lillian Goldman Charitable Trust, 1987, which gave more than $20 million to Yale U. Law School, believed to be the largest amount ever given to Amer. legal education (1992); $5 million to 92nd Street Y, NYC (1998); $1 million to Alzheimer's Association (2001); and about $1 million to renovate Kane St. Synagogue, Brooklyn (2002); also a major supporter of Breast Cancer Research Found., Parkinson's Disease Found., Natl. Multiple Sclerosis Soc., Lenox Hill Hospital, UJA-Fed. of N.Y., Educational Alliance, N.Y. Restoration Project, and other causes.

GOODMAN, WALTER, journalist, critic; b. NYC, Aug. 22, 1927; d. Valhalla, N.Y., Mar. 6, 2002. Educ.: Syracuse U. (BA); Reading U., England (MA). Ed., Foreign Broadcast Information Service, London, 1950s; freelance writer for magazines; ed., *N.Y. Times*, 1974–, mem., editorial bd., 1977–, critic, concentrating increasingly on television, 1983–, sr. writer, 1996–; exec. ed., WNET, 1979–80, dir., humanities programming, 1980–83. Au.: *The Clowns of Commerce* (1957); *All Honorable Men* (1963); *The Committee: The Extraordinary Career of the House Commit-*

tee on Un-American Activities (1968); *Black Bondage* (1969).

GOULD, STEPHEN JAY, paleontologist; b. NYC, Sept. 10, 1941; d. NYC, May 20, 2002. Educ.: Antioch Coll. (AB); Columbia U. (PhD). Asst. prof., geology, asst. curator, invertebrate paleontology, Harvard U., 1967–71, assoc. prof. and assoc. curator, 1971–73, prof. and curator, 1973–, Alexander Agassiz prof., zoology, 1982–; best known for theory of "punctuated equilibrium" to explain evolution. Au.: *Ontogeny and Phylogeny* (1977); *Ever Since Darwin* (1977); *The Panda's Thumb* (1980, Nat. Book Award for Science, Amer. Book Award for Science); *The Mismeasure of Man* (1981, Nat. Book Critics Circle Award for general nonfiction); *Hen's Teeth and Horse's Toes* (1983, Phi Beta Kappa Book Award); *The Flamingo's Smile* (1985); *Time's Arrow, Time's Cycle* (1987); *An Urchin in the Storm* (1987); *Wonderful Life* (1989, Phi Beta Kappa Book Award); *Bully for Brontosaurus* (1991); *Finders, Keepers* (1992); *Eight Little Piggies* (1993); *Questioning the Millennium* (1997); *The Structure of Evolutionary Theory* (2002). Ed. of, and contrib. to, numerous professional journals; also wrote regular column for nonspecialists in *Natural History,* 1974–2001. Rec. many awards, honors, prizes, including MacArthur Found. "genius" grant.

GREEN, ADOLPH, playwright; b. NYC, Dec. 2, 1914; d. NYC, Oct. 24, 2002. Educ.: NYU. Performed with Betty Comden at Village Vanguard, Blue Angel, Rainbow Room, NYC, 1937–44; wrote Broadway musicals in collaboration with Comden: *On the Town* (1944–45, Theater World Award); *Billion Dollar Baby* (1945); *Bonanza Bound* (1947); *Two on the Aisle* (1951); *Wonderful Town* (1953, Tony Award for outstanding musical); *Peter Pan* (1954); *Bells Are Ringing* (1956); *Say, Darling* (1958); *Do, Re, Mi* (1960); *Subways Are for Sleeping* (1961–62); *Fade Out—Fade In* (1964); *Hallelujah, Baby* (1967, Tony Awards for best score, lyrics, musical); *Applause* (1970–72, Tony Award for best musical); *On the Twentieth Century* (1978, Tony Awards for best book, best score); *The Madwoman of Central Park* (1979); *A Doll's Life* (1982); *Singin' in the Rain* (1985–86); *The Will Rogers Follies* (1991, Tony Award, best original score); also numerous screenplays with Ms. Comden, as well as stage

and film appearances. Named to Songwriters Hall of Fame, 1980.

GREEN, S. WILLIAM ("BILL"), congressman; b. NYC, Oct. 16, 1929; d. NYC, Oct. 14, 2002. Educ.: Harvard U. (AB, JD). Served U.S. Army (Judge Advocate General Corps). Law sec., Court of Appeals, Dist. of Columbia, 1955–56; assoc., Cleary, Gottlieb, Steen and Hamilton, NYC, 1956–66; mem., N.Y. State Assembly, 1965–68; assoc., Paul Weiss, Rifkind, Wharton and Garrison, NYC, 1966–68; regional administrator, U.S. Dept. of Housing and Urban Devel., 1970–77; mem., U.S. House of Reps. (for "silk stocking" district of Manhattan), 1978–93, serving on appropriations com.; mem., NYC Campaign Finance Bd., 1994–2000. Bd. mem., NYU Graduate School of Public Affairs; Cancer Research Inst.; New School for Social Research; F.D.R. Memorial Comm.; Montefiore Medical Center; U.S. Holocaust Memorial Comm.; N.Y. Fed. of Jewish Philanthropies; Jewish Assoc. for Services for the Aged (pres., 1994–95).

GUNTHER, GERALD, legal scholar; b. Usingen, Germany, May 26, 1927; d. Stanford, Cal., July 30, 2002; in U.S. since 1938. Educ.: Brooklyn Coll., CUNY (BA); Columbia U. (MA); Harvard U. (LLB). Law clerk, U.S. Court of Appeals, Second Circuit (Judge Learned Hand), 1953–54, U.S. Supreme Court Chief Justice Earl Warren, 1954–55; assoc., Cleary, Gottlieb, Friendly and Hamilton, NYC, 1955–56; assoc. prof, law, Columbia U., 1956–59, prof., 1959–62; prof., law, Stanford U., 1962–72, William Nelson Cromwell prof., 1972–95, emer., 1995–. Au.: *John Marshall's Defense of McColloch v. Maryland* (1969); *Constitutional Law* (14 ed., with K.M. Sullivan, 2001); *Learned Hand: The Man and the Judge* (1994, won Triennial Prize, Supreme Court Historical Soc.); *First Amendment Law* (1999). Mem. and officer of numerous professional assocs.; rec. of many awards.

KIPNIS, IGOR, musician; b. Berlin, Germany, Sept. 27, 1930; d. West Redding, Conn., Jan. 23, 2002; in U.S. since 1941. Educ.: Westport Music School; Harvard U. (AB). Record library asst., station WMCA, 1954–55; art and editorial dir., Westminster Records, 1955–59; dir., recorded music, Internat'l Good Music, 1959–61; after teaching himself to play harpsichord in 1959, performed and recorded widely; CBS contract, 1964, ultimately recording more than 80 albums; teacher, Baroque performance practice, Berkshire Music Center, summers, 1964–67; assoc. prof., fine arts, Fairfield U., 1971–75, artist-in-residence, 1975–77; solo harpsichord performances with many orchestras in U.S. and abroad, including N.Y. Philharmonic, Chicago Symphony, Pittsburgh Symphony, Natl. Symphony, Munich Philharmonic. Numerous awards and honors.

KOCH, KENNETH, poet; b. Cincinnati, Ohio, Feb. 27, 1925; d. NYC, July 6, 2002. Educ.: Harvard U. (AB); Columbia U. (MA, PhD). Served U.S. Army, WWII. Lecturer, English, Rutgers U., 1953–58, Brooklyn Coll., 1957–59; asst. prof., Columbia U., 1959–66, assoc. prof., 1966–71, prof., 1971–; dir., poetry workshop, New School for Social Research, 1958–66. Au.: more than 30 volumes of poems, plays, opera librettos, literary criticism, reflecting the sensibility of the "New York School" that he founded together with poets John Ashberry and Frank O'Hara and painters Jane Freilicher and Larry Rivers. Rec.: Nat. Inst. of Arts and Letters Award; Bollingen Prize for Poetry (Yale U.); Rebekah Johnson Bobbit Prize for Poetry (Library of Cong.); Fulbright Fellowship (three times); Guggenheim Fellowship.

LANDERS, ANN (ESTHER "EPPIE" LEDERER), advice columnist; b. Sioux City, Iowa, July 4, 1918; d. Chicago, Ill., June 23, 2002. Educ.: Morningside Coll., Sioux City. After spending 1939–55 as housewife and Democratic political activist, won contest to take over "Ask Ann Landers" advice column in *Chicago Sun-Times,* quickly becoming so popular that the column was syndicated and appeared all over the country, so that a 1978 *World Almanac* survey found her to be the most influential woman in the U.S.; moved to *Chicago Tribune,* 1987, and by the time of her death the column was carried in more than 1,200 papers worldwide, with readership of 90 million. Au.: *Since You Asked Me* (1962); *Ann Landers Talks to Teenagers about Sex* (1964); *Truth Is Stranger* (1968); *Ann Landers Speaks Out* (1975); *The Ann Landers Encyclopedia* (1978). Bd. mem., numerous health-related charitable orgs. Rec. many awards and honors.

LEWIS, FLORA, journalist; b. Los Angeles, Cal., July 29, 1922; d. Paris, France, June 2, 2002. Educ.: UCLA (BA); Columbia U. School of Journalism (MS). Reporter, Associated Press, N.Y., Washington, London, 1942–46; freelance and contract writer for numerous newspapers and magazines reporting from London, Warsaw, Berlin, The Hague, Mexico City, Tel Aviv, Prague, 1946–58; bureau chief, *Washington Post,* in Bonn, London, NYC, 1958–66; syndicated columnist, *Newsday,* 1967–72; bureau chief, *N.Y. Times,* Paris, 1972–80; European diplomatic correspondent, *N.Y. Times,* 1976–80, foreign affairs columnist, 1980–90, sr. columnist, 1990–94. Au.: *A Case History of Hope* (1958); *Red Pawn* (1964); *One of Our H-Bombs Is Missing* (1967); *Europe: A Tapestry of Nations* (1987); *Europe: A Road to Unity* (1992). Rec.: Overseas Press Club Award; Columbia U. School of Journalism 50th Anniversary Honor Award; George Washington U. School of Foreign Affairs Award for Distinguished Diplomatic Reporting.

MARCUS, STANLEY, business exec.; b. Dallas, Tex., Apr. 20, 1905; d. Dallas, Jan. 22, 2002. Educ.: Amherst Coll., Harvard U. (BA, year at business school). Began work with family firm, Neiman-Marcus, Dallas, 1926, merchandise mgr., sportswear shop, 1928, merchandise mgr., all apparel divs., 1929, exec. v.-pres., 1935–50, pres., 1950–72, chmn. bd., 1972–75, chmn. exec. com., 1975–77, chmn. emer., 1977–; Au.: *Minding the Store* (1974); *Quest for the Best* (1979); *His and Hers* (1982). Active in many civic and charitable causes.

MILLER, ISRAEL, rabbi, communal leader; b. Baltimore, Md., Apr. 6, 1918; d. Jerusalem, Mar. 21, 2002. Educ.: Yeshiva U. (BA, ordination); Columbia U. (MA). Chaplain, U.S. Air Force, WWII. Rabbi, Kingsbridge Heights Jewish Center, Bronx, N.Y., 1941–68, emer., 1968–. Prof., practical rabbinics, Yeshiva U. rabbinical school, 1968–80; asst. to pres., Yeshiva U., 1968–70, v.-pres., 1970–80, senior v.-pres., 1980–94, emer., 1994–. Pres., Rabbinical Council of Amer., 1964–66; chmn., Amer. Jewish Conf. on Soviet Jewry, 1965–67, Amer. Zionist Council, 1967–70; pres., Amer. Zionist Fed., 1970–74; chmn., Conf. of Presidents of Major Amer. Jewish Orgs., 1974–76; pres., Conf. on Jewish Material Claims Against Germany, 1982–, obtaining hundreds of millions of dollars for Holocaust survivors. Rec. numerous honors and awards.

NOZICK, ROBERT, philosopher; b. Brooklyn N.Y., Nov. 16, 1938; d. Cambridge, Mass., Jan 23, 2002. Educ.: Columbia U. (AB); Princeton U. (MA, PhD). Instr., philosophy, Princeton U., 1962–63, asst. prof., 1964–65; Fulbright scholar, Oxford U., 1963–64; asst. prof., philosophy, Harvard U., 1965–67, prof., 1969–, dept. chmn., 1981–84, Arthur Kingsley Porter prof., 1985–98, Pellegrino university prof., 1998–; asssoc. prof., Rockefeller U., 1967–69. Au.: *Anarchy, State, and Utopia* (1974, Natl. Book Award); *Philosophical Explanations* (1981, Ralph Waldo Emerson Award); *The Examined Life* (1989); *The Nature of Rationality* (1993); *Socratic Puzzles* (1997); *Invariances* (2001). Rec. fellowships from Guggenheim Found.; Rockefeller Found.; NEH; Center for Advanced Study in the Behavioral Sciences.

PEARL, DANIEL, reporter; b. Princeton, N.J., Oct. 10, 1963; d. Karachi, Pakistan, Jan. 31, 2002. Educ.: Stanford U. (BA). Reporter, *North Adams Transcript, Springfield Union-News, Berkshire Eagle* (all in Mass.), 1980s; *Wall Street Journal*, 1990–, reporting from London and Paris, then named South Asia bureau chief and stationed in Bombay; abducted Jan. 23, 2002, by Muslim extremists while investigating leads about "shoe bomber" Richard Reid; captors released videotape of his brutal murder Feb. 20.

PHILLIPS, WILLIAM, editor; b. NYC, Nov. 4, 1907; d. NYC, Sept. 13, 2002. Educ.: CCNY (BS); NYU (MA); Columbia U. Cofounder, with Philip Rahv, and ed., *Partisan Review*, 1934–, ed.-in-chief, 1969–, the magazine becoming an influential political and literary organ in 1940s and 1950s, publishing the early work of many writers who would become famous and maintaining an anticommunist leftwing posture; taught English at Sarah Lawrence Coll, U. Minn., NYU; prof., Rutgers U., 1963–78; prof., Boston U., 1978–. Au.: *A Sense of the Present* (1967); *A Partisan View: Five Decades of the Literary Life* (1983). Ed., *The Partisan Review Anthology* (1983); *Sixty Years of Great Fiction From the Partisan Review* (1997). Rec. grants and fellowships from Rockefeller Found.; NEH; Guggenheim Found.

POTOK, CHAIM, author; b. NYC, Feb. 17, 1929; d. Merion, Pa., July 23, 2002. Educ.: Yeshiva U. (BA); Jewish Theol. Sem. (ordination, MHL); U. Pa. (PhD). Chaplain, U.S. Army, in Korea. Dir., Camp Ramah, Ojai, Cal., 1957–59; scholar-in-residence, Har Zion Temple, Philadelphia, 1959–63; faculty, Teachers Inst., JTS, 1963–64; ed.-in-chief, Jewish Publ. Soc., 1965–74, special projects ed., 1974–. Au.: *The Chosen* (1967, Edward Lewis Wallant Award, made into feature film, 1981); *The Promise* (1969, Athenaeum Award); *My Name Is Asher Lev* (1972); *In the Beginning* (1975); *Wanderings* (1978); *The Book of Lights* (1981); *Davita's Harp* (1985); *The Gift of Asher Lev* (1990, Natl. Jewish Book Award); *I Am the Clay* (1992); *The Gates of November* (1996); *Old Men at Midnight* (2001). Literary ed., *JPS Torah Commentary* (1989–96).

RABB, MAXWELL, govt. official; b. Boston, Mass., Sept. 28, 1910; d. NYC, June 9, 2002. Educ.: Harvard U. (AB, LLB). Served U.S. Navy, WWII. Member, Rabb & Rabb law firm, Boston, 1935–37; asst. to U.S. Sen. Henry Cabot Lodge, 1937–43, asst. to Sen. Sinclair Weeks, 1944; practiced law, Boston, 1946–51; consultant, U.S. Senate Rules Com., 1952; exec. asst. to campaign manager, Eisenhower presidential campaign, 1952; asst. to Pres. Eisenhower and sec. to cabinet, 1953–58; partner, Stroock & Stroock and Lavan, NYC, 1958–81, of counsel, 1989–91; ambassador to Italy, 1981–89. Bd. mem. of corps.; trustee of charitable orgs. Pres., Cong. Emanu-El, NYC, 1973–81. Rec.: Grand Cross Order of Merit (Italy); Grand Cross of Order of Malta.

RABINOVE, SAMUEL, lawyer; b. NYC, Feb. 5, 1923; d. White Plains, N.Y., June 9, 2002. Educ.: CCNY (BA); Columbia U. (LLB). Served U.S. Navy, WWII. Natl. legal dir., Amer. Jewish Com., 1966–97, where he prepared precedent-setting briefs and advocated for church-state separation, religious pluralism, civil rights, civil liberties, freedom of expression, immigration reform; wrote numerous articles and op-eds in newspapers and magazines, as well as pamphlets and background papers. Active in Natl. Adv. Council of Americans United for Separation of Church and State; Internat'l. Acad. of Freedom of Religion and Belief; Natl. Council of

Churches Com. on Religious Liberty; Project Equality; Coalition Against Censorship; N.Y. State Adv. Com. to U.S. Civil Rights Comm. Rec.: Project Equality Pride and Excellence Award; Americans United for Separation of Church and State Religious Liberty Award; Amer. Jewish Com. Professional Leadership Award.

REISMAN, DAVID, sociologist; b. Philadelphia, Pa., Sept. 22, 1909; d. Binghamton, N.Y., May 10, 2002. Educ.: Harvard U. (AB, LLB). Research fellow, Harvard U., 1934–35; clerk to U.S. Supreme Court Justice Louis Brandeis, 1935–36; assoc., Lyne, Woodworth and Evarts, Boston, 1936–37; prof., law, U. Buffalo, 1937–41; deputy asst. district attorney, N.Y. County, 1942–43; exec., Sperry Gyroscope Co, 1943–46; assoc. prof., social sciences, U. Chicago, 1946–47, prof., 1949–58; dir., research project on mass communications, Yale U., 1948–49; Henry Ford II prof., social sciences, Harvard U., 1958–; Au.: *The Lonely Crowd: A Study of the Changing American Character* (1950); *Faces in the Crowd* (1952); *Thorstein Veblen* (1953); *Individualism Reconsidered and Other Essays* (1954); and several books on American higher education. *The Lonely Crowd,* which became an instant best seller (it has sold to date 1.4 million copies), developed a distinction between "inner-directed" and "other-directed" character types.

RIVERS, LARRY, artist; b. NYC, Aug. 17, 1923; d. Southampton, N.Y., Aug. 14, 2002. Educ.: NYU; Juilliard School of Music. Served briefly, U.S. Army Air Corps, WWII. While working as jazz musician and at odd jobs, began painting in 1945, first exhibit 1949; after studying in Paris, returned to U.S. and painted the influential *Washington Crossing the Delaware* (1953), a parody of a patriotic theme widely viewed as ushering in "Pop Art"; many one-man shows at museums all over U.S. and around the world; his work is in the permanent collections of major repositories and held by private collectors. Au.: *Drawings and Digressions* (1997); *What Did I Do?* (autobiography with Arnold Weinstein, 1993).

ROSTOW, EUGENE, legal scholar, govt. official; b. Brooklyn, N.Y., Aug. 25, 1913; d. Alexandria, Va., Nov. 26, 2002. Educ.: Yale U. (AB, LLB, AM). Private legal practice, NYC, 1937–38; adv., U.S. State Dept., 1942–44; asst. exec. sec., UN Economic Comm. for Europe, 1949–50; faculty, Yale U. Law School, 1938–, prof., 1944–84, Sterling prof., 1964–84, prof. emer. and research scholar, 1984–, dean, 1955–65. Under-sec. of state for political affairs, 1966–69; dir., Arms Control and Disarmament Agcy., 1981–83. Au.: *Planning for Freedom* (1959); *The Sovereign Prerogative* (1962); *Law, Power, and the Pursuit of Peace* (1968); *Peace in the Balance* (1972); *The Ideal in Law* (1978); *Toward Managed Peace* (1993). Rec. numerous honors and awards.

SPAISMAN, ZYPORA, actress; b. Lublin, Poland, Jan. 2, 1916; d. NYC, May 18, 2002; in U.S. since 1955. Educ.: Nursing School, Lublin. Worked as midwife from 1933; fled Nazi invasion of Poland to USSR, 1939, where she spent the war years in a Soviet camp delivering more than 1,000 babies and organizing Yiddish theater productions; after the war acted in Yiddish theater in Lodz, Paris, and Montreal, until allowed into U.S.; there she acted with the Folksbiene beginning 1956, achieving a formidable reputation for bringing characters to life and becoming exec. producer of the company, all the while supporting herself as recreation dir., Jewish Inst. for Geriatric Care; formed her own company, Yiddish Public Theater, 2000; appeared in cameo role in film *Enemies: A Love Story* (1989). Rec.: Obie Award; Drama Desk Award; NYC Lifetime Achievement Award.

TRIGÈRE, PAULINE, fashion designer; b. Paris, France, Nov. 4, 1908; d. NYC, Feb. 13, 2002; in U.S. since 1937. Educ.: Victor Hugo Coll., Paris. Asst. designer, Hattie Carnegie, NYC, 1937–42; founded and ran House of Trigère, 1942–94, which gained quick recognition in the fashion world and was first fashion house to employ black models; founded P.T. Concepts, marketing scarves and jewelry, 1994–2000. Rec.: Coty Amer. Fashion Critics Award; Neiman-Marcus Award; Filene's Award; Coty Hall of Fame Award; Silver Medal, City of Paris; Council of Fashion Designers Lifetime Achievement Award; French Legion of Honor.

WALLACH, JOHN, journalist, peace activist; b. NYC, June 18, 1943; d. NYC, July 9, 2002. Educ.: Middlebury Coll. (BA); New

School for Social Research (MA). State Dept. correspondent, Hearst Newspapers, Washington, 1968–74, White House correspondent, 1974–76, foreign ed., 1976–95; exec. dir., Elie Wiesel Found. for Humanity, 1995–96; sr. fellow, U.S. Inst. of Peace, 1997–98. Dir., Chautauqua Conf. on U.S.-Soviet Relations, 1983–87; dir., Seeds of Peace, summer camp brining together children from opposing sides of world conflicts, beginning with Jews and Arabs, 1993–, expanded to Jerusalem, 1999. Au.: *Still Small Voices: The Human Story Behind the Intifada* (1989); *Arafat: In the Eyes of the Beholder* (1990); *The New Palestinians* (1993); *The Enemy Has a Face: The Seeds of Peace Experience* (2000). Cont. ed., *Washingtonian* magazine, 1984–89. Rec.: Natl. Press Club Edwin Hood Award; Overseas Press Club Award; B'nai B'rith Humanitarian Award; Kingdom of Jordan Legion of Honor.

WASSERMAN, LEW, entertainment executive; b. Cleveland, Ohio, Mar. 22, 1913; d. Beverly Hills, Cal., June 3, 2002. Educ.: high school. Public relations dir., Music Corp. of Amer. (MCA), 1936–38, v-pres., 1938–39, given charge of motion picture div., 1940, pres., 1946–73, chmn. bd., 1973–90, emer., 1990–. During his tenure MCA acquired Decca Records, Universal Pictures; responsible for the production of such blockbuster films as *All About Eve; The Sting; Airport; Jaws; Star Wars; Indiana Jones; E.T.; Jurassic Park; Back to the Future;* and on television, *Alfred Hitchcock Presents; Marcus Welby, M.D.; Magnum P.I.; Miami Vice.* Extremely generous philanthropist, donating to Catholic charities, higher education for minorities, and Jewish causes—including Los Angeles Jewish Fed., Birthright Israel, Shoah Visual History Found., UCLA Hillel. Rec.: Presidential Medal of Freedom (1995).

WAXMAN, MORDECAI, rabbi; b. Albany, N.Y., Feb. 25, 1917; d. Great Neck, N.Y., Aug. 10, 2002. Educ.: U. Chicago (AB); Jewish Theol. Sem. (ordination, MHL). Chaplain, U.S. Army, WWII. Rabbi, Niagara Falls, N.Y., Chicago, 1940s, Temple Israel, Great Neck, N.Y., 1947–. Au.: *Tradition and Change: The Development of Conservative Judaism* (1958). Ed., *Conservative Judaism* (Rabbinical Assembly), 1969–74. Active in numerous Jewish orgs., especially noted for work in Jewish-Catholic relations—in 1987, as chmn., Internat'l. Jewish Com. on Interreligious Consultations (IJCIC), publicly confronted Pope John Paul II on anti-Semitism, and in 1998 pope named him knight commander of St. Gregory the Great

WELLSTONE, PAUL, senator; b. Washington, D.C., July 21, 1944; d. in plane crash over Minn. while campaigning for reelection, Oct. 25, 2002. Educ.: U. North Carolina (BA, PhD). Taught political science, Carleton Coll., Northfield, Minn., 1969–91; mem., Democratic Nat. Com., 1984; Minn. chmn, Jesse Jackson presidential campaign, 1988; U.S. Sen. from Minn. (Dem.), 1991–, known for political liberalism, maverick tendencies, opposition to Gulf, Iraq wars; served on foreign relations, small business, energy and natural resources, labor and human resources coms. Au.: *How the Rural Poor Got Power: Narrative of a Grass-Roots Organizer* (1972); *The Conscience of a Liberal* (2001).

WILDER, BILLY, film writer, director; b. Sucha, Austria (Galicia), June 22, 1906; d. Beverly Hills, Cal., Mar. 27, 2002; in U.S. since 1934. Educ.: U. Vienna. Served U.S. Army, Film Section, Psychological Div., WWII. Freelance reporter, silent-movie ghostwriter, Berlin, beginning 1926, first movie produced, *People on Sunday* (1930); worked for UFA, Berlin, 1931–33, writing nearly a dozen early sound films (in German); screenwriter in Paris, 1933–34; hired by Paramount Studios, U.S., 1936, collaborated (because his English was weak) on *Bluebeard's Eighth Wife* (1938); *Ninotchka* (1939); *Hold Back the Dawn* (1941); *Double Indemnity* (1944); *The Lost Weekend* (1945, Acad. Award, best dir.); *Sunset Boulevard* (1950); *Stalag 17* (1953); *Love in the Afternoon* (1957); *Some Like It Hot* (1959); *The Apartment* (1960, four Acad. Awards); *One, Two, Three* (1961); *The Fortune Cookie* (1966). Rec.: Acad. Awards (six); Irving Thalberg Award (Motion Picture Acad.); Laurel Award (twice); Film Soc. of Lincoln Center Award.

WURZBURGER, WALTER, rabbi; b. Munich, Germany, Mar. 29, 1920; d. NYC, Apr. 15, 2002; in U.S. since 1938. Educ.: Yeshiva U. (BA, ordination); Harvard U. (MA, PhD). Rabbi, Cong. Chai Odom,

Boston, 1944–53, Shaarei Shomayim Cong., Toronto, Canada, 1953–67, Shaaray Tefila Cong., Lawrence, N.Y., 1967–94; adj. prof., philosophy, Yeshiva U., 1967–. Au.: *Ethics of Responsibility: Pluralistic Approaches to Covenental Ethics* (1994); *God Is Proof Enough* (2000); numerous articles on Jewish theology and ethics. Ed., *Tradition* (Rabbinical Council of America), 1961–87; *A Treasury of Tradition* (1967, 1994); contrib. ed., *Shma.* Pres., Rabbinical Council of Amer., Rabbinical Council of Canada, Synagogue Council of Amer. Rec.: Natl. Rabbinic Leadership Award (Orthodox Union).

Calendars

SUMMARY JEWISH CALENDAR, 5763–5767 (Sept. 2002–Aug. 2007)

HOLIDAY	5763 — 2002	5764 — 2003	5765 — 2004	5766 — 2005	5767 — 2006
Rosh Ha-shanah, 1st day	Sa Sept. 7	Sa Sept. 27	Th Sept. 16	T Oct. 4	Sa Sept. 23
Rosh Ha-shanah, 2nd day	S Sept. 8	S Sept. 28	F Sept. 17	W Oct. 5	S Sept. 24
Fast of Gedaliah	M Sept. 9	M Sept. 29	S Sept. 19	Th Oct. 6	M Sept. 25
Yom Kippur	M Sept. 16	M Oct. 6	Sa Sept. 25	Th Oct. 13	M Oct. 2
Sukkot, 1st day	Sa Sept. 21	Sa Oct. 11	Th Sept. 30	T Oct. 18	Sa Oct. 7
Sukkot, 2nd day	S Sept. 22	S Oct. 12	F Oct. 1	W Oct. 19	S Oct. 8
Hosha'na' Rabbah	F Sept. 27	F Oct. 17	W Oct. 6	M Oct. 24	F Oct. 13
Shemini 'Azeret	Sa Sept. 28	Sa Oct. 18	Th Oct. 7	T Oct. 25	Sa Oct. 14
Simhat Torah	S Sept. 29	S Oct. 19	F Oct. 8	W Oct. 26	S Oct. 15
New Moon, Heshwan, 1st day	S Oct. 6	S Oct. 26	F Oct. 15	W Nov. 2	S Oct. 22
New Moon, Heshwan, 2nd day	M Oct. 7	M Oct. 27	Sa Oct. 16	Th Nov. 3	M Oct. 23
New Moon, Kislew, 1st day	T Nov. 5	T Nov. 25	S Nov. 14	F Dec. 2	T Nov. 21
New Moon, Kislew, 2nd day	W Nov. 6	W Nov. 26			W Nov. 22
Hanukkah, 1st day	Sa Nov. 30	Sa Dec. 20	W Dec. 8	M Dec. 26	Sa Dec. 16
New Moon, Tevet, 1st day	Th Dec. 5	Th Dec. 25	M Dec. 13	Sa Dec. 31	Th Dec. 21
New Moon, Tevet, 2nd day	F Dec. 6	F Dec. 26		S Jan. 1	F Dec. 22
Fast of 10th of Tevet	S Dec. 15	S 2004 Jan. 4	W Dec. 22	T 2006 Jan. 10	S Dec. 31

	2003	2004	2005	2006	2007
New Moon, Shevat	Sa Jan. 4	Sa Jan. 24	T Jan. 11	M Jan. 30	Sa Jan. 20
Hamishshah-ʿasar bi-Shevat	Sa Jan. 18	Sa Feb. 7	T Jan. 25	M Feb. 13	Sa Feb. 3
New Moon, Adar I, 1st day	S Feb. 2	S Feb. 22	W Feb. 9	T Feb. 28	S Feb. 18
New Moon, Adar I, 2nd day	M Feb. 3	M Feb. 23	Th Feb. 10	W Mar. 1	M Feb. 19
New Moon, Adar II, 1st day	T Mar. 4		F Mar. 11		
New Moon, Adar II, 2nd day	W Mar. 5		Sa Mar. 12		
Fast of Esther	M Mar. 17	Th Mar. 4	Th Mar. 24	M Mar. 13	Th Mar. 1
Purim	T Mar. 18	S Mar. 7	F Mar. 25	T Mar. 14	S Mar. 4
Shushan Purim	W Mar. 19	M Mar. 8	Sa Mar. 26	W Mar. 15	M Mar. 5
New Moon, Nisan	Th Apr. 3	T Mar. 23	S Apr. 10	Th Mar. 30	T Mar. 20
Passover, 1st day	Th Apr. 17	T Apr. 6	S Apr. 24	Th Apr. 13	T Apr. 3
Passover, 2nd day	F Apr. 18	W Apr. 7	M Apr. 25	F Apr. 14	W Apr. 4
Passover, 7th day	W Apr. 23	M Apr. 12	Sa Apr. 30	W Apr. 19	M Apr. 9
Passover, 8th day	Th Apr. 24	T Apr. 13	S May 1	Th Apr. 20	T Apr. 10
Holocaust Memorial Day	Tu Apr. 29	S Apr. 18	F May 6*	T Apr. 25	S Apr. 15
New Moon, Iyar, 1st day	F May 2	W Apr. 21	M May 9	F Apr. 28	W Apr. 18
New Moon, Iyar, 2nd day	Sa May 3	Th Apr. 22	T May 10	Sa Apr. 29	Th Apr. 19
Israel Independence Day	W May 7	M Apr. 26	Sa May 14†	W May 3	M Apr. 23
Lag Ba-ʿomer	T May 20	S May 9	F May 27	T May 16	S May 6
Jerusalem Day	F May 30*	W May 19	M June 6	F May 26*	W May 16
New Moon, Siwan	S June 1	F May 21	W June 8	S May 28	F May 18
Shavuʿot, 1st day	F June 6	W May 26	M June 13	F June 2	W May 23
Shavuʿot, 2nd day	Sa June 7	Th May 27	T June 14	Sa June 3	Th May 24
New Moon, Tammuz, 1st day	M June 30	Sa June 19	Th July 7	M June 26	Sa June 16
New Moon, Tammuz, 2nd day	T July 1	S June 20	F July 8	T June 27	S June 17
Fast of 17th of Tammuz	Th July 17	T July 6	S July 24	Th July 13	T July 3
New Moon, Av	W July 30	M July 19	Sa Aug. 6	W July 26	M July 16
Fast of 9th of Av	Th Aug. 7	T July 27	S Aug. 14	Th Aug. 3	T July 24
New Moon, Elul, 1st day	Th Aug. 28	T Aug. 17	S Sept. 4	Th Aug. 24	T Aug. 14
New Moon, Elul, 2nd day	F Aug. 29	W Aug. 18	M Sept. 5	F Aug. 25	W Aug. 15

*Observed Thursday, a day earlier, to avoid conflict with the Sabbath.
†Observed Thursday, two days earlier, to avoid conflict with the Sabbath.

CONDENSED MONTHLY CALENDAR
(2002–2004)

2002, Jan. 14–Feb. 12]   SHEVAṬ (30 DAYS)   [5762

Civil Date	Day of the Week	Jewish Date	SABBATHS, FESTIVALS, FASTS	PENTATEUCHAL READING	PROPHETICAL READING
Jan. 14	M	Shevaṭ 1	New Moon	Num. 28:1–15	
19	Sa	6	Bo'	Exod. 10:1–13:16	Jeremiah 46:13–28
26	Sa	13	Be-shallaḥ (Shabbat Shirah)	Exod. 13:17–17:16	Judges 4:4–5:31 *Judges 5:1–31*
28	M	15	Ḥamishah 'asar bi-Shevaṭ		
Feb. 2	Sa	20	Yitro	Exod. 18:1–20:23	Isaiah 6:1–7:6; 9:5–6 Isaiah 6: 1–13
9	Sa	27	Mishpaṭim (Shabbat Sheḳalim)	Exod. 21:1–24:18 Exod. 30:11–16	II Kings 12:1–17 *II Kings 11:17–12:17*
12	T	30	New Moon, first day	Num. 28: 1–15	

Italics are for Sephardi Minhag.

2002, Feb. 13– Mar. 13]   ADAR (29 DAYS)   [5762

Civil Date	Day of the Week	Jewish Date	SABBATHS, FESTIVALS, FASTS	PENTATEUCHAL READING	PROPHETICAL READING
Feb. 13	W	Adar 1	New Moon, second day	Num. 28:1–15	
16	Sa	4	Terumah	Exod. 25:1–27:19	I Kings 5:26–6:13
23	Sa	11	Teẓawweh (Shabbat Zakhor)	Exod. 27:20–30:10 Deut. 25:17–19	I Samuel 15:2–34 *I Samuel 15:1–34*
25	M	13	Fast of Esther	Exod. 32:11–14 Exod. 34:1–10 (morning and afternoon)	Isaiah 55:6–56:8 (afternoon only)
26	T	14	Purim	Exod. 17:8–16	Book of Esther (night before and in the morning)
27	W	15	Shushan Purim		
Mar. 2	Sa	18	Ki tissa' (Shabbat Parah)	Exod. 30:11–34:35 Num. 19: 1–22	Ezekiel 36:16–38 *Ezekiel 36:16–36*
9	Sa	25	Wa-yaḵhel, Peḵude (Shabbat Ha-ḥodesh)	Exod. 35:1–40:38 Exod. 12:1–20	Ezekiel 45:16–46:18 *Ezekiel 45:18–46:15*

Italics are for Sephardi Minhag.

Civil Date	Day of the Week	Jewish Date	SABBATHS, FESTIVALS, FASTS	PENTATEUCHAL READING	PROPHETICAL READING
Mar. 14	Th	Nisan 1	New Moon	Num. 28:1–15	
16	Sa	3	Wa—yiḳra'	Levit. 1:1–5: 26	Isaiah 43:21–44:24
23	Sa	10	Ẓaw (Shabbat Ha-gadol)	Levit. 6:1–8: 36	Malachi 3:4–24
27	W	14	Fast of Firstborn		
28	Th	15	Passover, first day	Exod. 12:21–51 Num. 28:16–25	Joshua 5:2–6:1, 27
29	F	16	Passover, second day	Levit. 22:26–23:44 Num. 28:16–25	II Kings 23:1–9, 21–25
30	Sa	17	Ḥol Ha-mo'ed, first day	Exod. 33:12–34:26 Num. 28:16–25	Ezekiel 37:1–14
31	S	18	Ḥol Ha-mo'ed, second day	Exod. 33:12–34:26 Num. 28:19–25	
Apr. 1	M	19	Ḥol Ha-mo'ed, third day	Exod. 22:24–23:19 Num. 28:19–25	
2	T	20	Ḥol Ha-mo'ed, fourth day	Num. 28: 19–25	
3	W	21	Passover, seventh day	Exod. 13:17–15:26 Num. 28:19–25	II Samuel 22:1—51
4	Th	22	Passover, eight day	Deut. 15:1–16:17 Num. 28:19 –25	Isaiah 10:32–12:6
6	Sa	24	Shemini	Levit. 9:1–11:47	II Samuel 6:1 –7:17 *II Samuel 6:1–19*
9	T	27	Holocaust Memorial Day		
12	F	30	New Moon, first day	Num. 28:1–15	

Italics are for Sephardi Minhag.

2002, Apr. 13– May 11]   IYAR (29 DAYS)   [5762

Civil Date	Day of the Week	Jewish Date	SABBATHS, FESTIVALS, FASTS	PENTATEUCHAL READING	PROPHETICAL READING
Apr. 13	Sa	Iyar 1	Tazria', Meẓora'; New Moon, second day	Levit. 12:1–15:33 Num. 28:9–15	Isaiah 66:1–24
17	W	5	Israel Independence Day		
20	Sa	8	Aḥare mot, Ḳedoshim	Levit. 16:1–20:27	Amos 9:7–15 *Ezekiel 20:2–20*
27	Sa	15	Emor	Levit. 21:1–24:23	Ezekiel 44:15–31
30	T	18	Lag Ba-'omer		
May 4	Sa	22	Be-har, Be-ḥuḳḳotai	Levit. 25:1–27:34	Jeremiah 16:19–17:14
10	F	28	Jerusalem Day*		
11	Sa	29	Be-midbar	Num 1:1–4:20	I Samuel 20:18–42

*Observed May 9, to avoid conflict with the Sabbath.

*Italics are for
Sephardi Minhag.*

2002, May 12– June 10]   SIWAN (30 DAYS)   [5762

Civil Date	Day of the Week	Jewish Date	SABBATHS, FESTIVALS, FASTS	PENTATEUCHAL READING	PROPHETICAL READING
May 12	S	Siwan 1	New Moon	Num. 28:1–15	
17	F	6	Shavu'ot, first day	Exod. 19:1–20:23 Num. 28:26–31	Ezekiel 1:1–28, Ezekiel 3:12
18	Sa	7	Shavu'ot, second day	Deut. 15:19–16: 17 Num. 28:26–31	Habbakuk 3:1–19 *Habbakuk 2:20–3:19*
25	Sa	14	Naso'	Num. 4:21–7:89	Judges 13:2–25
June 1	Sa	21	Be-ha'alotekha	Num. 8:1–12:16	Zechariah 2:14–4: 7
8	Sa	28	Shelaḥ lekha	Num. 13:1–15:41	Joshua 2:1–24
10	M	30	New Moon, first day	Num. 28:1–15	

Italics are for Sephardi Minhag.

2002, June 11– July 9] TAMMUZ (29 DAYS) [5762

Civil Date	Day of the Week	Jewish Date	SABBATHS, FESTIVALS, FASTS	PENTATEUCHAL READING	PROPHETICAL READING
Jun 11	T	Tammuz 1	New Moon, second day	Num. 28:1–15	
15	Sa	5	Ḳoraḥ	Num. 16:1–18:32	I Samuel 11:14–12:22
22	Sa	12	Ḥuḳḳat, Balaḳ	Num. 19:1–25:9	Micah 5:6–6:8
27	Th	17	Fast of 17th of Tammuz	Exod. 32:11–14 Exod. 34: 1–10 (morning and afternoon)	Isaiah 55:6–56:8 (afternoon only)
29	Sa	19	Pineḥas	Num. 25:10–30:1	Jeremiah 1:1–2:3
July 6	Sa	26	Maṭṭot Masʻe	Num. 30:2–36:13	Jeremiah 2:4–28 Jeremiah 3:4 *Jeremiah 2:4–28* *Jeremiah 4:1–2*

Italics are for
Sephardi Minhag.

2002, July 10–Aug. 8] AV (30 DAYS) [5762

Civil Date	Day of the Week	Jewish Date	SABBATHS, FESTIVALS, FASTS	PENTATEUCHAL READING	PROPHETICAL READING
July 10	W	Av 1	New Moon	Num. 28:1–15	
13	Sa	4	Devarim (Shabbat Ḥazon)	Deut. 1:1–3:22	Isaiah 1:1–27
18	Th	9	Fast of 9th of Av	Morning: Deut. 4:25–40 Afternoon: Exod. 32:1–14 Exod. 34:1–10	(Lamentations is read the night before) Jeremiah 8:13–9:23 (morning) Isaiah 55:6–56:8 (afternoon)
20	Sa	11	Wa-etḥannan (Shabbat Nahamu)	Deut. 3:23–7:11	Isaiah 40:1–26
27	Sa	18	ʿEḳev	Deut. 7:12–11:25	Isaiah 49:14–51:3
Aug. 3	Sa	25	Re'eh	Deut. 11:26–16:17	Isaiah 54:11–55:5
8	Th	30	New Moon, first day	Numbers 28:1– 15	

Italics are for Sephardi Minhag.

2002, Aug. 9–Sept. 6]   ELUL (29 DAYS)   [5762

Civil Date	Day of the Week	Jewish Date	SABBATHS, FESTIVALS, FASTS	PENTATEUCHAL READING	PROPHETICAL READING
Aug. 9	F	Elul 1	New Moon, second day	Num. 28:1–15	
10	Sa	2	Shofeṭim	Deut. 16:18–21:9	Isaiah 51:12–52:12
17	Sa	9	Ki teze'	Deut. 21:10–25:19	Isaiah 54:1–10
24	Sa	16	Ki tavo'	Deut. 26: 1–29:8	Isaiah 60:1–22
31	Sa	23	Niẓẓavim, Wa-yelekh	Deut. 29:9–31:30	Isaiah 61:10–63:9

Italics are for
Sephardi Minhag.

TISHRI (30 DAYS)

Civil Date	Day of the Week	Jewish Date	SABBATHS, FESTIVALS, FASTS	PENTATEUCHAL READING	PROPHETICAL READING
Sept. 7	Sa	Tishri 1	Rosh Ha-shanah, first day	Gen. 21:1–34 Num. 29:1–6	I Samuel 1:1–2:10
8	S	2	Rosh Ha-shana, second day	Gen. 22:1–24 Num. 29:1–6	Jeremiah 31:2–20
9	M	3	Fast of Gedaliah	Exod. 32:11–14 Exod. 34:1–10 (morning and afternoon)	Isaiah 55: 6–56:8 (afternoon only)
14	Sa	8	Ha'azinu (Shabbat Shuvah)	Deut. 32:1–52	Hosea 14:2–10 Micah 7:18–20 Joel 2:15–27 *Hosea 14:2–10* *Micah 7:18–20*
16	M	10	Yom Kippur	Morning: Levit. 16:1–34 Num. 29:7–11 Afternoon: Levit. 18:1–30	Isaiah 57:14–58:14 Jonah 1:1–4:11 Micah 7:18–20
21	Sa	15	Sukkot, first day	Levit. 22:26–23:44 Num. 29:12–16	Zechariah 14:1–21
22	S	16	Sukkot, second day	Levit. 22:26–23:44 Num. 29:12 –16	I Kings 8:2–21
23-26	M-Th	17-20	Ḥol Ha-mo'ed	M: Num. 29:17–25 T: Num. 29:20–28 W: Num. 29:23–31 Th: Num. 29:26–34	
27	F	21	Hosha'na' Rabbah	Num. 29:26–34	
28	Sa	22	Shemini 'Aẓeret	Deut. 14:22–16:17 Num. 29:35–30:1	I Kings 8:54–66
29	S	23	Simḥat Torah	Deut. 33:1–34:12 Gen. 1:1–2:3 Num. 29:35–30:1	Joshua 1:1–18 *Joshua 1:1–9*
Oct. 5	Sa	29	Be-re'shit	Gen. 1:1–6:8	I Samuel 20:18–42
6	S	30	New Moon, first day	Num. 28: 1–15	

Italics are for Sephardi Minhag.

2002, Oct. 7–Nov. 5] ḤESHWAN (30 DAYS) [5763

Civil Date	Day of the Week	Jewish Date	SABBATHS, FESTIVALS, FASTS	PENTATEUCHAL READING	PROPHETICAL READING
Oct. 7	M	Ḥeshwan 1	New Moon, second day	Num. 28:1–15	
12	Sa	6	Noaḥ	Gen. 6:9–11:32	Isaiah 54:1–55:5 *Isaiah 54:1–10*
19	Sa	13	Lekh lekha	Gen. 12:1–17:27	Isaiah 40:27–41:16
26	Sa	20	Wa-yera'	Gen. 18:11–22:24	II Kings 4:1–37 *II Kings 4:1–23*
Nov. 2	Sa	27	Ḥayye Sarah	Gen. 23:1–25:18	I Kings 1:1–31
5	T	30	New Moon, first day	Num. 28:1–15	

Italics are for Sephardi Minhag.

Civil Date	Day of the Week	Jewish Date	SABBATHS, FESTIVALS, FASTS	PENTATEUCHAL READING	PROPHETICAL READING
Nov. 6	W	Kislew 1	New Moon, second day	Num. 28:1–15	
9	Sa	4	Toledot	Gen. 25:19–28:9	Malachi 1:1–2:7
16	Sa	11	Wa-yeze'	Gen. 28:10–32:3	Hosea 12:13–14:10 *Hosea 11:7–12:12*
23	Sa	18	Wa-yishlaḥ	Gen. 32:4–36:43	Hosea 11:7–12:12 *Obadiah 1:1–21*
30	Sa	25	Wa-yeshev; Ḥanukkah, first day	Gen. 37:1–40:23 Num. 7:1–17	Zechariah 2:14–4:7
Dec. 1-4	S–W	26–29	Hanukkah, second to fifth days	S Num. 7:18–29 M Num. 7:24–35 T Num. 7:30–41 W Num. 7:36–41	
5	Th	30	New Moon, first day; Ḥanukkah, sixth day	Num. 28:1–15 Num. 7:42–47	

Italics are for Sephardi Minhag.

2002, Dec. 6–Jan. 3, 2003] ṬEVET (29 DAYS) [5763

Civil Date	Day of the Week	Jewish Date	SABBATHS, FESTIVALS, FASTS	PENTATEUCHAL READING	PROPHETICAL READING
Dec. 6	F	Ṭevet 1	New Moon, second day; Ḥanukkah, seventh day	Num. 28:1–15 Num. 7:48–59	
7	Sa	2	Mi-ḳeẓ; Ḥanukkah, eight day	Gen. 41:1–44:17 Num. 7:54–8:4	I Kings 7:40–50
14	Sa	9	Wa-yiggash	Gen. 44:18–47:27	Ezekiel 37:15–28
15	S	10	Fast of 10th of Ṭevet	Exod. 32:11–14 Exod. 34:1–10 (morning and afternoon)	Isaiah 55:6–56:8 (afternoon only)
21	Sa	16	Wa-yeḥi	Gen. 47:28–50:26	I Kings 2:1–12
28	Sa	23	Shemot	Exod. 1:1–6:1	Isaiah 27:6–28:13 Isaiah 29:22–23 *Jeremiah 1:1–2:3*

Italics are for
Sephardi Minhag.

2003, Jan. 4–Feb. 2]　　　　SHEVAṬ (30 DAYS)　　　　[5763

Civil Date	Day of the Week	Jewish Date	SABBATHS, FESTIVALS, FASTS	PENTATEUCHAL READING	PROPHETICAL READING
Jan. 4	Sa	Shevaṭ 1	Wa-'era'; New Moon	Exod. 6:2–9:35 Num. 28:9–15	Isaiah 66: 1–24
11	Sa	8	Bo'	Exod. 10:1–13:16	Jeremiah 46:13–28
18	Sa	15	Be-shallaḥ (Shabbat Shirah) Ḥamishar 'asar bi-Shevaṭ	Exod. 13:17–17:16	Judges 4:4–5:31 *Judges 5:1–31*
25	Sa	22	Yitro	Exod. 18:1–20:23	Isaiah 6:1–7:6; 9:5–6 *Isaiah 6: 1–13*
Feb. 1	Sa	29	Mishpaṭim	Exod. 21:1–24:18	1 Samuel 20: 18–42
2	S	30	New Moon, first day	Num. 28: 1–15	

Italics are for Sephardi Minhag.

2003, Feb. 3–Mar. 4] ADAR I (30 DAYS) [5763

Civil Date	Day of the Week	Jewish Date	SABBATHS, FESTIVALS, FASTS	PENTATEUCHAL READING	PROPHETICAL READING
Feb. 3	M	Adar I 1	New Moon, second day	Num. 28:1–15	
8	Sa	6	Terumah	Exod. 25:1–27:19	I Kings 5:26–6:13
15	Sa	13	Teẓawweh	Exod. 27:20–30:10	Ezekiel 43:10–27
22	Sa	20	Ki tissa'	Exod. 30:11–34:35	I Kings 18:1–39 *I Kings 18:20–39*
Mar. 1	Sa	27	Wa-yaḵhel (Shabbat Sheḵalim)	Exod. 35:1–38:20 Exod. 30:11–16	II Kings 12:1–17 *II Kings 11:17–12:17*
4	T	30	New Moon first day	Num. 28:1–15	

Italics are for Sephardi Minhag.

2003, Mar. 5–Apr. 2]   ADAR II (29 DAYS)   [5763

Civil Date	Day of the Week	Jewish Date	SABBATHS, FESTIVALS, FASTS	PENTATEUCHAL READING	PROPHETICAL READING
Mar. 5	W	Adar II 1	New Moon, second day	Num. 28:1–15	
8	Sa	4	Peḳude	Exod. 38:21–40:38	I Kings 7:51–8:21 *I Kings 7:40–50*
15	Sa	11	Wa-yiḳra' (Shabbat Zakhor)	Levit. 1:1–5:26 Deut. 25:17–19	I Samuel 15:2–34 *I Samuel 15:1–34*
17	M	13	Fast of Esther	Exod. 32:11–14 Exod. 34:1–10 (morning and afternoon)	Isaiah 55:6–56:8 (afternoon only)
18	T	14	Purim	Exod. 17:8–16	Book of Esther (night before and in the morning)
19	W	15	Shushan Purim		
22	Sa	18	Ẓaw (Shabbat Parah)	Levit. 6:1–8:36 Num. 19: 1–22	Ezekiel 36:16–38 *Ezekiel 36:16–36*
29	Sa	25	Shemini (Shabbat Ha-ḥodesh)	Levit. 9:1–11:47 Exod. 12:1–20	Ezekiel 45:16–46:18 *Ezekiel 45:18–46:15*

Italics are for Sephardi Minhag.

2003, Apr. 3– May 2]   NISAN (30 DAYS)   [5763

Civil Date	Day of the Week	Jewish Date	SABBATHS, FESTIVALS, FASTS	PENTATEUCHAL READING	PROPHETICAL READING
Apr. 3	Th	Nisan 1	New Moon	Num. 28:1–15	
5	Sa	3	Tazria'	Levit. 12:1–13:59	II Kings 4:42–5:19
12	Sa	10	Meẓora' (Shabbat Ha-gadol)	Levit. 14:1–15:33	Malachi 3:4–24
16	W	14	Fast of Firstborn		
17	Th	15	Passover, first day	Exod. 12:21–51 Num. 28:16–25	Joshua 5:2–6:1, 27
18	F	16	Passover, second day	Levit. 22:26–23:44 Num. 28:16–25	II Kings 23:1–9, 21–25
19	Sa	17	Ḥol Ha-moʿed, first day	Exod. 33:12–34:26 Num. 28:19–25	Ezekiel 37:1–14
20	S	18	Ḥol Ha-moʿed, second day	Exod. 13:1–16 Num. 28:19–25	
21	M	19	Ḥol Ha-moʿed, third day	Exod. 22:24–23:19 Num. 28:19–25	
22	T	20	Ḥol Ha-moʿed, fourth day	Num. 9: 1–14 Num. 28:19–25	
23	W	21	Passover, seventh day	Exod. 13:17–15:26 Num. 28:19–25	II Samuel 22:1—51
24	Th	22	Passover, eight day	Deut. 15:19–16:17 Num. 28:19–25	Isaiah 10:32–12:6
26	Sa	24	Aḥarei mot	Levit. 16:1–18:30	Amos 9:7–15 *Ezekiel 20:2–20*
29	T	27	Holocaust Memorial Day		
May 2	F	30	New Moon, first day	Num. 28:1–15	

Italics are for Sephardi Minhag.

2003, May 3– May 31]   IYAR (29 DAYS)   [5763

Civil Date	Day of the Week	Jewish Date	SABBATHS, FESTIVALS, FASTS	PENTATEUCHAL READING	PROPHETICAL READING
May 3	Sa	Iyar 1	Ḳedoshim; New Moon, second day	Levit. 19:1–20:27 Num. 28:9–15	Isaiah 66:1–24
7	W	5	Israel Independence Day		
10	Sa	8	Emor	Levit. 21:1–24:23	Ezekiel 44:15–31
17	Sa	15	Be-har	Levit. 21:1–26:2	Jeremiah 32:6–27
20	T	18	Lag Ba-'omer		
24	Sa	22	Be-ḥuḳḳotai	Levit. 26:3–27:34	Jeremiah 16:19–17:14
30	F	28	Jerusalem Day*		
31	Sa	29	Be-midbar	Num 1:1–4:20	I Samuel 20:18–42

*Observed May 29, to avoid conflict with the Sabbath.

Italics are for Sephardi Minhag.

SIWAN (30 DAYS)

Civil Date	Day of the Week	Jewish Date	SABBATHS, FESTIVALS, FASTS	PENTATEUCHAL READING	PROPHETICAL READING
June 1	S	Siwan 1	New Moon	Num. 28:1–15	
6	F	6	Shavu'ot, first day	Exod. 19:1–20:23 Num. 28:26–31	Ezekiel 1:1–28, 3:12
7	Sa	7	Shavu'ot, second day	Deut. 15:19–16: 17 Num. 28:26–31	Habbakuk 3:1–19 *Habbakuk 2:20–3:19*
14	Sa	14	Naso'	Num. 4:21–7:89	Judges 13:2–25
21	Sa	21	Be-ha'alotekha	Num. 8:1–12:16	Zechariah 2:14–4:7
28	Sa	28	Shelaḥ lekha	Num. 13:1–15:41	Joshua 2:1–24
30	M	30	New Moon, first day	Num. 28:1–15	

*Italics are for
Sephardi Minhag.*

TAMMUZ (29 DAYS)

Civil Date	Day of the Week	Jewish Date	SABBATHS, FESTIVALS, FASTS	PENTATEUCHAL READING	PROPHETICAL READING
July 1	T	Tammuz 1	New Moon, second day	Num. 28:1–15	
5	Sa	5	Ķoraḥ	Num. 16:1–18:32	I Samuel 11:14–12:22
12	Sa	12	Ḥuķķat, Balaķ	Num. 19:1–25:9	Micah 5:6–6:8
17	Th	17	Fast of 17th of Tammuz	Exod. 32:11–14 Exod. 34: 1–10 (morning and afternoon)	Isaiah 55:6–56:8 (afternoon only)
19	Sa	19	Pineḥas	Num. 25:10–30:1	Jeremiah 1:1–2:3
26	Sa	26	Maṭṭot Masʻe	Num. 30:2–36:13	Jeremiah 2:4–28 Jeremiah 3:4 *Jeremiah 2:4–28* *Jeremiah 4:1–2*

Italics are for
Sephardi Minhag.

2003, July 30–Aug. 29]   AV (30 DAYS)   [5763

Civil Date	Day of the Week	Jewish Date	SABBATHS, FESTIVALS, FASTS	PENTATEUCHAL READING	PROPHETICAL READING
July 30	W	Av 1	New Moon	Num. 28:1–15	
Aug. 2	Sa	4	Devarim (Shabbat Ḥazon)	Deut. 1:1–3:22	Isaiah 1:1–27
7	Th	9	Fast of 9th of Av	Morning: Deut. 4:25–40 Afternoon: Exod. 32:11–14 Exod. 34:1–10	(Lamentations is read the night before) Jeremiah 8:13–9:23 (morning) Isaiah 55:6–56:8 (afternoon)
9	Sa	11	Wa-etḥannan (Shabbat Nahamu)	Deut. 3:23–7:11	Isaiah 40:1–26
16	Sa	18	'Eḳev	Deut. 7:12–11:25	Isaiah 49:14–51:3
23	Sa	25	Re'eh	Deut. 11:26–16:17	Isaiah 54:11–55:5
28	Th	30	New Moon, first day	Numbers 28:1– 15	

Italics are for
Sephardi Minhag.

ELUL (29 DAYS) [5763

Civil Date	Day of the Week	Jewish Date	SABBATHS, FESTIVALS, FASTS	PENTATEUCHAL READING	PROPHETICAL READING
Aug. 30	F	Elul 1	New Moon, second day	Num. 28:1–15	
31	Sa	2	Shofeṭim	Deut. 16:18–21:9	Isaiah 51:12–52:12
Sept. 6	Sa	9	Ki teẓe'	Deut. 21:10–25:19	Isaiah 54:1–10
13	Sa	16	Ki tavo'	Deut. 26: 1–29:8	Isaiah 60:1–22
20	Sa	23	Niẓẓavim, Wa-yelekh	Deut. 29:9–31:30	Isaiah 61:10–63:9

Italics are for
Sephardi Minhag.

2003, Sept. 27–Oct. 26] TISHRI (30 DAYS) [5764

Civil Date	Day of the Week	Jewish Date	SABBATHS, FESTIVALS, FASTS	PENTATEUCHAL READING	PROPHETICAL READING
Sept. 27	Sa	Tishri 1	Rosh Ha-shanah, first day	Gen. 21:1–34 Num. 29:1–6	I Samuel 1:1–2:10
28	S	2	Rosh Ha-shana, second day	Gen. 22:1–24 Num. 29:1–6	Jeremiah 31:2–20
29	M	3	Fast of Gedaliah	Exod. 32:11–14 Exod. 34:1–10 (morning and afternoon)	Isaiah 55:6–56:8 (afternoon only)
Oct. 4	Sa	8	Ha'azinu (Shabbat Shuvah)	Deut. 32:1–52	Hosea 14:2–10 Micah 7:18–20 Joel 2:15–27 *Hosea 14:2–10* *Micah 7:18–20*
6	M	10	Yom Kippur	Morning: Levit. 16:1–34 Num. 29:7–11 Afternoon: Levit. 18:1–30	Isaiah 57:14–58:14 Jonah 1:1–4:11 Micah 7:18–20
11	Sa	15	Sukkot, first day	Levit. 22:26–23:44 Num. 29:12–16	Zechariah 14:1–21
12	S	16	Sukkot, second day	Levit. 22:26–23:44 Num. 29:12–16	I Kings 8:2–21
13-16	M-Th	17-20	Ḥol Ha-mo'ed	M: Num. 29:17–25 T: Num. 29:20–28 W: Num. 29:23–31 Th: Num. 29:26–34	
17	F	21	Hosha'na' Rabbah	Num. 29:26–34	
18	Sa	22	Shemini 'Aẓeret	Deut. 14:22–16:17 Num. 29:35–30:1	I Kings 8:54–66
19	S	23	Simḥat Torah	Deut. 33:1–34:12 Gen. 1:1–2:3 Num. 29:35–30:1	Joshua 1:1–18 *Joshua 1:1–9*
25	Sa	29	Be-re'shit	Gen. 1:1–6:8	I Samuel 20:18–42
26	S	30	New Moon, first day	Num. 28: 1–15	

Italics are for
Sephardi Minhag.

2003, Oct. 27–Nov. 25]   ḤESHWAN (30 DAYS)   [5764

Civil Date	Day of the Week	Jewish Date	SABBATHS, FESTIVALS, FASTS	PENTATEUCHAL READING	PROPHETICAL READING
Oct. 27	M	Ḥeshwan 1	New Moon, second day	Num. 28:1–15	
Nov. 1	Sa	6	Noaḥ	Gen. 6:9–11:32	Isaiah 54:1–55:5 *Isaiah 54:1–10*
8	Sa	13	Lekh lekha	Gen. 12:1–17:27	Isaiah 40:27–41:16
15	Sa	20	Wa-yera'	Gen. 18:11–22:24	II Kings 4:1–37 *II Kings 4:1–23*
22	Sa	27	Ḥayye Sarah	Gen. 23:1–25:18	I Kings 1:1–31
25	T	30	New Moon, first day	Num. 28:1–15	

Italics are for
Sephardi Minhag.

2003, Nov. 26–Dec. 25] KISLEW (30 DAYS) [5764

Civil Date	Day of the Week	Jewish Date	SABBATHS, FESTIVALS, FASTS	PENTATEUCHAL READING	PROPHETICAL READING
Nov. 26	W	Kislew 1	New Moon, second day	Num. 28:1–15	
29	Sa	4	Toledot	Gen. 25:19–28:9	Malachi 1:1–2:7
Dec. 6	Sa	11	Wa-yeẓe'	Gen. 28:10–32:3	Hosea 12:13–14:10 *Hosea 11:7–12:12*
13	Sa	18	Wa-yishlaḥ	Gen. 32:4–36:43	Hosea 11:7–12:12 *Obadiah 1:1–21*
20	Sa	25	Wa-yeshev; Ḥanukkah, first day	Gen. 37:1–40:23 Num. 7:1–17	Zechariah 2:14–4:7
21-24	S–W	26–29	Ḥanukkah, second to fifth days	S Num. 7:18–29 M Num. 7:24–35 T Num. 7:30–41 W Num. 7:36–41	
25	Th	30	New Moon, first day; Ḥanukkah, sixth day	Num. 28:1–15 Num. 7:42–47	

Italics are for Sephardi Minhag.

2003, Dec. 26–Jan. 23, 2004] ṬEVET (29 DAYS) [5764

Civil Date	Day of the Week	Jewish Date	SABBATHS, FESTIVALS, FASTS	PENTATEUCHAL READING	PROPHETICAL READING
Dec. 26	F	Ṭevet 1	New Moon, second day; Ḥanukkah, seventh day	Num. 28:1–15 Num. 7:48–53	
27	Sa	2	Mi-ḳeẓ; Ḥanukkah, eight day	Gen. 41:1–44:17 Num. 7:54–8:4	I Kings 7:40–50
2004 Jan. 3	Sa	9	Wa-yiggash	Gen. 44:18–47:27	Ezekiel 37:15–28
4	S	10	Fast of 10th of Ṭevet	Exod. 32:11–14 Exod. 34:1–10 (morning and afternoon)	Isaiah 55:6–56:8 (afternoon only)
10	Sa	16	Wa-yeḥi	Gen. 47:28–50:26	I Kings 2:1–12
17	Sa	23	Shemot	Exod. 1:1–6:1	Isaiah 27:6–28:13 Isaiah 29:22–23 *Jeremiah 1:1–2:3*

Italics are for
Sephardi Minhag.

Civil Date	Day of the Week	Jewish Date	SABBATHS, FESTIVALS, FASTS	PENTATEUCHAL READING	PROPHETICAL READING
Jan. 24	Sa	Shevaṭ 1	Wa-’era’; New Moon	Exod. 6:2–9:35 Num. 28:9–15	Isaiah 66: 1–24
31	Sa	8	Bo’	Exod. 10:1–13:16	Jeremiah 46:13–28
Feb. 7	Sa	15	Be-shallaḥ (Shabbat Shirah) Ḥamishar ‘asar bi-Shevaṭ	Exod. 13:17–17:16	Judges 4:4–5:31 *Judges 5:1–31*
14	Sa	22	Yitro	Exod. 18:1–20:23	Isaiah 6:1–7:6; 9:5–6 *Isaiah 6: 1–13*
21	Sa	29	Mishpaṭim (Shabbat Sheḳalim)	Exod. 21:1–24:18 30:11–16	1 Samuel 20: 18–42
22	S	30	New Moon, first day	Num. 28: 1–15	

*Italics are for
Sephardi Minhag.*

2004, Feb. 23–Mar. 22]   ADAR (29 DAYS)   [5764

Civil Date	Day of the Week	Jewish Date	SABBATHS, FESTIVALS, FASTS	PENTATEUCHAL READING	PROPHETICAL READING
Feb. 23	M	Adar 1	New Moon, second day	Num. 28:1–15	
28	Sa	6	Terumah	Exod. 25:1–27:19	I Kings 5:26–6:13
Mar. 4	Th	11	Fast of Esther	Exod. 32:11–14 Exod. 34:1–10 (morning and afternoon)	Isaiah 55:6–56:8 (afternoon only)
6	Sa	13	Teẓawweh (Shabbat Zakhor)	Exod. 27:20–30:10 Deut. 25:17–19	I Samuel 15:2–34 *I Samuel 15:1–34*
7	S	14	Purim	Exod. 17:8–16	Book of Esther (night before and in the morning)
8	M	15	Shushan Purim		
13	Sa	20	Ki tissa' (Shabbat Parah)	Exod. 30:11–34:35 Num. 19: 1–22	Ezekiel 36:16–38 *Ezekiel 36:16–36*
20	Sa	27	Wa-yaḵhel, Peḵude (Shabbat Ha-ḥodesh)	Exod. 35:1–40:38 Exod. 12:1–20	Ezekiel 45:16–46:18 *Ezekiel 45:18–46:15*

Italics are for Sephardi Minhag.

2004, Mar. 23–Apr. 21]   NISAN (30 DAYS)   [5764

Civil Date	Day of the Week	Jewish Date	SABBATHS, FESTIVALS, FASTS	PENTATEUCHAL READING	PROPHETICAL READING
Mar. 23	T	Nisan 1	New Moon	Num. 28:1–15	
27	Sa	5	Wa-yiḵra'	Levit. 1:1–5:26	Isaiah 43:21–44:24
Apr. 3	Sa	12	Ẓaw (Shabbat Ha-gadol)	Levit. 6:1–8:36	Malachi 3:4–24
5	M	14	Fast of Firstborn		
6	T	15	Passover, first day	Exod. 12:21–51 Num. 28:16–25	Joshua 5:2–6:1, 27
7	W	16	Passover, second day	Levit. 22:26–23:44 Num. 28:16–25	II Kings 23:1–9, 21–25
8	Th	17	Ḥol Ha-mo'ed, first day	Exod. 13:1–16 Num. 28:19–25	Ezekiel 37:1–14
9	F	18	Ḥol Ha-mo'ed, second day	Exod. 22:24–23:19 Num. 28:19–25	
10	Sa	19	Ḥol Ha-mo'ed, third day	Exod. 33:12–34:26 Num. 28:19–25	
11	S	20	Ḥol Ha-mo'ed, fourth day	Num. 9: 1–14 Num. 28:19–25	
12	M	21	Passover, seventh day	Exod. 13:17–15:26 Num. 28:19–25	II Samuel 22:1—51
13	T	22	Passover, eight day	Deut. 15:19–16:17 Num. 28:19–25	Isaiah 10:32–12:6
17	Sa	26	Shemini	Levit. 9:1–11:47	II Samuel 6:1–7:17 *II Samuel 6:1–19*
18	S	27	Holocaust Memorial Day		
21	W	30	New Moon, first day	Num. 28:1–15	

Italics are for Sephardi Minhag.

2004, Apr. 22– May 20]   IYAR (29 DAYS)   [5764

Civil Date	Day of the Week	Jewish Date	SABBATHS, FESTIVALS, FASTS	PENTATEUCHAL READING	PROPHETICAL READING
Apr. 22	Th	Iyar 1	New Moon, second day	Num. 28:1–15	
24	Sa	3	Tazria', Meẓora'	Levit. 12:1–15:33	II Kings 7:3–20
26	M	5	Israel Independence Day		
May 1	Sa	10	Aḥare Mot, Kedoshim	Levit. 16:1–20:27	Amos 9:7–15 *Ezekiel 20:2–20*
8	Sa	17	Emor	Levit. 21:1–24:23	Ezekiel 44:15–31
9	S	18	Lag Ba-'omer		
15	Sa	24	Be-har, Be-ḥukḳotai	Levit. 25:1–27:34	Jeremiah 16:19–17:14
19	W	28	Jerusalem Day		

Italics are for Sephardi Minhag.

2004, May 21–June 19]   SIWAN (30 DAYS)   [5764

Civil Date	Day of the Week	Jewish Date	SABBATHS, FESTIVALS, FASTS	PENTATEUCHAL READING	PROPHETICAL READING
May 21	F	Siwan 1	New Moon	Num. 28:1–15	
22	Sa	2	Be-midbar	Num. 1:1–4:20	Hosea 2:1–22
26	W	6	Shavu'ot, first day	Exod. 19:1–20:23 Num. 28:26–31	Ezekiel 1:1–28, 3:12
27	Th	7	Shavu'ot, second day	Deut. 15:19–16:17 Num. 28:26–31	Habbakuk 3:1–19 *Habbakuk 2:20–3:19*
29	Sa	9	Naso'	Num. 4:21–7:89	Judges 13:2–25
June 5	Sa	16	Be-ha'alotekha	Num. 8:1–12:16	Zechariah 2:14–4:7
12	Sa	23	Shelaḥ lekha	Num. 13:1–15:41	Joshua 2:1–24
19	Sa	30	Ḳoraḥ; New Moon, first day	Num. 16:1–18:13 Num. 28:9–15	Isaiah 66:1–24 *Isaiah 66:1–24* *I Samuel 20:18, 42*

Italics are for Sephardi Minhag.

2004, June 20– July 18]   TAMMUZ (29 DAYS)   [5764

Civil Date	Day of the Week	Jewish Date	SABBATHS, FESTIVALS, FASTS	PENTATEUCHAL READING	PROPHETICAL READING
June 20	S	Tammuz 1	New Moon, second day	Num. 28:1–15	
26	Sa	7	Ḥuḳḳat	Num. 19:1–22:1	Judges 11:1–33
July 3	Sa	14	Balaḳ	Num. 22:2–25:9	Micah 5:6–6:8
6	T	17	Fast of 17th of Tammuz	Exod. 32:11–14 Exod. 34: 1–10 (morning and afternoon)	Isaiah 55:6–56:8 (afternoon only)
10	Sa	21	Pineḥas	Num. 25:10–30:1	Jeremiah 1:1–2:3
17	Sa	28	Maṭṭot Masʿe	Num. 30:2–36:13	Jeremiah 2:4–28 Jeremiah 3:4 *Jeremiah 2:4–28* *Jeremiah 4:1–2*

Italics are for
Sephardi Minhag.

2004, July 19–Aug. 17]   AV (30 DAYS)   [5764

Civil Date	Day of the Week	Jewish Date	SABBATHS, FESTIVALS, FASTS	PENTATEUCHAL READING	PROPHETICAL READING
July 19	M	Av 1	New Moon	Num. 28:1–15	
24	Sa	6	Devarim (Shabbat Ḥazon)	Deut. 1:1–3:22	Isaiah 1:1–27
27	T	9	Fast of 9th of Av	Morning: Deut. 4:25–40 Afternoon: Exod. 32:11–14 Exod. 34:1–10	(Lamentations is read the night before) Jeremiah 8:13–9:23 (morning) Isaiah 55:6–56:8 (afternoon)
31	Sa	13	Wa-ethannan (Shabbat Naḥamu)	Deut. 3:23–7:11	Isaiah 40:1–26
Aug. 7	Sa	20	'Eḳev	Deut. 7:12–11:25	Isaiah 49:14–51:3
14	Sa	27	Re'eh	Deut. 11:26–16:17	Isaiah 54:11–55:5
17	T	30	New Moon, first day	Numbers 28:1–15	

Italics are for
Sephardi Minhag.

2004, Aug. 18–Sept. 15]   ELUL (29 DAYS)   [5764

Civil Date	Day of the Week	Jewish Date	SABBATHS, FESTIVALS, FASTS	PENTATEUCHAL READING	PROPHETICAL READING
Aug. 18	W	Elul 1	New Moon, second day	Num. 28:1–15	
21	Sa	4	Shofeṭim	Deut. 16:18–21:9	Isaiah 51:12–52:12
28	Sa	11	Ki teẓe'	Deut. 21:10–25:19	Isaiah 54:1–10
Sept. 4	Sa	18	Ki tavo'	Deut. 26: 1–29:8	Isaiah 60:1–22
11	Sa	25	Niẓẓavim, Wa-yelekh	Deut. 29:9–31:30	Isaiah 61:10–63:9

Italics are for Sephardi Minhag.

2004, Sept. 16–Oct. 15]   TISHRI (30 DAYS)   [5765

Civil Date	Day of the Week	Jewish Date	SABBATHS, FESTIVALS, FASTS	PENTATEUCHAL READING	PROPHETICAL READING
Sept. 16	Th	Tishri 1	Rosh Ha-shanah, first day	Gen. 21:1–34 Num. 29:1–6	I Samuel 1:1–2:10
17	F	2	Rosh Ha-shana, second day	Gen. 22:1–24 Num. 29:1–6	Jeremiah 31:2–20
18	Sa	8	Ha'azinu (Shabbat Shuvah)	Deut. 32:1–52	Hosea 14:2–10 Micah 7:18–20 Joel 2:15–27 *Hosea 14:2–10* *Micah 7:18–20*
19	S	3	Fast of Gedaliah	Exod. 32:11–14 Exod. 34:1–10 (morning and afternoon)	Isaiah 55:6–56:8 (afternoon only)
25	Sa	10	Yom Kippur	Morning: Levit. 16:1–34 Num. 29:7–11 Afternoon: Levit. 18:1–30	Isaiah 57:14–58:14 Jonah 1:1–4:11 Micah 7:18–20
30	Th	15	Sukkot, first day	Levit. 22:26–23:44 Num. 29:12–16	Zechariah 14:1–21
Oct. 1	F	16	Sukkot, second day	Levit. 22:26–23:44 Num. 29:12–16	I Kings 8:2–21
2	Sa	17–20	Ḥol Ha-mo'ed, first day	Exod. 33:12–34:26 Num. 29:17–22	Ezekiel 38:18–39:16
3-5	S-T	17–20	Ḥol Ha-mo'ed, second to fourth days	S: Num. 29:20–28 M: Num. 29:23–31 T: Num. 29:26–34	
6	W	21	Hosha'na' Rabbah	Num. 29:26–34	
7	Th	22	Shemini 'Aẓeret	Deut. 14:22–16:17 Num. 29:35–30:1	I Kings 8:54–66
8	F	23	Simḥat Torah	Deut. 33:1–34:12 Gen. 1:1–2:3 Num. 29:35–30:1	Joshua 1:1–18 *Joshua 1:1–9*
9	Sa	29	Be-re'shit	Gen. 1:1–6:8	Isaiah 42:5–43:10 *Isaiah 42:5–21*
15	F	30	New Moon, first day	Num. 28: 1–15	

Italics are for Sephardi Minhag.

2004, Oct. 16–Nov. 13]   HESHWAN (30 DAYS)   [5765

Civil Date	Day of the Week	Jewish Date	SABBATHS, FESTIVALS, FASTS	PENTATEUCHAL READING	PROPHETICAL READING
Oct. 16	Sa	Heshwan 1	Noaḥ; New Moon, second day	Gen. 6:9–11:32 Num. 28:1–15	Isaiah 66:1–24
23	Sa	8	Lekh lekha	Gen. 12:1–17:27	Isaiah 40:27–41:16
30	Sa	15	Wa-yera'	Gen. 18:1–22:24	II Kings 4:1–37 *II Kings 4:1–23*
Nov. 6	Sa	22	Ḥayye Sarah	Gen. 23:1–25:18	I Kings 1:1–31
13	Sa	29	Toledot	Gen. 25:19–28:9	I Samuel 20:18–42

Italics are for Sephardi Minhag.

2004, Nov. 14–Dec. 12]   KISLEW (30 DAYS)   [5765

Civil Date	Day of the Week	Jewish Date	SABBATHS, FESTIVALS, FASTS	PENTATEUCHAL READING	PROPHETICAL READING
Nov. 14	S	Kislew 1	New Moon,	Num. 28:1–15	
20	Sa	7	Wa-yeẓe'	Gen. 28:10–32:3	Hosea 12:13–14:10 *Hosea 11:7–12:12*
27	Sa	14	Wa-yishlaḥ	Gen. 32:4–36:43	Hosea 11:7–12:12 *Obadiah 1:1–21*
Dec. 4	Sa	21	Wa-yeshev;	Gen. 37:1–40:23	Amos 2:6–3:8
8–10	W–F	25–27	Ḥanukkah, first to third days	W: Num. 7:1–17 Th: Num. 7:18–29 F: Num. 7:24–35	
11	Sa	28	Mi-ḳeẓ Ḥanukkah, fourth day	Gen. 41:1–44:17 Num. 7:30–35	Zechariah 2:14–4:7
12	S	29	Ḥanukkah, fifth day	Num. 7:36–47	

Italics are for
Sephardi Minhag.

2004, Dec. 13–Jan. 20, 2005] ṬEVET (29 DAYS) [5765

Civil Date	Day of the Week	Jewish Date	SABBATHS, FESTIVALS, FASTS	PENTATEUCHAL READING	PROPHETICAL READING
Dec. 13	M	Ṭevet 1	New Moon; Ḥanukkah, sixth day	Num. 28:1–15 Num. 7:42–47	
14–15	T–W	2–3	Ḥanukkah, seventh and eight days	T: Num. 7:48–53 W: Num. 7:54–8:4	
18	Sa	6	Wa-yiggash	Gen. 44:18–47:27	Ezekiel 37:15–28
22	W	10	Fast of 10th of Ṭevet	Exod. 32:11–14 Exod. 34:1–10 (morning and afternoon)	Isaiah 55:6–56:8 (afternoon only)
25	Sa	13	Wa-yeḥi	Gen. 47:28–50:26	I Kings 2:1–12
Jan. 1 2005	Sa	20	Shemot	Exod. 1:1–6:1	Isaiah 27:6–28:13 Isaiah 29:22–23 *Jeremiah 1:1–2:3*
8	Sa	27	Wa-’era’	Exod. 6:2–9:35	Ezekiel 28:25–29:21

Italics are for Sephardi Minhag.

Index